Ray Rankins
Paul Bertucci
Chris Gallelli
Alex T. Silverstein

Microsoft®
SQL Server 2014®

UNLEASHED

SAMS | 800 East 96th Street, Indianapolis, Indiana 46240 USA

Microsoft® SQL Server 2014® Unleashed

ISBN-13: 978-0-672-33729-1

ISBN-10: 0-672-33729-0

Library of Congress Control Number: 2015900253

Printed in the United States of America

2 16

Trademarks

All terms mentioned in this book that are known to be trademarks or service marks have been appropriately capitalized. Sams Publishing cannot attest to the accuracy of this information. Use of a term in this book should not be regarded as affecting the validity of any trademark or service mark.

Warning and Disclaimer

Special Sales

For information about buying this title in bulk quantities, or for special sales opportunities (which may include electronic versions; custom cover designs; and content particular to your business, training goals, marketing focus, or branding interests), please contact our corporate sales department at corpsales@pearsoned.com or (800) 382-3419.

For government sales inquiries, please contact governmentsales@pearsoned.com.

For questions about sales outside the U.S., please contact international@pearsoned.com.

Editor-in-Chief
Greg Wiegand

Acquisitions Editor
Joan Murray

Development Editor
Mark Renfrow

Managing Editor
Kristy Hart

Project Editor
Elaine Wiley

Indexer
Lisa Stumpf

Proofreader
Debbie Williams

Technical Editors
Dan English
David Solomon

Publishing Coordinator
Cindy Teeters

Cover Designer
Mark Shirar

Compositor
Nonie Ratcliff

Contents at a Glance

> **NOTE**
>
> Chapters 48-51 are available online for readers of the printed edition of this book.
> You can register your book and access those chapters here:
> informit.com/title/9780672337291.

Table of Contents

NOTE

Chapters 48-51 are available online for readers of the printed edition of this book. You can register your book and access those chapters here: informit.com/title/9780672337291.

About the Authors

Ray Rankins is owner and president of Gotham Consulting Services, Inc. (http://www.gothamconsulting.com), near Saratoga Springs, New York. Ray has been working with Sybase and Microsoft SQL Server for more than 27 years and has experience in database administration, database design, project management, application development, consulting, courseware development, and training. He has worked in a variety of industries, including financial, manufacturing, health care, retail, insurance, communications, public utilities, and state and federal government. His expertise is in database performance and tuning, query analysis, advanced SQL programming and stored procedure development, database design, data architecture, and database application design and development, with recent specialization in Sybase to SQL Server migrations. Ray's presentations on these topics at user group conferences have been very well received. Ray is coauthor of *Microsoft SQL Server 2012 Unleashed, Microsoft SQL Server 2008 R2 Unleashed, Microsoft SQL Server 2005 Unleashed, Microsoft SQL Server 2000 Unleashed, Microsoft SQL Server 6.5 Unleashed, Sybase SQL Server 11 Unleashed*, and *Sybase SQL Server 11 DBA Survival Guide*, all published by Sams Publishing. As an instructor, Ray brings his real-world experience into the classroom, teaching courses on SQL, advanced SQL programming and optimization, database design, database administration, and database performance and tuning. Ray can be reached at rrankins@gothamconsulting.com.

Paul Bertucci is the founder of Data by Design, LLC (www.dataxdesign.com), a global database consulting firm with offices in the United States and Paris, France. He recently spent 6 years as the Chief Architect and Director of the global Shared Services team for Autodesk, Inc. running BI/DW/ODS, Big Data, Identity Management, SOA, Integration (EAI & ETL), MDM, Collaboration/Social, SaaS application platforms, and Enterprise Architecture teams. Prior to Autodesk, he was the Chief Data Architect at Symantec for 4 years. He is also co-founder and CTO for Diginome, Inc. (www.diginome.com), a data provenance/integrity software company. Paul has more than 30 years of experience with database design, data architecture, big data, data replication, performance and tuning, master data management (MDM), data provenance/DataDNA, distributed data systems, data integration, high-availability, enterprise architecture, identity management, SOA, SaaS, and systems integration for numerous Fortune 500 companies, including Intel, Coca-Cola, Apple, Toshiba, Lockheed, Wells Fargo, Safeway, Sony, Charles Schwab, Cisco Systems, Sybase, Symantec, Veritas, and Honda, to name a few. He has authored numerous database articles, data standards, and high-profile database courses, such as Sybase's "Performance and Tuning" and "Physical Database Design" courses. Other Sams Publishing books that he has authored include the highly popular *Microsoft SQL Server 2000 Unleashed, Teach Yourself ADO.NET in 24 Hours, Microsoft SQL Server High Availability, Microsoft SQL Server 2005 Unleashed, Microsoft SQL Server 2008 R2 Unleashed*, and *Microsoft SQL Server 2012 Unleashed*. Mr. Bertucci is a frequent speaker at industry conferences such as Informatica World, Oracle World, and the MDM Summit, and at Microsoft-oriented conferences such as SQL Saturday's, Silicon Valley Code-Camp, PASS conferences, Tech Ed's, and SQL Server User Groups. He has deployed numerous systems with Microsoft

SQL Server, Sybase, DB2, Postgres, MySQL, NoSQL, Paraccel, Hadoop and Oracle database engines, and he has designed/architected several commercially available tools in the database, data modeling, performance and tuning, data integration, digital DNA, and multi-dimensional planning spaces. Paul just finished a major "Master Data Management for Big Data" project with Intel Corporation that deployed MDS (with Profisee's Maestro) in a data mastering as a service architecture. Paul received his formal education in computer science and electrical engineering from UC Berkeley (Go Bears!). He lives in the great Pacific Northwest (Oregon) with his five children: Donny, Juliana, Nina, Marissa, and Paul Jr. Mr. Bertucci can be reached at pbertucci@dataxdesign.com or Bertucci@Alum.CalBerkeley.Org.

Chris Gallelli is the president of CGAL Consulting Services, Inc. His company focuses on consulting services in the areas of database administration, database tuning, advanced stored procedure development, Integration Services, Powershell development and database programming using Microsoft Visual Studio. Chris has more than 20 years of experience with SQL Server or Sybase and more than 25 years in the field of information technology. He has a bachelor's degree in electrical engineering and a master's degree in business administration from Union College. Chris currently lives near Albany, New York, with his lovely wife, Laura, and two beautiful daughters, Rachael and Kayla. Other Sams Publishing books that he has coauthored include *Microsoft SQL Server 2000 Unleashed, Microsoft SQL Server 2005 Unleashed, Microsoft SQL Server 2008 R2,* and *Microsoft SQL Server 2012 Unleashed.* Chris can be reached at cgallelli@gmail.com.

Alex T. Silverstein is owner and chief technologist of Unified Digital Group, LLC (http://unifieddigital.com), a custom software development firm headquartered near Saratoga Springs, New York. He specializes in designing high-availability software systems using SQL Server and Microsoft .NET. Alex has more than 18 years of experience providing application development, database administration, and training services worldwide to a variety of industries. He was also a coauthor of previous editions of this book. You can reach Alex anytime via email at alex@unifieddigital.com.

Dedications

*This book is dedicated to my loving wife of 28 years, Elizabeth Rankins,
for her patience and understanding during the long days, late nights,
and lost weekends spent working on yet another book. Elizabeth,
you are my soul mate and the light of my life. I'd also like to dedicate
this book to our son Jason—we are very proud of the bright,
responsible, and successful man you've become.*
—Ray Rankins

*Dedicated to my children and my parents, for the countless times
they have heard me say "No, not now, I'm writing chapters!"
Thanks Father Donald, Mother Jane, Paul Jr., Marissa, Nina, Juliana,
and Donny, I love you all very much! We sadly lost Mother Jane
to cancer this past year—love you Mom, rest well.*
—Paul Bertucci

*This book is dedicated to my two daughters, Rachael and Kayla Gallelli.
I am extremely proud of these two young ladies who are beautiful both inside
and out. Kayla is presently a sophomore in college and is excelling in her
pursuit of a degree in Speech Pathology. She is also a student ambassador
there and dedicates a great deal of time volunteering in her school
community. Rachael already graduated college with Cum Laude honors and
a degree in Clinical Research. She landed a job within weeks of graduating
and is shining in her new career in Clinical Research.*

...Your Mom and I are lucky to have you and we love you very much.
—Chris Gallelli - AKA Dad

*My work on this book is dedicated to my father, Harry Silverstein,
a fellow man of letters. For, while his stay with us on this planet was not
nearly long enough, he left us with a feeling of kindness and a call
to humanity and fellowship with all that has remained for a lifetime.
Thank you, Harry, for having been you.*
—Alex T. Silverstein

Acknowledgments

I would first like to thank my coauthors for their tireless efforts in helping to turn out a quality publication and their willingness to take on more work when needed to help keep things on track. I would also like to acknowledge my colleague and friend David Solomon for the thoughtful discussions and insightful questions which helped improve the content of this book, and also for developing the MS Word macro used to extract the code listings and examples presented in the chapters. His efforts made that task significantly easier.

I would also like to acknowledge my clients who not only keep me in business, but provide me with challenging opportunities that help me keep my skills sharp and provide the opportunity to work with and more fully understand the SQL Server technologies that are covered in this book. Specifically, I'd like to acknowledge Chris Cazer, Bob Paquette, and Jerry Lamb of Osprey Software Solutions, Inc., and George Javitz at NYS Dept. of Health.

—Ray Rankins

With any writing effort, there is always a huge sacrifice of time that must be made to properly research, demonstrate, and describe leading-edge subject matter. The brunt of the burden usually falls on those many people who are near and very dear to me. With this in mind, I desperately need to thank my family for allowing me to encroach on many months of what should have been my family's "quality time."

However, with sacrifice also comes reward in the form of technical excellence and high quality business relationships. Many individuals were involved in this effort, both directly and indirectly, starting with the other authors (thanks RR, CG, & AS!), Yves Moison (Data by Design & Database Architechs FRANCE), Rene Fluhler (RightShare, Switzerland), Anthony Vanlandingham (CSAA), Mark Ginnebaugh (DesignMind), Jack McElreath, Scott Smith, Kevin Kenan, Martin Sommer, and Bert Haberland. Their expertise in and knowledge of database engines, SQL, performance and tuning, data replication, database mirroring, database snapshots, business intelligence, data integration, SQL Clustering, Master Data Services, Data Quality Services, and high availability are unmatched. Special thanks to Profisee, Inc. for their permission to showcase Maestro in conjunction with MDS.

—Paul Bertucci

Writing a book of this size and scope requires a tremendous amount of time and dedication. The time and dedication apply not only to the authors who are writing the book but also to their family members. My wife and daughters were very understanding while I was holed up working on this book, and that understanding helped make this book happen. My love and thanks to them.

I would also like to thank many of my clients who embraced SQL Server 2014 and gave me the opportunity to use it in the real world. In particular, I would like to thank Ray McQuade and Spruce Computer Systems. Spruce has had tremendous success with SQL Server 2005, SQL Server 2008, SQL Server 2012, and now SQL Server 2014.

—Chris Gallelli

I would like to acknowledge the following people for their inspirational and personal character, experienced both in the field and at home, each helping in his/her own way to make my contributions to this book possible: Ray Rankins, Chris Gallelli, George Gamble, Al Evans, Vincent Nicotina, Gregory Abbruzzese, Jonathan Rubenstein, Linda Motzkin, Chris Trow, Dmitry Balianouski, Heather Carl, and all the wonderful customers who keep the Unified Digital Group in business.

—Alex T. Silverstein

We Want to Hear from You!

As the reader of this book, *you* are our most important critic and commentator. We value your opinion and want to know what we're doing right, what we could do better, what areas you'd like to see us publish in, and any other words of wisdom you're willing to pass our way.

We welcome your comments. You can email or write to let us know what you did or didn't like about this book—as well as what we can do to make our books better.

Please note that we cannot help you with technical problems related to the topic of this book.

When you write, please be sure to include this book's title and author as well as your name and email address. We will carefully review your comments and share them with the author and editors who worked on the book.

Email: consumer@samspublishing.com

Mail: Sams Publishing
ATTN: Reader Feedback
800 East 96th Street
Indianapolis, IN 46240 USA

Reader Services

Visit our website and register this book at informit.com/register for convenient access to any updates, downloads, or errata that might be available for this book.

Introduction

Throughout its lifetime, SQL Server has continued to establish itself as a robust and reliable database platform with performance, scalability, and reliability that meets the implementation needs of businesses and corporations from small desktop applications on up to multi-terabyte enterprise-wide systems. The updates and enhancements in SQL Server 2014 further solidify its position in the marketplace as a robust, high performing, enterprise system, providing a database engine foundation that can be available 24/7.

One of the challenges we face writing the *SQL Server Unleashed* series of books is how to provide comprehensive, in-depth coverage of all of the SQL Server features within a single book. Over the past few releases, the number of SQL Server features and components has increased, and many of these (for example, SQL Server Integration Services, Reporting Services, SQL Server Analysis Services, and .NET Framework integration) are complex enough to warrant separate titles of their own. To cover each topic sufficiently would require more information than could reasonably fit in print in a single volume. (In fact, there are a few chapters we still couldn't fit in the printed edition. See the note in the Table of Contents on accessing Chapters 48-51.) So, we had to make some hard decisions as to what topics to include in this edition.

We decided that this edition of the *SQL Server Unleashed* series would focus on the core database server features and the day-to-day administrative and management aspects and tools of SQL Server 2014, with a focus on SQL Server administration rather than SQL Server development. This way, we can provide sufficient in-depth information, tips, and guidelines to help get you started installing, monitoring, and maintaining your SQL Server 2014 environments. Another primary goal in writing this book was for it to be more than just a syntax reference. SQL Server Books Online is a fine resource as a syntax reference; however, it often lacks sufficient examples of how to use the features and commands in SQL Server. This book attempts to pick up where Books Online leaves off, by providing, in addition to syntax where necessary, valuable insight, tips, guidelines, and useful examples derived from our many years of experience working with SQL Server. Although this book does provide the core, and sometimes advanced, syntax elements for the SQL commands discussed, SQL Server Books Online provides a much more extensive syntax reference than would make sense to try to duplicate here. As a matter of fact, at times, we may even direct you to Books Online for more detail on some of the more esoteric syntax options available for certain commands.

We hope that we have succeeded in meeting the goals we set out for this book and that it becomes an essential reference and source of expert information for you as you work with SQL Server 2014.

Who This Book Is For

This *Unleashed* book is intended for intermediate-level to advanced-level users: SQL Server administrators who want to effectively manage and administer their SQL Server environments and developers who want a more thorough understanding of the inner workings of SQL Server to help them write better Transact-SQL (T-SQL) code and develop more robust SQL Server applications. If you are responsible for analysis, design, implementation, support, administration, or troubleshooting of SQL Server 2014, this book provides an excellent source of experiential information for you. You can think of this as a book of applied technology. The emphasis is on the more complex aspects of the product, including using the new tools and features, administering SQL Server, analyzing and optimizing queries, implementing data warehouses, ensuring high availability, and tuning SQL Server performance.

This book is primarily intended for SQL Server administrators who are new to SQL Server 2014 as well as those who are already familiar with prior versions of SQL Server. Each chapter provides a brief summary of the major changes or new features or capabilities of SQL Server related to that topic. If you are already familiar with SQL Server, you can refer to this summary to focus on the content that covers the new features and capabilities in more detail.

This book is intended to provide a behind-the-scenes look into SQL Server, showing you what goes on beneath the various wizards and GUI-based tools so that you can learn the underlying SQL commands. Although the GUI tools can make your average day-to-day operations much simpler, every database administrator should learn the underlying commands to fully unlock the power and capabilities of SQL Server.

What This Book Covers

The book is divided into the following parts:

 ▶ **Part I, "Welcome to Microsoft SQL Server"**—Chapters in this part introduce you to the Microsoft SQL Server 2014 environment, the various editions of SQL Server that are available, and the capabilities of each edition in the various Windows environments. In addition, it provides an overview of and introduction to the new features found in SQL Server 2014, which are covered in more detail throughout the rest of the book.

 ▶ **Part II, "SQL Server Tools and Utilities"**—Chapters in this part cover the tools and utility programs that SQL Server 2014 provides for you to administer and manage your SQL Server environments. You'll find information on the various management tools you use on a daily basis, such as SQL Server Management Studio and the SQLCMD command-line query tool, along with information on SQL Server Profiler. If you are not familiar with these tools, you should read this part of the book early on because these tools are often used and referenced throughout many of the other chapters in the book.

▶ **Part III, "SQL Server Administration"**—Chapters in this part discuss topics related to the administration of SQL Server at the database server level. It begins with an overview of what is involved in administering a SQL Server environment and then goes on to cover the tasks related to setting up and managing it, including installing and upgrading to SQL Server 2014 as well as installing SQL Server clients. These chapters also include coverage of database backup and restore, using the Database Mail facility, scheduling and notification using SQL Server Agent, implementing Policy-Based Management, and working with and deploying SQL Azure databases.

▶ **Part IV, "Database Administration"**—Chapters in this part delve into the administrative tasks associated with creating and managing a SQL Server 2014 database, including the creation and management of database objects such as tables, indexes, views, stored procedures, functions, and triggers. It also covers database snapshots and database maintenance tasks and responsibilities.

▶ **Part V, "SQL Server Performance and Optimization"**—Chapters in this part provide information to help you get the best performance out of SQL Server. It begins with a discussion of data structures and indexes—key items to understand to help ensure good database performance. It then builds on that information with chapters on query optimization and analysis, locking, database design and performance, and ways to manage workloads using the Resource Governor.

▶ **Part VI, "SQL Server High Availability"**—Chapters in this part cover topics related to achieving high availability for your SQL Server instances, including SQL Server high-availability fundamentals and best practices, as well as chapters on SQL Server replication, SQL Server failover clustering, and SQL Server 2014's AlwaysOn and Availability Groups features.

▶ **Part VII, "SQL Server Business Intelligence Features"**—Chapters in this part provide a comprehensive overview of SQL Server 2014's built-in business intelligence features: Analysis Services, Integration Services, and Reporting Services, enhancements to Master Data Services as well as an introduction to Data Quality Services and the Parallel Data Warehouse Appliance.

▶ **Book Materials on the Web**—Many of the code samples, scripts, sample databases and other materials that supplement various chapters of this book are available for download on the Web at www.informit.com/title/9780672337291. Please visit the web page periodically for any updated or additional code samples and bonus material as it becomes available.

Conventions Used in This Book

Names of commands and stored procedures are presented in a special monospaced computer typeface. We have tried to be consistent in our use of uppercase and lowercase for keywords and object names. However, because the default installation of SQL Server doesn't make a distinction between upper- and lowercase for SQL keywords or object names and data, you might find some of the examples presented in either upper- or lowercase.

Code and output examples are presented separately from regular paragraphs and are also in a monospaced computer typeface. The following is an example:

```
select object_id, name, type_desc
from sys.objects
where type = 'SQ'

object_id     name                               type_desc
-----------   --------------------------------   -------------
1977058079    QueryNotificationErrorsQueue       SERVICE_QUEUE
2009058193    EventNotificationErrorsQueue       SERVICE_QUEUE
2041058307    ServiceBrokerQueue                 SERVICE_QUEUE
```

When syntax is provided for a command, we have attempted to follow these conventions:

Syntax Element	Definition
command	These are command names, options, and other keywords.
placeholder	Monospaced italic indicates values you provide.
{}	You must choose at least one of the enclosed options.
<>	The enclosed value/keyword is a value you provide.
[]	The enclosed value/keyword is optional.
()	Parentheses are part of the command.
|	You can select only one of the options listed.
,	You can select any of the options listed.
[...]	The previous option can be repeated.

Consider the following syntax example:

```
grant {all | permission_list} on object [(column_list)]
      to {public | user_or_group_name [, [...]]}
```

In this case, object is required, but column_list is optional. Note also that items shown in plain computer type, such as grant, public, and all, should be entered literally, as shown. (One exception to this is any argument with the "_name" suffix, which is a placeholder for the specified object name that must be provided.) Placeholders are usually presented in monospaced italic, such as permission_list and user_or_group_name.

A *placeholder* is a generic term for which you must supply a specific value or values. Also, any values enclosed in angle brackets (<>) indicate a specific value that needs to be provided. The *ellipsis* ([...]) in the square brackets following `user_or_group_name` indicates that multiple user or group names can be specified, separated by commas. You can specify either the keyword `public` or one or more user or group names, but not both.

Most of the examples presented in this book make use of the `AdventureWorks2012` database, which is not automatically installed with SQL Server 2014 nor included with the SQL Server installation media. To install the `AdventureWorks2012` sample database, you must first download the installer from the Microsoft SQL Server Samples and Community Projects website at http://sqlserversamples.codeplex.com. A few chapters use the `AdventureWorks2014` sample database in the examples. `AdventureWorks2014` was made available a few months after the release of SQL Server 2014 so it also is not included with the SQL Server installation media. The download of the `AdventureWorks2014` sample database is available on the Microsoft SQL Server Database Product Samples website at https://msftdbprodsamples.codeplex.com.

Some of the chapters in Part VII, "SQL Server Business Intelligence Features," make use of a sample database called `CompSales`. The `CompSales` database provides a good star-schema model that represents a real-world production database. This database is provided on the website in the Code Listings and Sample Databases folder at www.informit.com/title/9780672337291. To install the `CompSales` database, follow these steps:

1. Copy the CompSales.mdf file into the SQL Server data folder where you want it to reside.

2. Ensure that the Read-Only property of the CompSales.mdf file is not enabled.

3. Attach the `CompSales` database by using a command similar to the following. (Edit the path to match the location of the CompSales.mdf file on your system.)

```
sp_attach_single_file_db 'CompSales',
    N'D:\MSSQL\DATA\MSSQL.1\MSSQL\Data\CompSales.mdf'
```

Good Luck!

If you have purchased this book, you are on your way to getting the most from SQL Server 2014. You have already chosen a fine platform for building database applications, one that can provide outstanding performance and rock-solid reliability and availability at a reasonable cost. With this book, you now have the information you need to make the best of it.

Many of us who worked on this book have been using SQL Server since it was first released. Writing about each new version challenges us to reassess our understanding of SQL Server and the way it works. It's an interesting and enjoyable process, and we learn a lot writing each of these books. We hope you get as much enjoyment and knowledge from reading this book as we have from writing it.

PART I

Welcome to Microsoft SQL Server

IN THIS PART

SQL Server 2014 Overview

Exactly what is SQL Server 2014? When you first install the product, what are all the components and features you get, what do they do, and which of them do you need?

At its core, SQL Server 2014 is an enterprise-class database management system (DBMS) that is capable of running anything from a personal database only a few megabytes in size on a handheld Windows Mobile device up to a multi-server database system managing terabytes of information. However, SQL Server 2014 is much more than just the Database Engine.

The SQL Server product is made up of a number of different components. This chapter describes each of the pieces that make up the SQL Server product and what role each plays. Each of these topics is dealt with in more detail later in the book. In addition, this chapter looks at the environments that support SQL Server 2014 and the features available in each of the various SQL Server editions.

SQL Server Components and Features

The main component of SQL Server 2014 is the Database Engine. Before you can use the other components and features of SQL Server 2014, which are discussed in the following sections, you need to have an instance of the Database Engine installed.

The SQL Server Database Engine

The Database Engine is the core application service in the SQL Server package for storing, processing, and securing data with SQL Server 2014. The SQL Server 2014 Database Engine is a Windows service that can be used to store and process data in a relational format, as XML documents, as spatial data, and as columnstore indexes. The following are the main responsibilities of the Database Engine:

▶ Provide reliable storage for data

▶ Provide a means to rapidly retrieve this data

▶ Provide consistent access to the data

▶ Control access to the data through security

▶ Enforce data integrity rules to ensure that the data is reliable and consistent

Each of these responsibilities is examined in greater detail in later chapters in this book. For now, this chapter provides just a brief overview on each of these points to show how Microsoft SQL Server fulfills these core responsibilities.

Reliable Storage

Reliable storage starts at the hardware level. This isn't the responsibility of the Database Engine, but it's a necessary part of a well-built database. Although you can put an entire SQL database on a single IDE or SATA drive (or even burn a read-only copy on a CD), it is preferable to maintain the data on some type of disk storage with redundancy, such as RAID arrays or SAN. The most common RAID array or SAN can survive hardware failures at the disk level without loss of data.

> **NOTE**
>
> For more information on the reliability characteristics and performance implications of the various RAID configurations and guidelines for implementing SAN and RAID configurations with SQL Server, see Chapter 38, "Database Design and Performance."

Using whatever hardware you have decided to make available, the Database Engine manages all the data structures necessary to ensure reliable storage of your data. Rows of data are stored in *pages*, and each page is 8KB in size. Eight pages make up an *extent*, and the Database Engine keeps track of which extents are allocated to which tables and indexes.

> **NOTE**
>
> A *page* is an 8KB chunk of a data file, the smallest unit of storage available in the database. An *extent* is a collection of eight 8KB pages.

Another key feature the Database Engine provides to ensure reliable storage is the transaction log. The transaction log makes a record of every change that is made to the database.

For more information on the transaction log and how it's managed, see Chapter 28, "Transaction Management and the Transaction Log."

> **NOTE**
>
> It is not strictly true that the transaction log records all changes to the database; some exceptions exist. Operations on binary large objects—data of type `image` and `text`—can be exempted from logging, and bulk copy loads into tables can be minimally logged to get the fastest possible performance.

Rapid Data Access

SQL Server allows the creation of indexes, enabling fast access to data. See Chapter 32, "Indexes and Performance," for an in-depth discussion of indexes.

Another way to provide rapid access to data is to keep frequently accessed data in memory. Excess memory for a SQL Server instance is used as a data cache. When pages are requested from the database, the SQL Server Database Engine checks to see if the requested pages are already in the cache. If they are not, it reads them off the disk and stores them in the data cache. If there is no space available in the data cache, the least recently accessed pages (that is, those that haven't been accessed in a while since they were read into memory) are flushed out of the data cache to make room for the newly requested pages. If the pages being flushed contain changes that haven't been written out yet, they are written to disk before being flushed from memory. Otherwise, they are simply discarded.

> **NOTE**
>
> With sufficient memory, an entire database can fit completely into memory, providing the best possible I/O performance for the database.

Consistent Data Access

Getting to your data quickly doesn't mean much if the information you receive is inaccurate. SQL Server follows a set of rules to ensure that the data you receive from queries is consistent.

The general idea with consistent data access is to allow only one client at a time to change the data and to prevent others from reading data from the database while it is undergoing changes. Data and transactional consistency are maintained in SQL Server by using transactional locking.

Transactional consistency has several levels of conformance, each of which provides a trade-off between accuracy of the data and concurrency. These levels of concurrency are examined in more detail in Chapter 37, "Locking and Performance."

Access Control

SQL Server controls access by providing security at multiple levels. Security is enforced at the server, database, schema, and object levels. Server-level access is enforced either by using a SQL Server username and password or through integrated network security, which uses the client's network login credentials to establish identity.

SQL Server security is examined in greater detail in Chapter 15, "Security and User Administration."

Data Integrity

Some databases have to serve the needs of more than a single application. A corporate database that contains valuable information might have a dozen different departments wanting to access portions of the database for different needs.

In this kind of environment, it is impractical to expect the developers of each application to agree on an identical set of standards for maintaining data integrity. For example, one department might allow phone numbers to have extensions, whereas another department may not need that capability. One department might find it critical to maintain a relationship between a customer record and a salesperson record, whereas another might care only about the customer information.

The best way to keep everybody sane in this environment—and to ensure that the data stays consistent and usable by everyone—is to enforce a set of data integrity rules within the database itself. This is accomplished through data integrity constraints and other data integrity mechanisms, such as triggers. See Chapter 23, "Implementing Data Integrity," and Chapter 27, "Creating and Managing Triggers," for more details.

SQL Server 2014 Administration and Management Tools

SQL Server 2014 provides a suite of tools for managing and administering the SQL Server Database Engine and other components. The following sections provide an overview of the primary tools for day-to-day administration, management, and monitoring of your SQL Server environments.

SQL Server Management Studio (SSMS)

SSMS is the central console from which most database management tasks can be coordinated. SSMS provides a single interface from which all servers in a company can be managed. SSMS is examined in more detail in Chapter 3, "SQL Server Management Studio."

Following are some of the tasks you can perform with SSMS. Most of these tasks are discussed in detail later in the book:

▶ Completely manage many servers in a convenient interface

▶ Set server options and configuration values, such as the amount of memory and number of processors to use, default language, and default location of the data and log files

▶ Manage logins, database users, and database roles

- ▶ Create, edit, and schedule automated jobs through the SQL Server Agent

- ▶ Back up and restore databases and define maintenance plans

- ▶ Create new databases

- ▶ Browse table contents

- ▶ Create and manage database objects, such as tables, indexes, and stored procedures

- ▶ Generate DDL scripts for databases and database objects

- ▶ Configure and manage replication

- ▶ Create, edit, execute, and debug Transact-SQL (T-SQL) scripts

- ▶ Define, implement, manage, and invoke SQL Server Policies

- ▶ Enable and disable features of SQL Server

- ▶ Manage and organize scripts into projects and save versions in source control systems such as Team Foundation Server (TFS)

NOTE

Much of SQL Server Managements Studio's interaction with SQL Server is done through standard T-SQL statements. For example, when you create a new database through the SSMS interface, behind the scenes, SSMS generates a CREATE DATABASE SQL statement to be executed in the target server. Essentially, whatever you can do through the SSMS GUI, you can do with T-SQL statements. As a matter of fact, nearly every dialog in SSMS provides the capability to generate the corresponding T-SQL script for the action(s) it performs. This capability can be very useful as a timesaver for tasks that you need to perform repeatedly, avoiding the need to step through the options presented in the GUI.

If you're curious about how SSMS is accomplishing something that doesn't provide the capability to generate a script, you can run SQL Profiler to capture the commands that SSMS is sending to the server. You can use this technique to discover some interesting internal information and insight into the SQL Server system catalogs.

SQL Server Configuration Manager

SQL Server Configuration Manager is a tool provided with SQL Server 2014 for managing the services associated with SQL Server and for configuring the network protocols used by SQL Server. Primarily, SQL Server Configuration Manager is used to start, pause, resume, and stop SQL Server services and to view or change service properties.

SQL Server Agent

SQL Server Agent is a scheduling tool integrated into SSMS that allows convenient definition and execution of scheduled scripts and maintenance jobs. SQL Server Agent also handles automated alerts—for example, if the database runs out of space.

SQL Server Agent is a Windows service that runs on the same machine as the SQL Server Database Engine. The SQL Server Agent service can be started and stopped through either SSMS, the SQL Server Configuration Manager, or the ordinary Windows Services Manager.

In enterprise situations in which many SQL Server machines need to be managed together, the SQL Server Agent can be configured to distribute common jobs to multiple servers through the use of multiserver administration. This capability is most helpful in a wide architecture scenario, in which many SQL Server instances are performing the same tasks with the databases. Jobs are managed from a single SQL Server machine, which is responsible for maintaining the jobs and distributing the job scripts to each target server. The results of each job are maintained on the target servers but can be observed through a single interface.

If you had 20 servers that all needed to run the same job, you could check the completion status of that job in moments instead of logging in to each machine and checking the status 20 times.

The SQL Server Agent also handles event forwarding. Any system events recorded in the Windows system event log can be forwarded to a single machine. This gives a busy administrator a single place to look for errors.

More information about how to accomplish these tasks, as well as other information on the SQL Server Agent, is available in Chapter 13, "SQL Server Agent."

SQL Server Profiler

The SQL Server Profiler is a GUI interface to the SQL Trace feature of SQL Server that captures the queries and results flowing to and from the Database Engine. It is analogous to a network sniffer, although it does not operate on quite that low a level. The Profiler can capture and save a complete record of all the T-SQL statements passed to the server and the occurrence of SQL Server events such as deadlocks, logins, and errors. You can use a series of filters to pare down the results when you want to drill down to a single connection or even a single query.

You can use the SQL Profiler to perform these helpful tasks:

▶ You can capture the exact SQL statements sent to the server from an application for which source code is not available (for example, third-party applications).

▶ You can capture all the queries sent to SQL Server for later playback on a test server. This capability is extremely useful for performance testing with live query traffic.

▶ If your server is encountering recurring access violations (AVs), you can use the Profiler to reconstruct what happened leading up to an AV.

▶ The Profiler shows basic performance data about each query. When your users start hammering your server with queries that cause hundreds of table scans, the Profiler can easily identify the culprits.

▶ For complex stored procedures, the Profiler can identify which portion of the procedure is causing the performance problem.

▶ You can audit server activity in real time.

More information on SQL Server Profiler is available in Chapter 5, "SQL Server Profiler."

> **NOTE**
>
> SQL Server Profiler, a favorite tool of database administrators (DBAs) and developers, is unfortunately listed as a deprecated feature in SQL Server 2014. It's still available and supported but is expected to be eliminated in some future version of SQL Server. The replacement for SQL Server Profiler is Extended Events. SQL Server 2014 provides a mechanism for creating, managing, and viewing Extended Events within SSMS. For more information on using Extended Events in SQL Server 2014, see Chapter 39, "Monitoring SQL Server Performance."

Replication

Replication is a server-based tool that you can use to synchronize data between two or more databases. Replication can send data from one SQL Server instance to another, or it can replicate data to Oracle, Access, or any other database that is accessible via ODBC or OLE DB.

SQL Server supports three kinds of replication:

▶ Snapshot replication

▶ Transactional replication

▶ Merge replication

The availability and functionality of replication might be restricted, depending on the edition of SQL Server 2014 you are running.

> **NOTE**
>
> Replication copies the changes to data from your tables and indexed views, but it does not normally re-create indexes or triggers at the target. It is common to have different indexes on replication targets than on the source to support different requirements.

Snapshot Replication

With snapshot replication, the server takes a picture, or snapshot, of the data in a table at a single point in time. Usually, if this operation is scheduled, the target data is simply replaced at each update. This form of replication is appropriate for small data sets, infrequent update periods (or for a one-time replication operation), or management simplicity.

Transactional Replication

Initially set up with a snapshot, the server maintains downstream replication targets by reading the transaction log at the source and applying each change at the targets. For every insert, update, and delete operation, the server sends a copy of the operation to every downstream database. This is appropriate if low-latency replicas are needed. Transactional replication can typically keep databases in sync within about five seconds of latency, depending on the underlying network infrastructure. Keep in mind that transactional replication does not guarantee identical databases at any given point in time. Rather, it guarantees that each change at the source will eventually be propagated to the targets. If you need to guarantee that two databases are transactionally identical, you should look into distributed transactions or database mirroring.

Transactional replication might be used for a website that supports a huge number of concurrent browsers but only a few updates, such as a large and popular messaging board. All updates would be done against the replication source database and would be replicated in near real time to all the downstream targets. Each downstream target could support several web servers, and each incoming web request would be balanced among the web farm. If the system needed to be scaled to support more read requests, you could simply add more web servers and databases and add the database to the replication scheme.

Merge Replication

With snapshot and transactional replication, a single source of data exists from which all the replication targets are replenished. In some situations, it might be necessary or desirable to allow the replication targets to accept changes to the replicated tables and merge these changes together at some later date.

Merge replication allows data to be modified by the subscribers and synchronized at a later time. This synchronization could be as soon as a few seconds, or it could be a day later.

Merge replication would be helpful for a sales database that is replicated from a central SQL Server database out to several dozen sales laptops. As the sales personnel make sales calls, they can add new data to the customer database or change errors in the existing data. When the salespeople return to the office, they can synchronize their laptops with the central database. Their changes are submitted, and the laptops get refreshed with whatever new data was entered since the last synchronization.

Immediate Updating

Immediate updating allows a replication target to immediately modify data at the source. This task is accomplished by using a trigger to run a distributed transaction. Immediate updating is performance intensive, but it allows for updates to be initiated from anywhere in the replication architecture.

More details on replication are available in Chapter 43, "Data Replication."

SQL Server AlwaysOn Features

For SQL Server high availability needs, SQL Server 2014 provides a feature referred to as AlwaysOn. The AlwaysOn features provide SQL Server administrators more power and flexibility in their efforts toward providing both high availability and disaster recovery. AlwaysOn is not a technology in and of itself but rather the grouping of the latest high-availability and disaster-recovery features in SQL Server.

The AlwaysOn features consist of AlwaysOn Availability Groups and AlwaysOn Failover Cluster Instances. The AlwaysOn Availability Groups feature is a high-availability and disaster-recovery solution that provides an enterprise-level alternative to database mirroring, which was designated as a deprecated feature in SQL Server 2012. An availability group can support a failover environment for a discrete set of user databases that fail over together. In addition, a single SQL Server instance can host multiple availability groups. In the event of a failure, each availability group can be configured to fail over to different SQL Server instances. For example, one availability group can fail over to instance 2, another availability group to instance 3, and so on. You no longer need to have a standby server that is capable of handling the full load of your primary server. You can distribute those workloads across multiple lower-powered servers.

An availability group consists of a set of one or more read-write primary databases and from one to four remote secondary copies. The remote secondary databases can be set up as read-only copies that you can run certain backup operations and reporting activity against, taking significant load off the primary server. The real advantage is that this can be done without the maintenance and overhead of creating snapshots of the secondary databases.

The other feature that is part of the AlwaysOn offering is AlwaysOn Failover Cluster Instances. This feature is an enhancement to the existing SQL Server failover clustering, which is based on Windows Server Failover Cluster (WSFC). AlwaysOn Failover Clustering provides higher availability of SQL Server instance after failover. Enhancements in AlwaysOn Failover Cluster Instance over the existing SQL Server failover clustering include the following:

▶ The ability to set up multisite failover clustering for improved site protection

▶ More flexible failover policies to better control instance failover

▶ Better and improved diagnostics capabilities

Within the AlwaysOn Failover Cluster feature, you can provide high availability through redundancy at the server-instance level, referred to as an AlwaysOn *Failover Cluster Instance* (FCI). An FCI is a SQL Server instance that is installed across nodes in a WSFC cluster with shared disk storage (via Fibre Channel or iSCSI SAN) and a shared virtual network name. Through this virtual network name, an FCI appears to your applications as a single instance of SQL Server running on a single computer. The FCI can failover automatically from one WSFC node to another if the current node becomes unavailable. In the event of a failover, the WSFC service transfers ownership of instance's resources to a designated failover node, and the SQL Server instance is then restarted on the failover node.

For more information on AlwaysOn Availability features and SQL Server Failover Clustering, see Chapters 44, "SQL Server Failover Clustering," and 45, "SQL Server AlwaysOn and Availability Groups."

SQL Server Service Broker

SQL Server Service Broker provides a native SQL Server infrastructure that supports asynchronous distributed messaging between database-driven services. Service Broker handles all the hard work of managing coordination among the constructs required for distributed messaging, including transactional delivery and storage, message typing and validation, multithreaded activation and control, event notification, routing, and security.

Service Broker is designed around the basic functions of sending and receiving messages. An application sends messages to a *service*, which is a name for a set of related tasks. An application receives messages from a *queue*, which is a view of an internal table. Service Broker guarantees that an application receives each message exactly once, in the order in which the messages were sent.

Service Broker can be useful for any application that needs to perform processing asynchronously or that needs to distribute processing across a number of computers. An example is a bicycle manufacturer and seller who must provide new and updated parts data to a company that implements a catalog management system. The manufacturer must keep the catalog information up-to-date with its product model data, or it could lose market share or end up receiving orders from distributors based on out-of-date catalog information. When the parts data is updated in the manufacturer's database, a trigger could be invoked to send a message to Service Broker with information about the updated data. Service Broker would then asynchronously deliver the message to the catalog service. The catalog service program would then perform the work in a separate transaction. When this work is performed in a separate transaction, the original transaction in the manufacturer's database can commit immediately. The application avoids system slowdowns that result from keeping the original transaction open while performing the update to the catalog database.

> **NOTE**
>
> There are no significant changes to Service Broker in SQL Server 2014 from what was available in SQL Server 2012 and this topic was deemed beyond the scope of this book. For more information on Service Broker, you can refer to the SQL Server 2014 Books Online reference or the *SQL Server 2012 Unleashed* book, which does include a chapter on Service Broker.

Full-Text and Semantic Search

SQL Server 2014 provides the optional feature to issue full-text queries against plain character-based data in your SQL Server tables. This capability is useful for searching large text fields, such as movie reviews, book descriptions, or case notes. Full-text queries can include words and phrases, or multiple forms of a word or phrase. Full-Text Search capabilities in Microsoft SQL Server 2014 are provided by the Microsoft Full-Text Engine for SQL Server (MSFTESQL). The MSFTESQL service works together with the SQL Server Database Engine. You specify tables or entire databases that you want to index. The full-text indexes are built and maintained outside the SQL Server database files in special full-text indexes stored in the Windows file system. You can specify how often the full-text indexes are updated to balance performance issues with timeliness of the data.

> **NOTE**
>
> Full-text search is an optional component of the SQL Server Database Engine that is not installed by default. For more information on installing this feature, see Chapter 8, "Installing SQL Server 2014."

The SQL Server Database Engine supports basic text searches against specific columns. For example, to find all the rows where a text column contained the word *guru*, you might write the following SQL statement:

```
select *
   from resume
   where description like '%guru%'
```

This statement finds all the rows in the resume table where the description contains the word *guru*. This method has a couple problems, however. First, the search is slow. Because the Database Engine can't index text columns, a full table scan has to be done to satisfy the query. Even if the data were stored in a varchar column instead of a text column, an index may not help because you're looking for *guru* anywhere in the column, not just at the beginning, so the index cannot be used to locate the matching rows. (Chapter 30, "Database Maintenance," contains more information on avoiding such situations.)

What if you wanted to search for the word *guru* anywhere in the table, not just in the description column? What if you were looking for a particular set of skills, such as "SQL" and "ability to work independently?" Full-text indexing addresses these problems. To perform the same search as before with full-text indexing, you might use a query like this:

```
select *
   from resume
   where contains(description, 'guru')
```

To perform a search that looks for a set of skills, you might use a query like this:

```
select *
   from resume
   where contains(*, 'SQL and "ability to work independently"')
```

Semantic Search was introduced in SQL Server 2012. Semantic Search builds upon the existing Full-Text Search feature in SQL Server but enables new scenarios that extend beyond keyword searches. Whereas Full-Text Search lets you query the words in a document, Semantic Search lets you query the meaning of the document. Semantic Search is also called *Statistical Semantic Search* because its intelligence is based on statistics. Semantic Search attempts to improve document searches by understanding the contextual meaning of the terms and tries to provide the most accurate answer from a given document repository. If you use a web search engine like Google, you are already familiar with Semantic Search technology.

The SQL Server Statistical Semantic Search builds its indexes using the indexes created by Full-Text Search. However, before you can use Statistical Semantic Search in SQL Server 2014, you will need to download, install, attach, and register the Semantic Language Statistics Database. This database contains the statistical language models that semantic search depends on.

When you have Semantic Search configured, you can go beyond just searching for specific words or strings in a document. Solutions are possible that include automatic tag extraction, related content discovery, and hierarchical navigation across similar content. For example, you can query the index of key phrases to build the taxonomy for an organization, or you can query the document similarity index to identify resumes that match a particular job description.

```
SELECT Name FROM semantickeyphrasetable (MyTable, *)
    INNER JOIN MyTable ON ID = document_key
    WHERE keyphrase = 'sql'
```

The following is an example of a query that counts the number of documents containing the keyword SQL:

```
SELECT COUNT(*) AS 'Number of SQL documents'
    FROM semantickeyphrasetable (MyTable,*)
    WHERE keyphrase = 'sql'
```

> **NOTE**
>
> There are no significant changes to Full-Text or Semantic Search in SQL Server 2014 from what was available in SQL Server 2012 and this topic was determined to be beyond the scope of this book. For more information on setting up and searching Full-Text Search indexes and using the Semantic Search feature, these topics are covered in the SQL Server 2014 Books Online and are also covered in Chapter 51 in *SQL Server 2012 Unleashed*.

SQL Server Integration Services (SSIS)

SSIS is a platform for building high-performance data integration solutions and workflow solutions. You can build extract, transform, and load (ETL) packages to update data warehouses, interact with external processes, clean and mine data, process analytical objects, and perform administrative tasks. Following are some of the features of SSIS:

▶ Graphical tools and wizards for building, debugging, and deploying SSIS packages

▶ Workflow functions, such as File Transfer Protocol (FTP), SQL statement execution, and more

- ▶ SSIS application programming interfaces (APIs)

- ▶ Complex data transformation for data cleansing, aggregation, merging, and copying

- ▶ An email messaging interface

- ▶ A service-based implementation

- ▶ Support for both native and managed code (C++ or any common language runtime [CLR]-compliant language, such as C# or J#)

- ▶ An SSIS object model

SSIS is a tool that helps address the needs of getting data—which is often stored in many different formats, contexts, file systems, and locations—from one place to another. In addition, the data often requires significant transformation and conversion processing as it is being moved around. Common uses of SSIS might include the following:

- ▶ Exporting data out of SQL Server tables to other applications and environments (for example, ODBC or OLE DB data sources, flat files)

- ▶ Importing data into SQL Server tables from other applications and environments (for example, ODBC or OLE DB data sources, flat files)

- ▶ Initializing data in some data replication situations, such as initial snapshots

- ▶ Aggregating data (that is, data transformation) for distribution to/from data marts or data warehouses

- ▶ Changing the data's context or format before importing or exporting it (that is, data conversion)

For more information on creating and using SSIS packages, see Chapter 47, "SQL Server Integration Services."

SQL Server Analysis Services (SSAS)

Within the SSAS capabilities, tabular and multidimensional solutions are built using SQL Server Data Tools and are intended for corporate BI projects that run on a standalone Analysis Services instance. Both solutions yield high performance analytical databases that integrate easily with Excel, Reporting Services reports, and other BI applications. Both solutions result in standalone databases that can be used by any client application that supports Analysis Services:

- ▶ Multidimensional and data mining solutions use OLAP modeling constructs (cubes and dimensions) and MOLAP, ROLAP, or HOLAP storage that uses disk as the primary data storage for pre-aggregated data.

- ▶ Tabular solutions use relational modeling constructs such as tables and relationships for modeling data and the in-memory analytics engine for storing and calculating data. Most, if not all, of the model is stored in RAM and is often much faster than its multidimensional counterpart.

SSAS provides a rich set of data mining algorithms to enable business users to mine data, looking for specific patterns and trends. These data mining algorithms can be used to analyze data through a Unified Dimensional Model (UDM) or directly from a physical data store.

For multidimensional, SSAS uses both server and client components to supply OLAP and data mining functionality for BI applications. SSAS consists of the analysis server, process-ing services, integration services, and a number of data providers. It has both server-based and client-/local-based analysis services capabilities. This essentially provides a complete platform for SSAS. The basic components within SSAS are all focused on building and managing data cubes.

SSAS allows you to build dimensions and cubes from heterogeneous data sources. It can access relational OLTP databases, multidimensional data databases, text data, and any other source that has an OLE DB provider available. You don't have to move all your data into a SQL Server database first; you just connect to its source. In addition, SSAS allows a designer to implement OLAP cubes, using a variety of physical storage techniques directly tied to data aggregation requirements and other performance considerations.

SSAS is commonly used to perform the following tasks:

▶ Perform trend analysis to predict the future. For example, based on how many widgets you sold last year, how many will you sell next year?

▶ Combine otherwise disconnected variables to gain insight into past performance. For example, was there any connection between widget sales and rainfall patterns? Searching for unusual connections between your data points is a typical data mining exercise.

▶ Perform offline summaries of commonly used data points for instant access via a web interface or custom interface. For example, a relational table might contain one row for every click on a website. SSAS can be used to summarize these clicks by hour, day, week, and month and then to further categorize them by business line.

Analysis Services in SQL Server 2014 includes PowerPivot for Excel and PowerPivot for SharePoint. PowerPivot for Excel and SharePoint are client and server components that integrate Analysis Services with Excel and SharePoint. PowerPivot for Excel is an add-in that allows you to create PowerPivot workbooks that can assemble and relate large amounts of data from different sources. PowerPivot workbooks typically contain large, multidimensional datasets that use PivotTables and PivotCharts in a worksheet. The PowerPivot add-in provides rapid calculations for the large data that you assemble.

PowerPivot for SharePoint extends SharePoint and Excel Services to add server-side processing, collaboration, and document management support for the PowerPivot workbooks that you publish to SharePoint.

Together, the PowerPivot client add-in and server components provide an end-to-end solution that furthers business intelligence data analysis for Excel users on the workstation and on SharePoint sites.

SSAS is a complex topic. For more information on MDX, data cubes, and ways to use data warehousing analysis services, see Chapter 46, "SQL Server 2014 Analysis Services."

SQL Server Reporting Services (SSRS)

SQL Server Reporting Services is a server-based reporting platform that delivers enterprise, web-enabled reporting functionality so you can create reports that draw content from a variety of data sources, publish reports in various formats, and centrally manage security and subscriptions.

Reporting Services includes the following core components:

▶ A complete set of tools you can use to create, manage, and view reports

▶ A report server component that hosts and processes reports in a variety of formats, including HTML, PDF, TIFF, Excel, CSV, and Open Office XML (Excel and Word formats)

▶ An API that allows developers to integrate or extend data and report processing into custom applications or to create custom tools to build and manage reports

There are two design tools for building reports: Report Designer, which is part of SQL Server Data Tools (SSDT), a powerful development tool system integrated with Visual Studio; and Report Builder 3.0 (RB3), which is a simpler point-and-click tool that you use to design ad hoc reports. Both report design tools provide a WYSIWYG experience.

Reports are described using the Report Definition Language (RDL). RDL contains the description of the report layout, formatting information, and instructions on how to fetch the data. After a report is defined, it can be deployed on the report server, where it can be managed, secured, and delivered to a variety of formats, including HTML, Excel, PDF, TIFF, and XML. Various delivery, caching, and execution options are also available, as are scheduling and historical archiving.

For more information on designing and deploying reports using SSRS, see Chapter 48, "SQL Server 2014 Reporting Services."

Master Data Services

Master Data Services (MDS) provides a much needed capability around the management of core data within a complex data environment. Microsoft recognized that key to delivering data to applications also meant developing technology around improving data quality. By using Microsoft's Master Data Services, organizations can align operational and analytical data across the enterprise and across lines of business systems with a guaranteed level of data quality for most core data categories (such as customer data, product data, and other core data of the business).

Microsoft has created data stewardship capabilities complete with workflows and notifications of any business user who might be impacted by core data change. Managing hierarchies is also an important part of mastering data that has a natural hierarchical structure, such as customer hierarchies (parent company to subsidiaries and so on). Each master data change within the system is treated as a transaction; and the user, date, and time of each change are logged, as well as pertinent audit details, such as type of change, member code, and prior versus new value. In addition to being a very useful audit trail, the transaction log can be used to selectively reverse changes. Customizable data quality rules create default values, enable data validation, and trigger actions such as email notifications and workflows. Rules can be built by IT professionals or business users directly from the stewardship portal. You can work with an easy to use MDS Excel plug-in or work directly with MDS via MDS web services/APIs using your favorite programming languages (C# and so on). There is also a browser-based capability that allows some drag-and-drop master data management along with extensive MDS configuration (see Chapter 50, "Master Data Services").

Data Quality Services

Within the same Master Data Management family is SQL Server Data Quality Services (DQS) that complements MDS and is usable by other key data manipulation components within the SQL Server environment. This feature allows you to build a knowledge base of data rules and use those to perform a variety of critical data quality tasks, including correction, enrichment, standardization, and de-duplication of your data. Microsoft has also tooled these data cleansing capabilities up by using cloud-based reference data services (provided by industry data providers). This also includes the ability to do some basic data profiling to better understand the integrity and overall data quality state of your core data.

There are two primary components to DQS: a Data Quality Server and Data Quality Client. The Data Quality Server is a SQL Server instance feature that consists of three SQL Server catalogs with data quality features and functionality. The Data Quality Client is a SQL Server shared feature that is usable by anyone needing to manage, analyze, or visualize their data quality. These features are available as a DQS Cleansing component in Integration Services and MDS data quality functionality. See Chapter 49, "Data Quality Services," for more on this feature.

SQL Server 2014 Editions

You can choose from several editions of SQL Server 2014. The edition you choose depends on your database and data processing needs, as well as the Windows platform on which you want to install it.

For actual deployment of SQL Server in a production environment, you can choose from any edition of SQL Server 2014 except the Developer Edition and the Evaluation Edition. Which edition you choose to deploy depends on your system requirements and need for SQL Server components.

The following sections examine the different editions of SQL Server and discuss their features and capabilities. Using this information, you can better choose which edition provides the appropriate solution for you.

SQL Server 2014 Standard Edition

The Standard Edition of SQL Server 2014 is the version intended for the masses—those running small- to medium-sized systems who don't require the performance, scalability, and availability features provided by Enterprise Edition. Standard Edition scalability is limited to the lesser of 4 sockets or 16 cores. The maximum amount of memory Server 2014 Standard Edition can utilize is 128GB.

SQL Server 2014 Standard Edition includes the following features:

▶ CLR procedures, functions, and data types

▶ SQL Server Analysis Services—Multidimensional

▶ Service Broker

▶ Reporting Services

▶ SQL Server Integration Services

▶ Full-Text Search

▶ Built-in XML support

▶ Spatial indexes

▶ SQL Server Profiler and performance analysis tools

▶ SQL Server Management Studio

▶ Policy-Based Management

▶ Replication

▶ Two-node failover clustering

▶ Database mirroring (safety full mode only)

▶ Log shipping

▶ Contained Databases

▶ Backup compression

▶ Encrypted Backups

▶ Buffer Pool Extension (64 bit only)

▶ Delayed Durability

The Standard Edition can be installed on any of the Windows Server 2008 SP2 and Windows Server 2012 platforms, as well as Windows 7 SP1 Ultimate, Enterprise, or Professional Editions, and Windows 8 and Windows 8.1.

The Standard Edition should meet the needs of most departmental and small to midsized applications. However, if you need more scalability, availability, advanced security or performance features, or comprehensive analysis features, you should implement the Enterprise Edition of SQL Server 2014.

SQL Server 2014 Enterprise Edition

The Enterprise Edition of SQL Server 2014 is the most comprehensive and complete edition available. It provides the most scalability and availability of all editions and is intended for systems that require high performance and availability, such as large-volume websites, data warehouses, and high-throughput online transaction processing (OLTP) systems.

SQL Server 2014 Enterprise Edition supports as much memory and as many CPUs as supported by the operating system on which it is installed. It can be installed on any of the Windows Server 2008 SP2 and Windows Server 2012 platforms.

In addition, SQL Server 2014 Enterprise Edition provides performance enhancements, such as parallel queries, table and index partitioning, In-Memory OLTP, Resource Governor, indexed views, and enhanced read-ahead scanning, as well as enhanced availability and security features.

Which version is right for you? The next section explores the feature sets of Enterprise and Standard Editions so that you can decide which one provides the features you need.

Differences Between the Enterprise and Standard Editions of SQL Server

For deploying SQL Server 2014 in a server environment, either the Standard Edition or Enterprise Edition of SQL Server is a logical choice. To help you decide between the two editions, Table 1.1 compares the major features that each edition supports.

TABLE 1.1   SQL Server 2014 Feature Comparison: Enterprise and Standard Editions

Feature	Enterprise Edition	Standard Edition
Max number of processors/cores	OS maximum	4 sockets or 16 cores
64-bit support	Yes	Yes
CLR runtime integration	Yes	Yes
Full-Text and Semantic Search	Yes	Yes
Native XML support	Yes	Yes
XML indexing	Yes	Yes
FILESTREAM support	Yes	Yes
FileTable	Yes	Yes
Spatial data support	Yes	Yes
SQL Server Integration Services	Yes	Yes
Database Mail	Yes	Yes
Policy-Based Management	Yes	Yes
SQL Profiler	Yes	Yes
Integration Services with Basic Transforms	Yes	Yes
Integration Services–Advanced Transforms	Yes	No

Feature	Enterprise Edition	Standard Edition
Star Join Query Optimization	Yes	No
Change Data Capture	Yes	No
Service Broker	Yes	Yes
Reporting Services	Yes	Yes
Change Tracking	Yes	Yes
Replication	Yes	Yes
Log Shipping	Yes	Yes
Database mirroring	Yes	Yes (single REDO thread with Safety FULL only)
Database snapshots	Yes	No
Contained databases	Yes	Yes
Indexed views	Yes	Yes (can be created, but automatic matching by Query Optimizer not supported)
Updatable distributed partitioned views	Yes	No
Table and index partitioning	Yes	No
Online index operations	Yes	No
Parallel index operations	Yes	No
Parallel DBCC	Yes	No
Online page and file restoration	Yes	No
Hot Add Memory and CPU	Yes	No
Buffer Pool Extension	Yes	Yes
In-Memory OLTP	Yes	No
Delayed Durability	Yes	Yes
xVelocity memory-optimized columnstore indexes	Yes	No
Fast recovery	Yes	No
Data compression	Yes	No
Compressed backups	Yes	Yes
Encrypted backups	Yes	Yes
Resource Governor	Yes	No
Fine-grained encryption	Yes	No
Transparent data encryption	Yes	No
Failover clustering	Yes	Yes (2-node only)
AlwaysOn Availability features	Yes	No
Multiple-instance support	50	50
PowerPivot for SharePoint	Yes	No

Feature	Enterprise Edition	Standard Edition
Master Data Services	Yes	No
Data Quality Services	Yes	No
Application and multiserver management	Yes	Yes (as a managed instance only)

Other SQL Server 2014 Editions

The Standard and Enterprise Editions of SQL Server 2014 are intended for server-based deployment of applications. In addition, the following editions are available for other specialized uses:

▶ Business Intelligence Edition

▶ Developer Edition

▶ Web Edition

▶ Express Edition

Business Intelligence Edition

The Business Intelligence Edition of SQL Server 2014 provides a comprehensive platform for building and deploying secure, scalable, and manageable BI solutions. The features supported by the Business Intelligence Edition fall somewhere between the Enterprise and Standard Editions. For example, the SQL Server Database Engine has the same memory and processor limits as the Standard Edition, but Analysis Services and Reporting Services support up to the OS maximum like the Enterprise Edition. The Business Intelligence Edition also fully supports all BI features supported by the Enterprise Edition such as PowerPivot for SharePoint, data-mining features, BI Semantic Model features, and all Reporting Services features.

The Business Intelligence Edition can be installed in any of the environments supported by the Enterprise Edition.

Developer Edition

The Developer Edition of SQL Server 2014 is a full-featured version intended for development and end-user testing only. It includes all the features and functionality of Enterprise Edition, at a much lower cost, but the licensing agreement prohibits production deployment of databases using Developer Edition.

To provide greater flexibility during development, Developer Edition can be installed in any of the following environments.

▶ Any Windows Server 2012 editions

▶ Any Windows Server 2008 R2 SP1 editions

▶ Any Windows Server 2008 SP2 editions

▶ Windows 8 or 8.1

▶ Windows 7 SP1

Web Edition

SQL Server 2014 Web Edition is a lower total-cost-of-ownership option, intended for small- to large-scale web hosts and websites.

Web Edition includes most of the core database features and capabilities of the SQL Server Standard Edition with the following key differences:

▶ The maximum memory per instance is limited to 64GB.

▶ It does not support failover clustering.

▶ It can participate in replication as a subscriber only.

▶ Database mirroring support is limited to being a witness only.

▶ It does not include Analysis Services.

▶ It supports Service Broker as a client only.

▶ It provides limited support for Integration Services and Reporting Services features.

Web Edition can be installed in any of the following environments:

▶ Any Windows Server 2012 editions

▶ Any Windows Server 2008 R2 SP1 editions

▶ Any Windows Server 2008 SP2 editions

Express Edition

SQL Server Express Edition is a free, lightweight, embeddable, and redistributable version of SQL Server 2014. It includes a stripped-down version of SQL Server Management Studio, called SQL Server Management Studio Express, for easily managing a SQL Server Express instance and its databases. The Express Edition of SQL Server 2014 is intended for users who are running applications that require a locally installed database, often on mobile systems, and who spend at least some time disconnected from the network. The core Database Engine of Express Edition is the same as the other SQL Server editions, so as your needs grow, your applications seamlessly work with the rest of the SQL Server product family.

There are three flavors of Express Edition: Express, Express with Tools, and Express with Advanced Services. The basic Express Edition is essentially just the Database Engine for a small-footprint installation. Express with Tools includes SSMS, and Express Edition with Advanced Services includes support for Full-Text and Semantic Search and limited support for Reporting Services. SQL Server 2014 also provides a version of SQL Server Express called SQL Server Express LocalDB. Express LocalDB is a lightweight version of Express that has all of its programmability features yet runs in user mode and has a fast, zero-configuration installation and a short list of prerequisites.

The Express Edition can be installed in any of the following environments:

▶ Any Windows Server 2012 editions

▶ Any Windows Server 2008 R2 SP1 editions

▶ Any Windows Server 2008 SP2 editions

▶ Windows 8 or 8.1

▶ Windows 7 SP1

Express Edition supports many of the same features as the Web Edition, with the following exceptions:

▶ It is limited to using a maximum of one socket (or four cores) and 1GB of memory.

▶ It limits the maximum database size to 10GB.

▶ It does not include Analysis Services.

▶ It does not include SQL Server Agent.

▶ It includes only limited support for SQL Server Integration Services.

▶ It supports Service Broker as a client only.

▶ It includes SSMS only if you install Express with Advanced Services or Express with Tools.

▶ It can participate in database mirroring as a witness only.

▶ It can participate in replication only as a subscriber.

If you need a bit more than the Express Edition offers, but not as much as the Standard Edition, Microsoft also provides the Express Edition with Advanced Services. The Express Edition with Advanced Services includes support for Full-Text Search and limited support of Reporting Services for web reporting.

SQL Server Licensing

In addition to feature sets, one of the determining factors in choosing a SQL Server edition is cost. There are two primary methods for licensing SQL Server: Server/Client Access License (CAL)-based licensing and Core-based Licensing.

> **NOTE**
>
> This section is intended to provide just an overview of SQL Server licensing options. In some environments, properly licensing SQL Server can be a complicated task. For more details and specifics on how to properly license your SQL Server environments, refer to the SQL Server 2014 Licensing Guide available at www.microsoft.com/sql.

Core-based license includes unlimited client device access. Additional server licenses, seat licenses, and Internet connector licenses are not required. In SQL Server 2014, core based licensing is based on the total number of processor cores in the server, with the minimum purchase of four core licenses per processor. When licensing a physical server, you must purchase a license for all the cores in the server. (Virtual server licensing is discussed later in this section.)

For those who prefer the more familiar server/CAL licensing or for environments in which the number of client devices connecting to SQL Server is small and known, two server/CAL-based licensing models are also available:

▶ **Device CALs**—A device CAL is required for a device (for example, PC, workstation, terminal, PDA, mobile phone) to access or use the services or functionality of Microsoft SQL Server. The server plus device CAL model is likely to be the more cost-effective choice if there are multiple users per device (for example, in a call center).

▶ **User CALs**—A SQL server user CAL is required for a user (for example, an employee, a customer, a partner) to access or use the services or functionality of Microsoft SQL Server. The server plus user CAL model is likely to be more cost effective if there are multiple devices per user (for example, a user who has a desktop PC, laptop, tablet device, and so forth).

The server/CAL licensing model requires purchasing a license for each system running SQL Server 2014 as well as a license for each client device or user that accesses any SQL Server 2014 installation. Each server license allows customers to run any number of SQL Server instances in a single system, either physical or virtual. Server/per-seat CAL licensing is intended for environments in which the number of clients per server is relatively low and access from outside the company firewall is not required, or when a fixed number of users will be accessing multiple SQL Server systems or new servers will be added over time. Once customers have purchased the necessary CALs, only additional server licenses are needed for new SQL Server system deployments.

To access a licensed SQL Server, each user or device must have a SQL Server CAL that is the same version or later than the version of SQL Server being accessed. For example, a SQL Server 2014 CAL provides access to any number of 2014 or previous versions of SQL Server instances that have a server license within the customer's organization, regardless of the platform (32-bit, 64-bit, or IA64) or product edition, including legacy SQL Server Workgroup and SQL Server for Small Business edition servers.

Be aware that using a middle-tier or transaction server that pools or multiplexes database connections does not reduce the number of CALs required. A CAL is still required for each distinct client workstation that connects through the middle tier. (Core-based licensing might be preferable in these environments due to its simplicity and affordability when the number of clients is unknown and potentially large.)

Web Edition Licensing

The Web Edition of SQL Server 2014 is available only for third party software service providers via a Services Provider License Agreement (SPLA).

Developer Edition Licensing

The Developer Edition of SQL Server 2014 is licensed per user, and its use is limited to designing, developing, and testing purposes only.

Express Edition Licensing

The Express Edition of SQL Server 2014 is available via free download from www.microsoft.com/sql. Developers can redistribute it with their applications at no cost by simply registering for redistribution rights with Microsoft. The Express Edition does not require a CAL when it is used on a standalone basis. If it connects to a SQL Server instance running Enterprise, Business Intelligence, or Standard Edition, a separate user or device CAL is required for the device running Express Edition unless the SQL Server instance it connects to is licensed using core-based licensing.

Choosing a Licensing Model

Which licensing model should you choose? Core-based licensing is generally required in instances in which the server will be accessed via the Web. This type of licensing includes servers used in Internet situations or servers that will be accessed from both inside and outside an organization's firewall. Core-based licensing might also be appropriate and cost effective for internal environments in which there are a very large number of users in relation to the number of SQL Server machines. An additional advantage to the core-based model is that it eliminates the need to count the number of devices connecting to SQL Server, which can be difficult to manage on an ongoing basis for a large organization.

Using the server/per-seat CAL model is usually the most cost-effective choice in internal environments in which client-to-server ratios are low. The CAL model is usually more cost effective when you have multiple SQL server systems and the number of users/devices can be easily quantified.

Mixing Licensing Models

You can mix both core-based and server/CAL licensing models in your organization. If the Internet servers for your organization are segregated from the servers used to support internal applications, you can choose to use core-based licensing for the Internet servers and server/CAL licensing for internal SQL Server instances and user devices.

Keep in mind that you do not need to purchase CALs to allow internal users to access a server already licensed via a server core license: The core licenses allow access to that server for all users.

Licensing SQL Server of High Availability

In SQL Server 2014, two or more servers can be configured in a high availability mode, such that if one server fails, its processing will be picked up, recovered, and continued by another server. SQL Server 2014 offers the following types of failover support:

▶ Database mirroring

▶ Two-node Failover clustering

▶ AlwaysOn Availability Groups

▶ Log shipping

If your environment uses an active/passive configuration in which at least one server in the failover configuration is truly passive, the secondary server does not need to be separately licensed if the primary server is licensed with Software Assurance (SA). A truly passive SQL Server instance cannot be serving SQL Server data to clients or running active SQL Server workloads unless processing has been failed over to it. If the secondary server is serving data, such as reports to clients running active SQL Server workloads, or performing any "work", such as additional backups being made from secondary servers, then separate SQL Server licenses must be acquired for the secondary server.

If SQL Server 2014 is licensed using the Per Core model, the total number of core licenses for an active/passive configuration must be based on the server that requires the higher number of licenses. If the number of cores on the passive server exceeds the number of cores on the active server, additional core licenses must be acquired for the number of additional cores on the passive computer so that the secondary server will be properly licensed in the event of a failover.

> **NOTE**
>
> Primary server licenses under Software Assurance provide support for only one secondary server. Any additional secondary servers must be separately licensed for SQL Server.

In an active/active failover configuration, all servers in the failover configuration regularly process information independently unless a server fails, at which point one server or more takes on the additional workload of the failed server. In this environment, all servers must be fully licensed using either per-core licensing or server/CAL licensing. Keep in mind that in some log shipping and database mirroring configurations, the standby (passive) server can be used as a read-only reporting server installation. Under this usage, the standby server is no longer "passive" and must be licensed accordingly.

When using AlwaysOn Availability Groups for SQL Server 2014 high availability, you can configure multiple databases that will failover as a unit, with support for up to eight active secondary servers and two synchronous secondary servers. The AlwaysOn Availability Groups feature provides the ability to use secondary servers for more than just passive failover support, such as improving the performance of primary, reporting and backup workloads by balancing workloads across instances. This capability helps provide a better return on hardware investment. Because secondary servers in AlwaysOn Availability Groups are often used to support these additional workload scenarios, the servers used for failover purposes are typically no longer truly passive, so all servers participating in AlwaysOn Availability Groups must be fully licensed.

Licensing SQL Server in a Virtual Environment

SQL Server is increasingly being deployed in virtual environments such as VMWare VSphere or Microsoft Hyper-V. A virtual environment exists when an operating system is somehow emulated (that is, does not run directly on the physical hardware). When you're running virtualization software on a system, one or several applications and their associated operating system environments can run on one physical server host inside their respective virtual environments.

When deploying SQL Server 2014 software in virtualized environments, you have the choice to license either individual virtual machines as needed, or to license for maximum virtualization in highly virtualized, private cloud, or dynamic environments.

When deploying SQL Server 2014 inside a virtual operating environment (OSE) that requires just a fraction of a physical server, you may want to consider licensing individual virtual machines (VMs). Purchasing a license for an individual virtual operating system environment allows you to run one or more instances of SQL Server 2014 within that virtual OSE only.

The license for a virtual OSE can be a server/CAL license or a core-based license. If using a core-based license, you must purchase a core license for each virtual core that is allocated to the virtual machine with a minimum of four cores per VM. If you are using the Server+CAL licensing model, which is available for SQL Server 2014 Standard and Business Intelligence editions, you need only purchase one server license for each VM running SQL Server 2014, regardless of the number of virtual processors allocated to the VM. As with the Server+CAL licensing on physical servers, each user or device accessing SQL Server 2014 in a VM will require a SQL Server 2014 CAL.

If you are running SQL Server 2014 Enterprise Edition and all physical cores in the machine have been licensed, but not under Software Assurance (SA), you may run an unlimited number of SQL Server instances within the OSEs within that VM host up to the total number of core licenses purchased. For example, if you have a server with 32 cores and have licensed all 32 cores, you can run SQL Server 2014 in up to 32 VMs regardless of the number of virtual cores assigned to each VM. If you need to run more VMs than permitted under maximum virtualization, you will need to purchase additional core licenses so that the total number of core licenses equals the number of VMs. If you wanted to run 36 SQL Server VMs in the 32 core server in the previous example, you would need to purchase 4 additional core licenses.

Maximum virtualization can be achieved by licensing the entire physical server with Enterprise Edition core licenses and covering those licenses with Software Assurance. With SA coverage on all Enterprise Edition core licenses, you can run any number of SQL Server 2014 instances in any number of OSEs within the VM host, enabling you to deploy an unlimited number of VMs to handle dynamic workloads and fully utilize your hardware computing capacity.

Summary

This chapter examined the various platforms that support SQL Server 2014 and reviewed and compared the various editions of SQL Server 2014 that are available. Which platform and edition are appropriate to your needs depends on scalability, availability, performance, licensing costs, and limitations. The information provided in this chapter should help start you in the right direction to making the appropriate choice.

Chapter 2, "What's New in SQL Server 2014," takes a closer look at the new features and capabilities provided with SQL Server 2014.

What's New in SQL Server 2014

With SQL Server currently on a 2-year release cycle, each release is more of an evolutionary change from the previous release than a revolutionary change. However, Microsoft SQL Server 2014 does introduce some interesting new features, primarily related to improving performance of critical OLTP applications, including memory-optimized tables, Buffer Pool Extension, and Delayed Durability. This chapter introduces the major new features provided in SQL Server 2014 and lists a number of the enhancements to previously available features. Most of these new features and enhancements are covered in more detail in the related chapters of this book.

New SQL Server 2014 Features

So what does SQL Server 2014 have to offer over SQL Server 2012? Following is an overview of the new features provided in SQL Server 2014:

▶ Memory-optimized tables/In-Memory OLTP and Natively Compiled Stored Procedures.

▶ New cardinality estimation logic.

▶ Delayed durability for transactions.

▶ Buffer Pool Extension.

The following sections take a closer look at each of these new features and, where appropriate, provide references to subsequent chapters where you can find more information and detail about the new features.

Memory-Optimized Tables/In-Memory OLTP

Memory-optimized tables are part of the new In-Memory OLTP feature in SQL Server 2014. In-Memory OLTP is a memory-optimized database engine integrated into the SQL Server engine and is designed as a means to significantly improve OLTP performance. In-Memory OLTP achieves significant performance and scalability gains by using:

▶ Algorithms that are optimized for accessing memory-resident data.

▶ Optimistic concurrency control that eliminates logical locks.

▶ Lock free objects that eliminate all physical locks and latches.

▶ Natively compiled stored procedures, which provide significantly better performance than interpreted stored procedures when accessing memory-optimized tables.

The creation and use of memory-optimized tables is covered in Chapter 33, "In-Memory Optimization and the Buffer Pool Extension." Natively complied stored procedures are covered in Chapter 25, "Creating and Managing Stored Procedures," and Chapter 33.

New Cardinality Estimation Logic

The release of SQL Server 2014 brings with it the first new re-design of the Cardinality Estimator since SQL Server 7.0. The cardinality estimation logic has been re-designed in SQL Server 2014 to improve the quality of query plans and ostensibly, query performance. The new cardinality estimator is based on in-depth cardinality estimation research based on what Microsoft has seen and learned over the past 15 years. The new cardinality estimator incorporates assumptions and algorithms that work well on modern OLTP and data warehousing workloads. A completed list of all changes has not been documented, and some are proprietary, but some of the changes are highlighted in Chapter 32, "Indexes and Performance," and Chapter 34, "Understanding Query Optimization."

Delayed Durability for Transactions

To help reduce transaction related latency, SQL Server 2014 introduces the ability to designate some or all transactions as delayed durable. Fully durable transactions, the default in SQL Server from the beginning, return control to the client only after the log records for the transaction have been written to disk. A delayed durable transaction, on the other hand, returns control to the client before the transaction log record has been written to disk. Transaction durability can be controlled at the database level, COMMIT level, or ATOMIC block level. A more in-depth comparison of fully durable and delayed durable transactions and how they are managed, as well as when and how to implement delayed durability, is covered in Chapter 28, "Transaction Management and the Transaction Log."

Buffer Pool Extension

The buffer pool extension feature, available for the 64-bit Enterprise, Developer, or Evaluation editions of SQL Server 2014, provides SQL Server the ability to define a solid-state drive (SSD) as a non-volatile RAM (NvRAM) buffer file location. When the buffer pool fills, the data and index pages are seamlessly written out to SSD. This helps to resolve I/O bottlenecks while improving overall I/O throughput, due to lower latency and better random I/O performance of SSDs versus normal mechanical disk drives. For more information on configuring and using the Buffer Pool Extension, see Chapter 33.

SQL Server Data Tools for Business Intelligence

The tools previously known as Business Intelligence Development Studio (BIDS) and SQL Server Data Tools (SSDT) have been replaced in SQL Server 2014 by SQL Server Data Tools for BI (SSDT BI). SSDT BI is used to create SQL Server Analysis Services (SSAS) models, SQL Server Reporting Services (SSRS) reports, and SQL Server Integration Services (SSIS) packages. SSDT BI is based on Microsoft Visual Studio 2012 and supports SSAS and SSRS for SQL Server 2014 and earlier, but SSIS projects are limited to SQL Server 2014. However, SSDT BI cannot be installed using the SQL Server 2014 Setup. Instead, you must download it separately from the Microsoft Download Center. The SQL Server Installation Center provides a link to the download on the Tools as described in Chapter 8, "Installing SQL Server 2014."

SQL Server 2014 Enhancements

In addition to the brand new features in SQL Server 2014, there are a number of enhancements to existing features provided with SQL Server 2014. The following sections provide an overview of some of the major enhancements.

Resource Governor Enhancements

In previous versions of SQL Server, the Resource Governor was limited to managing workloads based on CPU and memory resources. SQL Server 2014 added the ability to manage workloads based on physical I/O. This is a significant enhancement because physical I/O is often the main resource bottleneck in a SQL Server environment. For more information on these new enhancements to Resource Governor, see Chapter 41, "Managing Workloads with the Resource Governor."

Security Enhancements

SQL Server 2014 provides a number of security related enhancements as follows:

▶ CONNECT ANY DATABASE—A server-level permission that allows a login to connect to all databases that currently exist and any new databases that are created in the future.

▶ IMPERSONATE ANY LOGIN—A server-level permission that allows a middle-tier process to impersonate the account of clients connecting to the database.

▶ SELECT ALL USER SECURABLES—A server-level permission that allows a login to view data in all databases that the user can connect to.

▶ `ALTER ANY DATABASE EVENT SESSION`—A database-level permission typically used to give a role the ability to read metadata associated with a database for monitoring purposes.

For more information on these enhancements, see Chapter 15, "Security and User Administration."

Backup and Restore Enhancements

SQL Server 2014 offers the following three main backup and restore enhancements:

▶ **SQL Server Backup to URL**—This option enables SQL Server to perform backup and restore operations utilizing Windows Azure Blob Storage Service. SQL Server 2014 provides the ability to use SQL Server Management Studio to perform these operations via the Backup task or maintenance plans.

▶ **SQL Server Managed Backup to Windows Azure**—This option is built on SQL Server Backup to URL but it provides more automation around these types of backups utilizing a Windows service that SQL Server provides to manage and schedule database and log backups. This feature provides a great way to utilize cloud storage and get a reliable offsite backup of your database(s).

▶ **Encryption for Backups**—SQL Server 2014 provides the ability to create an encrypted database backup without having to encrypt the database itself.

See Chapters 11, "Database Backup and Restore" and 19, "Working with and Deploying to Azure SQL Database" for more information on these features.

Indexing Enhancements

SQL Server introduces the following indexing enhancements:

▶ Clustered columnstore indexes.

▶ Extended support for online index operations.

▶ Memory-optimized indexes.

▶ System View enhancements.

▶ Transact-SQL enhancements related to indexes.

Columnstore indexes, which were introduced in SQL Server 2012, offer a powerful way to accelerate data warehouse workloads. However, in SQL Server 2012, columnstore indexes were nonclustered only and were not updateable. In SQL Server 2014, clustered columnstore indexes can be defined that are updateable so your workloads can perform insert, update, and delete operations on clustered columnstore indexes. Also new to SQL Server 2014 is the ability to see columnstore indexes in SHOWPLAN displays and a new option to set archival data compression on a columnstore index. These new features are covered in more detail in Chapter 32, "Indexes and Performance," and Chapter 51, "Parallel Data Warehouse."

SQL Server 2014 also includes extended support for online index operations. In particular, the Progress Report: Online Index Operation event class has two new data columns named PartitionId and PartionNumber. These columns provide information about the partition being built during an Online Index operation. You can also now specify a lock priority for online re-index operations in the ALTER INDEX statement. In SQL Server 2014, you can specify how your re-index operation will handle being blocked. You can specify how long it will wait and what to do when the wait is over: terminate and move to the next table, or kill the blocking query, so your re-indexing can complete.

Memory-optimized indexes are new index structures introduced in SQL Server 2014 as well. These indexes are related to memory-optimized tables, which were also introduced in SQL Server 2014. These tables are not stored on disk and live in memory only. The same is true of the indexes on these tables. Memory-optimized tables and the related indexes are discussed in more detail in Chapter 33.

Finally, SQL Server 2014 includes Transact-SQL enhancements that provide the capability to create clustered and nonclustered indexes using an inline specification that is part of the table creation statements. These enhancements are covered in Chapter 22, "Creating and Managing Indexes."

Monitoring Enhancements

SQL Server 2014 also introduces a few new dynamic management views (DMVs) and enhancements to existing DMVs. These have mostly been in support of Availability Groups and managing the lock priority of online operations but have also added some additional columns to several other DMVs. The DMV enhancements include:

- ▶ `sys.xml_indexes`—Includes 3 new columns: `xml_index_type`, `xml_index_type_ description`, and `path_id`.

- ▶ `sys.dm_exec_query_profiles`—New DMV to monitor real time query progress while a query is in execution.

- ▶ `sys.column_store_row_groups`—New DMV that provides clustered columnstore index information on a per-segment basis to help the administrator make system management decisions.

- ▶ `sys.databases`—Includes 3 new columns: `is_auto_create_stats_incremental_on`, `is_query_store_on`, and `resource_pool_id`.

There are also a number of system view enhancements for In-Memory OLTP.

Information about the system view enhancements in SQL Server 2014 is covered in more detail in various chapters throughout the book where appropriate.

SQL Server AlwaysOn and Availability Groups Enhancements

Now, with a couple of years under their belt with these features, Microsoft is starting to open up several of the previously tight limitations such as the number of secondaries allowed. The enhancementes provided in SQL Server 2014 include:

▶ You can use AlwaysOn and Availability Groups with complex data managed through FILESTREAM, even when using Remote Blob Storage and FileTable.

▶ An increase from a max of 4 to up to 8 secondary replicas can be defined for any one availability group.

▶ There can now be up to 3 Synchronous Commit replicas.

▶ Client applications can now achieve failover across multiple subnets (as many as 64) almost as fast as they can achieve failover within a single subnet.

For more information on the AlwaysOn and Availability Groups Enhancements, see Chapter 45, "SQL Server AlwaysOn and Availability Groups."

New Transact-SQL Enhancements

What would a new SQL Server release be without a number of new T-SQL commands and constructs to further expand the power and capabilities of the T-SQL language? However, SQL Server 2014 seems to be the exception.

Besides the T-SQL constructs and syntax elements introduced to support In-Memory OLTP, the only other new T-SQL constructs provided in SQL Server 2014 include the following:

▶ Inline specification of CLUSTERED and NONCLUSTERED indexes in the CREATE TABLE command for disk-based tables. This feature is equivalent to issuing a create table followed by corresponding CREATE INDEX statements (this feature is covered in Chapter 21, "Creating and Managing Tables", and Chapter 22.

▶ The SELECT ... INTO statement can now operate in parallel.

The T-SQL enhancements to support In-Memory OLTP are covered in Chapter 33.

Deprecated and Discontinued Features

In addition to the new and enhanced features in SQL Server 2014, it's important to note the features for which support has been deprecated or discontinued. Deprecated features are ones that still exist in SQL Server 2014, but may not exist in the next or future release of SQL Server. Discontinued features are no longer available. Table 2.1 lists the features that were discontinued in SQL Server 2012 or 2014.

TABLE 2.1   Discontinued Features in SQL Server 2012 and 2014

Discontinued Feature	Replacement
`Makepipe.exe` and `readpipe.exe` commands	None
`BACKUP { DATABASE	LOG } WITH PASSWORD` and `BACKUP { DATABASE	LOG } WITH MEDIAPASSWORD`	None
SQL Mail	Database Mail
`sp_dboption`	`ALTER DATABASE`
90 compatibility level	Support provided only for compatibility levels 100 and higher
`*=` and `=*` `OUTER JOIN` syntax	`LEFT OUTER JOIN` or `RIGHT OUTER JOIN`
`FASTFIRSTROW` hint	`OPTION (FAST 1)`
32-bit Address Windowing Extensions (AWE) and 32-bit Hot Add memory support.	Use a 64-bit operating system
`DATABASEPROPERTY`	`DATABASEPROPERTYEX`
Database user aliases	Replace aliases with a combination of user accounts and database roles.
`COMPUTE / COMPUTE BY`	`ROLLUP`

Table 2.2 lists a number of the deprecated features in SQL Server 2014 along with their replacements, if any. Note that these features are still supported in SQL Server 2014, but may not be in the next or subsequent releases of SQL Server and should be replaced by supported features if possible.

TABLE 2.2   Deprecated Features in SQL Server 2014

Deprecated Feature	Replacement
SQL Server Profiler	Extended Events and the Extended Events GUI in SSMS
`Sqlmaint.exe`	SQL Server Maintenance Plan feature
`RESTORE { DATABASE	LOG } ... WITH DBO_ONLY`	`RESTORE { DATABASE	LOG } ... ... WITH RESTRICTED_USER`
SQL Mail	Database Mail
`sp_dboption`	`ALTER DATABASE`
Ability to return result sets from triggers	None
Database mirroring	AlwaysOn Availability Groups
`sp_dropgroup, sp_helpgroup)`	
`*=` and `=*` `OUTER JOIN` syntax	`LEFT OUTER JOIN` or `RIGHT OUTER JOIN`

Deprecated Feature	Replacement
Remote Servers and associated system procedures (sp_addserver, sp_remote-option, sp_helpremotelogin, and sp_addremotelogin)	Linked servers
SET ROWCOUNT for INSERT, UPDATE, and DELETE statements	TOP keyword
sp_dbcmptlevel	ALTER DATABASE ... SET COMPATIBILITY_LEVEL
BACKUP { DATABASE | LOG } TO TAPE	BACKUP { DATABASE | LOG } TO DISK
sp_helpdevice	sys.backup_devices
SET ANSI_NULLS OFF	ANSI_NULLS, ANSI_PADDING and
SET ANSI_PADDING OFF	CONCAT_NULLS_YIELDS_NULL will always be
SET CONCAT_NULL_YIELDS_NULL OFF	set to ON
SET OFFSETS	None
sp_addtype	CREATE TYPE
sp_droptype	DROP TYPE
'text in row' table option	Use varchar(max), nvarchar(max), and varbinary(max) data types
text, ntext, image data types	Use varchar(max), nvarchar(max), and varbinary(max) data types
CREATE DEFAULT	DEFAULT constraint
DROP DEFAULT	
sp_bindefault	
sp_unbindefault	
CREATE RULE	CHECK constraint
DROP RULE	
sp_bindrule	
sp_unbindrule	
Numerous sp_* system procedures	Related/replacement T-SQL commands
DBCC DBREINDEX	REBUILD option of ALTER INDEX
DBCC INDEXDEFRAG	REORGANIZE option of ALTER INDEX
SETUSER	EXECUTE AS

To help keep track of deprecated features so that you can identify potential future upgrade and compatibility problems, SQL Server 2014 provides the SQL Server: Deprecated Features performance counter and the Deprecation Announcement and Deprecation Final Support event classes, which you can monitor via SQL Server Profiler or SQL Trace.

Summary

SQL Server 2014 provides a number of new and long-awaited features and enhancements. This chapter provides an overview of the new features and enhancements that ship with SQL Server 2014. To learn more, refer to the other chapters referenced here.

The next chapter, Chapter 3, "SQL Server Management Studio" will introduce you to the GUI interface that will be used throughout this book for managing your SQL Server instances and databases.

PART II

SQL Server Tools and Utilities

IN THIS PART

SQL Server Management Studio

SQL Server Management Studio (SSMS) is an integrated application that provides access to most of the graphical tools you can use to perform administrative and development tasks on SQL Server 2014. SSMS was introduced with SQL Server 2005 and replaced the Enterprise Manager, Query Analyzer, and Analysis Manager that were available in SQL Server 2000. Microsoft consolidated all those tools into one, with a focus on providing a tool that suits the needs of both developers and database administrators (DBAs). They furthered this consolidation in SQL Server 2012 by leveraging the Visual Studio shell in SSMS. This integration with the Visual Studio shell is still present in SQL Server 2014.

SSMS is a complicated tool that provides an entry point to almost all of SQL Server's functionality. The functionality that is accessible from SSMS is entirely too much to cover in one chapter. The aim of this chapter is to give a basic overview of SSMS. Other chapters in this book discuss the components of SSMS and provide more detailed coverage.

This chapter first examines the features at the environmental level, focusing on how SSMS behaves and how to best utilize the environment. Next, it looks at the administrative tools and the capabilities to help you better manage your SQL Server environment. Finally, this chapter looks at the development tools available with SSMS and the features available to improve your SQL Server development experience.

What's New in SSMS

SSMS in SQL Server 2014 is essentially the same as it was in SQL Server 2012. There are, however, some features such as memory-optimized tables that are new to SQL Server 2014 and are accessible from SSMS. These new features are not covered in this chapter. They are covered in detail in other chapters in this book that are related to them. For example, refer to Chapter 33, "In-Memory Optimization and the Buffer Pool Extension," for a detailed discussion of memory-optimized tables.

The Integrated Environment

If you have been working with SQL Server for a long time, you may remember the SQL Enterprise Manager that came with SQL Server 6.5. In some respects, with SSMS, Microsoft has moved back to the paradigm that existed then. Like the SQL Server 6.5 Enterprise Manager, SSMS provides an integrated environment where developers and DBAs alike can perform the database tasks they need. The disparate tools such as Query Analyzer, Analysis Manager, and a number of other tools used in SQL Server 2000 are gone. Say hello to SSMS, which provides "one-stop shopping" for most of your database needs.

> **NOTE**
>
> SSMS is built upon the Visual Studio shell. This started with SQL Server 2012 and remains in effect with SQL Server 2014. This move has laid the groundwork to unify the database development environment found in Visual Studio and SSMS. There is some debate regarding which environment provides the best database development environment. There are advantages to each, but the good news is that the use of the Visual Studio shell in SSMS should help unify the Microsoft SQL Server development experience.

Window Management

Figure 3.1 shows a sample configuration for the SSMS main display. The environment and windows displayed are completely customizable, with the exception of the document window area. Figure 3.1 shows the document window area displaying the Object Explorer Details page. The Object Explorer Details page is the default, but other pages, such as a Query Editor window, can take the focus in this tab-oriented section of the SSMS display.

The dialogs that form the rest of the SSMS display are referred to as *components* and include the Registered Servers and Object Explorer windows shown in Figure 3.1, as well as a number of other components that can be displayed via the View menu found at the top of the SSMS display. You can configure each of the component windows in a number of ways; for example, you can have them float, or you can hide, dock, autohide, or display them as tabbed documents in the document window area.

The configuration that you choose for your SSMS display depends on the type of work you do with SQL Server as well as the type of person you are. The Auto Hide feature causes the component window to shrink to a tab along the left or right side of the display. When you mouse over the tab, the window automatically expands and stays expanded as long as the mouse cursor remains in the component window area. Auto Hide helps maximize the working real estate available in the document window for query development and the like. Docking many windows can clutter the screen, but this feature allows you to view many different types of information all at once. This is a matter of personal preference, and SSMS has made it very easy to change.

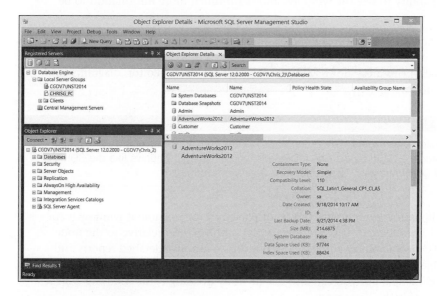

FIGURE 3.1   The SSMS main display.

You can reposition the component windows by dragging and dropping them to the desired locations. When you are in the middle of a drag and drop, rectangular icons with arrows are displayed at different locations on the SSMS window surface. If you mouse over one of these arrowed icons to select the window location, you see the window destination highlighted. If you release your mouse button while the destination is highlighted, the window docks in that position.

Some users at first ignore the arrow icons and keep hovering the window over the location where they want the window to go. Hovering the window over the desired location does not allow you to effectively dock it. You should save yourself some time and aggravation and use the arrow icons for drag-and-drop positioning.

The SSMS window environment also includes nonmodal windows that are sizable. The nonmodal windows allow you to perform multiple tasks at one time without needing to open another instance of the SSMS application. With SSMS, you can launch a backup with the Back Up Database dialog and then continue working with the Object Explorer or other components in SSMS while the backup is running. This capability is a great timesaver and helps improve overall productivity.

Your ability to size the dialog boxes is another user-friendly feature that may seem minor but is quite handy on certain windows. For example, the SQL Server 2000 Enterprise Manager Restore dialog had a fixed size. Viewing the backup set information in this relatively small (nonsizable) dialog box was a challenge. The Restore dialog in SQL Server 2014's SSMS can contain a slew of information related to the backup sets available for restore. The capability to size the windows allows for much more information to be displayed.

The tabbed document window area provides some usability improvements as well. This area, as described earlier, is fixed and is always displayed in SSMS. Component windows can be displayed in this area, along with windows for the Query Editor, diagrams, and other design windows.

> **NOTE**
>
> In earlier versions, you could change the environment from a tabbed display to multiple-document interface (MDI) mode. The MDI mode would manage windows like the SQL Server 2000 Query Analyzer. This option has been removed.

One particularly useful window that can be displayed in the document window is the Object Explorer Details page. This window displays information relative to the node selected in the Object Explorer and includes options to produce detailed reports and graphs. The Object Explorer Details page is displayed in the document window by default when SSMS is launched, but you can also display it by pressing F7 or choosing Object Explorer Details from the View menu.

The Object Explorer Details page was vastly improved in SQL Server 2008, and these improvements have been retained in SQL Server 2014. The right-hand side of Figure 3.1 shows the large amount of information that can be displayed in the Object Explorer Details window in SQL Server 2014. The nice part is that you can customize the information that is displayed and save those changes so that they are used the next time you open SSMS. For example, when you right-click a column heading (such as Name), you see all the columns available for display. Only a handful are displayed by default, but more than 30 columns that relate to databases are available. The columns that are available depend on the type of object selected in the Object Explorer window. Just right-click any of the column header names in the Object Explorer Details window, and you will see a list of all the available columns.

> **TIP**
>
> You can copy some or all of the information shown in the Object Explorer Details window and paste it into another application such as Excel for a quick and easy report. For example, you can select the `Databases` node in Object Explorer, highlight the data shown in the Object Explorer Details page, press Ctrl+C to copy the data, and then paste it into Excel. All the columns related to a database (including Headings) are captured and give you an easy way to review information about all your databases.

Another useful feature in the Object Explorer Details page is the Object Search box. The Object Search box, located at the top of the Object Explorer Details page (next to the Search label), allows you to search for objects by name. You can use wildcards (for example, `Product%`), or you can type a specific name you are looking for. The results are displayed in the Object Explorer Details page. Keep in mind that the objects that are searched depend on what is selected in the Object Explorer window. For example, if you highlight the `Databases` node, you search all the databases on your SQL Server instance. If you select a specific database, only that database is searched.

TIP

You can script multiple selections from the Object Explorer Details page. You hold down the Ctrl key and click only those items you want to script. After you select the items you want, you simply right-click one of the selected items and choose the preferred scripting option. This method works for many of the items displayed in the Object Explorer Details page including scheduled jobs.

Integrated Help

The integrated help, including Books Online documentation, changed significantly in SQL Server 2012 and those changes have been carried forward to SQL Server 2014. SQL Server provides a new Help Viewer that changes the way that you install and view the documentation. SQL Server 2014 Books Online now uses the Help Viewer that was originally released with Microsoft Visual Studio 2010 Service Pack 1 (SP1). Figure 3.2 shows an example of the Help Viewer. Note the content displayed on the right side of Figure 3.2; it describes some of the basic elements of the help facility in SQL Server 2014.

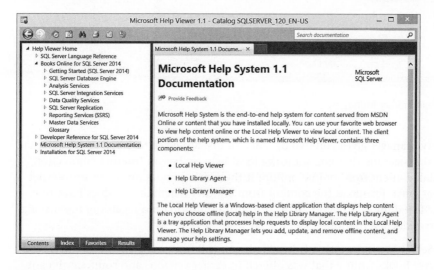

FIGURE 3.2   Microsoft Help Viewer.

You can choose to install the Help Viewer during the installation of SQL Server 2014, but the SQL Server documentation itself is no longer included with the installation media. You now have the options of viewing the documentation online or manually download-ing it to a local help collection. By default, the Help Viewer component uses the online SQL Server library. One of the benefits of using the online library is that you are always accessing the most recent version of the SQL Server documentation. However, if you prefer having the documentation installed locally, after installing the Documentation Components you can run the Help Library Manager to download the documentation to the computer locally.

To launch the Help Library Manager, select Microsoft SQL Server 2014 in the Windows Start menu, select Documentation and Community, and then click Manage Help Settings. Doing so launches the Help Library Manager, as shown in Figure 3.3. You can also launch the Help Library Manager by selecting Help from the SSMS menu and selecting Manage Help Settings.

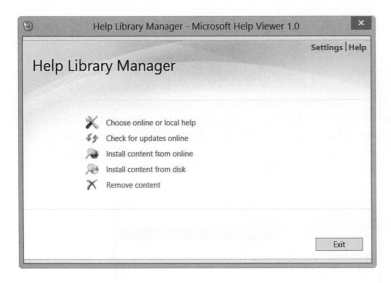

FIGURE 3.3   Help Library Manager.

The Help Library Manager gives you two options for installing the SQL Server documenta-tion locally. If the machine that you want the local help on has an Internet connection, choose the Install content from online option. If the machine does not have an Internet connection, you must download the content from another machine that does have one. See Chapter 8, "Installing SQL Server 2014," for further information regarding the installa-tion of SQL Server documentation.

Once the SQL Server Documentation is installed, you will find that there are some similar-ities to SQL Server Books Online that was offered in earlier versions and some significant differences. The similarities include a navigation pane on the right side of the help facility that includes Content, Index, and Favorites tabs. These tabs work in much the same way as they did in SQL Server Books Online from past versions.

The main differences in the SQL Server 2014 help facility are centered on searching the documentation and the ability to have multiple help tabs open at one time. Searches are now done using the Search Documentation field found in the upper-right portion of the form. The search text is entered in this field, and then results are displayed in the Results tab on the right side of the Help Viewer window. When you select one of the results from the Results tab, the related content is displayed in the selected tab on the right side.

Additional tabs of help information are created by selecting the smaller tab that is always positioned as the rightmost tab in the panel on the right. When you click this tab, a new tab (aptly titled New Tab) is created. To populate this new tab, just select it as the active tab and then choose the content that you want to display in the navigation panel. This can be useful when you have numerous help topics that you want to display all at once. Figure 3.4 shows an example of the Help Viewer with multiple tabs displayed, including one that is labeled New Tab that has not been populated with help content yet. This figure also shows the new Results tab with results returned when searching for the text "xml."

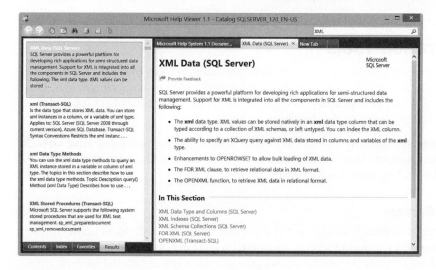

FIGURE 3.4   Multiple help tabs.

Microsoft has also made changes to the Books Online content in SQL Server 2014 that are intended to focus on features and tasks. These changes provide new reference content in the following areas:

▶ Feature descriptions

▶ How-to content

▶ Tool descriptions

▶ Language references, including SQL, DAX and MDX.

The integration of the help content in SSMS has changed as well. In earlier versions, Dynamic Help was available in SSMS. Dynamic Help is a carryover from the Visual Studio environment. It is a help facility that automatically displays topics in a Help window that are related to what you are doing in SSMS. This type of Dynamic Help is no longer available in SQL Server 2014, but there is some integration that can make your life easier. For example, click the F1 button while the SSMS window is in focus, and the Microsoft Help Viewer will display. You will also see Help icons displayed on many forms and dialog boxes that are displayed in SSMS. When you click these buttons, the Microsoft Help Viewer is displayed with the content that relates to the screen that you were on. This type of integration is available in other places such as the query window, which is discussed later in this chapter. When you are writing a query you can select an element of the query, click F1, and help for that element will be displayed in the Microsoft Help Viewer.

> **NOTE**
>
> There is a tremendous amount of SQL Server help available from Microsoft. Whether you get this content from online help or from local content, make sure that you get familiar with this powerful resource.

Administration Tools

The tools available with SSMS can be broadly categorized into tools that are used for administering SQL Server and tools that are used for developing or authoring new SQL Server objects. As a matter of practice, developers use some of the administrative tools, and administrators use some of the development tools.

SSMS comes with an expanded set of tools to help with SQL Server administrative tasks. It builds on the functionality that was available in SQL Server 2005 and adds some new tools and functionality to help ease the administrative burden.

Registered Servers

Registered servers is a concept in SQL Server 2014 that represents a division between managing servers and registering servers. Registered servers are displayed in the Registered Servers component window. Figure 3.5 shows an example of the Registered Servers window, with several server groups and their associated registered servers. You can add new groups or servers any time so that you have a handy way of organizing the servers you work with.

The servers listed in Figure 3.5 are all Database Engine servers. These server types are the conventional SQL Server instances. You can also register several other types of servers. The icons across the top of the Registered Servers window indicate the types of servers that are available. In addition to Database Engine servers, you can also register servers for Analysis Services, Reporting Services, and Integration Services. The Registered Servers window gives you one consolidated location to register all the different types of servers available in SQL Server 2014. You simply click the icon associated with the appropriate server type, and the registered servers of that type are displayed in the Registered Servers tree.

FIGURE 3.5   The Registered Servers window.

NOTE

The SQL Server 2014 Registered Servers window enables you to register servers that are running older version of SQL Server, including SQL Server 2012, 2008R2, 2008, and 2005. You can manage all the features of these prior versions with SQL Server 2014 tools. You can also have multiple sets of tools on one machine. The SQL Server tools from prior versions (starting with 2005) are compatible with SQL Server 2014 tools and function normally together.

Management tools from prior SQL Server versions cannot be used to manage all aspects of the SQL Server 2014 instances. For example, the SQL Server 2000 Enterprise Manager cannot be used to manage SQL Server 2014. You can connect the Query Analyzer to a SQL Server 2014 instance and run queries, but the Object Explorer and other tools are not compatible with SQL Server 2014.

When a server is registered, you have several options available for managing the server. You can right-click the server in the Registered Servers window to start or stop the related server, open a new Object Explorer window for the server, connect to a new query window, or export the registered servers to an XML file so that they can be imported on another machine.

TIP

The import/export feature can be a real timesaver, especially in environments where many SQL servers are managed. You can export all the servers and groups registered on one machine and save the time of registering them all on another machine. For example, you can right-click the `Database Engine` node, select Export, and then choose a location to store the XML output file. Then all you need to do to register all the servers and groups on another machine is move the file to that machine and import the file. Another option for bringing over registered servers occurs when you launch the SQL Server 2014 SSMS for the first time. If you had an earlier version installed on that same machine, the 2014 SSMS should prompt you and ask if you want to import the registered servers from the prior version.

Object Explorer

SQL Server 2014 continues to use an integrated Object Explorer that behaves similar to SQL Server 2008. The asynchronous population of the Object Explorer tree continues to be a time-saving feature. This may not hit home for folks who deal with smaller databases, but it can be a real time saver for those who are dealing with many databases on a single SQL Server instance or for those who work with databases that have a significant number of database objects. The Object Explorer tree in SSMS displays immediately and allows navigation in the tree and elsewhere in SSMS while the population of the tree is taking place.

The Object Explorer is adaptive to the type of server it is connected to. For a Database Engine server, the databases and objects such as tables, stored procedures, and so on are displayed in the tree. If you connect to an Integration Services server, the tree displays information about the packages defined on that type of server. Figure 3.6 shows an example of the Object Explorer with several different types of SQL Server servers displayed in the tree. Each server node has a unique icon that precedes the server name, and the type of server is also displayed in parentheses following the server name.

FIGURE 3.6   Multiple server types in Object Explorer.

The objects displayed in the Object Explorer tree can be filtered in SQL Server 2014. The number of filters is limited, but those that are available can be helpful. For example, you can filter the tables displayed in Object Explorer based on the name of the table, the schema that it belongs to, or the date on which it was created. In SQL Server 2014 you can also filter tables based on whether the table is memory optimized. Again, for those who deal with large databases and thousands of database objects, this feature is very helpful.

Administrators also find the enhanced scripting capabilities in the Object Explorer useful. The scripting enhancements are centered mostly on the administrative dialog boxes. These dialogs now include a script button that allows you to see what SSMS is doing behind the scenes to affect your changes. In older versions of SQL Server, the Profiler could be used to gather this information, but it was more time-consuming and less integrated than what is available now.

Figure 3.7 shows an example of an administrative dialog, with the scripting options selected at the top. You can script the commands to a new query window, a file, the Windows Clipboard, or a job that can be scheduled to run at a later time.

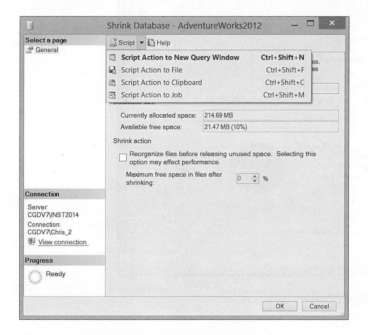

FIGURE 3.7   Scripting from administrative dialogs.

Many of the features and much of the functionality associated with the Object Explorer are similar to what was found in prior versions and are almost identical to what was found in SQL Server 2012. Keep in mind that the nodes that display in the Object Explorer tree are dependent on the version of SQL Server that you are connected to. For example, if you connect to a SQL Server 2012 or 2014 database engine then you will see the `AlwaysOn High Availability` and `Integration Services Catalogs` nodes at the root of the Object Explorer tree. If you connect to a SQL Server 2008 R2 database engine, these nodes will not be displayed because this version of SQL Server does not support these features.

One often-overlooked Object Explorer feature is the reports option that was added in SQL Server 2005 and still exists in SQL Server 2014. This option is available by right-clicking a node in the Object Explorer. Reports are not available for every node in the Object Explorer tree, but many of them do have this option. Most reports are found in the top-level nodes in the tree. For example, if you right-click a database in the Object Explorer tree and then select Reports and Standard Reports, you see more than a dozen available reports. These reports include Disk Usage, Backup and Restore Events, Top Transactions by Age, and a host of others. Graphs are included with some reports, and you can export or print all these reports. Figure 3.8 shows an example of the Disk Usage report for the AdventureWorks2012 database.

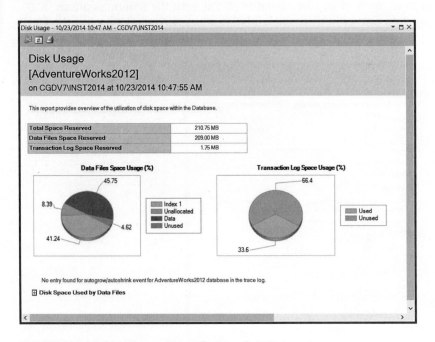

FIGURE 3.8   A Disk Usage Object Explorer Details report.

The graphs are easy to read, and some sections of the report can be expanded to provide more detail. Bullets at the bottom of a report are nodes that can be expanded. For example, the bullet Disk Space Used by Data Files at the bottom of Figure 3.8 can be expanded to display details about each of the data files.

Activity Monitor

The Activity Monitor saw some dramatic changes in SQL Server 2008 that were carried forward to SQL Server 2014. These changes build on the foundation established in SQL Server 2005 and help provide much more information related to the performance of your SQL Server instance.

Before we get into the details of the Activity Monitor, let's make sure you know where to find it. It is no longer found in the Management node of the Object Explorer. Instead, you right-click the name of the server instance in the Object Explorer, and you see a selection for Activity Monitor.

When the Activity Monitor launches, you see a new display with four different graphs, as shown in Figure 3.9. The graphs include % Processor Time (from SQL Server), Waiting Tasks, Database I/O, and Batch Requests. These graphs give you a quick performance snapshot for your SQL Server in one spot without having to launch System Monitor or some other monitoring tool to view this kind of information.

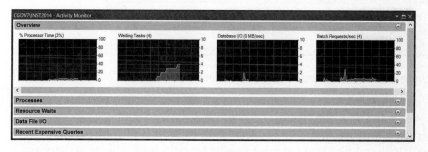

FIGURE 3.9   SQL Server 2014 Activity Monitor.

You also find more detailed performance information below the graphs. This information is grouped into four categories: Processes, Resource Waits, Data File I/O, and Recent Expensive Queries. Clicking the expand button for one of these categories presents the details you are looking for. These details contain drop-down headings that allow you to filter the results and view only the information you need.

The Processes Details window contains information similar to what was displayed in prior versions. These details include information similar to what is returned with the sp_who system stored procedure. The server process ID (SPID) is listed in a column named Session ID, and the related information for each SPID is displayed in the remaining columns. If you right-click a particular process, you can see the details of that process. You can then kill that process or launch the SQL Server Profiler to trace the activity for the process. Figure 3.10 shows an example of the expanded Processes details window.

TIP

If you need more space to view the Activity Monitor, you can click the Activity Monitory tab and drag it outside of SSMS. This will increase your overall real estate and allow you to view other SSMS data at the same time.

The Resource Waits window (that is displayed below the Process window) can help you identify bottlenecks on your server. It details the processes waiting for other resources on the server. The amount of time a process is waiting and the wait category (what the process is waiting for) are found in this display. If you click the Cumulative Wait Time column, the rows are sorted by this column, and you can find the wait category that has been waiting the longest. This sorting capability applies to all the columns in the display.

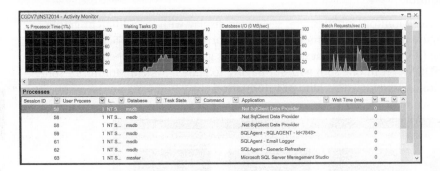

FIGURE 3.10   Processes Details window in the Activity Monitor.

The Data File I/O window lists each database and its related database files. The amount of disk I/O experienced by each of the files is detailed in the columns of this display. You can isolate the database and files that are most heavily hit with read or write activity as well as the databases that may be suffering from poor I/O response with this screen.

Finally, the Recent Expensive Queries window displays information similar to what you can obtain using catalog views. It provides statistics for all the databases on the instance and is a quick and easy way to find and tune expensive SQL statements. If you right-click a row in the display and click Edit Query Text, you can see the entire SQL text associated with the query. You are able to click one of the column headings such as CPU to sort the display according to the metric you feel defines cost. Best of all, you can right-click a row and choose Show Execution Plan, and you have the Query Plan ready for analysis.

TIP

When you mouse over the column headers in the detailed windows, ToolTips give you more information about the columns. This information includes the system view that the information is gathered from and where you can look in Books Online to obtain further information.

Log File Viewer

The Log File Viewer is another nonmodal window that is essential for administering your SQL Server. It can display log files that are generated from several different sources, including Database Mail, SQL Server Agent, SQL Server, and Windows NT. All of these log files contain critical information that is generated while the related item is running.

The Log File Viewer can be launched from the related node in the SSMS Object Explorer. For example, you can select the `Management` node and expand `SQL Server Error Logs`. If you double-click one of the error logs listed, a new Log File Viewer window is launched, displaying the SQL Server log file entries for the log type selected (see Figure 3.11).

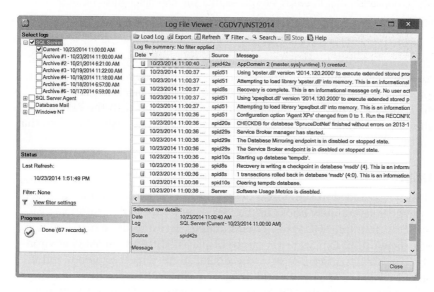

FIGURE 3.11   SQL Server logs displayed in the Log File Viewer.

NOTE

By default, entries are shown in the SQL Server Log File Viewer from newest to oldest. This is helpful for viewing the latest information but is counterintuitive for some people.

One of the first things you notice when you launch the Log File Viewer is that a tree structure at the top-left corner of the screen shows the log files you are viewing. You can see that there are four different log types available: Database Mail, SQL Server Agent, SQL Server, and Windows NT. You can choose to display multiple log files within a given log type (for example, the current SQL Server log and Archive #1), or you can select logs from different sources. For example, you can display all the current log entries for SQL Server and the current log entry for the SQL Server Agent.

When multiple logs are selected, you can differentiate between the rows shown on the right side of the Log File Viewer by looking at the Log Source column and the Log Type column. The Log Source values match up with the names shown in the tree structure where the log was selected. The Log Type column shows the type of log, such as SQL Agent or SQL Server. Rows from the different log types are displayed together and sorted according to the date on which the row was created. The sort order cannot be changed.

TIP

You can rearrange the order of the columns shown in the Log File Viewer. You simply click the column header and drag the column to the desired location. When you are viewing rows for more than one log type or multiple logs, it is best to drag the Log Type and Log Source columns to a location that is easily viewed so that you can distinguish between the entries.

Other noteworthy features in the Log File Viewer include the capability to filter and load a log from an external source. You can filter on dates, users, computers, the message text, and the source of the message. You can import log files from other machines into the view by using the Load Log facility. This facility works hand-in-hand with the Export option, which allows you to export the log to a file. These files can be easily shared so that others can review the files in their own Log File Viewer.

SQL Server Utility

The SQL Server Utility was added in SQL Server 2008 R2 and is geared toward multiserver management. It provides several new hooks in the SSMS environment that improve visibility and control across multiple SQL Server environments. Access to these new hooks is provided through a new Utility Explorer that can be displayed within your SSMS environment. This Utility Explorer has a tree-like structure similar to the Object Explorer, and it provides rich content related to the health and integrity of the SQL Server environments you have selected to manage using the SQL Server Utility. Figure 3.12 shows an example of the type of information the Utility Explorer can display.

The SQL Server Utility must first be configured to facilitate the display of information in the Utility Explorer. The configuration is relatively straightforward, but you must meet several requirements before starting it. The following requirements apply to the utility control point (UCP), which is the SQL Server instance capturing the information and the SQL Server instances being managed by the UCP:

▶ SQL Server must be version 10.50 or higher.

▶ The SQL Server instance type must be Database Engine.

▶ The SQL Server Utility must operate within a single Windows domain or domains with two-way trust relationships.

▶ On Windows Server 2003, the SQL Server Agent service account must be a member of Performance Monitor User group.

▶ The SQL Server service accounts on the UCP and all managed instances of SQL Server must have read permission to Users in Active Directory.

In addition, the UCP must be running the Developer, or Enterprise Edition of SQL Server.

When you have met these requirements, you are ready to start using the SQL Server Utility. The first steps are to establish a UCP and to enroll SQL Server instances for the UCP to manage. This is accomplished by selecting View on the SSMS menu bar and then selecting Utility Explorer. A content pane is displayed in SSMS that contains options for configuring the SQL Server Utility (see Figure 3.13). It also contains links to video that can guide you through each step.

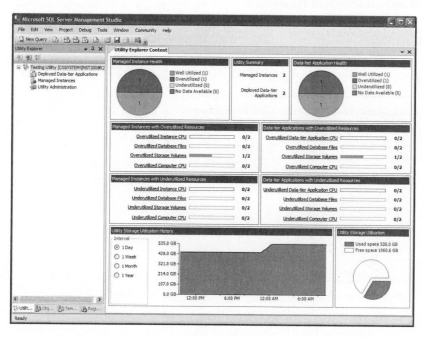

FIGURE 3.12   Utility Explorer content.

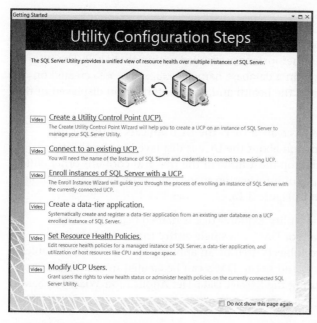

FIGURE 3.13
Utility Configuration Steps.

The first thing to do when configuring the SQL Server Utility is to click the Create a Utility Control Point (UCP) link on the Getting Started tab. This initiates a wizard that will guide you through a five-step process that creates the UCP. The first wizard screen that outlines these steps is shown in Figure 3.14.

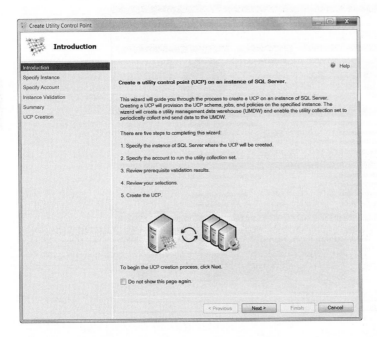

FIGURE 3.14   Create Utility Control Point Wizard screen.

The first step of the wizard is the most critical because you choose the SQL Server Instance that will be the UCP. The SQL Server instance you select in this step will store the information related to the UCP and any other instances enrolled within that UCP. The information collected by the UCP is stored in a database named `sysutility_mdw` created on the UCP instance. This database drives the health and status information displayed in the Utility Explorer.

After you complete the wizard steps to create a UCP, the UCP appears in the Utility Explorer Tree, and summary information about the UCP is displayed in the Utility Explorer Content tab. The UCP is the top-most node in the tree and contains other child nodes that contain the different types of information managed by the UCP. An example of the Utility Explorer tree is shown in Figure 3.15.

The first child node displayed in the Utility Explorer tree is named `Deployed Data-tier Applications`. A data-tier application, or DAC, is a single entity that contains all the database objects and related instance objects used by an application. This includes tables, stored procedures, SQL Server Logins, and so on. DACs can be created from a Visual Studio data-tier application project or by using the Extract Data-Tier Application Wizard in SSMS.

The full scope of DAC capabilities is beyond the scope of this chapter, but it is important to see how they fit into the Utility Explorer Display.

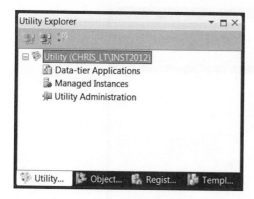

FIGURE 3.15   Utility Explorer tree.

> **NOTE**
>
> Two different SQL Server features use the same *DAC* acronym. The aforementioned *data-tier application* is one of them, but a *dedicated administrator connection* is also referred to as a DAC.

After creating a DAC deployment package, you can deploy it to another SQL Server instance. This deployment creates the related database, the database objects, along with the related server objects. If the server to which the DAC is deployed is managed by the UCP, you can show the deployed DAC information by clicking the `Deployed Data-tier Applications` node of the Utility Explorer.

The next node in the Utility Explorer tree, named `Managed Instances`, contains information about SQL Server instances enrolled in the UCP. Enrolling an instance essentially means you want to manage the instance through the UCP and gather information about it. You can easily enroll this instance by right-clicking the `Managed Instances` node and selecting Enroll Instance.

Each instance enrolled in the UCP is listed at the top of the Utility Explorer Content tab. When a managed instance is selected from this list, a set of resource and policy information is made available in the lower half of the window. The available tabs in this window, which define the type of information that is captured, include CPU Utilization, Storage Utilization, Policy Details, and Property Details. Figure 3.16 shows two managed instances and the related CPU Utilization graphs for the top-most SQL Server instance.

The last node, `Utility Administration`, can be used to manage policy, security, and data warehouse settings for a SQL Server Utility. These settings drive the SQL Server Utility summary screen and set thresholds across the entities defined in the utility.

Figure 3.17 shows an example of the policy information that can be managed with Utility Administration.

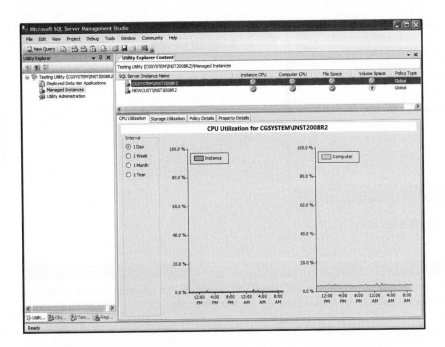

FIGURE 3.16   Managed instances.

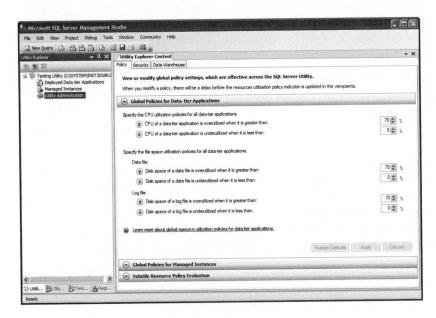

FIGURE 3.17   Utility Administration.

The Policy tab is one of three tabs available on the Utility Administration window. You can see in Figure 3.17 that there are also Security and Data Warehouse tabs. The Security tab allows you to manage permissions for logins that can administer or read from the UCP. Logins can be assigned to the Utility Reader role on this screen, which allows them to connect to the SQL Server Utility and read information from the Utility Explorer in SSMS. The Data Warehouse tab allows you to adjust the amount of time data will be retained in the UCP data warehouse. The default time period is one year.

Over time, the amount of data collected in the UCP data warehouse can be substantial. By default, each managed instance enrolled in the UCP sends configuration and performance data to the UCP every 15 minutes. Consequently, the space used by the utility management data warehouse (UMDW) needs to be monitored. The UMDW database, named `sysutility_mdw`, is listed as a user database in the Object Explorer.

Development Tools

SSMS delivers an equally impressive number of features for database developers. Many of the features were available with SQL Server 2008 or added in SQL Server 2012. T-SQL snippets, improved IntelliSense in the Query Editor, and enhanced debugging capabilities are a few of the changes made in SQL Server 2012 that are geared toward developers. These features and the other essential developer tools from SSMS are discussed in the following sections.

The Query Editor

The Query Editor sits at the top of the list for development tools in SSMS. The Query Editor, as its name indicates, is the editing tool for writing queries in SSMS. It contains much of the functionality that was contained in SQL Server 2000's Query Analyzer. The capability to write T-SQL queries, execute them, return results, generate execution plans, and use many of the other features that were in Query Analyzer are also available with the Query Editor.

> **NOTE**
>
> The biggest upside to the integration of the query-editing tool into the SSMS environment is that you can find almost anything you need to administer or develop on your SQL Server database in one spot. There is no need to jump back and forth between applications. One possible downside, however, is that SSMS may be much more than some database developers need.

Clicking the New Query button, opening a file, and selecting the Script to File option from a list of database objects in the Object Explorer are just a few of the ways to launch the Query Editor. Figure 3.18 shows the Query Editor window with a sample SELECT statement from the `AdventureWorks2012` database. The Query Editor window is displayed on the right side of the screen and the Object Explorer on the left side.

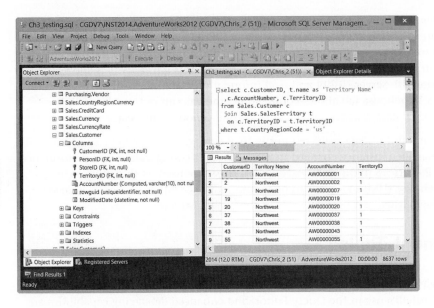

FIGURE 3.18   The Query Editor window in SSMS.

The basic editing environment within the Query Editor has remained the same in SQL Server. The top portion of the Query Editor window contains the query. The bottom portion contains the results of an executed query. The results can be displayed as text, displayed in a grid format, or output as XML. The results can then be copied or saved in a variety of formats including delimited files.

IntelliSense

IntelliSense finally made it to the SQL Server Query Editor in SQL Server 2008. This much-anticipated tool was slated for SQL Server 2005, but it was pulled before making it to the marketplace. Fortunately, it made it to SQL Server 2008 and continues to be a strong feature in 2014. In fact, there have been several improvements over the years. These improvements include the following:

▶ **Snippit integration**—T-SQL snippets were added in SQL Server 2012 and provide a starting point when building T-SQL statements. Once these snippets have been inserted into a script, IntelliSense helps with the completion of these scripts. Snippits are discussed later in the chapter.

▶ **Enhanced string matches**—A completion list will now suggest string matches based on partial words. In earlier versions, the matches were based on the first character.

▶ **Selective word match**—IntelliSense is more selective when identifying a match in the completion list. This gives the user more control when returning a match.

IntelliSense is a handy tool that helps you complete queries as you are typing them in the Query Editor window. Start typing, and you will see. For example, type SELECT * FROM A in the Query Editor window, and a drop-down appears in the Query Editor window after you start typing the first letter after the FROM clause. The drop-down, in this case, contains the databases and tables from which you can select data. If you type in a stored procedure name to execute, a drop-down shows you the parameters that the stored procedure accepts. Type sys. in the Query Editor window, and you see a drop-down of all the objects available in the sys schema. This includes catalog views and the related columns that these views contain. If you type in a query that is incorrect, IntelliSense places a red squiggly line under the part of the query that is syntactically incorrect.

The value of this tool will become more apparent as you use it. It can be confusing at times, but it will ultimately speed up your development time. It can also reduce the number of times you need to go to Books Online or some other help source and will make your development life easier.

NOTE

IntelliSense works only with database that are SQL Server 2008 or later. If you start typing a query against a database from a prior version, the handy IntelliSense drop-downs do not appear.

Query Editor Types

The Query Editor in SQL Server 2014 enables you to develop different types of queries. You are not limited to database queries based on SQL. You can use the Query Editor to develop all types of SQL Server Scripts, including those for SQL Server Analysis Services (SSAS) and SQL Server Database Engine. The SSAS queries come in three different flavors: multidimensional expressions (MDX), data mining expressions (DMX), and XML for analysis (XMLA). Only one selection exists for creating SQL Server Database Engine scripts.

You see these new query options when you create a new query. When you select New from the SSMS menu, you can choose what type of query to create. You use the Database Engine Query choice to create a T-SQL query against the Database Engine. The other new query options correspond to SSAS. The SSMS toolbar has icons that correspond to each type of query that can be created.

Each query type has a code pane that works much the same way across all the different types of queries. The code pane, which is the topmost window, color-codes the syntax that is entered, and it has sophisticated search capabilities and other advanced editing features that make it easy to use.

TIP

The ability to open and edit different types within a single SSMS instance is a powerful feature but can lead to a large number of open windows with limited screen real estate. SQL Server 2014 allows you to drag a tab from the query window outside of SSMS. Just click the tab you want and drag it outside of SSMS. In essence, it makes the individual tab a floating window. This can be useful when comparing code or viewing more of the code at once.

Disconnected Editing

SQL Server 2014 is able to use the code editor without a database connection. When creating a new query, you can choose to connect to a database or select Cancel to leave the code pane disconnected. To connect to the database later, you can right-click in the code pane window and select the Connect option. You can also disconnect the Query Editor at any time or choose the Change Connection option to disconnect and connect to another database all at once.

With SQL Server 2014, a new query window is opened every time a new file is opened. The new window approach is faster but can lead to many more open windows in the document window. You need to be careful about the number of windows/connections you have open. Also, you need to be aware that the tabbed display shows only a limited number of windows. Additional connections can exist even if their tabs are not in the active portion of the document window.

> **TIP**
>
> There is a drop-down arrow in the top-right corner of the query window that can be used to display all the query window tabs that are open in the query window. You can also use the Window menu in SSMS to list all the windows or tabs that are open.

Editing `sqlcmd` Scripts in SSMS

`sqlcmd` is a command-line utility introduced in SQL Server 2005. You can use it for ad hoc interactive execution of T-SQL statements and scripts. It is basically a replacement for the `ISQL` and `OSQL` utilities used in versions prior to SQL Server 2005. (`OSQL` still works with SQL Server 2014, but `ISQL` has been discontinued.)

You can write, edit, and execute `sqlcmd` scripts within the Query Editor environment. The Query Editor in SSMS treats `sqlcmd` scripts in much the same way as other scripts. The script is color-coded and can be parsed or executed. This is possible only if you place the Query Editor in SQLCMD mode, which you do by selecting Query, SQLCMD Mode or selecting the SQLCMD mode icon from the SSMS toolbar.

Figure 3.19 shows a sample `sqlcmd` script in SSMS that can be used to back up a database. This example illustrates the power and diversity of a `sqlcmd` script that utilizes both T-SQL and `sqlcmd` statements. It uses environment variables set within the script. The script variables DBNAME and BACKUPPATH are defined at the top of the script with the SETVAR command. The BACKUP statement at the bottom of the script references these variables using the convention `$(variablename)`, which substitutes the value in the command.

`sqlcmd` scripts that are edited in SSMS can also be executed within SSMS. The results are displayed in the results window of the Query Editor window, just like any other script. After you test a script, you can execute it by using the `sqlcmd` command-line utility. The `sqlcmd` command-line utility is a powerful tool that can help automate script execution. For more information on using `sqlcmd` in SSMS, refer to the Books Online topic "Edit SQLCMD Scripts with Query Editor." The `sqlcmd` command-line utility is discussed in more detail in Chapter 4, "SQL Server Command-Line Utilities."

FIGURE 3.19   Editing a `sqlcmd` script in SSMS.

Regular Expressions and Wildcards in SSMS

SSMS has a robust search facility that includes the use of regular expressions. Regular expressions provide a flexible notation for finding and replacing text, based on patterns within the text. Regular expressions are found in other programming languages and applications, including the Microsoft .NET Framework. The regular expressions in SSMS work in much the same way as these other languages, but there are some differences in the notation.

The option to use regular expressions is available whenever you are doing a find or replace within an SSMS script. You can use the find and replace option in the code pane or results window. You can use the Find and Replace option from the Edit menu or press either the Ctrl+F or Ctrl+H shortcut keys to launch the Find and Replace dialog box. Figure 3.20 shows an example of the Find and Replace dialog that utilizes a regular expression. This example is searching for the text *Customer*, preceded by the @ character and not followed by the Id characters. This kind of search could be useful for searching a large stored procedure where you want to find the customer references but don't want to see the variables that contain the word customer in the first part of the variable name.

You use regular expressions only when the Use check box in the Find and Replace dialog is selected. When this option is selected, you can choose either Regular Expressions or Wildcards. Wildcard searches work much the same way in SSMS as they do in file searches. For example, if you want to find any references to the word zip, you could enter `*zip*` in the Find What text box. The wildcard options are limited but very effective for simple searches.

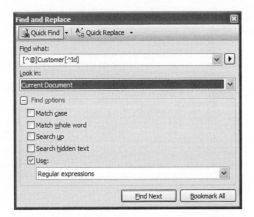

FIGURE 3.20   A find and replace with regular expressions.

Regular expressions have a much more extensive number of available search options. When you choose the option to use regular expressions, the arrow button is enabled to the right of the text box where you enter your search text. If you click this button, you are given an abbreviated list of regular expression characters that you can use in your searches. A brief description of what each character represents in the search is listed next to the character. For a complete list of characters, you can choose the Complete Character List option at the bottom of the list. This option brings you to the Books Online topic, "How to: Search with Regular Expressions," which gives a comprehensive review of all the characters.

TIP

SSMS also has a Find in Files option that is available in the Find and Replace window. The Quick Find option is displayed by default, so the Find in Files option is sometimes overlooked. Just click the drop-down arrow next to Quick Find and choose Find in Files. This is a powerful search option that enables you to search the contents of multiple files. The same search options are available with Find in Files, including Regular expressions. The results of the search are displayed in the query window results pane, and the resulting files can be quickly opened by double-clicking a find result.

Enhanced Performance Output

The Query Editor in SSMS has an extensive set of options available for capturing and distributing performance-related data. If you're familiar with the SQL Server 2012 performance output, you will find that the SQL Server 2014 performance output has changed very little. The Execution Plan tab that is displayed in the results window and the Results and Messages tab are still there in SQL Server 2014. The Execution Plan tab can be populated with two different types of plans: estimated plans and actual plans. The actual execution plan shows the plan that was used in generating the actual query results. The actual plan is generated along with the results when the Include Actual Execution Plan option is selected. This option can be selected from the SSMS toolbar or from the Query menu. Figure 3.21 shows an example of an actual execution plan generated for a query against the AdventureWorks2012 database.

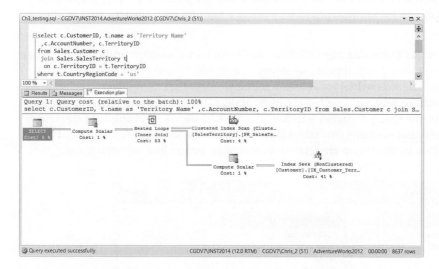

FIGURE 3.21   Displaying an actual execution plan in Query Editor.

The familiar treelike structure that was also present in past versions is still used in SQL Server 2014. The ToolTips displayed when you mouse over a node in the execution plan include additional information; you can see that information in a more static form in the Properties window if you right-click the node and select Properties. The display is generally easy to read and should be read from right to left.

Query plans generated in the Query Editor are easy to distribute in SQL Server 2014. You have several options for capturing query plan output so that you can save it or send it to someone else for analysis. If you right-click an empty section of the Execution Plan window, you can select the Save Execution Plan As option, which allows you to save the execution plan to a file. By default, the file has the extension .sqlplan. This file can be opened using SSMS on another machine to display the graphical output.

The query plan can also be output in XML format and distributed in this form. You make this happen by using the SET SHOWPLAN_XML ON option. This option generates the estimated execution plan in a well-defined XML document. The best way to do this is to turn off the display of the actual execution plan and execute the SET SHOWPLAN_XML ON statement in the code pane window. Next, you set the Query Editor to return results in grid format and then execute the statements for which you want to generate a query plan. If you double-click the grid results, they are displayed in the SSMS XML editor. You can also save the results to a file. If you save the file with the .sqlplan extension, the file displays the graphical plan when opened in SSMS.

Using the Query Designer in the Query Editor

A graphical query design tool is accessible from the Query Editor window where you write your queries. This tool was introduced in SQL Server 2005 and remains generally unchanged in SQL Server 2014. It provides a quick way for producing T-SQL statements that is particularly useful for individuals who are not familiar with the structure of the target database.

With SQL Server 2014, you can right-click in the Query Editor window and choose Design Query in Editor. A dialog box appears, allowing you to add tables to the graphical query designer surface. The selected tables are shown in a window that allows you to select the columns you want to retrieve. Selected columns appear in a SELECT statement displayed at the bottom of the Query Designer window. Figure 3.22 shows an example of the Query Designer window that contains two tables from the AdventureWorks2012 database. The two tables selected in this figure are related, as indicated by the line between them.

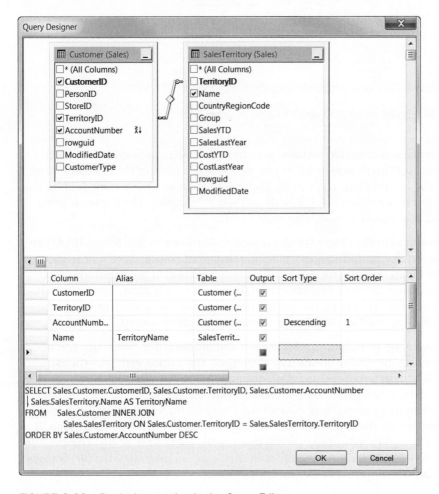

FIGURE 3.22   Designing queries in the Query Editor.

The T-SQL statements are generated automatically as you select various options on the Query Designer screen. If you select Sort Type, an ORDER BY clause is added. If you choose an alias for a column, it is reflected in the T-SQL. If tables are related, the appropriate joins are generated.

When you click OK on the Query Designer window, the related T-SQL is automatically placed in the Query Editor window. You can edit the T-SQL as needed or use it as is. You can imagine the time savings you can achieve by using this tool.

TIP

The Query Designer has a very impressive feature that allows you to view a T-SQL query visually. If you copy a valid T-SQL statement, open the Query Designer, and paste the T-SQL into the SQL pane at the bottom of the Query Designer, it tries to resolve the T-SQL into a graphical display. The tables in the FROM clause are shown in the designer panel, and information related to the selected columns is listed as well. The Query Designer cannot resolve all T-SQL statements and may fail to generate a visual display for some complex T-SQL.

Managing Projects in SSMS

Project management capabilities like those available in Visual Studio are available in SSMS. Building SSMS with the Visual Studio shell has aided in this integration. Queries, connections, and other files that are related can be grouped into projects. A project or set of projects is further organized or grouped as a solution. This type of organization is the same as in the Visual Studio environment.

Projects and solutions are maintained and displayed with the Solution Explorer. The Solution Explorer contains a tree-like structure that organizes the projects and files in the solution. It is a component window within SSMS that you launch by selecting View, Solution Explorer. Figure 3.23 shows an example of the Solution Explorer. The solution in this example is named EmployeeUpgrade, and it contains two projects, named Phase1 and Phase2. Each project contains a set of connections, a set of T-SQL scripts, and a set of miscellaneous files.

The first thing to do when using the project management capabilities in SSMS is to add a project. To do this, you select File, New, and when the New dialog appears, you select Project to add a new project. When adding the new project, you are given a choice of the type of project, and you must select either SQL Server Scripts, Analysis Services Scripts, or SQL Mobile Scripts. Each one of these project types is geared toward the respective SQL Server technology.

The solution that is related to the project is created at the same time that the project is created. The Solution Name is entered at the bottom of the New Project window, and an option to create a separate directory for the solution is provided. There is no option to create the solution separately.

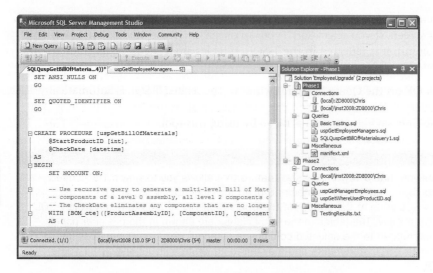

FIGURE 3.23   Solutions and projects listed in the Solution Explorer.

After the project is added, you can add the related connections and files. To add a new connection, you simply right-click the Connections node. The Connections entries allow you to store SQL Server connection information that relates to the project you are working on. For example, you could have a connection to your test environment and another connection to the production environment that relates to the project. When a connection is included in the project, you can double-click it, and a new query window for that connection is established.

SQL script files are added to a project in a similar fashion to connections: You right-click the Queries node and select the New Query option. A new Query Editor window appears, allowing you to enter the T-SQL commands. Any T-SQL script is viable for this category, including those that relate to database objects such as stored procedures, triggers, and tables.

You can also add existing files to a project. To do this, you right-click the project node, select Add, and then select Existing Item. The file types listed in the drop-down at the bottom of the Add Existing Item dialog include SQL Server files (*.sql), SQL deadlock files (*.xdl), XML files (*.xml), and execution plan files (*.sqlplan). SQL Server files are added, by default, to the Queries node. All the other file types are added to the Miscellaneous node. The connection entries are not stored in a separate file but are contained in the project file itself.

Integrating SSMS with Source Control

SSMS has the capability to integrate database project files into a source control solution. Source control provides a means for protecting and managing files. Source control applications typically contain features that allow you to track changes to files, control and track who uses the files, and provide a means for tagging the files with a version stamp so that the files can be retrieved at a later time, by version.

SSMS can integrate with a number of different source control applications. Visual SourceSafe is Microsoft's basic source control solution, but other source control applications can be used instead. The source control client application must be installed on the machine on which SSMS is running. When the installation is complete, you can set the source control application that SSMS will use within SSMS. To do this, you select Tools, Options and navigate to the `Source Control` node. The available source control clients are listed in the Current Source Control Plug-in drop-down.

The link between SSMS and the source control application is the database solution. After a solution is created, it can be added to the source control. To add a solution to a source control application, you open the Solution Explorer and right-click the solution or any of the projects in the solution. You then see the Add Solution to Source Control option. You must then log in to the source control application and select a source control project to add the solution to.

When the solution is added to a source control application, all the related projects and project files are added as well. The projects and files in the source control application have additional options available in the Solution Explorer. Figure 3.24 shows a sample solution added to a source control application. A subset of the source control options available when you right-click project files are shown in this figure as well.

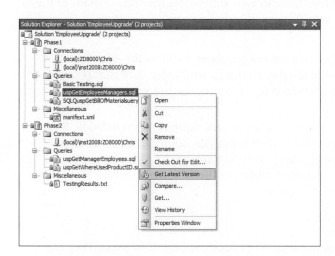

FIGURE 3.24   Source control options in the Solution Explorer.

The options related to source control are listed toward the bottom of the options list. The options that are available depend on the status of the selected file. For example, if a file has been checked out, additional options are displayed that relate to checking the file back in. Following are some of the common source control options:

▶ **Check Out for Edit**—This option allows you to get a copy of the file from the source control application so that you can modify the file. When you check out the file, the source control provider can keep track of the user who has checked out the file, and it can also prevent other users from checking out the file.

▶ **Check In**—This option copies the locally modified file into the source control solution. The file must first be checked out for editing before you can use the Check In option. A new version for the file is established, and any prior versions of the file are retained as well.

▶ **Get Latest Version**—This option gets a read-only copy of the latest version of the project file from the source control application. The file is not checked out with this option.

▶ **Compare**—This option enables you to compare versions of source control files. The default comparison that is shown is between the file in the source control application and the local file on your machine.

▶ **Get**—This option is similar to the Get Latest Version option, but it retrieves a read-only copy of the file. With this option, a dialog box appears, allowing you to select the file(s) you want to retrieve.

▶ **View History**—This option lists all versions of the files checked into the source control application. The History dialog box has many options that you can use with the different versions of the file. You can view differences between versions of the files, view the contents of a specific version, generate reports, or get an older version of the file.

▶ **Undo Checkout**—This option changes the checkout status in the source control application and releases the file to other source control users. Any changes made to the local copy of the file are not added to the source control version.

Other source control options are available via the Source Control menu in SSMS. You select an item in the Solution Explorer and then select File, Source Control. You can use this menu to check the status of a file by using the SourceSafe Properties option (if SourceSafe is being used), set source control properties, launch the source control application, and perform other source control operations.

Using SSMS Templates

Templates provide a framework for the creation of database objects in SSMS. They are essentially boilerplate files that help generate scripts for common database objects. They can speed up the development of these scripts and help enforce consistency in the generation of the underlying database objects.

The Template Browser is a component window available in SSMS that can be launched by selecting Template Browser from the View menu. Figure 3.25 shows the Template Browser and a portion of the available SQL Server template folders. Separate templates also exist for Analysis Services. You can view them by selecting the related icon at the top of the Template Browser.

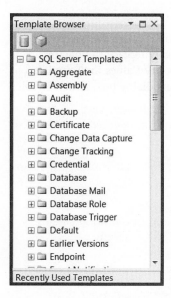

FIGURE 3.25   The SSMS Template Browser.

You access the available templates by expanding the template folder in the Template Browser tree. For example, if you expand the Index folder, you see six different types of index templates. If you double-click one of the templates, a new Query Editor window appears, populated with the template script. Figure 3.26 shows the template script displayed when you open the Create Index Basic template.

```
SQLQuery2.sql - (local)\INST2012.AdventureWorks2012 (chris_lt\chris (59))
-- =============================================
-- Create index basic template
-- =============================================
USE <database_name, sysname, AdventureWorks>
GO

CREATE INDEX <index_name, sysname, ind_test>
ON <schema_name, sysname, Person>.<table_name, sysname, Address>
(
    <column_name1, sysname, PostalCode>
)
GO
```

100 %
Conn...   (local)\INST2012 (11.0 SP1)   chris_lt\chris (59)   AdventureWorks2012   00:00:00   0 rows

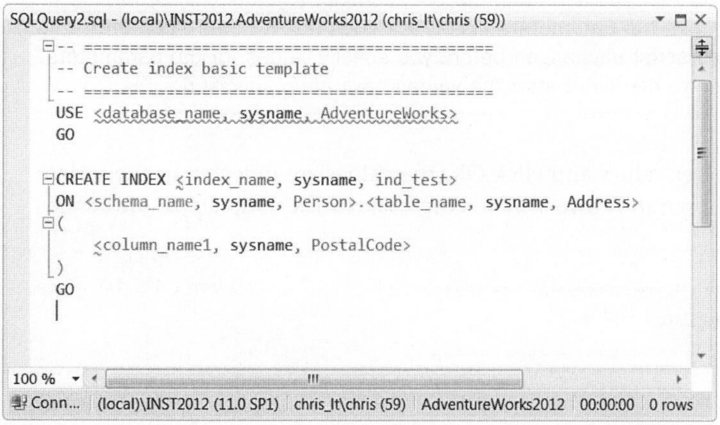

FIGURE 3.26   The template script for creating a basic index.

The template script contains template parameters that have the following format within the script:

```
<parameter_name, data_type, value>
```

You can manually replace these parameters in the script, or you can use the Specify Values for Template Parameters option from the Query menu to globally replace the parameters in the script with the desired values. Selecting Query, Specify Values for Template Parameters launches the Specify Values for Template Parameters dialog box, which enables you to enter the parameter values (see Figure 3.27).

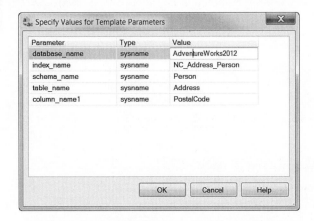

FIGURE 3.27   The Specify Values for Template Parameters dialog box.

TIP

When you use the Specify Values for Template Parameters option, some parameters may be missed if the parameter text has been altered. For example, if you add a carriage return after `parameter_name`, the Parameters dialog box does not list that parameter. It is best to leave the template script unchanged before you specify values for the parameters. You should make changes to the script after the values have been specified.

After you enter the parameter values and click OK, the values are reflected in the script. For example, the values shown in Figure 3.27 for the basic index template result in the following script:

```
-- ==========================================
-- Create index basic template
-- ==========================================
USE AdventureWorks2012
GO
CREATE INDEX NC_Address_Person
ON Person.Address
```

```
(
    PostalCode
)
GO
```

You also have the option of creating your own custom templates. These templates can contain parameters just like those available with the default templates. You can also create your own template folder that will be displayed in the Template Browser tree. To create a new template folder, you right-click the SQL Server Templates node in the Template Browser tree and select New, Folder. A new folder appears in the tree, and you can specify a new folder name. Figure 3.28 shows the Template Browser with a set of custom templates found under the _mytemplates folder. The code pane in this figure shows the contents of a new custom template named sys.objectSelectWithParameters. This custom template contains two parameter declarations: object_type and modify_date. When you select the Specify Values for Template Parameters options for this custom template, you have the opportunity to change the values, just as you can with the default templates.

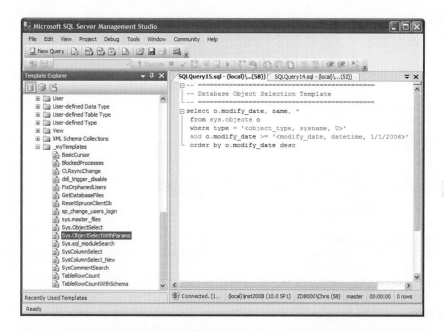

FIGURE 3.28   A custom template example.

NOTE

When you double-click a template in the Template Browser tree, you create a script based on the template. Changes made to the script do not affect the template; they affect only the script generated from the template. To change the actual template, you need to right-click the template and select Edit. After you complete your changes, you need to make sure to save the template.

Also, you should keep in mind that there is no requirement to have parameters in your templates. Templates are handy tools for accessing any code snippet you might use. After the code snippet is added as a template, you can open a new Query Editor window based on the template or simply drag and drop the template from the Template Browser to an existing Query Editor window, and the code for the template is pasted into the window.

Using SSMS Snippets

A T-SQL code snippet is a new type of template that was added in SQL Server 2012. The templates are another great starting point when writing new T-SQL statements in the Database Engine Query Editor. They are tightly integrated into the Query Editor window and are supported by IntelliSense.

Snippets can be accessed in a number of different ways in SSMS. One easy way to access them is to right-click in a Query Editor window and choose Insert Snippet, which displays the snippet picker tooltip, as shown in Figure 3.29.

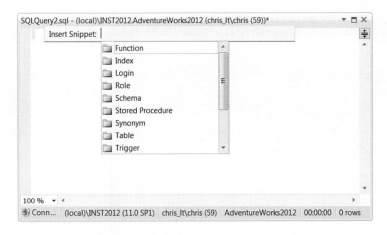

FIGURE 3.29   Snippet picker tooltip.

When you select the desired snippet, the related T-SQL statements are added to the Query Editor window. The T-SQL statements have replacement points that are highlighted and reflect areas in the script that must be updated for your specific needs. Figure 3.30 shows the resulting T-SQL statements for the Index snippet that are ready for completion.

The snippet statement has several display elements that help in the completion of the statement. The replacement points in the snippet statement are highlighted so that they are easy to identify. You can hover your mouse over the highlighted text, and a tooltip is visible as shown in Figure 3.30 below the column declaration for the index.

There are a number of ways to complete the snippet statement. You can use the Tab key to move from one replacement point to the next. You can also click Ctrl+Space to invoke IntelliSense, or you can manually select the text in the replacement point to provide the required value.

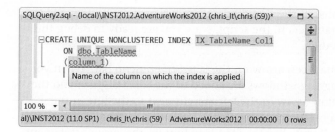

FIGURE 3.30 Completing the snippet statement.

There is also another flavor of snippet called a *surround-with snippet*. This kind of snippet is a template that you can use as a starting point when enclosing a set of T-SQL statements in a BEGIN, IF, or WHILE block. Simply right-click in the Query Editor window and choose Surround With from the context menu. After you choose the desired Surround With option, the related block of text will be inserted in the Query Editor window with replacements points where applicable.

T-SQL Debugging

The debugging capabilities that were introduced in SQL Server 2008 continue to mature in SQL Server 2014. The following are some of the enhanced capabilities:

▶ You can now debug Transact-SQL scripts running on instances of SQL Server 2005 Service Pack 2 (SP2) or later.

▶ Breakpoint conditions are now supported and conditionally determine whether the breakpoint is invoked.

▶ Breakpoint hit counts that specify the number of times a breakpoint is hit.

▶ Breakpoint filters that limit the breakpoint to operating only on specified computers, processes, or threads.

▶ Breakpoint actions that specify a custom task that is performed when the breakpoint is invoked.

▶ Breakpoint editing that allows the location of a breakpoint to be moved from one Transact-SQL statement to another.

▶ Quick Info pop ups that display the name of the expression and its current value when you move the cursor over a Transact-SQL identifier.

▶ Watch window and Quick Watch that now support watching Transact-SQL expressions.

The trickiest part of debugging may be starting the debugger. It is not all that difficult but may be less than obvious for some. For example, let's say you want to debug a stored procedure. To do this, you right-click the stored procedure in the Object Explorer and select Script Stored Procedure As, Execute To, New Query Editor Window, and a script for executing the procedure is generated. If the stored procedure has parameters, you add the SQL to assign a value to those parameters to the script. Now you are ready to debug this script and the related stored procedure.

To initiate debugging, you click the green arrow on the SQL Server menu bar. When you start debugging, several new debugging windows are added to the SSMS display, and the Query Editor window shows a yellow arrow in the left margin next to the line in the script that is about to be run. You can now use the debug toolbar at the top of the SSMS screen to step through your code. If you click the Step Into button, the current statement executes, and the script progresses to the next available statement. Figure 3.31 shows an example of the T-SQL Debugging Environment while debugging is in progress. The debugging environment enables you to view values assigned to variables, review the call stack, set breakpoints, and perform debugging much like you would do in development environments such as Visual Studio.

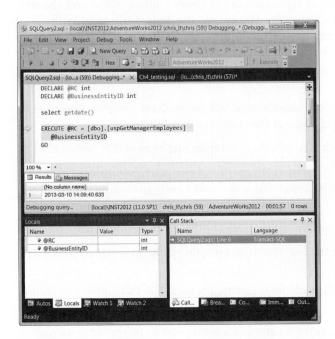

FIGURE 3.31   The T-SQL Debugging Environment.

Multiserver Queries

Another slick option available with SQL Server 2014 is the capability to execute a script on multiple servers at once. Multiserver queries allow the contents of a single Query Editor window to be run against all the servers defined in a given registered server group. After the group is created and servers are registered in the group, you can right-click the group and select the New Query option to create a query window that can be run against all the servers in the group. Click the Execute button, and the query is run against all the servers. Figure 3.32 shows a server group named `MyTestGroup` containing three servers registered in that group, a sample query to run against these servers, and a single result window that shows the results of the query for all servers in the group.

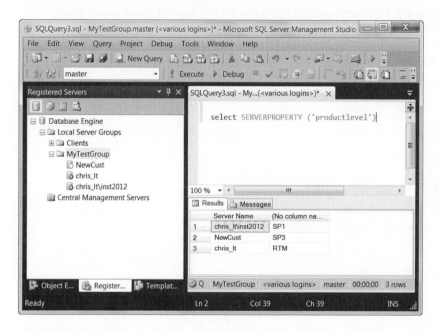

FIGURE 3.32   Multiserver query execution.

Multiserver queries are relatively easy to use. The results window includes a Server Name column that allows you to determine which server the result came from. These queries are backward compatible and allow you to run against prior versions of SQL Server. The only caveat is that you must first create a registered server group and the related registered servers before you run the query, but you already know that this task is also relatively easy.

Summary

The number of tools and features available in SSMS is extensive and can be daunting when you first enter the environment. Remember that you can customize this environment and hide many of the windows that are displayed. You can start with a fairly simple SSMS configuration that includes the Object Explorer and a Query Editor window. This configuration may allow you to accomplish a majority of your SQL Server tasks. As you become more familiar with the environment, you can introduce new tools and features to help improve your overall productivity.

The discussion of SSMS does not end with this chapter. Further details related to SSMS are covered throughout this book. You can use the new features described in this chapter as a starting point and look to other chapters for more detailed discussion of database features accessible through SSMS.

Chapter 4 looks at the SQL Server utilities that can be run from the command prompt. These tools allow you to perform some of the same tasks available in SSMS. The capability to launch these utilities from the command line can be useful when you're automating tasks or accessing SQL Server when a GUI tool such as SSMS is not available.

SQL Server Command-Line Utilities

This chapter explores various command-line utilities that ship with SQL Server. These utilities give administrators a different way to access the Database Engine and its related components. In some cases, they provide functionality that is also available with SQL Server Management Studio. Other command-line utilities provide functionality that is available only from the command prompt. For each utility, this chapter provides the command syntax along with the most commonly used options. For the full syntax and options available for the utility, see SQL Server Books Online.

> **NOTE**
>
> This chapter focuses on command-line utilities that are core to SQL Server and the SQL Server Database Engine. Several other command-line utilities that are used less frequently or geared toward other SQL Server services are not covered in this chapter. These utilities include `dtexec` and `dtutil`, which can be used with SQL Server Integration Services (SSIS). Reporting Services has the `rs`, `rsconfig`, and `rskeymgmt` command-line utilities. Lastly, there are several executable files documented as utilities in Books Online (such as `ssms`, which opens the SQL Server Management Studio) that have limited parameters and are basically used to launch their related applications.

Table 4.1 lists the command-line utilities discussed in this chapter. This table lists the default physical location of each utility's executable. The location is needed to execute the utility in most cases unless the associated path has been added to the `Path` system environment variable.

TABLE 4.1   Command-Line Utility Installation Locations

Utility	Install Location
bcp	c:\Program Files\Microsoft SQL Server\Client SDK\ODBC\110\Tools\Binn
dta	c:\Program Files (x86)\Microsoft SQL Server\120\Tools\Binn
sqlcmd	c:\Program Files\Microsoft SQL Server\Client SDK\ODBC\110\Tools\Binn
sqllocaldb	c:\Program Files\Microsoft SQL Server\120\Tools\Binn
sqldiag	c:\Program Files\Microsoft SQL Server\120\Tools\Binn
sqlservr	c:\Program Files\Microsoft SQL Server\MSSQL12.MSSQLSERVER\MSSQL\Binn
tablediff	c:\Program Files\Microsoft SQL Server\120\COM

> **NOTE**
>
> The install location shown in Table 4.1 is the default location for the utility, but it may be found in a different location. The location depends upon the operating system, the instance name, and the installation path chosen during the SQL Server installation. Also the tablediff utility is installed when SQL Server replication is installed. If you can't find the tablediff.exe in the location specified in Table 4.1, check to see whether the replication was installed.

When you are testing many of these utilities, it is often easiest to set up a batch file (.BAT) that contains a command to change the directory to the location shown in Table 4.1. After you make this directory change, you can enter the command-line utility with the relevant parameters. Finally, you should enter a PAUSE command so that you can view the output of the utility in the command prompt window. Following is an example you can use to test the sqlcmd utility (which is discussed in more detail later in this chapter). Change localhost below to your SQL Server instance name if you're not running this batch file on the server itself:

```
CD "C:\Program Files\Microsoft SQL Server\120\Tools\Binn"
SQLCMD -Slocalhost -E -Q "select @@servername"
pause
```

After you save the commands in a file with a .BAT extension, you can simply double-click the file to execute it. This approach is much easier than retyping the commands many times during the testing process.

What's New in SQL Server Command-Line Utilities

The SQL Server command-line utilities available in SQL Server 2014 are basically the same as those offered with SQL Server 2012. Functionality related to Azure SQL Database administration has been added to a few utilities, detailed in the following sections of this chapter. Overall, very little has changed in the syntax, and batch files or scripts you have used with these utilities in the past should continue to work unchanged.

One command-line utility has been added in SQL Server 2014, however, and some have been removed or deprecated. The `sqllocaldb` utility was new to SQL Server 2012. This utility is used to create and manage an instance of the Microsoft SQL Server 2014 Express LocalDB. This LocalDB is an execution mode of SQL Server that utilizes a minimal set of files to start the SQL Server Database Engine.

Utilities removed from SQL Server 2012 include `makepipe` and `readpipe`. These two utilities were used to test the integrity of the network named pipe services. The `sqlmaint` utility is deprecated in SQL Server 2014. This utility, which can be used for performing database maintenance, may be removed in a future version of SQL Server.

The `sqlcmd` Command-Line Utility

The `sqlcmd` command-line utility is the next generation of the `isql` and `osql` utilities that you may have used in prior versions of SQL Server. It provides the same type of functionality as `isql` and `osql`, including the capability to connect to SQL Server from the command prompt and execute T-SQL commands. The T-SQL commands can be stored in a script file, entered interactively, or specified as command-line arguments to `sqlcmd`.

> **NOTE**
>
> The `isql` and `osql` command-line utilities are not covered in this chapter. The `isql` utility was discontinued in SQL Server 2005 and is not supported in SQL Server 2014. The `osql` utility is still supported but will be removed in a future version of SQL Server. It is also not supported by Azure SQL Database, so make sure to use `sqlcmd` in place of `osql` to avoid unnecessary changes in the future.

The command-line options for `sqlcmd` are as follows:

```
sqlcmd
    -a packet_size
    -A (dedicated administrator connection)
    -b (terminate batch job if there is an error)
    -c batch_terminator
    -C (trust the server certificate)
    -d db_name
    -e (echo input)
    -E (use trusted connection)
    -f codepage | i:codepage[,o:codepage] | o:codepage[,i:codepage]
    -h rows_per_header
    -H workstation_name
    -i input_file
    -I (enable quoted identifiers)
    -k[1 | 2] (remove or replace control characters)
    -K application_intent
```

```
-l login_timeout
-L[c] (list servers, optional clean output)
-m error_level
-M multisubnet_failover
-N (encrypt connection)
-o output_file
-p[1] (print statistics, optional colon format)
-P password
-q "cmdline query"
-Q "cmdline query" (and exit)
-r[0 | 1] (msgs to stderr)
-R (use client regional settings)
-s col_separator
-S [protocol:]server[\instance_name][,port]
-t query_timeout
-u (unicode output file)
-U login_id
-v var = "value"
-V error_severity_level
-w column_width
-W (remove trailing spaces)
-x (disable variable substitution)
-X[1] (disable commands, startup script, environment variables and optional exit)
-y variable_length_type_display_width
-Y fixed_length_type_display_width
-z new_password
-Z new_password (and exit)
-? (show syntax summary)
```

The number of options available for `sqlcmd` is extensive, but many are not necessary for basic operations. To demonstrate the usefulness of this tool, we look at several different examples of the `sqlcmd` utility, from fairly simple (using few options) to more extensive.

NOTE

The -Z and -z `sqlcmd` options are not supported by Azure SQL Database. You must use the `ALTER LOGIN` command to change a user password.

TIP

To connect to an Azure SQL Database instance, use the following `sqlcmd` command-line syntax:

`C:\Program Files\Microsoft SQL Server\120\Tools\Binn>sqlcmd -S servername.database.windows.net -d master -U username@servername -P password`

The `username@servername` syntax shown in this example is required.

Executing the `sqlcmd` Utility

Before we get into the examples, it is important to remember that `sqlcmd` can be run in several different ways. It can be run interactively from the command prompt, from a batch file, or from a Query Editor window in SSMS. When run interactively, the `sqlcmd` program name is entered at the command prompt followed by the required options to connect to the database server. When the connection is established, a numbered row is presented, after which you enter your T-SQL commands. Multiple rows of T-SQL can be entered in a batch; they are executed only after the GO command has been entered. Figure 4.1 shows an example of a simple SELECT statement that was executed interactively with `sqlcmd`. The connection in this example was established by typing `sqlcmd` at the command prompt to establish a trusted connection to the default instance of SQL Server running on the machine on which the command prompt window is opened.

FIGURE 4.1   Executing `sqlcmd` from the command line.

The capability to edit and execute `sqlcmd` scripts was added to SSMS with SQL Server 2005. A `sqlcmd` script can be opened or created in a Query Editor window within SSMS. To edit these scripts, you must place the editor in SQLCMD Mode. You do so by selecting Query, SQLCMD Mode or by clicking the related toolbar button. When the editor is put in SQLCMD Mode, it provides color coding and the capability to parse and execute the commands within the script. Figure 4.2 shows a sample `sqlcmd` script opened in SSMS in a Query Editor window set to SQLCMD Mode. The shaded lines are `sqlcmd` commands.

FIGURE 4.2   Executing and editing `sqlcmd` scripts in SSMS.

The most common means for executing `sqlcmd` utility is via a batch file. This method can provide a great deal of automation because it allows you to execute a script or many scripts by launching a single file. The examples shown in this section are geared toward the execution of `sqlcmd` in this manner. The following simple example illustrates the execution of `sqlcmd`, using a trusted connection to connect to the local instance of SQL Server, and the execution of a simple query that is set using the -Q option:

```
sqlcmd -S (local) -E -Q"select getdate()"
```

You can expand this example by adding an output file to store the results of the query and add the -e option, which echoes the query that was run in the output results:

```
sqlcmd -S (local) -E -Q"select getdate()" -o c:\TestOutput.txt -e
```

The contents of the c:\TestOutput.txt file should look similar to this:

```
select getdate()
-----------------------
2014-12-10 20:29:05.645

 (1 rows affected)
```

Using a trusted connection is not the only way to use sqlcmd to connect to a SQL Server instance. You can use the -U and -P command-line options to specify the SQL Server user and password. sqlcmd also provides an option to specify the password in an environmental variable named SQLCMDPASSWORD, which can be assigned prior to the sqlcmd execution and eliminates the need to hard-code the password in a batch file.

sqlcmd also provides a means for establishing a dedicated administrator connection (DAC) to the server. The DAC is typically used for troubleshooting on a server that is having problems. It allows an administrator to get onto the server when others may not be able to. If the DAC is enabled on the server, a connection can be established with the -A option and a query can be run, as shown in the following example:

```
sqlcmd -S (local) -A -Q"select getdate()"
```

If you need to manage more complex T-SQL execution, it is typically easier to store the T-SQL in a separate input file. The input file can then be referenced as a sqlcmd parameter. For example, say that you have the following T-SQL stored in a file named c:\TestsqlcmdInput.sql:

```
BACKUP DATABASE Master
 TO DISK = 'c:\master.bak'

BACKUP DATABASE Model
 TO DISK = 'c:\model.bak'

BACKUP DATABASE MSDB
 TO DISK = 'c:\msdb.bak'
```

The sqlcmd execution, which accepts the C:\TestsqlcmdInput.sql file as input and executes the commands within the file, looks like this:

```
sqlcmd -S (local) -E -i"C:\TestsqlcmdInput.sql" -o c:\TestOutput.txt -e
```

The execution of the preceding example backs up three of the system databases and writes the results to the output file specified.

Using Scripting Variables with sqlcmd

sqlcmd provides a means for utilizing variables within sqlcmd input files or scripts. These scripting variables can be assigned as sqlcmd parameters or set within the sqlcmd script. To illustrate the use of scripting variables, let's change our previous backup example so that the database that will be backed up is passed as a variable. A new input file named c:\BackupDatabase.sql should be created, and it should contain the following command:

```
BACKUP DATABASE $(DatabaseToBackup)
 TO DISK = 'c:\$(DatabaseToBackup).bak'
```

The variable in the preceding example is named `DatabaseToBackup`. Scripting variables are referenced using the $( ) designators. These variables are resolved at the time of execution, and a simple replacement is performed. This allows variables to be specified within quotation marks, if necessary. The –v option is used to assign a value to a variable at the command prompt, as shown in the following example, which backs up the model database:

```
sqlcmd -S (local) -E -i"C:\BackupDatabase.sql" -v DatabaseToBackup = model
```

If multiple variables exist in the script, they can all be assigned after the –v parameter. These variables should not be separated by a delimiter, such as a comma or semicolon. Scripting variables can also be assigned within the script, using the :SETVAR command. The input file from the previous backup would be modified as follows to assign the `DatabaseToBackup` variable within the script:

```
:SETVAR DatabaseToBackup Model
BACKUP DATABASE $(DatabaseToBackup)
 TO DISK = 'c:\$(DatabaseToBackup).bak'
```

Scripts that utilize variables, `sqlcmd` commands, and the many available options can be sophisticated and can make your administrative life easier. The examples in this section illustrate some of the basic features of `sqlcmd`, including some of the features that go beyond what is available with `osql`.

The `dta` Command-Line Utility

`dta` is the command-line version of the graphical Database Engine Tuning Advisor. Both the command-line utility and graphical tool provide performance recommendations based on the workload provided to them. The syntax for `dta` is as follows:

```
dta [ -? ] |
[
    [ -S server_name[ \instance ] ]
    {
        { -U login_id [-P password ] }
        | -E              }
        { -D database_name [ ,...n ] }
            [-d database_name ]
            [ -Tl table_list | -Tf table_list_file ]
        {
            -if workload_file |
            -it workload_trace_table_name |
            -ip (take workload from plan cache)
            [ -ipf ] (filter query on database id (false))
        }
        { -s session_name | -ID session_ID }
            [ -F ]
```

```
              [ -of output_script_file_name ]
              [ -or output_xml_report_file_name ]
              [ -ox output_XML_file_name ]
              [ -rl analysis_report_list [ ,...n ] ]
              [ -ix input_XML_file_name ]
              [ -A time_for_tuning_in_minutes ]
              [ -n number_of_events ]
      [ -m minimum_improvement ]
              [ -fa physical_design_structures_to_add ]
              [ -fp partitioning_strategy ]
              [ -fk keep_existing_option ]
              [ -fx drop_only_mode ]
              [ -fi (consider filtered indexes for recommendations) ]
      [ -B storage_size ]
      [ -c max_key_columns_in_index ]
      [ -C max_columns_in_index ]
              [ -e | -e tuning_log_name ]
              [ -N online_option]
              [ -q ]
              [ -u ]
          [ -x ]
          [ -a ]
]
```

An extensive number of options are available with this utility, but many of them are not required to do basic analysis. At a minimum, you need to use options that provide connection information to the database, a workload to tune, a tuning session identifier, and the location to store the tuning recommendations. The connection options include -s for the server name, -D for the database, and either -E for a trusted connection or -U and -P, which can be used to specify the user and password.

> **NOTE**
>
> The Database Tuning Advisor and dta.exe are not supported by Azure SQL Database.

When using sqlcmd for database tuning, the workload to tune is either a workload file, workload table, or workload taken from the plan cache. The -if option is used to specify the workload file location, and the -it option is used to specify a workload table. The workload file must be a SQL Profiler trace file (.trc), SQL script (.sql) that contains T-SQL commands, or SQL Server trace file (.log). The workload table is a table that contains output from a workload trace. The table is specified in the form database_name.owner_name.table_name.

The tuning session must be identified with either a session name or session ID. The session name is character based and is specified with the -s option. If the session name is not provided, a session ID must be provided instead. The session ID is numeric and is set using the -ID option. If the session name is specified instead of the session ID, the dta generates an ID anyway.

The last options required for a basic dta execution identify the destination to store the dta performance recommendations, which can be stored in a script file or in XML. The -of option is used to specify the output script filename. XML output is generated when the -or or -ox option is used. The -or option generates a filename if one is not specified, and the -ox option requires a filename. The -F option can be used with any of the output options to force overwriting a file with the same name if one exists.

To illustrate the use of dta with basic options, let's look at an example of tuning a simple SELECT statement against the AdventureWorks2012 database. To begin, you use the following T-SQL, which is stored in a workload file named c:\myScript.sql:

```
USE AdventureWorks2012;
GO
select *
 from Production.TransactionHistory
 where TransactionDate = '9/1/08';
```

The following example shows the basic dta execution options that can be used to acquire performance recommendations:

```
dta -S servername -E -D AdventureWorks2012 -if c:\MyScript.sql
-s MySessionX -of C:\MySessionOutputScript.sql -F
```

> **NOTE**
>
> dta and other utilities executed at the command prompt are executed with all the options on a single line. The preceding example and any others in this chapter that are displayed on more than one line should actually be executed at the command prompt or in a batch file on a single line. They are broken here because the printed page can accommodate only a fixed number of characters.

The preceding example utilizes a trusted connection against the AdventureWorks2012 database, a workload file named c:\MyScript.sql, and a session named MySessionX, and it outputs the performance recommendations to a text file named c:\MySessionOutputScript.sql. The -F option is used to force a replacement of the output file if it already exists. The output file contains the following performance recommendations:

```
USE [AdventureWorks2012]
go

CREATE NONCLUSTERED INDEX [_dta_index_TransactionHistory_5]
 ON [Production].[TransactionHistory]
 (
    [TransactionDate] ASC
```

```
)
INCLUDE ( [TransactionID],
[ProductID],
[ReferenceOrderID],
[ReferenceOrderLineID],
[TransactionType],
[Quantity],
[ActualCost],
[ModifiedDate])
 WITH (SORT_IN_TEMPDB = OFF, IGNORE_DUP_KEY = OFF,
  DROP_EXISTING = OFF, ONLINE = OFF) ON [PRIMARY]
go
```

In short, the `dta` output recommends that a new index be created on the `TransactionDate` column in the `TransactionHistory` table. This is a viable recommendation, considering that there was no index on the `TransactionHistory.TransactionDate` column, and it was used as a search argument in the workload file.

Many other options (that go beyond basic execution) can be used to manipulate the way `dta` makes recommendations. For example, a list can be provided to limit which tables the `dta` looks at during the tuning process. Options can be set to limit the amount of time that the `dta` tunes or the number of events. These options go beyond the scope of this chapter, but you can gain further insight into them by looking at the graphical DTA, which contains many of the same types of options. You can refine your tuning options in the DTA, export the options to an XML file, and use the `-ix` option with the `dta` utility to import the XML options and run the analysis.

The `tablediff` Command-Line Utility

The `tablediff` utility enables you to compare the contents of two tables. It was originally developed for replication scenarios to help troubleshoot non-convergence, but it is also useful in other scenarios. When data in two tables should be the same or similar, this tool can help determine whether they are the same, and if they are different, it can identify which data in the tables are different.

The syntax for `tablediff` is as follows:

```
tablediff
[ -? ] |
{
        -sourceserver source_server_name[\instance_name]
        -sourcedatabase source_database
        -sourcetable source_table_name
    [ -sourceschema source_schema_name ]
    [ -sourcepassword source_password ]
    [ -sourceuser source_login ]
    [ -sourcelocked ]
```

```
        -destinationserver destination_server_name[\instance_name]
        -destinationdatabase subscription_database
        -destinationtable destination_table
   [ -destinationschema destination_schema_name ]
   [ -destinationpassword destination_password ]
   [ -destinationuser destination_login ]
   [ -destinationlocked ]
   [ -b large_object_bytes ]
   [ -bf number_of_statements ]
   [ -c ]
   [ -dt ]
   [ -et table_name ]
   [ -f [ file_name for SQL fix ] ]
   [ -o output_file_name ]
   [ -q (quick row count) ]
   [ -rc number_of_retries ]
   [ -ri retry_interval ]
   [ -strict (strict schema comparison) ]
   [ -t connection_timeouts ]
}
```

The `tablediff` syntax requires source and destination connection information to perform a comparison. This information includes the servers, databases, and tables that will be compared. Connection information must be provided for SQL Server authentication but can be left out if Windows authentication can be used. The source and destination parameters can be for two different servers or the same server, and the `tablediff` utility can be run on a machine that is neither the source nor the destination.

> **NOTE**
>
> Although Azure SQL Database does not support SQL Server Replication (instead, relying on its own methods of geo-distributed replication), the `tablediff` utility is supported on Azure SQL Database tables.

To illustrate the usefulness of this tool, let's look at a sample comparison in the `AdventureWorks2012` database. The simplest way to create some data for comparison is to select the contents of one table into another and then update some of the rows in one of the tables. The following SELECT statement makes a copy of the `AddressType` table in the `AdventureWorks2012` database to the `AddressTypeCopy` table:

```
select *
 into Person.AddressTypeCopy
 from Person.AddressType
```

In addition, the following statement updates two rows in the `AddressTypeCopy` table so that you can use the `tablediff` utility to identify the changes:

```
UPDATE Person.AddressTypeCopy
 SET Name = 'Billing New'
 WHERE AddressTypeId = 1

UPDATE Person.AddressTypeCopy
 SET Name = 'Shipping New',
  ModifiedDate = '20140918'
 WHERE AddressTypeId = 5
```

The `tablediff` utility can be executed with the following parameters to identify the differences in the `AddressType` and `AddressTypeCopy` tables:

```
tablediff -sourceserver "(local)" -sourcedatabase
"AdventureWorks2012"
-sourceschema "Person"-sourcetable "AddressType"
-destinationserver "(local)" -destinationdatabase
"AdventureWorks2012"
-destinationschema "Person" -destinationtable "AddressTypeCopy"
-f c:\TableDiff_Output.txt
```

The destination and source parameters are the same as in the previous example, except for the table parameters, which have the source `AddressType` and the destination `AddressTypeCopy`. The execution of the utility with these parameters results in the following output to the command prompt window:

```
User-specified agent parameter values:
-sourceserver (local)
-sourcedatabase AdventureWorks2012
-sourceschema Person
-sourcetable AddressType
-destinationserver (local)
-destinationdatabase AdventureWorks2012
-destinationschema Person
-destinationtable AddressTypeCopy
-f c:\TableDiff_Output

Table [AdventureWorks2012].[Person].[AddressType] on (local)
and Table [AdventureWorks2012].[Person].[AddressTypeCopy] on (local)
have 2 differences.
Fix SQL written to c:\TableDiff_Output.sql.
Err      AddressTypeID    Col
Mismatch         1        Name
Mismatch         5        ModifiedDate Name
The requested operation took 0.296875 seconds.
```

The output first displays a summary of the parameters used and then shows the comparison results. In this example, it found the two differences that are due to updates performed on `AddressTypeCopy`. In addition, the `-f` parameter used in the example caused the `tablediff` utility to output a SQL file that can be used to fix the differences in the destination table. The output file from this example looks as follows:

```
-- Host: (local)
-- Database: [AdventureWorks2012]
-- Table: [Person].[AddressTypeCopy]
SET IDENTITY_INSERT [Person].[AddressTypeCopy] ON
UPDATE [Person].[AddressTypeCopy]
 SET [Name]='Billing'
 WHERE [AddressTypeID] = 1
UPDATE [Person].[AddressTypeCopy]
 SET [ModifiedDate]='2014-06-01 00:00:00.000',
 [Name]='Shipping' WHERE [AddressTypeID] = 5
SET IDENTITY_INSERT [Person].[AddressTypeCopy] OFF
```

> **NOTE**
>
> The `tablediff` utility requires the source table to have at least one primary key, identity, or `ROWGUID` column. This gives the utility a key that it can use to try to match a corresponding row in the destination table. If the `-strict` option is used, the destination table must also have a primary key, identity, or `ROWGUID` column.

Keep in mind that several different types of comparisons can be done with the `tablediff` utility. The `-q` option causes a quick comparison that compares only record counts and looks for differences in the schema. The `-strict` option forces the schemas of each table to be the same when the comparison is run. If this option is not used, the utility allows some columns to be of different data types, as long as they meet the mapping requirements for the data type (for example, `INT` can be compared to `BIGINT`).

The `tablediff` utility can be used for many different types of comparisons. How you use this tool depends on several factors, including the amount and type of data you are comparing.

The `bcp` Command-Line Utility

You use the `bcp` (bulk copy program) tool to address the bulk movement of data. This utility is bidirectional, allowing for the movement of data into and out of a SQL Server database.

`bcp` uses the following syntax:

```
bcp [database_name.] schema.{table_name | view_name | "query" {in
data_file | out data_file | queryout data_file | format nul}
   [-a packet_size] [-b batch_size] [-c]
   [-C { ACP | OEM | RAW | code_page } ]
```

```
[-d database_name] [-e err_file] [-E]
[-f format_file] [-F first_row] [-h"hint [,...n]"]
[-i input_file] [-k] [-K application_intent]
[-L last_row] [-m max_errors] [-n]
[-N] [-o output_file]
[-P password] [-q] [-r row_term]
[-R] [-S [server_name[\instance_name]]
[-t field_term] [-T] [-U login_id]
[-v] [-V (80 | 90 | 100 )] [-w (wide character type) ]
[-x (generate xml format file) ]
/?
```

Some of the commonly used options—other than the ones used to specify the database, such as user ID, password, and so on—are the -F and -L options. These options allow you to specify the first and last row of data to be loaded from a file, which is especially helpful in large batches. The -t option allows you to specify the field terminator that separates data elements in an ASCII file. The -E option allows you to import data into SQL Server fields that are defined with identity properties. As with sqlcmd, the -S option also allows you to connect to Azure SQL Database instances.

TIP

The BULK INSERT T-SQL statement and SSIS are good alternatives to bcp. The BULK INSERT statement is limited to loading data into SQL Server, but it is an extremely fast tool for loading data. SSIS is a sophisticated GUI that allows for both data import and data export, and it has capabilities that go well beyond bcp.

This section barely scratches the surface when it comes to the capabilities of bcp. For a more detailed look at bcp, refer to the section, "Using bcp" in Chapter 47, "SQL Server Integration Services."

The `sqldiag` Command-Line Utility

sqldiag is a diagnostic tool that you can use to gather diagnostic information about various SQL Server services. It is intended for use by Microsoft support engineers, but you might also find the information it gathers useful in troubleshooting a problem. sqldiag collects the information into files that are written, by default, to a folder named SQLDIAG, which is created where the file sqldiag.exe is located (for example, C:\Program Files\ Microsoft SQL Server\120\Tools\Binn\SQLDIAG\). The folder holds files that contain information about the machine on which SQL Server is running in addition to the following types of diagnostic information:

▶ SQL Server configuration information

▶ SQL Server blocking output

▶ SQL Server Profiler traces

▶ Windows performance logs

▶ Windows event logs

The syntax for `sqldiag` changed quite a bit back with SQL Server 2005, but very little has changed since (`sqldiag` is also not supported by Azure SQL Database). Some of the options that were used in versions prior to SQL Server 2005 are not compatible with the current version. The full syntax for `sqldiag` is as follows:

```
sqldiag
    { [/?] }
    |
    { [/I configuration_file]
      [/O output_folder_path]
      [/P support_folder_path]
      [/N output_folder_management_option]
      [/M machine1 [ machine2 machineN]| @machinelistfile]
      [/C file_compression_type]
      [/B [+]start_time]
      [/E [+]stop_time]
      [/A SQLdiag_application_name]
      [/T { tcp [ ,port ] | np | lpc | via } ]
      [/Q] [/G] [/R] [/U] [/L] [/X] }
    |
    { [START | STOP | STOP_ABORT] }
    |
    { [START | STOP | STOP_ABORT] /A SQLdiag_application_name }
```

NOTE

Keep in mind that many of the options for `sqldiag` identify how and when the `sqldiag` utility will be run. The utility can be run as a service, scheduled to start and stop at a specific time of day, and configured to change the way the output is generated. The details about these options are beyond the scope of this chapter but are covered in detail in SQL Server Books Online. This section is intended to give you a taste of the useful information that this utility can capture.

By default, the `sqldiag` utility must be run by a member of the Windows Administrators group, and this user must also be a member of the sysadmin fixed SQL Server role. To get a flavor for the type of information that `sqldiag` outputs, open a command prompt window, change the directory to the location of the `sqldiag.exe` file, and type the following command:

```
sqldiag
```

No parameters are needed to generate the output. The command prompt window scrolls status information across the screen as it collects the diagnostic information. You see the message "SQLDIAG Initialization starting..." followed by messages that indicate what information is being collected. The data collection includes a myriad of system information from MSINFO32, default traces, and SQLDumper log files. When you are ready to stop the collection, you can press Ctrl+C.

If you navigate to the sqldiag output folder, you find the files created during the collection process. In this output folder, you should find a file with MSINFO32 in its name. This file contains the same type of information that you see when you launch the System Information application from Accessories or when you run MSINFO32.EXE. This is key information about the machine on which SQL Server is running. This information includes the number of processors, the amount of memory, the amount of disk space, and a slew of other hardware and software data.

You will also find a file named xxx_sp_sqldiag_Shutdown.out, where xxx is the name of the SQL Server machine. This file contains SQL Server–specific information, including the SQL Server error logs, output from several key system stored procedures, including sp_helpdb and sp_configure, and much more information related to the current state of SQL Server.

You find other files in the sqldiag output directory as well. Default trace files, log files related to the latest sqldiag execution, and a copy of the XML file containing configuration information are among them. Microsoft documentation on these files is limited, and you may find that the best way to determine what they contain is simply to open the files and review the wealth of information therein.

The sqlservr Command-Line Utility

The sqlservr executable is the program that runs when SQL Server is started. You can use the sqlservr executable to start SQL Server from a command prompt. When you do that, all the startup messages are displayed at the command prompt, and the command prompt session becomes dedicated to the execution of SQL Server.

> **CAUTION**
>
> If you start SQL Server from a command prompt, you cannot stop or pause it by using SSMS, Configuration Manager, or the Services applet in the Control Panel. You should stop the application only from the command prompt window in which SQL Server is running. If you press Ctrl+C or Ctrl+Break, you are asked whether you want to shut down SQL Server. If you close the command prompt window in which SQL Server is running, SQL Server is automatically shut down.

The syntax for the sqlservr utility is as follows:

```
sqlservr
    [-a<L2 buffer pool directory>,<size in GB>]
    [-c] (not as a service)
    [-d file] (alternative master data file)
    [-l file] (alternative master log file)
```

```
[-e file] (alternate errorlog file)
[-f] (minimal configuration mode)
[-m] (single user admin mode)
[-g number] (stack MB to reserve)
[-k <decimal number>] (checkpoint speed in MB/sec)
[-n] (do not use event logging)
[-s name] (alternate registry key name)
[-T <number>] (trace flag turned on at startup)
[-x] (no statistics tracking)
[-y number] (stack dump on this error)
[-B] (breakpoint on error (used with -y))
[-K] (force regeneration of service master key (if exists))
[-v] (list version information)
```

Most commonly, you start SQL Server from the command prompt if you need to trouble-shoot a configuration problem. The -f option starts SQL Server in minimal configuration mode. This allows you to recover from a change to a configuration setting that prevents SQL Server from starting. You can also use the -m option when you need to start SQL Server in single-user mode, such as when you need to rebuild one of the system databases.

SQL Server functions when started from the command prompt in much the same way as it does when it is started as a service. Users can connect to the server, and you can connect to the server by using SSMS. What is different is that the SQL Server instance running in the command prompt appears as if it is not running in some of the tools. SSMS and SQL Server Service Manager show SQL Server as being stopped because they are polling the SQL Server service, which is stopped when running in the command prompt mode.

> **TIP**
>
> If you simply want to start the SQL Server service from the command prompt, you can use the NET START and NET STOP commands. These commands are not SQL Server-specific but are handy when you want to start or stop SQL Server, especially in a batch file. The SQL Server service name must be referenced after these commands. For example, NET START MSSQLSERVER starts the default SQL Server instance.

The `sqlLocalDB` Command-Line Utility

sqllocaldb is used to create and manage instances of SQL Server Express LocalDB. LocalDB utilizes a minimal set of files to start a local copy of the SQL Server Database Engine. LocalDB offers developers a light weight option for deploying a SQL Server Express database without complicated configuration or setup. LocalDB is not a replacement of SQL Server Express. It utilizes the full SQL Server Express engine, but it is invoked directly from a client process.

The sqllocaldb utility is basically a Configuration Manager for LocalDB engine. It enables you to create and delete an instance of LocalDB. It can also be used to start or stop this instance and share the instance with other users. The syntax for the utility is as follows. Most parameter names do not allow for a leading hyphen unless they come after the specified instance name:

```
SqlLocalDB.exe
{
      [ create    | c ] <instance-name>  <instance-version> [-s ]
    | [ delete    | d ] <instance-name>
    | [ start     | s ] <instance-name>
    | [ stop      | p ] <instance-name>  [ -i ] [ -k ]
    | [ share     | h ] [" <user_SID> " | " <user_account> " ] "
<private-name> " " <shared-name> "
    | [ unshare   | u ] " <shared-name> "
    | [ info      | i ] <instance-name>
    | [ versions  | v ]
    | [ trace     | t ] [ on | off ]
    | [ -? ]
}
```

The `sqllocaldb` utility is not installed until LocalDB has been installed on the machine. The LocalDB binary files can be installed as part of the SQL Server Express install or by using the SQLLocalDB.msi program. The full SQL Server Express install and the SQLLocalDB.msi are both free downloads available from Microsoft. The SQLLocalDB.msi is a relatively small download that is specifically for the LocalDB install.

After you have the LocalDB binaries installed, you can find `Sqllocaldb.exe` in the Tools folders (for example, c:\Program Files\Microsoft SQL Server\120\Tools\Binn) along with several other command prompt utilities. To get started using the utility, open a command prompt using Administrator privileges. Navigate to the aforementioned tools folder and type the following at the command prompt to create a LocalDB instance:

```
SqlLocalDB.exe create "MyLocalDB" -s
```

This will create a LocalDB instance on the machine where this command was executed. The `-s` option also starts the instance so that it is ready to use. The SQL Server Express binaries that are used for this instance are the same as the version of `sqllocaldb` that was executed. You can also specify the version that you want to start by passing the version number to the `sqllocaldb` utility, as shown here:

```
SqlLocalDB.exe create "MyLocalDB" 12.0 -s
```

After the instance is started, you can use the `info` parameter to return important information about the instance. Figure 4.3 shows an example of the output that is returned with the `info` parameter:

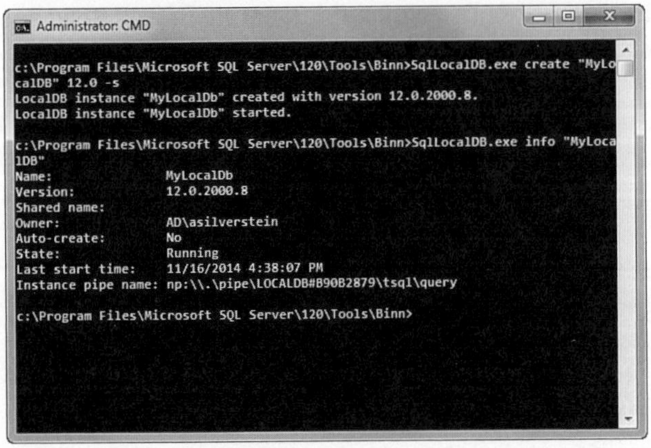

FIGURE 4.3   LocalDB information.

The Instance pipe name that is shown in Figure 4.3 is particularly important for connecting to the LocalDB if you are using a version of .NET that is earlier than 4.0.2. In this case, you must connect directly to the named pipe of the LocalDB. We can use one of the previously discussed utilities, sqlcmd, to make a connection to the new LocalDB using named pipes, as shown in the following example:

```
sqlcmd -S np:\\.\pipe\LOCALDB#331FD664\tsql\query
```

> **NOTE**
>
> In some connection scenarios, the sqllocaldb utility is not needed to establish a client connection to the LocalDB. One of these scenarios involves a connection that references a specific database file (for example, C:\mssql\MyDatabase.mdf). In this scenario, a LocalDB instance can be automatically created and started without the use of sqllocaldb.

Another common use of the sqllocaldb utility is to create a shared instance of LocalDB. Sharing an instance allows other users on the same machine to gain access to LocalDB, as shown in the following example:

```
SqlLocalDB.exe share "MyLocalDB" "EveryoneDb"
```

Summary

SQL Server provides a set of command-line utilities that allow you to execute some of the available SQL Server programs from the command prompt. Much of the functionality housed in these utilities is also available in graphical tools, such as SSMS. However, the capability to initiate these programs from the command prompt is invaluable in certain scenarios.

Chapter 5, "SQL Server Profiler," covers a tool that is critical for performance tuning in SQL Server 2014. SQL Server Profiler provides insight by monitoring and capturing the activity occurring on a SQL Server instance. Although deprecated, it is still a "go-to" tool for many DBAs and developers because of the wide variety of information it can capture.

4

SQL Server Profiler

This chapter explores the SQL Server Profiler, one of SQL Server's most powerful auditing and analysis tools. The SQL Server Profiler gives you a basic understanding of database access and helps you answer questions such as these:

▶ Which queries are causing table scans on my invoice history table?

▶ Am I experiencing deadlocks, and, if so, why?

▶ What SQL queries is each application submitting?

▶ Which were the 10 worst-performing queries last week?

▶ If I implement this alternative indexing scheme, how will it affect my batch operations?

SQL Server Profiler records activity that occurs on a SQL Server instance. The tool has a great deal of flexibility and can be customized for your needs. You can direct SQL Server Profiler to record output to a window, file, or table. You can specify which events to trace, the information to include in the trace, how you want that information grouped, and what filters you want to apply.

What's New with SQL Server Profiler

The SQL Server 2014 Profiler is essentially the same as the SQL Server 2012 Profiler. This is not surprising because many new features that were added in SQL Server 2005 and SQL Server 2008 addressed gaps identified in previous versions.

One surprising decision is that the SQL Server Profiler for Database Engine Trace Capture and Trace Replay remains on the deprecation list in SQL Server 2014. These features will be supported in the next version of SQL Server but will be removed in a later version. Microsoft has identified Extended Events as the replacement. Extended Events is a lightweight event-based infrastructure that is covered in more detail in Chapter 39, "Monitoring SQL Server Performance."

SQL Server Profiler Architecture

SQL Server 2014 has both a server and a client-side component for tracing activity on a server. The SQL trace facility is the server-side component that manages queues of events initiated by event producers on the server. Extended stored procedures can be used to define the server-side events that are to be captured. These procedures, which define a SQL trace, are discussed later in this chapter in the section, "Defining Server-Side Traces."

The SQL Server Profiler is the client-side tracing facility. It comes with a fully functional GUI that allows for real-time auditing of SQL Server events. When it is used to trace server activity, events that are part of a trace definition are gathered at the server. Any filters defined as part of the trace definition are applied, and the event data is queued for its final destination. The SQL Server Profiler application is the final destination when client-side tracing is used. The basic elements involved in this process are shown in Figure 5.1.

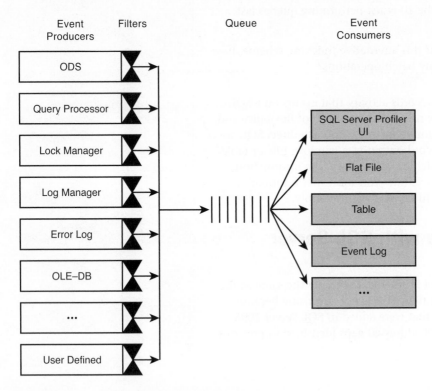

FIGURE 5.1   SQL Server Profiler's architecture.

This figure illustrates the following four steps in the process when tracing from the SQL Server Profiler:

1. Event producers, such as the Query Processor, Lock Manager, Open Data Services ODS, and so on, raise events for the SQL Server Profiler.

2. The filters define the information to submit to SQL Server Profiler. A producer will not send events if the event is not included in the filter.

3. SQL Server Profiler queues all the events.

4. SQL Server Profiler writes the events to each defined consumer, such as a flat file, a table, the Profiler client window, and so on.

In addition to obtaining its trace data from the event producers listed in step 1, you can also configure SQL Server Profiler so that it obtains its data from a previously saved location. This includes trace data saved in a file or table. The "Saving and Exporting Traces" section, later in this chapter, covers using trace files and trace tables in more detail.

Creating Traces

Because SQL Server Profiler can trace numerous events, it is easy to get lost when reading the trace output. You need to roughly determine the information you require and how you want the information grouped. For example, if you want to see the SQL statements that each user is submitting through an application, you could trace incoming SQL statements and group them by user and by application.

When you have an idea about what you want to trace, you should launch the SQL Server Profiler by selecting Start, then Microsoft SQL Server 2014, then Performance Tools, and finally SQL Server Profiler. You can also launch it from within SQL Server Management Studio (SSMS) from the Tools menu. When you launch the Profiler, the first window to appear allows you to enter the connection information for the server that you want to trace. After the connection is established, the General tab of the Trace Properties window (see Figure 5.2) is displayed.

The first place you should look when creating a new trace is at the trace templates. These templates contain predefined trace settings that address some common auditing needs. They have preset events, data columns, and filters targeted at specific profiling scenarios. The available trace templates, found in the template drop-down on the General tab of the Trace Properties window, are listed in Table 5.1.

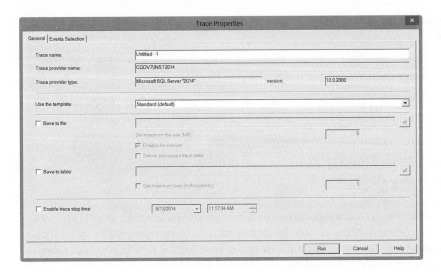

FIGURE 5.2   General trace properties.

TABLE 5.1   SQL Server Profiler Templates

Template	Description
SP_Counts	Tracks all the stored procedures as they start. No event except for the stored procedure starting is traced.
Standard	Traces the completion of SQL statements and Remote Procedure Calls (RPCs) as well as key connection information.
TSQL	Traces the start of SQL statements and RPCs. This template is useful for debugging client applications where some of the statements are not completing successfully.
TSQL_Duration	Traces the total execution time for each completed SQL statement or RPC.
TSQL_Grouped	Traces the start of SQL statements and RPCs, grouped by Application, NTUser, LoginName, and ClientProcessId.
TSQL_Locks	Traces the completion of SQL statements along with the key lock information that can be used to troubleshoot lock timeouts, deadlocks, and lock escalation issues.
TSQL_Replay	Captures profiling information that is useful for replay. This template contains the same type of information as the standard template, but it adds more detail, including cursor and RPC output details.
TSQL_SPs	Traces stored procedures in detail, including the start and completion of each stored procedure. The SQL statements within each procedure are traced as well.
Tuning	Performs a streamlined trace that tracks only the completion of SQL statements and RPCs. The completion events provide duration details that can be useful for performance tuning.

Keep in mind that the templates that come with SQL Server 2014 are not actual traces. They simply provide a foundation for you in creating your own traces. After you select a template, you can modify the trace setting and customize it for your own needs. You can then save the modified template as its own template file that will appear in the template drop-down list for future trace creation.

`Trace Name` is another property you can modify on the General tab. `Trace Name` is a relatively unimportant trace property for future traces. When you create a new trace, you can specify a name for the trace; however, this trace name will not be used again. For instance, if you have a trace definition you like, you can save the trace definition as a template file. If you want to run the trace again in the future, you can create a new trace and select the template file that you saved. You will not be selecting the trace to run based on the trace name you entered originally. `Trace Name` is useful only if you are running multiple traces simultaneously and need to distinguish between them more easily.

> **TIP**
>
> Do yourself a favor and save your favorite trace definitions in your own template. The default set of templates that come with SQL Server are good, but you will most likely want to change the position of a column or add an event that you find yourself using all the time. It is not hard to adjust one of the default templates to your needs each time, but if you save your own template with exactly what you need, it makes the task all the more easy. After you save your own template, you can set it as the default template, and it will be used by default every time you start the Profiler.

The Save to File and Save to Table options on the General tab of the Trace Properties page allow you to define where the trace output is stored. You can save the output to a flat file or SQL Server table. These options are discussed in more detail later in the chapter, in the section "Saving and Exporting Traces."

The last option on the General tab of the Trace Properties window is the Enable Trace Stop Time option. This scheduling-oriented feature allows you to specify a date and time at which you want to stop tracing. This capability is handy if you want to start a trace in the evening before you go home. You can set the stop time so that the trace will run for a few hours but won't affect any nightly processing that might occur later in the evening.

Events

The events and data columns that will be captured by your Profiler trace are defined on the Events Selection tab. An example of the Events Selection tab is shown in Figure 5.3.

The Events Selection tab consolidates the selection of events, data columns, and filters on one screen. One of the biggest advantages of the SQL Server 2014 Events Selection tab is that you can easily determine which data columns will be populated for each event by looking at the columns that have check boxes available for the event. For example, the Audit Login event has check boxes for `Text Data`, `ApplicationName`, and others but does not have a check box available for `CPU`, `Reads`, `Writes`, and other data columns that are not relevant to the event. For those data columns that have check boxes, you have the option of unchecking the box so that the data column will not be populated for the event when the trace is run.

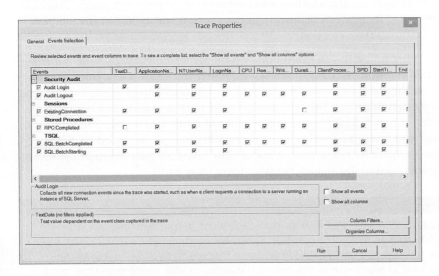

FIGURE 5.3   The Events Selection tab.

You may find that adding events in SQL Server 2014 is a bit confusing. When you select a template, the event categories, selected events in those categories, and selected columns are displayed in the Events Selection tab. Now, if you want to add additional events, how do you do it? The answer to this question lies in the Show All Events check box in the lower-right corner of the Events Selection tab. When you click this check box, all the available event categories are listed on the screen. The events and columns that you had previously selected may or may not be visible on the screen. They are not lost, but you may need to scroll down the Events Selection tab to find the event categories that contain the events you had selected prior to selecting the Show All Events check box.

You will also notice that all the events in the categories in which you had events selected are displayed. In other words, if you had only 2 events selected in the Security Audit category and then selected the Show All Events check box, you see all 42 events listed. The only 2 events selected are the ones you had selected previously, but you need to wade through many events to see them. One upside to this kind of display is that you can easily view all the events for a category and the columns that relate to the events. One possible downside is that the Events Selection tab can be very busy, and it may take a little extra time to find what you are looking for.

TIP

If you capture too many events in one trace, the trace becomes difficult to review. Instead, you can create several traces, one for each type of information that you want to examine, and run them simultaneously. You can also choose to add or remove events after the trace has started. Keep in mind that you can pause a running trace, change the selected events, and restart the trace without losing the output that was there prior to pausing the trace.

Your ability to select and view events is made easier by using the tree control available on each event. The tree control allows you to expand or collapse an event category. When you click the + icon next to a category, all the events are displayed. When you click the – icon, the event category is collapsed to a single row on the display. When an event has been selected for use within a category, the category name is shown in bold. If you want to add all the events in a category to your trace, you can simply right-click the category name and choose the Select Event Category option. You can also remove all events in a category by right-clicking the category name and choosing the Deselect Event Category option.

Understanding what each of the events captures can be a challenging task. You can refer to "SQL Server Event Class Reference" in Books Online for a detailed description, or you can use the simple Help facility available on the Events Selection tab. The Events Selection tab has a Help facility that describes each of the events and categories. The Help text is displayed on the Events Selection tab below the list of available events. When you mouse over a particular event or event category, a description of that item is shown. This puts the information you need at your fingertips.

NOTE

If you are going to use SQL Server Profiler, you should spend some time getting to know the events first and the type of output that Profiler generates. You should do this first in a development environment or standalone environment where the Profiler's effect on performance does not matter. It's a good idea to start a trace with a few events at a time and execute some relevant statements to see what is displayed for each event. You will soon realize the strength of the SQL Server Profiler and the type of valuable information it can return.

Data Columns

The columns of information captured in a Profiler trace are determined by the Data Columns selected. The Events Selection tab has the functionality you need to add columns, organize the columns, and apply filters on the data returned in these columns. As mentioned earlier, you can select and deselect the available columns for a particular event by using the check boxes displayed for the listed events. To understand what kind of information a column is going to return, you can simply mouse over the column and Help for that item is displayed in the second Help box below the event list. Figure 5.4 shows an example of the Help output. In this particular case, the mouse pointer is over the ApplicationName column returned for the SQL:BatchCompleted event. The first Help box displays information about the SQL:BatchCompleted event, and the second Help box shows information about the data column.

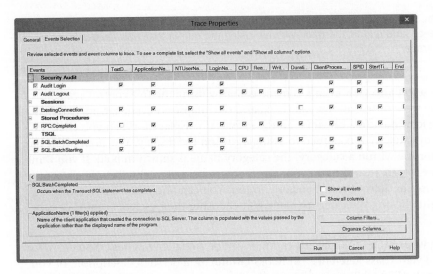

FIGURE 5.4   Help for data columns on the Events Selection tab.

Keep in mind that there is a default set of columns displayed for each event. You can view additional columns by selecting the Show All Columns check box. When you choose this option, an additional set of columns is displayed in the Events Selection tab. The additional columns are shown with a dark gray background, and you may need to scroll to the right on the Events Selection tab to be able to see them. Figure 5.5 shows an example of the additional columns displayed for the Performance event when the Show All Columns option is used. Some of the additional columns available for selection in this example are BigintData1 and BigintData2.

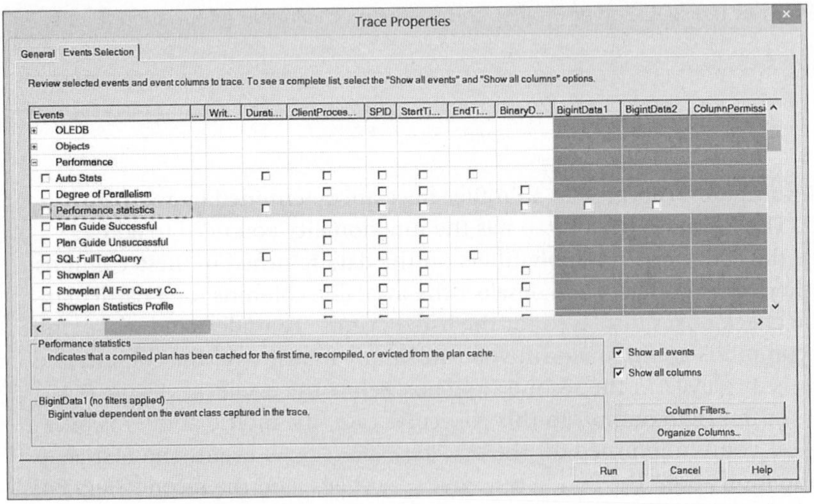

FIGURE 5.5   Additional columns displayed with the Show All Columns option.

To organize the columns you have selected, you can choose the Organize Columns selection on the Events Selection tab. This Organize Columns window allows you to change the order of the columns in the trace output as well as group the data by selected columns. Figure 5.6 shows an example of the Organize Columns window with the groups and columns selected by default when you use the TSQL_Grouped template.

To change the order of a column, you simply select the column in the list and use the Up or Down buttons to move it. The same movement can be done with columns selected for grouping. You add columns to groups by selecting the column in the data list and clicking the Up button until the column is moved out of the Columns list and into the Groups list. For example, in Figure 5.6, you can group the SPID column by selecting it and clicking the Up button until it moves into the Groups tree structure instead of the Columns tree structure.

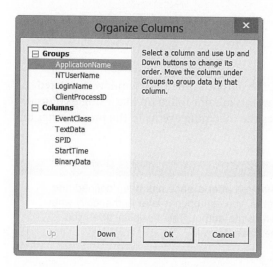

FIGURE 5.6   Organizing columns in the Events Selection tab.

The number of columns selected for grouping and the order of the columns are both important factors in the way the trace data will be displayed. If you choose only one column for grouping, the trace window displays events grouped by the values in the grouped data column and collapses all events under it. For example, if you group by DatabaseId, the output in the trace window grid displays DatabaseId as the first column, with a + sign next to each DatabaseId that has received events. The number displayed to the right of the event in parentheses shows the number of collapsed events that can be viewed by clicking on the + sign. Figure 5.7 shows an example of the trace output window that has been grouped by DatabaseId only. The database with a DatabaseId equal to 6 is shown at the bottom of the grid in this example. The grid has been expanded, and some of the events that were captured for this DatabaseId are shown.

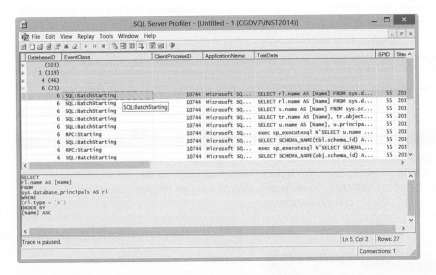

FIGURE 5.7   Grouping on a single column.

If you select multiple columns for grouping, the output in the trace window is ordered based on the columns in the grouping. The events are not rolled up like a single column, but the trace output grid automatically places the incoming events in the proper order in the output display.

TIP

The organization of columns in a trace can happen after a trace has been defined and executed. If you save the trace to a file or table, you can open it later and specify whatever ordering or grouping you want to reorganize the output. This flexibility gives you almost endless possibilities for analyzing the trace data.

Filters

Filters restrict the event data returned in your trace output. You can filter the events captured by the SQL Server Profiler via the Column Filters button on the Events Selection tab. An example of the Edit Filter window is shown in Figure 5.8. All the available columns for the trace are shown on the left side of the Edit Filter window. Those columns that have filters on them have a filter icon displayed next to the column in the column list.

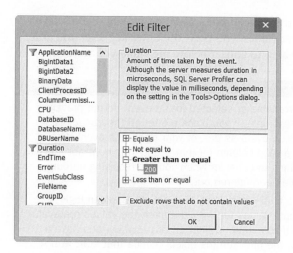

FIGURE 5.8   Editing filter properties.

The filtering options in SQL Server 2014 are similar to those available in prior versions. Which options are available depends on the type of column you are filtering on. The different filtering options are as follows:

▶ **Like/Not Like**—This option enables you to include or exclude events based on a wildcard. You should use the % character as your wildcard character. When you have completed a filter definition, you can press Enter to create an entry space for another filter definition. For example, with the ApplicationName filter, you can specify Like Microsoft%, and you get only those events related to applications that match the wildcard, such as Microsoft SQL Server Management Studio. This filtering option is available for text data columns and data columns that contain name information, such as NTUserName and ApplicationName.

▶ **Equals/Not Equal To/Greater Than or Equal/Less Than or Equal**—Filters with this option have all four of these conditions available. For the Equals and Not Equal To conditions, you can specify a single value or a series of values. For a series of values, you press Enter after each value is entered, and a new entry space is created for you to enter the next value. For the other conditional types, a single value is supplied. For example, you can filter on DataBaseID and input numeric values under the Equals To node of the filtering tree. This filtering option is available for numeric data columns such as Duration, IndexId, and ObjectId.

▶ **Greater Than/Less Than**—This type of filtering option is available only on time-based data columns. This includes StartTime and EndTime filters. These filters expect date formats of the form YYYY-MM-DD or YYYY-MM-DD HH:MM:SS.

Each data column can use one of these three filtering options. When you click the data column available for filtering, you see the filtering options for that column displayed in the right-hand pane of the Edit Filter window. You enter the values on which you want to filter in the data entry area on the filter tree. This input area is shown when you select a specific filtering option. For multiple filter values, you press the Enter key after you enter each value. This causes a new data entry area to appear below the value you were on.

CAUTION

Filters applied to columns that are not available or selected for an event do not prevent the event data from being returned. For example, if you place a filter on the `ObjectName` column and choose the `SQL:StmtStarting` event as part of your trace, the event data is not filtered because `ObjectName` is not a valid column for that event. This behavior may seem relatively intuitive, but it is something to consider when you are receiving output from a trace that you believe should have been filtered out.

Also, be careful when specifying multiple filter values and consider the Boolean logic applied to them. When you specify multiple values for the `Like` filter, the values are evaluated with an `OR` condition. For example, if you create a filter on `ObjectName` and have a `Like` filter with values of `A%`, `B%`, and `C%`, the filter returns object names that start with A or B or C. When you use the `Not Like` filter, the `AND` condition is used on multiple values. For example, `Not Like` filter values for `ObjectName` of `A%` and `C%` result in objects with names that do not start with A and object names that do not start with C.

Executing Traces and Working with Trace Output

After you define the events and columns you want to capture in a trace, you can execute the Profiler trace. To do so, you click the Run button on the Trace Properties window, and the Profiler GUI starts capturing the events you have selected. The GUI contains a grid that is centrally located on the Profiler window, and newly captured events are scrolled on the screen as they are received. Figure 5.9 shows a simple example of the Profiler screen with output from an actively running trace.

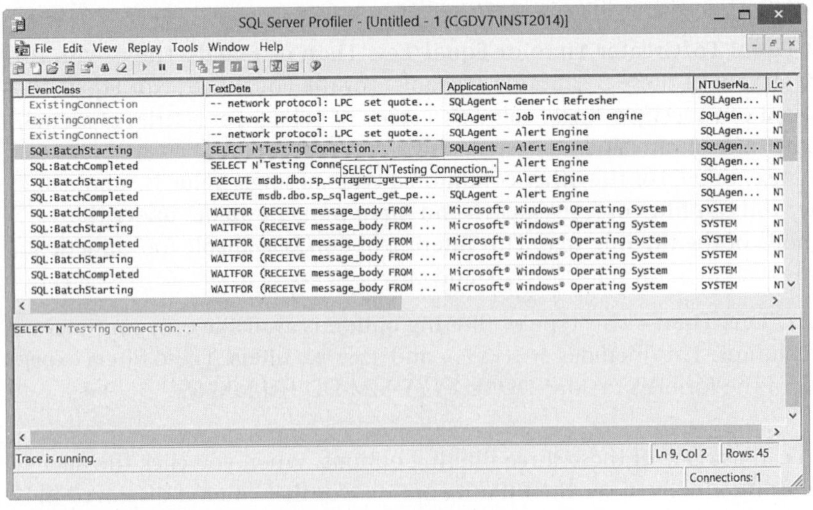

FIGURE 5.9   The Profiler GUI with an active trace.

The Profiler GUI provides many different options for dealing with an actively running trace. You can turn off scrolling on the trace, pause the trace, stop the trace, and view the properties of an actively running trace. You can find strings within the trace output, and you can even move the columns around in the display so that they are displayed in a different order. These options provide a great deal of flexibility and allow you to focus on the output that is most important to you.

Saving and Exporting Traces

In many cases, you want to save or export the trace output generated by a Profiler trace. The output can be analyzed, replayed, imported, or manipulated at a later time after it has been saved. Trace output can be saved as the trace is running or saved after it has been generated to the Profiler GUI. The Trace Properties window provides options for saving trace output while the trace is running. The options are defined using the Save to File and Save to Table options on the General tab of the Trace Properties window. You can save to a file, a table, or both a table and a file. Figure 5.10 shows an example of a trace that will save to both a file and table while it is executing.

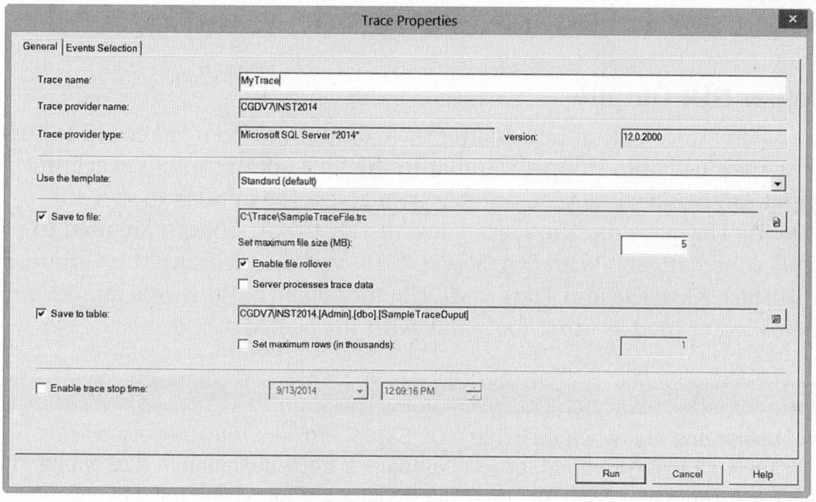

FIGURE 5.10   Saving trace output while a trace is running.

Saving Trace Output to a File

When you save a running trace to a file, you have several options for controlling the output. One option you should always consider is the Set Maximum File Size (MB) option. This option prevents a trace output file from exceeding the specified size. Controlling the size helps make the file more manageable, and, more importantly, it can save you from having a trace file gobble up all the disk space on the drive you are writing to. Remember that the amount of trace data written to a file on a busy production system can be extensive. You can also use this file size option in conjunction with the Enable File Rollover option. When the Enable File Rollover option is used, the trace does not stop when the file size maximum is met. Instead, a new trace file is created, and the output is generated to that file until it reaches the file size maximum.

Saving Trace Output to a Table

The Save to Table option writes the trace output directly to a SQL Server table as the trace is running. Having the data in a SQL table provides a great deal of flexibility for analyzing the data. You can use the full power of Transact-SQL against the table, including sorting, grouping, and more complex search conditions that are not available through the SQL Server Profiler filters.

You need to consider both the disk space requirements and impact on performance when the Save to Table option is used. The Profiler provides an option, Set Maximum Rows (in Thousands), to limit the amount of output generated from the trace. The performance impact depends on the volume of data being written to the table. Generally, you should avoid writing the trace output to a table when using high-volume SQL servers. Writing directly to a table adds an additional load on SQL Server that can be avoided.

The best option for high-volume servers is to first write the trace output to a file and then import the file to a trace table at a later time.

Saving the Profiler GUI Output

Another option for saving trace output occurs after trace output has been generated to the Profiler GUI and the trace has been stopped. Similar to the save options for an executing trace, the GUI output can be saved to a file or table. You access the options to save the GUI output by selecting File, Save As. The Trace File and Trace Table options are used to save to a file or table consecutively. With SQL Server 2014, you can also save the output to an XML file. The Trace XML File and Trace XML File for Replay options generate XML output that can be edited or used as input for replay with the SQL Server Profiler.

> **NOTE**
>
> Two distinct save operations are available in the SQL Server Profiler. You can save trace events to a file or table as just described, or you can save a trace definition in a template file. The Save As Trace Table and Save As Trace File options are for saving trace events to a file. The Save As Trace Template option saves the trace definition. Saving a trace template saves you the trouble of having to go through all the properties each time to set up the events, data columns, and filters for your favorite traces.

An alternative to saving all the event data associated with a particular trace is to select specific event rows from the SQL Server Profiler windows. You can capture all the trace information associated with a trace row by selecting a row in the trace output window of Profiler and choosing Edit, Copy. Or, you can just copy the event text (typically a SQL statement) by selecting the row, highlighting the text in the lower pane, and using the Copy option. You can then paste this data into SSMS or the tool of your choice for further execution and more detailed analysis. This capability can be particularly useful during performance tuning. After you identify the long-running statement or procedure, you can copy the SQL, paste it into SSMS, and display the query plan to determine why the query was running so long.

Importing Trace Files

A trace saved to a file or table can be read back into SQL Server Profiler at a later time for more detailed analysis or to replay the trace on the same SQL Server or another SQL Server instance. You can import data from a trace file or trace table by choosing File, Open and then selecting either a trace file or trace table. If you choose to open a trace file, you are presented with a dialog to locate the trace file on the local machine. If you choose to import a trace table, you are first presented with a connection dialog to specify the SQL Server name, the login ID, and the password to connect to it. When you are successfully connected, you are presented with a dialog to specify the database and name of the trace table you want to import from. After you specify the trace file or trace table to import into Profiler, the entire contents of the file or table are read in and displayed in a Profiler window.

You may find that large trace files or trace tables are difficult to analyze, and you may just want to analyze events associated with a specific application or table or specific types of queries. To limit the amount of information displayed in the Profiler window, you can filter out the data displayed via the Properties dialog. You can choose which events and data columns you want to display and also specify conditions in the Filters tab to limit the rows displayed from the trace file or trace table. These options do not affect the information stored in the trace file or trace table—only what information is displayed in the Profiler window.

Importing a Trace File into a Trace Table

Although you can load a trace file directly into Profiler for analysis, very large files can be difficult to analyze. Profiler loads an entire file. For large files, this process can take quite a while, and the responsiveness of Profiler might not be the best. Multiple trace output files for a given trace can also be cumbersome and difficult to manage when those files are large.

You can use the trace filters to limit which rows are displayed but not which rows are imported into Profiler. You often end up with a bunch of rows displayed with no data in the columns you want to analyze. In addition, while the filters allow you to limit which rows are displayed, they don't really provide a means of running more complex reports on the data, such as generating counts of events or displaying the average query duration.

> **TIP**
>
> Fortunately, SQL Server 2014 provides a way for you to selectively import a trace file into a trace table. When importing a trace file into a trace table, you can filter the data before it goes into the table as well as combine multiple files into a single trace table. When the data is in a trace table, you can load the trace table into Profiler or write your own queries and reports against the trace table for more detailed analysis than is possible in Profiler.

5

Microsoft SQL Server also includes some built-in user-defined functions for working with Profiler traces. The `fn_trace_gettable` function is used to import trace file data into a trace table. Following is the syntax for this function:

```
fn_trace_gettable( [ @filename = ] filename , [ @numfiles = ] number_files )
```

This function returns the contents of the specified file as a table result set. You can use the result set from this function just as you would any table. By default, the function returns all possible Profiler columns, even if no data was captured for the column in the trace. To limit the columns returned, you specify the list of columns in the query. If you want to limit the rows retrieved from the trace file, you specify your search conditions in the WHERE clause. If your Profiler trace used rollover files to split the trace across multiple files, you can specify the number of files you want it to read in. If the default value of default is used, all rollover files for the trace are loaded. Listing 5.1 provides an example of creating and populating a trace table from a trace file, using SELECT INTO, and then adding rows by using an INSERT statement. Note that this example limits the columns and rows returned by specifying a column list and search conditions in the WHERE clause.

LISTING 5.1   Creating and Inserting Trace Data into a Trace Table from a Trace File

```
/**************************************************************
*********
** NOTE - you will need to edit the path/filename on your
system if
**        you use this code to load your own trace files
**************************************************************
*********/

select EventClass,
       EventSubClass,
       TextData = convert(varchar(8000), TextData),
       BinaryData,
       ApplicationName,
       Duration,
       StartTime,
       EndTime,
       Reads,
       Writes,
       CPU,
       ObjectID,
       IndexID,
       NestLevel
    into TraceTable
    FROM ::fn_trace_gettable('c:\temp\sampletrace_
20140510_0622.trc', default)
    where TextData is not null
       or EventClass in (16, -- Attention
```

```
                           25, -- Lock:Deadlock
                           27, -- Lock:Timeout
                           33, -- Exception
                           58, -- Auto Update Stats
                           59, -- Lock:Deadlock Chain
                           79, -- Missing Column Statistics
                           80, -- Missing Join Predicate
                           92, -- Data File Auto Grow
                           93, -- Log File Auto Grow
                           94, -- Data File Auto Shrink
                           95) -- Log File Auto Shrink

Insert into TraceTable (EventClass, EventSubClass,
             TextData, BinaryData,
             ApplicationName, Duration, StartTime, EndTime,
Reads, Writes,
             CPU, ObjectID, IndexID, nestlevel)
      select EventClass, EventSubClass,
             TextData = convert(varchar(7900), TextData),
BinaryData,
             ApplicationName, Duration, StartTime, EndTime,
Reads, Writes,
             CPU, ObjectID, IndexID, nestlevel
        FROM ::fn_trace_gettable('c:\temp\sampletrace_
20140510_0205.trc', -1)
        where TextData is not null
           or EventClass in (16, --  Attention
                           25, -- Lock:Deadlock
                           27, -- Lock:Timeout
                           33, -- Exception
                           58, -- Auto Update Stats
                           59, -- Lock:Deadlock Chain
                           79, -- Missing Column
Statistics
                           80, -- Missing Join Predicate
                           92, -- Data File Auto Grow
                           93, -- Log File Auto Grow
                           94, -- Data File Auto Shrink
                           95) -- Log File Auto Shrink
go
```

After the trace file is imported into a trace table, you can open the trace table in Profiler or run your own queries against the trace table from a Query Editor window in SSMS. For example, the following query returns the number of lock timeouts encountered for each table during the period the trace was running:

```
select object_name(ObjectId), count(*)
    from TraceTable
    where EventClass = 27 -- Lock:Timout Event
    group by object_name(ObjectId)
go
```

Analyzing Trace Output with the Database Engine Tuning Advisor

In addition to being able to manually analyze traces in Profiler, you can also use the Database Engine Tuning Advisor to analyze the queries captured in a trace and recommend changes to your indexing scheme. You can invoke it from the Tools menu in SQL Server Profiler. The Database Engine Tuning Advisor can read in a trace that was previously saved to a table or a file. This feature allows you to capture a workload, tune the indexing scheme, and rerun the trace to determine whether the index changes improved performance as expected.

Because the Database Engine Tuning Advisor analyzes SQL statements, you need to make sure that the trace includes one or more of the following events:

```
SP:StmtCompleted
SP:StmtStarting
SQL:BatchCompleted
SQL:BatchStarting
SQL:StmtCompleted
SQL:StmtStarting
```

One of each class (one SP: and one SQL:) is sufficient to capture dynamic SQL statements and statements embedded in stored procedures. You should also make sure that the trace includes the text data column, which contains the actual queries.

The Database Engine Tuning Advisor analyzes the trace and gives you recommendations, along with an estimated improvement-in-execution time. You can choose to create indexes now or at a later time, or you can save the CREATE INDEX commands to a script file. The Database Engine Tuning Advisor is discussed in more detail in Chapter 40, "SQL Server Database Engine Tuning Advisor."

Replaying Trace Data

To replay a trace, you must have a trace saved to a file or a table. The trace must be captured with certain trace events to enable playback. The required events are captured by default if you use the Profiler template TSQL_Replay. You can define a trace to be saved when you create or modify the trace definition. You can also save the current contents of the trace window to a file or table by using the Save As Trace File or Save As Trace Table options in the File menu.

To replay a saved trace, you choose File and then Open to open a trace file or trace table. After you select the type of trace to replay, a grid with the trace columns selected in the original trace is displayed. At this point, you can either start the replay of the trace step-by-step or complete execution of the entire trace. The options for replaying the trace are found under the Replay menu. When you start the replay of the trace, the Connect to Server dialog is displayed, enabling you to choose the server that you want to replay the traces against. When you are connected to a server, a Replay Configuration dialog like the one shown in Figure 5.11 is displayed.

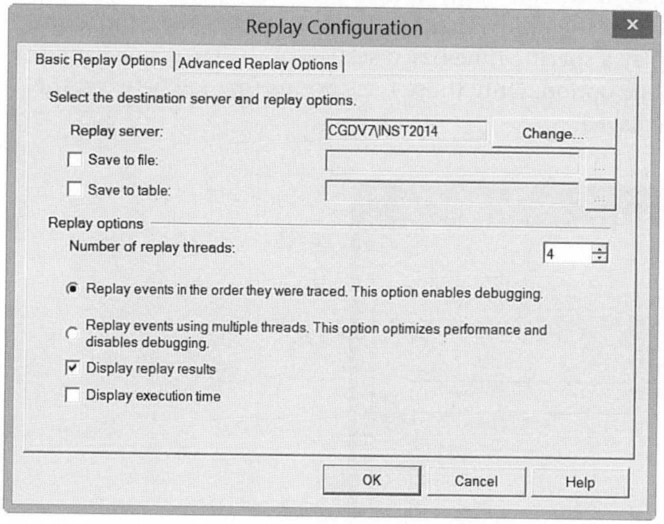

FIGURE 5.11   Basic replay options.

The first replay option, which is enabled by default, replays the trace in the same order in which it was captured and allows for debugging. The second option takes advantage of multiple threads; it optimizes performance but disables debugging. A third option involves specifying whether to display the replay results. You would normally want to see the results, but for large trace executions, you might want to forgo displaying the results and send them to an output file instead.

If you choose the option that allows for debugging, you can execute the trace in a manner similar to many integrated development environments. You can set breakpoints, step through statements one at a time, or position the cursor on a statement within the trace and execute the statements from the beginning of the trace to the cursor position.

> **NOTE**
>
> Automating testing scripts is another important use of the SQL Server Profiler Save and Replay options. For instance, a trace of a heavy production load can be saved and rerun against a new release of the database to ensure that the new release has similar or improved performance characteristics and returns the same data results. The saved traces can help make regression testing much easier.

You also have the option of specifying advanced replay options in SQL Server 2014. These options are found on the Advanced Replay Options tab of the Replay Configuration dialog (see Figure 5.12).

The first two options on the Advanced Replay Options tab relate to the system process IDs (SPIDs) targeted for replay. If the Replay System SPIDs option is selected, the trace events for every SPID in the trace file will be replayed. If you want to target activity for a specific SPID, you should choose the Replay One SPID Only option and select the SPID from the drop-down menu. You can also limit the events that will be replayed based on the timing of the events. If you want to replay a specific time-based section of the trace, you can use the Limit Replay by Date and Time option. Only those trace events that fall between the data range you specify will be replayed.

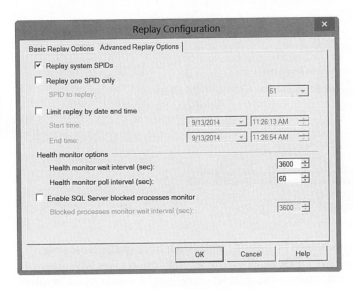

FIGURE 5.12   Advanced replay options.

The last set of advanced options is geared toward maintaining the health of the server on which you are replaying the trace. The Health Monitor Wait Interval (sec) option determines the amount of time a thread can run during replay before being terminated. This helps avoid an excessive drain on the server's resources. The Health Monitor Poll Interval (sec) option determines how often the health monitor will poll for threads that should be terminated. The last advanced option on the screen relates to blocked processes. When it is enabled, the monitor polls for blocked processes according to the interval specified.

> **NOTE**
>
> Extended Events can be used to capture trace data as well and this type of trace can then be replayed using the Distributed Replay feature. The Distributed Replay feature is more scalable than the SQL Server Profiler and allows for a workload to be replayed from multiple computers at one time. Microsoft recommends the use of this replay method because

it is more robust and because the SQL Server Profiler has been deprecated. Distributed Replay is discussed in more detail in Chapter 6, "SQL Distributed Replay."

Defining Server-Side Traces

Much of the SQL Server Profiler functionality can also be initiated through a set of system stored procedures. Through these procedures, you can define a server-side trace that can be run automatically or on a scheduled basis, such as via a scheduled job, instead of through the Profiler GUI. Server-side traces are also useful if you are tracing information over an extended period of time or are planning on capturing a large amount of trace information. The overhead of running a server-side trace is less than that of running a client-side trace with Profiler.

To start a server-side trace, you need to define the trace by using the trace-related system procedures. These procedures can be called from within a SQL Server stored procedure or batch. You define a server-side trace by using the following four procedures:

- ▶ **sp_trace_create**—This procedure is used to create the trace definition. It sets up the trace and defines the file to store the captured events. sp_trace create returns a trace ID number that you need to reference from the other three procedures to further define and manage the trace.

- ▶ **sp_trace_setevent**—You need to call this procedure once for each data column of every event that you want to capture.

- ▶ **sp_trace_setfilter**—You call this procedure once for each filter you want to define on an event data column.

- ▶ **sp_trace_setstatus**—After the trace is defined, you call this procedure to start, stop, or remove the trace. You must stop and remove a trace definition before you can open and view the trace file.

You will find that manually creating procedure scripts for tracing can be rather tedious. Much of the tedium is due to the fact that many numeric parameters drive the trace execution. For example, the sp_trace_setevent procedure accepts an eventid and a columnid that determine what event data will be captured. Fortunately, SQL Server 2014 provides a set of catalog views that contain these numeric values and what they represent. The sys.trace_categories catalog view contains the event categories. The sys.trace_events catalog view contains the trace events, and sys.trace_columns contains the trace columns. The following SELECT statement utilizes two of these system views to return the available events and their related categories:

```
select e.trace_event_id, e.name 'Event Name', c.name
'Category Name'
 from sys.trace_events e
  join sys.trace_categories c on e.category_id =
c.category_id
 order by e.trace_event_id
```

The results of this SELECT statement are shown in Table 5.2.

TABLE 5.2   Trace Events and Their Related Categories

trace_event_id	Event Name	Category Name
10	RPC:Completed	Stored Procedures
11	RPC:Starting	Stored Procedures
12	SQL:BatchCompleted	TSQL
13	SQL:BatchStarting	TSQL
14	Audit Login	Security Audit
15	Audit Logout	Security Audit
16	Attention	Errors and Warnings
17	ExistingConnection	Sessions
18	Audit Server Starts And Stops	Security Audit
19	DTCTransaction	Transactions
20	Audit Login Failed	Security Audit
21	EventLog	Errors and Warnings
22	ErrorLog	Errors and Warnings
23	Lock:Released	Locks
24	Lock:Acquired	Locks
25	Lock:Deadlock	Locks
26	Lock:Cancel	Locks
27	Lock:Timeout	Locks
28	Degree of Parallelism	Performance
33	Exception	Errors and Warnings
34	SP:CacheMiss	Stored Procedures
35	SP:CacheInsert	Stored Procedures
36	SP:CacheRemove	Stored Procedures
37	SP:Recompile	Stored Procedures
38	SP:CacheHit	Stored Procedures
40	SQL:StmtStarting	TSQL
41	SQL:StmtCompleted	TSQL
42	SP:Starting	Stored Procedures
43	SP:Completed	Stored Procedures
44	SP:StmtStarting	Stored Procedures
45	SP:StmtCompleted	Stored Procedures
46	Object:Created	Objects
47	Object:Deleted	Objects
50	SQLTransaction	Transactions

trace_event_id	Event Name	Category Name
51	Scan:Started	Scans
52	Scan:Stopped	Scans
53	CursorOpen	Cursors
54	TransactionLog	Transactions
55	Hash Warning	Errors and Warnings
58	Auto Stats	Performance
59	Lock:Deadlock Chain	Locks
60	Lock:Escalation	Locks
61	OLEDB Errors	OLEDB
67	Execution Warnings	Errors and Warnings
68	Showplan Text (Unencoded)	Performance
69	Sort Warnings	Errors and Warnings
70	CursorPrepare	Cursors
71	Prepare SQL	TSQL
72	Exec Prepared SQL	TSQL
73	Unprepare SQL	TSQL
74	CursorExecute	Cursors
75	CursorRecompile	Cursors
76	CursorImplicitConversion	Cursors
77	CursorUnprepare	Cursors
78	CursorClose	Cursors
79	Missing Column Statistics	Errors and Warnings
80	Missing Join Predicate	Errors and Warnings
81	Server Memory Change	Server
82	UserConfigurable:0	User configurable
83	UserConfigurable:1	User configurable
84	UserConfigurable:2	User configurable
85	UserConfigurable:3	User configurable
86	UserConfigurable:4	User configurable
87	UserConfigurable:5	User configurable
88	UserConfigurable:6	User configurable
89	UserConfigurable:7	User configurable
90	UserConfigurable:8	User configurable
91	UserConfigurable:9	User configurable
92	Data File Auto Grow	Database
93	Log File Auto Grow	Database
94	Data File Auto Shrink	Database

5

trace_event_id	Event Name	Category Name
95	Log File Auto Shrink	Database
96	Showplan Text	Performance
97	Showplan All	Performance
98	Showplan Statistics Profile	Performance
100	RPC Output Parameter	Stored Procedures
102	Audit Database Scope GDR Event	Security Audit
103	Audit Schema Object GDR Event	Security Audit
104	Audit Addlogin Event	Security Audit
105	Audit Login GDR Event	Security Audit
106	Audit Login Change Property Event	Security Audit
107	Audit Login Change Password Event	Security Audit
108	Audit Add Login to Server Role Event	Security Audit
109	Audit Add DB User Event	Security Audit
110	Audit Add Member to DB Role Event	Security Audit
111	Audit Add Role Event	Security Audit
112	Audit App Role Change Password Event	Security Audit
113	Audit Statement Permission Event	Security Audit
114	Audit Schema Object Access Event	Security Audit
115	Audit Backup/Restore Event	Security Audit
116	Audit DBCC Event	Security Audit
117	Audit Change Audit Event	Security Audit
118	Audit Object Derived Permission Event	Security Audit
119	OLEDB Call Event	OLEDB
120	OLEDB QueryInterface Event	OLEDB
121	OLEDB DataRead Event	OLEDB
122	Showplan XML	Performance
123	SQL:FullTextQuery	Performance
124	Broker:Conversation	Broker
125	Deprecation Announcement	Deprecation
126	Deprecation Final Support	Deprecation
127	Exchange Spill Event	Errors and Warnings
128	Audit Database Management Event	Security Audit
129	Audit Database Object Management Event	Security Audit
130	Audit Database Principal Management Event	Security Audit
131	Audit Schema Object Management Event	Security Audit

trace_event_id	Event Name	Category Name
132	Audit Server Principal Impersonation Event	Security Audit
133	Audit Database Principal Impersonation Event	Security Audit
134	Audit Server Object Take Ownership Event	Security Audit
135	Audit Database Object Take Ownership Event	Security Audit
136	Broker:Conversation Group	Broker
137	Blocked process report	Errors and Warnings
138	Broker:Connection	Broker
139	Broker:Forwarded Message Sent	Broker
140	Broker:Forwarded Message Dropped	Broker
141	Broker:Message Classify	Broker
142	Broker:Transmission	Broker
143	Broker:Queue Disabled	Broker
144	Broker:Mirrored Route State Changed	Broker
146	Showplan XML Statistics Profile	Performance
148	Deadlock graph	Locks
149	Broker:Remote Message Acknowledgement	Broker
150	Trace File Close	Server
151	Database Mirroring Connection	Database
152	Audit Change Database Owner	Security Audit
153	Audit Schema Object Take Ownership Event	Security Audit
154	Audit Database Mirroring Login	Security Audit
155	FT:Crawl Started	Full text
156	FT:Crawl Stopped	Full text
157	FT:Crawl Aborted	Full text
158	Audit Broker Conversation	Security Audit
159	Audit Broker Login	Security Audit
160	Broker:Message Undeliverable	Broker
161	Broker:Corrupted Message	Broker
162	User Error Message	Errors and Warnings
163	Broker:Activation	Broker
164	Object:Altered	Objects
165	Performance statistics	Performance

5

trace_event_id	Event Name	Category Name
166	SQL:StmtRecompile	TSQL
167	Database Mirroring State Change	Database
168	Showplan XML For Query Compile	Performance
169	Showplan All For Query Compile	Performance
170	Audit Server Scope GDR Event	Security Audit
171	Audit Server Object GDR Event	Security Audit
172	Audit Database Object GDR Event	Security Audit
173	Audit Server Operation Event	Security Audit
175	Audit Server Alter Trace Event	Security Audit
176	Audit Server Object Management Event	Security Audit
177	Audit Server Principal Management Event	Security Audit
178	Audit Database Operation Event	Security Audit
180	Audit Database Object Access Event	Security Audit
181	TM: Begin Tran starting	Transactions
182	TM: Begin Tran completed	Transactions
183	TM: Promote Tran starting	Transactions
184	TM: Promote Tran completed	Transactions
185	TM: Commit Tran starting	Transactions
186	TM: Commit Tran completed	Transactions
187	TM: Rollback Tran starting	Transactions
188	TM: Rollback Tran completed	Transactions
189	Lock:Timeout (timeout > 0)	Locks
190	Progress Report: Online Index Operation	Progress Report
191	TM: Save Tran starting	Transactions
192	TM: Save Tran completed	Transactions
193	Background Job Error	Errors and Warnings
194	OLEDB Provider Information	OLEDB
195	Mount Tape	Server
196	Assembly Load	CLR
198	XQuery Static Type	TSQL
199	QN: Subscription	Query Notifications
200	QN: Parameter table	Query Notifications
201	QN: Template	Query Notifications
202	QN: Dynamics	Query Notifications
212	Bitmap Warning	Errors and Warnings
213	Database Suspect Data Page	Errors and Warnings

trace_event_id	Event Name	Category Name
214	CPU threshold exceeded	Errors and Warnings
215	PreConnect:Starting	Sessions
216	PreConnect:Completed	Sessions
217	Plan Guide Successful	Performance
218	Plan Guide Unsuccessful	Performance
235	Audit Fulltext	Security Audit

The numeric IDs for the trace columns can be obtained from the `sys.trace_columns` catalog view, as shown in the following example:

```
select trace_column_id, name 'Column Name', type_name 'Data Type'
 from sys.trace_columns
 order by trace_column_id
```

Table 5.3 shows the results of this SELECT statement and lists all the available trace columns.

TABLE 5.3   Trace Columns Available for a Server-Side Trace

trace_column_id	Column Name	Data Type
1	TextData	text
2	BinaryData	image
3	DatabaseID	int
4	TransactionID	bigint
5	LineNumber	int
6	NTUserName	nvarchar
7	NTDomainName	nvarchar
8	HostName	nvarchar
9	ClientProcessID	int
10	ApplicationName	nvarchar
11	LoginName	nvarchar
12	SPID	int
13	Duration	bigint
14	StartTime	datetime
15	EndTime	datetime
16	Reads	bigint
17	Writes	bigint
18	CPU	int
19	Permissions	bigint

trace_column_id	Column Name	Data Type
20	Severity	int
21	EventSubClass	int
22	ObjectID	int
23	Success	int
24	IndexID	int
25	IntegerData	int
26	ServerName	nvarchar
27	EventClass	int
28	ObjectType	int
29	NestLevel	int
30	State	int
31	Error	int
32	Mode	int
33	Handle	int
34	ObjectName	nvarchar
35	DatabaseName	nvarchar
36	FileName	nvarchar
37	OwnerName	nvarchar
38	RoleName	nvarchar
39	TargetUserName	nvarchar
40	DBUserName	nvarchar
41	LoginSid	image
42	TargetLoginName	nvarchar
43	TargetLoginSid	image
44	ColumnPermissions	int
45	LinkedServerName	nvarchar
46	ProviderName	nvarchar
47	MethodName	nvarchar
48	RowCounts	bigint
49	RequestID	int
50	XactSequence	bigint
51	EventSequence	bigint
52	BigintData1	bigint
53	BigintData2	bigint
54	GUID	uniqueidentifier
55	IntegerData2	int
56	ObjectID2	bigint

trace_column_id	Column Name	Data Type
57	Type	int
58	OwnerID	int
59	ParentName	nvarchar
60	IsSystem	int
61	Offset	int
62	SourceDatabaseID	int
63	SqlHandle	image
64	SessionLoginName	nvarchar
65	PlanHandle	image
66	GroupID	int

You have to call the `sp_trace_setevent` procedure once for each data column you want captured for each event in the trace. Based on the number of events and number of columns, you can see that this can result in a lot of executions of the `sp_trace_setevent` procedure for a larger trace definition.

To set up filters, you must pass the column ID, the filter value, and numeric values for the logical operator and column operator to the `sp_trace_setfilter` procedure. The logical operator can be either 0 or 1. A value of 0 indicates that the specified filter on the column should be AND'ed with any other filters on the column, whereas a value of 1 indicates that the OR operator should be applied. Table 5.4 describes the values allowed for the column operators.

TABLE 5.4   Column Operator Values for `sp_trace_setfilter`

Value	Comparison Operator
0	= (equal)
1	<> (not equal)
2	> (greater than)
3	< (less than)
4	>= (greater than or equal)
5	<= (less than or equal)
6	LIKE
7	NOT LIKE

Fortunately, there is an easier way of generating a trace definition script. You can set up your traces by using the SQL Server Profiler GUI and script the trace definition to a file. After you define a trace with SQL Server Profiler GUI and specify the events, data columns, and filters you want to use, you select File, Export, Script Trace Definition. The SQL commands (including calls to the aforementioned system stored procedures) to define the trace, start the trace, and write the trace to a file are generated into one script file. You have the option to generate a script that works with SQL Server 2005, 2008, 2008 R2, 2012 and 2014. Listing 5.2 shows an example of a trace definition exported from the Profiler. It contains the trace definitions for the TSQL trace template. You must replace the text InsertFileNameHere with an appropriate filename, prefixed with its pathname, before running this script.

LISTING 5.2   A SQL Script for Creating and Starting a Server-Side Trace

```
/*****************************************************/
/* Created by: SQL Server 2014 Profiler             */
/* Date: 0512/08/2014   03:53:54 PM          */
/*****************************************************/


-- Create a Queue
declare @rc int
declare @TraceID int
declare @maxfilesize bigint
set @maxfilesize = 5

-- Please replace the text InsertFileNameHere, with an
appropriate
-- filename prefixed by a path, e.g., c:\MyFolder\MyTrace.
The .trc extension
-- will be appended to the filename automatically. If you
are writing from
-- remote server to local drive, please use UNC path and
make sure server has
-- write access to your network share

exec @rc = sp_trace_create @TraceID output, 0,
N'InsertFileNameHere', @maxfilesize, NULL
if (@rc != 0) goto error


-- Client side File and Table cannot be scripted

-- Set the events
declare @on bit
set @on = 1
exec sp_trace_setevent @TraceID, 14, 1, @on
exec sp_trace_setevent @TraceID, 14, 12, @on
exec sp_trace_setevent @TraceID, 14, 14, @on
exec sp_trace_setevent @TraceID, 15, 12, @on
exec sp_trace_setevent @TraceID, 15, 14, @on
exec sp_trace_setevent @TraceID, 17, 1, @on
```

```
exec sp_trace_setevent @TraceID, 17, 12, @on
exec sp_trace_setevent @TraceID, 17, 14, @on
exec sp_trace_setevent @TraceID, 11, 2, @on
exec sp_trace_setevent @TraceID, 11, 12, @on
exec sp_trace_setevent @TraceID, 11, 14, @on
exec sp_trace_setevent @TraceID, 13, 1, @on
exec sp_trace_setevent @TraceID, 13, 12, @on
exec sp_trace_setevent @TraceID, 13, 14, @on

-- Set the Filters
declare @intfilter int
declare @bigintfilter bigint

-- Set the trace status to start
exec sp_trace_setstatus @TraceID, 1

-- display trace id for future references
select TraceID=@TraceID
goto finish

error:
select ErrorCode=@rc
finish:


go
```

TIP

If you want to always capture certain trace events when SQL Server is running, such as auditing events, you can create a stored procedure that uses the `sp_trace` stored procedures to create a trace and specify the events to be captured. You can use the code in Listing 5.2 as a basis to create the stored procedure. Then you can mark the procedure as a startup procedure by using the `sp_procoption` procedure to set the `autostart` option. The trace automatically starts when SQL Server is started, and it continues running in the background.

Just be aware that although using server-side traces is less intrusive than using the SQL Server Profiler client, some overhead is necessary to run a trace. You should try to limit the number of events and number of columns captured to minimize the overhead as much as possible.

Monitoring Running Traces

SQL Server 2014 provides some additional built-in user-defined functions to get information about currently running traces. Like the `fn_trace_gettable` function discussed previously, these functions return the information as a tabular result. The available functions are as follows:

▶ `fn_trace_getinfo(trace_id)`—This function is passed a traceid, and it returns information about the specified trace. If passed the value of default, it returns information about all existing traces. An example of the output from this function is shown in Listing 5.3.

▶ `fn_trace_geteventinfo(trace_id)`—This function returns a list of the events and data columns being captured for the specified trace. Only the event and column ID values are returned. You can use the information provided in Tables 5.2 and 5.3 to map the IDs to the more meaningful event names and column names.

▶ `fn_trace_getfilterinfo(trace_id)`—This function returns information about the filters being applied to the specified trace. Again, the column ID and logical and comparison operator values are returned as integer IDs that you need to decipher. See Table 5.4 for a listing of the column operator values.

LISTING 5.3   An Example of Using the Built-in User-Defined Functions for Monitoring Traces

```
SELECT * FROM ::fn_trace_getinfo(default)

traceid     property     value
---------   ----------   --------------------------------

1           1            2
1           2            C:\Program Files\Microsoft SQL
Server\

MSSQL11.INST2012\MSSQL\Log\log_10.trc
1           3            20
1           4            NULL


select * from ::fn_Trace_getfilterinfo(2)

columnid    logical_operator comparison_operator value
---------   ---------------- ------------------- --------

3           0                0                   6
10          0                7                   Profiler
10          0                7                   SQLAgent
```

> **NOTE**
>
> You may be wondering why there is always a `traceid` with a value of 1 running when you run the `fn_trace_getinfo` procedure. This is the default trace that SQL Server automatically initiates when it starts. The default trace is enabled by default. You can identify which trace is the default by selecting from the `sys.traces` catalog view and examining

the `is_default` column. The default trace captures a number of different types of events, including object creates and drops, errors, memory and disk changes, security changes, and more. You can disable this default trace, but it is generally lightweight and should be left enabled.

The output from the functions that return trace information is relatively cryptic because many of the values returned are numeric. For example, the property values returned by `fn_trace_getinfo` are specified as integer IDs. Table 5.5 describes each of these property IDs.

TABLE 5.5   Description of Trace Property ID Values

Property ID	Description
1	Trace options specified in `sp_trace_create`
2	Trace filename
3	Maximum size of trace file, in MB
4	Date and time the trace will be stopped
5	Current trace status

Stopping Server-Side Traces

It is important to keep track of the traces you have running and to ensure that "heavy" traces are stopped. Heavy traces are typically traces that capture a lot of events and are run on a busy SQL Server. These traces can affect the overall performance of your SQL Server machine and write a large amount of information to the trace output file. If you specified a stop time when you started the trace, it automatically stops and closes when the stop time is reached. For example, in the SQL script in Listing 5.2, if you wanted the trace to run for 15 minutes instead of indefinitely, you would set the value for the `stoptime` variable at the beginning of the script, using a command similar to the following:

```
set @stoptime = dateadd(minute, 15, getdate())
```

To otherwise stop a running server-side trace, you use the `sp_trace_setstatus` stored procedure and pass it the trace ID and a status of 0. Stopping a trace only stops gathering trace information and does not delete the trace definition from SQL Server. Essentially, it pauses the trace. You can restart the trace by passing `sp_trace_setstatus` a status value of 1.

After you stop a trace, you can close the trace and delete its definition from SQL Server by passing `sp_trace_setstatus` the ID of the trace you want to stop and a status value of 2. After you close the trace, you must redefine it before you can restart it.

If you don't know the ID of the trace you want to stop, you can use the `fn_trace_getinfo` function or the `sys.traces` catalog view to return a list of all running traces and select the appropriate trace ID. The following example shows how to stop and close a trace with a trace ID of 2:

```
-- Set the trace status to stop
exec sp_trace_setstatus 2, 0
go


-- Close and Delete the trace
exec sp_trace_setstatus 2, 2
go
```

If you want to stop and close multiple traces, you must call sp_trace_setstatus twice for each trace. Listing 5.4 provides an example of a system stored procedure that you can create in SQL Server to stop a specific trace or automatically stop all currently running traces.

LISTING 5.4   A Sample System Stored Procedure to Stop Profiler Traces

```
use master
go
if object_id ('sp_stop_profiler_trace') is not null
    drop proc sp_stop_profiler_trace
go


create proc sp_stop_profiler_trace @TraceID int = null
as


if @TraceID is not null
begin
    -- Set the trace status to stop
    exec sp_trace_setstatus @TraceID, 0

    -- Delete the trace
    exec sp_trace_setstatus @TraceID, 2
end
else
begin
-- the following cursor does not include the default trace
    declare c1 cursor for
    SELECT distinct traceid FROM :: fn_trace_getinfo
(DEFAULT)
        WHERE traceId not in (select ID from sys.traces
where is_default = 1)
    open c1
    fetch c1 into @TraceID
    while @@fetch_status = 0
    begin
```

```
        -- Set the trace status to stop
        exec sp_trace_setstatus @TraceID, 0

        -- Delete the trace
        exec sp_trace_setstatus @TraceID, 2
        fetch c1 into @TraceID
    end
    close c1
    deallocate c1
end
```

Profiler Usage Scenarios

This chapter has already covered many of the technical aspects of SQL Server Profiler, but what about some practical applications? Beyond the obvious uses of identifying what SQL statements an application is submitting, the following sections look at a few scenarios in which the SQL Server Profiler can be useful. These scenarios are presented to give you some ideas about how SQL Server Profiler can be used. You'll see that the monitoring and analysis capabilities of SQL Server Profiler are limited only by your creativity and ingenuity.

Analyzing Slow Stored Procedures or Queries

After you identify that a particular stored procedure is running slowly, what should you do? You might want to look at the estimated execution plan for the stored procedure, looking for table scans and sections of the plan that have a high cost percentage. But what if the execution plan has no obvious problems? This is the time you should consider using the SQL Server Profiler.

You can set up a trace on the stored procedure that captures the execution of each statement within it, along with its duration, in milliseconds. Here's how:

1. Create a new trace, using the `TSQL_Duration` template.

2. Add the `SP:StmtCompleted` event from the stored procedure event class to the trace.

3. Add a filter on the `Duration` column with the duration not equal to `0`. You can also set the filter to a larger number to exclude more of the short-running statements.

If you plan to run the procedure from SSMS, you might want to add a filter on the `SPID` column as well. Set it equal to the process ID for your session; the SPID is displayed at the bottom of the SSMS window next to your username, in parentheses. This traces only those commands that are executed from your SSMS Query Editor window.

When you run the trace and execute the stored procedure, you see only those statements in the procedure that have nonzero duration. The statements are listed in ascending duration order. You need to look to the bottom of the Profiler output window to find your longer-running statements. You can isolate these statements, copy them to SSMS, and perform a separate analysis on them to determine your problem.

You can also add `showplan` events to your Profiler trace to capture the execution plan as the trace is running. SQL Server now has `showplan` events that capture the `showplan` results in XML format. Traces with this type of XML output can have a significant impact on server performance while they are running but make the identification of poorly performing statements much easier. When you are tracing stored procedure executions, it is a good idea to add a filter on the specific stored procedure you are targeting to help minimize the impact on performance.

After you run a trace with an XML `showplan` event, you can choose to extract the `showplan` events to a separate file. To do so, in the SQL Server Profiler you select File, Export, Extract SQL Server Events, Extract Showplan Events. At this point, you can save the `showplan` events in a single file or to a separate file for each event. The file(s) is saved with a `SQLPlan` file extension. This file can then be opened in SSMS, and the graphical query execution plan is displayed.

Deadlocks

Deadlocks are a common occurrence in database management systems (DMBSs). In simple terms, deadlocks occur when a process (for example, SPID 10) has a lock on a resource that another process (for example, SPID 20) wants. In addition, the second process (SPID 20) wants the resource that the first process has locked. This cyclic dependency causes the DBMS to kill one of the processes to resolve the deadlock situation.

Resolving deadlocks and identifying the deadlock participants can be difficult. In SQL Server 2014 and past versions, trace flag 1204 can be set to capture the processes involved in the deadlock. This can be set by execution `dbcc traceon (1204, 3605, -1)` from a Query Window. The output is text-based but provides valuable information about the types of locks and the statements that were executing at the time of the deadlock. In addition to this approach, SQL Server 2014 offers the capability to capture detailed deadlock information via the SQL Server Profiler. This type of tracing can be accomplished as follows:

1. Create a new trace, using a `Blank` template; this leaves the selection of all the events, data columns, and filters to you.

2. Add the `Locks:Deadlock graph` event to the trace from the `Locks` category. An additional tab named Event Extraction Settings appears on the Trace Properties window.

3. Click the Save Deadlock XML Events Separately check box and enter a filename that the XML data will be saved to. This causes the deadlock information to be written to a separate file. You could also export the results after the trace has been run by using the File, Export option.

When you run this trace, it captures any deadlock event that occurs and writes it to the XML file specified. To test this, you can open two Query Editor windows and execute the following statements, in the order listed, and in the query window specified:

```
-- In Query Window # 1
--Step1
USE ADVENTUREWORKS2012
GO
BEGIN TRAN
    UPDATE HumanResources.Employee SET ModifiedDate =
GETDATE()

-- In Query Window # 2
--Step2
USE ADVENTUREWORKS2012
GO
BEGIN TRAN
    UPDATE HumanResources.Department SET ModifiedDate =
GETDATE()
    SELECT * FROM  HumanResources.Employee

-- In Query Window # 1
--Step3
    SELECT * FROM  HumanResources.Department
```

When the deadlock occurs, the results pane for one of the query windows contains a message similar to the following:

```
Msg 1205, Level 13, State 51, Line 3
Transaction (Process ID 55) was deadlocked on lock resources
with another
process and has been chosen as the deadlock victim. Rerun
the transaction.
```

When the row with the `Deadlock graph` event is selected in the Profiler output grid, a graph like the one shown in Figure 5.13 is displayed.

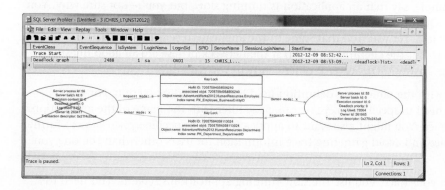

FIGURE 5.13   Output from the `Deadlock graph` event.

The `Deadlock graph` event contains a wealth of information about the deadlock occurrence. The oval nodes represent the processes involved in the deadlock. The oval with an X mark across it is the deadlock victim that had its process killed. The other oval represents the process that was allowed to complete when the deadlock was resolved. The boxes in the middle of the graph display lock information about the specific objects involved in the deadlock.

The graph is interactive and displays relevant information about the processes that were running when the deadlock occurred. For example, when you mouse over the oval nodes, pop-up text appears, displaying the SQL statement that was executing at the time of the deadlock. This is the same type of information that is displayed when the aforementioned trace flag is used, but the graph tends to be easier to decipher.

Identifying Ad Hoc Queries

One problem that can plague a production system is the execution of ad hoc queries against the production database. If you want to identify ad hoc queries, the application, and the users who are running them, SQL Server Profiler is your tool. You can create a trace as follows:

1. Create a new trace, using the `SQLProfilerStandard` template.

2. Add a new `ApplicationName` filter with `Like Microsoft%`.

When this trace is run, you can identify database access that is happening via SSMS, Microsoft Access, and other Microsoft applications that are accessing the database. The user, the duration, and the actual SQL statement are captured. An alternative would be to change the `ApplicationName` filter to trace application access for all application names that are not like the name of your production applications, such as `Not Like MyOrderEntryApp%`.

Identifying Performance Bottlenecks

Another common problem with database applications is identifying performance bottlenecks. For example, say that an application is running slow, but you're not sure why. You tested all the SQL statements and stored procedures used by the application, and they were relatively fast. Yet you find that some of the application screens are slow. Is it the database server? Is it the client machine? Is it the network? These are all good questions, but what is the answer? SQL Server Profiler can help you find out.

You can start with the same trace definition used in the preceding section. For this scenario, you need to specify an `ApplicationName` filter with the name of the application you want to trace. You might also want to apply a filter to a specific `NTUserName` to further refine your trace and avoid gathering trace information for users other than the one you have isolated.

After you start your trace, you use the slow-running application's screens. You need to look at the trace output and take note of the duration of the statements as they execute on the database server. Are they relatively fast? How much time was spent on the execution of the SQL statements and stored procedures relative to the response time of the application screen? If the total database duration is 1,000 milliseconds (1 second), and the screen takes 10 seconds to refresh, you need to examine other factors, such as the network or the application code.

With SQL Server 2014, you can also combine Performance Monitor (Perfmon) output with trace output to identify performance bottlenecks. This feature helps unite system-level metrics (for example, CPU utilization, memory usage) with SQL Server performance metrics. The result is a very impressive display that is synchronized based on time so that a correlation can be made between system-level spikes and the related SQL Server statements.

To try out this powerful feature, you open the Perfmon application and add a new User Defined Collector Set. For simplicity, you can just add one counter, such as `% Processor Time` from the Processor performance object. The Log Format should be changed to comma separated, and you want to set the interval to sample every second for this example. Now, you want to apply some kind of load to the SQL Server system. The following script does index maintenance on two tables in the AdventureWorks2012 database and can be used to apply a sample load:

```
USE [AdventureWorks2012]
GO
ALTER INDEX
[PK_SalesOrderDetail_SalesOrderID_SalesOrderDetailID]
 ON [Sales].[SalesOrderDetail]
 REORGANIZE WITH ( LOB_COMPACTION = ON )
GO
PRINT 'FIRST INDEX IS REBUILT'
WAITFOR DELAY '00:00:05'
USE [AdventureWorks2012]
GO
ALTER INDEX [PK_Person_BusinessEntityID]
 ON [Person].[Person] REBUILD WITH
 ( PAD_INDEX  = OFF, STATISTICS_NORECOMPUTE  = OFF,
   ALLOW_ROW_LOCKS  = ON, ALLOW_PAGE_LOCKS  = ON,
   SORT_IN_TEMPDB = OFF )
GO
PRINT 'SECOND INDEX IS REORGANIZED'
```

Next, you open the script in SSMS, but you don't run it yet. You open SQL Server Profiler and create a trace by using the Standard Profiler template. This template captures basic SQL Server activity and also includes the StartTime and EndTime columns that are necessary to correlate with the Perfmon counters. Now you are ready to start the performance log in Perfmon and the SQL Server Profiler trace. When they are running, you can run the sample load script. When the script has completed, you stop the performance log and Profiler trace. You save the Profiler trace to a file and then open the file in the Profiler application.

The correlation of the Perfmon log to the trace output file is accomplished from within the Profiler application. To do this, you select File, Import Performance Data. Then you select the performance log file that was just created; these files are located by default in the c:\perflogs folder. After you import the performance data, a new performance graph and associated grid with the performance counters is displayed in the Profiler, as shown in Figure 5.14.

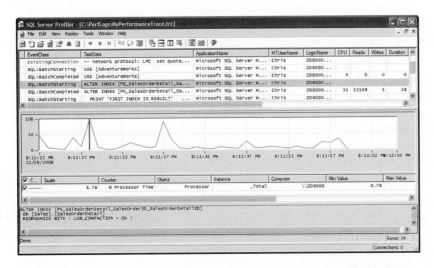

FIGURE 5.14   System Monitor counters correlated within a Profiler trace.

Now the fun begins! If you click one of the statements captured in the Profiler grid, a vertical red line appears in the Perfmon graph that reflects the time at which the statement was run. Conversely, if you click a location in the graph, the corresponding SQL statement that was run at that time is highlighted in the grid. If you see a spike in CPU in the Perfmon graph, you can click the spike in the graph and find the statement that may have caused the spike. This can help you quickly and efficiently identify bottlenecks and the processes contributing to it.

Monitoring Auto-Update Statistics

As discussed in Chapter 34, "Understanding Query Optimization," SQL Server updates index statistics automatically as data is changed in a table. In some environments, excessive auto-updating of statistics can affect system performance while the statistics are being updated. SQL Server Profiler can be used to monitor auto-updating of statistics as well as automatic statistics creation.

To monitor auto-updating of statistics, you create a trace and include the AutoStats event from the Performance event category. Then you select the TextData, Integer Data, Success, and Object ID columns. When the AutoStats event is captured, the Integer Data column contains the number of statistics updated for a given table, the Object ID is the ID of the table, and the TextData column contains names of the columns together with either an `Updated:` or `Created:` prefix. The `Success` column contains potential failure indication.

If you see an excessive number of `AutoStats` events on a table or index, and the duration is high, it could be affecting system performance. You might want to consider disabling auto-update for statistics on that table and schedule statistics to be updated periodically during nonpeak periods. You may also want to utilize the `AUTO_UPDATE_STATISTICS_ASYNC` database setting, which allows queries that utilize affected statistics to compile without having to wait for the update of statistics to complete.

Monitoring Application Progress

The 10 SQL Server Profiler user-configurable events can be used in a variety of ways, including for tracking the progress of an application or procedure. For instance, perhaps you have a complex procedure that is subject to lengthy execution. You can add debugging logic in this procedure to allow for real-time benchmarking via SQL Server Profiler.

The key to this type of profiling is the use of the `sp_trace_generateevent` stored procedure, which enables you to launch the `User configurable` event. The procedure needs to reference one of the `User configurable` event IDs (`82` to `91`) that correspond to the `User configurable` event `0` to `9`. If you execute the procedure with `eventid = 82`, then `User configurable` event `0` catches these events.

Listing 5.5 contains a sample stored procedure that (in debug mode) triggers the trace events that SQL Server Profiler can capture.

LISTING 5.5   A Stored Procedure That Raises User Configurable Events for SQL Server Profiler

```
CREATE PROCEDURE SampleApplicationProc (@debug bit = 0)
as
declare @userinfoParm nvarchar(128)
select @userinfoParm = getdate()

--if in debug mode, then launch event for Profiler
--    indicating Start of Application Proc
if @debug =1
begin
        SET @userinfoParm = 'Proc Start: ' +
convert(varchar(30),getdate(),120)
        EXEC sp_trace_generateevent @eventid = 83, @userinfo
= @userinfoparm
end

--Real world would have complex proc code executing here
--The WAITFOR statement was added to simulate processing
time
WAITFOR DELAY '00:00:05'
```

```
---if debug mode, then launch event indicating next
significant stage
if @debug =1
begin
        SET @userinfoParm = 'Proc Stage One Complete: '
                        +
convert(varchar(20),getdate(),120)
        EXEC sp_trace_generateevent @eventid = 83, @userinfo
= @userinfoparm
end

--Real world would have more complex proc code executing
here
--The WAITFOR statement was added to simulate processing
time
WAITFOR DELAY '00:00:05' --5 second delay

---if debug mode, then launch event indicating next
significant stage
if @debug =1
begin
        SET @userinfoParm = 'Proc Stage Two Complete: '
                        +
convert(varchar(30),getdate(),120)
        EXEC sp_trace_generateevent @eventid = 83, @userinfo
= @userinfoparm
end

--You get the idea

GO
```

Now you need to set up a new trace that includes the UserConfigurable:1 event. To do so, you choose the TextData data column to capture the User configurable output and any other data columns that make sense for your specific trace. After this task is complete, you can execute the sample stored procedure from Listing 5.5 and get progress information via SQL Server Profiler as the procedure executes. You can accumulate execution statistics over time with this kind of trace and summarize the results. The execution command for the procedure is as follows:

```
EXEC  SampleApplicationProc @debug = 1
```

The resulting SQL Server Profiler results are shown in Figure 5.15.

There are many other applications for User configurable events. How you use them depends on your specific need. As is the case with many Profiler scenarios, there are seemingly endless possibilities.

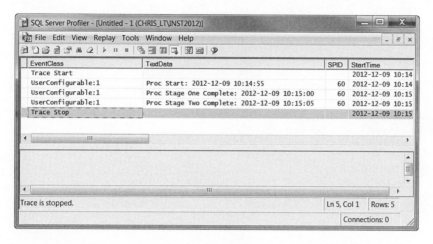

FIGURE 5.15   User configurable trace results.

Summary

Whether you are a developer or database administrator, you should not ignore the power of the SQL Server Profiler. It is often one of the most underused applications in the SQL Server performance toolkit, yet it is one of the most versatile. Its auditing capabilities and ability to unravel complex server processes define its value.

This chapter wraps up the introduction to the tools and utilities available with SQL Server. Now you should be equipped to start administering and working with SQL Server.

Chapter 6 delves into the aforementioned replay capabilities of this powerful tool.

Summary

CHAPTER 6

SQL Distributed Replay

If you have used the SQL Server Profiler, you might have wished for a mechanism in SQL Server that would replay a workload similar to what the database might experience in a production scenario. Such a mechanism could replay a captured database workload on multiple computers and better simulate a mission-critical application.

Fortunately, SQL Server 2014 has such a mechanism: Distributed Replay. Distributed Replay allows you to replay a captured trace from more than one computer. It builds upon the capabilities of the SQL Server Profiler that were discussed in the prior chapter. It does not replace the SQL Server Profiler. Instead, it provides a mechanism for taking the SQL Server Profiler replay capabilities to the next level.

> **NOTE**
>
> Distributed Replay is available in several Editions of SQL Server 2014 but the Enterprise Edition is the only one that supports replay on more than 1 client.

What's New for Distributed Replay

Distributed Replay was first introduced in SQL Server 2012. Very little has changed in SQL Server 2014. The one notable change in 2014 is that it can replay workloads that were captured in SQL Server 2014. This is not possible with the SQL Server 2012 Distributed Replay.

Overview of Distributed Replay

The SQL Server Profiler and Distributed Replay are two performance oriented tools that work hand in hand. In fact, there is some overlap in the functionality available with these tools. The overlap is centered on replaying a workload. Both tools can replay a workload but the capabilities surrounding the replay differ.

The SQL Server Profiler can only replay a workload on a single computer but it has replay capabilities that Distributed Replay does not. In particular, the SQL Server Profiler has debugging options that are common in a lot of Integrated Design Environments (IDEs). These debugging features include Step, Run To Cursor, and Breakpoint capabilities. These features are not available with Distributed Replay.

Distributed Replay can replay the same workload that SQL Server Profiler can replay but it can replay the load on multiple machines. This capability is paramount when evaluating concurrent workloads. Let's face it, the workload from a single user running a serial stream of statements against a database is a lot different than workloads from multiple machines running statements against the database at the same time. This concurrent database access is more indicative of the type of load that a SQL Server database will incur in a production environment.

In the following sections, you learn how to set up and configure Distributed Replay for use, how Distributed Replay works under the hood, and how you can use Distributed Replay to get a better understanding of how your database will perform with a concurrent workload.

Distributed Replay Components

Distributed Replay consists of four main components: Distributed Replay administrative tool, Distributed Replay controller, Distributed Replay clients, and the Target server. Understanding these four components and how they interact is important to understanding and using Distributed Replay. Figure 6.1 shows the Distributed Replay components and the flow of information between them.

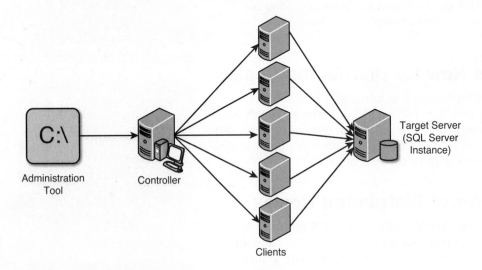

FIGURE 6.1   Overview of Distributed Replay.

Distributed Replay Administrative Tool

The *Distributed Replay administrative tool* is a console application that is used to communicate with the Distributed Replay controller. The executable file associated with this tool is named DReplay.exe and can be found in the SQL Server tools folder (for example C:\Program Files (x86)\Microsoft SQL Server\120\Tools\Binn).

The DReplay.exe application can be used to initiate, monitor and cancel replay operations. The syntax for using this application and performing these operations follows:

```
dreplay {preprocess|replay|status|cancel} [options] [-?]}
```

```
Usage:

  dreplay preprocess [-m controller] -i input_trace_file
    -d controller_working_dir [-c config_file] [-f status_interval]

  dreplay replay [-m controller] -d controller_working_dir [-o]
    [-s target_server] -w clients [-c config_file]
    [-f status_interval]

  dreplay status [-m controller] [-f status_interval]
  dreplay cancel [-m controller] [-q]
```

The following list contains a brief description of the *command-line* options associated with this application:

- ▶ **preprocess**—this option initiates the preprocess stage which causes the controller to prepare the input trace data that was captured.

- ▶ **replay**—this option initiates the event replay stage which causes the controller to dispatch replay data to the specified clients.

- ▶ **status**—this option queries the controller and displays the current status.

- ▶ **cancel**—this option cancels the current operation that is running on the controller.

Distributed Replay Controller

The Distributed Replay Controller manages the actions of the distributed replay clients. It is a Windows service that is named SQL Server Distributed Replay Controller. There is only one controller for each Distributed Replay environment.

The service associated with the Distributed Replay Controller can run on a computer that is separate from the other Distributed Replay components. Or, they can all run on the same machine. The Distributed Replay architecture provides a lot of flexibility in this area.

Distributed Replay Clients

The Distributed Replay Clients are one or more computers that are running a Windows service named SQL Server Distributed Replay client. The clients process the replay workloads and apply those workloads against the target server.

The service associated with the Distributed Replay Clients can run on a computer that is separate from the other Distributed Replay components. For optimal concurrent workload testing it is best to run multiple clients on computers other than the target server. This type of setup will apply a workload that is representative of real world database access.

Target Server

The final component in a Distributed Replay environment is the target server. The target server is the SQL Server instance where the Distributed Replay clients apply the replay workloads.

The target server must be running a version of SQL Server that is supported by Distributed Replay. SQL Server 2014 Distributed Replay supports target servers that are running SQL Server 2008, SQL Server 2008 R2, SQL Server 2012, and SQL Server 2014.

The version of SQL Server that was used to capture the trace data that will be replayed is important too. SQL Server 2014 Distributed Replay supports input trace data that was captured from SQL Server 2005 through SQL Server 2014. The captured trace file must be replayed on a target SQL Server that is running the same version as the version of SQL Server that was used to capture the trace file. For example, a trace file that was captured using the SQL Server 2012 Profiler can be replayed on a target server running SQL Server 2012 or SQL Server 2014 but it could not be run if the target server was SQL Server 2008.

Now that you have an understanding of the Distributed Replay components, let's put them into use by creating the configuration files that drive this process.

Configuring Distributed Replay

To begin using Distributed Replay you must create configuration files that relate to the Distributed Replay components. The configuration files, which are specified in XML, are shown in the following list:

1. Controller Configuration File (DReplayController.config).

2. Client Configuration File (DReplayClient.config).

3. Process Configuration File (DReplay.exe.preprocess.config).

4. Replay Configuration File (DReplay.exe.replay.config).

Default configuration files can be found in the SQL Server tools folder (for example C:\Program Files (x86)\Microsoft SQL Server\120\Tools\) or subfolders related to the specific component. These files have options related to the process that they are associated with. You can modify these files in any text editor but be careful when making changes because the file contents must have a valid XML format. It is a good idea to make a copy of these default files first before making any changes. Each of the files and the related options are described in the following sections.

Controller Configuration File

The Distributed Replay controller service loads the controller configuration file when it starts. This configuration file is relatively simple and contains only one option that determines the logging level that will be used by the service. The file is named `DReplayController.config` and it should be located in the same folder where you installed the Distributed Replay controller service. For example, C:\Program Files (x86)\Microsoft SQL Server\120\Tools\DReplayController. The contents of the default configuration file are as follows:

```
<?xml version="1.0" encoding="utf-8"?>
<Options>
    <LoggingLevel>CRITICAL</LoggingLevel>
</Options>
```

The available options for LoggingLevel are INFORMATION, WARNING, and CRITICAL.

NOTE

If you didn't install the Distributed Replay components on either the controller server or clients during the initial SQL Server install, you'll need to re-run the SQL Server Installer from the original SQL Server media and go through the process of adding features to an existing installation. For more infomration on running the SQL Server Installer, see Chapter 8, "Installing SQL Server 2014."

Client Configuration File

The Distributed Replay client service loads the controller configuration file when it starts. This configuration file has four different settings that control the Distributed Replay Client behavior. The file is named `DReplayClient.config` and it should be located in the same folder where you installed the Distributed Replay client service. For example, C:\Program Files (x86)\Microsoft SQL Server\120\Tools\DReplayClient. The contents of the default configuration file follow:

```
<?xml version="1.0" encoding="utf-8"?>
<Options>
  <Controller>cgdv7</Controller>
  <WorkingDirectory>C:\Program Files (x86)\Microsoft SQL Server\120\Tools\
DReplayClient\WorkingDir\</WorkingDirectory>
  <ResultDirectory>C:\Program Files (x86)\Microsoft SQL Server\120\Tools\
DReplayClient\ResultDir\</ResultDirectory>
  <LoggingLevel>CRITICAL</LoggingLevel>
</Options>
```

The Controller option specifies the name of the controller computers that will be sending the trace workload to the Distributed Replay client. It is imperative that each client machine that will be used in Distributed Replay properly references the name of the controller computer in the client configuration file. The Windows service (named 'SQL Server Distributed Replay Client') loads the client configuration file when it starts. During this process, the service validates that it can communicate with the specified controller. If you want to change the name of the controller that the client will use then you need to modify the configuration file and restart the SQL Server Distributed Replay Client service for it to recognize the new controller. If no value is specified, the client will attempt to register with the controller instance running on the local server.

The WorkingDirectory setting specifies the local path on the client where the dispatch files will be saved. The ResultDirectory is the local path on the client where the result trace file from the replay activity (for the client) will be saved. If no value is specified for either of these settings, the associated files will be saved in the same location as the default client configuration file. The directory specified must exist or the client service will not start. The files saved in both the WorkingDirectory and ResultDirectory are overwritten on the next invocation of a replay.

Preprocess Configuration File

The Distributed Replay administrative tool loads the preprocess configuration file when you use the tool to initiate the preprocessing stage. This configuration file has two different settings that control the preprocessing stage. The file is named DReplay.exe.preprocess.config and it should be located in the same folder where you installed the Distributed Replay administration tool. For example, C:\Program Files (x86)\Microsoft SQL Server\120\Tools\Binn. The contents of the default configuration file follow:

```
<?xml version="1.0" encoding="utf-8"?>
<Options>
    <PreprocessModifiers>
        <IncSystemSession>No</IncSystemSession>
        <MaxIdleTime>-1</MaxIdleTime>
    </PreprocessModifiers>
</Options>
```

The IncSystemSession setting specifies whether system session activities during the capture will be included during replay. The default is No - only user session activities will be included.

The MaxIdleTime setting specifies the max idle time, in seconds, between activities in a trace file to an absolute number. You can set this value to any number greater than or equal to -1. A value of -1 (the default) indicates that the time between activities should be the same as in the original trace file. A value of 0 indicates that activities in the trace file should be applied one after the other with no idle time between them.

Replay Configuration File

The Distributed Replay administrative tool loads the replay configuration file when you use the tool to initiate the replay stage. This configuration file has the most extensive number of settings. These settings control the replay stage. The default replay configuration file is named `DReplay.exe.replay.config` and it should be located in the same folder where you installed the Distributed Replay administration tool. For example, C:\Program Files (x86)\Microsoft SQL Server\120\Tools\Binn. You can use the administration tool -c parameter to specify the location of a modified replay configuration file rather than modify the default configuration file. If you do modify the default configuration file, you should first make a backup copy of it.

The contents of the default configuration file follow:

```
<?xml version="1.0" encoding="utf-8"?>
<Options>
    <ReplayOptions>
        <Server></Server>
        <SequencingMode>stress</SequencingMode>
        <ConnectTimeScale>100</ConnectTimeScale>
        <ThinkTimeScale>100</ThinkTimeScale>
        <HealthmonInterval>60</HealthmonInterval>
        <QueryTimeout>3600</QueryTimeout>
        <ThreadsPerClient>255</ThreadsPerClient>
        <EnableConnectionPooling>No</EnableConnectionPooling>
        <StressScaleGranularity>SPID</StressScaleGranularity>
    </ReplayOptions>
    <OutputOptions>
        <ResultTrace>
            <RecordRowCount>Yes</RecordRowCount>
            <RecordResultSet>No</RecordResultSet>
        </ResultTrace>
    </OutputOptions>
</Options>
```

The `ReplayOptions` settings available in the Replay Configuration file are as follows:

▶ **SequencingMode**—The options for this setting are "synchronization" and "stress." Synchronization mode is the mode you would typically use for testing application compatibility or for validating that recent changes haven't degraded performance. In this mode, the distributed replay controller makes sure that the events are replayed in the same sequence they were generated. In "Stress" mode, the controller only follows the sequence of events within each client, but not the event sequence of the entire trace. This mode is used for capacity, scalability, and stress testing. It allows you to increase the workload volume during the replay. The amount of the increase is controlled by the `ConnectTimeScale`, `ThinkTimeScale` and `StressScaleGranularity` settings.

9

▶ **ConnectTimeScale**—This setting, specified as a percentage, allows you to scale the amount of time that the trace should wait between the trace starting and the logging of events starting. A lower value will decrease the gap and help drive a higher volume of activity.

▶ **ThinkTimeScale**—This setting, specified as a percentage, controls the amount of time the distributed replay controller waits between the completion of one statement/batch before submitting the next. Lowering this value will increase transaction volume during the replay.

▶ **HealthmonInteral**—This setting, specified in seconds, configures how often a process wakes up to detect deadlocks.

▶ **QueryTimeout**—This setting specifies the max amount of time, in seconds, to wait for a query that's waiting on a resource (such as a lock request) before aborting the query.

▶ **ThreadsPerClient**—Specifies the number of replay threads to use for each replay client. Default is 255.

▶ **EnableConnectionPooling**—Specifies whether connection pooling will be enabled on each Distributed Replay client. Default is NO.

▶ **StressScaleGranularity**—By default, the captured workload is divided almost equally between all available clients in the distributed environment. The StressScaleGranularity parameter determines how the workload will be divided. This parameter can accept two possible values – SPID or CONNECTION. Specifying SPID instructs the controller to try to divide the workload among all the clients you have installed based on how much work each of them is "doing." So if you have 6 sessions that you want to replay and you have 3 clients and all of those 6 sessions have around the same number of events to be replayed, the DReplay controller will go ahead and divide your workload so that the 3 clients will have to replay each of the events from 2 sessions. The same applies if you enable the "connection" as parameter, but this time it will be 2 connections per client.

The `OutputOptions` settings specify what information should be recorded in the result trace files. RecordRowCount specifies whether the row count should be recorded for each result set. The default is Yes. RecordResultSet specifies whether the content of all result sets should be captured. The default is No. You may want to capture the result sets if you are doing compatibility testing so you can compare the results against a previous replay, however, it can make for a very large replay trace output file.

The components related to distributed replay can be run using the default configuration files. The configuration files just give you a relatively easy means to adjust the behavior of those components. Once you have the setting in the configuration file set the way you want you are ready to move to the next section where we replay a workload.

Replay the Trace Data

There are four basic steps required to capture and replay a workload using Distributed Replay:

1. Review and configure permissions/security related to Distributed Replay.

2. Capture a workload that can be processed and applied using the Distributed Replay Components. This is typically a trace file that has been captured using the SQL Server Profiler.

3. Preprocess the trace file from the first step using DReplay.exe with the preprocess option.

4. Apply the workload using DReplay.exe with the replay option.

There are other considerations, such as Firewall exceptions, that come into play with Distributed Replay but these 4 steps are core to the process. The following sections cover each one of these steps using examples from the AdventureWorks2012 database. As mentioned earlier, you can run all of the components involved in Distributed Replay on different computers. For simplicity sake, the examples in the following section will use only two computers. The Distributed Replay Administrative tool (DReplay.exe), the controller, and the client will run on one computer. The target server will run on another computer.

> **NOTE**
>
> In the real world you would likely want to run the workload using multiple client computers to realize the full power of Distributed Replay. There is, however, some benefit to establishing Distributed Replay on fewer computers in the beginning. There is less setup when you use fewer computers and it is easier to diagnose possible issues with the replay when fewer computers are used. Scaling out the number of machines involved in Distributed Replay is relatively easy to do after you have established that Distributed Replay is working on fewer computers.

Configure Permissions and Security

Distributed Replay, as the name indicates, can be distributed across multiple computers and requires special attention with regard to permissions and security. All of the computers involved must be able to talk to each other and the processes that run on these computers must have the appropriate permissions to run the Distributed Replay workload.

The network accounts that run the Distributed Replay services are at the center of Distributed Replay security. There is an account associated with the Controller Service (SQL Server Distributed Replay Controller) and the Client Service (SQL Server Distributed Replay Client). Two separate domain accounts can be used for these services if desired. For our example, we will use the same domain account and refer to it as DReplaySvcAcct. Open the Windows Services application on the machine(s) where these services will be running and set the Log On account to DReplaySvcAcct. The Distributed Replay services need to be restarted in order to complete this change.

Running Distributed Replay services using a domain account that has permissions to all the machines involved will provide a majority of the security that you will need to run this tool. There are, however, a few other security related changes you need to make. The first of these changes relates to the Distributed Component Object Model (DCOM). The network account that will be running the Controller Service needs to be given permission via the DCOM configuration tool (dcomcnfg). To do this, click on the Start menu, select Run, and type in dcomcnfg which will open Component Services (if you are running Windows Server 2012 or Windows 8 or 8.1, press Win+Q and type dcomcnfg.exe). Find the DReplayController in Component Services by navigating to Console Root -> Component Services -> Computers -> My Computer -> DCOM Config -> DReplayController. Right click on DReplayContoller and select properties. Select the Security tab, edit the Launch and Activation Permissions and grant the domain account the Replay Controller service is running under Local Activation and Remote Activation permissions. (See Figure 6.2.) Similarly, edit the Access Permissions and grant the domain user account Local Access and Remote Access permissions. The controller domain account should also be added to the Distributed COM Users group using the Computer Management Administrative tool. Again, this should all be done on the computer where the Controller Service will be running.

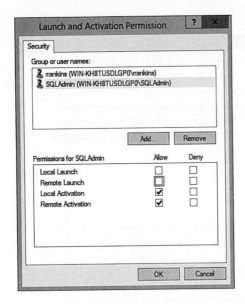

FIGURE 6.2   Setting DCOM Launch and Activation Permissions.

There is also an additional client oriented permission that must be considered. In particular, the Domain Account that is used for the Distributed Replay Client must be able to connect to SQL Server to run the replay workload. Ensure that this Domain account is a valid login on the target SQL Server instance and that this login has the necessary permissions to apply the workload.

Verifying the Configuration

Before attempting to run a replay session, you'll want to verify that the Replay Client is running and able to connect to the Replay Controller.

If you haven't already, start the Replay Client on the system where the client is installed and will be running with the following command:

```
NET START "SQL Server Distributed Replay Client"
```

Once the service is running, check the last log file for the Distributed Replay Client which should be in the folder "C:\Program Files (x86)\Microsoft SQL Server\120\Tools\ DReplayController\Log". If everything is configured correctly, the last line should read:

```
Registered with controller "YourControllerServerName".
```

If you had a "Failed to connect controller with error code" message, either the DCOM permissions aren't set correctly or there are firewall issues. If the Error code is 0x80070005, that indicates a DCOM access permission error. Review the steps above for configuring the DCOM permissions and verify they were done correctly.

If the error code is 0x800706BA, then it's likely a Firewall issue preventing the Distributed Replay Client from connecting to the controller. To add the rule for the Distributed Replay Controller, run the following command on the system where the replay controller resides modifying the pathname if necessary if you installed the tools in a different folder than the default:

```
NETSH advfirewall firewall add rule name="Allow DReplay Controller" dir=in
program="C:\Program Files (x86)\Microsoft SQL Server\120\Tools\DReplayController\
DReplayController.exe" action=allow
```

To add the rule for the Distributed Replay Clients, run the following command on each of the remote systems where the replay client is installed:

```
NETSH advfirewall firewall add rule name="Allow DReplay Client" dir=in program=
"C:\Program Files (x86)\Microsoft SQL Server\120\Tools\DReplayClient\DReplayClient.
exe" action=allow
```

Stop and restart the SQL Server Distributed Replay Client service and check the log file again to verify that it is now showing the "Registered with controller" message.

Capture the Workload

Use the SQL Server Profiler to capture a workload that will be applied by Distributed Replay. Use the Profiler template named TSQL_Replay. This template captures the columns and events that are needed to replay a workload. If you exclude any of them, you will not be able to preprocess your trace file. Also, it is highly recommended that you capture your workload using a server side trace rather than the Profiler GUI. Refer to Chapter 5 "SQL Server Profiler" for a more detailed discussion of SQL Server Profiler and how to capture a trace file.

Once you have started the Profiler Trace you are ready to apply a workload against the SQL Server instance. For demonstration purposes, the following statements were executed against the AdventureWorks2012 database while the Profiler was running:

```
SELECT * FROM [HumanResources].[Department]
GO


UPDATE [HumanResources].[Department]
 SET [ModifiedDate] = GETDATE()
GO


SELECT * FROM [HumanResources].[Department]
GO
```

This is a simple workload that is easy to apply and easy to confirm that the workload has been applied at a later time. You just need to check the date that is being updated on the HumanResources.Department table to confirm that the workload has been applied.

Once you have run your workload and generated the trace file, you need to make this file accessible to the Distributed Replay administrative tool that will be used in the next step.

Preprocess the Trace File

The workload file that was captured in the prior steps needs to be prepared before it can be used by the Distributed Replay Clients. This preparation is done using the dreplay.exe with the preprocess option. Preprocessing verifies that the workload file contains the necessary trace events and data to replay the workload, and will also remove any additional trace events that may have been captured that are not needed for the replay.To preprocess the workload file, you first need to copy it to the Controller computer then open up a command prompt window. Run the dreplay.exe application with the preprocess option as shown in the following example:

```
dreplay preprocess -i "C:\Trace\DReplay_Example.trc" -d "C:\Trace"
```

In this example, the workload file named DReplay_Example.trc has been copied to the C:\Trace folder and this same folder is being used as the working directory for this process. Figure 6.3 shows an example of the type of output that you will see when the preprocess of the trace file is successful.

Details related to the preprocess step can be found in the Distributed Replay Controller log folder. The default location for this log folder is C:\Program Files (x86)\Microsoft SQL Server\120\Tools\DReplayController\Log. A separate log file is written when the preprocess step is done. Refer to these log files if you encounter errors during this step.

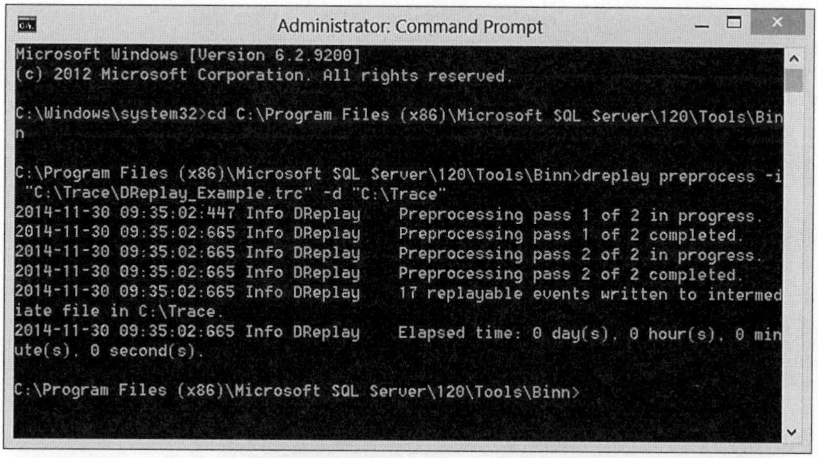

FIGURE 6.3   Preprocess Output.

There are two files that are generated when the preprocess step completes successfully. These files are named ReplayEvents.irf and TraceStats.xml. They are located in the working folder that was specified; for example C:\Trace. The controller will use these files during the Replay step discussed in the next section.

Apply the Workload

The output files that were created in the prior step can now be processed by the Distributed Replay Controller and run by the Distributed Replay Clients against the target server. This is done using the `dreplay.exe` with the `replay` option. You should get on the Controller computer then open up a command prompt window. Run the dreplay.exe application with the `replay` option as shown in the following example:

```
dreplay replay -s dreplaytarget\Inst2014 -w cgdv7 -f 10 -o -d "C:\trace"
```

In this example, the target SQL Server instance is set to dreplaytarget\Inst2014 using the `-s` option. The `-w` option is used to specify the client machines that you want to run the workload. In this example, there is only one client named `cgdv7` that is running the workload. Additional clients can be specified by passing a comma separated list of client computer names to the `-w` option. Figure 6.4 shows an example of the type of output that you will see when the replay of the trace file is successful.

> **TIP**
>
> If your workload file contains data modification operations (INSERTs/UPDATEs/DELETEs), you may want to make a backup of the target database before running the replay. That way, if you want to re-run the replay, you can restore the database back to its state prior to running the replay.

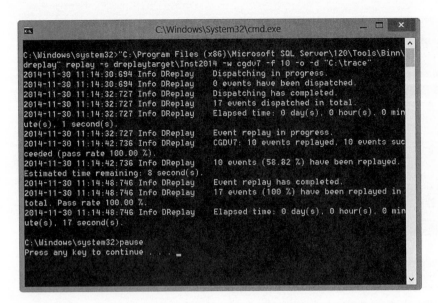

FIGURE 6.4   Replay Output.

You can monitor and assess the results of the replay in several different ways. The first place to look is the output displayed in the Command Prompt window. Look for the pass rate percentage that is displayed in the output text. If you see that the rate is 100 % then this is a good indication that the replay was successful. If, on the other hand, you see that the pass rate is 0 % then there is an underlying issue with the replay.

For a replay that takes longer to run than the one used in this example, you can monitor the status of the replay process in the Command Prompt window where the Distributed Replay Controller is running. The frequency of the status updates can be controlled using the –f command line switch to specify the number of seconds between each of the updates. The status updates provide information about each of the clients showing the total number of events that have been replayed, the success rate of the replay operations per client, as well as an estimate for the total amount of time remaining to complete the replay operation. When the replay completes, the controller will display the total elapsed time and overall pass rate for the events. You can obtain further information about the results of the replay by looking at the trace output file that is generated when the -o option is used. The default location for the trace output file is C:\Program Files (x86)\Microsoft SQL Server\120\Tools\DReplayClient\ResultDir on the client computer. Open up this trace file in SQL Server Profiler and you should see the execution of the commands that were part of your workload. Figure 6.5 shows the trace output file with the commands from the sample workload that we created earlier.

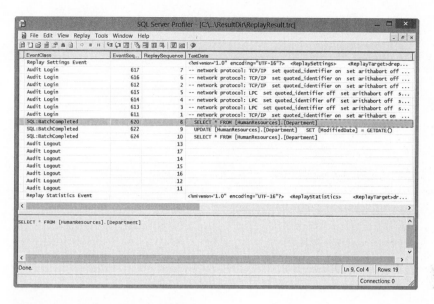

FIGURE 6.5   Replay Trace Output File.

The highlighted row in Figure 6.5 shows the first of three commands that were shown in our sample workload against the AdventureWorks2012 database. The subsequent UPDATE to the HumanResources.Department table can be seen in this figure as well. As mentioned earlier, this UPDATE gives us a relatively easy way to verify that the workload was applied successfully. You can also simply open up a Query Window in SSMS and SELECT the rows from the HumanResources.Department table. If you see that the ModifiedDate on this table corresponds with the time that you did your replay then you know you are in business.

Summary

Distributed Replay is a powerful tool that can give you a much better idea of how your database will perform under load. It builds off of the SQL Server Profiler's replay capability but it adds in the all-important capability of replaying concurrent workloads. Concurrent load testing will get you much closer to what you might see in the real world and it fits in with Microsoft's goal of providing predictable performance for your SQL Server applications.

Another key aspect of database performance is the administration and management of the SQL Server databases. The next chapter, "SQL Server System and Database Administration," provides guidelines for administering SQL Server databases and accessing the plethora of system information that is available within them.

PART III

SQL Server Administration

IN THIS PART

SQL Server
Administration

IN THIS PART

SQL Server System and Database Administration

This chapter outlines the role of a SQL Server system administrator and explores some of the methods that an administrator can use to query important system data. As with any other job, understanding the roles and responsibilities of the job is critical to doing the job well. The responsibilities of an administrator vary depending on the job, but there are some core responsibilities covered in this chapter.

You also need the right tools and right information to do the job well and do it efficiently. The system data covered in this chapter provides some of the key information. The methods discussed to access this information are among the tools you will need. System data discloses information that can be invaluable when assessing your SQL Server environment and is an essential part of administering a SQL Server database.

What's New in SQL Server System and Database Administration

The means for accessing system information has changed very little from SQL Server 2005 to SQL Server 2014. The system views that were introduced in SQL Server 2005 are still the preferred means for getting at that all-important system information. These views, which include catalog, compatibility, and dynamic views, are discussed in detail later in this chapter.

What is new in SQL Server 2014 is an enhanced set of system objects. There are some new system views such as sys.dm_exec_query_stats and sys.column_store_row_groups. There are also quite a few system objects that have been updated to capture information related to new functionality offered with SQL Server 2014. Most of the updates relate to the new In-Memory OLTP feature that is available in SQL Server 2014. Updates have been made to properties, System Views, System Stored Procedures, and Dynamic Management Views to capture data related to In-Memory OLTP.

System Administrator Responsibilities

A system administrator is responsible for the integrity and availability of the data in a database. This is a simple concept, but it is a huge responsibility. Some large corporations place a valuation on their data as high as $1 million per 100MB. The investment in dollars is not the only issue; many companies that lose mission-critical data simply never recover.

Job descriptions for system administrators vary widely. In small shops, the administrator might lay out the physical design of the database, install SQL Server, implement the logical design of the database, tune the installation, and then manage ongoing tasks, such as backups. At larger organizations tasks might be broken out into separate job functions. Managing users and backing up data are common examples. However, a lead administrator should still be in place to define policy and coordinate efforts.

Whether performed by an individual or as a team, the core administration tasks are as follows:

▶ Install and configure SQL Server.

▶ Plan and create databases.

▶ Manage data storage.

▶ Control security.

▶ Tune the database.

▶ Perform backup and recovery.

Another task sometimes handled by administrators is managing stored procedures. Because stored procedures for user applications often contain complex Transact-SQL (T-SQL) code, they tend to fall into the realm of the application developer. However, because stored procedures are stored as objects in the database, they are also the responsibility of the administrator. If an application calls custom stored procedures, the system administrator must be aware of this and coordinate with the application developers.

The system administration job can be stressful, frustrating, and demanding, but it is a highly rewarding, interesting, and respected position. As a system administrator, you are expected to know all, see all, and predict all, and should be well compensated for your efforts.

System Databases

SQL Server uses system databases to support different parts of the database management system (DBMS). Each database plays a specific role and stores information that SQL Server needs to do its job. The system databases are much like the user databases created in SQL Server. They store data in tables and contain the views, stored procedures, and other database objects that you also see in user databases. They also have associated database files (that is, `.mdf` and `.ldf` files) just like user databases. Table 7.1 lists system databases and their related database filenames.

TABLE 7.1   System Databases and Their Associated Database Files

Database	`.mdf` **Filename**	`.ldf` **Filename**
master	master.mdf	mastlog.ldf
resource	mssqlsystemresource.mdf	mssqlsystemresource.ldf
model	model.mdf	modellog.ldf
msdb	msdbdata.mdf	msdblog.ldf
distribution	distmdl.ldf	distmdl.mdf
tempdb	tempdb.mdf	templog.ldf

TIP

You can use the `sys.master_files` catalog view to list the physical locations of the system database files as well as the user database files. This catalog view contains a myriad of information, including the logical name, current state, and size of each database file.

The folder where each of these database files is located depends on the SQL Server installation. For SQL Server 2014, the installation process places these files in a default folder named `<drive>:\Program Files\Microsoft SQL Server\MSSQL12.MSSQLSERVER\MSSQL\DATA\`. You can change this location during the install. You can also move these files after the installation by using special procedures that are documented in the SQL Server Books Online topic, "Move System Databases."

The following sections describe the function of each system database.

The `master` Database

The `master` database contains server-wide information about the SQL Server system. This server-wide information includes logins, linked server information, configuration information for the server, and information about user databases created in the SQL Server instance. The actual locations of the database files and key properties that relate to each user database are stored in the `master` database.

SQL Server cannot start without a `master` database. This is not surprising, given the type of information it contains. Without the `master` database, SQL Server does not know the location of the databases it services and does not know how the server is configured to run.

The `resource` Database

The `resource` database contains all the system objects deployed with SQL Server 2014. These system objects include the system stored procedures and system views that logically appear in each database but are physically stored in the `resource` database. Microsoft moved all the system objects to the `resource` database to simplify the upgrade process. When a new release of the software is made available, upgrading the system objects is accomplished by simply copying the single `resource` database file to the local server. Similarly, rolling back an upgrade only requires overwriting the current version of the `resource` database with the older version.

You do not see the `resource` database in the list of system databases shown in SQL Server Management Studio (SSMS). You also cannot add user objects to the `resource` database. For the most part, an administrator has nothing to do with the `resource` database, but it does play an important role. It has database files named `mssqlsystemresources.mdf` and `mssqlsystemresources.ldf` that are located in the `Binn` folder, but you cannot access the database directly. In addition, you do not see the database listed when selecting databases using system views or with system procedures, such as `sp_helpdb` or `sys.databases`.

The `model` Database

The `model` database is a template on which all user-created databases are based. All databases must contain a base set of objects known as the *database catalog*. When a new database is created, the model is copied to create the requisite objects. Conveniently, objects can be added to the `model` database. For example, if you want a certain table created in all your databases, you can create the table in the `model` database, and it is then propagated to all subsequently created databases.

The `msdb` Database

The `msdb` database is used to store information for the SQL Server Agent, the Service Broker, Database Mail, log shipping, and more. When you create and schedule a SQL Server Agent job, the job's parameters and execution history are stored in `msdb`. Backups and maintenance plan information are stored in `msdb` as well. If log shipping is implemented, critical information about the servers and tables involved in this process are stored in `msdb`.

The `distribution` Database

The `distribution` database, utilized during replication, stores metadata and history information for all types of replication. It is also used to store transactions when transactional replication is utilized. By default, replication is not installed with SQL Server, and you do not see the `distribution` database listed in SSMS. However, the actual data files for the `distribution` database are installed by default.

Refer to Chapter 43, "Data Replication," for a more detailed discussion of the intricacies of replication.

The `tempdb` Database

The `tempdb` database stores temporary data and data objects. The temporary data objects include temporary tables, temporary stored procedures, and any other objects you want to create temporarily. The longevity of data objects in the temporary database depends on the type of object created. Ultimately, all temporary database objects are removed when the SQL Server service is restarted. The `tempdb` database is re-created, and all objects and data added since the last restart of SQL Server are lost.

The `tempdb` database can also be used for some of SQL Server's internal operations. Large sort operations are performed in `tempdb` before the result set is returned to the client. Certain index operations can be performed in `tempdb` to offload some of the space requirements or to spread I/O. SQL Server also uses `tempdb` to store row versions that are generated from database modifications in databases that use row versioning or snapshot isolation transactions. Refer to Chapter 37, "Locking and Performance," for a more detailed discussion of transaction isolation levels and row versioning.

Maintaining System Databases

You should give system databases the same attention you give your user databases. These databases should be backed up on a regular basis and secured in the event that one of them needs to be restored. All the system databases, with the exception of `tempdb` and `resource`, can be backed up. These same databases can also be restored to bring them back to a previous state.

> **NOTE**
>
> Although you cannot back up the `resource` database using SQL Server's BACKUP and RESTORE commands, you can make a backup copy of it by performing a file-based or disk-based backup of the `mssqlsystemresource.mdf` file (SQL Server must not be running at the time). Likewise, you can manually restore a backup copy of the `mssqlsystem-resource.mdf` file only when SQL Server is not running. You must be careful not to over-write the current `resource` database with a version for a different release level of SQL Server.

It's important that you monitor the size of your system databases too. The amount of data that accumulates in these databases can be significant. This is particularly true for the `tempdb`, `msdb`, and `distribution` databases. Large sort or index operations can increase the size of your `tempdb` database in a short period of time. The `msdb` and `distribution` databases contain a great deal of historical information. Consider, for example, a server with hundreds of databases that have log backups occurring every 15 minutes. The information captured for each individual backup is not significant, but the total number of databases and frequency of the backups cause many rows to be stored in the `msdb` database. Cleanup tasks and similar activities that remove older historical data can help keep the database size manageable.

System Tables

System tables contain data about objects in the SQL Server databases (that is, metadata) as well as information that SQL Server components use to do their job. Many of the system tables are now hidden (in the `resource` database) and are no longer available for direct access by end users. In SQL Server 2014, compatibility views, which are discussed later in this chapter, have the same names as the system tables that could be accessed directly in SQL Server 2000. For example, if you had a query in SQL Server 2000 that selected from `syscolumns`, this query continues to work in SQL Server 2014, but the results come from a view instead of a system table.

The system tables that you can view are now found in some of the system databases, such as `msdb` or `master`. You can use the Object Explorer in SSMS to view the system tables in these databases. Figure 7.1 shows the system tables listed for the `master` database in the Object Explorer.

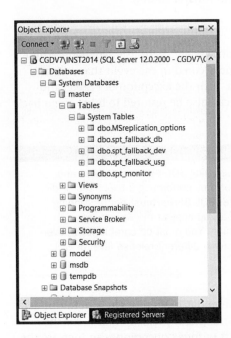

FIGURE 7.1   System tables listed in Object Explorer.

The `msdb` system database has the largest number of viewable system tables. The system tables in this database support backup and restore, log shipping, maintenance plans, Notification Services, the SQL Server Agent, and more. You can retrieve a tremendous amount of information from these system tables if you know what you are looking for. The following query selects from the system tables in `msdb` to report on recent restores for the `AdventureWorks2012` database:

```
select destination_database_name 'database', h.restore_date,
restore_type,
    cast((backup_size/1024)/1024 as numeric(8,0))
'backup_size MB',
    f.physical_device_name
 from msdb..restorehistory h (NOLOCK)
    LEFT JOIN msdb..backupset b (NOLOCK)
        ON h.backup_set_id = b.backup_set_id
    LEFT JOIN msdb..backupmediafamily f (NOLOCK)
        ON b.media_set_id = f.media_set_id
 where h.restore_date > getdate() - 5
    and UPPER(h.destination_database_name) =
'AdventureWorks2012'
 order by UPPER(h.destination_database_name),
h.restore_date desc
```

One of the challenges with using system tables is determining the relationships between them. Some vendors offer diagrams of these tables or views. You can also determine the relationships by reviewing the foreign keys on these tables and by referring to SQL Server 2014 Books Online, which describes the use for each column in the system table.

CAUTION

Microsoft does not recommend querying system tables directly. It does not guarantee the consistency of system tables across versions and warns that queries that may have worked against system tables in past versions may no longer work. Catalog views or information schema views should be used instead, especially in production code.

Queries against system tables are best used for ad hoc queries. The values in system tables should never be updated, and an object's structure should not be altered, either. Making changes to the data or structure could cause problems and cause SQL Server or one of its components to fail.

System Views

System views are virtual tables that expose metadata that relates to many different aspects of SQL Server. Several different types of views target different data needs. SQL Server 2014 offers an extended number of system views and view types that should meet most, if not all, your metadata needs.

The available system views can be shown in the Object Explorer in SSMS. Figure 7.2 shows the Object Explorer with the System Views node highlighted. There are far too many views to cover in detail in this chapter, but we cover each type of view and provide an example of each to give you some insight into their value. Each system view is covered in detail in SQL Server Books Online, which includes descriptions of each column in the view.

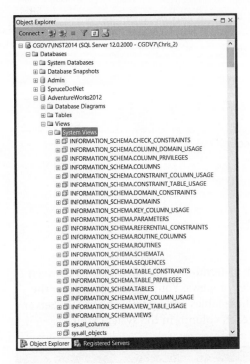

FIGURE 7.2   System views listed in Object Explorer.

Compatibility Views

Compatibility views were retained in SQL Server 2014 for backward compatibility. Many of the system tables available in SQL Server 2000 and prior versions of SQL Server are now implemented as compatibility views. These views have the same name as the system tables from prior versions and return the same metadata available in SQL Server 2000. They do not contain information that was added after SQL Server 2000.

You can find most of the compatibility views in the Object Explorer by looking for system views that have names starting with `sys.sys`. For example, `sys.syscolumns`, `sys.syscomments`, and `sys.sysobjects` are all compatibility views. The first part of the name indicates the schema that the object belongs to (in this case, `sys`). All system objects are part of this `sys` schema or the `INFORMATION_SCHEMA` schema. The second part of the name is the view name, which corresponds to the name of a system table in SQL Server 2000.

TIP

To see a list of compatibility views, use the index lookup in SQL Server 2014 Books Online and look for `sys.sysa`. The index is placed at the beginning of a list of compatibility views, starting with `sys.sysaltfiles`. Objects in the list that are compatibility views have the text `compatibility view` following the object name, so you can easily identify them and get help.

You also can use the IntelliSense feature available with SQL Server 2014 to obtain information about the compatibility views and other system views. Simply open a query window in SSMS and start typing a SELECT statement. When you start typing the name of the view that you want to select from (for example, sys.), the IntelliSense drop-down appears listing the views that start with the letters sys. You can also determine the columns available from the view by referencing the view or alias for the view in the column selection list. When you enter the period following the view or alias, the IntelliSense drop-down shows you the available columns.

You should transition from the use of compatibility views to the use of other system views, such as catalog views. The scripts that were created in SQL Server 2000 and reference SQL Server 2000 system tables should continue to function in SQL Server 2014, but this capability is strictly for backward compatibility. The compatibility views are slated to be removed in a future version of SQL Server. Table 7.2 provides a list of SQL Server 2000 system tables and alternative SQL Server 2014 system views you can use instead.

TABLE 7.2   SQL Server 2014 Alternatives for SQL Server 2000 System Tables

SQL Server 2000	SQL Server 2014 System View	View Type System Table
sysaltfiles	sys.master_files	Catalog view
syscacheobjects	sys.dm_exec_cached_plans	DMV
	sys.dm_exec_plan_attributes	DMV
	sys.dm_exec_sql_text	DMV
syscharsets	sys.syscharsets	Compatibility view
syscolumns	sys.columns	Catalog view
syscomments	sys.sql_modules	Catalog view
sysconfigures	sys.configurations	Catalog view
sysconstraints	sys.check_constraints	Catalog view
	sys.default_constraints	Catalog view
	sys.key_constraints	Catalog view
	sys.foreign_keys	Catalog view
syscurconfigs	sys.configurations	Catalog view
sysdatabases	sys.databases	Catalog view
sysdepends	sys.sql_dependencies	Catalog view
sysdevices	sys.backup_devices	Catalog view
sysfilegroups	sys.filegroups	Catalog view
sysfiles	sys.database_files	Catalog view
sysforeignkeys	sys.foreign_keys	Catalog view
sysfulltextcatalogs	sys.fulltext_catalogs	Catalog view
sysindexes	sys.indexes	Catalog view

SQL Server 2000	SQL Server 2014 System View	View Type System Table
	sys.partitions	Catalog view
	sys.allocation_units	Catalog view
	sys.dm_db_partition_stats	DMV
sysindexkeys	sys.index_columns	Catalog view
syslanguages	sys.syslanguages	Compatibility view
syslockinfo	sys.dm_tran_locks	DMV
syslocks	sys.dm_tran_locks	DMV
syslogins	sys.sql_logins (transact-sql)	Catalog view
sysmembers	sys.database_role_members	Catalog view
sysmessages	sys.messages	Catalog view
sysobjects	sys.objects	Catalog view
sysoledbusers	sys.linked_logins	Catalog view
sysopentapes	sys.dm_io_backup_tapes	DMV
sysperfinfo	sys.dm_os_performance_counters	DMV
syspermissions	sys.database_permissions	Catalog view
	sys.server_permissions	Catalog view
sysprocesses	sys.dm_exec_connections	DMV
	sys.dm_exec_sessions	DMV
	sys.dm_exec_requests	DMV
sysprotects	sys.database_permissions	Catalog view
	sys.server_permissions	Catalog view
sysreferences	sys.foreign_keys	Catalog view
sysremotelogins	sys.remote_logins	Catalog view
sysservers	sys.servers	Catalog view
systypes	sys.types	Catalog view
sysusers	sys.database_principals	Catalog view

Catalog Views

Catalog views are the preferred method for returning information used by the Microsoft SQL Server Database Engine. There is a catalog view to return information about almost every aspect of SQL Server. The number of catalog views is far too large to list here, but you can gain some insight into the range of information available by looking at Table 7.3, which shows the categories of information covered by catalog views:

TABLE 7.3   Catalog View Categories

AlwaysOn Availability Group	Linked Servers
Change Tracking	Messages (For Errors)
CLR Assembly	Object
Databases and Files	Partition Function
Database Mail Views	Policy-Based Management Views
Database Mirroring	Resource Governor
Data Collector Views	Scalar Types
Data Spaces	Schemas
Endpoints	Security
Extended Events	Service Broker
Extended Properties	Server-wide Configuration
FileTable	XML Schemas (XML Type System)
Full-Text Search and Semantic Search	

Some of the catalog views return information that is new to SQL Server 2014. Examples include the `sys.table_types` which now indicates if a table has been memory optimized and `sys.tables` which also has new columns related to memory-optimized tables. Other catalog views provide information that may have been available in prior versions through system tables, system procedures, and so on, but the new catalog views expand on the information returned and include elements that are new to SQL Server 2014.

To demonstrate the use of a catalog view, let's compare a simple SQL SELECT statement that returns object information using a compatibility view to a SELECT statement in SQL Server 2014 that returns similar information using a catalog view. The following example shows a SELECT statement written that uses a compatibility view to return any stored procedure created after a given date:

```
select o.crdate, o.name
 from sysobjects o
 where type = 'p'
  and crdate > '1/1/08'
 order by crdate, name
```

Now, compare this SELECT statement to one that uses a SQL Server 2014 catalog view. The `sys.objects` catalog view is an alternative to the SQL Server 2000 `sysobjects` system table. The following SELECT uses the `sys.all_objects` catalog view to return the same type of information as the preceding example:

```
select o.create_date, o.modify_date, name
 from sys.all_objects o
 where type = 'p'
 and create_date > '1/1/08'
 order by create_date, name
```

As you can see, the `modify_date` column has been added to the `SELECT` statement. This column did not exist with the `sysobjects` system table. The addition of this column allows you to identify objects that were created as well as objects that were modified or altered.

Let's look at an example of using a catalog view to return the same kind of information returned in SQL Server 2000 with a system procedure. The handy `sp_helpfile` system procedure returns information about database files associated with a given database. This SQL Server 2000 procedure is still available in SQL Server 2014. An alternative to this procedure is the new `sys.master_files` catalog view. This view returns all the information that `sp_helpfile` returns and more. The following example shows a `SELECT` statement using the `sys.master_files` catalog view to return the database files for the `AdventureWorks2012` database:

```
select *
 from sys.master_files
 where db_name(database_id) = 'AdventureWorks2012'
```

You have the distinct advantage of being able to select the database files for all the databases on your server by using this catalog view. You can also tailor your `SELECT` statement to isolate database files based on the size of the database or the location of the physical database files. For example, to return all database files that are found somewhere on your C: drive, you could use the following `SELECT`:

```
select db_name(database_id), physical_name
 from sys.master_files
 where physical_name like 'c:\%'
```

There are plenty of catalog views that provide information about SQL Server. When you are looking to return information about SQL Server components, you should look to the catalog views first. These views provide a great deal of flexibility and allow you to isolate the specific information you need.

Information Schema Views

Information schema views provide another option for accessing SQL Server metadata that is independent of system tables. This type of view was available in prior versions of SQL Server. Using information schema views is a viable alternative for accessing SQL Server metadata from a production application. The information schema views enable an application that uses them to function properly even though the underlying system tables may have changed. Changes to the underlying system tables are most prevalent when a new version of SQL Server is released (such as SQL Server 2014), but changes can also occur as part of service packs to an existing version.

> **CAUTION**
>
> Microsoft does its best to make information schema views backward compatible, but in some cases, changes are made to these views that break backward compatibility. Make sure to review any changes that may have been made to these views in new versions of the SQL Server or SQL Server service packs.

The information schema views also have the advantage of being SQL-92 compatible. Compliance with the SQL-92 standard means that SQL statements written against these views work with other DBMSs that also adhere to the SQL-92 standard. The SQL-92 standard supports a three-part naming convention, which SQL Server has implemented as `database.schema.object`.

In SQL Server 2014, all the information schema views are in the same schema, named `INFORMATION_SCHEMA`. The following information schema views or objects are available:

- CHECK_CONSTRAINTS
- COLUMN_DOMAIN_USAGE
- COLUMN_PRIVILEGES
- COLUMNS
- CONSTRAINT_COLUMN_USAGE
- CONSTRAINT_TABLE_USAGE
- DOMAIN_CONSTRAINTS
- DOMAINS
- KEY_COLUMN_USAGE
- PARAMETERS
- REFERENTIAL_CONSTRAINTS
- ROUTINES
- ROUTINE_COLUMNS
- SCHEMATA
- TABLE_CONSTRAINTS
- TABLE_PRIVILEGES
- TABLES
- VIEW_COLUMN_USAGE
- VIEW_TABLE_USAGE
- VIEWS

When you refer to information schema views in a SQL statement, you must use a qualified name that includes the schema name. For example, the following statement returns all the tables and columns in a given database, using the `tables` and `columns` information schema views:

```
select t.TABLE_NAME, c.COLUMN_NAME
 from INFORMATION_SCHEMA.TABLES t
  join INFORMATION_SCHEMA.COLUMNS c on t.TABLE_NAME =
c.TABLE_NAME
 order by t.TABLE_NAME, ORDINAL_POSITION
```

> **TIP**
>
> You can expand the `Views` node in a given database in the Object Explorer and open the `System Views` node to see a list of the available information schema views. The information schema views are listed at the top of the `System Views` node. If you expand

the `Column` node under each information schema view, you see the available columns to select from the view. You can then drag the column into a query window for use in a `SELECT` statement. You can also use IntelliSense in a query window to determine the columns.

Fortunately, the names of the information schema views are fairly intuitive and reflect the kind of information they return. The relationships between the information schema views can be derived from the column names shared between the tables.

Dynamic Management Views

Dynamic management views (DMVs), which were introduced in SQL Server 2005, provide a simple means for assessing the state of your SQL Server instance. These views provide a lightweight means for gathering diagnostic information without the heavy burden of some of the more complicated diagnostic tools. The diagnostic tools, such as heavy Profiler traces, Performance Monitor, DBCC executions, and the Database Engine Tuning Advisor are still available, but oftentimes, the information returned from the DMVs is enough to determine what may be ailing a SQL Server instance.

An extensive number of DMVs are available in SQL Server 2014. Some DMVs are scoped at the server level, and others are scoped at the database level. They are all found in the `sys` schema and have names that start with `dm_`. Table 7.4 lists the different types of DMVs. The DMVs in this table are categorized based on function as well as the starting characters in the DMV names. The naming convention gives you an easy means for identifying the type of each DMV.

TABLE 7.4   Types of DMVs

Category	Name Prefix	Information Captured
AlwaysOn Availability	dm_hadr	New AlwaysOn Availability Groups
Auditing	dm_audit	Auditing information
Change Data	dm_cdc	Change data capture information
CLR	dm_clr	CLR information, including the CLR loaded assemblies
Cryptographic	dm_cryptographic	Security-related data
Database	dm_db	Databases and database objects
Execution	dm_exec	Execution of user code
Extended Events	dm_xe	Event handling infrastructure
Filestream	dm_filestream	New FILESTREAM and FileTable features
Full-Text	dm_fts	Full-Text Search information
In-Memory OLTP	Dm_xtp	In-Memory optimization stats
I/O	dm_io	Input and output on network disks
Object	dm_sql	Object references

Category	Name Prefix	Information Captured
Operating system	dm_os	Low-level operating system information, including memory and locking information
Query Notification	dm_qn	Active Query Notification subscriptions
Replication	dm_repl	Replication information, including the articles, publications, and transaction involved in replication
Resource Governor	dm_resource_governor	Resource Governor configuration and monitoring
Server	dm_server	Server data
Service Broker	dm_broker	Server Broker statistics, including activated tasks and connections
TCP Listener	dm_tcp	New availability group TCP listeners
TDE	dm_database	Transparent data encryption
Transactions	dm_tran	SQL Server transactions

TIP

You can expand the Views node in a given database in the Object Explorer and open the System Views node to see a list of the available DMVs. The DMVs are all listed together and start with sys.dm_. If you expand the Columns node under each DMV, you see the available columns to select from the view. You can then drag the column into a query window to be included in a SELECT statement.

To illustrate the value of the DMVs, let's look at a performance scenario and compare the SQL Server 2000 approach to a SQL Server 2014 approach using DMVs. A common performance-related question is, "What stored procedures are executing most frequently on my server?" With SQL Server 2000, the most likely way to find out is to run a Profiler trace. You must have a Profiler trace that has already been running to capture the stored procedure executions, or you must create a new trace and run it for a period of time to answer the performance question. The trace takes time to create and can affect server performance while it is running.

With SQL Server 2014, you can use one of the DMVs in the execution category to answer the same performance question. The following example uses the sys.dm_exec_query_stats DMV along with a dynamic management function named dm_exec_sql_text. It returns the object IDs of the five most frequently executed stored procedures, along with the actual text associated with the procedure:

```
select top 5 q.execution_count, q.total_worker_time,
 s.dbid, s.objectid, s.text
 from sys.dm_exec_query_stats q
```

```
CROSS APPLY sys.dm_exec_sql_text (q.sql_handle) s
ORDER BY q.execution_count desc
```

The advantage of using a DMV is that it can return past information without having to explicitly create a trace or implement some other performance tool. SQL Server automatically caches the information so that you can query it at any time. The collection of the data starts when the SQL Server instance is started, so you can get a good cross-section of information if the instance has not been restarted for some time. Keep in mind that your results can change as the server continues to collect information over time.

Many of the performance scenarios such as those that relate to memory, CPU utilization, blocking, and recompilation can be investigated using DMVs. You should consider using DMVs to address performance problems before using other methods in SQL Server 2014. In many cases, you may be able to avoid costly traces and glean enough information from the DMV to solve your problem.

> **NOTE**
>
> Dynamic management functions return the same type of information as DMVs. The dynamic management functions also have names that start with `sys.dm_` and reside in the `sys` schema. You can find the dynamic management functions listed in the Object Explorer within the `master` database. If you select Function, System Functions, Table-Valued Functions, you see the dynamic management functions listed at the top.

DMVs are also a great source of information that does not relate directly to performance. For example, you can use the `dm_os_sys_info` DMV to gather important server information, such as the number of CPUs, the amount of memory, and so on. The following example demonstrates the use of the `dm_os_sys_info` DMV to return CPU and memory information:

```
select cpu_count, hyperthread_ratio, physical_memory_kb
 from sys.dm_os_sys_info

/* Results from prior select

cpu_count   hyperthread_ratio physical_memory_kb
----------- ----------------- ------------------------
8           8                 6281072
*/
```

The `cpu_count` column returns the number of logical CPUs, `hyperthread_ratio` returns the ratio between physical CPUs and logical CPUs, and the last column selected returns the physical memory on the SQL Server machine.

System Stored Procedures

System stored procedures have been a favorite of SQL Server Database Administrators (DBAs) since the inception of SQL Server. They provide a rich set of information that covers many different aspects of SQL Server. They can return some of the same types of information as system views, but they return a fixed set of information that you cannot modify as you can when using a SELECT statement against the system views. That is not to say that they are not valuable; they are valuable, and they are particularly useful for people who have been using SQL Server for a long time. System stored procedures such as sp_who2, sp_lock, and sp_help are tools for a database professional that are as basic as a hammer is to a carpenter.

System stored procedures have names that start with sp_, and they are found in the sys schema. They are global in scope, which allows you to execute them from any database, without qualifying the stored procedure name. They also run in the context of the database where you are working. In other words, if you execute sp_helpfile in the AdventureWorks2012 database, the database files for the AdventureWorks2012 database are returned. This same type of behavior exists for any stored procedure that is created in the master database with a name that starts with sp_. For example, if you create a procedure named sp_helpme in the master database and execute that procedure in the AdventureWorks2012 database, SQL Server ultimately finds and executes the procedure in the master database.

> **NOTE**
>
> It is often useful to create your own system stored procedures to make it easier to execute complex queries against the system views (or to provide information not provided by the built-in system procedures). For more information and tips on creating your own system stored procedures, refer to Chapter 25, "Creating and Managing Stored Procedures."

System stored procedures are listed in the Object Explorer, in the Programmability node within Stored Procedures and then System Stored Procedures. There are far too many system stored procedures to list or discuss them all here. A quick check of the master database lists more than 1,000 procedures. SQL Server Books Online provides detailed help on these procedures, which it groups into 18 different categories.

Useful System Stored Procedures

You are likely to use only a handful of system stored procedures on a regular basis. What procedures you use will depend on the type of work you do with SQL Server and your capacity to remember their names. Table 7.5 contains a sample set of system stored procedures that you may find useful.

TABLE 7.5 Useful System Stored Procedures

System Stored Procedure	Description
sp_configure	Displays or changes server-wide configuration settings.
sp_createstats	Creates statistics that are used by the Query Optimizer for all tables in a database.
sp_help	Provides details about the object that is passed to it. If a table name is passed to this procedure, it returns information on the columns, constraints, indexes, and more.
sp_helpdb	If no parameters are supplied, returns relevant database information (including the space used) for all the databases on an instance of SQL Server.
sp_helpfile	Lists the database files associated with the database you are connected to.
sp_lock	Displays current locking information for the entire SQL Server instance.
sp_spaceused	Provides the number of rows and disk space used by the table, indexed view, or queue passed to it.
sp_who	Lists current processes that are connected to an instance of SQL Server.

Many of the administrative functions performed by SSMS can also be accomplished with system stored procedures. Examples include procedures that start with sp_add and sp_delete, which can be used to add and delete database objects. In addition, more than 90 system stored procedures start with sp_help, which return help information on database objects.

> **TIP**
>
> You can use the sys.all_objects catalog view to search for available system stored procedures. This catalog view lists objects that are schema scoped as well as system objects. For example, the query SELECT * FROM sys.all_objects WHERE name LIKE 'sp_help%' returns all the system stored procedures that start with sp_help. You can turn to Books Online for detailed help on any of the system stored procedures. Just enter sp_ in the index search, and you see a list of them all.

Becoming familiar with some of the system stored procedures is well worth your while. Using them is a fast and effective means for gathering information from SQL Server. They do not require the formation of a SELECT statement, and using them is often the easiest way to get information via a query window.

Summary

Administering SQL Server can be a complex and time-consuming job. Understanding the SQL Server internals and some of the easy ways to obtain information about a SQL Server instance can make this job a lot easier. Taking the time to learn what makes SQL Server tick expands your knowledge of this comprehensive DBMS and helps you make better decisions when working with it.

Now that you know a bit about managing SQL Server, you may need to install an instance of SQL Server to administer. Take a look at Chapter 8, "Installing SQL Server 2014," which guides you through the installation process.

7

Installing SQL Server 2014

Installing SQL Server is the first and one of the easiest tasks you'll accomplish as an administrator. And even though it may take as little as 15 minutes to get SQL Server 2014 up and running by clicking through the install screens and accepting the defaults (Next, Next, Next...), it is crucial to first understand the meaning of each install option and its ramifications for your environment.

What's New in Installing SQL Server 2014

Except for some minor differences in some of the options available on the various screens, the installation process for SQL Server 2014 is relatively unchanged from SQL Server 2012 except for some minor re-ordering of the screens and some streamlining of the install process, skipping over pages where no input or attention is required.

Installation Requirements

Before you install SQL Server 2014 on your server, it's a good idea (even if you own the latest-and-greatest system) to review the hardware and software requirements. The next two sections gather all the fine print into a few conveniently organized tables.

> **NOTE**
>
> The SQL Server 2014 installer helps determine whether your system meets the minimum requirements by running the System Configuration Checker (SCC) early in the install process. SCC conveniently provides a savable (via a button click) report on its results (and displays them onscreen). SCC is covered in detail later in this chapter.

Hardware Requirements

To install SQL Server 2014, you must ensure your system possesses a few basic components:

▶ A minimum of 6GB of available hard disk space. (See Table 8.2 for detailed disk space requirements for specific SQL Server 2014 components.)

▶ A display device with resolution of at least 800x600.

▶ A DVD-ROM or CD-ROM drive (for installation from disc).

Table 8.1 lists server environment hardware requirements, by SQL Server edition, with reference to processor type and/or word length. This table lists the base minimum hardware requirements. In most installations, you want to have at least 4GB of memory and a 2GHz or faster processor. In addition, installation using a redundant array of disks (RAID) or Storage Area Network (SAN) on production systems is highly recommended.

Of course, faster editions of processors, increased RAM, and more disk space don't negatively impact any installation either. One final (and perhaps obvious) note: The more SQL Server components you install, the more disk space you need. Analysis Services, for example, requires an additional 345MB of disk space for the install.

The hard disk space requirements for SQL Server are dependent on which SQL Server components are installed. Table 8.2 breaks down the disk space requirements by feature.

TABLE 8.1   SQL Server 2014 Minimum Hardware Requirements, by Edition

SQL Server Editions	Memory (RAM)	Processors (CPU)
Enterprise, Business Intelligence, Standard, Web, and Developer	1GB	1GHz x86 1.4GHz x64
Express	512MB	1.0 GHz x86 1.4 GHz x64

TABLE 8.2   SQL Server 2014 Disk Space Requirements, by Feature

SQL Server Feature	Disk Space Requirement
Database Engine and data files, Replication, Full-Text Search, and Data Quality Services	811MB
Analysis Services and data files	345MB
Reporting Services and Report Manager	304MB
Integration Services	591MB
Master Data Services	243MB
Client Components	1823MB
SQL Server Books Online Components	375KB (an additional 200MB is required for downloaded BOL content)

Software Requirements

The following software prerequisites must be installed on any server running any SQL Server edition:

▶ Windows Installer 4.5 or later (sometimes distributed by Microsoft Windows Update services; also will be installed by the SQL Server Installation Center).

▶ Windows PowerShell 2.0. (This is not installed by SQL Server Installation Center. If the Installer reports it is not present, you will need to download and install it from the Windows Management Framework web page, http://support.microsoft.com/kb/968929.)

▶ .NET 3.5 SP1 and .Net 4.0, SQL Server Native Client and SQL Server Setup support files.

If not installed or enabled already, the .Net 4.0 Framework will be installed by the SQL Server 2014 Installation Center. However, .NET 3.5 is not installed automatically by SQL Server Setup. To avoid interruption during SQL Server Setup, you should download and install .NET 3.5 SP1 before starting the install. Table 8.3 lists the different operating systems and what you will need to do to install/enable .Net 3.5 before you can proceed with the SQL Server installation.

> **NOTE**
>
> The .NET Framework 4 is not included in the SQL Server Express installation media. If you are installing the SQL Server Express editions, you will need an Internet connection available so that SQL Server Setup can download and install .Net 4.0 if needed. If no Internet connection is available, you will need to manually download and install .Net 4.0 before running the SQL Server Setup.

TABLE 8.3   SQL Server 2014 .Net 3.5 Installation by OS

Operating System	.Net 3.5 Installation Procedure
Windows Server 2008 SP2	.Net 3.5 SP1 should be downloaded and installed before you run the Installer.
Windows Server 2008 R2 SP1 Windows 8.1 Windows 8 Windows 7	Enable .NET Framework 3.5 SP1 through the Windows Program and Features Control Panel before installing SQL Server 2014.
Windows Server 2012 Windows Server 2012 R2	Enable .NET Framework 3.5 by using the Add Roles and Features Wizards

NOTE

If you do not have Internet access from the system you are installing to, you will need to download and install .NET Framework 3.5 SP1 manually before you run the Installation Center.

Table 8.4 lists the software and operating system requirements for SQL Server 2014, by edition.

TABLE 8.4   SQL Server 2014 Software Requirements, by Edition

SQL Server Editions	Supported Operating Systems
Enterprise and Business Intelligence	Windows Server 2008 R2 SP1 Web, Standard, Enterprise, and Datacenter Editions
	Windows Server 2012 Foundation, Essentials, Standard, and Datacenter Editions
	Windows Server 2012 R2 Foundation, Essentials, Standard, and Datacenter Editions
Standard	Windows 7 SP1 Ultimate, Enterprise, and Professional Editions
	Windows 8 and Windows 8 Professional and Enterprise Editions
	Windows 8.1 and Windows 8.1 Professional and Enterprise Editions
	Windows Server 2008 R2 SP1 Foundation, Web, Standard, Enterprise, and Datacenter Editions
	Windows Server 2008 SP2 Foundation, Web, Standard, Enterprise, and Datacenter Editions
	Windows Server 2012 Foundation, Essentials, Standard, and Datacenter Editions
	Windows Server 2012 R2 Foundation, Essentials, Standard, and Datacenter Editions
Developer	Windows 7 SP1 Ultimate, Enterprise, Professional, and Home Editions
	Windows 8 and Windows 8 Professional and Enterprise Editions
	Windows 8.1 and Windows 8.1 Professional and Enterprise Editions
	Windows Server 2008 R2 SP1 Foundation, Web, Standard, Enterprise, and Datacenter Editions
	Windows Server 2008 SP2 Foundation, Web, Standard, Enterprise, and Datacenter Editions
	Windows Server 2012 Foundation, Essentials, Standard, and Datacenter Editions
	Windows Server 2012 R2 Foundation, Essentials, Standard, and Datacenter Editions

SQL Server Editions	Supported Operating Systems
Web	Windows Server 2008 SP2 Web, Standard, Enterprise, and Datacenter Editions
	Windows Server 2008 R2 SP1 Web, Standard, Enterprise, and Datacenter Editions
	Windows Server 2012 Foundation, Essentials, Standard, and Datacenter Editions
	Windows Server 2012 R2 Foundation, Essentials, Standard, and Datacenter Editions
Express	Windows 7 SP1 Ultimate, Enterprise, Professional, and Home Basic/Premium Editions
	Windows 8 and Windows 8 Professional and Enterprise Editions
	Windows 8.1 and Windows 8.1 Professional and Enterprise Editions
	Windows Server 2008 SP2 Web, Standard, Enterprise, and Datacenter Editions
	Windows Server 2008 R2 SP1 Web, Standard, Enterprise, and Datacenter Editions
	Windows Server 2012 Foundation, Essentials, Standard, and Datacenter Editions
	Windows Server 2012 R2 Foundation, Essentials, Standard, and Datacenter Editions

Network Protocol Support

The following network protocols are supported for all editions (where applicable):

- ▶ Shared memory (but not for failover clusters)
- ▶ Named pipes
- ▶ TCP/IP (required for SQL Server endpoint communications)

Running Multiple Simultaneous Editions

You can install multiple editions of SQL Server 2014 on the same machine and run them simultaneously. This capability comes in handy when you need to test code or other feature functionality on one edition versus another, such as when your development and deployment environments differ.

> **NOTE**
>
> You can quickly ascertain the SQL Server edition you're running by executing this T-SQL query:
>
> ```
> select serverproperty('edition')
> ```

8

Installation Walkthrough

The following sections walk you through a typical installation scenario step-by-step. We bring up important points of information along the way, providing a real-world perspective on the process. No past experience with SQL Server is required to understand these sections.

> **NOTE**
>
> The installation walkthrough presented in this chapter is for a new installation of SQL Server 2014 on a system that hasn't had SQL Server installed on it previously. The ordering of the installation screens may be different if you are installing an instance of SQL Server on a system that already has SQL Server installed. However, while the ordering of the screens may be different, the content and actions to be performed would be the same as those presented here.

> **NOTE**
>
> SQL Server 2014 is actually version 12 of the product, just as SQL Server 2012 is version 11. SQL Server 2008 R2 was version 10.50, SQL Server 2008 was version 10, SQL Server 2005 was version 9, and SQL Server 2000 was version 8, which succeeded SQL Server 7. Although versioning by year seems straightforward, it may obfuscate the reasoning behind the naming convention used for many installed items, such as shared folder names (for example, Microsoft SQL Server\120), SQL Server instance folder names (for example, \MSSQL12.MSSQLSERVER), and so on.

Install Screens, Step-by-Step

The first step in installing SQL Server 2014 is, of course, to launch the SQL Server Installation Center. You do this by inserting the install DVD in the drive (or mounting the downloaded ISO file) and double-clicking setup.exe in the root folder (if AutoPlay is enabled, setup runs automatically). If you're installing from a decompressed .iso file or network share, locate the root folder and double-click the setup.exe file in the root folder.

> **NOTE**
>
> If any prerequisites for the Installer need to be installed, you will likely need to restart the computer for the updates to take effect. After restarting, rerun `setup.exe` to continue the installation.

After any missing prerequisites are installed, the Installation Wizard runs the SQL Server Installation Center, as shown in Figure 8.1.

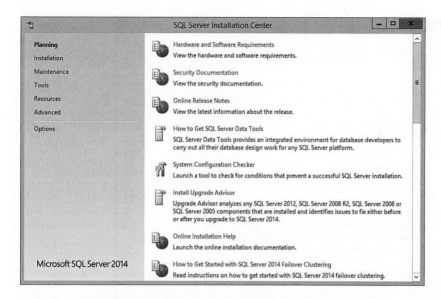

FIGURE 8.1   SQL Server 2014 Installation Center window.

> **NOTE**
>
> The same installation program is used whether you want to perform a full SQL Server installation, add features to an existing installation, or to install just the client tools. You have the option to choose which components to install on the Feature Selection screen, which is displayed after you install the Setup Support Files.

The first thing you'll notice is that there is a great deal of content immediately available from the SQL Server Installation Center Planning window, including documentation on hardware and software requirements, release notes, security and upgrade documentation, and the System Configuration Checker. You typically first want to run the System Configuration Checker to confirm that your system meets the minimum hardware and software requirements for installing SQL Server 2014. Click on the link for the System Configuration Checker to bring up the screen shown in Figure 8.2. This is essentially the Global Rules screen that also runs during the actual installation. It's better to find out now if there will be any issues with the installation before you get into the actual installation and have to cancel it and start over.

When the SCC scan is complete, overall status of the check is detailed at the top of the main window. You can click the Show Details button to view a detailed report of the checks performed. This report notes any issues found. If any checks fail, or a warning is raised, click the hyperlink in the Status column for more detailed report with specifics and suggestions for resolution. Click the View Detailed Report link to see the SCC results in an HTML report format, which is also saved to a file (see Figure 8.3).

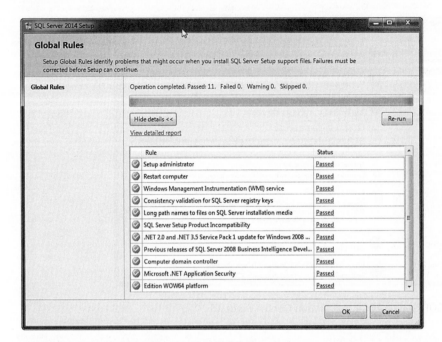

FIGURE 8.2   System Configuration Checker window.

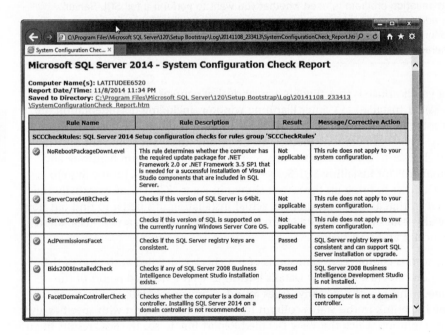

FIGURE 8.3   System Configuration Checker HTML report.

After you verify that the system configuration is sufficient to support the SQL Server 2014 installation, click OK to go back to the SQL Server Installation Center. Then click on the Installation option in the menu on the left of the SQL Server Installation Center. This brings up the installation options. To install a new instance of SQL Server, select the New Installation or Add Features to an Existing Installation option, as shown in Figure 8.4.

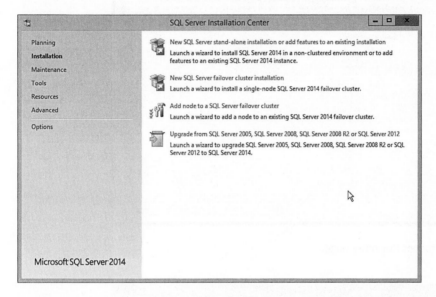

FIGURE 8.4   The New Installation or Add Features to an Existing Installation option in SQL Server Installation Center.

If this is the first time installing SQL Server on the system, the first screen you'll see is the Product Key page (see Figure 8.5). The Product Key page is where you'll need to enter any necessary product keys if you are installing a version of SQL Server 2014 that is not free.

After entering the product key (if needed), click Next to review the License Terms for SQL Server 2014 (see Figure 8.6). Note that you need to accept the license agreement; otherwise, you can't proceed.

NOTE

There is also a check box on the License Terms page to indicate whether you are willing to send information about your hardware and software environment and your usage of SQL Server 2014 and its components to Microsoft. If you enable this feature, SQL Server will automatically report errors and send data about how you use SQL Server software and services to Microsoft who uses this information to improve SQL Server. Any information sent is confidential. However, it does require access to the Internet, so if you are installing SQL Server on a system behind a firewall, you will not want to enable this option.

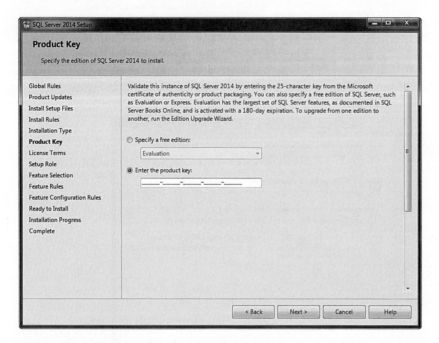

FIGURE 8.5   Product Key entry page.

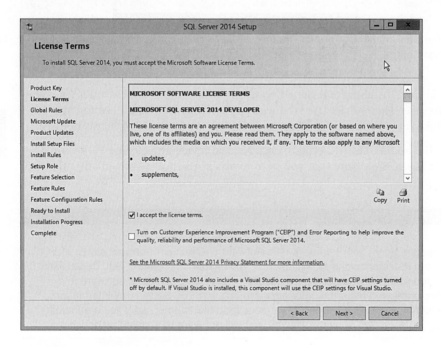

FIGURE 8.6   License Terms page.

After accepting the license terms, the installer will next need to install the setup support files. The first step of this installation is to run the Global Rules to identify any potential issues that might occur when the installer installs the SQL Server Setup support files. If any issues are found, the Installer will show the Global Rules pages which lists any items that may need to be corrected before Setup can continue. These checks may be different depending on the operating system you are installing to, but typically include the following:

▶ Whether the logged-in user is a system administrator (a must) with appropriate privileges

▶ Whether there are any reboots pending from other installers

▶ Whether the required .NET components are available

▶ Whether there is support for long pathnames where the installation media resides

▶ The consistency of any SQL Server Registry keys

Once the Global Rules have been evaluated, the Global Rules page will be displayed indicating if there are any issues or not. If any rule reports an error or warning, you can click the View Detailed Report link to see a more detailed report file (this screen is just like the one shown in Figure 8.2). You can also click the hyperlink in the Status column of the failed rule to view specifics on the failed rule. Correcting any of the items shown on this page will usually require exiting the installer and restarting the installation after fixing the issue, which is why it's recommended that you run the System Configuration Checker before starting the Install.

Once the Global Rules are successfully validated, click next to proceed to the Microsoft Update as shown in Figure 8.7. The Microsoft Update page allows you to have the installer run Microsoft Update to see if there are any recommended updates for Windows or SQL Server 2014 to be installed before continuing with the installation. If there are any updates available for SQL Server 2014 (for example, a new service pack), the Installer will display the Product Updates page and give you the opportunity to download the update and have it incorporated into the installation process (this is also referred to as a SlipStream installation).

If you do not want to include the updates, you can uncheck the Include SQL Server Product Updates check box on the Product Update page and click Next to continue the Setup Support Files installation. If you choose to install any updates, they will be downloaded first before proceeding.

If there are no recommended updates found, the Installer will skip the Product Updates page and skip ahead to the Install Setup Files page.

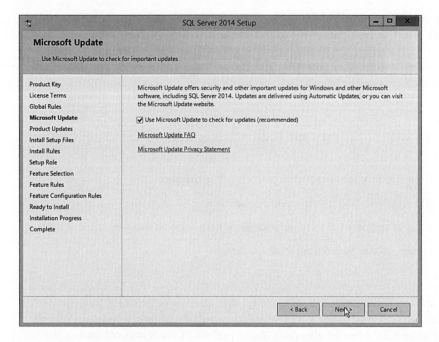

FIGURE 8.7   Microsoft Update page.

NOTE

At the time of this writing, there currently are no available updates for SQL Server 2014 so the Product Update page is skipped and not displayed.

The Install Setup Files page is only displayed briefly while the files are being installed, and if there are no errors, it will automatically go on to the Install Rules page (see Figure 8.8).

The Install Rules page runs additional checks to verify that the system will support the installation of SQL Server and its features and identifies any potential problems that might prevent a successful installation. Again, if any of the tests fail or a warning is generated, you typically need to address this situation before continuing to ensure a successful SQL Server installation. For example, Figure 8.8 shows a warning regarding Windows Firewall. Clicking the Warning hyperlink in the Status column brings up a dialog with more information about the warning. In this case, the warning indicates that if Windows Firewall is enabled, the network ports for SQL Server need to be opened to allow remote clients to access SQL Server on this machine.

If no tests have failed and all warnings have been reviewed or resolved, click Next to bring up the Setup Role page, as shown in Figure 8.9.

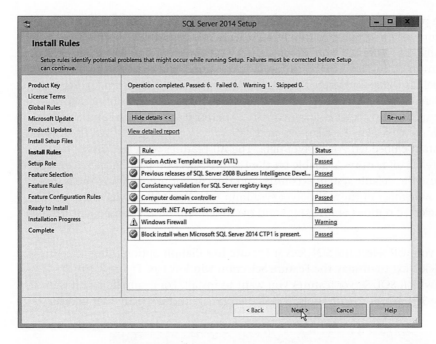

FIGURE 8.8   The Install Rules page.

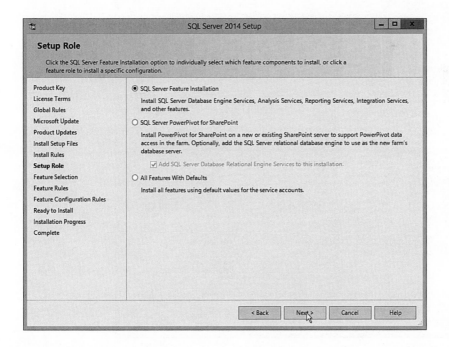

FIGURE 8.9   Setup Role page.

The Setup Role page lets you specify whether to use the Feature Selection page to select individual features to be installed or to select a feature role to install a specific configuration. For example, in Figure 8.9, you are presented with three options. The SQL Server Feature Installation option lets you select individual features and shared components to be installed, such as Database Engine Services, Analysis Services (native mode), Reporting Services, and Service Broker. The SQL Server PowerPivot for SharePoint option allows you to install Analysis Services server components in a Microsoft Office SharePoint Server farm. This option enables large-scale query and data processing for published Excel workbooks that contain embedded PowerPivot data. The All Features with Defaults option will automatically select all features available on the Feature Selection page. All services will be configured to use the default system accounts, and the current user running the install is provisioned as a member of the SQL Server sysadmin role. You will still have the option to review the selected options and settings and override them on the subsequent Installer pages.

In most cases, you will select the SQL Server Feature Installation option. After selecting this option, click Next to display the Feature Selection window (see Figure 8.10). Here, you can select which SQL Server features you want to install. For example, if you want to install only the SQL Server Client Tools, this is the place you can specify that choice.

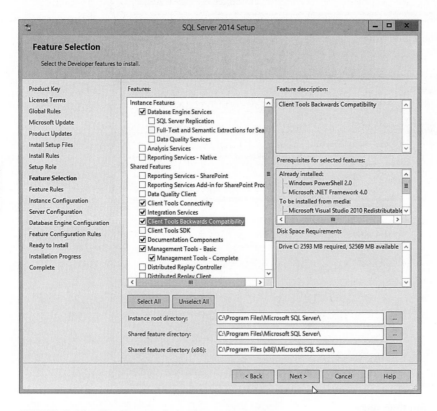

FIGURE 8.10   The Feature Selection page.

Following are the most commonly available features (detailed in subsequent chapters of this book):

▶ **Database Engine Services**—Includes the core Database Engine services, optional SQL Server Replication (see Chapter 43, "Data Replication"), Full-Text Search services, and Data Quality services (see Chapter 49, "Data Quality Services")

▶ **Analysis Services**—Includes the engine used to create business intelligence solutions that rely on OLAP and data mining (see Chapter 46, "SQL Server 2014 Analysis Services")

▶ **Reporting Services**—Includes the engine and tools used to generate and deploy data-centric reports (see Chapter 48, "SQL Server 2014 Reporting Services")

▶ **Shared Features**—Includes optional features shared among multiple SQL Server instances on the same system, such as Client Tools Connectivity components, Integration Services (Chapter 47), SQL Server Documentation Components, SQL Server Management Tools (Chapter 3), the Data Quality Client, the Distributed Replay Controller and Client (Chapter 6), and Master Data Services (Chapter 50).

If you are uncertain about the need for a specific feature, when you click on it in this window, a description of the feature and what will be installed is displayed in the Description pane on the right.

The Feature Selection page is also the place where you can change the installation location for the shared features (if this is the first time any of the shared features are being installed on the system). The default location is C:\Program Files\Microsoft SQL Server. In most production installations, you'll most likely want the shared features to remain in the Program Files folder.

While making your selections, you can review the Prerequisites for selected features window to identify if any feature prerequisites are already installed or will be installed from the installation media during the install process. After you finish making your selections, click Next to move on to the Feature Rules page (see Figure 8.11).

The Feature Rules page runs a check to determine whether there are any issues that will block the installation of the selected features. From this page, you can address any issues and rerun the rules until they all pass or only warning messages are displayed. Like the Global Rules page, this page enables you to get detailed information on the rule checks performed by clicking on the Show Details button. You can get more information on a specific rule by clicking the hyperlink in the Status column. A detailed HTML report can be generated as well by clicking on the View Detailed Report hyperlink.

If no errors are encountered on the Feature Rules page, the Installer will automatically advance to the Instance Configuration page (see Figure 8.12).

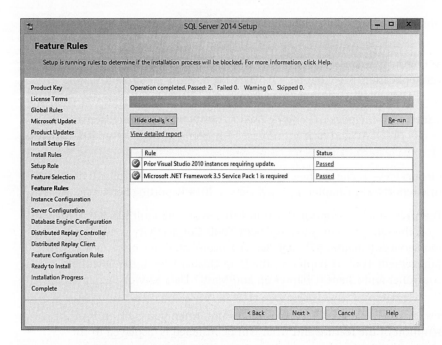

FIGURE 8.11   The Feature Rules page.

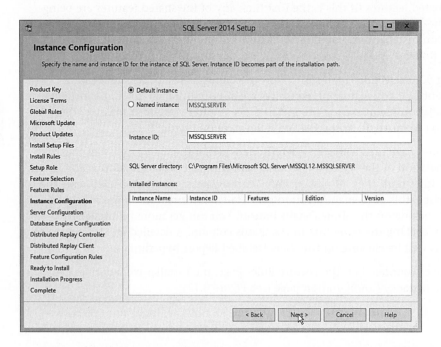

FIGURE 8.12   The Instance Configuration page.

On the Instance Configuration page, you can choose to install SQL Server as the default instance (if a default instance has not already been installed) or as a named instance. SQL Server supports multiple instances of SQL Server on a single server or workstation, but only one instance can be the default instance. The default instance can be an installation of any version of SQL Server from SQL Server 2000 through SQL Server 2014. All other instances must be named instances. The named instances can be different versions/editions of SQL Server. You can run multiple instances of SQL Server concurrently on the same machine with each instance running independently of other instances. You can also install SQL Server as a named instance without installing a default instance first. If any instances are already installed, they are listed in the Installed Instances list.

After you finish configuring the instance, click Next to bring up the Server Configuration page (see Figure 8.13).

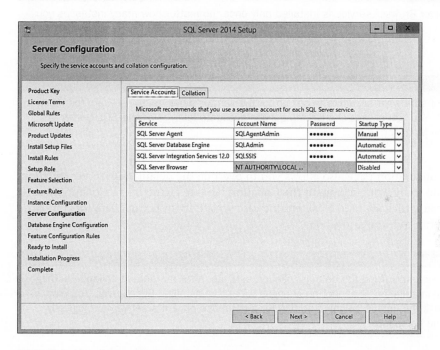

FIGURE 8.13   Server Configuration page.

On the Server Configuration page, you can specify the user accounts and passwords to use for the selected SQL Server services you chose to install. You can choose to use the same account for all SQL Server services; however, for improved security, it is recommended that you use multiple accounts, one for each service. This helps reinforce the least-privileged user account approach, which states that a user should have only the privileges required to get the job done—and no more. Having multiple accounts also makes it clearer for network administrators to determine which SQL Server services (as opposed to the multitude of other running services) are requesting access to a resource. If you don't specify a user account, the services by default are set up to run under separate local system accounts, which are accounts with local admin privileges that do not have access to any network resources. The Installer provides warnings if you specify a user account with insufficient privileges or credentials.

Also on the Service Accounts tab, you can select the server startup options for the SQL Server services being installed by selecting the startup type in the drop-down selection list to the right of the service. It is highly recommended to set the SQL Server Startup Type to Automatic so it's available when the system is started. (If necessary, you can change the startup options for the SQL Server services later, using the SQL Server Configuration Manager.)

NOTE

The SQL Server Browser service is installed only once, no matter how many instances you install.

NOTE

If you are not sure what accounts to set up for the various services, don't worry too much at this point. You can always change the service accounts later using the SQL Server Configuration Manager.

The Server Configuration page also allows you to override the default SQL Server collation settings. You do so by first clicking on the Collation tab (see Figure 8.14). Collations are important because they are used to determine case sensitivity of textual data for comparisons, sort order in indexes, and so on.

NOTE

Be careful when specifying the default collation settings. After the default collation setting is set during installation, it cannot be changed without reinstalling SQL Server. You also cannot change the default collation setting for a database once it's set without logically recreating the database.

If you're running Windows in the United States, the collation selection defaults to SQL_Latin1_General_CP1_CI_AS for the Database Engine. The default settings should be changed only if the collation setting for this installation of SQL Server needs to match the collation settings used by another instance of SQL Server, or if it needs to match the Windows system locale of another computer. If you need to change the collation settings, click on the Customize button. This brings up the Database Engine Collation Customization dialog, where you can select from standardized SQL Collations or customize your own by specifying a Windows collation setting and the desired sort options.

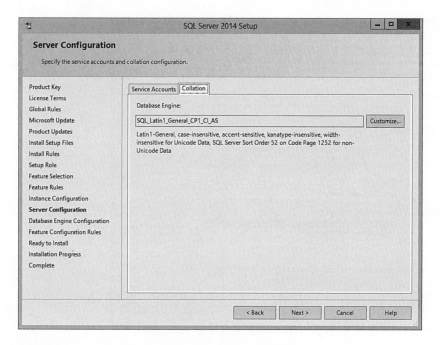

FIGURE 8.14   Server Configuration Collation setting.

After making your selections on the Server Configuration page, click Next to move onto the Database Engine Configuration page. On this page, you can specify the authentication mode to use for SQL Server. This is done on the Server Configuration tab (see Figure 8.15). The default setting is for Windows Authentication only. However, Mixed Mode authentication is required if you plan to have any clients authenticating to SQL Server 2014 but will not be authenticating to a Windows domain. If you do select Mixed Mode authentication, you also have to enter a password to use for the built-in SQL Server administration account (sa). A strong sa password is recommended. The Server Configuration page also provides the opportunity to specify local or domain accounts to be mapped to the sysadmin role in SQL Server. (You must provide at least one. You can click the Add Current User button to add the user account you are using to install SQL Server.) SQL Server administration accounts have unrestricted access to SQL Server for performing SQL Server administration and maintenance tasks. For more information on user accounts, passwords, and server roles, see Chapter 15, "Security and User Administration."

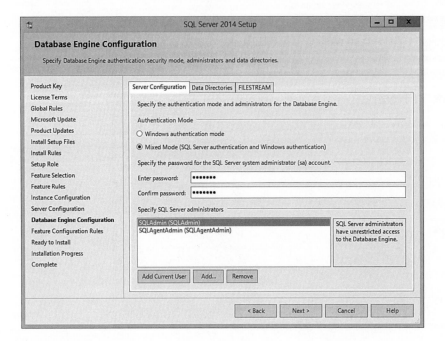

FIGURE 8.15   The Server Configuration tab.

On the Data Directories tab (see Figure 8.16), you can configure the data root directory and default directories where the user and tempdb data and log files will be created, as well as the default location for the Backup directory. Note that the System Database Directory cannot be changed here; you need to return to the Feature Selection page and modify the Instance Root directory. In a production installation, for performance reasons, you should set up multiple drives or drive arrays to store the data and log files. Typically, you do not want the system data files stored on the C: drive, especially buried in the Program Files folder. You likely want to locate the data files on a high-performance drive setup specifically for database files and away from the system swap file and other applications. For recoverability purposes, you also should keep your backup files on a separate drive from your data files. (For more information on database devices and performance, see Chapter 38, "Database Design and Performance.") As a general rule, you also should place the log files on separate disks from the data files, and placing tempdb on its own disk further helps improve performance

NOTE

If you are planning on installing multiple SQL Server instances on the same server, consider using separate subdirectories for each instance's data and log files. This way, you avoid potential conflicts between data and log filenames for databases with the same names created in more than one SQL Server instance. As you notice, by default, the SQL Server Installer creates subdirectories under the specified root directory name using the

SQL Server version number and instance name (for example, MSSQL12.MSSQLSERVER) and then an additional subdirectory for the services type (MSSQL for SQL Server, MSAS for Analysis Services, and MSRS for Reporting Services).

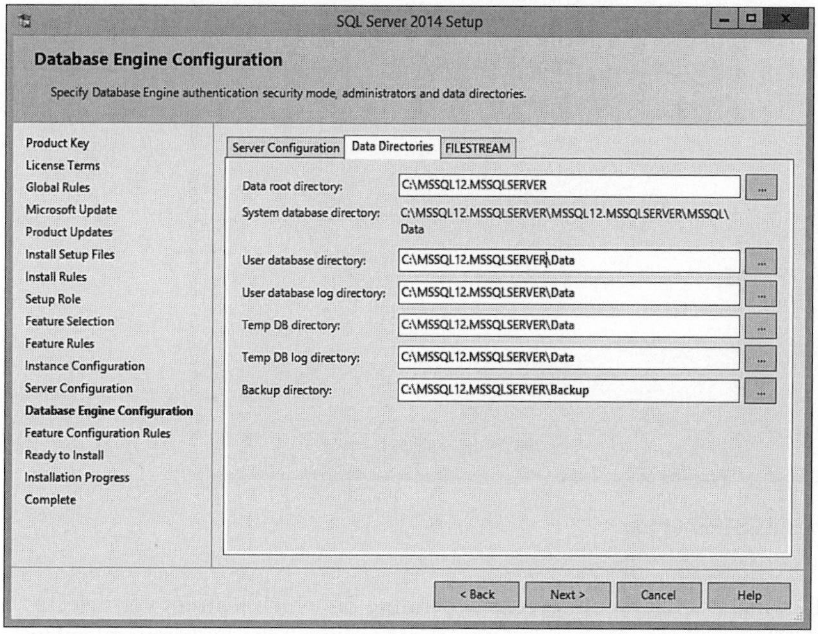

FIGURE 8.16   The Data Directories tab.

The final tab on the Database Engine Configuration tab is FILESTREAM (see Figure 8.17). The FILESTREAM data type is a column property available in SQL Server 2014. FILESTREAM storage is implemented as a varbinary(max) column, but the actual data is stored as BLOBs in the file system. Because of security considerations, FILESTREAM, by default, is disabled. If you want to use the FILESTREAM option, click the Enable FILESTREAM for Transact-SQL Access check box to enable FILESTREAM capabilities. This control must be checked before the other control options will be available. The Enable FILESTREAM for File I/O Streaming Access check box enables Win32 streaming access for FILESTREAM. If this option is selected, you can specify the name of the Windows share in which the FILESTREAM data will be stored. The Allow Remote Clients to Have Streaming Access to FILESTREAM Data check box determines whether to allow remote clients to access this FILESTREAM data on this server. For more information on defining and using FILESTREAM data in SQL Server 2014, see Chapter 21, "Creating and Managing Tables." If you are unsure whether you need or want to use FILESTREAM data, you can leave this option disabled during the install. You can enable FILESTREAM data at any time via the SQL Server Configuration Manager.

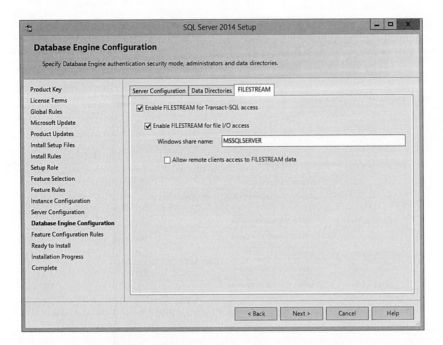

FIGURE 8.17   The FILESTREAM tab.

There may be additional configuration screens depending on which features you selected in the Feature Selection page. For example, if you chose to install the Distributed Replay Controller or Client, Analysis Services or Reporting Services, there will be configuration pages to specify the installation options for these features. For more information on configuring Analysis Services and Reporting Services, see Chapters 46 and 48,. As with the FILESTREAM option, you do not have to install Analysis Services or Reporting Services during the initial install. You can always run the SQL Server Installation Center later to add these features to an existing SQL Server instance.

After you finish making your selections, click Next to continue to the Feature Configuration Rules page, as shown in Figure 8.18.

The Feature Configuration Rules page runs a final set of checks to determine if there are any issues that will prevent a successful installation of SQL Server 2014. If no errors are reported, the Installer will automatically skip to the Ready to Install page (see Figure 8.19). This page displays a summary of the installation options chosen as well as the file locations specified. Review this information to ensure the features and file locations are what you intended. This page also displays the location of the Configuration file path where you can find the ConfigurationFile.ini file generated by the installer. This .ini file can be used for unattended installations, which are discussed later in this chapter. The ConfigurationFile.ini file is located in the same place where you can find the installation log files, which you can review if any problems occur during the installation.

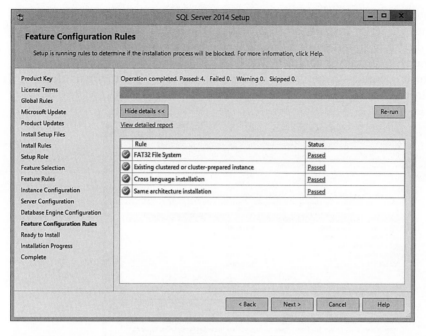

FIGURE 8.18   The Feature Configuration Rules page.

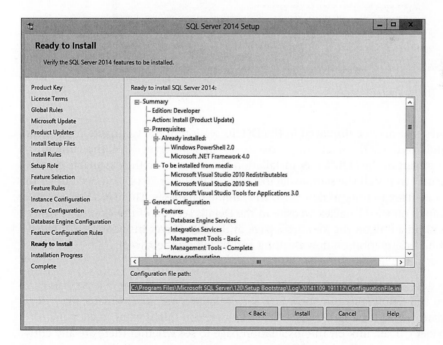

FIGURE 8.19   The Ready to Install page.

If everything looks satisfactory on the Ready to Install page, click the Install button to proceed with the SQL Server installation. This displays the Installation Progress screen, which shows a progress bar and messages to allow you to track the progress of the installation. When the setup process is complete, the Installer displays the Complete page (see Figure 8.20), which contains a hyperlink to the Installer log file and additional information about the installation.

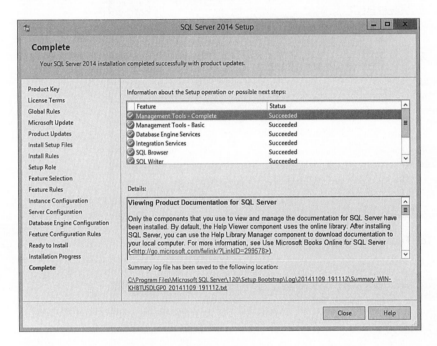

FIGURE 8.20   The Complete page.

One of the notes that may be displayed in the Details section of the Complete page refers to the installation of the SQL Server sample databases. In SQL Server 2014, the sample databases are not part of the SQL Server Installation Center, nor are they available on the installation media. To install the sample databases for SQL Server 2014, you need to go to the Microsoft CodePlex website to download the sample databases. There is a link to the SQL Server samples on the CodePlex website in the Details section of the Complete page, or you can also find a link on the Resources page of the SQL Server Installation Center. You can also find information on downloading and installing the AdventureWorks2012 sample database in the Introduction of this book.

The Details section also provides a link to the latest Release Notes for the release of SQL Server installed and a note regarding how SQL Server updates are now available via Microsoft Update. Before leaving the Installation Center, you might want to click the Search for Product Update link on the Installation page to see whether there are any critical hotfixes or service packs already available for your SQL Server installation.

Installing SQL Server Documentation

If you chose to install the Documentation Components when installing SQL Server 2014, be aware that this only installs the Help Viewer components that let you view and manage the SQL Server documentation, but not the actual documentation files. By default, the Help Viewer component uses the online SQL Server library. One of the benefits of using the online library is that you are always accessing the most recent version of the SQL Server documentation. However, if you prefer having the documentation installed locally, after installing the Documentation Components you can run the Help Library Manager to download the documentation to the computer locally.

To launch the Help Library Manager, select the Microsoft SQL Server 2014 folder in the Windows Start menu, select the Documentation and Community folder, and click on Manage Help Settings. This will launch the Help Library Manager, as shown in Figure 8.21. (If you are running Windows Server 2012 or Windows 8 or 8.1, launch the Windows Search and type in "manage help settings" to locate and launch the Help Library Manager.)

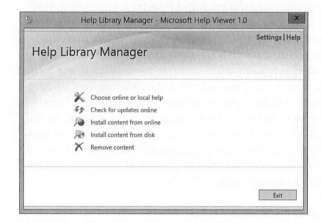

FIGURE 8.21   The Help Library Manager.

Within the Help Library Manager you can change the option to view help locally or online. If you do have the help content installed locally, you can run the Help Library Manager to check for and download updates to the local help files. If you select to use local help, the next step is to install the content. If you have access to the Internet, you can select the option to Install Content from Online. If you select this option, the Help Library Manager presents a list of content to download and install, as shown in Figure 8.22. For example, to install SQL Server content, scroll down until you see the SQL Server 2014 content and click on Add to add the content. After you've selected the content you want downloaded, click the Update button to begin the download and installation.

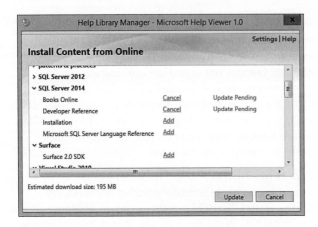

FIGURE 8.22   Install Content from Online screen.

If the system you want to install the documentation on is not directly connected to the Internet, you can install the content from disk. From a machine that does have Internet access, go to the Microsoft Download Center and locate the "Product Documentation for Microsoft SQL Server 2014 for firewall and proxy restricted environments" page (currently, the URL for this page is http://www.microsoft.com/en-us/download/details. aspx?id=42557). Click the Download button to download the self-extracting archive to media that you can then take and copy onto the system without Internet access. Extract the contents of the download to a folder or network share visible from the system. In the Help Library Manager, click the Install Content from Disk option, and browse to the location of SQL Server help content setup file (HelpContentSetup.msha). Click Next to view the Install Content from Disk screen to select the SQL Server documentation components that you want to Add and click Update to install them.

Other Options Available in the SQL Server Installation Center

Before leaving the SQL Server Installation Center, let's explore a few other utilities available from the main menu. The Maintenance menu provides tools to perform an edition upgrade (for example, from Standard Edition to Enterprise Edition), repair a corrupt installation, remove a node from a SQL Server 2014 cluster, or launch Windows Update. The Tools menu provides links to the System Configuration Checker, the Installed features discovery report that generates information regarding all SQL Server products and features installed on the local machine, the Microsoft Assessment and Planning Toolkit which can be used to map out a complete network inventory of SQL Server, Sybase, Oracle and MySQL instances to assist in migration to SQL Server 2014, or a link to assist you in installing SQL Server Data Tools for Business Intelligence (SQL Server Data Tools is no longer included with the SQL Server installation media).

The Resources menu provides a number of useful links, including a link to the SQL Server 2014 Books Online, SQL Server Tech and Developer Centers, a link to view the SQL Server 2014 license terms, and a link to the Codeplex samples where you can download the Adventureworks sample databases.

Finally, on the Advanced menu, there are options to prepare and complete a SQL Server failover cluster, to perform an install of a SQL Server 2014 instance using an existing configuration file, or to prepare or complete an installation of SQL Server 2014 from a prepared image (referred to as a SysPrep installation). Installing using an existing configuration file allows you to repeat an installation without having to go through all the individual steps and enter/select all the options you normally have to go through with the installation wizard. SQL Server SysPrep allows you to prepare an image for a stand-alone instance of SQL Server and to complete the configuration at a later time on that system or on multiple other computers.

Installing SQL Server Using a Configuration File

If you need to install SQL Server 2014 to multiple machines, you'll likely want to do so without having to manually select the same options over and over. Running the installer using a configuration file provides this much-needed timesaving feature. With the SQL Server 2014 installer, you have the option of running the installer with a configuration file in a couple of ways: using the Installer Wizard with options prefilled by the configuration file or using a fully automated and unattended installation from the command line. If you use the GUI with the options prefilled by the configuration file, you have the opportunity to review and change options along the way as necessary.

The ConfigurationFile.ini file is a text file composed of parameters in name/value pairs along with descriptive comments. Many of the parameter names correspond to the screens and screen options you would see when using the Installer Wizard. Here are some examples of the more common configuration settings:

▶ **INSTANCENAME**—Specifies a named instance name for the value or specifies the special value MSSQLSERVER to install the default instance.

▶ **FEATURES**—Specifies which features to install, uninstall, or upgrade. The list of top-level features include SQL, AS, RS, IS, and Tools. The SQL feature installs the Database Engine, Replication, and Full-Text. The Tools feature installs Management Tools, Books Online, and other shared components.

▶ **UPDATEENABLED**—Specifies whether the installer should check for and include product updates during the install.

▶ **INSTANCEDIR**—Specifies the installation directory for instance-specific components.

▶ **INSTALLSQLDATADIR**—Specifies the Database Engine root data directory.

▶ **SQLBACKUPDIR**—Specifies the default directory for the Database Engine backup files.

▶ **SQLUSERDBDIR**—Specifies the default directory for the Database Engine user databases.

▶ **SQLUSERDBLOGDIR**—Specifies the default directory for the Database Engine user database logs.

▶ **SQLTEMPDBDIR**—Specifies the directory for Database Engine tempdb files.

▶ **SQLCOLLATION or ASCOLLATION**—Specifies values to set the collation for SQL Server or Analysis Services.

▶ **SQLSVCACCOUNT**—Specifies the user account for the SQL Server service: domain\ user or system account.

▶ **TCPENABLED**—Specifies whether the TCP/IP protocol is enabled (1) or disabled (0).

▶ **NPENABLED**—Specifies whether the Named Pipes protocol is enabled (1) or disabled (0).

▶ **SECURITYMODE**—Specifies authentication mode for SQL Server. You can use the special value "SQL" here to override the default of Windows-only authentication.

The following example shows the contents of a configuration file for SQL Server 2014 generated by the installation walk through presented in this chapter:

```
;SQL Server 2014 Configuration File
[OPTIONS]

; Specifies a Setup work flow, like INSTALL, UNINSTALL, or UPGRADE. This is a
required parameter.
ACTION="Install"

; Use the /ENU parameter to install the English version of SQL Server on your
localized Windows operating system.
ENU="True"

; Parameter that controls the user interface behavior. Valid values are Normal for
the full UI,AutoAdvance for a simplied UI, and EnableUIOnServerCore for bypassing
Server Core setup GUI block.
UIMODE="Normal"

; Setup will not display any user interface.
QUIET="False"

; Setup will display progress only, without any user interaction.
QUIETSIMPLE="False"

; Specify whether SQL Server Setup should discover and include product updates. The
valid values are True and False or 1 and 0. By default SQL Server Setup will include
updates that are found.
UpdateEnabled="True"

; Specify if errors can be reported to Microsoft to improve future SQL Server
releases. Specify 1 or True to enable and 0 or False to disable this feature.
```

```
ERRORREPORTING="False"

; If this parameter is provided, then this computer will use Microsoft Update to
check for updates.
USEMICROSOFTUPDATE="True"

; Specifies features to install, uninstall, or upgrade. The list of top-level
features include SQL, AS, RS, IS, MDS, and Tools. The SQL feature will install the
Database Engine, Replication, Full-Text, and Data Quality Services (DQS) server. The
Tools feature will install Management Tools, Books online components, SQL Server
Data Tools, and other shared components.
FEATURES=SQLENGINE,IS,SSMS,ADV_SSMS

; Specify the location where SQL Server Setup will obtain product updates. The
valid values are "MU" to search Microsoft Update, a valid folder path, a relative
path such as .\MyUpdates or a UNC share. By default SQL Server Setup will search
Microsoft Update or a Windows Update service through the Window Server Update
Services.
UpdateSource="MU"

; Displays the command line parameters usage
HELP="False"

; Specifies that the detailed Setup log should be piped to the console.
INDICATEPROGRESS="False"

; Specifies that Setup should install into WOW64. This command line argument is not
supported on an IA64 or a 32-bit system.
X86="False"

; Specify the root installation directory for shared components.  This directory
remains unchanged after shared components are already installed.
INSTALLSHAREDDIR="C:\Program Files\Microsoft SQL Server"

; Specify the root installation directory for the WOW64 shared components.  This
directory remains unchanged after WOW64 shared components are already installed.
INSTALLSHAREDWOWDIR="C:\Program Files (x86)\Microsoft SQL Server"

; Specify a default or named instance. MSSQLSERVER is the default instance for
non-Express editions and SQLExpress for Express editions. This parameter is required
when installing the SQL Server Database Engine (SQL), Analysis Services (AS), or
Reporting Services (RS).
INSTANCENAME="MSSQLSERVER"

; Specify that SQL Server feature usage data can be collected and sent to Microsoft.
Specify 1 or True to enable and 0 or False to disable this feature.
```

```
SQMREPORTING="False"

; Specify the Instance ID for the SQL Server features you have specified. SQL Server
directory structure, registry structure, and service names will incorporate the
instance ID of the SQL Server instance.
INSTANCEID="MSSQLSERVER"

; Specify the installation directory.
INSTANCEDIR="C:\Program Files\Microsoft SQL Server"

; Agent account name
AGTSVCACCOUNT="SQLAgentAdmin"

; Auto-start service after installation.
AGTSVCSTARTUPTYPE="Manual"

; Startup type for Integration Services.
ISSVCSTARTUPTYPE="Automatic"

; Account for Integration Services: Domain\User or system account.
ISSVCACCOUNT="SQLSSIS"

; CM brick TCP communication port
COMMFABRICPORT="0"

; How matrix will use private networks
COMMFABRICNETWORKLEVEL="0"

; How inter brick communication will be protected
COMMFABRICENCRYPTION="0"

; TCP port used by the CM brick
MATRIXCMBRICKCOMMPORT="0"

; Startup type for the SQL Server service.
SQLSVCSTARTUPTYPE="Automatic"

; Level to enable FILESTREAM feature at (0, 1, 2 or 3).
FILESTREAMLEVEL="2"

; Name of Windows share to be created for FILESTREAM File I/O.
FILESTREAMSHARENAME="MSSQLSERVER"

; Set to "1" to enable RANU for SQL Server Express.
ENABLERANU="False"
```

```
; Specifies a Windows collation or an SQL collation to use for the Database Engine.
SQLCOLLATION="SQL_Latin1_General_CP1_CI_AS"

; Account for SQL Server service: Domain\User or system account.
SQLSVCACCOUNT="SQLAdmin"

; Windows account(s) to provision as SQL Server system administrators.
SQLSYSADMINACCOUNTS="SQLAdmin" "SQLAgentAdmin"

; The default is Windows Authentication. Use "SQL" for Mixed Mode Authentication.
SECURITYMODE="SQL"

; The Database Engine root data directory.
INSTALLSQLDATADIR="C:\MSSQL12.MSSQLSERVER"

; Default directory for the Database Engine backup files.
SQLBACKUPDIR="C:\MSSQL12.MSSQLSERVER\Backup"

; Default directory for the Database Engine user databases.
SQLUSERDBDIR="C:\MSSQL12.MSSQLSERVER\Data"

; Directory for Database Engine TempDB files.
SQLTEMPDBDIR="C:\MSSQL12.MSSQLSERVER\Data"

; Provision current user as a Database Engine system administrator for %SQL_PRODUCT_
SHORT_NAME% Express.
ADDCURRENTUSERASSQLADMIN="False"

; Specify 0 to disable or 1 to enable the TCP/IP protocol.
TCPENABLED="0"

; Specify 0 to disable or 1 to enable the Named Pipes protocol.
NPENABLED="0"

; Startup type for Browser Service.
BROWSERSVCSTARTUPTYPE="Disabled"
```

Depending on which options you chose during an install, other options or values may be listed in the configuration file, some of which are designed solely for clustered installs, Analysis Services, Reporting Services, Integration Services, or Tools.

To create a configuration file (sorry, no configuration file template is available on the installation media), run the installation program and follow the wizard all the way through to the Ready to Install page where the location of the Configuration.ini file generated is specified (see Figure 8.19). If you do not want to continue with an actual installation at this point, simply click the Cancel button to cancel the setup. At this point, you can copy the Configuration.ini file to another location so you can make edits to it.

> **NOTE**
>
> The Installer writes out all the appropriate parameters for the options and values specified, with the exception of sensitive information such as passwords. For an unattended install, these values can be provided at the command prompt when you run setup.exe. In addition, the /IAcceptSQLServerLicenseTerms parameter is also not written out to the configuration file and requires either you modify the configuration file or supply a value at the command prompt.

The setup.exe command-line program can be found at the root level of the installation media. To use a configuration file to install a standalone SQL Server instance, run the installation through the command-line setup.exe program and supply the ConfigurationFile.ini using the `ConfigurationFile` parameter, as in the following example:

```
Setup.exe /ConfigurationFile=CustomConfigurationFile.INI
```

If you want to override any of the values in the configuration file or provide values not specified in the configuration file, you can provide additional command-line parameters to setup.exe. For example, to avoid having to enter the service account passwords during the installation, you can enter them on the command line using the password parameters to config.exe:

```
Setup.exe /SQLSVCPASSWORD="mypassword"
/AGTSVCPASSWORD="mypassword"
 /ASSVCPASSWORD="mypassword" /ISSVCPASSWORD="mypassword"
 /RSSVCPASSWORD="mypassword" /ConfigurationFile=CustomConfigurationFile.INI
```

> **NOTE**
>
> The password parameters are required to run a fully unattended installation. Also, if the SECURITYMODE setting is set to SQL in the configuration file or via the command-line parameter, you need to provide the /SAPWD parameter to provide a password for the sa account.

Most of the other available setup.exe command-line parameters are the same as the parameter names used in the configuration file as listed previously. For a complete list of the available setup.exe parameters, you can run "setup.exe /?", or refer to SQL Server Books Online.

Running an Automated or Manual Install

When installing SQL Server from the command prompt, you can also specify what level of the installer interface you want to run, either silent, basic, or full interaction. SQL Server supports full quiet mode by using the /Q parameter or Quiet Simple mode by using the /QS parameter. The /Q switch is intended for running unattended installations. With this switch provided, Setup runs in quiet mode without any user interface. The /QS switch only shows progress via the GUI; it does not accept any input and displays no error messages if encountered.

Regardless of the installation method chosen, you are required to confirm acceptance of the software license terms as an individual or on behalf of an entity, unless your use of the software is governed by a separate agreement such as a Microsoft volume licensing agreement or a third-party agreement with an ISV or OEM. For full unattended installations (using the /Q or /QS parameters) with SQL Server 2014, you must include the /IACCEPTSQLSERVERLICENSETERMS parameter to avoid the display of the License Terms page. Following is a sample command line for running an unattended installation of SQL Server 2014:

```
D:\setup.exe /configurationfile=customconfigurationfile.ini /Q
/IACCEPTSQLSERVERLICENSETERMS  /SQLSVCPASSWORD="mypasswd"
 /AGTSVCPASSWORD="mypasswd"  /SAPWD="mypasswd"
```

SQL Server 2014 provides an option to the setup.exe that allows you to run a somewhat more attended mode of the installation that gives you a bit more control over the install than the /Q and /QS parameters, while streamlining the install somewhat. You can specify the /UIMODE parameter instead of the /Q or /QS switches. The /UIMODE parameter specifies whether to present the full set of Installer Wizard pages for review and confirmation while running the setup or to present a minimum number of pages during setup. /UIMODE=Normal, the default option, presents all setup dialog boxes for the selected features, allowing you to review the values or manually enter values not provided in the configuration file (such as service account passwords). You can specify the /UIMODE=AutoAdvance option to skip nonessential dialogs (primarily the rules and information pages that do not require any user supplied values) and auto-advances through a number of pages, including the Ready to Install page.

NOTE

If you want to control the interface mode with the /Q, /QS/, or /UIMODE command-line options, be sure to clear these options settings from the configurationfile.ini file, or the configuration file settings will override the command-line settings.

NOTE

To avoid the User Access Control dialog from popping up when running the installer from the command line in quiet or unattended mode, you need to run setup.exe from a command prompt invoked as administrator.

Installing SQL Server Using Sysprep

The Microsoft System Preparation (Sysprep) tool provides a way to capture a customized installer disk image that you can reuse throughout an organization to simplify the task of performing multiple installations. The Windows SysPrep tool is used to prepare Windows operating system images.

SQL Server SysPrep allows you to prepare one or more images of a stand-alone instance of SQL Server. Preparing a SQL Server image with sysprep installs all the necessary binaries for the features you select without actually completing the installation. This makes installation of one or more instance on the same system easier by only having to specify the usable features (such as the instance name, service accounts, data file directories, etc.) during the completion of a prepared image without having to walk through the full installation process each time.

Creating a SQL Server image with SQL Server SysPrep involves a two-step process:

▶ Step 1, Prepare Image: Stops the installation process after the product binaries are installed, without configuring the computer, network, or account-specific information for the instance of SQL Server that is being prepared.

▶ Step 2, Complete Image: Completes the configuration of a prepared instance of SQL Server, having you provide the computer, network, and account-specific information not applied when preparing the image.

Preparing a SQL Server Sysprep Image

To prepare a SQL Server Sysprep image, launch the SQL Server Installation Wizard, click on the Advanced page, and select "Image Preparation of a stand-alone instance of SQL Server" (see Figure 8.23). This will launch the SQL Server sysprep installation wizard.

The Sysprep installation wizard is similar to the normal installation wizard with some minor differences and a stripped down set of screens and installation options. Like a normal installation, it first runs the System Configuration Checker Global Rules and then the Product Updates check to see if there are any SQL Server updates to include in the installation (see the next section in this chapter for an example of including a service pack or cumulative update in a SQL Server installation).

After installing the required Setup Files, it will run the Prepare Image Rules to verify that the system supports the preparation of a sysprep image. If the Prepare Image Rules pass, the installer wizard will automatically advance to the License Terms page. You will need to select the check box to acknowledge acceptance of the license terms, then click on Next to advance to the Features Selection page (see Figure 8.24).

The Sysprep Feature selection page again is similar to the standard feature selection page during a regular installation but with only Sysprep compatible features listed. After completing the selection of features you want to include in the sysprep image, click Next to run the Features Rules. If all Feature Rules are passed, the installer will automatically move onto the Instance Configuration page.

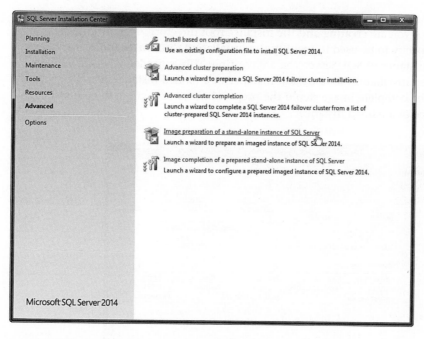

FIGURE 8.23   Launching the SQL Server 2014 Sysprep Installation Wizard.

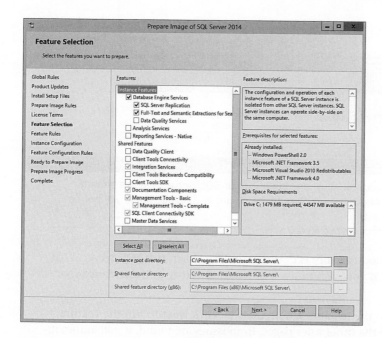

FIGURE 8.24   The SQL Server Sysprep Feature Selection page.

On the Instance Configuration page (see Figure 8.25), you specify the Instance ID for the prepared instance you are creating and the instance root directory. The Instance ID is a name you can specify to be used to identify the installation directories and registry keys for the sysprep instance of SQL Server you are creating. This is needed whether you are creating a sysprep installation for a default instance or a named instance. You will actually specify during the complete image step if the prepared instance is going to be installed as a default instance or a named instance.

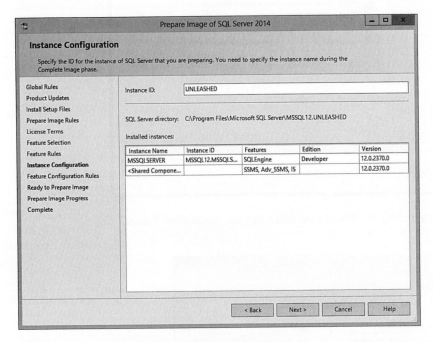

FIGURE 8.25   The SQL Server Sysprep Instance Configuration page.

NOTE

The Installed instances grid will show any instances of SQL Server that are already installed on the system where the Prepare Image wizard is running. These will not be included in the Sysprep image.

By default, the instance root directory is C:\Program Files\Microsoft SQL Server\120\. You can change this here if you wish to use a different directory as the instance root directory.

Once you have completed the Instance Configuration, click Next to run the Feature Configuration Rules. Like the other rules pages, if no issues are found, it will automatically advance to the Ready to Prepare Image page. This page is similar to the Ready to Install page as shown in Figure 8.19 and lists the specifics about the image being prepared including the SQL Server edition and features to be included in the sysprep image. If everything looks okay, click the Prepare button to prepare the sysprep image.

The Prepare Image Progress page will be displayed while the image is being generated. Once complete, the wizard will automatically advance to the Complete page. Click Close to exit the wizard. At this point, all of the necessary binaries have been installed to the system to support the creation of a SQL Server instance with the selected features. To create an instance from this sysprep image, you need to run the Image Completion wizard.

Completing a SQL Server Sysprep Image

There are two ways to complete a prepared sysprep instance of SQL Server 2014:

▶ You can use the shortcut installed on the Start menu by the Prepare Image process. The shortcut is added to the Configuration Tools folder under the Microsoft SQL Server 2014 folder in the Programs menu. (In Windows Server 2012 or later or Windows 8 or 8.1, launch the Windows Search and type in "complete sql server 2014 installation")

▶ You can click on the "Image completion of a prepared stand-alone instance item" on the Advanced page of the Installation Center (see Figure 8.23)

NOTE

It's unclear whether this is a bug or not, but there is a minor difference between invoking the completion of the sysprep image from the shortcut versus invoking it from the Installation center option, especially if installing the Developer edition. When running it from the Start menu shortcut, the product key is not automatically filled in. However, if you launch SQL Server setup from the ISO image and choose the "Image completion" option from the advanced page, it will automatically fill-in your product key for you.

When you first launch the Complete image wizard, you'll be presented with the Product Key page which is similar to the one shown in Figure 8.5. If the product key is not automatically filled in, you'll need to enter it here, or you have the option of installing a free version of SQL Server 2014. You also have the option of performing an edition upgrade at this point by specifying the appropriate product key for the edition you wish to install.

After entering or verifying the product key, click Next to review and access the License Terms (again, this screen is similar to the one shown in Figure 8.6).

After accepting the License terms, click Next to run the Global Rules check. If all rules pass, the wizard will auto-advance to the Microsoft Update page. Here you'll have the option to once again check for updates to SQL Server 2014 and if any are available, have the option of including them. Click Next to run the Complete Image Rules. If no rules fail and you've reviewed any warnings displayed (like the ubiquitous Windows Firewall warning), click Next to advance to the Select Prepared Features page (see Figure 8.26).

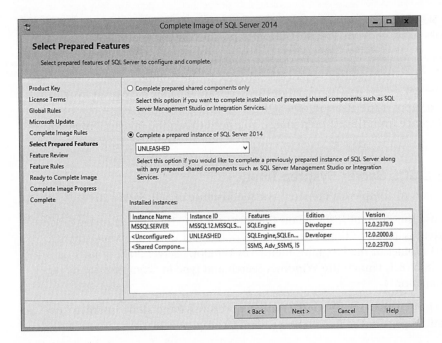

FIGURE 8.26   The Select Prepared Features page.

On the Select Prepared Features page, you can choose which sysprep image you want to complete by selecting the appropriate Image ID that you specified during the Prepare Image process. Again, note that the Installed instances grid will show any instances of SQL Server that are already installed on the system along with any unconfigured sysprep images that exist. You also have the option of only installing the prepared shared components such as SSMS or SSIS. Once you've selected the Instance ID you want to configure and complete, click Next to move to the Feature Review page. This page is displayed for information purposes only to see what features will be installed. You cannot modify any options on this page. Click Next to continue.

If the sysprep image to be completed included the Database Engine feature, you'll next be presented with the Instance Configuration page, as shown in Figure 8.27. This is where you can specify the instance name, or to install it as the default instance if not default instance already exists. Click Next to continue to the Server Configuration page, where you specify the service accounts to use and the SQL Server Collation, similar to the page shown in Figure 8.13.

Once you've specified the collation and service account information, click Next to continue to the Database Engine Configuration page, which is where you'll specify the authentication mode, administrator accounts, data directories, Filestream settings, similar to those shown in Figures 8.15 through 8.17. Once all values have been entered, click Next to run the Feature Rules. If all rules pass, the wizard will auto advance to the Ready to Complete Image page where you can review the configuration settings specified in the previous screens. If everything looks okay, click Complete to complete the image and create the configured SQL Server instance. The Complete Image Progress screen will be displayed and once finished, it will advance to the Complete page which will summarize the features installed and the installation status (see Figure 8.28).

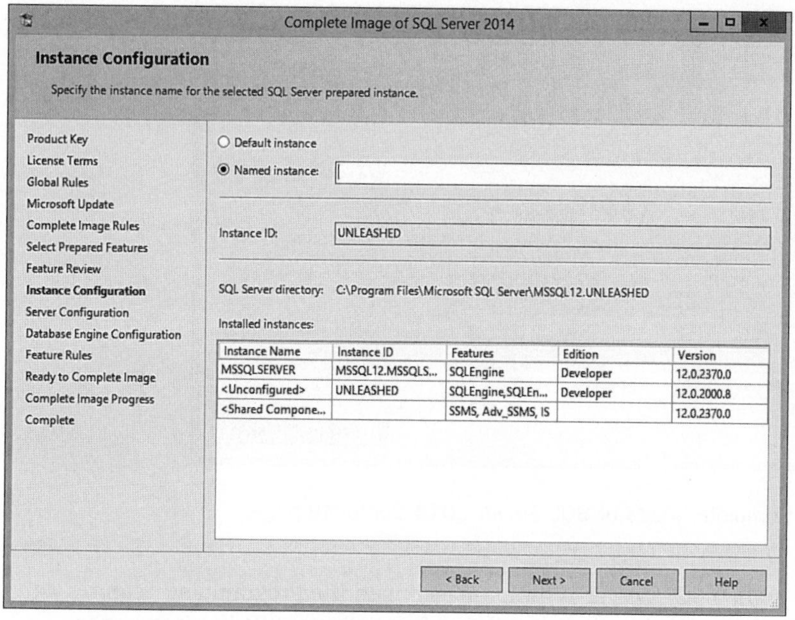

Complete Image of SQL Server 2014

Instance Configuration

Specify the instance name for the selected SQL Server prepared instance.

Product Key
License Terms
Global Rules
Microsoft Update
Complete Image Rules
Select Prepared Features
Feature Review
Instance Configuration
Server Configuration
Database Engine Configuration
Feature Rules
Ready to Complete Image
Complete Image Progress
Complete

○ Default instance
◉ Named instance: [   ]

Instance ID: UNLEASHED

SQL Server directory: C:\Program Files\Microsoft SQL Server\MSSQL12.UNLEASHED

Installed instances:

Instance Name	Instance ID	Features	Edition	Version
MSSQLSERVER	MSSQL12.MSSQLS...	SQLEngine	Developer	12.0.2370.0
<Unconfigured>	UNLEASHED	SQLEngine,SQLEn...	Developer	12.0.2000.8
<Shared Compone...		SSMS, Adv_SSMS, IS		12.0.2370.0

< Back   Next >   Cancel   Help

FIGURE 8.27   The Complete Image Instance Configuration page.

Modifying a SQL Server Sysprep Image

Once you've created a SQL Server Sysprep image, you can add or remove features from the image without having to drop and recreate it.

To add features to a SQL Server Sysprep image, run the Image preparation of a stand-alone instance of SQL Server on the Advanced page of the Installation Wizard. Step through the screens until you get to the Prepare Image Type page. On that page, select Add features to an existing prepared instance of SQL Server option. Select the specific prepared instance you want to add features to from the drop down list of available prepared instances and click Next to continue. On the Feature Selection page, specify the features you want to add to the prepared instance. Click Next and continue through the Prepare Image wizard as you would when preparing a new image. On the Complete page, it will list the features added and whether they succeeded or not. Click Close to exit the Wizard.

> **NOTE**
>
> The Prepare Image Type page will only be available if there is a prepared image available that hasn't been used to complete an image. You cannot modify a Sysprep image that has been used to create a SQL Server instance.

8

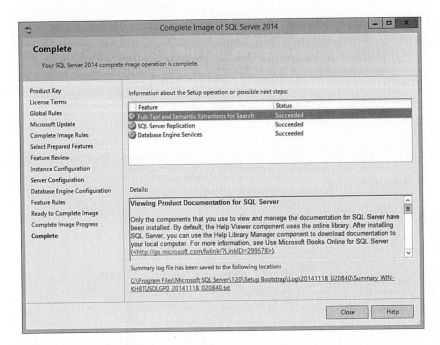

FIGURE 8.28   The Complete Image of SQL Server 2014 Complete page.

To remove features from a SQL Server Sysprep Image, open the Program and Features control panel in Windows. Double click on Microsoft SQL Server 2014 to invoke the Remove SQL Server 2014 wizard. On the Select Instance page, select the unconfigured prepared instance you want to remove features from and click Next. On the Select Features page, specify the features to remove from the SQL Server instance you specified and click Next to continue. The Removal rules will run to verify that the operation can complete successfully and if so, advance to the Ready to Remove page. Click Remove to begin the removal process. On the Complete page you can review the completion status of the operation. Click close to exit the removal wizard.

Common Uses of SQL Server Sysprep Images

You can use the SQL Server SysPrep capability in a number of ways including the following:

▶ You can prepare one or more unconfigured instances of SQL Server on the same system. You can select which of the prepared instances to configure and install by selecting the appropriate Instance ID when running the Complete Image wizard on the same computer.

▶ You can use the SQL Server Setup configuration file generated by a prepared instance and use it to prepare additional unconfigured SQL Server instances on other systems for configuration at a future date.

▶ In combination with the Windows SysPrep, you can create an image of the operating system and also include the unconfigured prepared instances of SQL Server also created on the source computer. After you deploy and configure the operating system image to one or more computers, you can configure the prepared SQL Server instances included with the Windows SysPrep image by running the Complete Image step of SQL Server Setup. This makes it easier to deploy a number of similar SQL Server configurations across multiple systems.

Installing Service Packs and Cumulative Updates

After the official release of a product, Microsoft will occasionally release updates to the product as either service packs or cumulative updates. It is highly recommended that you apply SQL Server services packs when they become available because they often contain critical fixes to the product and sometimes new or enhanced features. You should especially consider applying the latest services pack when performing a new SQL Server installation. As of this writing, no service packs are yet available for SQL Server 2014.

Cumulative updates provide one or more hotfixes that are released to the public on a scheduled delivery basis. Each cumulative update release contains all the hotfixes and security fixes that were in the previous updates. The hotfixes contained in cumulative update have not undergone full testing. Therefore, cumulative updates should only be applied if they provide a fix for any issues you are currently experiencing with SQL Server 2014 as described in the related Microsoft Knowledge Base articles. If your system is not affected by any of the problems addressed by the fixes in the cumulative update, it is recommended that you wait for the next service pack that contains the fixes contained in the cumulative update. The service pack will include a fully tested version of the fixes in the cumulative update. Also, it is strongly recommended that you install and test a cumulative update before applying it to a production environment.

Applying a Service Pack or Cumulative Update During a New Installation

With the available preconfigured slipstream installation downloads and the new Product Update feature, Microsoft has made it easier to apply service packs during a SQL Server 2014 installation. You can choose to download and run a SQL Server slipstream installation package that already includes the latest service pack or choose to have the latest product updates downloaded and included during the SQL Server installation. The new Product Update feature actually replaces the slipstream functionality that was introduced in SQL Server 2008 SP1, so there is no reason anymore to create or configure your own slipstream installation.

To apply a cumulative update when performing a new SQL Server installation, you need to download the cumulative update and after extracting it, copy it to a folder that is accessible by the SQL Server install utility. Invoke the installer from the command line and specify the directory where the cumulative update resides with the /UpdateSource option along with the `Action="Install"` option. For example, if you copied the cumulative update to the `C:\SQL2014_CU` folder, the command to execute is as follows:

```
setup.exe /ACTION="Install" /UpdateEnabled="true" /UpdateSource="C:\sql2014_CU"
```

This command invokes the SQL Server installer and begins the SQL Server installation. After getting past the SQL Server Setup Support rules, it will display the Product Updates page. If any product updates are installed in the specified UpdateSource folder, you will see a screen similar to that shown in Figure 8.29.

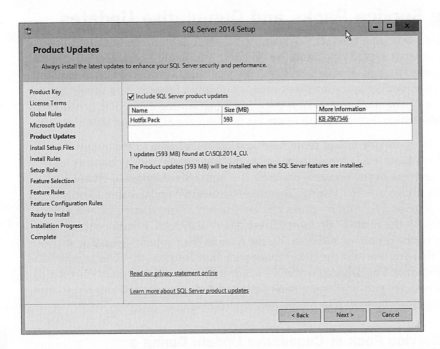

FIGURE 8.29   SQL Server 2014 Product Update screen with updates available in the UpdateSource folder.

Click on Next to continue the installation, and the Installer will extract the hotfix/cumulative update/service pack and integrate it with the installation. While the update is being extracted and installed, you'll see a screen like that shown in figure 8.30. Depending on the files affected by the updates, you may see a dialog box stating that a restart is required after installation to apply the updates. After stepping through the subsequent setup screens to specify the SQL Server configuration, you can confirm that the desired update is being applied by checking the Product Update feature on the Ready to Install screen, as shown in Figure 8.31. If everything looks okay, click Install to proceed with the installation.

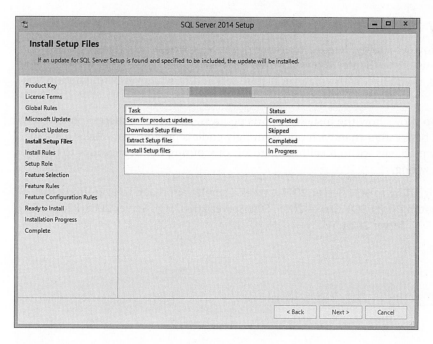

FIGURE 8.30   SQL Server 2014 Install Setup Files screen.

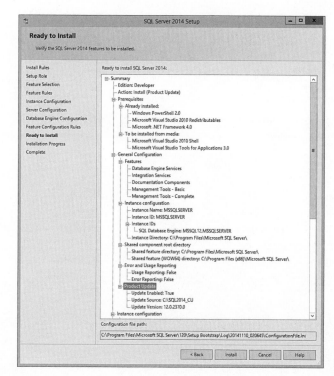

FIGURE 8.31   Verifying the product update in the Ready to Install screen.

Summary

This chapter provides a fairly detailed overview of the SQL Server 2014 install process from start to finish. The chapter shows how the Installer Wizard makes it easy to install as many instances as you like, with whatever feature sets and in whatever configuration you choose.

The chapter also shows how the installer reports progress, failure, and success on an individual task basis rather than with one seemingly endless progress bar, making it a lot easier to rectify problems without calling Microsoft or scouring the newsgroups to figure out what went wrong.

Chapter 9, "Upgrading to SQL Server 2014," takes a similar approach to examining the process of upgrading from SQL Server 2005, SQL Server 2008, SQL Server 2008 R2, or SQL Server 2012 to SQL Server 2014.

Upgrading to SQL Server 2014

SQL Server 2014 offers a number of new features and improvements that make upgrading desirable. You can upgrade instances of SQL Server 2005 through SQL Server 2012 to SQL Server 2014. Whether you're a gung-ho developer or the most conservative of administrators, there's an upgrade path to suit your comfort level. This chapter provides best practices and recommendations for upgrading to SQL Server 2014 with minimal issues.

What's New in Upgrading SQL Server

The installer program for performing installations and upgrades for SQL Server 2014 is not much different from the installer provided with SQL Server 2012, except for some minor changes and reorganization.

> **NOTE**
>
> The focus of this chapter is on upgrade options and best practices rather than a screen-by-screen walkthrough of the upgrade process. An upgrade installation is not much different from a new installation. See Chapter 8, "Installing SQL Server 2014," for a detailed walkthrough and description of the installer screens and options.

The SQL Server 2014 Upgrade Matrix

No software upgrade section would be complete without an illustrative table showing the versions and editions of SQL Server for which direct upgrades are supported. They are presented in Table 9.1.

TABLE 9.1   Supported Upgrade Paths to SQL Server 2014

Previous SQL Server	Supported Upgrades
SQL Server 2005 SP4 Enterprise	SQL Server 2014 Enterprise
	SQL Server 2014 Business Intelligence
SQL Server 2005 SP4 Developer	SQL Server 2014 Developer
SQL Server 2005 SP4 Standard	SQL Server 2014 Standard
	SQL Server 2014 Enterprise
	SQL Server 2014 Business Intelligence
SQL Server 2005 SP4 Workgroup	SQL Server 2014 Standard
	SQL Server 2014 Enterprise
	SQL Server 2014 Business Intelligence
	SQL Server 2014 Web
SQL Server 2005 SP4 Express	SQL Server 2014 Express
	SQL Server 2014 Standard
	SQL Server 2014 Enterprise
	SQL Server 2014 Business Intelligence
	SQL Server 2014 Web
SQL Server 2008 SP3 Enterprise	SQL Server 2014 Enterprise
	SQL Server 2014 Business Intelligence
SQL Server 2008 SP3 Developer	SQL Server 2014 Developer
SQL Server 2008 SP3 Standard	SQL Server 2014 Standard
	SQL Server 2014 Enterprise
	SQL Server 2014 Business Intelligence
SQL Server 2008 SP3 Workgroup	SQL Server 2014 Web
	SQL Server 2014 Standard
	SQL Server 2014 Enterprise
	SQL Server 2014 Business Intelligence
SQL Server 2008 SP3 Web	SQL Server 2014 Web
	SQL Server 2014 Standard
	SQL Server 2014 Enterprise
	SQL Server 2014 Business Intelligence
SQL Server 2008 SP3 Express	SQL Server 2014 Express
	SQL Server 2014 Web
	SQL Server 2014 Standard
	SQL Server 2014 Enterprise
	SQL Server 2014 Business Intelligence
SQL Server 2008 R2 SP2 Datacenter	SQL Server 2014 Enterprise
	SQL Server 2014 Business Intelligence
SQL Server 2008 R2 SP2 Enterprise	SQL Server 2014 Enterprise
	SQL Server 2014 Business Intelligence

Previous SQL Server	Supported Upgrades
SQL Server 2008 R2 SP2 Developer	SQL Server 2014 Developer
SQL Server 2008 R2 SP2 Standard	SQL Server 2014 Standard
	SQL Server 2014 Enterprise
	SQL Server 2014 Business Intelligence
SQL Server 2008 R2 SP2 Workgroup	SQL Server 2014 Web
	SQL Server 2014 Standard
	SQL Server 2014 Enterprise
	SQL Server 2014 Business Intelligence
SQL Server 2008 R2 SP2 Web	SQL Server 2014 Web
	SQL Server 2014 Standard
	SQL Server 2014 Enterprise
	SQL Server 2014 Business Intelligence
SQL Server 2008 R2 SP2 Express	SQL Server 2014 Express
	SQL Server 2014 Web
	SQL Server 2014 Standard
	SQL Server 2014 Enterprise
	SQL Server 2014 Business Intelligence
SQL Server 2012 SP1 Enterprise	SQL Server 2014 Enterprise
	SQL Server 2014 Business Intelligence
SQL Server 2012 SP1 Developer	SQL Server 2014 Developer
SQL Server 2012 SP1 Standard	SQL Server 2014 Standard
	SQL Server 2014 Enterprise
	SQL Server 2014 Business Intelligence
SQL Server 2012 SP1 Web	SQL Server 2014 Web
	SQL Server 2014 Standard
	SQL Server 2014 Enterprise
	SQL Server 2014 Business Intelligence
SQL Server 2012 SP1 Express	SQL Server 2014 Express
	SQL Server 2014 Web
	SQL Server 2014 Standard
	SQL Server 2014 Enterprise
	SQL Server 2014 Business Intelligence
SQL Server 2012 SP1 Business Intelligence	SQL Server 2014 Enterprise
	SQL Server 2014 Business Intelligence

SQL Server 32-bit editions can only be upgraded to 32-bit versions of SQL Server 2014 or on the 32-bit subsystem (WOW64) of a 64-bit server. You cannot upgrade a 32-bit installation of SQL Server to native 64-bit using SQL Server Setup. Likewise, SQL Server 64-bit versions can be upgraded to SQL Server 2014 64-bit server only. You can upgrade databases from a 32-bit edition to a 64-bit edition by backing up or detaching the databases from a 32-bit instance of SQL Server and then restoring or attaching them to a new instance of SQL Server (64-bit).

> **NOTE**
>
> As you see in Table 9.1, direct upgrades from versions prior to SQL Server 2005 SP4 are not supported. Options for migrating databases from these versions of SQL Server are presented later in this chapter.

Identifying Products and Features to be Upgraded

Before you start the process of upgrading to SQL Server 2014, it is a good idea to identify what SQL Server products and features you already have installed on the system you are planning on upgrading. This way you will know for sure what may be affected by the upgrade.

To easily identify the SQL Server products and features installed on your systems, you can run the "Installed SQL Server features discovery report," which is on the Tools page of the SQL Server Installation Center (see Figure 9.1).

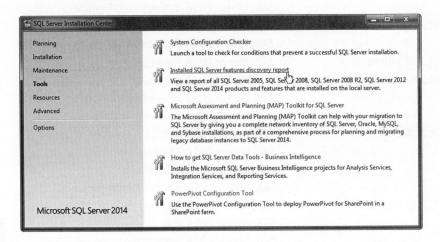

FIGURE 9.1   Running the Installed SQL Server features discovery report.

When you click the hyperlink for the features discovery report, it will search the system for any SQL Server installed features and display a report of all features found, the instance names, the product level, edition, and version number, similar to the report shown in Figure 9.2.

Once you know what products and features are installed and available for upgrade, the next step may be to run the SQL Server Upgrade Advisor to identify any database objects or components that may present compatibility issues after upgrading.

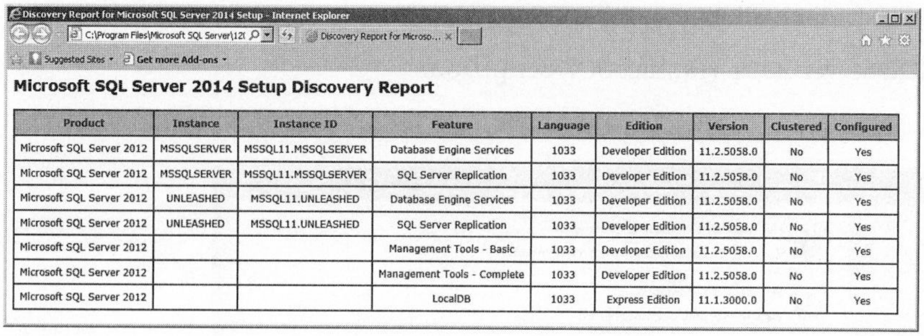
Discovery Report for Microsoft SQL Server 2014 Setup - Internet Explorer

C:\Program Files\Microsoft SQL Server\12(Discovery Report for Microso...

Suggested Sites Get more Add-ons

Microsoft SQL Server 2014 Setup Discovery Report

Product	Instance	Instance ID	Feature	Language	Edition	Version	Clustered	Configured
Microsoft SQL Server 2012	MSSQLSERVER	MSSQL11.MSSQLSERVER	Database Engine Services	1033	Developer Edition	11.2.5058.0	No	Yes
Microsoft SQL Server 2012	MSSQLSERVER	MSSQL11.MSSQLSERVER	SQL Server Replication	1033	Developer Edition	11.2.5058.0	No	Yes
Microsoft SQL Server 2012	UNLEASHED	MSSQL11.UNLEASHED	Database Engine Services	1033	Developer Edition	11.2.5058.0	No	Yes
Microsoft SQL Server 2012	UNLEASHED	MSSQL11.UNLEASHED	SQL Server Replication	1033	Developer Edition	11.2.5058.0	No	Yes
Microsoft SQL Server 2012			Management Tools - Basic	1033	Developer Edition	11.2.5058.0	No	Yes
Microsoft SQL Server 2012			Management Tools - Complete	1033	Developer Edition	11.2.5058.0	No	Yes
Microsoft SQL Server 2012			LocalDB	1033	Express Edition	11.1.3000.0	No	Yes

FIGURE 9.2 Viewing the results of the Installed SQL Server features discovery report.

Using the SQL Server Upgrade Advisor (UA)

It would be a daunting task indeed to try to test every stored procedure and function, every table and view, every online analytical processing (OLAP) cube, every Data Transformation Services (DTS) or SQL Server Integration Services (SSIS) package, and so on that your team has built to make sure they still work after you migrate them to SQL Server 2014.

With the availability of the SQL Server Upgrade Advisor (UA), you can relax a bit and let the combined experience and testing of early adopters and the SQL Server development team go to work for you.

The UA advises on which aspects of your current setup should or need to be changed to become compatible with SQL Server 2014. Let's look at how it works.

NOTE

Even though the UA is a great tool, if you have the resources to do so, it is a good idea to set up an additional test environment just for SQL Server 2014. Also, you should thoroughly test your upgraded objects and code *after the upgrade* on a dry run, just to be sure you don't miss anything. Remember to make full backups!

Getting Started with the UA

Before running the Upgrade Advisor, you must first install it. The easiest way to install the Upgrade Advisor is to start the SQL Server 2014 Installer. On the Installer Landing page is an option to install the Upgrade Advisor (see Figure 9.3). Alternatively, the Upgrade Advisor is available in the `Servers\redist\Upgrade Advisor` folder of the SQL Server installation media or from the Microsoft Download Center. The Upgrade Advisor has the following system requirements:

- Windows Server 2008 SP2, Windows 7, or Windows Server 2008 R2 SP1
- Windows Installer beginning with version 4.5 (required by the .NET Framework; you can install Windows Installer from the Windows Installer website)

▶ Microsoft .NET Framework 4

▶ Microsoft SQL Server 2014 Transact-SQL ScriptDom

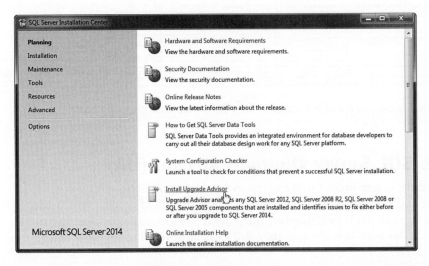

FIGURE 9.3   Installing the Upgrade Advisor from the SQL Server 2014 Installer.

TIP

Although not listed in the documentation as a requirement for running the Upgrade Advisor, you may find that the installer for the Upgrade Advisor may fail with the following error message if Microsoft SQL Server 2014 Transact-SQL ScriptDom is not available:

```
Setup is missing
prerequisites:
 -Microsoft SQL Server 2014 Transact-SQL ScriptDom, which is not installed by
Upgrade Advisor Setup. To continue, install SQL Server 2014 Transact-SQL
ScriptDom from below hyperlink and then run the Upgrade Advisor Setup operation
again:
Go to http://go.microsoft.com/fwlink/?LinkID=296473.
```

The Transact-SQL ScriptDom is a .NET Framework API that provides parsing and scripting services for Transact-SQL. It's essentially what allows the Upgrade Advisor to parse and interpret your database objects (such as stored procedures, functions, triggers, and so on) to identify possible compatibility issues. The link provided in the error message will take you to the SQL Server 2014 Feature Pack page in the Microsoft Download Center. Click on the Download button, scroll through the list of files available to download, and locate either ENU\x64\SqlDom.msi (for 64 bit platforms, about 1/3 of the way down in the list) or ENU\x86\SqlDom.msi (for 32 bit platforms, 80-85% of the way down in the list). Download and run the installer for the ScriptDom appropriate for your platform (32- or 64-bit), and you should then be able to successfully run the installer for the Upgrade Advisor.

> **NOTE**
>
> If not installed already, the .NET Framework 4 is available on the SQL Server 2014 product media, and from the SDK, redistributable, and service pack download website. To install the .NET Framework 4 from the SQL Server 2014 media, locate the root of the disk drive. Then double-click the `\redist` folder, double-click the `DotNetFrameworks` folder, and run `dotNetFx40_Full_x86_x64.exe` for 32-bit or 64-bit operating systems.

If you run the SQL Server Installer, it installs the Windows Installer and .NET Framework requirements automatically if they are not detected.

> **NOTE**
>
> The location where you can install SQL Server Upgrade Advisor depends on what you will be analyzing. Upgrade Advisor supports remote analysis of all supported components except Reporting Services. If you are not scanning instances of Reporting Services, you can install Upgrade Advisor on any computer that can connect to your instance of SQL Server and that meets the Upgrade Advisor prerequisites. If you are scanning instances of Reporting Services, you must install Upgrade Advisor on the Report Server.

As described in the following sections, the UA has two main functional areas: the Analysis Wizard and Report Viewer. The first time you use Upgrade Advisor, run the Upgrade Advisor Analysis Wizard to analyze SQL Server components. When the wizard finishes the analysis, you can view the resulting reports in the Upgrade Advisor Report Viewer.

The Analysis Wizard

You'll be glad to know that the analysis process does not modify any code or data; that is left for you to do (or not do) at a later time. As an example, let's run the UA's Analysis Wizard against all the SQL Server components of a locally installed SQL Server 2008 R2 instance. The Analysis Wizard examines objects that can be accessed, such as scripts, stored procedures, triggers, and trace files. Upgrade Advisor cannot analyze desktop applications or encrypted stored procedures.

To start the process, launch the SQL Server 2014 Upgrade Advisor from the Windows Start menu and then click the Launch Upgrade Advisor Analysis Wizard hyperlink at the bottom of the Welcome page (see Figure 9.4). When the Analysis Wizard's Welcome page appears, click Next. When you reach the SQL Server Components screen, choose the components to be analyzed by checking their corresponding check boxes (see Figure 9.5).

Be sure to select only components that are actually installed on the server being upgraded; otherwise, the Upgrade Advisor stalls at the appropriate feature screen with an error message that the feature could not be found on the specified server. This is where it is useful to have run the Installed SQL Server features discovery report, as described in the previous section. You can also click on the Detect button next to the Server name you are analyzing, and it will detect which components are available on that server for upgrade analysis.

FIGURE 9.4   The Upgrade Advisor Welcome page.

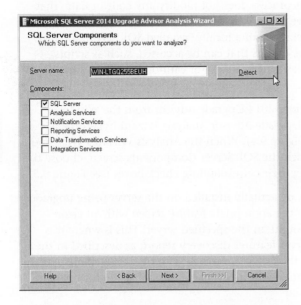

FIGURE 9.5   Choosing the components to be analyzed by the UA's Analysis Wizard.

NOTE

Interestingly, while the Analysis Wizard has a check box for Data Transformation Services, if you select it, the UA Analysis Wizard displays a warning that Data Transformation Services is removed in SQL Server 2014 and will not let you continue until you uncheck it. Apparently, this option is there to make it clear that Data Transformation Services (DTS) packages are not supported in SQL Server 2014. SQL Server 2014 lacks the Legacy Components feature that was available in SQL Server 2008 and SQL Server 2008 R2 and is unable to run DTS packages directly. SQL Server 2014 also lacks the Package Migration Wizard that was provided in previous versions of SQL Server. If you still have DTS packages in use in the SQL Server instances you are upgrading to SQL Server 2014, you will have to convert them to SQL Server Integration Services (SSIS) packages using the Package Migration Wizard available in SQL Server 2005, SQL Server 2008, or SQL Server 2008 R2 before you can bring the functionality they previously provided into SQL Server 2014.

After selecting components, click Next and the Connection Parameters screen appears. This is where you need to specify the target SQL Server Instance name and specify an authentication method. If using SQL Server authentication, enter a username and password with sysadmin privileges so that the UA can connect to the instance with sufficient rights to perform the analysis. When finished, click Next, and if you selected to analyze the SQL Server component (see Figure 9.5), the SQL Server Parameters screen, shown in Figure 9.6, appears, which allows you to choose which (if any) of the databases within the SQL Server instance to analyze.

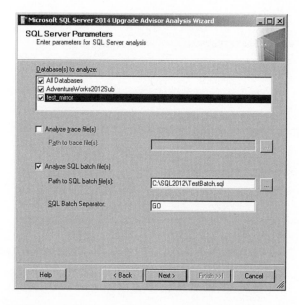

FIGURE 9.6   Choosing the databases and files for the UA to analyze.

> **NOTE**
>
> Since SQL Server 2014 only supports upgrading from SQL Server 2005 SP4 and later, any databases to be analyzed have to be at compatibility level 90 or later. Compatibility level 90 relates to SQL Server 2005 (which was also considered SQL Server version 9.0).

You can also use this screen to ask the UA to analyze one or more SQL Profiler trace (`.trc`) files. This feature is useful for analyzing the actual T-SQL statements submitted from one or more applications for any deprecated or discontinued features. You would want to set up and run a trace in SQL Profiler ahead of time to capture a representative sample of the T-SQL executed against the server by your applications. You can also scan T-SQL batch files (maintenance scripts, procedures, functions, triggers, and so on) to check for deprecated or discontinued features used in the SQL scripts.

For this example, create a SQL batch file that contains the following T-SQL commands, most of which are deprecated in SQL Server 2014, just to test the UA:

```
use AdventureWorks2012
go

if DATABASEPROPERTY('Adventureworks2012', 'IsTruncLog') <> 1
    EXEC sp_dboption 'AdventureWorks2012', 'trunc. log on chkpt', 'true'
go

SELECT * FROM master..syslockinfo
go

select * from Sales.SalesOrderDetail with (FASTFIRSTROW)
    where ProductID = 1234

if @@ROWCOUNT = 0
      raiserror 50001 'No rows found'
go

Set rowcount 100
select  SalesOrderID, ProductID, OrderQty, UnitPrice
   from Sales.SalesOrderDetail
     order by SalesOrderID
     compute SUM(OrderQty) by SalesOrderID
     compute sum(OrderQty)
Set rowcount 0
go

SELECT substring(name,1,25) AS Name,
      single_pages_kb,
      single_pages_in_use_kb
```

```
FROM sys.dm_os_memory_cache_counters
    order by single_pages_kb desc
go
```

When you're ready, click Next, and the Upgrade Advisor presents screens for any of the other SQL Server components you selected previously (refer to Figure 9.5) asking for login information or to select packages to analyze. For example, if you selected to analyze SSIS packages, the SSIS Parameters screen (shown in Figure 9.7) is presented to give you the option to analyze all the packages stored in the target server instance or to specify one or more package files stored in operating system files to be analyzed.

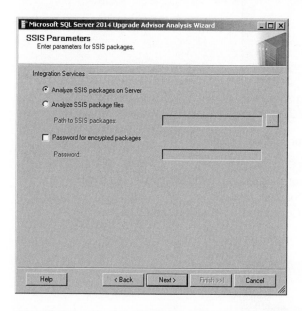

FIGURE 9.7   Choosing the SSIS packages to analyze.

> **NOTE**
>
> If you selected a component, but that component isn't installed on the server you are upgrading, the Upgrade Advisor reports that no instances of that component could be found on the server, and you cannot proceed until you go back and deselect the component.

When you're all set with your SSIS selections, click Next to reach the Confirm Upgrade Advisor Settings screen where you can confirm the options selected to be analyzed on the previous screens (see Figure 9.8). Make sure that all the SQL Server services you are analyzing are running and (if you're happy with your selections) click the Run button to begin the analysis.

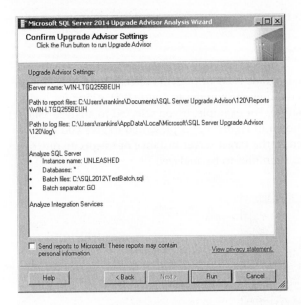

FIGURE 9.8   The Confirm Upgrade Advisor Settings screen.

As you can see from the Upgrade Advisor Progress screen that appears (see Figure 9.9), the wizard performs a task-based study of each component, providing per-step reporting, similar to the installer and the System Configuration Checker (both discussed in Chapter 8).

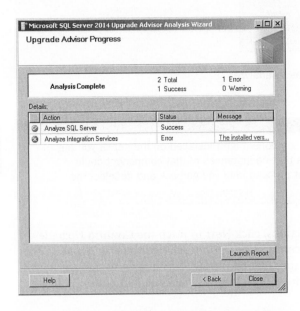

FIGURE 9.9   The Upgrade Advisor Progress screen.

When the analysis is complete, the UA Progress screen presents a Launch Report button. The output of the UA Analysis Wizard is an XML report that you can view via the second major component of the UA, the Report Viewer, described in the next section.

You can launch the Report Viewer to figure out what to do about the issues the UA may have uncovered. Click the Launch Report button to proceed.

The Report Viewer

The Report Viewer is one of the most important tools in the upgrade process because it provides per-issue messaging, resolution tracking, and (in many cases) hyperlinks to the compiled help documentation distributed with the UA.

Issues are organized in the Report Viewer on a per-server and then per-component basis. They can be filtered by type (that is, all issues, all upgrade issues, pre-upgrade issues, all migration issues, resolved issues, and unresolved issues), and you can track your resolution progress by checking the This Issue Has Been Resolved check boxes. Figure 9.10 shows the main user interface of the Report Viewer.

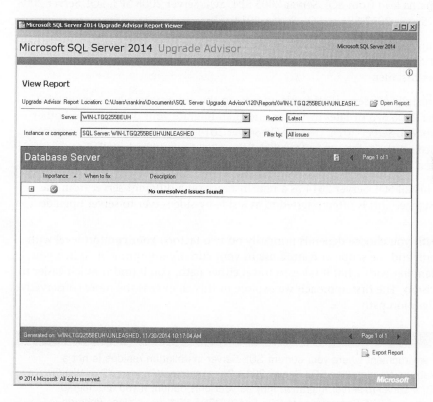

FIGURE 9.10   SQL Server UA's Report Viewer.

You can view previously generated reports by launching the Upgrade Advisor Report Viewer from the UA welcome screen (see Figure 9.4). By default, the UA Report Viewer displays the most recently generated report. To open a previously generated report, click on the Open Report link in the upper-right corner of the Report Viewer to bring up the Open Report File dialog. UA reports are saved by default to the `MyDocuments\SQL Server Upgrade Advisor\120\Reports\`*Servername* folder. The files are broken down into separate XML files by component and include a timestamp in the filename representing the time the report was generated (for example, `AS_YYYY-MM-DD_HH-MM-SS.xml` for Analysis Services, `DE_YYYY-MM-DD_HH-MM-SS.xml` for the Database Engine).

Destination: SQL Server 2014

Now that you have become familiar with how to use the helpful Upgrade Advisor, you're ready to begin your extensive pre-upgrade testing phase. After you resolve all the issues you can, it's time to take the next step: install SQL Server 2014 (in your test and development environments first, of course).

Four different paths lead from SQL Server 2005 SP4, SQL Server 2008 SP3, SQL Server 2008 R2 SP2, or SQL Server 2012 SP1 to SQL Server 2014:

▶ You can upgrade your existing SQL Server 2005 SP4 or later, SQL Server 2008 SP3 or later, SQL Server 2008 R2 SP2, and SQL Server 2012 SP1 instances in-place, using the SQL Server Installer.

▶ You can install SQL Server 2014 side by side on the same system as your current SQL Server 2008 SP3 or later instances and then migrate your databases and other content to SQL Server 2014. (Note: SQL Server 2014 and SQL Server 2005 cannot be installed on the same computer.) SQL Server 2014 would be installed as a new instance on the same server as the current SQL Server instance.

▶ You can install SQL Server 2014 as a new instance on a different server from the target instance. This is often referred to as a side-by-side server-to-server upgrade.

The upgrade path you choose depends primarily on two factors: your comfort level with the new platform and the scope of feature use in your current environment. When you have become familiar with what it takes to travel either path, you'll find it much easier to make your decision. The first approach we explore in this chapter is the more conservative side-by-side migration path.

> **NOTE**
>
> If the server environment where your current SQL Server installation resides is not a supported platform for installing SQL Server 2014 (for example, Windows XP or Windows Server 2003), a server-to-server migration may be your only option. If you are upgrading from a version of SQL Server prior to SQL Server 2005 SP4, an in-place upgrade is not supported without first upgrading to one of the supported versions, and a side-by-side server-to-server migration may be the better option. For a list of supported in-place upgrade paths, see the "Upgrading In-Place" section, later in this chapter.

Side-by-Side Upgrades

SQL Server 2014 can coexist on the same servers as any existing SQL Server 2008, 2008 R2, or SQL Server 2012 instances. This means you can install one or more instances of SQL Server 2014 without performing an in-place upgrade of any pre-2014 instances. You don't have to worry about whether you're breaking existing functionality. Side-by-side migration is therefore an easy option to investigate, especially if you don't have a spare server available to install SQL Server 2014 on its own separate server and perform a server-to-server upgrade.

> **NOTE**
>
> If you are performing a side-by-side installation on the same server, be sure your server has sufficient resources (CPU, memory, disk space) to support running multiple instances of SQL Server.

Many administrators favor the side-by-side or server-to-server approach to upgrading because it gives everyone on the development team (including eager software folks) a chance to get comfortable with the new features in the new SQL Server release before committing to it fully, while at the same time, allowing development work and/or bug fixes to continue in the previous SQL Server version.

In addition, it is far easier to roll back to your previous-version SQL Server components because installing a separate instance of SQL Server 2014 leaves the previous version instances intact (unlike upgrading in-place, which replaces them). When you are reasonably comfortable with the new SQL Server release, you can go forward confidently in migrating all of your environments (presuming that if you're leaving previous versions intact, you're also ready to perform the other necessary tasks, such as changing connection strings, server aliases, and so on, to redirect users and applications to the new instances).

The key point to be aware of when performing a side-by-side upgrade either on the same server or separate servers, is that you must manually transfer databases and other supporting objects from the older instance of SQL Server to the new instance of SQL Server 2014. The objects and items that you will need to transfer may include, but not be limited to, the following:

- ▶ Databases and database objects
- ▶ SQL Server configuration settings
- ▶ Security settings and logins
- ▶ SQL Server Agent jobs, alerts, and operators
- ▶ Database maintenance plans
- ▶ SSIS packages
- ▶ Replication publications and subscriptions

▶ Resource Governor resource pools and workload groups

▶ SQL Server policies

▶ Linked server definitions

▶ SQL Server Analysis Services (SSAS) databases

The main steps that you must perform when doing a side-by-side upgrade of SQL Server 2005 SP4, SQL Server 2008 SP3, SQL Server 2008 R2 SP2, or SQL Server 2012 SP1 to SQL Server 2014 are as follows:

1. Install a new instance of SQL Server 2014 on the existing server or on a separate server.

2. Run the SQL Server 2014 Upgrade Advisor against the current instance and resolve any upgrade issues it finds.

3. Suspend any update activity on the legacy instance so that you can make a clean backup or detach the source database.

4. Transfer databases to the instance of SQL Server 2014 using backup and restore or detach/copy/attach method.

5. Migrate additional SQL Server objects such as SQL Server Agent jobs, security settings, logins, configuration settings.

6. Migrate/Upgrade SSIS packages.

7. Run validation scripts and user-acceptance tests against the new instance.

8. Redirect applications and users to the new instance.

9. Maintain your legacy instance for recovery/rollback purposes until you are confident that no problems exist on the new production database instance.

The primary advantage of performing a side-by-side upgrade is that you can take advantage of the new platform, while retaining the legacy server as a fallback if you encounter any showstopper type of problems. This method can also potentially reduce upgrade downtime by having the new server and instances tested, up, and running without affecting the current server and its workloads. You can test and address any problems encountered as a result of the new version without incurring any downtime of the current system.

The downside of performing a side-by-side upgrade is the increased manual intervention required to move databases and other SQL Server objects over to the new instance. It typically requires additional effort to make sure all critical components from the existing system are migrated to the new instance and are functioning as expected.

If you decide to go ahead with a side-by-side installation on the same server, you simply run the SQL Server Installation Center and choose to install a New SQL Server stand-alone installation. (See Chapter 8 for a walk through of an installation of a new SQL Server instance.) When you reach the Instance Configuration screen, you'll typically need to choose the Named instance radio button and install a new named instance of SQL Server 2014, as there is likely already a default instance of SQL Server installed. If a default instance does already exist and you try to install SQL Server 2014 as the default instance, the page will raise a validation error and require you to install it as named instance with a unique instance name.

If you do not already have a default instance of SQL Server installed on the system (that is, all existing instances already installed are named instances, or you are installing SQL Server 2014 on a new server to perform a server-to-server upgrade), you can install SQL Server 2014 as the default instance.

Figure 9.11 shows an example of specifying a new instance name, SQLUNLSHD_2014, during the installation of a new instance. Note that the screen lists any existing installed instances to make it easier for you to make sure you provide a unique instance name for the new installation.

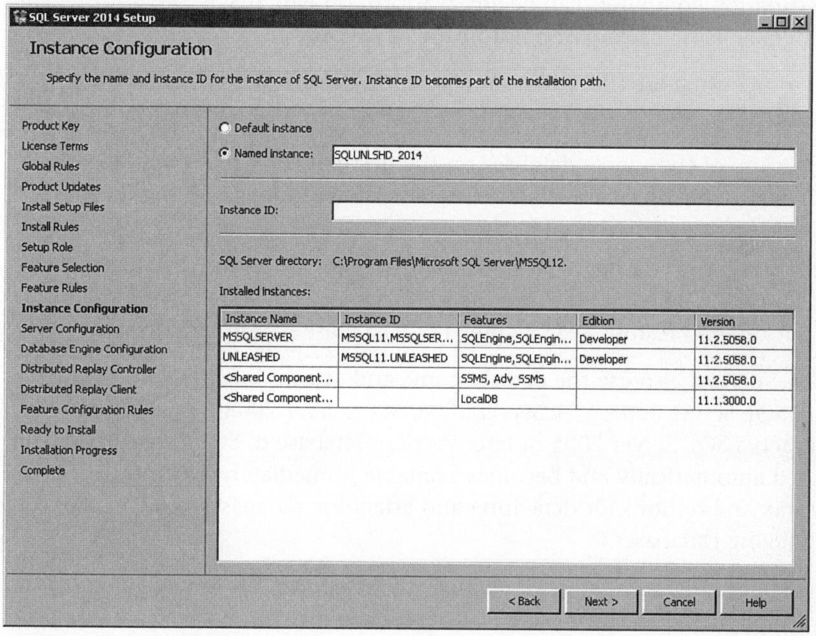

FIGURE 9.11   Installing a new named SQL Server 2014 instance.

After completing the installation of the new SQL Server 2014 instance, you can begin the task of migrating databases and other features and components from the previous version to the new 2014 instance.

Migrating Databases

Once you have your new SQL Server 2014 instance available, it's time for the most important task: migrating your databases to SQL Server 2014. One method of migrating to SQL Server 2014 is by backing up your SQL Server 2005, 2008, 2008 R2, and 2012 databases and restoring them to SQL Server 2014. Another method is to detach, copy, and attach a database from a prior version of SQL Server to SQL Server 2014. When you migrate using either of these methods, the database is upgraded automatically during the attach/restore process.

NOTE

Database backups created by using SQL Server 2000 or earlier are in an incompatible format and cannot be restored in SQL Server 2014. For information on how to migrate a database from versions of SQL Server prior to SQL Server 2005 to SQL Server 2014, see the section, "Upgrading from Pre-SQL Server 2005 Versions," later in this chapter.

When you use backup and restore to copy a database to another instance of SQL Server, the source and destination computers can be any platform on which SQL Server runs. The general steps to upgrade using backup and restore are as follows:

1. Back up the source database that resides on an instance of SQL Server 2005, SQL Server 2008, SQL Server 2008 R2, or SQL Server 2012.

2. Restore the backup of the source database on the destination SQL Server. Restoring the database automatically creates all the database files and upgrades the database.

When restoring the database, you might need to use the MOVE option to relocate the database files to the data path where data files for the new instance are stored. For more information on using backup and restore, see Chapter 11, "Database Backup and Restore."

In SQL Server 2014, you can also use the detach, copy, and attach operations to migrate a user database from SQL Server 2005, SQL Server 2008, SQL Server 2008 R2, or SQL Server 2012. After you attach a SQL Server 2005 or later version database to SQL Server 2014, the database is upgraded automatically and becomes available immediately. For more information on the syntax and options for detaching and attaching databases, see Chapter 20, "Creating and Managing Databases."

Another method of migrating an existing database is by using the SQL Server Copy Database Wizard to copy databases from one SQL Server instance to another.

TIP

Before you use any of the methods described here, Microsoft recommends you run the appropriate DBCC consistency checks to make sure there is no data corruption within the databases to be migrated.

Using the Copy Database Wizard

The Copy Database Wizard is another method you can use to migrate your databases to SQL Server 2014, especially if for some reason, the backup and restore or detach/copy/attach methods are not an option (for example, if you need to keep the source database online during the upgrade/migration). The Copy Database Wizard can perform a logical migration of the database, essentially scripting out and creating each table and database object and then migrating the data. The Copy Data Wizard also provides a mechanism to migrate other SQL Server features such as logins, SQL Agent jobs, and SSIS packages.

To run the Copy Database Wizard using SQL Server Management Studio (SSMS), connect the Object Explorer to your previous SQL Server version's instance. Expand `Databases` and then select and right-click the database you want to copy (or move) into SQL Server 2014. Then select Tasks, Copy Database.

When the wizard's initial Welcome page is displayed, click Next and then select your source server (the SQL Server 2005 or later instance). Click Next again and select your destination server (your newly installed SQL Server 2014 instance). Click Next again to bring up the Select the Transfer Method screen. This screen provides two options for copying or moving your databases to SQL Server 2014:

▶ **Detach and Attach**—This option is the same as the detach/attach method described previously. It's fast, but it takes the database offline during the migration process.

▶ **Use the SQL Server Management Objects (SMO) to Import the Database**—This option is slower, but it keeps the source database online during the process.

NOTE

When you use the detach and attach method, SSIS uses the service account of SQL Server Agent that is running on the SQL Server 2014 (destination) instance. This account must be able to access the file systems of both servers; otherwise, the wizard will fail.

Select the option that works best for you and then click Next. The Select Databases screen appears, and, as Figure 9.12 shows, you should check the Copy (not Move) check boxes for the databases you want to migrate.

CAUTION

After a pre-2008 database is upgraded (in case you choose the Move Database option or you perform an attach or restore and delete the original), it cannot be downgraded back to its former version—not even if you attempt to detach/attach or restore it to SQL 2000 or 2005. Thus, it is especially important to create full backup copies of all your databases before you upgrade. It's also a good idea to back up the entire `Program Files/ Microsoft SQL Server` directory tree.

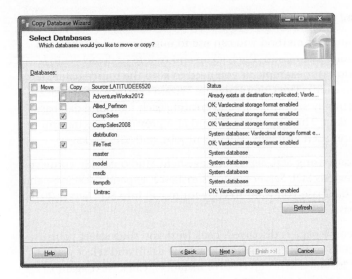

FIGURE 9.12   Selecting the databases to copy to SQL Server 2014.

After you make your database selections, click Next, and the Configure Destination Database screen appears for each database you selected in the previous step. This screen allows you to rename the database on the destination server if you so desire (see Figure 9.13). It also provides options to overwrite any existing databases or MDF (data) and LDF (log) files on the destination server or to create new ones in the folders of your choice. Make your selections and click Next to configure any additional databases. Once all databases have been configured, clicking Next will bring up the Select Server Objects screen.

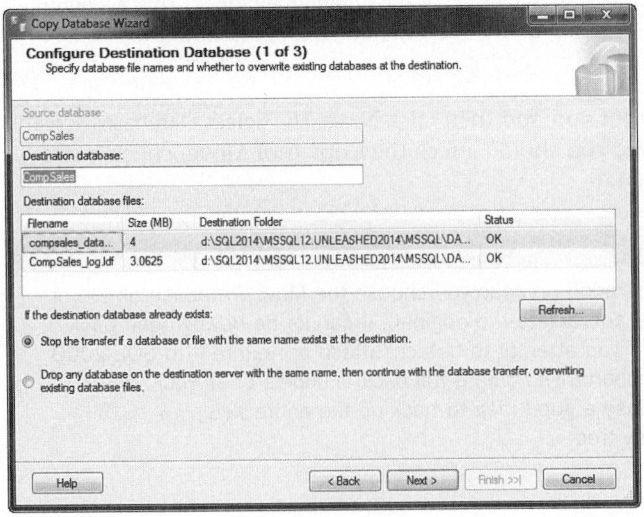

FIGURE 9.13   Copy Database Wizard Configure Destination Database screen.

The Select Server Objects screen (see Figure 9.14) provides some real power because it allows the server-wide objects (those stored in the system databases) to be imported. These objects include user-defined stored procedures residing in `master`, SQL Server Agent jobs, custom user-defined error messages, SSIS packages, any SQL Server logins used by the selected databases, and SQL Server connection endpoints such as database mirror endpoints. You need to click the ellipsis button to choose the specific objects you want to import for any of the items (rather than choosing them all, which is the default).

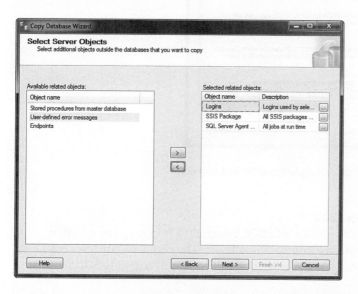

FIGURE 9.14   Importing server-wide objects using the Copy Database Wizard.

When you're finished selecting the objects you want brought over, click Next again. The Configure the Package screen that appears next provides the opportunity to name and save the SSIS package created for migrating the database and to specify how you want to log the messages generated during the transfer (Windows event log or text file). Click Next to present the Schedule the Package screen, which allows you to run the transfer immediately or schedule it to run at a specific time. You are also given an opportunity to specify an SSIS proxy account to use to run the transfer (you should make sure it's an account that has appropriate permissions on both the source and destination servers to ensure a successful transfer).

After you make your scheduling choices, click Next to display the Complete the Wizard screen (see Figure 9.15). Here, you have an opportunity to review the choices you've made on the prior screens. If everything looks okay, click Finish to complete the wizard and start or schedule the Copy Database package.

9

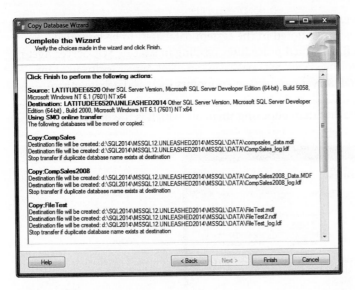

FIGURE 9.15   The Copy Database Complete the Wizard screen.

Setting Database Compatibility Level

Migrating databases from prior versions into SQL Server 2014 brings up the question of compatibility issues and database compatibility levels. The compatibility level is a per-database setting that controls T-SQL execution behavior with regard to SQL Server's versioning system.

The T-SQL execution engine is flexible insofar as it has the capacity to switch between varying, version-dependent behaviors according to the current compatibility-level setting.

When a database is upgraded to SQL Server 2014 from any earlier version of SQL Server, the database retains its existing compatibility level if it is at least compatibility level 100 (SQL Server 2008). When a SQL Server 2005 database is upgraded to SQL Server 2014, the database compatibility level will be changed from 90 to 100.

Compatibility level affects behaviors only for the specified database, not for the entire server. An important point to understand about database compatibility levels, however, is that the database compatibility-level setting is intended to provide only partial backward compatibility with earlier versions of SQL Server. It does not prevent the use of new T-SQL features available in SQL Server 2014 such as any new data types or syntax elements.

The compatibility-level setting is provided primarily as an interim migration aid to work around version differences in the behaviors that are controlled by the relevant compatibility-level setting. Essentially, it allows T-SQL code that may be using deprecated features or expects pre-SQL Server 2014 (level 120) behaviors for certain commands to continue operating as they did in the corresponding version of SQL Server. Using the compatibility-level setting should not be viewed as a permanent solution. It should be used only until the T-SQL code affected by behavioral differences in SQL Server 2014 can be converted to work properly in SQL Server 2014. Then you can use ALTER DATABASE to change the compatibility level to 120.

You can find a full list of the behavioral differences between the compatibility-level settings in the Microsoft Help Viewer article associated with the "ALTER DATABASE Compatibility Level" topic. This option can be used to set the compatibility level for a particular database.

To view the current compatibility level of a database, you can query the compatibility_level column in the sys.databases catalog view:

```
select compatibility_level from sys.databases where name = db_name()
go


compatibility_level
-------------------
100
```

Upgrading In-Place

Now that you've seen how to migrate your databases to SQL Server 2014 by following the side-by-side migration path, let's look at the alternative: upgrading in-place. Unlike a side-by-side install, an in-place upgrade permanently modifies the SQL Server components, data, and metadata objects, and there is no going back. You will likely be more comfortable taking the side-by-side migration path than doing an in-place upgrade, unless a side-by-side migration is not possible because of disk space limitations, you have very few SQL Server features in use, or you are fairly confident about the potential success of the upgrade process because you've done extensive issue resolution with the assistance of the Upgrade Assistant.

The advantages of performing an in-place upgrade include the following:

▶ An in-place upgrade can be easier and faster, especially for small systems, because databases, logins, configuration options, SQL Agent jobs, and so on do not have to be manually transferred to a new server.

▶ Upgrading is mostly an automated process.

▶ The resulting upgraded instance has the same name as the original, so applications continue to connect to the same instance name.

▶ No additional hardware is required because only the one instance is involved, although additional disk space is required by the setup process.

The main disadvantages of performing an in-place upgrade include the following:

▶ You can only upgrade the entire instance or a major SQL Server component. For example, you cannot upgrade only a single database.

▶ You must address all compatibility issues before running the SQL Server 2014 upgrade.

▶ You don't have two instances running side by side to compare before and after upgrade differences.

▶ Rollback of an upgraded instance and its databases can be complex and time-consuming.

> **NOTE**
>
> There are a couple of restrictions to be aware of when running an in-place upgrade. The first is that all SQL Server components will be upgraded together. You cannot upgrade only an instance of the Database Engine without also upgrading the associated Analysis Services component. You also cannot upgrade from a 32-bit instance of SQL Server 2005/2008/2008 R2/2012 to a 64-bit instance of SQL Server 2014, or vice versa. You'll have to perform a side-by-side upgrade to change platforms.

If you decide to go forward with an in-place upgrade of the Database Engine, it is strongly recommended that you first do the following:

▶ Create full, verified backups of your existing SQL Server databases.

▶ Run the appropriate DBCC consistency checks (for example, DBCC CHECKDB and DBCC CHECKFILEGROUP).

▶ Make sure the system databases on your pre-2014 instances (for example, master, msdb, tempdb, and model) are all set to auto-grow and have sufficient free space to grow.

▶ Disable any startup stored procedures that get kicked off when the SQL Server service starts.

▶ Quit all applications and services that access the SQL Server being upgraded as the upgrade might fail if applications are connected to the instance during the upgrade.

▶ Disable database replication and empty the replication log.

After you perform all these actions, you are ready to begin the upgrade process.

Upgrading the Database Engine

You perform an in-place upgrade by running the SQL Server Installation Center. On the Installation page, you can invoke the Upgrade Wizard to upgrade from SQL Server 2005, 2008, 2008 R2, or 2012 (see Figure 9.16). The major steps performed by the SQL Server 2014 Installer program when performing an in-place upgrade include the following:

1. First, the SQL Server 2014 Setup prerequisites (Microsoft .NET Framework 3.5 Service Pack 1 (SP1) or a later version, SQL Server Native Client, and so on) are installed.

2. The Installer checks for issues that would prevent an upgrade. If it finds any, it will list them, and you must fix them and restart the upgrade process.

3. Setup installs the required SQL Server 2014 executables and support files.

4. Setup stops the legacy SQL Server service.

5. SQL Server 2014 updates the selected instance databases and components.

6. Setup removes the prior version executables and support files.

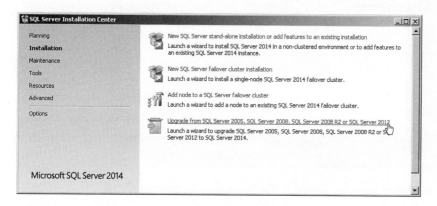

FIGURE 9.16   Running the Upgrade Wizard from the Installation Center.

After prompting for the Product Key, running the Global Rules check, Checking for Product Updates, installing the Setup Support Files, and running an Upgrade Rules check, the Upgrade Wizard essentially runs the installation process. (The installation process and all its screens are described in Chapter 8 under the heading, "Install Screens, Step by Step.") The key differences between running a new install versus an upgrade is that during the upgrade process, you choose an existing default or named instance on the Select Instance screen (see Figure 9.17).

After selecting the instance to upgrade, you see the Feature Selection page. The features to be upgraded are preselected. You cannot change the features to be upgraded, and you cannot add features during an upgrade operation. To add features, you need to run the Installation Center again after the upgrade operation is complete.

After reviewing the selections on the Feature Selection page, step through the Instance Configuration and Server Configuration screens, making changes as necessary. On the Instance Configuration page, you can specify the Instance ID for the instance of SQL Server. By default, the instance name is the same as the Instance ID. The Instance ID is used to identify the installation directories and registry keys for your instance of SQL Server. To specify a different value for the instance ID (and thus have the upgrade process install to a different folder), specify a value in the Instance ID text box.

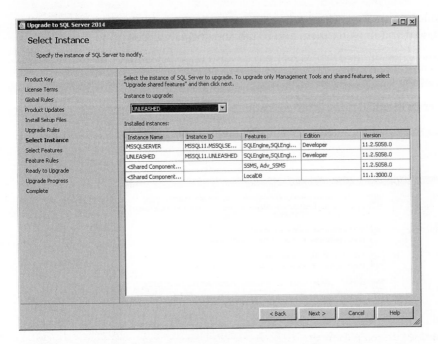

FIGURE 9.17   The Select Instance screen in the SQL Server Installation Center.

On the Server Configuration page, the default service accounts are displayed for SQL Server services. The actual services that can be configured on this page depend on which features are being upgraded. Typically, the authentication and login information are carried forward from the previous instance of SQL Server.

Next, you are presented with options for upgrading your full-text catalogs. Three options are available for upgrading your existing full-text catalogs:

▶ **Import**—This is the default option. SQL Server imports the data from the old index structures to the new structures without resetting or rebuilding the indexes. Because of this, an imported full-text catalog does not use the new and enhanced word breakers introduced in SQL Server 2014, so you might want to rebuild your full-text catalogs eventually if not during the upgrade.

▶ **Rebuild**—With this option, SQL Server 2014 will rebuild all full-text indexes, triggering a full population using the new and improved word breakers, but this rebuilding of indexes can take a while and could be very CPU and memory intensive.

▶ **Reset**—When you choose this option, the SQL Server full-text catalog files are removed, but the metadata for full-text catalogs and full-text indexes is retained. In addition, full-text indexes are disabled for change tracking, and crawls are not started automatically. The catalog remains empty until you manually issue a full population after the upgrade completes.

After choosing your full-text upgrade option, the Feature Rules check is run to validate your system configuration with the options and features chosen during the upgrade process. If all the rules pass, the Installer will auto-advance to the Ready to Upgrade page where you can review the upgrade operation. This page also displays the path to the upgrade configuration file, which is useful for setting up and performing unattended upgrades from the command line, as discussed later in this chapter. If everything looks okay, click Upgrade to begin the upgrade process. The upgrade process automatically upgrades all objects that are common to all databases, including the following:

▶ Tables, views, indexes, and constraints

▶ Stored procedures, functions, and triggers

▶ User-defined types, rules, and defaults

▶ Logins, users, and permissions

▶ Database diagrams

You can monitor the upgrade progress on the Upgrade Progress screen. Depending on your hardware configuration and the features to be upgraded, the upgrade operation can take from approximately 30 minutes to a few hours. The databases on the instance being upgraded remain unavailable until the upgrade is complete.

When the upgrade finishes, it displays the upgrade status of each component and also provides the location of the upgrade log. A system restart may be required in some cases if any upgraded components were in use during the upgrade process.

When your upgrade of the Database Engine is complete, it is recommended that you perform the following on all databases (also recommended for side-by-side migration):

▶ Repopulate your full-text catalogs if you chose not to rebuild them during the upgrade.

▶ Run the DBCC UPDATEUSAGE command for all databases to update statistics and page and row counts.

▶ Reregister your server in SSMS.

Installing Product Updates (Slipstreaming) During Upgrades

If you are upgrading to SQL Server 2014, you may want to include any available service packs and/or the latest cumulative update. Prior to SQL Server 2008 R2, this meant running the upgrade and then running any service pack and cumulative update separately. This process was tedious and time consuming. Fortunately, the SQL Server 2014 Installer provides the Product Updates feature. Product Updates allows you to include the latest publicly available product updates with the main product installation media so that the original media and the update are installed at the same time.

Microsoft also makes available installation media that already includes the latest service pack. This is essentially a prebuilt slipstream installation where the service pack is already included with the installation media so that it doesn't need to be downloaded first.

Near the beginning of the installation, if any updates are available, you'll be presented with the Product Updates screen. The installer will check online for any available service packs or updates. If you select to include SQL Server product updates, when you click Next the installer will automatically download the updates and incorporate them into the upgrade files.

If the system you are installing on is behind a firewall without access to the Internet, or you want to include a cumulative update when performing the upgrade, you can download the service pack or cumulative update manually and, after extracting it, copy it to a folder that is accessible by the SQL Server install utility. You can then invoke the installer from the command line and specify the directory where the cumulative update resides with the /UpdateSource option along with the Action="Upgrade" option. For example, if you copied the updates to the C:\SQL2014 folder, the command to execute is as follows:

```
setup.exe /ACTION="Upgrade" /UpdateEnabled="true" /UpdateSource="C:\sql2014"
```

This command invokes the SQL Server installer and begins the SQL Server upgrade process. After getting past the Global Rules page, it will display the Product Updates page if any product updates exist in the specified UpdateSource folder with the downloaded updates listed.

Click on Next to continue the upgrade, and the installer will extract the update or service pack and integrate it with the upgrade process.

Upgrading Using a Configuration File

If you need to upgrade multiple SQL Server 2014 instances, you'll likely want to do so without having to run the Installation Center utility each time and manually select the same options over and over. Fortunately, you can run an upgrade via the Installation Center using a configuration file. Using a configuration file, you have a couple options for how you run the upgrade: using the Upgrade Wizard with options prefilled by the configuration file or as a fully automated and unattended installation from the command line. If you run using the GUI with the options prefilled by the configuration file, you have the opportunity to review and change options along the way as necessary.

NOTE

If you've never run a SQL Server installation using the setup feature of SQL Server, you should refer to the "Installing SQL Server Using a Configuration File" section in Chapter 8 for a detailed description of the process and options available.

Following are a few of the parameters relevant to running an upgrade using a configuration file:

▶ /ACTION=UPGRADE—Specifies that you are running an upgrade.

▶ /INSTANCENAME—Specifies the SQL Server instance to be upgraded. For the default instance, you use the special value MSSQLSERVER.

▶ /CONFIGURATIONFILE—Specifies the configuration file to use for the upgrade.

▶ /INSTANCEDIR—Specifies a nondefault installation directory for shared components to be upgraded.

▶ /UIMODE—Specifies whether to present only the minimum number of dialog boxes during setup. Normal presents all setup dialogs; AutoAdvance skips nonessential dialog boxes.

▶ /FTUPGRADEOPTION—Specifies the full-text catalog upgrade option. Valid values are REBUILD, RESET, and IMPORT.

▶ /UPDATEENABLED—Specifies whether the installer should check for and include product updates during the install.

To create an upgrade configuration file, run the Upgrade Wizard as described previously and follow it all the way through to the Ready to Install page where the location of the generated Configuration.ini file is specified. At this point, you can click the Cancel button if you don't want to actually perform the upgrade. Then copy the Configuration.ini file to another location so you can make any necessary edits to it.

To run an upgrade using a configuration file, you need to run the setup.exe program, which can be found at the root level of the installation media. If you want to override any of the values in the configuration file or provide values not specified in the configuration file, you can provide additional command-line parameters. For example, to avoid having to enter the service account passwords during the installation, you can enter them on the command line using the password parameters to config.exe. Following is a sample execution to upgrade the default instance and specify the account and password for Reporting Services and the service account for Integration Services:

```
Setup.exe /q /ACTION=upgrade /INSTANCENAME=MSSQLSERVER
/RSUPGRADEDATABASEACCOUNT="myRSaccount" /RSUPGRADEPASSWORD="myRSpassword"
/ISSVCAccount="NT Authority\Network Service" /IACCEPTSQLSERVERLICENSETERMS
```

Note also that the preceding example specifies the /q parameter, which runs the upgrade in Full Quiet mode, which is intended for running unattended installations. With this switch provided, Setup runs without any user interface. Another option is to run with the /QS switch, which shows progress via the GUI but does not accept any input and displays no error messages if encountered.

Upgrading from Pre-SQL Server 2005 Versions

SQL Server 2014 supports upgrading from SQL Server 2005 SP4 and later versions. Upgrading directly from SQL Server 2000 or earlier versions is not supported. The only migration path available is to first migrate your SQL Server 2000 (or earlier) databases to a supported upgrade version, such as SQL Server 2005 SP4 or SQL Server 2008 SP3, and then upgrade from one of these versions to SQL Server 2014.

If you have a SQL Server 2005 SP4 instance available, the easiest way to upgrade your SQL Server 2000 or earlier databases is to detach them from the source server and then attach the databases to an instance running SQL Server 2005 SP4. When the database is attached, it is upgraded to SQL Server 2005, and then you can upgrade the database to SQL Server 2014.

Upgrading Other SQL Server Components

Now that you've seen how to migrate databases, jobs, logins, custom error messages, and full-text catalogs, let's discuss how you can migrate the rest of your SQL Server objects. First, let's look at Analysis Services.

Upgrading Analysis Services

The following sections highlight some important considerations you should be aware of when upgrading Analysis Services.

Upgrading SQL Server Analysis Services

You can upgrade an existing instance of SQL Server 2005, 2008, 2008 R2, or 2012 Analysis Services to SQL Server 2014 Analysis Services using the Upgrade Wizard. The wizard automatically migrates existing databases from the old instance to the new instance. The metadata and binary data is compatible between SQL Server 2005/2008/2008 R2/2012 and SQL Server 2014, so the data is retained after you upgrade. You do not have to manually migrate the data. To upgrade an existing instance of Analysis Services, run the Upgrade Wizard and specify the name of the existing Analysis Services instance as the name of the new AS instance. The AS databases are upgraded automatically.

> **NOTE**
>
> When upgrading from a 64-bit edition of SQL Server to a 64-bit edition of SQL Server 2014, you must upgrade Analysis Services before you upgrade the Database Engine.

Upgrading Reporting Services

SQL Server 2014 supports upgrading from the following earlier editions of Reporting Services:

- ► SQL Server 2005 Reporting Services
- ► SQL Server 2008 Reporting Services

▶ SQL Server 2008 R2 Reporting Services

▶ SQL Server 2012 Reporting Services

You can choose to perform an in-place upgrade or migrate a Reporting Services Installation to SQL Server 2014. You can run the Upgrade Advisor tool on the Report Server computer to determine any issues that might prevent a successful upgrade. Known upgrade issues currently include the following:

▶ There is no support for earlier versions of the Reporting Services WMI provider because the Reporting Services WMI provider is not backward compatible with previous versions.

▶ You cannot use the SQL Server 2014 Reporting Services WMI provider with earlier versions of Reporting Services.

Performing an In-Place Upgrade of Reporting Services

If you've run the Upgrade Advisor and it doesn't report any issues that would prevent a successful upgrade (or you've addressed any issues it raises), you can perform an in-place upgrade of any instance of SQL Server 2005 SP4 Reporting Services, SQL Server 2008 SP3 Reporting Services, SQL Server 2008 R2 SP2, or SQL Server 2012 SP1 Reporting Services.

Before upgrading Reporting Services, you should first back up the following:

▶ The symmetric key (by using the RSKEYMGMT tool)

▶ Your Report Server databases

▶ Configuration files: Rsreportserver.config, Rswebapplication.config, Rssvrpolicy.config, Rsmgrpolicy.config, Reportingservicesservice.exe.config, Web.config (for both the Report Server and Report Manager ASP.NET applications), and Machine.config (for ASP.NET if you modified it for Report Server operations)

▶ Any customizations to existing Reporting Services virtual directories in IIS

▶ Your reports

To upgrade Reporting Services, run the Installation Center and select your existing instance for upgrade at the appropriate screen. The Installation Center upgrades the instance in-place, including all its components and any published reports and snapshots.

Upgrading Reporting Services also requires updates to your Report Server databases. Because the Report Server database schema can change with each new release of Reporting Services, it is required that the database version match the version of the Report Server instance you are using. In most cases, a Report Server database can be upgraded automatically with no specific action on your part. The following list identifies all the conditions under which a Report Server database is upgraded:

▶ After a Reporting Services instance is upgraded, the database schema is automatically upgraded after service startup, and the Report Server determines that the database schema version does not match the server version.

▶ At service startup, the Report Server checks the database schema version to verify that it matches the server version. If the database schema version is an older version, it is automatically upgraded to the schema version that is required by the Report Server. Automatic upgrade is especially useful if you restored or attached an older Report Server database. A message is entered in the Report Server trace log file indicating that the database schema version was upgraded.

▶ The Reporting Services Configuration tool upgrades a local or remote Report Server database when you select an older version to use with a newer Report Server instance, as long as it is a native instance of SSRS (i.e., it is not SharePoint Integrated). In this case, you must confirm the upgrade action before it happens.

> **NOTE**
>
> The Reporting Services Configuration tool no longer provides a separate Upgrade button or upgrade script. Those features are obsolete starting in SQL Server 2008 due to the automatic upgrade feature of the Report Server service.

After the database schema is updated, you cannot roll back the upgrade to an earlier version. Always back up the Report Server database in case you need to re-create a previous installation.

If you are unable to perform an in-place upgrade of your existing installation for any reason, your other option is to install a new instance of SQL Server 2014 Reporting Services and then migrate your Report Server database and configuration files to the new instance.

Migrating to Reporting Services 2014

The migration process for Reporting Services includes a combination of manual and automated steps. The following tasks are required to perform a Reporting Services migration:

▶ Back up your Report Server databases, applications, and configuration files.

▶ Back up the encryption key.

▶ If it is not installed already, install a new instance of SQL Server 2014.

▶ Move your Report Server database(s) from your existing SQL Server 2005 SP4 or later installation to your new installation using the detach/copy/attach or backup/restore method.

▶ Move any custom report items, assemblies, or extensions to the new installation.

▶ Configure the Report Server.

▶ Edit the RSReportServer.config file to include any custom settings from your previous installation.

▶ Optionally, configure custom Access Control Lists (ACLs) for the new Reporting Services Windows service group.

▶ Remove unused applications and tools after you have confirmed that the new instance is fully operational.

When you are backing up the Report Server configuration files, the files to back up include

▶ `Rsreportserver.config`

▶ `Rswebapplication.config`

▶ `Rssvrpolicy.config`

▶ `Rsmgrpolicy.config`

▶ `Reportingservicesservice.exe.config`

▶ `Web.config` for both the Report Server and Report Manager ASP.NET applications

▶ `Machine.config` for ASP.NET if you modified it for Report Server operations

During the install of your new instance of Reporting Services, when you reach the Reporting Services screen, you need to be sure to select the Install but Do Not Configure option. After moving your Report Server databases, launch the new Reporting Services Configuration tool and select the Report Server database that you've moved from the previous installation to automatically upgrade it. Then restore your backed-up encryption key.

Just as with an in-place upgrade, to upgrade the reports themselves, all you need to do is open them in the Report Designer, which automatically converts them to the new Report Definition Language format.

After you successfully migrate your Report Server to a SQL Server 2014 Reporting Services instance, you might want to perform the following steps to remove programs and files that are no longer necessary:

▶ Uninstall the previous version of Reporting Services if it's no longer needed.

▶ Remove IIS if you no longer need it on the computer (it's no longer needed as of Reporting Services 2008).

▶ Remove any files or objects not deleted by uninstalling Reporting Services such as any virtual directories for Report Manager and the report server, Report Server Log file, the old Report Server database, and any Report Server service accounts.

Upgrading SSIS Packages

When you upgrade an instance of SQL Server 2005, 2008, 2008 R2, or 2012 to SQL Server 2014, the new SQL Server 2014 SSIS files, service, and tools are installed, and your SSIS packages are moved into the new system catalogs, but your existing SQL Server Integration Services packages are not automatically upgraded to the package format that SQL Server

2014 Integration Services uses. You have to manually upgrade your SSIS packages created in prior versions.

There are multiple methods to upgrade SQL Server packages from SQL Server 2005 through 2012. Some of the methods are only temporary. For others, the upgrade is permanent. Table 9.2 lists each of the upgrade methods and whether the upgrade is temporary or permanent.

TABLE 9.2   SSIS Upgrade Methods

Upgrade Method	Type of Upgrade
Using the `dtexec` utility installed with SQL Server 2014	The package upgrade and script migration are temporary. The changes are not saved.
Open a SQL Server 2005 or later package file in SQL Server 2014 Data Tools (SSDT)	The package upgrade and script migration are permanent if you save the package; otherwise, it is only temporary.
Adding a SQL Server 2005 or later package to an existing project in SQL Server 2014 Data Tools	The package upgrade and script migration are permanent.
Using the SSIS Package Upgrade Wizard	The package upgrade and script migration are permanent.

The SSIS Package Upgrade Wizard is the recommended approach for upgrading your SSIS packages. Because you can configure the wizard to back up your original packages, you can continue to use the original packages if you experience upgrade difficulties. You can run the SSIS Package Upgrade Wizard from SQL Server Management Studio, from SQL Server Data Tools, or from the command prompt.

TIP

If you haven't already, it is recommended that you run the Upgrade Advisor to review your SSIS packages before you attempt to upgrade them. The Upgrade Advisor will report issues that you might encounter when migrating your existing Integration Services packages to the new package format that SQL Server 2014 uses. For more information on using the Upgrade Advisor, see the section on using the Upgrade Advisor earlier in this chapter.

To run the wizard from SQL Server Management Studio, connect to Integration Services, expand the `Stored Packages` node, right-click the `File System` or `MSDB` node, and then click Upgrade Packages. At the command prompt, run the `SSISUpgrade.exe` file from the `C:\Program Files\Microsoft SQL Server\120\DTS\Binn` folder. To run the wizard from SQL Server Data Tools, create or open an Integration Services project and in the Solution Explorer, right-click the SSIS Packages node and then click Upgrade All Packages to upgrade all the packages under that node.

> **NOTE**
>
> If you open an SSIS project that contains SQL Server 2005 SSIS or SQL Server 2008 SSIS packages, the SSIS Package Upgrade Wizard will be launched automatically.

In SQL Server 2014, the names of some providers have changed and require different values in the connection strings for your SQL Server 2005 or SQL Server 2008 SSIS packages. To update the connection strings in your SQL Server 2005 and SQL Server 2008 packages, use one of the following procedures:

▶ Use the SSIS Package Upgrade Wizard to upgrade the package and select the Update connection strings to use new provider names option.

▶ In SQL Server Data Tools (SSDT), on the General page of the Options dialog box, select the Update connection strings to use the new provider names option.

▶ In SQL Server Data Tools (SSDT), open the package and manually change the text of the ConnectionString property.

Migrating DTS Packages

Support for running DTS packages is not provided with SQL Server 2014, and there is no method available for migrating DTS packages to SSIS. If you are still using DTS packages and want to bring the functionality into SQL Server 2014, you have the following two options for migrating DTS packages:

▶ Migrate the packages first to SQL Server 2005 SSIS or SQL Server 2008 SSIS using the DTS Package Migration Wizard available with those versions and then upgrade the SSIS packages generated by these tools to SQL Server 2014 Integration Services using the SQL Server 2014 SSIS Package Upgrade Wizard.

▶ Re-create your DTS packages from scratch using SQL Server 2014 SSIS.

Summary

Now that you've taken in a great deal of information to help your organization transition to SQL Server 2014, it's time to put that knowledge to work by actively taking the plunge.

If you need even more documentation, you can look to the many other chapters in this book and even more resources on the Web that can assist you. Of course, there's an abundance of content on Microsoft's website (after all, it's in Microsoft's interests that customers upgrade to SQL Server 2014), including webcasts, TechNet, and online learning courses available to MSDN subscribers.

When your new environment is ready to go, you can move on to Chapter 10, "Client Installation and Configuration," to learn how to get your clients up and running with your new installation of SQL Server 2014.

Client Installation and Configuration

SQL Server 2014 offers a robust client/server architecture that provides speed and security, simple configuration and maintenance, and enhanced management capabilities.

This chapter contains the latest information on how to install, configure, and connect to SQL Server 2014 from the client side, and it offers key server-side insights that will help provide a complete understanding of what you need to do to establish a database connection.

What's New in Client Installation and Configuration

Client installation and configuration in SQL Server 2014 is very similar to SQL Server 2012. The SQL Server Native Client (abbreviated SNAC or SNAC11) net-library introduced with SQL Server 2012 is the same one distributed with SQL Server 2014—there is no new version. This native client (SNAC11) is a single dynamic link library (DLL) containing both the SQL Server OLE DB provider and SQL Server ODBC driver. It builds on the data access component distribution strategy introduced in SQL Server 2005 that was simply called SQL Native Client (SNAC or SNAC9). The SNAC11 driver contains features such as support for AlwaysOn, SQL Server Express LocalDB, Azure SQL Database, and performance improvements for developers.

NOTE

Several versions of the SNAC library were released with different versions of SQL Server. Each version has a number associated with it that can be used to easily reference it. SNAC9 is associated with SQL Server 2005. SNAC10 is associated with SQL Server 2008 and SQL Server 2008 R2. The version that ships with SQL Server 2014 is generally referred to as the SQL Server Native Client in the Microsoft documentation. It can be abbreviated as SNAC11 and will be referred to this way in the rest of this book.

The good news is that your applications can continue to access SQL Server 2014 with the older SNAC components. SNAC9, SNAC10, and SNAC11 can be used on the same client system. SNAC9 and SNAC10 are not able to reference new features in SQL Server 2012 and 2014, however, so you have to upgrade to SNAC11 to gain access to them.

A big change in SQL Server 2014 is the deprecation of the ODBC driver in SQL Server Native client. The SQL Server 2012 version is the final version. Microsoft ODBC Driver 11 for SQL Server, included with SQL Server 2014, is its replacement.

A noteworthy addition to SNAC11, the SQL Server ODBC driver for Linux allows direct access to SQL Server from applications that run on 64-bit SUSE Enterprise Linux, and 64-bit Red Hat Enterprise Linux. Two other drivers were updated in 2012 so that they support SQL Server 2012 features. The Microsoft JDBC driver 4.1 provides access to SQL Server from any Java application and allows access to new features in SQL Server 2012 such as AlwaysOn. Updates were also made to the PHP driver for SQL Server. The PHP driver for SQL Server (version 3.1) includes improvements for developing PHP/SQL Server applications and also provides access to the latest features.

One final change in SQL Server 2014 that is worth noting is the deprecation of the SQL Server Native Client OLE DB provider. This provider is still available in SQL Server 2012 but not in SQL Server 2014. The version that ships with SQL Server 2012 provides access to its latest features, but it will not be updated.

Client/Server Networking Considerations

Before we delve into the features on the client side in SQL Server, it's important to make note of a few server-side features. This information will help you gain an understanding of which networking features are initially configured on the server (after an installation or upgrade) as well as how incoming connections are dealt with. Such knowledge can be invaluable in diagnosing connectivity issues.

If you've been following along chapter by chapter, you've learned how to install or upgrade an instance of SQL Server 2014. To get your clients up and running fast, you must be sure the Database Engine is listening for them.

The following sections describe how to set up the server's basic network configuration, including configuring it to accept remote connections, learning which protocols it supports, and understanding how it listens for and responds to client requests.

Server Network Protocols

The first and most basic step after a SQL Server installation or upgrade is to make sure the appropriate network protocols are configured on the server.

> **NOTE**
>
> Note that the term server is used here to refer to an instance of the SQL Server 2014 Database Engine. The term client is used generally to mean any program that needs to communicate with a server. The server and client may reside on the same physical machine (especially when using SQL Server LocalDb, Compact, and Express Editions).

First, you should ensure that the protocols your clients once used to connect to SQL Server 7, 2000 or 2005 (or that your clients would like to use) are still supported by SQL Server 2014 and are configured.

You might be surprised to learn that the following protocols that were supported as recently as SQL Server 2000 are not supported by SQL Server 2014:

- ▶ AppleTalk
- ▶ Banyan VINES
- ▶ Multiprotocol
- ▶ NW Link IPX/SPX
- ▶ VIA

If you were using these protocols and you've upgraded from an earlier version of SQL Server, your clients are no longer able to connect. Following are the only protocols that SQL Server 2014 supports:

- ▶ Named pipes
- ▶ Shared memory
- ▶ TCP/IP

If you were using any of these protocols and you just upgraded, Setup copies your pre-upgrade settings over to SQL Server 2014, including the enabled state, IP addresses, TCP ports, pipe names, and so on. Clients can simply test their connections to be sure the upgrade was successful, and in most cases, no changes need to be made.

10

> **NOTE**
>
> The Shared memory protocol works only for connections both to and from the same machine hosting the Database Engine. Shared memory is used by client tools such as SQL Server Management Studio (SSMS) and SQLCMD, and it's also a good choice for use by locally running custom applications because it is secure by design. (It is the default protocol used by local applications that do not specify otherwise.)

All remote connections to SQL Server are thus disabled by default. The following is an extremely common client-side error message illustrating connection failure due to disabled remote connectivity:

```
A network-related or instance-specific error occurred while
establishing a connection to SQL Server. The server was not found
or was not accessible. Verify that the instance name is correct and
that SQL Server is configured to allow remote connections.
```

The exact wording of this message varies slightly, depending on the particular client or connection method used. The same type of error also occurs when the Database Engine service is stopped.

In SQL Server 2014, remote connections must be enabled for each network protocol on which you want the server to communicate. This is easily accomplished using the SQL Server Configuration Manager (SSCM) application. In SSCM, you expand SQL Server Network Configuration and then select the Protocols entry for the SQL Server instance that you want to configure. In the Details pane, right-click on one of the available protocols (for example, Named Pipes) and select Enable to allow connections for this protocol (see Figure 10.1). SSCM serves many purposes and is discussed in detail later in this chapter.

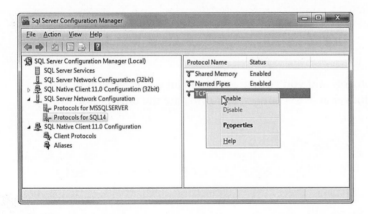

FIGURE 10.1   Enabling remote connections over TCP/IP using SSCM.

When the protocol is enabled, SQL Server is configured to listen for connections from clients using the same protocol. You must restart the SQL Server instance for the changes to take effect and for SQL Server to actually start listening for connections. You can verify that SQL Server is listening on the protocol that you have enabled by looking at the SQL Server error log. Each time the SQL Server instance is restarted, messages are written to the log indicating which protocols it is listening on. The following sample error log messages show what SQL Server is listening for:

```
Server is listening on [ 'any' <ipv4> 1719].
Server named pipe provider is ready to accept connection on
[ \\.\pipe\MSSQL$SQL14\sql\query ].
```

SQL Server listens on all configured protocols simultaneously, giving no preference or priority to any. This is in contrast to the explicitly prioritized manner in which clients attempt to connect via all configured protocols. The client configuration is discussed in detail later in this chapter.

> **NOTE**
>
> In SQL Server 2005, the Surface Area Configuration (SAC) tool also could be used to allow remote connections and to configure the protocols on which they communicate. The SAC tool was removed in SQL Server 2008, so you need to look to the SSCM to configure your protocols.

The Server Endpoint Layer

A networking feature in SQL Server 2014 adds an additional layer to the client/server network structure: Tabular Data Stream (TDS) endpoints. When you install (or upgrade to) SQL Server 2014, a default system endpoint is created on the server for each available protocol on the server. These endpoints cannot be dropped, and they are created regardless of whether the protocol is disabled or otherwise unavailable.

> **NOTE**
>
> The term endpoint in this context refers to the combination of a protocol selection, one or more IP addresses (or pipe names), and any associated port numbers.

These are the default system endpoints:

- ▶ TSQL Local Machine (for shared memory)
- ▶ TSQL Named Pipes
- ▶ TSQL Default TCP
- ▶ Dedicated Admin Connection (also known as the DAC)

You can view these endpoints and check their status by executing the following T-SQL statement:

```
Use Master
GO
SELECT * FROM sys.endpoints WHERE principal_id = 1
```

10

By default, all users are granted access to these endpoints (except the DAC, which is only for members of the sysadmin role). Administrators can create new endpoints on the server to increase connection security by stopping (or disabling) the default system endpoints and then creating new user-defined endpoints that only specific clients can access. (Creating a new system endpoint automatically revokes permission on the default endpoint of the same protocol to the public group.)

> **NOTE**
>
> Only one named pipe and one shared memory endpoint can exist per instance, but multiple TCP endpoints (with different port and address settings) can coexist.

Each endpoint communicates with clients via TDS packets, which are formatted on the server side by SNAC and on the client side by SNAC or another of the net-libraries.

Administrators have the option of stopping and starting endpoints while sessions are still active, preventing new connections from being made while still supporting existing ones.

An administrator can grant or revoke endpoint access to specific users or groups (for example, preventing backdoor access through client tools). It is therefore important for clients to know that this structure exists and to learn how they receive permission to connect to endpoints through a server-side process known as *provisioning*.

Client Access Provisioning

There are three fairly straightforward rules of access provisioning. If any one of these rules is met by an incoming client, that client may access the endpoint. If none are met, the client is denied access. These are the rules:

▶ If the client specifies an IP address and a TCP port that match those of a specific endpoint, the client may connect to it if the client has permission to do so.

▶ If only the TCP port specified by the client matches that of a specific endpoint, and the endpoint is configured to listen on all IP addresses, the client may connect to it if the client has permission to do so.

▶ If neither the TCP port nor IP address is specified, but the default endpoint for the protocol is enabled, the client may attempt to connect to the endpoint.

> **NOTE**
>
> If the endpoint to which access is successfully provisioned is currently stopped, or if the user does not have permission to connect to it, no further endpoints are tried, and the client cannot continue.

For example, let's say a server has three TCP/IP endpoints defined:

▶ The default (TSQL Default TCP), which listens on all IP addresses and Port 1433 (a default SQL Server 2014 instance)

▶ A user-created endpoint called TCP_UserCreated 101_91, configured to listen on internal IP address 192.168.1.101 and Port 91

▶ A second user-created endpoint, called TCP_UserCreated Any_91, which is configured to listen on all IP addresses and Port 91

A client attempts to connect specifically to 192.168.1.101:91. Because this is an exact address and port match, the client can try to connect to TCP_UserCreated 101_91. Having an exact address and port match meets the first provisioning rule.

A second client attempts to connect to any IP address on Port 91. Because there is no exact address match, the client cannot attempt to connect to TCP_UserCreated 101_91. However, the client can attempt to connect to TCP_UserCreated Any_91 because it is configured to listen on all IP addresses. This meets the second provisioning rule.

A third client attempts to connect on any port and any address. If TSQL Default TCP is started, the client is granted permission to attempt to connect. This meets the third provisioning rule.

NOTE

Settings such as IP addresses and TCP ports are used to implicitly connect to specific endpoints. These values are specified by clients in connection strings, data source names (DSNs), and server aliases, all of which are discussed later in this chapter in the "Client Configuration" section.

TIP

If at any time you want to discover which protocol and endpoint a connected client is currently using, you can run the following T-SQL to list the current connections and related protocols. The session_id identifies the server process ID (SPID), and an additional WHERE clause can be added to the SELECT statement that selects only the SPID you are interested in:

```
SELECT name, net_transport, session_id, e.endpoint_id
FROM sys.dm_exec_connections d
JOIN sys.endpoints e
ON e.endpoint_id = d.endpoint_id;
GO
-- T-SQL Output:
name                    net_transport    session_id    endpoint_id
TSQL Default TCP    TCP    51            4
```

The following is an example of the client-side error message that results if the TSQL Default TCP endpoint is stopped and you try to connect to it:

```
A connection was successfully established with the server, but then an error
occurred during the login process
```

Now that you know a bit about endpoints, let's go a bit deeper and explore how client connections are facilitated on the server.

The Role of SQL Browser

You might be surprised to learn that when clients try to connect to SQL Server 2014, their first network access is made over UDP Port 1434 to the SQL Browser service.

NOTE

Regardless of the encryption status of the connection itself, login credentials are always encrypted when passed to SQL Server 2014 (to foil any malicious packet sniffing). If a certificate signed by an external authority (such as VeriSign) is not installed on the server, SQL Server automatically generates a self-signed certificate for use in encrypting login credentials.

SQL Browser is the upgrade to the old SQL Server Resolution Protocol (SSRP), and its job is to hand out instance names, version numbers, and connection information for each (non-hidden) instance of the Database Engine (and Analysis Services) residing on a server—not only for SQL Server 2014 instances, but for SQL Server 2000, 2005, and 2008 instances as well.

When clients connect by name, SQL Browser searches for that name in its list and then hands out the connection data for that instance. It can also provide a list of available servers and help make connections to the correct server instance or to make a connection on the dedicated administrator connection (DAC).

Ports, Pipes, and Instances

Default instances of SQL Server 2014 are automatically configured (just as in previous editions) to listen on all IP addresses and TCP Port 1433.

Named instances, on the other hand, are automatically configured to listen on all IP addresses, using dynamic TCP port numbers that change when the Database Engine is restarted. (Most often, these change only when the port number last used by the service is in use by a different application.)

If the SQL Browser service is not running, the client might need to provide additional connection information to be able to connect to SQL Server. The additional connection information includes the specific port or pipe that the SQL Server instance may be listening on. The only exception to this is if the server is listening on the default port of 1433. Otherwise, the client must specify the port when connecting with TCP/IP. When dynamic ports are used, the port number can change at any given time and cause your clients to have to change their port to match the new server port.

SQL Browser, therefore, is configured to auto-start on servers that contain one or more named instances so that clients can connect by simply providing the server name. The complexity associated with providing additional port or pipe information is avoided when the SQL Browser service is running. SQL Browser is also required for enumerating the server lists used to connect with client tools such as SMSS.

> **NOTE**
>
> If named instances have fixed port numbers known to clients, or if a pipe name is well known, SQL Browser is not required to connect.

> **NOTE**
>
> For named pipes, the default instance's pipe name is \sql\query; for named instances, the pipe name is MSSQL$instancename\sql\query.

When a link is made, endpoint provisioning kicks in to finalize (or reject) the connection.

Client Installation

Now that you have acquired some knowledge about the most important server-side networking considerations, it's time to learn how to install and configure the client-side half of the equation.

Installing the Client Tools

To install the SQL Server 2014 client tools, you start Setup normally and follow the prompts as described in Chapter 8, "Installing SQL Server 2014." When the Feature Selection screen appears, you check only the Client Tools Connectivity check box, as shown in Figure 10.2.

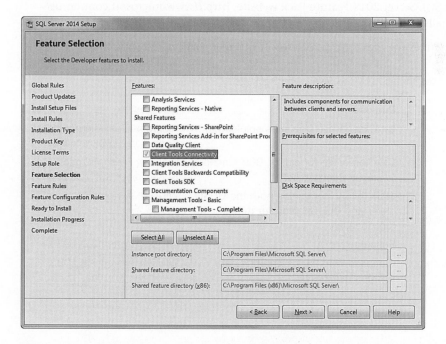

FIGURE 10.2   Performing a client-tools-only installation.

The same kind of install can be done quietly from the command line, as shown in the following example:

```
driveletter:\Setup.exe /q /ACTION=Install /FEATURES=CONN
 /INSTANCENAME=your_instance_name
```

That's all there is to it!

You will be happy to learn that the SQL Server 2014 client tools can safely be installed side by side with your SQL Server 2008 R2 or 2012 client tools. You can even access databases and other objects created in either edition by using either toolset.

The sections that follow describe how to install and use a few of the client tools for client configuration and testing.

Installing SNAC

This section shows how easy it is to install SNAC, the key net-library for SQL Server.

As mentioned earlier, both the SQL Server 2014 Database Engine and the client tools depend on SNAC11. SNAC is installed when you install the SQL Server connectivity tools, or you can simply launch it on its own from the SQL Server installation media. Keep in mind that SNAC hasn't changed for SQL Server 2014—the installer's window title still contains SQL Server 2012. The `sqlncli.msi` installer is found in several locations on the media, including `driveletter:\1033_ENU_LP\x64\Setup\x64`. You can just search for the sqlncli.msi to find the location on your media. You can also download the installer from the Microsoft SQL Server 2014 Feature Pack website, http://www.microsoft.com/en-us/download/details.aspx?id=42295.

Table 10.1 describes the files that the Microsoft Installer (MSI) package installs.

TABLE 10.1   Files Installed by the SNAC MSI Package

Filename	Purpose	Installed To
Sqlncli.h	C++ header file (replaces sqloledb.h)	Program Files\Microsoft SQL Server\110\SDK\Include
sqlncli11.lib	C++ library file for calling BCP functions (replaces odbcbcp.lib)	Program Files\Microsoft SQL Server\110\SDK\Lib\x64
sqlncli11.dll	Main library, containing both the ODBC driver and OLE DB provider (houses all functionality)	WINDIR\system32
sqlnclir11.rll	Resource file	WINDIR\system32\1033
s11ch_sqlncli.chm	Compiled help file for creating data sources using SNAC	WINDIR\system32\1033

TIP

For detailed information on how to write C++ code by using the header and library files included in the SNAC software development kit (SDK), see the Books Online topic "Using the SQL Native Client Header and Library Files."

The SNAC11 installer has two primary options (shown in Figure 10.3):

▶ Install SNAC by itself

▶ Install the SNAC SDK files along with it

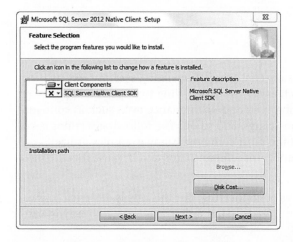

FIGURE 10.3   SNAC's installation options.

NOTE

The network protocols that are enabled by default depend on the edition of SQL Server that is installed. In all instances, the Shared Memory protocol is enabled for all editions on the client during installation.

That's all there is to installing SNAC!

Redistributing SNAC with Custom Client Applications

If you build an application that relies on SNAC, you need to be aware that it can be redistributed in two ways:

▶ As part of any SQL Server 2014 installation or upgrade

▶ As a custom application installation dependency

When you are building MSI files for an application, it is important that you register sqlncli.msi as a package dependency (and, of course, to install it as well, if it is not present

10

on the destination machine). This helps ensure that SNAC will not be accidentally uninstalled from the destination machine without first flashing a warning to users, indicating that any application that relies on it will break. To do this, you execute the following command early in your application's installation process:

```
msiexec /i sqlncli.msi APPGUID={unique identifier for your product}
```

NOTE

The program name for SNAC found in the Add or Remove Programs Control Panel applet is Microsoft SQL Server 2012 Native Client, not SQL Native Client, as it is commonly known.

Client Configuration

Client configuration is a many-leveled beast, consisting of operating system tasks such as installing protocols; application tasks such as choosing or coding to a specific Application Programming Interface (API), provider, or driver; and maintenance tasks such as configuring network settings, building connection strings, and so on. The following sections cover a broad range of these tasks, focusing on the most common. Many examples utilize TCP/IP both because it is the default protocol for remote clients and because it is the most widely used.

No chapter can cover all the possible ways of connecting, but this one is designed to give you the tools you need to get set up right from the start and to navigate your way in case specific issues arise.

The first client configuration tool we look at is SSCM.

Client Configuration Using SSCM

The Client Network Utility available prior to SQL Server 2005 has been decommissioned, and all its functionality is now built into SSCM. This includes the capability to create server aliases, to enable and prioritize network protocols, to control the various SQL Server services, and more.

NOTE

One thing Microsoft is keen on including in Books Online is that neither Setup nor `sqlncli.msi` installs the actual network protocols themselves, nor do they enable them at the operating system level. This means that if you do not have TCP/IP installed and you need to start using it, you have to first set it up by using the Network Connections Control Panel applet (if you're using Windows, that is).

You can launch SSCM directly from its Start menu icon (which points to target file c:\Windows\SysWOW64\SQLServerManager12.msc), or you can access it in the Services and Applications node of the Computer Management console. When you have SSCM up and running, to access its client-side functionality, you expand its top-level node (SQL Server Configuration Manager (*server_name*)) and then you click the SQL Native Client 11.0 Configuration node. Below it, you click the Client Protocols node to reveal the enabled state and priority order of each protocol, in grid format, in the right-hand pane (see Figure 10.4).

FIGURE 10.4   SSCM's Client Protocols screen.

From this screen, you can right-click any of the protocols to change their enabled state, view Properties pages, or change the default connection order (except that of shared memory, which is always tried first and whose order cannot be changed). The following is the default connection order for clients connecting without the benefit of a server alias, connection string, or other means:

▶ Shared memory

▶ TCP/IP

▶ Named pipes

When you are connecting remotely, TCP/IP is the first protocol attempted because shared memory is local only.

> **NOTE**
>
> When a client does not specify a connection protocol, SNAC automatically tries each protocol in the list in sequence, according to the Order column. The first protocol to connect successfully wins.
>
> If the winning connection is subsequently rejected by the server for any reason, no other protocols are tried.
>
> Note also that local clients using MDAC 2.8 or lower cannot connect using shared memory, and they are automatically switched to named pipes if they attempt to do so.

10

Let's examine one of the protocols. To start, you need to double-click TCP/IP under the Name column to open the TCP/IP Properties screen (see Figure 10.5).

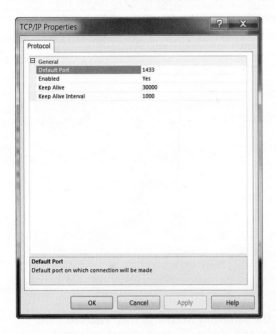

FIGURE 10.5   The TCP/IP Properties screen.

The values stored here are used by TCP/IP clients as default connection values, and they are applied only when a specific server alias or other configuration mechanism is not in use. They are also used by the client tools when shared memory is not available.

As you can see, the default port, 1433, is set up to connect to the more commonly configured default instances of SQL Server. By editing the values on this page, you can change the default port number, enabled state, keep-alive values, and other settings that are displayed when editing other protocols. You should edit and enable the protocols according to your specific needs.

Server Aliases

A server alias is a name that is used like a server name that represents a group of server settings for use by connecting clients. Server aliases are handy because of the way they simplify connection parameters: Clients need only specify the alias name, and SNAC pulls the rest of the information (such as the IP address, TCP port number, and pipe name) at connection time.

To create a server alias, you right-click the Aliases node under SQL Native Client Configuration and choose New Alias. On the Alias - New screen that appears (see Figure 10.6), you specify the alias name, protocol (except shared memory, for which you cannot create an alias), and server name (`local`, `.`, and `localhost` also work for local connections over TCP/IP or named pipes).

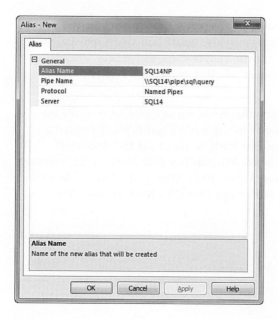

FIGURE 10.6   Alias properties for a new named pipe server alias.

When you make your protocol selection, the grid rows change to dynamically reveal the settings particular to that protocol. When you are finished, you click OK, and your alias is ready for use.

Connection Encryption

With SQL Server 2014, it is easy to set up Secure Sockets Layer (SSL) encrypted client/ server communication over all protocols. The SNAC net-library handles the tasks of encryption and decryption on both the server and client ends. (Note that this process does cause a slight decrease in performance.) Setting it up requires both server-side and client-side configuration changes; this section covers only the client-side changes in detail.

SQL Server 2014 enables encryption using two types of certificates:

▶ Certificates generated by and obtained from an external certification authority such as VeriSign, Thawte, Comodo, and others

▶ Certificates generated by SQL Server 2014 (known as self-signed certificates)

The bit strength of the encryption (for example 128-bit) depends on the bit strength of the operating systems of the computers involved in the connection.

10

To set up the server for encryption, your administrator registers a certificate on the server operating system (using the Certificates Management console) and then installs it in the Database Engine.

If an externally signed certificate is not installed on the server, SQL Server uses its built-in self-signed certificate. (A server administrator may also create and save a self-signed certificate by using SQL Server 2014 via the CREATE CERTIFICATE and BACKUP CERTIFICATE T-SQL syntax.) It is also up to the server to decide whether encryption is required or optional for connecting clients.

The client's half of the job is to have installed what is known as a root-level certificate that is issued by the same certification authority as the server's certificate. To install a root-level certificate, you right-click the certificate itself (a .cer or .crt file) and select Install Certificate to launch the Certificate Import Wizard. You click Next on the welcome screen to reach the Certificate Store screen (see Figure 10.7). Then you select the first radio button (Automatically Select the Certificate Store) and then click Next. Finally, you click Finish.

FIGURE 10.7   Importing a certificate on the client computer using the Certificate Import Wizard.

Next, you launch SSCM, right-click the SQL Native Client 11.0 Configuration node, and then select Properties. The Flags tab appears (see Figure 10.8) in the Properties window.

You set the Force Protocol Encryption property value to Yes. This causes clients to request an SSL-encrypted connection when communicating with the Database Engine. If the server does not respond in kind, the connection is killed.

The Trust Server Certificate property gives clients a choice in how they deal with server certificates:

▶ To use a self-signed certificate, you set the property value to Yes. This option prevents SNAC from validating the server's certificate.

▶ To use an externally signed certificate, you set the property value to No, which causes SNAC to validate the server's certificate.

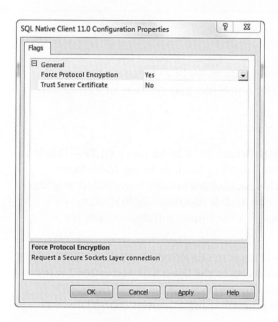

FIGURE 10.8   Forcing clients to request an encrypted connection using SSCM.

SSMS can also connect over an encrypted connection. When connecting using the Connect to Server dialog, you click the Options button and then click the Connection Properties tab. Then you choose your database and protocol and, at the bottom left, check the Encrypt Connection check box.

Client Data Access Technologies

The question of which data access technology to use with SQL Server 2014 is a common one, with a seemingly easy answer: You use SNAC because it has all the latest functionality, all rolled into one. (You learn how to use SNAC in the sections that follow.) A more correct answer is that your choice depends on which software technologies your clients currently use and what their specific needs are.

Your data access options consist of providers and drivers, whose functionality is often encapsulated inside code libraries known as net-libraries (such as SNAC's `sqlncli11.dll`). In addition to these net-libraries, supporting services such as MDAC's OLE DB Core Services are also available, providing useful functionality not found in the net-libraries, such as connection pooling. (ADO.NET also functions as a service, to a certain degree.)

10

> **NOTE**
>
> The Microsoft Data Access Components (MDAC) has a new name that started with the Vista operating system. The data access components are now called Windows Data Access Components or Windows DAC or WDAC. References to MDAC in this chapter also apply to the Windows DAC.

Provider Choices

A provider is software used for accessing various data stores in a consistent manner conforming to a specification, such as OLE DB. A provider may contain an API. Clients that use providers are known as consumers.

The following providers are available:

▶ **ASP.NET Session State Provider for SQL Server 2014 In-Memory OLTP**—This is a brand new provider that enables ASP.NET web applications to use In-Memory OLTP for session state management. This package is available from NuGet at URL: https://www.nuget.org/packages/Microsoft.Web.SessionState.SqlInMemory. Full source code is also available at CodePlex at URL: https://msftdbprodsamples.codeplex.com/releases/view/125282.

▶ **SQL Native Client OLE DB provider**—This is the final version of the OLE DB provider built into SNAC11. It provides access to the latest SQL Server 2012 features as well as earlier versions of SQL Server. However, SNAC11 is the last version. Microsoft is encouraging developers to program using Microsoft ODBC Driver 11 for SQL Server instead.

▶ **.NET Framework data provider for SQL Server**—This data provider is built in to the System.Data.SqlClient namespace in the .NET Framework. Managed code applications (such as Microsoft Visual Basic or Visual C#) should use it to access the latest SQL Server functionality.

▶ **Microsoft OLE DB provider for SQL Server (SQLOLEDB)**—This data provider supports access to Microsoft SQL Server 2014 and prior versions of SQL Server. SNAC11 is the final version of this provider.

Driver Choices

A *driver* in this context can be defined as software that conforms to a standard such as Open Database Connectivity (ODBC) and provides an API for accessing a specific type of data store. osql.exe is a good example of an application that uses an ODBC driver (the SNAC driver).

These are the available drivers:

▶ **SQL Native Client ODBC driver**—This is the ODBC driver built into SNAC11. It complies with the Microsoft Win32 ODBC specification.

▶ **Microsoft ODBC Driver 11 for SQL Server**—This ODBC driver is housed in a single dynamic link library and provides support for applications using native-code APIs for accessing SQL Server databases. Applications should use this driver to access SQL Server 2014, or they can switch to the SNAC ODBC driver for the latest functionality. This driver also provides access to SQL Server 7, 2000, 2005, 2008, 2008 R2, and 2012 databases.

▶ **Java Database Connectivity (JDBC) driver**—The JDBC driver was built specifically for accessing SQL Server data from Java code. The latest 4.1 driver supports new features in SQL Server 2012, including SQL Server AlwaysOn and support for SQL Server Parallel Data Warehouse.

▶ **PHP driver for SQL Server 3.1**—The 3.1 PHP driver allows applications that use the PHP open source server-side scripting language to connect to SQL Server 2014. It supports new features in SQL Server 2012, including SQL Server AlwaysOn, buffered queries, and support for LocalDB access.

▶ **SQL Server ODBC driver for Linux**—This driver allows native C and C++ applications that are running on Linux to connect directly to SQL Server 2014.

CAUTION

Although it is still possible to connect to SQL Server 2014 by using DB-library and Embedded SQL, Microsoft has deprecated them both, and they will not be supported in future editions.

Connecting Using the Various Providers and Drivers

Now that you know what your options are in terms of providers and drivers, the following sections detail them one by one, with a special focus on putting the features in SQL Server 2014 to work.

Using SNAC

SNAC is a net-library that contains both the latest OLE DB provider and ODBC provider for using the rich features in SQL Server 2014 databases. It is compatible for accessing SQL Server 7, 2000, 2005, 2008, 2008 R2, and 2012 databases as well.

The code for SNAC is contained in the single dynamic link library `sqlncli11.dll`, and it serves as provider, driver, and API for applications that call its underlying COM functions from unmanaged code (that is, from C or C++).

The bottom line with SNAC is that if you're building applications that need to exploit the latest features of SQL Server 2014, you need to use its APIs. If you don't, your application will continue to work without SNAC, but those new features will not be available.

10

NOTE

A large number of connection keywords are available for use with SNAC connections. A few of them are illustrated in the examples that follow, but for a complete reference, see the Books Online topic, "Using Connection String Keywords with SQL Native Client."

Using OLE DB with SNAC   Applications that call the COM APIs for OLE DB need to have the connection provider value changed from SQLOLEDB to SQLNCLI11. You also need to use the SNAC header file, as in the following example:

```
include "sqlncli.h";
```

sqlncli.h contains the latest function prototypes and other definitions for use with SNAC. This file is named the same as it was in SQL Server 2012, but it is installed in a different location.

NOTE

The SNAC OLE DB provider is OLE DB version 2.0 compliant.

Using ODBC with SNAC   To connect to SQL Server 2014 using ODBC, you use a connection string or a DSN that is accessible to the client application at runtime. The ODBC driver used with SQL Server 2000 (simply called SQL Server) can still be used but is not the best option for SQL Server versions that were released since then. To get the latest SNAC functionality, you must use the driver called SQL Native Client 11.0 (for example, DRIVER={SQL Native Client 11.0}).

To create a SNAC ODBC DSN, you run the Data Sources (ODBC) applet found in your operating system's administrative tools. You should first select the Drivers tab in this applet to ensure that the latest SNAC driver is installed on the machine. Figure 10.9 shows the drivers tab which includes the SQL Server Native Client 11.0 driver. After the driver has been verified, you create a system, file, or user DSN. When adding one of these DSNs, you need to be sure to select the SQL Server Native Client 11.0 driver on the Create New Data Source screen that appears.

You finish the wizard by entering the configuration data as you normally would, and you can use your new DSN just as you would any other. For more information on building COM applications that utilize SNAC, see the Books Online topic, "Creating a SQL Native Client ODBC Driver Application."

Using the .NET Framework Data Provider for SQL Server

.NET applications that use the System.Data.SqlClient namespace rely on the .NET Framework data provider and ADO.NET. To use this provider, you simply add the following statement to your C# code file:

```
using System.Data.SqlClient;
```

For VB .NET, you use this:

```
Imports System.Data.SqlClient
```

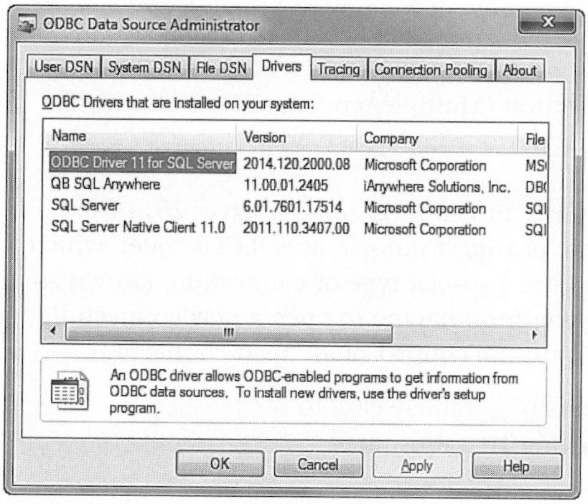

FIGURE 10.9   ODBC Data Source drivers.

Note that the .NET provider supports a variety of connection string styles, including ODBC, OLE DB, and OLE DB/SNAC, and you can mix and match some of their respective connection string keywords. For example, Database and Initial Catalog mean the same thing to ADO.NET, and so do Server and Data Source. But don't let this fool you: Under the covers, only the .NET provider is always in use. (This is probably why changing the value passed to the Provider keyword seems to have no noticeable effect.)

Applications built on .NET Framework 3.0, 3.5, and 4.0 can access SQL Server 2014 databases without issue. The only caveat is that earlier versions of ADO.NET can't make use of newer SQL Server features, such as asynchronous command execution, cache synchronization, bulk copy, and the new data types. (However, implicit conversions such as from varchar to xml and from UDTs to varbinary allow their use as T-SQL input from .NET Framework 1.1 applications.) ADO.NET 4.5 applications, however, have access to the full gamut of new functionality in SQL Server 2012 and 2014.

The following is an example of two connection strings (in different styles) that both turn on the Multiple Active Result Sets (MARS) feature for ADO.NET applications, which allows client applications to keep more than one data set or data reader open simultaneously using a single connection:

The following is in ODBC style:

```
Driver={SQL Native Client 11.0}; Server=MyServer/SQL14;
Database=AdventureWorks2012;
Encrypt=yes; Trusted_Connection=yes; MARS_Connection=yes
```

10

The following is in OLE DB style:

```
Provider=SQLNCLI11; Server=MyServer/SQL14;
Database=AdventureWorks2012;
Encrypt=yes; Trusted_Connection=yes;
MultipleActiveResultSets=true
```

Notice the use of the keywords MARS_Connection (MultipleActiveResultSets also works) and Encrypt (which requests connection encryption from the server).

The SQLCLR Context Connection   When you need to connect to SQL Server 2014 from within a managed stored procedure, function, or trigger (known as SQLCLR code), which is possible only with .NET 2.0 or greater, you use a special type of connection, known as a context connection. This feature prevents you from having to open a new connection because the code itself is already running within the context of an open connection.

The connection string for context connections is extremely easy to use ("context connection=true"), as the C# example in Listing 10.1 illustrates.

LISTING 10.1   Using the Context Connection from a Managed Stored Procedure

```csharp
using System;
using System.Data;
using System.Data.SqlClient;
using System.Data.SqlTypes;
using Microsoft.SqlServer.Server;

public partial class StoredProcedures
{
    [Microsoft.SqlServer.Server.SqlProcedure]
    public static void ContextConnectionTest()
    {
        using (SqlConnection Context =
            new SqlConnection("context connection=true"))
        {
            using (SqlCommand TestCommand =
                new SqlCommand("SELECT TOP 10 * FROM
Person.Person", Context))
            {
                using (SqlDataAdapter Adapter =
                    new SqlDataAdapter(TestCommand))
                {
                    using (DataSet MyData = new DataSet())
                    {
                        Adapter.Fill(MyData);
                    }
                }
            }
```

```
                }
            }
        }
    }
}
```

Using Windows DAC

Windows DAC (WDAC, formerly known as MDAC) contains the OLE DB provider for SQL Server (SQLOLEDB) and the ODBC driver for SQL Server. WDAC is officially part of the operating system, and, as mentioned earlier, WDAC and SNAC are distributed and developed on separate tracks: WDAC with the operating system and SNAC with SQL Server. They do interrelate, however, in that applications that use SNAC can make use of the core services provided by WDAC, including support for connection pooling, client-side cursors, ADO support, and memory management. As mentioned earlier, to make use of the latest SQL Server functionality, you need to use SNAC.

> **TIP**
>
> If at any time you want to discover which version of WDAC is installed on a machine, you can simply check the value of the following Registry key (using regedit.exe or from code):
>
> `HKEY_LOCAL_MACHINE\SOFTWARE\Microsoft\DataAccess\Version`

If you choose to upgrade from WDAC to SNAC, it's important to note some key differences between the two that could affect your applications:

▶ Return values from SQL Server 2014 to WDAC applications are implicitly type converted, as shown in Table 10.2.

▶ Warning and error messages and message handling differ between WDAC and SNAC.

▶ SNAC requires that T-SQL parameters begin with the @ character; WDAC does not.

▶ SNAC, unlike WDAC, is not compatible with Visual Studio Analyzer or PerfMon.

TABLE 10.2   Implicit Type Conversions for SQL Server 2014 Data Types

SQL Server 2014 Data Type	Converted to Data Type
varbinary(MAX)	Image
xml	ntext
nvarchar(MAX)	ntext
varchar(MAX)	text
UDTs	varbinary

For further details, see the Books Online topic, "Updating an Application to SQL Native Client from MDAC."

Using ODBC with WDAC   You can configure an ODBC connection by using a connection string or DSN that specifies the Microsoft ODBC driver for SQL Server.

For connection strings, you use the keyword-value pair Provider={SQL Server}.

To use a DSN, you run the Data Sources (ODBC) applet, as mentioned earlier. When choosing a driver, you select the one simply named SQL Server.

Using OLE DB with WDAC   You can access SQL Server 2014 databases by using the Microsoft OLE DB provider for SQL Server (SQLOLEDB). In connection strings or property values, you use the Provider keyword and the value SQLOLEDB.

> **NOTE**
>
> Unlike with SNAC's OLE DB provider, with SQLOLEDB you can access both SQL Server data and data from non–SQL Server data sources. Also, SNAC is not dependent on any particular version of WDAC because it expects that a compatible WDAC version will be present on the operating system, as enforced by its own installation requirements.

Using JDBC   Microsoft released a freely downloadable, JDBC 4.1-compliant, Type 4 driver for use with SQL Server 2014. It can be used from all types of Java programs and servers via the J2EE connection API.

The following is the basic syntax for a JDBC connection string:

```
jdbc:sqlserver://ServerName\InstanceName:port;property=value[;property=value]
```

For complete details on using JDBC, check out Microsoft's JDBC product documentation at http://msdn.microsoft.com/library/ms378749.aspx.

General Networking Considerations and Troubleshooting

This section provides guidelines for solving some common connectivity issues. You can perform the following steps as a first line of defense when your connections fail:

1. Check whether the server is configured (via SSCM, as detailed earlier in this chapter, in the section, "Server Network Protocols") to accept remote connections.

2. Ensure that the SQL Browser service is started.

3. Determine whether clients are specifying the correct port (for using fixed ports with named instances) in the server alias or connection string.

4. Check whether the client's network protocols are enabled and configured to correctly handshake with those of the server. They should use SSCM on both sides, as explained earlier in this chapter, in the section, "Client Configuration Using SSCM."

5. Be sure you have permission to connect to the server's endpoints.

6. When using encryption, be sure the server and client certificates match (that is, check their Common Name (CN) and any other relevant attributes) and are installed and configured correctly on both sides. (See the section, "Connection Encryption," earlier in this chapter.)

7. Make certain that your firewalls are configured to permit the required network traffic. (See the following section, "Firewall Considerations.")

8. Check to see whether your users have permission to log in to the server and access the specified database.

9. Make sure that your clients' choices of providers support the SQL Server features they are trying to use.

10. Make sure the provider, driver, DSN, server alias, or other connection mechanism is still valid and hasn't been altered or removed from the system.

11. Network administrators are no longer added to the SQL Server sysadmin role by default. If the user trying to connect is a network administrator, he or she must be granted explicit permission with SQL Server 2014. See the topic named "Database Engine Configuration - Account Provisioning" in Books Online for more information.

Firewall Considerations

For clients to successfully connect through a firewall, it must be configured to allow the following:

▶ **Bidirectional traffic on UDP Port 1434**—This is required only for communications to and from the SQL Browser service; when SQL Browser is not in use, you can close this port.

▶ **Bidirectional traffic on any TCP port used by SQL Server**—Be sure to open port 1433 for default instances and also open any fixed ports assigned to your named or default instances. (TCP high port numbers must be opened only when dynamic ports are used by named instances. Using dynamic port numbers for named instances is not recommended.) You can determine the ports currently in use via SSCM.

When using Windows Firewall, you can easily open these ports. To do this, you run Windows Firewall from the Control Panel. Click on the Inbound Rules selection on the left-hand side of the Windows Firewall with Advanced Security window then select the option to add a new rule. This will launch the New Inbound Rule Wizard that will guide you through the creation of a new firewall rule. Figure 10.10 shows the wizard screen where you can enter the port associated with the rule. The next screen in the wizard allows you to define the action such as allowing connections on the port specified.

10

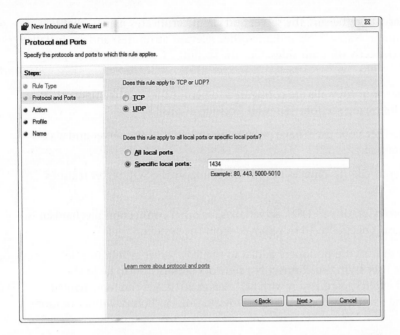

FIGURE 10.10   Creating port exceptions for SQL Server 2014 using Windows Firewall.

Tools for Testing Connections

It's always helpful to have a few tools on your belt for testing client connectivity.

SSCM is a tool that is usually easily accessible, and you can use its Connect to Server dialog to select a protocol to test (as described earlier in this chapter in the section, "Client Data Access Technologies"). You can also use SQLCMD with the -s parameter to connect to a particular server. This is the syntax:

```
SQLCMD -S [protocol:]server[\instance_name][,port]-
```

In this syntax, `protocol_prefix` takes one of the following values:

▶ `np` (for named pipes)

▶ `tcp` (for TCP/IP)

▶ `lpc` (for shared memory)

In the following example, -E indicates the use of a trusted connection to a SQL Server instance named INST2014:

```
SQLCMD -S tcp:.\INST2014,1435 -E
```

When all else fails, you can use telnet client to test the openness of a port on the firewall. Here's an example:

```
telnet IP_Address Port_Number
```

Summary

This chapter covered a lot of ground regarding client-side (and even a bit of server-side) communication with SQL Server 2014. Some of the sections are admittedly dense enough to bear rereading, and you probably have questions about your specific setup. You can always refer to the sections presented in this chapter to pick up tips on how to best configure and troubleshoot the varying environments you may encounter.

Now that your client configuration is complete, you can move on to Chapter 11, "Database Backup and Restore," to learn how to safeguard your databases.

CHAPTER 11

Database Backup and Restore

You need to perform database backups to protect your investment in data. Making backups may seem mundane, but consider Murphy's law ("If anything can go wrong, it will") when you are considering your backup plan. For example, if you forget to add a new database to your backup plan, that database will crash. If you neglect to run a test restore of your backups, those backups will not restore properly. This type of thinking may seem a bit defeatist, but it can help you create a robust backup solution that allows you to sleep comfortably knowing you have a good plan.

Fortunately, SQL Server comes with many different backup and restore options you can use to develop a robust backup plan and avoid those worst-case scenarios. This chapter covers the key considerations in developing a backup and restore plan and then covers the options available with SQL Server to implement that plan.

What's New in Database Backup and Restore

SQL Server 2014 offers the following three main enhancements that are geared towards Backup and Restore:

▶ **SQL Server Backup to URL**—This option enables SQL Server to perform backup and restore operations utilizing Windows Azure Blob Storage Service. It was introduced in SQL Server 2012 SP1 CU2 but the operations could only be initiated through T-SQL, PowerShell, or SQL Server Management Objects (SMO). In SQL Server 2014 you can use SQL Server

Management Studio to perform these operations. This can be done via the Backup task or maintenance plans.

▶ **SQL Server Managed Backup to Windows Azure**—This option is built on SQL Server Backup to URL but it provides more automation around these types of backups. It utilizes a Windows service that SQL Server provides to manage and schedule database and log backups. You determine the retention period for your backups and the service determines the type and frequency of backups that will be stored on the Windows Azure Blob Storage Service. This is a great way to utilize cloud storage and get a reliable offsite backup of your database(s).

▶ **Encryption for Backups**—SQL Server 2014 has the ability to create an encrypted database backup. The backup is created using an encryption algorithm and an encryptor which is either a certificate or an asymmetric key. The available encryption algorithms include AES 128, AES 192, AES 256, and Triple DES, which are industry standard.

Encryption for Backups is discussed in more detail later in the chapter. SQL Server Backup to URL and SQL Server Managed Backup to Windows Azure are not covered in detail in this chapter. Please refer to Chapter 19, "Working with and Deploying to Azure SQL Database" for more detailed information.

Developing a Backup and Restore Plan

Developing a solid backup and restore plan for SQL Server is one of the most critical tasks an administrator performs. Simply put, if you are a database administrator (DBA) and have a significant loss of data in a database you are responsible for, your job may be on the line. You need to carefully examine the backup needs of your organization, document your needs, and deliver a plan that defines how your backup and restore plan will meet those needs.

The best place to start in identifying the backup requirements is to ask the right questions. The following questions can help drive out the answers you need:

▶ How much data loss is acceptable? For example, if you choose to do only full database backups each night, would it be acceptable to lose all the data added to the database during the next day? This could happen if you had a failure and had to restore to the last full backup.

▶ What is the nature of the database? For example, is the database used for a data warehouse, or is it used for a high-volume transaction processing system?

▶ How often does the data in the database change? Some databases may change very little or not at all during the day but sustain heavy batch updates during the evening.

▶ What is the acceptable recovery time in the event a database must be restored from previous backups? This question is directly related to the amount of downtime acceptable for the applications using the database.

▶ Is there a maintenance window for the application/database? The maintenance window is typically a period of time when the database or server can be taken offline. What are the exact times of the maintenance windows?

▶ What is the size of the database(s) you need to back up?

▶ What media is available for backup, and where is the media located?

▶ What is the budget for database backup and recovery? If no budget has been established, the answers to some of the preceding questions drive the cost of the solution.

Some of the questions that need to be asked to come up with a good backup and restore plan may raise some eyebrows. For example, you may find that the answer you get for the question, "How much data loss is acceptable?" is "None!" Don't panic. There are sensible responses for these types of answers. The reality is that you can deliver a solution that virtually eliminates the possibility of data loss—but that comes at a cost. The cost may come in the form of real dollars as well as other costs, such as performance or disk space. As with many other technical solutions, you need to consider trade-offs to come up with the right plan.

> **NOTE**
>
> Many of the questions that relate to database backup and restore are related to system backups as well. System-wide file or image backups, which happen independently of SQL Server backups, capture all or most of the files on a server and write them to appropriate media. These server backups are often performed by DBAs, system administrators, and the like. You should consider having the person or persons responsible for the system backups present when asking the database backup and restore questions. This will help with the coordination and timing of the backups.

When you have the answers to these questions, you need to document them, along with your recommended solutions. You should identify any assumptions and make sure to outline any portion of the plan that has not met the requirements.

The good news is that the implementation of the plan is often less difficult than coming up with the plan itself. Microsoft provides a number of tools to create database backups that can meet the needs of your organization. The remainder of this chapter focuses on the details required to finalize a solid backup and recovery plan.

Types of Backups

SQL Server offers several different types of backups you can use to restore a database to a former state. Each of these backups uses a file or set of files to capture the database state. The files are found outside the SQL Server database and can be stored on media such as tape or hard disk.

As described in the following sections, these backup types are available with SQL Server 2014:

- ► Full database backups

- ► Differential database backups

- ► Partial backups

- ► Differential partial backups

- ► File and filegroup backups

- ► Copy-only backups

- ► Transaction log backups

Full Database Backups

A full database backup is an all-inclusive backup that captures an entire database in one operation. This full backup can be used to restore a database to the state it was in when the database backup completed. The backup is transactionally consistent, contains the entire database structure, and contains the related data stored in these structures.

As with many other backups, SQL Server allows for updates to the database while a full backup is running. It keeps track of the changes occurring during the backup by capturing a portion of the transaction log in the database backup. The backup also records the log sequence number (LSN) when the database backup is started, as well as the LSN when the database backup completes. The LSN is a unique sequential number you can use to determine the order in which updates occur in the database. The LSNs recorded in the backup are used in the restore process to recover the database to a point in time that has transactional consistency.

A full database backup is often used in conjunction with other backup types; it establishes a base for these other types if a restore operation is needed. The other backup types are discussed in the following sections, but it is important not to forget about the full backup that must be restored first in order to utilize other backup types. For example, let's say you are making hourly transaction log backups. If the database is to be recovered using those transaction log backups, the last full database backup must be restored first, and then the subsequent log backups can be applied.

Differential Database Backups

Differential database backups capture changes to any data extent that happened since the last full database backup. The last full database backup is referred to as the *differential base* and is required to make the differential backup useful. Each data extent that is monitored consists of eight physically contiguous data pages. As changes are made to the pages in an extent, a flag is set to indicate that a change has been made to the extent. When the differential database backup is executed, only those extents that have had pages modified are written to the backup.

Differential database backups can save backup space and improve the overall speed of recovery. The savings in space and time are directly related to the amount of change that occurs in the database. The amount of change in the database depends on the amount of time between differential backups. When the number of database changes since the last backup is relatively small, you achieve the best results. If, however, a significant number of changes occur to the data between differential backups, the value of this type of backup is diminished.

Ultimately the number of data pages that are affected by the changes determine the number of pages that must be included in the differential backup. The number of pages is affected by the indexing structure as well as the nature of the updates. If for example, there are many rows that are changed but those rows are all clustered on a limited number of data pages, then the differential backup will not be that large.

Partial Backups

Partial backups provide a means for eliminating read-only data from a backup. In some implementations, a portion of the data in a database may not change and is strictly used for inquiry. If this data is placed on a read-only filegroup, you can use partial backups to back up everything except the read-only data. This technique reduces the size of your backup and the time it takes to complete the backup. The read-only filegroups should still be backed up, but this needs to occur only after the read-only data is loaded.

Differential Partial Backups

Differential partial backups work like differential database backups but are focused on the same type of data as partial backups. The extents that have changed in filegroups that are not read-only are captured in this type of backup. This includes the primary filegroup and any read/write filegroups defined at the time of the backup. Like differential database backups, these backups also require a differential base, but it must be a single differential base. In other words, multiple base backups that have been taken at different times for different database files will not work. You must use a single base backup that encompasses all of the database files.

File and Filegroup Backups

File and filegroup backups are targeted at databases that contain more than one filegroup. In these situations, the filegroup or files in the filegroups can be backed up independently. If a filegroup is backed up, all the files defined in the filegroup are backed up.

File and filegroup backups are often used for larger databases where the creation time for a full database backup takes too long or the resulting backup is too large. In these situations, you can stagger the backups of the files or filegroups and write them to different locations.

The main disadvantage of this type of backup is the increase in administrative overhead. Each of the files in the database must be backed up, and a complete set of these files must be retained to restore the database. For a full recovery model, the transaction log backups must also be retained.

NOTE

SQL Server 2014 supports file and filegroup backups for all recovery models, including simple recovery. The catch with simple recovery is that the files and filegroups are limited to read-only secondary filegroups. SQL Server 2000 did not allow these types of backups with simple recovery.

Copy-Only Backups

Copy-only backups allow a backup of any type to be taken without affecting any other backups. Normally, a database backup is recorded in the database itself and is identified as part of a chain that can be used for restore. For example, if a full database backup is taken, any subsequent differential database backups use this full database backup as their base. A restore process utilizing the differential database backups would have a reference to the full database backup, and that backup would have to be available.

Copy-only backups do not affect the restore chain. They are useful in situations in which you simply want to get a copy of the database for testing purposes or things of this nature. Microsoft has made it easier to make this kind of backup by adding the Copy Only Backup check box when performing a backup using SQL Server Management Studio (SSMS). In SQL Server 2005, the Copy Only Backup had to be performed via the Transact-SQL (T-SQL) BACKUP command. An example of the copy-only backup is provided later in this chapter, in the section, "Backing Up a Database."

Transaction Log Backups

Transaction log backups capture records written to the transaction log file(s) defined for a database. The full and bulk-logged recovery models are the only models that support transaction log backups. These models cause transaction events to be retained in the transaction log so that they can be backed up. Simple recovery mode causes the transaction log to be truncated periodically and thus invalidates the usefulness of the transaction log backups.

The transaction log backups and their strong ties to the recovery model are discussed in more detail in the next section.

Recovery Models

Each database has a recovery model that determines how transactions will be written to the transaction log. The recovery model you choose has a direct impact on your ability to recover from a media failure. These following three recovery models are available with SQL Server 2014:

▶ Full recovery

▶ Bulk-logged

▶ Simple

You set the recovery model via T-SQL or the Database Properties window in SSMS. The following example shows the T-SQL command you can use to change the AdventureWorks2012 database to the bulk-logged model:

```
ALTER DATABASE [AdventureWorks2012] SET RECOVERY BULK_LOGGED WITH NO_WAIT
```

Figure 11.1 shows the Options page on the Database Properties window, which also allows you to select a recovery model.

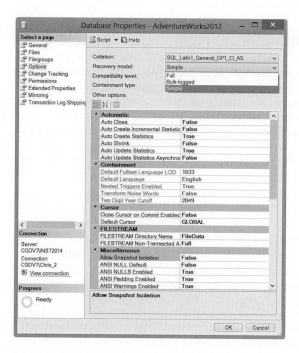

FIGURE 11.1   Setting the recovery model in SSMS.

Full Recovery

The full recovery model gives you the most protection against data loss. A database set to full recovery will have all database operations written to the transactions log. These operations include insertions, updates, and deletions, as well as any other statements that change the database. In addition, the full recovery model captures any database inserts that are the result of a BCP command or BULK INSERT statement.

In the event of a media failure, a database that is in full recovery can be restored to the point in time at which the failure occurred. Your ability to restore to a point in time is dependent on your database backup plan. If a full database backup is available, along with the transaction log backups that occurred after the full database backup, you can recover to the point of the last transaction log backup. In addition, if your current transaction log is available, you can restore up to the point of the last committed transaction in the transaction log.

This recovery model is the most comprehensive, but in some respects, it is the most expensive. It is expensive in terms of the transaction log space needed to capture all the database operations. The space can be significant with databases that have a lot of update activity or with databases that have large bulk load operations. It is also expensive in terms of server overhead because every transaction is captured and retained in the transaction log so that they can be recovered in the event of a failure.

TIP

A common problem in SQL Server environments involves a database that is set to full recovery but whose transaction log is never backed up. In this scenario, the transaction log can grow to the point that it fills up the drive on which the transaction log is located. You need to ensure that you have regularly scheduled backups of the transaction log if you have set your database to full recovery. The transaction log backups allow you to recover from a media failure and also remove the inactive portion of the transaction log so that it does not need to grow.

Bulk-Logged Recovery

The bulk-logged recovery model is similar to full recovery, but it differs in the way that bulk operations are captured in the transaction log. With full recovery mode, SQL Server writes every row to the transaction log including those rows that are inserted with bulk import operations. Bulk import operations include BCP and BULK INSERT. The SELECT INTO, CREATE INDEX, and ALTER INDEX can also be bulk import operations when certain conditions are met.

In contrast, bulk-logged recovery only keeps track of the extents that have been modified by a bulk load operation but does not write each row to the transaction log; this is also referred to as *minimal logging*. This reduces the overall size of the transaction log during bulk load operations and still allows the database to recover after a bulk load operation has occurred.

TIP

It is possible to get some INSERT INTO ... SELECT statements to be minimally logged. This can significantly reduce transaction log file growth resulting from these kinds of inserts. To accomplish these minimally logged inserts the following must be true:

1. The database is in bulk-logged or simple recovery mode.
2. A table level lock is acquired on the target table.
3. The table has no indexes or only an empty clustered index.
4. The table is not being replicated.

The biggest downside to setting a database to bulk-logged recovery is that log backups for the databases can be large. The log backups are large because SQL Server copies all the data extents that have been affected by bulk load operations since the last backup of the transaction log. Remember that data extents consist of eight data pages each, and each page is 8KB in size. This may not seem like much by today's standards, but it can be significant when you're bulk loading a large table. For example, consider a table occupying 1GB of space that is truncated each week and reloaded with a bulk insert. The bulk insert operation goes relatively fast because the rows are not being written to the transaction log, but the backup of the transaction log is much larger.

> **NOTE**
>
> In testing we did on a table with approximately 2.4 million rows (that occupied 500MB of space), the log file grew over 2GB during a bulk insert operation that reloaded all rows in a full recovery mode database. In contrast, the same bulk insert operation on the database with bulk-logged recovery grew the log by only 9MB. However, the backup of the 9MB transaction log was approximately 500MB. This is much larger than the actual log itself because the bulk operation caused all the modified extents from the bulk insert operation to be stored in the log backup as well.

The other downside to bulk-logged recovery is that with it, you may sacrifice the ability to restore to the most recent point in time. This situation occurs if a bulk insert operation has occurred since the last database backup and a media failure occurs. In this case, any outstanding changes that were retained in the transaction log cannot be applied. The reason is that bulk operations are not written to the log directly in this model and cannot be recovered. Only bulk operations captured in a backup can be restored.

If transactions have occurred in a database since the last backup, and no bulk insert operations have occurred, you can recover those pending transactions as long as the media containing the transaction log is still available. The tail of the transaction log can be backed up and applied during a restore operation. The tail of the log and other restore scenarios are discussed in the "Restore Scenarios" section, later in this chapter.

Simple Recovery

The simple recovery model is the easiest to administer, but it is the option that has the greatest possibility for data loss. In this mode, your transaction log is truncated automatically based on a checkpoint in the database. These checkpoints happen often, and they cause the data in the transaction log to be truncated frequently.

> **NOTE**
>
> Prior to SQL Server 2000, the `truncate log on checkpoint` database option was used to truncate the log on a checkpoint and produce the same type of behavior as simple recovery. This database option and the equivalent backup options `NO_LOG` and `TRUNCATE_ONLY` are no longer supported. The only supported method for truncating the transaction log in SQL Server 2014 is to switch the database to use the simple recovery model.

The most important point to remember about the simple recovery model is that with it, you cannot back up the transaction log that captures changes to your database. If a media failure occurs, you are not able to recover the database activity that has occurred since the last database backup. This is a major exposure, so simple recovery is not recommended for production databases. However, it can be a good option for development databases where the loss of some transactions is acceptable. In these types of environments, simple recovery can equate to saved disk space because the transaction log is constantly truncated. The administration in these environments is reduced as well because the transaction log backups are not an option and thus do not need to be managed.

For a more detailed discussion of the transaction log, see Chapter 28, "Transaction Management and the Transaction Log."

Backup Devices

A backup device is used to provide a storage destination for the database backups created with SQL Server. Backups can be written to logical or physical devices. A logical device is essentially an alias to the physical device and makes it easier to refer to the device when performing database backups. The physical backup devices that SQL Server can write to include files on local disks, tape, and network shares.

Disk Devices

A disk device is generally stored in a folder on a local hard drive. This should not be the same hard drive where your data is stored! Disk devices have several advantages, including speed and reliability. If you have ever had a backup fail because you forgot to load a tape, you can appreciate the advantage of disk backups. On the other hand, if backups are stored on a local disk and the server is destroyed, you lose your backups as well.

> **NOTE**
>
> Disks have become increasingly popular media as the prices have fallen. Storage area networks (SANs) and other large-scale disk solutions have entered mainstream usage and offer a large amount of storage at a relatively inexpensive price. They also offer redundancy and provide fault tolerance to mitigate the chance of losing data on a disk. Finally, increased network bandwidth across LANs and WANs has allowed for the movement of backups created on disk to alternate locations. This is a simple way to achieve additional fault tolerance.

Tape Devices

Tape devices are used to back up to tape. Tape devices must be directly connected to the server, and parallel backups to multiple drives are supported to increase throughput. Tape backups have the advantage of being scalable, portable, and secure. Scalability is important as a database grows; available disk space often precludes the use of disk backups for large databases. Because tapes are removable media, they can easily be transported offsite, where they can be secured against theft and damage.

SQL Server supports the Microsoft Tape Format (MTF) for backup devices, which means that SQL Server backups and operating system backups can share the same tape. This capability is convenient for small sites with shared use servers and only one tape drive. You can schedule your SQL Server backups and file backups without having to be onsite to change the tape.

Network Shares

SQL Server 2014 allows the use of both mapped network drives and Universal Naming Convention (UNC) paths in the backup device filename. A mapped network drive must be mapped as a network drive in the session in which SQL Server is running. This is prone to error and generally not recommended. UNC paths are much simpler to administer. With UNC backup devices, the SQL Server service account must be able to see the UNC path on the network. This can be accomplished by granting the service account full control permission on the share or by making the service account a member of the `Administrators` group on the remote computer.

Keep in mind that backups performed on a network share should be done on a dedicated or high-speed network connection, and the backup should be verified to avoid potential corruption introduced by network error. The time it takes a backup to complete over the network depends on network traffic, so you need to take this factor into consideration when planning your backups.

Media Sets and Families

When you're backing up to multiple devices, the terms *media set* and *media family* are used to describe the components of the backup. A *media set* is the target destination of the database backup and comprises several individual media. All media in a media set must be of the same type (for example, all tape or all disk). A *media family* is the collection of media associated with an individual backup device. For example, a media family could be a collection of five tapes contained in a single tape device.

The first tape in the media family is referred to as the *initial* media, and the subsequent tapes are referred to as *continuation* media. All the media families combined are referred to as the *media set*. If, for example, a backup is written to 3 backup devices (each with 4 tapes), the media set would contain 3 media families and consist of a total of 12 tapes. It is recommended to use the MEDIANAME parameter of the BACKUP command to specify a name for the media set. This parameter associates the multiple devices as members of the media set. The MEDIANAME parameter can then be referenced in future backup operations.

Creating Backup Devices

You can create logical backup devices by using T-SQL or SSMS. The T-SQL command for creating these logical backup devices is `sp_addumpdevice`, which has the following syntax:

```
sp_addumpdevice [ @devtype = ] 'device_type'
        , [ @logicalname = ] 'logical_name'
        , [ @physicalname = ] 'physical_name'
```

```
    [ , { [ @cntrltype = ] controller_type |
        [ @devstatus = ] 'device_status' }
    ]
```

The following sample script demonstrates the creation of the different types of backup devices:

```
-- Local Disk
EXEC sp_addumpdevice 'disk', 'diskdev1',
    'c:\mssql\backup\AdventureWorks2012.bak'
-- Network Disk
EXEC sp_addumpdevice 'disk', 'networkdev1',
    '\\myserver\myshare\AdventureWorks2012.bak'
-- Tape
EXEC sp_addumpdevice 'tape', 'tapedev1', '\\.\tape0'
```

To create backup devices with SSMS, you navigate to the Server Objects node in the Object Explorer and right-click Backup Devices and then New Backup Device; the Backup Device screen appears. This screen includes a text box for the device name, along with a section to select the destination for the device. This is the physical location, and you can select either Tape or File.

Backing Up a Database

Now that you know the types of backups, the recovery models they relate to, and the devices you can write to, you are ready to back up your database. You can create backups with SQL Server 2014 by using either the SSMS or T-SQL. Some backups are supported only through T-SQL, but the vast majority can be accomplished with either tool.

Creating Database Backups with SSMS

The backup options in SSMS are accessible through the Object Explorer. For example, you can right-click the AdventureWorks2012 database in the SSMS Object Explorer, select Tasks and Backup, and a backup window like the one shown in Figure 11.2 appears.

The Source section on the Back Up Database window contains information relative to the database that will be backed up. The source database is displayed in the first drop-down, along with the recovery model set for the database. The backup types available in the drop-down are dependent on the recovery model. For simple recovery, only full and differential backup types are available. For full recovery and bulk-logged recovery models, all backup types are available in the drop-down.

The Backup Set section allows you to give the backup a meaningful name and specify when the backup set will expire. When the backup set expires, the backup can be over-written and is no longer retained. If the backup is set to expire after 0 days, it will never expire.

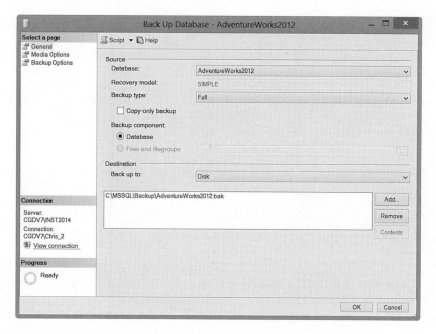

FIGURE 11.2 The Back Up Database window in SSMS.

The Destination section identifies the disk or tape media that will contain the backup. You can specify multiple destinations in this section by clicking the Add button. For disk media, you can specify a maximum of 64 disk devices. The same limit applies to tape media. If multiple devices are specified, the backup information is spread across those devices. All the devices must be present for you to be able to restore the database. If no tape devices are attached to the database server, the Tape option is disabled.

You can select several different types of options for a database backup. Figure 11.3 shows the options page available when you back up a database by using SSMS.

The Overwrite Media section allows you to specify options relative to the destination media for the backup. Keep in mind that a given media set can contain more than one backup. This can occur if the Append to the Existing Backup Set options is selected. With this option, any prior backups contained on the media set are preserved, and the new backup is added to it. With the Overwrite All Existing Backup Sets option, the media set contains only the latest backup, and no prior backups are retained.

You can use the options in the Reliability section to ensure that the backup that has been created can be used reliably in a restore situation. Verifying the backup when finished is highly recommended, but doing so causes the backup time to be extended during the verification. Similarly, the Perform Checksum Before Writing to Media option helps ensure that you have a sound backup, but again, it causes the database backup to run longer.

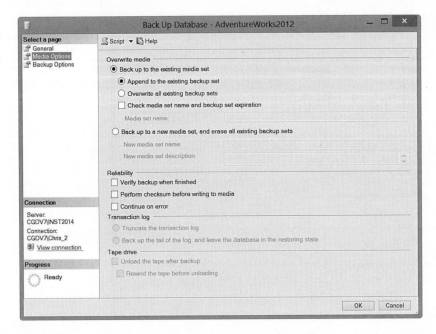

FIGURE 11.3   The Back Up Database Options page in SSMS.

The options in the Transaction Log section are available for databases in the full recovery or bulk-logged model. These options are disabled in the simple recovery model. The Truncate the Transaction Log option causes any inactive portion of the transaction log to be removed after the database backup is complete. The inactive portion of the log and other details of the transaction log are discussed in more detail in Chapter 28. This option, the default, helps keep the size of the transaction log manageable. The Back Up the Tail of the Log option is related to point-in-time restores and is discussed in more detail in the "Restore Scenarios" section later in this chapter.

The set of options in the Tape Drive section are enabled only when tape has been selected for the destination media. Selecting the Unload the Tape After Backup option causes the media tape to be ejected when the backup completes. This option can help identify the end of a backup and prevent the tape from being overwritten the next time the backup runs. The Rewind the Tape Before Unloading option is self-explanatory; it causes the tape to be released and rewound before you unload the tape. The last set of options relate to compressed database backups. The options for compressed backups are discussed in detail in the "Compressed Backups" section later in this chapter.

> **NOTE**
>
> Keep in mind that all backups can be performed while the database is in use. SQL Server is able to keep track of the changes occurring during the backup and can maintain transactional consistency as of the end of the backup. You need to consider that there is some

performance overhead during the actual backup, but the backup can occur during active database hours. However, it is still a good idea to schedule your database backups during off-hours, when database activity is at a minimum.

Creating Database Backups with T-SQL

The T-SQL BACKUP command offers a myriad of options to perform all the backup operations available in SSMS. However, SSMS does not support some backup operations that can be performed only with T-SQL.

The BACKUP command comes in three different flavors. The first flavor involves the backup of a database. The command syntax starts with BACKUP DATABASE, followed by the relevant parameters and options. The second flavor involves the backup of a file or filegroup that is part of the database. The command syntax for this type of backup also utilizes the BACKUP DATABASE command, but a file or filegroup is specified after the database name to identify which parts of the database should be backed up. The last flavor involves the backup of the database's transaction log. The syntax for backing up the transaction log starts with BACKUP LOG. Each flavor shares many of the same options. The basic syntax for backing up a database follows:

```
BACKUP DATABASE { database_name | @database_name_var }
TO < backup_device > [ ,...n ]
[ [ MIRROR TO < backup_device > [ ,...n ] ] [ ...next-mirror
] ]
[ WITH
     [ BLOCKSIZE = { blocksize | @blocksize_variable } ]
     [ [ , ] { CHECKSUM | NO_CHECKSUM } ]
     [ [ , ] COMPRESSION | NO_COMPRESSION]
     [ [ , ] COPY_ONLY ]
     [ [ , ] { STOP_ON_ERROR | CONTINUE_AFTER_ERROR } ]
     [ [ , ] DESCRIPTION = { 'text' | @text_variable } ]
     [ [ , ] DIFFERENTIAL ]
     [ [ , ] EXPIREDATE = { date | @date_var }
     | RETAINDAYS = { days | @days_var } ]
     [ [ , ] PASSWORD = { password | @password_variable } ]
     [ [ , ] { FORMAT | NOFORMAT } ]
     [ [ , ] { INIT | NOINIT } ]
     [ [ , ] { NOSKIP | SKIP } ]
     [ [ , ] MEDIADESCRIPTION = { 'text' | @text_variable } ]
     [ [ , ] MEDIANAME = { media_name | @media_name_variable
} ]
     [ [ , ] MEDIAPASSWORD = { mediapassword |
@mediapassword_variable } ]
     [ [ , ] NAME = { backup_set_name | @backup_set_name_var
} ]
     [ [ , ] { NOREWIND | REWIND } ]
```

```
    [ [ , ] { NOUNLOAD | UNLOAD } ]
    [ [ , ] RESTART ]
    [ [ , ] STATS [ = percentage
 ] ]
]
```

The number of options is extensive, but many of them are optional. A BACKUP DATABASE command can be as simple as the following example:

```
BACKUP DATABASE [AdventureWorks2012]
  TO  DISK = N'C:\mssql\backup\AdventureWorks2012_COPY.bak'
```

The first part of the BACKUP command is related to the database you want to back up (database_name), followed by the location to which you want to write the backup (backup_device). The remainder of the syntax relates to the options that can be specified following the WITH clause. These options determine how your backup will be created and the properties of the resulting backup. Table 11.1 outlines these options.

TABLE 11.1   BACKUP DATABASE Options

Option	Description
BLOCKSIZE	The physical block size that will be used to create the backup. The default is 64KB.
BUFFERCOUNT	Sets the total number of I/O buffers that will be used for the backup operation.
CHECKSUM | NO_CHECKSUM	When CHECKSUM is specified, a checksum is calculated before the backup is written to validate that the backup is not corrupt. The default is NO_CHECKSUM.
COMPRESSION | NO_COMPRESSION	This option causes the backup file to be compressed. It was introduced in SQL Server 2008 and was only available with the Enterprise or Developer Edition. SQL Server 2014 supports backup compression in the Enterprise, Business Intelligence and Standard Editions. The default is NO_COMPRESSION.
COPY_ONLY	This option allows a backup to be made without affecting the normal sequence of backups.
DESCRIPTION	This is a 255-character description of the backup set.
DIFFERENTIAL	This option causes a differential backup to occur, which captures changes only since the last backup.
ENCRYPTION	Used to specify the encryption options that will be used for the backup. These options are new to SQL Server 2014 and are discussed in detail later in the chapter.
EXPIREDATE	This option specifies the date on which the backup set will expire and be overwritten.

Option	Description
FORMAT | NOFORMAT	FORMAT causes the existing media header and backup set to be overwritten. The default is NOFORMAT.
INIT | NOINIT	The INIT option causes a backup set to be overwritten. The backup set is not overwritten if the backup set has not expired or if it does not match the media name specified with the NAME option. NOINIT, which is the default, causes the backup set to be appended to the existing media.
MAXTRANSFERSIZE	Sets the largest unit of transfer (in bytes) to be used between SQL Server and the backup media.
MEDIADESCRIPTION	This is a 255-character description for the entire backup media containing the backup sets.
MEDIANAME	This is a 128-character name for the backup media. If it is specified, the target media must match this name.
MEDIAPASSWORD	This is a password for the media set. When media is created with this password, the password must be supplied to be able to create a backup set on that media or to restore from that media.
NAME	This is a 128-character name for the backup set.
NORECOVERY | STANDBY = undo_file_name } | NO_TRUNCATE	These options are used with the BACKUP LOG option and are discussed in more detail later in this chapter.
NOREWIND | REWIND	This option is used for tape operations. REWIND, which is the default, causes the tape to be released and rewound after it fills.
NOSKIP | SKIP	NOSKIP, which is the default, allows backup sets to be over-written if they have expired. The SKIP option skips expiration and media name checks and is used to prevent the overwriting of backup sets.
NOUNLOAD | UNLOAD	This option is used for tape operations. NOUNLOAD, which is the default, causes the tape to remain in the tape drive after a backup completes. UNLOAD causes the tape to be rewound and unloaded when the backup completes.
PASSWORD	This is a password that must be specified when restoring the backup set.
RESTART	This option has no effect and is in place only for backward compatibility.
RETAINDAYS	This option specifies the number of elapsed days before the backup set can be overwritten.
STATS	This option causes completion statistics to be displayed at the specified interval to assess progress.
STOP_ON_ERROR | CONTINUE_AFTER_ERROR	This option is used in conjunction with the CHECKSUM option. The STOP_ON_ERROR option, which is the default, causes the backup to fail if the checksum cannot be validated.

The "Backup Scenarios" section, later in this chapter, provides some examples of how to use these options.

Backing Up the Transaction Log

As discussed, the full and bulk-logged recovery models cause transactions to be written to the database's transaction log. These transactions should be backed up periodically for two main reasons. First, the transaction log backups can be used in case of a media failure to restore work completed in the database. These backups limit your exposure to data loss and enable you to reapply changes that have occurred.

The second reason for backing up the transaction log is to keep the size of the log manageable. Keep in mind that SQL Server is a write-ahead database management system (DBMS) and thus writes most changes to the transaction log first, before it updates the actual data files. This type of DBMS is great for recovery purposes, but it can be a real headache if you do not periodically clear those transactions from the log. Without a backup or manual truncation, the log can fill to a point where it will use up all the space on your disk.

Creating Transaction Log Backups with SSMS

The same backup screen utilized for database backups in SSMS can also be used for transaction log backups. Figure 11.4 shows the Back Up Database window with Transaction Log selected as the backup type. A device must be selected to write the backup to, and some additional options on the Media Options page that relate to the transaction log are enabled.

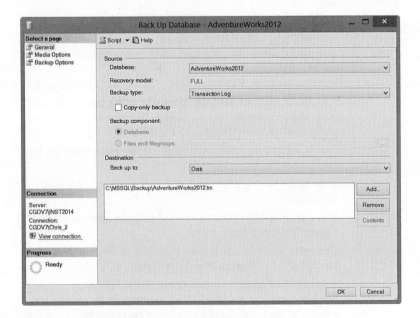

FIGURE 11.4   Backing up the transaction log in SSMS.

Creating Transaction Log Backups with T-SQL

When you back up a transaction log by using T-SQL, you use the BACKUP LOG command, which includes all the previously listed options except the DIFFERENTIAL option. (Differential backups do not apply to transaction logs.) Several additional options are available for transaction log backups. The following abbreviated syntax for the BACKUP LOG command shows the options used exclusively for backing up transaction logs:

```
BACKUP LOG { database_name | @database_name_var }
TO < backup_device > [ ,...n ]
[ [ MIRROR TO < backup_device > [ ,...n ] ] [ ...next-mirror
] ]
[ WITH
......
     [ [ , ] NO_TRUNCATE ]
     [ [ , ] { NORECOVERY | STANDBY = undo_file_name } ]
```

The options specific to BACKUP LOG are discussed in detail in the following sections.

The NO_TRUNCATE Option

You use the NO_TRUNCATE option when the log is available, but the database is not. This option prevents the truncation of the transaction log after a backup occurs. Under normal circumstances, the BACKUP LOG command not only writes to the transaction log, but also signals a checkpoint for the database to flush any dirty buffers from memory to the database files. This behavior becomes a problem when the media containing the database is unavailable and you must capture the current contents of a log to a backup file for recovery. If you last did a log backup four hours ago, this would mean the loss of all the input since then. If your log is on a separate disk that is not damaged, you have those four hours of transactions available to you, but BACKUP LOG fails because it can't run a checkpoint on the data files. You run BACKUP LOG with the NO_TRUNCATE option, and the log is backed up, but the checkpoint is not run because the log is not actually cleared. You now have this new log backup to restore as well, enabling recovery to the time of failure. The only transactions lost are those that were not yet committed.

The NORECOVERY | STANDBY= undo_file_name Options

The NORECOVERY option causes the tail of the log to be backed up and leaves the database in a RESTORING state, which allows additional transaction logs to be applied, if necessary. The tail of the log is the active portion of the log that contains transactions not yet backed up. This "tail" is critical in restore situations in which all committed transactions are reapplied. Typically, the NORECOVERY option is used with the NO_TRUNCATE option to retain the contents of the log.

The STANDBY option also backs up the tail of the log, but it leaves the database in a read-only/standby state. The read-only state allows inquiry on the database and allows additional transaction logs to be applied to the database as well. undo_file_name must be supplied with the STANDBY command so that transactions not committed and rolled back at the time of the backup can be reapplied if additional transaction logs are applied to the database. This STANDBY option produces the same results as executing BACKUP LOG WITH NORECOVERY followed by a RESTORE WITH STANDBY command.

> **NOTE**
>
> As mentioned earlier, Microsoft has removed the NO_LOG and TRUNCATE_ONLY options available with earlier versions of SQL Server, including SQL Server 2005. Setting a database to use the simple recovery model is the alternative to these options.

Backup Scenarios

Typically, several different types of backups are used in a comprehensive backup plan. These backups are often combined to produce maximum recoverability while balancing the load on the system and amount of time to recover the database. The following backup scenarios outline some of the ways SQL Server backups are used.

> **NOTE**
>
> Many of the examples that follow utilize a backup directory named c:\mssql\backup. If you are interested in running some of these examples on your own system, you need to create this directory on the database server first before running the scripts that reference this directory. You can use backup and data directories different from the default directory to simplify the directory structure for the SQL Server files. Typically, these directories should not be on the c: drive, but the c: drive is used here for simplicity.

Full Database Backups Only

A full database backup, without the use of other type of database backups, is often found in nonproduction environments where the loss of transactional data is relatively unimportant. Some development environments are good examples of this. In these environments, a nightly full backup is sufficient to ensure that recent Data Definition Language (DDL) changes and the related development data for the day are captured. If a catastrophic failure occurs during the day and causes a restore to occur, the database can be restored from the prior night's backup. The following example shows a full backup of the AdventureWorks2012 database:

```
--Full Database Backup to a single disk device
BACKUP DATABASE [AdventureWorks2012]
 TO  DISK = N'C:\mssql\backup\AdventureWorks2012.bak'
 WITH NOFORMAT, INIT,  NAME = N'AdventureWorks2012-Full
Database Backup',
 SKIP, NOREWIND, NOUNLOAD,  STATS = 10
```

The sole use of daily full database backups needs to be carefully considered. The benefits of limited administration and limited backup space requirements have to be weighed against the costs of losing an entire day's transactions.

Full Database Backups with Transaction Log Backups

Compared to making a full database backup only, a more comprehensive approach to database backups includes the use of transaction log backups to augment the recoverability of full database backups. Transaction log backups that are taken periodically capture incremental database activity that can be applied to a full database backup during database restore.

You need to measure the frequency of the transaction log backup against the tolerance for data loss. For example, if the requirement is to prevent no more than one hour's worth of work, the transaction log backups should be taken hourly. If the media on which the backup is stored is accessible, you should lose no more than one hour's worth of data.

As mentioned earlier, the database must be placed in full or bulk-logged recovery mode to capture transaction log backups. Listing 11.1 shows the commands necessary to place the AdventureWorks2012 database in full recovery mode, the required backup to establish a base, followed by the command to perform the actual transaction log backup.

LISTING 11.1   Full Backups with Transaction Logs

```
--First need to change the recovery model from simple to full
--so that the tlogs are available for backup
ALTER DATABASE [AdventureWorks2012] SET RECOVERY FULL WITH
NO_WAIT

--*** A Full database backup must be taken after the
--*** recovery mode has been changed
--*** in order to set a base for future tlog backups.
--*** If the full backup is not taken
--*** then tlog backups will fail.
--The Following full backup utilizes two devices on the same drive.
--Often times multiple devices are backed up to different drives.
--Backing up to different drives
-- can speed up the overall backup
time and help when you are running low on space on a drive
-- where your backups are written.

BACKUP DATABASE [AdventureWorks2012]
 TO  DISK =
N'C:\mssql\backup\AdventureWorks2012_Full_Dev1.bak',
    DISK =
N'C:\mssql\backup\AdventureWorks2012_Full_Dev2.bak'
 WITH NOFORMAT, NOINIT, SKIP, NOREWIND, NOUNLOAD,  STATS =
10

--Transaction log backups can be taken now that a base has been established
--The following tlog backup is written to a single file
BACKUP LOG [AdventureWorks2012]
```

```
 TO  DISK =
N'C:\mssql\backup\log\AdventureWorks2012_FirstAfterFull.trn'
 WITH NOFORMAT, INIT,  NAME = N'AdventureWorks2012-
Transaction Log  Backup',
 SKIP, NOREWIND, NOUNLOAD,  STATS = 10, CHECKSUM
```

Differential Backups

Differential backups can be used to reduce the amount of time required to restore a database and can be particularly useful in environments where the amount of data that changes is limited. Differential backups capture only the database extents that have changed since the last database backup—typically, a full database backup.

The addition of differential backups to a plan that includes full database backups and transaction log backups can significantly improve the overall recovery time. The differential database backup eliminates the need to apply any transaction log backups that have occurred from the time of the last full backup up until the completion of the differential backup. Figure 11.5 depicts a backup plan that includes full database backups, transaction log backups, and differential backups. The differential backups are executed on a daily basis between the full backups.

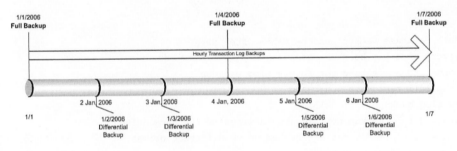

FIGURE 11.5   A backup plan that includes differential backup.

It is important to remember that differential backups are cumulative and contain all changes since the last differential base. There is no need to apply differential backups that were taken prior to the one that you are restoring. For example, in the backup plan shown in Figure 11.5, if a media failure occurred in the middle of the day on January 3, the differential backup that would be used is the one taken at the beginning of the day on January 3; the differential backup that occurred on January 2 would not be needed. The full backup from January 1, the differential from January 3, and any transaction log backups that had occurred since the differential on January 3 would be used to restore the database.

You can create differential backups by using SSMS or T-SQL. The following example demonstrates the creation of a differential backup for the AdventureWorks2012 database using T-SQL:

```
BACKUP DATABASE [AdventureWorks2012]
 TO  DISK = N'C:\mssql\backup\AdventureWorks2012_Diff2.bak'
 WITH  DIFFERENTIAL , NOFORMAT, INIT,
 NAME = N'AdventureWorks2012-Differential Database Backup',
 SKIP, NOREWIND, NOUNLOAD,   STATS = 10
```

Partial Backups

Partial backups are useful when read-only files or filegroups are part of a database.
Listing 11.2 contains the commands necessary to add a read-only filegroup to the
AdventureWorks2012 database. The commands in Listing 11.2 do not perform a partial
backup, but they do modify a sample database so that a partial backup would make sense.

LISTING 11.2   Adding a Read-Only Filegroup to a Database

```
--Need to add a read only filegroup first to demonstrate
ALTER DATABASE AdventureWorks2012
ADD FILEGROUP ReadOnlyFG1
GO
-- Add a file to the Filegroup
ALTER DATABASE AdventureWorks2012
ADD FILE
(    NAME = AdventureWorks2012_ReadOnlyData,
     FILENAME =
'C:\mssql\data\AdventureWorks2012_ReadOnlyData.ndf',
     SIZE = 5MB,
     MAXSIZE = 100MB,
     FILEGROWTH = 5MB) TO FILEGROUP ReadOnlyFG1
go
--Create a table on the ReadOnly filegroup
CREATE TABLE AdventureWorks2012.dbo.MyReadOnlyTable
  ( FirstName varchar(50),
    LastName varchar(50),
    EMailAddress char(1000) )
ON ReadOnlyFG1

--Insert some data into the new read only Filegroup
insert AdventureWorks2012.dbo.MyReadOnlyTable
 select LastName, FirstName, 'xxx'
 from AdventureWorks2012.person. person

--Make the filegroup readonly
 ALTER DATABASE [AdventureWorks2012] MODIFY FILEGROUP [ReadOnlyFG1] READONLY
```

When you have a filegroup that contains read-only data, a partial backup can be valuable. The partial backup by default excludes any read-only filegroups and backs up only the read/write data that could have changed.

Listing 11.3 contains three separate backup commands that relate to the partial backup. The first backup command is not a partial backup but instead backs up the read-only filegroup. If the read-only filegroup is not backed up prior to the partial backup, the read-only filegroup is backed up, as is part of the partial backup. The second backup command creates the actual partial backup. The key parameter in this backup is READ_ WRITE_FILEGROUPS, which causes the backup to skip the read-only data. The third backup command in Listing 11.3 shows that it is possible to perform a partial backup that includes the read-only data as well. This command includes a specific reference to the read-only filegroup, which causes it to be backed up as well.

LISTING 11.3   Making a Partial Backup

```
--Need to backup the readonly filegroup that was created
-- or it will be included in the partial backup
BACKUP DATABASE [AdventureWorks2012]
 FILEGROUP = N'ReadOnlyFG1'
 TO  DISK =
N'C:\mssql\backup\AdventureWorks2012_ReadOnlyFG.bak'
 WITH NOFORMAT, NOINIT,  NAME = N'AdventureWorks2012-Full
Filegroup Backup',
 SKIP, NOREWIND, NOUNLOAD,  STATS = 10


--Create the Partial Database Backup
--It will not contain the data from readonly filegroup
--The partial database backup can be restored without
affecting
-- the data in the readonly filegroup
BACKUP DATABASE [AdventureWorks2012] READ_WRITE_FILEGROUPS
 TO  DISK =
N'C:\mssql\backup\AdventureWorks2012_Partial.bak'
 WITH NOFORMAT, INIT,  NAME = N'AdventureWorks2012-Partial
Database Backup',
 SKIP, NOREWIND, NOUNLOAD,  STATS = 10


--It is possible to backup the readonly filegroup(s) as well
--by listing the readonly filegroups in the backup command
as shown in the
--following backup command
BACKUP DATABASE [AdventureWorks2012] FILEGROUP =
'ReadOnlyFG1',
 READ_WRITE_FILEGROUPS
 TO  DISK =
N'C:\mssql\backup\AdventureWorks2012_Partial_WithReadOnly.
```

```
bak'
 WITH NOFORMAT, INIT,  NAME = N'AdventureWorks2012-Partial
Database Backup',
  SKIP, NOREWIND, NOUNLOAD,  STATS = 10
```

File/Filegroup Backups

Much of our discussion thus far has focused on backing up an entire database, but it is possible to back up only particular files or a group of files in a filegroup. A SQL Server database, by default, has only two files: the data file (with the file extension .mdf) and the log file (with the extension .ldf). You can add additional files and filegroups that contain these files to extend the database beyond the original two files. These additional files are often data files added to larger databases that require additional space. With very large databases, performing a full backup that contains all the database files can take too much time. In such a case, the individual files or filegroups can be backed up separately, enabling you to spread out the backup.

Listing 11.4 shows the T-SQL command that can be used to back up the read-only file you added to the AdventureWorks2012 database in Listing 11.3.

LISTING 11.4   Creating a File Backup

```
BACKUP DATABASE [AdventureWorks2012] FILE =
'AdventureWorks2012_ReadOnlyData'
 TO  DISK =
N'C:\mssql\backup\AdventureWorks2012_ReadOnlyData.bak'
 WITH NOFORMAT, INIT,  NAME = N'AdventureWorks2012-Readonly
File Backup',
  SKIP, NOREWIND, NOUNLOAD,  STATS = 10
```

There is some additional administrative overhead associated with file and filegroup backups. Unlike a full database backup that produces one file that contains the entire database, the file backups do not stand by themselves and require other backups to be able to create the entire database. You need to keep the following points in mind when performing file and filegroup backups:

▶ A file or filegroup backup does not back up any portion of the transaction log. To restore a file or filegroup backup, you must have the transaction log backups since the last file or filegroup backup, including the tail of the log, for the database system to ensure transactional consistency. This also implies that the database must be in full or bulk-logged recovery because these are the only models that support transaction log backups.

▶ Individual file or filegroup backups can be restored from a full database backup.

▶ Point-in-time recovery is not permitted with file or filegroup backups.

▶ Differential backups can be combined with file or filegroup backups. These differential backups capture only those extents that have changed since the file or filegroup backup was made.

File and filegroup backups can be powerful options for very large databases, but you need to ensure that the relevant backups can be accounted for. In all backup situations, the key to a successful plan is testing your backup strategy; this is particularly true with file and filegroup backups.

Mirrored Backups

The use of mirrored backups can help diminish the possibility of losing a database backup. Database backups can be your lifeline to recovery, and you do not want to lose them. Mirrored backups simultaneously write the backup information to more than one media set. You can mirror the backup to two, three, or four different media sets. Listing 11.5 gives an example of a mirrored backup that writes two different media sets.

LISTING 11.5   Creating a Mirrored Backup

```
BACKUP DATABASE AdventureWorks2012
TO disk = 'C:\mssql\backup\AdventureWorks2012_Mirror1a.bak',
    disk = 'C:\mssql\backup\AdventureWorks2012_Mirror1b.bak'
MIRROR TO disk =
'c:\mssql\backup\AdventureWorks2012_Mirror2a.bak',
    disk = 'C:\mssql\backup\AdventureWorks2012_Mirror2b.bak'
WITH FORMAT,
    MEDIANAME = 'AdventureWorks2012MirrorSet'
```

The example in Listing 11.5 is simplistic but demonstrates the backup's capability to write to two different locations. At the end of the backup example, four files will exist. Each pair of files can be used to restore the database. In the real world, a backup like that in Listing 11.5 would typically write to two different disk or tape drives. Storing the media on the same drive is very risky and does not give you all the advantages a mirror can afford.

Copy-Only Backups

If you want a backup that will not affect future or past backups, copy-only backups are for you. The copy-only backup allows you to make a database or log backup without identifying the backup as one that should be included in a restore sequence.

Contrast this with a full database backup: If a full database backup is taken, the information related to this backup is captured in the system tables. This backup can form the base for other backups, such as transaction log backups or differential backups, and must be retained to be able to restore the backups that depend on the base.

The following example shows a copy-only backup; the COPY_ONLY parameter is the key to creating this kind of backup:

```
BACKUP DATABASE [AdventureWorks2012]
 TO  DISK = N'C:\mssql\backup\AdventureWorks2012_COPY.bak'
WITH COPY_ONLY
```

Compressed Backups

How would you like to create a backup file that is smaller and takes less time to create? Sign me up. This has got to be an option that the average database user would love to use. Compressed backups are smaller in size than uncompressed backups. The reduced size of a compressed backup typically requires less device I/O and can therefore reduce backup times significantly.

There are some trade-offs, however. The creation of a compressed backup can impact the performance of concurrent operations on your database server while the backup is being created. Specifically, CPU usage increases during the backup. This may or may not be an issue for you. Consider that many full database backups are taken during off-hours, so there are more CPU cycles available during this time. Either way, you should monitor the CPU usage using compression versus not using compression to evaluate the impact. Another option is to create low-priority compressed backups in a session whose CPU usage is limited by the Resource Governor. (For more information on using the Resource Governor, see Chapter 41, "Managing Workloads with the Resource Governor.")

> **NOTE**
>
> There are some situations where the size of the database backup is not reduced by much. For example, compressed backups of encrypted databases might not reduce the size very much. Encrypted data compresses much less than the equivalent unencrypted data. You may also find that databases that contain a significant amount of binary data do not compress much. Binary data includes data found in columns defined with the Image data type. In the end the type of data you have stored in your database will determine the amount of compression that you will see in your compressed backup.

When you get past these hurdles, the creation of a compressed backup is straightforward. One option is to set a server option so that all backups are created as compressed files by default. You can do this in SSMS by right clicking on the instance name in the SSMS object explorer and enabling the Compress backup option on the Database Settings page. You can also use the sp_configure stored procedure to set the backup compression default. If this is set to true, future backups will be created in a compressed format unless the backup is specifically created with the NO_COMPRESS option.

You also have the option of creating a compressed backup regardless of the server option. This is done using the new COMPRESSION option available with the T-SQL BACKUP command. The following example shows how to create an AdventureWorks2012 backup in the compressed format:

```
BACKUP DATABASE [AdventureWorks2012]
TO  DISK =
N'C:\MSSQL\Backup\AdventureWorks2012_compressed.bak'
```

```
WITH NOFORMAT, NOINIT,
 NAME = N'AdventureWorks2012-Full Database Backup',
SKIP, NOREWIND, NOUNLOAD, COMPRESSION,  STATS = 10
```

The compression is quite impressive. In some simple tests performed on the `AdventureWorks2012` database, the compressed backup was one fourth the size of a noncompressed backup. The compression ratio varies depending on the type of data in the database that you are backing up but can be as good as or better than 4:1.

Encrypted Backups

One of the core Backup and Restore enhancements in SQL Server 2014 is the ability to create an encrypted backup. Backup encryption allows for the use of several encryption algorithms that help secure your backup files. The available encryption algorithms include AES 128, AES 192, AES 256, and Triple DES.

In order to create an encrypted backup you must choose one of the aforementioned encryption algorithms and you must also choose an encryptor which is a certificate or asymmetric key. Encrypted backups can be created using the Back Up Database Wizard, the Maintenance Plan Wizard, or with T-SQL. This section focuses on the T-SQL commands that can be used to create an encrypted backup.

The first step in creating an encrypted backup with T-SQL is the creation of a database master key. An example of the commands to create the database master key and store the password in the Master database follows:

```
USE master;
GO
CREATE MASTER KEY ENCRYPTION BY PASSWORD = 'somecomplexpassword';
GO
```

The password that you provide when creating the master key above should be complex and secured so that you have it for the future. After you have created the master key you can move along to the creation of a backup certificate as shown in the following example:

```
USE master;
GO
CREATE CERTIFICATE ExampleDBBackupCert
WITH SUBJECT = 'Example Database Backup Certificate'
GO
```

You should immediately back up the certificate and the private key associated with the certificate. If the certificate ever becomes unavailable or if you must restore or attach the database on another server, you must have backups of both the certificate and the private key or you will not be able to open the database. The following example backs up the certificate that we created in the previous example:

```
USE master;
GO
BACKUP CERTIFICATE ExampleDBBackupCert
  TO FILE = 'C:\mssql\Backup\ExampleDBBackupCert.cert'
    WITH PRIVATE KEY ( FILE = 'c:\mssql\Backup\ExampleDBBackupCert.privatekey' ,
    ENCRYPTION BY PASSWORD = 'SomeComplexCertPassword')
GO
```

Once you have the certificate and private key you can now create an encrypted database backup. The following example shows the creation of an encrypted backup for the AdventureWorks2012 database.

```
BACKUP DATABASE [AdventureWorks2012]
  TO  DISK = N'C:\mssql\backup\AdventureWorks2012_Encrypted.bak'
  WITH COMPRESSION,
ENCRYPTION(ALGORITHM = AES_128,
SERVER CERTIFICATE = [ExampleDBBackupCert]), STATS = 10
GO
```

The encrypted backup can be restored on the same server just like any other backup. There are no additional steps or syntax options needed to restore the backup in this scenario. If, however, you attempt to restore the encrypted database backup on another server it will fail unless the backup certificate is created on the server where the backup will be restored. The certificate can be created on the destination server by restoring a backup of the certificate and the private key. The following example restores the certificate that was created in a previous example:

```
create CERTIFICATE ExampleDBBackupCert
  FROM FILE = 'C:\mssql\Backup\ExampleDBBackupCert.cert'
    WITH PRIVATE KEY ( FILE = 'c:\mssql\Backup\ExampleDBBackupCert.privatekey' ,
    DECRYPTION BY PASSWORD = 'SomeComplexCertPassword')
GO
```

> **NOTE**
>
> The SQL Server Backup to URL and SQL Server Managed Backup to Windows Azure are two other new backup and restore enhancements in SQL Server 2014. These enhancements are centered on backup and restore with a Windows Azure Blob Storage Service. Please refer to Chapter 19 for more detailed information.

System Database Backups

The system databases are the master, model, msdb, resource, tempdb, and distribution databases. SQL Server uses these databases as part of its internal workings. All these databases should be part of your backup plan, except for resource and tempdb. You can find detailed descriptions of these databases in Chapter 7, "SQL Server System and Database Administration." The important point to remember about all these databases is that they contain key information about your SQL Server environment. The `msdb` database contains information about backups and scheduled jobs. The `master` database contains information about all the user databases stored on the server. This information can change over time.

To ensure that you do not lose the information the system databases contain, you should back up these databases as well. Typically, nightly full database backups of these databases suffice. You can use the same backup T-SQL syntax or SSMS screens that you use for a user database to accomplish this task.

Restoring Databases and Transaction Logs

A database restore allows a database or part of a database to be recovered to a state that it was in previously. This state includes the physical structure of the database, configuration options, and data contained in the database. The options you have for recovery are heavily dependent on the backup plan you have in place and way you have configured your database. Databases that are set to simple recovery mode have limited options for database restore. Databases that are in full recovery mode and have frequent backups have many more restore options. Following are the basic options for restore:

- ▶ Restore an entire database.

- ▶ Perform a partial restore.

- ▶ Restore a file or page from a backup.

- ▶ Restore a transaction log.

- ▶ Restore a database to a point in time by using a database snapshot.

The following sections delve further into the restore options listed here. They focus on the means for accomplishing these restores and some of the common restore scenarios you might encounter.

Restores with T-SQL

The command to restore a database in SQL Server is aptly named RESTORE. The RESTORE command is similar to the BACKUP command in that it can be used to restore a database, part of a database, or a transaction log. You restore an entire database or part of a database by using the RESTORE DATABASE syntax. You do transaction log restores by using the RESTORE TRANSACTION syntax.

Database Restores with T-SQL

Listing 11.6 shows the full syntax for RESTORE DATABASE.

LISTING 11.6   RESTORE DATABASE Syntax

```
--To Restore an Entire Database from a Full database backup
(a Complete Restore):
RESTORE DATABASE { database_name | @database_name_var }
[ FROM <backup_device> [ ,...n ] ]
[ WITH
    [ { CHECKSUM | NO_CHECKSUM } ]
    [ [ , ] { CONTINUE_AFTER_ERROR | STOP_ON_ERROR } ]
    [ [ , ] ENABLE_BROKER ]
    [ [ , ] ERROR_BROKER_CONVERSATIONS ]
    [ [ , ] FILE = { file_number | @file_number } ]
    [ [ , ] KEEP_REPLICATION ]
    [ [ , ] MEDIANAME = { media_name | @media_name_variable }
]
    [ [ , ] MEDIAPASSWORD = { mediapassword |
                    @mediapassword_variable } ]
    [ [ , ] MOVE 'logical_file_name' TO
'operating_system_file_name' ]
                [ ,...n ]
    [ [ , ] NEW_BROKER ]
    [ [ , ] PARTIAL ]
    [ [ , ] PASSWORD = { password | @password_variable } ]
    [ [ , ] { RECOVERY | NORECOVERY | STANDBY =
          {standby_file_name | @standby_file_name_var }
    } ]
    [ [ , ] REPLACE ]
    [ [ , ] RESTART ]
    [ [ , ] RESTRICTED_USER ]
    [ [ , ] { REWIND | NOREWIND } ]
    [ [ , ] STATS [ = percentage ] ]
    [ [ , ] { STOPAT = { date_time | @date_time_var }
    | STOPATMARK = { 'mark_name' | 'lsn:lsn_number' }
            [ AFTER datetime ]
    | STOPBEFOREMARK = { 'mark_name' | 'lsn:lsn_number' }
            [ AFTER datetime ]
    } ]
    [ [ , ] { UNLOAD | NOUNLOAD } ]
]
```

Once again, there are many available options for restoring a database, but a simple restore is fairly straightforward. The following example demonstrates a full restore of the AdventureWorks2012 database:

```
RESTORE DATABASE [AdventureWorks2012]
FROM  DISK =
N'C:\mssql\backup\AdventureWorks2012_FullRecovery.bak'
WITH  FILE = 1,  NOUNLOAD,  REPLACE,  STATS = 10
```

For more sophisticated restores, you can specify options following the WITH clause. Table 11.2 briefly describes these options. Many of the options are the same as for the BACKUP command and provide similar functionality.

TABLE 11.2   RESTORE DATABASE Options

Option	Description
BLOCKSIZE	The physical block size used for the restore. The default is 64KB.
CHECKSUM | NO_CHECKSUM	When CHECKSUM is specified, a checksum is calculated before the backup is restored. If the checksum validation fails, the restore fails as well. The default is NO_CHECKSUM.
STOP_ON_ERROR | CONTINUE_AFTER_ERROR	The STOP_ON_ERROR option, which is the default, causes the backup to fail if an error is encountered. CONTINUE_AFTER_ERROR allows the restore to continue if an error is encountered.
ENABLE_BROKER	This option starts the Service Broker so that messages can be received.
ERROR_BROKER_CONVERSATIONS	Service Broker conversations with the database being restored are ended, with an error stating that the database is attached or restored.
FILE = { file_number | @file_number }	This option identifies the backup set number to be restored from the backup media. The default is 1, which indicates the latest backup set.
KEEP_REPLICATION	This option prevents replication settings from being removed during a restore operation. This is important when setting up replication to work with log shipping.
MEDIANAME	This is a 128-character name for the backup media. If it is specified, the target media must match this name.
MEDIAPASSWORD	This is a password for the media set. If the media was created with a password, the password must be supplied to restore from that media.
MOVE	This option causes the specified logical_file_name to be moved from its original file location to another location.
NEW_BROKER	This option creates a new service_broker_guid.
PARTIAL	This option causes a partial restore to occur that includes the primary filegroup and any specified secondary filegroup(s).
PASSWORD	This password is specific to the backup set. If a password was used when creating the backup set, a password must be used to restore from the media set.

Option	Description
RECOVERY | NORECOVERY | STANDBY	The RECOVERY option, which is the default, restores the database so that it is ready for use. NORECOVERY renders the database inaccessible but able to restore additional transaction logs. The STANDBY option allows additional transaction logs to be applied but the database to be read. These options are discussed in more detail later in this section.
REPLACE	This option causes the database to be created with the restore, even if the database already exists.
RESTART	This option allows a previously interrupted restore to restart where it was stopped.
RESTRICTED_USER	This option restricts access to the database after it has been restored. Only members of the db_owner, dbcreator, or sysadmin role can access it.
REWIND | NOREWIND	This option is used for tape operations. REWIND, which is the default, causes the tape to be released and rewound.
STATS	This option causes completion statistics to be displayed at the specified interval to assess progress.
STOPAT | STOPATMARK | STOPBEFOREMARK	This option causes a restore to recover to a specified date/time or to recover to a point defined by a specific transaction. The STOPAT option restores the database to the state it was in at the date and time. The STOPATMARK and STOPBEFOREMARK options restore based on the specified marked transaction or LSN.
UNLOAD | NOUNLOAD	This option is used for tape operations. NOUNLOAD cause the tape to remain in the tape drive after a restore completes. UNLOAD, which is the default, causes the tape to be rewound and unloaded when the restore completes.

Various options are utilized in the "Restore Scenarios" section, later in this chapter. Those restore scenarios provide a frame of reference for the options and further meaning about what they can accomplish.

Transaction Log Restores with T-SQL

The syntax details and options for restoring a transaction log backup are similar to those for RESTORE BACKUP. The options not available with RESTORE LOG include ENABLE_BROKER, ERROR_BROKER_CONVERSATIONS, NEW_BROKER, and PARTIAL.

The RECOVERY | NORECOVERY | STANDBY options are particularly important when performing transaction log restores and also when restoring a database that will have transaction logs applied. If these options are used incorrectly, you can render your database inaccessible or unable to restore subsequent transaction log backups. With the RECOVERY option, any uncommitted transactions are rolled back, and the database is made available for use. When a restore (of either a database or transaction log) is run with this option, no further transaction logs can be applied. The NORECOVERY and STANDBY options do allow subsequent transaction logs to be applied. When the NORECOVERY option is specified, the database is completely unavailable after the restore and is left in a restoring state. In this state, you cannot read the database, update the database, or obtain information about the database, but you can restore transaction logs.

With the STANDBY option, the database is left in a read-only state that allows some database access. standby_file_name must be specified with the STANDBY option. The standby file contains uncommitted transactions rolled back to place the database in a consistent state for read operations. If subsequent transaction log backups are applied to the STANDBY database, the uncommitted transactions in the standby file are reapplied to the database.

CAUTION

Take note of the standby_file_name name used when restoring with the STANDBY option and make sure the file is secure. If another restore operation is performed and the same standby_file_name is used, the previous standby file is overwritten. The database cannot be fully recovered without the standby file, so you have to perform all the restore operations again.

We speak from personal experience on this one. During a data recovery drill, for a large database (approximately 1TB), we spent hours restoring the transaction logs on a set of log-shipped databases. We manually restored the last log to be applied to place the database in STANDBY mode. Another database also in the data recovery drill was also placed in STANDBY, and unfortunately, the same standby file was used on this database. This caused more than one person a very long night. Be careful!

Some of the other options of the RESTORE DATABASE command are covered in the "Restore Scenarios" section, later in this chapter. Once again, many of these options are not required for most types of restores. For example, the following command uses basic options to restore a transaction log backup to the AdventureWorks2012 database:

```
RESTORE LOG [AdventureWorks2012] FROM
DISK =
N'C:\mssql\backup\AdventureWorks2012\AdventureWorks2012_back
up_201406091215.trn'
WITH  FILE = 1,  NOUNLOAD,  STATS = 10, NORECOVERY
```

Typically, the individual restore commands you will use are along the lines of the preceding example. The restores become more complicated when many restores of different types are involved in a recovery option. Fortunately, SSMS can help ease this pain.

Restoring by Using SSMS

The restore capabilities in SSMS are comprehensive and can reduce the amount of time needed to perform a restore and limit the number of errors. This is partly due to the fact that SSMS keeps track of the backups that have occurred on a server. When a restore operation is requested for a database, SQL Server reads from its own system tables and presents a list of backups that it knows about that can be restored. In situations in which many files need to be restored, SSMS can be an invaluable tool.

You access the restore functions in SSMS by right-clicking the database in the Object Explorer and selecting Tasks and then Restore. The options available for restore include Database, File and Filegroups, and Transaction Log. Which restore options are enabled depends on the state of the database being restored. The Transaction Log option is disabled for databases that were restored with the RECOVERY option or are set to simple recovery mode. Figure 11.6 shows an example of the restore screen that is displayed when you select a database restore for the AdventureWorks2012 database.

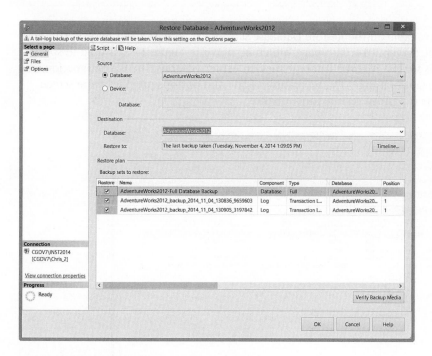

FIGURE 11.6   A database restore with SSMS.

The Restore Database window can show more than one type of backup, depending on what is available. The first backup shown in Figure 11.6 is a full backup, followed by transaction log and differential backups. The beauty of this screen is that the backups are shown in the order in which they should be applied. This order is very important with restores because they must be applied in the order in which they occurred. You can choose to apply all the backups or selectively choose the backups you want to apply. If you uncheck the first full database backup, all subsequent log backups are unchecked as well. If you recheck the full database backup and click one of the transaction log backups toward the bottom of the list, all the required backups that happened prior to the selected backups are also selected.

CAUTION

The order of items on the Restore Database screen was changed in SQL Server 2012. In earlier versions, the Destination section was displayed at the top of the General page followed by the Source section. Starting with SQL Server 2012, the order of these sections has been reversed. The Source section is at the top followed by the Destination section. This is a small change but could be disastrous if the source and destination were selected incorrectly.

The Files page available on the Restore Database screen was added in SQL Server 2012 and still exists in SQL Server 2014. This page, which is shown in Figure 11.7, is used to specify the file locations for the restored database files. In earlier versions, the file designation occurred on the Options page. The separation of File and options provides more screen real estate for the expanded restore functionality.

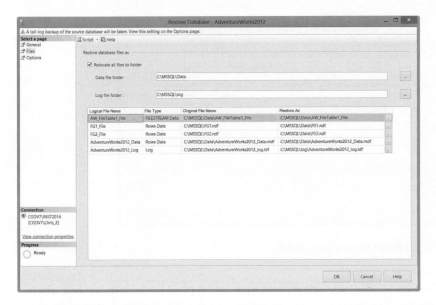

FIGURE 11.7   SSMS Restore Database - Files page.

The Files page is relatively straightforward. The grid on this screen contains a list of database files that are associated with the related backup. The Original File Name column in the grid shows where the files were located when the backup was taken. The Restore As column reflects where the database files will be located on the machine where the restore is happening. You can manually change the Restore As location by typing in the grid or by clicking the ellipsis. You can also use the Relocate All Files to Folder option to change the location. When this option is checked, the Data File folder and Log file folder fields are enabled. The folder names that are specified in these fields are then used for the Restore As folders. This provides an easy way to get a consistent location on the destination server without having to edit each one of the files individually.

Figure 11.8 shows an example of the SSMS Restore Database - Options page. The Options page allows you to specify many of the T-SQL RESTORE options reviewed previously. The Overwrite the Existing Database option is equivalent to the REPLACE parameter and forces a replacement of the restored database if it exists already. The Preserve the Replication Settings option is equivalent to KEEP_REPLICATION. The Restrict Access to the Restored Database option is the same as using the RESTRICTED_USER option with the T-SQL RESTORE command.

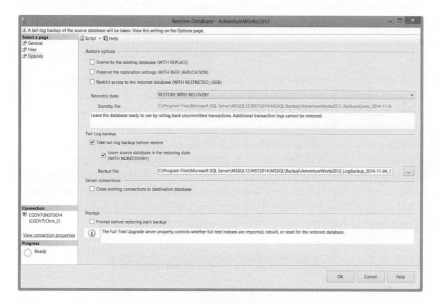

FIGURE 11.8   SSMS Restore Database - Options page.

The bottom portion of the Options page was changed in SQL Server 2012. The Recovery State and Standby file relate to the last backup set that will be restored. The RESTORE WITH RECOVERY selection is synonymous with the RECOVERY option, the RESTORE WITH NORECOVERY is the same as NORECOVERY, and the last option (RESTORE WITH STANDBY) is equivalent to the STANDBY option. The standby filename must be supplied with the STANDBY option and defaults to the default backup directory for the server. By default, the name of the file contains the name of the database being restored.

The Tail-Log backup and Server connections options were added in SQL Server 2012. When the Tail-Log backup option is checked, the tail or portion of the transaction log file that has been written to since the last backup is backed up before the restore is performed. This is a nice feature to help ensure that the tail is not mistakenly lost. The Server connection option is a powerful feature that should be used with caution. When checked, all connections to the destination database are killed. This option will help you get around the error message that is generated when someone is still using the database when a restore is attempted.

The last option on the page is the Prompt Before Restoring Each Backup option. This option does not have a T-SQL equivalent; it displays a prompt before restoring each backup set to ask whether you want to restore it. It is a particularly useful option when you are restoring from tape and need to swap the tape during the restore process.

TIP

You should click the Script button available on the Restore Database window if you want to see what is going on under the hood of the SSMS restores or want to run a restore later. You can learn a lot about the T-SQL options and how they work by scripting out the commands.

The Database Recovery Advisor is another way to perform a restore using SSMS. This new tool was introduced in SQL Server 2012 and is intended to simplify the restore process. The Database Recovery Advisor is launched by clicking the Timeline button on the General page of the Restore Database screen. Figure 11.9 shows the main Database Recovery Window with a sample backup timeline of 1 hour. In this figure, the option to recover to a specific date and time was chosen. This option enables the Date and Time fields. You can manually enter the date and time, but a more convenient option is to click on the timeline to select the point which you want the database restored. When you click on the timeline, a red vertical line is displayed on the timeline indicating the selected restore time. The Time field is also updated when you click on the timeline.

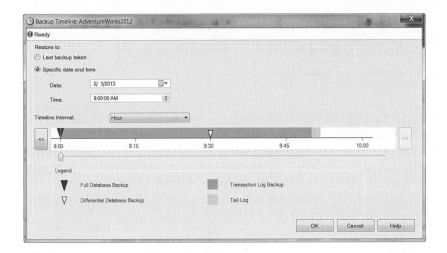

FIGURE 11.9   The Database Recovery Advisor.

The timeline can also be used to display information related to the files that will be restored. Simply mouse over the timeline, and file specifics will be displayed in a window below the timeline. The individual full and differential backups are easy to identify on the timeline and are designated with inverted triangles. The transaction log and tail log backups are reflected via colored sections of the timeline. Multiple transaction log backups can be included in a section between two full or differential backups, but this will just appear as one shaded area on the timeline.

The beauty of the Database Recovery Advisor is that you really don't need to concern yourself that much with the backup files associated with the restore. You can use the timeline to select what point in time that you want to restore the database, click OK, and then the files needed to accomplish this restore will be populated on the General page of the Restore Database screen. It's that easy.

Restore Information

Backup files and system tables contain a wealth of information about what can be restored or already has been restored. You can retrieve information from the backup files by using variations of the RESTORE command. These variations do not actually perform the restore operation but provide information about the backups that can be restored. The RESTORE commands and some useful system tables are detailed in the following sections.

The RESTORE FILELISTONLY Command

The RESTORE FILELISTONLY command returns a result set that contains a list of the database and log files contained in the backup. An example of this command follows:

```
RESTORE FILELISTONLY
FROM DISK = 'C:\mssql\backup\AdventureWorks2012_Partial.bak'
```

The results from this type of restore include the logical and physical filenames, the type of each file, and the size of each file.

The RESTORE HEADERONLY Command

The RESTORE HEADERONLY command returns a result set that contains the backup header data for all backup sets on the specified backup device. This command is useful when multiple backup sets are written to the same device. An example of this command follows:

```
RESTORE HEADERONLY
FROM DISK = 'C:\mssql\backup\AdventureWorks2012_Partial.bak'
```

More than 50 columns are returned in the result set. Some particularly useful pieces of information include the start and finish time for the backup, recovery mode when the backup was taken, type of backup, and name of the computer from which the backup was performed.

The RESTORE VERIFYONLY Command

The RESTORE VERIFYONLY command verifies that a backup set is complete and readable. The restore does not attempt to verify the structure of the data in the backups, but it has been enhanced to run additional checks on the data. The checks are designed to increase the probability of detecting errors. An example of this command follows:

```
RESTORE VERIFYONLY
FROM DISK = 'C:\mssql\backup\AdventureWorks2012_Partial.bak'

/*Result from the prior RESTORE VERIFYONLY command
The backup set on file 1 is valid.
*/
```

The results from the prior example show that the RESTORE VERIFYONLY command does not contain much output, but the value of this command is in helping ensure that the backups are sound.

Backup and Restore System Tables

The system tables for backups and restores are found predominantly in the msdb system database. These system tables are used to keep historical information about the backups and restores that have occurred on the server. These system tables are listed in Table 11.3.

TABLE 11.3   Backing Up and Restoring System Tables

msdb System Table	Description
backupfile	Contains one row for each data or log file of a database.
backupfilegroup	Contains one row for each filegroup in a database at the time of backup.
backupmediafamily	Contains a row for each media family.
backupmediaset	Contains one row for each backup media set.
backupset	Contains a row for each backup set.
logmarkhistory	Contains one row for each marked transaction that has been committed.
restorefile	Contains one row for each restored file. These include files restored indirectly, by filegroup name.
restorefilegroup	Contains one row for each restored filegroup.
restorehistory	Contains one row for each restore operation.
suspect_pages	Contains one row per page that failed with an 824 error (with a limit of 1,000 rows).
sysopentapes	Contains one row for each currently open tape device.

Refer to "Backup and Restore Tables" in the "System Tables" section of SQL Server Books Online for a detailed description of each table, including each column that can be retrieved.

You are able to query these tables to obtain a variety of information related to backups and restores. You can tailor these queries to look at a specific database or a specific time frame. The following example retrieves restore information for the AdventureWorks2012 database:

```
select destination_database_name 'database', h.restore_date,
restore_type,
 cast((backup_size/1024)/1024 as numeric(8,0)) 'backup_size
MB',
  f.physical_device_name
 from msdb..restorehistory h (NOLOCK)
   LEFT JOIN msdb..backupset b (NOLOCK)
   ON h.backup_set_id = b.backup_set_id
   LEFT JOIN msdb..backupmediafamily f (NOLOCK)
   ON b.media_set_id = f.media_set_id
 where h.restore_date > getdate() - 5
    and UPPER(h.destination_database_name) =
'AdventureWorks2012'
 order by UPPER(h.destination_database_name), h.restore_date desc
```

This example displays information related to restores that have been executed in the past five days for the AdventureWorks2012 database. The restore date, type of restore, size of the backup, and physical location of the file used for the restore are displayed when you run this query.

CAUTION

Queries against system tables are acceptable and can provide a wealth of information, but you need to exercise caution whenever you are dealing with a system table. SQL Server uses these tables, and problems can occur if the values in them are changed or their physical structure is altered.

Backup and Restore Report

A set of standard reports that come with SQL Server 2014 provide a variety of information about your databases, including recent restores and backups. You can access these reports by right-clicking on a database in the SSMS Object Explorer, then Reports, and then Standard Reports. You see over a dozen reports ready for you to run.

A report particularly useful for obtaining restore and backup information is named Backup and Restore Events. This report details the latest backup and restore events that have occurred on a particular database. An example of this report is shown in Figure 11.10.

The interactive report allows you to drill down into each backup or restore event to obtain more information. For example, the restore information shown in Figure 11.10 was obtained by clicking on the plus button next to the Successful Restore Operations label. You can then drill down into an individual restore to obtain more information, including the physical files involved in the operation.

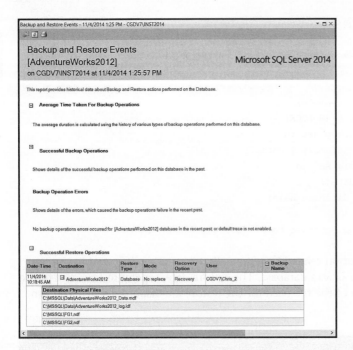

FIGURE 11.10   Backup and Restore Events report.

Restore Scenarios

Restore scenarios are as varied as the backup scenarios that drive them. The number of scenarios is directly related to the types of backups taken and frequency of those backups. If a database is in simple recovery mode and full database backups are taken each night, your restore options are limited. Conversely, full recovery databases that have multiple filegroups and take a variety of different types of backups have a greater number of options that can be used to restore the database.

The following sections describe a number of restore scenarios to give you a taste of the types of restores you may encounter. The scenarios include some restores performed with T-SQL and others performed with SSMS.

Restoring to a Different Database

You can restore a database backup to a different database. The database you're restoring to can be on the same server or a different server, and the database can be restored to a different name, if needed. These types of restores are common in development environments where a production backup is recovered on a development server or multiple copies of the same development database are restored to different database names for use by different groups.

Listing 11.7 shows the T-SQL RESTORE command you can use to create a new database named AdventureWorks2012_COPY from the backup of the AdventureWorks2012 database. Take note of the MOVE options that specify where the database files for the new AdventureWorks2012_COPY database will exist. Each MOVE option must refer to the logical name for the file and include a physical file location that is a valid location on the server. In addition, the referenced file cannot be used by another database. The only exception is when you are restoring to the database that is using the files and the REPLACE option is used.

LISTING 11.7   Restore to a Different Database

```
RESTORE DATABASE [AdventureWorks2012_COPY]
 FROM  DISK = N'C:\mssql\backup\AdventureWorks2012.bak'
 WITH  FILE = 1,
 MOVE N'AdventureWorks2012_Data' TO
N'C:\mssql\data\AdventureWorks2012_Copy.mdf',
 MOVE N'AdventureWorks2012_Log' TO
N'C:\mssql\data\AdventureWorks2012_Copy_log.ldf',
  NOUNLOAD,  STATS = 10
```

TIP

A restore of a database backup taken from another server can cause problems after the restore completes. The problems are caused by broken relationships between the database users captured in the backup file and the associated logins on the server to which the backup is restored. The relationships are broken because each login receives a unique ID assigned to it when it is added. These unique IDs can and will be different across servers, even though the logins may have the same name. The unique ID from the login is stored with each database user in order to identify the login that the user is associated with. When the unique ID for the login is different or not found, you get spurious errors when trying to connect to the database with these users or when trying to administer these users in SSMS.

The sp_change_users_login system stored procedure is designed to correct these broken relationships. You can run this procedure with the "report" option in the database in question to help identify any problems (that is, sp_change_users_login "report"). The stored procedure also has options to fix the broken relationships. For example, sp_change_users_login "autofix", "myuser" fixes the relationship for the "myuser" database user. You should check SQL Server Books Online for further options and details on this stored procedure.

Another quick-and-dirty means for fixing orphaned database users is to delete the users from the database and then re-create them. Of course, the login must exist on the server, and all the permissions associated with the database user must be re-established. Permissions can be overlooked or missed with this method, so it is safer to stick with the sp_change_users_login procedure.

Restoring a Snapshot

Database snapshots, which were introduced in SQL Server 2005, provide a fast method for capturing a transactionally consistent view of a database. The snapshot is created as another read-only database linked to the original database from which the snapshot was taken. As changes are made to the original database, the Database Engine uses a copy-on-write method to keep the snapshot consistent.

After a snapshot is taken, you can revert back to the snapshot at a later time and restore the original database to the state it was in when the snapshot was taken. You do not create the snapshot by backing up a database, but you can restore it using methods similar to restoring a backup. The following example shows the syntax to revert a database back to a database snapshot:

```
RESTORE DATABASE { database_name | @database_name_var }
FROM DATABASE_SNAPSHOT database_snapshot_name
```

Database snapshots are available only with the Enterprise or Development Editions of SQL Server. They are discussed in more detail in Chapter 29, "Database Snapshots."

Restoring a Transaction Log

Transaction log restores deserve special attention because of their dependency on other backup types. Typical transaction log restores occur after a full or differential database restore has occurred. After this base is established, the transaction log restores must be done in the same sequential order as the backups that were taken.

Fortunately, SSMS does a good job of presenting the available backups in the order in which they must be applied. You can do the entire restore sequence with SSMS, including a full restore followed by a restore of any other backups, including transaction log backups. To restore transaction log backups (independent of other backups), you can select the Restore Transaction Log option. This option is only available if the prior restore was done with the NORECOVERY or STANDBY option. Figure 11.11 shows a sample screen for restoring transaction logs in the AdventureWorks2012 database.

The transaction logs shown in Figure 11.11 are listed in the order in which they were taken and the order in which they need to be applied. You can uncheck some of the available backups, but you are not allowed to select backups that are not in the correct sequence. In other words, you can uncheck backups from the bottom of the list, but if you uncheck backups toward the top of the list, all backups found below that item are unchecked as well.

It is important to remember that you can restore transaction log backups only to a database that is in the NORECOVERY or STANDBY state. Make sure that every restore prior to the last one uses one of these options. When you restore the last transaction log, you should use the RECOVERY option so that the database is available for use.

FIGURE 11.11   Transaction log restore.

Restoring to the Point of Failure

A disk failure on a drive that houses database files is a reality that some database administrators must deal with. This situation can give pause to the most seasoned administrators, but it is a situation that can be addressed with little or no data loss. Don't panic! You need to first identify the available backups.

> **NOTE**
>
> Hopefully, the disk that experienced a failure is not the same disk that houses your backups. Database backups should always be stored on separate media. One of the best approaches is to write the backups to a drive that does not contain any other SQL Server files and write the contents of that drive to tape. This minimizes the possibility of losing one of those all-important backups.

The backup components that you need to restore to the point of failure include the following:

▶ A backup of the tail of the transaction log

▶ A full database backup or file/filegroup backup to establish a base

▶ The full sequence of transaction log backups created since the full database backup

The following sections describe the detailed steps for recovery that relate to these backup components.

> **NOTE**
>
> The restore steps outlined in the following sections do not address the recovery of the actual disk that failed. The recovery of hardware, such as a disk, is beyond the scope of this book, but it needs to be addressed to get your environment back to the state it was in prior to the failure.

Backing Up the Tail of the Transaction Log

The first thing you should do in the event of a damaged database is to back up the tail of the transaction log. The tail of the transaction log is found in the active SQL Server transaction log file(s). This tail is available only for databases that are in full or bulk-logged recovery mode. This tail contains transactions not backed up yet. The following example shows how to back up the tail of the log for the AdventureWorks2012 database using T-SQL:

```
BACKUP LOG [AdventureWorks2012]
 TO  DISK =
N'C:\mssql\backup\log\AdventureWorks2012_Tail.trn'
 WITH  NO_TRUNCATE
```

NO_TRUNCATE prevents the transactions in the log from being removed and allows the transaction log to be backed up, even if the database is inaccessible. This type of backup is possible only if the transaction log file is accessible and was not on the disk that had the failure.

Recovering the Full Database Backup

After you back up the tail of the transaction log, you are ready to perform a full database restore. This restore, which is based on a full database backup or a file/filegroup backup, overwrites the existing database. It is imperative that the full database restore be done with the NORECOVERY option so that the transaction log backups and tail of the log can be applied to the database as well. The following example restores a full backup of the AdventureWorks2012 database, using the T-SQL RESTORE command:

```
RESTORE DATABASE [AdventureWorks2012]
 FROM  DISK = N'C:\mssql\backup\AdventureWorks2012.bak'
 WITH  FILE = 1,  NORECOVERY,  NOUNLOAD,  REPLACE,  STATS =
10
```

Upon completion of this type of restore, the database appears in the SSMS Object Explorer with "(Restoring...)" appended to the end of the database name. The database is now ready for transaction log backups to be applied.

Restoring the Transaction Log Backup

The final step in recovery is to apply the transaction log backups. These backups include all the transaction log backups since the last full backup plus the tail of the log you backed up after the media failure. If differential backups were taken since the last full backup, you can apply the last differential backup and apply only those transaction log backups that have occurred since the last differential backup.

You can restore transaction log backups by using T-SQL or SSMS. To restore with SSMS, you can right-click the database in the restoring state and select the Transaction Log Restore option. The Restore Transaction Log screen lists the available transaction log backups, including the backup of the transaction log tail. You need to select all the transaction logs, including the tail. You should make sure to go to the Options tab and select the Recovery option so that your database is available after the restore completes.

Alternatively, you can use T-SQL to perform the transaction log backup restores. The following example shows a series of transaction log restores. The first two restores are done with the NORECOVERY option. The last command restores the tail of the log and uses the RECOVERY option to make the database available for use:

```
RESTORE LOG [AdventureWorks2012]
  FROM  DISK =
N'C:\mssql\backup\AdventureWorks2012_backup_201406180922.trn
'
  WITH  FILE = 1,  NORECOVERY,  NOUNLOAD,  STATS = 10
GO
RESTORE LOG [AdventureWorks2012]
  FROM  DISK =

N'C:\mssql\backup\AdventureWorks2012_backup_201406180923.trn
'
  WITH  FILE = 1,  NORECOVERY,  NOUNLOAD,  STATS = 10
GO
RESTORE LOG [AdventureWorks2012]
  FROM  DISK =
  N'C:\mssql\backup\log\AdventureWorks2012_Tail.trn'
  WITH  FILE = 3, RECOVERY, NOUNLOAD,  STATS = 10
GO
```

When many transaction log backups are involved, using T-SQL to perform the restores can be challenging. The restores must occur in the proper order and refer to the proper location of the backup file(s). Restores done with SSMS are typically less prone to error.

Restoring to a Point in Time

Databases in the full or bulk-logged recovery models can be restored to a point in time. This type of restore is similar to the point-of-failure scenario covered previously, but it allows for a more precise restore operation. These restores allow the database to be recovered to a time prior to a particular event. Malicious attacks or erroneous updates are some examples of events that would justify a point-in-time restore.

NOTE

There are some limitations on point-in-time restores of databases set to the bulk-logged recovery model. Point-in-time restores are not possible on transaction log backups that contain bulk load operations. Point-in-time restores can occur using transaction log backups that occurred prior to the bulk load operation, as long as a bulk load did not occur during the time of these backups.

A point-in-time restore can be done using one of the following:

▶ A specific date/time within the transaction log backup

▶ A specific transaction name inserted in the log

▶ An LSN

Point-in-time restores can be done with T-SQL or SSMS. The easiest way to perform a point-in-time restore is to use the new Database Recovery Advisor. After it is launched, choose the Specific Date and Time option, and then select the point in time where you want to recover the database on the timeline displayed. Figure 11.12 shows the General page that is displayed after the date/time has been selected using the Database Recovery timeline. The specific date and time is shown in the Restore To field along with all the backup settings required to accomplish the point-in-time restore.

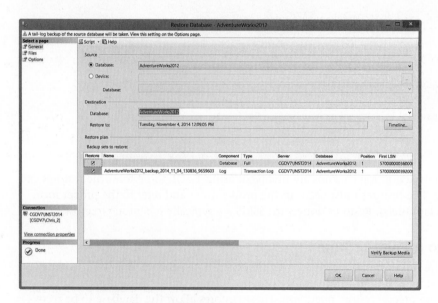

FIGURE 11.12   A point-in-time restore.

Online Restores

Online restores were new to SQL Server 2005 and continue to be supported in SQL Server 2014. They allow a filegroup, file, or specific page within a file to be restored while the rest of the database is online. The file or filegroup that is being restored to must be offline during the duration of the online restore.

> **TIP**
>
> You should take a full backup of a database immediately before taking a read-only file offline. This simplifies the online restore process and eliminates the need to apply a bunch of transaction log backups prior to the online restore. This applies only to databases in full or bulk-logged recovery.

The following example demonstrates how to take a read-only file offline:

```
ALTER DATABASE AdventureWorks2012
MODIFY FILE (NAME = 'AdventureWorks2012_ReadOnlyData',
OFFLINE)
```

When the file is offline, you can perform a restore to that file without affecting the rest of the database. The following example shows an example of an online restore of a read-only file to the AdventureWorks2012 database:

```
RESTORE DATABASE [AdventureWorks2012]
 FILE = N'AdventureWorks2012_ReadOnlyData'
 FROM  DISK =
N'C:\mssql\backup\AdventureWorks2012_ReadOnlyData.bak'
 WITH  FILE = 1,  NOUNLOAD,  STATS = 10, RECOVERY
```

Restoring the System Databases

The SQL Server 2014 system databases that can be restored are the master, msdb, model, and distribution databases. Each of these databases performs an essential role in the operation of SQL Server. If these databases are damaged or lost, they can be restored from database backup files in a similar fashion to user databases.

The master database, which contains information about other databases and is required to start SQL Server, has some special restore considerations. It must be operational before restores of other system databases can be considered. When you are restoring the master database, there are two basic scenarios. The first scenario involves a restore of the master database when the master database currently used by SQL Server is operational. For example, if someone inadvertently made changes to the master database and you wanted to restore the database to a point in time prior to the change. In the second scenario, the master database is unavailable, and SQL Server is unable to start.

The first `master` database restore scenario is less involved and typically less stressful than the second. In the first scenario, your SQL Server can be up and running until the time you want to do the restore. When you are ready to do the restore, the SQL Server instance must be running in single-user mode. The server can be started in single-user mode via a command prompt window. You stop the currently running SQL Server service, open a command prompt window, navigate to the directory where the `sqlservr.exe` file exists (typically `C:\Program Files\Microsoft SQL Server\MSSQL11\MSSQL\Binn\`), and run the following command:

```
sqlservr.exe -m
```

When this command is executed, the SQL Server instance is running in the command prompt window. This window must be kept open for the SQL Server instance to keep running. The service for SQL Server appears as stopped, but the Database Engine is truly running.

The `-m` parameter places the server in single-user mode and allows a single administrator connection to the server. You can use that one connection to connect to the server to use the Object Explorer, a database query window in SSMS, SQLCMD, or any other tool that allows you to establish a connection and run commands against the database server. If you use the SSMS Object Explorer connection, you can right-click on the `master` database and select the Restore option. You need to enter **master** for the database to restore and select the overwrite option. You can instead run a T-SQL `RESTORE` command to achieve the same result.

When the restore of the `master` database is complete, SQL Server is automatically shut down. If you performed the restore using Object Explorer, you can expect to get an error message at the end of the restore process because SQL Server was shut down. You can simply close the command prompt window you used earlier and establish a new connection to the database server. All the databases, logins, and so on that were present prior to the backup are re-established.

In the second scenario, the `master` database is damaged or unavailable, and SQL Server cannot start. If SQL Server is unable to start, you must re-establish a base environment like that which existed when SQL Server was initially installed. Using the `REBUILDDATABASE` option in `setup.exe` is one way to re-create all the system databases and reestablish this base environment. The `REBUILDDATABASE` parameter is part of a SQL Server installation that is done from the command prompt. You need the installation media for the edition of SQL Server installed on the machine. After you insert the disk and when you have access to the installation files, you can use the following syntax to launch the Setup program from a command prompt window:

```
start /wait <CD or DVD Drive>\setup.exe /qn
INSTANCENAME=<InstanceName> REINSTALL=SQL_Engine
/SQLSYSADMINACCOUNTS=accounts
REBUILDDATABASE=1 SAPWD=<NewStrongPassword>
```

InstanceName should be set to MSSQLSERVER for a default instance of SQL Server or the name of the instance, if it is not the default. A new SA password needs to be supplied for the SAPWD parameter as well as an administrator account for the SQLSYSADMINACCOUNTS parameter. The /qn parameter suppresses all the setup dialog boxes and error messages and causes the installation to run silently. If you want to receive more information during the installation, you can specify the /qb parameter.

NOTE

If you get a message about a missing Windows Installer, you can find that software on the SQL Server media in the Redist folder. You may also find that the setup.exe file is not found on the root of your installation media. If this is the case, you need to change the directory in the command prompt window to the location of the setup.exe file on the installation media prior to executing the command to launch the setup program. Finally, remember to reinstall any service packs or patches you may have installed. The execution of the command prompt setup reverts the server back to the original software release.

At the end of the installation, all the system database files are installed to their original locations. This includes the original master.mdf, mastlog.ldf, msdbdata.mdf, and msdblog.ldf files, as well as the related database files for the other system databases. Any of the user databases you may have added to the server are no longer known by the master database and in turn are not available in the Object Explorer or other database tools.

If you have a backup of the master database, you can restore it after the command prompt installation is complete. You follow the procedures outlined in the first scenario, earlier in this section, to restore the master database from a backup. At the completion of the restore, any user databases present at the time of the master database backup are now available. You can also run restores for other system databases at this time, including the msdb database, which contains all your scheduled jobs and history.

If you do not have a backup of the master database, this is not the end of the world. You still have the option of manually attaching your user databases or restoring them from backup files. Attaching the database is typically much faster than restores from backup files and is the preferred method. You must also re-establish logins, backup devices, server triggers, and any other server-level objects stored in the master database. Depending on your environment, this can be a lengthy operation, but you can easily avoid it by making those all-important system database backups.

Additional Backup Considerations

A sound backup plan goes beyond the commands and tools described thus far in this chapter. There are several other things you want to consider as well, as detailed in the following sections.

Frequency of Backups

How often you back up your databases depends on many factors, including the following:

▶ The size of your databases and your backup window (that is, the time allocated to complete the task of backing up the database)

▶ The frequency of changes to the data and method by which it is changed

▶ The acceptable amount of data loss in the event of a failure

▶ The acceptable recovery time in the event of a failure

First, you must establish what your backup window will be. Because SQL Server allows dynamic backups, users can still access the database during backups; however, this affects performance. This means you should still schedule backups for low-activity periods and have them complete in the shortest possible time.

After you establish your backup window, you can determine your backup method and schedule. For example, if it takes 4 hours for a full backup to complete, and the database is quiescent between midnight and 6:00 a.m., you have time to perform a full backup each night. On the other hand, if a full backup takes 10 hours, and you have a 2-hour window, you should consider monthly or weekly backups, perhaps in conjunction with filegroup, differential, and transaction log backups. In many decision-support databases populated with periodic data loads, it might suffice to back up once after each data load.

Backup frequency is also directly tied to acceptable data loss. In the event of catastrophic failure, such as a fire in the server room, you can recover data only up to the point of the last backup moved offsite. If it is acceptable to lose a day's worth of data entry, nightly backups might suffice. If your acceptable loss is an hour's worth of data, hourly transaction log backups would have to be added to the schedule.

Your backup frequency affects your recovery time. In some environments, a weekly full backup plus transaction log backups taken every 10 minutes provide an acceptable data loss factor. A failure a few days after backup would require a full database restore and the application of hundreds of transaction logs. Adding a daily differential backup in this case would vastly improve restore time. The full and differential backups would be restored, and then six logs would be applied for each hour between the differential backup and the time of failure.

In the end it is a bit of a balancing act between the time and space taken to create the backups and the time it takes to recover the backups. Full backups and differential backups generally take longer, and the resulting backup files are larger. Transaction log backups are smaller and take less space if they are taken on a more frequent basis. The transaction volume in your database and the amount of data that is changing will drive the best backup solution.

Using a Standby Server

If the ability to quickly recover from failure is crucial to your operation, you might consider implementing a standby server. Implementing a standby server involves backing up the production server and then restoring it to the standby server, leaving it in recovery mode. As transaction logs are backed up on the production server, they are applied to the standby server. If a failure occurs on the production server, the standby server can be recovered and used in place of the production server. If the production server is still running, you should not forget to back up the current log with the NO_TRUNCATE option and restore it to the standby server as well before bringing it online.

> **NOTE**
>
> Another advantage of restoring backups to a standby server is that it immediately validates your backups so you can be assured of whether they are valid. There is nothing worse than finding out during a recovery process that one of the backup files is damaged or missing.

The STANDBY =undo_file_name option plays a key role in the application of transaction logs to the standby server. When the database and subsequent log backups are restored to the standby server with this option, the database is left in recovery mode but is available as a read-only database. Now that the standby database is available for queries, it can actually reduce load on the production database by acting as a reporting database. Database Consistency Checks (DBCC) can be run on it as well, further reducing the load on the production system.

For the database to be available for reads, the data must be in a consistent state. This means that all uncommitted transactions must be rolled back. This rollback is usually handled by the RECOVERY option during a restore. In the case of a standby server, this would cause a problem because you would intend to apply more logs, which could, in fact, commit those transactions. This situation is handled by the undo_file_name clause of the STANDBY option. The file specified here holds a copy of all uncommitted transactions rolled back to bring the standby server to a consistent, read-only state. If those transactions subsequently commit a log restore, this undo information can be used to complete the transaction.

The application of hundreds or thousands of transaction logs to the standby server can be challenging. Fortunately, SQL Server 2014 includes log shipping, which automates the transfer of logs to the standby server. Log shipping, which can be configured in SSMS, uses SQL Server Agent jobs on the primary server to back up the transaction log and copy it to a folder on the standby server. SQL Server Agent on the standby server then executes a load job to restore the log. Automating your standby server with log shipping reduces administration and helps to ensure that the standby database is up-to-date. For further details on log shipping, see Chapter 43, "Data Replication." Log shipping isn't a form of replication but is covered in Chapter 43 as an alternative to replication.

Snapshot Backups

Snapshot backups are developed in conjunction with independent hardware and software vendors. These backups are not related to SQL Server database snapshots and are not accessible from any of the SQL Server tools. They utilize backup and restore technology and can provide relatively fast backup and restore operations. Snapshot backups are typically utilized on very large databases that are unable to perform database backups and restores in a timely fashion using SQL Server's conventional backup and restore resources.

Considerations for Very Large Databases

When it comes to backup and recovery, special consideration must be given to very large databases, which are known as VLDBs. A VLDB has the following special requirements:

▶ **Storage**—Size might dictate the use of tape backups instead of network or disk.

▶ **Time**—As your time to backup increases, the frequency of backups might have to be adjusted.

▶ **Method**—How you back up your database is affected by its size. Differential or file and filegroup backups might have to be implemented.

▶ **Recovery**—Partial database recovery, such as restoring a file or filegroup, might be required due to the prohibitive time required to restore the entire database.

When designing a VLDB, you must integrate your backup plan with storage, performance, and availability requirements. Larger databases take longer to back up because the backup sizes are larger, and restores on this type of database can take much longer to complete than with a smaller database.

Maintenance Plans

SQL Server includes maintenance plans that provide database maintenance tasks, including optimization, integrity checks, and backups. The backup options available in the maintenance plans are comprehensive and include the capability to regularly schedule full, differential, and transaction log backups. This type of automation is essential to ensure that your backups are taken with a reliable tool at regular intervals.

You can create maintenance plans from within SSMS. If you open the Management node in the Object Explorer, you see a node named Maintenance Plans. If you right-click this node, you can select New Maintenance Plan to create a plan from scratch, or you can select Maintenance Plan Wizard to have a wizard guide you through the creation of a new maintenance plan. The following options that relate to backups are available as part of a maintenance plan:

▶ Back Up Database (Full)

▶ Back Up Database (Differential)

▶ Back Up Database (Transaction Log)

Using these tasks in a maintenance plan is a great start to a solid backup and recovery plan. Refer to Chapter 30, "Database Maintenance," for further details about creating a maintenance plan.

Summary

Having a database environment without a solid backup and recovery plan is like owning a home without an insurance policy to protect it. If you develop a plan to minimize the possibility of losing a database, you have essentially bought an insurance policy for your data. In the event of a problem, you can call on the backups that you have invested in and recover the loss with a minimal amount of cost.

Chapter 12, "Database Mail," explores a comprehensive mail feature offered with SQL Server 2014. Database Mail allows you to send email notifications from SQL Server. These notifications can be tied to scheduled jobs and alerts within SQL Server, including jobs that can execute those all-important database backups.

11

Database Mail

Database Mail is SQL Server 2014's emailing component, built as the replacement for SQL Mail. SQL Mail has been completely removed from SQL Server 2014. However, it's a simple task to convert any legacy SQL Mail code and SQL Agent Mail notifications to use Database Mail. This chapter shows you how.

What's New in Database Mail

SQL Mail has been removed, and for good reason: it was quite capable of crashing the database engine process. You must use Database Mail to send notifications and other kinds of mail messages from SQL Server.

Database Mail is an enterprise-class implementation designed with all the features you'd expect from this next-generation database server, most of which are not available in SQL Mail. These features include support for multiple email profiles and accounts, asynchronous (queued) message delivery via a dedicated process in conjunction with Service Broker, cluster-awareness, 64-bit compat-ibility, greater security options (such as governing of mail attachment size and prohibition of file extensions), and simplified mail auditing. Database Mail also utilizes the industry-standard Simple Mail Transfer Protocol (SMTP), signaling the end of reliance on Extended Messaging Application Programming Interface (Extended MAPI).

Database Mail has more capabilities and is more scalable and reliable than SQL Mail, especially when stressed with the heavier usage scenarios common today. And, thankfully, it's a good deal easier to successfully configure than its predecessor.

Setting Up Database Mail

Setting up profiles and accounts for use with Database Mail is easy to accomplish, thanks mainly to the Database Mail Configuration Wizard, found in the SQL Server Management Studio (SSMS) Object Browser. You can use this wizard both to set up and manage Database Mail. Before using it, you need to switch on the Database Mail feature, which is off by default, in keeping with Microsoft's secure-by-default approach. Follow these steps to do so.

Configure the `Database Mail XPs` configuration option by running the following T-SQL code in a new query window (while logged in as `sysadmin`, of course):

```
use Master
GO
sp_configure 'show advanced options', 1;
GO
RECONFIGURE;
GO
sp_configure 'Database Mail XPs', 1;
GO
RECONFIGURE
GO
Configuration option 'show advanced options' changed from 0
to 1. Run the
RECONFIGURE statement to install.
Configuration option 'Database Mail XPs' changed from 0 to
1. Run the
RECONFIGURE statement to install.
```

If you ever want to disable Database Mail, you can run this:

```
sp_configure 'Database Mail XPs', 0;
```

This statement prevents Database Mail from starting in response to a call to `sysmail_start_sp` (discussed later in this chapter). If Database Mail is running when you make this call, it sends unsent queued mail until the mail sending process (`DatabaseMail.exe`) has been idle for the duration of the `DatabaseMailExeMinimumLifeTime` configuration setting (discussed later in this chapter); then it stops.

You also need to enable Service Broker in `msdb` (if not done already) because Database Mail relies on it as part of its implementation. To do this, stop the SQL Server Agent service and then execute the following script:

```
USE master
GO
ALTER DATABASE msdb SET SINGLE_USER WITH ROLLBACK IMMEDIATE
```

```
GO
ALTER DATABASE msdb SET ENABLE_BROKER
GO
ALTER DATABASE msdb SET MULTI_USER
```

You can check the status of Service Broker on `msdb` by using the following code:

```
USE Master
GO
SELECT is_broker_enabled
FROM sys.databases
WHERE name = 'msdb'
GO
is_broker_enabled
-----------------
1
(1 row(s) affected)
```

To receive message send requests from outside the SQL Server instance, you need to create an endpoint (preferably a certificate-secured one) associated with Service Broker. To accomplish this, consult the "Create Endpoint" Service Broker topic in Books Online.

To complete this configuration, you need to return to SSMS and establish a connection to the same SQL Server instance for which you just enabled Database Mail. You connect the Object Browser to that instance and expand the Management folder to reveal the `Database Mail` node. Then right-click the `Database Mail` node and select the Configure Database Mail menu option to launch the Database Mail Configuration Wizard.

Creating Mail Profiles and Accounts

After you pass the Database Mail Configuration Wizard's welcome screen, you are presented with the opportunity to set up Database Mail ("for the first time"). You can achieve this by creating the required profiles, profile security settings, SMTP accounts, and system-wide mail settings. You should leave the first radio button (Set Up Database Mail by Performing the Following Tasks) selected and then click Next.

NOTE

In Database Mail, you use mail profiles. A *mail profile* is simply a securable container for a group of SMTP accounts that is used when sending mail. You can set up multiple profiles containing multiple accounts, allowing for finer-grained administrative control. You can create one profile for administrators and another for regular users, for example, or create distinct profiles dedicated to various software applications.

Note also that to use Database Mail, you no longer need to run the SQL Server or SQL Server Agent Windows services under user accounts (rather than using the default, LocalSystem), nor do you need to install Microsoft Outlook (or any other Extended MAPI client) on the machine hosting SQL Server 2014.

In the New Database Mail Account screen that appears after you click the Add button (see Figure 12.1), you name (using a valid `sysname`) and describe your first profile in the provided text boxes, and then you click Add to add your first SMTP account. This process is much like the process of setting up the SMTP (or sending) portion of your email accounts with your regular email client software. To create the SMTP account, you specify a name, an optional description, a user display name, an email address, an optional reply address, a server name, a port, and an authentication mode, which is used to authenticate to the specified SMTP server (as required by your SMTP provider). For many non-Windows SMTP providers, anonymous (no authentication) or basic (simple user name/password) authentication is usually required. If your provider requires Windows Authentication, the credentials under which the SQL Server Windows service runs are supplied to the SMTP server at runtime.

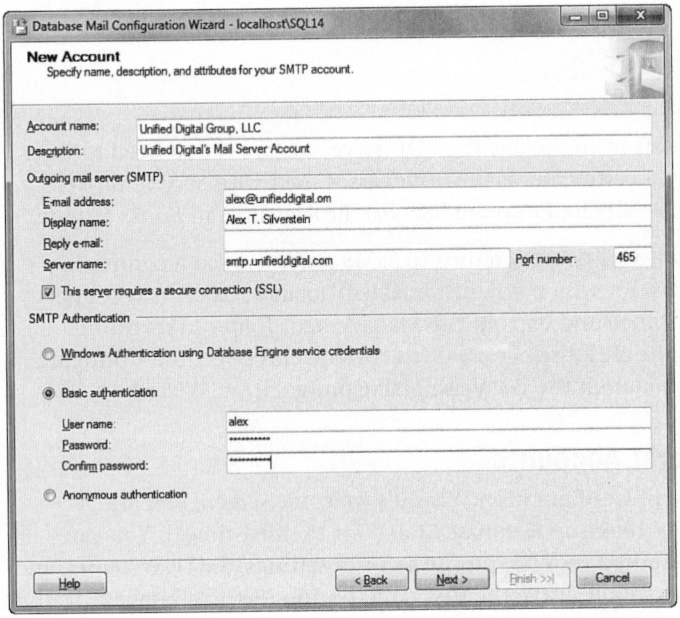

FIGURE 12.1   Using the Database Mail Configuration Wizard to set up SMTP accounts.

Instead of using the wizard, you can add a new profile via T-SQL. For example, the following three examples introduce the Database Mail stored procedures `sysmail_add_profile_sp`, `sysmail_add_account_sp`, and `sysmail_add_profileaccount_sp`.

The first script creates the new profile:

```
EXEC msdb.dbo.sysmail_add_profile_sp
    @profile_name = 'Default SQL 2014 Profile',
    @description = 'Used for general-purpose emailing.'
```

The second script creates the new SMTP account:

```
EXEC msdb.dbo.sysmail_add_account_sp
    @account_name = 'UnleashedMailAcct1',
    @description = 'The first SMTP Account.',
    @email_address = 'sql2014@unifieddigital.com',
    @display_name = 'SQL 2014 Mail Account 1',
    @mailserver_name = 'smtp.unifieddigital.com' ;
```

The third script associates this new account with the new profile:

```
EXEC msdb.dbo.sysmail_add_profileaccount_sp
    @profile_name = 'Default SQL 2014 Profile',
    @account_name = 'UnleashedMailAcct1',
    @sequence_number = 1;
```

The great thing you'll find when adding SMTP accounts is that Database Mail allows you to provide more than one SMTP account for the same profile. You can order the SMTP accounts by priority (using the Move Up/Move Down buttons) so that if a mail send via the top-level (or first) account fails, the second account will be used to retry sending, and so on. This is called *SMTP failover priority*, and there are two mail settings that control how it works. These settings, found on the Configure System Parameters screen of the wizard, are `AccountRetryAttempts` and `AccountRetryDelay`. `AccountRetryAttempts` specifies how many mail send retries Database Mail will make before failing over to the SMTP account of next-highest priority. `AccountRetryDelay` specifies (in seconds) how long to wait between mail send retries.

After adding the new account to the profile, click Next to set up the profile security settings on the Manage Profile Security screen. Database Mail profiles have two levels of security (with two corresponding tabs on the wizard screen):

▶ **Public**—The profile can be used by all `msdb` users.

▶ **Private**—The profile can be used only by specific users or members of a specific role. (Note that to send mail, users must have `DatabaseMailUserRole` membership in `msdb`. Use `sp_addrolemember` to accomplish this.) Specify these users on the Private Profiles tab of the Manage Profile Security screen.

In this case, check the box under the Public column of the data grid on the Public tab; then click the word No under the Default Profile column. A drop-down list appears, allowing you to make the profile the default (by changing the selection to Yes). The default profile on the server is used when you invoke `sp_send_dbmail` (the successor to `xp_sendmail`) without specifying any profile name for the `@profile_name` parameter. It's a good idea to have a default profile set up for general mailing purposes, especially when testing.

To set profile security using T-SQL, run the following call to the stored procedure `sysmail_add_principalprofile_sp`:

```
EXEC msdb.dbo.sysmail_add_principalprofile_sp
    @profile_name = 'Default SQL 2014 Profile',
    @principal_name = 'public',
    @is_default = 1 ;
```

A third way to configure all the previously mentioned mail objects (in the form of a T-SQL script) is to use an SMSS Database Mail query template. To do this, you open the Template Browser via the View menu (or by pressing Ctrl+Alt+T), and then you expand to the Database Mail folder and double-click Simple Mail Database Configuration. Then you connect to your SQL Server instance and, from the Query menu, select the Specify Values for Template Parameters option (or press Ctrl+Shift+M) to fill in the desired parameter values, which correspond to the parameters of the stored procedures mentioned previously.

Using T-SQL to Update and Delete Mail Objects

To delete or update profiles, accounts, profile-account associations, and profile security settings (note: do so in reverse order), you use the stored procedures shown in Table 12.1.

TABLE 12.1   T-SQL Stored Procedures

Stored Procedure Name	Purpose
sysmail_delete_profile_sp	Delete a profile
sysmail_delete_account_sp	Delete an account
sysmail_delete_principalprofile_sp	Delete the association between a profile and a user or role (revokes permission for the principal on use of the profile)
sysmail_delete_profileaccount_sp	Delete the association between a profile and an account
sysmail_update_profile_sp	Update a profile
sysmail_update_account_sp	Update an account
sysmail_update_principalprofile_sp	Update the association between a profile and a user or role
sysmail_update_profileaccount_sp	Update the association between a profile and an account

For example, to delete a profile, you execute this:

```
EXEC msdb.dbo.sysmail_delete_profile_sp @profile_name='Undesireable Profile Name'
```

To update a profile's security, changing it from the default to the nondefault profile, you execute the following:

```
EXEC msdb.dbo.sysmail_update_principalprofile_sp
    @profile_name = 'Default SQL 2014 Profile',
    @principal_name = 'public',
    @is_default = 0;
```

Alternatively, you can simply return to the wizard and select one of the Manage options to alter or drop any of the settings or objects. (Of course, under the covers, the wizard probably uses all these stored procedures.)

Setting System-Wide Mail Settings

You use the Configure System Parameters screen in the Database Mail Configuration Wizard to configure the system-wide Database Mail settings. (Click Next on the Select Configuration Task screen to reach this screen, if you haven't already.) You've seen the first two settings that appear in the grid (AccountRetryAttempts and AccountRetryDelay) in an earlier section ("Creating Mail Profiles and Accounts") as they relate to SMTP failover priority. These are the other four:

▶ **Maximum File Size (Bytes)**—This setting specifies the maximum size of any one email attachment.

▶ **Prohibited Attachment File Extensions**—This setting specifies which potentially dangerous or undesirable attachment types to ban from exchanged emails.

▶ **Database Mail Executable Minimum Lifetime (seconds)**—This setting specifies how long (minimally) the database mail process (that is, DatabaseMail.exe, which is activated by Service Broker) should run idly before closing after it finishes emptying the mail send queue.

▶ **Logging Level**—This setting specifies the quality of email auditing to use, and it can be set to Normal (errors only), Extended (errors, warnings, and informational messages; this is the default), or Verbose (the same as Extended, plus success messages and other messages that are useful when you debug problems with DatabaseMail.exe). To view Database Mail's primary log, right-click the Database Mail folder in the Object Browser and then click the View Database Mail Log menu option. Examine and maintain the log by using the Log File Viewer that is launched. You can also use the built-in stored procedure sysmail_delete_log_sp to clear the log, or query the msdb sysmail_event_log view to see its contents in tabular format.

To change any of these configuration settings via T-SQL script, use the sysmail_configure_sp stored procedure. sysmail_configure_sp takes two parameters: the name of the setting (minus any spaces) and its new value. The following example uses the sysmail_configure_sp procedure to change AccountRetryDelay to two minutes:

```
exec msdb.dbo.sysmail_configure_sp 'AccountRetryDelay', 120
```

Testing Your Setup

The final step in setting up Database Mail is to ask SQL Server to send a test email. To do this, right-click the `Database Mail` folder in the Object Browser and then click the Send Test E-mail menu option.

If the test fails, click Troubleshoot, and SMSS opens the "Troubleshooting Database Mail" Books Online topic, which provides a solid set of troubleshooting steps to get you started.

If the mail is sent by SQL Server and successfully received in your client software's inbox, you can proceed to the next section to learn how to use the `sp_send_dbmail` stored procedure to send email from T-SQL. Otherwise, look for more troubleshooting help in the "Related Views and Procedures" section of this chapter.

Sending and Receiving with Database Mail

If you're building client applications that rely heavily on Database Mail, it's crucial to gain an in-depth understanding of its underlying architecture. The following sections provide detailed information on its inner workings.

The Service Broker Architecture

As noted earlier, SQL Server relies on Service Broker (SSB) to activate the Database Mail process (`DatabaseMail.exe`) used to send mail. `DatabaseMail.exe` uses ADO.NET to connect to SQL Server and to read from and write to SSB queues (found in `msdb`) that hold send requests and send statuses in the form of typed SSB messages. You can view these queues (`InternalMailQueue` and `ExternalMailQueue`) in the Object Browser by selecting `Service Broker` and then the `Queues` folder. If you look a bit further in the Object Browser, you see how the mail transmission architecture is implemented (in part) as an SSB application, as you find the corresponding internal and external Database Mail SSB services (`InternalMailService` and `ExternalMailService`), SSB message types (`SendMail` and `SendMailStatus`), and a single SSB contract (`SendMail/v1.0`).

SSB's involvement with Database Mail works like this:

1. `sp_send_dbmail` (as the SSB *initiator*) is invoked and returns immediately. Under the covers, this adds an SSB message of type `SendMail` to the SSB mail queue, activating the undocumented internal stored procedure `sp_ExternalMailQueueListener`. Note that the mail message itself is saved to one or more of the `msdb` tables (such as `sysmail_unsentitems` and `sysmail_attachments`) if there are any attachments.

2. SSB launches `DatabaseMail.exe` (running under the credentials of the SQL Server service), which, in turn, connects back to SQL Server, using Windows Authentication.

3. `DatabaseMail.exe` reads the queued SSB send message, retrieves the mail message data, sends the email, and, finally (acting as the SSB *target*), places a message of type `SendMailStatus` in the mail status queue, reporting on the mail sending success or failure.

4. When there's nothing left to be sent in the outbound queue, and the maximum process idle time has been reached, `DatabaseMail.exe` exits.

By using SSB, Database Mail inherits the reliability of the SSB message transmission architecture. If you want to learn more about Service Broker and how its constructs work, consult the SQL Server Service Broker topics in Books Online.

Sending Email

The SSB queues that Database Mail uses must first be enabled before you can send mail from a session. You do this by executing the `msdb` stored procedure `sysmail_start_sp`. This procedure is similar to its predecessor, `xp_startmail` (as it must be called before sending), except that it has no parameters and, of course, has nothing to do with MAPI. It returns `0` or `1`, indicating success or failure. If you don't call this procedure, you receive this error message:

```
Mail not queued. Database Mail is stopped. Use
sysmail_start_sp to
start Database Mail.
```

To temporarily disable SSB's activation of the mail process, you execute `sysmail_stop_sp` (also with no parameters), which returns 0 or 1. If you send mail from code after disabling this process, these messages will be queued. The external process is not started until `sysmail_start_sp` is called again. To check on the status of Database Mail, you can execute `sysmail_help_status_sp` (with no parameters). To check on the status of the queues, you execute `sysmail_help_queues_sp`.

After you execute `sysmail_start_sp`, you're ready to begin sending mail using the `sp_send_dbmail` stored procedure. It has 21 parameters, most of which are optional. As the query engine will tell you if you try to execute it with no or too few parameters, at least one of the following parameters must be specified: `@body`, `@query`, `@file_attachments`, or `@subject`. You also must specify one of the following: `@recipients`, `@copy_recipients`, or `@blind_copy_recipients`.

> **NOTE**
>
> For the following T-SQL examples to work, you must first configure a default profile using either the Database Mail Configuration Wizard or Database Mail stored procedures, as detailed earlier.

A minimally parameterized test call might look like the following:

```
EXEC msdb.dbo.sp_send_dbmail @body='Testing...', @subject='A
Test',
@recipients='test@unifieddigital.com'
go
Mail Queued.
```

Table 12.2 describes the many parameters, their types, and the `xp_sendmail` parameters to which they may correspond, to help you along in converting your existing T-SQL code.

TABLE 12.2   Parameters for Database Mail Stored Procedure `sp_send_dbmail`

Parameter	Description	xp_sendmail Parameter to Which It Corresponds
@profile_name	The `sysname` of the profile whose SMTP accounts will be used to send.	Not available in `xp_sendmail`.
@recipients	A `varchar(max)` semicolon-delimited list of the recipients' email addresses.	Same as `xp_sendmail`.
@copy_recipients	A `varchar(max)` semicolon-delimited list of the carbon copy recipients' email addresses.	Same as `xp_sendmail`.
@blind_copy_recipients	A `varchar(max)` semicolon-delimited list of the blind carbon copy recipients' email addresses.	Same as `xp_sendmail`.
@subject	The `nvarchar(255)` email subject.	Same as `xp_sendmail`.
@body	The `nvarchar(max)` email body.	Was `@message` in `xp_sendmail`.
@body_format	One of the two `varchar (20)` email format type strings, either `'HTML'` or `'TEXT'` (the default).	Not available in `xp_sendmail`.
@importance	One of the three `varchar (6)` email importance strings, either `'Low'`, `'Normal'` (the default), or `'High'`.	Not available in `xp_sendmail`.
@sensitivity	One of the four `varchar (12)` email sensitivity strings, either `'Normal'` (the default), `'Personal'`, `'Private'`, or `'Confidential'`.	Not available in `xp_sendmail`.
@file_attachments	An `nvarchar(max)` semicolon-delimited list of absolute paths to files to attach.	Was `@attachments` in `xp_sendmail`.
@query	An `nvarchar(max)` T-SQL code string to be executed when the message is sent. The code is executed in a different session than the calling session, so variable scope is a consideration.	Same as `xp_sendmail`.
@execute_query_database	The `sysname` of the database in which the T-SQL in `query` is to be executed.	Was `@dbuse` in `xp_sendmail`.

Parameter	Description	xp_sendmail Parameter to Which It Corresponds
@attach_query_result_as_file	A bit value indicating whether the results of the T-SQL in query should be an attachment (1) or appended to the body (0; the default).	Was @attach_results in xp_sendmail.
@query_attachment_filename	The nvarchar(255) filename for the attached query results (as per @query and @attach_query_result_as_file). If not specified, the generated filename is arbitrary (usually QueryResults [some number].txt)	In xp_sendmail, the first filename in @attachments was used.
@query_result_header	A bit value indicating whether the query result (1; the default) should include the column headers.	Was @no_header in xp_sendmail.
@query_result_width	An int value (defaulting to 256; you specify a number between 10 and 32767) indicating how wide a line in the query results should be before line wrapping occurs.	Was @width in xp_sendmail.
@query_result_separator	A char(1) value (defaulting to a space) that indicates the query results column separator.	Was @separator in xp_sendmail.
@exclude_query_output	A bit value that indicates whether to suppress the query output (such as rowcounts, print statements, and so forth) from being printed on the query console. 0 (do not suppress) is the default.	Was @no_output in xp_sendmail.
@append_query_error	A bit value that indicates whether to send the email if the query to be executed raises an error. If set to 1, the error message is appended to the query output, and the query window for the session also displays the error ("A severe error occurred on the current command. The results, if any, should be discarded."). If set to 0 (the default), the message is not sent, and sp_send_dbmail returns 1.	Not available in xp_sendmail, but similar to @echo_error.

12

Parameter	Description	xp_sendmail Parameter to Which It Corresponds
@query_no_truncate	A `bit` value that indicates whether to truncate query results having long values (such as `varchar(max)`, `text`, `xml`, and so on) greater than 256. It defaults to `0` (off). Microsoft warns that using this can slow things down, but it is the only way to properly send these types.	Not available in `xp_sendmail`.
@mailitem_id	An output parameter, an `int` value indicating the unique `mailitem_id` of the message. You see this as a column in the views discussed in the section, "Related Views and Procedures," later in this chapter.	Not available in `xp_sendmail`.

Note that the `@type` and `@set_user` parameters for `xp_sendmail` are not available. `@type`, of course, is obsolete because it is MAPI-specific. `@set_user` is also obsolete because the content of the T-SQL to be executed may contain an EXECUTE AS statement.

Now that you're familiar with the flurry of mail sending options, let's look at a few examples and then examine how to track your sent messages by using the system views. Both of the following examples rely on sending via the default profile of the current user context. If the user has a default private profile assigned, it is used. If not, the default public profile is used (as in these examples). If there is no default public profile, an error is raised.

The example shown in Listing 12.1 sends an email containing an `xml` result to a recipient as an attached Extensible Application Markup Language (XAML) document, retrieved from the `AdventureWorks2012.Production.Illustration` column.

LISTING 12.1   Sending XML as an Attachment with Database Mail

```
USE AdventureWorks2012
GO
DECLARE
    @subject nvarchar(255),
    @body varchar(max),
    @query nvarchar(max),
    @IllustrationId int,
    @query_attachment_filename nvarchar(255),
    @mailitem_id int
```

```
SELECT
    @IllustrationId = pi.IllustrationId,
    @subject = 'XAML for "' + pm.Name + '" attached. '
FROM Production.Illustration pi
JOIN Production.ProductModelIllustration pmi
ON pmi.IllustrationId = pi.IllustrationId
JOIN Production.ProductModel pm
ON pm.ProductModelID = pmi.ProductModelID

SELECT
    @body =
        N'Attached, please find the XAML diagram for illustration #' +
        CAST(@IllustrationId as nvarchar(10)) +
        '. A XAML browser plug-in is required to view this file.'

SELECT @query =
    N'SELECT Diagram FROM Production.Illustration
    WHERE IllustrationId = ' + CAST(@IllustrationId as nvarchar(10))

SELECT @query_attachment_filename = N'PM_' +
    CAST(@IllustrationId as nvarchar(10)) + '.xaml'

exec msdb.dbo.sp_send_dbmail
    @subject=@subject,
    @body=@body,
    @recipients='test@samspublishing.com',
    @query=@query,
    @execute_query_database='AdventureWorks2012',
    @attach_query_result_as_file=1,
    @query_attachment_filename=@query_attachment_filename,
    @query_no_truncate=1,
    @exclude_query_output=1,
    @query_result_width=32767,
    @mailitem_id=@mailitem_id OUTPUT

SELECT sent_status, sent_date
FROM msdb.dbo.sysmail_allitems
WHERE mailitem_id = @mailitem_id
GO
sent_status sent_date
----------- ---------
unsent      NULL
 (1 row(s) affected)
```

Note that you must set @query_no_truncate to 1 and @query_result_width to the maximum (to be safe) value for the attached query results to contain consistently well-formed XML. In addition, you should not include any carriage returns or line feeds in the body of the message, or the SMTP servers may not be able to send it.

The example in Listing 12.2 sends some query results as a comma-separated value (CSV) file that can be imported into programs such as Microsoft Excel. (You need to use the Get External Data command to accomplish this with Excel 9.)

LISTING 12.2   Sending CSV Data as an Attachment with Database Mail

```
USE AdventureWorks2012
GO
DECLARE @mailitem_id int, @tab char(1)
SET @tab = char(13)

exec msdb.dbo.sp_send_dbmail
    @subject='D. Margheim, Contact Info',
    @body='Attached is Diane Margheim''s contact info, in
CSV format.',
    @recipients='test@samspublishing.com',
    @query=N'SELECT BusinessEntityID, Title, FirstName,
MiddleName, LastName
        FROM Person.Person
        WHERE BusinessEntityId = 8',
    @execute_query_database='AdventureWorks2012',
    @attach_query_result_as_file=1,
    @query_attachment_filename='DMargheim.csv',
    @exclude_query_output=1,
    @query_result_separator=',',
    @mailitem_id=@mailitem_id OUTPUT

SELECT sent_status, sent_date
FROM msdb.dbo.sysmail_allitems
WHERE mailitem_id = @mailitem_id
GO
sent_status sent_date
----------- ---------
unsent      NULL
 (1 row(s) affected)
```

Notice that in both of these code listings, the values selected from the sent_status and sent_date columns of sysmail_allitems indicate that the mail has not yet been sent. The reason is that mail sending (like all other SSB messaging) is asynchronous: The message is immediately queued, and the Mail process later picks it up and sends it. To find out more about system views such as `sysmail_allitems`, see the section, "Related Views and Procedures," later in this chapter.

Receiving Email

Database Mail does not support receiving incoming messages because there is no IMAP or POP3 support. This may have something to do with the fact that receiving email can represent a major security risk. Imagine what a denial-of-service attack on a database cluster could do to an organization. Or consider the danger of an incoming email request resulting in the execution of a query such as `DROP DATABASE x`. Most SQL Server data is too precious to jeopardize in this manner. Plus, there are many better alternatives to using this methodology, such as using .NET CLR-integrated assembly code, or building a dedicated Service Broker application.

Using SQL Server Agent Mail

As with SQL Server 2000, SQL Server 2014's Agent has the capability to send email notifications. They may be triggered by alerts or scheduled task completions, such as jobs. As with Database Mail, SQL Server Agent Mail is turned off by default, and you must configure it via SMSS or T-SQL, as described in the following sections.

Job Mail Notifications

The following sections show an example in which you create a SQL Server Agent Mail operator that SQL Server Agent will notify when a job completes.

Creating an Operator

First, you need to create an operator. To do so, using the Object Browser, you expand the `SQL Server Agent` node and then right-click the `Operators` folder and select New Operator. Then you should name this new operator `Test Database Mail Operator` and provide an email address for testing purposes in the Email Name text box. You can use any valid email address you can access with your email client software. You click OK to save the new operator.

Enabling SQL Agent Mail

Next, you need to enable SQL Server Agent to use Database Mail. You right-click the `SQL Server Agent` node and then select Properties. On the left side of the Properties dialog that appears (see Figure 12.2), you click the Alert System link. Under the Mail Session group, you check the Enable Mail Profile check box. In the Mail System drop-down list, you select Database Mail. In the Mail Profile drop-down list, you select the default SQL 2014 profile you created earlier and then click OK. By doing this, you are telling SQL Server Agent to use the SMTP servers in your default profile to send email. You need to restart SQL Server Agent by using the right-click menu. Additionally, you may need to enable SQL Server Agent's extended stored procedures by executing the following commands:

```
sp_configure 'show advanced options', 1;
GO
RECONFIGURE;
GO
sp_configure 'Agent XPs', 1;
GO
RECONFIGURE
GO
```

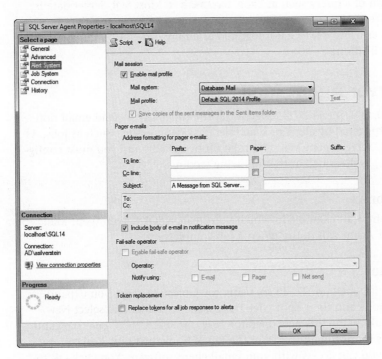

FIGURE 12.2   Using the SQL Server Agent Properties dialog to configure Database Mail.

Creating the Job

Next, you need to create the job. You begin by right-clicking the Jobs folder and then selecting New Job. You should name the job Database Mail Test Job and select an owner. Then you should check the Enabled check box near the bottom of the dialog and click the Steps link on the left side of the dialog. Next, you click the New button and add a step named Test Mail Step 1. You should leave the type as Transact-SQL and then change the database selection to AdventureWorks2012. In the Command text box, you enter the following code:

```
RAISERROR('This is simply a test job.', 10, 1)
```

Next, you click the Advanced link on the left side of the dialog, and in the On Success Action drop-down list, you select Quit the Job Reporting Success. Then you click the Notifications link on the left side of the dialog. Next, under Actions to Perform When the Job Completes, you check the Email check box and select the operator you just created. From the drop-down to the right, you select When the Job Completes and then click OK to save the job.

Testing the Job-Completion Notification

To test the email configuration and notification you just set up, you right-click the job name under the `Jobs` folder and then select Start Job. If everything is set up properly, an email message appears in your inbox, indicating the job's successful completion. Its body text might look something like this:

```
JOB RUN:     'Database Mail Test Job' was run on 11/7/2014 at
8:37:22 PM
DURATION:    0 hours, 0 minutes, 0 seconds
STATUS:      Succeeded
MESSAGES:    The job succeeded.  The Job was invoked by User
[TestUser].
     The last step to run was step 1 (Test Mail Step 1).
```

Alert Mail Notifications

As another example, in the following sections, you'll create a simple user-defined alert that you can trigger directly from T-SQL script.

Creating an Alert

You start by creating an alert. To do this, you use the Object Browser to expand the `SQL Server Agent` node; then you right-click the `Alerts` node and select New Alert. In the Alert Properties dialog that appears (see Figure 12.3), you name the new alert `Database Mail Test Alert` and make sure the Enable check box is checked. For the Event type, you leave the selection on SQL Server Event Alert. Under Event Alert Definition, select `AdventureWorks2012` from the Database Name drop-down list, and then click the Severity option button and choose 010 - Information. Next, check the Raise Alert When Message Contains check box and type the phrase `This is a Test` in the Message Text text box.

On the left side of the alert properties dialog, you click the Response link. Then you check the Notify Operators check box and, in the Operator list, check the Email check box to the right of the Test Database Mail Operator grid row. Finally, you click OK to close and save the new custom alert.

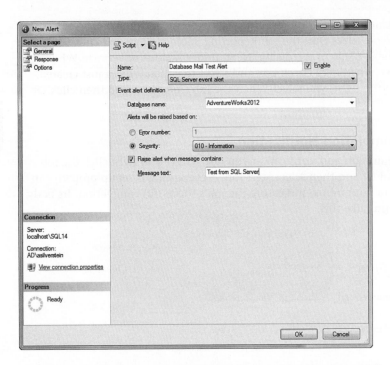

FIGURE 12.3   Creating a SQL Server event alert with a Database Mail notification.

Testing the Alert Notification

To test your new alert notification, you open a new query window in SMSS and enter the following code:

```
USE AdventureWorks2012
go
RAISERROR('This is an alert mail test', 10, 1) WITH LOG
go
'This is an alert mail test'
```

Because you specified WITH LOG, this simple statement writes an event to the Windows Event log, which in turn triggers the alert because the database context, message text, and severity all match the conditions of the alert. An email message should have appeared in your inbox, indicating the alert's successful triggering. This message should contain body text such as this:

```
DATE/TIME:    11/7/2014 9:00:45 PM
DESCRIPTION:    Error: 50000 Severity:  10 State: 1 This is an alert
    mail test
COMMENT:    (None)
JOB RUN:    (None)
```

Related Views and Procedures

To report on the status of all your Database Mail objects without relying on wizards and properties pages, you need some tabular views and stored procedures. msdb contains many system tables, views, and corresponding stored procedures that make this task easy. The following section lists the tables (or views) and their columns, noting the stored procedure (if any) that you can use to read from them.

Viewing the Mail Configuration Objects

The first set of msdb objects we'll review are those related to system objects such as profiles, profile security, and accounts:

- ▶ **sysmail_profile**—Contains basic profile data, including the unique profile_id, name, description, last_mod_datetime, and last_mod_user name. You execute sysmail_help_profile_sp to retrieve this data by @profile_name or @profile_id.

- ▶ **sysmail_principalprofile**—Contains profile security settings, including the profile_id, associated principal (or user) (principal_SID), profile default status (is_default: 1 for yes or 0 for no), last_mod_datetime, and last_mod_user name. You execute sysmail_help_principalprofile_sp to retrieve this data by @profile_name, @profile_id, @principal_name, or @principal_id (not principal SID). Here's an example:

```
exec msdb.dbo.sysmail_help_principalprofile_sp
    @profile_name='Default SQL 2014 Profile'
```

- ▶ **sysmail_account**—Contains basic account data, including the unique account_id, name, description, email_address, display_name, replyto_address, last_mod_datetime, and last_mod_user name. You execute sysmail_help_account_sp to retrieve this data by @account_id or @account_name.

- ▶ **sysmail_server**—Contains account SMTP server data, including the unique related account_id and servertype, servername, port, server username, server authentication data (credential_id), SSL status (enable_SSL), last_mod_datetime, and last_mod_user name. (sysmail_help_account_sp returns data from this table as well.)

- ▶ **sysmail_servertype**—Contains servertype data for accounts' servers. (SMTP is the only currently supported type, although it seems this system was built for extensibility, as the columns is_incoming and is_outgoing may leave the door open for adding POP or IMAP servers sometime in the future.) Also includes last_mod_datetime and last_mod_user name. (sysmail_help_account_sp returns data from this table as well.)

To join sysmail_account, sysmail_server, and sysmail_servertype (as sysmail_help_account_sp seems to do), you can try a query such as the following:

```
SELECT *
FROM msdb.dbo.sysmail_account a
JOIN msdb.dbo.sysmail_server s
```

```
ON a.account_id = s.account_id
JOIN msdb.dbo.sysmail_servertype st
ON st.servertype = s.servertype
```

▶ **sysmail_profileaccount**—Maintains the profile-account relationship, including the `profile_id`, `account_id`, `account priority sequence_number`, `last_mod_datetime`, and `last_mod_user` name. You execute `sysmail_help_profileaccount_sp` to retrieve this data by `@account_id`, `@account_name`, `@profile_id`, or `@profile_name`.

▶ **sysmail_configuration**—Contains the system-wide mail configuration settings (`paramname`, `paramvalue`, `description`), and when and by whom each was last modified (`last_mod_datetime` and `last_mod_user` name). You execute `sysmail_help_configure_sp` to query this data by `@parameter_name`. Here's an example:

```
exec msdb.dbo.sysmail_help_configure_sp
    @parameter_name='accountretrydelay'
```

Viewing Mail Message Data

The second set of `msdb` objects (and perhaps the more important ones) we'll review are those used to discover the status of mail messages.

The first thing you need to do is to check on the status of the mail messages you've attempted to send, without relying on inboxes to tell you if they've been received. Several views in `msdb` enable this, most of which may be filtered by mail account, sending user, send date, status, and more. To begin this process, you query the view `sysmail_allitems`, which contains all the data about your messages (subjects, recipients, importance, and so on) as well as `send_request_date`, `sent_date`, and `sent_status`. Here's an example:

```
SELECT mailitem_id, subject, sent_status
FROM msdb.dbo.sysmail_allitems
go
mailitem_id    subject                                                        sent_status
-------------------------------------------------------------------------------------

1              Database Mail Test                                             sent
2              C. Adams, Contact Info                                         sent
3              XAML for HL Touring Seat/Saddle attached.                      sent
4              SQL Server Job System: 'Database Mail Test Job'                sent

(4 row(s) affected)
```

Because all these messages have a `sent_status` of sent, the contents of this recordset are analogous to what you'd find if you queried the view `sysmail_sentitems`. But suppose your `sent_status` column read failed. In that case, you'd start by querying the `sysmail_faileditems` view (a subset of `sysmail_allmailitems`) in conjunction with `sysmail_event_log` (which contains the detailed textual reasons why failures have occurred). Here's an example:

```
SELECT f.subject, f.mailitem_id, l.description
FROM msdb.dbo.sysmail_event_log l
JOIN msdb.dbo.sysmail_faileditems f
ON f.mailitem_id = l.mailitem_id
WHERE event_type = 'error'
ORDER BY log_date
go
subject                 mailitem_id     description
--------------------------------------------------------------------------------
Database Mail Test      3               The mail could not be sent because [...] the
string is not in the form required for an e-mail address

(1 row(s) affected)
```

Note that the quality of the contents of `sysmail_event_log` depends on the Log Level system-wide mail configuration setting (discussed earlier in the section "Setting System-wide Mail Settings"). The Log File Viewer also uses this table's contents. To permanently delete its contents, you use the stored procedure `sysmail_delete_log_sp`.

To query how many messages are queued (waiting to be sent) and for how long, you use the `sysmail_unsentitems` view. Here's an example:

```
SELECT
    mailitem_id,
    subject,
    DATEDIFF(hh, send_request_date, GETDATE()) HoursSinceSendRequest
FROM msdb.dbo.sysmail_unsentitems
```

If you're unsure why messages aren't being sent, you can try the following:

▶ Execute `sysmail_help_queue_sp`, whose resulting `state` column tells the state of the mail transmission queues: INACTIVE (off) or RECEIVES_OCCURRING (on). To see the status for only the `mail` (outbound) or `status` (send status) queues, you use the `@queue_type` parameter.

▶ Execute `sysmail_help_status_sp`, whose resulting `status` column tells you the state of Database Mail itself: STOPPED or STARTED.

Summary

This chapter showed how Database Mail has elevated the status of emailing with SQL Server from somewhat difficult to use to enterprise class. Microsoft has achieved this goal by relying on cross-platform industry standards, by making configuration easy, by providing a comprehensive set of system objects for storage and tracking, by adding failover capability, and by utilizing the Service Broker infrastructure.

Chapter 13, "SQL Server Agent," digs much deeper into configuring SQL Server Agent jobs and alerts, as well as using Database Mail for job and alert notifications.

CHAPTER 13

SQL Server Agent

Automation is the key to efficiency, and the SQL Server Agent is your automation tool in SQL Server 2014. This chapter delves into the administrative capabilities of the SQL Server Agent and its capability to schedule server activity and respond to server events.

The SQL Server Agent, which runs as a Windows service, is responsible for running scheduled tasks, notifying operators of events, and responding with predefined actions to errors and performance conditions. The SQL Server Agent can perform these actions without user intervention, utilizing the following:

▶ **Alerts**—*Alerts* respond to SQL Server or user-defined errors, and they can also respond to performance conditions. An alert can be configured to run a job as well as notify an operator.

▶ **Jobs**—A *job* is a predefined operation or set of operations, such as transferring data or backing up a transaction log. A job can be scheduled to run on a regular basis or called to run when an alert is fired.

▶ **Operators**—An *operator* is a user who should be notified when an alert fires or a job requests notification. The operator can be notified by email, by pager, or via the NET SEND command.

▶ **Schedules**—A *schedule* determines when a job will run. *Schedules* can be applied to a single job or shared across many jobs. You can also apply more than one schedule to a given job.

NOTE

The SQL Server Agent is not supported with the SQL Server Express Edition or SQL Server Express Advanced Edition. It is supported in all the other editions of SQL Server 2014, however. You can use the Windows Task Scheduler as an alternative for scheduling when using the SQL Server Express Editions. The Task Scheduler has basic scheduling capabilities but does not compare to the robust features found in the SQL Server Agent.

What's New in Scheduling and Notification

There are very few changes in the SQL Server Agent in SQL Server 2014. Changes are isolated to minor adjustments to the related screens. Those who have used the SQL Server Agent in SQL Server 2012 will find that almost all the screens and functionality are the same in SQL Server 2014. In fact, the SQL Server agent has changed very little since SQL Server 2005.

Configuring the SQL Server Agent

The primary configuration settings for the SQL Server Agent are located within the Object Explorer and SQL Server Configuration Manager. Most of the settings that define how the SQL Server Agent will execute are defined via the SQL Server Agent Properties accessible from the Object Explorer. The SQL Server Configuration Manager contains settings related to the SQL Server Agent's service. The service settings are limited but contain important properties such as the Startup Account for the SQL Server Agent.

Configuring SQL Server Agent Properties

Figure 13.1 shows the SQL Server Agent Properties dialog that appears when you right-click and select Properties on the SQL Server Agent node located on the root of the Object Explorer tree.

You can set several different types of properties in the SQL Server Agent Properties dialog. The General options are displayed by default, and they include the capability to set the auto restart options and define an error log for the SQL Server Agent. Selecting the option Auto Restart SQL Server Agent If It Stops Unexpectedly is best for most installations. There is usually a heavy dependency on the Agent performing its actions, and you probably want the service to be restarted if it has been inadvertently stopped.

The Advanced page contains options for event forwarding and idle CPU conditions. The event forwarding options are discussed in detail in the section "Event Forwarding," later in this chapter. The idle CPU options define conditions related to the execution of jobs that have been set up to run when the CPU is idle. You can define idle CPU conditions such as the average CPU percentage that the CPU must be below to be considered idle.

The Alert System page is related to configuring email notification and is discussed in the "Configuring Email Notification" section, later in this chapter.

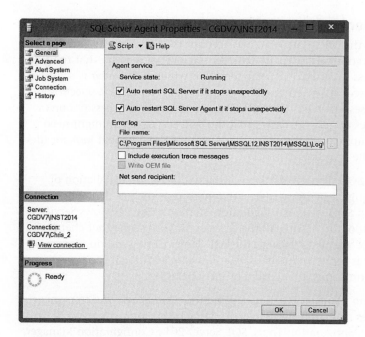

FIGURE 13.1   SQL Server Agent properties.

The Job System page has an option to set the shutdown time-out interval. This option determines the amount of time the SQL Server Agent waits for jobs to complete before finalizing the shutdown process. There is also an option related to proxy accounts discussed in the "SQL Server Agent Proxy Account" section, later in this chapter.

The Connection page includes an option to set an alias for the local host server. This option is useful if you cannot use the default connection properties for the local host and need to define an alias instead.

The History page options are related to the amount of job history that will be retained. You have the option to limit the size of the job history log and/or remove job history that is older than a set period of time.

TIP

Careful attention should be given to the amount of history that is retained. Every time a job is run, the history of that execution and the related detail is saved. The need for careful monitoring is particularly true when dealing with SQL Server instances that have a large number of databases. The `msdb` database contains the job history records and can become sizable over time if the history is not removed. For example, we have seen environments where close to 700 databases were installed on one SQL Server instance. The company was performing SQL Server log backups every 15 minutes on each of these databases and full backups each night. When you do the math (4 log backups/hour * 700 databases = 2800 backups/hour), you can see that the amount of history written to the `msdb` database can be significant.

Configuring the SQL Server Agent Startup Account

The startup account defines the Microsoft Windows account the SQL Server Agent service uses. The selection of this account is critical in defining the level of security that the SQL Server Agent will have. Access to resources on the server on which SQL Server is running and access to network resources are determined by the startup account. This selection is particularly important in cases in which the SQL Server Agent needs to access resources on other machines. Examples of network access that the SQL Server Agent might need include jobs that write backups to a drive on another machine and jobs that look for files found on other servers on the network.

The startup account for the SQL Server Agent is set initially during the installation of SQL Server, but you can change it by using several different tools such as the Windows Service Control Manager and SQL Server Configuration Manager. The Windows Service Control Manager is a good tool for viewing all the services on your server, but changes to the SQL Server services are better made through the SQL Server Configuration Manager. The Configuration Manager is more comprehensive and makes additional configuration settings, such as Registry permissions, that ensure proper operation.

The SQL Server Configuration Manager is a consolidated tool that allows you to manage network options and services related to SQL Server. To launch this tool, you select Start, Microsoft SQL Server 2014, Configuration Tools, SQL Server 2014 Configuration Manager. Figure 13.2 shows an example of the Configuration Manager with the SQL Server Services selected for viewing.

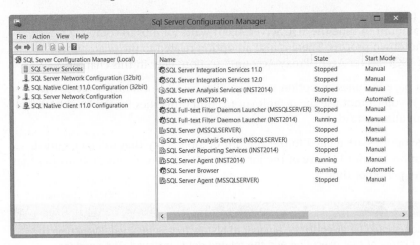

FIGURE 13.2   SQL Server Configuration Manager.

You can view the properties associated with the SQL Server Agent service by right-clicking on its service in the SQL Server Configuration Manager and selecting properties. Figure 13.3 shows an example of the SQL Server Agent properties screen. The Log On tab displays the startup account that the SQL Server Agent Server will use. This startup account is initially determined during the installation of SQL Server. You have the option of choosing one of several built-in accounts, or you can select a domain account. The built-in accounts are available by default and do not require any network administration to use them. These accounts, however, should be used with caution because they can provide network access to the SQL Server Agent that may not be desired. Generally, you want to provide the minimum amount of security necessary for the SQL Server Agent to perform its tasks.

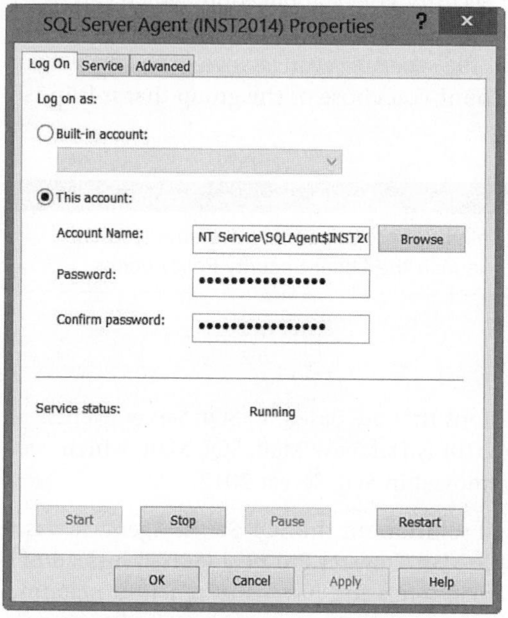

FIGURE 13.3   SQL Server Agent Service properties.

The recommended startup account for the SQL Server Agent is a Windows account. You specify a Windows startup account for SQL Server Agent by using the This Account option on the Service Properties window. The Windows account can be a local user account or domain user account. In either case it must be a member of the SQL Server sysadmin fixed server role on the local SQL Server instance. The use of this type of startup account provides the most flexibility and allows you to tailor the network and local resources that the SQL Server Agent has permission to access.

The Windows account does not have to be a member of the Windows administrators group. In fact, exclusion from the administrators group is recommended in most cases. This approach adheres to the principle of least privileges, which says that you should limit the amount of security provided to only that which is needed. In many cases, inclusion in the administrators group is not needed and only increases exposure to security threats.

The Windows account you choose with the This Account option must have certain security rights to be able to function as the startup account for SQL Server. The required Windows permissions are shown in the following list:

▶ Log on as a service

▶ Replace a process-level token

▶ Bypass traverse checking

▶ Adjust memory quotas for a process

You can set these permissions using the Local Security Policy application, which can be found under Administrative Tools. You select the Local Policies node and then select User Rights Assignment to display a list of all the security settings, including Log On as a Service Policy. You should make sure the account you chose or the group that it is in is included in this policy.

TIP

The Local Security Policy editor can be hard to find. In most operating systems, you can click Start, Run and then enter secpol.msc to launch the Local Security Policy editor.

Configuring Email Notification

The SQL Server Agent can send email notifications that are based on SQL Server events. The only available Mail System in SQL Server 2014 is Database Mail. SQL Mail, which was available in prior version of SQL Server, was removed in SQL Server 2012.

Database Mail has been the recommended mail solution for the SQL Server Agent. It was added in SQL Server 2005, and it utilizes Simple Mail Transfer Protocol (SMTP) instead of Extended MAPI to send mail. This simplifies email setup and has many benefits, including the following:

▶ There is no requirement that an email client be installed on the SQL Server machine.

▶ Email is queued for later delivery if the mail server stops or fails.

▶ Multiple SMTP servers can be specified so that mail continues to be delivered in the event that one of the SMTP servers stops.

▶ Database Mail is cluster aware.

Database Mail is disabled by default in SQL Server 2014 but can be enabled using the Database Mail Configuration Wizard. This wizard provides a comprehensive means for configuring Database Mail. The Database Mail Configuration Wizard is not launched from the SQL Server Agent node. Instead, you can launch it by expanding the Management node in the Object Explorer, right-clicking Database Mail, and selecting Configure Database Mail. This wizard guides you through the configuration of mail profiles, SMTP accounts, and other options relevant to Database Mail. The Configuration Wizard and many other details related to Database Mail are discussed in detail in Chapter 12, "Database Mail."

After you set up Database Mail and confirm that it is working properly, you can select it as your mail system for the SQL Server Agent to send mail. You do this by right-clicking the SQL Server Agent node in the Object Explorer and selecting Properties. Then you select the Alert System page in the SQL Server Agent Properties dialog, and the screen shown in Figure 13.4 appears. In this figure, Database Mail is selected as the mail system, along with a mail profile for Database Mail created with the Database Mail Configuration Wizard. The mail profile you select can have multiple SMTP accounts assigned to it. This allows for redundancy in the event that the mail cannot be sent to one of the SMTP accounts.

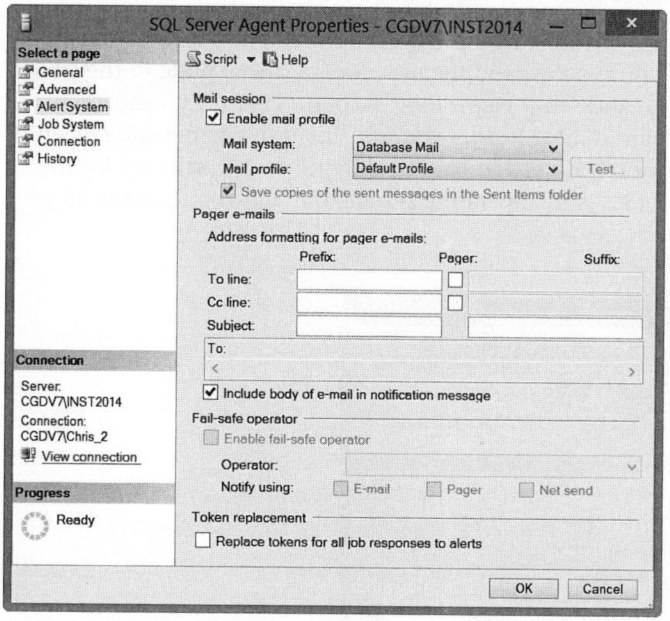

FIGURE 13.4   The Alert System page of the SQL Server Agent Properties dialog.

To ensure proper functioning of the alert system, you should restart the SQL Server Agent service after the alert system has been configured. If you experience problems sending notifications via the SQL Server Agent, you should check the service account that SQL Server is running under. If the SQL Server Agent is running with the local system account, resources outside the SQL Server machine will be unavailable; this includes mail servers that are on other machines. You should change the service account for the SQL Server Agent to a domain account to resolve this issue. Chapter 12 provides more information on using Database Mail in SQL Server 2014.

SQL Server Agent Proxy Account

Proxy accounts allow non–Transact-SQL (non–T-SQL) job steps to execute under a specific security context. By default, only users in the sysadmin role can execute these job steps. Non-sysadmin users can be assigned to a proxy account to allow them to run the special job steps. With SQL Server 2014, multiple proxy accounts can be established, each of which can be assigned to a different SQL Server Agent subsystem.

To establish a proxy account for the SQL Server Agent, you must first create a credential. A *credential* contains the authentication information necessary to connect to a resource outside SQL Server. The credential is typically linked to a Windows account that has the appropriate rights on the server. To create a credential, you open the `Security` node in the Object Explorer, right-click the `Credentials` node, and select New Credential. You give the credential a name, enter an identity value that corresponds to a valid Windows account, and provide a password for the account.

After creating a credential, you can create a new proxy account and link it to the credential. To create a new proxy account, you expand the `SQL Server Agent` node in the Object Explorer tree, right-click `Proxies`, and select New Proxy Account. Figure 13.5 shows an example of the New Proxy Account dialog. In this example, the proxy name and credential name are the same, but they do not need to be. The only subsystem selected for the sample proxy account in Figure 13.5 is the operating system, but a proxy account can be linked to multiple subsystems.

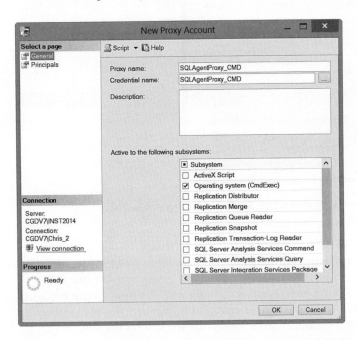

FIGURE 13.5   Creating a new proxy account.

After a proxy account is created, a `sysadmin` can assign one or more SQL logins, `msdb` roles, or server roles to the proxy. You do this by using the Principals page of the New Proxy Account dialog. A proxy account can have zero or many principals assigned to it. Conversely, a principal can be assigned to many different proxies. Linking non-admin principals to the proxy allows the principal to create job steps for subsystems that have been assigned to the proxy.

Proxy accounts are referenced within a SQL Server Agent job step. The General page of the Job Step Properties dialog contains a Run As drop-down that lists valid accounts or proxies that can be used to run the particular job step. After you add a proxy account, you see it in this drop-down list. Keep in mind that the proxy account is not visible for a T-SQL job step because it cannot utilize a proxy account. Steps that utilize the T-SQL subsystem execute under the job owner's context, and they do not utilize a proxy account.

Viewing the SQL Server Agent Error Log

The SQL Server Agent maintains an error log that records information, warnings, and error messages concerning its operation. A node named Error Logs is located in the SQL Server Agent tree in the Object Explorer. The Error Logs node contains multiple versions of the SQL Server Agent error log. By default, a maximum of 10 versions of the error log are displayed under the Error Logs node. The versions displayed include the current error log and the last 9 versions. Each time the SQL Server Agent is restarted, a new error log is generated, with a name that includes a time stamp. The first part of the current version's name is Current. Names of older logs start with Archive #, followed by a number; the newer logs have lower numbers. The SQL Server error log works in much the same way as the SQL Server Agent's error log.

TIP

You can cycle the error log at any time without stopping and starting the SQL Server Agent. To do so, you right-click the Error Logs node in the Object Explorer and select Recycle; a new error log is then generated. You can also use the msdb.dbo.sp_cycle_agent_errorlog stored procedure to cycle the error log. You need to remember to also select the Refresh option to show the latest available error logs.

To view the contents of any of the logs, you need to double-click the particular log. Double-clicking on a log file launches the Log File Viewer. The Log File Viewer contains the SQL Server Agent error logs in addition to logs that are associated with other SQL Server components, including Database Mail, SQL Server, and Windows NT. Figure 13.6 shows a sample Log File Viewer screen with the current SQL Server Agent error log selected for display. The Log File Viewer provides filtering capabilities that allow you to focus on a particular type of error message, along with other viewing capabilities that are common to all the logs available for viewing.

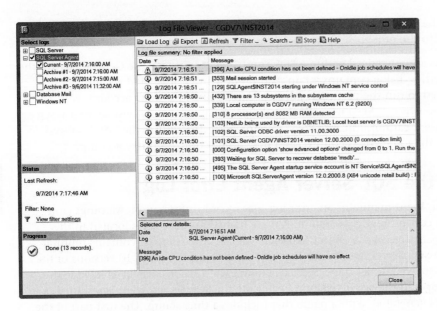

FIGURE 13.6   The SQL Server Agent error log.

SQL Server Agent Security

Many changes were made to the security model related to the SQL Server Agent in SQL Server 2005. In versions prior to 2005, everyone could view the SQL Server Agent. Starting in SQL Server 2005, logins must be a part of the sysadmin server role or assigned to one of three msdb database roles to be able to view and modify the SQL Server Agent. The SQL Server Agent node does not appear in the Object Explorer tree if the login does not have the appropriate permissions. Following are the msdb database roles and their basic permissions:

▶ **SQLAgentUserRole**—Users with this permission can create and manage local jobs and job schedules that they own. They cannot create multiserver jobs or manage jobs that they do not own.

▶ **SQLAgentReaderRole**—Users with this permission can view jobs that belong to other users in addition to all the permissions associated with SQLAgentUserRole.

▶ **SQLAgentOperatorRole**—Users with this permission can view operators and alerts and control jobs owned by other users. The job control on jobs owned by other users is limited to stopping or starting and enabling or disabling those jobs. SQLAgentOperatorRole also has all the permissions available to SQLAgentUserRole and SQLAgentReaderRole.

SQLAgentUserRole has the fewest privileges, and each subsequent role has increasing levels of security. In addition, each subsequent role inherits the permissions of the roles with fewer permissions. For example, SQLAgentReaderRole can do everything that

`SQLAgentUserRole` can do and more. Refer to the topic "SQL Server Agent Fixed Database Roles" in SQL Server Books Online for a detailed list of all the permissions related to the new database roles.

Managing Operators

Operators are accounts that can receive notification when an event occurs. These accounts are not linked directly to the user and login accounts that are defined on the server. They are basically aliases for people who need to receive notification based on job execution or alerts. Each operator can define one or more electronic means for notification, including email, pager, and the `NET SEND` command.

To add a new operator, you expand the `SQL Server Agent` node in the Object Explorer and right-click the `Operators` node. Then you select New Operator from the right-click menu. Figure 13.7 shows the New Operator screen, with many of the fields populated for the creation of a new operator named `LauraG`.

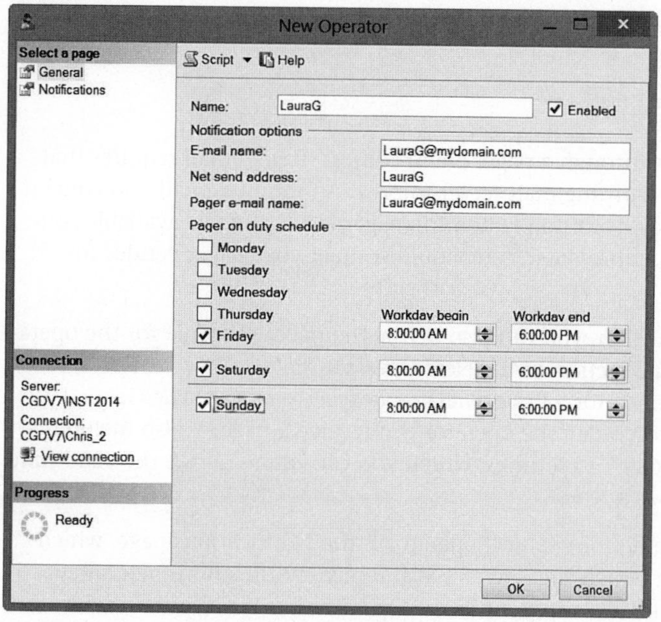

FIGURE 13.7   Creating a new operator.

The General page of the New Operator screen allows you to enter the name of the operator, the notification options, and the "on duty" scheduled for the operator. The operator name can be any name, but it must be unique within the SQL Server instance and must be no more than 128 characters. The operator name can be the same as another login or user on the server, but this is not required.

The notifications options are the key to operators. You create operators so that you can then define notification options and have messages sent from SQL Server.

If you use the email notification option, the email address you specify must be a valid address that can be reached via Database Mail. Database Mail must be configured before the email functionality will work. If Database Mail is configured, the email is sent via an SMTP server.

The NET SEND notification option causes a pop-up window to appear on the recipient's computer; this window contains the notification text. In the Net Send Address text box, you specify the name of the computer or user that is visible on the network to the SQL Server machine. For NET SEND to work, the Messenger service on SQL Server must be started. This Messenger service must also be started on the machine that is receiving the NET SEND message. You can test the basic NET SEND capabilities by executing NET SEND at the command prompt. The basic syntax for NET SEND follows:

```
NET SEND {name | * | /domain[:name] | /users} message
```

The following example uses the NET SEND command to send the message "Test net send message" to the operator LauraG:

```
NET SEND LauraG "Test net send message"
```

The final notification option is through a pager email address. Pager email requires that third-party software be installed on the mail server to process inbound email and convert it to a pager message. The methods for implementing pager email and the available software are dependent on the pager provider. You should contact your pager vendor for implementation details.

If you implement pager notification, you can also define the pager schedule for the operator. The Pager on Duty Schedule section of the New Operator dialog allows you to define the days and times when the operator will be available to receive a page. The General page includes a check box for each day the operator can receive a page. It also includes the Workday Begin and Workday End settings, which you can use to define the valid time periods to receive a page.

The other page available when defining a new operator is the Notifications page, which displays the alerts and jobs for which the operator will receive notifications. For a new operator, the Alert List or Job List is empty. After the Operator has been set to receive notifications, you can view them on the Notifications page as shown in Figure 13.8.

You'll have a better understanding of the usefulness of operators after you read the following discussions of jobs and alerts. Jobs and alerts can have operators linked to them for notification purposes.

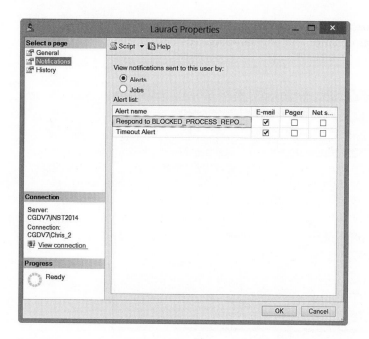

FIGURE 13.8   The Notifications page of the New Operator dialog.

Managing Jobs

A *job* is a container for operations that can be executed by the SQL Server Agent. Jobs can be run once or scheduled to run on a regular basis. Jobs provide the basis for SQL Server automation and allow for the execution of many different types of operations, including T-SQL, SQL Server Integration Services (SSIS) packages, and operating system commands.

Defining Job Properties

The Jobs node is located under SQL Server Agent in the Object Explorer. You right-click the Jobs node and select New Job to create a new SQL Server Agent job. A New Job dialog like the one shown in Figure 13.9 appears.

> **NOTE**
>
> Only logins that are part of one of the msdb fixed database roles or are members of the sysadmin fixed server role are able to create or modify jobs.

The General properties page shown in Figure 13.9 contains the basic information about the job, including the name and description. The owner of the job defaults to the login for the person creating the job; however, if the login of the person creating the job is part of the sysadmin fixed server role, the default can be changed. You use the Category selection to group or organize jobs. There are several predefined categories for selection, including Database Maintenance and Log Shipping. The default category is set to [Uncategorized(local)].

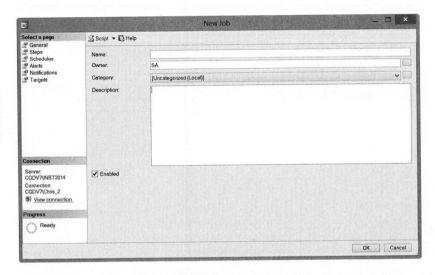

FIGURE 13.9   The New Job dialog.

Defining Job Steps

After you add the general information for a new job, you are ready to add the job steps that actually perform the work. To do this, you select the Steps page on the left side of the New Job dialog, and the job steps for this job are listed. To create a new job step, you click the New button, and a New Job Step dialog like the one shown in Figure 13.10 appears.

A step name is the first piece of information you need to provide for the job step. It can be up to 128 characters long and must be unique within the job. Then you need to select a job step type. The SQL Server Agent can run a variety of types of job steps, including the following:

- ActiveX script (Visual Basic, Java, Perl script)
- Operating System (CmdExec)
- PowerShell
- Replication Distributor
- Replication Merge
- Replication Queue Reader
- Replication Snapshot
- Replication Transaction Log Reader

▶ SQL Server Analysis Services Command

▶ SQL Server Analysis Services Query

▶ SQL Server Integration Services Package

▶ Transact-SQL script (T-SQL)

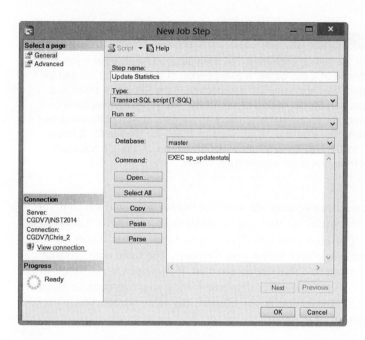

FIGURE 13.10   The New Job Step dialog.

The Step properties page displays different information, depending on the type of step selected. When the Transact-SQL script (T-SQL) type is selected, you see a window similar to the one shown in Figure 13.10. If you choose the SQL Server Integration Services Package type, the Step properties page changes to allow you to enter all the relevant information needed to execute an SSIS package.

In many cases (including T-SQL), a command window is available to input the step commands. With a T-SQL command, you can enter the same type of commands you would enter in a query window. You click the Parse button to validate the SQL and ensure proper syntax. The Operating system (CmdExec) type allows you to enter the same types of commands that you can enter in a command prompt window. Each step type has its own command syntax that you can test in the native environment to ensure proper operation.

You can select the Advanced page to configure job flow information and other information related to the job step. On Success Action allows you to specify the action to perform when the current job step completes. Actions include the execution of the next job step (if one exists) and the ability to set job status based on the step completion. The same selection options also exist for On Failure Action.

The Retry options define the options that relate to retrying the job step in the event that the job step fails. Retry Attempts defines the number of times the job step will be re-executed if it fails. Retry Intervals (Minutes) defines the amount of time (in minutes) between retry attempts.

TIP

The Retry options are useful for polling scenarios. For example, you might have a job step that tests for the existence of a file during a given period of the day. The job can be scheduled to start at a time of day when the file is expected. If the file is not there and the step fails, Retry Attempts can be set to poll again for the file. Retry Interval determines how often it retries and the combination of Retry Attempts and Retry Interval determines the total polling window. For example, if you want to check for the file for 2 hours, you can set Retry Attempts to 24 with a Retry Interval of 5 minutes. If the job step fails more than the number of retries, the step completes in failure.

The last set of options on the Advanced page relate to the output from the job step. Job step output can be saved to an output file that can be overwritten each time the job step is run, or the output can be appended each time. The Log to Table option writes the job step output to the `sysjobstepslogs` table in the `msdb` database. The table contains one row for each job step with the Log to Table option enabled. If Append Output to Existing Entry in Table is enabled, the `sysjobstepslogs` data row for the step can contain output for more than one execution. If this option is not selected, the table contains only execution history for the last execution of the step.

CAUTION

If you choose the Append Output to Existing Entry in Table option, the size of the `sysjobstepslogs` table will grow over time. You should consider using the `sp_delete_jobsteplog` stored procedure to remove data from the `sysjobstepslogs` table. This stored procedure has several different parameters that allow you to filter the data that will be removed. You can use these parameters to remove log data by job, job step, date, or size of the log for the job step.

Defining Multiple Job Steps

You can define multiple job steps in a single job. This allows you to execute multiple dependent job actions. The job steps run one at a time (serially), and you can specify the order of the job steps. The job order and the related dependencies are called *control of flow*.

Figure 13.11 shows an example of a job that has multiple dependent job steps. Take note of the On Success and On Failure columns, which define the control of flow. For example, if step 1 succeeds, the next step occurs. If step 1 fails, no further steps are executed, and the job quits, reporting a job failure. The control of flow is slightly different for the second step, whereby the control of flow passes to the next step on success but flows to the fourth step if a failure occurs.

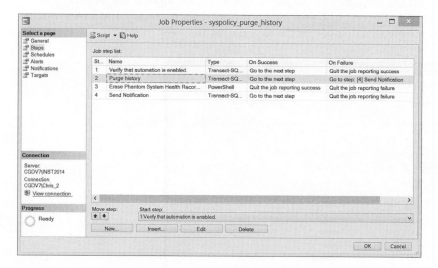

FIGURE 13.11   Multiple job steps.

The control of flow is defined on each job step. As discussed earlier in this chapter, the Advanced tab of the New Job Step dialog provides drop-down lists that allow you to specify the actions to take on success and on failure. In addition, the Steps page that lists all of a job's steps allows you to specify the start step for the job. The drop-down box at the bottom of the Steps page provides this function. You can also use the Move Step arrows to change the start step. Manipulating the start step is useful when you're restarting a job manually, as in the case of a job failure; in this situation, you might want to set the job to start on a step other than the first step.

> **NOTE**
>
> SSIS provides the same type of flow control capabilities as the SQL Server Agent. In fact, maintenance plans that contain multiple related actions (such as optimization, backup, and reporting) utilize SSIS packages. A scheduled job starts an SSIS package, which executes the package in a single step, but the actual maintenance steps are defined within the package. The SSIS Designer utilizes a graphical tool that depicts the flow of control and allows you to modify the individual steps.

Defining Job Schedules

The SQL Server Agent contains a comprehensive scheduling mechanism you can use to automate the execution of your jobs. A job can have zero, one, or more schedules assigned to it. You can view the schedules associated with a job by selecting the Schedules page of the Job Properties screen. To create a new schedule for a job, you can click the New button at the bottom of the Schedules page. Figure 13.12 shows the New Job Schedule Properties page, with a sample schedule and options defined. The options on this screen vary, depending on the frequency of the job schedule. For example, if the frequency of the schedule shown in Figure 13.12 were changed from daily to weekly, the screen would change to allow for the selection of specific days during the week to run the job.

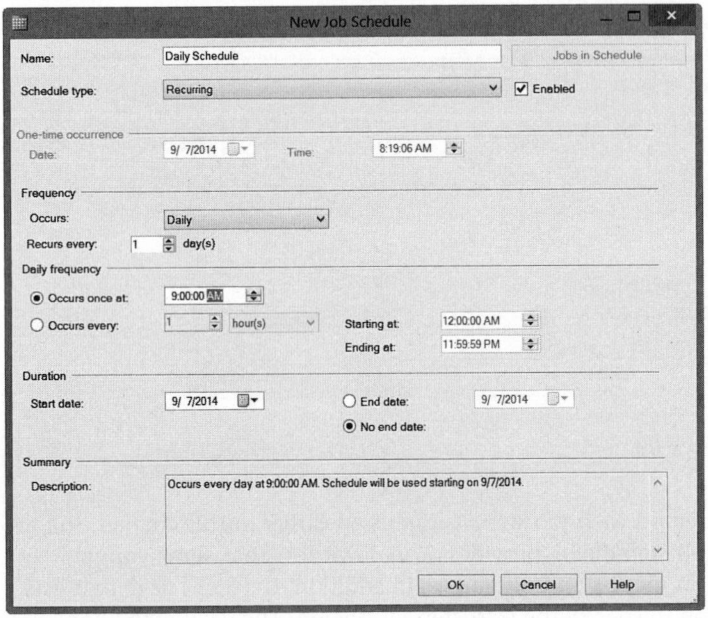

FIGURE 13.12   The New Job Schedule Properties page.

You have the ability to share job schedules so that one job schedule can be utilized by more than one job. When you select the Schedule page, a Pick button is available at the bottom of the page. If you click the Pick button, a screen appears showing all the defined schedules. If you highlight one of the schedules in the list and click OK, the schedule is linked to the related job. You can also view all the jobs associated with a particular schedule by editing the schedule and clicking the Jobs in Schedule button in the top-right portion of the Job Schedule Properties screen.

Tracking multiple job schedules and schedule execution can be challenging in an environment that has many jobs and schedules. The sp_help_jobs_in_schedule, and sp_help_jobactivity stored procedures are helpful system stored procedures that are found in the msdb database. The sp_help_jobs_in_schedule stored procedure provides information about the relationship between jobs and schedules. The sp_help_jobactivity stored procedure provides point-in-time information about the runtime state of SQL Server jobs. This stored procedure returns a lot of information, including recent job executions, the status of those executions, and the next scheduled run date.

Defining Job Notifications

The Notifications page of the Job Properties dialog, as shown in Figure 13.13, allows you to define the notification actions to perform when a job completes.

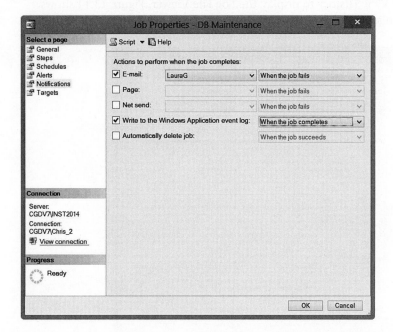

FIGURE 13.13   The Notifications page of the Job Properties dialog.

As discussed earlier in this chapter, notifications can be sent via email, pager, or NET SEND command. The notifications for a Schedule Job can be sent based on the following events:

▶ When the job succeeds

▶ When the job fails

▶ When the job completes

Each of these events can have a different notification action defined for it. For example, a notification might send an email if the job succeeds but page someone if it fails.

You also have the option of writing notification information into the Windows Application event log or automatically deleting the job when it completes. These two options are also available on the Notifications page. Writing events to the Application log is a useful tracking mechanism. Monitoring software is often triggered by events in the application log. The automatic job deletion options are useful for jobs that will be run only once. As with the other notification options, you can set up the delete job action such that it is deleted only when a specific job event occurs. For example, you might want to delete the job only if the job succeeds.

Viewing Job History

You view job history via the Log File Viewer, which is a comprehensive application that allows for many different types of logs to be viewed. You right-click a job in the SQL Server Agent and select View History to display the Log File Viewer. Figure 13.14 shows the Log File Viewer with several examples of job history selected for viewing.

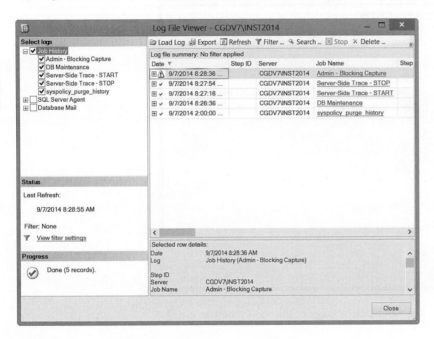

FIGURE 13.14   Job history shown in the Log File Viewer.

Compared to viewing job history in SQL Server versions prior to SQL Server 2005, the current form of the Log File Viewer has some distinct advantages for viewing job history. In the Log File Viewer, you can select multiple jobs for viewing at one time. To view job step details, you expand the job entries and select a job step. You can use the row details shown below the log file summary to troubleshoot job errors and isolate problems. The Log File Viewer also has filtering capabilities that allow you to isolate the jobs to view. Click on the Filter button, and the Filter Settings dialog appears. You can filter jobs by using a number of different settings, including User, Start Date, and Message Text. You must click the Apply Filter button for the selected filtering option to take effect.

The amount of history that is kept is based on the history settings defined for the SQL Server Agent. You access the history settings by right-clicking the SQL Server Agent node, selecting Properties, and then selecting the History page on the left part of the screen. The settings available on the History page are shown in Figure 13.15. By default, the job history log is limited to 1,000 rows, with a maximum of 100 rows per job. You can also select the Automatically Remove Agent History option and select a period of time to retain history. This setting causes the SQL Server Agent to periodically remove job history from the log. This is a good approach for keeping the size of the log manageable.

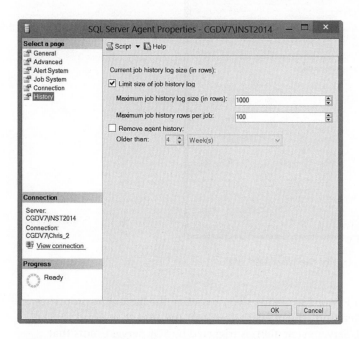

FIGURE 13.15 Job history settings.

Managing Alerts

The SQL Server Agent can monitor events that occur on the database server and automatically respond to these events with alerts. Alerts can be fired based on SQL Server events, performance conditions, and Windows Management Instrumentation (WMI) events. After an alert is fired, the SQL Server Agent can respond by notifying an operator or executing a job. This provides a proactive means for identifying and reacting to critical conditions on a database server.

Defining Alert Properties

To define alerts, you select the SQL Server Agent node in the Object Explorer tree and then right-click on the Alerts node and select New Alert. Figure 13.16 shows an example of the New Alert dialog that appears.

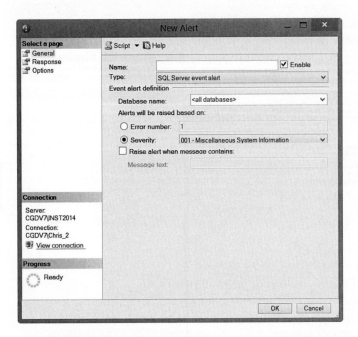

FIGURE 13.16   The General page of the New Alert dialog.

The General page selected in Figure 13.16 allows you to define the basic alert properties, including the name of the alert and type of event you want the alert to respond to. The default type of alert, the SQL Server event alert, is triggered by SQL Server events that write to the Windows Application event log. SQL Server writes to the Application event log when the following events occur:

▶ When sysmessages errors with a severity of 19 or higher are generated. You can use the sys.sysmessages catalog view to view all the sysmessages that are stored in the server. You can create new user-defined messages by using the sp_addmessage stored procedure; they must have a msg_id (or error number) that is greater than 50,000. The error message must be created before you can reference the error number in an alert.

▶ When sysmessages errors are generated by the Database Engine. These messages have error numbers lower than 50,000 and are installed by default.

▶ When any RAISERROR statement is invoked with the WITH LOG option. The WITH LOG statement forces the event to be written to the Application event log. Messages generated with RAISERROR that have a severity level greater than 18 are required to write to the Application event log.

▶ When sysmessages have been altered with the sp_altermessage statement to write to the application log. The sp_altermessage command has a write_to_log parameter that you can use to modify error numbers found in sys.messages. When the write_to_log parameter is set to WITH_LOG, these message automatically write to the

Application event log, regardless of whether the WITH_LOG option is used when the error is raised.

▶ When application calls are made to xp_logevent to log an event to the application log.

The bottom portion of the General page of the New Alert dialog allows you to define which events in the Application event log the alert should respond to. You can have the event respond to a specific error number, the error severity level, or specific text that is contained in the error message. The sys.sysmessages catalog view contains a complete list of all the error message details for all the supported languages. You can use the following SELECT statement to list the error messages for the English language:

```
SELECT * FROM SYS.SYSMESSAGES
where msglangid = 1033
order by msglangid, error
```

You can define an alert for hundreds of messages. For example, you can define an alert that responds to changes to database options. You do this by selecting error number 5084, which is triggered whenever a change is made to the database options. You can also narrow the scope of the alert to look at a specific database by using the Database Name drop-down. This limits the alert to errors that occur in the specific database you choose. The default option is to look at all databases.

The two other types of alerts you can define are SQL Server performance condition alerts and WMI event alerts. A SQL Server performance condition alert reacts to performance conditions on the server. Figure 13.17 shows an example of this type of alert.

When you select a SQL Server performance condition alert, you need to select the performance object and counter for that object to monitor. The SQL Server performance objects and counters available on the General page of the New Alert dialog are a subset of those available in the Windows Performance Monitor application. These performance metrics encompass key indicators, such as memory, CPU, and disk space.

After selecting the object and counter, you need to define the performance threshold for the alert at the bottom of the General page, below the Alert if Counter label. In the example shown in Figure 13.17, the alert is monitoring the transaction log file for the AdventureWorks2012 database. The threshold has been set such that the alert will fire if the transaction log for this database rises above 2000KB.

The WMI event alerts use WMI to monitor events in an instance of SQL Server. The SQL Server Agent can access SQL Server events by using the WMI provider for server events by issuing WMI Query Language (WQL) statements. WQL is a scaled-down version of SQL that contains some WMI-specific extensions. When a WMI query is run, it essentially creates an event notification in the target database so that a related event will fire. The number of WMI events is extensive. Refer to the "WMI Provider for Server Events Classes and Properties" topic in SQL Server Books Online for a complete list.

13

FIGURE 13.17   A SQL Server performance condition alert on the General page.

Figure 13.18 shows an example of a WMI event alert. This example uses a WQL query that detects any Data Definition Language (DDL) changes to any of the databases on the server. After the alert is created, you can test it by running a DDL statement against a database (for example, `alter table Person.address add newcol int null`).

Defining Alert Responses

The definition of an alert has two primary components. As discussed earlier in this chapter, the first component involves the identification of the event or performance condition that will trigger the alert. The second part of an alert definition involves the desired response when the alert condition is met. You can define an alert response by using the Response page on the alert's Properties screen. Figure 13.19 shows a sample response that has been configured to execute a job and NET SEND a message to the operator named ChrisG.

Operator notification and job execution are the two responses to an alert. Operator notification allows for one or more operators to be notified via email, pager, or the NET SEND command. Job execution allows for the execution of a job that has been defined in the SQL Server Agent. For example, you could execute a job that does a database backup for an alert that is triggered based on database size. You can define both job execution and operator notification in a single alert; they are not mutually exclusive.

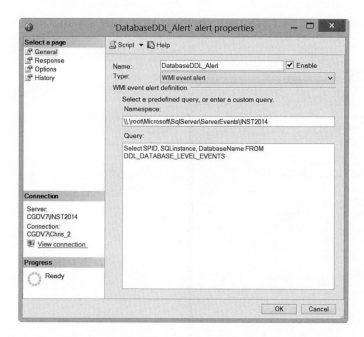

FIGURE 13.18   The General page showing a WMI event alert.

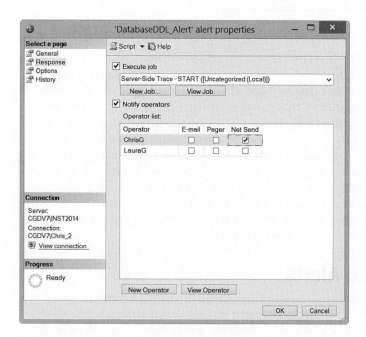

FIGURE 13.19   Configuring an alert response.

You can further define an alert response by using the Options page of an alert's Properties window (see Figure 13.20).

FIGURE 13.20   Alert options.

You can include an alert's error text in the operator notification message on this page. This alert error text provides further details about why the alert was fired. For example, if you have an alert that is triggered by changes to database options, the alert error text would include the actual option that was changed. You can also define additional notification text that is included when the message is sent. This message could include directives for the operators or additional instructions. Finally, you can define the amount of time that the alert will wait before responding to the alert condition again. You do this by using the Delay Between Responses drop-downs (Minutes and Seconds) to set the wait time. This capability is useful in situations in which an alert condition can happen repeatedly within a short period of time. You can define a response delay to prevent an unnecessarily large number of alert notifications from being sent.

Scripting Jobs and Alerts

SQL Server has options that allow for the scripting of jobs and alerts. As with many of the other objects in SQL Server, you might find that it is easier and more predictable to generate a script that contains the jobs and alerts on the server. You can use these scripts to reinstall the jobs and alerts or deploy them to another server. You can right-click the job or alert you want to script and choose a scripting option to generate the T-SQL for the individual object. You can also select the Job or Alerts node to view the Object Explorer Details that lists all the objects. You can also display the Object Explorer Details through the View menu or by selecting it as the active tab. When Object Explorer Details is selected, you have the option of selecting one or more jobs to script. You can select multiple jobs by holding down the Ctrl key and clicking the jobs you want to script.

Figure 13.21 shows a sample Object Explorer Details for jobs, with several of the jobs selected for scripting. To generate the script, you simply right-click one of the selected jobs and select the Script Job As menu option to generate the desired type of script.

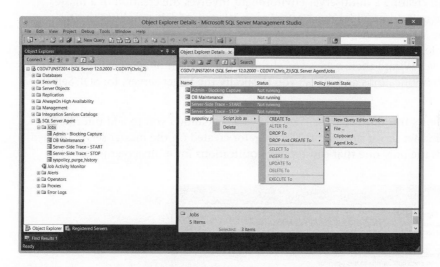

FIGURE 13.21   Script generation for jobs.

> **NOTE**
>
> With SQL Server 2014, you can also filter the jobs you want to script by using the filtering capabilities that are available on the Object Explorer Details. For example, you can filter on jobs whose names contain specific text. After you filter the jobs, you can script the jobs that are displayed. The filtering options and the capability to selectively script jobs are particularly useful in environments in which many jobs and alerts exist.

Multiserver Job Management

Multiserver job management allows you to centralize the administration of multiple *target* servers on a single *master* server. The master server is a SQL Server instance that contains the job definitions and status information for all the enlisted target servers. The target servers are SQL Server instances that obtain job information from the master server and continually update the master server with job statistics.

Multiserver job management is beneficial in SQL Server environments in which there are many instances to manage. You can establish jobs, operators, and execution schedules one time on the master server and then deploy them to all the target servers. This promotes consistency across the enterprise and can ease the overall administrative burden. Without multiserver job management, administrative jobs must be established and maintained on each server.

Creating a Master Server

The first step in creating a multiserver environment involves the creation of a master server. SQL Server 2014 provides the Master Server Wizard, which simplifies this task. You launch the Master Server Wizard by right-clicking the SQL Server Agent node in the Object Explorer and selecting Multi Server Administration and Make This a Master. The Master Server Wizard then guides you through the creation of an operator to receive multiserver job notifications and allows you to specify the target servers for SQL Server Agent jobs.

Figure 13.22 shows the Master Server Wizard screen that allows you to add information related to the master server's operator. The operator created on the master server, named MSXOperator, is the only one that can receive notifications for multiserver jobs.

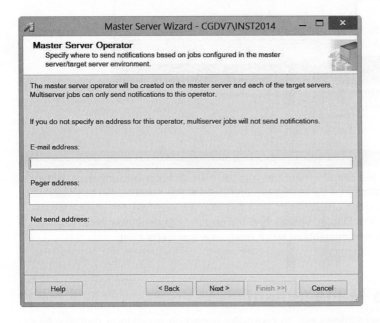

FIGURE 13.22   The Master Server Wizard.

The Master Server Wizard also validates the service accounts that the SQL Server Agent uses on the target servers. These accounts are typically Windows domain accounts that are in the same domain as the master server. The service accounts are important because the target servers utilize Windows security to connect to the master server and download jobs for the SQL Server Agent. The validation process and security considerations are simplified if the master server and target servers are run with the same domain account.

Enlisting Target Servers

The Master Server Wizard allows you to enlist one or more target servers. Enlisting a target server identifies it to the master server and allows the master server to manage the administration of its jobs. You can also enlist additional target servers after the wizard completes. You do this by right-clicking the SQL Server Agent node of the target server and then selecting Multi Server Administration and then Make This a Target. Doing so launches the Target Server Wizard, which guides you through the addition of another target server. The Target Server Wizard performs some of the same actions as the Master Server Wizard, including the following:

▶ It ensures that the SQL Server versions on the two servers are compatible.

▶ It ensures that the SQL Server Agent on the master server is running.

▶ It ensures that the Agent Startup account has rights to log in as a target server.

▶ It enlists the target server.

Creating Multiserver Jobs

After setting up the master and target servers, you can create jobs on the master server and specify which target servers they should run on. Periodically, the target servers poll the master server. If any jobs defined for them have been scheduled to run since the last polling interval, the target server downloads the jobs and runs them. When a job completes, the target server uploads the job outcome status to the master server.

Event Forwarding

Event forwarding is another multiserver feature that allows a single SQL Server instance to process events for other servers in your SQL Server environment. This involves the designation of an alerts management server to which other servers can forward their events. You enable the alerts management server by right-clicking the SQL Server Agent node and selecting Properties. When the Properties page appears, you click the Advanced page (see Figure 13.23).

To configure event forwarding, you select the Forward Events to a Different Server option on the Advanced page. You can then enter the SQL Server instance you want as the alerts management server. You can choose to forward unhandled events, all events, or only a subset of the events. The default is to send all unhandled events, but you can customize this for your needs. You can further limit the messages that are forwarded by specifying the severity level that the message must have in order to be forwarded. For example, you can configure the servers to forward only fatal error messages that have a severity greater than or equal to Level 19. In this scenario, you could define alerts on the alerts management server that respond to these fatal errors and notify operators that specialize in their resolution.

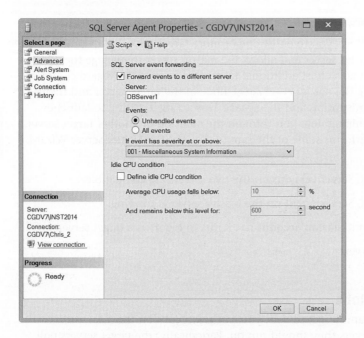

FIGURE 13.23   Configuring event forwarding.

You need to consider a number of trade-offs when using event forwarding. You need to weigh the benefits of central administration and a lack of redundancy against the disadvantages of having a single point of failure and increased network traffic. The available network bandwidth, number of servers involved in event forwarding, and stability of the alerts management server are some of the key factors you need to think about in making your decision.

Summary

The SQL Server Agent in SQL Server 2014 delivers a powerful set of tools to make your administrative life easier. It provides automation in the form of jobs, operators, and alerts that help you deliver a consistent and healthy database environment. After you have set up the appropriate automation with the SQL Server Agent, you can rest assured that you have been proactive in managing your database environment.

PowerShell is another tool to help with your automation needs. This new tool, which was integrated into SQL Server 2014, provides a powerful command-line facility you can use to access SQL Server objects. This tool is discussed in Chapter 14, "SQL Server Policy-Based Management."

SQL Server Policy-Based Management

Policy-Based Management enables an organization to define policies to manage one or more SQL Server instances, databases, or objects within the enterprise. In addition, policies can be evaluated against target systems to ensure that the standard configuration settings are not out of compliance. Policy-Based Management was developed in response to the following industry trends:

▶ Increasing amounts of data being stored

▶ Data center consolidation and virtualization

▶ Growing product capabilities

▶ Proliferation of SQL Server systems within the enterprise

▶ Need for a way to manage SQL Server settings from a holistic perspective

▶ Regulatory compliance demanding secure and standardized settings

What's New in Policy-Based Management

Except for two new facets related to the SQL Server 2014 Smart Admin feature (Smart Admin and Smart Admin State), Policy-Based Management is relatively unchanged from what was provided with SQL Server 2012.

Introduction to Policy-Based Management

A data explosion has been occurring over the past several years. This data explosion often results in a proliferation of SQL servers, often requiring DBAs to do more, frequently with less. In addition, the increasing complexities of the SQL Server product set are forcing DBAs to focus on efficient, scalable management and standardization. Due to the large numbers of SQL servers involved, management by automation becomes critical as well to lessen the administrative burden. Monitoring also becomes more important to provide proactive support.

A well-managed SQL Server enterprise that follows best practices offers the following advantages:

▶ **Standardization**—Every SQL Server will have a common disk layout and settings, as well as consistent naming standards. As a result, DBAs moving from one SQL Server to another will not be surprised by different disk layouts or unusual settings that could account for a performance problem.

▶ **Best practices**—Microsoft internal studies have shown that 80% of the support calls to their Customer Service and Support (CSS) could have been avoided if the customer had been following best practices. Best practices not only offer performance advantages but also lead to fewer failure events caused by poorly configured SQL Servers and security breaches due to SQL Servers that have not been hardened (security holes not locked down).

▶ **Ease of deployment**—A well-managed data center will have automated procedures for building SQL Servers (that is, unattended installations using configuration files) that require less time to build and minimal administrative interaction, resulting in fewer mistakes in a build and a reduction in administrative tasks.

▶ **Regulatory compliance**—By maintaining controlled and standardized settings, organizations can easily adhere to the demanding requirements of regulations such as Sarbanes-Oxley, the Health Insurance Portability and Accountability Act (HIPAA), and Payment Card Industry (PCI) standards.

The intent of Policy-Based Management is to provide a management framework that allows DBAs to automate management in their enterprise according to their own set of predefined standards. By implementing Policy-Based Management within a SQL Server infrastructure, organizations can reap the following benefits: total cost of ownership associated with managing SQL Server systems will be reduced, configuration changes to the SQL Server system can be monitored, unwanted system configuration changes can be prevented, and policies will ensure compliance.

The stated goals of Policy-Based Management fall into three categories:

▶ **Management by intent**—Allows DBAs to enforce standards and best practices from the start rather than in response to a performance problem or failure event

▶ **Intelligent monitoring**—Allows DBAs to detect changes that have been made to their SQL Server environments that deviate from the desired configuration

▶ **Virtualized management**—Provides a scalable framework that allows for management across the enterprise

Microsoft SQL Server 2014 ships with several predefined policies. These policies are not automatically imported into a default installation of SQL Server 2014. However, you can manually import them into SQL Server and use them as is or as a foundation for defining your own similar policies. These sample policies can be found in `C:\Program Files\Microsoft SQL Server\120\Tools\Policies\DatabaseEngine\1033` (or `C:\Program Files (x86)\Microsoft SQL Server\120\Tools\Policies\DatabaseEngine\1033` if you are running in a 64 bit environment). Note that there are also policies for Reporting Services and Analysis Services, which can be found in the `ReportingServices` and `AnalysisServices` subdirectories of the `Policies` directory. Also note that Policy-Based Management can be used to manage prior versions of SQL Server as well.

Policy-Based Management Concepts

There are a few key concepts you need to understand before diving into the setup and implementation of policies in your system. These concepts include

▶ Facets

▶ Conditions

▶ Policies

▶ Categories

▶ Targets

▶ Execution mode

▶ Central Management Servers

Facets

A *facet* is a logical grouping of predefined SQL Server 2014 configuration settings. When a facet is coupled with a condition, a policy is formed and can be applied to one or more SQL Server instances and systems. Common facets include Surface Area Configuration, Server Audit, Database File, and Databases. Table 14.1 illustrates the complete list of predefined facets that can be selected, along with an indication of how each facet can be automated. Check On Schedule uses a SQL Server Agent job to evaluate a policy. Check On Change uses event notification to evaluate based on when changes occur. Facets are included with SQL Server 2014 and cannot be modified.

TABLE 14.1   Facets for Policy-Based Management

Facet Name	Check on Change: Prevent	Check on Change: Log	Check on Schedule
Application Role	X	X	X
Asymmetric Key	X	X	X
Audit			X
Availability Database			X
Availability Group			X
Availability Group State			X
Availability Replica			X
Backup Device			X
Broker Priority			X
Broker Service			X
Certificate			X
Credential			X
Cryptographic Provider			X
Data File			X
Database			X
Database Audit Specification			X
Database DDL Trigger			X
Database Maintenance			X
Database Option		X	X
Database Performance			X
Database Replica State			X
Database Role	X	X	X
Database Security			X
Default			X
Endpoint	X	X	X
Filegroup			X
Full Text Catalog			X
Full Text Index			X
Full Text Stop List			X
Index			X
Linked Server			X

Facet Name	Check on Change: Prevent	Check on Change: Log	Check on Schedule
Log File			X
Login			X
Login Options	X	X	X
Message Type			X
Multipart Name	X	X	X
Name			X
Partition Function			X
Partition Scheme			X
Plan Guide			X
Remote Service Binding			X
Resource Governor			X
Resource Pool	X	X	X
Rule			X
Schema	X	X	X
Search Property List		X	X
Sequence	X	X	X
Server			X
Server Audit			X
Server Audit Specification			X
Server Configuration		X	X
Server DDL Trigger			X
Server Information			X
Server Installation Settings			
Server Performance			X
Server Protocol Settings			X
Server Role	X	X	
Server Security			X
Server Selection			
Server Settings			X
Service Contract			X
Service Queue			X
Service Route			X

14

Facet Name	Check on Change: Prevent	Check on Change: Log	Check on Schedule
Smart Admin			X
Smart Admin State			X
Statistic			X
Stored Procedure	X	X	X
Surface Area Configuration		X	X
Surface Area Configuration for Analysis Services			
Surface Area Configuration for Reporting Services			
Symmetric Key			X
Synonym			X
Table			X
Table Options	X	X	X
Trigger			X
User			X
User Defined Aggregate			X
User Defined Data Type			X
User Defined Function	X	X	X
User Defined Table Type			X
User Defined Type			X
User Options	X	X	X
View			X
View Options	X	X	X
Workload Group	X	X	X
Xml Schema Collection			X

The complete list of facets can be viewed in SQL Server 2014 Management Studio by expanding the Management folder, the Policy Management node, and then the Facets folder. Alternatively, to view facets applied to a specific database, you can right-click the database and select Facets.

Conditions

A *condition* is a Boolean expression that dictates an outcome or desired state of a specific management condition, also known as a facet. Condition settings are based on properties, comparative operators, and values such as String, equal, not equal, LIKE, NOT LIKE, IN, or NOT IN. For example, a check condition could verify that data and log files reside on separate drives, that the state of the database recovery model is set to Full Recovery, that database file sizes are not larger than a predefined value, and that Database Mail is disabled.

Policies

A policy is a standard for a single setting of an object. It ultimately acts as a verification mechanism of one or more conditions of the required state of SQL Server targets. Typical scenarios for creating policies include imposing Surface Area Configuration settings, enforcing naming conventions on database objects, enforcing database and transaction log placement, and controlling recovery models. As mentioned earlier, a tremendous number of policies can be created against SQL Server 2014 systems. Surface Area Configurations are a common policy, especially because the SQL Server 2005 Surface Area Configuration tool no longer ships with SQL Server 2008 and later.

> **NOTE**
>
> A policy can contain only one condition and can be either enabled or disabled.

Categories

Microsoft recognized that although you may want to implement a set of rigid standards for your internal SQL Server development or deployments, your enterprise may have to host third-party software that does not follow your standards. Although your internally developed user databases will subscribe to your own policies, the third-party user applications will subscribe to their own categories. To provide flexibility, you can select which policies you want a table, database, or server to subscribe to and group them into groups called *categories*, and then have a database subscribe to a category and unsubscribe from a group of other policies if necessary. A policy can belong to only one policy category.

Targets

A *target* is one or more SQL Server instances, databases, or database objects that you want to apply your categories or policies to. Targets can be only SQL Server 2014, 2012, 2008 R2, 2008, 2005, or 2000 systems. All targets in a server instance form a target hierarchy. A target set is the set of targets that results from applying a set of target filters to the target hierarchy—for example, all the tables in a database contained in a specific schema.

Execution Modes

When you are implementing policies, there are three types of execution modes. The On Change mode has two variations:

- ▶ **On Demand**—The On Demand policy ensures that a target or targets are in compliance. This task is invoked manually by right-clicking on the policy in the Management folder, Policy Management folder, Policies folder, and selecting Evaluate. The policy is not enforced and is only verified against all targets that have been subscribed to that policy. You can evaluate a policy also by right-clicking on the database and selecting Policies and Evaluate.

▶ **On Schedule**—Policies can be evaluated on a schedule. For example, a policy can be scheduled to check all SQL Server 2014 systems once a day. If any anomalies arise, these out-of-compliance policies are logged to a file. This file should be reviewed on a periodic basis.

▶ **On Change Prevent**—The On Change Prevent execution mode prevents changes to server, server object, database, or database objects that would make them out of compliance. For example, if you select a policy that restricts table names to only those that begin with the prefix tbl, and you attempt to create a table called MyTable, you get the following error message, and your table is not created:

```
Policy 'table name' has been violated by
'/Server/(local)/Database/iFTS/Table/dbo.mytable'.
This transaction will be rolled back.
Policy description: ''
Additional help: '' : ''.
Msg 3609, Level 16, State 1, Procedure sp_syspolicy_
dispatch_event, Line 50
The transaction ended in the trigger.
The batch has been aborted.
```

▶ **On Change Log Only**—If you select On Change Log Only, a policy condition that is evaluated as failed is logged in the SQL Server Error log. The change does not prevent out-of-compliance changes.

Central Management Servers

In large enterprises, organizations most likely have more than one SQL Server system they want to effectively manage from a Policy-Based Management perspective. Therefore, if DBAs want to implement policies on multiple servers, they have two options. The first option includes exporting the policy and then importing it into different SQL Server systems. After the policy is imported, it must be configured to be evaluated on demand, on schedule, or on change.

The second option includes creating one or more Central Management Servers in SQL Server 2014. Basically, by registering one or more SQL Servers with a Central Management Server, a DBA can deploy multiserver policies and administration from a central system.

For example, you could create two Central Management Servers, one called OLAP and another called OLTP, and then register servers into each Central Management Server, import the different policies into each Central Management Server, and then evaluate the polices on each different Central Management Server. So, on your OLTP Central Management Server, the servers OLTP1, OLTP2, OLTP3, which are registered in the OLTP Central Management Server, would have the OLTP policies evaluated on them.

Creating a Central Management Server

Follow these steps to register a Central Management Server:

1. In SQL Server Management Studio, click on the View menu and select Registered Servers.

2. In Registered Servers, expand the Database Engine node, right-click Central Management Servers, and then select Register Central Management Server.

3. In the New Server Registration dialog, specify the name of the desired Central Management Server.

4. If necessary, specify additional connection properties on the Connection Properties tab or click Save.

Registering SQL Server Instances in a Central Management Server

The next task registers SQL Server instances to be associated with a Central Management Server. The following steps outline this task:

1. Right-click on the Central Management Server with which you want to associate your SQL Server instance.

2. Select New Server Registration.

3. In the New Server Registration dialog, specify the name of the SQL Server Instance and the proper connection information and click Save.

4. Repeat steps 1-3 for all SQL Server instances that you want to register with this Central Management Server.

After following these steps, SSMS should display information in the Registered Servers panel similar to that shown in Figure 14.1, which illustrates a Central Management Server with one Server Group and four SQL Server instances registered.

FIGURE 14.1   Central Management Server with Registered SQL Server instances.

Importing and Evaluating Polices to the Central Management Server

After the Central Management Server is established, the Server Group is created, and the desired SQL Server instances are registered, it is time to import and evaluate policies. You can import policies for multiple instances by right-clicking the Central Management Server or Server Group and selecting Import Policies. After the policies are imported, the next step is to evaluate the policies by right-clicking the Central Management Server or Server Group and selecting Evaluate. The output indicates the status of policies associated with all the SQL Server instances associated with the Central Management Server or Server Group.

> **NOTE**
>
> Importing, exporting, and evaluating policies are covered throughout the rest of the chapter.

Implementing Policy-Based Management

Now that you understand the basic purpose and concepts behind Policy-Based Management, let's look at how to administer Policy-Based Management, applying it to a server, and then a group of servers.

There are essentially five steps to implementing and administering Policy-Based Management:

- ▶ Creating a condition based on a facet
- ▶ Creating a policy based on that condition
- ▶ Creating a category
- ▶ Subscribing to a category
- ▶ Exporting or importing a policy

Let's look at each of these steps in turn. The upcoming sections explain each step in its entirety.

Creating a Condition Based on a Facet

When you are creating conditions, the general principle includes three elements: selecting a property, an operator, and then a value. The following example walks through the steps to create a condition based on a facet, which will enforce a naming standard on a table:

1. To create a condition, connect to a SQL Server 2014 instance on which you want to create a policy.

2. Launch SQL Server Management Studio (SSMS). In Object Explorer, expand the server instance, expand the Management folder, expand the Policy Management folder, and then expand the Facets folder.

3. Within the `Facets` folder, browse to the desired facet on which you want to create the policy (in this case, the Table facet).

4. To invoke the Create New Condition window, right-click the facet and select New Condition.

5. In the Create New Condition dialog, type a name for the condition (for example, `Table Name Convention`) and ensure that the facet selected is correct.

6. In the Expression section, perform the following tasks:

   a. In the Field column, select the property on which you want to create your condition. For this example, use the `@Name` property.

   b. In the Operator drop-down box, select the `NOT LIKE` operator.

   c. In the value text box, enter `'tbl%'`. (The single quotes are required for any strings.)

7. Repeat step 6 for any additional expressions. For this example, the following expressions were entered, as displayed in Figure 14.2.

AndOr	Field	Operator	Value
	@Name	NOT LIKE	'tbl%'
AND	Len(@Name)	<=	50
AND	@Name	NOT LIKE	'%s'

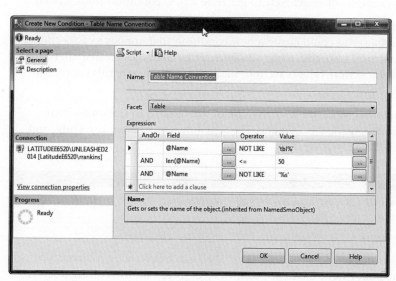

FIGURE 14.2   Creating a condition based on a facet.

8. Click OK to finalize the creation of the condition. You may have to click on the Field text box again for the OK button to be enabled.

NOTE

You can create conditions that query Windows Management Instrumentation (WMI) (using the `ExecuteWSQL` function) or SQL Server (using the `ExecuteSQL` function). For example, you can create conditions to check on available disk space or number of processors on the server. WMI allows you to issue SQL-like queries against management objects, which can return information on the physical machine hosting SQL Server and configuration and performance information, which is not accessible from within SQL Server itself.

Creating a Policy

After creating the condition or conditions, you need to create the policy. The policy is a standard that can be enforced on one or more SQL Server instances, systems, server objects, databases, or database objects. Follow these steps to create a policy with SQL Server Management Studio:

1. In Object Explorer, expand the `Management` folder, expand the `Policy Management` folder, and then click on `Policies`.

2. Right-click on the `Policies` folder and select New Policy.

3. On the General tab of the Create New Policy dialog, enter a name for the new policy, such as `Check Table Naming Conventions`.

4. In the Check Condition drop-down box, select a condition, such as the one created in the previous example, or select New to generate a new condition from scratch.

5. The Against Targets section indicates which objects the policy should be evaluated against. For example, you could create a new condition that applies to a specific database, all databases, a specific table, all tables, or to databases created after a specific date. In the Action Targets section, indicate which targets this condition should apply to.

6. Specify the Evaluation Mode by selecting one of the options in the drop-down menu. The options include On Demand, On Schedule, On Change Log Only, and On Change Prevent.

NOTE

If On Schedule is selected for the Evaluation Mode, specify a schedule from the predefined list or enter a new schedule.

7. The final drop-down box is Server Restriction. You can restrict which servers you do not want the policy to be evaluated against or enforced on by creating a server condition. Create a server restriction or leave the default setting None. An example of the policy settings for checking table name conventions is displayed in Figure 14.3.

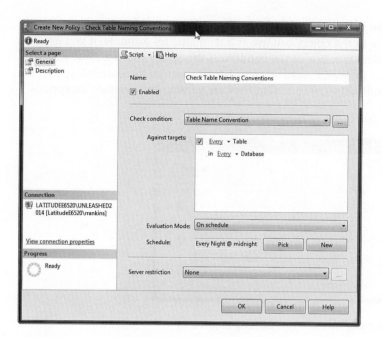

FIGURE 14.3   The Create New Policy dialog.

8. If you selected an Evaluation mode other than On Demand (for example, On Schedule), before you close the Create New Policy dialog, ensure that the policy is enabled (the Enabled check box is selected).

9. Next, click on the Description page. The Description page allows you to categorize your policy, but it also allows you to display a custom text message when a policy is violated and a hyperlink where the DBA/developer can go for more information about the policy.

10. Click OK to finalize the creation of the new policy.

An Alternative to Creating Policies

As you can imagine, for complex policies you might need to create many conditions. In some cases it may be easier to create a table, database, or server that is configured to conform to the policy you want to create and then right-click on the specific object and select Facets. This brings up the View Facets page. This brings up a dialog showing all the properties of the object selected that can be managed via facets. Make sure that the values correspond to the standards you want to set and then click on the Export Current State as Policy button. This exports a policy and a single condition to which the existing object will conform.

Figure 14.4 illustrates the dialog that prompts you for a policy name and condition name as well as where you want to store the policy. You can store it in the file system and then import it to a Central Management Server or other servers where you want the policy to be evaluated, or you can store it directly in the local server. Note that this policy will contain conditions specific to the object you use as a template; for example, if you use the AdventureWorks2012 database, one of the conditions the policy will test for is whether the database name is equal to AdventureWorks2012. For this feature to be useful, you likely need to edit the conditions to ensure that they are generic and evaluate exceptions correctly.

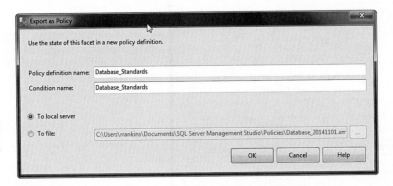

FIGURE 14.4   Exporting a policy based on an existing object.

Creating a Category

After you create a policy, it should be categorized. Categorization allows you to group policies into administrative or logical units and then allow database objects to subscribe to specific categories. It is worth mentioning that server objects can't subscribe to policies.

To create a category, click on the Description page in the Create New Policy dialog or the Policy properties dialog. Policies can be placed in the default category or a specific category, or you can create a new category. The dialog to specify or create a new category is illustrated in Figure 14.5.

You can also create categories by right-clicking on Policy Management and selecting Manage Categories.

If you choose to create a new category, click on the New button. This presents a dialog that allows you to name the category. By default, the current policy is parked in the new category.

You can select which category you want policies to belong to by selecting a specific category in the drop-down box. After you categorize your policies, you can select which categories you want your database to subscribe to. Right-click on the Policy Management folder and select Manage Categories. The Manage Policy Categories dialog (illustrated in Figure 14.6) appears. Check the categories to which you want all databases on your server to subscribe and deselect the ones that you do not want your server databases to be subscribed to by default.

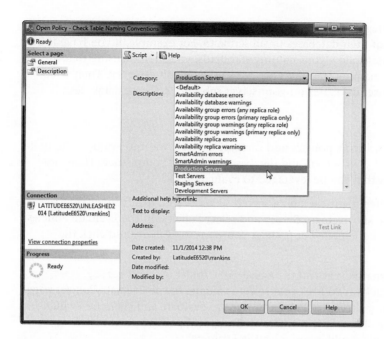

FIGURE 14.5   The category selection dialog.

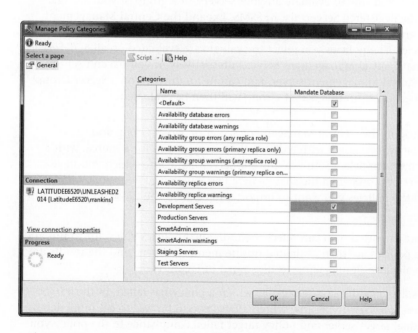

FIGURE 14.6   The Manage Policy Categories dialog.

Other than the default category, DBAs can select which category (and policies belonging to that category) they want their databases to subscribe to. For example, if you have third-party software that does not follow your naming standards, you should ensure that the policies that enforce your naming standards are not in the default category. Then selectively have each of your user databases on your server subscribe to these databases.

Evaluating Policies

After you create an organization's policies and categories, you'll want to evaluate the policies to determine which of your servers and databases are out of compliance. There are three management points that can be leveraged to evaluate policies:

▶ For the first alternative, right-click on a server, server object, database, or database object in SQL Server Management Studio and select Policies. In the Evaluate Policies page displayed, check the policy or policies you want to evaluate and click the Evaluate button.

▶ For the second alternative, expand the Management folder, expand Policy Management, right-click on Policies, and select Evaluate. In the Evaluate Policies page displayed, check the policy or policies you want to evaluate and click the Evaluate button. It is also possible to just evaluate an individual policy by right-clicking on the Policy in the Policies folder and selecting Evaluate.

▶ Finally, the preferred way to evaluate all your servers, or a group of your servers, is to display the Registered Servers list in SSMS. Expand the Central Management Servers node and right-click on the name of a Central Management Server and select Evaluate Policies. The policies you select to evaluate are evaluated on all SQL Servers defined on that Central Management Server. Alternatively, if you haven't set up servers in a Central Management server, you can just right-click on a Server Group; and all member servers in that Server Group will then be evaluated.

When you right-click on the Central Management Server or Server Group and select Evaluate Polices, you are presented with a dialog that prompts you for a source, with a Choose Source prompt. For Select Source, enter the server name into which you have defined your policies or browse to a file share where you have saved your policy definitions. Highlight all the policies you want to import and click on the Close button to close the dialog.

After the policies are imported, you can select the individual policies you want to run and click Evaluate. The policies are then evaluated on the member servers, and the results are displayed in the Evaluation Results pane, as illustrated in Figure 14.7.

The Evaluation Results pane displays servers for which a policy has failed. In the Target Details section, there is a View hyperlink, which allows you to browse to get more details on why the individual target server and policy target failed compliance to the policy you evaluated.

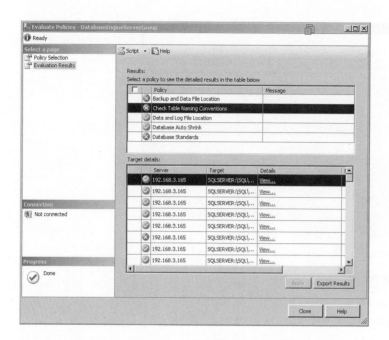

FIGURE 14.7   The Evaluation Results pane.

Importing and Exporting Policies

In some situations a DBA might want to export one or many policies with their conditions from one or many SQL Server systems and import them to another SQL Server instance or system. Fortunately, you can perform this task easily with an export and import wizard that generates or reads the policy definitions as XML files.

Follow these steps to export a policy with SQL Server Management Studio:

1. In Object Explorer, expand the `Management` folder, expand the `Policy Management` node, and then expand the `Policies` folder.

2. Within the `Policies` folder, right-click a desired policy to export and then select Export Policy.

3. In the Export Policy dialog, specify a name and path for the policy and click Save.

Importing a policy from an XML file is just as simple. Follow these steps to import a policy with SQL Server Management Studio:

1. In Object Explorer, expand the `Management` folder, expand the `Policy Management` node, and then select `Policies`.

2. Right-click on the `Policies` folder and select Import Policy... to bring up the dialog shown in Figure 14.8

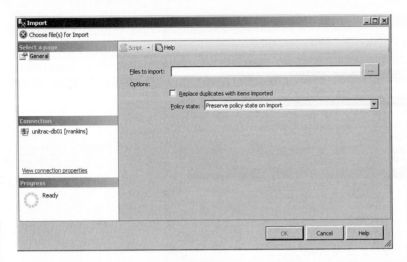

FIGURE 14.8   The Import Policy dialog.

3. The import screen has three options you need to be aware of:

   a. First, provide the path of the file to import.

   b. Second, enable the option Replace duplicates with items imported.

   c. Finally, in the Policy State drop-down box, specify the state of the policy being imported. The options include Preserve Policy State on Import, Enable All Policies on Import, and Disable All Policies on Import.

Sample Templates and Real-World Examples

The following sections illustrate the sample policy templates included with SQL Server 2014 and real-world examples for using Policy-Based Management.

Sample Policy Templates

SQL Server 2014 includes a plethora of predefined sample policies, which can be leveraged by importing them into a SQL Server 2014 system. The policies available for import are located in the default installation drive, which is usually located at `C:\Program Files\Microsoft SQL Server\120\Tools\Policies\DatabaseEngine\1033` (or `C:\Program Files (x86)\Microsoft SQL Server\120\Tools\Policies\DatabaseEngine\1033` if you are running in a 64-bit environment). As mentioned earlier, you can import the desired policies by right-clicking the `Policies` node and selecting Import Policy... The sample templates are categorized by SQL Server feature such as Database Engine, Reporting Services, and Analysis Services.

Evaluating Recovery Models

Recovery models determine how SQL Server uses the transaction log. On OLTP systems, the most appropriate recovery model is generally the Full Recovery model. For OLAP systems, the most appropriate recovery model is generally the bulk-logged or simple recovery model. For most development environments, the most appropriate recovery model is usually the simple recovery model.

For mission-critical databases, or databases where point-in-time recovery is important, having a transaction log backed up very frequently may be required. Policy-Based Management can be used to determine whether the appropriate recovery model is in place for each user database for each server type. Central Management Servers could be created for each server type, and a policy can be created to ensure that the appropriate recovery model is in place across all servers managed within a management server.

Ensuring Object Naming Conventions

Your company may have standards for how database objects should be named. For example, stored procedures must start with the prefix `usp`, tables must start with the prefix `tbl`, and functions must start with the prefix `ufn`. Policy-Based Management can be used to ensure that all objects are compliant with this policy. This policy can be implemented to execute as On Change Prevent, which prevents the creation of such noncompliant objects.

Checking Best Practices Compliance

You can implement policies that check for SQL Server best practices. For example, databases can be configured with the autoclose and autoshrink options. Although these options have their place on some systems, they are not recommended to be enabled in production environments because the autoclose option causes a time delay while a closed database is opened by the first connection trying to access it. This can lead to timeouts and overall performance degradation. The autoshrink option can lead to fragmentation and is in general not recommended. A policy can check for these settings and other settings to ensure that all your databases are following best practices.

Policy-Based Management Best Practices

Following are some best practices to consider when implementing Policy-Based Management in SQL Server 2014:

- ▶ When deploying Policy-Based Management in your environment, you should be very careful about using On Change Prevent. For example, a policy that prevents stored procedure creation with the `sp_` prefix prevents the enabling of replication on a SQL Server.

- ▶ When you create a policy that you want enforced on all user databases, you should place this policy in the default category so that all databases are subscribed to it. Otherwise, you need to manually subscribe all databases to the categories that contain the policies you want enforced.

▶ You should make use of multiple Central Management Servers or Server Groups to group your SQL Servers according to logical groupings on which you want to enforce your policies.

▶ Importing policies into centralized SQL Server 2014 servers makes it easier to deploy groups of policies against groups of servers using Central Management Servers—for example, to store data warehouse policies on Server A. You should use this server as a source when selecting policies to evaluate against your data warehouse servers registered in the Data Warehousing Central Management Server.

▶ You might find that your environment contains third-party user applications/ databases that are not in compliance with the policies you have created for your enterprise. Policy-Based Management uses the opt-in metaphor such that all policies are enforced by default. For databases on which you do not want the policy to be enforced, you need to tag the database, perhaps with an extended property or a specially named table that the server exception category or target will detect and exempt that server or database from the policy.

▶ You should use the ExecuteWSQL task to issue WMI queries to extend conditions and policies beyond the SQL Server environment—for example, to check what other services may be running on a server hosting SQL Server.

Summary

Policy-Based Management is a feature available in SQL Server 2014 that allows you to manage your SQL Server 2000 through SQL Server 2014 servers by creating policies that can be used to enforce compliance to best practices or to report on out-of-compliance servers. It provides a highly granular, flexible, and extensible toolset that allows you to manage all aspects of your SQL Server. Properly used, it is a great tool to enforce standardization in your environment and to ease the management burden.

The next chapter, Chapter 15, "Security and User Administration," explores the importance of implementing robust security standards and practices in your SQL Server environments and how to go about doing so.

Security and User Administration

Securing your database environment and providing the right type of access to your users are critical administrative tasks. This chapter examines the security features in SQL Server 2014 that relate to user administration and the objects that users can access.

What's New in Security and User Administration

Several new security enhancements have been added to SQL Server 2014 to help make it more secure than any prior version. These enhancements build upon the myriad of security-related changes made in the three prior versions and follow the policy of "least privileges" that Microsoft has been pushing. Several of these new changes follow:

▶ CONNECT ANY DATABASE—A server-level permission that allows a login to connect to all databases that currently exist and any new databases that are created in the future.

▶ IMPERSONATE ANY LOGIN—A server-level permission that allows a middle-tier process to impersonate the account of clients connecting to the database.

▶ SELECT ALL USER SECURABLES—A server-level permission that allows a login to view data in all databases that the user can connect to.

▶ ALTER ANY DATABASE EVENT SESSION—A database-level permission typically used to give a role the ability to read metadata associated with a database for monitoring purposes.

An Overview of SQL Server Security

The SQL Server 2014 security model is the best place to start to understand SQL Server security. This model is based on three categories that separate the basic elements of security:

▶ **Principals**—Principals are the entities that request security to SQL Server resources. They include Windows users, SQL Server users, and database users.

▶ **Securables**—Securables are the SQL Server resources to which permissions can be granted.

▶ **Permissions**—Permissions link principals with securables.

There are a limited number of principals that can be assigned permissions is this model. These principals are divided into three main categories: Windows-level, SQL Server-level and Database-level. Each of these categories and the available principals are shown below:

Windows-level principals

▶ Windows Domain Login

▶ Windows Local Login

SQL Server-level principals

▶ SQL Server Login

▶ Server Role

Database-level principals

▶ Database User

▶ Database Role

▶ Application Role

There are many more securables available than there are principals. The securables are scoped at three different levels: Server, Database, and Schema. In addition, some securables are nested such that a given securable can have other securables that are contained within it. Table 15.1 has a column for each of the securable scopes along with the related securables:

TABLE 15.1   SQL Server Securables

Server Scope	Database Scope	Schema Scope
Endpoint	User	Type
Login	Database role	XML schema collection
Server role	Application role	Object – The object class has the following members:
Database	Assembly	Aggregate
	Message type	Function
	Route	Procedure
	Service	Queue
	Remote Service Binding	Synonym
	Fulltext catalog	Table
	Certificate	View
	Asymmetric key	
	Symmetric key	
	Contract	
	Schema	

The last element of the security model is made up of the actual permissions. The number of permissions is extensive, and there are far too many to list in this chapter. Microsoft has created a poster that does a good job of depicting all the permissions and simplifies the complex relationship between these permissions. The poster is available at http://go.microsoft.com/fwlink/?LinkId=229142. It also depicts the inherent hierarchy within permissions and is a good resource.

Another way to break down the security model it to use the `fn_builtin_permissions` function. This function can be used to return a complete list of grantable permissions or you can use it to return the permissions that are available at a more granular level. To return all the permissions, you use the function in the following way:

```
SELECT * FROM fn_builtin_permissions(default)
```

To refine your search of permissions, you can provide a particular class of object to the function as shown in the following example, which retrieves all the permissions associated with routes:

```
SELECT permission_name, parent_class_desc
 ,parent_covering_permission_name
FROM fn_builtin_permissions('route')

-- Results from the proceeding query
/*
permission_name   parent_class_desc parent_covering_permission_name
----------------  ----------------- -------------------------------
VIEW DEFINITION   DATABASE          VIEW DEFINITION
ALTER             DATABASE          ALTER ANY ROUTE
TAKE OWNERSHIP    DATABASE          CONTROL
CONTROL           DATABASE          CONTROL
*/
```

The implementation of the security model is relatively straightforward. Most permission statements have the following format:

```
AUTHORIZATION PERMISSION ON SECURABLE::NAME TO PRINCIPAL
```

There are four main components in the preceding statement. Three of them (`Permission`, `Securable`, and `Principal`) are the key elements of the security model that have already been covered. The first component (`Authorization`) is specified as either GRANT, REVOKE, or DENY. The following is an example of implementing security using all four components of the permission statement:

```
GRANT INSERT ON SCHEMA :: HumanResources TO guest
```

In the preceding example, GRANT is the authorization, INSERT is the permission, `HumanResources` is the securable name, and the principal name is `guest`. It should be noted that there are some permissions that do not require the ON SECURABLE::NAME component of the permission statement. The following is an example of this kind of permission:

```
GRANT CREATE TABLE TO KaylaG
```

In the end, the assignment of permissions is relatively simple, but a level of complexity has been introduced, based on the hierarchical nature of some of the security components. Security can be established on these hierarchical components, which in turn cascades the security to the underlying components. In addition, not all the permission components apply to every securable. Many of the securables have a set number of permissions that apply to them; conversely, many permissions apply only to a set number of securables. For example, SELECT permission is applicable to securables such as tables and views but would not be appropriate for stored procedures.

The following sections discuss the tiers of the security model and their underlying components.

Authentication Methods

The first level of security encountered when accessing SQL Server is known as *authentication*. The authentication process performs the validation needed to allow a user or client machine to connect to SQL Server. This connection can be granted via a Windows login or SQL Server login.

Windows Authentication Mode

Windows Authentication mode validates the account name and password, using information stored in the Windows operating system. A Windows account or group must be established first, and then security can be established for that account in SQL Server. This mode has the advantage of providing a single login account and the capability to leverage domain security features, such as password length and expiration, account locking, encryption, and auditing. Microsoft recommends this approach.

Mixed Authentication Mode

Mixed authentication allows for both Windows authentication and SQL Server authentication. SQL Server authentication is based on a login that is created in SQL Server and lives in SQL Server only. No Windows account is involved with SQL Server authentication. The account and password are established and maintained in SQL Server. SQL Server logins can be created with stronger password enforcement that help better protect the login. This topic is discussed in more detail in the section, "Managing SQL Server Logins," later in this chapter.

SQL Server authentication is useful in environments in which a Windows domain controller does not control network access. It can also be useful for Web applications or legacy applications, where it may be cumbersome to establish a Windows user account for every connection to the database server.

Setting the Authentication Mode

You can select the authentication mode when you install SQL Server, and you can change it after the installation. To change the authentication mode after installation, you right-click the server node in the Object Explorer in SSMS and choose the Properties option. When the Server Properties dialog appears, you select the Security page (see Figure 15.1). The Security page allows you to specify Windows Authentication mode or SQL Server and Windows Authentication mode (that is, mixed authentication). Any changes to the authentication mode require a restart of SQL Server to make the change effective.

15

FIGURE 15.1   Changing the authentication mode.

Managing Principals

Principals are the entities that can request permission to SQL Server resources. They are made up of groups, individuals, or processes. Each principal has its own unique identifier on the server and is scoped at the Windows, server, or database level. The principals at the Windows level are Windows users or groups. The principals at the SQL Server level include SQL Server logins and server roles. The principals scoped at the database level include database users, data roles, and application roles.

Logins

Generally, every principal granted security to SQL Server must have an associated login. The login provides access to SQL Server and can be associated with principals scoped at the Windows and server levels. These logins can be associated with Windows accounts, Windows groups, or SQL Server logins.

> **NOTE**
>
> Contained databases and their related users were introduced in SQL Server 2012. The users associated with a contained database do not have to have an associated login. This supports the principal behind a contained database which is to keep all elements of the database scoped at the database level. All references, including logins, which are

outside the scope of the database, are removed. The users associated with a contained database are discussed in the "SQL Server Security: Users" section later in the chapter. Contained databases are discussed in more detail in Chapter 20, "Creating and Managing Databases."

Logins are stored in the `master` database and can be granted permission to resources scoped at the server level. Logins provide the initial permission needed to access a SQL Server instance and allow you to grant access to the related databases. Permissions to specific database resources must be granted via a database user. The important point to remember is that logins and users are related to each other but are different entities. It is possible to create a new login without creating an associated database user, but a new database user must have an associated login except in the case of a contained database user.

To better understand logins, you can look at the `sys.server_principals` catalog view. This view contains a row for every server-level principal, including each server login. The following example selects from this view and displays the results:

```
select left(name,25) name, type, type_desc
  from sys.server_principals AS log
WHERE (log.type in ('U', 'G', 'S', 'R'))
  order by 3,1


/*Results from previous query
name                      type type_desc
------------------------- ---- -----------
bulkadmin                 R    SERVER_ROLE
dbcreator                 R    SERVER_ROLE
diskadmin                 R    SERVER_ROLE
processadmin              R    SERVER_ROLE
public                    R    SERVER_ROLE
securityadmin             R    SERVER_ROLE
serveradmin               R    SERVER_ROLE
setupadmin                R    SERVER_ROLE
sysadmin                  R    SERVER_ROLE
sa                        S    SQL_LOGIN
DBSVRXP\LocalUser1        U    WINDOWS_LOGIN
HOME\Administrator        U    WINDOWS_LOGIN
NT AUTHORITY\SYSTEM       U    WINDOWS_LOGIN
*/
```

The results from the `sys.server_principals` selection include the name of the server principal as well as the type of principal. The rows that have a `type_desc` value of `SQL_LOGIN`, `WINDOWS_GROUP`, or `WINDOWS_LOGIN` are all logins established on the SQL Server instance. A login with a `type_desc` of `SQL_LOGIN` represents a login created with SQL Server authentication. Logins with a `type_desc` of `WINDOWS_GROUP` or `WINDOWS_LOGIN` are Windows

15

groups or individual Windows users granted logins to SQL Server. The other entries with type_desc of SERVER_ROLE are fixed server roles discussed later in this chapter.

The logins established for Windows logins or groups can be part of the local domain of the SQL Server machine, or they can be part of another domain. In the previous example, DBSVRXP\LocalUser1 is a login established for a local user on a database server named DBSVRXP. The HOME\Administrator login is also a Windows login, but it is part of a network domain named HOME. Both logins are preceded by the domain that they are part of and are displayed this way in SQL Server.

NOTE

In SQL Server 2000, logins were stored in the syslogins system table in the master database. The syslogins table is still available for selection as a view, but it is available only for backward compatibility. The catalog views (including sys.server_principals) are recommended for use instead.

You might have noticed in the earlier sys.server_principals output that two other logins are listed that we have not discussed yet. These logins (SA and NT AUTHORITY\SYSTEM) are system accounts installed by default at installation time. Each of these accounts serves a special purpose in SQL Server.

The SA account is a SQL_LOGIN assigned to the sysadmin fixed server role. The SA account and members of the sysadmin fixed server role have permission to perform any activity within SQL Server. The SA account cannot be removed, and it can generally be used to gain access to SQL Server.

NOTE

If the SQL Server instance has been set to Windows Authentication Only then SQL Server logins including SA will not be able to access the instance. The SA account can be explicitly disabled or denied access and this will also prevent the SA account from being used to access the instance.

The SA account should always have a strong password to prevent malicious attacks, and it should be used only by database administrators. Users or logins requiring full administrative privileges can be assigned a separate SQL Server login that is assigned to the sysadmin fixed server role. This improves the audit trail and limits the amount of use on the SA account.

The NT AUTHORITY\SYSTEM login is an account related to the local system account under which SQL Server services can run. It is also added as a member of the sysadmin fixed server role and has full administrative privileges in SQL Server. This account can also be removed if the SQL Server services are not running with the local system account. This should be done with caution, however, because it can affect applications such as Reporting Services.

One other special account was not listed, but it would have been in SQL Server 2005. The BUILTIN\Administrators login is a Windows group that corresponds to the local administrators group for the machine that SQL Server is running on. The BUILTIN\Administrators group is no longer added by default as a SQL Server login during installation. In SQL Server 2005, it was also added as a member of the sysadmin fixed server role, but this is no longer the case. This change improves the security of SQL Server out of the box by limiting the number of people that have access (by default) to the SQL Server instance.

> **NOTE**
>
> The BUILTIN\Administrators group can be manually added in SQL Server 2014 if desired. This allows domain administrators and anyone else who has been added to the local administrators group to have sysadmin privileges. Adding this group is not recommended but can be done if you want to set network privileges that are similar to past versions of SQL Server.

SQL Server Security: Users

Database users are principals scoped at the database level. Database users generally establish a link between logins (which are stored at the server level) and users (which are stored at the database level). Database users are required to use the database and are also required to access any object stored in the database.

Generally, the login name and database username are the same, but this is not a requirement. If desired, you could add a login named Chris and assign it to a user named Kayla. This type of naming convention would obviously cause some confusion and is not recommended, but SQL Server has the flexibility to allow you to do it. In addition, a user can be associated with a single person or a group of people. This capability is tied to the fact that a login can be related to a single account or group. For example, a login named training could be created and tied to a Windows group (that is, domain\training) that contains all the training personnel. This login could then be tied to a single database user. That single database user would control database access for all the users in the Windows group.

> **TIP**
>
> The relationship between logins and users can be broken when databases are moved or copied between servers. The reason is that a database user can contain a reference to the associated login. Logins are referenced based on a unique identifier called a security identifier (SID). When a database is copied from one server to another, the users in that database contain references to logins that may not exist on the destination server or that may have different SIDs.
>
> You can use the sp_change_users_login system stored procedure to identify and fix these situations. You can run the following command against a newly restored or attached database to check for orphaned users: EXEC sp_change_users_login 'Report'

15

If orphaned users are shown in the results, you can rerun the procedure and fix the problems. For example, if the results indicate that a user named Chris is orphaned, you can run the following command to add a new login named Chris and tie the orphaned database user to this newly created login: `EXEC sp_change_users_login 'Auto_Fix', 'Chris', NULL, 'pw'` Refer to SQL Server Books Online for full documentation on the `sp_change_users_login` system stored procedure.

You can use the `sys.database_principals` catalog view to list all the users in a given database. The following example shows a `SELECT` statement using this view and its results:

```
SELECT
left(u.name,25) AS [Name],
type,
left(type_desc,15) as type_desc
FROM
sys.database_principals AS u
WHERE
(u.type in ('U', 'S', 'G'))
ORDER BY 1

/*Results from previous query
Name                      type type_desc
------------------------- ---- ---------------
dbo                       S    SQL_USER
DBSVRXP\LocalUser1        U    WINDOWS_USER
guest                     S    SQL_USER
INFORMATION_SCHEMA        S    SQL_USER
sys                       S    SQL_USER
*/
```

The `SELECT` statement in this example returns five rows (that is, five users). This `SELECT` was run against the `AdventureWorks2012` database, and the only user explicitly added to the database was the Windows user DBSVRXP\LocalUser1. The other users are special users who are added by default to each database. These users do not have corresponding server logins named the same and are discussed in the following sections.

The dbo User

The `dbo` user is the database owner and cannot be deleted from the database. Members of the `sysadmin` server role are mapped to the `dbo` user in each database, which allows them to administer all databases. Objects owned by `dbo` that are part of the `dbo` schema can be referenced by the object name alone. When an object is referenced without a schema name, SQL Server first looks for the object in the default schema for the user that is connected. If the object is not in the user's default schema, the object is retrieved from the `dbo` schema. Users can have a default schema that is set to `dbo`.

Schemas and their relationship to users are discussed in more detail in the section "User/Schema Separation," later in this chapter.

The guest User

The guest user is created by default in each database when the database is created. This account allows users that do not have a user account in the database to access it. By default, the guest user does not have permission to connect to the database. To allow logins without a specific user account to connect to the database, you need to grant CONNECT permission to the guest account. You can run the following command in the target database to grant the CONNECT permission:

```
GRANT CONNECT TO GUEST
```

When the guest account is granted CONNECT permission, any login can connect to the database. This opens a possible security hole. The default permissions for the guest account are limited by design. You can change the permissions for the guest account, and all logins that use it will be granted those permissions. Generally, you should create new database users and grant permissions to these users instead of using the guest account.

If you want to lock down the guest account, you can. You cannot drop the guest user, but you can disable it by revoking its CONNECT permission. The following example demonstrates how to revoke the CONNECT permission for the guest user:

```
REVOKE CONNECT FROM guest
```

If you decide to grant additional access to the guest account, you should do so with caution. The guest account can be used as a means for attacking your database.

The INFORMATION_SCHEMA User

The INFORMATION_SCHEMA user owns all the information schema views installed in each database. These views provide an internal view of the SQL Server metadata that is independent of the underlying system tables. Some examples of these views include INFORMATION_SCHEMA.COLUMNS and INFORMATION_SCHEMA.CHECK_CONSTRAINTS. The INFORMATION_SCHEMA user cannot be dropped from the database.

The sys User

The sys account gives users access to system objects such as system tables, system views, extended stored procedures, and other objects that are part of the system catalog. The sys user owns these objects. Like the INFORMATION_SCHEMA user, it cannot be dropped from the database.

TIP

If you are interested in viewing the specific objects owned by any of the special users discussed in these sections, you can use a SELECT statement like the following:

```
--Find all objects owned by a given user
SELECT name, object_id, schema_id, type_desc
FROM sys.all_objects
WHERE OBJECTPROPERTYEX(object_id, N'OwnerId') =
USER_ID(N'sys')
ORDER BY 1
```

The SELECT in this example shows all the objects owned by the sys user. To change the user, you simply change the parameter of the USER_ID function in the SELECT statement from 'sys' to whatever user you want.

User/Schema Separation

The changes to schema security introduced in SQL Server 2005 are still valid in SQL Server 2014. Versions of SQL Server before SQL Server 2005 had schemas, but they did not conform to the American National Standards Institute (ANSI) definition of schemas. ANSI defines a schema as a collection of database objects that one user owns and that forms a single namespace. A single namespace is one in which each object name is unique and there are no duplicates. So, for example, if you have two tables named customer, they cannot exist in the same namespace.

To fully understand the user/schema separation, you need to understand how schemas were used in prior versions of SQL Server. In SQL Server 7.0 and 2000, a default schema was created for each user, and it had the same name as the user. For example, if you created a new user named Rachael, a corresponding schema named Rachael would be created as well. There was no option in those releases to change the default schema for a user, and each user was forever bound to a schema with the same name. When the user created new objects, the objects were created by default in that user's schema, which is always the name of the user. So, if Rachael created an object named customer, it was placed in the Rachael schema, and the object was owned by Rachael. When Rachael wanted to reference the object, she could use a three-part name with the format database.owner.object. If a linked server was used, according to the SQL Server 2000 documentation, the object in the linked server could be referenced with the four-part name linked_server.catalog.schema.object. (for example myserver. AdventureWorks2012.Rachael.Customer). You can see that the schema name is used prior to the object name when the object is outside the local server. The bottom line is that the schema and owner were basically the same thing in SQL Server 7.0 and 2000.

Starting in SQL Server 2005, the owner and schema have been separated. This is made possible in part by allowing a database user to have a default schema different from the name of the user. For example, our sample user Rachael could be assigned the default schema Sales. When Rachael creates objects in the database, her objects are created, by default, in the `Sales` schema. If `Rachael` wants to reference an object that she created, she can reference the table in a number of different ways. She can use the full four-part name (`server.database.schema.object`) that includes the `Sales` schema name to reference the object via a linked server. She can simply refer to the object with the object name alone, and the `Sales` schema will be searched first for the object. If the object name is not found in the `Sales` schema, the `dbo` schema will be searched. She also has the option of using a two part name (schema.object) or a three part name (database.schema.object). This concept is illustrated in the following sample `SELECT` statements that all retrieve the same rows from the Region table that was created by Rachael in the `AdventureWorks2012` database.

```
select * from region
select * from sales.region
select * from AdventureWorks2012.Sales.Region
```

The important point to remember is that owners and schemas are different from one another in SQL Server 2014. For example, you can have a customer table created in the Sales schema, and that table can be owned by a user named Chris. The object should be referenced with the schema name qualifier, such as `Sales.Customer`, not `Chris.Customer`. This has the distinct advantage of allowing object ownership to change without affecting the code that references the object. The reason is that database code that references an object uses the schema name instead of the object owner.

The schema capabilities in SQL Server 2014 go well beyond the user/schema separation. Schemas are an integral part of all the database objects that exist in SQL Server. As we delve into more details about SQL Server security and the assignment of permissions, you will see that schemas play an important part.

Roles

Roles provide a consistent yet flexible model for security administration. Roles are similar to the groups used in administering networks. Permissions are applied to a role, and then members are added to the role. Any member of the role has all the permissions that the role has.

The use of roles simplifies the administrative work related to security. Roles can be created based on job function, application, or any other logical group of users. With roles, you do not have to apply security to each individual user. Any required changes to permissions for the role can be made to the role security, and the members of the role receive those changes.

SQL Server has the following four types of roles:

▶ **Fixed server and fixed database roles**—These roles are installed by default and have a predefined set of permissions.

▶ **User-defined database roles**—These roles are created in each database, with a custom set of permissions for each set of users assigned to it.

▶ **User-defined server roles**—These roles were added in SQL Server 2012 and add the same type of role flexibility at the server level that has existed at the database level for some time.

▶ **Application roles**—These special roles can be used to manage database access for an application.

These roles are discussed in the following sections.

Fixed Server Roles

Fixed server roles are scoped at the server level, which means that the permissions for these roles are oriented toward server-level securables. These roles contain a variety of fixed permissions geared toward common administrative tasks. Logins (not users) are assigned to these roles.

The same fixed server roles that were available since SQL Server 2008 are still available in SQL Server 2014. The only relatively new role is `public`, which was added in SQL Server 2008. Server principals, by default, are granted the permissions that have been granted to the `public` role. There are a limited number of permissions that are initially granted to the `public` role, but you can change the permissions if you like. A complete list of all the fixed server roles and their related permissions is shown in Table 15.2.

TABLE 15.2   Fixed Server Roles

Role	Permission
bulkadmin	Allowed to run the BULK INSERT statement.
dbcreator	Allowed to use CREATE, ALTER, DROP, and RESTORE on any database.
diskadmin	Allowed to manage disk files that are used by SQL Server.
processadmin	Allowed to terminate SQL Server processes.
public	Assigned to all logins. Permissions granted to this role are assigned to every login by default.
securityadmin	Allowed to use GRANT, DENY, and REVOKE permissions for logins at the server and database levels. Members of this role can reset passwords for SQL Server logins.
serveradmin	Allowed to change server-wide configuration properties and shut down the server if needed.
setupadmin	Allowed to add and remove linked servers and execute some system stored procedures.
sysadmin	Allowed to perform any activity in the server.

A single login can be assigned to one or more of these fixed server roles. When multiple roles are assigned, the combination of all the permissions is granted to the login.

> **NOTE**
>
> Keep in mind that when a login is assigned to certain fixed server roles, they have implied permissions that cascade to the database level. For example, if a login is assigned to the `sysadmin` role, that login can perform any activity on the server, and it can also perform any action on any database on that server. Similarly, if a login is added to the `securityadmin` role, the login can change permissions at the database level as well as the server level.

All the fixed server roles are listed in the SQL Server Management Studio (SSMS) Object Explorer. Figure 15.2 shows the Object Explorer with the `Server Roles` node expanded. You can right-click any of the roles and select Properties to display the logins that are currently members of the role.

FIGURE 15.2   Fixed server roles in Object Explorer.

Fixed Database Roles

SQL Server provides fixed roles that define a common set of permissions at the database level. These fixed database roles are assigned to database users. The permissions defined for the fixed database roles cannot be changed. Table 15.3 lists the fixed database roles and their permissions.

TABLE 15.3   Fixed Database Roles

Role	Permission
db_accessadmin	Allowed to add or remove database access for logins.
db_backupoperator	Allowed to back up the database.
db_datareader	Allowed to read all user table data.
db_datawriter	Allowed to change the data in all user tables.
db_ddladmin	Allowed to run any Data Definition Language (DDL) command against the database. This includes commands to create, alter, and drop database objects.
db_denydatareader	Denied the right to read all user table data.
db_denydatawriter	Denied the right to change the data in any of the user tables.
db_owner	Allowed to perform any action on the database. Members of the sysadmin fixed server role are mapped to this database role.
db_securityadmin	Allowed to manage permissions for database users, including membership in roles.
public	Granted: SELECT on system views

NOTE

You can find a more granular breakdown of permissions associated with fixed database roles by using the sp_dbfixedrolepermission. If you run this system procedure without any parameters, it returns a list of all the permissions for all the fixed database roles. You can also pass a specific fixed database role to the procedure to return only the permissions for that role. For example, for the db_backupoperator role you will see that it is granted the BACKUP DATABASE, BACKUP LOG, and CHECKPOINT permissions. This gives you more insight into what the members of this role can do. Some fixed database roles have a large number of permissions defined for them, such as db_ddladmin, which has more than 30 individual permissions. The types of permissions and improved granularity available with SQL Server 2014 are discussed in the "Managing Permissions" section, later in this chapter.

You can also find a list of fixed database roles in the Object Explorer. Figure 15.3 shows the fixed database roles for the AdventureWorks2012 database. The roles are found under the Security node within each database. You can right-click a fixed database role and select Properties to view the member users.

Fixed database roles and schemas are related. Figure 15.3 shows the expanded Schemas node for the AdventureWorks2012 database. You can see that there is a corresponding schema for each of the fixed database roles. These schemas are automatically created, and each is owned by the related database role.

FIGURE 15.3   The fixed database roles in Object Explorer.

The `public` Role

The `public` role is a special database role that is like a fixed database role except that its permissions are not fixed. The permissions for this role can be altered. Every user in a database is automatically made a member of the `public` role and in turn receives any permissions that have been granted to the `public` role. Database users cannot be removed from the `public` role.

The `public` role is similar in function to the `guest` user that is installed by default in each database. The difference is that the permissions granted to the `guest` user are used by any login that does not have a user account in the database. In this case, the login is allowed to enter the database via the `guest` account. In the case of the `public` role, the login has been added as a user of the database and in turn picks up any permissions that have been granted to the `public` role.

To view the permissions associated with the `public` role, you can use a `SELECT` statement like the following:

```
SELECT top 5 g.name,
    object_name(major_id) as 'Object',
    permission_name
 from sys.database_permissions p
```

```
join sys.database_principals g
  on p.grantee_principal_id = g.principal_id
    and g.name = 'public'
order by 1,2

/*Results from the previous select
name    Object          permission_name
------  --------------  ---------------
public  all_columns     SELECT
public  all_objects     SELECT
public  all_parameters  SELECT
public  all_sql_modules SELECT
public  all_views       SELECT
*/
```

This SELECT utilizes two catalog views that contain security information and returns only the first five permissions for the public role, but the TOP clause can be removed to return all the permissions.

User-Defined Database Roles

SQL Server enables you to create your own custom database roles. Like the fixed roles, user-defined roles can be used to provide a common set of permissions to a group of users. The key benefit behind using user-defined roles is that you can define your own set of custom permissions that fit your needs. User-defined roles can have a broad range of permissions, including the more granular set of permissions made available with SQL Server 2014.

To demonstrate the power of a user-defined database role, let's look at a simple example. Let's say that you have a group of users who need to read all the tables in a database but should be granted access to update only one table. If you look to the fixed database roles, you have the db_datareader and db_datawriter roles, which give you a partial solution. You can use the db_datareader role to allow the read capability you need, but the db_datawriter role gives write permission to all the tables—not just one.

One possible solution would be to give every user in the group membership to the db_datareader group and assign the specific UPDATE permission to each user as well. If the group contains hundreds of users, you can see that this would be rather tedious. Another solution might be to create a Windows group that contains every user who needs the permissions. You can then assign a login and database user to this group and grant the appropriate permissions. The Windows group is a viable solution but can sometimes be difficult to implement in a complex Windows domain.

Another approach to this challenge is to use a user-defined database role. You can create the role in the database that contains the tables in question. After you create the role, you can include it in the db_datareader role, and you can establish the UPDATE permission to the single table. Finally, you can assign the individual users or group of users to the role. Any future permission changes for this set of users can be administered through the user-defined database role. The script in Listing 15.1 steps through a process that demonstrates and tests the addition of a database role. This is similar to the example we just walked through. Parts of the script need to be run by an administrator, and other parts should be run in a Query Editor window that is connected to the database with the newly created testuser.

LISTING 15.1   An Example of User-Defined Database Roles

```
--The following statements must be run by an administrator to add
--a login and database user with no explicit permissions granted
CREATE LOGIN [TestUser] WITH PASSWORD=N'pw',
DEFAULT_DATABASE=[master], CHECK_EXPIRATION=OFF, CHECK_POLICY=OFF
GO


GO
USE [AdventureWorks2012]
GO
CREATE USER [TestUser] FOR LOGIN [TestUser]
go
--the following statement fails when executed by the TestUser
--which has no explicit permissions defined in the AdventureWorks2012 database
select top 5 * from person.person
UPDATE person.person SET suffix = 'Jr.'
 WHERE FirstName = 'Ken'
--The following statement is run by an administrator to:
--1)add a new TestDbRole with permission to UPDATE
--2)grant UPDATE permission on the Person.person table
--3)add the TestUser to the TestDbRole database role
USE [AdventureWorks2012]
GO
--1)
CREATE ROLE [TestDbRole] AUTHORIZATION [dbo]
--2)
GRANT UPDATE ON [Person].[Person] TO [TestDbRole]
GRANT SELECT ON [Person].[Person] TO [TestDbRole]
--3)
EXEC sp_addrolemember N'TestDbRole', N'TestUser'

--the following statements now succeed when executed
--by the TestUser because the role that it
--was added to has SELECT and UPDATE permission
--on that table
select top 5 * from person.person
UPDATE person.person SET suffix = 'Jr.'
 WHERE BusinessEntityID = 1
```

```
--the following select fails because 'testdbrole'
--does not permit SELECT on any table but person.person
select * from person.ContactType
--The following statement is run by an administrator
--to add the TestDbRole database role to the db_datareader
--fixed-database role
EXEC sp_addrolemember N'db_datareader', N'TestDbRole'
GO
--Finally, the testuser can update the Person.person table
-- and select from any other table in the database
select * from person.ContactType
```

Database roles and permissions are discussed in more detail later in this chapter, in the sections, "Managing Database Roles" and "Managing Permissions."

User-Defined Server Roles

User-defined server roles were added in SQL Server 2012. They provide the same type of flexibility that is available with user-defined database roles. The difference with user-defined server roles is that server-level permissions are used to customize the rights for this role instead of permissions that are scoped at the database level.

Prior to SQL Server 2012, administrators were limited to using the fixed server roles when granting server side permission. The fixed server roles offer security for many of the common administrative tasks, but there is no way to customize the underlying permissions. Without the ability to customize, administrators would sometimes add logins to fixed server roles that had more rights to the server than were actually needed.

Now, with user-defined server roles you can define a role with only the permissions that are required. Suppose, for example, that you want to grant permission to a login so that they can only ALTER or CREATE a database. Prior to SQL Server 2012 you could add the login to the dbcreator fixed server role, but this would also allow the login to drop databases, restore databases, and more. With user-defined server roles, the new role can be added with only the permission to ALTER or CREATE a database. The means for adding and managing these new roles is discussed later in this chapter in the section, "Managing Server Roles."

Application Roles

Unlike other roles, application roles contain no database users. When an application role is created (see the section "Managing Database Roles," later in this chapter), rather than add a list of users who belong to the role, you specify a password. To obtain the permissions associated with the role, the connection must set the role and supply the password. This is done using the stored procedure sp_setapprole. You set the role to the sales application role (with the password PassW0rd) as follows:

```
EXEC sp_setapprole 'sales', 'PassW0rd'
```

You can also encrypt the password:

```
EXEC sp_setapprole 'sales', {ENCRYPT N ' PassW0rd'}, 'odbc'
```

When an application role is set, all permissions from that role apply, and all permissions inherited from roles other than public are suspended until the session is ended.

So why is it called an application role? The answer is in how it is used. An application role is used to provide permissions on objects through an application—*and only through the application*. Remember that you must use `sp_setapprole` and provide a password to activate the role; this statement and password are not given to the users; rather, they are embedded in the application's CONNECT string. This means that the user can get the permissions associated with the role only when running the application. The application can have checks and balances written into it to ensure that the permissions are being used for the forces of good and not evil.

Managing Securables

Securables are the entities in SQL Server on which permissions can be granted. In other words, principals (for example, users or logins) obtain permission to securables. This chapter describes many examples of securables, including tables, databases, and many entities that have been part of the SQL Server security model in past versions. SQL Server 2014's security model contains a granular set of securables for applying permissions.

Securables are hierarchical in nature and are broken down into nested hierarchies of named scopes. Three scopes are defined: at the server, database, and schema levels. Table 15.4 lists the securables for each scope.

TABLE 15.4   SQL Server 2014 Securables

Server Scope	Database Scope	Schema Scope
Endpoint	User	Type
Login	Database role	XML schema collection
Server role	Application role	Object – The object class has the following members:
Database	Assembly	Aggregate
	Message type	Function
	Route	Procedure
	Service	Queue
	Remote Service Binding	Synonym
	Fulltext catalog	Table
	Certificate	View
	Asymmetric key	

Server Scope	Database Scope	Schema Scope
	Symmetric key	
	Contract	
	Schema	

As mentioned earlier, a hierarchy exists within each scope; in addition, relationships cross scope boundaries. Servers contain databases, databases contain schemas, and schemas contain a myriad of objects that are also hierarchical. When certain permissions are granted on a securable at the server level, the permissions cascade; meaning permission is granted at the database and schema levels. For example, if a login is granted `control` permission at the server level, `control` is implicitly granted at the database and schema levels. The relationships between securables and permissions can be complicated. The next section details the different types of permissions and sheds some light on how these permissions affect securables.

Managing Permissions

Database security is mainly about managing permissions. Permissions are the security mechanisms that tie principals (for example, logins) to securables (for example, tables). With SQL Server 2014, permissions can be applied at a granular level that provides a great deal of flexibility and control.

Permissions in SQL Server 2014 revolve around three commands: GRANT, REVOKE, and DENY. These three commands have been around since SQL Server 2000. When permission is granted, the user or role is given permission to perform an action, such as creating a table. The DENY statement denies permission on an object and prevents the principal from gaining GRANT permission based on membership in a group or role. The REVOKE statement removes a permission that was previously granted or denied.

When specifying permissions, you need to carefully consider the hierarchy that exists between GRANT, REVOKE, and DENY. This is particularly important when the principal (for example, user or login) is part of a group or role and permissions have been granted on securables at different scopes of the security model. Following are some examples of the precedence that exists between these statements:

▶ A GRANT of a permission removes any REVOKE or DENY on a securable. For example, if a table has SELECT permission denied on it and then the SELECT permission is granted, the DENY permission is then removed on that table.

▶ DENY and REVOKE remove any GRANT permission on a securable.

▶ REVOKE removes any GRANT or DENY permission on a securable.

▶ Permissions denied at a higher scope in the security model override grants on that permission at a lower scope. Keep in mind that the security model has the server scope at the highest level, followed by database and schema. So if INSERT permission is denied on tables at the database level, and INSERT on a specific table in that database is granted at the schema level, the result is that INSERT is denied on all tables. In this example, a database-level DENY overrides any GRANT at the lower schema level.

▶ Permissions granted at a higher scope in the security model are overridden by a DENY permission at a lower level. For example, if INSERT permission is granted on all tables at the database scope, and INSERT is denied on a specific table in the database (schema scope), INSERT is then denied on that specific table.

The assignment of a permission includes the GRANT, DENY, or REVOKE statements plus the permission that these statements affect. The number of available permissions increased in SQL Server 2014. Familiar permissions such as EXECUTE, INSERT, and SELECT that have been around since SQL Server 2000 are still around, plus four new permissions that were added in SQL Server 2014. Following are some of the new permissions that were added in SQL Server 2014 (grouped by the feature they support):

▶ **CONNECT ANY DATABASE**—A server-level permission that allows a login to connect to all databases that currently exist and any new databases that are created in the future.

▶ **IMPERSONATE ANY LOGIN**—A server-level permission that allows a middle-tier process to impersonate the account of clients connecting to the database.

▶ **SELECT ALL USER SECURABLES**—A server-level permission that allows a login to view data in all databases that the user can connect to.

▶ **ALTER ANY DATABASE EVENT SESSION**—A database-level permission typically used to give a role the ability to read metadata associated with a database for monitoring purposes.

The combination of available permissions and the securables that they can be applied to is extensive. The permissions that are applicable depend on the particular securable. SQL Server Books Online lists the permissions for specific securables. You can use the index feature in Books Online to look for "permissions [Database Engine]." There, you will find a section named "Permissions Related to Specific Securables" as well as a section named "SQL Server Permissions" that lists each securable and its related permissions.

You can also view the available permissions by using system functions and catalog views. The following example uses the sys.fn_builtin_permissions function to retrieve a partial listing of all the available permissions:

```
SELECT top 5 class_desc, permission_name, parent_class_desc
 FROM sys.fn_builtin_permissions(default)
order by 1,2
/* Results from previous query
```

```
class_desc              permission_name parent_class_desc
----------------        --------------- -----------------
APPLICATION ROLE        ALTER           DATABASE
APPLICATION ROLE        CONTROL         DATABASE
APPLICATION ROLE        VIEW DEFINITION DATABASE
ASSEMBLY                ALTER           DATABASE
ASSEMBLY                CONTROL         DATABASE
*/
```

The granularity with which permissions can be applied with SQL Server 2014 is impressive and, to some degree, challenging. When you look at all the available permissions, you will see that some planning is needed to manage them. In the past, fixed database roles were simple to use but in many cases provided permissions that went beyond what the user needed. Microsoft has supplied the tools to facilitate the concept of "least privileges," which means providing only the privileges that are needed and nothing more. The tools to help you manage permissions are discussed later in this chapter, in the section, "Managing SQL Server Permissions."

Managing SQL Server Logins

You can create and administer logins easily using SSMS. You can use T-SQL as well, but the GUI screens are often the best choice. The GUI screens present the configurable properties for a login, including the available options, databases, and securables that can be assigned to a login. The number of configurable options is extensive and can be difficult to manage with T-SQL.

Using SSMS to Manage Logins

The visual tools for managing logins in SSMS are accessible via the Object Explorer. You need to expand the Security node in Object Explorer and right-click the Logins node. Then you select the New Login option, and the new login screen, shown in Figure 15.4, appears.

The default authentication mode for a new login is Windows Authentication. If you want to add a login with Windows Authentication, you need to type the name of your Windows user or group in the Login Name text box. You can also click the Search button to search for Windows logins. In either case, the login entered for Windows Authentication should be in the form <DOMAIN>\<UserName> (for example, mydomain\ Chris) or in the form user@company.com.

With Windows Authentication, you have an option to restrict access to the server for the new login when it is created. If you select Deny Server Access, a command to deny access to SQL Server is issued immediately after the login is created (for example, DENY CONNECT SQL TO [DBSVRXP\Chris]). This option can be useful for staging new logins and waiting until all the appropriate security has been applied prior to allowing the login to access your SQL Server instance. After you complete the security setup for the login, you can select the login properties and choose the GRANT SERVER ACCESS option.

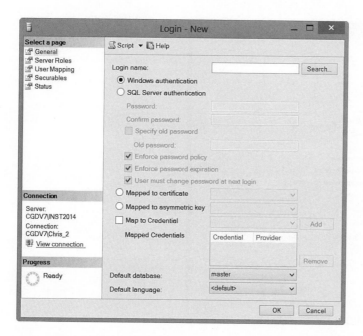

FIGURE 15.4   Creating a login in SSMS with Windows Authentication.

You can also use the same new login screen shown in Figure 15.4 to add a login with SQL Server Authentication. Again, you need to provide a login name, but with the standard SQL Server login, there is no domain associated with the user. The login is independent of any Windows login and can be named as desired. The login and password for SQL Server Authentication are stored and maintained in SQL Server.

When SQL Server Authentication is selected, several options related to passwords are enabled. These options, as shown in Figure 15.5, include Enforce Password Expiration, Enforce Password Policy, and User Must Change Password at Next Login. These options are all associated with a more rigid password policy. They are similar to options available with Windows accounts and provide a more robust security solution for SQL Server logins. In past versions, the catch was that the new password options were enforced only on the Windows Server 2003 operating system and later versions. This is not a problem with SQL Server 2014 because it requires an operating system later than Windows Server 2008.

The next set of options on the General page of the new login allows you to map the login to a certificate, asymmetric key, or credential. The certificate and asymmetric key selections allow you to create a certificate-mapped login or an asymmetric key-mapped login. A certificate-mapped login and an asymmetric key-mapped login are used only for code signing and cannot be used to connect to SQL Server. If these options are used, the certificate or asymmetric key must exist on the server before you map the logins to them. The capability to map the login to a credential on the General page was added in SQL Server 2008. This option simply links the login to an existing credential, but its capabilities may be expanded.

FIGURE 15.5   Creating a login in SSMS with SQL Server Authentication.

The default database and default language are the final options located on the General page of the new login screen. These options are available regardless of the authentication method selected. The default database is the database that the login will connect to by default. The master database is selected, but it is generally not the best database to select for your default. You should choose the default database that your login will use most often and avoid using any of the system databases as your default. This helps prevent database users from executing statements against the wrong database, and it also removes the step of having to change the database every time the user connects. You should make sure that the login is given access to whatever database you select as the default. (The Database Access page is discussed later in this chapter.)

The default language determines the default language used by the login. If no default language is specified and the <default> entry is left in the Language drop-down, the server's default language is used. The default language for the server can be retrieved or set by using the sp_configure system stored procedure. The language selection affects many things, including date formats, month names, and names of days. To see a list of languages available on the server and the related options, you use the sys.syslanguages catalog view.

The new login screen has four other pages available for selection when creating your new login: Server Roles, User Mapping, Securables, and Status. The Server Roles page allows you to select one or more fixed server roles for the login to participate in. Figure 15.6 shows the new login screen with the Server Roles page selected. For a more detailed review of the permissions related to each server role, refer to the section, "Fixed Server Roles," earlier in this chapter.

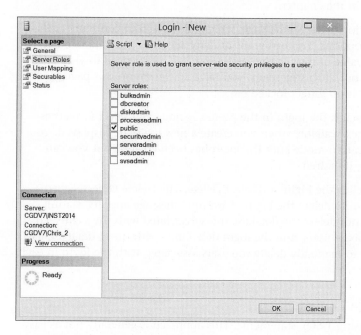

FIGURE 15.6   Choosing a server role.

The User Mapping page allows you to select the databases that the login will have access to. When the Map check box is selected for a database, the default schema and User cells are enabled. The default schema is the schema that will contain the database objects created by the login. The login can create objects in schemas other than the default if the login has permission to use the other schemas. If no schema is specified, the default schema is used. The default schema also comes into play when you're retrieving database objects. If no schema is specified on database retrievals, the default schema is searched first for the database object. If no default schema is specified on the Database Access screen, the default schema is set to dbo. The User data entry area allows you to enter a database username that is different from the login name. By default, the database user-name is the same as the login name, but you can change it.

The other thing that happens when you select the Map check box on the database is that the list of database roles is enabled in the bottom portion of the screen. You can select one or more database roles for the login. Both fixed and user-defined database roles are available for selection. The public database role is selected by default and cannot be deselected.

The Securables page allows you to select server objects for login permissions. The server objects are limited to object types scoped at the server level. They include Availability

Groups, Servers, Endpoints, Logins, and Server Roles object types. The management of all permissions, including those for Logins, is discussed in detail in the "Managing Permissions" section, earlier in the chapter.

The last page listed for selection is the Status page, which allows you to configure authorization and authentication options. You can grant or deny access to the Database Engine on this page, and you can enable or disable the login. You also might need to visit this page if the login gets locked out. If this happens, you have an option on this page to re-enable the login so that it is no longer locked out.

To modify a login, you right-click the login in the Security node and select Properties. The same set of property pages available when you create a new login are displayed. You cannot change the authentication mode after the login has been created, but you can change all the other settings, if desired.

To delete a login, you right-click the login and select Delete. The Delete Object screen appears, and you can click OK to delete the login. A warning message appears, stating "Deleting server logins does not delete the database users associated with the logins." If the login has associated database users, and the login deletion is performed, database users are orphaned, and you have to manually delete the users associated with the login in each database.

Using T-SQL to Manage Logins

You can manage logins by using T-SQL statements. This approach is generally not as easy as using the user-friendly GUI screens that come with SSMS, but sometimes using T-SQL is better. For example, with installations and upgrades that involve changes to logins, you can use T-SQL to script the changes and produce a repeatable process.

SQL Server 2014 includes system stored procedures and an ALTER LOGIN statement that you can use to manage logins. The same system stored procedures available in prior versions are still available in SQL Server 2014, but they have been deprecated and will not be available in a future version. Table 15.5 lists the available system stored procedures and the basic function and current state of each one. The state indicates whether the procedure has been deprecated and whether an alternative exists in SQL Server 2014.

TABLE 15.5   System Stored Procedures for Managing Logins

Store Procedure	Function	Status
sp_addlogin	Add a SQL Server login.	Deprecated; use CREATE LOGIN instead.
sp_defaultdb	Change the default database.	Deprecated; use ALTER LOGIN instead.
sp_defaultlanguage	Change the default language.	Deprecated; use ALTER LOGIN instead.
sp_denylogin	Deny server access to a Windows login.	Deprecated. use ALTER LOGIN instead.

Store Procedure	Function	Status
sp_droplogin	Drop a SQL Server login.	Deprecated; use DROP LOGIN instead.
sp_grantlogin	Add a Windows login.	Deprecated. use CREATE LOGIN instead.
sp_password	Change a login's password.	Deprecated; use ALTER LOGIN instead.
sp_revokelogin	Drop a Windows login.	Deprecated; use DROP LOGIN instead.

The system stored procedures have a variety of parameters, which are documented in Books Online. Because they have been deprecated, they are not the focus of this section. Instead, this section focuses on a number of examples that utilize the CREATE, ALTER, and DROP statements. The following example creates a SQL Server login with a password that must be changed the first time the login connects:

```
CREATE LOGIN Laura WITH PASSWORD=N'mypassw0rd$'
  MUST_CHANGE, CHECK_EXPIRATION=ON
```

You can then use the following ALTER LOGIN statement to change the default database, language, and password for the new Laura login:

```
ALTER LOGIN [Laura] WITH
 DEFAULT_DATABASE=[AdventureWorks2012],
 DEFAULT_LANGUAGE=[British],
 PASSWORD=N'myStr0ngPW'
```

Finally, you can drop the Laura login by using the following:

```
DROP LOGIN [Laura]
```

As you can see, the T-SQL statements for logins are relatively easy to use. To simplify matters, you can generate T-SQL statements from SSMS. To do so, you click the Script button available on the screen that appears after you specify a login action. For example, if you right-click a login and select Delete, the Delete Object screen appears. At the top of this screen is a Script button. When you click this button, SSMS scripts the related T-SQL statements into a Query Editor window for you to review and execute.

Managing SQL Server Users

SSMS has a set of friendly user interfaces to manage SQL Server users as well. The screens are similar to the screens for logins and are also launched from the Object Explorer. You can also use a set of T-SQL statements to manage users.

Using SSMS to Manage Users

To manage users via SSMS, you open the Object Explorer and expand the `Security` node followed by the `Users` node. The `Users` node contains a list of the current database users. To add a new database user, you can right-click the `Users` node and select New User. Figure 15.7 shows the Object Explorer window with the option to create a new user selected for the `AdventureWorks2012` database.

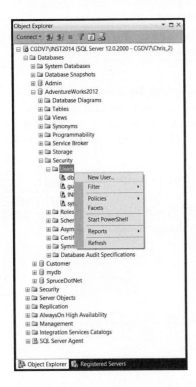

FIGURE 15.7   The New User option in Object Explorer.

Figure 15.8 shows the dialog box that is displayed after you select the New User option. The New User dialog box has changed quite a bit in SQL Server 2014. In earlier versions, the Owned Schemas and Membership information was displayed at the bottom of the General page. In SQL Server 2014, there are two new pages that are available for selection to configure schemas and membership for the user.

Another change to the New User dialog box in SQL Server 2014 is the User type drop-down. The options available are SQL User with Login, SQL User Without Login, User Mapped to a Certificate, User Mapped to an Asymmetric Key, and Windows User. In Figure 15.8, the user type that has been selected from the drop-down is SQL User with Login. With this option, the login must exist before you can create the user. You can click the ellipsis button next to the login name to view a list of available logins. After you click the ellipsis, you can click the Browse button to see the logins that have already been added to SQL Server.

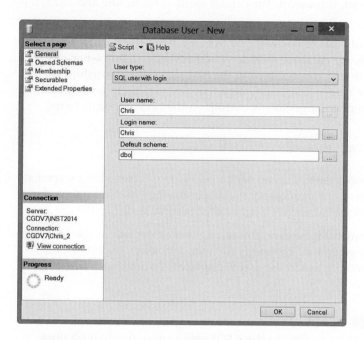

FIGURE 15.8   Using SSMS to create a new user.

NOTE

The username and login name shown in Figure 15.8 are the same, but this is not a requirement. The username can be changed to a name that does not match the login name, but this can cause some confusion. It is a good practice to leave the names the same.

When the SQL User Without Login option is chosen from the User Type drop-down, the login does not need to exist. This option was added in SQL Server 2012 to support contained databases, which were new in SQL Server 2012 as well. The authentication of these types of users happens at the database level. Applications that connect to the database with this type of user must specify the contained database as the initial catalog.

The user type of Windows User is another option for connecting to a contained database. This type of user will be contained if the corresponding account for Windows Authentication does not exist as a SQL Server login when the user is created. If the related login already exists in SQL Server when the user is created in the contained database, then the user will be linked to the login, and the database will no longer be contained.

The default schema is available if you select either SQL User with Login, SQL User Without Login, or Windows User as the user type. The default schema must be a valid schema created in the database. If the default schema is left blank, it defaults to dbo. After the default schema has been set, it is used as the default location for storing and retrieving database objects.

You can select one or more schemas to be owned by the user, but a given schema can be owned by only one user in the database. When a schema is selected for ownership for a user, the previous owner loses ownership, and the new user gains ownership. The following example shows the type of T-SQL statement that you can run to accomplish the ownership change. This example changes the ownership on the Person schema to the user Laura:

```
ALTER AUTHORIZATION ON SCHEMA::[Person] TO [Laura]
```

When you select the Permissions page, you can assign permissions to securables scoped at the database and schema levels. The management of all permissions, including those for users, is discussed in detail in the "Managing Permissions" section, earlier in the chapter.

To modify or delete an existing database user, you can right-click the user in the Object Explorer and choose the related option. To modify the user, you select Properties, and a screen similar to the one you use to add the user is displayed. To delete the user, you select the Delete option.

Using T-SQL to Manage Users

CREATE USER, ALTER USER, and DROP USER are the T-SQL commands you use most often to manage database users. These commands are replacements for the system stored procedures used in prior versions. The system stored procedures, such as sp_adduser, sp_dropuser, sp_grantdbaccess, and sp_revokedbaccess, have been deprecated and will be removed in a future version. They are still available for use now, but you should avoid them when possible.

The following example demonstrates the use of the CREATE USER statement to create a new database user named Laura, with a default schema Sales:

```
CREATE USER Laura FOR LOGIN Laura
    WITH DEFAULT_SCHEMA = Sales
```

You can use the ALTER USER statement to change the default schema or the username. The following example uses the ALTER USER statement to change the name of the database user currently named Laura to LauraG:

```
ALTER USER Laura WITH NAME = LauraG
```

If you want to delete a database user, you use the DROP USER command. The following example demonstrates how to delete the LauraG from the previous example:

```
DROP USER [LauraG]
```

When dropping database users, you must keep in mind that you cannot drop them if they are the owners of database objects. An object's ownership must be transferred to another database user before that object can be deleted. This applies to schemas that can be owned by the user as well.

Managing Database Roles

Database roles are custom roles that you can define to group your users and simplify the administration of permissions. Generally, custom database roles (nonfixed) are created if the fixed database roles do not meet the security needs of the administrator. (The assignment of logins and users to fixed server and fixed database roles is covered earlier in this chapter.)

Using SSMS to Manage Database Roles

You can find database roles in the Object Explorer for each database, under the `Security` node, which contains a `Roles` node. The `Roles` node contains a `Database Roles` node, which lists both fixed and nonfixed database roles. To add a new custom database role (nonfixed), you right-click the `Database Roles` node and select New Database Role. A new database role dialog box appears, as shown in Figure 15.9.

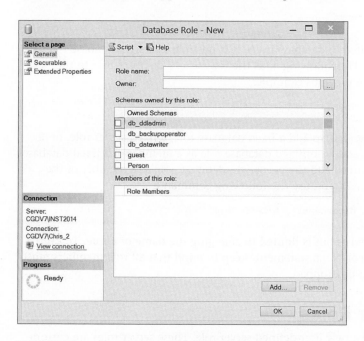

FIGURE 15.9   The new database role dialog box.

You need to enter a name for the role and name for the owner of the role. Like a database user, a database role can also own schemas. If you click the Add button, you can add database users from the current database to the role.

If you select the Permissions page, you can define the permission for the database role. This definition includes the selection of database objects scoped at the database and schema levels. These permissions are discussed in detail in the "Managing Permissions" section, earlier in this chapter.

Using T-SQL to Manage Database Roles

Some of the T-SQL system stored procedures used in prior versions to manage roles have been deprecated, including `sp_addrole` and `sp_droprole`. The `sp_addrolemember` and `sp_droprolemember` procedures were recently deprecated as well and will be removed in a future version of SQL Server.

The `CREATE ROLE` and `DROP ROLE` statements are the new replacements for `sp_addrole` and `sp_droprole`. The following example uses the `CREATE ROLE` statement to create a new database role named `DevDbRole`:

```
CREATE ROLE [DevDbRole]
```

To assign a user named Chris to the new `DevDbRole` role, you can use the following:

```
ALTER ROLE DevDbRole ADD MEMBER chris
```

Role membership is not limited to database users. It is possible to assign database roles as members of another role. The following adds the `TestDbRole` database role to the `DevDbRole` role created in the previous example:

```
EXEC sp_addrolemember N'DevDbRole', N'TestDbRole'
```

You cannot use `sp_addrolemember` to add a fixed database role, a fixed server role, or `dbo` to a role. You can, however, add a nonfixed database role as a member of a fixed database role. If, for example, you want to add the `DevDbRole` database role as a member of the fixed database role `db_dataread`, you use the following command:

```
EXEC sp_addrolemember N'db_datareader', N'DevDbRole'
```

The `ALTER ROLE` statement exists but is limited to changing the name of a role. To drop a database role, you use the `DROP ROLE` statement. Keep in mind that all role members must be dropped before a role can be dropped.

Managing Server Roles

SQL Server 2012 introduced a new user-defined server role. These server roles are custom roles that you can define to group your logins and simplify the administration of permissions at the server level. Generally, custom server roles (nonfixed) are created if the fixed server roles do not meet the security needs of the administrator and more granular control of permissions is needed.

Using SSMS to Manage Server Roles

You can find server roles in the Object Explorer under the `Security` node, which contains a `Server Roles` node. The `Server Roles` node lists both fixed and nonfixed server roles. To add a new custom server role (nonfixed), you right-click the `Server Roles` node and select New Server Role. A new Server Role dialog box appears, as shown in Figure 15.10.

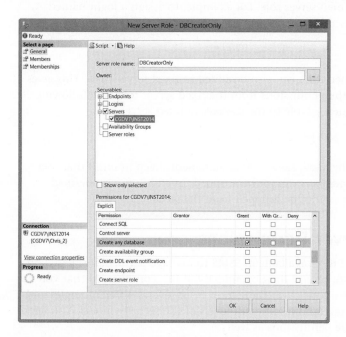

FIGURE 15.10   The new Server Role dialog box.

You need to enter a name for the role and name for the owner of the role. In Figure 15.10 the new server role name has been set to `DbCreatorOnly`. A specific server instance has been selected as well, which causes the Permissions grid at the bottom of the page to be populated with the available permissions for this securable. The securables and related permissions that are available are scoped at the server level.

After you have selected the permissions you want to assign the server role, you can use the Members page to assign logins or other server roles to the server role. You can also use the Memberships page to make the new server role a member of one of the fixed server roles. This will give the new server role all the permissions associated with the fixed server role in addition to any of the permissions that were manually configured for this role on the General page.

Using T-SQL to Manage Server Roles

The `CREATE SERVER ROLE`, `ALTER SERVER ROLE`, and `DROP SERVER ROLE` statements were added in SQL Server 2014 to facilitate the management of the new user-defined server roles. The following example uses the CREATE SERVER ROLE statement to create a new Server Role named DbCreatorOnly:

```
CREATE SERVER ROLE [DbCreatorOnly]
```

The ALTER SERVER ROLE statement can be used to change the membership of a server role or change names of a user—defined server role. For example, to assign a login named Chris to the new DbCreatorOnly role, you can use the following:

```
ALTER SERVER ROLE [DbCreatorOnly] ADD MEMBER [Chris]
```

As mentioned earlier, user-defined roles can also be added to fixed server roles. This gives the user-defined server role all the permissions from the fixed server role. The following example adds the new DbCreatorOnly role to the diskadmin fixed server role:

```
ALTER SERVER ROLE [diskadmin] ADD MEMBER [DbCreatorOnly]
```

To drop a server role, you use the DROP SERVER ROLE statement. Keep in mind that user-defined server roles that have members cannot be dropped. In addition, user-defined server roles that own securables cannot be dropped from the server

Managing SQL Server Permissions

You can use T-SQL or the visual tools available in SSMS to manage permissions. Based on the number of available permissions and their complexity, it is recommended that you use the SSMS tools. The following sections cover these tools from several different angles and look at the management of permissions at different levels of the security model. You learn how to use T-SQL to manage the permissions as well.

Using SSMS to Manage Permissions

The Object Explorer in SSMS enables you to manage permissions at many different levels of the permission hierarchy. You can manage permissions at a high level, such as the entire server, or you can manage permissions at the very lowest level, including a specific object, such as a table or stored procedure. The degree of granularity you use for permissions depends on your security needs. To demonstrate the scope of permissions, let's look at managing permissions at several different levels, starting at a high level and working down to the object level.

> **NOTE**
>
> There are many different ways to achieve a security goal in SSMS. For example, you can manage permissions for a database user from the database or from the user. You can apply permissions on schema objects for the entire schema or to individual objects. You should always try to choose the permission solution that allows you to achieve your security goals with the least amount of administrative overhead.

Using SSMS to Manage Permissions at the Server Level

Logins can be granted explicit permissions at the server level. Earlier we looked at fixed server roles as one means for assigning permissions, but you can manage individual server-level securables as well. Figure 15.11 shows the Login Properties window for a login named Chris. You launch this window by right-clicking the login and selecting Properties or just double click on the login. Figure 15.11 shows the Securables page, which allows you to add specific securables to the grid.

FIGURE 15.11   Server-level permissions.

NOTE

You can open a Permissions page like the one shown in Figure 15.11 from many different places in the Object Explorer. The title of the dialog box and the content of the grid vary, depending on the object selected, but the screen is generally the same, no matter where it is launched. This provides consistency and simplifies the overall management of permissions.

You can click the Search button shown toward the top of Figure 15.11 to add objects to the securables grid. When you click this button, the Add Objects window shown in Figure 15.12 is displayed. This window allows you to choose the types of objects you want to add. If you select Specific Objects, you are taken directly to the Select Objects window. If you choose All Objects of the Types, you are taken to an intermediate screen that allows you to select the type of objects you want to assign permissions to.

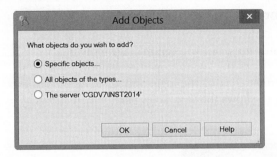

FIGURE 15.12 The Add Objects window.

Again, the Add button and the means for adding objects are fairly consistent for all permissions. What varies is the object types available for selection. For example, at the server level, the types of objects available to assign permissions are scoped at the server level. Figure 15.13 shows the Select Object Types window displayed when you choose the All Objects of the Types option at the server level. You can see that the available objects are all scoped at the server level.

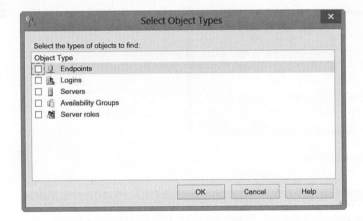

FIGURE 15.13 Server-level object types.

If the endpoints objects are selected, the securables grid is populated with all the available endpoints that have permissions to manage. Figure 15.14 shows the Login Properties window with the endpoints securables populated. The TSQL Named Pipes securable is selected, which allows you to specify the explicit permissions for the securable in the bottom grid. In this example, the Grant and With Grant check boxes have been selected for the control permission. This gives the login named Chris the right to control the Named Pipes endpoint and also allows him to grant this control right (because With Grant is selected) to other logins.

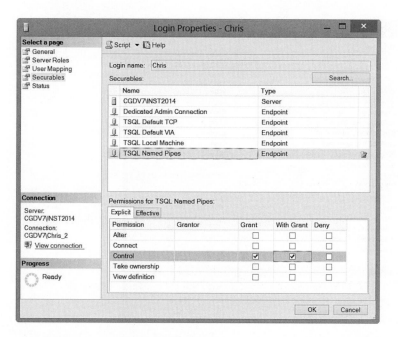

FIGURE 15.14   Server-level securables.

The examples we just walked through are related to the assignment of explicit permission on a specific instance of a securable. You can also apply server permissions at a higher level. For example, you might want to specify permissions for a login to allow that login to control all server endpoints instead of specific endpoints. You can accomplish this in several ways. One way to do it is to select the Server object from the list of object types when adding permissions for a specific login. Another way is to right-click the server name in the Object Explorer and select Properties. The Server Properties window that appears has a Permissions page that lists all the logins for the server, along with the macro-level permissions scoped for the server. Figure 15.15 shows the Server Properties window with the login Chris selected. The explicit permissions listed in this case are at a higher level and are not just for one instance. The example shown in Figure 15.15 allows the login Chris to alter any endpoint on the server. This is based on the Grant check boxes selected.

Using SSMS to Manage Permissions at the Database Level

The same type of hierarchy exists with permissions at the database level as at the server level. You can apply permissions at a high level to affect many objects of a particular type, or you can apply them on a specific object. You can also manage the permissions at the database level on a specific database user, or you can manage them on the database across many users.

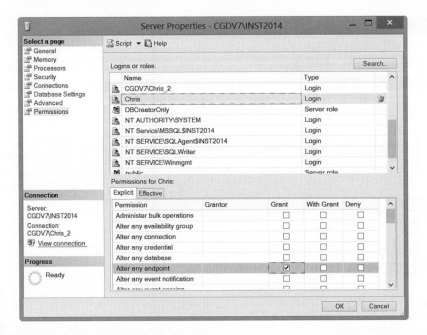

FIGURE 15.15   The Server Properties window's Permissions page.

To demonstrate the differences between object types available at the database level, let's first look at managing permissions for a specific database user. As with logins, you can right-click a database user and select Properties. On the Properties window that appears, you select the Securables page, and you get a screen to assign permissions that is similar to the login permissions screen. The difference at the database level is in the object types available for selection. Figure 15.16 shows the object types available when you choose the All Objects of Types choice during the addition of securables for a database user.

When a low-level object type such as a table or stored procedure is selected, you are able to apply explicit permissions to a specific object instance. Figure 15.17 shows an example of low-level securables available when the Tables object type is selected.

To apply permissions at a higher level in the database, you choose the object type Databases. With this securable added to the permissions grid, you can apply permissions to a group of objects by selecting a single permission. Figure 15.18 shows the AdventureWorks2012 database selected as the securable and the related permissions available. In this example, the login Chris has been granted INSERT, SELECT, and UPDATE permissions to all the tables in the AdventureWorks2012 database.

FIGURE 15.16 Database-level object types.

FIGURE 15.17 Low-level database securables.

FIGURE 15.18 High-level database securables.

Using SSMS to Manage Permissions at the Object Level

The last permission assignment we look at is the object level. SSMS enables you to select a specific object instance in the Object Explorer and assign permissions to it. This method allows you to navigate to the object you want via the Object Explorer tree and assign permissions accordingly. Figure 15.19 shows the Object Explorer tree expanded to the Stored Procedures node. A specific stored procedure has been right-clicked, and the Properties option has been selected.

The Properties window has a page dedicated to permissions. You can select the Permissions page and then select the users or roles you want to add for the specific object, such as a stored procedure. Figure 15.20 shows the Permissions page with a user named Chris added to the Users or Roles window at the top of the page. The bottom portion of the page shows explicit permissions for the user Chris, which includes a DENY permission to alter the stored procedure selected.

> **NOTE**
>
> The methods described here for managing permissions in SSMS are by no means the only ways you can manage permissions in SSMS. You will find that the assignment of permissions pervades SSMS and that SSMS allows you to assign permissions in many different ways. The point to keep in mind is that server roles, application roles, schemas, and other objects in the security model all have similar methods for assigning permissions.

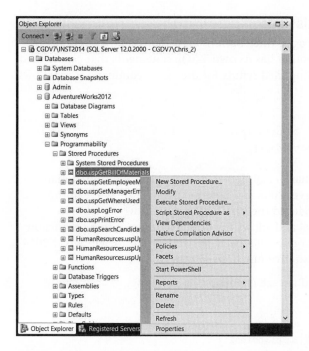

FIGURE 15.19   Object-level permissions selected via Object Explorer.

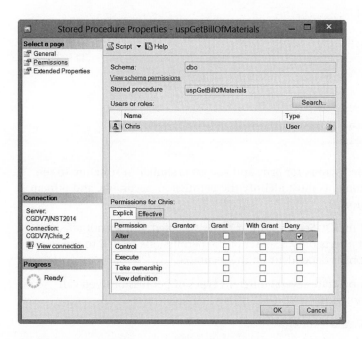

FIGURE 15.20   Object-level permissions.

Using T-SQL to Manage Permissions

As you saw in the SSMS Permissions pages, three options exist for assigning every permission: GRANT, DENY, and REVOKE. Each option has its own T-SQL statements that can be used to manage permissions as well. The simplified syntax for the GRANT command is as follows:

```
GRANT { ALL [ PRIVILEGES ] }
      | permission [ ( column [ ,...n ] ) ] [ ,...n ]
      [ ON [ class :: ] securable ] TO principal [ ,...n ]
      [ WITH GRANT OPTION ] [ AS principal ]
```

This basic GRANT syntax is similar to that in SQL Server 2000, but the addition of many permissions and securables in SQL Server 2005 and newer expanded the scope of the command. SQL Server 2005 also introduced the WITH GRANT option, which allows a permission to be granted to a principal and allows the principal to grant that permission to another principal. The WITH GRANT option has been carried forward to SQL Server 2014 and is a good way to delegate administrative functions to others.

The simplified syntax for the DENY and REVOKE commands is as follows:

```
DENY { ALL [ PRIVILEGES ] }
      | permission [ ( column [ ,...n ] ) ] [ ,...n ]
      [ ON [ class :: ] securable ] TO principal [ ,...n ]
      [ CASCADE] [ AS principal ]


REVOKE [ GRANT OPTION FOR ]
      {
        [ ALL [ PRIVILEGES ] ]
        |
                permission [ ( column [ ,...n ] ) ] [ ,...n ]
      }
      [ ON [ class :: ] securable ]
      { TO | FROM } principal [ ,...n ]
      [ CASCADE] [ AS principal ]
```

You can see that the simplified syntax for DENY and REVOKE is similar in structure to the GRANT statement. All the statements must identify the permission, securable, and principal that will receive the permission.

The ALL clause is deprecated in SQL Server 2014. If ALL is specified, it does not affect all permissions on the object; it affects only a subset of the permissions related to the securable. The subset of permissions is dependent on the securable.

The following examples demonstrate several different types of permissions you can manage by using T-SQL commands:

```
--Grant permissions to create a table
-- to a user named Chris
GRANT CREATE TABLE TO Chris
```

```
--Grant ALL permissions on a stored procedure
-- to a database role named TestDBRole
GRANT ALL ON dbo.uspGetBillOfMaterials TO TestDBRole

--DENY UPDATE permission on the Customer table
-- to user named Laura
DENY UPDATE ON OBJECT::sales.customer TO Laura

--REVOKE UPDATE permissions on the Customer table
-- to user named Laura.
REVOKE UPDATE ON OBJECT::sales.customer TO Laura
```

There are many different flavors of the GRANT, DENY, and REVOKE statements, depending on the securable they are affecting. Books Online outlines the syntax for each securable and the permissions that can be applied.

Remember that you can use the Script option to generate the T-SQL from SSMS. The Script button is available when you're managing permissions, and using it is a great way to familiarize yourself with the T-SQL that is used to effect changes. You can select the permissions you want to apply via the GUI screen and then click the Script button to generate the T-SQL.

The Execution Context

The execution context determines what permissions are checked when statements are executed or actions are performed on the database server. By default, the execution context is set to the principal connected to the server or database. If a user named Chris connects to the AdventureWorks2012 database, the permissions assigned to Chris are checked.

In SQL Server 2014, you can change the execution context so that permissions are checked for a principal other than that to which you are connected. You can make this change in execution context (called *context switching*) explicitly or implicitly.

Explicit Context Switching

With explicit context switching, you can use the EXECUTE AS statement to change the user or login used to check permissions. This is similar to the SET USER statement available in prior versions. It is extremely useful for administrators who are testing the permissions they have set for users or logins. The following example demonstrates the use of the explicit EXECUTE AS statement:

```
--Assume that you are connected as an administrator (DBO)
--and want to prevent members of the Public role from
--selecting from the Sales.Customer table
DENY SELECT ON sales.customer TO Public
```

```
--We can check that user Laura cannot select from the
-- Sales.Customer table using the EXECUTE AS statement
EXECUTE AS USER = 'laura'
SELECT TOP 1 * FROM sales.customer

-- Revert to the previous execution context.
REVERT
```

You can also do explicit context switching at the login level. You can use the EXECUTE AS statement to switch the execution context to another login instead of a user.

Context switching is linked to the IMPERSONATE permission. As an administrator, you can grant IMPERSONATE to a login or user to enable that user to execute as that user. For example, an administrator can temporarily enable another login to run in the same execution context by using the IMPERSONATE permission and EXECUTE AS statement. The following example demonstrates the assignment of the IMPERSONATE permission to a login named Laura:

```
--Chris grants the right to Laura to impersonate him
GRANT IMPERSONATE ON LOGIN::[chris] TO [laura]
GO

--Laura can then connect with her login and use
-- the EXECUTE AS command to run commands that
-- normally only Chris has permission to run
EXECUTE AS Login = 'Chris'
DBCC CHECKDB (AdventureWorks2012)
SELECT USER_NAME()
--Revert back to Laura's execution context
REVERT
SELECT USER_NAME()
```

Laura can now use EXECUTE as Chris, who is an administrator. This capability can be particularly useful when a user or login has many custom permissions that would take a lot of time to establish for another user or login.

Implicit Context Switching

With implicit context switching, the execution context is set within a module such as a stored procedure, trigger, or user-defined function. The EXECUTE AS clause is placed in the module and is set to the user that the module will be run as. The context switch is implicit because the user who runs the module does not have to explicitly specify the context before running the module. The context is set within the module.

The EXECUTE AS clause has several different options to establish the execution context. All modules are able to set the context to a specific user or login. Functions, stored procedures, and Data Manipulation Language (DML) triggers can also execute as CALLER, SELF, or OWNER. DDL triggers can run as CALLER or SELF. Queues can run as SELF or OWNER. The

CALLER option is the default, and it runs the module in the context of the user who called the module. The SELF option causes the module to run in the context of the user or login that created the procedure. The OWNER option causes the module to run in the context of the current owner of the module.

The following example demonstrates the creation and execution of a stored procedure with the EXECUTE AS clause on a specific user named Chris:

```
CREATE PROCEDURE dbo.usp_TestExecutionContext
WITH EXECUTE AS 'chris'
AS SELECT USER_NAME() as 'User'

--Set the user to someone other than chris to test the
-- implicit EXECUTE AS
EXECUTE AS 'DBO'
EXEC usp_TestExecutionContext

/*Results of the prior execution
User
------
chris
*/
```

This example shows that the USER_NAME retrieved in the stored procedure is Chris, regardless of who executed the procedure.

Implicit execution context can be particularly useful in situations in which permissions cannot be granted to a user directly. For example, TRUNCATE TABLE permissions cannot be granted explicitly to a user, but a database owner can run this command. Instead of granting dbo rights to a user needing TRUNCATE permissions, you can create a stored procedure that does the truncation. You can create the stored procedure with the execution context of dbo, and you can grant the user rights to execute the stored procedure that does the truncation. When you use this method, the user can perform the truncation but does not have any of the other permissions related to a database owner.

Summary

SQL Server 2014 continues the trend of providing more security and more flexible security to the SQL Server database environment. Several new enhancements have been added to SQL Server 2014 that add to the slew of security changes added since SQL Server 2005. The granularity of the permissions and the other security-related features covered in this chapter allow you to keep your SQL Server environment safe.

Chapter 16, "Data Encryption," looks at another aspect of SQL Server that helps secure your database environment. It covers encryption methods that can be implemented to further protect your data from unauthorized access.

Data Encryption

With all the concern about identity theft these days, there has been increasingly more attention paid to how all the personally identifiable information (PII) and other sensitive information stored in databases is being protected. It is necessary to secure and protect this data to avoid any potential liability should the PII or sensitive data fall into the wrong hands, and in some cases, doing so may even be required by law (for example, Health Insurance Portability and Accountability Act, or HIPAA, requirements).

Chapter 15, "Security and User Administration," discussed methods to secure and control the access to your SQL Server data via login and user security. This type of security is usually sufficient to prevent access to the data by anyone other than properly authorized users. But what if you need to prevent authorized users, such as your database or server administrators, from viewing sensitive data? How can you protect sensitive data from hackers or in the event that a database backup is stolen?

One method is to encrypt the data. This chapter looks at two methods provided in SQL Server 2014 for encrypting data: column-level encryption and transparent data encryption (TDE). In addition to describing how to implement both methods, the chapter presents the features and limitations of each of these methods to help you decide which data encryption method may help you meet your data security needs.

> **NOTE**
>
> Both column-level and transparent data encryption are available only in the Enterprise and Developer Editions of SQL Server 2014.

What's New in Data Encryption

There really are no notable differences with data encryption in SQL Server 2014 compared to what was available in SQL Server 2012. However, SQL Server 2014 now supports encryption for backups, without requiring implementation of TDE for the database itself. Setting up a database master key (DMK) in the master database and creating a certificate or asymmetric key is still a prerequisite for encrypting a backup. For more information on encrypting backups, see Chapter 11, "Database Backup and Restore."

An Overview of Data Encryption

Even if you follow the recommended best practices for securing your SQL Server environment, you still can be vulnerable to access control problems. Data encryption provides a means of enhancing data security by limiting data loss even in the rare occurrence that access controls are bypassed and a malicious user obtains access to sensitive data such as credit card numbers. Data encryption is the process of obfuscating data through the use of an encryption key or password. This can make the data unreadable without the corresponding decryption key or password. Encryption does not solve your access control problems, but it can enhance data security by limiting access to data, even if access controls are bypassed.

Encryption is actually the conversion of readable plaintext into ciphertext, which cannot be easily understood by unauthorized people. The concrete procedure of carrying out the encryption is called an algorithm. Decryption is the process of converting ciphertext back into its original form so it can be understood. Both encryption and decryption require a key, which must be kept secret because it enables the holder to carry out the decryption.

There are two primary methods of encryption: symmetric key encryption and asymmetric key encryption. Symmetric key encryption uses the same key for both encryption and decryption. Asymmetric key encryption, also called public-key encryption, uses two different keys for encryption and decryption, which together form a key pair. The key used for encryption is called a *public key*. The key used for decryption is referred to as a *private key*.

Symmetric key encryption is inherently less secure because it uses the same key for both encryption and decryption operations, and the exchange of data requires transfer of the key, which introduces a potential for its compromise. This can be avoided with an asymmetric key because individuals encrypting and decrypting data have their own, separate keys. However, asymmetric encryption is based on algorithms that are more complex, and its impact on performance is more significant, making it often unsuitable in scenarios involving larger amounts of data. However, it is possible to take advantage of the strengths of both methods by encrypting data with a symmetric key and then protecting the symmetric key with asymmetric encryption.

One solution to the dilemma of key distribution is to use digital certificates. A certificate is a digitally signed piece of software that associates a public key with the identity of the private key owner, assuring its authenticity. There is an inherent problem with this approach—namely, how to assure the identity of the certificate issuer. To resolve this issue, Microsoft provides a number of trusted certificate authorities (known as Trusted Root Certification Authorities) with the operating system. These certificate authorities are responsible for verifying that organizations requesting certificates are really what they claim to be.

Typically, the algorithms used for encryption are industry standard, such as the Advanced Encryption Standard (AES). The fact that the algorithms are published doesn't make them weaker, but rather helps ensure they are strong and robust. Because these algorithms have been reviewed by thousands of experts around the globe, they have stood the test of time. SQL Server 2014 allows administrators and developers to choose from among several algorithms, including DES, Triple DES, TRIPLE_DES_3KEY, RC2, RC4, 128-bit RC4, DESX, 128-bit AES, 192-bit AES, and 256-bit AES. No one algorithm is ideal for all situations, and a discussion on the merits of each is beyond the scope of this chapter. However, the following general principles apply:

▶ Strong encryption generally consumes more CPU resources than weak encryption.

▶ Long keys generally yield stronger encryption than short keys.

▶ Asymmetric encryption is stronger than symmetric encryption using the same key length, but it is slower.

▶ Long, complex passwords are stronger than short passwords.

▶ If you are encrypting lots of data, you should encrypt the data using a symmetric key and encrypt the symmetric key with an asymmetric key.

However, what really protects your data from third parties is not so much the algorithm but the encryption key, which you must keep secure. Keys must be stored securely and made available only on a need-to-know basis. Ideally, authorized people or systems should be able to use but not necessarily have a copy of the key. It's also a security best practice to implement key rotation, changing keys periodically in case a key has been compromised. For greater key security, you can also make use of Extensible Key Management, allowing keys to be managed by an external source such as Hardware Security Module.

SQL Server 2014 provides support for not only encryption of data, but also encryption of user network connections and stored procedures. The remainder of this chapter discusses the two methods of data encryption, column-level encryption and transparent data encryption. Client network encryption is covered in Chapter 10, "Client Installation and Configuration." Encryption of stored procedure code is discussed in Chapter 25, "Creating and Managing Stored Procedures."

16

> **NOTE**
>
> Although encryption is a valuable tool to help ensure security, it does incur overhead and can affect performance, and any use of encryption requires a maintenance strategy for your passwords, keys, and certificates.
>
> Therefore, encryption should not be automatically considered for all data or connections. When you are deciding whether to implement encryption, consider how users access the

data. If access is over a public network, data encryption may be required to increase data security. However, if all access is via a secure intranet configuration, encryption may not be required.

This chapter describes the encryption methods available in SQL Server 2014 along with the pros and cons of implementing these encryption methods. This information should help you to determine whether using encryption is appropriate for implementing your data security solutions.

SQL Server Key Management

SQL Server 2014 provides rich support for various types of data encryption using symmetric and asymmetric keys and digital certificates. As an administrator, you probably need to manage at least the upper level of keys in the hierarchy shown in Figure 16.1. Each key protects its child keys, which in turn protect their child keys, down through the tree. The one exception is when a password is used to protect a symmetric key or certificate. This is how SQL Server lets users manage their own keys and take responsibility for keeping the key secret.

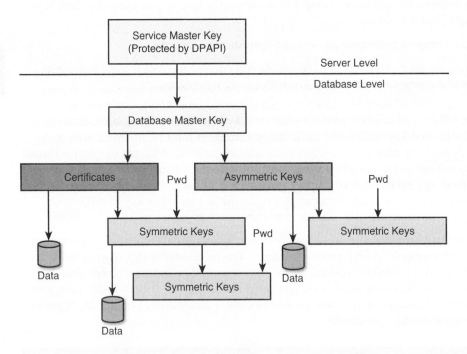

FIGURE 16.1   Key hierarchy in SQL Server 2014.

Each SQL Server instance has its *service master key*. The service master key is the one key that rules them all. It is a symmetric key created automatically during SQL Server installation and is encrypted and protected by the Data Protection API (DPAPI), which is provided by the underlying Windows OS, using the credentials of the SQL Server service account. Protection of this key is critical because if it is compromised, an attacker can eventually decipher every key in the server managed by SQL Server. SQL Server manages the service master key for you, although you can perform maintenance tasks on it to dump it to a file, regenerate it, and restore it from a file. However, most of the time you will not need or want to make any of these changes to the key, although administrators are advised to back up their service master keys in the event of key corruption.

The main purpose of the server master key is to secure system data, such as passwords used in instance-level settings such as linked servers or connection strings. The service master key is also used to secure each of the *database master keys*. Within each database, the database master key serves as the basis for creating certificates or asymmetric keys, which subsequently can be applied to protect data directly or to further extend the encryption hierarchy (for example, by creating symmetric keys). Creation, storage, and other certificate and key management tasks can be handled internally without resorting to features of the operating system or third-party products.

Each database can have a single master key. You must create a database master key before using it by using the CREATE MASTER KEY Transact-SQL statement with a user-supplied password:

```
CREATE MASTER KEY ENCRYPTION BY PASSWORD = 'R@nD0m!T3%t'
```

SQL Server encrypts the database master key using an AES key derived from the password as well as the service master key. The first copy is stored in the database, and the second is stored in the master database. Having the database master key protected by the server master key makes it possible for SQL Server to decrypt the database master key automatically when required. The application or user does not need to open the master key explicitly using the password. This is a major benefit of having the keys protected in the hierarchy.

16

> **NOTE**
>
> Detaching a database with an existing master key and moving it to another server can be an issue. The problem is that the new server's database master key is different from that of the old server. As a result, the server cannot automatically decrypt the database master key. This situation can be circumvented by opening the database master key with the password with which it is encrypted and using the ALTER MASTER KEY statement to encrypt it with the new server's database master key.

When the database master key exists, developers can use it to create any of three types of keys, depending on the type of encryption required:

▶ Asymmetric keys

▶ Symmetric keys

▶ Certificates

TIP

Microsoft recommends against using certificates or asymmetric keys for encrypting data directly. Asymmetric key encryption is many times slower, and the amount of data that you can protect using this mechanism is limited, depending on the key modulus. It is recommended that you protect certificates and asymmetric keys using a password instead of with the database master key.

Extensible Key Management

SQL Server 2014 makes use of Extensible Key Management (EKM) to provide greater key security. EKM enables you to manage your encryption keys via an external provider. This allows for flexibility and choice in encryption providers as well as common key management across your enterprise.

With the growing demand for regulatory compliance and concern for data privacy, organizations are taking advantage of encryption as a way to provide a "defense in depth" solution. As organizations increasingly use encryption and keys to secure their data, key management becomes more complex. Some high security databases use thousands of keys, and you must employ a system to store, retire, and regenerate these keys. This approach is often impractical using only database encryption management tools. As a solution, various hardware vendors provide products to store encryption keys on hardware or software modules. These products also provide a more secure key management solution because the encryption keys do not reside with encryption data. They also move the key management workload from SQL Server to a dedicated key management system.

Extensible key management in SQL Server 2014 also supports the use of Hardware Security Module, which enables the encryption keys used to protect your data to be stored in an off-box device such as a smartcard, USB device, or EKM/HSM module, providing a physical separation of keys from data. SQL Server 2014 Extensible Key Management enables third-party EKM/HSM vendors to register their modules in SQL Server. When registered, SQL Server users can use the encryption keys stored on EKM modules. This enables SQL Server to access the advanced encryption features these modules support such as bulk encryption and decryption, and key management functions such as key aging and key rotation.

SQL Server 2014 Extensible Key Management also provides data protection from database administrators. Data can be encrypted by using encryption keys that only the database user has access to on the external EKM/HSM module.

To summarize, SQL Server 2014 Extensible Key Management provides the following benefits:

▶ An additional authorization check that enables separation of duties between database administration and key management

▶ Improved performance through hardware-based encryption/decryption rather than software-based encryption/decryption

▶ External encryption key generation

▶ Physical separation of data and keys

▶ Encryption key retrieval

▶ External encryption key retention and encryption key rotation

▶ Easier encryption key recovery

▶ Manageable encryption key distribution

▶ Secure encryption key disposal

When possible, it is highly recommended that you use EKM with both database- and column-level encryption for more comprehensive key management and hardware-based cryptography.

Column-Level Encryption

Column-level encryption (sometimes referred to as cell-level encryption) was introduced in Microsoft SQL Server 2005 and is still fully supported in SQL Server 2014. Column-level encryption offers a more granular level of encryption than TDE, allowing you to encrypt specific data columns in the context of specific users.

Column-level encryption is implemented as a series of built-in functions and a key management hierarchy. Implementing column-level encryption is a manual process that requires a re-architecture of the application to call the encryption and decryption functions explicitly when storing or retrieving data. In addition, the tables must be modified to store the encrypted data as `varbinary`. The data is then recast back to the appropriate data type when it is read.

Column-level encryption and decryption are provided by pairs of functions that complement each other:

▶ `EncryptByCert()` and `DecryptByCert()`—Encrypts and decrypts data using the public key of a certificate to generate a private asymmetric key

▶ `EncryptByAsymKey()` and `DecryptByAsymKey()`—Encrypts and decrypts data using an asymmetric key

▶ `EncryptByKey()` and `DecryptByKey()`—Encrypts and decrypts data by using a symmetric key

▶ `EncryptByPassphrase()` and `DecryptByPassphrase()`—Encrypts and decrypts data by using a passphrase to generate a symmetric key

Before you can begin generating keys to encrypt columns, you must first make sure a database master key has been created:

16

```
USE AdventureWorks2012;
GO


--If there is no master key, create one now.
IF NOT EXISTS
    (SELECT * FROM sys.symmetric_keys
            WHERE symmetric_key_id = 101)
    CREATE MASTER KEY ENCRYPTION
        BY PASSWORD = 'Th15i$aS7riN&ofR@nD0m!T3%t'
GO
```

Encrypting Columns Using a Passphrase

As our first example, let's keep things simple and look at how to encrypt a column using a passphrase. To do so, let's look at the Sales.CreditCard table, which currently stores card numbers in cleartext:

```
select top 5 * from Sales.CreditCard
go


/* Result
CreditCardID CardType      CardNumber      ExpMonth ExpYear ModifiedDate
------------ ------------- --------------- -------- ------- ------------
1            SuperiorCard  33332664695310 11        2006    2007-08-30
2            Distinguish   55552127249722 8         2005    2008-01-06
3            ColonialVoice 77778344838353 7         2005    2008-02-15
4            ColonialVoice 77774915718248 7         2006    2007-06-21
5            Vista         11114404600042 4         2005    2007-03-05
*/
```

Credit card numbers really should not be stored in their cleartext form in the database, so to fix this, first create a copy of the Sales.CreditCard table and define the CardNumber_encrypt column as a varbinary(256) so you can store the encrypted credit card numbers in the column (encrypted columns in SQL Server 2014 can be stored only as varbinary values):

```
USE AdventureWorks2012;
GO


select CreditCardID,
       CardType,
       CardNumber_encrypt = CONVERT(varbinary(256), CardNumber),
       ExpMonth,
       ExpYear,
       ModifiedDate
```

```
into Sales.CreditCard_encrypt
from Sales.CreditCard
where 1 = 2
```

Now, you can populate the `CreditCard_encrypt` table with rows from the original `CreditCard` table using the `EncryptByPassPhrase` function to encrypt the credit card numbers as the rows are copied over:

```
declare @passphrase varchar(128)
set @passphrase = 'unencrypted credit card numbers are bad, um-kay'
insert Sales.CreditCard_encrypt (
        CardType,
        CardNumber_encrypt,
        ExpMonth,
        ExpYear,
        ModifiedDate
)
select top 5
        CardType,
        CardNumber_encrypt = EncryptByPassPhrase(@passphrase, CardNumber),
        ExpMonth,
        ExpYear,
        ModifiedDate
from Sales.CreditCard
```

Now, try a query against the `CreditCard_encrypt` table without decrypting the data and see what it returns (note, for display purposes, the values in the `CardNumber_encrypt` column have been truncated):

```
select * from Sales.CreditCard_encrypt
go

/* Result
CreditCardID CardType      CardNumber_encrypt      ExpMonth ExpYear ModifiedDate
------------ ------------- --------------------- -------- ------- -----------
1            SuperiorCard  0x010000007C65089E... 11       2006    2007-08-30
2            Distinguish   0x010000000C624987... 8        2005    2008-01-06
3            ColonialVoice 0x01000000AA8761A0... 7        2005    2008-02-15
4            ColonialVoice 0x010000002C2857CC... 7        2006    2007-06-21
5            Vista         0x0100000095F6730D... 4        2005    2007-03-05
*/
```

In the preceding results, you can see that the credit card numbers have been encrypted as a varbinary value, and no meaningful information can be obtained from this. To view the data in its unencrypted form, you need to use the `DecryptByPassPhrase` function and convert the value back to an `nvarchar(25)`:

```
declare @passphrase varchar(128)
set @passphrase = 'unencrypted credit card numbers are bad, um-kay'
select CreditCardID,
       CardType,
       CardNumber = convert(nvarchar(25), DecryptByPassPhrase(@passphrase,
 CardNumber_encrypt)),
       ExpMonth,
       ExpYear,
       ModifiedDate
from Sales.CreditCard_encrypt
GO


/* Result
CreditCardID  CardType       CardNumber      ExpMonth ExpYear ModifiedDate
------------  -------------  --------------- -------- ---------------------

1             SuperiorCard   33332664695310 11        2006    2007-08-30
2             Distinguish    55552127249722 8         2005    2008-01-06
3             ColonialVoice  77778344838353 7         2005    2008-02-15
4             ColonialVoice  77774915718248 7         2006    2007-06-21
5             Vista          11114404600042 4         2005    2007-03-05
*/
```

So that's a simple example showing how to encrypt a column. You may be thinking, however, using a passphrase like this probably isn't very secure. The passphrase used to encrypt the column would have to be shared with all users and applications that need to store or retrieve data in the CreditCard_encrypt table. A shared passphrase like this can be easily compromised, and then the data is visible to anyone who can gain access to the database. It is usually more secure to encrypt data using a symmetric key or certificate.

Encrypting Columns Using a Certificate

One solution to the problem of encrypting using a shared passphrase is to encrypt the data using a certificate. A primary benefit of certificates is that they relieve hosts of the need to maintain a set of passwords for individual subjects. Instead, the host merely establishes trust in a certificate issuer, which may then sign an unlimited number of certificates.

Certificates can be created within SQL Server 2014 using the CREATE CERTIFICATE command. The certificate created is a database-level securable that follows the X.509 standard and supports X.509 V1 fields. The CREATE CERTIFICATE command can load a certificate from a file or assembly, or it can also generate a key pair and create a self-signed certificate. The ENCRYPTION BY PASSWORD option is not required; the private key of the certificate is encrypted using the database master key. When the private key is encrypted using the database master key, you do not have to specify a decryption password when retrieving the data using the certificate.

The first step is to create the certificate with the CREATE CERTIFICATE command:

```
USE AdventureWorks2012;
CREATE CERTIFICATE BillingDept01
    WITH SUBJECT = 'Credit Card Billing'
GO
```

After you create the certificate, the next step is to create a symmetric key that will be encrypted by the certificate. You can use many different algorithms for encrypting keys. The supported encryption algorithms for the symmetric key are DES, TRIPLE_DES, RC2, RC4, RC4_128, DESX, AES_128, AES_192, and AES_256. The following code creates a symmetric key using the AES_256 encryption algorithm and encrypts it using the BillingDept01 certificate:

```
USE AdventureWorks2012;
CREATE SYMMETRIC KEY BillingKey2014 WITH ALGORITHM = AES_256
    ENCRYPTION BY CERTIFICATE BillingDept01;
GO
```

Now empty out the rows inserted previously in the CreditCard_encrypt table using the PassPhrase encryption method by truncating it:

```
USE AdventureWorks2012;
Truncate table Sales.CreditCard_encrypt
```

Next reinsert rows from the CreditCard table, this time using the symmetric key associated with the certificate to encrypt the data using the EncryptByKey function. The EncryptByKey function requires the GUID of the symmetric key as the first parameter. You can look up this identifier by running a query against the sys.symmetric_keys table or simply use the KEY_GUID() function, as in this example:

```
USE AdventureWorks2012;
-- First, decrypt the key using the BillingDept01 certificate
OPEN SYMMETRIC KEY BillingKey2014
    DECRYPTION BY CERTIFICATE BillingDept01
-- Now, insert the rows using the symmetric key
-- encrypted by the certificate
insert Sales.CreditCard_encrypt (
    CardType,
    CardNumber_encrypt,
    ExpMonth,
    ExpYear,
    ModifiedDate
)
select top 5
    CardType,
    CardNumber_encrypt = EncryptByKey(KEY_GUID('BillingKey2014'),
                                       CardNumber),
```

16

```
        ExpMonth,
        ExpYear,
        ModifiedDate
from Sales.CreditCard
```

If you examine the contents of the `CreditCard_encrypt` table, you can see that they have been encrypted:

```
select * from Sales.CreditCard_encrypt
go
```

```
/* Result
CreditCardID CardType        CardNumber            ExpMonth ExpYear ModifiedDate
------------ --------------- --------------------- -------- ------- ------------

1            SuperiorCar     0x00570501EC516D4D 11          2006    2007-08-30
2            Distinguish     0x00570501EC516D4D 8           2005    2008-01-06
3            ColonialVoice   0x00570501EC516D4D 7           2005    2008-02-15
4            ColonialVoice   0x00570501EC516D4D 7           2006    2007-06-21
5            Vista           0x00570501EC516D4D 4           2005    2007-03-05
*/
```

Now, an authorized user that specifies the appropriate certificate can retrieve the data by using `DecryptByKey` function:

```
USE AdventureWorks2012;
OPEN SYMMETRIC KEY BillingKey2014
    DECRYPTION BY CERTIFICATE BillingDept01
select CardType,
        CardNumber = convert(nvarchar(25), DecryptByKey(CardNumber_encrypt)),
        ExpMonth,
        ExpYear,
        ModifiedDate
from Sales.CreditCard_encrypt
go
```

```
/* Result
CreditCardID CardType        CardNumber       ExpMonth ExpYear ModifiedDate
------------ --------------- --------------- -------- ------- -----------

1            SuperiorCard    33332664695310 11        2006    2007-08-30
2            Distinguish     55552127249722 8         2005    2008-01-06
3            ColonialVoice   77778344838353 7         2005    2008-02-15
4            ColonialVoice   77774915718248 7         2006    2007-06-21
5            Vista           11114404600042 4         2005    2007-03-05
*/
```

When you are done using a key, it is good practice to close the key using the CLOSE SYMMETRIC KEY statement:

```
CLOSE SYMMETRIC KEY BillingKey2014
```

The keys defined in a database can be viewed through the system catalog table, sys.symmetric_keys:

```
select name,
       pvt_key_encryption_type,
       issuer_name,
       subject,
       expiry_date = CAST(expiry_date as DATE),
       start_date = CAST(start_date as DATE)
  from sys.certificates
go


/* Result
name           pvt_key_encryption_type issuer_name
subject                  expiry_date start_date
------------- --------------------- -------------------
------------------- ----------- ----------
BillingDept01 MK                     Credit Card Billing
Credit Card Billing 2015-11-01      2014-11-01
*/
```

The certificates defined in a database can be viewed through the system catalog tables, sys.certificates:

```
select name,
       key_length,
       key_algorithm,
       algorithm_desc,
       create_date = CAST(create_date as DATE),
       modify_date = CAST(create_date as DATE),
       key_guid
    from sys.symmetric_keys
go


/* Result
name                     key_length  key_algorithm algorithm_desc create_date
modify_date key_guid
----------------------- ----------- ------------- -------------- ----------- ------
##MS_DatabaseMasterKey## 256         A3            AES_256        2014-11-01 2014-
11-01  ED812900-C36B-4FA2-A818-5BF622C1EE9B
BillingKey2014           256         A3            AES_256        2014-11-01 2014-
11-01  331E4100-570F-496D-9906-B0B9E001219D
*/
```

16

If the usage of the key and certificate are no longer needed, they should be dropped from the database:

```
DROP SYMMETRIC KEY BillingKey2014
DROP CERTIFICATE BillingDept01
```

> **NOTE**
>
> There is a lot more information about column-level encryption and key management that could be discussed at this point, but such discussion would be beyond the scope of this chapter; our intent here is to merely introduce the concepts of data encryption. For more information on column-level encryption, refer to SQL Server 2014 Books Online.

Transparent Data Encryption

As mentioned previously, transparent data encryption (TDE) is available in SQL Server 2014. TDE allows an entire database to be encrypted. Unlike column-level encryption, in TDE the encryption and decryption of data is performed automatically by the Database Engine, and this is fully transparent to the end user and applications. No changes to the database or applications are needed. Consequently, TDE is the simpler choice when bulk encryption of data is required to meet regulatory compliance or corporate data security standards.

The encryption of a database using TDE helps prevent the unauthorized access of data in the scenario in which physical media or backups have been lost or stolen. Transparent data encryption uses a database encryption key (DEK) for encrypting the database. The DEK is stored in the database boot record and is secured by a certificate stored in the master database. The database master key is protected by the service master key, which is in turn protected by the Data Protection API. When TDE is enabled on a database, attaching data files to another SQL Server instance or the restoring of a backup to another SQL Server instance is not permitted until the certificate that was used to secure the DEK is available.

> **NOTE**
>
> Optionally, the DEK can be secured by an asymmetric key that resides in a Hardware Security Module with the support of Extensible Key Management. The private key of the certificate is encrypted with the database master key that is a symmetric key, which is usually protected with a strong password.

For example, if a hard drive that contains database files is stolen, without TDE, those database files can be attached in another SQL Server instance, thus allowing access to the nonencrypted data in those files. With TDE, the data and log files are automatically encrypted, and the data within these files cannot be accessed without an encryption key. Additionally, backups of databases that have TDE enabled are also encrypted automatically. We're all familiar with stories about how backup tapes containing sensitive information have been lost or stolen. With TDE, the data in the backup files is completely useless without also having access to the key used to encrypt that data.

The encryption and decryption of data with TDE are performed at the page level as data moves between the buffer pool and disk. Data residing in the buffer pools is not encrypted. TDE's specific purpose is to protect data at rest by encrypting the physical files of the database, rather than the data itself. These physical files include the database files (.mdf and .ndf), transaction log file (.ldf), and backup files (.bak). Data pages are encrypted as they are written from the buffer pool to the database files on disk. Conversely, the data is decrypted at the page level when the data is read in from the files on disk into the buffer pool. The encryption and decryption are done using a background process transparent to the database user. Although additional CPU resources are required to implement TDE, overall, this approach offers much better performance than column-level encryption. According to Microsoft, the performance hit averages only about 3% to 5%.

TDE supports several different encryption options, such as AES with 128-bit, 192-bit, or 256-bit keys or 3 Key Triple DES. You can choose the encryption option when implementing TDE.

Implementing Transparent Data Encryption

Like many encryption scenarios, TDE is dependent on an encryption key. The TDE database encryption key is a symmetric key that secures the encrypted database. The DEK is protected using a certificate stored in the master database of the SQL Server instance where the encrypted database is installed.

Implementing TDE for a specific database is accomplished by following these steps:

▶ Create a master key.

▶ Create or obtain a certificate protected by the master key.

▶ Create a database encryption key and protect it by the certificate.

▶ Configure the database to use encryption.

Listing 16.1 demonstrates the commands needed to encrypt the AdventureWorks2012 database, including the creation of a master key, certificate, and DEK protected by the certificate.

LISTING 16.1   Encrypting the AdventureWorks2012 Database

```
USE master;
GO

--Create the master key which is stored in the master database
CREATE MASTER KEY ENCRYPTION BY PASSWORD = 'Mystr0ngp@ssword$$';
GO
```

```
-- Create a certificate that is also stored in the master
-- database. This certificate will be used to encrypt a user database
CREATE CERTIFICATE MyCertificate
 with SUBJECT = 'Certificate stored in Master Db'
GO


-- Create a Database Encryption Key (DEK) that is based
-- on the previously created certificate
-- The DEK is stored in the user database
USE AdventureWorks2012
GO
CREATE DATABASE ENCRYPTION KEY
WITH ALGORITHM = AES_256
ENCRYPTION BY SERVER CERTIFICATE MyCertificate
GO


-- Turn the encryption on for the AdventureWorks2012
ALTER DATABASE AdventureWorks2012
SET ENCRYPTION ON
GO
```

After you enable TDE, you might want to monitor the progress of the encryption. This can be done by running the following query:

```
SELECT DBName = DB_NAME(database_id), encryption_state
FROM sys.dm_database_encryption_keys ;
GO


/* Result
DBName                encryption_state
------------------ ----------------
tempdb                     3
AdventureWorks2012         2
*/
```

This query returns the database encryption state. A database encryption state of 2 means that encryption has begun, and an encryption state of 3 indicates that encryption has completed. When the tempdb database and user database you are encrypting reach a state of 3, the entire user database and tempdb database are encrypted.

When TDE is enabled for a given database, encryption is applied to a variety of files related to the database, including the following:

- **Database Data Files**—All data files that contain the database data are encrypted. These files typically have the extension .mdf or .ndf.

- **Database Log Files**—The transaction log files are encrypted so that no clear text is visible in the files. These files typically have the extension .ldf.

▶ **Database Backups**—All database backups, including full, differential, and log, are encrypted.

▶ **Tempdb**—If any databases on a server are encrypted with TDE, the `tempdb` database is also encrypted so that any data from an encrypted database that is inserted into work tables or temporary tables remains encrypted.

In addition to these files, you can also manually enable TDE on the distribution and subscriber database involved in replication. This encrypts a portion of data involved in replication, but there are still some unencrypted files. Snapshots from snapshot replication as well as the initial distribution of data for transactional and merge replication are not encrypted.

Managing TDE in SSMS

You can also view and manage transparent data encryption in SQL Server Management Studio. To do so, right-click on the database in the Object Explorer for which you want to configure TDE and select Tasks; then select Manage Database Encryption. If you are setting up the initial configuration for TDE in a database, you see a dialog like that shown in Figure 16.2.

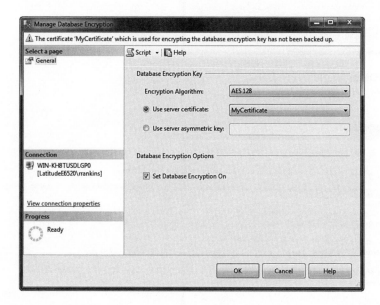

FIGURE 16.2   Enabling TDE in SSMS.

The options available in this dialog correspond to commands shown in Listing 16.1. You specify the encryption algorithm to be used and the server certificate used to protect the database encryption key. When you are ready to enable TDE for the database, put a check-mark in the Set Database Encryption On check box.

If TDE is already enabled for a database, the dialog changes to provide you with options to re-encrypt the database encryption key and to regenerate the DEK using a different encryption algorithm. You can also enable/disable database encryption (see Figure 16.3). A second page displays the current TDE properties and encryption state of the database (see Figure 16.4).

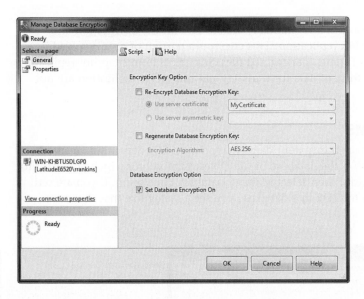

FIGURE 16.3   Modifying TDE properties in SSMS.

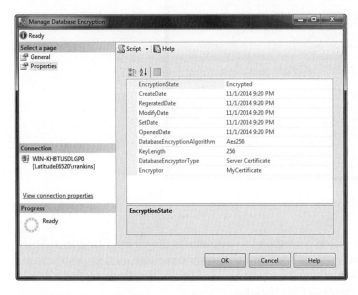

FIGURE 16.4   Viewing TDE properties in SSMS.

Backing Up TDE Certificates and Keys

The most important issue to consider when using TDE is that you must back up and retain the certificate and private key associated with the encryption. If these things are lost or unavailable, you are not able to restore or attach the encrypted database files on another server. The following warning message displayed after creating a certificate drives home this point:

```
Warning: The certificate used for encrypting the database
encryption key has not been backed up. You should immediately
back up the certificate and the private key associated with the
certificate. If the certificate ever becomes unavailable or if you
must restore or attach the database on another server, you must have
backups of both the certificate and the private key or you will not
be able to open the database.
Backup up the certificate and private key
```

Backing up the certificate, private key, and master key for the server is relatively straight-forward. An example of backing up the master key is shown in the following SQL statement:

```
BACKUP MASTER KEY TO FILE = 'c:\mssql\backup\masterkey'
    ENCRYPTION BY PASSWORD = 'S0mekeyb@ckuppassword$$'
```

Backing up the certificate and associated private key also uses the BACKUP command. The following example backs up the certificate created in Listing 16.1:

```
USE MASTER;
GO
BACKUP CERTIFICATE MyCertificate TO FILE = 'c:\mssql\backup\MyCertificate'
    WITH PRIVATE KEY ( FILE = 'c:\mssql\backup\MyCertificatePrivateKey' ,
    ENCRYPTION BY PASSWORD = 'S0mecertb@ckuppassword$$' );
```

If you want to restore a database backup on another server instance, a master key for the server must exist. If one does not exist, you can create one by using the CREATE MASTER KEY ENCRYPTION syntax. After creating the master key, you are able to create the TDE certificate from a backup of the certificate from the original SQL Server instance, as shown in the following example:

```
CREATE CERTIFICATE MyCertificate
    FROM FILE = 'd:\sql2014\backup\MyCertificate'
    WITH PRIVATE KEY (FILE = 'd:\sql2014\backup\MyCertificatePrivateKey',
    DECRYPTION BY PASSWORD = 'S0mecertb@ckuppassword$$')
```

16

After the certificate is restored on the other server instance, you can restore the encrypted database backup. At this point, the restore can be performed just as you would restore any unencrypted database backup. The restored database is also encrypted and behaves like the original TDE database.

TDE is a relatively simple and effective way to encrypt and protect your data. Other encryption methods that exist with SQL Server can protect different elements of your database. Encryption can be applied to columns of data, an entire table, as well as the communication that occurs between databases and the clients that access them. The level of encryption and need to use it depend on the type of data you are securing.

The Limitations of TDE

Although TDE offers many benefits over column-level encryption, it has some of its own limitations, which are important to consider. They include

▶ TDE is not granular like column-level encryption. The entire database is encrypted, but only on disk. Sensitive data such as Social Security numbers or credit card numbers can be seen by anyone who has permission to access those columns. TDE also does not prevent DBAs from viewing any data in the database.

▶ TDE does not protect communications between client applications and SQL Server. Network encryption methods should be used to protect sensitive data flowing over the network.

▶ FILESTREAM data is not encrypted.

▶ When any one database on a SQL Server instance has TDE enabled, the `tempdb` database is also automatically encrypted. This can affect performance for both encrypted and nonencrypted databases running on the same instance.

▶ Encrypted data compresses significantly less than equivalent unencrypted data. If TDE is used to encrypt a database, backup compression will not be able to significantly compress the backup. For this reason, using TDE and backup compression together is not recommended.

Column-Level Encryption Versus Transparent Data Encryption

So is column-level encryption or transparent data encryption the right solution for your systems? Both column-level encryption and transparent data encryption provide a means of obfuscating sensitive data to protect it from unauthorized access. However, they do so in different ways.

TDE prevents the unauthorized access of the contents of the database files and backups but does not protect sensitive data within the database from being viewed by authorized users or database administrators. Column-level encryption provides more granular control over the data being encrypted but is not transparent to your applications.

Table 16.1 lists the similarities and differences between column-level encryption and TDE.

TABLE 16.1   Comparison of Column-Level Encryption and Transparent Data Encryption

Features/Limitations	Column-Level Encryption	Transparent Data Encryption
Data is encrypted on disk and backups	Yes	Yes
Supports EKM/HSM modules	Yes	Yes
Data level of encryption	Granular, at the column level	Encrypts the entire database only
User level of encryption	Encrypted data can be restricted at the user level on a need-to-know basis	Any user with sufficient database access permissions can view encrypted data
Impact on applications	Database applications need to be modified	Completely transparent to applications and end users
Indexing of encrypted data	Encrypted columns cannot be indexed	No restrictions on indexes
Performance impact	May be significant depending on the type of encryption key used	Small impact on performance (3–5%)

For some organizations, you might want to consider implementing both column-level encryption along with TDE for a database. Although this combination is more complex to set up and administer, it offers greater security and encryption granularity than does either method used alone. TDE protects the database files and backups from unauthorized access, whereas column-level encryption protects sensitive data within the database from being accessed by authorized users, including DBAs. Implementing TDE in conjunction with column-level encryption provides a layered approach to data security, which enhances its effectiveness.

The main disadvantage to implementing column-level encryption is that it isn't transparent to the end-user applications. In addition to requiring changes to the database schema, it also requires changes in the applications to include the proper function calls to encrypt and decrypt the data as it is stored and retrieved. Another issue with column-level encryption is that you cannot index encrypted columns, nor can you generate statistics on the encrypted columns. This can affect query performance because search arguments that reference encrypted columns cannot be optimized. For this reason, typically only the most sensitive columns of a table that do not need to be indexed are encrypted.

16

Summary

Chapter 15 discussed methods to secure and control the access to your SQL Server data via login and user security to prevent unauthorized users from accessing your SQL Server instances and databases. Column-level encryption, as discussed here, takes these protections a step further by preventing authorized users, such as your database or server administrators, from viewing sensitive data within a database. Transparent data encryption protects all your data from being accessed by unauthorized users in the event that your database files or backups are lost or stolen.

In the next chapter, "Managing Linked Servers," we continue our discussion of SQL Server Administration topics with an overview of setting up and managing Linked Servers.

CHAPTER 17

Managing Linked Servers

As your databases grow in size, complexity, or geographic distribution, you might need to spread your data across multiple servers and locations. You might also need to bring together disparate data that is not all on one server or is not all in the same type of data container (Access, Excel, text files, and other RDBMSs) to fulfill a business need. SQL Server has long had the capability to perform server-to-server communication even when they are different data containers (like Excel, Access, and so on). This can be done using the linked server capabilities. In versions of SQL Server prior to 7.0, the only option was to use Remote Procedure Calls (RPC) and remote servers. An RPC was the execution of a stored procedure on a local server that actually resides on a remote server. Linked servers to the rescue! As linked server capabilities were introduced (with SQL Server 7.0 onward), using the remote servers approach became fairly obsolete because of their inherent limitations.

SQL Server 2014 provides the capability to link together servers (of the same or different data containers), allowing you to join information together across servers or simply access data on another server. Access to the remote tables can be to another SQL Server or to any other data source with an OLE DB provider. You can also define distributed partitioned views that can pull data together from multiple servers into a single view. For end-user queries that use these views, it appears as if the data is coming from a single local table. For more information on distributed partitioned views, see Chapter 24, "Creating and Managing Views."

This chapter provides an overview of linked servers in SQL Server 2014. Keep in mind that Microsoft is also telling folks to convert any remote server implementations they currently have to linked server implementations. Deprecating remote servers was also announced in SQL Server 2005; however, due to the outcry from many customers, it was not dropped in SQL Server 2008 R2.

What's New in Managing Linked Servers

With SQL Server 2014, there are no significant changes to the linked servers' capabilities. Of the few changes for linked servers, the following are the most significant:

▶ Remote servers are officially deprecated, and this means system stored procedures such as `sp_addserver`, `sp_remoteoption`, `sp_helpremotelogin`, and `sp_addremotelogin` are gone.

▶ System variable `@@REMSERVER` and server-wide settings such as `SET REMOTE_PROC_TRANSACTIONS` are also gone.

▶ More DATA providers are now certified with Microsoft. This includes flat files, DB2, Informix, and Oracle providers used with linked servers.

Linked Servers

Linked servers enable SQL Server–based applications to include most any other type of data source to be part of a SQL statement execution, including being able to directly reference remote SQL servers (as shown in Figure 17.1). They also make it possible to issue distributed queries, updates, deletes, inserts, commands, and full transactions on heterogeneous data sources across your entire company (network). SQL Server essentially acts as the master query manager. Then, via OLE DB providers and OLE DB data sources, any compliant data source is easily referenced from any valid SQL statement or command. For each data source, either they are directly referenced, or SQL Server creates provider-specific sub-queries issued to a specialized provider. This is very close to being a federated data management capability across most heterogeneous data sources.

Unlike remote servers, linked servers have two simple setup steps:

1. Define the remote (linked) server on the local server.

2. Define the method for mapping remote logins on the local server.

All linked server configurations are performed on the local server. The mapping for the local user to the remote user is stored in the local SQL Server database. In fact, you don't need to configure anything in the remote database. Using linked servers also allows SQL Server to use OLE DB to link to many data sources other than just SQL Server.

OLE DB is an API that allows COM/.NET applications to work with databases as well as other data sources, such as text files and spreadsheets. This capability lets SQL Server have access to a vast amount of different types of data as if these other data sources were local SQL Server tables or views. This is extremely powerful.

Linked servers also allow distributed queries and transactions.

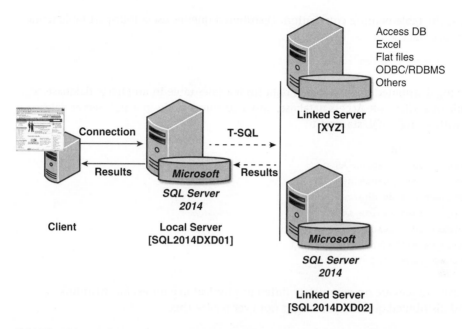

FIGURE 17.1 A remote server of most any kind can be accessed through the local server via linked servers. The client has to maintain only a single connection to the local server.

TRULY A LINKED SERVER

Keep in mind that when you define linked servers, SQL Server really keeps these data resources linked in many ways. Most importantly, it keeps the schema definitions linked. In other words, if the schema of a remote table on a linked server changes, any server that has links to it also knows the change (that is, gets the change). Even when the linked server's schema comes from something such as Excel, if you change the Excel spreadsheet in any way that change is automatically reflected back at the local SQL Server that has defined that Excel spreadsheet within their linked server connection. This is extremely significant from a metadata and schema integrity point of view. This is what is meant by "completely linked."

Distributed Queries

Distributed queries access data stored in OLE DB data sources. SQL Server treats these data sources as if they contained SQL Server tables. Basically, via a provider such as OLE DB, the data source is put in terms of recordsets. Recordsets are the way SQL Server needs to see any data. The Microsoft SQL Native Client OLE DB provider (with PROGID sqlncli) is the official OLE DB provider for SQL Server 2014. You can view or manipulate data through this provider by using the same basic Data Manipulation Language (DML) syntax as for T-SQL for SQL Server (SELECT, INSERT, UPDATE, or DELETE statements). The main difference is the table-naming convention. Distributed queries use a four-part table name syntax for each data source as follows:

```
linked_server_name.catalog.schema.object_name
```

The following distributed query accesses data from a sales table in an Oracle database, a region table in a Microsoft Access database, and a customer table in a SQL Server database—all with a single SQL statement:

```
SELECT s.sales_amount
FROM access_server...region AS r,
oracle_server..sales_owner.sale AS s,
sql_server.customer_db.dbo.customer AS c
where r.region_id=s.region_id
and s.customer_id=c.customer_id
and r.region_name='Southwest'
and c.customer_name='ABC Steel'
```

All these data sources are on completely different physical machines. But with linked servers and distributed queries, you might not ever realize this.

Distributed Transactions

With SQL Server distributed transaction coordinator, it is possible to manipulate data from several different data sources in a single transaction. Distributed transactions are supported if the OLE DB provider has built in the XA transactional functionality. For example, suppose two banks decide to merge. The first bank (let's call it OraBank) stores all checking and savings accounts in an Oracle database. The second bank (let's call it SqlBank) stores all checking and savings accounts in a SQL Server 2014 database. A customer has a checking account with OraBank and a savings account with SqlBank. What would happen if the customer wanted to transfer $100 from the savings account to the checking account? You can handle this task by using the following code while maintaining transactional consistency:

```
BEGIN DISTRIBUTED TRANSACTION
-- One hundred dollars is subtracted from the savings account.
UPDATE oracle_server..savings_owner.savings_table
  SET account_balance = account_balance - 100
WHERE account_number = 12345
-- One hundred dollars is added to the checking account.
UPDATE sql_server.checking_db.dbo.checking_table
  SET account_balance = account_balance + 100
WHERE account_number = 98765
COMMIT TRANSACTION;
```

The transaction is either committed or rolled back on both databases.

Adding, Dropping, and Configuring Linked Servers

The next few sections show how to add, drop, and configure linked servers through system stored procedures. All these configuration options can also be done very easily with SQL Server Management Studio. The following sections occasionally describe that capability but focus on the SQL commands method because you will usually use this method in real-life production systems. But before we look at an example of a local server connecting to a linked server, let's first set up a database in another SQL Server instance that will be the target of our linked server examples, create a sample table, and create a stored procedure to execute on the linked server. You can grab the `CustomersPlusSQLTable.sql` SQL script for this purpose in the sample files and code listings folder for this book on the Web. The `CustomersPlusSQLTable.sql` script contains a `create database` statement that creates a database named `UnleashedRemoteDB`, creates a table named `CustomersPlus` in this database, and populates the table with about 90 rows of test data. You should go ahead and grab the script now and execute it on the target remote server (`SQL2014DXD02` in this example). You will need to edit the `create database` statement (`FILENAME` parameter) for your own environment. Now we are ready to get going.

sp_addlinkedserver

Before you can access an external data source through SQL Server, it must be registered inside the database as a linked server. Essentially, you must capture (register) the connection information and specific data source information within SQL Server. After it is registered, the data source can simply be referenced within the SQL statement by a single logical name. You use the `sp_addlinkedserver` stored procedure for this registering purpose. Only users with the sysadmin or setupadmin fixed server roles can run this procedure.

SQL Server 2014 ships with a number of OLE DB providers, including providers for Oracle, DB2, Informix, Access, and other SQL Server 6.5/7.0/2000/2005/2008 R2/2012 databases, as well as databases that can be reached through ODBC. Others include the following:

OLE DB Provider	Value (PROGID)
SQL Server	SQLNCLI (OLE DB provider)
SQL Server	SQLOLEDB
Access DB/Jet	Microsoft.Jet.OLEDB.4.0 (32-bit only)
Excel spreadsheets	Microsoft.Jet.OLEDB.4.0 (32-bit only)
ODBC	MSDASQL
DB2	DB2OLEDB
Oracle	MSDAORA (32-bit only)
Oracle, Version 8 or later	OraOLEDB.Oracle (32-bit only)
File system	MSIDXS (through Indexing Service)

17

Microsoft puts each of these providers through extensive testing to certify them. We have found that sometimes a provider isn't available on the 64-bit version of SQL Server 2014 yet. So as a precaution, check the list of 64-bit providers before you upgrade your SQL Server to the 2014 64-bit version. If you are not using a Microsoft-certified provider, however, you might still be able to use that provider if it is compliant with the OLE DB provider specifications.

OLE DB Provider	Value
SQL Server	Network name of the SQL Server
Access DB/Jet	Full pathname to the file
Excel spreadsheet	Full pathname to spreadsheets
ODBC	System DSN or ODBC connection string
Oracle	SQL*Net alias
Oracle, Version 8 or later	Alias for the database
DB2	Catalog name of the database
File System	Indexing Service catalog name (Indexing Service)

> **TIP**
>
> When a linked server is created using `sp_addlinkedserver`, a default self-mapping is added for all local logins. This means that for non–SQL Server providers, SQL Server authenticated logins may be able to gain access to the provider under the SQL Server service account. If you want, you can issue the `sp_droplinkedsrvlogin` command to remove these mappings.

Figure 17.2 depicts the overall technical architecture of what is being enabled via linked servers and providers. There is a SQL Server 2014 side set of provider DLLs, along with a client-side provider that communicates directly with the data sources. Clients usually connect to SQL Server 2014 via the native SQLNCLI provider (OLE DB) or via the ODBC provider.

This provider architecture allows data sources to be accessed from within SQL Server with the highest degree of efficiency and integrity possible.

Some of the arguments for `sp_addlinkedserver` are needed only for certain OLE DB providers. Because of the number of different options and settings available, you should always double-check the documentation for the OLE DB provider to determine exactly which arguments must be provided and what strings are to be specified. Following is the `sp_addlinkedserver` procedure:

```
sp_addlinkedserver [@server =] 'server'
    [, [@srvproduct =] 'product_name']
    [, [@provider =] 'provider_name']
    [, [@datasrc =] 'data_source']
```

```
[, [@location =] 'location']
[, [@provstr =] 'provider_string']
[, [@catalog =] 'catalog']
```

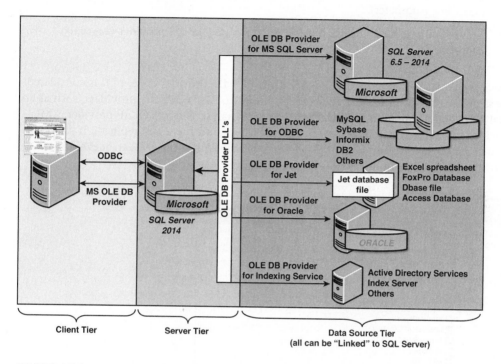

FIGURE 17.2   Linked servers provider architecture.

Following are the elements of this syntax:

▶ **server**—The name of the linked server that will be added (@server parameter).

▶ **product_name**—The product name of the OLE DB provider (@srvproduct parameter). If this argument is set to 'SQL Server', only the @server argument is required. For all other OLE DB providers delivered with SQL Server, you can ignore this parameter.

▶ **provider_name**—The unique programmatic identifier (PROGID). This value must match the PROGID in the Registry for the particular OLE DB provider (@provider parameter). The following are the OLE DB providers delivered with SQL Server and the corresponding values for the provider_name argument:

▶ **data_source**—A data source that points to the particular version of the OLE DB source (@datasrc parameter). For example, for setting up an Access linked server, this argument holds the path to the file. For setting up a SQL Server linked server, this argument holds the machine name of the linked SQL Server. Following are the OLE DB providers delivered with SQL Server and the corresponding values for this argument:

▶ `location`—The location string, possibly used by the OLE DB provider (`@location` parameter).

▶ `provider_string`—The connection string, possibly used by the OLE DB provider (`@provstr` parameter).

▶ `catalog`—The catalog string, possibly used by the OLE DB provider (`@catalog` parameter).

The `SQLNCLI` native SQL provider uses the same OLE DB provider code, so it is considered the same provider as `SQLOLEDB`. There are also many other "certified" providers, such as an Analysis Services data mining model provider, an Analysis Services OLAP provider, XML providers, SSIS (DTS) providers, PostgreSQL providers, and even data replication providers. Figure 17.3 shows the entire list of providers available within the `Linked Servers` node of SQL Server Management Studio (32-bit providers).

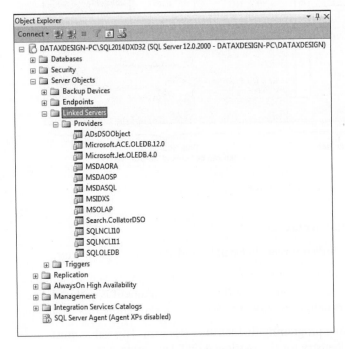

FIGURE 17.3   Linked server 32-bit providers supplied by Microsoft with SQL Server 2014.

The following example adds an Oracle linked server called `'ORACLE_DATABASE'` that connects to the database specified by the SQL*Net string `'my_sqlnet_connect_string'`:

```
EXEC sp_addlinkedserver @server='ORACLE_DATABASE',
@srvproduct='Oracle', @provider='MSDAORA',
@datasrc='my_sqlnet_connect_string'
```

The next example creates a linked server reference for an Access database called
`CustomersPlus.mdb`. As you can see in Figure 17.4, this Microsoft Access database is an
Access 2010 file format database.

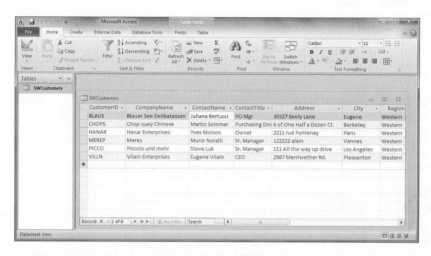

FIGURE 17.4   The `CustomersPlus.mdb` Microsoft Access database.

The following example adds an Access database linked server entry called `'ACCESS_
DATABASE_CUSTOMERS'` that establishes a connection to the database `'CustomersPlus.mdb'`
stored in the `C:\SQL2014DB` directory (or any local directory):

```
EXECUTE sp_addlinkedserver @server='ACCESS_DATABASE_CUSTOMERS',
  @srvproduct='Access',
  @provider='Microsoft.Jet.OLEDB.4.0',
  @datasrc='C:\SQL2014DB\CustomersPlus.mdb'
```

The `CustomersPlus.mdb` Access database is available in the Sample Files and Code Listings
folder for this book on the Web. For this example, download this Access database file
onto the same server machine on which you have SQL Server installed. The Microsoft
Access client provider also needs to be present on this machine (which it will be if you
have installed Microsoft Office on the system). Once you run the `sp_addlinkedserver`
statement, you will be able to reference this linked server directly from a SQL statement.
`sp_addlinkedserver` and all other SQL statements for this linked server set of examples are
also in the sample files and code listings folder for this book on the Web in the script file
`LinkedServerSQL.sql`. Here is a small sample of SQL code that selects all values from this
Access database linked server entry:

```
SELECT CustomerID, ContactName, City, Country
FROM ACCESS_DATABASE_CUSTOMERS...SWCustomers
ORDER BY ContactName
Go
```

```
CustID ContactName           City        Country
------ -------------------- ---------- ---------------
VILLN  Eugene Vilain        Pleasanton  USA
BLAUS  Juliana Bertucci     Eugene      USA
CHOPS  Martin Sommer        Berkeley    USA
MEREP  Munir Noralli        Vannes      FRANCE
PICCO  Steve Luk            Los Angeles USA
HANAR  Yves Moison          Paris       FRANCE

(6 row(s) affected)
```

Note that you can see the fully qualified link server reference as the table name.

Here's an example that adds a "SQL Server" linked server that points to the `'DATAXDESIGN-PC\SQL2014DXD02'` machine and a specific SQL Server instance:

```
EXECUTE sp_addlinkedserver @server='DATAXDESIGN\SQL2014DXD02',
@srvproduct='SQL Server'
```

In the code samples for this chapter, you can quickly create a test database and sample table that correspond to these examples. Go ahead and grab these now and create them (in the file named CustomersPlusSQLTable.sql).

Then you select data from a table on that linked server:

```
---------------------------------------------------
-- Selecting data from the Linked Server directly --
---------------------------------------------------
SELECT TOP 10
       [CustomerID]
     , [ContactName]
     ,sum([YTDBusiness]) as 'YTD Sales'
  FROM [DATAXDESIGN-PC\SQL2014DXD02].[UnleashedRemoteDB].[dbo].[CustomersPlus]
GROUP BY [CustomerID]
         , [ContactName]
ORDER BY 3 desc
go
CustomerID   ContactName                                  YTD Sales
----------   ------------------------------------------   -------------
BERTU        Juliana Bertucci                             200039.80
QUICK        Horst Kloss                                  117483.39
SAVEA        Jose Pavarotti                               115673.39
ERNSH        Roland Mendel                                113236.68
HUNGO        Patricia McKenna                              57317.39
RATTC        Paula Wilson                                  52245.90
HANAR        Mario Pontes                                  34101.15
```

```
FOLKO       PJ Bertucci                                 32555.55
MEREP       Jean Fresniére                              32203.90
KOENE       Philip Cramer                               31745.75

(10 row(s) affected)
```

This example adds an Excel 8.0 spreadsheet as a linked server:

```
/* Set up of an Excel linked server */
EXEC sp_addlinkedserver
    'ExcelSW',     /* linked server name you want to use*/
    'Jet Excel',   /* product name - can be anything */
    'Microsoft.Jet.OLEDB.4.0', /* OLE provider name */
    'c:\SQL2014DB\SWCustomers.xls',  /* datasource name */
    NULL,  /* location not needed in this case */
    'Excel 8.0',  /* Provider string if needed */
    NULL    /* catalog name if needed */
go
```

This next example adds an ODBC data source as a linked server called 'ODBC_with_DATA_ SOURCE'. The ODBC connection string must be registered on the local server to use this linked server:

```
EXEC sp_addlinkedserver
  @server='ODBC_with_DATA_SOURCE',
  @srvproduct='ODBC',
  @provider='MSDASQL',
  @datasrc='My_ODBC_connection_string'
```

This example adds an ODBC data source as a linked server called 'ODBC_with_PROVIDER_ STRING'. Unlike with the previous example, an ODBC data source does not need to exist. The information normally stored as an ODBC data source is stored in the provstr argument:

```
EXEC sp_addlinkedserver
  @server='ODBC_with_PROVIDER_STRING',
  @srvproduct='ODBC',
  @provider='MSDASQL',
  @provstr='DRIVER={SQL Server}; SERVER=MyServer; UID=sa;PWD=;'
```

Following is an example of a distributed query that accesses multiple tables via linked servers we set up. Try it:

```
SELECT substring(CustomerID,1,5) as 'CustID',
       substring(ContactName,1,18) as ContactName,
       substring(City,1,10) as 'City',
       substring(Country,1,15) as 'Country'
```

17

```
FROM [Linked ExcelSW]...[SWCustomers$]
UNION
SELECT substring(CustomerID,1,5) as 'CustID',
       substring(ContactName,1,18) as ContactName,
       substring(City,1,10) as 'City',
       substring(Country,1,15) as 'Country'
FROM ACCESS_DATABASE_CUSTOMERS...SWCustomers
go
CustID ContactName         City        Country
------ ------------------- ----------  ---------------

BLAUS  John Monroe         Concord     USA
BLAUS  Juliana Bertucci    Eugene      USA
CHOPS  Martin Sommer       Berkeley    USA
HANAR  Yves Moison         Paris       FRANCE
MEREP  Munir Noralli       Vannes      FRANCE
PICCO  Donald Renato       Los Angeles USA
PICCO  Steve Luk           Los Angeles USA


(7 row(s) affected)
```

In that example, we united (Unioned) customers from the Access database with customers from the Excel spreadsheet, all as a single SQL statement within SQL Server.

sp_linkedservers

To see the linked servers defined within a SQL Server instance, you simply use sp_linkedservers:

```
EXEC sp_linkedservers
Go
```

The sp_linkedservers execution provides the list of all linked servers on this SQL Server:

```
SRV_NAME                    SRV_PROVIDERNAME        SRV_PRODUCT SRV_DATASOURCE
--------------------------- ----------------------- ----------- ----------------------
ACCESS_DATABASE_CUSTOMERS Microsoft.Jet.OLEDB.4.0 Access  C:\SQL2014DB\CustomersPlus.
mdb
DATAXDESIGN-PC\SQL2014DXD02     SQLNCLI         SQL Server DATAXDESIGN-PC\SQL2014DXD02
DATAXDESIGN-PC\SQL2014DXD32     SQLNCLI         SQL Server DATAXDESIGN-PC\SQL2014DXD32



Linked ExcelSW          Microsoft.Jet.OLEDB.4.0 Jet Excel
C:\ SQL2014DB\SWCustomers.xls


(4 row(s) affected)
```

Option Name	Description
`'collation compatible'`	If `optvalue` is set to TRUE, SQL Server assumes that the linked server has the same character set and collation sequence. Set this option to TRUE only if you are sure the character sets and collation are identical.
`'connect timeout'`	The length of time, in seconds, to wait before timing out the connection attempt to the linked server. If set to 0, this option uses the `sp_configure` default value.
`'data access'`	If `optvalue` is set to TRUE and if the OLE DB provider supports them, distributed queries are allowed. If `optvalue` is set to FALSE, distributed queries are disabled on this linked server.
`'lazy schema validation'`	If `optvalue` is set to TRUE, the check of the schema for remote tables will be skipped at the beginning of the query.
`'query timeout'`	Length of time, in seconds, to wait before timing out queries against linked server. If set to 0, this option uses the `sp_configure` default value.
`'rpc'`	If the `optvalue` is set to TRUE, this option allows RPCs from the linked server.
`'rpc out'`	If the `optvalue` is set to TRUE, this option allows RPCs to the linked server.
`'use remote collation'`	If the `optvalue` is set to TRUE, this option uses the collation of remote columns for SQL Server data sources or the specified `collation name` for non–SQL Server sources. If set to FALSE, this option uses the local server default collation.
`'collation name'`	If `use remote collation` is set to TRUE and the linked server is not a SQL Server, this option specifies the name of the collation to be used on the linked server. Use this option when the OLE DB data source has a collation that matches one of the SQL Server collations.

Since the introduction of SQL Server 2005, you can also get the same information via system views set up for this purpose. In this case, you can query the system catalog view `sys.servers` directly to get your information on linked servers:

```
select server_id,
       substring(name,1,28) as 'name',
       substring(product,1,10) as 'Product',
       substring(provider,1,24) as 'Provider',
       substring(data_source,1,25) as 'Source'
from sys.servers
order by server_id
go
```

```
id    name                          Product     Provider                  Source
----  ----------------------------  ----------  ------------------------  ---------------
0     DATAXDESIGN-PC\SQL2014DXD32   SQL Server  SQLNCLI
DATAXDESIGN-PC\SQL2014DXD32
1     ACCESS_DATABASE_CUSTOMERS     Access      Microsoft.Jet.OLEDB.4.0
C:\SQL2014DB\CustomersPlu
2     DATAXDESIGN-PC\SQL2014DXD02   SQL Server  SQLNCLI
DATAXDESIGN-PC\SQL2014DXD02
3     Linked ExcelSW                Jet Excel   Microsoft.Jet.OLEDB.4.0
C:\SQL2014DB\SWCustomers.
```

```
(4 row(s) affected)
```

sp_dropserver

To unregister linked servers, you can use sp_dropserver. Only members of the sysadmin and setupadmin fixed server roles can execute this stored procedure:

```
sp_dropserver [@server =] 'server' [, [@droplogins =] {'droplogins' | NULL}]
```

The elements of the syntax are as follows:

▶ **server**—The linked server that will be unregistered.

▶ **droplogins**—An argument that specifies the logins associated with the server should be dropped. If this argument is not specified, the server is dropped only if logins do not exist for this linked server.

The following example unregisters Oracle, Access, and SQL Server databases:

```
EXECUTE sp_dropserver @server='ORACLE_DATABASE', @droplogins='droplogins'
EXECUTE sp_dropserver @server='ACCESS_DATABASE_CUSTOMERS'
EXECUTE sp_dropserver @server='DATAXDESIGN-PC\SQL2014DXD02'',@
droplogins='droplogins'
```

sp_serveroption

You can configure linked servers by using sp_serveroption. This affects how distributed queries behave at the linked server provider level. In other words, the options you set with the sp_serveroption procedure are for a particular linked server entry only. Only users with the sysadmin or setupadmin fixed server roles can run this procedure, which has the following syntax:

```
sp_serveroption [[@server =] 'server']
  [, [@optname =] 'option_name']
  [, [@optvalue =] 'option_value']
```

The elements of the syntax are as follows:

▶ `server`—The linked server affected by this option.

▶ `option_name`—The name of the option to be configured. The valid option names follow.

▶ `option_value`—The value of this option. Valid values are TRUE (or ON) and FALSE (or OFF), a non-negative integer for the `connect timeout` and `query timeout` options, or a collation name for the `collation name` option.

The following example disables distributed queries to the ORACLE_DATABASE linked server:

```
EXECUTE sp_serveroption @server='ORACLE_DATABASE',
@optname='data access', @optvalue='FALSE'
```

The following example enables Remote Procedure Calls to the SQL_SERVER_DB linked server:

```
EXECUTE sp_serveroption @server='SQL_SERVER_DB',
@optname='rpc out', @optvalue='TRUE'
```

To set the query timeout to 60 seconds for the SQL Server data source, you execute the following command:

```
EXECUTE sp_serveroption  'DATAXDESIGN-PC\SQL2014DXD02', 'query timeout', 60
```

To display the options currently enabled for a linked server, you use sp_helpserver:

```
EXECUTE sp_helpserver @server='DATAXDESIGN-PC\SQL2014DXD02'
GO
name                        network_name                             status  id connect..
------------------          --------------------------------         ------  -- ---------
DATAXDESIGN-PC\SQL2014DXD02 DATAXDESIGN-PC\SQL2014DXD02 rpc..  0       0  60
```

Mapping Local Logins to Logins on Linked Servers

For a user to gain access to a linked server, the linked server must validate the user for security reasons. The requesting server (that is, the local server) provides a login name and password to the linked server on behalf of the local server user. For this to work, you need to map the local logins with the linked server logins you are going to use. Remember that sp_addlinkedserver creates a default self-mapping for all local logins to the linked server. You use sp_addlinkedsrvlogin to specifically control the logins that you want to use the linked server.

sp_addlinkedsrvlogin

SQL Server provides the `sp_addlinkedsrvlogin` system stored procedure to map local logins to logins on the linked servers. This stored procedure can be executed by members of the sysadmin and securityadmin fixed server roles. Its syntax is as follows:

```
sp_addlinkedsrvlogin [@rmtsrvname =] 'rmtsrvname'
 [, [@useself =] 'useself']
 [, [@locallogin =] 'locallogin']
 [, [@rmtuser =] 'rmtuser']
 [, [@rmtpassword =] 'rmtpassword']
```

The elements in this syntax are as follows:

▶ **rmtsrvname**—The linked server that will use this login setting (`@rmtsrvname` parameter).

▶ **useself**—The setting that determines whether a user or group of users will use their own usernames and passwords to log in to the linked server (`@useself` parameter). There are two possible settings:

  ▶ **'true'**—Local server logins use their own usernames and passwords to log in to the linked server. Consequently, the `rmtuser` and `rmtpassword` arguments are ignored. For example, the local `jdoe` user with a password of `shrek` would attempt to log in to the linked server with the `jdoe` username and `shrek` password.

  ▶ **'false'**—Local server logins use the arguments specified in `rmtuser` and `rmtpassword` to log in to the linked server. For a linked server that does not require usernames and passwords (such as Microsoft Access), these arguments can be set to `NULL`.

▶ **locallogin**—The local logins affected by this mapping (`@locallogin` parameter). You can designate either an individual login or all local logins. To specify that all logins be affected, you pass a `NULL` to this argument.

▶ **rmtuser**—The username used to connect to the linked server if `@useself` is set to `FALSE` (`@rmtuser` parameter).

▶ **rmtpassword**—The password used to connect to the linked server if `@useself` is set to `FALSE` (`@rmtpassword` parameter).

As noted earlier, by default, after you run `sp_addlinkedserver`, all local logins automatically attempt to use their own usernames and passwords to log in to the new linked server. Essentially, SQL Server runs the following statement after `sp_addlinkedserver`:

```
EXECUTE sp_addlinkedsrvlogin @rmtsrvname='My_Linked_Server',
@useself='true', @locallogin=NULL
```

You can delete this default mapping by using `sp_droplinkedsrvlogin`, which is described in the next section.

In Windows Authentication mode, SQL Server submits the Windows username and password to the linked server if the provider supports Windows authentication and if security account delegation is available on both the client and server.

The following example connects all users to the `'ORACLE_DATABASE'` linked server, using the `'guest'` username and `'confio'` password:

```
EXECUTE sp_addlinkedsrvlogin @rmtsrvname='ORACLE_DATABASE',
@useself='false', @rmtuser='guest', @rmtpassword='confio'
```

The following example connects all users to the `'DATAXDESIGN-PC\SQL2014DXD32'` linked server, using their own local usernames and passwords:

```
EXECUTE sp_addlinkedsrvlogin @rmtsrvname='DATAXDESIGN-PC\SQL2014DXD32',
@useself='true'
```

The following example logs in the local `'RobinOrdes'` user as the remote user `'ROrdes'` with the `'new_orleans'` password to the `'ORACLE_DATABASE'` linked server:

```
EXECUTE sp_addlinkedsrvlogin @rmtsrvname='ORACLE_DATABASE',
@useself='false', @locallogin='RobinOrdes', @rmtuser='ROrdes',
@rmtpassword='new_orleans'
```

The following example logs in the Windows user `'Domain1\DonLarson'` as the remote user `'DLarson'` with the `'five_sons'` password:

```
EXECUTE sp_addlinkedsrvlogin @rmtsrvname='ORACLE_DATABASE',
@useself='false', @locallogin='Domain1\DonLarson',
@rmtuser='DLarson', @rmtpassword='five_sons'
```

The following example connects all users to the `'ACCESS_DATABASE_CUSTOMERS'` linked server without providing a username or password:

```
EXECUTE sp_addlinkedsrvlogin @rmtsrvname='ACCESS_DATABASE_CUSTOMERS',
@useself='false', @rmtuser=NULL, @rmtpassword=NULL
```

sp_droplinkedsrvlogin

You can delete mappings for linked servers by using `sp_droplinkedsrvlogin`. Members of the `sysadmin` and `securityadmin` fixed server roles can execute this stored procedure:

```
sp_droplinkedsrvlogin [@rmtsrvname =] 'rmtsrvname',
[@locallogin =] 'locallogin'
```

The elements of this syntax are as follows:

▶ **rmtsrvname**—The linked server that will lose this login mapping (`@rmtsrvname` parameter).

17

▶ **locallogin**—The local login that will lose the mapping to the linked server (@local-login parameter). You can designate either an individual login or all local logins. To specify that all logins should be affected, you pass a NULL to this argument.

The following example removes the login mapping for the `'RobinOrdes'` user to the `'ORACLE_DATABASE'` linked server:

```
EXECUTE sp_droplinkedsrvlogin @rmtsrvname='ORACLE_DATABASE',
 @locallogin='RobinOrdes'
```

The following example removes the default login mapping for all users using the `'SQL_SERVER_DB'` linked server:

```
EXEC sp_droplinkedsrvlogin @rmtsrvname='SQL_SERVER_DB',
 @locallogin=NULL
```

sp_helplinkedsrvlogin

To determine the current linked server login settings, you run the sp_helplinkedsrvlogin procedure, which has the following syntax:

```
sp_helplinkedsrvlogin [[@rmtsrvname =] 'rmtsrvname',]
 [[@locallogin =] 'locallogin']
```

The elements of this syntax are as follows:

▶ **rmtsrvname**—The linked server that will have its login settings displayed.

▶ **locallogin**—The local login mappings that will be displayed.

The following example shows the sp_helplinkedsrvlogin output if no arguments are provided:

```
EXECUTE sp_helplinkedsrvlogin
GO
Linked Server            Local Login   Is Self Mapping Remote Login
----------------------------------------------------------------
ACCESS_DATABASE_CUSTOMERS       NULL         1           NULL
DATAXDESIGN-PC\SQL2014DXD02      NULL         1           NULL
DATAXDESIGN-PC\SQL2014DXD32      NULL         1           NULL
Linked ExcelSW                   NULL         1           NULL
```

This example displays one line for each linked server login mapping. The first column (Linked Server) shows which linked server owns this mapping. The second column (Local Login) shows which user is affected by this mapping. If set to NULL, this mapping applies to all users who do not have specific mappings. The third column (Is Self Mapping) displays a 1 if the local username and password will be attempted on the remote server. If it displays a 0, the value in the last column (Remote Login) will be used to log in to the remote server. Note that the remote password is not listed for security reasons.

The next example shows the sp_helplinkedsrvlogin output if only the rmtsrvname argument is provided:

```
EXECUTE sp_helplinkedsrvlogin @rmtsrvname='DATAXDESIGN-PC\SQL2014DXD02'
GO


Linked Server     Local Login   Is Self Mapping  Remote Login
-------------     -----------   ---------------  ------------
DATAXDESIGN-PC\SQL2014DXD02NULL            0                NULL
```

The output for this example is identical to that of the preceding example except that only the entries for the specified server are displayed.

Obtaining General Information About Linked Servers

You can use both SQL Server Management Studio and the system stored procedures to gather information about linked servers and the referenced data sources. Following are some of the most-often-used system stored procedures:

- ▶ **sp_linkedservers**—This returns a list of linked servers defined on the local server.

- ▶ **sp_catalogs**—This displays a list of catalogs and descriptions for a specified linked server.

- ▶ **sp_indexes**—This shows index information for a specified remote table.

- ▶ **sp_primarykeys**—This returns the primary key columns for the specified table.

- ▶ **sp_foreignkeys**—This lists the foreign keys defined for the remote table.

- ▶ **sp_tables_ex**—This displays table information from the linked server.

- ▶ **sp_columns_ex**—This returns column information for all columns or a specified column for a remote table.

- ▶ **sp_helplinkedsrvlogin**—This displays the linked server login mappings for each linked server.

For example, at query prototyping time, it is useful to see all the ways the linked server objects and columns are being referenced (especially when you're dealing with other data sources, such as Excel spreadsheets).

First, the exact linked object name is displayed via the sp_tables_ex system stored procedure. In this case, you would see the following for the ACCESS_DATABASE_CUSTOMERS linked server just created:

```
EXECUTE sp_tables_ex 'ACCESS_DATABASE_CUSTOMERS'
go
TABLE_CAT  TABLE_SCHEM  TABLE_NAME          TABLE_TYPE    REMARKS
---------  -----------  ------------        ------------  -------

NULL       NULL         MSysAccessObjects   ACCESS TABLE
NULL       NULL         MSysACEs            SYSTEM TABLE
NULL       NULL         MSysObjects         SYSTEM TABLE
NULL       NULL         MSysQueries         SYSTEM TABLE
NULL       NULL         MSysRelationships   SYSTEM TABLE
NULL       NULL         SWCustomers         TABLE
```

Then you can see all the table columns of that linked server's data source by using the sp_columns_ex system stored procedure. The following command provides the column definitions for the SWCustomers Access table for the linked server 'ACCESS_DATABASE_CUSTOMERS':

```
EXECUTE sp_columns_ex 'ACCESS_DATABASE_CUSTOMERS'
go
TABLE_CAT  TABLE_SCH  TABLE_NAME         COLUMN_NAME   TYPE_NAME   SIZE
---------  ---------  ------------       ------------  ----------  -------

NULL       NULL       MSysAccessObjects  Data          VarBinary   3992
NULL       NULL       MSysAccessObjects  ID            Long        10
NULL       NULL       SWCustomers        CustomerID    VarChar     255
NULL       NULL       SWCustomers        CompanyName   VarChar     255
NULL       NULL       SWCustomers        ContactName   VarChar     255
NULL       NULL       SWCustomers        ContactTitle  VarChar     255
NULL       NULL       SWCustomers        Address       VarChar     255
NULL       NULL       SWCustomers        City          VarChar     255
NULL       NULL       SWCustomers        Region        VarChar     255
NULL       NULL       SWCustomers        PostalCode    Double      15
NULL       NULL       SWCustomers        Country       VarChar     255
NULL       NULL       SWCustomers        Phone         VarChar     255
NULL       NULL       SWCustomers        Fax           VarChar     255
```

Executing a Stored Procedure via a Linked Server

Executing a stored procedure is possible via a linked server. The server hosting the client connection accepts the client's request and sends it to the linked server. The EXECUTE statement must contain the name of the linked server as part of its syntax:

```
EXECUTE servername.dbname.owner.procedure_name
```

The following example executes the sp_helpserver system stored procedure on the linked server 'DATAXDESIGN-PC\SQL2014DXD02', which simply shows the server configuration information on that remote server:

```
EXEC [DATAXDESIGN-PC\SQL2014DXD02].[master].[dbo].[sp_helpserver]
```

The final example executes the user-created stored procedure on the remote linked server `'DATAXDESIGN-PC\SQL2014DXD02'` that will return the top 10 customers in the CustomersPlus table there:

```
EXEC [DATAXDESIGN-PC\SQL2014DXD02].[UnleashedRemoteDB].[dbo].[Top10Customers];
CustomerID CompanyName                         City             Country          YTDBusiness
---------- ---------------------------------   --------------   --------------   ---------------
BERTU      Bertucci Villa                      ilano            Italy            200039.80
QUICK      QUICK-Stop                          Cunewalde        Germany          117483.39
SAVEA      Save-a-lot Markets                  Boise            USA              115673.39
ERNSH      Ernst Handel                        Graz             Austria          113236.68
HUNGO      Hungry Owl All-Night Grocers        Cork             Ireland           57317.39
RATTC      Rattlesnake Canyon Grocery          Albuquerque      USA               52245.90
HANAR      Yves Moison                         Paris            France            34101.15
FOLKO      Folk och fä HB                      Bräcke           Sweden            32555.55
MEREP      Munir Nuralli                       Vannes           France            32203.90
KOENE      Königlich Essen                     Brandenburg      Germany           31745.75

(10 row(s) affected)
```

Setting Up Linked Servers Using SQL Server Management Studio

Although you can set up linked servers and login mappings by directly executing system stored procedures, you can also set them up easily through SQL Server Management Studio.

To create a "SQL Server" linked server, you follow these steps:

1. Open SQL Server Management Studio with a connection to a local server (DATAXDESIGN-PC\SQL2014DXD32 in this example).

2. Expand the Server Objects node and then the Linked Servers node.

3. Right-click the Linked Servers node and choose New Linked Server.

4. You are presented with a properties page where you must specify all the connection properties for the linked server. For this example, create a SQL Server database linked server entry. As shown in Figure 17.5, provide the linked server name DATAXDESIGN-PC\SQL2012DXD02 (or whatever your server and instance name might be) and click the SQL Server radio button. All the other fields are not needed (and are grayed out).

5. After you finish the linked server specification, click OK. An entry is added under the Linked Server node in SQL Server Management Studio. You may receive an error message complaining about not having the proper authentication for the linked server access. Not to worry; we'll fix that in a minute. The linked server can be used

17

by a SQL query based on the default local logins being mapped to the linked server. However, you really want to control the access to this linked server.

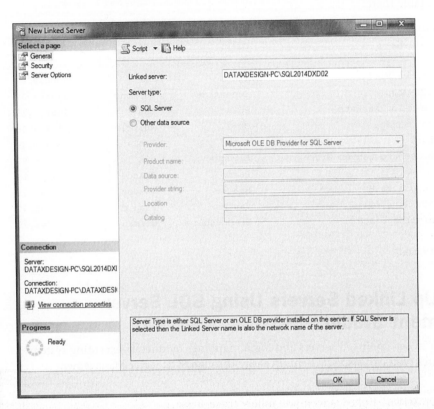

FIGURE 17.5   Creating a "SQL Server" linked server entry through SQL Server Management Studio.

6. Right-click the newly created linked server entry and choose Properties. When the properties page comes up, select the Security entry on this page. Figure 17.6 shows explicitly a local login on the local server (DATAXDESIGN-PC\DATAXDESIGN) that you can use to impersonate your login at the linked server (where you are already a valid Windows user on the linked server). Now, also indicate that for any logins not in this list, connections will be made using the login's current security context. This locks it down as tightly as you need it. Click OK, and you are ready to test the linked server.

Figure 17.7 shows the successful execution of a query by user DATAXDESIGN-PC\ DATAXDESIGN, using the linked server.

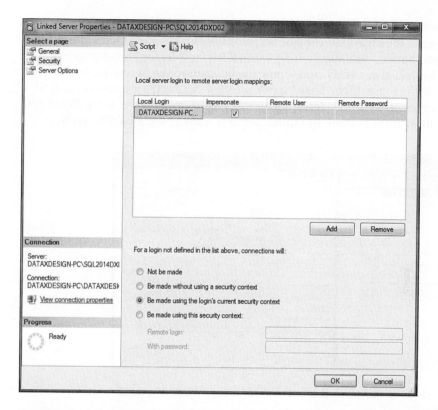

FIGURE 17.6   Specifying the security properties of a new linked server entry.

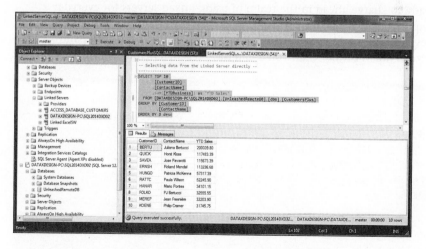

FIGURE 17.7   Execution of a SQL query referencing the new linked server entry.

Figure 17.8 shows an example of creating an Access database linked server entry. As you can see, you specify the linked server name ACCESS_DATABASE_CUSTOMERS, click the Other Data Source radio button, pick Microsoft Jet 4.0 OLE DB Provider for Provider, specify Access for the Product Name entry, and supply the full path to the Access database for which you are trying to create the linked server entry (c:\SQL2014DB\CustomerPlus.mdb). There is no need to specify a provider string for this type of linked server entry. When you click the OK button at the bottom, this linked server is ready to use for a SQL query.

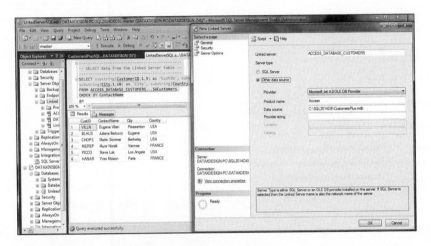

FIGURE 17.8   Creating an Access database linked server through SQL Server Management Studio.

You are now ready to charge ahead in the realm of using linked servers for everyday purposes. As you can see in Figure 17.9, linked servers can take their place in your SQL Server data access layer alongside any traditional SQL table. This capability expands your data access horizons much further than you could have reached before.

FIGURE 17.9   Several different linked servers from SQL Server Management Studio.

Summary

In this chapter, you learned how distributed queries and transactions work with linked servers. Specifically, you learned how to set up, configure, and gather information on linked servers by using the system stored procedures, including sp_addlinkedserver, sp_dropserver, sp_serveroption, sp_linkedserver, sp_table_ex, sp_column_ex, sp_addlinkedsrvlogin, sp_droplinkedsrvlogin, and sp_helplinkedsrvlogin. Finally, you learned how to configure linked servers through SQL Server Management Studio and tighten up the security access around the use and execution of linked servers. These foundational skills are the cornerstone of helping your organization expand its reach to data, no matter where it resides.

Keep in mind that although linked servers provide a method to access data in other data sources beyond SQL Server, at times you might need to work with data in a data source that cannot be linked. In these rare circumstances, you can still use Bulk Copy Program (BCP) to import data files that have been exported from other data sources into local SQL Server tables or create SSIS packages to periodically pull, push, and transform data to other locations.

SQL Server Configuration Options

This chapter delves into what can be done with the SQL Server configurable options—particularly what can be improved that SQL Server isn't automatically tuning already. By setting the values of several key SQL Server configuration parameters, you can fine-tune SQL Server to provide excellent performance and throughput. Note that with each release of SQL Server, less needs to be tuned from a SQL Server configuration point of view. With the advent of self-tuning or self-configuring options, it is only a matter of time before most of your server tuning time will be spent elsewhere, such as with the operating system, disk systems, and network interfaces—and only because SQL Server can't reach there (yet). As you also see in Chapter 39, "Monitoring SQL Server Performance," many SQL Server components can be monitored and tuned to yield high performance. Some of the options discussed here also surface in that chapter, from a monitoring point of view.

What's New in Configuring, Tuning, and Optimizing SQL Server Options

There are a couple of new configuration options in SQL Server 2014. One of these is the backup checksum default option related to guaranteeing the integrity of database backups. Another one is the change in SQL Server 2012 for the startup parameter of the SQL Server database engine that provides an amount of memory to reserve (-g option). However, you must be warned that there are options available that are not obsolete yet but have no effect (even if you set them). We identify them in this chapter as they come up.

SQL Server 2000 had a total of 36 options. With SQL Server 2005, the number of options nearly doubled, with a total of 64 (basic and advanced) active options. There are now 70 basic and advanced options in SQL Server 2014. Not all are usable, and some apply only to certain OS platforms (64-bit) or SQL Server editions.

> **NOTE**
>
> You can't use Locks, Remote proc trans, Allow Updates, Open Objects, or the Set Working Set Size `sp_configure` options. They have become obsolete and have no effect in SQL Server 2014, even though they are still listed. The Web Assistant Procedures option doesn't exist anymore either. In addition, Microsoft has announced that all the `ft_crawl` and `ft_notify` options (ft = File Text) will be deprecated. Oh, and SQL Server 2005 compatibility level is no longer supported (database compatibility level 90).

This chapter discusses the configuration options only.

SQL Server Instance Architecture

Figure 18.1 illustrates the address space architecture of an instance of SQL Server 2014. When you fire up a SQL Server instance, two main areas are allocated: the code area and memory pool area. The code area is mostly static executable code of the SQL Server kernel; SQL Server .NET Library DLLs; Open Data Services code; the stack space; and a variable code area that contains distributed query OLE DB providers, OLE automation objects, and extended stored procedures as they are needed by user requests.

The memory pool area of SQL Server is the most dynamically changing part of an instance. Even now, the once-static system data structures and user connection structures (connection context) are controlled by user requests and dynamically allocate structures as they are needed. Then, there are the primary SQL Server databases master, tempdb, msdb, and model. There is another system database called a *resource database* that is present in each SQL Server instance. This read-only database contains system objects that are included with SQL Server. System objects are physically persisted in the resource database, but they logically appear in the sys schema of every database and provide the results to system-level information such as server properties (SERVERPROPERTY) and object definitions (OBJECT_DEFINITION). Of these system-wide databases, tempdb has the most significance for performance because it is the heart of all internal tables, indexing, sorting, grouping, and other worktable activity for the entire SQL Server instance.

By default, SQL Server tries to keep the amount of virtual memory allocations on a computer at 4MB to 10MB less than the physical memory available. The rest of the memory pool area is divided into procedure cache, data cache (buffer cache), and log cache. SQL Server actively adjusts these for optimal performance. Previously, the system administrator had to do all this manually. Many of the configurable options directly relate to optimizing this address space. There is a caching framework that utilizes internal and external clocks to determine how the caches are managed.

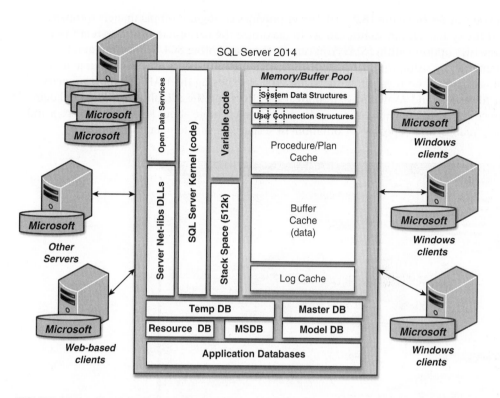

FIGURE 18.1   The SQL Server 2014 instance architecture.

Configuration Options

With SQL Server 2014, many options may affect the performance of individual SQL statements or the overall performance of a SQL Server instance. There are instance-wide configuration options (set using the `sp_configure` system stored procedure or with the server properties dialog within SSMS), database-level options (set with `ALTER DATABASE`), database compatibility levels (using the `sp_dbcmptlevel` system stored procedure), batch-level options (using the `SET` command for things such as `SET ANSI_NULLS`), and statement-level options (such as table hints, query hints, and join hints). Always remember that a hint overrides a `SET` option, a `SET` option overrides a database option, and a database option overrides an instance-wide option.

For SQL Server 2014, this chapter discusses the instance-wide configurable options in two distinct categories: basic options and advanced options. The advanced options are a superset of the basic options. As each option is discussed, this chapter notes whether it is self-configuring. A *self-configuring option* is an option that adjusts itself dynamically, according to the needs of the system. In most cases, this eliminates the need for setting the values manually. Sometimes you don't want to rely on certain self-configuring values, depending on how SQL Server is being used. This chapter identifies self-configuring values.

18

As you can see in Figure 18.2, SQL Server provides configuration parameters (properties) that the system administrator can set to maximize the performance of a system from the properties option within SSMS. You can set these and other SQL Server configuration parameters by using the `sp_configure` system stored procedure as well. A couple new things changed on these property pages, such as exposing the HADR Enabled property for AlwaysOn and Availability Group features, lowering the default of the Remote Login Timeout from 20 down to 10 seconds, showing a bit more about FILESTREAM access and share names, and exposing a Containment section specific to databases.

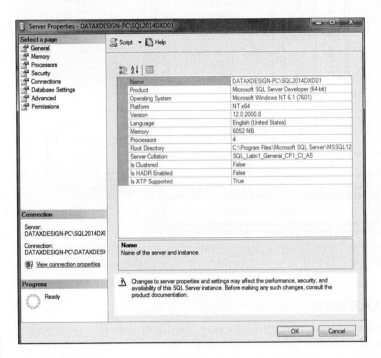

FIGURE 18.2   The SQL Server 2014 Configuration Properties dialog from SSMS.

Now, the only questions that need to be answered are "What configuration options do I need to set that aren't already fine?" and "How do I set them?"

To answer the "what" question, you first need to determine for what purpose the applications are using SQL Server. The answer must include understanding variables such as the number of potential connections to support, resources available on the box, size of the database, type of data accesses occurring, and workload being put on SQL Server. When you know all this, it is easy to determine the configuration option setting to adjust.

The following shows a generalization of the types of applications you might find in the real world that would be implemented using SQL Server 2014 and the general behavior they elicit:

▶ **Online transaction processing (OLTP)**—Mix of reads, writes, updates, and deletes. Large number of concurrent users.

▶ **Data warehouse**—Incremental loads (deltas), aggregation/transformation processing, then primarily read-only. Medium number of users.

▶ **Online analytical processing (OLAP)**—Big loads, then primarily read-only. Medium to large number of simultaneous users.

▶ **Mixed server**—Mix of reads, writes, updates, deletes, big loads, and big extracts. Large number of users.

This is not a complete list, just a generalized list. Because these configuration options are set at the SQL Server level, it is important to know the combined behavior of all application processing. For each SQL Server configuration option discussed in this chapter, we recommend an appropriate setting, based on these generalized application processing behavior types.

Now let's answer the "How do I set them?" question. The next few sections describe all the types of configuration options available on SQL Server 2014. These sections show how to set these configuration options using both SSMS and the sp_configure system stored procedure. The rule is that you can certainly set a configuration option using SSMS, but you should keep an sp_configure version of that setting change as a backup in case you need to rebuild the entire server configuration from scratch. In addition, keeping an sp_configure version around in a file provides a great audit trail of what you did and why. If you simply execute sp_configure without parameters, you are given a list of options that can be addressed. When you have just installed a SQL Server instance, you can see only the basic configuration options.

SQL Server 2014 has 18 basic configuration options available:

```
exec sp_configure
go
```

name	minimum	maximum	config_value	run_value
allow updates	0	1	0	0
backup checksum default	0	1	0	0
backup compression default	0	1	0	0
clr enabled	0	1	0	0
contained database authentication	0	1	0	0
cross db ownership chaining	0	1	0	0
default language	0	9999	0	0
filestream access level	0	2	0	0
max text repl size (B)	-1	2147483647	65536	65536
nested triggers	0	1	1	1
remote access	0	1	1	1
remote admin connections	0	1	0	0
remote login timeout (s)	0	2147483647	10	10

18

remote proc trans	0	1	0	0
remote query timeout (s)	0	2147483647	600	600
server trigger recursion	0	1	1	1
show advanced options	0	1	0	0
user options	0	32767	0	0

By default, all SQL Server users have permission to run the `sp_configure` system stored procedure, but only users who have sysadmin and serveradmin fixed server roles (such as sa) can actually set the value of a parameter.

The proper syntax of the `sp_configure` command is as follows:

```
exec sp_configure  [parameter_name [, parameter_value ]]
```

In this syntax, `parameter_name` is the name of the configuration parameter you want to set, and `parameter_value` is the value for the parameter. Both of these parameters are optional. Parameters set by `sp_configure` take effect at the server level.

Following is a brief explanation of the output of the `sp_configure` command. As you can see, the output consists of five columns:

- ▶ **Name**—This is the name of the configurable option.

- ▶ **Minimum**—This is the minimum legal value allowed for this parameter. Passing an illegal value causes SQL Server to return an error.

- ▶ **Maximum**—This is the maximum legal value allowed for this parameter. Passing an illegal value causes SQL Server to return an error.

- ▶ **Config_value**—This column reflects the values that will take effect the next time SQL Server is started. If you change static parameters, the new values are listed under this column.

- ▶ **Run_value**—This column reflects the values that SQL Server is currently using. If you change any dynamic parameters, the new values are listed in this column. At the time of SQL Server startup, `config_value` for all the parameters is copied into `run_value`. Immediately after restart, both columns (`run_value` and `config_value`) should display the same values, corresponding to each parameter.

If you specify a parameter name, SQL Server returns the current configuration value for that particular parameter, as in this example:

```
exec sp_configure 'clr enabled'
go
name                                minimum     maximum     config_value run_value
----------------------------------- ----------- ----------- ------------ ---------
clr enabled                         0           1           0            0
```

There are many more than 18 basic configuration options. In fact, there are 70 configuration options in total. They consist of the original 18 basic options plus 52 advanced options (including a few for 64-bit processing). To see a complete list of all options, you turn on the show advanced option configuration option with the value 1.

In addition, when using sp_configure to change a setting, you use the RECONFIGURE WITH OVERRIDE statement to make the change take effect immediately. You can also choose to use just the RECONFIGURE statement. Depending on the configuration option, it may take effect immediately, or it may not take effect until the server has been restarted.

The following commands set the show advanced options configuration option and then retrieve the complete list of all configuration options:

```
exec sp_configure 'Show Advanced Options', 1     /* Advanced config options */
go
RECONFIGURE WITH OVERRIDE                        /* to have it take effect immediately */
go
sp_configure
go
```

name	minimum	maximum	config_value	run_value
access check cache bucket count	0	65536	0	0
access check cache quota	0	2147483647	0	0
Ad Hoc Distributed Queries	0	1	0	0
affinity I/O mask	-2147483648	2147483647	0	0
affinity mask	-2147483648	2147483647	0	0
affinity64 I/O mask	-2147483648	2147483647	0	0
affinity64 mask	-2147483648	2147483647	0	0
Agent XPs	0	1	0	0
allow updates	0	1	0	0
backup checksum default	0	1	0	0
backup compression default	0	1	0	0
blocked process threshold (s)	0	86400	0	0
c2 audit mode	0	1	0	0
clr enabled	0	1	0	0
common criteria compliance enabled	0	1	0	0
contained database authentication	0	1	0	0
cost threshold for parallelism	0	32767	5	5
cross db ownership chaining	0	1	0	0
cursor threshold	-1	2147483647	-1	-1
Database Mail XPs	0	1	0	0
default full-text language	0	2147483647	1033	1033
default language	0	9999	0	0
default trace enabled	0	1	1	1
disallow results from triggers	0	1	0	0
EKM provider enabled	0	1	0	0
filestream access level	0	2	0	0
fill factor (%)	0	100	0	0
ft crawl bandwidth (max)	0	32767	100	100

18

ft crawl bandwidth (min)	0	32767	0	0
ft notify bandwidth (max)	0	32767	100	100
ft notify bandwidth (min)	0	32767	0	0
index create memory (KB)	704	2147483647	0	0
in-doubt xact resolution	0	2	0	0
lightweight pooling	0	1	0	0
locks	5000	2147483647	0	0
max degree of parallelism	0	32767	0	0
max full-text crawl range	0	256	4	4
max server memory (MB)	128	2147483647	2147483647	2147483647
max text repl size (B)	-1	2147483647	65536	65536
max worker threads	128	65535	0	0
media retention	0	365	0	0
min memory per query (KB)	512	2147483647	1024	1024
min server memory (MB)	0	2147483647	0	16
nested triggers	0	1	1	1
network packet size (B)	512	32767	4096	4096
Ole Automation Procedures	0	1	0	0
open objects	0	2147483647	0	0
optimize for ad hoc workloads	0	1	0	0
PH timeout (s)	1	3600	60	60
precompute rank	0	1	0	0
priority boost	0	1	0	0
query governor cost limit	0	2147483647	0	0
query wait (s)	-1	2147483647	-1	-1
recovery interval (min)	0	32767	0	0
remote access	0	1	1	1
remote admin connections	0	1	0	0
remote login timeout (s)	0	2147483647	10	10
remote proc trans	0	1	0	0
remote query timeout (s)	0	2147483647	600	600
Replication XPs	0	1	0	0
scan for startup procs	0	1	0	0
server trigger recursion	0	1	1	1
set working set size	0	1	0	0
show advanced options	0	1	1	1
SMO and DMO XPs	0	1	1	1
transform noise words	0	1	0	0
two digit year cutoff	1753	9999	2049	2049
user connections	0	32767	0	0
user options	0	32767	0	0
xp_cmdshell	0	1	0	0

Microsoft suggests that only very experienced SQL Server administrators change these advanced configuration options. In general, this is good advice because most of these options are set to where you might want them as you start out. As you learn more about your application and the other things happening in your SQL Server instance, you will change them more and more. You have been warned!

With SQL Server 2014, you can see all the configuration options and their current settings via system views. The `sys.configurations` view shows the option, a description, and the current value in use for each configuration option. The following example shows what you might expect to see if you query the `sys.configurations` view:

```
SELECT convert(varchar(10),value_in_use) AS 'Value in Use',
substring (name,1,30) AS 'Configuration Option',
substring (description,1,30) AS 'Description'
FROM sys.configurations
ORDER BY 2
Go
```

Value in Use	Configuration Option	Description
0	access check cache bucket coun	Default hash bucket count for
0	access check cache quota	Default quota for the access c
0	Ad Hoc Distributed Queries	Enable or disable Ad Hoc Distr
0	affinity I/O mask	affinity I/O mask
0	affinity mask	affinity mask
0	affinity64 I/O mask	affinity64 I/O mask
0	affinity64 mask	affinity64 mask
0	Agent XPs	Enable or disable Agent XPs
0	allow updates	Allow updates to system tables
0	backup checksum default	Enable checksum of backups by
0	backup compression default	Enable compression of backups
0	blocked process threshold (s)	Blocked process reporting thre
0	c2 audit mode	c2 audit mode
0	clr enabled	CLR user code execution enable
0	common criteria compliance ena	Common Criteria compliance mod
0	contained database authenticat	Enables contained databases an
5	cost threshold for parallelism	cost threshold for parallelism
0	cross db ownership chaining	Allow cross db ownership chain
-1	cursor threshold	cursor threshold
0	Database Mail XPs	Enable or disable Database Mai
1033	default full-text language	default full-text language
0	default language	default language
1	default trace enabled	Enable or disable the default
0	disallow results from triggers	Disallow returning results fro
0	EKM provider enabled	Enable or disable EKM provider
0	filestream access level	Sets the FILESTREAM access lev
0	fill factor (%)	Default fill factor percentage
100	ft crawl bandwidth (max)	Max number of full-text crawl
0	ft crawl bandwidth (min)	Number of reserved full-text c

18

100	ft notify bandwidth (max)	Max number of full-text notifi
0	ft notify bandwidth (min)	Number of reserved full-text n
0	index create memory (KB)	Memory for index create sorts
0	in-doubt xact resolution	Recovery policy for DTC transa
0	lightweight pooling	User mode scheduler uses light
0	locks	Number of locks for all users
0	max degree of parallelism	maximum degree of parallelism
4	max full-text crawl range	Maximum crawl ranges allowed
2147483647	max server memory (MB)	Maximum size of server memory
65536	max text repl size (B)	Maximum size of a text field i
0	max worker threads	Maximum worker threads
0	media retention	Tape retention period in days
1024	min memory per query (KB)	minimum memory per query (kByt
16	min server memory (MB)	Minimum size of server memory
1	nested triggers	Allow triggers to be invoked w
4096	network packet size (B)	Network packet size
0	Ole Automation Procedures	Enable or disable Ole Automati
0	open objects	Number of open database object
0	optimize for ad hoc workloads	When this option is set, plan
60	PH timeout (s)	DB connection timeout for full
0	precompute rank	Use precomputed rank for full-
0	priority boost	Priority boost
0	query governor cost limit	Maximum estimated cost allowed
-1	query wait (s)	maximum time to wait for query
0	recovery interval (min)	Maximum recovery interval in m
1	remote access	Allow remote access
0	remote admin connections	Dedicated Admin Connections ar
10	remote login timeout (s)	remote login timeout
0	remote proc trans	Create DTC transaction for rem
600	remote query timeout (s)	remote query timeout
0	Replication XPs	Enable or disable Replication
0	scan for startup procs	scan for startup stored proced
1	server trigger recursion	Allow recursion for server lev
0	set working set size	set working set size
1	show advanced options	show advanced options
1	SMO and DMO XPs	Enable or disable SMO and DMO
0	transform noise words	Transform noise words for full
2049	two digit year cutoff	two digit year cutoff
0	user connections	Number of user connections all
0	user options	user options
0	xp_cmdshell	Enable or disable command shel

Dynamically changing configuration options are also updated so that their values are visible through the system views.

Fixing an Incorrect Option Setting

Setting a parameter value too high might cause SQL Server to crash during startup. For example, if you set the value of the memory option to a value that is higher than the physical memory on the machine, SQL Server does not start. In this case, you start SQL Server with the `-f` option, which causes SQL Server to start with the default parameter values (the same values used by the Setup program when you installed SQL Server). After SQL Server is running, you can change the incorrect value to the correct one and restart SQL Server without the `-f` option.

Setting Configuration Options with SSMS

As mentioned previously, you can set SQL Server configuration options by using SSMS. You simply invoke SSMS from the Microsoft SQL Server program group and right-click the `Server` folder. In Figure 18.2, you can see the SQL Server Properties pane, the different server categories of options that are available (General, Processors, Memory, and so on), and the selected option category properties that can be adjusted. Keep in mind that some of these options are not configuration options that correspond to `sp_configure` (for example, the Root Directory or Platform properties of the General Server Instance properties options). However, as you will see, Microsoft has done a nice job of organizing and presenting the option information. In addition, you can look at either the configured option value or the running values. If you are manipulating these, they may not be the same.

Not all 70 configuration options can be set from SMSS; only about half of them can. It's therefore best to get to know the `sp_configure` system stored procedure. Remember that you must have `sysadmin` and `serveradmin` fixed server roles to make changes.

All the `sp_configure` settings and options used in this chapter are included in a SQL script named `SQLConfigOptions.sql` that you can find in the sample files and code listings folder for this book on the Web.

Obsolete Configuration Options

Many configuration options available in SQL Server 7.0 or SQL Server 2000 have become obsolete or do not function any longer. Some options, such as `time slice`, were introduced in SQL Server 7.0 and then immediately became obsolete.

The following configuration options are obsolete in SQL Server 2014:

▶ `Allow Update` (remains listed but cannot be set)

▶ `set working set size` (remains listed but has no effect)

▶ `Open Objects` (remains listed but has no effect)

From a historical perspective, one of the all-time favorite options in SQL Server 7.0 was `max async IO`. The reason that option became obsolete is that it is completely automated with SQL Server 2014. Previously, `max async IO` was used to specify the number of simultaneous disk I/O requests that SQL Server 7.0 (and earlier versions) could submit to the Windows OS during a checkpoint operation. It invariably helped overall throughput on systems that used RAID devices that had extensive disk cache mechanisms. SQL Server 2014 adjusts these options automatically.

Configuration Options and Performance

The following sections explain essential information about many of the most significant SQL Server configuration options and their impact on SQL Server performance. Some of the options don't have performance implications and therefore may not be addressed in much detail—or at all. As part of each option's explanation, an indication of whether the option is advanced or basic is given, along with the option's default value and whether the option is self-configuring. Recommended values are usually indicated for the different types of generalized application processing that the SQL Server is used for (that is, OLTP, OLAP, data warehouse, and mixed). For some configuration options, there may not be recommended values, but perhaps there may be notes that further explain how they can be used. Remember that there are 70 configuration options; this chapter focuses on the essential ones in alphabetical order (how they are listed in SQL Server).

`access check cache bucket count`

Type: Advanced Option

Default Value: 0

When any database object is accessed by SQL Server, the access check is cached in an internal structure named `access check result cache`. The `access check cache bucket count` option controls the number of entries and number of hash buckets used for `access check result cache`.

Possible performance gains can be made by changing these options (in rare circumstances). In general, you should leave this one alone.

The following is an example of this option:

```
exec sp_configure 'access check cache bucket count', 0
go
RECONFIGURE
Go
```

`access check cache quota`

Type: Advanced Option

Default Value: 0

In conjunction with `access check cache bucket count` option, when SQL server accesses any database object, the access check is cached in an internal structure named `access check result cache`. The `access check cache bucket count` option, along with the access check cache quota option, controls the number of entries and number of hash buckets used for access check result cache.

Possible performance gains can be made by changing these options (in rare circumstances). But, in general, you should leave this one alone also.

The following is an example of this option:

```
exec sp_configure 'access check cache quota', 0
go
RECONFIGURE
Go
```

ad hoc distributed queries

Type: Advanced Option

Default Value: 0

SQL Server does not allow ad hoc distributed queries using OPENROWSET and OPENDATASOURCE against providers other than the SQL Native Client OLE DB provider. When the ad hoc distributed queries option is set to 1, SQL Server allows ad hoc access against other providers. When it is set to 0, SQL Server does not allow any ad hoc access.

Ad hoc distributed queries use the OPENROWSET and OPENDATASOURCE functions to connect to remote data sources using OLE DB. OPENROWSET and OPENDATASOURCE should be used only to reference OLE DB data sources that are accessed infrequently. For any data sources that will be accessed more than a few times, you should define a linked server. Enabling the use of ad hoc queries means that any authenticated login to SQL Server can access the provider. SQL Server administrators should enable this feature only for highly trusted providers that are safe to be accessed by any local login.

The following is an example of this option:

```
exec sp_configure 'Ad Hoc Distributed Queries', 1
go
RECONFIGURE
Go
```

18

affinity I/O mask

Type: Advanced option; requires a reboot of SQL Server to take effect

Default value: 0

In Windows Servers, multitasking sometimes requires that process threads move among different processors. This type of movement of processing threads can reduce Microsoft SQL Server performance under heavy system loads because each processor cache is repeatedly reloaded with data. Assigning processors to specific threads can improve performance by eliminating processor reloads; such an association between a thread and a processor is called processor affinity. SQL Server 2014 supports processor affinity by means of two affinity mask options: `affinity mask` (to deal with the processor affinity needs) and `affinity I/O mask` (to address I/O-related affinity). Affinity support for servers with 33 to 64 processors is available only on 64-bit operating systems.

The `affinity I/O mask` option binds SQL Server disk I/O to a specified subset of CPUs. In high-end SQL Server OLTP environments, this extension can enhance the performance of SQL Server threads issuing I/Os. This enhancement does not support hardware affinity for individual disks or disk controllers.

Bitmask	Processors Used
00000001 (1)	0
00000011 (3)	0, 1
00000111 (7)	0, 1, 2
00001111 (15)	0, 1, 2, 3
00011111 (31)	0, 1, 2, 3, 4
00111111 (63)	0, 1, 2, 3, 4, 5
01111111 (127)	0, 1, 2, 3, 4, 5, 6

The value for `affinity I/O mask` specifies which CPUs in a multiprocessor computer are eligible to process SQL Server disk I/O operations. The mask is a bitmap in which the rightmost bit specifies the lowest-order CPU (0), the bit to its immediate left specifies the next-lowest-order CPU (1), and so on. To configure more than 32 processors, you set both `affinity I/O mask` and `affinity64 I/O mask`. When all bits are set to 0 (or `affinity I/O mask` is not specified), SQL Server disk I/O is scheduled to any of the CPUs eligible to process SQL Server threads.

The values for `affinity I/O mask` are as follows:

▶ A 1-byte `affinity I/O mask` value covers up to 8 CPUs in a multiprocessor computer.

▶ A 2-byte `affinity I/O mask` value covers up to 16 CPUs in a multiprocessor computer.

▶ A 3-byte `affinity I/O mask` value covers up to 24 CPUs in a multiprocessor computer.

▶ A 4-byte `affinity I/O mask` value covers up to 32 CPUs in a multiprocessor computer.

To cover more than 32 CPUs, you configure a 4-byte `affinity I/O mask` value for the first 32 CPUs and up to a value-byte `affinity64 I/O mask` value for the remaining CPUs.

A 1 bit in the affinity I/O pattern specifies that the corresponding CPU is eligible to perform SQL Server disk I/O operations; a 0 bit specifies that no SQL Server disk I/O operations should be scheduled for the corresponding CPU.

An example of the bitmask values for the first seven processors of an eight-processor system follows (with decimal values shown in parentheses):

Bitmask	Processors Used
00000001 (1)	0
00000011 (3)	0, 1
00000111 (7)	0, 1, 2
00001111 (15)	0, 1, 2, 3
00011111 (31)	0, 1, 2, 3, 4
00111111 (63)	0, 1, 2, 3, 4, 5
01111111 (127)	0, 1, 2, 3, 4, 5, 6

Because setting the SQL Server `affinity I/O mask` option is a specialized operation, it should be used only when necessary. When specifying the `affinity I/O mask` option, you must use it with the `affinity mask` configuration option. You should not enable the same CPU in both the `affinity I/O mask` switch and the `affinity mask` option. The bits corresponding to each CPU should be in one of the following three states:

▶ 0 in both the `affinity I/O mask` option and the `affinity mask` option

▶ 1 in the `affinity I/O mask` option and 0 in the `affinity mask` option

▶ 0 in the `affinity I/O mask` option and 1 in the `affinity mask` option

In SQL Server 2014, reconfiguring the `affinity I/O mask` option requires a restart of the SQL Server instance.

The following is an example of this option:

```
exec sp_configure 'affinity I/O mask', 1
go
RECONFIGURE
Go
```

`Affinity64 I/O mask` is available only in the 64-bit version of SQL Server but is used for the same thing as `affinity I/O` mask.

affinity mask

Type: Advanced option

Default value: 0

When a server is experiencing a heavy load because other applications are running on the same server, it might be desirable to bind thread affinity to a processor.

`affinity mask` is a bitmapped field that provides SQL Server threads an affinity to processors. This is typically used in conjunction with the `affinity I/O mask` option just

18

described. Starting from the least-significant digit, each bit that is set to 1 represents the processor on which SQL Server will spawn its threads. Processors are numbered from 0 to 7. You usually leave the eighth processor alone because many system processes—such as domain controllers—default to that processor.

For example, if you want to create the affinity for one SQL Server instance's threads to use four processors of an eight-processor system, you would set this bitmask to be 15 (00001111). As a result, SQL Server would spawn its threads only on those processors, thus reducing overall reloading of the processor cache. This can be especially evident during heavy system loads.

The following is an example of this option:

```
exec sp_configure 'affinity mask', 15
go
RECONFIGURE
Go
```

In general, the default `affinity` value is able to provide ample load balancing across processors. You should allocate CPUs based on your particular processing load and application types. `affinity64 mask` is available only on the 64-bit version of SQL Server but is used for the same thing as affinity mask.

Following is a general recommendation of what to specify based on the different application types you are running:

▶ **OLTP**—Use the default value, 0.

▶ **Data warehouse**—Potentially use 75% of available processors to maximize the huge data loads, large reporting, and number of users.

▶ **OLAP**—Use the default value, 0.

▶ **Mixed**—Use the default value, 0.

From SSMS, you select SQL Server Properties, open the Processor tab, and select the targeted processors in the Enable Processors section, as shown in Figure 18.3.

Agent XP

Type: Advanced

Default value: 0

The `Agent XP` option enables SQL Server 2014 Agent extended stored procedures for this server. If enabled, the SQL Server Agent is available in SSMS. If not enabled, the SQL Server Agent is not available in SSMS and cannot be used to start or stop the service. This option changes to 1 when SQL Server Agent is started. This option also supports direct execution of CLR assemblies. It is not optimized to do so; it just supports this.

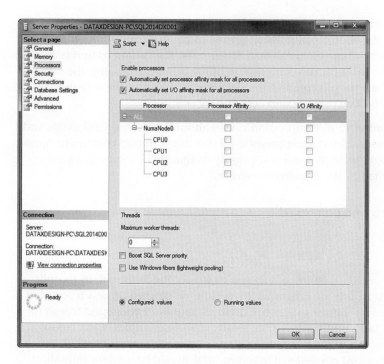

FIGURE 18.3   SQL Server 2014 processor's configuration from SSMS.

A 0 value indicates that SQL Server Agent extended stored procedures are not available (the default). A value of 1 indicates that the SQL Server Agent extended stored procedures are available.

backup checksum default

Type: Basic (NEW)

Default value: 0

With SQL Server 2014, you can use the BACKUP and RESTORE Transact-SQL statement WITH CHECKSUM. Doing a checksum verifies the backups file integrity (same size). However, when you install SQL Server 2014, the backup checksum default is set to 0, which makes backup/restore checksum off by default. To change the default to CHECKSUM, you set the backup checksum default to 1. To revert the default to NO_CHECKSUM, set the backup checksum default back to 0.

backup compression default

Type: Basic

Default value: 0

With SQL Server 2014 Enterprise and Standard editions, you can use the BACKUP Transact-SQL statement to select the backup compression setting to use WITH COMPRESSION or WITH NO_COMPRESSION. However, when you install SQL Server 2014, the backup compression default is set to 0, which makes backup compression off by default. To change the default to COMPRESSION, you set the backup compression default to 1. To revert the default to NO_COMPRESSION, set the backup compression default back to 0.

From a performance point of view, compression can significantly increase CPU usage, and the additional CPU consumed by the compression process might impact concurrent operations. Therefore, you might want to create low-priority compressed backups in a session whose CPU usage is limited by the Resource Governor.

blocked process threshold

Type: Advanced

Default value: 0

The blocked process threshold option allows you to specify the threshold, in seconds, at which blocked process reports are generated. By default, no blocked process reports are produced. blocked process threshold uses the deadlock monitor background thread to walk through the list of tasks waiting for a time greater than or multiples of the configured threshold. This option is useful when debugging systems with many deadlock situations. However, there is a cost of overhead involved, so it should be used for only short periods of time.

c2 audit mode

Type: Advanced; requires a reboot of SQL Server to take effect

Default value: 0

C2 audit mode can be configured through SSMS or with the c2 audit mode option in sp_configure. This feature is still available. Selecting this option configures the server to record both failed and successful attempts to access statements and objects. This information can help you profile system activity and track possible security policy violations. The C2 security standard has been superseded by common criteria compliance features. Much of the detail-level auditing is now done with SQL Auditing (covered in the SQL Server Security chapters) and is far more robust than this feature. C2 audit mode data is saved in a file in the default data directory of the instance. If the audit log file reaches its size limit of 200MB, SQL Server creates a new file, closes the old file, and writes all new audit records to the new file. This process continues until the audit data directory fills up or auditing is turned off. To determine the status of a C2 trace, you query the sys.traces catalog view. Be aware that C2 audit mode saves a large amount of event information to the log file, which can grow quickly. If the data directory in which logs are being saved runs out of space, SQL Server shuts itself down! If auditing is set to start automatically, you must either restart the instance with the -f flag (which bypasses auditing) or free up additional disk space for the audit log.

clr enabled

Type: Basic

Default value: 0

SQL Server 2014 supports direct execution of CLR assemblies. It is not optimized to do so; it just supports this capability.

A 0 value for clr enabled indicates that these CLR assemblies are not allowed to run on this SQL Server instance. A value of 1 allows this type of execution. The setting takes effect immediately after sp_configure is run, with no restart of the SQL Server instance required. When RECONFIGURE is run and the run value of the clr enabled option is changed from 1 to 0, all application domains containing user CLR assemblies are immediately unloaded. CLR assembly execution is not supported under lightweight pooling, so you must disable one of two options: clr enabled or lightweight pooling.

common criteria compliance enabled

Type: Advanced; requires a reboot of SQL Server to take effect

Default value: 0

The common criteria compliance enabled option enables three areas (or elements) of what is termed *common criteria*. The first is Residual Information Protection (RIP), which overwrites memory with a known pattern of bits before memory is reallocated to a new resource. This meets the RIP standard and contributes to improved security. The downside of this improvement is a slowing in performance. The second enables login auditing to occur. Each time a user successfully logs in to SQL Server, information about the last successful login time, the last unsuccessful login time, and the number of attempts between the last successful and current login times is made available. These login statistics can be viewed by querying the sys.dm_exec_sessions dynamic management view. And lastly, this option enables the behavior that a column-level GRANT should not override a table-level DENY. In other words, when enabled, a table-level DENY takes precedence over a column-level GRANT.

contained database authentication

Type: Basic

Default value: 0

Use the contained database authentication option to enable contained databases on the instance of SQL Server Database Engine.

This server option enables you to control contained database authentication.

- ▶ When contained database authentication is off (0) for the instance, contained databases cannot be created or attached to the Database Engine.

- ▶ When contained database authentication is on (1) for the instance, contained databases can be created or attached to the Database Engine.

18

A contained database includes all database settings and metadata required to define the database and has no configuration dependencies on the instance of the Database Engine where the database is installed. Users can connect to the database without authenticating a login at the Database Engine level.

Isolating the database from the Database Engine makes it possible to easily move the database to another instance of SQL Server. Including all the database settings in the database enables database owners to manage all the configuration settings for the database.

Contained databases allow users with the ALTER ANY USER permission, such as database owners, to authorize new users of the database. This reduces the access control of the sysadmin fixed server role. Before allowing contained databases, you should understand the risks associated with contained databases.

The following is an example of this option:

```
sp_configure 'contained database authentication', 1;
GO
RECONFIGURE;
GO
```

cost threshold for parallelism

Type: Advanced

Default value: 5

SQL Server 2014 supports parallel query execution. Before a query is executed, SQL Server's cost-based optimizer estimates the cost of execution for a serial plan (that is, a plan that uses a single thread). The option to set the cost threshold for parallelism allows you to specify a threshold in seconds; if the cost of the serial execution plan (in seconds) is greater than the value specified by this parameter, SQL Server considers a parallel query execution plan. A query does not become a candidate for parallel query execution simply based on this fact. Because parallel query execution is supported only on multiprocessor servers, the cost threshold for parallelism value is ignored for single-processor hardware. For an application that uses many complex queries, you should set this value to a lower number so that you can take advantage of the parallel query execution capabilities of SQL Server.

The following is an example of this option:

```
exec sp_configure 'cost threshold for parallelism', 2
go
RECONFIGURE
Go
```

The following is a general recommendation of what to specify based on the different application types you are running:

- ▶ **OLTP**—Use the default value, 5.

- ▶ **Data warehouse**—Many complex queries are candidates for parallelism. Set to a low value, such as 2 (seconds).

- ▶ **OLAP**—Use the default value, 5.

- ▶ **Mixed**—Use the default value, 5.

cross db ownership chaining

Type: basic

Default value: 0

You use the `cross db ownership chaining` option to configure cross-database ownership chaining for an instance of Microsoft SQL Server. This server option allows you to control cross-database ownership chaining at the database level or to allow cross-database ownership chaining for all databases. In other words, when this option is off for the instance, it is disabled for all databases. This server-wide option can be more selectively set at the individual database level. Our recommendation is to turn it off at the server instance level and then explicitly allow cross-database ownership chaining using the SET clause of the ALTER DATABASE statement.

cursor threshold

Type: Advanced

Default value: -1

The `cursor threshold` option allows you to specify when SQL Server should generate a cursor result set asynchronously. If the optimizer estimates that the number of rows returned by the cursor is greater than the value specified by this parameter, it generates the result set asynchronously. The optimizer makes this decision based on the distribution statistics for each table that is participating in the join in the cursor.

To determine the optimal value for this parameter, you need to make sure that statistics are up-to-date (by running update statistics) for the tables used in the cursors. By default, SQL Server generates a cursor result set synchronously. If you are using a fair number of cursors that return a large number of result sets, setting this value to a higher value results in better performance. Setting this value to 0 forces SQL Server to always generate a cursor result set asynchronously.

The following is an example of this option:

```
exec sp_configure 'cursor threshold', 100000
go
RECONFIGURE
go
```

18

The following is a general recommendation of what to specify based on the different application types you are running (where -1 indicates to let SQL Server decide when to do cursor result sets asynchronously):

▶ **OLTP**—Use the default value, `-1`.

▶ **Data warehouse**—A data warehousing environment is the largest potential user of this option due to the high volume of result rows returned by applications using data warehouses. Setting this value to `100,000` is a good starting point.

▶ **OLAP**—Use the default value, `-1`.

▶ **Mixed**—Use the default value, `-1`.

Database Mail XPs

Type: Advanced

Default value: `0`

Use the `Database Mail XPs` option to enable Database Mail on this server.

The possible values are as follows:

▶ `0`, indicating Database Mail is not available

▶ `1`, indicating Database Mail is available

The setting takes effect immediately without a server stop and restart.

After enabling Database Mail, you must configure a Database Mail host database to use Database Mail. Configuring Database Mail using the Database Mail Configuration Wizard enables the Database Mail extended stored procedures in the `msdb` database. If you use the Database Mail Configuration Wizard, you do not have to use `sp_configure`. Setting the `Database Mail XPs` option to `0` prevents Database Mail from starting. If it is running when the option is set to `0`, it continues to run and send mail until it is idle for the time configured in the `DatabaseMailExeMinimumLifeTime` option.

The following is an example of this option:

```
sp_configure 'Database Mail XPs', 1;
GO
RECONFIGURE
GO
```

default full-text language

Type: Advanced

Default value: `1033`

The `default full-text language` option is used to specify a default language value for full-text indexed columns. Linguistic analysis is performed on all data that is full-text indexed and is strictly dependent on the language of the data. The default value of this option is the language of the server.

The value of the `default full-text language` option is used when no language is specified for a column through the LANGUAGE option in the CREATE FULLTEXT INDEX or ALTER FULLTEXT INDEX statements. If the `default full-text language` option is not supported or the linguistic analysis package is not available, the CREATE or ALTER operation doesn't work, and SQL Server returns an `invalid language specified` error message. To see the list of linguistic analysis packages that are part of SQL Server 2014, you query the system view `sys.fulltext_languages`, as in this example:

```
SELECT * FROM sys.fulltext_languages
order by 2
Go
lcid        name
----------  -----------------------------
1025        Arabic
1093        Bengali (India)
1046        Brazilian
2057        British English
1026        Bulgarian
1027        Catalan
3076        Chinese (Hong Kong SAR, PRC)
5124        Chinese (Macau SAR)
4100        Chinese (Singapore)
1050        Croatian
1043        Dutch
1033        English
1036        French
1031        German
1095        Gujarati
1037        Hebrew
1081        Hindi
1039        Icelandic
1057        Indonesian
1040        Italian
1041        Japanese
1099        Kannada
1042        Korean
1062        Latvian
1063        Lithuanian
1086        Malay - Malaysia
1100        Malayalam
1102        Marathi
0           Neutral
```

18

1044	Norwegian (Bokmål)
2070	Portuguese
1094	Punjabi
1048	Romanian
1049	Russian
3098	Serbian (Cyrillic)
2074	Serbian (Latin)
2052	Simplified Chinese
1051	Slovak
1060	Slovenian
3082	Spanish
1053	Swedish
1097	Tamil
1098	Telugu
1054	Thai
1028	Traditional Chinese
1058	Ukrainian
1056	Urdu
1066	Vietnamese

If setting to other than the default, the `sp_configure` command would look like this (when set to French):

```
exec sp_configure 'default full-text language', 1036
go
RECONFIGURE
Go
```

default language

Type: Basic

Default value: `0`

The `default language` option specifies the language ID currently in use by SQL Server. The default value is `0`, which specifies the U.S. English system. As you add languages on the server, SQL Server assigns a new ID for each language. You can then use these IDs to specify the default language of your choice. You can add languages by using the SQL Server Setup program. Adding a language allows SQL Server to display error messages and date/time values in the format that is appropriate for that language. You set this option in the SQL Server instance Properties: Advanced settings page.

You can override the default language for a login by using `sp_addlogin` or `sp_default-language`. The default language for a session is the language for that session's login, unless overridden on a per-session basis by using the ODBC or OLE DB APIs. To see the languages supported for your SQL Server instance, you use the system view `sys.syslanguages`.

```
SELECT langid, substring(name,1,20) AS name,
            substring(alias,1,20) AS alias,
      lcid
FROM sys.syslanguages
order by 3
Go
```

langid	name	alias	lcid
31	Arabic	Arabic	1025
27	Português (Brasil)	Brazilian	1046
23	British	British English	2057
20	Bulgarian		1026
16	hrvatski	Croatian	1050
12		Czech	1029
4	Dansk	Danish	1030
7	Nederlands	Dutch	1043
0	us_english	English	1033
24	eesti	Estonian	1061
10	Suomi	Finnish	1035
2	Français	French	1036
1	Deutsch	German	1031
19		Greek	1032
13	magyar	Hungarian	1038
6	Italiano	Italian	1040
3		Japanese	1041
29		Korean	1042
25		Latvian	1062
26		Lithuanian	1063
8	Norsk	Norwegian	2068
14	polski	Polish	1045
9	Português	Portuguese	2070
15	română	Romanian	1048
21		Russian	1049
30		Simplified Chinese	2052
17		Slovak	1051
18	slovenski	Slovenian	1060
5	Español	Spanish	3082
11	Svenska	Swedish	1053
32		Thai	1054
28		Traditional Chinese	1028
22	Türkçe	Turkish	1055

Setting the default language to something other than the default would look like this (again, when set to French):

18

```
exec sp_configure 'default language', 2
go
RECONFIGURE
Go
```

You can change the language for a session during the session through the SET LANGUAGE statement. From SSMS, you can easily see the current default language and default full-text language settings, as shown in Figure 18.4.

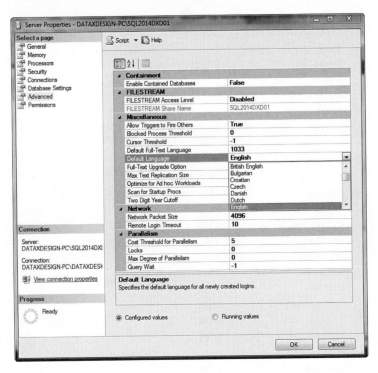

FIGURE 18.4   SQL Server 2014 server properties: advanced settings: language setting.

default trace enabled

Type: Advanced

Default value: 1

Use the default trace enabled option to enable or disable the default trace log files. The default trace functionality provides a rich, persistent log of activity and changes primarily related to the configuration options. This feature will be removed in a future version of Microsoft SQL Server. Avoid using this feature in new development work and plan to modify applications that currently use this feature. Use Extended Events instead!

disallow results from triggers

Type: Advanced

Default value: 0

Use the disallow results from triggers option to control whether triggers return result sets. Triggers that return result sets may cause unexpected behavior in applications that are not designed to work with them. This feature will be removed in a future version of Microsoft SQL Server. We recommend that you set this value to 1.

EKM provider enabled

Type: basic

Default value: 0

The EKM provider enabled option controls Extensible Key Management (EKM) device support in SQL Server. By default, this option is off. SQL Server 2014 Extensible Key Management enables third-party EKM/HSM vendors to register their modules in SQL Server. When registered, SQL Server 2014 users can use the encryption keys stored on EKM modules. This enables SQL Server to access the advanced encryption features these modules support, such as bulk encryption and decryption, and key management functions such as key aging and key rotation.

The following is an example of this option:

```
exec sp_configure 'EKM provider enabled', 1
go
RECONFIGURE
go
```

filestream_access_level

Type: basic

Default value: 0

You use the filestream_access_level option to change the FILESTREAM access level. Before this option has any effect, the Windows administration settings for FILESTREAM must be enabled. You can also enable these settings when you are installing SQL Server or by using SQL Server Configuration Manager (SSCM) for a specific SQL Server instance. Setting the value to 0 disables this option. A value of 1 enables FILESTREAM for T-SQL access only. A value of 2 enables FILESTREAM for both T-SQL and Win32 streaming access.

FILESTREAM integrates the SQL Server Database Engine with an NTFS file system by storing varbinary(max) binary large object (BLOB) data as files on the file system. T-SQL statements can insert, update, query, search, and back up FILESTREAM data.

18

The following is an example of this option:

```
exec sp_configure 'filestream_access_level', 2
go
RECONFIGURE
```

fill factor

Type: Basic

Default value: 0

The `fill factor` option allows you to define the percentage of free space on a data page or an index page when you create an index or a table. The value can range from 1 to 100. Setting the value to 80 would mean each page would be 80% full at the time of the `create index`. SQL Server also allows you to specify the value of `fill factor` at the server level by providing a `fill factor` parameter.

The following is an example of this option:

```
exec sp_configure 'fill factor', 80
go
RECONFIGURE
Go
```

The following is a general recommendation of what to specify based on the different application types you are running:

▶ **OLTP**—This is a good candidate for leaving space free in pages due to the update, delete, and insert characteristics. Try 80% full value first and watch the page split activity.

▶ **Data warehouse**—Use the default value, 0.

▶ **OLAP**—Use the default value, 0.

▶ **Mixed**—Use the default value, 0, or about a 90% full value.

index create memory

Type: Advanced, self-configuring

Default value: 0

The `index create memory` option is used to control the amount of memory used by index creation sorts. It is a self-configuring option and usually doesn't need to be adjusted. However, if you are having problems with the creation of large indexes, you might want to try specifying a KB value here that will contain the sort portion of the `index create`. Zero (0) means "self-configuring" by SQL Server.

The following is an example of this option:

```
exec sp_configure 'index create memory', 1000
go
RECONFIGURE
go
```

in-doubt xact resolution

Type: Advanced

Default value: 0

The in-doubt xact resolution option changes the behavior of the default outcome for transactions that the Microsoft Distributed Transaction Coordinator (MS DTC) is unable to resolve. This helps prevent MS DTC–related downtime and provides clarity to transaction outcomes across database servers. A value of 1 is a *presume commit* directive. In other words, any MS DTC in-doubt transactions are presumed to have committed. A value of 2 is a *presume abort* directive, which means any MS DTC in-doubt transactions are presumed to have aborted.

The following is an example of this option:

```
exec sp_configure 'in-doubt xact resolution', 2
go
RECONFIGURE
go
```

lightweight pooling

Type: Advanced

Default value: 0

Lightweight pooling is relevant to multiprocessor environments that have excessive context switching. By flipping the lightweight pooling switch, you might get better throughput by performing the context switching inline, thus helping to reduce user/kernel ring transitions. The lightweight pooling option actually causes SQL Server to switch to fiber mode scheduling. CLR execution is not supported under lightweight pooling. You can disable one of two options: clr enabled or lightweight pooling.

The following is an example of this option:

```
exec sp_configure 'lightweight pooling', 1
go
RECONFIGURE
go
```

The following is a general recommendation of what to specify based on the different application types you are running:

18

- ▶ **OLTP**—This is a good candidate for use on a multiprocessor machine.

- ▶ **Data warehouse**—This has a good potential for usage on a multiprocessor machine.

- ▶ **OLAP**—Use the default value, 0.

- ▶ **Mixed**—Use the default value, 0.

locks

Type: Advanced, self-configuring

Default value: 0

In SQL Server 2014 and future releases, this feature is deprecated. Making a change to this value will have no effect.

max degree of parallelism

Type: Advanced

Default value: 0

The max degree of parallelism option specifies the number of threads to be used for parallel query execution. On a single-processor server, this value is always ignored. For multiprocessor servers, a default value of 0 signifies that all the CPUs will be used for parallel query execution. When SQL Server 2014 runs on a machine that has more than one processor, it detects the best degree of parallelism. If you set this value to 1, all query plans are serialized. If the affinity mask option is on, parallel query execution takes place only on the CPUs for which the affinity mask bit is turned on. In that way, these two options can be used in conjunction. The application types assessment is the same as described for the affinity mask option.

The following is an example of this option:

```
sp_configure 'max degree of parallelism', 4
go
RECONFIGURE
go
```

max server memory **and** min server memory

Type: Advanced, self-configuring

Default values: 2147483647 and 1024

The max server memory option specifies the maximum amount of memory (in megabytes) available to SQL Server. It is used in conjunction with min server memory, and they essentially establish upper and lower bounds for memory allocation. SQL Server uses this memory for user connections, locks, internal data structures, and caching of the data. This is the memory pool described earlier. The default value of 2147483647 for the max server memory option means that SQL Server performs dynamic allocation of memory from the operating system, based on available physical memory on the machine. The default value of 1024 for the min server memory option means that SQL Server starts allocation memory as it is needed and then never goes below the minimum value after it is reached.

The SQL Server lazywriter process is responsible for making sure enough memory is available to SQL Server for the optimal number of buffers and Windows so that no excess paging occurs at the operating system level. The lazywriter process frequently checks physical memory available on the machine. If the memory available is greater than 5MB, lazywriter assigns excess memory to the SQL Server buffer cache.

You should watch the Working Set performance counter, which shows the amount of memory used by a process (SQL Server in this case). If this number is consistently below the amount of memory for which SQL Server is configured, SQL Server is configured for more memory than it needs. You can also adjust the set working set size configuration option.

If SQL Server is the only application running on a machine, you might want to perform static memory allocation. You need to be careful when you allocate fixed memory to SQL Server. If you allocate more memory to SQL Server than the machine has, SQL Server fails to start. You use the -f option during startup to bring up SQL Server with the default configuration. You can then change the value to the correct value and restart SQL Server.

The following is an example of this option:

```
exec sp_configure 'max server memory', 200000
go
RECONFIGURE
Go
exec sp_configure 'min server memory', 1024
go
RECONFIGURE
go
```

Because memory is managed dynamically, these settings basically create the lower and upper bounds within which SQL Server must operate. When SQL Server is started, it uses the minimum server memory amount to pre-allocate space to SQL Server. If the load on the server never requires allocating the amount of memory specified in the minimum server memory option, SQL Server runs with less memory.

Figure 18.5 shows both the minimum server memory and maximum server memory settings on the SQL Server Properties: Memory page.

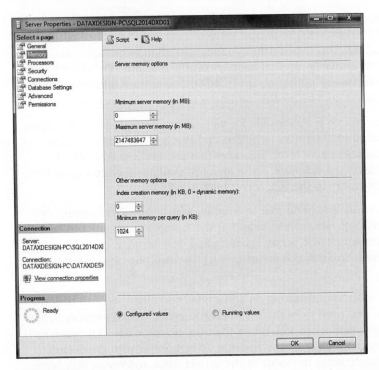

FIGURE 18.5   Accessing the minimum and maximum server memory configuration settings in SSMS.

The following is a general recommendation of what to specify based on the different application types you are running:

▶ **OLTP**—For those with heavy loads, this is a good candidate for high minimum memory settings.

▶ **Data warehouse**—Use the default values.

▶ **OLAP**—Use the default values.

▶ **Mixed**—For those with heavy loads, this is a good candidate for high minimum memory settings.

max text repl size

Type: Basic

Default value: 65536

The max text repl size parameter specifies the maximum size of the text, ntext, varchar(max), nvarchar(max), and image data types for columns participating in replication during single insert, update, writetext, and updatetext statements. You might need to raise this value if the image sizes your application deals with are consistently large and the data is part of a replication configuration.

The following is an example of this option:

```
exec sp_configure 'max text repl size', 131072
go
RECONFIGURE
go
```

max worker threads

Type: Advanced

Default value: 0

SQL Server uses native operating system threads. The max worker threads parameter specifies the maximum number of threads available for SQL Server processes. One or more threads are used for supporting each network protocol (for example, TCP/IP, named pipes). SQL Server is configured to listen. The checkpoint and lazywriter processes also consume threads. A pool of threads is used to handle user connections. When the number of connections is lower than the max worker threads parameter value, a thread is created for each connection. When more connections are on the server than the value defined by the max worker threads parameter, SQL Server provides thread pooling for efficient resource utilization. The default value of 0 autoconfigures the number of max worker threads to be (256 + ((number of processors – 4) × 8)) for a 32-bit processor and twice that for a 64-bit processor. So, for an 8 processor 32-bit machine, the max worker threads value would be autoconfigured to be (256 + ((8 – 4) × 8)) = 288.

More threads can create overhead on the system processors. Therefore, lowering this value might sometimes improve the performance of a system. For a system with a few hundred user connections, a reasonable value for this parameter is 288. You might want to experiment with various values to determine the appropriate setting for this parameter. A multiprocessor environment can easily handle more threads, and you can increase the number of threads accordingly.

The following is an example of this option:

```
exec sp_configure 'max worker threads', 288
go
RECONFIGURE
go
```

The following is a general recommendation of what to specify based on the different application types you are running:

▶ **OLTP**—For multiprocessor environments, set the value upward because those environments can handle servicing more threads. This yields performance gains.

▶ **Data warehouse**—Use the default value, 0.

▶ **OLAP**—Use the default value, 0.

▶ **Mixed**—For multiprocessor environments, set the value upward because those environments can handle servicing more threads. This yields performance gains.

media retention

Type: Advanced, requires a restart of SQL Server.

Default value: 0

The media retention option specifies the length of time to retain each backup set. The option helps protect backups from being overwritten until the specified number of days has elapsed. After you configure the media retention option, you do not have to specify the length of time to retain system backups each time you perform a backup. The default value is 0 days, and the maximum value is 365 days.

The media retention option can be overridden by using the RETAINDAYS clause of the backup statement.

The following is an example of this option:

```
EXEC sp_configure 'media retention', 60
GO
RECONFIGURE
GO
```

min memory per query

Type: Advanced

Default value: 1024

The min memory per query option specifies the minimum amount of memory (KB) that will be allocated for the execution of a query. Normally, the SQL Server query processor attempts to determine the optimal amount of memory for a query. This option allows the sysadmin role to specify this value instead. Increasing this value usually improves queries that handle hash and sort operations on a large volume of data.

The following is an example of this option:

```
exec sp_configure 'min memory per query', 2048
go
RECONFIGURE
go
```

Looking back at Figure 18.5 showing the Memory page of the Server Properties dialog, you can see the min memory per query option set at 1024 (the default).

The following is a general recommendation of what to specify based on the different application types you are running:

▶ **OLTP**—Use the default value, `1024`.

▶ **Data warehouse**—This is a good opportunity to better service numerous canned queries in this environment. Set the value higher than the default.

▶ **OLAP**—Use the default value, `1024`.

▶ **Mixed**—Use the default value, `1024`.

nested triggers

Type: Basic

Default value: `1`

As the name suggests, `nested triggers` specifies whether a trigger event on a table will fire another trigger (that is, cascade). The nesting level of triggers is `32`. If you reach this limit of `32`, SQL Server gives an error and rolls back the transaction. The default value of `1` means that a trigger on a table can cause another trigger to fire.

network packet size

Type: Basic

Default value: `4096`

The `network packet size` parameter specifies the default network packet size for SQL Server. Setting this value to a higher number (which should be divisible by 512) can improve the performance of applications that involve a large amount of data transfer from the server. Check your network configuration and set an appropriate value for this parameter. You can also improve performance by lowering the size value for applications that are small in data transfer size. However, the usual scenario is to increase this size to accommodate large amounts of data transfer, as with bulk loads.

The following is an example of this option:

```
exec sp_configure 'network packet size', 8192
go
RECONFIGURE
go
```

> **TIP**
>
> You can also specify the network packet size from the client when you connect to SQL Server (using the -a option for isql, osql, and bcp). Setting the network packet size from a client can be useful when the default network packet size is adequate for general application needs. However, a larger packet size might be needed for some specific operations, such as bulk copy. You can also call OLE DB, ODBC, and DB-Library functions to change the packet size.

18

The following is a general recommendation of what to specify based on the different application types you are running:

- ▶ **OLTP**—Possibly decrease this size to `512` if all queries deal with small amounts of data transfer, which is often the case in OLTP or ATM applications.

- ▶ **Data warehouse**—Perhaps increase this to `8192` or larger to handle the consistently large data transfers in this environment.

- ▶ **OLAP**—Use the default value, `4096`.

- ▶ **Mixed**—Use the default value, `4096`.

Ole Automation Procedures

Type: Advanced

Default value: `0`

Use the `Ole Automation Procedures` option to specify whether OLE Automation objects can be instantiated within Transact-SQL batches. This option can also be configured using the Policy-Based Management or the `sp_configure` stored procedure.

The `Ole Automation Procedures` option can be set to the following values:

- ▶ `0`, to disable OLE Automation Procedures

- ▶ `1`, to enable OLE Automation Procedures

When OLE Automation Procedures are enabled, a call to `sp_OACreate` will start the OLE shared execution environment.

The following is an example of this option:

```
sp_configure 'Ole Automation Procedures', 1;
GO
RECONFIGURE;
GO
```

optimize for ad hoc workloads

Type: Advanced

Default value: `0`

The `optimize for ad hoc workloads` option is used to improve the efficiency of the plan/procedure cache for workloads that contain many single-use ad hoc batches. When this option is set to `1`, the Database Engine stores a small compiled plan stub in the plan/procedure cache when a batch is compiled for the first time, instead of the full compiled plan. This helps to relieve memory pressure by not allowing the plan/procedure cache to become filled with compiled plans that are not reused. The compiled plan stub allows SQL Server to recognize that this ad hoc batch has been compiled before but has stored only a compiled plan stub, so when this batch is invoked (compiled or executed) again, SQL Server compiles the batch, removes the compiled plan stub from the plan/procedure cache, and adds the full compiled plan to the plan/procedure cache. Setting `optimize for ad hoc workloads` to 1 affects only new plans; plans that are already in the plan/procedure cache are unaffected. The compiled plan stub is one of the cache object types displayed by the `sys.dm_exec_cached_plans` catalog view.

The following is an example of this option:

```
exec sp_configure 'optimize for ad hoc workloads',1
go
RECONFIGURE
go
```

PH_timeout

Type: Advanced

Default value: 60

You use the full-text protocol handler timeout option (`PH timeout`) to specify the time, in seconds, that the handler should wait to connect to a database before timing out. The default value is 60 seconds. Increase the value when connection attempts are timing out due to temporary network issues or increased workloads. The full-text protocol handler is hosted in the filter daemon host and is used to fetch the data to be full-text indexed.

The following is an example of this option:

```
exec sp_configure 'PH_timeout', 120
go
RECONFIGURE
Go
```

priority boost

Type: Advanced

Default value: 0

In SQL Server 2014 and future releases, this feature is deprecated. Making a change to this value will have no effect.

Looking back at Figure 18.3, you can see the Boost SQL Server Priority on Windows option in the Processors page of the Server Properties dialog. Use care when applying this option.

query governor cost limit

Type: Advanced

Default value: 0

Queries are often the cause of major performance problems. SQL Server can handle queries, but many are poorly written and don't restrict the search criteria enough. This can result in runaway queries that return large result sets, and they can adversely affect the entire server's performance. One way to control this situation is to cut off the query at the pass by specifying a maximum cost limit to queries, in seconds. If any query's cost, in seconds, is greater than this maximum value, the query is not allowed to execute. The query governor cost limit value is server-wide and cannot be applied to just one query. Remember, though, that 0 (the default) for this option turns off the query governor, and all queries are allowed to run without any time limitation.

The following is an example of this option:

```
exec sp_configure 'query governor cost limit', 300
go
RECONFIGURE
Go
```

To change the value on a per-connection basis, you use the SET QUERY_GOVERNOR_COST_LIMIT statement.

The following is a general recommendation of what to specify based on the different application types you are running:

 ▶ **OLTP**—Use the default value, 0.

 ▶ **Data warehouse**—This is a must-have option for this environment. Try setting this value to 300 seconds and then get ready for the users to scream at you. On the positive side, the server won't get bogged down or freeze again.

 ▶ **OLAP**—For OLAP systems that use SQL Server storage, set this value to 600 seconds to get started and then reduce it over time.

 ▶ **Mixed**—You have the same protection opportunity here as for OLAP. This won't affect the OLTP queries, so it is safe to apply.

query wait

Type: Advanced

Default value: -1

Queries that are memory intensive and involve huge sorts might take a long time to execute, based on the available memory during execution. SQL Server internally calculates the timeout interval for such queries. Usually, this is quite a large number. You can override this value by specifying a value (in seconds) for the `query wait` parameter in SQL Server. If you set this value too low, you risk more frequent query timeouts when your system is under a heavy load and a highly concurrent environment. If `-1` is specified (the default), the timeout is calculated as 25 times of the estimated query cost.

The following is an example of this option:

```
exec sp_configure 'query wait', 20
go
RECONFIGURE
go
```

recovery interval

Type: Advanced, self-configuring

Default value: `0`

The `recovery interval` parameter is used to specify the maximum time (in minutes) that SQL Server requires to recover a database during startup. During startup, SQL Server rolls forward all the changes committed during a SQL Server crash and rolls back the changes that were not committed. Based on the value specified for this parameter, SQL Server determines when to issue a checkpoint in every database of SQL Server so that in the event of a crash, SQL Server can recover the databases in the time specified by `recovery interval`. If the value of the `recovery interval` parameter is low, SQL Server issues check-points more frequently to allow a recovery to be faster; however, frequent checkpoints can slow down performance. Setting `recovery interval` too high creates a longer recovery time for databases in the event of a crash. The default value of `0` leaves this option open to SQL Server to determine the best value.

The following is an example of this option:

```
exec sp_configure 'recovery interval', 10
go
RECONFIGURE
go
```

The following is a general recommendation of what to specify based on the different application types you are running:

- ▶ **OLTP**—Use the default value, `0`.

- ▶ **Data warehouse**—This is an opportunity to save on checkpoints and not degrade performance in this mostly read-only environment. Set this value high.

- ▶ **OLAP**—In this read-only environment, you have the same performance opportunity here as in a data warehouse.

- ▶ **Mixed**—Use the default value, `0`.

18

remote access

Type: Basic, requires a restart of SQL Server

Default value: 1

The `remote access` option controls the execution of stored procedures from local or remote servers on which instances of SQL Server are running. This grants permission to run local stored procedures from remote servers or remote stored procedures from the local server. To prevent local stored procedures from being run from a remote server or remote stored procedures from being run on the local server, set the option to 0.

This feature will be removed in the next version of Microsoft SQL Server. Use `sp_addlinkedserver` instead.

remote admin connections

Type: Basic

Default value: 0

Microsoft SQL Server 2014 provides a dedicated administrator connection (DAC). The DAC lets an administrator access a running server to be able to execute diagnostic functions or T-SQL statements, or troubleshoot problems on the server, even when the server is locked or running in an abnormal state and not responding to any other type of user connection. By default, the DAC is available only from a client on the server. But if you set the `Remote Admin connections` option to 1, the DAC is available from a remote connection as well. By default, the DAC listens only on the loopback IP address (127.0.0.1), port 1434.

The following is an example of this option:

```
exec sp_configure 'remote admin connections', 1
go
RECONFIGURE
Go
```

remote login timeout

Type: Basic

Default value: 10

You use the `remote login timeout` option to specify the number of seconds to wait before returning from a failed attempt to log in to a remote server. If you are attempting to log in to a remote server and that server is down, `remote login timeout` ensures that you do not have to wait indefinitely before your computer ceases its attempts to log in.

This option affects connections to OLE DB providers made for heterogeneous queries. The default setting for remote login timeout is 20 (seconds). A value of 0 allows for an infinite wait.

The following is an example of this option:

```
exec sp_configure 'remote login timeout', 30
go
RECONFIGURE
Go
```

remote proc trans

Type: Basic

Default value: 0

In SQL Server 2014 and future releases, this feature is deprecated. Making a change to this value will have no effect.

remote query timeout

Type: Basic

Default value: 600

You use the `remote query timeout` option to specify how long (in seconds) a remote operation can take before Microsoft SQL Server times out. The default is 600, which allows a 10-minute wait. This value applies to an outgoing connection initiated by the Database Engine as a remote query. This value has no effect on queries received by the Database Engine.

For heterogeneous queries, `remote query timeout` specifies the number of seconds (initialized in the command object using the DBPROP_COMMANDTIMEOUT rowset property) that a remote provider should wait for result sets before it times out. This value is also used to set DBPROP_GENERALTIMEOUT, if supported by the remote provider. This setting causes any other operations to time out after the specified number of seconds.

The following is an example of this option:

```
exec sp_configure 'remote query timeout', 300
go
RECONFIGURE
Go
```

scan for startup procs

Type: Advanced

Default value: 0

When the `scan for startup procs` option is set to 1, SQL Server scans for and executes all automatically executed stored procedures on the server on startup. To set a stored procedure to become automatically executed, you use the `sp_procoption` system stored procedure. Typically, a stored procedure is executed at startup time when you want to have certain processing occur that creates the proper working environment for all subsequent database processing on the server. You also can execute at startup when you want to make sure that certain stored procedures' execution plans (with proper optimizer decisions) are already in the procedure cache before anyone else requests their execution.

The following is an example of this option:

```
exec sp_configure 'scan for startup procs', 1
go
RECONFIGURE
go
```

show advanced options
Type: Basic

Default value: 0

By default, you do not see the advanced configuration parameters of SQL Server. If you set show advanced options to 1, you can see all the SQL Server parameters that can be set by the sp_configure command.

user connections
Type: Advanced, self-configuring

Default value: 0

The user connections option specifies the number of concurrent users allowed on SQL Server. When the value is 0 (which is the default), SQL Server can configure the needed user connections dynamically as they are needed (unlimited). If you specify a value, you are limited to that maximum number of user connections until you specify a larger value. If you specify a value other than 0, the memory allocation for user connections is allocated at SQL Server startup time, and it burns up portions of the memory pool. Each connection takes up 40KB of memory space. For instance, if you configure SQL Server for 100 connections, SQL Server pre-allocates 4MB (40KB ¥ 100) for user connections. You can see that setting this value too high might eventually impact performance because the extra memory could instead be used to cache data. In general, user connections are best left to be self-configuring.

The following is an example of this option:

```
exec sp_configure 'user connections', 300
go
RECONFIGURE
go
```

In Figure 18.6, you can see the current setting of 0 (unlimited) for the user connections value within SSMS. If you plan to set this option, the value must be between 5 and 32,767.

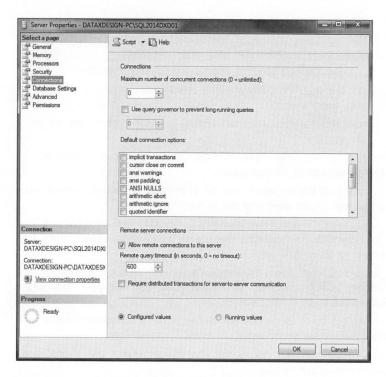

FIGURE 18.6   The Connections page of the Server Properties dialog in SSMS.

user options

Type: Basic

Default value: 0

The user options parameter allows you to specify certain defaults for all the options allowed with the SET T-SQL command. Individual users can override these values by using the SET command. You are essentially able to establish these options for all users unless the users override them for their own needs. User options is a bitmask field, and each bit represents a user option. Table 18.1 outlines the values you can set with this parameter.

TABLE 18.1   Specifying User Options Values

Bitmask Value	Description
1	DISABLE_DEF_CNST_CHK controls interim/deferred constraint checking.
2	IMPLICIT_TRANSACTIONS controls whether a transaction is started implicitly when a statement is executed.
4	CURSOR_CLOSE_ON_COMMIT controls the behavior of cursors after a commit has been performed.
8	ANSI_WARNINGS controls truncation and nulls in aggregate warnings.

Bitmask Value	Description
16	`ANSI_PADDING` controls padding of fixed-length variables.
32	`ANSI_NULLS` controls null handling when using equality operators.
64	`ARITHABORT` terminates a query when an overflow or divide-by-zero error occurs during query execution.
128	`ARITHIGNORE` returns `NULL` when an overflow or divide-by-zero error occurs during a query.
256	`QUOTED_IDENTIFIER` differentiates between single and double quotation marks when evaluating an expression.
512	`NOCOUNT` turns off the message returned at the end of each statement that states how many rows were affected by the statement.
1024	`ANSI_NULL_DFLT_ON` alters the session's behavior to use ANSI compatibility for nullability. New columns that are defined without explicit nullability are defined to allow `NULL` values.
2048	`ANSI_NULL_DFLT_OFF` alters the session's behavior to not use ANSI compatibility for nullability. New columns defined without explicit nullability are defined not to allow `NULL` values.
4096	`CONCAT_NULL_YIELDS_NULL` has SQL Server return a `NULL` when concatenating a `NULL` value with a string.
8192	`NUMERIC_ROUNDABORT` has SQL Server generate an error if loss of precision ever occurs in an expression.
16344	`XACT_ABORT` has SQL Server roll back a transaction if a T-SQL statement raises a runtime error.
	For remote stored procedures, `remote query timeout` specifies the number of seconds that must elapse after sending a remote `EXEC` statement before the remote stored procedure times out.

For a given user connection, you can use the `@@options` global variable to see the values that have been set.

The following is an example of this option:

```
exec sp_configure 'user options', 256
go
RECONFIGURE
Go
```

Again, a user can override these values with the `SET` command during a session.

XP-Related Configuration Options

Type: Advanced

Default: 0

A handful of advanced options are available with SQL Server 2014 to more granularly address the execution of extended stored procedures within different SQL server components:

Agent XPs

Database Mail XPs

Replication XPs Option

SMO and DMO XPs

SQL Mail XPs

`xp_cmdshell`

Each of these options defaults to 0, which means external stored procedures for these areas are not available in the instance. If you enable these options, you should fully understand that doing so opens these extended stored procedures to all on the instance.

As SQL Server 2014 expands in use, some of these options will probably be highlighted in more detail as more real-world examples support their use and attention.

Summary

Dealing with the large number of configurable options in SQL Server is a big undertaking. You not only need to know about the internal address space of SQL Server, but also need to understand what types of applications will be running on the server so that the configuration decisions you make are not counterproductive.

Many of the configurable options have a direct effect on the most dynamic part of SQL Server: the memory pool. This is truly where all the action is. Whether you have chosen to let SQL Server help you manage this space dynamically via self-configuring options or you have decided to manage this yourself, you must constantly monitor the current settings and be prepared to modify them at any time. In general, you can start with the default values given to the server at installation time and then slowly enhance those options over time.

18

Working with and Deploying to Azure SQL Database

This chapter provides an introduction to the cloud platform for SQL Server, Azure SQL Database (ASD). ASD is a highly available, multitenant, database-as-a-service architecture that enables you to scale your data both vertically (by adding instances) and horizontally (by federating these instances) to a seemingly limitless extent.

Relying on ASD means that you no longer have to buy and maintain your own server hardware, pay for network bandwidth, or purchase SQL Server and perform its inevitable upgrades. However, the liberation from maintenance that it offers also brings fresh challenges. It requires you to adapt to a new way of thinking about how you administer your data, monitor and adjust resource usage, and manage your budget.

The sections that follow guide you in the most efficient, practical way possible, beyond the hype and into the tools and techniques you need to use ASD today.

Setting Up Subscriptions, Servers, and Databases

Before using ASD, you must sign up for a Windows Azure subscription. Azure is the core infrastructural platform on which ASD is built. Its heart is a fault-tolerant, geographically distributed network of Microsoft-powered data centers whose online services are available to you on a fee-for-use basis. It provides the backbone operating system, network, and security layers that your database instances need to stay online, healthy, and protected.

Your first steps with ASD include creating your account, provisioning one or more cloud-based servers and instances, and, as a side-effect of accomplishing these tasks, mastering its online toolset.

Setting Up Your Windows Azure Subscription

Signing up for a Windows Azure subscription is a simple process that takes only a few steps.

To begin, visit http://azure.microsoft.com and sign in with your Microsoft account. Next, click on the Try it Free button, after which you'll be redirected to a screen where you will enter your registration details. Even though you may be entitled to a free trial (or other discount, usually bundled with an MSDN subscription or Visual Studio purchase), you might still need to provide a credit card in the next sign-up step. Be aware that billing charges (at the rates effective at the time of billing) begin to accrue immediately after your trial period ends for all of the services you configure. (Costs are covered in detail in the section, "Understanding SQL Database Billing.")

After submitting the registration form, you are taken to the account Summary screen, where you can choose to upgrade your subscription (if you are using a trial account) to a Pay-As-You-Go account by clicking the Upgrade Now button, then selecting the Yes radio button, then clicking the checkmark icon at bottom right (illustrated in Figure 19.1). In order to complete the examples in this chapter, you don't need to upgrade; a trial account is sufficient.

> **NOTE**
>
> When you are done testing ASD, be sure to delete your storage accounts, servers, and databases *and* cancel your subscription, unless, of course, you want to continue using them for other projects. Otherwise, after your free trial's end date, your account will continue to accrue billing charges at current rates.

Once you've completed sign-up, you are redirected to the Azure subscription home page. From here, click on the Account Menu link and make sure your subscription matches what you selected during sign-up (illustrated in Figure 19.2).

Having verified your subscription, your next step is to click on the blue Portal button at screen right to access the Azure portal management dashboard. If this is your first time through, a quick five-step tour of the management interface is brought into focus in the web UI. This tour-style tutorial is actually quite useful, as it illustrates how to use the menu system to manage your account and perform related tasks, including creating services and resources, executing global commands, and viewing onscreen notifications. (You'll complete most of these actions as you follow along with this chapter's exercises.)

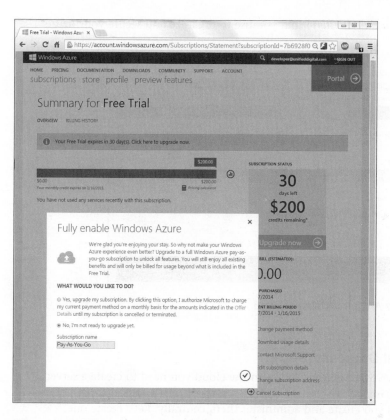

FIGURE 19.1   Windows Azure's Account Summary screen, with upgrade option in focus.

FIGURE 19.2   Windows Azure account screen showing current subscription.

After you complete the tour, you land on your Azure dashboard, also known as the *current portal* or *management portal*, which (as of this writing) is at stable version V11 (illustrated in Figure 19.3). Your dashboard contains a list of logical directories (including your automatically-created *default directory*) that you use to organize and secure your Azure objects.

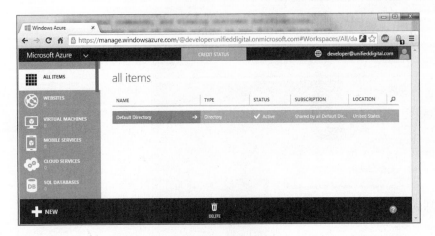

FIGURE 19.3   Windows Azure's portal dashboard.

Creating a Logical Database Server

Just as with on-premises SQL Server editions, in the cloud you need to create a server before creating a database. In the context of ASD, a server is just a logical construct used to group the databases you create and administer them centrally. Let's create one.

Using the left menu, click SQL Databases. Under the primary page heading (SQL Databases) you will find three links (acting more akin to tabs, and so referred to as such from this point): Databases, Servers, and Deleted Databases. You can create a server as a discrete task, or you can create a server when you create a database by selecting New SQL Database Server in the New SQL Database dialog. You can also create a database in a slightly different manner by clicking the +New menu button at the bottom of the screen and then following the links Data Services, SQL Database, Custom Create.

To keep things simple, let's create a server first so that you get the feel of each individual task. Click the Servers tab and then click Create a Database Server. Enter a login name and a strong password (according to the restrictions shown in the balloon help), select the geographical region nearest you (to ensure lowest network latency), check the box to allow the Azure online tools access to your server, and then click the checkmark icon to save all your information (see Figure 19.4).

The account you just created is your central administration account, also known as your *server login* or *server-level principal*. You can create additional logins and assign them to the built-in roles available with ASD (covered later in the section, "Managing Logins, Users, and Roles").

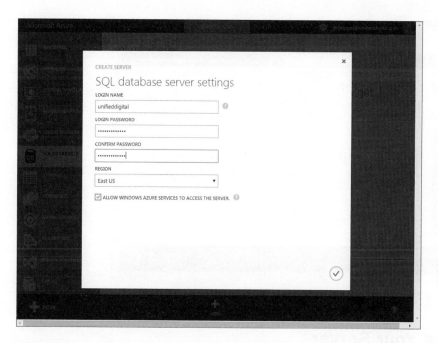

FIGURE 19.4   Configuring Windows Azure SQL Database server settings.

Upon saving your new SQL Server, the system navigates back to your dashboard with the Servers tab loaded with your new server listed in the grid. You will notice that your server has been given a system-generated name that ensures uniqueness at the DNS level. Click it to reveal the Common Tasks area (shown in Figure 19.5) and then click Manage Server, after which the screen dims and, at screen bottom, a dialog asks whether to add your current IP address to the list of allowed addresses in the firewall rules (covered in more detail in the section, "Configuring Your Firewall"). In future sessions, if you visit the portal from another IP address, the Configure page will recognize your new IP and ask whether you want to add it as well. Be sure to answer in the affirmative; otherwise, you will not be able to manage your new SQL Server. Answer yes, as well, to the subsequent dialog that asks whether to begin administering your server.

At this point, you will likely need to allow the WindowsAzure.com domain to display pop-up windows in your browser. This is essential to experiencing the UI as designed. If you miss the first pop-up window, it's okay; just click Manage Server in the Common Tasks area to navigate to the server login screen. Alternatively, you can click on SQL Databases using the left menu, and then, under SQL Databases, click the autogenerated name of your new server.

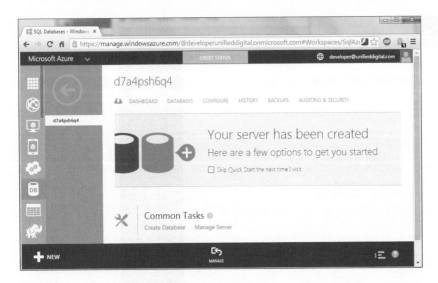

FIGURE 19.5   Windows Azure SQL Database Server common tasks.

Managing Your Server

Your server's name is a unique string that forms the first subdomain portion of its fully qualified domain name (a.k.a. its *hostname*). You will use this hostname to connect to your databases and to manage your server (using the Management Portal over HTTPS). These addresses always take the following form:

```
alphanumxx.database.windows.net
```

Where `alphanumxx` is your server's 10-character name.

NOTE

The autogenerated name given to your ASD server cannot be changed. However, there is a simple workaround if you don't want to have to live with it (on your local network, at least), although it could be argued that using an unusual server name offers a modicum of security (via obfuscation). Using SQL Server Configuration Manager (SSCM), create an alias of your choosing (in both the 32-bit and 64-bit alias sections) that points to your server using TCP/IP over port 1433. For example, if your server name is `asdfghjkl7.database. windows.net`, add an alias called something like `mycompany.database.windows.net`. Be sure to do this consistently on all of your local computers or use Group Policy to push down a Registry entry (using the key `[HKEY_LOCAL_MACHINE\SOFTWARE\[Wow6432Node\]` `Microsoft\MSSQLServer\Client\ConnectTo]`). Alternatively, you can use your DNS management system to create a CNAME record, pointing a subdomain of your domain to the autogenerated name).

Take a moment to see if you can connect to your server using the tried-and-true telnet method. (You can install the telnet client using Windows Add/Remove Features.) Fire up a command line and type the following:

```
telnet alphanumxx.database.windows.net 1433
```

When you press Enter, the screen should clear (go black), indicating a successful connection (use the key sequence Ctrl+] to exit, then quit telnet). If you receive a connection failed message, log in to the Management Portal, navigate to your SQL Server's settings, and then click on the Configure tab, where you will add your machine to the list of allowed clients. Let's take a moment to explore this screen in depth (see Figure 19.6).

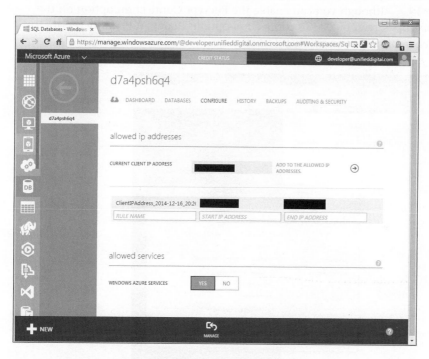

FIGURE 19.6   Windows Azure SQL Database firewall configuration.

19

Configuring Your Firewall

On the Configure screen, you can create named firewall rules that allow individual IP addresses and IP address ranges access to your server.

It's important to understand that ASD only allows client access over TCP/IP port 1433 (the default SQL Server port) using an encrypted connection. By default, no clients are allowed to access your server; you must grant access explicitly. You must also configure your local machines by enabling TCP/IP (using Configuration Manager) and by opening outgoing port 1433 on your firewall (incoming port 1433 usually need not be enabled, as allowed outgoing port requests usually enable incoming traffic on the same port).

Use the Configure screen to add the IP addresses you need to connect to ASD (be sure to use your router's external IP), and then, on your local machine, fire up SQL Server Management Studio (SSMS). (SSMS edition 2008 R2 or later is required to connect to ASD.)

Using SQL Server Management Studio

Because ASD supports the same Tabular Data Stream (TDS) protocol as standard SQL Server, you can connect to your new server using its hostname (or any alias you may have created) in the usual manner, using the server login and password you created earlier, as shown in Figure 19.7. Although you can enable the Encrypt Connection option on the Connection Properties screen of SSMS's connection options dialog, it is not necessary to do so, as Azure encrypts the connection automatically.

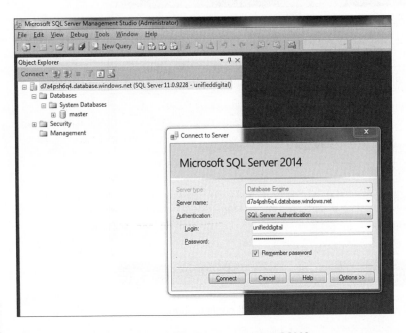

FIGURE 19.7   Connecting to SQL Database using SSMS.

When you've connected to your server, view it using Object Explorer and expand the databases node. As you can see, a few things set ASD instances apart from standard SQL Server instances in the UI: The server icon is tinted blue, and the right-click menu offers greatly reduced functionality. The only possible actions are to connect, disconnect, refresh, open a new query window, or run a custom (local) SQL Server Reporting Services (SSRS) report. Notice also that master is the only available (and the only system) data-base. All the administrative T-SQL commands you execute with ASD must be done in the context of `master`. `master` is also the default database that clients will connect to if they do not specify a database in their connection options.

Let's take a moment to explore the system views and commands required for managing client connectivity. Open a new query window by right-clicking the `master` database and then enter the T-SQL specified in Listing 19.1. (You will notice that, unfortunately, IntelliSense is not yet available in SSMS for ASD instances.)

LISTING 19.1   Using T-SQL to View, Add, and Delete SQL Database Firewall Rules

```
SELECT *
FROM sys.firewall_rules
ORDER BY id;

EXEC sys.sp_set_firewall_rule
     @name=N'test_firewall_rule',
     @start_ip_address='4.2.2.2',
     @end_ip_address='4.2.2.3';


EXEC sys.sp_delete_firewall_rule @name=N'test_firewall_rule';
```

Notice first in Listing 19.1 the absence of a `USE` statement; in ASD, the `USE` statement is not supported (other than to specify the current database). All statements not executed in the context of a database to which a client has explicitly connected are executed in the context of `master`.

The first statement in Listing 19.1 reveals the `sys.firewall_rules` system view. Its columns include an auto-incremented primary key, row created and last modified dates, the name of the firewall rule, and its IP address range. To add a new firewall rule programmatically, you call the system extended stored procedure `sys.sp_set_firewall_rules`, specifying a name and IP address range for your rule. To delete an existing firewall rule, you call the system extended stored procedure `sys.sp_delete_firewall_rule`, specifying the name of the rule to delete. Keep in mind that these T-SQL statements perform exactly the same functions offered by the Configure screen of the online portal. You can use whichever method you prefer.

Now that you've had a taste of how easy it is to work with SQL Database using SSMS, let's return to the online portal to complete our overview.

Using Management Portal

The Server Settings screen in Management Portal includes seven important configuration tabs: Common Tasks (represented at far left by a cloud icon), Dashboard, Databases, Configure, History, Backups, and Auditing & Security:

- ▶ **Common Tasks**—Lists server management tasks.

- ▶ **Dashboard**—Shows the number of databases in use and available. As of this writing, you can create up to 150 databases per server, including the `master` database.

This screen also allows you to reset your administrator login password, view your server status and region, and view basic subscription information. The Dashboard tab also shows your database usage quota, expressed using the proprietary Database Throughput Unit (DTU) measure (covered in this chapter in the section "Understanding SQL Database Service Tiers"). You can also use this page to reset your server login password.

▶ **Databases**—Enables database creation, modification, and deletion.

▶ **Configure**—Allows you to configure firewall rules for external clients and for Azure platform utility access.

▶ **History**—Allows you to view history records for any data import or export process you performed on ASD.

▶ **Backups**—Covered in the section "Backing Up and Restoring Databases" in this chapter.

▶ **Auditing & Security**—Allows you to audit ASD usage, including the following events: Data Access, Schema Changes, Data Changes, Security Failures, Grant/Revoke Permissions. Also allows you to download audit logs to an Excel Power View and Power Pivot spreadsheet for further analysis.

Click on each tab to familiarize yourself with all of the available options.

Our tutorial continues by showing you how to create and manage user databases by using the Management Portal and also with T-SQL.

Working with Databases

Using Management Portal, begin by clicking on the Databases tab and then click Create a SQL Database. On the ensuing dialog, enter a database name (our example screens use the name FirstSQLDB), select a collation (the default is a fine choice), select the subscription against which the database will be billed (use the free trial if you have one), and make sure that your server name is selected in the last drop-down. The Service Tiers and Performance Level form options require some explanation before you make your selections.

Understanding SQL Database Service Tiers

ASD comes in three new tiers: Basic, Standard, and Premium. The older Web and Business editions are still available, but these will be retired in September 2015, so we don't recommend using them with a new database. Each tier has a maximum database size along with a Database Throughput Unit (DTU) capacity rating. DTU is a proprietary (Microsoft) measure of server power that incorporates CPU, RAM, and IO thresholds. (Further details are available from MSDN here: http://msdn.microsoft.com/library/dn741336.aspx.)

The Basic tier is targeted at small (usually application- or website-specific) data-usage scenarios. It has a maximum database size of 2GB with a performance level fixed at 5 DTUs.

The Standard edition, more appropriate for data supporting multiple applications, has a maximum database size of 250GB, and you can select from 10, 20, and 50-DTU capacities (known as performance levels S1, S2, and S3, respectively).

The Premium tier, for large enterprise-level storage, has a maximum database size of 500GB, and you can select from 100, 200, and 800-DTU capacities (known as performance levels P1, P2, and P3, respectively).

Be aware that your database tier's maximum size is somewhat fixed—SQL Database won't automatically expand your database or change your tier to fit new growth. However, you can easily do this yourself using the Scale options on your ASD database's context page (as described below). Once your database reaches its maximum size, you can no longer create tables, routines, and views, or perform inserts or updates; however, you can still perform deletions and truncations, drop tables and indexes, and rebuild indexes (in an effort to reclaim disk space).

It's important (from both a billing and a data management perspective) to know which objects are included in the maximum size calculation. User tables, views, stored routines, and indexes are all included. System tables, system views, system stored routines, and the master database are all excluded.

Now that you understand the ramifications of the database creation options, you can make selections from the remaining two selections (Service Tiers and Performance Level) on the new database dialog box in Management Portal. For our examples, enter the name FirstSQLDB, then select the Basic tier and click the checkmark icon at bottom right. The final state of the dialog box should resemble Figure 19.8.

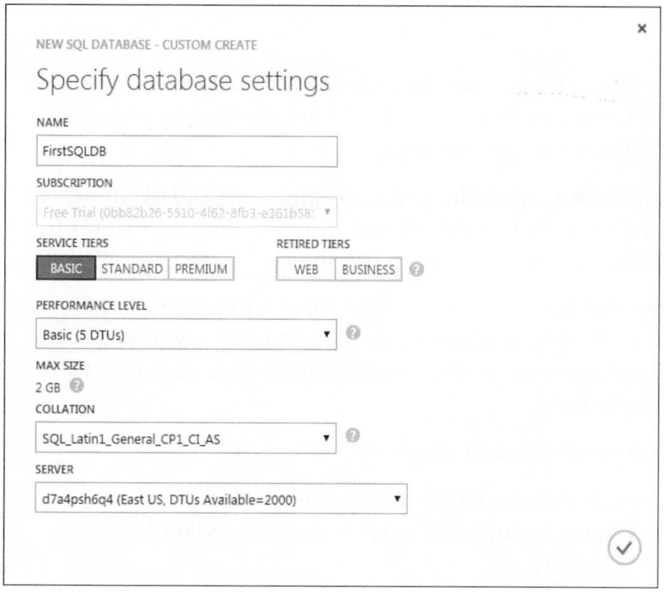

FIGURE 19.8   Using the Custom Create dialog to create a Basic tier SQL database.

After a few moments of preparation, your new database will appear in the grid on the Databases tab. Click the database name to reveal its management tabs. Clicking the Dashboard tab reveals a graph showing storage, connections, and deadlocks, plotted over a configurable time period. (Some of this data is available in the system view `master.sys.database_connection_stats`.) Below it your database disk usage is shown. To the right, you can click Show Connection Strings to reveal client applications connection strings for your database (making it easy for developers to connect), as well as links to view related applications and ASD documentation.

When you click the Monitor tab, you see the same graph that is depicted at the top of the Dashboard tab, although this version includes statistical counters of tracked events in its footer.

Clicking the Scale tab allows you to change your database's service tier, enabling a quick scale-up of your plan (just click the new tier's name, then click Save in the footer at page bottom).

Using the Configure tab, you can set up automatic exports of your database, on a schedule of your choosing, to an Azure storage account. (Learn more about Azure storage accounts here: http://azure.microsoft.com/en-us/documentation/articles/storage-whatis-account/.)

On the Geo-Replication tab, if you subscribed to the Standard or Premium tiers, you can configure replication settings for your databases, either across Azure regions or within the same region. (For more information about regions, see this article: http://azure.microsoft.com/en-us/regions/.)

Finally, using the Auditing & Security tab, you can set up auditing of events including data access and modifications, schema changes, security, and permission changes.

Using the Database Workspace

You can use the online database design tools to create tables in your database. To do this, click the cloud icon to reveal the Common Tasks view, then click the Design Your SQL Database link near the bottom of the main content area.

When you arrive at the ASD login screen, enter the username and password of the server login you previously created and then click Log On. (It may take a minute or two for the next screen to load, especially if this is your first visit to the site.)

The UI that loads is known as the Database Workspace. The three tabs at bottom left provide features that enable you to design, administer, and get an overview of your database. When you click your database name using the breadcrumb links at page top, two tabs are revealed in the right content pane:

▶ **Summary**—Provides database statistics and usage.

▶ **Query Performance**—Shows all recent queries, the number of times run, duration, and I/O metrics. (The display is similar to what is shown in SSMS's Activity Monitor.)

When you click an individual query statement in Query Performance, the Query Details content pane is revealed. It also has two tabs:

▶ **Query Plan Details**—Displays your query with general statistics and advanced metrics.

▶ **Query Plan**—Displays a graphical query execution plan, including a set of tabs on the left that lets you locate, filter, and get statistics on various plan operations. You can click each operation to reveal its details, as shown in Figure 19.9. This is the closest thing to SQL Profiler currently offered by Azure (V11).

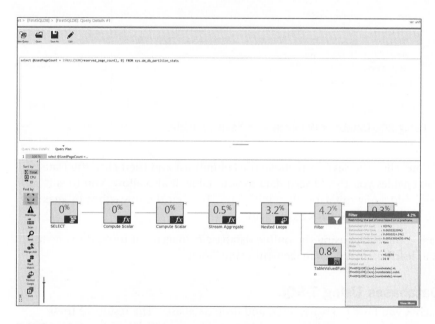

FIGURE 19.9   Viewing query plan details using the SQL Database Workspace.

As you click through various tasks in the Database Workspace, new entries appear at top left representing each task. You can use these to navigate from task to task. When you click the topmost My Work entry, an icon view of each task is presented. Click any icon to return to its task.

You can use the Database Workspace to develop your databases. Click the Design tab at bottom left to reveal the Database Design Workspace. In in the right content pane, three tabs appear, allowing you to design tables, views, and stored procedures using the Silverlight-based online tools. Let's take a few moments to create a table.

Click the Tables tab and then click New Table. This reveals three tabs you use to add and alter these familiar database objects: Columns, Indexes and Keys, and Data. The Columns tab loads by default. The interface is straightforward and similar to the design surface in SSMS. Add a few columns, being sure to mark one of them as the primary key. A clustered index is required for all ASD tables. (Heaps are not supported; although you can create them, you cannot use them until a clustered index is created.) Figure 19.10 illustrates a simple table that has an incremental primary key, a required (non-null) string field, and a nullable datetime field with a default value of GETDATE().

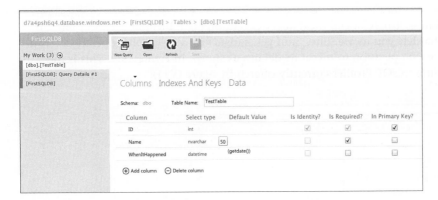

FIGURE 19.10   Using SQL Database Workspace to design a table.

When you are done, click the Save icon above the column list and then click the Data tab. The Data tab enables you to add seed data to your table; it also allows you to edit any existing rows. Add a few rows and then click Save. Test out the row editor by making modifications to a row and then click Save again.

Now that you are comfortable using the online database management tools, it's time to return to SSMS to learn basic ASD management using T-SQL.

Managing Databases Using T-SQL

This section teaches you how to create, alter, and drop databases. The results of these T-SQL operations are the same as what you achieved using the ASD UI. The syntax will be familiar to you from your experience with standard SQL Server, although the options available are more restricted.

When you created your ASD server, the master system database was also generated for you. Whenever you execute a CREATE, ALTER, or DROP DATABASE command in T-SQL, as explained in the following examples, you must do so while in the context of master.

Creating Databases

When you create a database using T-SQL, it defaults to the Basic tier. You can, however, specify tier options using the EDITION, SERVICE_OBJECTIVE, and MAXSIZE keywords (as shown in Listing 19.2). If you specify the MAXSIZE keyword, but not the EDITION keyword, you will end up creating a Web or Business edition database—don't do this because these are retired editions. (See this article for more details on creating Azure databases using T-SQL: http://msdn.microsoft.com/en-us/library/dn268335.aspx.)

> **NOTE**
>
> For every database you host in Standard and Premium tiers, ASD creates and manages at least three replicas (one primary and at least two secondaries). Every transaction is written to the primary and the secondary replicas before a commit is considered to be complete. In the event the primary replica fails, ASD automatically fails over to one of the secondary replicas. If any replica fails, a new one is automatically created. In addition, ASD keeps these copies available for restore using the Backups tab of your database context page. This high-availability service is provided transparently and requires no additional setup actions.

The syntax for CREATE DATABASE does not allow you to specify filegroups, attachments, Service Broker settings, database snapshots, or access options. This is in keeping with the set of limitations in effect for ASD as a whole (see the later section, "Understanding SQL Database Limitations," for more details). Remember, you must be in the context of the master database to execute CREATE, ALTER, or DROP DATABASE statements.

LISTING 19.2   Creating a Standard Tier S1 Performance Level Database Using T-SQL

```
CREATE DATABASE MySecondDB
(
        EDITION = 'standard',
        SERVICE_OBJECTIVE = 'S1'
);
```

Modifying Databases

You can change the maximum size and edition of your database on-the-fly using the ALTER DATABASE syntax (just as you can by using Management Portal). The example code in Listing 19.3 shows you how to use the MODIFY clause to change the database you just created from Standard tier to Premium tier. Note that this upgrade operation is not possible when using a free trial subscription.

LISTING 19.3   Altering a Database's Tier, Maximum Size, and Performance Level Using T-SQL

```
ALTER DATABASE MySecondDB
MODIFY
(
        EDITION = 'premium',
        SERVICE_OBJECTIVE = 'P1',
        MAXSIZE = 500GB
);
```

Dropping Databases

When necessary, you can easily drop your database using the following familiar syntax:

```
DROP DATABASE MySecondDB;
```

All service tiers allow you to recover a deleted database during the tier's retention period, covered in the section "Using SQL Database Backup, Replication, and Recovery."

Migrating Data into SQL Database

A number of options exist for importing existing SQL Server (and other platform) data into ASD. They include the following:

▶ Executing a T-SQL script that includes object declarations and data insertion statements. You can create these scripts using the Generate and Publish Scripts Wizard, launched by right-clicking a standard SQL Server database in SSMS and then choosing Tasks, Generate Scripts.

▶ Importing a data-tier application export package (DACPAC) file (covered later in the section, "Backing Up and Restoring Databases")

▶ Using SSMS, including the Azure Deployment wizard and script generation

▶ Using the SQL Server Migration Assistant (SSMA)

▶ Using a custom-built SQL Server Integration Services (SSIS) package

▶ Using the bcp utility (a good choice for reliably importing large quantities of data)

▶ Using the SQL Database Migration Wizard (an excellent open-source tool available at https://sqlazuremw.codeplex.com/)

No matter which import method you select, keep in mind the set of limitations listed in the section, "Understanding SQL Database Limitations," as several generally used features supported by most standard SQL Server editions will not work with ASD.

The simplest way to get your existing databases into ASD is by using SSMS. SSMS 2014 includes a right-click option to bring any (well, any Azure-compatible) database objects into ASD. Connect to your on-premises server using SSMS, right click the database of your choice and select Tasks, Deploy Database to Windows Azure SQL Database. The ASD deployment wizard launches, shown in Figure 19.11, connected to our test Azure instance with our local database ready to be uploaded. As of this writing, this wizard only allows you to select from the two retired ASD editions (Web and Business). For now, we'll choose Web and then change to Basic tier later using our Azure dashboard's Scale tab settings. If your database is fairly simple, there should be no problems getting it into Azure.

Another convenient data import choice is to use the Generate and Publish Scripts Wizard in SSMS. To test your database's compatibility with ASD, right-click it and select Generate Scripts to launch the wizard for any existing database you have. When you reach the second wizard step (Choose Objects), select the Script Specific Database Objects radio button and check all the check box options except Users and XML Schema Collections. Complete the rest of the wizard steps and then save your script to a file.

When your script file is ready, connect to your destination SQL database (i.e., any SQL database other than master) using SSMS. (To do this, you use the connection dialog's Options tab to select a database in the Connect to Database drop-down list before

connecting.) Next, open your wizard-generated script in SSMS and remove any CREATE
DATABASE or USE statements. Attempt to execute the remainder of your script. Observe any
warnings or errors you experience and cross-reference them against the list of limitations
cataloged in the "Understanding SQL Database Limitations" section, later in this chapter.
Modify your script accordingly until your database successfully creates.

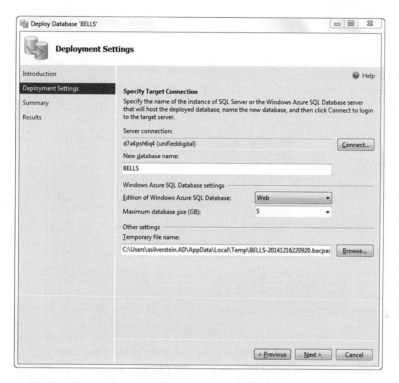

FIGURE 19.11   Using SSMS to copy an on-premises database to ASD.

One bonus that comes with migrating to ASD is that inbound bandwidth is free (although
outbound and cross-region bandwidth is not), so you don't have to worry about failures
and restarts costing you money during your import process. See the following article for
current pricing details: http://azure.microsoft.com/en-us/pricing/details/data-transfers/.

Copying Databases

ASD supports easy copying of existing SQL databases using the AS COPY OF clause of the
CREATE DATABASE statement (keep in mind that you cannot copy the master database
using this technique), shown in Listing 19.4. You can even use this syntax to create a
copy of a database on a different ASD server (provided the source and target servers reside
in the same geographical region) simply by prefixing the name of the source server to the
name of the source database.

19

LISTING 19.4   Copying an Existing SQL Database Using T-SQL

```
CREATE DATABASE AdventureWorks2012_Copy
AS COPY OF AdventureWorks2012;
GO
WAITFOR DELAY '00:02:00'; -- two-minute delay; allows time to copy data

DECLARE @DBID INT =
        (
                SELECT database_id
                 FROM sys.databases
                  WHERE name = 'AdventureWorks2012_Copy'
        );

SELECT
        c.database_id,
        name,
        state,
        state_desc,
        percent_complete,
        create_date
FROM sys.dm_database_copies c
JOIN sys.databases d
ON c.database_id = d.database_id
WHERE c.database_id = @DBID;
```

The CREATE DATABASE AS COPY OF statement is an asynchronous process that executes and returns immediately. You can monitor its progress by querying the system views sys.dm_database_copies and sys.databases, as shown at the bottom of Listing 19.4. Keep in mind that any copies you create are billed at standard rates; no discount is made for storing database copies, no matter how inactive.

Exporting Databases

ASD includes built-in capabilities for exporting databases to Azure Blob storage, and for creating ASD databases from these stored export results (a.k.a. BACPAC files, covered in the later section "Using BACPAC Files for Backup and Restore"). You can think of the Azure Export Service as a fully cloud-based, lightweight backup solution, however, because it relies on the uptime of different Azure service, it is not necessarily considered to be as reliable as the automatic, geo-replicated backups built into ASD. (The latter allows you to perform point-in-time restore [covered in the next section], while the former does not.) Let's take a quick look at how to perform an ASD export.

The first step is to create an Azure Storage account. To do this, locate and click the Storage link on the far left portal menu, then click Create a Storage Account in the right content area. On the entry form shown at page bottom, enter a unique subdomain name in the URL text box, choose a location (closest to you), then choose the Read-Access Geo-Redundant (RA-GRS) replication option from the Replication drop-down. Azure storage supports four different replication options and RA-GRS is the most robust. It allows read-only data access from the secondary replica, in addition to geo-replication across two regions. (To learn more about these options, see "Azure Storage Redundancy Options" at http://msdn.microsoft.com/en-us/library/azure/dn727290.aspx.)

Once your storage account has been created, return to your database context page by clicking SQL Databases on the far left menu, then click your target database name, then click the Configure tab. To set up automatic exports, click the Automatic button to the right of Export Status, select your storage account, configure a schedule of your choosing, then click the Save button at page bottom. Figure 19.12 illustrates this screen configured to perform a daily export (note the warning icon—Azure is kindly letting us know that this will be expensive).

FIGURE 19.12   Configuring an Azure Export Service schedule.

Once the service has created at least one export, you can then use this screen to create an ASD database from it, simply by clicking the Create Database button.

Backing Up and Restoring Databases

The backup and restore scenarios for ASD are fairly simple when compared with standard SQL Server methodologies. There are three primary approaches to creating a reliable system: The first is to use the built-in backup, replication, and recovery options provided in ASD. The second is a bit more manual—it makes use of the database copies you learned how to create in the previous section. The third relies on data-tier application features built into SSMS. We'll examine the built-in approach first.

Using SQL Database Backup, Replication, and Recovery

It's comforting to know that ASD automatically creates database backups for you (without any user intervention) on the following schedule: full backups once a week (automatically replicated across regions), daily differentials, and transaction logs every 5 minutes. Of course, the retention and recovery options for these backups vary by service tier.

Table 19.1 summarizes several key aspects of ASD's backup and restore capabilities according to service tier, including retention duration, recovery options, data loss duration, and replication options.

TABLE 19.1   Backup and Recovery Options by Service Tier

	Basic Tier	Standard Tier	Premium Tier
Backup retention duration	7 Days	14 Days	35 Days
Point-in-time restore available?	Yes	Yes	Yes
Point-in-time recovery option	Any restore point during the retention period	Any restore point during the retention period	Any restore point during the retention period
Geo-restore available?	Yes	Yes	Yes
Geo-restore's max data loss duration	24 hours	24 hours	24 hours
Geo-replication available?	No	Yes	Yes
Geo-replication's max data loss duration	No	30 minutes	30 minutes
Active geo-replication available?	No	No	Yes
Able to restore a deleted database?	Yes	Yes	Yes

Let's take a look at these features in detail. First, all tiers provide backup retention, differing only in by retention duration (7 for Basic, 14 for Standard, or 35 days for Premium). You can perform point-in-time database restoration using any of these backups. To do this, navigate to your database list page in the ASD Management Portal, click the database you wish to restore, then click the Restore button found at page bottom. In the ensuing dialog, confirm the source database and target server, then use the Restore Point slider to set the UTC date and time to which you want to recover (or just enter the date and time in the text boxes). Finally, click the checkmark icon to execute. This is illustrated in Figure 19.13.

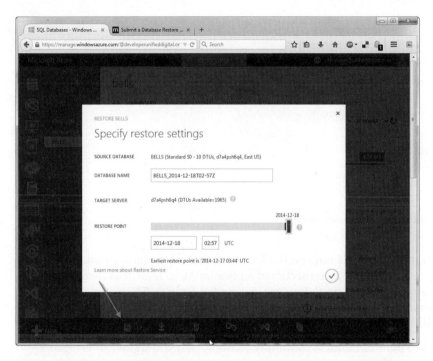

FIGURE 19.13   Point-in-Time restore of a live database.

All tiers even support restoring a backed-up (but currently deleted) database. To do this, navigate to your database list page, then click on the Deleted Databases tab. Click the database you wish to restore, then click the Restore button at page bottom. The ensuing dialog (shown in Figure 19.14) is very similar to the one shown in Figure 19.13.

All tiers provide *geo-restoration* capability, which can be defined as the ability to restore a backup from a different datacenter (region) in the event of a regional failure. All databases are backed up to Azure Blob storage and then these storage units are replicated to different datacenters. This brings with it a maximum 24-hour data loss potential (depending upon the time of the last automatic backup, relative to the time of the regional failure). To perform a so-called *geo-restore*, navigate to the Servers tab in the Management Portal, then click the server at fault. The ensuing screen (Geo-Redundant Backups) takes you to a list of backups that you can choose to restore, using the same steps previously described.

The Standard and Premium tiers also offer a *geo-replication* feature. When a primary database starts to fail (i.e., enters the *degraded* state) you can initiate failover to one of its offline, secondary replicas. This brings the selected replica online and the problematic database offline. The maximum data loss duration with geo-replication is 30 minutes.

19

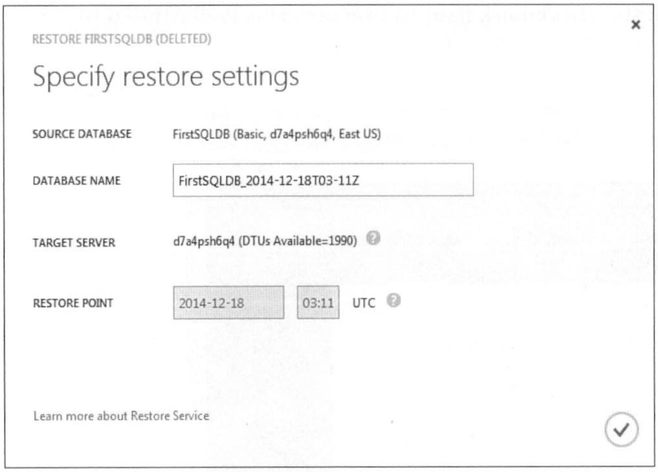

FIGURE 19.14   Restoring a deleted database.

Active geo-replication (available only on the Premium tier) takes multi-region replication a step further, by providing online transactional replication (also known as *continuous copy*) from your primary database to up to four geo-distributed replicas. These readable replicas can act as a high-availability cluster, enabling high-throughput distributed database reads (and failover capability) across regions.

Even with all these built-in business continuity technologies, you should still consider learning a few manual backup and restore techniques to complement your redundancy strategy.

Using Database Copies for Backup and Restore

You've already seen how to create database copies using the CREATE DATABASE AS COPY OF command. You can also use database copying as a simple backup and restore methodology. To do this you first create a T-SQL backup script that works against your SQL databases. Next you incorporate this script into a scheduled job that executes using your local installation of SQL Agent. One example might resemble the following scenario.

Every evening your backup script creates a fresh copy of your production database, naming it with a suffix indicating the current day, month, and year (e.g., MyDatabase_12_14_2014). After accumulating the desired maximum number of copies, your script drops the oldest copy before creating the next new copy (just as in a log rotation scenario). When the time comes to restore your production database from one of the copies, you use the ALTER DATABASE command (in the context of the master database) to rename the live version and the copy. To prevent the wrong copy of the database from being modified by clients, it is best to halt all incoming connections performing the rename (as illustrated in Listing 19.5).

LISTING 19.5   Restoring a Database Copy Using ALTER DATABASE

```
ALTER DATABASE MyDatabase -- the production database
MODIFY NAME = MyDatabase_BeforeRestore_12_13_2014; -- keep a pre-restore copy
GO
WAITFOR DELAY '00:20:00'; -- a twenty-minute delay
                          -- allows connections to drop off over time
GO
ALTER DATABASE MyDatabase_12_13_2014 -- restore yesterday's copy to production
MODIFY NAME = MyDatabase;
```

As soon as these statements complete, your live database is switched to its copy from the previous evening. The state of the live database prior to the switch is also preserved.

Using BACPAC Files for Backup and Restore

Database administrators tasked with deploying databases to remote servers can use data-tier applications (DACs, introduced with SQL Server 2008 R2) to rapidly and reliably create the schemas, tables, views, and other objects that make up application databases to any number of target environments.

DACs rely on backup package (BACPAC) files that contain all the logic necessary to re-create a database and its dependencies. The BACPAC functionality provided out-of-the-box in SSMS enables you to easily transfer databases into and out of ASD as a simple means of backup and restore.

Creating BACPAC Files

To export a complete database from ASD to a local file, complete the following steps:

1. Connect to your SQL database of choice using SSMS.

2. Right-click the database name in Object Explorer and then select Tasks, Export Data-Tier Application. This launches the BACPAC creation wizard.

3. On the Settings tab of the Export Settings screen, select the Save to Local Disk radio button and then browse to a local or network storage location.

4. Give your new .bacpac file a name, click Save, and then click the Advanced tab.

5. Make sure that all the tables you want backed up are selected and then click Next.

6. Click Finish after reviewing the contents of the Summary screen.

Figure 19.15 illustrates the Summary screen as it appears when exporting the Azure version of the AdventureWorks2012 database (available as a free download from CodePlex.com).

19

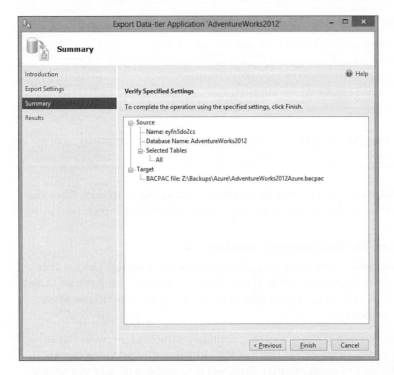

FIGURE 19.15   Viewing the Summary screen of the BACPAC Creation Wizard.

> **NOTE**
>
> To successfully export the Azure version of `AdventureWorks2012`, you must first create a clustered index on its `DatabaseLog` table.

You can automate BACPAC creation (and restoration) by building (and scheduling the execution of) a custom .NET application that works with the Windows Azure SQL Database Management API. For more information, see the MSDN article, "Managing Azure SQL Databases with REST API."

Restoring BACPAC Files

Restoring a BACPAC file is also a simple task. Just complete the following steps:

1. Connect to your SQL database server using SSMS, right-click on the Databases folder in Object Explorer, and select Import Data-Tier Application to launch the wizard.

2. On the Import Settings screen, select the Import from Local Disk option, browse to the file you created using the BACPAC Export Wizard, and then click Open.

3. Click Next.

4. Under New Database Name, enter a name for the destination database.

5. You can overwrite an existing database (by entering the name of an existing database) or create a new one on-the-fly (by entering a new name). You can also set the MAXSIZE, SERVICE_OBJECTIVE, and EDITION options (covered in the previous section, "Managing Databases Using T-SQL") for the database by using the drop-downs under the Azure SQL Database Settings heading.

6. Click Next, review your settings on the Summary screen, and then click Finish.

Your SQL database has just been restored to your local SQL Server instance using a BACPAC file.

Managing Logins, Users, and Roles

ASD includes support for the same T-SQL login, user, and role-management commands available in standard SQL Server, with some restrictions. In keeping with the other T-SQL commands you learned about earlier in this chapter, you can only execute login and database management statements in the context of the master system database, although you can also create users in the context of other databases as well.

Understanding Roles

The first step in working with logins and users is to understand the roles available in ASD. This set of roles is distinctly smaller than what is available with standard SQL Server. In fact, there are only two roles you need to learn about:

▶ dbmanager—Includes the permissions necessary to manage databases

▶ loginmanager—Includes the permissions necessary to manage server logins and database users

These two roles are created in the master database when you set up your ASD server. You can view them by querying the system view sys.database_principals, as shown in Listing 19.6.

LISTING 19.6 Viewing the Built-In SQL Database Roles Using T-SQL

```
SELECT DISTINCT
        p.principal_id,
        p.type_desc,
        p.name as role_name,
        p.create_date
FROM sys.database_principals p
WHERE p.type_desc = 'DATABASE_ROLE'
AND p.is_fixed_role = 0
AND p.principal_id > 0
ORDER BY p.principal_id;
```

19

To assign a login to a role, you execute the system stored procedure `sp_addrolemember`; to remove a login from a role, you execute `sp_droprolemember`. Although these two procedures are both deprecated, the newer `ALTER ROLE` syntax you might want to use instead is not yet completely supported for ASD. The following example removes a login from the `loginmanager` role and then adds that same user to the `dbmanager` role:

```
EXEC sp_droprolemember 'loginmanager', 'unifieddigital';
EXEC sp_addrolemember 'dbmanager', 'unifieddigital';
```

Now that you know how to work with ASD roles, you can create logins and users.

Managing Logins and Users

As mentioned earlier in this chapter, all ASD logins must use SQL Authentication. In addition to not supporting Windows Authentication, a few other ASD restrictions apply: You cannot use an email address as a login or user name, Microsoft user accounts are not supported (although you must have one to manage your Azure subscription), and all other custom authentication tweaks (including the use of `LOGON` triggers) are unsupported.

Managing Logins

The login you are already familiar with is that of the server-level principal (SLP). This is the login you created when you set up your ASD server. At creation time, it is made a member of both the `dbmanager` and `loginmanager` roles. In addition, it is also a member of the hidden `db_owner` role, aliased to the hidden `dbo` user, set up very much like the `sa` user in standard SQL Server editions.

To create a login using T-SQL for a user named Developer, open a connection to the `master` database and execute the following:

```
CREATE LOGIN Developer WITH PASSWORD='strong as !?#1B password';
```

As the example implies, you must provide a strong password that is at least nine characters long and includes both uppercase and lowercase letters and at least one number or symbol.

To view the logins on your server, you can query the system view `sys.sql_logins`, which you can also join to `sys.database_principals` and `sys.database_role_members` to view the roles currently assigned to these logins (as shown in Listing 19.7).

LISTING 19.7   Viewing the SQL Database Logins and Roles Using T-SQL

```
SELECT
        p.principal_id,
        l.name,
        l.create_date,
        l.default_database_name,
        l.default_language_name,
        s.role_principal_id,
        r.name as role_name
```

```
FROM sys.sql_logins l
JOIN sys.database_principals p
ON p.principal_id = l.principal_id
LEFT JOIN sys.database_role_members s
ON s.member_principal_id = p.principal_id
LEFT JOIN sys.database_principals r
ON r.principal_id = s.role_principal_id;
```

To modify a login you use the ALTER LOGIN statement. The following four T-SQL statements show how to rename a login (changing Developer to CTO), change its password, disable it, and then re-enable it:

```
ALTER LOGIN Developer WITH NAME = CTO;
GO
ALTER LOGIN CTO WITH PASSWORD = 'AE*(si@222';
GO
ALTER LOGIN CTO DISABLE;
GO
ALTER LOGIN CTO ENABLE;
```

To drop a login, simply use the DROP LOGIN statement, as follows:

```
DROP LOGIN CTO;
```

You can always use SSMS to view the logins, roles, and users in your system using Object Explorer by expanding the Security folder at the root level to view server principals and the Security folder at the database level for database users. Let's examine how to create the latter.

Managing Users

Working with ASD users is quite simple. To create a user, connect to the database of choice using a login that is in the loginmanager role (you can do this in SSMS by right-clicking your database and selecting New Query) and then execute a CREATE USER T-SQL statement similar to the following:

```
CREATE USER CTO FROM LOGIN CTO;
```

You can use ALTER USER to change the login associated with a user, switch a user's default schema (if in the context of the master database), and change a user's name. The following T-SQL statements exemplify these three actions:

```
ALTER USER CTO WITH NAME = CEO;
ALTER USER CEO WITH DEFAULT_SCHEMA = master;
ALTER USER CEO WITH LOGIN = Manager;
```

To view the users in any database you can query the `sys.sysusers` system view, as follows:

```
SELECT name, hasdbaccess, islogin
from sys.sysusers
WHERE name = 'CEO' AND islogin = 1;
```

Considerations for SQL Database Client Applications

Before letting the development team loose on ASD, it's important to understand that the connectivity model ASD presents is not quite the same as they've come to rely on using on-premises SQL Server editions.

Connectivity Limitations

For one thing, connectivity to ASD is never 100% guaranteed. Almost, but not quite. This may seem shocking, given that the ASD service level agreement (SLA) includes a 99.99% uptime clause (see the "Service Level Agreements" article for details: http://azure. microsoft.com/en-us/support/legal/sla/). However, there are a few client-side usage patterns that will result in interrupted connectivity and even forced disconnections.

Here are some typical situations your development team should be aware of before they build custom applications that depend on ASD:

▶ Connections that have been idle for more than 30 minutes will be automatically closed (this is also true for SSMS).

▶ Connections may be automatically closed (temporarily) in the event of an internal database failover or replica re-creation.

▶ Connections that generate vast amounts of network traffic may be closed or limited. (For more details on ASD's connection-throttling mechanism, see the TechNet article, "Windows Azure SQL Database Performance and Elasticity Guide," at http://social.technet.microsoft.com/wiki/contents/articles/3507.windows-azure-sql-database-performance-and-elasticity-guide.aspx.)

▶ Connections with long-running explicit transactions may be automatically closed.

▶ *Any* general network outage may automatically close connections.

There is also a special scenario to watch for related to database growth: If your SQL database reaches its maximum size threshold and, in response, you immediately upsize it, data modification (insert and update) queries may continue to fail (and continue to report errors, as if the database had not been upsized) until the database has been successfully replicated by ASD (as described earlier). Of course, the amount of time this actually takes depends on your database size.

Handling Intermittent Connectivity in Code

To deal with such scenarios, your custom applications' data access code should always include connection-retry logic. Developers should strongly consider unit testing the data access layer (DAL) by simulating lost connections and monitoring the attempts to reopen connections.

Connection String Differences

ASD client connection strings have a few unique aspects you should also familiarize yourself with:

▶ The segment `Encrypt=True` is required. This tells your application to use an encrypted connection.

▶ The segment `Trusted_Connection=False` is optional. This tells your application not to attempt Windows authentication.

▶ The `Server` segment specifies the hostname of your ASD server, prefixed by `tcp:`, which forces a TCP/IP connection. It is also suffixed with `,1433`, indicating the port to use. Both the prefix and suffix are optional, since TCP/IP is the default protocol and 1433 is the default port.

Now that you've have a taste of how to prepare applications that rely on ASD, it's time to learn how to estimate how much it will cost to use the service.

Understanding SQL Database Billing

ASD is billed using a pay-as-you-go model. The fees involved establish the baseline costs for the two primary services you need: database storage and bandwidth utilization. Prior to April 2014, new subscribers received discounts against the baseline free schedule by signing up for a long-term commitment plan and paying in advance; sadly, this offer has been discontinued and all newcomers must pay-as-you-go as well.

The next few sections explain your plan options and related pricing so you know roughly how much to budget. We also show you how to monitor your daily use so you can calculate (and verify the correctness of) your bill at any time.

Baseline Billing

The first tool available to help you estimate your billing is the online Billing Calculator, available at http://azure.microsoft.com/en-us/pricing/calculator/. This calculator enables you to estimate monthly costs based on database size, bandwidth quantity, and choice of support plan (if any). You simply adjust the slider controls to estimate your monthly bill. While this UI provides a convenient way to get a quick cost evaluation, it lacks the level of detail you need to truly understand how you will be invoiced.

Calculating Database Billing

There are three keys to understanding database billing:

▶ The cost of your database is calculated on a per-hour basis, according to service tier and performance level. Think of this measure as *database-hours*.

▶ The per-hour cost is billed daily.

▶ If you have multiple databases, simply sum your per-database costs.

Table 19.2 lists the current database-hour rates (as of this writing).

TABLE 19.2   SQL Database Pricing, by Service Tier and Performance Level

Service Tier (Abbreviation)	Performance Level (in DTUs)	Database-Hourly Rate
Basic (B)	5	$0.0067
Standard (S0)	10	$0.0202
Standard (S1)	20	$0.0403
Standard (S2)	50	$0.1008
Premium (P1)	100	$0.625
Premium (P2)	200	$1.25
Premium (P3)	800	$5.00

Calculating Bandwidth Billing

Bandwidth charges are also simple to calculate. The first point of importance is that bandwidth is classified according to its direction: inbound (or *ingress*) for data going into Azure; outbound (or *egress*) for data leaving Azure; and within (or *across*) for data that never enters or leaves Azure (i.e., data that is neither uploaded to nor downloaded from Azure).

All inbound bandwidth is free. All data transfer within Azure is also free if all the components involved (say, an ASD accessed from an Azure .NET application) are hosted within the same geographical region. Outbound bandwidth, the cost that most often comes as a surprise to customers, is free for the first 5GB/month and then calculated according to the region (or *zone*) where your data resides. These zones are simply named Zone 1, 2, and 3. Zone 1 includes all data centers in North America and Europe; Zone 2 covers Asia; Zone 3 covers southern Brazil. Outbound bandwidth from one zone to another is also billed at the outbound rate of the source zone. Table 19.3 lists the per-gigabyte prices for each zone according to the applicable monthly outbound thresholds.

TABLE 19.3   SQL Database Bandwidth Pricing, According to Zone

Outbound Monthly Threshold	Zone 1 Price-Per-GB	Zone 2 Price-Per-GB	Zone 3 Price-Per-GB
0-5GB	$0	$0	$0
5GB-10TB	$.0087	$0.138	$0.181
10-50TB	$.0083	$0.135	$0.175
50-150TB	$0.07	$0.13	$0.17
150-500TB	$0.05	$0.12	$0.16

Tracking Your Usage

Now that you know how to calculate costs, you're ready to start tracking (and correlating) your SQL database usage. You can perform this task using a spreadsheet you can download from the Management Portal and by querying system tables.

Usage Tracking Using Management Portal

To track your usage using the Management Portal, complete these steps:

1. Navigate to your subscription dashboard at https://account.windowsazure.com/Subscriptions.

2. Once there, click the button (or heading) showing the name of your subscription. Figure 19.16 illustrates the ensuing subscription detail page.

3. Click the Download Usage Details link, located at bottom right.

4. On the Billing History screen, click the Download Usage link for the period you are interested in studying.

5. Download and then open the comma-delimited (CSV) usage file in Excel.

   The content of the usage file is organized into an account header area, followed by two primary data regions. The header area includes all of your essential subscription information. The first data region includes your actual monthly statement, broken down according to the types of Azure services your account consumed, priced according to service and regional rate, then summarized by cost and time utilized. The second data region lists your Azure system usage by service, unit, and day, including all costs and times utilized.

6. To locate your data-specific costs, search the contents of the document for the text SQL Database (your server name and database name will be located in the Component column of the report).

7. To locate your bandwidth consumption costs, search the file for Data Transfer.

All of your service utilization total times are found under the Consumed column headers in both the first and second data regions.

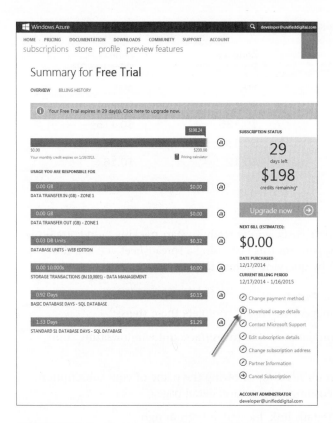

FIGURE 19.16   Viewing subscription details using the Management Portal.

Usage Tracking with System Views

To track your SQL database usage using T-SQL, you can query the `sys.database_usage` and `sys.bandwidth_usage` system views. One way you might consider for automating regular monitoring of your daily usage would be to create a local SQL Agent job that connects to ASD and executes a query (in the context of the `master` database) such as the one shown in Listing 19.8.

LISTING 19.8   Querying the System Views to Track SQL Database Usage

```
SELECT [time] as event_date_day,
       sku as edition,
       SUM(quantity) as total_database_quantity
FROM sys.database_usage
WHERE DATEPART(DAY, [time]) = DATEPART(DAY, GETDATE())
GROUP BY sku, [time]
WITH ROLLUP;
```

```
SELECT [time] as event_date_hour,
       database_name,
       direction,
       SUM(quantity) as total_bandwidth_kb_quantity
FROM sys.bandwidth_usage
WHERE DATEPART(DAY, [time]) = DATEPART(DAY, GETDATE())
GROUP BY direction, database_name, [time]
WITH ROLLUP;
```

The first query in this listing calculates your total number of databases in use by edition for the current day. The second query calculates your total bandwidth used per database by transfer direction for the current day. If you have specific budgeting thresholds in mind, you can use the results of these queries to set off alerts in your system using SQL Agent or custom code.

Understanding SQL Database Limitations

Although ASD supports a wide variety of commonly used standard SQL Server features and tools, there are several limitations you should keep in mind before you develop new ASD-dependent applications and before you import your existing data.

Unsupported and Partially Supported Functionality

This section covers the features and utilities that are not compatible with ASD. Most of these limitations simply make sense, due to the cloud-based nature of ASD (such as the absence of filegroups), since they are more tailored toward traditional server infrastructure management.

You can refer to the following list (and the set of MSDN articles found after it in the "References" section) whenever you have a question about ASD feature support. Keep in mind, this list is changing quickly as the Azure platform evolves. Items supported in the next version of ASD (V12) are marked as such below.

Unsupported XML Features

▶ Creating or using XML schema collections (V12)

▶ Managing XML indexes (V12)

▶ Using OPENXML and the related system stored procedures sp_xml_prepare_document and sp_xml_remove_document (although you can use the near-equivalent .nodes() XML data type method).

Unsupported Data Types and Functions

▶ Deploying or using custom SQLCLR objects (although the built-in hierarchyid and spatial data types are supported) (V12)

▶ Using the FILESTREAM data type

19

▶ Selecting data from external or distributed data sources, using operators such as OPENQUERY, OPENROWSET, and OPENDATASOURCE

▶ Using certain full-text functions, such as FREETEXTTABLE, CONTAINS, CONTAINSTABLE, as well as semantic search

▶ Using certain text and image data type functions, such as TEXTPTR and TEXTVALID (V12)

▶ Creating or using large user-defined types and aggregates (V12)

▶ Using database metadata functions, such as FILEPROPERTY, DATABASEPROPERTY, and KEY_NAME

▶ Using system statistical functions, such as @@CONNECTIONS, @@PACKET_ERRORS, and @@IDLE

Unsupported Database Features

▶ Taking database snapshots

▶ Using database mirroring (which is deprecated anyway)

▶ Using replication (although data is internally geo-replicated)

▶ Using log shipping

▶ Using database compression

▶ Using SQL Server audit, although SQL Database has its own auditing feature

▶ Using Change Data Capture

▶ Using Transparent Data Encryption

▶ Performing standard backup and restore procedures (although you can use the techniques described in the section, "Backing Up and Restoring Databases")

▶ Designing maintenance plans

▶ Attaching databases

▶ Using the SET options typical for database creation, other than the following V12-supported additions: ANSI_DEFAULTS, CONCAT_NULL_YIELDS_NULL, CONTEXT_INFO, OFFSETS

▶ Using the TRUSTWORTHY database option

▶ Using the USE *DATABASE* statement

▶ Managing filegroups (although DBCC CHECKFILEGROUP is V12-supported)

▶ Partitioning tables

▶ Using global temporary tables

▶ Using distributed queries and transactions

▶ Working with several system tables, views, and stored procedures (to see which are available, expand the `master` database folder in SSMS's Object Explorer window and then examine its child nodes)

▶ Using any table that lacks a clustered index (V12)

▶ Creating or altering extended stored procedures; using Extended Events (V12)

▶ Using application roles

Unsupported Networking Features

▶ Using named pipes protocol

▶ Using dynamic ports

▶ Connecting on ports other than 1433

▶ Connecting using an unencrypted connection

▶ Using SQL Browser

Unsupported Server Management Features

▶ Monitoring Extended Events (V12)

▶ Setting trace flags

▶ Using Policy-Based Management

▶ Using Service Broker

▶ Using Resource Governor

▶ Working with Master Data Services

▶ Using SQL Agent (although you can connect to your ASD server using your locally installed version)

▶ Using SQL Profiler (although you can use the online Query Plan feature described in the section, "Using the Database Workspace," as well as the V12-supported Dynamic Management Views (DMVs), detailed in the article "Monitoring Azure SQL Database Using Dynamic Management Views" at URL http://msdn.microsoft.com/library/azure/ff394114.aspx)

Unsupported Authentication and Authorization Features

▶ Creating a login named `sa`, `admin`, `administrator`, `guest`, or `root`

▶ Using many of the system and database roles found in standard SQL Server

▶ Creating and modifying custom server roles

▶ Using Windows authentication

19

References

Be sure to refer to the following MSDN articles for more detailed and up-to-date information on supported ASD functionality:

▶ "Azure SQL Database Transact SQL Reference"

▶ "Azure SQL Database Tools and Utilities Support"

▶ "System Stored Procedures (Azure SQL Database)"

▶ "Azure SQL Database General Guidelines and Limitations"

Summary

In this chapter, you learned how to use ASD to design, manage, administer, and scale out databases on the Windows Azure cloud platform.

The next chapter teaches you the essentials of creating and managing standard SQL Server databases.

PART IV

Database
Administration

IN THIS PART

PART IV

Database Administration

IN THIS PART

CHAPTER 20

Creating and Managing Databases

A database is a collection of tables and related objects that help protect and organize data. It must exist before you can create all database objects, including tables, indexes, and stored procedures. This chapter focuses on how to create a sound database that can house database objects and how to manage the database after the objects are created. The creation and management of the various database objects is discussed in the remaining chapters in Part IV, "Database Administration."

> **NOTE**
>
> It is important to remember that SQL Server actually uses its own set of databases that are installed by default when SQL Server is installed. These databases are referred to as *system databases*. The databases that users create are aptly named *user databases*. The system databases include `master`, `model`, `msdb`, `tempdb`, and `resource`. Each of these databases performs a key function in the operation of SQL Server. For example, the `master` database contains an entry for every user database created and contains server-wide information critical to the operation of SQL Server. The `model` database is basically a template database for any newly created databases. Each system database is based on a structure similar to user databases and contain database objects like those contained in user databases. The system databases are discussed in detail in Chapter 7, "SQL Server System and Database Administration."

What's New in Creating and Managing Databases

The features and functionality related to creating and managing databases have changed very little in SQL Server 2014. There have been some changes to the objects that are contained within a 2014 database but those will be discussed in chapters that cover those objects.

Data Storage in SQL Server

A database is a storage structure for database objects. It is made up of at least two files. One file, referred to as a *data file*, stores the database objects, such as tables and indexes. The second file, referred to as the *transaction log file*, records changes to the data. A data file or log file can belong to only one database.

SQL Server stores data on the data file in 8KB blocks, known as pages. A *page* is the smallest unit of input/output (I/O) that SQL Server uses to transfer data to and from disk. An 8KB page is equal to 1024 bytes times 8, or 8192 bytes. There is some overhead associated with each data page, so the maximum number of bytes of data that can be stored on a page is 8060 bytes. The overhead on a data page includes a 96-byte page header that contains system information about the page. This system information includes the page number, page type, and amount of free space on the page.

Generally, a row of data in a SQL Server database is limited to the 8060-byte maximum. With SQL Server 2014, there are some exceptions to this 8060-byte limit if the table contains columns that have the data types `text/image`, `varchar`, `nvarchar`, `varbinary`, or `sql variant`. With these data types, SQL Server can store the data in a separate data structure when the size of the row exceeds the 8060-byte limit. When the 8060-byte limit is exceeded, SQL Server stores a pointer to the separate data structure so that the information in these columns can be accessed.

Another exception to the 8060-byte limit is a table with `FILESTREAM` columns. `FILESTREAM` storage is implemented as a `varbinary(max)` column that has the `FILESTREAM` attribute enabled. With a `FILESTREAM` column, the data is stored as BLOBs in the file system. There is no fixed limit to the size of the BLOBs stored in these columns. You are limited only by the amount of space available on your file system.

In an effort to reduce internal operations and increase I/O efficiency, SQL Server, when allocating space to a table or an index, allocates space in extents. An extent is eight contiguous pages, or 64KB of storage. There are actually two types of extents. Every table or index is initially allocated space in a mixed extent. As the name implies, mixed extents store pages from more than one object. When an index or a table is first created, it is assigned an index allocation map (IAM), which is used to track space usage for the object, and at least one data page. The IAM and data page are assigned to a mixed extent in an effort to save space because dedicating an extent to a table with a few small rows would be wasteful. Up to eight initial pages are assigned this way. When an object requires more than eight pages of storage, all further space is allocated from uniform extents. A *uniform extent* stores pages for only a single index or table. This allows SQL Server to optimize read and write operations and reduce fragmentation because the data is stored in units of 64KB (that is, eight pages) as opposed to individual 8KB pages being scattered throughout the data file.

For more detailed information on the internal storage structures and how to manage them in SQL Server databases, see Chapter 31, "Understanding SQL Server Data Structures."

Database Files

SQL Server maps a database over a set of operating system files that are visible to the SQL Server instance. Microsoft recommends that the files be located on a storage area network (SAN), on an iSCSI-based network, or on a locally attached disk. These three storage options provide the best performance and reliability for a SQL Server database. You have an option of storing database files on a network, but this option must be used with caution. Network storage that has high latency can lead to consistency issues in the database and is not supported.

> **NOTE**
>
> In SQL Server 2008 and earlier versions, you had to enable trace flag 1807 to allow for data and log files to be located on network storage. This trace flag was removed in SQL Server 2008 R2. Databases created with this version and newer can be created using files that are found on network storage without having to use this trace flag.

Each database can contain a maximum of 32,767 files. This limitation does not apply to files that are associated with filestream. Each database file serves a different purpose for the Database Engine. These files have a standard layout that allows SQL Server to organize and read the data within the files. SQL Server needs to keep track of the allocated space in each data file; it does so by allocating special pages in the first extent of each file. Because the data stored on these pages is dense and the files are accessed often, they are usually found in memory; therefore, they can be retrieved quickly.

The first page (page 0) in every file is the file header page. This page contains information about the file, such as the database to which the file belongs, the filegroup it is in, the minimum size, and its growth increment.

The second page (page 1) in each file is the page free space (PFS) page. The PFS page keeps track of the other pages in the database file. The PFS uses 1 byte for each page. This byte keeps track of whether the page is allocated, whether it is empty, and if it is not empty, how full the page is. A single PFS page can keep track of 8,080 contiguous pages. Additional PFS pages are created as needed.

The third page (page 2) in each file is the global allocation map (GAM) page. This page tracks allocated extents. Each GAM page tracks 64,000 extents or 4GB (64,000 * 64KB), and additional GAM pages are allocated as needed. The GAM page contains 1 bit for each extent, which is set to 0 if the extent is allocated to an object and to 1 if it is free.

The fourth page (page 3) is the secondary GAM (SGAM) page. The SGAM page tracks allocated mixed extents. Each SGAM page tracks 64,000 mixed extents, and additional SGAM

20

pages are allocated as needed. A bit set to 1 for an extent indicates a mixed extent with pages available.

Primary Files

The *primary data file* is the data file that keeps track of all the other data files used by the database. It is an operating system file that typically has the file extension .mdf. SQL Server does not require that it have this .mdf extension, but it is recommended for consistency. The primary data file is the first file created for a database. Each database must have only one primary file. This file stores data for any database objects mapped to it, and it contains references to any other database files created.

In many cases, the primary data file is the only data file. There is no requirement to have more than one data file, and often, a database contains only one primary data file (for example, C:\mssql\mydb.mdf) and only one log file (for example, C:\mssql\mydb_log.ldf).

Secondary Files

You can create zero or more secondary data files in a database. These files, by default, are identified with the .ndf extension, but the extension can be different. Secondary data files provide an opportunity to spread the data that SQL Server stores over more than one physical file. This capability can be particularly useful for larger databases and can help with performance and management of database files. Consider, for example, a situation in which a database server has four physical drives available for the data file(s). Each drive is 1TB in size, but the database you are creating is 2TB. In this example, the database will not fit on one drive. A solution to this problem is to create a primary data file on one of the drives and a secondary data file on each of the three remaining drives. SQL Server automatically spreads the 2TB database across the four data files located on four separate drives.

Secondary files also provide some added flexibility for backing up or copying databases. This is most apparent with large databases. For example, let's say you have a 100GB database, and it contains only a primary data file. If you want to move this database to another environment, you must have a drive that is at least 100GB to store the primary data file. If you want to copy the database to a server that has 10 50GB drives, you cannot do it. You have the space across all 10 drives, but you do not have a single drive that can hold the primary data file. If, however, you create the database with several secondary files, you have the option of placing each of the secondary files on a separate drive.

> **TIP**
>
> You can use the sys.master_files catalog view to list the database files for all the databases. For example, SELECT db_name(database_id),* from sys.master_files order by 1 returns all the database files, ordered by the name of the database they belong to. You can change the sort order for the SELECT statement and order it by physical_name to quickly locate a database file and find which database is using that file.

Using Filegroups

Filegroups allow you to align certain database objects with specific data files. Tables, indexes, and large object (LOB) data can be assigned to a filegroup. A filegroup can be associated with one or more data files. The alignment of data and indexes to filegroups can provide performance benefits and improve manageability. Each database has at least one filegroup, called the *primary filegroup*. This filegroup, by default, contains the primary data file and any other secondary data files that have not been specifically aligned with another filegroup. Any database object that you create without specifying a filegroup is created in the primary filegroup.

Additional filegroups can be created and aligned with secondary data files. There is no requirement to have more than one filegroup, but additional filegroups give you added flexibility. Filegroups can be aligned with data files that can be stored on separate disk drives to improve data access. This improvement is facilitated by concurrent disk access across the disk drives assigned to the filegroups.

TIP

If too many outstanding I/Os are causing bottlenecks in the disk I/O subsystem, you might want to consider spreading the files across more disk drives. Performance Monitor can identify I/O bottlenecks by monitoring the `PhysicalDisk` object and `Disk Queue Length` counter. You should consider spreading the files across multiple disk drives if the `Disk Queue Length` counter is greater than two times the number of spindles on the disk. For more information on monitoring SQL Server performance, see Chapter 39, "Monitoring SQL Server Performance."

For example, you could create a filegroup called `UserData_FG`, consisting of three files spread over three physical drives. You could create another filegroup named `Index_FG`, with a single file, on a fourth drive. Then, when you create the tables, you can create them on the `UserData_FG` filegroup. You can create indexes on the `Index_FG` filegroup. This reduces contention between tables because the data is spread over three disks and can be accessed independently of the indexes. If more storage is required in the future, you can easily add additional files to the index or data filegroup, as appropriate.

You can create filegroups at the time the database is created, or you can add them after the database is created. When you create filegroups along with the database, the definition for the filegroup is contained in the CREATE DATABASE statement. Following is an example of a CREATE DATABASE statement with filegroup definitions:

```
CREATE DATABASE [mydb] ON  PRIMARY
( NAME = N'mydb',
    FILENAME = N'C:\mssql\data\mydb.mdf' ,
    SIZE = 4MB , FILEGROWTH = 1MB ),
 FILEGROUP [Index_FG]
( NAME = N'mydb_index1',
    FILENAME = N'I:\mssql\data\mydb_index1.ndf' ,
    SIZE = 2048KB , FILEGROWTH = 1024KB ),
```

```
FILEGROUP [UserData_FG]
( NAME = N'mydb_userdata1',
        FILENAME = N'D:\mssql\data\mydb_userdata1.ndf' ,
        SIZE = 2048KB , FILEGROWTH = 1024KB ),
( NAME = N'mydb_userdata2',
        FILENAME = N'E:\mssql\data\mydb_userdata2.ndf' ,
        SIZE = 2048KB , FILEGROWTH = 1024KB ),
( NAME = N'mydb_userdata3',
        FILENAME = N'F:\mssql\data\mydb_userdata3.ndf' ,
        SIZE = 2048KB , FILEGROWTH = 1024KB )
 LOG ON
( NAME = N'mydb_log',
        FILENAME = N'L:\mssql\log\mydb_log.ldf' ,
        SIZE = 1024KB , FILEGROWTH = 10%)
```

This example creates a database named mydb that has three filegroups. The first filegroup, PRIMARY, contains the .mdf file. Index_FG contains one file: I:\mssql\data\mydb_index1. ndf. The third filegroup, UserData_FG, contains three data files located on the D:, E:, and F: drives. This example demonstrates the relationship between databases, filegroups, and the underlying operating system files. (The T-SQL for creating a database is discussed in detail later in this chapter.)

After you create a database with multiple filegroups, you can then create a database object on a specific filegroup. In the preceding example, you could use the filegroup named UserData_FG to hold user-defined tables, and you could use the filegroup named Index_FG for the database indexes. You assign database objects at the time you create the object. The following example demonstrates the creation of a user-defined table on the UserData_FG filegroup and the creation of an index for that table on the Index_FG filegroup:

```
CREATE TABLE dbo.Table1
    (TableId int NULL,
    TableDesc varchar(50) NULL)
  ON [UserData_FG]


CREATE CLUSTERED INDEX [CI_Table1_TableID] ON [dbo].[Table1]
( [TableId] ASC)
  ON [Index_FG]
```

Any objects not explicitly created on a filegroup are created on the default filegroup. The PRIMARY filegroup is the default filegroup when a database is created. You can change the default filegroup if necessary. If you want to change the default group to another group, you can use the ALTER DATABASE command. For example, the following command changes the default filegroup for the mydb database:

```
ALTER DATABASE [mydb] MODIFY FILEGROUP [UserData_FG] DEFAULT
```

You can also change the default filegroup by right-clicking the database in the Object Explorer, choosing Properties, and selecting the Filegroups page. Then you select the check box labeled Default to make the given filegroup the default. Figure 20.1 shows the filegroups for the `AdventureWorks2012` database, with the primary filegroup selected as the default.

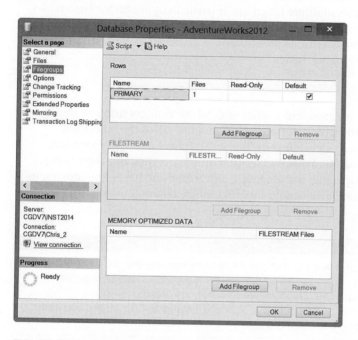

FIGURE 20.1   Setting the default filegroup in SQL Server Management Studio (SSMS).

When creating filegroups, you should keep in mind the following restrictions:

▶ You can't move a data file to another filegroup after it has been added to the database.

▶ Filegroups apply only to data files and not to log files.

▶ A data file can be part of only one filegroup and cannot be spread across multiple filegroups.

▶ You can have a maximum of 32,767 filegroups for each database.

20

NOTE

Using a SAN or RAID array for the database disk subsystem diminishes the need for filegroups. SAN and RAID systems typically have many disks mapped to a single data drive. This inherently allows for concurrent disk access without requiring the creation of a filegroup with multiple data files.

Using Partitions

Partitioning in SQL Server 2014 allows for a single table or index to be aligned to more than one filegroup. This capability was introduced in SQL Server 2005. Prior to SQL Server 2005, you could use filegroups to isolate a table or an index to a single filegroup, but the table or index could not be spread across multiple filegroups or data files. The ability to spread a table or an index across multiple filegroups is particularly useful for large tables. You can partition a table across multiple filegroups and have data files live on separate disk drives to improve performance. Table partitioning is discussed in more detail in Chapter 21, "Creating and Managing Tables."

Transaction Log Files

A *transaction* is a mechanism for grouping a series of database changes into one logical operation. SQL Server keeps track of each transaction in a file called the *transaction log*. This log file usually has the extension .ldf, but it can have a different extension. Typically, there is only one log file. You can specify multiple log files, but these files are accessed sequentially. If multiple files are used, SQL Server fills one file before moving to the next. You realize no performance benefit by using multiple files, but you can use them to extend the size of the log.

> **NOTE**
>
> The transaction log file is not a text file that can be read by opening the file in a text editor. The file is proprietary, and you cannot easily view the transactions or changes within it. However, you can use the undocumented DBCC LOG (database name) command to list the log contents. The output is relatively cryptic, but it can give you some idea of the type of information that is stored in the log file.

Because the transaction log file keeps track of all changes applied to a database, it is very important for database recovery. The transaction log is your friend: It can prevent significant data loss and provide recovery that is not possible without it. Consider, for example, a case in which a database is put in simple recovery mode. In short, this causes transaction detail to be automatically removed from the transaction log. This option is often selected because the transaction log is seen as taking too much disk space. The problem with simple mode is that it limits your ability to recover transactions. If a catastrophic failure occurs, you can restore your last full database backup, but that may be it. If that backup was taken the night before, all the database work done that day is lost.

If your database is not in simple mode (Full or Bulk-Logged), and the transaction log is intact, you have much better recovery options. For example, if you back up your transaction log periodically (for example, every hour) and a catastrophic error occurs, your data loss is limited. You still need to restore your last database backup, but you have the option of applying all the database changes stored in your transaction log. With hourly backups, you should lose no more than an hour's worth of work. This topic is covered in detail in Chapter 11, "Database Backup and Restore."

How the Transaction Log Works

SQL Server utilizes a write-ahead log. As changes are made to data through transactions, those changes are written immediately to the transaction log when the transaction is complete. The write-ahead log guarantees that all data modifications are written to the log prior to being written to disk. By writing each change to the transaction log before it is written to the database, SQL Server can increase I/O efficiency to the data files and ensure data integrity in case of system failure.

To fully understand the write-ahead log, you must first understand the role of SQL Server's cache or memory as it relates to database updates. SQL Server does not write updates directly to the data page on disk. Instead, SQL Server writes a change to a copy of the data page that has been placed in memory. Pages changed in memory and not yet written to disk are called *dirty pages*. The same basic approach is used for transaction log updates. The update to the log is performed in the log cache first, and it is written to disk at a later time. The time when the updates are actually written from cache to disk is called a *checkpoint*. The checkpoint occurs periodically, and SQL Server ensures that dirty pages are not written to disk before the corresponding log entry is written to disk.

The write-ahead log was designed for performance reasons, and it is critical for the recovery process after a system failure. If SQL Server shuts down unexpectedly, an automatic recovery process is initiated when SQL Server restarts. This recovery process can use the checkpoint marker in the log file as a starting point for recovery. SQL Server examines all transactions after the checkpoint. If they are committed transactions, they are rolled forward; if they are incomplete transactions, they are rolled back, or undone.

> **NOTE**
>
> Changes were made in SQL Server 2005 that improved the availability of the database during the recovery process. These changes have been carried forward to SQL Server 2014. In versions prior to SQL Server 2005, the database was not available until it was completely recovered and the roll-forward and roll-back processes were complete. In versions following SQL Server 2005, the database is made available right after the roll-forward process. The roll-back or undo process can occur while users are in the database. This feature, known as Fast Recovery, is available only with the Enterprise Edition of SQL Server 2014.

For more detailed information on this topic, see Chapter 28, "Transaction Management and the Transaction Log."

Creating Databases

Database creation is a relatively straightforward operation that you can perform by using T-SQL statements or SSMS. Because the data and log files are created at the time the database is created, the time it takes for the database to be created depends on the size and number of files you specify when you create the database. If there is not enough disk space to create any of the files specified, SQL Server returns an error, and none of the files are created.

> **NOTE**
>
> Enhancements that were added in SQL Server 2005 and still exist in SQL Server 2014 have reduced the amount of time it takes to create a database. The reduction in creation time is attributed to a change in the way the database files are initialized. The initialization of the file with binary zeros is now deferred until the file is accessed via SQL queries. This results in much faster database creation and expansion. For example, we created a database with a 1GB data file on a machine running SQL Server 2014. The database was created in approximately 1 second. This same operation took significantly longer in versions prior to SQL Server 2005.

Using SSMS to Create a Database

The Object Explorer in SSMS makes creating a database simple. You right-click the `Databases` node and select New Database. The New Database dialog appears, as shown in Figure 20.2. The General page is selected by default. It allows you to select the essential information needed to create a database, including the database name, database owner, and location of the database files.

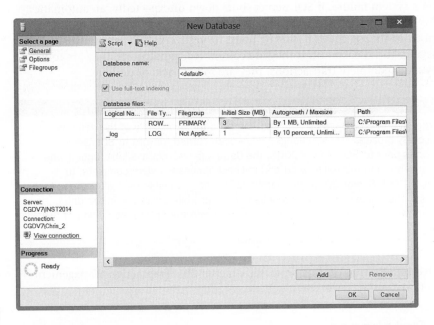

FIGURE 20.2   Creating a database by using SSMS.

Some related information is populated when you enter the database name. For example, the default logical names and locations of the database files are populated using the database name. The data file (which is identified with the file type `Data`) is named the same as the database. The log file (file type `Log`) has a database name with the suffix `_log`. The logical filename can be changed, but it must be unique within the database.

The location of the database files is an important decision. The location for each file is entered in the Path column in the Database Files grid. This column, located on the right side of the Database Files grid, includes an ellipsis that can help you navigate the directory structure on your server. When you select the location of these files, you should keep in mind the following:

▶ **Disk space**—Databases, by nature, grow over time. You need to make sure the location where you place your database files has sufficient space for growth.

▶ **Performance**—The location of your database files can affect performance. Generally, the data and log files should be placed on separate disk drives (with separate controllers) to maximize performance.

▶ **Organization**—Choosing a common location or directory for your database files can help keep things organized. For example, you could choose to place your data files in directories named \mssql\data\ and \mssql\log instead of using the long pathname that SQL Server uses by default.

There are several restrictions related to the database files specified. Each filename must be unique and cannot be used by another database. The files specified for a database should be located on a local drive of the machine where SQL Server is installed, a SAN drive, or an iSCSI-based network drive to optimize SQL Server performance and reliability. Finally, you need to make sure the path specified exists on the drive prior to creating the database.

> **NOTE**
>
> The default path for the database files is populated based on database settings values specified in the Server Properties dialog. To open this dialog, you right-click the server in the Object Explorer and choose Properties. When the Server Properties dialog appears, you choose the Database Settings page, where you see the database default locations. If the database default locations for the log and data files are not specified, the paths to the master database files are used. You can determine the paths to the master database files by looking at the startup parameters for the SQL Server instance. You can view these startup parameters within the SQL Server Configuration Manager. After you open this application, you right-click the SQL Server service and select Properties. On the Advanced tab of the Properties dialog that appears, you find the setting named Startup Parameters. The -d parameter identifies the location of the data file for the master database. The -1 parameter identifies the location of the log file for the master database.

The remaining pages in the New Database dialog allow you to set database options, utilize filegroups, and set extended properties. The Options page contains many settings discussed in the "Setting Database Options" section later in this chapter. Three settings at the top of the Options page deserve special attention: Collation, Recovery Model, and Compatibility Level. Figure 20.3 shows the Options page.

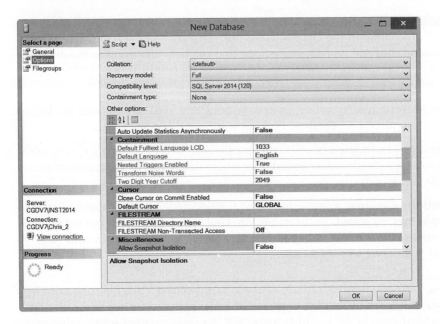

FIGURE 20.3   The Options page for creating a database.

Collation specifies how strings are sorted and compared. The selection of collation is language-dependent and addresses differences in the way characters are ordered. The default collation for a database is based on the server default, which is set during the installation of SQL Server. The server default for many U.S.-based installations is SQL_Latin1_General_CP1_CI_AS. The collation name provides some insight into how the collation will work. For example, CI is an acronym for Case Insensitive, and AS indicates that the collation will be Accent Sensitive. The following SELECT statement can be used to list all the available collations and relates details about how the collation behaves:

```
SELECT * from ::fn_helpcollations()
```

The Recovery Model setting is critical in determining how much data can be recovered in the event of a media failure. The default is Full, which provides the greatest level of recovery. With Full recovery, all changes to the database (inserts, updates, and deletions) are written to the transaction log, and so are any changes that may have occurred using BCP or BULK INSERT. If a failure occurs on one of the database files, you can restore the database by using the last full backup. All the changes captured in the transaction log since the last full backup can be reapplied to the database as well.

The Bulk-Logged recovery setting is similar to Full recovery but has some differences in the way that operations (BCP or BULK INSERT) are logged. With Bulk-Logged recovery, you can still restore all the transaction log backups to recover your database but there are some limitations for point in time recovery. Refer to Chapter 11, "Database Backup and Restore" for more details on Recovery models including Bulk-Logged recovery.

NOTE

When either the Full recovery or Bulk-Logged setting is selected, it is important to set up a job or maintenance plan that performs periodic backups of the transaction log. A backup of the transaction log removes data from the log and keeps the size of the transaction log manageable. If regular backups of the transaction log are not made, the transaction log will continue to grow as every change in the database is written to it.

Simple recovery mode offers the simplest backup/recovery model but the greatest possibility of losing changes to the database. This is based on the fact that changes recorded in the transaction log are automatically truncated when the database is placed in Simple recovery mode. Recovery with Simple mode is limited to using full or differential database backups that have been taken. Simple recovery mode is a good option for read-only databases and for development databases that can afford the loss of changes since the last database backup. All the recovery models are discussed in detail in Chapter 11.

The last setting on the Options page that deserves special attention is Compatibility Level. The Compatibility Level determines the level of backward compatibility the Database Engine uses. For many newly created databases in SQL Server 2014, the default of SQL Server 2014 (110) will suffice. With this setting, all the new features available with SQL Server 2014 are utilized. In some situations, however, you might want a SQL Server 2014 database to behave as though it were a SQL Server 2008 database or SQL Server 2005 database. You can accomplish this by setting Compatibility Level to SQL Server 2014 (120), SQL Server 2012 (110), SQL Server 2008 (100) or SQL Server 2005 (90). The SQL Server 2005 (90) compatibility level has actually been discontinued in SQL Server 2014. If you choose this compatibility level, you will get an error when creating the database. Generally, you select older compatibility levels to allow code that was developed for prior versions of SQL Server to work as it did with those versions.

NOTE

The Compatibility Level setting is intended to allow a database to behave as if it were running in a previous version of SQL Server by providing similar query behavior or by allowing deprecated features to still work as they did in the previous version. However, setting the Compatibility Level to a prior version does not prevent new SQL Server 2014 features from being implemented in the database. The intent of this functionality is to provide a means for moving a database and application developed for a previous release of SQL Server to SQL Server 2014 and allow it to work as it did while enabling you to start taking advantage of new features and capabilities as you migrate the system to SQL Server 2014.

20

Using T-SQL to Create Databases

Instead of using SSMS, you can use T-SQL to create a database. The T-SQL command to do this is CREATE DATABASE. The CREATE DATABASE syntax is extensive and is best illustrated with an example. Listing 20.1 shows a sample script to create a database called `mydb`. This script was generated using the Script option available on the New Database screen.

LISTING 20.1   Using T-SQL to Create a Database

```
CREATE DATABASE [mydb] ON  PRIMARY
( NAME = N'mydb', FILENAME = N'C:\mssql\data\mydb.mdf' ,
    SIZE = 2048KB , FILEGROWTH = 1024KB )
 LOG ON
( NAME = N'mydb_log', FILENAME = N'C:\mssql\log\mydb_log.ldf',
    SIZE = 1024KB , FILEGROWTH = 10%)
GO
```

The database created in Listing 20.1 is relatively simple. It is named `mydb` and contains one data file and one log file. The data file is created on the PRIMARY filegroup; it is named `mydb.mdf` and is created in the `C:\mssql\data` folder. The `mydb.mdf` file is initially created with a size of 2048KB, or 2MB. If the database utilizes the entire 2MB, the file can be expanded by the amount specified in the FILEGROWTH parameter. In this case, the file can grow in 1MB increments. (Managing file growth is discussed in the section, "Managing Databases," later in this chapter.)

The log file is defined using the LOG ON clause in the CREATE DATABASE command. The `mydb` database created in Listing 20.1 has a log file named `mydb_log.ldf` that is also created in the `C:\mssql\data` folder. The initial size of the file is 1MB, and it can expand by 10% of the current log file size. You need to use caution with large databases when using a percentage to define FILEGROWTH. For example, you may have problems if you have a large database that has a 30GB log file and a FILEGROWTH of 10%. If the database file is set to autogrow, and the 30GB log file is full, it attempts to expand the log file by 3GB. An expansion of this size could be detrimental to performance, and the disk drive where the log file is located might not have that much disk space remaining.

You can specify many of the other options that define a database after the database is created by using the ALTER DATABASE statement. The T-SQL scripting option available on the CREATE DATABASE screen generates the basic CREATE DATABASE syntax shown in Listing 20.1, and then it generates a series of ALTER DATABASE commands that further define the database. These options are discussed in the next section.

Setting Database Options

You can use an abundance of database options to refine the behavior of a database. These options fall into the following categories, which are part of the option specification:

▶ Auto Options

▶ Change Tracking Options

▶ Containment Options

▶ Cursor Options

- ▶ Database Mirroring Options

- ▶ Database Encryption

- ▶ Database Availability Options

- ▶ Date Correlation Optimization Options

- ▶ External Access Options

- ▶ FILESTREAM

- ▶ High Availability

- ▶ Parameterization Options

- ▶ Recovery Options

- ▶ Service Broker Options

- ▶ Snapshot Isolation Options

- ▶ SQL Options

For each category, you can set one or more options. You can find a full list of options for each category in the section, "Alter Database Set Options," in SQL Server Books Online. Some of the options are discussed in further detail in the chapters of this book that relate to the option category. For example, the recovery options are discussed in detail in Chapter 11.

The following section focuses on the database options displayed on the Options page in SSMS.

The Database Options

You can access many of the most common database options via the Options page of the Database Properties dialog. To get to this dialog, you right-click a database in the SSMS Object Explorer and select Properties. When the dialog appears, you select the Options page from the list on the left side of the Database Properties dialog. Figure 20.4 shows the Options page for the AdventureWorks2012 database. The options listed under Other Options can be listed alphabetically or by category. The default display mode is by category.

The default settings for these options suffice for most installations. However, some options deserve special attention. The options listed under the Automatic category are among these options. The Auto Close option could cause problems in prior versions of SQL Server. This option is intended for desktop implementations in which the database does not need to be online all the time. When users are not accessing the database and this option is selected, the database files are closed. When the first user accesses the database, the database is brought back online. The problem in prior versions was that the synchronous operation of opening and closing the database files caused performance problems. This issue was addressed in SQL Server 2008 and is no longer an issue because

20

the operations are now performed asynchronously. The Auto Close option defaults to `true` only for the Express Edition and should generally be left set to `false` for all other versions.

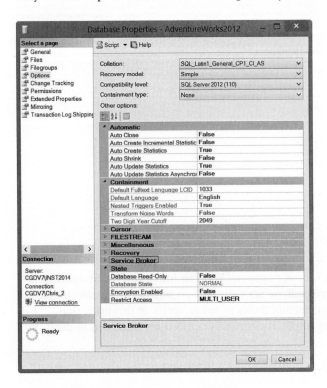

FIGURE 20.4   Database options in SSMS.

The Auto Create Statistics and Auto Update Statistics options also deserve special attention in situations in which the creation or updating of statistics is affecting performance. Generally, the creation or updating of statistics improves performance. These statistics enable the Query Optimizer to make the best decisions when determining the access path to the data. In some rare circumstances, there may be performance problems at the time statistics are created or updated automatically. When these situations arise, you can turn off the Auto Statistics options and schedule the statistics operations to occur during off-hours. You can address this performance issue by using the Auto Update Statistics Asynchronously option. With this option, the Query Optimizer does not wait for the update of statistics to complete before it compiles queries. The query can continue while the statistics are updated in the background asynchronously.

Enabling the Auto Shrink option is a good idea for keeping a nonproduction database as small as possible. This option automatically performs a database shrink operation against the database files when more than 25% of a file contains unused space. The default setting is `false` because this option can cause performance problems (related to the timing of the shrink operation) in a production database. Because the operation is automatic, it can run at any time, including times when there may be heavy production load.

The Page Verify option in the Recovery category was enhanced in SQL Server 2005. That enhancement came in the form of a new CHECKSUM option. This CHECKSUM option is the default; it causes a checksum calculation to occur across the entire database page. Prior to the availability of the CHECKSUM option, page verification was done with TORN_PAGE_DETECTION. Both of these options help detect damaged database pages, but CHECKSUM is the method that Microsoft recommends. The CHECKSUM calculation can be complicated, but it basically tells SQL Server to calculate a number based on the contents of each data / index page. The CHECKSUM value is stored in the page header when it is written to disk. When the page is read from the disk, the checksum is computed again and compared to the value in page header to help ensure that the contents of each page are valid.

Database Read-Only and Restrict Access are two other commonly used options in the State category. You can set Database Read-Only to true to prevent updates from occurring in the database. Databases used for reference and not updated are perfect candidates for this option. The Restrict Access options are handy when you're executing system maintenance or mass updates in which you want to restrict users from accessing the database. Single User allows only one user to access the database. The Restricted User option allows only members of db_owner, dbcreator, and sysadmin to access the database. With the Restricted User option, there is no limit on the number of users in these groups that can access the database.

You can easily set up the options reviewed in this section as well as the other options mentioned by using the Database Properties dialog. The current value for each option is shown in the right-hand column. To set an option to another value, you click the current value, and a drop-down arrow appears. When you click the drop-down arrow, you can select from the list of valid values for the option. After making all your option changes, you can click OK for the changes to take effect immediately, or you can click the Script button to generate the T-SQL code to change the options. The T-SQL code used to change the options is discussed in the next section.

Using T-SQL to Set Database Options

If you prefer to use T-SQL, or if the option you need to set doesn't appear in the Database Properties dialog, you can use the ALTER DATABASE command to set options. For example, the following command sets AUTO_UPDATE STATISTICS to OFF in the AdventureWorks2012 database:

```
ALTER DATABASE [AdventureWorks2012] SET AUTO_UPDATE_STATISTICS OFF WITH NO_WAIT
```

Prior to SQL Server 2012, you could also change some of the options by using the system stored procedure sp_dboption. The sp_dboption was removed in SQL Server 2012. This system procedure was an essential tool for DBA's in the past. Make sure to update any scripts or other places that you may have use this procedure so that they use the ALTER DATABASE statement instead.

Setting a database to single-user mode is useful when you're performing certain database operations. For example, you might set a database to single-user mode prior to renaming the database with the sp_renamedb system procedure. It is important to break old habits

20

and move on to using the ALTER DATABASE command. The single-user option and database name change have both been integrated into the ALTER DATABASE syntax. The following example shows how to set the single-user mode option and change the database name by using ALTER DATABASE:

```
ALTER DATABASE [AdventureWorks2012] SET  SINGLE_USER WITH NO_WAIT
GO
ALTER DATABASE [AdventureWorks2012] MODIFY NAME = [AdventureWorks2012_New]
GO
```

As you can see, using ALTER DATABASE is fairly straightforward and offers a consistent approach for modifying a database and its options.

TIP

Databases can be brought offline in SQL Server 2014 using SSMS or the T-SQL ALTER DATABASE command. When databases are offline no one can access them, and the related database files can be moved. For example, you use the following T-SQL command to take the AdventureWorks2012 database offline:

```
ALTER DATABASE [AdventureWorks2012] SET OFFLINE WITH NO_WAIT
```

You can also specify an option with the ALTER DATABASE command that sets the database into an emergency state. This state marks the database as read-only, logging is disabled, and access to the database is limited to members of the sysadmin fixed server role. This option quickly prevents normal users from getting at the database but leaves the database available for inquiry for administrators. This is particularly useful when a database had been marked as suspect and is inaccessible. An example of setting a database to the emergency state follows:

```
ALTER DATABASE [AdventureWorks2012] SET emergency WITH NO_WAIT
```

The offline option and emergency options can be invaluable when you want to quickly prevent or limit access to you database.

Retrieving Option Information

You can retrieve database settings by using several different methods. You can use the Database Properties dialog in SSMS (as described in the preceding section) to display commonly accessed options. You can also use the DATABASEPROPERTYEX function or the sys.databases catalog view to display individual database options. As mentioned previously, sp_dboption was removed, so the DATABASEPROPERTYEX function is preferred. This function accepts input values for the database name and the option for which you want to retrieve the value. The following is an example of a SELECT statement you can use to retrieve the Auto Shrink option for the AdventureWorks2012 database:

```
SELECT DATABASEPROPERTYEX ('AdventureWorks2012', 'IsAutoShrink')
```

This function returns a value of 1 or 0 for Boolean values—with 1 being "on" or "true"—and returns the actual value for non-Booleans. Table 20.1 lists the valid properties for the DATABASEPROPERTYEX function.

TABLE 20.1   DATABASEPROPERTYEX Properties

Property	Explanation
Collation	This is the default collation name for the database.
ComparisonStyle	This is the Windows comparison style of the collation.
Edition	The database edition; such as Web or Business
IsAnsiNullDefault	The database follows SQL-92 rules for allowing null values.
IsAnsiNullsEnabled	All comparisons to a null evaluate to unknown.
IsAnsiPaddingEnabled	Strings are padded to the same length before comparison or insertion.
IsAnsiWarningsEnabled	Error or warning messages are issued when standard error conditions occur.
IsArithmeticAbortEnabled	Queries are ended when an overflow or divide-by-zero error occurs during query execution.
IsAutoClose	The database shuts down cleanly and frees resources after the last user exits.
IsAutoCreateStatistics	Existing statistics are automatically updated when the statistics become out-of-date because the data in the tables has changed.
IsAutoShrink	Database files are candidates for automatic periodic shrinking.
IsAutoUpdateStatistics	The AUTO_UPDATE_STATISTICS database option is enabled.
IsCloseCursorsOnCommitEnabled	Cursors that are open when a transaction is committed are closed.
IsFulltextEnabled	The database is full-text enabled.
IsInStandBy	The database is online as read-only, with the restore log allowed.
IsLocalCursorsDefault	Cursor declarations default to LOCAL.
IsMemoryOptimizedElevateTo-SnapshotEnabled	Memory-optimized tables are accessed using SNAPSHOT isolation.
IsMergePublished	The tables in a database can be published for merge replication if replication is installed.
IsNullConcat	The null concatenation operand yields NULL.
IsNumericRoundAbortEnabled	Errors are generated when loss of precision occurs in expressions.

20

Property	Explanation
IsParameterizationForced	The PARAMETERIZATION database SET option is FORCED.
IsPublished	The tables of the database can be published for snapshot or transactional replication if replication is installed.
IsQuotedIdentifiersEnabled	Double quotation marks can be used on identifiers.
IsRecursiveTriggersEnabled	Recursive firing of triggers is enabled.
IsSubscribed	The database is subscribed to a publication.
IsSyncWithBackup	The database is either a published database or a distribution database and can be restored without disrupting transactional replication.
IsTornPageDetectionEnabled	The SQL Server Database Engine detects incomplete I/O operations caused by power failures or other system outages.
LCID	This is the Windows locale ID (LCID) for the collation.
MaxSizeInBytes	The maximum database size in bytes.
Recovery	This is the recovery model for the database.
SQLSortOrder	This indicates the SQL Server sort order ID supported in earlier versions of SQL Server.
Status	This is the database status.
Updateability	This indicates whether data can be modified.
UserAccess	This indicates which users can access the database.
Version	This is the internal version number of the SQL Server code with which the database was created. It is for internal use only by SQL Server tools and in upgrade processing.

If you would like to retrieve all the options set for a database, you have a couple of choices. The option that has been around for a while is sp_helpdb. You can pass to this system stored procedure the database name, and it returns several pieces of information about the database, including the options set. The database options are returned in the first result set from sp_helpdb in a column named Status. The database options are displayed in a comma-delimited format in the Status column. All Boolean options that are set to ON are returned in the Status column, and all non-Boolean values are returned with the value to which they are set.

The syntax for sp_helpdb is as follows:

```
sp_helpdb database_name
```

The sys.databases catalog view is another good resource for displaying all the database options. This catalog view has a separate column for each of the database options and is much easier to read than the `sp_helpdb` output. The view also has the added flexibility of allowing you to choose a set of options to return. The following example shows a SELECT statement that uses the `sys.databases` catalog view to return a common set of options:

```
select name, is_auto_close_on, is_auto_shrink_on,
    is_auto_create_stats_on, is_auto_update_stats_on
from sys.databases
where name = 'AdventureWorks2012'
```

The results from this SELECT statement return Boolean values in each column, indicating whether the option is set to on or off. The number of columns available for selection is extensive and similar to those options available with the DATABASEPROPERTYEX function.

TIP

Selecting the column you want from the `sys.databases` catalog view is easier when you use the Object Explorer. To review the columns, you go to the `master` database and expand the `Views` node, followed by the `System Views` node. When you see the `sys.databases` view listed under `System Views`, you expand the columns for the `sys.databases` view to see a list of all the available columns. You can then drag the options you want to view into a database query window for use in a SELECT statement.

You can also use the IntelliSense feature available in the SQL Server 2014 query window. When creating a SELECT statement that retrieves from the `sys.databases` catalog view (or any other catalog view), you are given a drop-down list of available columns when you reference the view in the select list. See Chapter 3, "SQL Server Management Studio," for a more in-depth discussion of the Object Explorer and IntelliSense.

Managing Databases

After you create a database, you have the ongoing task of managing it. At the database level, this task generally involves manipulating the file structure and setting options appropriate for the usage of the database.

Managing File Growth

As discussed earlier in this chapter, SQL Server manages file growth by automatically growing files by preset intervals when a need for additional space arises. However, this is a very loose definition of the word *manages*. What actually happens is that when the database runs out of space, it suspends all update activity, checks whether it is allowed additional space, and if space is available, it increases the file size by the value defined by FILEGROWTH. When the database fills up again, the whole process starts over.

When all the files in a filegroup are full and are configured to autogrow, SQL Server automatically expands one file at a time in a round-robin fashion to accommodate more data. For example, if a filegroup consists of multiple files, and no free space is available in any file in the filegroup, the first file is expanded by the specified file-growth setting. When the first file is full again, and there is no more free space elsewhere in the filegroup, the second file is expanded. When the second file is full, and there is no more free space else-where in the filegroup, the third file is expanded, and so on.

Because FILEGROWTH can be defined as small as 64KB, automatically increasing the file size can be detrimental to performance if it happens too frequently. When you think of managing file growth, you can think of the database administrator proactively monitoring the size of files and increasing the size before SQL Server runs out of space when allocating new extents. That's not to say automatic file growth is a bad thing; it is, in fact, a great "safety valve" to accommodate unpredictable data growth or a lack of attention on the part of the administrator.

Expanding Databases

As previously discussed, databases can be expanded automatically, or you can intervene and expand them manually. The manual expansion can be accomplished by adding more files to the database or by increasing the size of the existing files. The database expansions can be accomplished with either SSMS or T-SQL.

To expand the size of the data files using SSMS, you right-click the database in the Object Explorer and select Properties. When the Database Properties dialog appears, you select the Files page to list all the files associated with the database. The Initial Size (MB) column displays the current disk allocation for each file. You can enter the new size directly into the column or use the up arrow to increase the size. After establishing the new size, you can simply click OK to expand the database file, or you can script the change by using the Script button at the top of the Database Properties window.

You can also use the Files page of the Database Properties dialog in SSMS to add files to a database. You do this by clicking the Add button, which adds a new file entry row into the Database Files grid. You must supply a logical name for the new file, which typically contains the database name. In addition, you must supply the other data values in the row, including the file type, filegroup, initial size, autogrowth parameters, and path to the file.

The T-SQL ALTER DATABASE command is another option you can use for expanding a data-base. Listing 20.2 shows an ALTER DATABASE example that increases the size of a data file in the AdventureWorks2012 database to 200MB.

LISTING 20.2   Using T-SQL to Increase the Size of a Database File

```
ALTER DATABASE [AdventureWorks2012]
 MODIFY FILE ( NAME = N'AdventureWorks2012_Data', SIZE = 200MB )
GO
```

You can also use the ALTER DATABASE command to add a new file to a database. Listing 20.3 shows an example that adds a new data file to the AdventureWorks2012 database.

LISTING 20.3   Using T-SQL to Add a New Database File

```
ALTER DATABASE [AdventureWorks2012]
 ADD FILE ( NAME = N'AdventureWorks2012_Data2',
FILENAME = N'C:\MSSQL\DATA\AdventureWorks2012_Data2.ndf',
  SIZE = 2048KB , FILEGROWTH = 1024KB ) TO FILEGROUP [PRIMARY]
GO
```

Shrinking Databases

Shrinking database files is a bit more involved than expanding them. Generally, you do database shrink operations manually, using DBCC commands. SQL Server does have the AUTOSHRINK database option, but it is usually reserved for development databases and should not be used in production. The reason it is not recommended for production is that the AUTOSHRINK operation can run at peak usage time and affect performance. AUTOSHRINK is executed when more than 25% of a file contains unused space. This event can occur, for example, after a large deletion.

If you want to shrink a database manually, you can do so by using DBCC SHRINKDATABASE, DBCC SHRINKDATAFILE, or SSMS. The following sections describe these three methods.

> **NOTE**
>
> Generally, you should avoid shrinking database files if you believe that the files are going to grow to the same larger size again. The continual expansion of a database can affect performance while the expansion is occurring. Also, if a database file is repeatedly shrunk and expanded, the database file itself can become fragmented within the file system, which can degrade I/O performance for the file.

Using DBCC SHRINKDATABASE to Shrink Databases

The DBCC SHRINKDATABASE statement attempts to shrink all the files in a database and leave a specified target percentage of free space. The following is an example of the DBCC SHRINKDATABASE syntax and running the command against the AdventureWorks2012 database:

```
DBCC SHRINKDATABASE
( 'database_name' | database_id | 0
    [ ,target_percent ]
    [ , { NOTRUNCATE | TRUNCATEONLY } ]
)
[ WITH NO_INFOMSGS ]
--Shrink Example
DBCC SHRINKDATABASE (AdventureWorks2012, 25)
```

The first parameter of the DBCC SHRINKDATABASE command is the database_name or database_id. If this parameter is set to 0 then the current database will be used. The second parameter is the desired percentage that will be left free. In the preceding example,

20

an attempt will be made to shrink the database file and leave 25% free space in the files. This operation is done one data file at a time, and the log files are treated as one unit and shrunk together.

There are quite a few things to consider when you use the DBCC SHRINKDATABASE command. The following are some of the most important considerations:

▶ DBCC SHRINKDATABASE does not shrink a file smaller than its minimal size. The minimal size is the size of the file when it was initially created or the size of the file after it was explicitly resized. Explicit resizing can be accomplished with the DBCC SHRINKFILE command.

▶ The TRUNCATEONLY option frees any unused space at the end of a file but does not attempt any page movement within the file. The target percentage is ignored when this option is specified.

▶ The NOTRUNCATE option attempts to move pages in the files to push all free space to the end of the file. This option does not actually return the space to the operating system, and the physical file does not end up smaller when this option is used.

▶ If neither the NOTRUNCATE nor TRUNCATEONLY options are specified, this is equivalent to running DBCC SHRINKDATABASE WITH NOTRUNCATE followed by DBCC SHRINKDATABASE WITH TRUNCATEONLY. The first part attempts to push all the free space to the end of the file; then the free space is released to the operating system, and the file ends up smaller.

▶ The database files can never be shrunk to a size smaller than the data contained within them.

For smaller databases, the DBCC SHRINKDATABASE command is often considered to be a good choice because it is all inclusive and applies to all the database files. For larger databases or situations in which you need more control, you should consider using the DBCC SHRINKFILE command, which is discussed in the next section.

Using DBCC SHRINKFILE to Shrink Databases

The DBCC SHRINKFILE command operates on individual database files. For databases that contain many database files, you must execute multiple commands to shrink the entire database. This task requires some extra work, but the increased control is often worth the effort. This, combined with the fact that you can shrink a file below its minimum specified size, makes it a very good option.

The following example shows the syntax for the DBCC SHRINKFILE command and a simple example for the AdventureWorks2012 database:

```
DBCC SHRINKFILE
(
    { ' file_name ' | file_id }
    { [ , EMPTYFILE]
```

```
  | [ [ , target_size ] [ , { NOTRUNCATE | TRUNCATEONLY } ] ]
  }
)
[ WITH NO_INFOMSGS ]

-- sample shrink command
USE [AdventureWorks2012]
GO
DBCC SHRINKFILE (N'AdventureWorks2012_Data' , 180)
GO
DBCC SHRINKFILE (N'AdventureWorks2012_Log' , 10)
GO
```

Note that with this option, a filename or an ID is supplied, rather than the database
name. DBCC SHRINKFILE must be run in the database that the file belongs to. You specify
TARGET_SIZE in megabytes; this is the desired size for the file after the shrink completes.
If TARGET_SIZE is not specified or the target size is too small, the command tries to shrink
the file as much as possible. The EMPTYFILE option migrates all data in the file to other
files in the same filegroup. No further data can be placed on the file. The file can subsequently be dropped from the database. This capability can be useful when you want to
migrate a data file to a new disk. The NOTRUNCATE and TRUNCATEONLY options for DBCC
SHRINKDATAFILE work the same way as with DBCC SHRINKDATABASE. Refer to the previous
section for details.

TIP

If you would like to shrink every database file by using the DBCC SHRINKFILE command,
you can generate the commands by using a SELECT statement. The following SELECT is an
example of this:

```
SELECT 'PRINT ''LOGICAL NAME: ' + rtrim(name) +
   ' FILENAME: ' + rtrim(filename) + '''' + char(10) +
   'go' + char(10) +
   ' DBCC SHRINKFILE (' + convert(varchar(8),fileid) + ',1)' +
char(10) + 'go' + char(10)
from sysfiles  order by fileid
```

The results from this SELECT produce the DBCC SHRINKFILE commands for all the files
in the database that it is run against. You can then paste the results into another query
window and execute them. This particular example uses a fixed target size of 1MB, but
you can adjust this size in the SELECT statement. You could also modify this SELECT
statement so that it uses the sys.master_files catalog view instead of using sysfiles.

Shrinking the Log File

The data file most likely to grow beyond a normal size and require periodic shrinking is the transaction log file. If a user process issues a large update transaction, the log file grows to the size needed to hold the records generated by the transaction. This could be significantly larger than the normal growth of the transaction log.

As with data files, shrinking of the log file in SQL Server 2014 can take place only from the end of the log file. However, you must first back up or truncate the log to remove the inactive log records and reduce the size of the logical log. You can then run the DBCC SHRINKFILE or DBCC SHRINKDATABASE command to release the unused space in the log file.

Transaction log files are divided logically into segments, called virtual log files. The Database Engine chooses the size of the virtual log files dynamically while it is creating or extending log files. Transaction log files can only be shrunk to a virtual log file boundary. It is therefore not possible to shrink a log file to a size smaller than the size of a virtual log file, even if the space is not being used. The size of the virtual log files in a transaction log increase as the size of the log file increases. For example, a database defined with a log file of 1GB may have virtual log files 128MB in size. Therefore, the log can be shrunk to only about 128MB.

Because of the overhead incurred when the autoshrink process attempts to shrink database files, it is not recommended that you enable this option for the transaction log because it could be triggered numerous times during the course of a business day. It is better to schedule the shrinking of the log file to be performed during normal daily maintenance, when production system activity is at a minimum.

Using SSMS to Shrink Databases

In addition to shrinking a database by using T-SQL, you can do so through SSMS. In the Object Explorer, you right-click the database you want to shrink, and then you choose Tasks, followed by Shrink. You can then select either Database or Files. Selecting the Database option displays the Shrink Database dialog (see Figure 20.5). The currently allocated size and free space for the database are shown. You have the option of selecting the Shrink Action and checking the Reorganize Files Before Releasing Unused Space check box.

You can click the Script button to generate the T-SQL that will be used to perform the database shrink operation. When you do, a DBCC SHRINKDATABASE command is generated.

If you want to shrink database files, you choose the Files option instead of Database. Figure 20.6 shows the Shrink File dialog displayed when you select Files. You can shrink one database file at a time using this window. If you choose the shrink option Release Unused Space, SMSS uses the DBCC SHRINKFILE command with the TRUNCATEONLY option. If you choose the Reorganize Pages Before Releasing Unused Space option, SMSS uses the DBCC SHRINKFILE command without the TRUNCATEONLY or NOTRUNCATE option. As mentioned earlier, this causes page movement to free as much space as possible. A TRUNCATE operation then releases the free space back to the operating system.

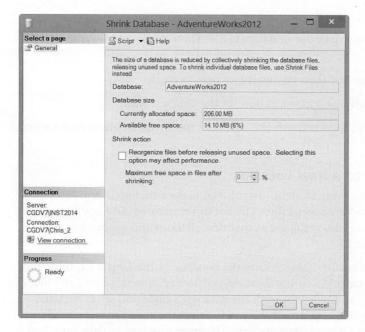

FIGURE 20.5   Shrinking an entire database using SSMS.

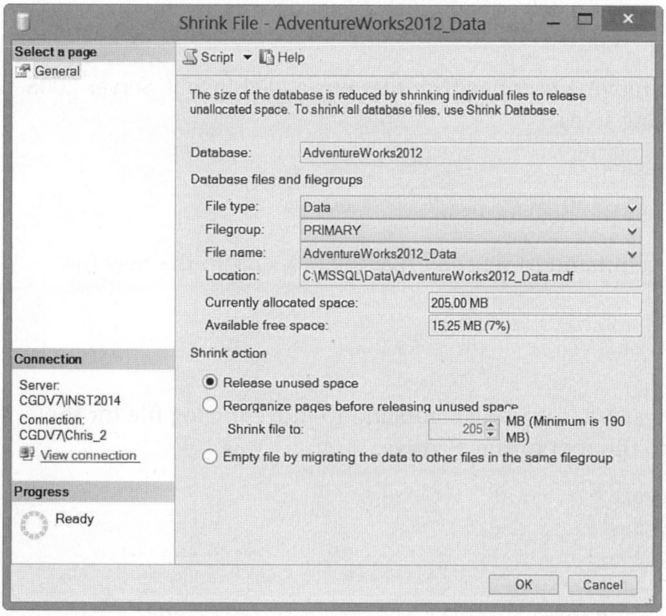

FIGURE 20.6   Shrinking database files in SSMS.

Moving Databases

Sometimes you need to move a database or database file. There are several ways to accomplish this task:

▶ Make a database backup and then restore it to a new location.

▶ Alter the database, specifying a new location for the database file.

▶ Detach the database and then reattach the database, specifying an alternate location.

Restoring a Database to a New Location

The database backup option is fairly straightforward. You make a backup of the database, which writes the backup to a file or set of files. The backup is restored, and any changes to the location of the database files are made at that time. Backup and restoration are discussed in detail in Chapter 11.

You can easily detach a database by right-clicking the database in the Object Explorer and choosing Tasks and then Detach. When the database is detached, you can move the file(s) to the desired location. You can then right-click the database's node and select Attach. The Attach Databases screen that appears allows you to select the .mdf file and change the file location for any of the related database files. The steps involved in detaching and attaching a database are discussed in detail in the later section, "Detaching and Attaching Databases."

Using ALTER DATABASE

The ALTER DATABASE option for moving user database files was added in SQL Server 2005. This option involves the following steps:

1. Take the database offline.

2. Manually move the file(s) to the new location.

3. Run the ALTER DATABASE command to set the FILENAME property to the new file location.

4. Bring the database online.

The following example uses the ALTER DATABASE command to move the log file for the AdventureWorks2012 database to the root of the c: drive.

```
ALTER DATABASE AdventureWorks2012
  MODIFY FILE (NAME = AdventureWorks2012_Log,
    FILENAME = 'C:\AdventureWorks2012_log.ldf')
```

> **CAUTION**
>
> Use caution when specifying the FILENAME parameter to move a database log file. If the FILENAME setting specified in the ALTER DATABASE command is incorrect and the file does not exist, the command still completes successfully. When the database is brought back online, a message stating that the file can't be found appears, and a new log file is created for you. This invalidates the old log file.

Detaching and Attaching Databases

A convenient way to move or copy database files is to detach and attach databases. Detaching database files removes the database from an instance of SQL Server but leaves the database files intact. After the database is detached, the files associated with the database (that is, .mdf, .ndf, and .ldf files) can be copied or moved to an alternate location. You can then reattach the relocated files by using the CREATE DATABASE command with the FOR ATTACH option.

> **TIP**
>
> The process of detaching and attaching a database is extremely fast. It is therefore a good alternative to use BACKUP and RESTORE when you're copying a database to another location. The catch with detaching a database is that all users must be disconnected from the database, and the database is unavailable during the detach and copy of the database files.

To detach a database, you right-click the database in Object Explorer and select Tasks and then Detach. Figure 20.7 shows an example of the Detach Database dialog box for detaching the AdventureWorks2012 database. You can specify several options, including a handy option (called Drop Connections) to kill any user processes (SPIDs) that may still be connected to the database when the detach operation is running. If you do not select the Drop Connections option and users are still connected to the database, the detach operation fails.

Other options available during the detach operation are also useful. The Update Statistics option updates out-of-date statistics for all the database tables before you detach the database. The statistics update can take some time on larger databases, so this slows down the overall detach operation. The other option, Keep Full Text Catalogs, was added in SQL Server 2008. It allows you to detach any full-text catalogs associated with the database. These detached full-text catalogs are then reattached along with the database when the files are attached.

The attach operation is simple to execute through SMSS. In Object Explorer, you simply right-click the database's node and select the Attach option. The Attach Databases dialog box appears, allowing you to specify the database file(s) you want to attach. You need to click the Add button to be able to select a database file for restoration. When you select the main .mdf file associated with the database, the associated file information for the other related database files is populated as well.

20

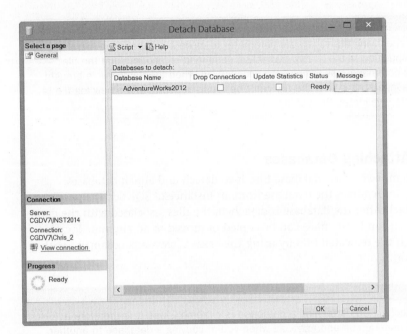

FIGURE 20.7   Detaching a database by using SSMS.

Figure 20.8 shows the Attach Databases dialog box for the AdventureWorks2012 database. The top portion of the dialog box lists the main (.mdf) database file selected for the AdventureWorks2012 database. The bottom portion lists the related files. You have an option to attach the database with a different name by changing the Attach As name located at the top of the screen. You can also edit the database details at the bottom of the screen and enter the location of the database files that will be attached. The Current File Path column displays the original file locations determined from the .mdf file. If the files were moved to a new location, this is the place to change the current file path to the new location.

You can also accomplish the detach and attach operations by using T-SQL. You perform the detach operation with the sp_detach_db system stored procedure. You perform the attach operation with the CREATE DATABASE command, using the FOR ATTACH option. The following is an example of T-SQL commands for detaching and attaching the AdventureWorks2012 database:

```
--Detach the database
EXEC master.dbo.sp_detach_db
 @dbname = N'AdventureWorks2012', @keepfulltextindexfile=N'false'
GO
--Attach the database
CREATE DATABASE [AdventureWorks2012] ON
( FILENAME = 'C:\Program Files\Microsoft SQL
Server\MSSQL12\MSSQL\Data\AdventureWorks2012_Data.mdf' ),
```

```
( FILENAME = 'C:\Program Files\Microsoft SQL
Server\MSSQL12\MSSQL\Data\AdventureWorks2012_log.LDF' )
  FOR ATTACH
```

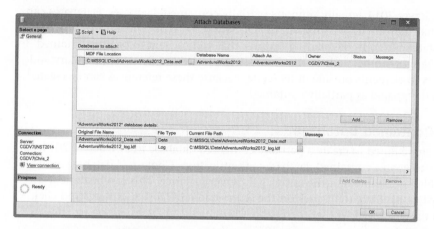

FIGURE 20.8   Attaching a database by using SSMS.

> **NOTE**
>
> You can use the `sp_attach_db` procedure to attach a database, but Microsoft recommends that you use the `CREATE DATABASE ... FOR ATTACH` command instead. The `sp_attach_db` procedure has been deprecated and is slated for removal in a future release of SQL Server.

SQL Server 2014 has the capability to attach a database without all the log files. You do this by using the `ATTACH_REBUILD_LOG` clause when creating the database. When you use this clause, SQL Server rebuilds the log files for you. This capability is useful on large databases that may have large logs that are not needed in the environment where the database files are attached. For example, a `READ_ONLY` database would not need the log files that may be associated with its production counterpart. The following example uses the `ATTACH_REBUILD_LOG` clause to create a copy of the `AdventureWorks2012` database:

```
CREATE DATABASE [AdventureWorks2012Temp] ON
( FILENAME = 'C:\Temp\AdventureWorks2012_Data.mdf' )
  FOR ATTACH_REBUILD_LOG
```

Contained Databases

There is a set of features that was introduced in SQL Server 2012 that allow for the creation of a contained database. By definition, a *contained database* is one that is isolated from other databases and from the instance of SQL Server that it is running on. When contained, no relationship exists between the database and the instance of SQL Server that

20

it is running on. So the database can be moved from one server to another without affecting the usability of the database. Issues such as orphaned database users where the user/login relationship is broken are eliminated with the use of a contained database.

In reality, SQL Server 2014 actually supports partially contained databases. Databases can be created so that they are fully contained in SQL Server 2014, but there is nothing to prevent the database from implementing features that will cause it to be noncontained. In other words, changes can be made to the database that cross the database boundary and create references to elements outside of its scope. Because these references can be created, the database is designated as partially contained.

Creating a Contained Database

Two key steps are required to create a partially contained database in SQL Server 2014. The first step is to enable contained database authentication. Contained database authentication is enabled or disabled for the entire SQL Server instance. This can be done using SSMS or via T-SQL. In SSMS, right-click on the server name in Object Explorer and click Properties. On the Advanced tab, set the Enable Contained Databases option to True, as shown in Figure 20.9.

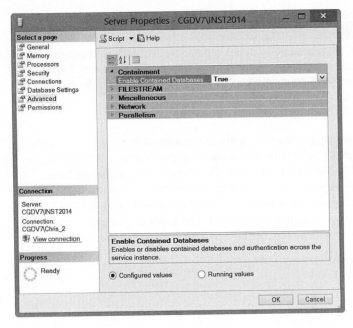

FIGURE 20.9   Enabling contained database authentication.

The following T-SQL statements can also be used to enable contained database authentication:

```
EXEC sys.sp_configure N'contained database authentication', N'1'
GO
RECONFIGURE WITH OVERRIDE
GO
```

The next step is to configure the database for containment. In SSMS, right-click on the database and select properties. Choose the Options page, click the Containment Type drop-down, and select Partial, as shown in Figure 20.10.

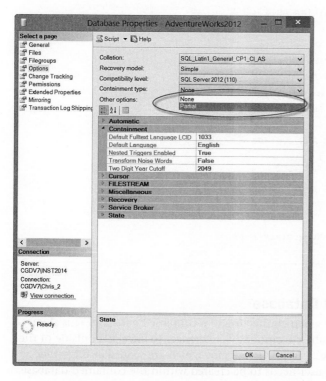

FIGURE 20.10   Configuring a database for partial containment.

The T-SQL for configuring the database for partial containment follows:

```
USE [master]
GO
ALTER DATABASE [mydb] SET CONTAINMENT = PARTIAL WITH NO_WAIT
GO
```

The first thing that you should do after you have chosen a database for containment is to check whether the database is truly contained. The sys.dm_db_uncontained_entities dynamic management view is a good tool for assessing containment. This view returns database objects that cross the database boundary and are thus uncontained. The view

20

returns the IDs of the objects that are uncontained. Listing 20.4 contains T-SQL that utilizes this view. It contains joins to several other system views so that the related names of these objects are displayed as well.

LISTING 20.4   T-SQL to Verify Database Containment

```
SELECT e.feature_name, COALESCE(o.name, a.name, t.name, tr.name, i.name, r.name,
p.name ) Name,
 class, class_desc
FROM   sys.dm_db_uncontained_entities AS e
 LEFT OUTER JOIN sys.objects AS o
  ON e.major_id = o.[object_id] AND e.class = 1
 LEFT OUTER JOIN sys.database_principals AS p
  ON e.major_id = p.principal_id AND e.class = 4
 LEFT OUTER JOIN sys.assemblies AS a
  ON e.major_id = a.assembly_id AND e.class = 5
 LEFT OUTER JOIN sys.types AS t
  ON e.major_id = t.user_type_id AND e.class = 6
 LEFT OUTER JOIN sys.indexes AS i
  ON e.major_id = i.index_id AND e.class = 7
 LEFT OUTER JOIN sys.triggers AS tr
  ON e.major_id = tr.object_id AND e.class = 12
 LEFT OUTER JOIN sys.routes AS r
  ON e.major_id = r.[route_id] AND e.class = 19
 GO
```

Connecting to a Contained Database

Some special considerations apply when connecting to a contained database. This stems from the fact that a contained database cannot have references to elements outside of the scope of the database. This includes references to logins which are scoped at the server level. To address this, a contained user needs to be created within the contained database. To create a contained user, expand the database node in Object Explorer, right-click on Users, and then click on New User. To create a contained SQL Server Authentication user, choose the user type of SQL User Without Login, as shown in Figure 20.11.

You can also create a contained user that utilizes Windows Authentication. The user will be contained if the corresponding account for Windows Authentication does not exist as a SQL Server login when the user is created. If the related login already exists in SQL Server when the user is created in the contained database, the user will be linked to login, and the database will no longer be contained.

After the user is created in the contained database, you can connect to this database using that user in much the same way as you connect to noncontained databases. Users connecting to a contained database will only see the databases they have access to. System databases and other elements that are scoped at the server level will not be visible to the contained user.

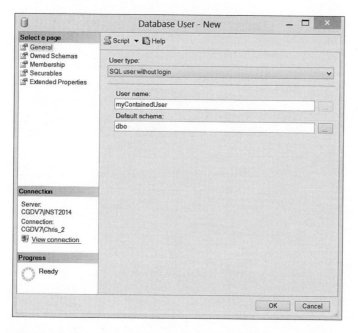

FIGURE 20.11   Contained SQL Server Authentication user.

There are many advantages to contained databases as well as some pitfalls. The biggest advantage is the portability of the database and the ability to easily move the database from one server to another. This portability makes these databases good candidates for high availability solutions such as the new AlwaysOn Availability Groups as well as database mirroring. With these solutions, it is possible for the database to be running on different servers where the location of the database is dependent on the state of availability. With contained databases, the authentication to these databases is independent of the server they are running on; thus reducing the amount of administrative overhead.

Summary

The steps involved in creating and managing databases are by no means limited to the topics in this chapter. A database consists of many database objects and has a myriad of other features discussed throughout this book. The next chapter, "Creating and Managing Tables," delves into one of the most basic elements of a database: the table.

20

Creating and Managing Tables

Tables are logical constructs used for the storage and manipulation of data in databases. Tables contain *columns*, which describe data, and *rows*, which are instances of table data. Basic relational database design determines the table and column names as well as the distribution of columns within tables.

This chapter gives you the administrative knowledge you need to create tables and manage them within your enterprise. It focuses on the basic constructs for tables and the table-level features that can make your tables robust and efficient objects to house your data.

What's New in SQL Server 2014

The good news is that overall, the management of tables and their related columns has remained relatively unchanged in SQL Server 2014. You will find that the facilities available in the SQL Server Management Studio are as familiar and as easy to use as they were in SQL Server 2012. However, SQL Server 2014 does introduce the new concept of memory optimized tables as part of the new In-Memory OLTP features. Memory-optimized tables reside entirely in memory with a second copy of the table data maintained on disk, but only for durability purposes. Because memory-optimized tables are so tightly integrated with the other In-Memory OLTP features, creation, altering, and maintaining memory optimized tables is discussed in detail in Chapter 33, "In-Memory Optimization and the Buffer Pool Extension."

Creating Tables

SQL Server 2014 supports the creation of tables using T-SQL, the SQL Server Management Studio (SSMS) Object Explorer and the SSMS Database Diagram Editor. Regardless of the tool you choose, creating a table involves naming the table, defining the columns, and assigning properties to the columns. The visual tools (such as Object Explorer and database diagrams) are usually the best starting point for creating tables. These tools offer drop-down boxes that allow you to choose the data types for your columns and check boxes that allow you to define their nullability.

This chapter first looks at the visual tools and then delves into the specific parameters related to the underlying T-SQL statements that ultimately create a table.

Using Object Explorer to Create Tables

The Object Explorer in SSMS has a `Tables` node under each database listed. You can add tables via the Object Explorer by right-clicking this `Tables` node. Figure 21.1 shows the New Table option displayed after you right-click the `Tables` node in Object Explorer. The top-right side of the screen shown in Figure 21.1 is the table creation screen that allows you to enter the column name and data type and to set the Allow Nulls option.

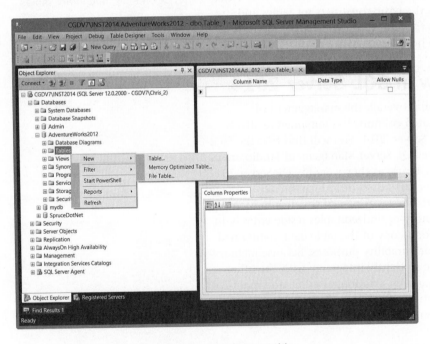

FIGURE 21.1   Using Object Explorer to create a table.

The data entry area under Column Name is a free-form area where you can define a column name. You can select the data type from the Data Type drop-down, which displays the data types available with SQL Server. The Allow Nulls option is Boolean in nature and is either checked or not checked. For each column selected, a Column Properties section is displayed in SSMS, providing a myriad of additional properties that you can assign to each column. These properties are discussed in more detail in the "Defining Columns" section, later in this chapter.

Using Database Diagrams to Create Tables

You can use the database diagrams for a more robust visual representation of your tables. You view them from within SSMS, and they give you the distinct advantage of being able to display multiple tables and the relationships between these tables. The Database Diagram Editor behaves similarly to other data modeling tools that allow you to move related tables around in the diagram and group them accordingly.

Figure 21.2 shows several screens related to database diagrams. The left side of Figure 21.2 shows the Object Explorer and the resulting New Database Diagram option that is displayed if you right-click the `Database Diagrams` node. The right side of the screen shows the diagram design window. In this example, the existing `Department` table from the `AdventureWorks2012` database was added to the diagram, and a new `Printer` table was added as well. The printer table was added by right-clicking in the diagram design window and selecting the New Table option.

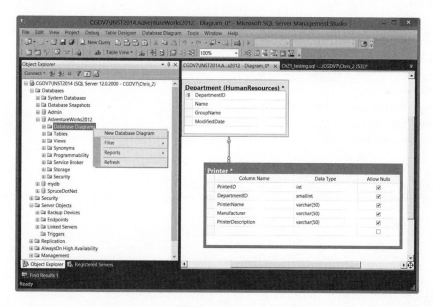

FIGURE 21.2   Using database diagrams to create a table.

The column names and related attributes for the new `Printer` table in Figure 21.2 were added using the table entry fields. The data entry screen for the table is similar to the one provided with the Object Explorer. You enter column names, along with their associated data types and nullability option.

The advantage of database diagrams is that you can define relationships and show them with a visual representation. This visual view provides a much easier way to view the table structures in a database. In the example shown in Figure 21.2, the line drawn between the Department and Printer tables represents a relationship between these two tables. You define such a foreign key relationship in the database diagram by dragging the related column from one table to the other related table. Table relationships and constraints are discussed later in this chapter, in the section, "Defining Table Constraints."

Using T-SQL to Create Tables

Ultimately, all the tables created with the visual tools can also be created by using T-SQL. As with many of the SSMS tools, database objects can be resolved or scripted into T-SQL statements. Let's examine the T-SQL syntax to better understand some of the table creation options; then we can discuss the definition of the columns in each table.

The full T-SQL CREATE TABLE syntax is extensive. It includes options to define table constraints, indexes, and index options. The SQL Server Books Online topic named "CREATE TABLE (Transact-SQL)" shows the full syntax and describes each of these options in detail. Listing 21.1 shows the basic T-SQL syntax; the first part of the syntax is listed in Books Online. This syntax is enough to enable you to create a table with its associated column definitions.

LISTING 21.1   Basic T-SQL CREATE TABLE Syntax

```
CREATE TABLE
    [ database_name . [ schema_name ] . | schema_name . ] table_name
    [ AS FileTable ]
    ( { <column_definition> | <computed_column_definition>
        | <column_set_definition> | [ <table_constraint> ] [ ,...n ] } )
    [ ON { partition_scheme_name ( partition_column_name ) | filegroup
        | "default" } ]
    [ { TEXTIMAGE_ON { filegroup | "default" } ]
    [ FILESTREAM_ON { partition_scheme_name | filegroup
        | "default" } ]
    [ WITH ( <table_option> [ ,...n ] ) ]
[ ; ]


<column_definition> ::=
column_name <data_type>
    [ FILESTREAM ]
    [ COLLATE collation_name ]
    [ NULL | NOT NULL ]
    [
        [ CONSTRAINT constraint_name ] DEFAULT constant_expression ]
        | [ IDENTITY [ ( seed ,increment ) ] [ NOT FOR REPLICATION ] ]
    ]
```

```
    [ ROWGUIDCOL ] [ <column_constraint> [ ...n ] ]
    [ SPARSE ]

<data type> ::=
[ type_schema_name . ] type_name
    [ ( precision [ , scale ] | max |
        [ { CONTENT | DOCUMENT } ] xml_schema_collection ) ]
```

The number of options in this basic syntax can be daunting, but the reality is that you can exclude many of the options and execute a relatively simple statement. Listing 21.2 is an example of a simple statement you can use to create a table. This listing shows a CREATE TABLE statement that you can use to create the Printer table that was shown in Figure 21.2.

LISTING 21.2   A Basic T-SQL CREATE TABLE Example

```
CREATE TABLE Printer
    (
    PrinterID int NOT NULL,
    DepartmentID smallint NOT NULL,
    PrinterName varchar(50) NOT NULL,
    Manufacturer varchar(50) NOT NULL,
    PrinterDescription varchar(250) NULL
    )
```

The CREATE TABLE statement in Listing 21.2 specifies the table to create, followed by an ordered list of columns to add to the table. The following section describes the specifics related to defining the columns.

TIP

SSMS provides several methods for generating the T-SQL code to create tables. Therefore, you rarely need to type the CREATE TABLE statements from scratch. Instead, you can use the friendly graphical user interface (GUI) screens that enable you to define the table, and then you can generate the T-SQL script. For example, you can right-click a new table in the database diagram and select Generate Change Script to generate the associated T-SQL for the table.

One of the important considerations during table creation is schema assignment. *Schemas* allow you to logically group objects (including tables) and define ownership, independent of the individual users in the database. Schema enhancements introduced in SQL Server 2005 are still available in SQL Server 2014 and can play a significant role in the definition of tables in a database. Consider, for example, the AdventureWorks2012 database that ships with SQL Server 2014. The tables in this database have been assigned to schemas that group the tables according to their functional areas. The schemas in the AdventureWorks2012 database include Sales, Purchasing, Person, Production, HumanResources, and dbo. Some sample tables in the Person schema include the Person and Address tables. The Purchasing schema includes tables that relate to purchasing, including the PurchaseOrderHeader and Vendor tables.

The designation of a schema in the CREATE TABLE statement is relatively simple. Listing 21.3 includes a three-part table name for the creation of a Printer table in the HumanResources schema. The database name (AdventureWorks2012) is the first part of the name, followed by a schema name (HumanResources) and then the table name. The last part of Listing 21.3 shows a sample SELECT statement against the Printer table that is owned by the HumanResources schema. The schema name must precede the table, when referenced. The only exceptions to this rule are tables that belong to the default schema assigned to the user executing the query.

LISTING 21.3   Using T-SQL CREATE TABLE in a Schema

```
CREATE TABLE AdventureWorks2012.HumanResources.Printer
    (
    PrinterID int NOT NULL,
    DepartmentID smallint NOT NULL,
    PrinterName varchar(50) NOT NULL,
    Manufacturer varchar(50) NOT NULL,
    PrinterDescription varchar(250) NULL
    )
go
 select * from HumanResources.Printer
```

The creation of schemas and assignment of tables to schemas requires some forethought. This task, which is permission-oriented, is discussed in more detail in Chapter 15, "Security and User Administration."

Defining Columns

A *table* is defined as a collection of columns. Each column represents an attribute of the database table and has characteristics that define its scope and the type of data it can contain. In defining a column, you must assign a name and a data type. For consistency and readability, the column names should adhere to a naming convention that you define for your environment. Naming conventions often use a set of standard suffixes that indicate the type of data the column will contain. For example, you can add the Date suffix to a column name (for example, OrderDate) to identify it as a column that contains date/time data, or you can add the suffix ID (for example, PrinterID) to indicate that the column contains a unique identifier.

When creating and naming columns, you need to keep the following restrictions in mind:

▶ You can define up to 1,024 columns (nonsparse + computed) for each table. This number is increased to 30,000 columns if the table has a defined column set using sparse columns.

▶ Column names must be unique within a table.

▶ A row can hold a maximum of 8,060 bytes. Some data types can be stored off the 8KB data page to allow a row to exceed this limit.

▶ A data type must be assigned to each column.

These restrictions provide a framework for a column definition. The next consideration in defining a column is the data type. The following section discusses the various data types.

Data Types

SQL Server 2014 has an extensive list of data types to choose from. Each data type is geared toward a specific type of data that will be stored in the column. Table 21.1 provides a complete list of the data types available in SQL Server 2014.

TABLE 21.1   Table Data Types

Data Type	Range/Description	Storage
bigint	-2^{63} (−9,223,372,036,854,775,808) to 2^{63-1} (9,223,372,036,854,775,807)	8 bytes
binary (n)	Binary data with a length of n bytes, up to 8,000	The number of bytes specified by n
bit	An integer data type that can take a value of 1, 0, or NULL	1 byte for every eight columns that are defined as bits on the table
char(n)	Non-Unicode characters up to max of 8,000	The number of bytes specified by n
date	January 1, 0001 through December 31, 9999	3 bytes
datetime	January 1, 1753 through December 31, 9999; accurate to 3.33 milliseconds	8 bytes
datetime2[(n)]	January 1, 0001 through December 31, 9999; accurate to 100 nanoseconds with default fractional seconds precision of 7	6-8 bytes depending on optional precision specified by n
datetimeoffset[(n)]	January 1, 0001 through December 31, 9999 plus a time zone offset; accurate to 100 nanoseconds with default fractional seconds precision of 7	8-10 bytes depending on optional precision specified by n
decimal[(p[,s])]	-10^{38+1} to 10^{38-1}; precision from 1 to 38. Default precision is 18	5–17 bytes depending on the precision

Data Type	Range/Description	Storage
float[(n)]	−1.79E + 308 to −2.23E − 308, 0 and 2.23E − 308 to 1.79E + 308	4 or 8 bytes, depending on optional mantissa specified by n
geography	.NET CLR data type representing round-earth data such as GPS latitude and longitude coordinates	
geometry	.NET CLR data type representing data in a Euclidean (flat) coordinate system	
hierarchyid	User defined nodes and levels	Up to 892 bytes
image	Variable-length binary data up to 2^{31-1} (2,147,483,647) bytes	16 bytes plus the number of bytes entered up to the max
int	-2^{31} (−2,147,483,648) to 2^{31-1} (2,147,483,647)	4 bytes
money	−922,337,203,685,477.5808 to 922,337,203,685,477.5807	8 bytes
nchar(n)	Unicode characters up to max of 4,000	2 bytes times the number of characters specified by n
ntext	Unicode characters up to max of 2^{30-1} (1,073,741,823) characters	2 bytes times the number of characters entered up to the max
numeric[(p[,s])]	-10^{38+1} to 10^{38-1}; precision from 1 to 38. Default precision is 18	5-17 bytes depending on the precision
nvarchar(n)	Unicode characters up to a max of 4,000	2 bytes plus 2 bytes times the number of characters entered up to n
nvarchar(max)	Unicode characters up to the max of 2^{30-1} (1,073,741,823) characters	2 bytes plus 2 bytes times the number of characters entered up to max
real	− 3.40E + 38 to −1.18E − 38, 0 and 1.18E − 38 to 3.40E + 38	4 bytes
rowversion	Automatically generated unique binary numbers within a database; generally used for version stamping rows	8 bytes
smalldatetime	January 1, 1900, through June 6, 2079; accurate to 1 minute	4 bytes
smallint	-2^{15} (−32,768) to 2^{15-1} (32,767)	2 bytes
smallmoney	−214,748.3648 to 214,748.3647	4 bytes
sql_variant	A data type that stores values of various SQL Server–supported data types, except text, ntext, image, timestamp, and sql_variant	Up to 8,016 bytes

Data Type	Range/Description	Storage
text	Up to 2^{31-1} (2,147,483,647) characters	1 byte per character entered up to the max
time[(n)]	00:00:00.0 to 23:59:59.9999999; default fractional seconds precision is 7	3-5 bytes depending on specified fractional seconds precision
tinyint	0 to 255	1 byte
uniqueidentifier	A 16-byte globally unique identifier (GUID)	16 bytes
varbinary(n)	Binary data with a length of n bytes up to a max of 8,000	2 bytes plus the number of bytes entered up to n
varbinary(max)	Binary data up to the max of 2^{31-1} (2,147,483,647) bytes	2 bytes plus the number of bytes entered
varchar (n)	Non-Unicode characters up to 8,00 characters max	2 bytes plus 1 byte per character entered up to n
varchar (max)	Non-Unicode characters up to the max of 2^{31-1} (2,147,483,647) characters	2 bytes plus 1 byte per character entered
xml	XML instances or a variable of XML type	Number of bytes entered up to max of 2GB

NOTE

Several of the data types listed will not be supported in a future version of SQL Server. The text, ntext, and image data types will be supported in the next version of SQL Server but will be removed in a later version. The varchar(max), nvarchar(max), and varbinary(max) data types should be used instead.

The data type you select is important because it provides scope for the column. For example, if you define a column as type int, you can be assured that only integer data will be stored in the column and that character data will not be allowed. The advantages of data typing are fairly obvious but sometimes overlooked.

Columns should be defined with data types that match the type of data that the column will contain. For example, columns that contain dates should be defined with a date-oriented data type such as DateTime and not defined as varchar. As mentioned earlier in this chapter, the visual tools provide a great way for you to select a data type: you simply select a data type from a drop-down selection box that lists the available data types.

TIP

The Object Explorer has a categorized list of all the system data types. To get to it, you open the Programmability node under your database and then expand the Types node. You then see a node named System Data Types that lists all the data type categories, including Exact Numbers, Approximate Numbers, and Date and Time. The data types for each category are listed under each category node. If you click on the data type and then mouse over it, you will see a brief description, including the valid range of values.

Some data types in SQL Server 2014 deserve special attention. The following sections discuss these data types.

The xml Data Type

The xml data type (introduced in SQL Server 2005) enables you to store XML documents and XML fragments in a SQL Server database. (An XML fragment is an XML instance that is missing a single top-level element.)

The hierarchyid Data Type

The hierarchyid data type was introduced in SQL Server 2008. The hierarchyid data type is a variable-length system data type used to represent a position in a tree hierarchy. A column of type hierarchyid does not automatically represent a tree. It is up to the application to generate and assign hierarchyid values in such a way that the desired relationship between rows is reflected in the values.

Spatial Data Types

Spatial data types provide a comprehensive, high-performance, and extensible data storage solution for spatial data, enabling organizations of any scale to integrate geospatial features into their applications and services.

Spatial data types can be used to store and manipulate location-based information and come in the form of two data types: geography and geometry. The geography data type is a .NET CLR data type that provides a storage structure for geodetic data, sometimes referred to as round earth data because it assumes a roughly spherical model of the world. It provides a storage structure for spatial data that is defined by latitude and longitude coordinates using an industry standard ellipsoid such as WGS84, the projection method used by Global Positioning System (GPS) applications. The geometry data type is a .NET CLR data type that supports the planar model/data, which assumes a flat projection and is therefore sometimes called flat earth. geometry data is represented as points, lines, and polygons on a flat surface, such as maps and interior floor plans where the curvature of the earth does not need to be taken into account.

Large-Value Data Types

Three large-value data types allow you to store a significant amount of data in a single column. They allow you to store up to 2^{31-1} bytes of non-Unicode data and 2^{30-1} bytes of Unicode data. All these data types have the (max) designator: varchar(max), nvarchar(max), and varbinary(max).

The great thing about these data types is that they are much easier to work with than large object (LOB) data types. LOB data types (which include text, ntext, and image) require special programming when retrieving and storing data. The large-value data types do not have these restrictions. They can be used much like their smaller counterparts varchar(n), nvarchar(n), and varbinary(n) that are defined without the max keyword. So if you want to select data from a varchar(max) column, you can simply execute a SELECT statement against it, regardless of the amount of data stored in it. Consider, for example, the following SELECT statement, executed against a varchar(max) column named DocumentSummary in the AdventureWorks2012.Production.Document table:

```
select Title, substring(DocumentSummary,1,30) 'DocumentSummary'
from production.document
where LEFT(DocumentSummary,30) like 'Reflector%'

/* results from previous select statement
Title                                                DocumentSummary
--------------------------------------------------   ------------------------------
Front Reflector Bracket Installation                 Reflectors are vital safety co
*/
```

This works fine with the varchar(max) column, but the LEFT function used in the WHERE clause would cause an error if the column were a text column instead.

The large-value data types can be stored in the data row or in a separate data page, based on the setting of the sp_tableoption 'large value types out of row' option. If the option is set to OFF, up to 8 K can be stored in this column in the actual data row. If the option is set to ON, data for this column is stored in a separate data page if its length would result in the data row exceeding 8,060 bytes. The actual location of the column data is transparent to any user accessing the table.

Large Row Support

The maximum amount of data that SQL Server can store on a single data page is 8,060 bytes, but SQL Server can dynamically manage rows that may exceed the 8,060-byte limit. This dynamic behavior is designed for columns that are defined as varchar, nvarchar, varbinary, or sql_variant. If the values in these columns cause the total size of the row to go beyond the 8,060-byte limit, SQL Server moves one or more of the variable-length columns to pages in the ROW_OVERFLOW_DATA allocation unit. A pointer to this separate storage location, rather than the actual data, is kept in the data row. If the data row shrinks below the 8,060-byte limit at a later time, SQL Server dynamically moves the data from the ROW_OVERFLOW_DATA allocation unit back into the data page.

The following example creates a table that has columns that could exceed the 8,060-byte limit, with a total of 9,000 characters:

```
CREATE TABLE t1
(col1 varchar(4000), col2 varchar(5000))

insert t1
select replicate('x', 4000),replicate('x', 5000)
```

If you execute the CREATE TABLE statement, you do not get any warning message related to the 8,060-byte limit. After the table is created, you can execute an insert into the table that exceeds the 8,060-byte limit. The insert succeeds, and the dynamic allocation previously described is handled automatically.

User-Defined Data Types

User-defined data types allow you to create custom data types that are based on the existing system data types. These data types are also called *alias data types* in SQL Server 2014. You create a user-defined data type and give it a unique name that you can then use in the definitions of tables. For example, you can create a user-defined data type named ShortDescription, defined as varchar(20), and assign it to any column. This promotes data type consistency across your tables.

You can create user-defined data types by using T-SQL in a couple of different ways. Using the sp_addtype system stored procedure and using the CREATE TYPE command are two possibilities. The sp_addtype system stored procedure is slated to be removed in a future version of SQL Server, so using the CREATE TYPE command is preferred. The following example shows how to create the ShortDescription user-defined data type:

```
CREATE TYPE [dbo].[ShortDescription] FROM [varchar](20) NOT NULL
```

After a user-defined data type is created, you can use it in the definition of tables. The following is an example of a table created with the new ShortDescription user-defined data type:

```
CREATE TABLE [dbo].CodeTable
  (TableId int identity,
   TableDesc ShortDescription)
```

When you look at the definition of the CodeTable table in Object Explorer, you see the TableDesc column displayed with the ShortDescription data type as well as the underlying data type varchar(20).

You can use the Object Explorer to create user-defined data types as well. To do so, expand the Programmability folder, and then expand the Types folder and right-click the User-Defined Data Types node. Then you choose the New User-Defined Data Type option, and you can create a new user-defined data type through a friendly GUI screen. If you create a user-defined data type in the model database, this user-defined data type can be created in any newly created database.

CLR User-Defined Types

SQL Server 2014 continues support for user-defined types (UDTs) implemented with the Microsoft .NET Framework common language runtime (CLR). CLR UDTs enable you to extend the type system of the database and also enable you to define complex structured types.

A UDT may be simple or structured and of any degree of complexity. A UDT can encapsulate complex, user-defined behaviors. You can use CLR UDTs in all contexts where you can use a system type in SQL Server, including in columns in tables, in variables in batches, in functions or stored procedures, as arguments of functions or stored procedures, or as return values from functions.

A UDT must first be implemented as a managed class or structure in any one of the CLR languages and compiled into a .NET Framework assembly. You can then register it with SQL Server by using the CREATE ASSEMBLY command, as in the following example:

```
CREATE ASSEMBLY latlong FROM 'c:\samplepath\latlong.dll'
```

After registering the assembly, you can create the CLR UDTs by using a variation of the CREATE TYPE command shown previously:

```
CREATE TYPE latitude EXTERNAL NAME latlong.latitude
CREATE TYPE longitude EXTERNAL NAME latlong.longitude
```

When a CLR UDT is created, you can use it in the definition of tables. The following example shows a table created with the new latitude and longitude UDTs:

```
CREATE TABLE [dbo].StoreLocation
 (StoreID int NOT NULL,
  StoreLatitude latitude,
  StoreLongitude longitude)
```

Column Properties

Name and data type are the most basic properties of a column, but many other properties can be defined for a column. You do not have to specify these properties to be able to create the columns, but you can use them to further refine the type of data that can be stored within a column. Note that many of the available column properties relate to indexes and constraints that are beyond the scope of this section. The following sections describe some of the column properties you are most likely to encounter.

The NULL and NOT NULL Keywords

When you are defining tables, it is always good idea to explicitly state whether a column should or should not contain nulls. You do this by specifying the NULL or NOT NULL keywords after the column data type. If the nullability option is not specified, the SQL Server default is to allow nulls unless the ANSI_NULL_DFLT_OFF option is enabled for the session or no setting is specified for the session, and the ANSI_NULL_DEFAULT option for the database is set to OFF. Because of this uncertainty, it is best to always explicitly specify the desired nullability option for each column. Listing 21.4 creates a new table named PrinterCartridge that has the NULL or NOT NULL property specified for each column.

LISTING 21.4   Defining Column NULL Properties by Using CREATE TABLE

```
CREATE TABLE dbo.PrinterCartridge
    (
    CartridgeId int NOT NULL,
    PrinterID int NOT NULL,
```

```
    CartridgeName varchar(50) NOT NULL,
    CartridgeColor varchar(50) NOT NULL,
    CartrideDescription varchar(255) NULL,
    InstallDate datetime NOT NULL
    )
GO
```

NOTE

It is beyond the scope of this section to debate whether columns should ever allow nulls. In some organizations, nulls are heavily used, and in others they are not allowed. There is no right answer, but it is important for a development team to be aware of the existence of nulls so that it can create appropriate code to handle them.

Identity Columns

A property commonly specified when creating tables is IDENTITY. This property automatically generates a unique sequential value when it is assigned to a column. It can be assigned only to columns that are of the following types:

▶ decimal(p,0)

▶ int

▶ numeric(p,0)

▶ smallint

▶ bigint

▶ tinyint

Only one identity column can exist for each table, and that column cannot allow nulls.

When implementing the IDENTITY property, you supply a seed and an increment. The *seed* is the starting value for the numeric count, and the *increment* is the amount by which it grows. A seed of 10 and an increment of 10 would produce values of 10, 20, 30, 40, and so on. If not specified, the default seed value is 1, and the increment is 1. Listing 21.5 adds an IDENTITY value to the PrinterCartridge table used in the previous example.

LISTING 21.5   Defining an Identity Column by Using CREATE TABLE

```
IF  EXISTS (SELECT * FROM dbo.sysobjects
WHERE id = OBJECT_ID(N'dbo.PrinterCartridge')
AND OBJECTPROPERTY(id, N'IsUserTable') = 1)
DROP TABLE dbo.PrinterCartridge

CREATE TABLE dbo.PrinterCartridge
    (
```

```
      CartridgeId int IDENTITY (1, 1) NOT NULL,
      PrinterID int NOT NULL,
      CartridgeName varchar(50) NOT NULL,
      CartridgeColor varchar(50) NOT NULL,
      CartrideDescription varchar(255) NULL,
      InstallDate datetime NOT NULL
      )
GO

insert PrinterCartridge
 (PrinterID, CartridgeName, CartridgeColor, CartrideDescription, InstallDate)
values (1, 'inkjet', 'black','laser printer cartridge', '8/1/14')

select CartridgeId, PrinterID, CartridgeName
 from PrinterCartridge

/* results from previous SELECT statement
CartridgeId PrinterID    CartridgeName
----------- -----------  --------------------------------------------------
1            1           inkjet
*/
```

In this listing, the seed value has been set to 1, and the increment has been set to 1. An insert into the `PrinterCartridge` table and a subsequent `SELECT` from that table follows the `CREATE TABLE` statement in the listing. Notice that the results of the `SELECT` show a value of 1 for the identity column `CartridgeID`. This is the seed or starting point that is defined.

ROWGUIDCOL Columns

An alternative to an identity column is a column defined with the `ROWGUIDCOL` property. Like the `IDENTITY` property, the `ROWGUIDCOL` property is autogenerating and unique. The difference is that the `ROWGUIDCOL` option generates column values that will be unique on any networked database anywhere in the world. The identity column generates values that are unique only within the table that contains the column.

You can have only one `ROWGUIDCOL` column per table. You must create this `ROWGUIDCOL` column with the `uniqueidentifier` data type, and you must assign a default of `NEWID()` to the column to generate the unique value. Keep in mind that users can manually insert values directly into columns defined as `ROWGUIDCOL`. These manual inserts could cause duplicates in the column, so a `UNIQUE` constraint should be added to the column as well to ensure uniqueness.

Listing 21.6 shows the creation of a table with a `ROWGUIDCOL` column. Several rows are inserted into the newly created table, and those rows are selected at the end of the listing.

LISTING 21.6   Defining a ROWGUIDCOL Column

```
CREATE TABLE SomeUniqueTable
    (UniqueID    UNIQUEIDENTIFIER      DEFAULT NEWID(),
    EffectiveDate datetime )
GO
INSERT INTO SomeUniqueTable (EffectiveDate) VALUES ('7/1/09')
INSERT INTO SomeUniqueTable (EffectiveDate) VALUES ('8/1/09')
GO
select * from SomeUniqueTable
/* Results from previous select statement
UniqueID                             EffectiveDate
----------------------------------- -----------------------
614181BC-D7B9-4108-B2BD-C2F39E999424 2009-07-01 00:00:00.000
62368A2D-3557-4727-9DD3-FBCA38705B1B 2009-08-01 00:00:00.000
*/
```

You can see that the ROWGUIDCOL values are fairly large. They are 16-byte binary values that are significantly larger than most of the data types used for identity columns. For example, an identity column defined as data type int occupies only 4 bytes. You need to consider the storage requirements for ROWGUIDCOL when you select this data type.

> **NOTE**
>
> SQL Server 2012 added a new sequence object that is another option for implementing an auto-incrementing column similar to an Identity column. A sequence is created independent of the table by using the Create Sequence statement. Once created, the sequence object generates a sequence of numeric values according to the specification with which the sequence was created. When rows are inserted in a table, the Insert statement can reference the sequence object to obtain the next value in the sequence. The sequence has two real benefits. First, if you plan to use a single identifier across multiple tables with no overlap. Second it allows you to capture the sequence value in advance of the insert, so you don't need to use a trigger or output table to capture the value in single-row insert cases.

Computed Columns

A *computed column* is a column whose value is calculated based on other columns. Generally speaking, the column is a virtual column because it is calculated on the fly, and no value is stored in the database table. With SQL Server 2014, you have an option of actually storing the calculated value in the database. You do so by marking the column as persisted. If the computed column is persisted, you can create an index on this column as well.

Listing 21.7 includes several statements that relate to the creation of a computed column. It starts with an ALTER TABLE statement that adds a new computed column named SetRate to the Sales.CurrencyRate table in the AdventureWorks2012 database. The new rate column is based on an average of two other rate columns in the table. A SELECT statement is executed after that; it returns several columns, including the new SetRate computed column. The results are shown after the SELECT. Finally, an ALTER TABLE statement is used to change the newly added column so that its values are stored in the database. This is accomplished with the ADD PERSISTED option.

LISTING 21.7   Defining a Computed Column

```
--Add a computed column to the Sales.CurrencyRate Table named SetRate
ALTER TABLE Sales.CurrencyRate
 ADD SetRate AS ( (AverageRate + EndOfDayRate) / 2)
go
--Select several columns including the new computed column
select top 5 AverageRate, EndOfDayRate , SetRate
 from sales.currencyrate

/*Results from previous SELECT statement
AverageRate             EndOfDayRate            SetRate
--------------------    --------------------    --------------------
1.00                    1.2                     1.1
1.5491                  1.55                    1.5495
1.9379                  1.9419                  1.9399
1.4641                  1.4683                  1.4662
8.2781                  8.2784                  8.2782
*/

--Alter the computed SetRate column to be PERSISTED
ALTER TABLE Sales.CurrencyRate
 alter column SetRate ADD PERSISTED
```

NOTE

You can use the sp_spaceused stored procedure to check the space allocated to the Sales.CurrencyRate table. You need to check the size before the column is persisted, and then you need to check the space allocated to the table after the column is persisted. As you would expect, the space allocated to the table is increased only after the column is persisted.

FILESTREAM Storage

SQL Server 2008 introduced FILESTREAM storage for storing unstructured data, such as documents, images, and videos. In previous versions of SQL Server, there were two ways of storing unstructured data. One method was to store it in the database as a binary large object (BLOB) in an image or varbinary(max) column. The other method was to store the data outside the database, separate from the structured relational data, storing a reference or pathname to the unstructured data in a varchar column in a table. Neither of these methods is ideal for unstructured data.

FILESTREAM storage helps to solve the issues with using unstructured data by integrating the SQL Server Database Engine with the NTFS file system for storing the unstructured data, such as documents and images, on the file system with the database storing a pointer to the data. Although the actual data resides outside the database in the NTFS file system, you can still use T-SQL statements to insert, update, query, and back up FILESTREAM data, while maintaining transactional consistency between the unstructured data and corresponding structured data with same level of security.

To specify that a column should store data on the file system when creating or altering a table, you specify the FILESTREAM attribute on a varbinary(max) column. This causes the Database Engine to store all data for that column on the file system, but not in the database file. After you complete these tasks, you can use Transact-SQL and Win32 to manage the FILESTREAM data.

> **NOTE**
>
> To use FILESTREAM storage, you must first enable FILESTREAM storage at the Windows level as well as at the SQL Server Instance level. You can enable FILESTREAM at the Windows level during installation of SQL Server 2014 or at any time using SQL Server Configuration Manager. After you enable FILESTREAM at the Windows level, you next need to enable FILESTREAM for the SQL Server Instance. You can do this either through SQL Server Management Studio or via T-SQL.

Sparse Columns and Column Sets

SQL Server 2014 provides a space-saving storage option referred to as *sparse columns*. Sparse columns can provide optimized and efficient storage for columns that contain predominately NULL values. If the value of a column defined as a sparse column is NULL, it doesn't consume any space at all. The space savings of sparse columns come with a trade-off, however, requiring extra space when storing non-null values in the sparse column. Fixed-length and precision data types require 4 extra bytes, and variable-length data types require 2 extra bytes. For this reason, you should consider using sparse columns only when the space saved is at least 20% to 40%. However, the consensus rule of thumb that is emerging from experience with sparse columns is that it is best to use them only when more than 90% of the values are NULL.

SQL Server stores sparse columns in a single XML column that appears to external applications and end users as a normal column. Storing the sparse columns in a single XML column allows up to 30 sparse columns in a single table, exceeding the limitation of 1,024 columns if sparse columns are not used. In addition, because sparse columns have many null-valued rows, they are good candidates for filtered indexes. A filtered index on a sparse column can index only the rows that have non-null values stored in the column. This creates smaller and more efficient indexes. (For more information on filtered indexes, see Chapters 22, "Creating and Managing Indexes," and 31, "Understanding SQL Server Data Structures.")

Sparse columns can be defined using any SQL Server data type and behave like any other column with the following exceptions and restrictions:

▶ A sparse column cannot be defined on columns with user-defined data type or any of the following system data types—`text`, `ntext`, `image`, `timestamp`, `geometry`, or `geography`

▶ A sparse column must be nullable and cannot have the `ROWGUIDCOL` or `IDENTITY` properties.

▶ You can't define `varbinary(max)` fields that use `FILESTREAM` storage as sparse columns.

▶ A sparse column cannot be defined with a default value.

▶ A sparse column cannot be bound to a rule.

▶ A computed column cannot be defined as a sparse column, but you can use a sparse column in the calculation of a computed column.

▶ A sparse column cannot be part of a clustered index or a unique primary key index.

▶ A sparse column cannot be used as a partition key of a clustered index or heap. However, a sparse column can be used as the partition key of a nonclustered index.

▶ Sparse columns are incompatible with data compression. Therefore sparse columns cannot be added to compressed tables, nor can any tables containing sparse columns be compressed.

▶ A table cannot have more than 1,024 non-sparse columns.

▶ Although sparse columns allow up to 30 columns per table, the total row size is reduced to 8,018 bytes due to the additional overhead for sparse columns. When the number of sparse columns in a table is large and operating on them individually is cumbersome, you may want to define a column set.

Column Sets

Column sets provide an alternative way to view and work with all the sparse columns in a table. The sparse columns are aggregated into a single untyped XML column, which simplifies working with many sparse columns in a table. The XML column used for a column set is similar to a calculated column in that it is not physically stored, but unlike calculated columns, it is updateable. Applications may see some performance improvement when they select and insert data by using column sets on tables that have lots of columns.

There are some restrictions on column sets:

▶ You cannot add a column set to a table that already has sparse columns.

▶ You can define only one column set per table.

▶ Constraints or default values cannot be defined on a column set.

▶ Computed columns cannot contain column set columns.

▶ A column set cannot be changed; you must delete and re-create the column set. However, sparse columns can be added to the table after a column set has been defined and is automatically included in the column set.

▶ Distributed queries, replication, and Change Data Capture do not support column sets.

▶ A column set cannot be part of any kind of index, including XML indexes, full-text indexes, and indexed views.

NOTE

Sparse columns and column sets are defined by using the CREATE TABLE or ALTER TABLE statements. This chapter focuses on using and working with sparse columns.

Working with Sparse Columns

Querying and manipulation of sparse columns is the same as for regular columns, with one exception described later in this chapter. There's nothing functionally different about a table that includes sparse columns, except the way the sparse columns are stored. You can still use all the standard INSERT, UPDATE, and DELETE statements on tables with sparse columns just like a table that doesn't have sparse columns. You can also wrap operations on a table with sparse columns in transactions as usual.

To work with sparse columns, let's first create a table with sparse columns. The following example creates a version of the Product table in the AdventureWorks2012 database and then populates the table with data from the Production.Product table. The Color, Weight, and SellEndDate columns are defined as sparse columns (the source data contains a significant number of NULL values for these columns). These columns are also defined as part of the column set, ProductInfo.

```
USE AdventureWorks2012
GO
CREATE TABLE Product_sparse
(
    ProductID INT NOT NULL PRIMARY KEY,
    ProductName NVARCHAR(50) NOT NULL,
    Color NVARCHAR(15) SPARSE NULL,
    Weight DECIMAL(8,2) SPARSE NULL,
    SellEndDate DATETIME SPARSE NULL,
    ProductInfo XML COLUMN_SET FOR ALL_SPARSE_COLUMNS
)
GO
INSERT INTO Product_sparse
(ProductID, ProductName, Color, Weight, SellEndDate)
SELECT ProductID, Name, Color, Weight, SellEndDate
FROM Production.Product
GO
```

You can reference the sparse columns in your queries just as you would any type of column:

```
SELECT productID, productName, Color, Weight, SellEndDate
FROM Product_sparse
where ProductID < 320
go
```

productID	productName	Color	Weight	SellEndDate
1	Adjustable Race	NULL	NULL	NULL
2	Bearing Ball	NULL	NULL	NULL
3	BB Ball Bearing	NULL	NULL	NULL
4	Headset Ball Bearings	NULL	NULL	NULL
316	Blade	NULL	NULL	NULL
317	LL Crankarm	Black	NULL	NULL
318	ML Crankarm	Black	NULL	NULL
319	HL Crankarm	Black	NULL	NULL

Note, however, that if you use SELECT * in a query and the table has a column set defined for the sparse columns, the column set is returned as a single XML column instead of the individual columns:

```
SELECT *
FROM Product_sparse
where ProductID < 320
go
```

ProductID	ProductName	ProductInfo
1	Adjustable Race	NULL
2	Bearing Ball	NULL
3	BB Ball Bearing	NULL
4	Headset Ball Bearings	NULL
316	Blade	NULL
317	LL Crankarm	<Color>Black</Color>
318	ML Crankarm	<Color>Black</Color>
319	HL Crankarm	<Color>Black</Color>

You need to explicitly list the columns in the SELECT clause to have the result columns returned as relational columns.

When the column set is defined, you can also operate on the column set by using XML operations instead of relational operations. For example, the following code inserts a row into the table by using the column set and specifying a value for Weight as XML:

```
INSERT Product_sparse(ProductID, ProductName, ProductInfo)
  VALUES(5, 'ValveStem', '<Weight>.12</Weight>')
go


SELECT productID, productName, Color, Weight, SellEndDate
FROM Product_sparse
where productID = 5
go


productID    productName Color Weight SellEndDate
----------- ----------- ----- ------ -----------
5            ValveStem   NULL  0.12   NULL
```

Notice that NULL is assumed for any column omitted from the XML value, such as `Color` and `SellEndDate` in this example.

When updating a column set using an XML value, you must include values for all the columns in the column set you want to set, including any existing values. Any values not specified in the XML string are set to NULL. For example, the following query sets both `Color` and `Weight` where `ProductID` = 5:

```
Update Product_sparse
set ProductInfo = '<Color>black</Color><Weight>.20</Weight>'
where productID = 5


SELECT productID, productName, Color, Weight, SellEndDate
FROM Product_sparse
where productID = 5
go


productID    productName Color Weight SellEndDate
----------- ----------- ----- ------ -----------
5            ValveStem   black 0.20   NULL
```

Now, if you run another update but only specify a value for `Weight` in the XML string, the `Color` column is set to NULL:

```
Update Product_sparse
set ProductInfo = '<Weight>.10</Weight>'
where productID = 5


SELECT productID, productName, Color, Weight, SellEndDate
FROM Product_sparse
where productID = 5
go
```

```
productID    productName Color Weight SellEndDate
-----------  ----------- ----- ------ -----------
5            ValveStem   NULL  0.10   NULL
```

However, if you reference the sparse columns explicitly in an UPDATE statement, the other values remain unchanged:

```
Update Product_sparse
set Color = 'silver'
where ProductID = 5


SELECT productID, productName, Color, Weight, SellEndDate
FROM Product_sparse
where productID = 5
go


productID    productName Color  Weight SellEndDate
-----------  ----------- ------ ------ -----------
5            ValveStem   silver 0.10   NULL
```

Column sets are most useful when you have many sparse columns in a table (for example, hundreds) and operating on them individually is cumbersome. Your client applications may more easily and efficiently generate the appropriate XML string to populate the column set rather than your having to build an UPDATE statement dynamically to determine which of the sparse columns need to be included in the SET clause. Applications might actually see some performance improvement when they select, insert, or update data by using column sets on tables that have lots of columns.

Sparse Columns: Good or Bad?

There is some disagreement in the SQL Server community whether or not sparse columns are appropriate. A number of professionals are of the opinion that any table design that requires sparse columns is a bad design that does not follow good relational design guidelines. Sparse columns, by their nature, are heavily denormalized. On the other hand, many times you have to live in the real world and make the best of a bad database design that you've inherited. Sparse columns can help solve performance and storage issues in databases that may have been poorly designed.

Although sparse columns can solve certain kinds of problems with database design, you should never use them as an alternative to proper database and table design. As cool as sparse columns are, they aren't appropriate for every scenario, particularly when you're tempted to violate normalization rules to be able to cram more fields into a table.

Defining Sparse Columns in SSMS

To specify a column as a sparse column using SQL Server Management Studio (SSMS), set the Is Sparse property to Yes in the column properties for the selected column (see

Figure 21.3). Similarly, if a column needs to be declared as column set, set the `Is Columnset` property to Yes in the column properties.

FIGURE 21.3   Setting a column as a sparse column.

Defining Table Location

As databases scale in size, the physical location of database objects, particularly tables and indexes, becomes crucial. Consider two tables, `Authors` and `Titles`, that are always queried together. If they are located on the same physical disk, contention for hardware resources may slow performance. SQL Server addresses this issue by enabling you to specify where a table (or an index) is stored.

The mechanism for specifying the physical table location is the filegroup. Filegroups are aligned to physical data files. By default, each database has a primary filegroup and a data file that matches the name of the database. You can create additional filegroups and align them to other data files. When these filegroups are created, SQL Server enables you to create your database tables on a specific filegroup.

> **NOTE**
>
> Using partitioned tables is a way to specify table location. This SQL Server 2014 feature allows you to divide a table into partitions and align those partitions with filegroups. This concept is discussed in detail in the "Using Partitioned Tables" section, later in this chapter.

The placement of tables on separate filegroups has some distinct advantages, including performance benefits. You can achieve performance improvements by storing filegroups on different disks. You can also achieve some manageability improvements by using filegroups because you can back up and manipulate filegroups separately. This capability is particularly important for large tables.

You specify the location of a table by using the ON clause during table creation. Listing 21.8 shows an example of creating two filegroups in the AdventureWorks2012 database, followed by the creation of two new tables on those filegroups. Note that the filegroups must exist before the tables are created. For more information on filegroups, see Chapter 20, "Creating and Managing Databases."

LISTING 21.8   An Example of Creating Tables on Specific Filegroups

```
--Add the filegroups
ALTER DATABASE AdventureWorks2012 ADD FILEGROUP FG1
ALTER DATABASE AdventureWorks2012 ADD FILEGROUP FG2
GO
--Add files to the filegroups
ALTER DATABASE AdventureWorks2012 ADD FILE
(   NAME = FG1_File,
    FILENAME = 'C:\MSSQL\FG1.ndf',
    SIZE = 2MB) TO FILEGROUP FG1
go


ALTER DATABASE AdventureWorks2012 ADD FILE
(   NAME = FG2_File,
    FILENAME = 'C:\MSSQL\FG2.ndf',
    SIZE = 2MB) TO FILEGROUP FG2
go


CREATE TABLE [Person].[authors](
    [au_id] int NOT NULL,
    [au_lname] [varchar](40) ,
    [au_fname] [varchar](20) ,
    [phone] [char](12),
    [address] [varchar](40)  NULL,
    [city] [varchar](20)  NULL,
    [state] [char](2)  NULL,
    [zip] [char](5)  NULL,
    [contract] [bit] NOT NULL,
) ON FG1
go


CREATE TABLE [Sales].[titles](
    [title_id] int NOT NULL,
    [title] [varchar](80)  NOT NULL,
```

```
    [type] [char](12)  NOT NULL,
    [pub_id] [char](4)  NULL,
    [price] [money] NULL,
    [advance] [money] NULL,
    [royalty] [int] NULL,
    [ytd_sales] [int] NULL,
    [notes] [varchar](400)  NULL,
    [pubdate] [datetime] NOT NULL,
) ON FG2
GO
```

Defining Table Constraints

Constraints provide a means to enforce data integrity. In addition to NULL/NOT NULL, discussed earlier in this chapter, SQL Server provides five constraint types: PRIMARY KEY, FOREIGN KEY, UNIQUE, CHECK, and DEFAULT. These constraints help further define the type of data you can store in tables.

Constraints are covered in detail in Chapter 23, "Implementing Data Integrity." This chapter introduces the basic means for adding constraints to a table. You can add constraints at the time of table creation, or you can add them after a table has been created by using the ALTER TABLE statement.

Listing 21.9 shows a CREATE TABLE statement that has an example of each one of the five constraint types listed. The PRIMARY KEY constraint is created at the bottom of the script and is named PK_TitleHistory. The FOREIGN KEY constraint is created on the title_id column and is named FK_titles_titleHistory. The UNIQUE constraint is part of the primary key and can be identified with the UNIQUE keyword. The CHECK constraint is created on the price column; it checks to make sure the price is greater than zero. Finally, a DEFAULT constraint is created on the modify_user column; it sets the user to the value of system if no explicit value is specified.

LISTING 21.9   Example of Creating Constraints with CREATE TABLE

```
CREATE TABLE Sales.TitleHistory(
    title_id int
        CONSTRAINT FK_titles_titleHistory
        REFERENCES Sales.titles (title_id) NOT NULL,
    change_date datetime NOT NULL,
    title varchar(80) NOT NULL,
    type char(12)  NOT NULL,
    price money NULL
        CONSTRAINT CK_TitleHistory_Price CHECK  (Price>0),
    modify_user nchar(10) NOT NULL
        CONSTRAINT DF_TitleHistory_modify_user  DEFAULT (N'system'),
```

21

```
CONSTRAINT PK_TitleHistory UNIQUE CLUSTERED
( title_id ASC,
   change_date ASC ) )
```

You can create the same constraints as in Listing 21.9 by using the ALTER TABLE statement. This means you can first create the table (without the constraints) and then add the constraints afterward. Listing 21.10 shows the creation of the same titleHistory table, with the constraints added later via the ALTER TABLE statement.

LISTING 21.10   Example of Creating Constraints with ALTER TABLE

```
IF  EXISTS (SELECT * FROM sys.objects
WHERE object_id = OBJECT_ID(N'[sales].[TitleHistory]')
AND OBJECTPROPERTY(object_id, N'IsUserTable') = 1)
DROP TABLE [sales].[TitleHistory]
go

CREATE TABLE sales.TitleHistory(
   title_id int NOT NULL,
   change_date datetime NOT NULL,
   title varchar(80) NOT NULL,
   type char(12) NOT NULL,
   price money NULL,
   modify_user nchar(10) NOT NULL )
GO


--PRIMARY KEY/UNIQUE CONSTRAINT
ALTER TABLE sales.TitleHistory
   ADD  CONSTRAINT PK_TitleHistory UNIQUE CLUSTERED
    (
      title_id ASC,
      change_date ASC
    )WITH (SORT_IN_TEMPDB = OFF, ONLINE = OFF)
go
--FOREIGN KEY CONSTRAINT
ALTER TABLE sales.TitleHistory  WITH CHECK
   ADD  CONSTRAINT FK_titles_titleHistory FOREIGN KEY(   title_id)
    REFERENCES sales.titles (title_id)
GO
--CHECK CONSTRAINT
ALTER TABLE sales.TitleHistory  WITH CHECK
   ADD  CONSTRAINT CK_TitleHistory_Price CHECK  ((Price>(0)))
GO
--DEFAULT CONSTRAINT
```

```
ALTER TABLE sales.TitleHistory
   ADD   CONSTRAINT DF_TitleHistory_modify_user
      DEFAULT (N'system') FOR modify_user
```

Modifying Tables

You often need to modify database tables after you create them. Fortunately, you can use several tools to accomplish this task. These tools are the same set of tools you can use to add, modify, and delete tables: the SSMS Object Explorer, Table Designer, Database Diagram Editor, and T-SQL. The following sections touch on each of these tools but focus most heavily on the use of T-SQL.

Regardless of the method you use, you must always exercise caution when modifying tables, particularly in a production environment. Table relationships and the impact to data that may already exist in a table are key considerations in modifying a table. A visual tool such as a database diagram can assist you in determining the impact to related tables and can be used to generate the T-SQL script. The following section looks at the underlying T-SQL that can be used to modify a table, and then we delve into the visual tools that can simplify your life and generate some of the T-SQL for you.

Using T-SQL to Modify Tables

You can modify tables in many different ways, including making changes to the columns, constraints, and indexes associated with a table. Some of the changes have a bigger impact on the database than others. Some modifications require that the modified table be dropped and re-created to effect the change. Fortunately, you can use the T-SQL ALTER TABLE statement to mitigate the database impact and help streamline many of the most common modifications. You can make the following types of changes by using the ALTER TABLE statement:

▶ Change a column property, such as a data type or NULL property.

▶ Add new columns or drop existing columns.

▶ Add or drop constraints.

▶ Enable or disable CHECK and FOREIGN KEY constraints.

▶ Enable or disable triggers.

▶ Reassign partitions.

▶ Alter an index associated with a constraint.

The following sections discuss a few examples of these types of changes to familiarize you with the ALTER TABLE command. The full syntax for the ALTER TABLE command is extensive, and you can find it in SQL Server Books Online.

Changing a Column Property

You can use the ALTER COLUMN clause of the ALTER TABLE command to modify column properties, including the NULL property or the data type of a column. Listing 21.11 shows an example of changing the data type of a column.

LISTING 21.11   Changing the Data Type of a Column by Using ALTER TABLE

```
alter table sales.titles
  alter column notes varchar(400) null
```

You must be aware of several restrictions when you modify the data type of a column. The following rules apply when altering columns:

▶ You cannot modify a text, image, ntext, or timestamp column.

▶ The column cannot be the ROWGUIDCOL for the table.

▶ The column cannot be a computed column or be referenced by a computed column.

▶ The column cannot be a replicated column.

▶ If the column is used in an index, the column length can only be increased in size. In addition, it must be of varchar, nvarchar, or varbinary data type, and the data type cannot change.

▶ If statistics have been generated using CREATE STATISTICS, the statistics must first be dropped before the column can be altered.

▶ The column cannot have a PRIMARY KEY or FOREIGN KEY constraint or be used in a CHECK or UNIQUE constraint. The exception is that a column with a CHECK or UNIQUE constraint, if defined as variable length, can have the length altered.

▶ A column with a default defined for it can have only the length, nullability, or precision and scale altered.

▶ If a column has a schema-bound view defined on it, the same rules that apply to columns with indexes apply.

TIP

Changing some data types can result in changing the data. For example, changing from nchar to char could result in any extended characters being converted. Similarly, changing precision and scale could result in data truncation. Other modifications, such as changing from char to int, might fail if the data doesn't match the restrictions of the new data type. Before you change data types, you should always validate that the data conforms to the desired new data type.

Adding and Dropping Columns

You add columns to a table by using the ADD COLUMN clause. Listing 21.12 illustrates the addition of a new column named ISBN to the titles table.

LISTING 21.12   Adding a Column by Using ALTER TABLE

```
ALTER TABLE sales.titles
   add ISBN int null
```

When you use the ALTER TABLE statement to add a column, the new column is added at the end of the table. In most cases, this location is acceptable. The location of the column in the table generally has no bearing on the use of the table. There are, however, situations in which it is desired to have the new column added in the middle of the table. The ALTER TABLE statement does not work for this situation. To add a column in the middle of the table, you need to create a new version of the table with a different name and the columns in the desired order, copy the data from the old table, drop the old table, and rename the new table with the old table name. Alternatively, you can also accomplish this by using SSMS, as described in the following section.

There are also some issues you need to consider with regard to the null option specified for a new column. In the case of a column that allows nulls, there is no real issue: SQL Server adds the column and allows a NULL value for all rows. If NOT NULL is specified, however, the column must be an identity column or have a default specified. Note that even if a default is specified, if the column allows nulls, the column is not populated with the default if no value is provided for the column. You use the WITH VALUES clause as part of the default specification to override this and populate the column with the default.

With some restrictions, columns can also be dropped from a table. Listing 21.13 shows the syntax for dropping a column. You can specify to drop multiple columns, separated by commas.

LISTING 21.13   Dropping a Column by Using ALTER TABLE

```
alter table sales.titles
   drop column ISBN
```

The following columns cannot be dropped:

▶ A column in a schema-bound view

▶ An indexed column

▶ A replicated column

▶ A column used in a CHECK, FOREIGN KEY, UNIQUE, or PRIMARY KEY constraint

▶ A column associated with a default or bound to a default object

▶ A column bound to a rule

> **NOTE**
>
> Be careful when using ALTER TABLE to modify columns that hold existing data. When you add, drop, or modify columns, SQL Server places a schema lock on the table, preventing any other access until the operation completes. Changes to columns in tables that have many rows can take a long time to complete and generate a large amount of log activity.

As mentioned earlier, the ALTER TABLE statement is not the only T-SQL statement you can use to modify tables. You accomplish some table changes by using T-SQL that drops and re-creates the tables that are being modified. The following sections look at some examples of these types of changes.

Using Object Explorer and the Table Designer to Modify Tables

The Object Explorer in SSMS is your window into the various tables available for modification in a database. You expand the Tables node in the Object Explorer tree and right-click the table you would like to modify. Then you select the Design option, and a Table Designer window appears, showing all the table columns. In addition, a Table Designer menu option appears at the top of the SSMS window. The Table Designer menu includes many options, including Insert Columns, Delete Columns, and Remove Primary Key. The full list of available options is shown in Figure 21.4. A Table Designer window for the Sales.Titles table is shown as the active tab on the right side of Figure 21.4.

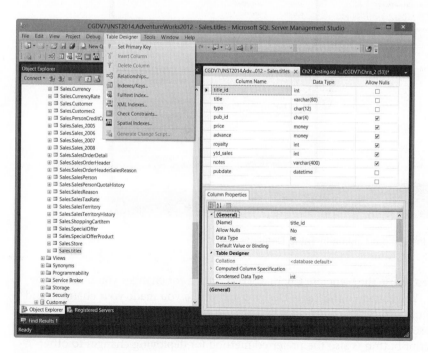

FIGURE 21.4   The Table Designer.

To illustrate the power of the Table Designer, let's add a new column to the `titles` table. You can add the column to the middle of the table, just prior to the `price` column. You do this by highlighting the entire `price` row in the Table Designer grid and then selecting Table Designer, Insert Column. A new data entry row is added to the Table Designer grid, where you can specify the name of the new column, the data type, and a null option. For this example, you can name the new column ISBN, with a data type of `varchar(30)` and ALLOW NULLS unchecked, and set a default value of 'N/A'. Figure 21.5 shows the Table Designer grid with the newly added ISBN column highlighted. In addition, the figure shows the Table Designer menu options with the newly enabled Generate Change Script option selected.

FIGURE 21.5   Inserting a column in Table Designer.

You do not need to use the Generate Change Script option for changes you make in the Table Designer. You can close the Table Designer tab where you made your changes, and the Table Designer makes the changes for you behind the scenes. Sometimes, though, you might want to script the changes and see exactly what is going to happen to the database. Clicking the Script button is also the preferred method for deploying changes to other environments. You can save a script in a change repository and execute it in your target environments. This approach ensures that you have a repeatable, well-documented means for making table changes.

Listing 21.14 shows the contents of a script that would be generated based on the new ISBN column you added to the titles table. For the sake of space, some of the initial script options and the triggers associated with the titles table have been removed from the script. The important point to note is how extensive this script is. A new temporary titles table is created, and it includes the new column; the data from the current titles table is copied into the temporary table; and then the table is renamed. In addition, the script must manage the constraints, indexes, and other objects associated with the titles table. The good news is that Table Designer does most of the work for you.

LISTING 21.14   Changing Script Generated from the Table Designer

```
BEGIN TRANSACTION
GO
CREATE TABLE Sales.Tmp_titles
        (
        title_id int NOT NULL,
        title varchar(80) NOT NULL,
        type char(12) NOT NULL,
        pub_id char(4) NULL,
        ISBN varchar(30) NOT NULL,
        price money NULL,
        advance money NULL,
        royalty int NULL,
        ytd_sales int NULL,
        notes varchar(400) NULL,
        pubdate datetime NOT NULL
        )  ON FG2
GO
ALTER TABLE Sales.Tmp_titles SET (LOCK_ESCALATION = TABLE)
GO
ALTER TABLE Sales.Tmp_titles ADD CONSTRAINT
        DF_titles_ISBN DEFAULT 'N/A' FOR ISBN
GO
IF EXISTS(SELECT * FROM Sales.titles)
        EXEC('INSERT INTO Sales.Tmp_titles (title_id, title, type, pub_id, price,
advance, royalty, ytd_sales, notes, pubdate)
            SELECT title_id, title, type, pub_id, price, advance, royalty, ytd_
sales, notes, pubdate FROM Sales.titles WITH (HOLDLOCK TABLOCKX)')
GO
ALTER TABLE Sales.TitleHistory
        DROP CONSTRAINT FK_titles_titleHistory
GO
DROP TABLE Sales.titles
```

```
GO
EXECUTE sp_rename N'Sales.Tmp_titles', N'titles', 'OBJECT'
GO
ALTER TABLE Sales.titles ADD CONSTRAINT
        PK__titles__1062D9771F100A34 PRIMARY KEY CLUSTERED
        (
        title_id
        ) WITH( STATISTICS_NORECOMPUTE = OFF, IGNORE_DUP_KEY = OFF, ALLOW_ROW_LOCKS =
ON, ALLOW_PAGE_LOCKS = ON) ON FG2

GO
COMMIT
BEGIN TRANSACTION
GO
ALTER TABLE Sales.TitleHistory ADD CONSTRAINT
        FK_titles_titleHistory FOREIGN KEY
        (
        title_id
        ) REFERENCES Sales.titles
        (
        title_id
        ) ON UPDATE  NO ACTION
         ON DELETE  NO ACTION

GO
ALTER TABLE Sales.TitleHistory SET (LOCK_ESCALATION = TABLE)
GO
COMMIT
```

You will find that you can make most of the changes you want to make by using the Table Designer. To make other changes, you can use the same approach you just used to add a column. This approach involves making the changes via the Table Designer menu options and then using the option to script the change. This is a great way to evaluate the impact of your changes and to save those changes for later execution.

Using Database Diagrams to Modify Tables

Database diagrams offer an excellent visual depiction of your database tables that you can also use to modify tables. You do this by adding the table you want to modify to a new or existing database diagram. Oftentimes, it is best to also add all the related tables to the diagram as well. You can easily do this by right-clicking the table and choosing the Add Related Tables option.

With a database diagram, you have the same options that you have with the Table Designer, plus you have diagramming options. Both the Table Designer and Database Diagrams menus are shown when a database diagram is in focus. These menus disappear if you change the tabbed window to a Database Engine query window, so remember that you must select the diagram window to be able to display the menu options.

Figure 21.6 shows a database diagram for the `HumanResouces.Department` table, along with its related table. The Database Diagram menu is selected to show that it is available when you work with a database diagram. You must have one of the tables selected to enable all the menu options. In Figure 21.6, the `Department` table has been highlighted, and a new `ModifiedUser` column has been added to the table. Figure 21.6 also shows that the Table Designer menu is available for selection. This menu and the Database Diagram menu include options to manipulate the tables within the diagram.

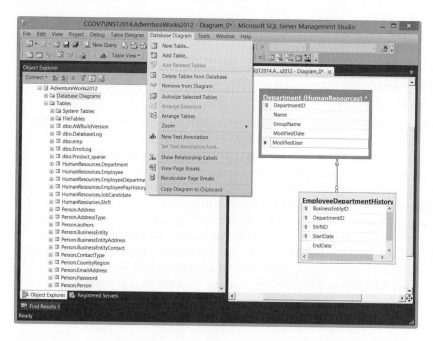

FIGURE 21.6   Modifying tables by using a database diagram.

The same scripting options are available with a database diagram as are available in the Table Designer. You can make your changes from within the diagram and then choose the Generate Change Script menu option. Listing 21.15 shows the change script generated based on the addition of the `ModifiedUser` column to the end of the `Department` table. As expected, this change is accomplished with an `ALTER TABLE` statement.

LISTING 21.15   The Change Script Generated from a Database Diagram

```
ALTER TABLE HumanResources.Department ADD
    ModifiedUser varchar(20) NULL
GO
```

The use of the ALTER TABLE statement in this listing brings us full circle, back to our initial method for making table modifications. Using all the tools discussed in this section together will usually give you the best results.

Dropping Tables

There are several different methods for dropping (or deleting) a table. You can right-click the table in the SSMS Object Explorer and select Delete, you can right-click a table in a database diagram and choose Delete Tables from Database, or you can use the old-fashioned method of utilizing T-SQL. Here's an example of the T-SQL DROP TABLE statement:

```
DROP TABLE [HumanResources].[Department]
```

You can reference multiple tables in a single DROP TABLE command by separating the table names with commas. Any triggers and constraints associated with the table are also dropped when the table is dropped.

A big consideration when dropping a table is the table's relationship to other tables. If a foreign key references the table that you want to drop, the referencing table or foreign key constraint must be dropped first. In a database that has many related tables, dropping elements can get complicated. Fortunately, a few tools can help you through this. The system stored procedure sp_helpconstraint is one of these tools. This procedure lists all the foreign key constraints that reference a table. Listing 21.16 shows an execution of this stored procedure for the Sales.Store table in the AdventureWorks2012 database. The procedure results include information about all the constraints on the table. The results to focus on are those that follow the heading, Table Is Referenced by Foreign Key. The partial results shown in Listing 21.16 for the Sales.Store table indicate that FK_StoreContact_Store_CustomerID must be dropped first before you can drop the Sales.Store table.

LISTING 21.16   Using sp_helpconstraint to Find Foreign Key References

```
sp_helpconstraint [Sales.Store]

/*partial results of sp_helpconstraint execution
Table is referenced by foreign key
-----------------------------------------------------------------
AdventureWorks2012.Sales.Customer: FK_Customer_Store_StoreID
 */
```

Two other approaches are useful for identifying foreign key references prior to dropping a table. The first is using a database diagram. You can create a new database diagram and add the table that you are considering for deletion. After the table is added, you right-click the table in Object Explorer and select Add Related Tables. The related tables, including those that have foreign key references, are then added. You can then right-click the relationship line connecting two tables and select Delete Relationships from Database. When you have deleted all the foreign key relationships from the diagram, you can right-click the table you want to delete and select Generate Change Script to create a script that can be used to remove the foreign key relationship(s).

The other approach is to right-click the table in Object Explorer and choose View Dependencies. The dialog that appears gives you the option of viewing the objects that depend on the table or viewing the objects on which the table depends. If you choose the option to view the objects that depend on the table, all the dependent objects are displayed, but you can focus on the objects that are tables.

Using Partitioned Tables

In SQL Server 2014, tables are stored in one or more partitions. Partitions are organizational units that allow you to divide data into logical groups. By default, a table has only a single partition that contains all the data. The power of partitions comes into play when you define multiple partitions for a table that is segmented based on a key column. This column allows the data rows to be horizontally split. For example, a date/time column can be used to divide each month's data into a separate partition. These partitions can also be aligned to different filegroups for added flexibility, ease of maintenance, and improved performance.

The important point to remember is that you access tables with multiple partitions (which are called partitioned tables) the same way you access tables with a single partition. Data Manipulation Language (DML) operations such as INSERT and SELECT statements reference the table the same way, regardless of partitioning. The difference between these types of tables has to do with the back-end storage and the organization of the data.

Generally, partitioning is most useful for large tables. Large is a relative term, but these tables typically contain millions of rows and take up gigabytes of space. Often, the tables targeted for partitioning are large tables experiencing performance problems because of their size. Partitioning has several different applications, including the following:

▶ **Archival**—Table partitions can be moved from a production table to another archive table that has the same structure. When done properly, this partition movement is very fast and allows you to keep a limited amount of recent data in the production table while keeping the bulk of the older data in the archive table.

▶ **Maintenance**—Table partitions that have been assigned to different filegroups can be backed up and maintained independently of each other. With very large tables, maintenance activities on the entire table (such as backups) can take a prohibitively long time. With partitioned tables, these maintenance activities can be performed at the partition level. Consider, for example, a table that is partitioned by month: All the new activity (updates and insertions) occurs in the partition that contains the current month's data. In this scenario, the current month's partition would be the focus of the maintenance, thus limiting the amount of data you need to process.

▶ **Query performance**—Partitioned tables joined on partitioned columns can experience improved performance because the Query Optimizer can join to the table based on the partitioned column. The caveat is that joins across partitioned tables not joining on the partitioned column may actually experience some performance degradation. Queries can also be parallelized along the partitions.

Now that we have discussed some of the reasons to use partitioned tables, let's look at how to set up partitions. There are three basic steps:

1. Create a partition function that maps the rows in the table to partitions based on the value of a specified column.

2. Create a partition scheme that outlines the placement of the partitions in the partition function to filegroups.

3. Create a table that utilizes the partition scheme.

These steps are predicated on a good partitioning design, based on an evaluation of the data within the table and the selection of a column that will effectively split the data. If multiple filegroups are used, those filegroups must also exist before you execute the three steps in partitioning. The following sections look at the syntax related to each step, using simple examples. These examples utilize the AdventureWorks2012 database.

Creating a Partition Function

A partition function identifies values within a table that will be compared to the column on which you partition the table. As mentioned previously, it is important that you know the distribution of the data and the specific range of values in the partitioning column before you create the partition function. The following query provides an example of determining the distribution of data values in the SalesOrderDetail table by year:

```
--Select the distinct yearly values
SELECT year(modifiedDate) as 'year', count(*) 'rows'
 FROM [AdventureWorks2012].[Sales].[SalesOrderDetail]
 GROUP BY year(modifiedDate)
 ORDER BY 1
go
```

```
     year        rows
----------- -----------
    2005        5151
    2006       19353
    2007       51237
    2008       45576
```

You can see from the results of the SELECT statement that there are four years' worth of data in the SalesOrderDetail. Because the values specified in the CREATE PARTITION FUNCTION statement are used to establish data ranges, at a minimum, you would need to specify at least three data values when defining the partition function, as shown in the following example:

```
--Create partition function with the yearly values to partition the data
CREATE PARTITION FUNCTION SalesOrderDetailPF1 (datetime)
    AS RANGE RIGHT FOR VALUES
    ('01/01/2006', '01/01/2007',
       '01/01/2008')
GO
```

In this example, four ranges, or partitions, would be established by the three RANGE RIGHT values specified in the statement:

- ▶ **values < 01/01/2006**—This partition includes any rows prior to 2006.

- ▶ **values >= 01/01/2006 AND values < 01/01/2007**—This partition includes all rows for 2006.

- ▶ **values >= 01/01/2007 AND values < 01/01/2008**—This partition includes all rows for 2007.

- ▶ **values > 01/01/2008**—This includes any rows for 2008 or later.

This method of partitioning would be more than adequate for a static table that is not going to be receiving any additional data rows for different years than already exist in the table. However, if the table is going to be populated with additional data rows after it has been partitioned, it is good practice to add additional range values at the beginning and end of the ranges to allow for the insertion of data values less than or greater than the existing range values in the table. To create these additional upper and lower ranges, you would want to specify five values in the VALUES clause of the CREATE PARTITION FUNCTION, as shown in Listing 21.17. The advantages of having these additional partitions are demonstrated later in this section.

LISTING 21.17   Creating a Partition Function

```
if exists (select 1 from sys.partition_functions where name = '
SalesOrderDetailPF1')
    drop partition function SalesOrderDetailPF1
go
--Create partition function with the yearly values to partition the data
Create PARTITION FUNCTION SalesOrderDetailPF1 (datetime)
    AS RANGE RIGHT FOR VALUES
    ('01/01/2005', '01/01/2006', '01/01/2007',
       '01/01/2008', '01/01/2009')
GO
```

In this example, six ranges, or partitions, are established by the five range values specified in the statement:

▶ `values < 01/01/2005`—This partition includes any rows prior to 2005.

▶ `values >= 01/01/2005 AND values < 01/01/2006`—This partition includes all rows for 2005.

▶ `values >= 01/01/2006 AND values < 01/01/2007`—This partition includes all rows for 2006.

▶ `values >= 01/01/2007 AND values < 01/01/2008`—This partition includes all rows for 2007.

▶ `values >= 01/01/2008 AND values < 01/01/2009`—This partition includes all rows for 2008.

▶ `values >= 01/01/2009`—This partition includes any rows for 2009 or later.

An alternative to the `RIGHT` clause in the `CREATE PARTITION FUNCTION` statement is the `LEFT` clause. The `LEFT` clause is similar to `RIGHT`, but it changes the ranges such that the `<` operands are changed to `<=`, and the `>=` operands are changed to `>`.

TIP

Using `RANGE RIGHT` partitions for `datetime` values is usually best because this approach makes it easier to specify the limits of the ranges. The `datetime` data type can store values only with accuracy to 3.33 milliseconds. The largest value it can store is 0.997 milliseconds. A value of 0.998 milliseconds rounds down to 0.997, and a value of 0.999 milliseconds rounds up to the next second.

If you used a `RANGE LEFT` partition, the maximum time value you could include with the year to get all values for that year would be `23:59:59.997`. For example, if you specified `12/31/2006 23:59:59.999` as the boundary for a `RANGE LEFT` partition, it would be rounded up so that it would also include rows with `datetime` values less than or equal to 01/01/2007 00:00:00, which is probably not what you would want. You would redefine the example shown in Listing 21.19 as a `RANGE LEFT` partition function as follows:

```
CREATE PARTITION FUNCTION SalesOrderDetailPF1 (datetime)
    AS RANGE LEFT FOR VALUES
    ('12/31/2004 23:59:59.997', '12/31/2005 23:59:59.997',
     '12/31/2006 23:59: 59.997', '12/31/2007 23:59:59.997',
     '12/31/2008 23:59:59.997')
```

As you can see, it's a bit more straightforward and probably less confusing to use `RANGE RIGHT` partition functions when dealing with `datetime` values or any other continuous-value data types, such as `float` or `numeric`.

Creating a Partition Scheme

After you create a partition function, the next step is to associate a partition scheme with the partition function. A partition scheme can be associated with only one partition function, but a partition function can be shared across multiple partition schemes.

The core function of a partition scheme is to map the values defined in the partition function to filegroups. When creating the statement for a partition scheme, you need to keep in mind the following:

▶ A single filegroup can be used for all partitions, or a separate filegroup can be used for each individual partition.

▶ Any filegroup referenced in the partition scheme must exist before the partition scheme is created.

▶ There must be enough filegroups referenced in the partition scheme to accommodate all the partitions. The number of partitions is one more than the number of values specified in the partition function.

▶ The maximum number of partitions is 15,000 for 64 bit.

▶ The filegroups listed in the partition scheme are assigned to the partitions defined in the function based on the order in which the filegroups are listed.

Listing 21.18 creates a partition scheme that references the partition function created in Listing 21.17. This example assumes that the referenced filegroups have been created for each of the partitions. (For more information on creating filegroups and secondary files, see Chapter 20.)

> **NOTE**
>
> If you would like to create the same filegroups and files used by the examples in this section, check out the script file called Create_Filegroups_and_Files_for_Partitioning.sql on the Web in the code listings directory for this chapter. If you run this script, it creates all the necessary filegroups and files referenced in the examples. Note that you need to edit the script to change the FILENAME value if you need the files to be created in a directory other than C:\MSSQL\DATA.

LISTING 21.18   Creating a Partition Scheme

```
--Create a partition scheme that is aligned with the partition function
CREATE PARTITION SCHEME SalesOrderDetailPS1
    AS PARTITION SalesOrderDetailPF1
    TO ([Older_data], [2005_data], [2006_data],
        [2007_data], [2008_data], [2009_data])
GO
```

Alternatively, if all partitions are going to be on the same filegroup, such as the PRIMARY filegroup, you could use the following:

```
Create PARTITION SCHEME SalesOrderDetailPS1
    as PARTITION SalesOrderDetailPF1
    ALL to ([PRIMARY])
go
```

Notice that `SalesOrderDetailPF1` is referenced as the partition function in Listing 21.18. This ties together the partition scheme and partition function. Figure 21.7 shows how the partitions defined in the function would be mapped to the filegroup(s). At this point, you have made no changes to any table, and you have not even specified the column in the table that you will partition. The next section discusses those details.

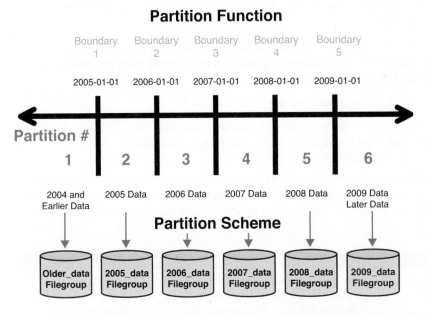

FIGURE 21.7   Mapping of partitions to filegroups, using a RANGE RIGHT partition function

Creating a Partitioned Table

Tables are partitioned only when they are created. This is an important point to keep in mind when you are considering adding partitions to a table that already exists. Sometimes, performance issues or other factors may lead you to determine that a table you have already created and populated may benefit from being partitioned.

The re-creation of large tables in a production environment requires some forethought and planning. The data in the table must be retained in another location for you to re-create the table. Bulk copying the data to a flat file and renaming the table are two possible solutions for retaining the data. After you determine the data retention method, you can re-create the table with the new partition scheme. For simplicity's sake, the example in Listing 21.19 creates a new table named `SalesOrderDetail_Partitioned` instead of using the original `SalesOrderDetail` table. The second part of Listing 21.19 copies the data from the `SalesOrderDetail` table into the `SalesOrderDetail_ Partitioned` table.

LISTING 21.19   Creating a Partitioned Table

```sql
CREATE TABLE [Sales].[SalesOrderDetail_Partitioned](
        [SalesOrderID] [int] NOT NULL,
        [SalesOrderDetailID] [int] IDENTITY(1,1) NOT NULL,
        [CarrierTrackingNumber] [nvarchar](25) NULL,
        [OrderQty] [smallint] NOT NULL,
        [ProductID] [int] NOT NULL,
        [SpecialOfferID] [int] NOT NULL,
        [UnitPrice] [money] NOT NULL,
        [UnitPriceDiscount] [money] NOT NULL,
        [LineTotal]   AS (isnull(([UnitPrice]*((1.0)-[UnitPriceDiscount]))*[Order
Qty],(0.0))),
        [rowguid] [uniqueidentifier] ROWGUIDCOL  NOT NULL,
        [ModifiedDate] [datetime] NOT NULL,
) ON SalesOrderDetailPS1 (ModifiedDate) --this statement is key to Partitioning the
table

GO
--Insert data from the SalesOrderDetail table into the new SalesOrderDetail_
partitioned table
SET IDENTITY_INSERT Sales.SalesOrderDetail_Partitioned ON
GO
INSERT INTO [Sales].[SalesOrderDetail_Partitioned]
            ([SalesOrderID]
                ,[SalesOrderDetailID]
            ,[CarrierTrackingNumber]
            ,[OrderQty]
            ,[ProductID]
            ,[SpecialOfferID]
            ,[UnitPrice]
            ,[UnitPriceDiscount]
            ,[rowguid]
            ,[ModifiedDate])
select
            [SalesOrderID]
                ,[SalesOrderDetailID]
            ,[CarrierTrackingNumber]
            ,[OrderQty]
            ,[ProductID]
            ,[SpecialOfferID]
            ,[UnitPrice]
            ,[UnitPriceDiscount]
            ,[rowguid]
            ,[ModifiedDate]
```

```
from Sales.SalesOrderDetail
GO
SET IDENTITY_INSERT Sales.SalesOrderDetail_Partitioned OFF
GO
```

The key clause to take note of in this listing is `ON SalesOrderDetailPS1 (ord_date)`. This clause identifies the partition scheme on which to create the table (`SalesOrderDetailPS1`) and the column within the table to use for partitioning (`ModifiedDate`).

After you create the table, you might wonder whether the table was partitioned correctly. Fortunately, there are some catalog views related to partitions that you can query for this kind of information. Listing 21.20 shows a sample `SELECT` statement that utilizes the `sys.partitions` view. The results of the statement execution are shown immediately after the `SELECT` statement. Notice that there are six numbered partitions and that the estimated number of rows for each partition corresponds to the number of rows you saw when you selected the data from the unpartitioned `SalesOrderDetail` table.

LISTING 21.20   Viewing Partitioned Table Information

```
select convert(varchar(16), ps.name) as partition_scheme,
       p.partition_number,
       convert(varchar(10), ds2.name) as filegroup,
       convert(varchar(19), isnull(v.value, ''), 120) as range_boundary,
       str(p.rows, 9) as rows
  from sys.indexes i
  join sys.partition_schemes ps on i.data_space_id = ps.data_space_id
  join sys.destination_data_spaces dds
       on ps.data_space_id = dds.partition_scheme_id
  join sys.data_spaces ds2 on dds.data_space_id = ds2.data_space_id
  join sys.partitions p on dds.destination_id = p.partition_number
                       and p.object_id = i.object_id and p.index_id = i.index_id
  join sys.partition_functions pf on ps.function_id = pf.function_id
  LEFT JOIN sys.Partition_Range_values v on pf.function_id = v.function_id
          and v.boundary_id = p.partition_number - pf.boundary_value_on_right
  WHERE i.object_id = object_id('Sales.SalesOrderDetail_partitioned')
    and i.index_id in (0, 1)
  order by p.partition_number

/* Results from the previous SELECT statement
partition_scheme partition_number filegroup  range_boundary       rows
---------------- ---------------- ---------- -------------------- ---------
SalesOrderDetail              1 Older_Data                              0
SalesOrderDetail              2 2005_Data  2005-01-01 00:00:00      5151
SalesOrderDetail              3 2006_Data  2006-01-01 00:00:00     19353
SalesOrderDetail              4 2007_Data  2007-01-01 00:00:00     51237
```

| SalesOrderDetail | | 5 | 2008_Data | 2008-01-01 00:00:00 | 45576 |
| SalesOrderDetail | | 6 | 2009_Data | 2009-01-01 00:00:00 | 0 |

```
*/
```

Adding and Dropping Table Partitions

One of the most useful features of partitioned tables is that you can add and drop entire partitions of table data in bulk. If the table partitions are set up properly, these commands can take place in seconds, without the expensive input/output (I/O) costs of physically copying or moving the data. You can add and drop table partitions by using the SPLIT RANGE and MERGE RANGE options of the ALTER PARTITION FUNCTION command:

```
ALTER PARTITION FUNCTION partition_function_name()
{ SPLIT RANGE ( boundary_value ) | MERGE RANGE ( boundary_value ) }
```

Adding a Table Partition

The SPLIT RANGE option adds a new boundary point to an existing partition function and affects all objects that use this partition function. When this command is run, one of the function partitions is split in two. The new partition is the one that contains the new boundary point. The new partition is created to the right of the boundary value if the partition is defined as a RANGE RIGHT partition function or to the left of the boundary if it is a RANGE LEFT partition function. If the partition is empty, the split is instantaneous.

If the partition being split contains data, any data on the new side of the boundary is physically deleted from the old partition and inserted into the new partition. In addition to being I/O intensive, a split is also log-intensive, generating log records that are four times the size of the data being moved. In addition, an exclusive table lock is held for the duration of the split. If you want to avoid this costly overhead when adding a new partition to the end of the partition range, it is recommended that you always keep an empty partition available at the end and split it before it is populated with data. If the partition is empty, SQL Server does not need to scan the partition to see whether there is any data to be moved.

> **NOTE**
>
> Avoiding the overhead associated with splitting a partition is the reason the code in Listing 21.19 defined the SalesOrderDetailPF1 partition function with a partition for 2009, even though there is no 2009 data in the SalesOrderDetail_partitioned table. As long as you split the partition before any 2009 data is inserted into the table and the 2009 partition is empty, no data needs to be moved, so the split is instantaneous.

Before you split a partition, a filegroup must be marked to be the NEXT USED partition by the partition scheme that uses the partition function. You initially allocate filegroups to partitions by using a CREATE PARTITION SCHEME statement. If a CREATE PARTITION SCHEME statement allocates more filegroups than there are partitions defined in the CREATE

PARTITION FUNCTION statement, one of the unassigned filegroups is automatically marked as NEXT USED by the partition scheme, and it will hold the new partition.

If there are no filegroups currently marked NEXT USED by the partition scheme, you must use ALTER PARTITION SCHEME to either add a filegroup or designate an existing filegroup to hold the new partition. This can be a filegroup that already holds existing partitions. Also, if a partition function is used by more than one partition scheme, all the partition schemes that use the partition function to which you are adding partitions must have a NEXT USED filegroup. If one or more do not have a NEXT USED filegroup assigned, the ALTER PARTITION FUNCTION statement fails, and the error message displays the partition scheme or schemes that lack a NEXT USED filegroup.

The following SQL statement adds a NEXT USED filegroup to the SalesOrderDetailPS1 partition scheme. Note that in this example, the filegroup specified is a new filegroup, 2010_DATA:

```
ALTER PARTITION SCHEME SalesOrderDetailPS1 NEXT USED '2010_Data'
```

Now that you have specified a NEXT USED filegroup for the partition scheme, you can go ahead and add the new range for 2010 and later data rows to the partition function, as in the following example:

```
--Alter partition function with the yearly values to partition the data
ALTER PARTITION FUNCTION SalesOrderDetailPF1 () SPLIT RANGE ('01/01/2010')
GO
```

Figure 21.8 shows the effects of splitting the 2009 table partition.

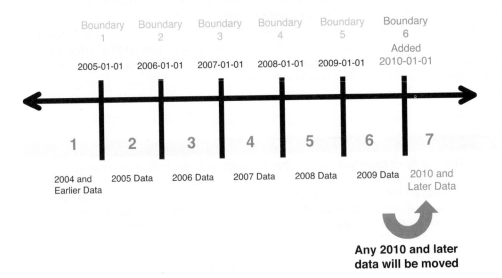

FIGURE 21.8   The effects of splitting a RANGE RIGHT table partition.

You can also see the effects of splitting the partition on the system catalogs by running the same query as shown earlier, in Listing 21.20:

```
/* New results from the SELECT statement in Listing 21.20
partition_scheme partition_number filegroup  range_boundary       rows
---------------- ---------------- ---------  -------------------- ---------
SalesOrderDetail                1 Older_Data                              0
SalesOrderDetail                2 2005_Data 2005-01-01 00:00:00        5151
SalesOrderDetail                3 2006_Data 2006-01-01 00:00:00       19353
SalesOrderDetail                4 2007_Data 2007-01-01 00:00:00       51237
SalesOrderDetail                5 2008_Data 2008-01-01 00:00:00       45576
SalesOrderDetail                6 2009_Data 2009-01-01 00:00:00           0
SalesOrderDetail                7 2010_Data 2010-01-01 00:00:00           0

*/
```

Dropping a Table Partition

You can drop a table partition by using the ALTER PARTITION FUNCTION ... MERGE RANGE command. This command essentially removes a boundary point from a partition function as the partitions on each side of the boundary are merged into one. The partition that held the boundary value is removed. The filegroup that originally held the boundary value is removed from the partition scheme unless it is used by a remaining partition or is marked with the NEXT USED property.

Any data that was in the removed partition is moved to the remaining neighboring partition. If a RANGE RIGHT partition boundary was removed, the data that was in that boundary's partition is moved to the partition to the left of boundary. If it was a RANGE LEFT partition, the data is moved to the partition to the right of the boundary.

The following command merges the 2005 partition into the Old_Data partition for the SalesOrderDetail_partitioned table:

```
ALTER PARTITION FUNCTION SalesOrderDetailPF1 () MERGE RANGE ('01/01/2005')
```

Figure 21.9 demonstrates how the 2005 RANGE RIGHT partition boundary is removed and the data is merged to the left, into the Old_Data partition.

> **CAUTION**
>
> Splitting or merging partitions for a partition function affects all objects using that partition function.

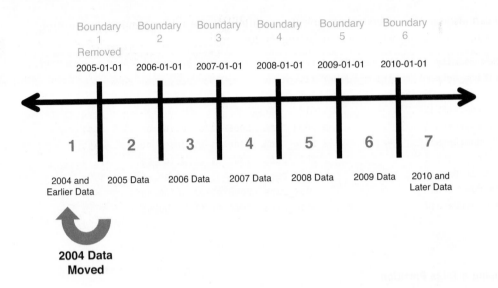

FIGURE 21.9   The effects of merging a RANGE RIGHT table partition.

You can also see the effects of merging the partition on the system catalogs by running the same query as shown in Listing 21.20:

```
/* New results from the SELECT statement in Listing 21.20
partition_scheme   partition_number  filegroup    range_boundary        rows
----------------   ----------------  ---------    ------------------    ---------
SalesOrderDetail                   1 Older_Data                             5151
SalesOrderDetail                   2 2006_Data  2006-01-01 00:00:00        19353
SalesOrderDetail                   3 2007_Data  2007-01-01 00:00:00        51237
SalesOrderDetail                   4 2008_Data  2008-01-01 00:00:00        45576
SalesOrderDetail                   5 2009_Data  2009-01-01 00:00:00            0
SalesOrderDetail                   6 2010_Data  2010-01-01 00:00:00            0

*/
```

Like the split operation, the merge operation occurs instantaneously if the partition being merged is empty. The process can be very I/O-intensive if the partition has a large amount of data in it. Any rows in the removed partition are physically moved into the remaining partition. This operation is also very log-intensive, requiring log space approximately four times the size of data being moved. An exclusive table lock is held for the duration of the merge.

If you no longer want to keep the data in the table for a partition you are merging, you can move the data in the partition to another empty table or empty table partition by using the SWITCH PARTITION option of the ALTER TABLE command. This option is discussed in more detail in the following section.

Switching Table Partitions

One of the great features of table partitions is that they enable you to instantly swap the contents of one partition to an empty table, the contents from a partition on one table to a partition in another table, or an entire table's contents into another table's empty partition. This operation performs changes only to metadata in the system catalogs for the affected tables/partitions, with no actual physical movement of data.

For you to switch data from a partition to a table or from a table into a partition, the following criteria must be met:

▶ The source table and target table must both have the same structure (that is, the same columns in the same order, with the same names, data types, lengths, precisions, scales, nullabilities, and collations). The tables must also have the same primary key constraints and settings for ANSI_NULLS and QUOTED_IDENTIFIER.

▶ The source and target of the ALTER TABLE...SWITCH statement must reside in the same filegroup.

▶ If you are switching a partition to a single, nonpartitioned table, the table receiving the partition must already be created, and it must be empty.

▶ If you are adding a table as a partition to an already existing partitioned table or moving a partition from one partitioned table to another, the receiving partition must exist, and it must be empty.

▶ If you are switching a partition from one partitioned table to another, both tables must be partitioned on the same column.

▶ The source must have all the same indexes as the target, and the indexes must also be in the same filegroup.

▶ If you are switching a nonpartitioned table to a partition of an already existing partitioned table, the nonpartitioned table must have a constraint defined on the column corresponding to the partition key of the target table to ensure that the range of values fits within the boundary values of the target partition.

▶ All indexes on the table have to be partitioned using the same partition function and partition scheme (you can't have any nonpartitioned indexes).

▶ If the target table has any FOREIGN KEY constraints, the source table must have the same foreign keys defined on the corresponding columns, and those foreign keys must reference the same primary keys that the target table references.

If you are switching a partition of a partitioned table to another partitioned table, the boundary values of the source partition must fit within those of the target partition. If the boundary values do not fit, a constraint must be defined on the partition key of the source table to make sure all the data in the table fits into the boundary values of the target partition.

CAUTION

If the tables have IDENTITY columns, partition switching can result in the introduction of duplicate values in IDENTITY columns of the target table and gaps in the values of IDENTITY columns in the source table. You can use DBCC_CHECKIDENT to check the identity values of tables and correct them if necessary.

When you switch a partition, data is not physically moved. Only the metadata information in the system catalogs indicating where the data is stored is changed. In addition, all associated indexes are automatically switched, along with the table or partition.

To switch table partitions, you use the ALTER TABLE command:

```
ALTER TABLE table_name SWITCH [ PARTITION source_partition_number_expression ]
    TO target_table [ PARTITION target_partition_number_expression ]
```

You can use the ALTER TABLE...SWITCH command to switch an unpartitioned table into a table partition, switch a table partition into an empty unpartitioned table, or switch a table partition into another table's empty table partition. The code shown in Listing 21.21 creates a table to hold the data from the 2006 partition and then switches the 2006 partition from the SalesOrderDetail_partitioned table to the new table.

LISTING 21.21   Switching a Partition to an Empty Table

```
CREATE TABLE [Sales].[SalesOrderDetail_2006](
        [SalesOrderID] [int] NOT NULL,
        [SalesOrderDetailID] [int] IDENTITY(1,1) NOT NULL,
        [CarrierTrackingNumber] [nvarchar](25) NULL,
        [OrderQty] [smallint] NOT NULL,
        [ProductID] [int] NOT NULL,
        [SpecialOfferID] [int] NOT NULL,
        [UnitPrice] [money] NOT NULL,
        [UnitPriceDiscount] [money] NOT NULL,
        [LineTotal]   AS (isnull(([UnitPrice]*((1.0)-[UnitPriceDiscount]))*[Order
Qty],(0.0))),
        [rowguid] [uniqueidentifier] ROWGUIDCOL  NOT NULL,
        [ModifiedDate] [datetime] NOT NULL
)
ON '2006_data' -- required in order to switch the partition to this table
GO
alter table Sales.SalesOrderDetail_partitioned
    switch partition $PARTITION.SalesOrderDetailPF1 ('1/1/2006')
    to Sales.SalesOrderDetail_2006

go
```

Note that Listing 21.21 uses the $PARTITION function. You can use this function with any partition function name to return the partition number that corresponds with the specified partitioning column value. This prevents you from having to query the system catalogs to determine the specific partition number for the specified partition value.

You can run the query from Listing 21.20 to show that the 2006 partition is now empty:

```
partition_scheme  partition_number  filegroup   range_boundary         rows
----------------  ----------------  ----------  --------------------   ---------
SalesOrderDetail                 1  Older_Data                              5151
SalesOrderDetail                 2  2006_Data   2006-01-01 00:00:00            0
SalesOrderDetail                 3  2007_Data   2007-01-01 00:00:00        51237
SalesOrderDetail                 4  2008_Data   2008-01-01 00:00:00        45576
SalesOrderDetail                 5  2009_Data   2009-01-01 00:00:00            0
SalesOrderDetail                 6  2010_Data   2010-01-01 00:00:00            0
```

Now that the 2006 data partition is empty, you can merge the partition without incurring the I/O cost of moving the data to the Older_data partition:

```
ALTER PARTITION FUNCTION SalesOrderDetailPF1 () merge RANGE ('1/1/2006')
```

Rerunning the query in Listing 21.20 now returns the following result set:

```
partition_scheme  partition_number  filegroup   range_boundary         rows
----------------  ----------------  ----------  --------------------   ---------
SalesOrderDetail                 1  Older_Data                              5151
SalesOrderDetail                 2  2007_Data   2007-01-01 00:00:00        51237
SalesOrderDetail                 3  2008_Data   2008-01-01 00:00:00        45576
SalesOrderDetail                 4  2009_Data   2009-01-01 00:00:00            0
SalesOrderDetail                 5  2010_Data   2010-01-01 00:00:00            0
```

To demonstrate switching a table into a partition, you can update the date for all the rows in the SalesOrderDetail_2006 table to 2009 and switch it into the 2009 partition of the SalesOrderDetail_partitioned table. Note that before you can do this, you need to copy the data to a table in the 2009_data filegroup and also put a check constraint on the ModifiedDate column to make sure all rows in the table are limited to values that are valid for the 2009_data partition. Listing 21.22 shows the commands you use to create the new table and switch it into the 2009 partition of the SalesOrderDetail_partitioned table.

LISTING 21.22   Switching a Table to an Empty Partition

```
CREATE TABLE Sales.SalesOrderDetail_2009(
        [SalesOrderID] [int] NOT NULL,
        [SalesOrderDetailID] [int] IDENTITY(1,1) NOT NULL,
        [CarrierTrackingNumber] [nvarchar](25) NULL,
        [OrderQty] [smallint] NOT NULL,
        [ProductID] [int] NOT NULL,
        [SpecialOfferID] [int] NOT NULL,
```

```
        [UnitPrice] [money] NOT NULL,
        [UnitPriceDiscount] [money] NOT NULL,
        [LineTotal]  AS (isnull((([UnitPrice]*((1.0)-[UnitPriceDiscount])))*[Order
Qty],(0.0))),
        [rowguid] [uniqueidentifier] ROWGUIDCOL  NOT NULL,
        [ModifiedDate] [datetime] NOT NULL
        constraint CK_SalesOrderDetail_2009_ModifiedDate
            check (ModifiedDate >= '1/1/2009' and ModifiedDate < '1/1/2010')

) ON '2009_data'  -- required to switch the table to the 2009 partition
go
set identity_insert Sales.SalesOrderDetail_2009 on
go
INSERT INTO [Sales].[SalesOrderDetail_2009]
            ([SalesOrderID]
                , [SalesOrderDetailID]
            , [CarrierTrackingNumber]
            , [OrderQty]
            , [ProductID]
            , [SpecialOfferID]
            , [UnitPrice]
            , [UnitPriceDiscount]
            , [rowguid]
            , [ModifiedDate])
 select
            [SalesOrderID]
                , [SalesOrderDetailID]
            , [CarrierTrackingNumber]
            , [OrderQty]
            , [ProductID]
            , [SpecialOfferID]
            , [UnitPrice]
            , [UnitPriceDiscount]
            , [rowguid]
            ,dateadd(yy, 3, [ModifiedDate])
 from Sales.SalesOrderDetail_2006
 GO
 go
 set identity_insert Sales.SalesOrderDetail_2009 off
 go

 alter table Sales.SalesOrderDetail_2009
   switch to Sales.SalesOrderDetail_partitioned
   partition $PARTITION.SalesOrderDetailPF1 ('1/1/2009')
 go
```

Rerunning the query from Listing 21.20 now returns the following result:

```
partition_scheme partition_number filegroup  range_boundary       rows
---------------- ---------------- ---------  -------------------  ---------
SalesOrderDetail                1 Older_Data                          5151
SalesOrderDetail                2 2007_Data 2007-01-01 00:00:00      51237
SalesOrderDetail                3 2008_Data 2008-01-01 00:00:00      45576
SalesOrderDetail                4 2009_Data 2009-01-01 00:00:00      19353
SalesOrderDetail                5 2010_Data 2010-01-01 00:00:00          0
```

TIP

Switching data into or out of partitions provides a very efficient mechanism for archiving old data from a production table, importing new data into a production table, or migrating data to an archive table. You can use SWITCH to empty or fill partitions very quickly. As you've seen in this section, split and merge operations occur instantaneously if the partitions being split or merged are empty first. If you must split or merge partitions that contain a lot of data, you should empty them first by using SWITCH before you perform the split or merge.

Using FILESTREAM Storage

FILESTREAM storage, introduced in SQL Server 2008, helps to solve the issues with storing unstructured data in SQL Server by integrating the SQL Server Database Engine with the NTFS file system for storing unstructured data such as documents and images on the file system with a pointer to the data in the database. The file pointer is implemented in SQL Server as a varbinary(max) column, and the actual data is stored in files in the file system.

In addition to enabling client applications to leverage the rich NTFS streaming APIs and the performance of the file system for storing and retrieving unstructured data, other advantages of FILESTREAM storage include the following:

▶ You are able to use T-SQL statements to insert, update, query, and back up FILESTREAM data even though the actual data resides outside the database in the NTFS file system.

▶ You are able to maintain transactional consistency between the unstructured data and corresponding structured data.

▶ You are able to enforce the same level of security on the unstructured data as with your relational data using built-in SQL Server security mechanisms.

▶ FILESTREAM uses the NT system cache for caching file data rather than caching the data in the SQL Server buffer pool, leaving more memory available for query processing.

▶ FILESTREAM storage also eliminates the size limitation of BLOBS stored in the database. Whereas standard `image` and `varbinary(max)` columns have a size limitation of 2GB, the sizes of the FILESTREAM BLOBs are limited only by the available space of the file system.

Columns with the `FILESTREAM` attribute set can be managed just like any other BLOB column in SQL Server. Administrators can use the manageability and security capabilities of SQL Server to integrate FILESTREAM data management with the rest of the data in the relational database—without needing to manage the file system data separately. This includes maintenance operations such as backup and restore, complete integration with the SQL Server security model, and full-transaction support to ensure data-level consistency between the relational data in the database and the unstructured data physically stored on the file system. The database administrator does not need to manage the file system data separately

Whether you should use database storage or file system storage for your BLOB data is determined by the size and use of the unstructured data. If the following conditions are true, you should consider using FILESTREAM:

▶ The objects being stored as BLOBS are, on average, larger than 1MB.

▶ Fast read access is important.

▶ You are developing applications that use a middle tier for application logic.

Enabling FILESTREAM Storage

If you decide to use FILESTREAM storage, it first needs to be enabled at both the Windows level as well as at the SQL Server Instance level. FILESTREAM storage can be enabled automatically during SQL Server installation or manually after installation.

If you are enabling FILESTREAM during SQL Server installation, you need to provide the Windows share location where the FILESTREAM data will be stored. You can also choose whether to allow remote clients to access the FILESTREAM data. For more information on how to enable FILESTREAM storage during installation, see Chapter 8, "Installing SQL Server 2014."

If you did not enable the FILESTREAM option during installation, you can enable it for a running instance of SQL Server 2014 at any time using SQL Server Configuration Manager (SSCM). In SSCM, right-click on the SQL Server Service and select Properties.

Then select the FILESTREAM tab, which provides similar options as those displayed during SQL Server installation (see Figure 21.10). This enables SQL Server to work directly with the Windows file system for storing FILESTREAM data. You have three options for how FILESTREAM functionality will be enabled:

▶ Allowing only T-SQL access (by checking only the Enable FILESTREAM for Transact-SQL Access option).

▶ Allowing both T-SQL and Win32 access to FILESTREAM data (by checking the Enable FILESTREAM for File I/O Streaming Access option and providing a Windows share name to be used to access the FILESTREAM data). This allows Win32 file system interfaces to provide streaming access to the data.

▶ Allowing remote clients to have access to the FILESTREAM data that is stored on this share (by selecting the Allow Remote Clients to Have Streaming Access to FILESTREAM Data option).

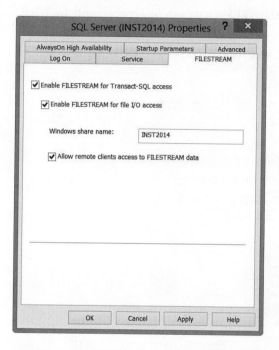

FIGURE 21.10   Setting FILESTREAM options in SQL Server Configuration Manager.

NOTE

You need to be Windows Administrator on a local system and have `sysadmin` rights to enable FILESTREAM for SQL Server.

After you enable FILESTREAM in SQL Server Configuration Manager, a new share is created on the host system with the name specified. This share is intended only to allow very low-level streaming interaction between SQL Server and authorized clients. It is recommended that only the service account used by the SQL Server instance should have access to this share. Also, because this change takes place at the OS level and not from within SQL Server, you need to stop and restart the SQL Server instance for the change to take effect.

After restarting the SQL Server instance to enable FILESTREAM at the Windows OS level, you next need to enable FILESTREAM for the SQL Server Instance. You can do this either through SQL Server Management Studio or via T-SQL. To enable FILESTREAM for the SQL Server instance using SQL Server Management Studio, right-click on the SQL Server instance in the Object Explorer, select Properties, select the Advanced page, and set the Filestream Access Level property as shown in Figure 21.11. The available options are

▶ **Disabled (0)**—FILESTREAM access is not permitted.

▶ **Transact SQL Access Enabled (1)**—FILESTREAM data can be accessed only by T-SQL commands.

▶ **Full Access Enabled (2)**—Both T-SQL and Win32 access to FILESTREAM data are permitted.

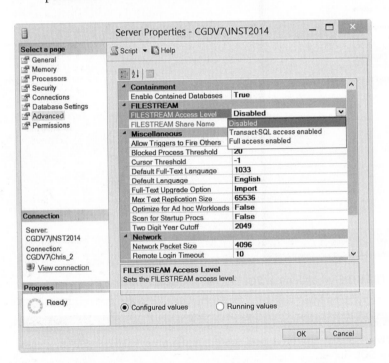

FIGURE 21.11   Enabling FILESTREAM for a SQL Server Instance in SSMS.

You can also optionally enable FILESTREAM for the SQL Server instance using the sp_ configure system procedure, specifying the 'filestream access level' as the setting and passing the option of 0 (disabled), 1 (T-SQL access), or 2 (Full access). The following example shows full access being enabled for the current SQL Server instance:

```
EXEC sp_configure 'filestream access level', 2
GO
RECONFIGURE
GO
```

After you configure the SQL Server instance for FILESTREAM access, the next step is to set up a database to store FILESTREAM data.

Setting Up a Database for FILESTREAM Storage

After you enable FILESTREAM for the SQL Server instance, you can store FILESTREAM data in a database by creating a FILESTREAM filegroup. You can do this when creating the database or by adding a new filegroup to an existing database. The filegroup designated for FILESTREAM storage must include the CONTAINS FILESTREAM clause and be defined. The code in Listing 21.23 creates the Customer database and then adds a FILESTREAM filegroup.

LISTING 21.23   Setting Up a Database for FILESTREAM Storage

```
Use Master;
go
CREATE DATABASE Customer
ON ( NAME='Customer_Data',
     FILENAME='C:\MSSQL\Data\Customer_Data1.mdf',
     SIZE=50,
     MAXSIZE=100,
     FILEGROWTH=10)
LOG ON ( NAME='Customer_Log',
     FILENAME='C:\MSSQL\Data\Customer_Log.ldf',
     SIZE=50,
     FILEGROWTH=20%)
GO

ALTER DATABASE Customer
 ADD FILEGROUP Cust_FSGroup CONTAINS FILESTREAM
GO

ALTER DATABASE Customer
 ADD FILE  ( NAME=custinfo_FS,
          FILENAME = 'c:\SQLData\custinfo_FS')
TO FILEGROUP Cust_FSGroup
GO
```

Notice in Listing 21.23 the FILESTREAM filegroup points to a file system folder rather than an actual file. This folder must not exist already (although the path up to the folder must exist); SQL Server creates the FILESTREAM folder (for example, in Listing 21.23, the custinfo_FS folder is created automatically by SQL Server in the C:\SQLData folder). The FILESTREAM files and file data actually end up being stored in the created folder. A FILESTREAM filegroup is restricted to referencing only a single file folder.

Using FILESTREAM Storage for Data Columns

Once FILESTREAM storage is enabled for a database, you can specify the FILESTREAM attribute on a varbinary(max) column to indicate that a column should store data in the FILESTREAM filegroup on the file system. When columns are defined with the FILESTREAM attribute, the Database Engine stores all data for that column on the file system instead of in the database file. In addition to a varbinary(max) column with the FILESTREAM attribute, tables used to store FILESTREAM data also require the existence of a UNIQUE ROWGUIDCOL, as shown in Listing 21.24, which creates a custinfo table on the FILESTREAM filegroup. CUSTDATA is defined as the FILESTREAM column, and ID is defined as the unique ROWGUID column.

LISTING 21.24   Creating a FILESTREAM-Enabled Table

```
Use Customer
Go
CREATE TABLE CUSTINFO
(ID UNIQUEIDENTIFIER ROWGUIDCOL NOT NULL UNIQUE,
CUSTDATA VARBINARY (MAX) FILESTREAM NULL )
FILESTREAM_ON Cust_FSGroup
GO
```

Each table created with a FILESTREAM column(s) creates a new subfolder in the FILESTREAM filegroup folder, and each FILESTREAM column in the table creates a separate subfolder under the table folder. These column folders are where the actual FILESTREAM files are stored. Initially, these folders are empty until you start adding rows into the table. A file is created in the column subfolder for each row inserted into the table with a non-NULL value for the FILESTREAM column.

> **NOTE**
>
> For more detailed information on how FILESTREAM data is stored and managed, see Chapter 31.

To ensure that SQL Server creates a new, blank file within the FILESTREAM storage folder for each row inserted in the table, you can specify a default value of 0x for the FILESTREAM column:

```
alter table CUSTINFO add constraint custdata_def default 0x for CUSTDATA
```

Creating a default is not required if all access to the FILESTREAM data is going to be done through T-SQL. However, if you will be using Win32 streaming clients to upload file contents into the FILESTREAM column, the file needs to exist already. Without the default to ensure creation of a "blank" file for each row, new files would have to be created first by inserting contents directly through T-SQL before they could be accessed via Win32 client streaming applications.

To insert data into a FILESTREAM column, you use a normal INSERT statement and provide a varbinary(max) value to store into the FILESTREAM column:

```
INSERT CUSTINFO (ID, CUSTDATA)
VALUES (NEWID(),  CONVERT(VARBINARY(MAX), REPLICATE ('CUST DATA', 100000)))
```

To retrieve FILESTREAM data, you can use a simple T-SQL SELECT statement, although you may need to convert the varbinary(max) to varchar to be able to display text data:

```
select ID, CONVERT(varchar(40), CUSTDATA) as CUSTDATA
 from CUSTINFO
go


ID                                    CUSTDATA
------------------------------------  ----------------------------------------
67C2166C-B88C-489E-9437-00FCC8603CB0 CUST DATACUST DATACUST DATACUST DATACUST
```

The preceding examples work fine if the FILESTREAM data is essentially text data; however, neither SQL Server Management Studio nor SQL Server itself really has any user interface, or native way, to let you stream the contents of an actual file into a table that's been marked with the FILESTREAM attribute on one of your varbinary(max) columns. In other words, if you have a .jpg or .mp3 file that you want to store within SQL Server, there's no native functionality to convert that image's byte stream into something that you could put, for example, into a simple INSERT statement. To read or store this type of data, you need to use Win32 to read and write data to a FILESTREAM BLOB. Following are the steps you need to perform in your client applications:

1. Read the FILESTREAM file path.

2. Read the current transaction context.

3. Obtain a Win32 handle and use the handle to read and write data to the FILESTREAM BLOB.

Each cell in a FILESTREAM table has a file path associated with it. You can use the PATHNAME property to retrieve the file path of a varbinary(max) column in a T-SQL statement:

```
DECLARE @filePath varchar(max)

SELECT @filePath = CUSTDATA.PathName()
FROM CUSTINFO
WHERE ID = '67C2166C-B88C-489E-9437-00FCC8603CB0'

PRINT @filepath
go
```

```
/* output
\\LATITUDEE6520\MSSQLSERVER\v02-A60EC2F8-2B24-11DF-9CC3-
AF2E56D89593\Customer\dbo\CUSTINFO\CUSTDATA\67C2166C-B88C-489E-9437-
00FCC8603CB0\VolumeHint-HarddiskVolume3
*/
```

Next, to obtain the current transaction context and return it to the client application, use the GET_FILESTREAM_TRANSACTION_CONTEXT() T-SQL function:

```
BEGIN TRAN
SELECT GET_FILESTREAM_TRANSACTION_CONTEXT()
```

After you obtain the transaction context, the next step in your application code is to obtain a Win32 file handle to read or write the data to the FILESTREAM column. To obtain a Win32 file handle, you call the OpenSqlFilestream API. The returned handle can then be passed to any of the following Win32 APIs to read and write data to a FILESTREAM BLOB:

- ▶ ReadFile
- ▶ WriteFile
- ▶ TransmitFile
- ▶ SetFilePointer
- ▶ SetEndOfFile
- ▶ FlushFileBuffers

To summarize, the steps you perform to upload a file to a FILESTREAM column are as follows:

1. Start a new transaction and obtain the transaction context ID that can be used to initiate the Win32 file-streaming process.

2. Execute a SqlDataReader connection to pull back the full path (in SQL Server) of the FILESTREAM file to which you will be uploading data.

3. Initiate a straight file-streaming operation using the System.Data.SqlTypes. SqlFileStream class.

4. Create a new System.IO.FileStream object to read the file locally and buffer bytes along to the SqlFileStream object until there are no more bytes to transfer.

5. Close the transaction.

> **NOTE**
>
> Because you're streaming file contents via a Win32 process, you need to use integrated security to connect to SQL Server because native SQL logins can't generate the needed security tokens to access the underlying file system where the FILESTREAM data is stored.

To retrieve data from a FILESTREAM column to a file on the client, you primarily follow the same steps as you do for inserting data; however, instead you pull data from a SqlFileStream object into a buffer and push it into a local FILESTREAM object until there are no more bytes left to retrieve.

> **TIP**
>
> Refer to the "Create Client Applications for FILESTREAM Data" topic in SQL Server 2014 Books Online for specific C#, Visual Basic, and Visual C++ application code examples showing how to obtain a Win32 file handle and use it to read and write data to a FILESTREAM column.

Using FileTables

A *FileTable* is a new type of table that was added in SQL Server 2012. It builds upon and uses the SQL Server FILESTREAM technology that was introduced in SQL Server 2008. Like FILESTREAM, the FileTable provides a means for accessing and storing files in the Windows file system using SQL Server. The main difference between FILESTREAM and FileTable is that the files that are stored in a FileTable can also be accessed from Windows applications as if they were stored in the file system.

Each FileTable represents a hierarchy of files and folders located on the Windows file system. The hierarchy starts from the root node of the folder configured for the FileTable. Each row in the FileTable represents either a file or folder in the hierarchy. The row also contains key information related to the file or folder including a FILESTREAM column, a file_id, path information, and 10 file attributes that describe the file or folder.

FileTable Prerequisites

Two main prerequisites must be satisfied before a FileTable can be created. The first prerequisite is at the server level and involves enabling FILESTREAM on the SQL Server instance. The means for enabling FILESTREAM is covered in the "Enabling FILESTREAM Storage" section earlier in this chapter.

The second prerequisite involves enabling directory name and nontransactional access on the database where the FileTable will be located. This is accomplished by right-clicking on the target database, selecting Properties, and then configuring the FILESTREAM Directory Name and FILESTREAM Non-Transacted Access options, as shown in Figure 21.12. The FILESTREAM directory name that is entered on this page must exist on the file system before setting this property. Choose either the Full or ReadOnly option for FILESTREAM Non-Transacted Access to facilitate FileTable usage.

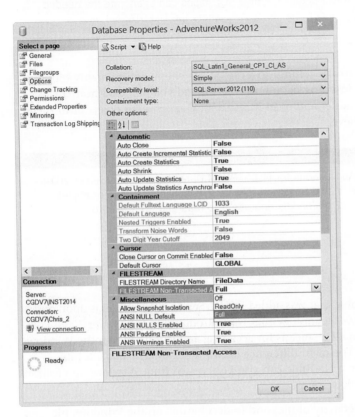

FIGURE 21.12   FILESTREAM directory and non-transacted access.

There is one other implied prerequisite for FileTables that relates to FILESTREAM. Because FileTable utilizes FILESTREAM, a FILESTREAM filegroup and related database file must exist. This is more of a prerequisite for FILESTREAM, but it also applies for a FileTable. The SQL statements shown in Listing 21.25 create the filegroup and database file that will be used in subsequent FileTable examples.

LISTING 21.25   Creating a Filegroup and File for FileTable

```
USE [master]
GO
ALTER DATABASE [AdventureWorks2012]
ADD FILEGROUP [AW_FileTable1_FG] CONTAINS FILESTREAM
GO
ALTER DATABASE [AdventureWorks2012]
ADD FILE ( NAME = N'AW_FileTable1_File',
```

```
FILENAME = N'C:\MSSQL\Data\AW_FileTable1_File' ) TO FILEGROUP
[AW_FileTable1_FG]
GO
```

Creating FileTables

FileTables can be created using SSMS or T-SQL. To create one using SSMS, you right-click on the Tables node in the Object Explorer and select New FileTable. This opens up a query window with a template script that you can modify with the FileTable specifics. The following example shows an example of creating the FileTable directly with T-SQL using the FILESTREAM filegroup created previously:

```
USE [AdventureWorks2012]
GO
CREATE TABLE FileTable1 AS FILETABLE
GO
```

It is as simple as that. There are additional parameters that you can also specify (such as FILETABLE_DIRECTORY and FILETABLE_COLLATE_FILENAME), but they are not required.

Copying Files to the FileTable

You can copy files to the FileTable using Windows Explorer or a similar program that uses a Windows API to access the file system. Before copying files, make sure that you know where the folder exists on your file system. This can be easily accomplished using the FileTableRootPath function, as shown in the following example. The first parameter of this function is the FileTable_Name. The second parameter sets an option that determines how the path will be returned; option #2 returns the complete server path:

```
select FileTableRootPath ( 'dbo.FileTable1', 2 )
--Sample results from FileTableRootPath
\\CGDV7\INST2014\FileData\FileTable1
```

You can also easily navigate to the FileTable folder by right-clicking on the FileTable name in the Object Explorer and choosing Explore FileTable Directory, as shown in Figure 21.13.

After you select Explore FileTable, a new Windows Explorer window appears such as the one shown in Figure 21.14.

The two files that are shown in Figure 21.14 were manually copied using Windows Explorer. Once files have been copied to the FileTable Directory, you can verify that the FileTable is aware of the files by selecting from the FileTable, as shown in the following example:

```
SELECT LEFT([name],20) name
      ,LEFT([file_type], 10) file_type
      ,[is_directory]
  FROM [AdventureWorks2012].[dbo].[FileTable1]
```

```
--Results from previous SELECT statement
name                    file_type   is_directory
--------------------    ---------   ------------

Sample.pdf              pdf         0
Notes.docx              docx        0
```

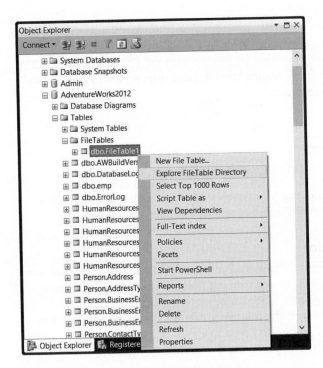

FIGURE 21.13   Explore FileTable Directory.

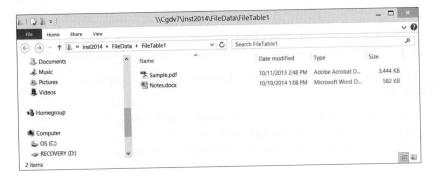

FIGURE 21.14   FileTable Directory in Windows Explorer.

Creating Temporary Tables

A temporary table is a special type of table that is automatically deleted when it is no longer used. Temporary tables have many of the same characteristics as permanent tables and are typically used as work tables that contain intermediate results.

You designate a table as temporary in SQL Server by prefacing the table name with a single pound sign (#) or two pound signs (##). Temporary tables are created in `tempdb`; if a temporary table is not explicitly dropped, it is dropped when the session that created it ends or the stored procedure it was created in finishes execution.

If a table name is prefaced with a single pound sign (for example, `#table1`), it is a *private* temporary table, available only to the session that created it.

A table name prefixed with a double pound sign (for example, `##table2`) indicates that it is a *global* temporary table, which means it is accessible by all database connections. A global temporary table exists until the session that created it terminates. If the creating session terminates while other sessions are accessing the table, the temporary table is available to those sessions until the last session's query ends, at which time the table is dropped.

A common way of creating a temporary table is to use the SELECT INTO method as shown in the following example:

```
SELECT* INTO #Person2 FROM Person.Person
```

This method creates a temporary table with a structure like the table that is being selected from. It also copies the data from the original table and inserts it into this new temporary table. All of this is done with this one simple command.

> **NOTE**
>
> Table variables are a good alternative to temporary tables. These variables are also temporary in nature and have some advantages over temporary tables. Table variables are easy to create, are automatically deleted, cause fewer recompilations, and use fewer locking and logging resources. Generally speaking, you should consider using table variables instead of temporary tables when the temporary results are relatively small. Parallel query plans are not generated with table variables, and this can impede overall performance when you are accessing a table variable that has a large number of rows.

Tables created without the # prefix but explicitly created in `tempdb` are also considered temporary, but they are a more permanent form of a temporary table. They are not dropped automatically until SQL Server is restarted and `tempdb` is reinitialized.

Summary

Tables are the key to a relational database system. When you create tables, you need to pay careful attention to choosing the proper data types to ensure efficient storage of data, adding appropriate constraints to maintain data integrity, and scripting the creation and modification of tables to ensure that they can be re-created, if necessary.

Good table design includes the creation of indexes on a table. Tables without indexes are generally inefficient and cause excessive use of resources on your database server. Chapter 22, "Creating and Managing Indexes," covers indexes and their critical role in effective table design.

Creating and Managing Indexes

Just like the index in this book, an index on a table or view allows you to efficiently find the information you are looking for in a database. SQL Server does not require indexes to be able to retrieve data from tables because it can perform a full table scan to retrieve a result set. However, doing a table scan is analogous to scanning every page in this book to find a word or reference you are looking for.

This chapter introduces the different types of indexes available in SQL Server 2014 to keep your database access efficient. It focuses on creating and managing indexes by using the tools Microsoft SQL Server 2014 provides. For a more in-depth discussion of the internal structures of indexes and designing and managing indexes for optimal performance, see Chapter 31, "Understanding SQL Server Data Structures" and Chapter 32, "Indexes and Performance."

What's New in Creating and Managing Indexes

The creation and management of indexes are among the most important performance activities in SQL Server. You will find that indexes and the tools to manage them in SQL Server 2014 are very similar to those in SQL Server 2012. There are, however, some minor changes to the index-oriented GUI screens. These changes include the ability to select the type of index that you want to create directly from the New Index menu and some organizational changes in the New Index screen.

Columnstore indexes were enhanced in SQL Server 2014. These indexes offer a powerful way to accelerate data warehouse workloads. You can now create a clustered columnstore index in SQL Server 2014. Also new to SQL Server 2014 is the ability to see columnstore indexes in SHOWPLAN displays and a new option to set archival data compression on a columnstore Index. Finally, clustered columnstore indexes are updateable in SQL Server 2014. These new indexes are covered in more detail in Chapter 32 and Chapter 51, "Parallel Data Warehouse."

SQL Server 2014 has also extended support for online index operations. In particular, the Progress Report: Online Index Operation event class has two new data columns named PartitionId and PartionNumber. These columns provide information about the partition being built during an Online Index operation. Memory-optimized indexes are new to SQL Server 2014 as well. These indexes are related to memory-optimized tables which were introduced in SQL Server 2014. These tables are not stored on disk and live in memory only. The same is true of the indexes on these tables. Memory-optimized tables and the related indexes are discussed in more detail in Chapter 33, "In-Memory Optimization and the Buffer Pool Extension."

Finally, SQL Server 2014 has Transact-SQL enhancements and System View enhancements that relate to indexes. You can now create clustered and nonclustered indexes using an inline specification that is part of the table creation statements. The System View enhancements include the addition of 3 new columns to the `sys.xml_indexes` view; `xml_index_type`, `xml_Index_type_description`, and `path_id`. A new `sys.column_store_row_groups` System View was also added in SQL Server 2014. This view provides information related to clustered columnstore indexes.

Types of Indexes

SQL Server has two main types of indexes: clustered and nonclustered. They both help the query engine get at data faster, but they have different effects on the storage of the underlying data. The following sections describe these two main types of indexes and provide some insight into when to use each type.

Clustered Indexes

Clustered indexes sort and store the data rows for a table, based on the columns defined in the index. For example, if you were to create a clustered index on the `LastName` and `FirstName` columns in a table, the data rows for that table would be organized or sorted according to these two columns. This has some obvious advantages for data retrieval. Queries that search for data based on the clustered index keys have a sequential path to the underlying data, which helps reduce I/O.

A clustered index is analogous to a filing cabinet where each drawer contains a set of file folders stored in alphabetical order, and each file folder stores the files in alphabetical order. Each file drawer contains a label that indicates which folders it contains (for example, folders A–D). To locate a specific file, you first locate the drawer containing the appropriate file folders, then locate the appropriate file folder within the drawer, and then scan the files in that folder in sequence until you find the one you need.

A clustered index is structured as a balanced tree (B-tree). Figure 22.1 shows a simplified diagram of a clustered index defined on a last name column.

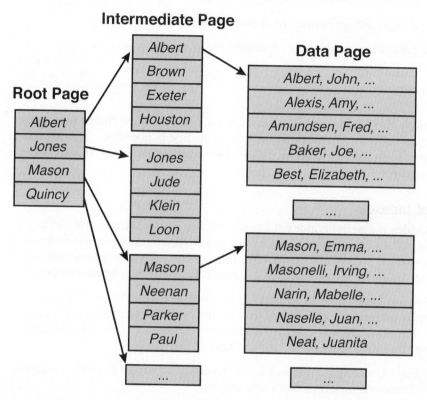

FIGURE 22.1   A simplified diagram of a clustered index.

The top, or root, node is a single page where searches via the clustered index are started. The bottom level of the index is the leaf nodes. With a clustered index, the leaf nodes of the index are also the data pages of the table. Any levels of the index between the root and leaf nodes are referred to as *intermediate nodes*. All index key values are stored in the clustered index levels in sorted order. To locate a data row via a clustered index, SQL Server starts at the root node and navigates through the appropriate index pages in the intermediate levels of the index until it reaches the data page that should contain the desired data row(s). It then scans the rows on the data page until it locates the desired value.

There can be only one clustered index per table. This restriction is driven by the fact that the underlying data rows can be sorted and stored in only one way. With very few exceptions, every table in a database should have a clustered index. The selection of columns for a clustered index is very important and should be driven by the way the data is most commonly accessed in the table. You should consider using the following types of columns in a clustered index:

▶ Those that are often accessed sequentially

▶ Those that contain a large number of distinct values

▶ Those that are used in range queries that use operators such as BETWEEN, >, >=, <, or <= in the WHERE clause

▶ Those that are frequently used by queries to join or group the result set

When you are using these criteria, it is important to focus on the most critical data access: the queries that are run most often or that must have the best performance. This approach can be challenging but ultimately reduces the number of data pages and related I/O for the queries that matter.

Nonclustered Indexes

A nonclustered index is a separate index structure, independent of the physical sort order of the data rows in the table. You are therefore not restricted to creating only 1 nonclustered index per table; in fact, in SQL Server 2014 you can create up to 999 nonclustered indexes per table. This is an increase from SQL Server 2005, which was limited to 249.

A nonclustered index is analogous to an index in the back of a book. To find the pages on which a specific subject is discussed, you look up the subject in the index and then go to the pages referenced in the index. With nonclustered indexes, you may have to jump around to many different nonsequential pages to find all the references.

A nonclustered index is also structured as a B-tree. Figure 22.2 shows a simplified diagram of a nonclustered index defined on a first name column.

As with a clustered index, in a nonclustered index, all index key values are stored in the nonclustered index levels in sorted order, based on the index key(s). This sort order is typically different from the sort order of the table itself. The main difference between a nonclustered index and clustered index is that the leaf row of a nonclustered index is independent of the data rows in the table. The leaf level of a nonclustered index contains a row for every data row in the table, along with a pointer to locate the data row. This pointer is either the clustered index key for the data row, if the table has a clustered index on it, or the data page ID and row ID of the data row if the table is stored as a heap structure (that is, if the table has no clustered index defined on it).

To locate a data row via a nonclustered index, SQL Server starts at the root node and navigates through the appropriate index pages in the intermediate levels of the index until it reaches the leaf page, which should contain the index key for the desired data row. It then scans the keys on the leaf page until it locates the desired index key value. SQL Server then uses the pointer to the data row stored with the index key to retrieve the corresponding data row.

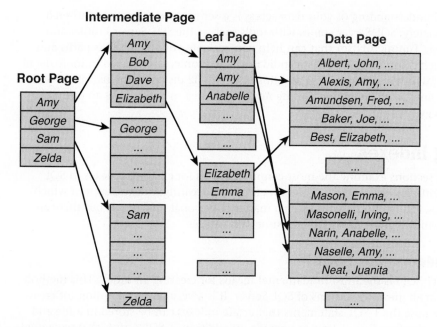

FIGURE 22.2   A simplified diagram of a nonclustered index.

> **NOTE**
>
> For a more detailed discussion of clustered tables versus heap tables (that is, tables with no clustered indexes) and more detailed descriptions of clustered and nonclustered index key structures and index key rows, as well as how SQL Server internally maintains indexes, see Chapter 31.

The efficiency of the index lookup and the types of lookups should drive the selection of nonclustered indexes. In the book index example, a single page reference is a simple lookup for the book reader and requires little work. If, however, many pages are referenced in the index, and those pages are spread throughout the book, the lookup is no longer simple, and much more work is required to get all the information.

You should choose your nonclustered indexes with the book index example in mind. You should consider using nonclustered indexes for the following:

▶ Queries that do not return large result sets

▶ Columns that are frequently used in the WHERE clause that return exact matches

▶ Columns that have many distinct values (that is, high cardinality)

▶ All columns referenced in a critical query (a special nonclustered index called a *covering index* that eliminates the need to go to the underlying data pages)

Having a good understanding of your data access is essential to creating nonclustered indexes. Fortunately, SQL Server comes with tools such as the SQL Server Profiler and Database Engine Tuning Advisor that can help you evaluate your data access paths and determine which columns are the best candidates. SQL Profiler is discussed in more detail in Chapter 5, "SQL Server Profiler." In addition, Chapter 32 discusses the use of the SQL Server Profiler and Database Engine Tuning Advisor to assist in developing an optimal indexing strategy.

Creating Indexes

The following sections examine the most common means for creating indexes in SQL Server. Microsoft provides several different methods for creating indexes, each of which has advantages. The method used is often a matter of personal preference, but there are situations in which a given method has distinct advantages.

Creating Indexes with T-SQL

Transact-SQL (T-SQL) is the most fundamental means for creating an index. This method was available in all previous versions of SQL Server. It is a very powerful option for creating indexes because the T-SQL statements that create indexes can be stored in a file and run as part of a database installation or upgrade. In addition, T-SQL scripts that were used in prior SQL Server versions to create indexes can be reused with very little change.

You can create indexes by using the T-SQL CREATE INDEX command. Listing 22.1 shows the basic CREATE INDEX syntax. Refer to SQL Server 2014 Books Online for the full syntax.

LISTING 22.1   CREATE INDEX Syntax

```
CREATE [ UNIQUE ] [ CLUSTERED | NONCLUSTERED ] INDEX index_name
    ON <object> ( column [ ASC | DESC ] [ ,...n ] )
    [ INCLUDE ( column_name [ ,...n ] ) ]
    [ WHERE <filter_predicate> ]
    [ WITH ( <relational_index_option> [ ,...n ] ) ]
```

Table 22.1 lists the CREATE INDEX arguments.

TABLE 22.1   Arguments for CREATE INDEX

Argument	Explanation
UNIQUE	Indicates that no two rows in the index can have the same index key values. Inserts into a table with a UNIQUE index will fail if a row with the same value already exists in the table.
CLUSTERED | NON-CLUSTERED	Defines the index as clustered or nonclustered. NON-CLUSTERED is the default. Only one clustered index is allowed per table.

Argument	Explanation
`index_name`	Specifies the name of the index to be created.
`object`	Specifies the name of the table or view to be indexed.
`column_name`	Specifies the column or columns that are to be indexed.
`ASC	DESC`	Specifies the sort direction for the particular index column. `ASC` creates an ascending sort order and is the default. The `DESC` option causes the index to be created in descending order.
`INCLUDE (column [ ,... n ] )`	Allows a column to be added to the leaf level of an index without being part of the index key. This is a new argument.
`WHERE <filter_predicate>`	This argument, new to SQL Server 2008, is used to create a filtered index. The `filter_predicate` contains a `WHERE` clause that limits the number of rows in the table that are included in the index.
`relational_index_option`	Specifies the index option to use when creating the index.

Following is a simple example using the basic syntax of the `CREATE INDEX` command:

```
CREATE NONCLUSTERED INDEX [NC_Person_LastName]
ON [Person].[Person]
(
[LastName] ASC
)
```

This example creates a nonclustered index on the `person.person` table, based on the `LastName` column. The `NONCLUSTERED` and `ASC` keywords are not necessary because they are the defaults. Because the `UNIQUE` keyword is not specified, duplicates are allowed in the index (that is, multiple rows in the table can have the same `LastName`).

Unique indexes are more involved because they serve two roles: They provide fast access to the data via the index's columns, but they also serve as a constraint by allowing only one row to exist on a table for the combination of column values in the index. They can be clustered or nonclustered. Unique indexes are also defined on a table whenever you define a unique or primary key constraint on a table. The following example shows the creation of a nonclustered unique index:

```
CREATE UNIQUE NONCLUSTERED INDEX [AK_CreditCard_CardNumber]

ON [Sales].[CreditCard]
(
        [CardNumber] ASC
)
```

This example creates a nonclustered index named AK_CreditCard_CardNumber on the Sales.CreditCard table. This index is based on a single column in the table. When it is created, this index prevents credit card rows with the same credit card number from being inserted into the CreditCard table.

The relational index options listed in Table 22.2 allow you to define more sophisticated indexes or specify how an index is to be created.

TABLE 22.2   Relational Index Options for CREATE INDEX

Argument	Explanation
PAD_INDEX = {ON | OFF}	Determines whether free space is allocated to the non-leaf-level pages of an index. The percentage of free space is determined by FILLFACTOR.
FILLFACTOR = fillfactor	Determines the amount of free space left in the leaf level of each index page. The fillfactor values represent a percentage, from 0 to 100. The default value is 0. If fillfactor is 0 or 100, the index leaf-level pages are filled to capacity, leaving only enough space for at least one more row to be inserted.
SORT_IN_TEMPDB = {ON | OFF}	Specifies whether intermediate sort results that are used to create the index are stored in tempdb. Using them can speed up the creation of the index (if tempdb is on a separate disk), but it requires more disk space.
IGNORE_DUP_KEY = {ON | OFF}	Determines whether multirow inserts will fail when duplicate rows in the insert violate a unique index. When this option is set to ON, duplicate key values are ignored, and the rest of the multirow insert succeeds. When it is OFF (the default), the entire multirow insert fails if a duplicate is encountered.
STATISTICS_NO_RECOMPUTE = {ON | OFF}	Determines whether distribution statistics used by the Query Optimizer are recomputed. When ON, the statistics are not automatically recomputed.
DROP_EXISTING = {ON | OFF}	Determines whether an index with the same name is dropped prior to re-creation. This can provide some performance benefits over dropping the existing index first and then creating. Clustered indexes see the most benefit.
ONLINE = {ON | OFF}	Determines whether the index is built such that the underlying table is still available for queries and data modification during the index creation. This new feature is discussed in more detail in the "Online Indexing Operations" section, later in this chapter.
ALLOW_ROW_LOCKS = {ON | OFF}	Determines whether row locks are allowed when accessing the index. The default for this new feature is ON.

Argument	Explanation
`ALLOW_PAGE_LOCKS = {ON	OFF}`	Determines whether page locks are allowed when accessing the index. The default for this new feature is ON.
`MAXDOP = number of processors`	Determines the number of processors that can be used during index operations. The default for this feature is 0, which causes an index operation to use the actual number of processors or fewer, depending on the workload on the system. This can be a useful option for index operations on large tables that may impact performance during the operation. For example, if you have four processors, you can specify MAXDOP = 2 to limit the index operation to use only two of the four processors. The MAXDOP index option overrides the max degree of parallelism configuration for the given index operation.
`DATA_COMPRESSION = { NONE	ROW	PAGE} [ON PARTITIONS ({ <partition_number_expression> | <range> } [, ...n])`	Determines whether data compression is used on the specified index. The compression can be done on the row or page level and specific index partitions can be compressed if the index uses partitioning.

The following example creates a more complex index that utilizes several of the index options described in Table 22.2:

```
CREATE NONCLUSTERED INDEX [
IX_Person_LastName_FirstName_MiddleName] ON [Person].[Person]
(
    [LastName] ASC,
    [FirstName] ASC,
    [MiddleName] ASC
)WITH (SORT_IN_TEMPDB = OFF, IGNORE_DUP_KEY = OFF, DROP_EXISTING = OFF,
FILLFACTOR=80)
```

This example creates a nonclustered composite index on the person's last name (LastName), first name (FirstName), and middle name (MiddleName). It utilizes some of the commonly used options and demonstrates how multiple options can be used in a single CREATE statement.

TIP

SQL Server Management Studio (SSMS) has several methods for generating the T-SQL code that creates indexes. You therefore rarely need to type index CREATE statements from scratch. Instead, you can use the friendly GUI screens that enable you to specify the common index options, and then you can generate the T-SQL script that can be executed to create the index.

Creating Indexes with SSMS

SQL Server 2014 has many options for creating indexes within SSMS. You can create indexes within SSMS via the Database Engine Tuning Advisor, database diagrams, the Table Designer, and several places within the Object Explorer. The means available from the Object Explorer are the simplest to use and are the focus of this section. The other options are discussed in more detail in related chapters of this book.

Index creation in the Object Explorer is facilitated by the New Index screen. You can launch this screen from SMSS by expanding the database tree in the Object Explorer and navigating to the `Indexes` node of the table that you want to add the index to. Then you right-click the `Indexes` node, select New Index, and then select the type of index that you want to create. If you select the option to create a new nonclustered index, a screen like the one shown in Figure 22.3 will display.

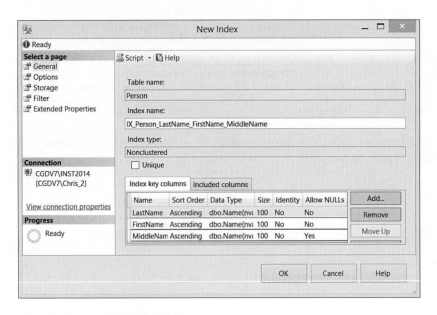

FIGURE 22.3   Using Object Explorer to create indexes.

The name and options that are populated in Figure 22.3 are based on the person index created in the previous T-SQL section. The `LastName`, `FirstName`, and `MiddleName` columns were selected and added as part of this new index by clicking the Add button, which displays a screen with all the columns in the table that are available for the index. You simply select the column(s) you want to include on the index. This populates the Index Key Columns grid on the default General page.

Included columns are managed on the General page as well. In SQL Server 2014, a separate tab named Included columns can be found next to the Index key columns tab. This tab allows you to select columns that you want to include in the leaf-level pages of the index but don't need as part of the index key. For example, you could consider using included columns if you have a critical query that often selects last name, first name, and address from a table but uses only the last name and first name as search arguments in the WHERE clause. This may be a situation in which you would want to consider the use of a covering index that places all the referenced columns from the query into a nonclustered index. In the case of our critical query, the address column can be added to the index as an included column. It is not included in the index key, but it is available in the leaf-level pages of the index so that the additional overhead of going to the data pages to retrieve the address is not needed.

You can select other options for an index by changing the Select a Page options available on the top-left side of the New Index screen. The Options, Storage, Filter, Spatial and Extended Properties pages each provide a series of options that relate to the corresponding category and are utilized when creating the index. The Spatial page can be used to set properties for spatial indexes on a column that is defined as a spatial data type; that is either type geometry or geography. If your table contains a column of this data type, you can right-click on the Indexes node in Object Explorer, choose New Index, and then choose Spatial Index. After this is done, you can add a column that is defined as a spatial data type to the index. Finally, you can select the Spatial option page, as shown in Figure 22.4, that allows you to fully define a spatial index. The meanings of the parameters on this page are beyond the scope of this chapter but are discussed in more detail in Chapter 32.

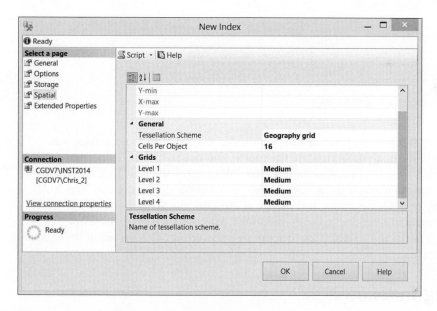

FIGURE 22.4   Spatial Index options page.

The Filter option page allows you to define a filtering criterion to limit the rows that are included in the index. The page, shown in Figure 22.5, is relatively simple with a single input area that contains your filtering criterion. This criterion is basically the contents of a WHERE clause that is similar to what you would use in a query window to filter the rows in your result. The filter expression shown in Figure 22.5 was defined for an index on the PersonType column, which is found in the Person.Person table of the AdventureWorks2012 sample database. Many of the rows in this table have a PersonType value equal to 'IN' so a filtered index that does not include rows with this value will dramatically reduce the size of the index and make searches on values other than 'IN' relatively fast.

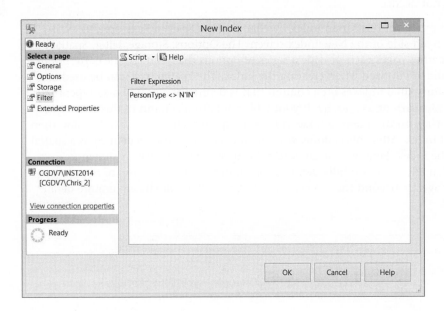

FIGURE 22.5   Filter Index options page.

After selecting all the options you want for your index via the New Index screen, you have several options for actually creating the index. You can script the index, schedule the index creation for a later time, or simply click OK to allow the New Index screen to add the index immediately. As mentioned earlier, it is a good idea to use this New Index screen to specify the index options, and then you can click the Script button to generate all the T-SQL statements needed to create the index. You can then save this script to a file to be used for generating a database build script or for maintaining a record of the indexes defined in a database.

Managing Indexes

There are two different aspects to index management. The first aspect is the management of indexes by the SQL Server Database Engine. Fortunately, the engine does a good job of managing the indexes internally so that limited manual intervention is required. This is predicated on a well-designed database system and the use of SQL Server features, such as automatic updates to distribution statistics.

The other aspect of index management typically comes into play when performance issues arise. Index adjustments and maintenance of these indexes make up the bulk of this effort.

Managing Indexes with T-SQL

One of the T-SQL features available with SQL Server 2014 is the ALTER INDEX statement. This statement simplifies many of the tasks associated with managing indexes. Index operations such as index rebuilds and changes to fill factor can be performed using the ALTER INDEX statement. The basic syntax for ALTER INDEX is as follows:

```
ALTER INDEX {index_name | ALL}
    ON [{database_name.[schema_name]. | schema_name.}]
    {table_or_view_name}
    { REBUILD [WITH(<rebuild_index_option>[,...n])]
    | REORGANIZE [ WITH( LOB_COMPACTION = {ON | OFF})]
    | DISABLE
    | SET (<set_index_option>[,...n]) }
```

Let's look at a few examples that demonstrate the power of the ALTER INDEX statement. The first example simply rebuilds the primary key index on the Production.Product table:

```
ALTER INDEX [PK_Product_ProductID] ON [Production].[Product] REBUILD
```

The REBUILD operation is equivalent to the DBCC DBREINDEX command. The specified index is dropped and re-created using the fillfactor that was specified when the index was created. This removes fragmentation from all of the index pages. The rebuild is done dynamically, without the need to drop and re-create constraints that reference any of the affected indexes. If it is run on a clustered index, the data pages of the table are defragmented as well. If you specify the ALL option for the ALTER INDEX command, all indexes as well as the data pages of the table (if the table has a clustered index) are defragmented.

> **NOTE**
>
> If the REBUILD option is run on a heap table (that is, a table with no clustered index), the REBUILD operation does not affect the underlying table. Only the specified nonclustered indexes are rebuilt.

For added flexibility, you can also specify index options as part of the REBUILD operation. The options available with the REBUILD command are the same options available when you are creating indexes. The only exception is that the DROP EXISTING option is not available with the REBUILD operation. (Table 22.2, earlier in this chapter, provides detailed descriptions of the options.) The following example rebuilds the clustered index on the Production.Product table and specifies several of the available REBUILD options:

```
ALTER INDEX [PK_Product_ProductID]
ON [Production].[Product] REBUILD WITH ( PAD_INDEX  = OFF,
  STATISTICS_NORECOMPUTE = OFF,
```

```
ALLOW_ROW_LOCKS = ON,
  ALLOW_PAGE_LOCKS = ON, ONLINE = OFF, SORT_IN_TEMPDB = OFF,
  DATA_COMPRESSION = NONE )
```

An alternative to the REBUILD operation is the REORGANIZE operation. The REORGANIZE operation is equivalent to the DBCC INDEX DEFRAG command. During the REORGANIZE operation, the leaf-level pages of the index are physically reordered to match the logical order of the index keys. The indexes are not dropped. The REORGANIZE operation is always an online operation and does not require long-term table locks to complete.

> **TIP**
>
> The REORGANIZE operation can generate a large number of transaction log records during its execution. You need to be sure to carefully evaluate the amount of space available in the transaction log and monitor the free space during this operation. If the transaction log is set to AUTOGROW, you need to make sure you have adequate free space on the drive where your transaction log lives. This is especially true for very large tables. Several options are available for mitigating the growth of the log during these operations, such as setting the recovery model on the database to BULK-LOGGED or SIMPLE recovery.

The REORGANIZE operation has just one option: LOB_COMPACTION. When the LOB_COMPACTION option is set to ON, the data for columns with large object (LOB) data types is compacted. This consolidates the data and frees disk space. LOB data types include image, text, ntext, varchar(max), nvarchar(max), varbinary(max), and xml. The following example performs a REORGANIZE operation on the clustered index of the Production.Product table with the LOB_COMPACTION option set to ON:

```
ALTER INDEX [PK_Product_ProductID] ON [Production].[Product]
REORGANIZE WITH ( LOB_COMPACTION = ON )
```

Disabling an index can also be accomplished with the ALTER INDEX statement. When the DISABLE option is used on an index, the index is no longer available for retrieving data from a table and the index keys are no longer maintained. If a clustered index is disabled, the entire table is made unavailable. The data remains in the table, but no Data Manipulation Language (DML) operations can be performed on the table until the index is dropped or rebuilt. Unlike dropping an index, when an index is disabled, SQL Server retains the index definition in metadata so it can easily be re-enabled; index statistics are still maintained for nonclustered indexes that have been disabled.

After an index is disabled, you can re-enable it only by re-creating the index. You can accomplish this using the ALTER INDEX REBUILD command or CREATE INDEX WITH DROP_EXISTING command.

Disabling indexes can be particularly useful for testing purposes. Let's say you have a nonclustered index on a table that you believe is used very little. You can disable the index initially before removing it to evaluate the change. The definition of the index is still contained in the database. If you ultimately determine that the index is still needed, you can simply rebuild the index to make it available again. You don't have to worry about keeping the INDEX CREATE script around in order to recreate it.

Disabling can also be useful when you have to perform a large number of INSERT/UPDATE/DELETE operations on a table. The overhead of maintaining the nonclustered indexes can slow down the inserts/updates/deletes and also potentially lead to excessive index fragmentation. Since you may have to rebuild the index after the operations are completed anyway, it can speed up the entire operation to disable the indexes first and then rebuild them to re-enable them.

TIP

Another reason for disabling a nonclustered index is to reduce the space requirements when rebuilding the index. If an index to be rebuilt is not disabled, SQL Server requires enough temporary disk space in the database to store both the old and new versions of the index. However, if the index is disabled first, SQL Server can reuse the space required for the disabled index to rebuild it. No additional disk space is necessary except for temporary space required for sorting, which is only about 20% of the index size.

The following example disables a nonclustered index on the `Production.Product` table:

```
ALTER INDEX [AK_Product_Name] ON [Production].[Product] DISABLE
```

One point to keep in mind when an index is disabled is that it is not readily apparent in SSMS that the index has been disabled. The index still appears in the Object Explorer tree under the `Indexes` node, and there are no indicators on the index display to alert you to the fact that it has been disabled. You can, however, use other methods to determine if the index has been disabled. The `sys.indexes` catalog view is one of these methods. Refer to the `is_disabled` column returned with this view. A value of 1 in the `is_disabled` column indicates that it has been disabled, and a value of 0 indicates that it is enabled. The following `SELECT` statement shows an example of how to use the `sys.indexes` catalog view:

```
select  is_disabled,* from sys.indexes
 where object_name(object_id) = 'Product'
```

You can also easily change options on an index with the `ALTER INDEX` statement. The following example sets several of the available options for a nonclustered index on the product table:

```
ALTER INDEX [AK_Product_ProductNumber] ON [Production].[Product]
 SET (
    ALLOW_PAGE_LOCKS = ON,
    ALLOW_ROW_LOCKS = OFF,
    IGNORE_DUP_KEY = ON,
    STATISTICS_NORECOMPUTE = ON
    )
```

Other options exist for managing indexes with T-SQL, but the ALTER INDEX statement provides the bulk of what you need. Many of the other T-SQL options that you may have used for managing indexes in previous versions of SQL Server, such as DBCC DBREINDEX, are still available in SQL Server 2014 for backward compatibility.

For more information and guidelines on managing indexes for performance, such as why and when to rebuild an index, see Chapter 32.

Managing Indexes with SSMS

Several tools are available in SSMS for managing indexes. You can use tools such as the Database Engine Tuning Advisor, database diagrams, and the Table Designer to view indexes and make modifications. These tools have many features that are geared toward specific tasks, but again, in most cases the Object Explorer provides the simplest means for managing indexes.

Figure 22.6 shows the index options available by right-clicking an index in the Object Explorer. Many of these options are geared toward index management, including the options Rebuild, Reorganize, and Disable.

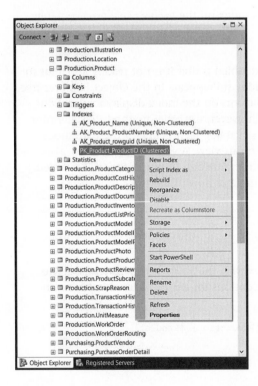

FIGURE 22.6   Using Object Explorer to manage indexes.

Similar options are also available from the Indexes node of the Object Explorer that enable you to rebuild, reorganize, or disable all the indexes for the table.

> **TIP**
>
> You can right-click an index in the Object Explorer and choose Properties to display the index columns and other relevant information. You can also run the SP_HELPINDEX command on any table in a database to list all the indexes on the table and their related columns. This command must be run in a Database Engine query window. For example, sp_helpindex [Production.Product] returns all the indexes for the Product table in the AdventureWorks2012 database. Make sure to enclose the table name with brackets when including the schema name.

Dropping Indexes

You can drop indexes by using T-SQL or via tools in the SSMS. To drop indexes with T-SQL, use the DROP INDEX command, a simple example of which follows:

```
DROP INDEX [IX_WorkOrder_ScrapReasonID] ON [Production].[WorkOrder]
```

This command drops the index named IX_WorkOrder_ScrapReasonID on the Production. WorkOrder table.

Using the Object Explorer in SSMS is the simplest alternative for dropping indexes. In the Object Explorer, you simply right-click the index you want to drop and then select Delete. The same execution options available for adding and modifying indexes are also available after you select Delete. This includes the option to script the T-SQL statements like that shown in the preceding DROP INDEX example.

> **NOTE**
>
> If you drop a clustered index on a table, SQL Server needs to rebuild all the remaining nonclustered indexes on the table. The reason is that when a clustered index exists on a table, the nonclustered indexes include the clustered index key in the nonclustered index rows as a pointer to the corresponding data rows. When the clustered index is dropped, the clustered index key needs to be replaced with page and row pointers. If a large number of nonclustered indexes exist on the table, the operation to rebuild the nonclustered indexes can be time consuming and I/O-intensive. For more information on the internal structures of clustered and nonclustered indexes, see Chapter 31.

Online Indexing Operations

One of the great features available with SQL Server 2014 is online indexing. This feature, available only with the Enterprise or Developer Edition, allows you to create, rebuild, or drop indexes without having exclusive access to the index or table. This means that users can continue to access the underlying tables and indexes while the index operation is in progress. This bodes well for high-availability applications and databases that have limited downtime available for offline operations.

NOTE

SQL Server 2014 continues to offer extended support for online index operations. In versions prior to SQL Server 2012, indexes that include large object (LOB) or XML data, or clustered indexes on tables with LOB or XML columns, could not be rebuilt online. This restriction was removed in SQL Server 2012 so that indexes with these types of columns can be built, rebuilt, or dropped online.

Following is an example of the T-SQL syntax for an online index operation:

```
ALTER INDEX [PK_Product_ProductID] ON [Production].[Product]
REBUILD WITH ( ONLINE = ON)
```

The ONLINE = ON parameter is the key to making the index operation an online operation.

To accomplish online indexing, SQL Server must maintain the old and new versions of the affected indexes during the operation. The old version (referred to as the *source*) includes any table or indexes that are affected by the index operation. For example, if a clustered index is part of the online operation, the clustered index and all the nonclustered indexes that reference the clustered index are maintained as part of the source. The new version (referred to as the *target*) is the new index or indexes that are being created or rebuilt. In the case of a table without a clustered index, a structure known as a heap is used as the source and target.

During online index operations, the following three phases occur:

▶ **Preparation**—Concurrent activity is temporarily suspended while a snapshot of the source index structure is taken and written as an empty structure to the target.

▶ **Building**—The source index structures are scanned, sorted, merged, and inserted into the target. User SELECT statements are satisfied via the source. Insertions, updates, and deletions to the affected table are written to both the source and target.

▶ **Final**—Concurrent activity is temporarily suspended while the source is replaced by the newly created structures (target).

When the final phase is complete, all the query and update plans that were using the old structures are invalidated. Future queries utilize the newly created index structures after this point.

When considering online indexing, you need to account for the following:

▶ **Disk space**—Generally, the disk space requirements for online operations are the same as those for offline operations. The exception to this is online index operations on clustered indexes. These operations use a temporary mapping index that requires additional disk space. The temporary mapping index contains one row for each record in the table.

▶ **Performance**—Online index operations are generally slower and take more system resources than offline operations. Primarily, the reason is that the old and new index structures are maintained during the index operation. Heavy updates to the tables involved in the index operation can cause an overall decrease in performance and a spike in CPU utilization and I/O as the two index structures are maintained.

▶ **Transaction log**—Online index operations are fully logged. You may therefore encounter a heavy burden on your transaction log during online index operations for large tables. This can cause your transaction log to fill quickly. The transaction log can be backed up, but it cannot be truncated during online index operations. You need to make sure you have enough space for your log to grow; otherwise, the online index operation could fail.

Indexes on Views

SQL Server 2014 supports the creation of indexes on views. Like indexes on tables, indexes on views can dramatically improve the performance of the queries that reference the views. By nature, a view is a virtual table and does not have a separate data structure as does a table, even though it can be referenced like a table. After an index is created on a view, the result set of the view is stored in the database, just as it would be for a table. The indexed view is no longer virtual because it requires maintenance as rows are added to, deleted from, or modified in the tables referenced by the view. Refer to Chapter 24, "Creating and Managing Views," for a more detailed discussion of views.

The first index created on a view must be a unique clustered index. After that is created, other nonclustered indexes can be built on the view for additional performance gains.

The most difficult part of the index creation process is identifying a view that is valid for index creation. Many requirements must be met for a view to qualify. Refer to the SQL Server Books Online documentation for a complete list of all the restrictions. The following is a partial list of the most common requirements:

▶ All the tables in the view must be in the same database as the view and have the same owner as the view.

▶ The view must not reference any other views.

▶ The view must be created with SCHEMABINDING, and any function referenced in the view must also be created with SCHEMABINDING.

▶ A two-part name with the schema prefix must be used for every table or user-defined function referenced in the view.

▶ Many SET options, including ANSI_NULLS, ANSI_PADDING, ANSI_WARNINGS, ARITHABORT, CONCAT_NULL_YIELDS_NULL, and QUOTED_IDENTIFIER must be set to ON.

▶ Any functions referenced in the view must be deterministic. (See Chapter 26, "Creating and Managing User-Defined Functions," for more information on deterministic functions.)

▶ Views with aggregate functions must also include COUNT_BIG(*).

The following example shows a view definition from the AdventureWorks2012 database that can have an index created on it:

```
CREATE VIEW [Person].[vStateProvinceCountryRegion]
WITH SCHEMABINDING
AS
SELECT
    sp.[StateProvinceID]
    ,sp.[StateProvinceCode]
    ,sp.[IsOnlyStateProvinceFlag]
    ,sp.[Name] AS [StateProvinceName]
    ,sp.[TerritoryID]
    ,cr.[CountryRegionCode]
    ,cr.[Name] AS [CountryRegionName]
FROM [Person].[StateProvince] sp
    INNER JOIN [Person].[CountryRegion] cr
    ON sp.[CountryRegionCode] = cr.[CountryRegionCode]
GO
```

The SCHEMABINDING clause and database schema qualifier (person) for each table are necessary in the view definition to be able to make the view valid for index creation. The following example shows the index creation statement for an index on the Person. vStateProvinceCountryRegion view in the AdventureWorks2012 database:

```
CREATE UNIQUE CLUSTERED INDEX [IX_vStateProvinceCountryRegion] ON [Person].
[vStateProvinceCountryRegion]
(
    [StateProvinceID] ASC,
    [CountryRegionCode] ASC
)
GO
```

After the index is created, you can manage it in much the same way that you manage the indexes on tables. You can use both T-SQL and SSMS to manage these indexes.

For more information and guidelines on creating and using indexed views, see Chapter 24.

Summary

Index creation is an important part of managing a database. Creating useful indexes can vastly improve query performance and should not be overlooked. Fortunately, SQL Server 2014 makes the creation and management of indexes quite easy.

In Chapter 23, "Implementing Data Integrity," you see how you can use indexes and other methods to enforce data integrity. Subsequent chapters cover the internal working of indexes and give you more insight into their role in performance.

Implementing Data Integrity

The value of your data is determined by its integrity. You may have heard the phrase "garbage in, garbage out." In the database world, "garbage in" refers to data that has been loaded into a database without validation or without data integrity. This "garbage" data can then be retrieved ("garbage out"), and erroneous decisions can result because of it.

Implementing good data integrity measures is your best defense against the "garbage in, garbage out" scenario. This involves identifying valid values for tables and columns and deciding how to enforce the integrity of those values. This chapter covers the different types of data integrity and the methods for enforcing them.

What's New in Data Integrity

Much of the functionality related to data integrity has remained the same in SQL Server 2014. Several features that were added in SQL Server 2005, such as cascading integrity constraints, are still supported in SQL Server 2014. The lack of change in this area is generally a blessing. The tools available to enforce data integrity were comprehensive in 2005 and remain so in 2014.

Keep in mind that bound defaults, which were deprecated in SQL Server 2005, are still available in SQL Server 2014. For now, you can still use this statement to create a default that is bound to one or more columns. Microsoft recommends using the DEFAULT keyword with ALTER TABLE or CREATE TABLE instead.

Types of Data Integrity

How integrity is enforced depends on the type of integrity being enforced. As described in the following sections, the types of data integrity are domain, entity, and referential integrity.

Domain Integrity

Domain integrity controls the validation of values for a column. You can use domain integrity to enforce the type, format, and possible values of data stored in a column. SQL Server provides several mechanisms to enforce domain integrity:

- ▶ You can control the type of data stored in a column by assigning a data type to the column.

- ▶ You can use CHECK constraints and rules to control the format of the data.

- ▶ You can control the range of values stored in a column by using FOREIGN KEY constraints, CHECK constraints, default definitions, nullability, and rules.

Entity Integrity

Entity integrity requires that all rows in a table be unique. You can enforce entity integrity in SQL Server by using PRIMARY KEY constraints, UNIQUE constraints, and IDENTITY properties.

Referential Integrity

Referential integrity preserves the defined relationships between tables. You can define such a relationship in SQL Server by relating foreign key columns on one table to the primary key or unique key of another table. When it is defined, referential integrity ensures that values inserted in the foreign key columns have corresponding values in the primary table. It also controls changes to the primary key table and ensures that related foreign key rows are not left orphaned.

Enforcing Data Integrity

You can enforce data integrity by using declarative or procedural methods. Implementing declarative data integrity requires little or no coding. Implementing procedural data integrity is more flexible but requires more custom coding.

Implementing Declarative Data Integrity

Declarative integrity is enforced within the database schema, using constraints, rules, and defaults. This is the preferred method of enforcing integrity because it has low overhead and requires little or no custom programming. It can be centrally managed in the database, and it provides a consistent approach for ensuring the integrity of data.

Implementing Procedural Data Integrity

Procedural integrity can be implemented with stored procedures, triggers, and application code. It requires custom programming that defines and enforces the integrity of the data. The biggest benefits of implementing procedural data integrity are flexibility and control. You can implement the custom code in many different ways to enforce the integrity of your data. The custom code can also be a detriment. Any lack of consistency and potential inefficiencies in the way the data integrity is performed can be a real problem.

In general, declarative data integrity should be used as the primary means for control. Procedural data integrity can be used to augment declarative data integrity, if needed.

Using Constraints

Constraints—including PRIMARY KEY, FOREIGN KEY, UNIQUE, CHECK, and DEFAULT—are the primary method used to enforce data integrity. They are relatively easy to implement, and they constrain or limit the values that are allowed in SQL Server tables.

The PRIMARY KEY Constraint

The PRIMARY KEY constraint is one of the key methods for ensuring entity integrity. When this constraint is defined on a table, it ensures that every row can be uniquely identified with the primary key value(s). The primary key can have one or more columns as part of its definition. None of the columns in the primary key definition are allowed to have null values. When multiple columns are used in the definition of the primary key, the combination of the values in all the primary key columns must be unique. Duplication can exist in a single column that is part of a multicolumn primary key as long as the combination of other columns in the key is not duplicated in the tables.

There can be only one primary key defined for each table. When a primary key is defined on a table, a unique index is automatically created as well. This index contains all the columns in the primary key and ensures that the rows in this index are unique. Generally, every table in a database should have a primary key. The primary key and its associated unique index provide fast access to a database table.

Figure 23.1 shows the AdventureWorks2012 database HumanResources.Employee table, which is an example of a table that has a primary key defined. The primary key in this table is BusinessEntityID, and it is denoted in the dialog shown in Figure 23.1 with a key symbol in the leftmost column.

The existing primary key on the Employee table in the AdventureWorks2012 database was generated as a T-SQL script, as shown in the following example:

```
ALTER TABLE [HumanResources].[Employee]
  ADD  CONSTRAINT [PK_Employee_BusinessEntityID] PRIMARY KEY CLUSTERED
(BusinessEntityID ASC)
```

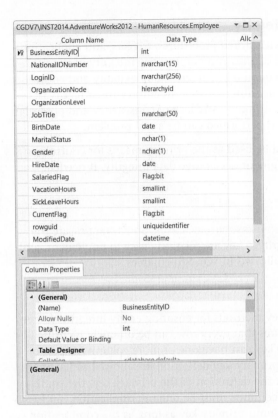

FIGURE 23.1   A primary key example.

NOTE

The example in Figure 23.1 includes the name of the primary key. The name is not required, but if the name of the primary key is not provided, then a unique name will automatically get generated. The problem with the unique name is that it is relatively cryptic and contains numbers at the end of the name to make it unique. This is also true for other types of constraints such as Foreign Keys. In general, always provide a name for your constraints and it will make it much easier to manage your database.

In general, you try to choose a primary key that is relatively short. BusinessEntityID, for example, is a good choice because it is an integer column and takes only 4 bytes of storage. This is particularly important when the primary key is CLUSTERED, as in the case of PK_Employee_BusinessEntityID. The key values from the clustered index are used by all nonclustered indexes as lookup keys. If the clustered key is large, this consumes more space and affects performance.

Surrogate keys are often good choices for primary keys. The BusinessEntityID column in the Person.BusinessEntity table is an example of a surrogate key. Surrogate keys consist of a single column that automatically increments and is inherently unique, as in the case of an identity column. Surrogate keys are good candidates for primary keys because they are implicitly unique and relatively short in length. You should avoid using large, multicolumn indexes as primary keys. They can impede performance because fewer index rows can be stored on each index page. The performance implications related to primary key indexes and other indexes are discussed in more detail in Chapter 32, "Indexes and Performance."

> **NOTE**
>
> Over the years, there has been much debate over the use of surrogate keys for primary keys. One school of thought is to avoid surrogate keys because insertions always occur at the end of the primary key index and are not evenly distributed. This can lead to "hot spots" in the index because the insert activity is always on the last page of the index. In addition, surrogate keys have no real meaning and are less intuitive than primary keys that have meaning, such as `lastname` and `firstname`.
>
> The other school of thought, in favor of using surrogate keys for primary keys, emphasizes the importance of defining primary keys that are not based on meaningful columns. If meaningful columns are used and the definitions of those columns change, this can have a significant impact on the table that contains the primary key and any tables related to it. Those in favor of using surrogate keys as primary keys also focus on the relatively small key size, which is good for performance and reduces page splits because the values are always inserted into the index sequentially.

The UNIQUE Constraint

The UNIQUE constraint is functionally similar to PRIMARY KEY. It also uses a unique index to enforce uniqueness, but unlike PRIMARY KEY, it allows nulls in the columns that participate in the UNIQUE constraint. The definition of a UNIQUE constraint with columns that are nulls is generally impractical. The value of NULL is considered a unique value, so you are limited to the number of rows that can be inserted with NULL values. For example, only one row with a NULL value in the constraint column can be inserted if the UNIQUE constraint is based only on a single column. UNIQUE constraints with multiple nullable columns can have more than one row with null values in the constraint keys, but the number of rows is limited to the combination of unique values across all the columns.

The alternate unique key on the Sales.SalesTaxRate table is a good example of a unique constraint in the AdventureWorks2012 database. The AK_SalesTaxRate_StateProvinceID_TaxType index contains the StateProvinceId and TaxType columns. Each of these columns is defined as NOT NULL. In simple terms this means that the values in the TaxType column must be unique within each state or province. If, however, the StateProvinceID were nullable, then you could have one row for a given TaxType that is null, and then all other rows for that tax type must have the StateProvinceID to make the combination of StateProvinceId and TaxType unique.

You generally use a UNIQUE constraint when a column other than the primary key must be guaranteed to be unique. For example, consider the Employee table example used in the previous section. The primary key on the identity column BusinessEntityID ensures that a unique value will be assigned to each employee row, but it does not prevent duplication in any of the other columns. For example, every row in the Employee table could have the same LoginID setting if no other UNIQUE constraints were found on this table. Generally, each employee should have his or her own unique LoginID. You can enforce this policy by adding a UNIQUE constraint on the LoginID column. The following example demonstrates the creation of a UNIQUE constraint on the LoginID column:

```
ALTER TABLE [HumanResources].[Employee]
 ADD CONSTRAINT AK_Employee_LoginID
  UNIQUE NONCLUSTERED (LoginID ASC)
```

As with PRIMARY KEY constraints, a unique index is created whenever a UNIQUE constraint is created. If you drop the UNIQUE constraint, you drop the unique index as well. Conversely, if you drop the unique index, you indirectly drop the UNIQUE constraint, too. You can implement a UNIQUE constraint as a constraint or an index. To illustrate this, the following example shows the creation of the same UNIQUE constraint on Employee_LoginID as before, this time using an index:

```
CREATE UNIQUE NONCLUSTERED INDEX [AK_Employee_LoginID]
 ON [HumanResources].[Employee]
(LoginID ASC)
```

> **NOTE**
>
> Although UNIQUE constraints and unique indexes achieve the same goal, they must be managed based on how they were created. In other words, if you create a UNIQUE constraint on a table, you cannot directly drop the associated unique index. If you try to drop the unique index directly, you get a message stating that an explicit DROP INDEX is not allowed and that it is being used for unique key constraint enforcement. To drop the UNIQUE constraint, you must use the DROP CONSTRAINT syntax associated with the ALTER TABLE statement. Similarly, if you create a unique index, you cannot drop that index by using a DROP CONSTRAINT statement; you must use DROP INDEX instead.

You can have more than one unique constraint per table. When creating unique constraints, you have all the standard index-creation options available. These options include how the underlying index is clustered, the fill factor, and a myriad of other index options.

The FOREIGN KEY Referential Integrity Constraint

The basic premise of a relational database is that tables are related. These relationships are maintained and enforced via referential integrity. FOREIGN KEY constraints are the declarative means for enforcing referential integrity in SQL Server. You implement FOREIGN KEY constraints by relating one or more columns in a table to the columns in a primary key or unique index. The columns in the referencing table can be referred to as *foreign key columns*. The table with the primary key or unique index can be referred to as the *primary table*. Figure 23.2 shows a relationship between the `BusinessEntityAddress` table and `AddressType` table. The foreign key in this example is `AddressTypeID` on the `BusinessEntityAddress` table. `AddressTypeID` on this table is related to the primary key on the `AddressTypeID` table. The foreign key relationship in this diagram is denoted by the line between these two tables.

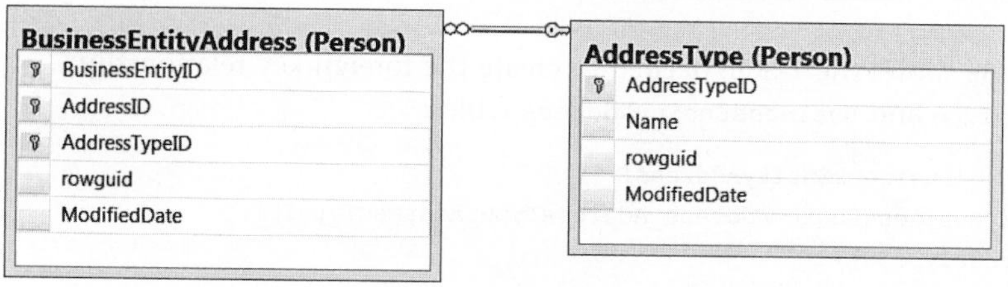

BusinessEntityAddress (Person)
- BusinessEntityID
- AddressID
- AddressTypeID
- rowguid
- ModifiedDate

AddressType (Person)
- AddressTypeID
- Name
- rowguid
- ModifiedDate

FIGURE 23.2   A foreign key constraint on the `BusinessEntityAddress` table.

Once defined, a foreign key, by default, enforces the relationship between the tables in the following ways:

▶ Values in the foreign key columns must have a corresponding value in the primary table. If the new values in the foreign key columns do not exist in the primary table, the insert or update operation fails. Keep in mind that foreign key columns can be defined as nullable so they can contain null values in that situation.

▶ Values in the primary key or unique index that are referenced by the foreign key table cannot be deleted. If an attempt is made to delete a referenced value in the primary table, the delete fails.

▶ Values in the primary key or unique index that are referenced by the foreign key table cannot be modified. If an attempt is made to change a referenced value in the primary table, the update fails.

In the case of the `AddressType/BusinessEntityAddress` relationship shown in Figure 23.2, any `AddressTypeID` used in the `BusinessEntityAddress` table must have a corresponding value in the `AddressType` table. Listing 23.1 shows an `INSERT` statement in the `BusinessEntityAddress` table that does not have a valid `AddressTypeID` entry in the `AddressType` table. The statement fails, and the resulting message is shown after the `INSERT` statement. A similar error message is displayed if an attempt is made to delete or update values in the primary key or unique index that does not satisfy the foreign key constraint.

LISTING 23.1   A Foreign Key Conflict with `INSERT`

```
INSERT Person.BusinessEntityAddress
 (BusinessEntityID,AddressID, AddressTypeID, rowguid, ModifiedDate)
 VALUES (1,249, 9, NEWID(), GETDATE())
/* RESULTS OF INSERT FOLLOW
```

```
Msg 547, Level 16, State 0, Line 1
The INSERT statement conflicted with the FOREIGN KEY
constraint "FK_BusinessEntityAddress_AddressType_AddressTypeID".
The conflict occurred in database "AdventureWorks2012",
table "Person.AddressType", column 'AddressTypeID'.
The statement has been terminated.*/
```

The following example shows the T-SQL needed to create the foreign key relationship between the AddressType and BusinessEntityAddress tables:

```
ALTER TABLE [Person].[BusinessEntityAddress]
ADD  CONSTRAINT [FK_BusinessEntityAddress_AddressType_AddressTypeID]
  FOREIGN KEY([AddressTypeID])
REFERENCES [Person].[AddressType]
([AddressTypeID])
```

When you create a FOREIGN KEY constraint, the related primary key or unique index must exist first. In the case of the AddressType/BusinessEntityAddress relationship, the AddressType table and primary key on AddressTypeID must exist before you can create the FK_BusinessEntityAddress_AddressType_AddressTypeID foreign key. In addition, the data types of the related columns must be the same. The related columns in the two tables can actually have different names, but in practice the columns are usually named the same. Naming the columns the same makes your database much more intuitive.

NOTE

In addition to relating two different tables with a foreign key, you can also relate a table to itself. These self-referencing relationships are often found in organization tables or employee tables. For example, you could have an Employee table with a primary key of BusinessEntityID. This table could also have a ManagerID column. In this case, ManagerID on the Employee table has a relationship to the primary key index on BusinessEntityID. The manager is an employee, so it makes sense that they should have a valid BusinessEntityID. A foreign key on the Employee table will enforce this relationship and ensure that any ManagerID points to a different row in the table with a valid BusinessEntityID.

Cascading Referential Integrity

Cascading referential integrity has been around for some time and was introduced with SQL Server 2000. This type of integrity allows for updates and deletions on the primary table to be cascaded to the referencing foreign key tables. By default, a FOREIGN KEY constraint prevents updates and deletions to any primary key or unique index values referenced by a foreign key. With cascading referential integrity, you can bypass this restriction and are able to define the type of action you want to occur when the updates and deletions happen.

You define the cascading actions on the FOREIGN KEY constraint, using the ON DELETE and ON UPDATE clauses. The ON DELETE clause defines the cascading action for deletions to the primary table, and the ON UPDATE clause defines the actions for updates. These clauses are used with the CREATE TABLE or ALTER TABLE statements and are part of the REFERENCES clause of these statements.

You can specify the same cascading actions for updates and deletions:

▶ **NO ACTION**—This action, the default, causes deletions and updates to the primary table to fail if the rows are referenced by a foreign key.

▶ **CASCADE**—This option causes updates and deletions to cascade to any foreign key records that refer to the affected rows in the primary table. If the CASCADE option is used with the ON DELETE clause, any records in the foreign key table that refer to the deleted rows in the primary table are also deleted. When CASCADE is used with the ON UPDATE clause, any updates to the primary table records are also made in the related rows of the foreign key table.

▶ **SET NULL**—This option is similar to the CASCADE option except that the affected rows in the foreign key table are set to NULL when deletions or updates are performed on the related primary table. The value of NULL is assigned to every column that is defined as part of the foreign key and requires that each column in the foreign key allow null values.

▶ **SET DEFAULT**—This option is similar to the CASCADE option except that the affected rows in the foreign key table are set to the default values defined on the columns when deletions or updates are performed on the related primary table. If you want to set this option, each column in the foreign key must have a default definition assigned to it, or it must be defined as nullable. If no default definition is assigned to the column, NULL is used as the default value. It is imperative that the primary table have related records for the default entries that can result from the cascading action. For example, if you have a two-column foreign key, and each column has a default of 1, a corresponding record with the key values of 1 and 1 needs to exist in the primary table, or the cascade action fails. The integrity of the relationship must be maintained.

To illustrate the power of cascading actions, consider the AddressType/BusinessEntity Address relationship used in previous examples. Let's say you want to remove the associated BusinessEntityAddress records when an AddressType record is deleted. The addition of the ON DELETE CASCADE clause at the bottom of the following foreign key definition achieves this result:

```
ALTER TABLE [Person].[BusinessEntityAddress]
ADD  CONSTRAINT [FK_BusinessEntityAddress_AddressType_AddressTypeID]
  FOREIGN KEY([AddressTypeID])
REFERENCES [Person].[AddressType]
([AddressTypeID])
ON DELETE CASCADE
```

23

Keep in mind that other factors affect the successful execution of a cascading deletion. If other foreign keys exist on the table, and they do not have ON DELETE CASCADE specified, the cascading actions do not succeed if a foreign key violation occurs on these tables. In addition, you need to consider the existence of triggers that may prevent deletions from occurring. Finally, you need to consider that a series of cascading actions can be initiated by a single DELETE statement. This happens when you have many related tables, each of which has cascading actions defined. This approach works fine as long as there are no circular references that cause one of the tables in the cascading tree to be affected by a table lower in the tree.

If you want to specify the cascading action for updates, you can add an additional ON UPDATE clause, along with the ON DELETE clause. For example, you can change the foreign key in the previous example so that BusinessEntityAddress records are set to NULL when an update is made to the related key on the primary table. This can be accomplished with the following foreign key definition:

```
ALTER TABLE [Person].[BusinessEntityAddress]
ADD  CONSTRAINT [FK_BusinessEntityAddress_AddressType_AddressTypeID]
  FOREIGN KEY([AddressTypeID])
REFERENCES [Person].[AddressType]
([AddressTypeID])
ON DELETE CASCADE
 ON UPDATE SET NULL
```

You can see that cascading referential integrity is a powerful tool. However, it must be used with caution. Consider the fact that foreign keys without cascading actions may prevent erroneous actions. For example, if a DELETE statement is mistakenly executed against the entire AddressType table, the deletion would fail before the records could be deleted because foreign key tables are referencing the AddressType table. This failure would be a good thing. If, however, the ON DELETE CASCADE clause were used in the foreign key definitions, the erroneous deletion would succeed, and all the foreign key records would be deleted as well.

The CHECK Constraint

You can use the CHECK constraint to enforce domain integrity and to provide a means for restricting the values that can be entered in a column. A CHECK constraint is implemented as a Boolean expression, and it must not be FALSE if the insertion or update is to proceed. The Boolean expression can reference other columns in the same table, but it cannot reference other tables. Foreign keys and triggers can be used to reference columns in other tables, if needed. The expression can also include functions that do not return results. A CHECK constraint that is defined on a specific column can reference only the values in the column.

CHECK constraints are good for ensuring the format of data inserted in a column and for defining a list of acceptable values. Columns with phone numbers or Social Security numbers are good candidates for CHECK constraints that enforce formatting restrictions. Columns that have the data types money or integer can use CHECK constraints to ensure that the values are always greater than or equal to zero. A column that has a small fixed number of valid values is also a good candidate for a CHECK constraint. A fixed number of values can be defined in the CHECK constraint, and no additional table lookup or coding is necessary to ensure that the valid values are inserted. The following example shows a CHECK constraint on the Employee table that checks the values for the Gender column:

```
ALTER TABLE [HumanResources].[Employee]  WITH CHECK
  ADD  CONSTRAINT [CK_Employee_Gender]
  CHECK  ((upper([Gender])='F' OR upper([Gender])='M'))
```

The CHECK constraint in this example ensures that only F or M is inserted in this column. These types of CHECK constraints are relatively fast and are preferred over FOREIGN KEY constraints when the values are fixed.

> **NOTE**
>
> Be careful with CHECK constraint expressions that can evaluate to NULL. CHECK constraints allow insertions and updates to the table to proceed when the CHECK constraint expression does not evaluate to FALSE. A NULL value is considered to be unknown and does not evaluate to FALSE, so the insertion or update succeeds. For example, if you have a nullable column that has a constraint specifying that the value must be greater than or equal to zero, this constraint does not prevent a NULL value from being inserted into the column.

Keep in mind that the creation of a CHECK constraint on a table that already has data in it may fail. This is due to a validation performed when the constraint is created. If existing data violates the constraint, the constraint is not created. The only exception is to create the constraint by using the NOCHECK option. When this option is used, the existing data is not checked, but any future updates or insertions are. The following example shows the creation of a CHECK constraint on the Employee table:

```
ALTER TABLE [HumanResources].[Employee]  WITH NOCHECK
ADD  CONSTRAINT [CK_Employee_Gender_F]
CHECK  ((upper([Gender])='F'))
```

The constraint is on the Gender column that already has a check constraint on it, which ensures that the data values are only F or M. The new constraint on the Gender column specifies that the value must be F. The existing data has values of F and M, but the NOCHECK option allows you to add the constraint anyway.

Any new rows added to the Employee table after the new CK_Employee_Gender_F CHECK constraint has been added are then checked. With multiple CHECK constraints defined on a column, the constraints are evaluated in the order in which they were added to the table. In the preceding example, the CK_Employee_Gender constraint is evaluated first, and then the new CK_Employee_Gender_F constraint is evaluated. If a Gender value of F is entered, both constraints evaluate to TRUE, and the change is accepted. If a value of M is inserted in the Gender column, the CK_Employee_Gender constraint succeeds, but the CK_Employee_Gender_F constraint fails, and the change is rejected.

23

Creating Constraints

You can define constraints on a single column or on multiple columns. Single-column constraints are referred to as *column-level* constraints. You can define this type of constraint when you create the column on the table. Constraints that reference multiple columns must be defined on the table and are considered *table-level* constraints. Table-level constraints must be defined after all the referenced columns in the table are created.

Using T-SQL to Create Constraints

You can create constraints with T-SQL by using the CREATE TABLE or ALTER TABLE statement. When you create a column-level constraint by using the CREATE TABLE statement, the CONSTRAINT keyword and constraint definition are included immediately after the column definition. Table-level constraints defined with the CREATE TABLE statement are specified after the column list in the table definition.

The Customer table in the AdventureWorks2012 database is a good example of a table that has several different types of constraints. Listing 23.2 shows the CREATE TABLE command, along with the constraint definitions for a table named Customer2 that is modeled after the Customer table. All the constraints in this example have been included in the CREATE TABLE statement. The constraints on this table include PRIMARY KEY, FOREIGN KEY, and CHECK constraints. You can find all the constraints in the CREATE TABLE statement by looking for the CONSTRAINT keyword.

LISTING 23.2   Creating Constraints by Using a CREATE TABLE Statement

```
CREATE TABLE [Sales].[Customer2](
    [CustomerID] [int] IDENTITY(1,1) NOT FOR REPLICATION NOT NULL,
    [TerritoryID] [int] NULL,
    [AccountNumber]  AS
        (isnull('AW'+[dbo].[ufnLeadingZeros]([CustomerID]),'')),
    [CustomerType] [nchar](1) NOT NULL
        CONSTRAINT CK_Customer_CustomerType2 CHECK
        ((upper([CustomerType])='I' OR upper([CustomerType])='S')),
    [rowguid] [uniqueidentifier] ROWGUIDCOL  NOT NULL
        CONSTRAINT [DF_Customer_rowguid2]  DEFAULT (newid()),
    [ModifiedDate] [datetime] NOT NULL
        CONSTRAINT [DF_Customer_ModifiedDate2]  DEFAULT (getdate()),
  CONSTRAINT [PK_Customer_CustomerID2] PRIMARY KEY CLUSTERED
    ([CustomerID] ASC),
  CONSTRAINT FK_Customer_SalesTerritory_TerritoryID2 FOREIGN KEY
    ([TerritoryID])
    REFERENCES [Sales].[SalesTerritory] ([TerritoryID])
)
GO
```

Generally, it is easier to manage constraints by using the ALTER TABLE statement than by integrating them into the CREATE TABLE statement. One of the biggest reasons is that the scripting capability in SQL Server Management Studio (SSMS) generates ALTER TABLE statements for many of the constraints. You can easily script a table and its constraints by using SSMS, and you will find that SSMS uses the ALTER TABLE statement extensively. Listing 23.3 includes a statement to remove the Customer2 table and a subsequent set of statements that re-creates the Customer2 table and utilizes the ALTER TABLE statement to create several of the constraints. The statements to re-create the Customer2 table were generated using the Object Explorer in SSMS. Some of the constraints are created within the initial CREATE TABLE statement, and some are created with the ALTER TABLE statement.

LISTING 23.3   Creating Constraints by Using ALTER TABLE

```
IF  EXISTS (SELECT * FROM dbo.sysobjects WHERE id
   = OBJECT_ID(N'[Sales].[Customer2]') AND OBJECTPROPERTY(id, N'IsUserTable') = 1)
 DROP TABLE [Sales].[Customer2]
go


CREATE TABLE [Sales].[Customer2](
   [CustomerID] [int] IDENTITY(1,1) NOT FOR REPLICATION NOT NULL,
   [TerritoryID] [int] NULL,
   [AccountNumber]  AS (isnull('AW'+[dbo].[ufnLeadingZeros]([CustomerID]),'')),
   [CustomerType] [nchar](1) COLLATE SQL_Latin1_General_CP1_CI_AS NOT NULL,
   [rowguid] [uniqueidentifier] ROWGUIDCOL  NOT NULL
    CONSTRAINT [DF_Customer_rowguid2]  DEFAULT (newid()),
   [ModifiedDate] [datetime] NOT NULL
    CONSTRAINT [DF_Customer_ModifiedDate2]  DEFAULT (getdate()),
 CONSTRAINT [PK_Customer_CustomerID2] PRIMARY KEY CLUSTERED
(
   [CustomerID] ASC
) ON [PRIMARY]
) ON [PRIMARY]


GO
ALTER TABLE [Sales].[Customer2]  WITH CHECK
 ADD  CONSTRAINT [FK_Customer_SalesTerritory_TerritoryID2]
  FOREIGN KEY(   [TerritoryID])
   REFERENCES [Sales].[SalesTerritory] (   [TerritoryID])
GO
ALTER TABLE [Sales].[Customer2]  WITH CHECK
 ADD  CONSTRAINT [CK_Customer_CustomerType2]
  CHECK  ((upper([CustomerType])='I' OR upper([CustomerType])='S'))
```

Using SSMS to Create Constraints

Most of the examples used so far in this chapter use T-SQL to demonstrate constraints. SSMS simplifies the administration of constraints by providing a user-friendly interface that allows you to view and manage constraints. The visual tools available for managing constraints in SSMS include the Object Explorer, Database Diagram Editor, and Table Designer.

Figure 23.3 shows the Object Explorer with the Constraints node expanded for the Employee table and the New Constraint option selected. The Constraints node contains the CHECK and DEFAULT constraints for the table. Notice in the Object Explorer that some of the constraints (PRIMARY KEY, UNIQUE, and FOREIGN KEY) are actually contained under the Keys node.

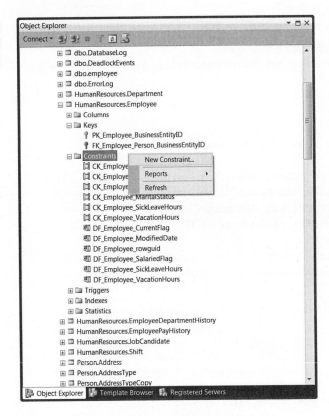

FIGURE 23.3   Constraints in Object Explorer.

When you select the New Constraint option from the Object Explorer, the Check Constraints dialog, shown in Figure 23.4, appears. This dialog gives you the option to define a new CHECK constraint on the table selected. You simply fill in a valid expression for the constraint, give it a unique name, and select the options you want.

Similarly, you can right-click the Keys node and select New Foreign Key to add a new FOREIGN KEY constraint. Figure 23.5 shows the Foreign Key Relationships dialog displayed after you select New Foreign Key. You click the ellipsis to the right of Tables and Columns Specification, and you can select the primary key table you want the foreign key to relate to. Finally, you select the desired options, and you are ready to add your new FOREIGN KEY constraint.

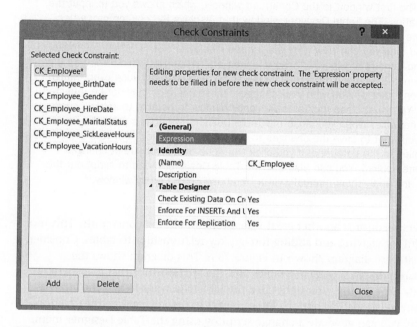

FIGURE 23.4   A new CHECK constraint in Object Explorer.

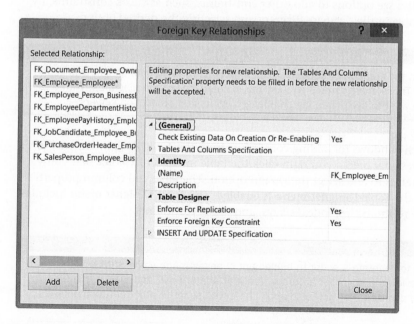

FIGURE 23.5   A new FOREIGN KEY constraint in Object Explorer.

When you use the Object Explorer to add or modify constraints, two windows are important to this process. The first window is the Constraint window, which allows you to input the constraint information. The Table Designer window that displays the column properties for the table is the other window that is important to the change process. It is launched in the background, and you can view it on the tabbed display of SSMS. When you make changes using the Constraint window, those changes are not applied via SSMS until the Table Designer window is closed. This may cause some confusion because even though you close your Constraint window with your changes, those changes may not be reflected in the database. You must close the Table Designer window to be able to actually make the changes to the table. When you close the Table Designer window, a prompt appears, asking whether you want to save the changes to the table. If you click Yes, your constraint changes are applied to the database. If you click No, none of the constraint changes you have made are applied. You can also use the Table Designer menu to script out the related changes and apply them manually via a Database Engine query window.

The Database Diagram Editor is another great visual tool for adding constraints. This tool is particularly useful for viewing and adding foreign key relationships to tables. Consider, for example, the database diagram shown in Figure 23.6. This diagram shows the `AddressType` and `BusinessEntityAddress` tables and the relationships that exist between them. To add a new relationship, you right-click the table you want to add the foreign key to and select the Relationships option. After you fill in the appropriate information for the relationship, you can generate a change script by using the Table Designer menu, or you can simply close the database diagram window and respond to the prompt to save changes. You can also see options to add other constraints, such as CHECK constraints, by right-clicking the table in the database diagram and selecting the desired option.

Keep in mind that the creation of database diagrams does render some simple changes to the database. These changes help support the maintenance of the diagrams. With this in mind, you may want to avoid creating database diagrams on production servers.

You can also launch windows for adding constraints from the Table Designer menu. To enable the Table Designer menu, you right-click the table in Object Explorer that you want to add constraints to and select the Design option. The table and column properties are displayed, and the Table Designer menu is enabled. The Table Designer menu includes options to manage relationships, indexes/keys, and CHECK constraints.

It is a good idea to generate a script to implement changes made using SSMS visual tools. You can review the script for accuracy, run it at a later time, and save it in a file to keep track of the changes. You can also apply the saved script to other environments if needed.

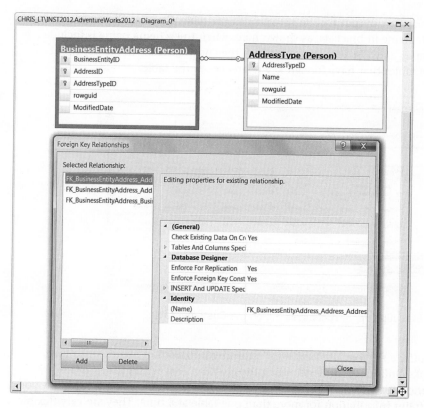

FIGURE 23.6   Adding constraints by using a database diagram.

Managing Constraints

Managing constraints consists of gathering information about constraints, disabling and re-enabling constraints, and dropping constraints. These actions are discussed in the following sections.

Gathering Constraint Information

You can obtain information about constraints by using the visual tools, system stored procedures, and `information_schema` views. The visual tools (including the Object Explorer, Table Designer, and database diagrams) were introduced in the previous section. These tools offer a simple, user-friendly means for obtaining information related to constraints. These tools allow you to view a table's constraints and display the relative information.

The `sp_help` and `sp_helpconstraint` system stored procedures are another good source of information about constraints. Like the visual tools, these procedures allow you to gather constraint information about a specific table. The `sp_helpconstraint` procedure provides the most concise information related to constraints. Figure 23.7 shows the `sp_helpconstraint` output for the `Sales.Customer` table. You need to make sure to enclose the table name in brackets, as shown here, when the schema name is included. The output from `sp_helpconstraint` includes all the constraints for the table, and it supplies a list of tables that have foreign key references to the table.

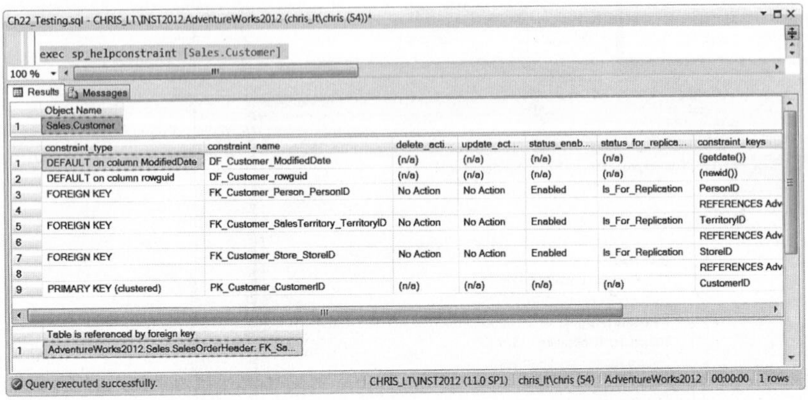

FIGURE 23.7   Executing `sp_helpconstraint` on the Customer table.

Catalog views offer a flexible alternative for returning information about constraints. SQL Server Books Online recommends using the `sys.key_constraints`, `sys.check_constraints`, and `sys.default_constraints` catalog views. These catalog views allow you to obtain constraint information for more than one table at a time. They are very flexible and allow you to customize the type of data you want to return simply by adjusting the selection criterion.

Listing 23.4 shows a sample `SELECT` statement for each of the catalog views related to constraints and the resulting output. The `SELECT` statements in this example have a `WHERE` clause in them that limits the results to the `SalesTax` table, but you can remove this clause to retrieve constraints for all the tables.

LISTING 23.4   Using Catalog Views to Display Constraint Information

```
select LEFT(name,30) NAME, type from sys.key_constraints
    where object_name(parent_object_id) = 'SalesTaxRate'
    order by 1

select LEFT(name,30) NAME, type from sys.check_constraints
    where object_name(parent_object_id) = 'SalesTaxRate'
    order by 1

select LEFT(name,30) NAME, type from sys.default_constraints
    where object_name(parent_object_id) = 'SalesTaxRate'
    order by 1
```

```
INSERT Sales.Customer
 (TerritoryID, CustomerType)
 SELECT TOP 1 TerritoryID, null
  from Sales.SalesTerritory
```

The insertion in this example succeeds, and the null value is stored in the `CustomerType` column that has a default defined on it.

To remove a declarative default constraint, you use `ALTER TABLE` with the `DROP CONSTRAINT` clause. The following example removes the `DF_Customer_CustomerType` constraint from the `Sales.Customer` table:

```
ALTER TABLE Sales.Customer DROP CONSTRAINT DF_Customer_CustomerType
```

Bound Defaults

Bound defaults are similar to rules in that you first create a bound default and then bind it to a column or set of columns. Bound defaults are also similar to rules in that they are slated for removal in a future version of SQL Server. This section covers the basics of bound defaults, but you should keep in mind that Microsoft recommends you avoid using them for new development work.

You use the `CREATE DEFAULT` command to establish a default that can be bound to a column at a later time. The `CREATE DEFAULT` syntax is as follows:

```
CREATE DEFAULT [ schema_name . ] default_name
AS constant_expression [ ; ]
```

`constant_expression` can include any constant, built-in function, or mathematical expression. It cannot include user-defined functions. Character and data values that are part of the expression should be enclosed in single quotation marks. Monetary, integer, and floating-point constants do not require the single quotation marks.

The following example creates a default named `password_df` that can be used to supply a default password for any password-oriented columns:

```
CREATE DEFAULT password_df AS 'defaultpw'
```

After you create a default, you can bind it to a column. The following example binds the `password_df` default to the `passwordSalt` column on the `person.password` table:

```
sp_bindefault password_df, 'person.password.PasswordSalt'
```

As you can see, a bound default appears to require an extra step, but after it is created, it offers an advantage: You can bind it to other columns. This capability provides some consistency across all the columns that the default is bound to and reduces the overall number of database objects.

When a Default Is Applied

Defaults are applied only when no value is specified for a column during an insertion. They can also be applied during insertions and updates when the DEFAULT keyword is used. To demonstrate the application of defaults, consider the following examples:

```
CREATE TABLE test_default
(id int IDENTITY NOT NULL,
 tmstmp timestamp NOT NULL,
 password char(13) NOT NULL DEFAULT 'defaultpw',
 Shortdesc VARCHAR(50) NULL)
```

The table in this example has a unique characteristic: each column has some sort of default value associated with it. One column has a default of NULL because it is nullable. The IDENTITY and TIMESTAMP columns automatically generate values because of their data type, and the password column has an explicit default definition. In this scenario, you can supply the keywords DEFAULT VALUES in the INSERT statement to insert a row of data, as shown in the following example:

```
INSERT test_default DEFAULT VALUES
select * from test_default
/* results from previous select statement
id            tmstmp              password        Shortdesc
----------    ------------------  -------------   -------------------------
1             0x00000000000007D1  defaultpw       NULL
*/
```

You can see from the results of the SELECT statement in this example that a row was inserted in the new table, and this row includes default values for all the columns. If you want to supply values for some of the columns and allow the defaults to be used for other columns, you can simply exclude the columns with defaults from the column listing in the INSERT statement. The following example demonstrates how to do this:

```
INSERT test_default (ShortDesc)
 VALUES('test default insertion')
SELECT * FROM test_default
 where ShortDesc = 'test default insertion'

/* results from previous select statement
id  tmstmp              password    Shortdesc
--- ------------------  ----------  -----------------------
2   0x00000000000007D2  defaultpw   test default insertion
*/
```

The DEFAULT keyword can also be listed explicitly in the VALUE listing of the INSERT statement, as shown in the following example:

```
INSERT test_default (tmstmp, password, ShortDesc)
 VALUES(DEFAULT, DEFAULT, DEFAULT)
SELECT * FROM test_default where id = @@identity
/*
(1 row(s) affected)
id  tmstmp              password       Shortdesc
--- ------------------- -------------- ----------
3   0x00000000000007D5 defaultpw      NULL
*/
```

All the examples so far have dealt with INSERT statements, but there is one scenario in which a default value can be applied with an UPDATE statement. This scenario is similar to the preceding example and requires the use of the DEFAULT keyword. The following example demonstrates the use of the DEFAULT keyword in an UPDATE statement:

```
UPDATE top (1) test_default
 SET PASSWORD = DEFAULT
GO
SELECT top 1 * from test_default
/*
id          tmstmp              password       Shortdesc
----------- ------------------- -------------- -----------
1           0x00000000000007DE defaultpw      NULL
*/
```

Keep in mind that default values are not used for updates unless the DEFAULT keyword is explicitly referenced in the SET clause of the UPDATE statement.

Restrictions on Defaults

When creating defaults, you need to keep in mind the following restrictions:

▶ A default cannot be created on columns that have been defined with TIMESTAMP, IDENTITY, or ROWGUIDCOL properties.

▶ Only one default can be assigned to a given column. This restriction applies to both declarative and bound defaults.

▶ Only one default can exist per column.

▶ The default value must be compatible with the data type of the column.

▶ A default that is bound cannot be dropped if the default is currently bound to a column. The default must be unbound from the column first.

▶ The expression in a default cannot include the names of any columns or other database objects.

There are also some considerations related to the interaction of rules, defaults, and constraints:

▶ If a column has both a rule and default, the default is not inserted if it violates the rules.

▶ If a default value violates a CHECK constraint, the default is not inserted. Ultimately, all the rules, defaults, and constraints that are active are validated. If the change to the data violates any of them, it is rejected.

Summary

This chapter covers the basic tools you can use to ensure the integrity of the data in a database. The integrity of data is directly related to its value; remember the concept of "garbage in, garbage out." If you take the time to implement the constraints and other methods discussed in this chapter, you provide a solid foundation for the storage of data and avoid the headaches related to dealing with "garbage" data.

Chapter 24, "Creating and Managing Views," discusses a means for virtually accessing the data in tables. Virtual tables, or views, allow you to selectively choose the data elements on one or more tables that you want to present as a single window into your data.

Creating and Managing Views

V iews offer a window into your data that does not require physical storage. They are essentially virtual tables that are defined by a SELECT statement. This chapter describes the benefits and advantages of these powerful database objects.

What's New in Creating and Managing Views

Much of the core functionality associated with standard views has remained unchanged in SQL Server 2014.

Definition of Views

Views are a logical way of viewing data in the underlying physical tables. They are tied to a SELECT statement that retrieves data from one or more tables or views in the same database or a different database. In most cases, no physical storage of data is associated with the view, and the SELECT that is associated with the view is run dynamically whenever the view is referenced.

The following T-SQL statement can be used to create a simple view in the AdventureWorks2012 database:

```
CREATE VIEW [dbo].[vw_CustomerAddress]
AS
SELECT    Sales.Customer.CustomerID, Sales.Customer.AccountNumber,
 Person.Address.AddressLine1,
 Person.Address.StateProvinceID, Person.Address.City,
 Person.Address.PostalCode
FROM Sales.Customer
 INNER JOIN Person.Person
  ON Sales.Customer.PersonID = Person.Person.BusinessEntityID
 INNER JOIN Person.BusinessEntityAddress
  ON Person.Person.BusinessEntityID = Person.BusinessEntityAddress.BusinessEntityID
  INNER JOIN Person.Address    ON Person.BusinessEntityAddress.AddressID = Person.
Address.AddressID
```

The `vw_CustomerAddress` view in this example selects from four different tables in the `AdventureWorks2012` database: `Sales.Customer`, `Person.Person`, `Person.Business EntityAddress`, and `Person.Address`. After the view is created, it can be used in the FROM clause of another SELECT statement. The following data-retrieval example uses the newly created view:

```
select c.AccountNumber, s.OrderDate, c.city , c.StateProvinceId
  from vw_CustomerAddress c
    INNER JOIN Sales.SalesOrderHeader s
    ON c.CustomerID = s.CustomerID
 WHERE StateProvinceId = 14
  AND s.OrderDate = '9/21/05'
 ORDER BY c.city
```

```
AccountNumber OrderDate                 city              StateProvinceId
AW00011333    2005-09-21 00:00:00.000   Newcastle upon Tyne 14
AW00020060    2005-09-21 00:00:00.000   Runcorn             14
```

You can see from the sample SELECT that the view is treated much like a table that is referenced in a SELECT statement. The view can be joined to other tables, individual columns from the view can be selected, and those columns can be included in the ORDER BY clause. All the retrieval is done dynamically when the view is referenced, and the underlying tables that are part of the view definition are implicitly accessed without the need to know the underlying structure of the view.

Using Views

Views are useful in many scenarios. Some of the most common scenarios include the following:

- ▶ Simplifying data manipulation

- ▶ Focusing on specific data

- ▶ Abstracting data

- ▶ Controlling access to data

Simplifying Data Manipulation

Views can be used to simplify data access. Common queries that utilize complex joins, UNION queries, and more involved SQL can be defined as views. This minimizes the amount of complex code that must be written or rewritten and provides a simple way of organizing your common data access.

SQL Server 2014 comes with a set of system views that demonstrate the views' capability to mask complex queries and simplify data manipulation. These system views include catalog views, information schema views, and compatibility views. In many cases, the definition of these views is hidden, but some of them can be analyzed using the sp_helptext system procedure. For example, sys.triggers, a catalog view defined in SQL Server 2014, has the following definition associated with it:

```
CREATE VIEW sys.triggers AS
  SELECT o.name,
         object_id = o.id,
         parent_class = o.pclass,
         parent_class_desc = pc.name,
         parent_id = o.pid,
         type = o.type,
         type_desc = n.name,
         create_date = o.created,
         modify_date = o.modified,
         is_ms_shipped = sysconv(bit, o.status & 1),        -- OBJALL_MSSHIPPED
         is_disabled = sysconv(bit, o.status & 256),        -- OBJTRG_DISABLED
         is_not_for_replication = sysconv(bit, o.status & 512),  -- OBJTRG_NOTFORREPL
         is_instead_of_trigger = sysconv(bit, o.status & 1024)   -- OBJTRG_INSTEADOF
  FROM sys.sysschobjs o
  LEFT JOIN sys.syspalnames n ON n.class = 'OBTY' AND n.value = o.type
  LEFT JOIN sys.syspalvalues pc ON pc.class = 'UNCL' AND pc.value = o.pclass
  WHERE o.type IN ('TA','TR') AND o.pclass <> 100 -- x_eunc_Server
        AND has_access('TR', o.id, o.pid, o.nsclass) = 1
```

To select the relevant data from the sys.triggers view, you need only reference the columns in the view that are of interest, and the complexity of the view is hidden. The following query demonstrates the simplicity of a SELECT statement against the sys.triggers view:

24

```
select name, type, create_date
 from sys.triggers
 where name like 'i%'
```

You can see from the `sys.triggers` example why the folks at Microsoft are big proponents of views. Complex queries such as the `sys.triggers` view can be written and tested once, and subsequent data retrieval can be accomplished by selecting from the view.

Focusing on Specific Data

Views allow users or developers to focus on the specific data elements they need to work with. Tables that contain hundreds of columns or columns that have limited value for the end user can be filtered with a view such that only the relevant data elements are returned. Views can also filter the rows of data that are returned. This can be particularly useful for tables that have a large number of rows. The View can contain a WHERE clause that limits the number of rows that are returned.

The `HumanResources.vEmployee` view in the `AdventureWorks2012` database is a good example of a view that focuses on specific data and simplifies data access. The view definition follows:

```
CREATE VIEW [HumanResources].[vEmployee]
AS
SELECT
     e.[BusinessEntityID]
    ,p.[Title]
    ,p.[FirstName]
    ,p.[MiddleName]
    ,p.[LastName]
    ,p.[Suffix]
    ,e.[JobTitle]
    ,pp.[PhoneNumber]
    ,pnt.[Name] AS [PhoneNumberType]
    ,ea.[EmailAddress]
    ,p.[EmailPromotion]
    ,a.[AddressLine1]
    ,a.[AddressLine2]
    ,a.[City]
    ,sp.[Name] AS [StateProvinceName]
    ,a.[PostalCode]
    ,cr.[Name] AS [CountryRegionName]
    ,p.[AdditionalContactInfo]
FROM [HumanResources].[Employee] e
    INNER JOIN [Person].[Person] p
    ON p.[BusinessEntityID] = e.[BusinessEntityID]
    INNER JOIN [Person].[BusinessEntityAddress] bea
    ON bea.[BusinessEntityID] = e.[BusinessEntityID]
```

```
INNER JOIN [Person].[Address] a
ON a.[AddressID] = bea.[AddressID]
INNER JOIN [Person].[StateProvince] sp
ON sp.[StateProvinceID] = a.[StateProvinceID]
INNER JOIN [Person].[CountryRegion] cr
ON cr.[CountryRegionCode] = sp.[CountryRegionCode]
LEFT OUTER JOIN [Person].[PersonPhone] pp
ON pp.BusinessEntityID = p.[BusinessEntityID]
LEFT OUTER JOIN [Person].[PhoneNumberType] pnt
ON pp.[PhoneNumberTypeID] = pnt.[PhoneNumberTypeID]
LEFT OUTER JOIN [Person].[EmailAddress] ea
ON p.[BusinessEntityID] = ea.[BusinessEntityID];
```

The `HumanResources.vEmployee` view filters out much of the data that is sensitive or superfluous when gathering the basic information about an employee.

Abstracting Data

Data abstraction, in its simplest form, isolates the client code from changes to the underlying structure. A view can be used to implement data abstraction within your database schema. If, for example, you have client code that will retrieve data from a database table that is likely to change, you can implement a view that retrieves data from the underlying table. The client code can then reference the view and never refer to the underlying table directly. If the underlying tables change or the source of the data for the view changes, these changes can be isolated from the referencing client code.

To demonstrate this scenario, let's look at the following SELECT statement, which retrieves data directly from the `Sales.SalesOrderHeader` table:

```
select TerritoryID, sum(TotalDue)
 from Sales.SalesOrderHeader
  group by TerritoryID
order by TerritoryID
```

The client code could certainly utilize this kind of query to retrieve the territory data. You may find, however, that the data retrieval would be better placed within a view if the summarized territory data were slated to be rolled up into an aggregate table at a later time. In this scenario, a view like the following could be created initially:

```
CREATE VIEW vw_TerritoryOrders AS
select TerritoryID, sum(TotalDue) 'TotalSales'
 from Sales.SalesOrderHeader
  group by TerritoryID
```

The client code that needs the territory data would then reference the `vw_TerritoryOrders` view. If the source of the territory data changes and it is rolled up in an aggregate table, the view can be changed to reflect the new source for the data, but the client code remains unchanged. The following example alters the `vw_TerritoryOrders` view such that the source of the data is changed to use an aggregate table:

```
ALTER VIEW vw_TerritoryOrders AS
select TerritoryID, SalesYTD 'TotalSales'
 from Sales.SalesTerritory
```

Changing a single view in these types of scenarios can be much easier than changing the client code that has direct references to the table. This type of abstraction also applies to partitioned views, which are discussed later in this chapter.

Controlling Access to Data

Views can be used as a security mechanism to limit a user's access to specific data. This type of view security can be used to limit the columns or the rows that the user has access to. A view that limits the accessible columns can be referred to as *vertical security*, or *column-level security*. A view that restricts the rows that are returned is referred to as *horizontal security*, or *row-level security*.

With vertical security, a view is created that contains only the data elements or columns that you want to make visible. Columns that are sensitive in nature (for example, payroll data) can be excluded from a view so that they are not seen when the user selects from the view.

After the view is created, security can be granted on the view. If the owner of the objects referenced in the view is the same as the owner of the view itself, the user who is granted permission to the view does not need to have permission granted to the underlying objects. Listing 24.1 gives an example of this scenario.

LISTING 24.1   Security with Views

```
USE AdventureWorks2012
go
CREATE LOGIN OwnerLogin WITH PASSWORD = 'pw'
CREATE USER OwnerLogin FOR LOGIN OwnerLogin
EXEC sp_addrolemember N'db_owner', N'OwnerLogin'

CREATE LOGIN NonOwnerLogin WITH PASSWORD = 'pw'
CREATE USER NonOwnerLogin FOR LOGIN NonOwnerLogin

--Connect as the OwnerLogin at this point
Go

CREATE VIEW OwnerView as
  select LoginID, JobTitle, BirthDate, Gender, HireDate, SalariedFlag
   from HumanResources.Employee go
```

```
GRANT SELECT ON [dbo].[OwnerView] TO [NonOwnerLogin]

--Connect as the NonOwnerLogin at this point

--The following select succeeds because the owner of the
--view that was granted permission is the same as the underlying
--table in the view
select * from OwnerView

--The following SELECT against the underlying table fails
--because the NonOwnerLogin does not have permission to
--select from the table.  He can only select through the view
select * from HumanResources.Employee
```

Listing 24.1 outlines a scenario where one login creates a view that selects specific columns from the `HumanResources.Employee` table. The `Employee` table is part of the `HumanResources` schema, and it is owned by DBO. The view that is created is also owned by DBO because the login (`OwnerLogin`) that created the view is a member of the db_owner role. Ultimately, `NonOwnerLogin` is granted permission to the view. When the `NonOwnerLogin` user connects to the database, that user can select rows from the view and will see only the columns in the `Employee` table that have been selected in the view. If that user tries to select rows directly from the underlying `HumanResources.Employee` table, a permission-related error fires. Ownership chaining is the key to making this scenario work.

With ownership chaining, SQL Server allows access to the underlying tables, views, or functions referenced in the view. This happens only if the view has the same owner as the underlying objects and the user has been granted permission to the view. If, however, you have various owners of the underlying objects that a view references, permissions must be checked at each level. If access is denied at any level, access to the view is denied. Ownership chaining was available in prior versions and is still available in SQL Server 2014 for backward compatibility.

Horizontal security can also be implemented with a view. With horizontal security, a WHERE clause is included in the view's SELECT statement to restrict the rows that are returned. The following example demonstrates a simple view that utilizes horizontal security:

```
CREATE VIEW EmpViewHorizontal
  as
 select LoginID, BirthDate, Gender, HireDate, SalariedFlag
  from HumanResources.Employee
 where HireDate >  '3/1/07'
--Sample SELECT results from the view:
```

LoginID	BirthDate	Gender	HireDate	SalariedFlag
adventure-works\syed0	1969-02-11	M	2007-04-15	1
adventure-works\lynn0	1965-04-18	F	2007-07-01	1
adventure-works\rachel0	1969-08-09	F	2007-07-01	1

Only the rows in the Employee table with a HireDate value greater than March 1, 2007, are returned when you select everything from the view. Separate views can be created based on geography, demographics, or any other data element that requires a different set of security.

Keep in mind that additional conditions can be applied when selecting from a view. You can utilize another WHERE clause in the SELECT statement that uses a view. This is demonstrated in the following example:

```
select * from EmpViewHorizontal
 where HireDate >= '7/1/07'
  and BirthDate > '1/1/69'
```

LoginID	BirthDate	Gender	HireDate	SalariedFlag
adventure-works\rachel0	1969-08-09	F	2007-07-01	1

As you can see, a view with horizontal security restricts your initial result set but does not prevent you from applying additional conditions to obtain the desired result.

Creating Views

You can create several different types of views in SQL Server 2014, including standard views, indexed views, and partitioned views. Standard views are like those that have been discussed thus far in this chapter; they let you achieve most of the benefits associated with views. An indexed view has a unique clustered index defined on it that causes the view to be materialized. In other words, the creation of the index causes physical storage of the data related to the view's index. Partitioned views join horizontally partitioned data from a set of distinct tables. They can be locally partitioned, meaning that the tables are on the same server; or they can be distributed, meaning that some of the tables exist on other servers. Partitioned views and indexed views are discussed in detail later in this chapter.

All types of views share a common set of restrictions:

▶ Every column (including derived columns) must have a unique name.

▶ The SELECT statement used in the view cannot include the INTO keyword.

▶ The SELECT statement used in the view cannot include the ORDER BY clause unless there is a TOP clause in the SELECT list.

▶ The SELECT statement used in the view cannot contain temporary tables or table variables.

▶ You cannot associate AFTER triggers with views, but you can associate INSTEAD OF triggers.

► You cannot associate rules or default definitions with a view.

► You cannot define a full-text index on a view.

A view can have a maximum of 1,024 columns. When you create a view, you can select all the columns from a table by using a SELECT * statement, but you need to use some caution when doing so. In particular, you must keep in mind that the view will not display columns that have been added to the view's underlying tables after the view has been created. The fact that the new columns are not displayed can be a good thing but is sometimes overlooked. You can prevent changes to the underlying objects (for example, tables) by creating the view with SCHEMABINDING. SCHEMABINDING is discussed in the next section.

If you want the changes to the underlying objects to be reflected in the views, you can use the sp_refreshview stored procedure. This stored procedure updates the metadata for the specified non-schema-bound view.

24

TIP

SQL Server Books Online lists a handy script that can be used to update any view that has a dependency on an object. The script is shown in the sp_refreshview examples. The script, listed here, is coded such that it will generate output that can be run to generate the sp_refreshview statements for the Person.Person table in the AdventureWorks2012 database:

```
SELECT DISTINCT 'EXEC sp_refreshview ''' + name + ''''
FROM sys.objects AS so
   INNER JOIN sys.sql_expression_dependencies AS sed
       ON so.object_id = sed.referencing_id
   WHERE so.type = 'V'AND sed.referenced_id = OBJECT_ID('Person.Person')
```

To generate the executions for another object, you simply change the name of the object (that is, Person.Person) found at the end of the script to the name of the object you want to investigate.

With these guidelines in mind, you are now ready to create your view. Views can be created in SQL Server 2014 using T-SQL or SQL Server Management Studio (SSMS).

Creating Views Using T-SQL

The CREATE VIEW statement is used to create views with T-SQL. The syntax for the CREATE VIEW statement follows:

```
CREATE VIEW [ schema_name . ] view_name [ (column [ ,...n ] ) ]
[ WITH <view_attribute> [ ,...n ] ]
AS select_statement [ ; ]
[ WITH CHECK OPTION ]
```

```
<view_attribute> ::=
{
    [ ENCRYPTION ]
    [ SCHEMABINDING ]
    [ VIEW_METADATA ]        }
```

This statement and the related options are the same in SQL Server 2014 as they were in SQL Server 2012 and prior versions. We first look at a simple example for creating a view with T-SQL and then delve into several other examples that utilize the view attributes. Listing 24.2 shows a sample T-SQL statement for creating a simple view.

LISTING 24.2   Creating a Simple View with T-SQL

```
CREATE VIEW Sales.vw_OrderSummary as
select datepart(yy, orderdate) as 'OrderYear',
    datepart(mm, orderdate) as 'OrderMonth',
    sum(TotalDue) as 'OrderTotal'
 from Sales.SalesOrderHeader
 group by datepart(yy, orderdate), datepart(mm, orderdate)
```

There are several important aspects to notice in the example in Listing 24.2. First, all the columns in the SELECT statement are derived columns and do not simply reference a column in a table. You do not need to have a derived column in your view, but if you do, the derived column(s) must have a name or an alias assigned to it to be able to create the view. The column name allows you to reference the derived column when selecting from the view. If the derived columns in the SELECT statement are not named, the CREATE VIEW statement will fail.

Another notable characteristic of the simple view example is that an aggregate is used in the SELECT statement. Aggregates are allowed in views and are common implementations of views. Views with aggregates can be used instead of summary tables. Summary tables denormalize data, use additional disk space, and cause more write activity in your database. Views that contain aggregate statements will cause some extra work at read time, but the view is typically a better option than the summary table.

Keep in mind that the results of any view (including those with aggregates) are not returned in any particular order. Views cannot be created with the ORDER BY clause unless the TOP clause is used, but the ORDER BY clause can be utilized in a SELECT statement that references the view. The following example shows the first five rows of the vw_OrderSummary view created in Listing 24.2:

```
select top 5 * from Sales.vw_OrderSummary
```

```
OrderYear    OrderMonth   OrderTotal
-----------  -----------  -------------
2006         9            3638980.3689
2007         4            2660723.7481
2007         10           3767722.1252
2006         3            2350568.1264
2005         10           1518540.2014
```

You can see from the results of SELECT that the summarized order information is not returned in any particular order. If you want to sort the results, you can treat the view like a table in a SELECT statement and use the ORDER BY clause to produce the desired results. The following example shows a SELECT statement from the vw_OrderSummary view and the ordered results:

```
select top 5 *
 from Sales.vw_OrderSummary
 where OrderYear >= 2008
 order by OrderYear, OrderMonth
```

```
OrderYear    OrderMonth   OrderTotal
-----------  -----------  -------------
2008         1            3359927.2196
2008         2            4662655.6183
2008         3            4722357.5175
2008         4            4269365.0103
2008         5            5813557.453
```

> **TIP**
>
> In many cases, it is best to create views that include the primary key columns from the underlying tables. This allows the views to be joined to other tables. Consider, for example, a view created on the Person.Address table in the AdventureWorks2012 database. If you want to join that view to another table (such as Person.AddressType), you need the primary key of the table (that is, AddressID) in the view.

Views can also be created with the following special view attributes: ENCRYPTION, SCHEMABINDING, and VIEW_METADATA. Each of these attributes and some other specialized views are discussed in the following sections.

ENCRYPTION

The ENCRYPTION attribute causes the view definition to be stored as encrypted text. Without encryption, the definition would be viewable via SSMS or by using the sys. syscomments or sys.sql_modules catalog views. This feature is also available for stored

24

procedures and other database code that you may want to protect. One issue to consider when you create a view using the ENCRYPTION option is that this option prevents the view from being published as part of SQL Server replication.

The following example shows the creation of one of the prior views with the ENCRYPTION attribute:

```
IF  EXISTS (SELECT * FROM sys.views WHERE
object_id = OBJECT_ID(N'[Sales].[vw_OrderSummary]'))
DROP VIEW [Sales].[vw_OrderSummary]
GO


CREATE VIEW Sales.vw_OrderSummary
    WITH ENCRYPTION AS
select datepart(yy, orderdate) as 'OrderYear',
    datepart(mm, orderdate) as 'OrderMonth',
    sum(TotalDue) as 'OrderTotal'
 from Sales.SalesOrderHeader
 group by datepart(yy, orderdate), datepart(mm, orderdate)
go
```

The following SELECT statement from sys. sql_modules retrieves the text related to the encrypted view and shows that the view definition is not visible in the definition column:

```
SELECT object_id, OBJECT_NAME(object_id) 'ViewName', definition
FROM sys.sql_modules

 WHERE OBJECT_NAME(object_id) LIKE '%vw_OrderSummary%'


Object_id   ViewName            definition
---------  -------------- ----  -----------------------------------------------------

695673526   vw_OrderSummary     NULL
```

SCHEMABINDING

The SCHEMABINDING attribute binds a view to the schema of the underlying table(s) referenced in the view's SELECT statement. This binding action prevents any changes to the underlying tables that would affect the view definition. For example, if you have a view that includes the Employee.JobTitle column, this column cannot be altered or dropped in the Employee table. If schema changes are attempted on the underlying tables, an error message is returned, and the change is not allowed. The only way to make the change is to drop the view or alter the view to remove the SCHEMABINDING attribute.

TIP

Views created with SCHEMABINDING have been used in the past to simply prevent changes to the underlying schema. Any table for which you wanted to prevent schema changes was included in a view, and this essentially locked the definition of the table. This approach is no longer needed because you can accomplish the same thing using DDL triggers, which can react to schema changes and prevent them if desired.

VIEW_METADATA

When the VIEW_METADATA option is specified, SQL Server returns information about the view, as opposed to the base tables. This happens when browse-mode metadata is requested for a query that references the view via a database API. Browse-mode metadata is additional information returned by SQL Server to client-side DBLIB, ODBC, and OLE DB APIs, which allows them to implement client-side updatable cursors.

WITH CHECK OPTION

WITH CHECK OPTION forces all data modifications made through a view to adhere to the conditions in the view. The example shown in Listing 24.3 shows a view created using WITH CHECK OPTION.

LISTING 24.3   View using a WITH CHECK OPTION

```
CREATE VIEW HumanResources.vw_MaleEmployees
 AS
SELECT LoginID, Gender
 FROM HumanResources.Employee
 WHERE Gender = 'M'
 WITH CHECK OPTION
```

The following UPDATE statement fails when executed against the view created in Listing 24.3 because the Gender change would cause it to no longer be seen by the view:

```
UPDATE HumanResources.vw_MaleEmployees
 SET Gender = 'F'
 WHERE LoginId = 'adventure-works\taylor0'
```

Updates and other modifications made though a view are discussed further in the "Data Modifications and Views" section, later in this chapter.

Creating Views Using the View Designer

SQL Server 2014 provides a graphical tool, called the View Designer, you can use to create views. This tool can be an invaluable aid when you are creating or modifying a view. The View Designer is equipped with four panes that provide the information relative to the view. Figure 24.1 shows the View Designer display for the Person.vStateProvince-CountryRegion view installed in the AdventureWorks2012 database. To view an existing view in the View Designer, right-click on the view listed in the Object Explorer and select Design. To create a new view via the View Designer, right-click the Views node in the Object Explorer and select New View. An empty View Designer is displayed.

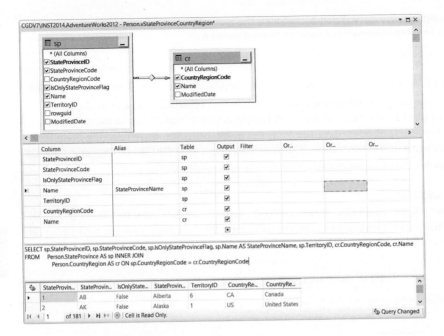

FIGURE 24.1   The View Designer window.

The View Designer has these four panes:

▶ **Diagram pane**—Gives a graphical view of the tables that are part of the view. This includes the columns in the tables and relationships between the tables contained in the view.

▶ **Criteria pane**—Displays all the columns selected in the view and allows for sorting, filtering, and other related column-oriented criteria.

▶ **SQL pane**—Renders the T-SQL associated with the view.

▶ **Results pane**—Shows the results of that view's SELECT statement.

The panes in the View Designer are dependent on each other. If you add a WHERE clause in the SQL pane, the corresponding Filter value is added in the Criteria pane. Similarly, if you right-click in the Diagram pane and add a table to the view, the Criteria and SQL panes are updated to reflect this change.

TIP

One of the most amazing features of the View Designer is the capability to render a SQL statement into its graphical form. You can copy T-SQL into the SQL pane, and the View Designer reverse-engineers the tables into the Diagram pane, giving you a graphical display of the query. Some complex SQL statements cannot be rendered, but many of them can. Give it a try; you will be impressed.

You can control the View Designer via the Query Designer menu option as well. Adding a new table, verifying the T-SQL, and changing the panes displayed are just some of the options available on this menu.

> **NOTE**
>
> The View Designer does not allow you to set every attribute of a view. It is a great starting point for creating a view, but you need to set some attributes using T-SQL after creating the view. For example, you cannot specify WITH CHECK OPTION in the View Designer, but you can set it by altering the view after it has been created.
>
> There is also no option to script a view from the View Designer. You must close the View Designer first, and then you are asked whether you want to save the view. If you click Yes, a prompt allows you to specify a name.

The Properties window displays information about the view and also allows you to enter additional view properties. If this window is not visible, you can select the Properties window from the View menu or simply press F4. The properties you can set on the view include (but are not limited to) a description, the schema that owns the view, and whether to bind the view to the schema. Figure 24.2 shows the Properties window for the Person.vStateProvinceCountryRegion view that we looked at earlier.

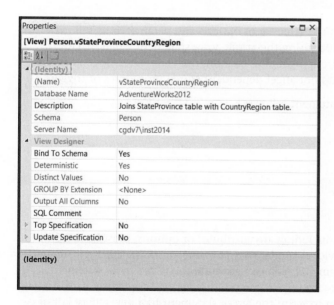

FIGURE 24.2   The view's Properties window.

After defining a view using the panes in the View Designer and setting its properties, you can choose to save the view. You are prompted to give it a name. After you save the view, it appears in the Object Explorer tree.

Managing Views

After creating your view, you can manage the view via T-SQL or the View Designer. The T-SQL commands for managing views are the ALTER VIEW and DROP VIEW statements. The ALTER VIEW statement is used to modify the properties or definition of the view, and the DROP VIEW statement is used to remove the view from the database.

Altering Views with T-SQL

The ALTER VIEW syntax follows:

```
ALTER VIEW [ schema_name . ] view_name [ ( column [ ,...n ] ) ]
[ WITH <view_attribute> [ ,...n ] ]
AS select_statement [ ; ]
[ WITH CHECK OPTION ]


<view_attribute> ::=
{
    [ ENCRYPTION ]
    [ SCHEMABINDING ]
    [ VIEW_METADATA ]
}
```

The ALTER VIEW statement utilizes the same set of options and parameters as the CREATE VIEW statement. You should consider using the ALTER VIEW statement when making changes to your view instead of dropping and re-creating the view. Altered views retain their associated permissions and do not affect dependent stored procedures or triggers.

An example of the ALTER VIEW statement follows:

```
ALTER VIEW [dbo].[vw_employee]
with SCHEMABINDING
AS
SELECT TITLE, GENDER
    FROM HumanResources.Employee
WITH CHECK OPTION
```

The entire definition of the view, including any attributes or options, must be listed in the ALTER VIEW statement. This behavior is similar to that of the ALTER PROCEDURE statement and some of the other ALTER statements. You can generate the ALTER VIEW statement from the Object Explorer by right-clicking the view and selecting Script View As and then choosing Alter To. This allows you to script the ALTER statement to a new Query Editor window, a file, or the Clipboard.

Dropping Views with T-SQL

You can drop views from a database by using the DROP VIEW statement. The syntax for DROP VIEW follows:

```
DROP VIEW [ schema_name . ] view_name [ ...,n ] [ ; ]
```

You can drop more than one view by using one DROP VIEW statement and listing all the targeted views, separated by commas. You should consider running the sp_depends stored procedure against the targeted views before dropping them. This procedure lists the objects dependent on the view you are dropping.

TIP

You can also drop more than one view via SSMS. Simply select the Views node in Object Explorer and then activate the Object Explorer Details window. The Object Explorer Details window displays all the views and allows you to select multiple views that are displayed. After selecting the views you want to delete, you can right-click a selection and choose Delete to remove all the views selected.

24

Managing Views with SSMS

You can use the Object Explorer in SQL Server Management Studio to alter or drop views as well. To do so, you right-click a view in the Object Explorer and choose Design to launch the View Designer. The View Designer allows you to modify a view in an easy-to-use graphical interface. Refer to the "Creating Views Using the View Designer" section, earlier in this chapter, for a detailed review of the View Designer.

To drop a view, you right-click the view in the Object Explorer and choose Delete. You can drop the view by clicking OK on the Delete Object screen, or you can script the drop statement for later execution.

Data Modifications and Views

Data modifications are allowed through a view under certain circumstances. When you execute DML statements against the view then the underlying tables are affected. Views that meet these criteria are sometimes called *updatable views*. Updatable views can be referenced in an INSERT, UPDATE, or DELETE statement, and these statements ultimately affect the underlying table(s) in the view.

The following example contains a SQL statement to create an updatable view, followed by an UPDATE statement that performs a data modification using the view:

```
CREATE VIEW vw_CreditCard
AS
SELECT     CreditCardID, CardType, CardNumber, ExpMonth, ExpYear
FROM       Sales.CreditCard
```

```
UPDATE vw_CreditCard
 SET ExpYear = ExpYear + 1
 WHERE ExpYear < 2006
```

In general, updatable views are similar to the previous example. The following specific conditions allow a view to be updatable:

▶ Any data modification via a view must reference columns from a single base table. This does not restrict a view to only one table, but the columns referenced in the data modification can be for only one of the tables defined in the view.

▶ The columns affected by the data modification must directly reference the underlying tables. They cannot be derived through an aggregate function (for example, AVG, COUNT, SUM) and cannot contain computations from an expression that utilizes columns from another table.

▶ The TOP clause cannot be part of the SELECT statement that defines the view when the WITH CHECK OPTION clause is used.

▶ The columns affected by the data modification cannot be affected by GROUP BY, HAVING, or DISTINCT clauses in the view definition.

You can overcome these restrictions by using INSTEAD OF triggers to perform the data modifications. You can create INSTEAD OF triggers on a view, and the logic within the triggers performs the actual database updates. INSTEAD OF triggers are discussed in detail in Chapter 27, "Creating and Managing Triggers."

Partitioned views are another means for performing data modifications via a view. Partitioned views can be updatable and are not subject to all the restrictions listed for conventional views. However, some additional restrictions apply to partitioned views. These additional restrictions and other details about partitioned views are discussed in the next section.

Partitioned Views

Partitioned views are used to access data that has been horizontally split, or partitioned, across multiple tables. These tables can be in the same or different databases—or even spread across multiple servers. Partitioning of tables is done to spread the I/O and processing load of large tables across multiple disks or servers.

You combine the tables in a partitioned view by using a UNION ALL statement that causes the data from the separate tables to appear as if they were one table. These separate tables are referred to as member tables or base tables. The member tables in a SELECT statement of the view must all be structured in the same way, and the view must adhere to the following restrictions:

▶ All the columns from the member tables should be included in the view definition.

▶ Columns with the same ordinal position in the SELECT list should have the same data type.

▶ The same column cannot be used multiple times in the SELECT list.

▶ A partitioning column that segments the data must be identified and needs to have the same ordinal position across all the member table SELECT statements.

▶ The partitioning column cannot be a computed column, an identity, a default, or a time stamp.

▶ The data values in the partitioning column cannot overlap in the underlying tables.

▶ The partitioning column must be part of the primary key of the member table.

▶ The member tables in the partitioned view need a CHECK constraint on the partitioning column.

▶ A table can appear only once as part of the UNION ALL statement.

▶ The member tables cannot have indexes created on computed columns in the table.

▶ The number of columns in the member table primary key constraints should be the same.

▶ All member tables should have the same ANSI PADDING setting when created.

The list of restrictions for creating partitioned views is extensive, but the creation of a partitioned view is relatively straightforward and intuitive. Consider, for example, the Sales.SalesOrderHeader table in the AdventureWorks2012 database. This table is relatively small, but it is the type of table that could have a large number of rows and experience heavy utilization. To balance the workload against this table, you could use a partitioned view that utilizes base tables that each contain a separate year's data. Listing 24.4 shows the CREATE TABLE statements to create the base tables for each year. The yearly tables are intended to hold summarized daily numbers, and each contains only a subset of the columns in the Sales.SalesOrderHeader table.

LISTING 24.4   Creating the Base Tables for a Partitioned View

```
CREATE TABLE Sales.Sales_2005
(
    OrderDay datetime NOT NULL
        CHECK (OrderDay BETWEEN '20050101' AND '20051231'),
    SubTotal money NOT NULL ,
    TaxAmt money not null,
    Freight money not null,
 CONSTRAINT PK_Sales_2005_OrderDay PRIMARY KEY CLUSTERED (OrderDay ASC)
)


CREATE TABLE Sales.Sales_2006
(
    OrderDay datetime NOT NULL,
        CHECK (OrderDay BETWEEN '20060101' AND '20061231'),
```

```
    SubTotal money NOT NULL ,
    TaxAmt money not null,
    Freight money not null,
 CONSTRAINT PK_Sales_2006_OrderDay PRIMARY KEY CLUSTERED (OrderDay ASC)
)


CREATE TABLE Sales.Sales_2007
(
    OrderDay datetime NOT NULL
        CHECK (OrderDay BETWEEN '20070101' AND '20071231'),
    SubTotal money NOT NULL ,
    TaxAmt money not null,
    Freight money not null,
 CONSTRAINT PK_Sales_2007_OrderDay PRIMARY KEY CLUSTERED (OrderDay ASC)
)


CREATE TABLE Sales.Sales_2008
(
    OrderDay datetime NOT NULL
        CHECK (OrderDay BETWEEN '20080101' AND '20081231'),
    SubTotal money NOT NULL ,
    TaxAmt money not null,
    Freight money not null,
 CONSTRAINT PK_Sales_2008_OrderDay PRIMARY KEY CLUSTERED (OrderDay ASC)
)
```

Notice that each table has a primary key on OrderDay, the partitioning column. Also notice that a CHECK constraint is defined for each table; it ensures that only orders for the given year can be stored in the table. The CHECK constraint is not a requirement but is critical for maintaining the integrity of the data and getting the best query plan.

To demonstrate the power of a partitioned view, it is best to populate the base tables that will be used by the view. Listing 24.5 contains a series of INSERT statements that select from the Sales.SalesOrderHeader table and populate the base tables. The SELECT statements summarize several key columns by day and contain a WHERE clause that limits the result to orders for the respective years.

LISTING 24.5   Populating the Base Tables for a Partitioned View

```
INSERT Sales.Sales_2005
   SELECT CONVERT(VARCHAR(8),OrderDate,112),
      SUM(SubTotal), SUM(TaxAmt), SUM(Freight)
   FROM Sales.SalesOrderHeader
   WHERE OrderDate between '20050101' AND '20051231'
   GROUP BY CONVERT(VARCHAR(8),OrderDate,112)
```

```
INSERT Sales.Sales_2006
   SELECT CONVERT(VARCHAR(8),OrderDate,112),
      SUM(SubTotal), SUM(TaxAmt), SUM(Freight)
   FROM Sales.SalesOrderHeader
   WHERE OrderDate between '20060102' AND '20061231'
   GROUP BY CONVERT(VARCHAR(8),OrderDate,112)

INSERT Sales.Sales_2007
   SELECT CONVERT(VARCHAR(8),OrderDate,112),
      SUM(SubTotal), SUM(TaxAmt), SUM(Freight)
   FROM Sales.SalesOrderHeader
   WHERE OrderDate between '20070101' AND '20071231'
   GROUP BY CONVERT(VARCHAR(8),OrderDate,112)

INSERT Sales.Sales_2008
   SELECT CONVERT(VARCHAR(8),OrderDate,112),
      SUM(SubTotal), SUM(TaxAmt), SUM(Freight)
   FROM Sales.SalesOrderHeader
   WHERE OrderDate between '20080102' AND '20081231'
   GROUP BY CONVERT(VARCHAR(8),OrderDate,112)
```

Now that you have the populated base table, you can create a partitioned view and ensure that the view is selecting only from the base tables that it needs.

Two types of partitioned views are discussed in this chapter: local and distributed. A local partitioned view utilizes base tables found on the same server. A distributed partitioned view contains at least one base table that resides on a different (remote) server. The focus in the section is on local partitioned views; distributed partitioned views are discussed later in this chapter. The T-SQL for creating a local partitioned view named Sales.vw_Sales_Daily is shown in Listing 24.6.

LISTING 24.6   Creating a Local Partitioned View

```
Create View Sales.vw_Sales_Daily
 as
      SELECT * FROM Sales.Sales_2005
        UNION ALL
      SELECT * FROM Sales.Sales_2006
        UNION ALL
      SELECT * FROM Sales.Sales_2007
        UNION ALL
      SELECT * FROM Sales.Sales_2008
```

The best way to validate that a partitioned view is working properly is to run a conditional SELECT against the view and display the execution plan. If the partitioned view is functioning properly, it should be accessing only the base tables it needs to satisfy the SELECT and should not access all the tables in the view unless it needs to. The following example shows a sample SELECT against the new partitioned view:

```
SELECT * FROM Sales.vw_Sales_Daily
 WHERE OrderDay > '20080701'
   and SubTotal > 2000
```

If you execute this statement and review the actual execution plan, you see that an index seek is performed against the Sales.Sales_2008 table. This is the correct result, given that the SELECT statement is targeting order data from 2008.

NOTE

SQL Server Books Online states that the recommended method for partitioning data on a local server in SQL Server 2014 is through the use of partitioned tables and indexes. Partitioned tables and indexes are discussed in Chapter 21, "Creating and Managing Tables."

Modifying Data Through a Partitioned View

You can modify data via a partitioned view if the SQL statement performing the modification meets certain conditions, as described here:

▶ All columns in the partitioned view must be specified in the INSERT statement. Columns that include a DEFAULT constraint or allow nulls are also subject to this requirement.

▶ The DEFAULT keyword cannot be used on inserts to partitioned views or on updates to partitioned views.

▶ Inserts and updates to a partitioned view are not allowed if the view contains a time stamp.

▶ Identity columns in a partitioned view cannot be modified by an INSERT or UPDATE statement.

▶ INSERT, UPDATE, and DELETE statements are not allowed against a partitioned view if there is a self-join with the same view or with any of the member tables in the statement.

NOTE

Data can be modified through partitioned views only in the Enterprise and Developer Editions of SQL Server 2014.

In addition to the conditions shown in this list, you must also satisfy any restrictions that apply to the member tables. Check constraints, foreign key constraints, and any other table-level restrictions must be accounted for in the modification statement. The user executing the modification against the partitioned view must have the appropriate INSERT, UPDATE, or DELETE permissions on the member tables for the update to succeed.

Distributed Partitioned Views

Microsoft provides distributed partitioned views (DPVs) as a primary means to scale out a database server. Scalability allows an application or a database to utilize additional resources, which allows it to perform more work. There are two kinds of scalability: scaleup and scaleout. A scaleup solution focuses on a single server scaled to provide more processing power than its predecessor. An example of scaleup would be migrating from a server with a single dual-core processor to a machine with 4-quad-core processors. Scaleout solutions include the addition of servers to augment the overall processing power.

DPVs are similar to local partitioned views, but they utilize one or more tables located on a remote server. The placement of partitioned data on remote servers allows the processing power of more than one server to be utilized. The partitioning is intended to be transparent to the application and allow for additional partitions and servers as the application's needs scale.

The following list outlines the basic requirements for creating a DPV:

▶ A linked server definition is added to each member server that will contain the partitioned data. The linked server contains the connection information required to run distributed queries on another member server.

▶ The lazy schema validation option is set to true on each of the member servers, using sp_serveroption. This option is set for performance reasons and allows the query processor to skip schema checking of remote tables if the query can be satisfied on a single member server.

▶ A DPV is created on each member server. This DPV references the local tables in addition to the tables found on the other member servers.

Listing 24.7 shows SQL commands that can be used to satisfy the requirements in the preceding list. The DPV created in the last portion of the script is similar to the local partitioned view created in the previous section. The key difference in this DPV example is the inclusion of a distributed query that retrieves records for Sales.Sales_2006 from a remote server. The remote server in this example is named chrisg_pc.

LISTING 24.7   Creating a Distributed Partitioned View

```
Exec sp_addlinkedserver @server='chrisg_pc',
     @srvproduct='',
     @provider='MSDASQL',
     @provstr='DRIVER={SQL Server};
SERVER=chrisg_pc;UID=linklogin;PWD=pw;Initial Catalog=AdventureWorks2012'

--Set the server option for improved DPV performance
exec sp_serveroption chrisg_pc, 'lazy schema validation', true
```

```
Create View Sales.vw_Sales_Daily
 as
      SELECT * FROM Sales.Sales_2005
       UNION ALL
      SELECT * FROM chrisg_pc.AdventureWorks2012.Sales.Sales_2006
       UNION ALL
      SELECT * FROM Sales.Sales_2007
       UNION ALL
      SELECT * FROM Sales.Sales_2008
```

The DPV created in Listing 24.7 contains only one remote table. The example could be further expanded to have each table in the UNION clause on a different remote server. Keep in mind that the DPV CREATE statement needs to be adjusted when run on the remote server(s). The tables that are local on one server are now remote on the other server, and those that are remote can now be local.

If the DPVs are properly defined, SQL Server 2014 attempts to optimize their performance by minimizing the amount of data transferred between member servers. The query processor retrieves the CHECK constraint definitions from each member table. This allows the query processor to map the specified search arguments to the appropriate table(s). The query execution plan then accesses only the necessary tables and retrieves only the remote rows needed to complete the SQL statement.

Data can be modified through a DPV as well. Updatable DPVs, which were introduced in SQL Server 2000, are still available in SQL Server 2014. Data modifications are performed against a view, allowing true transparency. The view is accessed as if it was a base table, and the user or application is unaware of the actual location of the data. If it is configured properly, SQL Server determines via the WHERE clause specified in the update query which partition defined in the view must be updated rather than updating all tables in the join.

> **NOTE**
>
> Data can be modified through distributed partitioned views only in the Enterprise and Developer Editions of SQL Server 2014.

Indexed Views

You establish indexed views by creating a unique clustered index on the view itself, independent of the member tables that it references. The creation of this unique index transforms a view from an object that is virtual in nature to one that has physical storage associated with it. Like all other indexes, the index on a view takes up physical storage and creates some database overhead when rows change and the index must be updated to reflect that change. These factors must be considered but the performance benefits of the Indexed view can justify its creation.

Creating Indexed Views

Indexed views were first available for creation in SQL Server 2000 and continue to be a viable means for improving query performance in SQL Server 2014. An index can be created on a view in all versions of SQL Server 2014, but there are limitations on some of the versions. The Developer and Enterprise Editions of SQL Server 2014 are the only editions that support the use of indexed views for queries that don't specifically reference the views. Other editions of SQL Server must reference the view by name in the SQL statements and must also use the NOEXPAND keyword in the query. The details of NOEXPAND are discussed in the section, "To Expand or Not to Expand," later in this chapter.

Regardless of the edition of SQL Server you are running, some basic requirements must be satisfied for you to create an indexed view. These requirements, which follow, are detailed in SQL Server 2014 Books Online:

▶ The ANSI_NULLS and QUOTED_IDENTIFIER options must be set to ON when the CREATE VIEW statement is executed.

▶ The ANSI_NULLS option must be set to ON for the execution of all CREATE TABLE statements that create tables referenced by the view.

▶ The view must not reference any other views, only base tables.

▶ All base tables referenced by the view must be in the same database as the view and have the same owner as the view.

▶ The view must be created with the SCHEMABINDING option. Schema binding binds the view to the schema of the underlying base tables.

▶ User-defined functions referenced in the view must be created with the SCHEMABINDING option.

▶ Tables and user-defined functions must be referenced via two-part names (schema and object) in the view. One-part, three-part, and four-part names are not allowed.

▶ All functions referenced by expressions in the view must be deterministic.

▶ If the view definition uses an aggregate function, the SELECT list must also include COUNT_BIG (*).

▶ CLR functions can appear only in the SELECT list of the view and can reference only fields that are not part of the clustered index key. They cannot appear in the WHERE clause of the view or the ON clause of a JOIN operation in the view.

▶ CLR functions and methods of CLR user-defined types used in the view definition must have the properties set as DETERMINISTIC = TRUE, PRECISE = TRUE, DATA ACCESS = NO SQL, and EXTERNAL ACCESS = NO.

▶ If GROUP BY is specified, the view SELECT list must contain a COUNT_BIG(*) expression, and the view definition cannot specify HAVING, CUBE, or ROLLUP.

24

▶ The view cannot contain any of the T-SQL elements shown in the following list:

* or `tablename.*`	An expression on a column found in the `GROUP BY` clause	A derived table
A common table expression (CTE)	A rowset function	The `UNION`, `EXCEPT`, or `INTERSECT` operators
Subqueries	Outer joins or self-joins	The `TOP` clause
The `ORDER BY` clause	The `DISTINCT` keyword	`COUNT` (`COUNT_BIG` is allowed)
`MAX`, `MIN`, `STDEV`, `STDEVP`, `VAR`, or `VARP`	A `SUM` function that references a nullable expression	A CLR user-defined aggregate function
The full text predicate	`COMPUTE` or `COMPUTE BY` `CONTAINS` or `FREETEXT`	`CROSS APPLY` or `OUTER APPLY` operators
Table hints	Join hints	`OFFSET`

You can see from this list that the number of requirements is extensive. It can therefore be difficult to determine whether all the requirements have been met for a particular view. To simplify this determination, you can query the `IsIndexable` property, using the `OBJECTPROPERTY` function. The following example demonstrates the use of the `IsIndexable` property against the `sys.views` catalog view:

```
SELECT name AS ViewName
  ,SCHEMA_NAME(schema_id) AS SchemaName
  ,OBJECTPROPERTYEX(object_id,'IsIndexed') AS IsIndexed
  ,OBJECTPROPERTYEX(object_id,'IsIndexable') AS IsIndexable
  ,create_date
  ,modify_date
FROM sys.views;
```

The `IsIndexable` property returns a 1 (or `TRUE`) if an index can be created on the view and a 0 if it is not indexable. Most of the views in the `AdventureWorks2012` database are not indexable, but the database does contain a couple of examples of views that have been indexed. The following example shows the `CREATE` statement for an index that already exists on the `Production.vProductAndDescription` view in the `AdventureWorks2012` database. The `SET` options required when creating the index are included in the example as well:

```
SET ARITHABORT ON    for 80 compatibility or earlier
SET CONCAT_NULL_YIELDS_NULL ON
SET QUOTED_IDENTIFIER ON
SET ANSI_NULLS ON
SET ANSI_PADDING ON
SET ANSI_WARNINGS ON
SET NUMERIC_ROUNDABORT OFF
GO
```

```
CREATE UNIQUE CLUSTERED INDEX [IX_vProductAndDescription]
 ON [Production].[vProductAndDescription]
(
      [CultureID] ASC,
      [ProductID] ASC
)
```

The following example shows the `Production.vProductAndDescription` view that the index was created on:

```
CREATE VIEW [Production].[vProductAndDescription]
WITH SCHEMABINDING
AS
View (indexed or standard) to display products
and product descriptions by language.
SELECT
    p.[ProductID]
    ,p.[Name]
    ,pm.[Name] AS [ProductModel]
    ,pmx.[CultureID]
    ,pd.[Description]
FROM [Production].[Product] p
    INNER JOIN [Production].[ProductModel] pm
    ON p.[ProductModelID] = pm.[ProductModelID]
    INNER JOIN [Production].[ProductModelProductDescriptionCulture] pmx
    ON pm.[ProductModelID] = pmx.[ProductModelID]
    INNER JOIN [Production].[ProductDescription] pd
    ON pmx.[ProductDescriptionID] = pd.[ProductDescriptionID];
```

> **TIP**
>
> You can use the sp_helpindex system stored procedure to list the indexes on a view. This is done in the same manner as a table except that the view name is passed to the stored procedure. For example, `sp_helpindex '[Production].[vProductAndDescription]'` can be used to list the existing indexes on the `Production.vProductAndDescription` view.

Indexed Views and Performance

Adding indexes to tables is a generally accepted means for improving database performance. Indexes provide a keyed lookup to rows of data that can improve database access and avoid the performance nightmare of a table scan where the entire contents of a table are searched. The same basic principles apply to indexes on views, but indexed views are best utilized to increase performance in the following scenarios:

▶ Aggregations such as SUM or AVG can be precomputed and stored in the index to minimize the potentially expensive computations during query execution.

▶ Large table joins can be persisted to eliminate the need to write a join when retrieving the data.

▶ A combination of aggregations and large table joins can be stored.

The performance improvements from the aforementioned scenarios can be significant and can justify the use of an index. The Query Optimizer can use the precomputed results stored in the view's index and avoid the cost of aggregating or joining the underlying tables. Keep in mind that the Query Optimizer may still use the indexes found on the member tables of the view instead of the index on the view. The Query Optimizer uses the following conditions in determining whether the index on the view can be utilized:

▶ The tables in the query FROM clause must be a superset of the tables in the indexed view's FROM clause. In other words, the query must contain all the tables in the view, and it can contain additional tables not contained in the view.

▶ The join conditions in the query must be a superset of the view's join conditions.

▶ The aggregate columns in the query must be derivable from a subset of the aggregate columns in the view.

▶ All expressions in the query SELECT list must be derivable from the view SELECT list or from the tables not included in the view definition.

▶ All columns in the query search condition predicates that belong to tables in the view definition must appear in the GROUP BY list, the SELECT list if there is no GROUP BY, or the same or equivalent predicate in the view definition.

NOTE

Predicting the Query Optimizer's use of an indexed view can be complicated and depends on the complexity of the view that is indexed and the complexity of the query that may utilize the view. A detailed discussion of these scenarios is beyond the scope of this chapter, but the Microsoft TechNet article, "Improving Performance with SQL Server 2008 Indexed Views," provides that detail. This article includes more than 20 examples that illustrate the use of indexed views and the conditions the Query Optimizer uses in selecting an indexed view. As you can see from the title, this article was written for SQL Server 2008, but the content is still relevant for SQL Server 2014.

The flip side of performance with indexes (including those on views) is that there is a cost in maintaining an index. This cost can adversely affect the performance of data modifications against objects that have these indexes. Generally speaking, indexes should not be placed on views that have underlying data sets that are frequently updated. Caution must be exercised when placing indexes on views that support online transaction processing (OLTP) applications. A balance must be struck between improving the performance of database modification and improving the performance of database inquiry. Indexed views improve database inquiry. Databases used for data warehousing and decision support are usually the best candidates for indexed views.

The impact of data modifications on indexed views is exacerbated by the fact that the complete result set of a view is stored in the database. When the clustered index is created on a view, you specify the clustered index key(s) in the CREATE UNIQUE CLUSTERED INDEX statement, but more than the columns in the key are stored in the database. As in a clustered index on a base table, the B-tree structure of the clustered index contains only the key columns, but the data rows contain all the columns in the view's result set.

The increased space utilized by the index view is demonstrated in the following examples. This first example creates a view and an associated index view similar to the AdventureWorks2012 Production.vProductAndDescription view used in a prior example:

```
CREATE VIEW [Production].[vProductAndDescription_2]
WITH SCHEMABINDING
AS
SELECT
    p.[ProductID]
    ,pmx.[CultureID]
FROM [Production].[Product] p
    INNER JOIN [Production].[ProductModel] pm
    ON p.[ProductModelID] = pm.[ProductModelID]
    INNER JOIN [Production].[ProductModelProductDescriptionCulture] pmx
    ON pm.[ProductModelID] = pmx.[ProductModelID]
    INNER JOIN [Production].[ProductDescription] pd
    ON pmx.[ProductDescriptionID] = pd.[ProductDescriptionID];
go
CREATE UNIQUE CLUSTERED INDEX [IX_vProductAndDescription_2]
  ON [Production].[vProductAndDescription_2]
(
    [CultureID] ASC,
    [ProductID] ASC
)
```

The difference with this new view is that the result set returns only the two columns in the clustered index; there are no additional columns in the result set.

When the new view and associated index are created, you can compare the amount of physical storage occupied by each. The following example shows the sp_spaceused commands for each view and the associated results:

```
exec sp_spaceused 'Production.vProductAndDescription'
/* results
name                        rows     reserved    data      index_size    unused

vProductAndDescription      1764     592 KB      560 KB    16 KB         16 KB
*/
```

24

```
exec sp_spaceused 'Production.vProductAndDescription_2'
/* results
name                        rows        reserved      data        index_size   unused

vProductAndDescription_2    1764        64 KB         48 KB       16 KB        0 KB
*/
```

Take note of the reserved space and data results for each view. The indexed view with only two result columns takes much less space than the view that has five result columns. You need to consider the overhead of storing these additional result columns along with the index when creating the view and related index. Changes made to any of the columns in the base tables that are part of the view results must also be maintained for the index view as well.

Nonclustered indexes can be created on a view, and they can also provide added query performance benefits when used properly. Typically, columns that are not part of the clustered index key on a view are added to the nonclustered index. Like nonclustered indexes on tables, the nonclustered indexes on the view provide additional options for the Query Optimizer when it is choosing the best query path. Common search arguments and foreign key columns that may be joined in the view are common targets for nonclustered indexes.

To Expand or Not to Expand

The expansion of a view to its base tables is a key consideration when evaluating the use of indexes on views. The SQL Server Query Optimizer can expand a view to its base tables or decide to utilize indexes that are found on the view itself. The selection of an index on a view is directly related to the edition of SQL Server 2014 you are running and the expansion options selected for a related query.

As mentioned earlier, the Enterprise and Developer Editions are the only editions that allow the Query Optimizer to use an indexed view to solve queries that structurally match the view, even if they don't refer to the view by name. For other editions of SQL Server 2014, the view must be referenced in the query, and the NOEXPAND hint must be used as well for the Query Optimizer to consider the index on the view. The following example demonstrates the use of the NOEXPAND hint:

```
SELECT *
FROM Production.vProductAndDescription (NOEXPAND)
 WHERE cultureid = 'he'
```

When this example is run against the AdventureWorks2012 database, the execution plan indicates that a clustered index seek will be performed, using the index on the view. If the NOEXPAND hint is removed from the query, the execution plan will ignore the index on the view and return the results from the base table(s). The only exception to this is when the Enterprise or Developer Edition is used. These editions can always consider indexed views but may or may not choose to use them.

SQL Server also has options to force the Query Optimizer to use the expanded base tables and ignore indexed views. The (EXPAND VIEWS) query hint ensures that SQL Server will process a query by accessing data directly from the base tables. This option might seem counterproductive, but it can be useful in situations in which contention exists on an indexed view. It is also handy for testing indexed views and determining overall performance with and without the use of indexed views.

The following example, which utilizes the same view as the previous example, demonstrates the use of the (EXPAND VIEWS) query hint:

```
SELECT *
FROM Production.vProductAndDescription
 WHERE cultureid = 'he'
 OPTION (EXPAND VIEWS)
```

The query plan in this example shows the use of the base tables, and the index on the view is ignored. For more information on query optimization and indexes, see Chapter 22, "Creating and Managing Indexes."

Summary

Views provide a broad spectrum of functionality, ranging from simple organization to improved overall query performance. They can simplify life for developers and users by filtering the complexity of a database. They can help organize data access and provide a security mechanism that helps keep a database safe. Finally, they can provide performance improvements via the use of partitioned views and indexed views that help keep your database fast.

Some of the same advantages, including performance and security benefits, can also be achieved through the use of stored procedures. Chapter 25, "Creating and Managing Stored Procedures," delves into these useful and powerful database objects.

Creating and Managing Stored Procedures

A stored procedure is one or more SQL commands stored in a database as an executable object. Stored procedures can be called interactively, from within client application code, from within other stored procedures, and from within triggers. Parameters can be passed to and returned from stored procedures to increase their usefulness and flexibility. A stored procedure can also return a number of result sets and a status code.

What's New in Creating and Managing Stored Procedures

SQL Server 2014 doesn't introduce any significant changes to the creation and functionality of stored procedures over what was available in SQL Server 2012, but does add the concept of natively compiled stored procedures. Natively compiled stored procedures are stored procedures that access memory-optimized tables and can be compiled to native code, allowing for more efficient execution of queries and business logic. This chapter provides only an overview of natively compiled stored procedures. For more details on creating and using natively compiled stored procedures, see Chapter 33, "In-Memory Optimization and the Buffer Pool Extension."

Advantages of Stored Procedures

Using stored procedures provides many advantages over executing large and complex SQL batches from client applications. Following are some of them:

▶ **Modular programming**—Subroutines and functions are often used in ordinary 3GL and 4GL languages (such as C, C++, and Microsoft Visual Basic) to break code into smaller, more manageable pieces. The same advantages are achieved when using stored procedures, with the difference that the stored procedure is stored in SQL Server and can be called by any client application.

▶ **Restricted, function-based access to tables**—A user can have permission to execute a stored procedure without having permissions to operate directly on the underlying tables.

▶ **Reduced network traffic**—Stored procedures can consist of many individual SQL statements but can be executed with a single statement. This allows you to reduce the number and size of calls from the client to the server.

▶ **Provides a finite code base**—If all database access is encapsulated in stored procedures, you know exactly every piece of code executing against your schema, making it easier to know what code needs to be modified when making schema changes or when migrating a database or tuning database performance.

▶ **Faster execution**—Stored procedures' query plans are kept in memory after the first execution. The code doesn't have to be reparsed and re-optimized on subsequent executions.

▶ **Enforced consistency**—If users modify data only through stored procedures, problems that often result from ad hoc modifications (such as omitting a crucial WHERE clause) are eliminated.

▶ **Reduced operator and programmer errors**—Because less information is being passed, complex tasks can be executed more easily, with less likelihood of SQL errors.

▶ **Automating complex or sensitive transactions**—If all modifications of certain tables take place in stored procedures, you can guarantee the data integrity on those tables.

Some of the disadvantages of using stored procedures (depending on the environment) are as follows:

▶ **Increase in server processing requirements**—Using stored procedures to process business logic can increase the amount of processing that takes place on the server. In a large user environment with considerable activity in the server, it may be more desirable to offload some of the business logic processing to the client workstation or application server.

▶ **Less cross-DBMS portability**—Although the ANSI-99 SQL standard provides syntax and support for stored procedures in database management systems (DBMSs), the format and structure are different from the syntax used for SQL Server stored procedures. Most of your SQL Server stored procedures would need to be rewritten to be compatible with another DBMS environment.

Should you use stored procedures? The answer is (as it often is): It depends.

If you are working in a two-tier environment, using stored procedures is often advantageous. The trend is shifting to three- (or more) tier environments. In such environments, business logic is often handled in some middle tier (possibly ActiveX objects managed by Microsoft Transaction Server). If you operate in that type of environment, you might want to restrict the stored procedures to performing basic data-related tasks, such as retrievals, insertions, updates, and deletions.

> **NOTE**
>
> You can use stored procedures to make a database sort of a "black box" as far as the developers and the application code are concerned. If all database access is managed through stored procedures, the applications are shielded from possible changes to the underlying database structures.
>
> For example, one organization found the need to split one table across multiple databases. By simply modifying the existing stored procedures to handle querying across multiple tables, the company was able to make this change without requiring any changes to the front-end application code.

25

Creating Stored Procedures

To create a stored procedure, you need to give the procedure a unique name within the schema and then write the sequence of SQL statements to be executed within the procedure. Following is the basic syntax for creating stored procedures:

```
CREATE { PROC | PROCEDURE } [schema_name.]procedure_name
    [ { @parameter [ schema_name.]data_type }
        [ VARYING ] [ = default ] [ OUT | OUTPUT ] [READONLY]
    ] [ ,...n ]
[ WITH  {  [ ENCRYPTION ]
        , [ RECOMPILE ]
        , [ EXECUTE_AS_Clause ]
        [ ,...n] ]
[ FOR REPLICATION ]
AS
[BEGIN]
    SQL_Statements
[   RETURN scalar_expression ]
[END]
```

It is good programming practice to always end a procedure with the RETURN statement and to specify a return status other than 0 when an error condition occurs. Listing 25.1 shows a simple stored procedure that returns employees and the names of the departments they work in.

LISTING 25.1   A Sample Stored Procedure

```
use AdventureWorks2012
go
IF EXISTS ( SELECT * FROM sys.procedures
                WHERE schema_id = schema_id('dbo')
                  AND name = N'Emp_Dept')
    DROP PROCEDURE dbo.Emp_Dept
GO
CREATE PROCEDURE Emp_Dept
AS
BEGIN
    SELECT p.Lastname, p.FirstName, d.Name
      FROM HumanResources.Department d
      JOIN HumanResources.EmployeeDepartmentHistory edh
        ON d.DepartmentID = edh.DepartmentID
        AND edh.EndDate IS null
      JOIN person.Person p
        ON p.BusinessEntityID = edh.BusinessEntityID
        ORDER BY d.departmentID
    RETURN 0
END
GO
```

> **NOTE**
>
> Unless stated otherwise, all examples in this chapter run in the context of the
> `AdventureWorks2012` database.

Creating Procedures in SSMS

To create a stored procedure in SSMS, open the object tree for the database in which
you want to create the procedure, open the `Programmability` folder, right-click the
`Stored Procedures` folder, and from the context menu, choose New Stored Procedure.
SSMS opens a new query window, populated with code that is based on a default template
for stored procedures. Listing 25.2 shows an example of the default template code for a
stored procedure that would be opened into a new query window.

LISTING 25.2   An Example of a New Stored Procedure Creation Script Generated by SSMS

```
-- =============================================
-- Template generated from Template Browser using:
-- Create Procedure (New Menu).SQL
--
-- Use the Specify Values for Template Parameters
-- command (Ctrl+Shift+M) to fill in the parameter
```

```
-- values below.
--
-- This block of comments will not be included in
-- the definition of the procedure.
-- ================================================
SET ANSI_NULLS ON
GO
SET QUOTED_IDENTIFIER ON
GO
-- =============================================
-- Author:       <Author,,Name>
-- Create date: <Create Date,,>
-- Description: <Description,,>
-- =============================================
CREATE PROCEDURE <Procedure_Name, sysname, ProcedureName>
    -- Add the parameters for the stored procedure here
    <@Param1, sysname, @p1> <Datatype_For_Param1, , int> = <Default_Value_For_
Param1, , 0>,
    <@Param2, sysname, @p2> <Datatype_For_Param2, , int> = <Default_Value_For_
Param2, , 0>
AS
BEGIN
    -- SET NOCOUNT ON added to prevent extra result sets from
    -- interfering with SELECT statements.
    SET NOCOUNT ON;

    -- Insert statements for procedure here
    SELECT <@Param1, sysname, @p1>, <@Param2, sysname, @p2>
END
GO
```

You can modify the template code as necessary to set the procedure name and to specify the parameters, return value, and procedure body. When you are finished, you can execute the contents of the query window to create the procedure. After you have created the procedure successfully, it is recommended that you save the source code to a file by choosing the Save or Save As option from the File menu. This way, you can re-create the stored procedure from the file if it is accidentally dropped from the database.

TIP

When you create a new stored procedure in SSMS via a Query window, the procedure does not show up in the `Stored Procedures` folder in the Object Browser unless you right-click the `Stored Procedures` folder and choose the Refresh option.

One thing you might notice about the stored procedure template is that it contains template parameters for parameter names, procedure name, author name, create date, and so on. These template parameters are in the format `<parameter, type, value>`:

▶ `parameter_name` is the name of the template parameter in the script.

▶ `data_type` is the optional data type of the template parameter.

▶ `value` is the default value to be used to replace every occurrence of the template parameter in the script.

You can auto substitute values for template parameters by selecting Query, Specify Values for Template Parameters or by pressing Ctrl+Shift+M. This brings up the dialog shown in Figure 25.1.

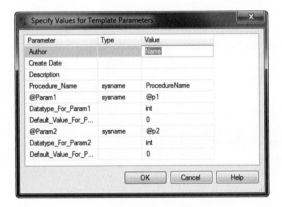

FIGURE 25.1   Using the Specify Values for Template Parameters dialog in SSMS.

Enter the substitution values for the template parameters in the Value column and then click OK. SSMS then substitutes any values you specified wherever the template parameter is used within the template.

An alternative way to create a stored procedure from a template is to use the Template Browser in SSMS. You can open the Template Browser by selecting View, Template Browser in SSMS or by pressing Ctrl+Alt+T. The Template Browser window appears in SSMS, as shown in Figure 25.2.

You can double-click the name of the stored procedure template you want to use or right-click the desired template and then select Open. SSMS opens a new query window, populated with the template code.

NOTE

It is also possible to edit the provided stored procedure templates available in the Template Browser by right-clicking them and selecting the Edit option. You can then customize the templates to include code fragments, comments, or structure that is more to your preference and save the changes to the template file. However, it is generally recommended that you not modify the Microsoft provided templates and instead create and save your own custom templates.

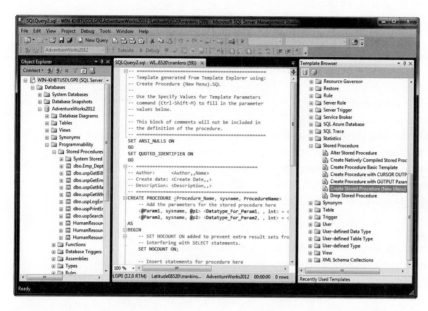

FIGURE 25.2   Using the Template Browser for creating stored procedures in SSMS.

Creating Custom Stored Procedure Templates

To create a custom stored procedure template, right-click the `Stored Procedure` folder in the Template Browser and select New. SSMS then creates an entry in the Template Browser, and you can specify the name for the template.

To begin adding code to the template, right-click the template and select Edit. This opens a query window in which you can start entering the new template code. Probably the best way to get started is to copy the template code from one of the templates provided with SQL Server 2014 and then modify it as you desire. When you are satisfied with your edits, select File, Save to save the template code to a file locally on your computer.

Listing 25.3 shows an example of a new stored procedure template.

LISTING 25.3   An Example of Custom Stored Procedure Template

```
-- ================================================
-- Create basic stored procedure template
-- ================================================

-- Drop stored procedure if it already exists
IF EXISTS (
```

```
  SELECT *
    FROM sys.procedures
   WHERE schema_id = schema_id('dbo')
     AND name = N'<Proc_Name, sysname, myproc>'
)
   DROP PROCEDURE <Schema_Name, sysname, dbo>.<Proc_Name, sysname, myproc>
GO
-- ===============================================
-- Author:         <Author,,Name>
-- Create date: <Create Date,,>
-- Description:    <Description,,>
-- ===============================================
CREATE PROCEDURE <Schema_Name, sysname, dbo>.<Proc_Name, sysname, myproc>
    -- Add the parameters for the stored procedure here
    <@param1, sysname, @p1> <param1_type, , int> = <param1_default, , 0>,
    <@param2, sysname, @p2> <param2_type, , int> = <param2_default, , 0>,
    <@param3, sysname, @p3> <param3_type, , int>  OUTPUT
AS
BEGIN
    -- SET NOCOUNT ON added to prevent extra result sets from
    -- interfering with SELECT statements.
    SET NOCOUNT ON;

    DECLARE @trancnt int
    SELECT @trancnt = @@TRANCOUNT

    if @trancnt = 0
        BEGIN TRAN <Proc_Name, sysname, myproc>
    else
        SAVE TRAN <Proc_Name, sysname, myproc>

    /* Insert processing code here */

    if (@@error != 0) -- check for error condition
    begin
        -- rollback to savepoint, or begin tran
        rollback tran <Proc_Name, sysname, myproc>
        -- return error code indicating rollback
        return -101
    end

    /* Insert more processing here if required */


    -- set value of output parameter
    set <@param3,sysname, @p3> = <@param1,sysname, @p1> + <@param2,sysname, @p2>
```

```
    if @trancnt = 0      -- this proc issued begin tran
      -- commit tran, decrement @@trancount to 0
      commit tran <Proc_Name, sysname, myproc>
    -- commit not required with save tran


    return 0 /* successful return */

END
GO



-- ===========================================
-- Example to execute the stored procedure
-- ===========================================
DECLARE <@output_variable, sysname, @p3_output> <output_datatype, , int>

EXECUTE <Schema_name, sysname, dbo>.<Proc_name, sysname, myproc>
        <@param1, sysname, @p1> = <param1_value, , 1>,
        <@param2, sysname, @p2> = <param2_value, , 1>,
        <@param3, sysname, @p3> = <@output_variable, sysname, @p3_output> OUTPUT

SELECT <@output_variable, sysname, @p3_output>
GO
```

After you define a custom stored procedure template, you can use it as you would use the built-in templates. You can double-click it or right-click and select Open, and SSMS opens a new query window with a new stored procedure creation script based on the custom template. If you use the default values for the template parameters, after the parameter substitution, the CREATE PROCEDURE script looks like the one in Listing 25.4.

LISTING 25.4 An Example of a CREATE PROCEDURE Script Generated from the Custom Stored Procedure Template

```
-- ===========================================
-- Create basic stored procedure template
-- ===========================================


-- Drop stored procedure if it already exists
IF EXISTS (
  SELECT *
    FROM sys.procedures
   WHERE schema_id = schema_id('dbo')
     AND name = N'myproc'
)
  DROP PROCEDURE dbo.myproc
GO
```

```
-- =================================================
-- Author:          Name
-- Create date:
-- Description:
-- =================================================
CREATE PROCEDURE dbo.myproc
    -- Add the parameters for the stored procedure here
    @p1 int = 0,
    @p2 int = 0,
    @p3 int   OUTPUT
AS
BEGIN
    -- SET NOCOUNT ON added to prevent extra result sets from
    -- interfering with SELECT statements.
    SET NOCOUNT ON;

    DECLARE @trancnt int
    SELECT @trancnt = @@TRANCOUNT

    if @trancnt = 0
        BEGIN TRAN myproc
    else
        SAVE TRAN myproc

    /* Insert processing code here */

    if (@@error != 0) -- check for error condition
    begin
        -- rollback to savepoint, or begin tran
        rollback tran myproc
        -- return error code indicating rollback
        return -101
    end

    /* Insert more processing here if required */


    -- set value of output parameter
    set @p3 = @p1 + @p2

    if @trancnt = 0       -- this proc issued begin tran
      -- commit tran, decrement @@trancount to 0
      commit tran myproc
    -- commit not required with save tran
```

```
          return 0 /* successful return */

END
GO



-- =============================================
-- Example to execute the stored procedure
-- =============================================
DECLARE @p3_output int

EXECUTE dbo.myproc
        @p1 = 1,
        @p2 = 1,
        @p3 = @p3_output OUTPUT

SELECT @p3_output
GO
```

Executing Stored Procedures

To execute a stored procedure, you simply invoke it by using its name (the same way you probably have already executed system stored procedures, such as sp_help). If the execution of the stored procedure isn't the first statement in a batch, you need to precede the procedure name with the EXEC keyword. Following is the basic syntax for executing stored procedures:

```
[EXEC[UTE]] [@status =] [schema].procedure_name[; number]
  [[@param_name =] expression [output][, ... ]]
[WITH RECOMPILE
  | { RESULT SETS UNDEFINED }
  | { RESULT SETS NONE }
  | { RESULT SETS ( <result_sets_definition> [,...n ] ) }
]
```

> **NOTE**
>
> The reason you need the EXEC keyword when invoking a stored procedure in a batch or other stored procedure is quite simple. SQL Server parses the commands sent to it in a batch by searching for keywords. Stored procedure names aren't keywords. If SQL Server finds a procedure name among the SQL statements, chances are that SQL Server will return an error message because it tries to treat it as part of the preceding command.

Sometimes the execution is successful, but SQL Server doesn't execute what you want. Consider this example:

```
SELECT * FROM titles
sp_help
```

The SELECT statement runs fine, but the procedure is not executed. The reason is that sp_help ends up being used as a table alias for the titles table in the SELECT statement.

However, if you precede the procedure name with EXEC, like this, you get the expected behavior:

```
SELECT * FROM titles
EXEC sp_help
```

Why don't you have to put EXEC in front of the procedure name if the procedure is the first statement in a batch? If SQL Server doesn't recognize the first string in a batch, it simply assumes that it is a name of a stored procedure. For example, execute the following string and notice the error message:

```
Dsfdskgkghk
go

Msg 2812, Level 16, State 62, Line 1
Could not find stored procedure 'Dsfdskgkghk'.
```

As good programming practice, it is best to always precede stored procedures with the EXEC keyword. This way, it will always work as expected, whether or not it's the first statement in a batch.

Executing Procedures in SSMS

To execute a stored procedure in SSMS, open the object tree for the database, open the Programmability folder, and open the Stored Procedures folder. Then right-click the stored procedure and from the context menu, choose Execute Stored Procedure. SSMS then presents you with the Execute Procedure dialog, as shown in Figure 25.3. In this window, you can enter values for any parameters contained in the stored procedure. If you want to pass a NULL value to a parameter, you need to be sure to place a checkmark in the Pass Null Value check box for that parameter.

After you specify values for all the parameters, SSMS opens a new query window with the generated execute statement and automatically executes it. It displays any results in the Results window. If the stored procedure contains output parameters, SSMS generates local variables for the output parameters and uses a SELECT statement to display the values returned to the output parameters. Listing 25.5 shows an example of the execute script and its results for the procedure invoked in Figure 25.3 (this procedure is the one generated from the custom procedure template, as shown in Listing 25.4).

FIGURE 25.3   Using the Execute Procedure dialog in SSMS.

LISTING 25.5   A Procedure Execution Script Generated by SSMS

```
USE [AdventureWorks2012]
GO


DECLARE @return_value int,
        @p3 int

EXEC @return_value = [dbo].[myproc]
        @p1 = 100,
        @p2 = 200,
        @p3 = @p3 OUTPUT

SELECT @p3 as N'@p3'

SELECT 'Return Value' = @return_value

GO

/* output
        @p3
```

```
-----------
       300

Return Value
-----------
         0
*/
```

Execution Context and the EXECUTE AS Clause

In order to execute a stored procedure created by another user, the user executing the procedure must be granted execute permission on the procedure. By default, however, permissions on objects referenced within the stored procedure are not automatically inherited from the procedure owner if the objects referenced within the stored procedure are not also owned by the creator of the stored procedure. The current user executing the procedure must also have the necessary permissions granted on the referenced objects in order to successfully execute the procedure. The only exception to this occurs when the objects referenced by a stored procedure are also owned by the same user who owns the stored procedure. For example, if the owner of a stored procedure also owns the table that it references, permissions are not checked when there is no change in object ownership. The user executing the stored procedure will automatically have access to the referenced table within the execution context of the stored procedure, without having to be granted explicit rights on the table by the table owner.

However, there are limitations to using ownership chaining alone for inheriting access permissions:

▶ The rights inherited by ownership chaining apply only to DML statements: SELECT, INSERT, UPDATE, and DELETE.

▶ The owner of the procedure and referenced objects must be the same.

▶ The rights inherited by ownership chaining do not apply to dynamic queries inside the stored procedure.

In SQL Server 2014, you can explicitly define the execution context of functions (except inline table-valued functions), stored procedures, and triggers by specifying the EXECUTE AS clause. The EXECUTE AS clause allows you to go beyond ownership chaining to specify the security context under which a stored procedure will execute and what access rights the user will have on the referenced objects. The EXECUTE AS clause allows you to specify explicitly the security context under which the stored procedure will execute. In other words, it allows you to specify which user account SQL Server should use to validate permissions on the database objects referenced by the stored procedure. The user executing the stored procedure, in effect, impersonates the user specified in the EXECUTE AS clause within the context of the execution of the stored procedure.

The EXECUTE AS clause can be specified when the stored procedure is created to set the default security context for all users when executing the stored procedure. Alternatively, the EXECUTE AS clause can be specified explicitly within the stored procedure code or within each individual user session. When specified in a user session, the security context switches to that specified until the connection is closed, a REVERT statement is run, or another EXECUTE AS statement is run.

The syntax of the EXECUTE AS clause for stored procedures is as follows:

```
{ EXEC | EXECUTE } AS { CALLER | SELF | OWNER | 'user_name' }
```

You can specify the following security context options when using the EXECUTE AS clause:

- ▶ **CALLER**—This option specifies that the statements inside the stored procedure are executed in the context of the caller of the module (that is, the current user). The user executing the stored procedure must have execute permission on the stored procedure and also permissions on any database objects that are referenced by the stored procedure that are not owned by the procedure creator. CALLER is the default behavior for all stored procedures.

- ▶ **SELF**—This option is equivalent to EXECUTE AS user_name, where the specified user_name is the person creating or modifying the stored procedure.

- ▶ **OWNER**—This option specifies that the statements inside the stored procedure execute in the context of the current owner of the stored procedure. If the procedure does not have a specified owner, the owner of the schema in which the procedure was created is used. OWNER must map to a single user account and cannot be a role or group.

- ▶ **'user_name'**—This option specifies that the statements inside the stored procedure execute in the context of the user_name specified. Permissions for any objects within the stored procedure are verified against this user. The user specified must exist in the current database and cannot be a group, role, certificate, key, or built-in account.

To determine the execution context of a stored procedure, you can query the execute_as_principal_id column in either the sys.sql_modules or sys.assembly_modules catalog view.

Specifying an execution context for a stored procedure can be very useful when you want to define custom permission sets. For example, some actions, such as TRUNCATE TABLE, cannot be explicitly granted to other users. However, if you use the EXECUTE AS clause to set the execution context of a stored procedure to a user who does have truncate table permissions (for example, a user who has permissions to alter the table), you can then incorporate the TRUNCATE TABLE statement within the procedure. Any user to whom you then grant EXECUTE permission on the stored procedure is able to run it to execute the TRUNCATE TABLE command contained in it.

25

> **TIP**
>
> When using the `EXECUTE AS` clause to customize the permission set for a stored procedure, it is good security policy to specify a login or user that has the least privileges required to perform the operations defined in the stored procedure. Do not specify an account such as a database owner account unless those permissions are required.

To specify the `EXECUTE AS` clause when you create or modify a stored procedure and specify a user account other than your own, you must have impersonate permissions on the specified user account in addition to having permissions to create or alter the stored procedure. When no execution context is specified or `EXECUTE AS CALLER` is specified, impersonate permissions are not required.

The following example demonstrates how the user context changes when you use the `EXECUTE AS` clause in the creation of a stored procedure:

```
use AdventureWorks2012
go
sp_addlogin fred, fred2012
go
sp_grantdbaccess fred
go

create proc test_execute_as
with EXECUTE AS 'fred'
as
select user_name() as 'User context within proc'
go

select user_name() as 'User context before EXEC'
exec test_execute_as
GO

/* output
User context before EXEC
-------------------------------
dbo

User context within proc
-------------------------------
Fred
*/
```

Using the `WITH RESULT SETS` Clause

Often, stored procedures are used to return result sets. Although this is a very useful feature, you might sometimes want greater control over the names and data types of the columns being returned as part of the result set. SQL Server 2014 provides the WITH RESULT SETS clause, which enables you to redefine the names, data types, and properties of the columns being returned from the stored procedure.

Modifying the names, data types, or properties of the columns being returned from a stored procedure result set can be useful when you want to modify the results for a specific report or application. The WITH RESULT SETS clause allows you to modify the name, data type, nullability, and collation of each column returned, but you cannot modify the number of columns returned, the column order, or the number of result sets.

For example, if you execute the uspGetEmployeeManagers stored procedure in AdventureWorks2012, you get the following results by default:

```
EXEC uspGetEmployeeManagers 16
go


/* output
RecursionLevel BusinessEntityID FirstName
LastName                                     OrganizationNode
ManagerFirstName                             ManagerLastName
-------------- ---------------- -------------------------------------------------- -
------------------------------------------------ ------------------------------------
-------------------------------------------------------------------------------------
-------------------------------------------------------------------------------------
---------------------------------------------------- -------------------------------
-------------------- ------------------------------------------------------------
             0               16 David
Bradley                                      /2/
Ken                                          Sánchez
*/
```

Using the WITH RESULT SETS clause, you can provide more meaningful column names and modify the data values to something that better meets your needs:

```
EXEC uspGetEmployeeManagers 16
WITH RESULT SETS
(
    ([Level] tinyint NOT NULL,
    [Emp ID] int NOT NULL,
    [Employee FName] nvarchar(10) NOT NULL,
    [Employee LName] nvarchar(10) NOT NULL,
    [Mgr ID] nvarchar(6) NOT NULL,
    [Mgr FName] nvarchar(10) NOT NULL,
    [Mgr LName] nvarchar(10) NOT NULL )
);
```

```
/* output
Level       Emp ID Employee FName Employee LName Mgr ID Mgr FName   Mgr LName
-----  ----------- -------------- -------------- ------ ---------- ----------
    0        16 David          Bradley          /2/    Ken         Sánchez
*/
```

The WITH RESULT SETS clause can also be used with a stored procedure that returns multiple result sets, and you can define the column names and data types for each result set separately.

As an example of using WITH RESULT SETS for a procedure that returns multiple result sets, you can create the product_sales_detail procedure in AdventureWorks2012 as shown in Listing 25.6.

LISTING 25.6   Stored Procedure that Returns Multiple Result Sets

```
CREATE PROC [dbo].[product_sales_detail]
@ProductID int
AS
SELECT p.ProductID, p.Name, p.ProductNumber, p.ListPrice
 FROM production.Product p
WHERE p.ProductID = @ProductID

SELECT total_sales = SUM(OrderQty)
   FROM Sales.SalesOrderDetail sod
   WHERE sod.ProductID = @ProductID

RETURN
```

To use the WITH RESULT SETS clause with multiple result sets, each result set definition is enclosed in parentheses and separated by a comma, as shown in the following example:

```
EXEC [product_sales_detail] 858
WITH RESULT SETS
(
    (
    ProdID smallint,
    ProductName nvarchar(25),
    ProdNumber nvarchar(10),
    ListPrice money
    ),
    (
    TotalSales bigint
    )
)
GO
```

```
/* output
ProdID ProductName                    ProdNumber           ListPrice
------ ----------------------------- ---------- ---------------------
   858 Half-Finger Gloves, S         GL-H102-S               24.49


        TotalSales
-------------------
             2188
*/
```

If you use the WITH RESULT SETS clause for a procedure that returns multiple result sets, you have to provide a definition for each result set; otherwise, you'll receive the following error:

```
Msg 11535, Level 16, State 1, Procedure ProductList, Line 8
EXECUTE statement failed because its WITH RESULT SETS clause specified 1 result
set(s), and the statement tried to send more result sets than this.
```

Also, the data types you specify for the result columns must be compatible with the data type of the column in the result set or must be a type that SQL Server can implicitly convert to. If the data type is incompatible, you'll receive an error similar to the following:

```
Msg 11538, Level 16, State 1, Procedure ProductList, Line 4
EXECUTE statement failed because its WITH RESULT SETS clause specified type 'date'
for column #1 in result set #1, and the corresponding type sent at run time was
'int'; there is no conversion between the two types.
```

If you do not specify a definition for each column in the procedure result set, you'll get an error similar to the following:

```
Msg 11537, Level 16, State 1, Procedure product_sales_detail, Line 4
EXECUTE statement failed because its WITH RESULT SETS clause specified 3 column(s)
for result set number 1, but the statement sent 4 column(s) at run time.
```

Deferred Name Resolution

In SQL Server 2014, the objects referenced within a stored procedure do not have to exist at the time the procedure is created. SQL Server creates the stored procedure and the references to missing objects are validated when the stored procedure is executed. No error or warning message is issued about the missing objects when the stored procedure is created. One exception is when a stored procedure references another stored procedure that doesn't exist. In that case, a warning message is issued, but the stored procedure is still created (see Listing 25.7). The other exception is when the stored procedure references an object through a linked server connection. The linked server must exist and be accessible, as well as the referenced database, schema, and object or the create will fail with an error.

LISTING 25.7   Procedure Name Resolution During Stored Procedure Creation

```
create proc p2
as
exec p3
go


/* output
The module 'p2' depends on the missing object 'p3'. The module will still be
created; however, it cannot run successfully until the object exists.
*/
```

When a table or view *does* exist at procedure creation time, the column names in the referenced table are validated. If a column name is mistyped or doesn't exist, an error message is issued, and the procedure is not created (see Listing 25.8).

LISTING 25.8   Column Name Validation in Stored Procedures

```
IF EXISTS ( SELECT * FROM sys.procedures
                WHERE schema_id = schema_id('dbo')
                AND name = N'get_employees_and_dept')
    DROP PROCEDURE dbo.get_employees_and_dept
GO
create proc get_employees_and_dept
as

select p.FirstName, p.LastName, d.deptname
    from Person.Person p
    join HumanResources.EmployeeDepartmentHistory edh
        ON p.BusinessEntityID = edh.BusinessEntityID
        AND GETDATE() BETWEEN edh.StartDate AND edh.EndDate
    JOIN HumanResources.Department d
        ON edh.DepartmentID = d.DepartmentID
return
go


/* output
Msg 207, Level 16, State 1, Procedure get_employees_and_dept, Line 4
Invalid column name 'deptname'.
*/
```

One advantage of deferred name resolution is the increased flexibility when creating stored procedures; the order of creating procedures and the tables they reference does not need to be exact. Deferred name resolution is an especially useful feature when a stored procedure references a temporary table that isn't created within that stored procedure.

However, at other times, it can be frustrating to have a stored procedure create successfully only to have it fail when it runs due to a missing table, as shown in Listing 25.9.

LISTING 25.9   Runtime Failure of a Stored Procedure with an Invalid Object Reference

```
IF EXISTS ( SELECT * FROM sys.procedures
              WHERE schema_id = schema_id('dbo')
                AND name = N'get_employees_and_dept')
    DROP PROCEDURE dbo.get_employees_and_dept
GO
create proc get_employees_and_dept
as

select p.FirstName, p.LastName, d.deptname
    from Person.Person p
    join HumanResources.EmployeeDepartmentHistory edh
        ON p.BusinessEntityID = edh.BusinessEntityID
        AND GETDATE() BETWEEN edh.StartDate AND edh.EndDate
    JOIN HumanResources.Departments d
        ON edh.DepartmentID = d.DepartmentID
return
GO

EXEC get_employees_and_dept
go

/* output
Msg 208, Level 16, State 1, Procedure get_employees_and_dept, Line 4
Invalid object name 'HumanResources.Departments'.
*/
```

Another issue to be careful of with deferred name resolution is that you can't rename objects referenced by stored procedures and have the stored procedure continue to work. When the object names are resolved at execution time, the procedure fails at the statement referencing the renamed object. For the stored procedure to execute successfully, it needs to be altered to specify the new object name.

Identifying the Objects Referenced Within Stored Procedures

Because changing the name of a table can cause stored procedures to no longer work, you might want to identify which stored procedures reference a specific table so you know which stored procedures will be affected by changes to the table name or columns. You can view the dependencies between database objects by querying the sys.sql_dependencies object catalog view. Unfortunately, all you really see if you query the sys.sql_dependencies view is a bunch of numbers—just the IDs of the objects and columns that have a dependency relationship, along with some additional status information.

The better way to display a list of stored procedures that reference a specific table or view, or to display a list of objects referenced by a stored procedure, is to use the `sys.dm_sql_referencing_entities` and `sys.dm_sql_referenced_entities` dynamic management functions.

```
sys.dm_sql_referencing_entities ( ' schema_name.table_or_view_name ' , ' OBJECT ' )
sys.dm_sql_referenced_entities ( ' schema_name.proc_name ' , ' OBJECT ' )
```

For example, to display the stored procedures, triggers, functions, and views that reference the Employee table, you execute the following:

```
select referencing_schema_name, referencing_entity_name
 From sys.dm_sql_referencing_entities ( 'HumanResources.Employee' , 'OBJECT' )
go
```

In the `AdventureWorks2012` database, the Employee table is referenced by the following:

```
referencing_schema_name    referencing_entity_name
-----------------------    ------------------------------
dbo                        ufnGetContactInformation
dbo                        uspGetEmployeeManagers
dbo                        uspGetManagerEmployees
HumanResources             CK_Employee_BirthDate
HumanResources             CK_Employee_Gender
HumanResources             CK_Employee_HireDate
HumanResources             CK_Employee_MaritalStatus
HumanResources             CK_Employee_SickLeaveHours
HumanResources             CK_Employee_VacationHours
HumanResources             Employee
HumanResources             uspUpdateEmployeeHireInfo
HumanResources             uspUpdateEmployeeLogin
HumanResources             uspUpdateEmployeePersonalInfo
HumanResources             vEmployee
HumanResources             vEmployeeDepartment
HumanResources             vEmployeeDepartmentHistory
Sales                      vSalesPerson
Sales                      vSalesPersonSalesByFiscalYear
```

To display the objects referenced by the `usp_GetManagerEmployees` stored procedure, you could execute the following:

```
select DISTINCT referenced_schema_name,
                referenced_entity_name AS tablename,
                referenced_minor_name AS columnName
 From sys.dm_sql_referenced_entities ( 'dbo.uspGetManagerEmployees' , 'OBJECT' )
go
```

In the current database, the specified object references the following:

```
referenced_schema_name   tablename     columnName
-----------------------   -----------   ------------------
HumanResources           Employee      NULL
HumanResources           Employee      BusinessEntityID
HumanResources           Employee      OrganizationNode
OrganizationNode         GetAncestor   NULL
OrganizationNode         ToString      NULL
Person                   Person        NULL
Person                   Person        BusinessEntityID
Person                   Person        FirstName
Person                   Person        LastName
```

You can also see dependency information in SSMS by right-clicking an object and choosing View Dependencies. This brings up the Object Dependencies window, as shown in Figure 25.4. You can view either the objects that depend on the selected object or objects on which the selected object depends. You can also expand the dependency tree for the objects listed in the Dependencies pane.

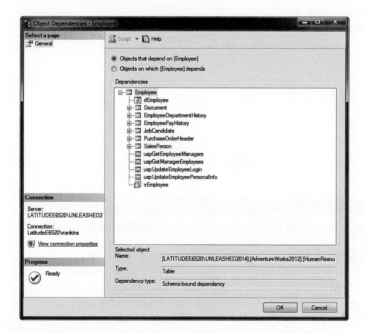

FIGURE 25.4   Viewing object dependencies in SSMS.

Viewing Stored Procedures

You can view the source code for stored procedures in SQL Server 2014 in a number of different ways. You can query the definition column of the object catalog view sys.sql_modules, use the system procedure sp_helptext, or use the object_definition() function. Listing 25.10 provides an example of using the sp_helptext stored procedure. However, sp_helptext returns the data in rows representing the way the procedure text is stored in the system tables. There will be some extra line breaks in the result, possibly in the middle of a keyword or object name.

LISTING 25.10   Viewing Code for a Stored Procedure by Using sp_helptext

```
EXEC sp_helptext Emp_Dept
GO

/* output
Text
-------------------------------------------------------------
CREATE PROCEDURE Emp_Dept
AS
BEGIN
    SELECT p.Lastname, p.FirstName, d.Name
        FROM HumanResources.Department d
        JOIN HumanResources.EmployeeDepartmentHistory edh
            ON d.DepartmentID = edh.DepartmentID
            AND edh.EndDate IS null
        JOIN person.Person p
            ON p.BusinessEntityID = edh.BusinessEntityID
            ORDER BY d.departmentID
    RETURN 0
END
*/
```

> **TIP**
>
> If you are running these queries to display the procedure code in a query window in SSMS, you probably need to modify the query results options to have the procedures display correctly and clearly. From the Query menu, select Query Options. Expand the Results item and select Text. Enter a value up to 8192 for the Maximum Number of Characters Displayed in Each Column setting and click OK.
>
> You probably also want to have the results displayed as text rather than in the grid. To make this change, under the Query menu, select the Results To submenu and then select Results to Text. As a shortcut, you can press Ctrl+T to switch to Results to Text. You can press Ctrl+D to switch back to Results to Grid. If you are using grid results, you'll typically have to select all grid cells and then copy and paste the results into a Query window or some other Text editor in order to view the full procedure code in a readable manner.

By default, all users have permission to execute sp_helptext to view the SQL code for the stored procedures in a database. If you want to protect the source code of stored procedures and keep its contents from prying eyes, you can create a procedure by using the

WITH ENCRYPTION option. When this option is specified, the source code stored in the database is encrypted.

NOTE

If you use encryption when creating stored procedures, be aware that although SQL Server can internally decrypt the source code, no mechanisms exist for the user or for any of the end-user tools to decrypt the stored procedure text for display or editing. With this in mind, make sure that you store a copy of the source code for those procedures in a file in case you need to edit or re-create them. Also, procedures created by using the WITH ENCRYPTION option cannot be published as part of SQL Server replication.

In addition, encrypting a stored procedure prevents the ability to step into the code of a stored procedure when debugging your code via the SSMS debugger.

Another way to view stored procedure code is with a query that retrieves the definition column from the sys.sql_modules object catalog view, which returns the entire procedure definition:

```
select definition
    from sys.sql_modules
    where object_id = object_id('dbo.Emp_Dept')
go

/* output
definition
-----------------------------------------------------------------
CREATE PROCEDURE Emp_Dept
AS
BEGIN
    SELECT p.Lastname, p.FirstName, d.Name
        FROM HumanResources.Department d
        JOIN HumanResources.EmployeeDepartmentHistory edh
            ON d.DepartmentID = edh.DepartmentID
            AND edh.EndDate IS null
        JOIN person.Person p
            ON p.BusinessEntityID = edh.BusinessEntityID
            ORDER BY d.departmentID
    RETURN 0
END
*/
```

Finally, one other method of displaying the source code for a stored procedure is to use the object_definition() function. This function takes the object ID as a parameter. If you, like most other people, do not know the object ID of the procedure in question, you can use the object_id() function. The following is an example of using the object_definition() function:

```
select object_definition(object_id('dbo.Emp_Dept'))
go

/* output

--------------------------------------------------------------------------------
------
CREATE PROCEDURE Emp_Dept
AS
BEGIN
    SELECT p.Lastname, p.FirstName, d.Name
        FROM HumanResources.Department d
        JOIN HumanResources.EmployeeDepartmentHistory edh
            ON d.DepartmentID = edh.DepartmentID
            AND edh.EndDate IS null
        JOIN person.Person p
            ON p.BusinessEntityID = edh.BusinessEntityID
            ORDER BY d.departmentID
    RETURN 0
END
*/
```

Modifying Stored Procedures

You can modify the text of a stored procedure by using the ALTER PROCEDURE statement. The syntax for ALTER PROCEDURE is similar to the syntax for CREATE PROCEDURE (see Listing 25.11). Using ALTER PROCEDURE has a couple advantages over dropping and re-creating a procedure to modify it. The main advantage is that you don't have to drop the procedure first to make the change, so it remains available, even if the ALTER PROCEDURE command fails due to a syntax or object reference error. The second advantage is that because you don't have to drop the procedure, you don't have to worry about reassigning permissions to it after modifying it.

LISTING 25.11   Modifying a Stored Procedure by Using ALTER PROCEDURE

```
Alter PROCEDURE Emp_Dept @dept_name nvarchar(50) = '%'
AS
BEGIN
    SELECT p.Lastname, p.FirstName, d.Name
        FROM HumanResources.Department d
        JOIN HumanResources.EmployeeDepartmentHistory edh
            ON d.DepartmentID = edh.DepartmentID
            AND edh.EndDate IS null
        JOIN person.Person p
            ON p.BusinessEntityID = edh.BusinessEntityID
```

```
        WHERE d.name LIKE @dept_name
        ORDER BY d.departmentID
    RETURN 0
END
```

Viewing and Modifying Stored Procedures with SSMS

You can also use SSMS to create, view, and modify stored procedures.

To edit a stored procedure in SSMS, expand the `Programmability` folder and then the `Stored Procedures` folder, right-click the name of the procedure you want to modify, and select Modify (see Figure 25.5).

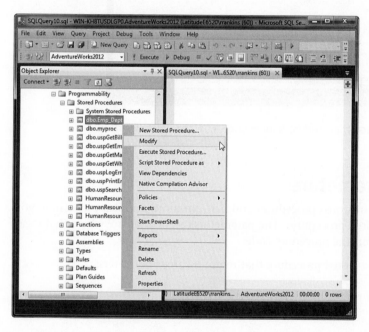

FIGURE 25.5   Modifying stored procedures in SSMS.

SSMS then extracts the `ALTER PROCEDURE` statement for the selected procedure into a new query window. Here, you can edit the procedure code as needed and then execute the contents of the query window to modify the procedure. In addition, the Object Browser in SSMS provides other options for extracting the stored procedure source code. It can generate code to create, alter, or drop the selected stored procedure. You can script the stored procedure source code to a new window, to a file, or to the Windows Clipboard by right-clicking the stored procedure name in the Object Browser and choosing the appropriate option (see Figure 25.6).

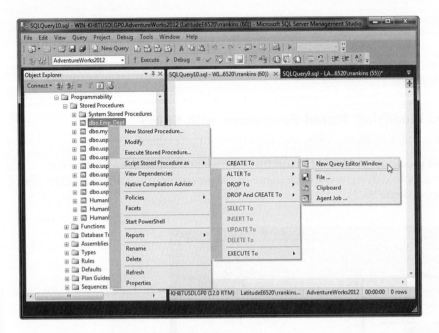

FIGURE 25.6   Extracting stored procedure source code to a new query window.

Using Input Parameters

To increase the flexibility of stored procedures and perform more complex processing, you can pass parameters to stored procedures. The parameters can be used anywhere that local variables can be used within the procedure code.

The following example is a stored procedure that requires three parameters:

```
CREATE PROC paramproc
 @parm1 int, @parm2 int, @parm3 int
AS
-- Processing goes here
RETURN
```

If you want to help identify the data values for which the parameters are defined, it is recommended that you give your parameters meaningful names. Parameter names, like local variables, can be up to 128 characters in length, including the @ sign, and they must follow SQL Server rules for identifiers. Up to 2,100 parameters can be defined for a stored procedure.

When you execute a procedure, you can pass the parameters by position or by name:

```
--Passing parameters by position
EXEC paramproc 1, 2, 3
--Passing parameters by name
```

```
EXEC paramproc @parm2 = 2, @parm2 = 1, @parm3 =3
--Passing parameters by position and name
EXEC paramproc 1, @parm3 =3, @parm2 = 2
```

After you specify one parameter by name, you must pass all subsequent parameters for the procedure in that EXECUTE statement by name as well. You cannot pass any of the subsequent parameters by position. If you want to skip parameters that are not the last parameter(s) in the procedure and have them take default values (as described in the next section), you also need to pass parameters by name or use the DEFAULT keyword in place of the parameter value.

> **TIP**
>
> When you are embedding calls to stored procedures in client applications and script files, it is advisable to pass parameters by name. Reviewing and debugging the code becomes easier that way. One time, half a day was spent debugging a set of nested stored procedures to figure out why they weren't working correctly, only to find the problem was due to a missed parameter; all the parameter values were shifted over one place, and the wrong values ended up being passed to the wrong parameters. This resulted in the queries not finding any matching values. Had the parameters been passed by name, this issue would not have occurred. This was a lesson learned the hard way!

25

Values passed in through input parameter can be only explicit constant values, local variables, parameters, or, table-valued parameters. You cannot specify a function or another expression as an input parameter value. You would have to store a return value from the function or expression in a local variable and pass the local variable into the input parameter. Likewise, you cannot use a function or another expression as a default value for a parameter.

Setting Default Values for Parameters

You can assign a default value to a parameter by specifying a value in the definition of the parameter, as shown in Listing 25.12.

LISTING 25.12   Assigning a Default Value for a Parameter in a Stored Procedure

```
Alter PROCEDURE Emp_Dept @dept_name nvarchar(50) = '%'
AS
BEGIN
    SELECT p.Lastname, p.FirstName, d.Name
        FROM HumanResources.Department d
        JOIN HumanResources.EmployeeDepartmentHistory edh
            ON d.DepartmentID = edh.DepartmentID
            AND edh.EndDate IS null
        JOIN person.Person p
            ON p.BusinessEntityID = edh.BusinessEntityID
```

```
        WHERE d.name LIKE @dept_name
        ORDER BY d.departmentID
    RETURN 0
END
```

You can have SQL Server apply the default value for a parameter during execution by not specifying a value or by specifying the DEFAULT keyword in the position of the parameter, as shown in Listing 25.13.

LISTING 25.13   Applying a Default Value for a Parameter When Executing a Stored Procedure

```
EXEC Emp_Dept
EXEC Emp_Dept DEFAULT
EXEC Emp_Dept @dept_name = DEFAULT
```

TIP

If you are involved in creating stored procedures that other people will use, you probably want to make the stored procedures as easy to use as possible.

If you leave out a parameter that is required, SQL Server presents an error message. The paramproc procedure, shown earlier in this section, requires three parameters: @parm1, @parm2, and @parm3:

```
    EXEC ParamProc

    /* output
    Msg 201, Level 16, State 4, Procedure paramproc, Line 0
    Procedure or function 'paramproc' expects parameter '@parm1', which was not
    supplied.
    */
```

Note that SQL Server complains only about the first missing parameter. The programmer passes the first parameter, only to find out that more parameters are required. This is a good way to annoy a programmer or an end user.

When you execute a command-line program, you probably expect that you can use /? to obtain a list of the parameters the program expects. You can program stored procedures in a similar manner by assigning NULL (or some other special value) as a default value to the parameters and checking for that value inside the procedure. The following is an outline of a stored procedure that presents the user with information about the parameters expected if the user doesn't pass parameters:

```
    CREATE PROC ParamProc2
      @parm1 int = NULL, @parm2 int = 32, @parm3 int = NULL
    AS
    IF (@parm1 IS NULL or @parm1 NOT BETWEEN 1 and 10) OR
       @parm3 IS NULL
    PRINT 'Usage:
     EXEC MyProc2
```

```
   @parm1 int,    (Required: Can be between 1 and 10)
   @parm2 = 32,   (Optional: Default value of 32)
   @parm3 int,    (Required: Any number within range)'
-- Processing goes here
RETURN
GO


EXEC ParamProc2
GO


/* output
Usage:
 EXEC MyProc2
  @parm1 int,    (Required: Can be between 1 and 10)
  @parm2 = 32,   (Optional: Default value of 32)
  @parm3 int,    (Required: Any number within range)
*/
```

You can develop your own standards for the way the message is presented to the user, but what is important is that the information is presented at all.

To display the parameters defined for a stored procedure, you can view them in the SSMS Object Explorer (see Figure 25.7) or by executing the sp_help stored procedure, as shown in Listing 25.14. (Note that the output has been edited to fit the page.)

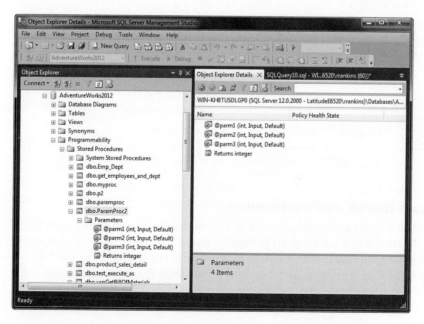

FIGURE 25.7   Displaying stored procedure parameters in SSMS.

LISTING 25.14   Displaying Stored Procedure Parameters by Using `sp_help`

```
sp_help 'dbo.Emp_Dept'
GO


/* output
Name             Owner        Type                              Created_datetime
---------------  ----------   -------------------------------   -----------------------
Emp_Dept         dbo          stored procedure                  2014-11-02 16:16:02.587



Parameter_name   Type         Length Prec Scale Param_order Collation
---------------  ----------   ------ ---- ----- ----------- -------------------------
----
@dept_name       nvarchar        100   50  NULL           1 SQL_Latin1_General_CP1_CI_AS
*/
```

You can also view parameter information for a stored procedure using the `sys.parameters` catalog view:

```
select substring(p.name,1, 20) as Parameter_name,
       substring (t.name, 1, 10) as Data_Type,
       p.max_length as Length,
       parameter_id as param_order,
       default_value
from sys.parameters p
inner join sys.types t
    on p.user_type_id = t.user_type_id
where p.object_id = object_id('dbo.Emp_Dept')
order by parameter_id
GO


/* output
Parameter_name        Data_Type   Length param_order default_value
-------------------   ----------  ------ ----------- --------------
@dept_name            nvarchar       100           1 NULL*/
```

Passing Object Names as Parameters

In SQL Server 2014, if you pass an object name as a parameter to a stored procedure, SQL Server attempts to treat it as a table-valued parameter unless the object name is used either as an argument in a WHERE clause or in a dynamic SQL query. For example, the code in Listing 25.15 generates an error message when you try to create the stored procedure.

LISTING 25.15   Attempting to Create a Stored Procedure by Using a Parameter to Pass in a Table Name

```
CREATE  proc find_data @table varchar(128)
as


select * from @table


GO


/* output
Msg 1087, Level 16, State 1, Procedure find_data, Line 4
 Must declare the table variable "@table".
*/
```

As you can see, when the parameter is used in the FROM clause, SQL Server expects it to be defined as a table variable. To use the value in the parameter as a table name, you can build a dynamic SQL query similar to the example shown in Listing 25.16.

LISTING 25.16   Passing a Table as a Parameter to a Stored Procedure for Dynamic SQL Execution

```
CREATE  proc find_data @table varchar(128)
as

exec ('select * from ' + @table)
return
go


exec find_data @table = 'Person.ContactType'
go


/* output
ContactTypeID Name                             ModifiedDate
------------- -------------------------------- ------------
            1 Accounting Manager               2002-06-01
            2 Assistant Sales Agent            2002-06-01
            3 Assistant Sales Representative   2002-06-01
            4 Coordinator Foreign Markets      2002-06-01
...
           19 Sales Manager                    2002-06-01
           20 Sales Representative             2002-06-01
*/
```

Using Wildcards in Parameters

Wildcards can be included in `varchar`-based input parameters and used in a `LIKE` clause in a query to perform pattern matching. However, you should not use the `char` data type for parameters that will contain wildcard characters because SQL Server pads spaces onto the value passed in to the parameter to expand it to the specified size of the `char` data type. For example, if you declared an `@lastname` parameter as `char(40)` and passed in `'s%'`, SQL Server would search not for a string starting with `'s'` but for a string starting with `'s'`, any characters, and ending with up to 38 spaces. This would likely not match any actual data values.

Also, to increase the flexibility of a stored procedure that searches for character strings, you can default the parameter to `'%'`, as in the following example:

```
IF EXISTS ( SELECT * FROM sys.procedures
              WHERE schema_id = schema_id('dbo')
                AND name = N'find_Person')
   DROP PROCEDURE dbo.find_Person
GO
 create proc find_Person @lastname varchar(50) = '%'
as
    select BusinessEntityID, LastName, FirstName
        from Person.Person
        where LastName like @lastname
        order by LastName, FirstName
```

This procedure, if passed no parameter, returns data for all persons in the `Person` table. If passed a string containing wildcard characters, this procedure returns data for all persons matching the search pattern specified. If a string containing no wildcards is passed, the query performs a search for exact matches against the string value.

Unfortunately, wildcard searches can be performed only against character strings. If you want to have similar flexibility searching against a numeric value, such as an integer, one option is to default the value to `NULL` and when the parameter is `NULL`, compare the column with itself, as shown in the following example:

```
IF EXISTS ( SELECT * FROM sys.procedures
              WHERE schema_id = schema_id('dbo')
                AND name = N'find_products_by_weight')
   DROP PROCEDURE dbo.find_products_by_weight
GO
create proc find_products_by_weight @weight decimal(8,2) = null
as
    select Name, ProductNumber, ListPrice, Weight
        from Production.Product
        where weight = ISNULL(@weight, weight)
```

However, the problem with this approach is that the procedure does not return any rows in which weight contains a NULL value. The reason is that NULL is never considered equal to NULL; you cannot compare an unknown value with another unknown value. To return all rows, including those in which weight is NULL, you need to implement a dual-query solution, as in the following example:

```
IF EXISTS ( SELECT * FROM sys.procedures
              WHERE schema_id = schema_id('dbo')
                AND name = N'find_products_by_weight')
   DROP PROCEDURE dbo.find_products_by_weight
GO
create proc find_products_by_weight @weight decimal(8,2) = null
AS
   IF @weight IS null
       select Name, ProductNumber, ListPrice, Weight
           from Production.Product
   ELSE
       select Name, ProductNumber, ListPrice, Weight
           from Production.Product
           where weight = ISNULL(@weight, weight)
```

Using Table-Valued Parameters

Table-valued parameters, which were introduced in SQL Server 2008, allow you to pass table variables to stored procedures. Table-valued parameters provide more flexibility and, in many cases, better performance than temporary tables as a means to pass result sets between stored procedures.

Table-valued parameters provide many of the same performance advantages as table data types. Table-valued parameters also share some of the same restrictions as table variables, such as SQL Server not maintaining statistics on table-valued parameters and table-valued parameters not permitted as the target of a SELECT INTO or INSERT EXEC statement. In addition, table-valued parameters can be passed only as READONLY input parameters to stored procedures. DML operations, such as UPDATE, INSERT, and DELETE, cannot be performed on table-valued parameters within the body of a stored procedure.

To create and use table-valued parameters, you must first create a user-defined table type and define the table structure. You do so using the CREATE TYPE command, as in the following example:

```
if exists (select * from sys.systypes t where t.name = 'ProductTableType'
              and t.uid = USER_ID('dbo'))
     drop type ProductTableType
go
CREATE TYPE ProductTableType AS TABLE
(ProductID int NOT NULL,
 name nvarchar(50) NOT null,
 ListPrice money NOT null,
```

```
Size nvarchar(5) null ,
Weight DECIMAL(8,2) NULL,
Color nvarchar(15) NULL,
SellStartDate datetime NOT null)
Go
```

After the table data type is created, you can use it for declaring local table variables and for stored procedure parameters. To use the table-valued parameter in a procedure, you create a procedure to receive and access data through a table-valued parameter:

```
/* Create a procedure to receive data for the table-valued parameter. */
if OBJECT_ID('tab_parm_test') is not null
    drop proc tab_parm_test
go
create proc tab_parm_test
        @SellStartDate datetime = null,
        @ListPrice money = $0.0,
        @Product_tab ProductTableType READONLY
as
set nocount on

if @SellStartDate is null
    -- if no date is specified, set date to last year
    set @SellStartDate = dateadd(month, -12, getdate())

select * from @Product_tab
where SellStartDate >= @SellStartDate
and ListPrice >= @ListPrice
return
go
```

Then, when calling that stored procedure, you declare a local table variable using the table data type defined previously, populate the table variable with data, and then pass the table variable to the stored procedure:

```
/* Declare a variable that references the type. */
declare @Product_tab ProductTableType

/* Add data to the table variable. */
insert @Product_tab
    select ProductID, Name, ListPrice, Size, Weight, Color, SellStartDate
      from Production.Product

/* Pass the table variable populated with data to a stored procedure. */
exec tab_parm_test '7/1/2007', $2000, @Product_tab
go
```

```
/* output
ProductID name                     ListPrice Size  Weight Color   SellStartDate
--------- ------------------------ --------- ----- ------ ------- -------------
      954 Touring-1000 Yellow, 46  2384.07   46    25.13  Yellow  2007-07-01
      955 Touring-1000 Yellow, 50  2384.07   50    25.42  Yellow  2007-07-01
      956 Touring-1000 Yellow, 54  2384.07   54    25.68  Yellow  2007-07-01
      957 Touring-1000 Yellow, 60  2384.07   60    25.90  Yellow  2007-07-01
      966 Touring-1000 Blue, 46    2384.07   46    25.13  Blue    2007-07-01
      967 Touring-1000 Blue, 50    2384.07   50    25.42  Blue    2007-07-01
      968 Touring-1000 Blue, 54    2384.07   54    25.68  Blue    2007-07-01
      969 Touring-1000 Blue, 60    2384.07   60    25.90  Blue    2007-07-01
*/
```

Using Output Parameters

If a calling batch passes a variable as a parameter to a stored procedure and that parameter is modified inside the procedure, the modifications are not passed to the calling batch unless they are defined as OUTPUT parameters. To define a parameter as an OUTPUT parameter, you need to specify the keyword OUTPUT in the parameter definition when creating the procedure. The following example shows a stored procedure that accepts two parameters, one of which is defined as an output parameter:

```
IF EXISTS ( SELECT * FROM sys.procedures
             WHERE schema_id = schema_id('dbo')
               AND name = N'product_sales')
   DROP PROCEDURE dbo.product_sales
GO
CREATE PROC product_sales
@ProductID int, @total_sales int OUTPUT
AS
SELECT @total_sales = SUM(OrderQty)
   FROM Sales.SalesOrderDetail sod
   WHERE sod.ProductID = @ProductID
RETURN
GO
```

The calling batch (or stored procedure) needs to declare a variable to store the returned value. The execute statement must include the OUTPUT keyword as well, or the modifications won't be reflected in the calling batch's variable:

```
DECLARE @totSales  int
EXEC product_sales 870, @totSales OUTPUT
PRINT 'Total Sales of productID 870: ' +
      CONVERT(VARCHAR(10), @totSales) + '.'
GO
```

25

```
/* output
Total Sales of productID 870: 6815.
*/
```

You can also pass the output parameter by name:

```
DECLARE @totSales  int
EXEC product_sales @ProductID = 870,
     @total_sales = @totSales OUTPUT
PRINT 'Total Sales of productID 870: ' +
       CONVERT(VARCHAR(10), @totSales) + '.'
GO
```

Note that when you pass an output parameter by name, the parameter name (@total_sales, in this example) is listed on the left side of the expression, and the local variable (@totSales), which is set equal to the value of the output parameter, is on the right side of the expression. An output parameter can also serve as an input parameter.

Output parameters can also be passed back and captured in a client application by using ADO, ODBC, OLE DB, and so on.

Returning Procedure Status

Most programming languages are able to pass a status code to the caller of a function or subroutine. A value of 0 generally indicates that the execution was successful. SQL Server stored procedures are no exception.

SQL Server automatically generates an integer status value of 0 after successful completion of a stored procedure. If SQL Server detects a system error, a status value between -1 and -99 is returned. You can use the RETURN statement to explicitly pass a status value less than -99 or greater than 0. The calling batch or procedure can set up a local variable to retrieve and check the return status.

In Listing 25.17, the product_sales2 stored procedure returns the total sales for a given product ID as a result set. If the product does not exist, to avoid just returning an empty result set, the procedure instead returns the status value -101. In the calling batch or stored procedure, you need to create a variable to hold the return value so you can check to see if it's non-zero. The return value is passed back into the local variable by the EXECUTE statement and can then be checked within the SQL code to determine if the procedure executed successfully.

LISTING 25.17   Returning a Status Code from a Stored Procedure

```
IF EXISTS ( SELECT * FROM sys.procedures
              WHERE schema_id = schema_id('dbo')
                AND name = N'product_sales2')
   DROP PROCEDURE dbo.product_sales2
GO
```

```
CREATE PROC product_sales2
@ProductID int
AS
IF NOT EXISTS (SELECT * FROM Sales.SalesOrderDetail WHERE ProductID = @ProductID)
    RETURN -101
SELECT total_sales = SUM(OrderQty)
   FROM Sales.SalesOrderDetail sod
   WHERE sod.ProductID = @ProductID
RETURN
GO


-- Execute the procedure
DECLARE @status int
EXEC @status = product_sales2 870
IF @status = -101
    PRINT 'No Product with that ID found.'
go

/* output
total_sales
-----------
      6815
*/


-- Execute the procedure
DECLARE @status int
EXEC @status = product_sales2 9999
IF @status = -101
    PRINT 'No Product with that ID found.'
go

/* output
No Product with that ID found.
*/
```

Return values can also be passed back and captured by client applications developed in ADO, ODBC, OLE DB, and so on.

Debugging Stored Procedures Using SQL Server Management Studio

The Transact-SQL debugger in SQL Server Management Studio enables you to step through Transact-SQL scripts, stored procedures, triggers, and functions as they are running. The Transact-SQL debugger allows you to do the following:

▶ Step through the Transact-SQL statements in the Query Editor line by line or set breakpoints to stop at specific lines.

▶ Step into or over Transact-SQL stored procedures, functions, or triggers run by the code in the Query Editor window.

▶ Watch the values assigned to variables and observe system objects such as the call stack and threads.

If you want to run the T-SQL Debugger, the Query Editor window must be connected to SQL Server through a user account that is a member of the `sysadmin` server role.

NOTE

Debugging of T-SQL code should be done only on a test or development server, not on a production server. Debugging sessions can often run for long periods of time while you are investigating the operations of your Transact-SQL statements. If the code being debugged involves a multistatement transaction, locks acquired by the session could be held for extended periods while the code is paused in the debugger, until the debugging session is ended, or the transaction is committed or rolled back. This could lead to extensive locking contention or blocking for other applications accessing production data.

You start the debugger in a Query Editor window by either clicking the Debug button on the Query toolbar or by clicking Start Debugging on the Debug menu, as shown in Figure 25.8.

FIGURE 25.8   Invoking the T-SQL debugger in SSMS.

When the Query Editor window enters debug mode, the debugger initially stops on the first executable line of code in the query window. You can then set any breakpoints and run to the breakpoints or step through the code one line at a time. You can press F10 to step through the code one line at a time. If the SQL code invokes a stored procedure or function, or a DML statement invokes a trigger, you can press F11 to step into the called routine. If you step into a routine in the T-SQL Debugger, SQL Server Management Studio opens a new Query Editor window populated with the source code for the routine, places the window into debug mode, and then pauses execution on the first statement in the routine, as shown in Figure 25.9. You can then step through or set breakpoints in the code for that routine.

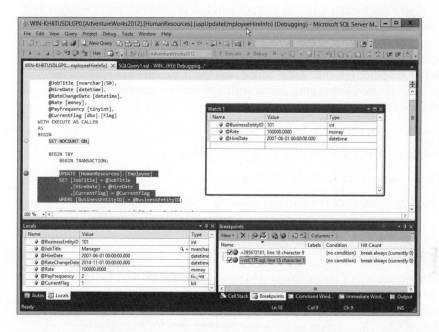

FIGURE 25.9   Debugging a T-SQL stored procedure in SSMS.

Located near the bottom of the debugger window are some useful information windows. The first group of windows is the Locals/Watch window, which displays the contents of local variables or any watch expressions you have defined. The Locals window displays the current values in all the local variables within the current scope. You can also modify the values of the variables in the Locals window to test various scenarios or to adjust data values so the code executes differently. To modify the value of a variable, right-click the row and select Edit Value.

In the Watch windows, you can add variables or expressions whose values you want to watch, such as the global variables @@NESTLEVEL, @@FETCH_STATUS, or @@ROWCOUNT. To add an expression to a Watch window, you can either right-click a variable and select Add

Watch or simply enter the name of the expression in the Name column of an empty row in a Watch window. The Watch windows, like the other tabbed windows in the debugger, can be set as docked or floating windows, allowing you to view multiple windows simultaneously (Figure 25.9 shows an example of the Watch1 window set as a floating window).

The second group of windows is the Call Stack, Breakpoints, Output, and Results and Messages windows. The Call Stack window displays the current execution location and also displays information about how execution passed from the original Query Editor window to the current execution location through any other functions, procedures, or triggers. The Breakpoints window lets you view information about the breakpoints you have set. From this window, you can also jump to the source code where the breakpoint is set or disable or delete the breakpoint. The Output window displays various messages and program data, including system messages from the debugger. The Results and Messages tabs on the Query Editor window display the results of previously executed Transact-SQL statements within the debugging session. The Query Editor window stays in debug mode until either the last statement in the Query Editor window is executed or you manually stop debugging. You can stop debugging, along with any further statement execution, using any one of the following methods:

▶ On the Debug menu, click Stop Debugging.

▶ On the Debug toolbar, click the Stop Debugging button.

▶ On the Query menu, click Cancel Executing Query.

▶ On the Query toolbar, click the Cancel Executing Query button.

Startup Procedures

A SQL Server administrator can create stored procedures that are marked for execution automatically whenever SQL Server starts. They are often referred to as *startup procedures*. Startup procedures are useful for performing housekeeping-type tasks or starting up a background process when SQL Server starts. Some possible uses for startup procedures include the following:

▶ Automatically perform system or maintenance tasks in `tempdb`, such as creating a global temporary table.

▶ Enable custom server side SQL Server Profiler traces automatically whenever SQL Server is running. (For more information on SQL Server Profiler traces, see Chapter 5, "SQL Server Profiler.")

▶ Automatically start other external processes on the SQL Server machine, using `xp_cmdshell`.

▶ Prime the data cache with the contents of your critical, frequently used tables.

▶ Prime the plan cache by executing procedures or functions you want to have compiled and cached before applications start using them.

To create a startup procedure, log in as a system administrator and create the procedure in the `master` database. Then set the procedure startup option to `true` by using sp_procoption:

```
sp_procoption procedure_name, startup, true
```

If you no longer want the procedure to run at startup, remove the startup option by executing the same procedure and changing the value to `false`.

By default, a startup procedure runs in the context of the system administrator account in the master database, but it can use SETUSER or the EXECUTE AS option to impersonate another account during execution, if necessary. If you need to reference objects in other databases from within a startup procedure, you need to fully qualify the object with the appropriate database and schema names.

Startup procedures are launched asynchronously; that is, SQL Server doesn't wait for them to complete before continuing with additional startup tasks. This allows a startup procedure to execute in a loop for the duration of the SQL Server process, or it allows several startup procedures to be launched simultaneously. While a startup procedure is running, it runs within a separate worker thread.

25

TIP

If you need to execute a series of stored procedures in sequence during startup, you can nest the stored procedure calls within a single startup procedure. This approach consumes only a single worker thread.

Any error messages or print statements generated by a startup procedure are written to the SQL Server error log. For example, consider the following whimsical but utterly useless startup procedure:

```
use master
go
create procedure good_morning
as
print 'Good morning, Dave'
return
go
sp_procoption good_morning, startup, true
go
```

When SQL Server is restarted, you'll see entries similar to the following displayed in the error log:

```
2014-11-02 20:13:55.280 spid8s        Launched startup procedure 'good_morning'.

2014-11-02 20:13:55.280 spid31s       Good morning, Dave
```

Any result sets generated by a startup procedure vanish into the infamous bit bucket. If you need to return result sets from a startup procedure, the procedure should be written to insert the results into a table. The table needs to be a permanent table and not a temporary table because a temporary table would be automatically dropped when the startup procedure finished executing.

The following example is a startup procedure that could preload all tables within the Sales and Purchasing schemas in the AdventureWorks2012 database into data cache memory on SQL Server startup:

```
use master
go
create procedure prime_cache
as
declare @tablename varchar(128),
        @schemaname varchar(128)

declare c1 cursor for
select s.name, o.name
    from AdventureWorks2012.sys.objects o
    join AdventureWorks2012.sys.schemas s
        on o.schema_id = s.schema_id
    where type = 'U'
    and s.name in ('Sales', 'Purchasing')

open c1
fetch c1 into @schemaname, @tablename
while @@fetch_status = 0
begin
    print 'Loading ''' + @schemaname + '.' + @tablename + ''' into data cache'
    exec ('select * from AdventureWorks2012.' + @schemaname + '.' + @tablename)
    fetch c1 into @schemaname, @tablename
end
close c1
deallocate c1
return
go


sp_procoption prime_cache, startup, true
go
```

The error log output from this startup procedure would be similar to the following:

```
2014-11-02 20:17:13.390 spid15s       Recovery is complete. This is an informational
message only. No user action is required.
2014-11-02 20:17:13.390 spid15s       SQL Server is now ready for client connections.
This is an informational message; no user action is required.
```

```
2014-11-02 20:17:13.400 spid24s      Loading 'Purchasing.ShipMethod' into data cache
2014-11-02 20:17:13.400 spid24s      Loading 'Sales.ShoppingCartItem' into data
cache
2014-11-02 20:17:13.400 spid24s      Loading 'Sales.SpecialOffer' into data cache
2014-11-02 20:17:13.410 spid24s      Loading 'Sales.SpecialOfferProduct' into data
cache
2014-11-02 20:17:13.410 spid24s      Loading 'Sales.Store' into data cache
2014-11-02 20:17:13.420 spid24s      Loading 'Purchasing.ProductVendor' into data
cache
2014-11-02 20:17:13.420 spid24s      Loading 'Purchasing.Vendor' into data cache
2014-11-02 20:17:13.420 spid24s      Loading 'Sales.CountryRegionCurrency' into data
cache
2014-11-02 20:17:13.430 spid24s      Loading 'Purchasing.PurchaseOrderDetail' into
data cache
2014-11-02 20:17:13.430 spid24s      Loading 'Sales.CreditCard' into data cache
2014-11-02 20:17:13.440 spid24s      Loading 'Sales.Currency' into data cache
2014-11-02 20:17:13.450 spid24s      Loading 'Purchasing.PurchaseOrderHeader' into
data cache
2014-11-02 20:17:13.450 spid24s      Loading 'Sales.CurrencyRate' into data cache
2014-11-02 20:17:13.460 spid24s      Loading 'Sales.Customer' into data cache
2014-11-02 20:17:13.520 Server       Software Usage Metrics is disabled.
2014-11-02 20:17:13.540 spid24s      Loading 'Sales.SalesOrderDetail' into data
cache
2014-11-02 20:17:13.650 spid24s      Loading 'Sales.SalesOrderHeader' into data
cache
2014-11-02 20:17:13.680 spid24s      Loading 'Sales.SalesOrderHeaderSalesReason'
into data cache
2014-11-02 20:17:13.690 spid24s      Loading 'Sales.SalesPerson' into data cache
2014-11-02 20:17:13.690 spid24s      Loading 'Sales.SalesPersonQuotaHistory' into
data cache
2014-11-02 20:17:13.690 spid24s      Loading 'Sales.SalesReason' into data cache
2014-11-02 20:17:13.690 spid24s      Loading 'Sales.SalesTaxRate' into data cache
2014-11-02 20:17:13.690 spid24s      Loading 'Sales.PersonCreditCard' into data
cache
2014-11-02 20:17:13.700 spid24s      Loading 'Sales.SalesTerritory' into data cache
2014-11-02 20:17:13.700 spid24s      Loading 'Sales.SalesTerritoryHistory' into data
cache
```

If you want to disable the automatic execution of all startup procedures, you can use the sp_configure system procedure to disable the scan for startup procs configuration option. Setting this option to 0 disables the running of startup procedures on subsequent SQL Server restarts.

If SQL Server is not currently running and you want to skip running the startup procedures when you start it up, you can specify Trace Flag 4022 as a startup parameter. You can set the trace flag for a SQL Server instance by using the SQL Server Configuration Manager. In SQL Server Configuration Manager, perform the following steps:

1. Click SQL Server Services.

2. In the right pane, right-click the SQL Server instance you want to set the trace flag for and select Properties.

3. Select the Startup Parameters tab.

4. Type -T4022 in the Specify a startup Parameter text box and click Add (see Figure 25.10).

5. Click OK or Apply.

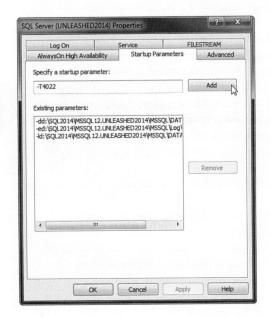

FIGURE 25.10   Setting Trace Flag 4022 to prevent startup procedures from executing.

Also, if you start SQL Server with minimal configuration (by using the -f flag), the startup stored procedures are not executed.

Natively Compiled Stored Procedures

SQL Server 2014 introduces In-Memory OLTP, which also introduces the concept of native compilation. SQL Server 2014 can now natively compile stored procedures that access memory-optimized tables. Native compilation allows faster data access and more efficient query execution than normal T-SQL Stored procedures which are processed as interpreted Transact-SQL.

The main difference between interpreted stored procedures and natively compiled stored procedures is that an interpreted stored procedure isn't compiled until its first execution whereas a natively compiled stored procedure is compiled when it is created. That compile process first translates the stored procedure code into C code, and then into machine language and the code is stored as a DLL in a special folder on the SQL Server machine. This special folder is located in the SQL Server default data directory. You can identify the location of the DLLs with the following query:

```
SELECT name,description
FROM   sys.dm_os_loaded_modules
WHERE description = 'XTP Native DLL'
GO
```

Because the code is compiled into machine code and can be run directly by the CPU without interpretation, it executes more efficiently than normally created stored procedures, and uses fewer machine instructions.

Currently, natively compiled stored procedures do not implement the full Transact-SQL programmability features. There are a number of Transact-SQL constructs that currently cannot be used inside natively compiled stored procedures, including the following:

▶ Cursors are not supported.

▶ The MERGE statement is not supported.

▶ Use of tempdb is not supported.

▶ OUTER joins, including LEFT join is not supported.

▶ OR and NOT are not supported.

▶ CASE statements are not supported.

▶ ALTER PROCEDURE is not allowed (to modify a natively compiled stored procedure, you have to drop and recreate it).

▶ No support for these clauses: OUTPUT, INTO, INTERSECT, EXCEPT, APPLY, PIVOT, UNPIVOT, IN, LIKE, UNION, DISTINCT, PERCENT, WITH TIES, UDFs, WITH RECOMPILE.

▶ Use of Views is not supported.

▶ Cannot reference user-defined functions or table valued functions.

▶ Cannot use multi-row insert statements.

▶ Cannot use common table expressions.

▶ Cannot use subqueries.

To help you determine which of the many T-SQL features in an existing T-SQL stored procedure are not supported for compiling the procedure as a natively compiled stored procedure, you can use the Native Compilation Advisor in SSMS. The Advisor will provide a report of which features used in the stored procedure are not supported in natively compiled procedures. To invoke the Native Compilation Advisor, right click on the procedure name in the Object Explorer in SSMS and select Native Compilation Advisor (see Figure 25.11). This will bring up the Native Compilation Advisor. If the procedure contains elements that disqualify it from being natively compiled, you'll see a screen similar to the one shown in Figure 25.12, which provides a list of the elements within the procedure code that are not supported.

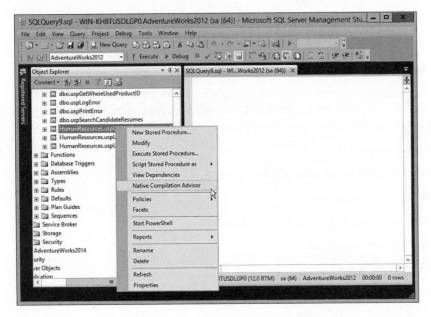

FIGURE 25.11   Invoking the Native Compilation Advisor in SSMS.

While there are a large number of restrictions on the T-SQL features allowed in natively compiled stored procedures, there are also a number of Transact-SQL features that are only supported within natively compiled stored procedures:

▶ Atomic blocks. For more information, see Atomic Blocks.

▶ NOT NULL constraints on parameters of and variables in natively compiled stored procedures. You cannot assign NULL values to parameters or variables declared as NOT NULL. For more information, see DECLARE @local_variable (Transact-SQL).

▶ Schema binding of natively compiled stored procedures.

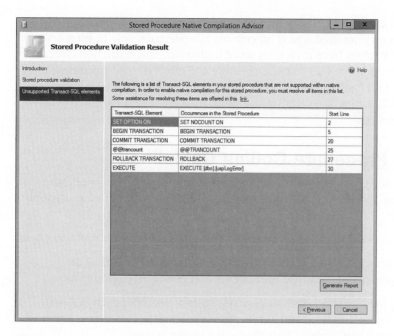

FIGURE 25.12   Native Compilation Advisor report for the `uspUpdateEmployeeHireInfo` Stored Procedure.

The following is an example of a natively compiled stored procedure:

```
create procedure dbo.OrderInsert(@OrdNo integer, @CustCode nvarchar(5))
with native_compilation, schemabinding, execute as owner
as
begin atomic with
(transaction isolation level = snapshot,
language = N'English')

  declare @OrdDate datetime = getdate();
  insert into dbo.Ord (OrdNo, CustCode, OrdDate) values (@OrdNo, @CustCode, @
OrdDate);
end
go
```

The NATIVE_COMPILATION keyword in the WITH clause indicates that the Transact-SQL stored procedure is a natively compiled stored procedure. The SCHEMABINDING and EXECUTE AS clauses are also required, as well as the new BEGIN ATOMIC clause. BEGIN ATOMIC is part of the ANSI SQL standard. Atomic blocks are single blocks of T-SQL statements that are executed (atomically) within the transaction. Either all statements in the block succeed or the entire block will be rolled back.

The biggest restriction, and potential showstopper, to using natively compiled stored procedures is that natively compiled stored procedures can reference only in-memory tables. In-Memory OLTP tables have their own set of limitations and restrictions. Because of the restrictions on In-Memory OLTP tables, the time and effort needed to convert old tables into In-Memory OLTP tables along can be significant. For more detailed information on In-Memory OLTP tables and creating and using natively compiled stored procedures, please see Chapter 33.

T-SQL Stored Procedure Coding Guidelines

Transact-SQL (T-SQL) stored procedures should be treated just like reusable application code. You should follow these suggested guidelines to ensure that your stored procedures are solid and robust:

▶ Check all parameters for valid values and return an error message if a problem exists.

▶ Be sure that the parameter data types match the column data types they are compared against to avoid data type mismatches and poor query optimization.

▶ Use `Try...Catch` logic or check the `@@error` system function after each SQL statement, especially `insert`, `update`, and `delete`, to verify that the statements executed successfully. Return a status code other than `0` if a failure occurs.

▶ Be sure to comment your code so that when you or others have to maintain it, the code is self-documenting.

▶ Consider using a source code management system, such as Microsoft Visual Studio SourceSafe, CVS, or Subversion, to maintain versions of your stored procedure source code.

▶ Avoid using `select *` in your stored procedure queries. If someone were to add columns to or remove columns from a table, the stored procedure would generate a different result set, which could cause errors with the applications. Specify explicit column lists in your SELECT statements.

▶ When using `INSERT` statements in stored procedures, you should always provide the column list associated with the values being inserted. This allows the procedure to continue to work if the table is ever rebuilt with a different column order or additional columns are added to the table.

▶ A stored procedure cannot directly create schemas, views, triggers, defaults, rules, aggregates, functions, or stored procedures. You can, however, execute dynamic SQL that creates the object

```
CREATE PROC create_other_proc AS
   EXEC ('CREATE PROC get_au_lname AS
         SELECT au_lname from authors
         RETURN')
```

> **TIP**
>
> If you are using dynamic SQL to create objects in stored procedures, be sure to qualify each object with the name of the object schema if users other than the stored procedure owner will be executing the stored procedure.

▶ You can create tables in stored procedures. Generally, as a good practice, only temporary tables are created in stored procedures. Temporary tables created in stored procedures are dropped automatically when the procedure terminates. Global temporary tables, however, exist until the connection that created them terminates.

▶ If you don't qualify object names within a stored procedure, they default to the schema of the stored procedure. It is recommended that objects in stored procedures be fully qualified with the appropriate schema name to avoid confusion and to promote query plan reuse.

▶ You cannot drop a table and re-create another table with the same name within the procedure unless you use dynamic SQL to execute a dynamically built command that creates the table.

▶ A stored procedure cannot issue the USE statement to change the database context in which it is running; the database context for execution is limited to a single database. If you need to reference an object in another database, you have to fully qualify the object name with the database name in your procedure code.

25

Summary

Stored procedures are among the premier features of Microsoft SQL Server. They provide a number of benefits over using ad hoc SQL, including faster performance; restricted, function-based access to tables; protection of application code from database changes; and the ability to simplify complex tasks into a simple stored procedure call.

In the next chapter, you learn how to expand the capabilities of your T-SQL code by creating and using user-defined functions developed in T-SQL.

Creating and Managing User-Defined Functions

SQL Server provides a number of predefined functions that are built in to the T-SQL language. The supplied functions help extend the capabilities of T-SQL, providing the ability to perform string manipulation, mathematic calculations, data type conversions, and so on within T-SQL code. Although SQL Server provides a reasonably extensive set of functions, you might sometimes wish you had available a function that is not provided. You could create a stored procedure to perform custom processing, but you can't use the result of a stored procedure in a WHERE clause or as a column in a SELECT list. For this type of situation, SQL Server 2014 provides user-defined functions.

A user-defined function can return a single scalar value, like the majority of the built-in functions, or it can return a result set as a table result, similarly to a table variable.

This chapter takes a look at how to create and manage user-defined functions as well as some guidelines to help determine whether to use stored procedures versus functions.

Why Use User-Defined Functions?

The main benefit of user-defined functions is that you are not limited to just the functions SQL Server provides. You can develop your own functions to meet your specific needs or to simplify complex SQL code. For example, the getdate() function returns the current system date and time. It always includes both a date component and time component, with accuracy down to the milliseconds. What if you wanted to return a datetime value with just the date and have the time always set to midnight? To do this, you would have to pass the result from getdate() through some other functions to zero out the time component. The following is one possible solution:

```
select convert(datetime, convert(date, getdate()))
```

Each time you wanted just the date, with the time always set to midnight, you would have to perform this same conversion operation on the result of the getdate() function. As an alternative, you could create a user-defined function that performs the operations on getdate() automatically and always returns the current date, with a time value of midnight, as in this example:

```
CREATE FUNCTION getonlydate ()
RETURNS datetime
AS
BEGIN    RETURN (select convert(datetime, convert(date, getdate())))
END
GO
```

You could then use the user-defined function in your SQL code in place of the more complex conversion operation on the getdate() function each time. Like the built-in system functions, user-defined functions can be used in SELECT lists, SET clauses of UPDATE statements, VALUES clauses of INSERT statements, as default values, and so on. For example, the following query uses the user-defined function getonlydate() to return the current date, with a time of midnight:

```
select dbo.getonlydate()
```

The following examples show how you could use the getonlydate() user-defined function in other statements:

```
CREATE TABLE Orders (
        OrderID int IDENTITY (1, 1) NOT NULL Primary Key,
        CustomerID nchar (5) COLLATE SQL_Latin1_General_CP1_CI_AS NULL ,
        EmployeeID int NULL ,
        OrderDate datetime NULL default dbo.getonlydate(),
        RequiredDate datetime NULL ,
        ShippedDate datetime NULL
)
go


insert Orders (CustomerID, EmployeeID, RequiredDate)
    values ('BERGS', 3, dbo.getonlydate() + 7)
go


update Orders
    set ShippedDate = dbo.getonlydate()
    where OrderID = 1
```

```
go

select OrderDate,
       RequiredDate,
       ShippedDate
    from Orders
  where OrderDate = dbo.getonlydate()
go

/* result
OrderDate              RequiredDate           ShippedDate
---------------------- ---------------------- ----------------------
2014-10-01 00:00:00.000 2014-10-09 00:00:00.000 2014-10-02 00:00:00.000
*/
```

If you use the `getonlydate()` function consistently when you want to store only dates with a time value of midnight, searching against datetime columns is easier because you don't have to concern yourself with the time component. For example, if you use `getdate()` instead of `getonlydate()`, you have to account for the time component in your queries against `OrderDate` to ensure that you find all records for a particular day:

```
SELECT OrderDate,
       RequiredDate,
       ShippedDate
    from Orders
  where OrderDate >= convert(varchar(10), getdate(), 110)
    and OrderDate < convert(varchar(10), getdate() + 1, 110)
```

From this example, you can see how much using the `getonlydate()` user-defined function can simplify your queries.

TIP

Another way to avoid the issues related to storing a time component in your date-valued columns in SQL Server 2014 is to use the DATE data type instead of DATETIME.

In addition to functions that return scalar values, you can define functions that return table results. You can use functions that return table results anywhere in queries that a table or view can be used, including joins, subqueries, and so on. The following examples show how to use a user-defined table-valued function that returns a list of job titles:

```
use adventureworks2012
go
create function valid_job_titles()
returns TABLE
as
return (SELECT distinct jobtitle from HumanResources.Employee e)
```

```
go

select * from dbo.valid_job_titles()
go
Insert INTO HumanResources.Employee
SELECT * from  EmployeeImport e
where e.JobTitle in (select jobtitle from dbo.valid_job_titles())
```

Essentially, this example reduces a query to a simple function that you can now use anywhere a table can be referenced.

With a few restrictions—which are covered later in this chapter, in the "Creating and Managing User-Defined Functions" section—you can write all types of functions in SQL Server to perform various calculations or routines. For example, you could create a T-SQL function that returns a valid list of code values, a function to determine the number of days items are backordered, a function to return the average price of all books, and so on. Plus, with the capability to create CLR-based functions, you can create significantly more powerful functions than what can be accomplished using T-SQL alone. Examples of CLR-based functions include a more robust soundex() function, a function to return the factorial of a number, and an address comparison function. The possibilities are nearly endless. As you have seen, user-defined functions significantly increase the capabilities and flexibility of T-SQL.

Types of User-Defined Functions

SQL Server supports three types of user-defined functions:

- ▶ Scalar functions
- ▶ Inline table-valued functions
- ▶ Multistatement table-valued functions

The next few sections take an in-depth look at the differences between the function types and how and where you can use them.

Scalar Functions

A scalar function is like the standard built-in functions provided with SQL Server. It returns a single scalar value that can be used anywhere a constant expression can be used in a query. (You saw an example of this in the earlier description of the getonlydate() function.)

A scalar function typically takes zero or more arguments and returns a value of a specified data type. Every T-SQL function must return a result using the RETURN statement. The value to be returned can be contained in a local variable defined within the function, or the value can be computed in the RETURN statement. The following two functions are variations of a function that returns the average salary calculated for a specified job title from the Employee and EmployeePayHistory tables:

```
CREATE FUNCTION AveragePayRate(@jobtitle nvarchar(50) = '%')
RETURNS money
AS
BEGIN
    DECLARE @avg money
    SELECT @avg = avg(Rate)
    FROM HumanResources.EmployeePayHistory eph
                JOIN
        HumanResources.Employee e
        ON e.BusinessEntityID = eph.BusinessEntityID
        AND eph.RateChangeDate =
                (SELECT MAX(ratechangedate)
                    FROM HumanResources.EmployeePayHistory ephmax
                    WHERE ephmax.BusinessEntityID = eph.BusinessEntityID)
    WHERE e.JobTitle like @jobtitle

    RETURN @avg
END
go


CREATE FUNCTION AveragePayRate2(@jobtitle nvarchar(50)= '%')
RETURNS money
AS
BEGIN
    RETURN ( SELECT avg(eph.Rate)
    FROM HumanResources.EmployeePayHistory eph
        JOIN
        HumanResources.Employee e
        ON e.BusinessEntityID = eph.BusinessEntityID
        AND eph.RateChangeDate = (SELECT MAX(ratechangedate) FROM HumanResources.
EmployeePayHistory ephmax
                                        WHERE ephmax.BusinessEntityID = eph.
BusinessEntityID)
    WHERE e.JobTitle like @jobtitle)
END
Go
```

As mentioned earlier in this chapter, a scalar function can be used anywhere a constant expression can be used. For example, SQL Server doesn't allow aggregate functions in a WHERE clause unless they are contained in a subquery. The AveragePayRate function lets you compare against the average salary without having to use a subquery in your main query:

```
select e.JobTitle, e.HireDate, eph.rate
FROM HumanResources.Employee e
INNER JOIN HumanResources.EmployeePayHistory eph
```

26

```
ON e.BusinessEntityID = eph.BusinessEntityID
where eph.Rate > dbo.AveragePayRate('Vice%')
GO


/* result
JobTitle                              HireDate      rate
----------------------------   ----------   ---------
Chief Executive Officer        2003-02-15    125.50
Vice President of Production    2003-03-07    84.1346
*/
```

When invoking a user-defined scalar function, you must include the schema name. If you omit the schema name, you get the following error, even if the function is created in your default schema or exists only in the dbo schema in the database:

```
SELECT AveragePayRate('Vice%')
GO


Msg 195, Level 15, State 10, Line 1
'AveragePayRate' is not a recognized built-in function name.
```

You can return the value from a user-defined scalar function into a local variable in three ways. You can assign the result to a local variable by using the SET statement or an assignment select, or you can use the EXEC statement. The following commands are functionally equivalent:

```
declare @avg1 money,
        @avg2 money,
        @avg3 money
select @avg1 = dbo.AveragePayRate('Vice%')
set @avg2 = dbo.AveragePayRate('Vice%')
exec @avg3 = dbo.AveragePayRate 'Vice%'
select @avg1 as avg1, @avg2 as avg2, @avg3 as avg3
go


/* result
          avg1              avg2              avg3
---------------  ---------------  ---------------
       73.2371          73.2371          73.2371
*/
```

Notice, however, that when you use a function in an EXEC statement, you invoke it similarly to the way you invoke a stored procedure, and you do not use parentheses around the function parameters. To avoid confusion, you should stick to using the EXEC statement for stored procedures and invoke scalar functions as you would normally invoke a SQL Server built-in function.

Table-Valued Functions

A table-valued user-defined function returns a rowset instead of a single scalar value. You can invoke a table-valued function in the FROM clause of a SELECT statement, just as you would a table or view. In some situations, a table-valued function can almost be thought of as a view that accepts parameters, so the result set is determined dynamically. A table-valued function specifies the keyword TABLE in its RETURNS clause.

Table-valued functions are of two types: inline and multistatement. The two types of table-valued functions return the same thing, and they are also invoked the same way. The only real difference between them is the way the function is written to return the rowset. The next couple sections look at each of these types of table-valued functions.

Inline Table-Valued Functions

An inline table-valued function specifies only the TABLE keyword in the RETURNS clause, without table definition information. The code inside the function is a single RETURN statement that invokes a SELECT statement. For example, you could create an inline table-valued function that returns a rowset of all job titles and the average pay rate for each job title, where the average pay rate exceeds the value passed into the function:

```
CREATE FUNCTION AveragePayRatebyJobTitle (@rate money = 0.0)
RETURNS table
AS
    RETURN ( SELECT e.JobTitle, avg(Rate) as avg_rate
        FROM HumanResources.EmployeePayHistory eph
            JOIN
            HumanResources.Employee e
            ON e.BusinessEntityID = eph.BusinessEntityID
            AND eph.RateChangeDate =
            (SELECT MAX(ratechangedate) FROM HumanResources.EmployeePayHistory ephmax
              WHERE ephmax.BusinessEntityID = eph.BusinessEntityID)
        group by e.JobTitle
        having avg(rate) > @rate )
go
```

You can invoke the function by referencing it in a FROM clause as you would a table or view:

```
select * from AveragePayRatebyJobTitle (75.00)
go

/* result
JobTitle                    avg_rate
--------------------------- --------
Chief Executive Officer     125.50
Vice President of Production 84.1346
*/
```

Notice that when you invoke a table-valued function, you do not have to specify the schema name as you do with a user-defined scalar function if the function is created in your default schema. However, it is good practice to always fully qualify the function name with the schema name.

Multistatement Table-Valued Functions

Multistatement table-valued functions differ from inline functions in two major ways:

▶ The RETURNS clause specifies a table variable and its definition.

▶ The body of the function contains multiple statements, at least one of which populates the table variable with data values.

You define a table variable in the RETURNS clause by using the TABLE data type. The syntax to define the table variable is similar to the CREATE TABLE syntax. Note that the name of the table variable comes before the TABLE keyword:

```
RETURNS @variable TABLE ( column definition | table_constraint [, ...] )
```

The scope of the table variable is limited to the function in which it is defined. Although the contents of the table variable are returned as the function result, the table variable itself cannot be accessed or referenced outside the function.

Within the function in which a table variable is defined, that table variable can be treated like a regular table. You can perform any SELECT, INSERT, UPDATE, or DELETE statement on the rows in a table variable, except for SELECT INTO. Here's an example:

```
INSERT INTO @table SELECT au_lname, au_fname from authors
```

The following example defines the inline table-valued function AveragePayRatebyJobTitle() as a multistatement table-valued function called AveragePayRatebyJobTitle2():

```
CREATE FUNCTION AveragePayRatebyJobTitle2 (@rate money = 0.0)
RETURNS @table table (JobTitle nvarchar(50) null, avg_rate money null)
AS
BEGIN
 INSERT @table
  SELECT e.JobTitle, avg(Rate) as avg_rate
   FROM HumanResources.EmployeePayHistory eph
     JOIN
     HumanResources.Employee e
     ON e.BusinessEntityID = eph.BusinessEntityID
     AND eph.RateChangeDate =
     (SELECT MAX(ratechangedate) FROM HumanResources.EmployeePayHistory ephmax
     WHERE ephmax.BusinessEntityID = eph.BusinessEntityID)
   group by e.JobTitle
```

```
            having avg(rate) > @rate
  RETURN
END
Go
```

Notice the main differences between this version and the inline version: in the multistatement version, you have to define the structure of the table rowset you are returning and also have to include the BEGIN and END statements as wrappers around the multiple statements that the function can contain. Other than that, both functions are invoked the same way and return the same rowset:

```
select * from AveragePayRatebyJobTitle2 (75.00)
go


/* result
JobTitle                    avg_rate
--------------------------- --------
Chief Executive Officer     125.50
Vice President of Production 84.1346
*/
```

Why use multistatement table-valued functions instead of inline table-valued functions? Generally, you use multistatement table-valued functions when you need to perform further operations (for example, inserts, updates, or deletes) on the contents of the table variable before returning a result set. You would also use them if you need to perform more complex logic or additional processing on the input parameters of the function before invoking the query to populate the table variable.

Creating and Managing User-Defined Functions

In the preceding sections of this chapter, you saw some examples of creating functions. The following sections discuss in more detail the CREATE FUNCTION syntax and the types of operations allowed in functions. These sections also show how to create and manage T-SQL functions by using SQL Server Management Studio (SSMS).

Creating User-Defined Functions

You create T-SQL functions by using T-SQL statements. You can enter the T-SQL code in sqlcmd, SSMS, or any other third-party query tool that allows you to enter ad hoc T-SQL code. The following sections first show the basic syntax for creating functions and then show how you can create functions by using the features of SSMS.

Creating T-SQL Functions

User-defined functions can accept 0 to 2,100 input parameters but can return only a single result: either a single scalar value or table result set.

The T-SQL syntax for the CREATE FUNCTION command for scalar functions is as follows:

```
CREATE FUNCTION [ schema_name. ] function_name
    ( [ { @parameter_name [AS] [ schema_name.]scalar_datatype [ = default ] [
READONLY ] }
      [ ,...n ] ] )
RETURNS scalar_datatype
[ WITH { [ ENCRYPTION ]
        [ , SCHEMABINDING ]
        [ , RETURNS NULL ON NULL INPUT | CALLED ON NULL INPUT ]
        [ , EXECUTE_AS_Clause ]
      } ]
 [ AS ]
BEGIN
    SQL_Statements
    RETURN scalar_expression
END
```

The syntax for the CREATE FUNCTION command for inline table-valued functions is as follows:

```
CREATE FUNCTION [ schema_name. ] function_name
    ( [ { @parameter_name [AS] [ schema_name.]scalar_datatype [ = default ] [
READONLY ] }
      [ ,...n ] ] )
RETURNS TABLE
[ WITH { [ ENCRYPTION ]
        [ , SCHEMABINDING ]
        [ , RETURNS NULL ON NULL INPUT | CALLED ON NULL INPUT ]
        [ , EXECUTE_AS_Clause ]
      } ]
[ AS ]
RETURN [ ( ] select-stmt [ ) ]
```

The syntax for the CREATE FUNCTION command for multistatement table-valued functions is as follows:

```
CREATE FUNCTION [ schema_name. ] function_name
    ( [ { @parameter_name [AS] [ schema_name.]scalar_datatype [ = default ] [
READONLY ] }
      [ ,...n ] ] )
RETURNS @table_variable TABLE ( { column_definition | table_constraint }
                                  [ ,...n ] )
[ WITH { [ ENCRYPTION ]
        [ , SCHEMABINDING ]
        [ , RETURNS NULL ON NULL INPUT | CALLED ON NULL INPUT ]
        [ , EXECUTE_AS_Clause ]
```

```
        } ]
   [ AS ]
BEGIN
      SQL_Statements
      RETURN
END
```

The types of SQL statements allowed in a function include the following:

▶ DECLARE statements to define variables and cursors that are local to the function.

▶ Assignments of values to variables that are local to the function, using the SET command or an assignment select.

▶ Cursor operations on local cursors that are declared, opened, closed, and de-allocated within the function. FETCH statements must assign values to local variables by using the INTO clause.

▶ Control-of-flow statements such as IF, ELSE, WHILE, GOTO, and so on, excluding the TRY...CATCH statements.

▶ UPDATE, INSERT, and DELETE statements that modify table variables defined within the function.

▶ EXECUTE statements that call an extended stored procedure. (Any results returned by the extended stored procedure are discarded.)

▶ Other user-defined functions, up to a maximum nesting level of 32.

If you specify the ENCRYPTION option, the SQL statements used to define the function are stored encrypted in the system catalog. This prevents anyone from viewing the function source code in the database.

NOTE

If you choose to encrypt the function code, you should be sure to save a copy of the script used to create the function to a file outside the database, in case you ever need to modify the function or re-create it. After the source code for the function is encrypted, you cannot extract the original unencrypted source code from the database.

If a function is created with the SCHEMABINDING option, the database objects that the function references cannot be altered or dropped unless the function is dropped first or the schema binding of the function is removed, using the ALTER FUNCTION command without specifying the SCHEMABINDING option. A CREATE FUNCTION statement with the SCHEMABINDING option specified fails unless all the following conditions are met:

▶ Any user-defined functions and views referenced within the function are also schema bound.

26

▶ Any objects referenced by the function are referenced using a two-part name (`schema.object_name`).

▶ The function and the objects it references belong to the same database.

▶ The user executing the CREATE FUNCTION statement has REFERENCES permission on all database objects that the function references.

You can specify the SCHEMABINDING option only for T-SQL functions, not for CLR functions. The following example modifies the `AveragePayRatebyJobTitle2` function by specifying the SCHEMABINDING option:

```
Alter FUNCTION AveragePayRatebyJobTitle2 (@rate money = 0.0)
RETURNS @table table (JobTitle nvarchar(50) null, avg_rate money null)
WITH SCHEMABINDING
AS
BEGIN
    INSERT @table
        SELECT e.JobTitle, avg(Rate) as avg_rate
            FROM HumanResources.EmployeePayHistory eph
                JOIN
                HumanResources.Employee e
                ON e.BusinessEntityID = eph.BusinessEntityID
                AND eph.RateChangeDate =
                    (SELECT MAX(ratechangedate)
                        FROM HumanResources.EmployeePayHistory ephmax
                        WHERE ephmax.BusinessEntityID = eph.BusinessEntityID)
            group by e.JobTitle
            having avg(rate) > @rate
    RETURN
END
Go
```

The following example shows what happens if you try to modify a column in the titles table referenced by the function:

```
alter table HumanResources.EmployeePayHistory alter column rate smallmoney NULL
go

Msg 5074, Level 16, State 1, Line 1
The object 'CK_EmployeePayHistory_Rate' is dependent on column 'rate'.
Msg 5074, Level 16, State 1, Line 1
The object 'AveragePayRatebyJobTitle2' is dependent on column 'rate'.
Msg 4922, Level 16, State 9, Line 1
ALTER TABLE ALTER COLUMN rate failed because one or more objects access this column.
```

If the RETURNS NULL ON NULL INPUT option is specified, the function automatically returns NULL as a result if a NULL value is passed as an input parameter, without invoking the function body. If this option is not specified, the default option of CALLED ON NULL INPUT is applied. The following example shows the difference between these two options:

```
CREATE FUNCTION striptime (@datetimeval datetime)
RETURNS datetime
AS
BEGIN
    DECLARE @dateval datetime
    SELECT @dateval = convert(date, isnull(@datetimeval, getdate()))
    RETURN @dateval
END
GO




CREATE FUNCTION striptime2(@datetimeval datetime)
RETURNS datetime
WITH RETURNS NULL ON NULL INPUT
AS
BEGIN
    DECLARE @dateval datetime
    SELECT @dateval = convert(date, isnull(@datetimeval, getdate()))
    RETURN @dateval

END
GO
select dbo.striptime(NULL), dbo.striptime2(NULL)

/* result

----------------------- -----------------------
2014-11-01 00:00:00.000 NULL

*/
```

The EXECUTE AS clause allows you to specify the security context under which the user-defined function will execute. This way, you can control which user account SQL Server uses to validate permissions on any database objects referenced by the function. This option cannot be specified for inline table-valued functions.

Another key restriction on user-defined functions is that SQL statements within a function cannot generate side effects; that is, a user-defined function cannot generate permanent changes to any resource whose scope extends beyond the function. For example, a function cannot modify data in a table, operate on cursors not local to the function, create or drop database objects, issue transaction control statements, or generate a result set other than the defined function result via a SELECT statement. The only changes that can be made by the SQL statements in a function are to the objects local to the function, such as local cursors or variables.

In SQL Server 2014, you can also include most built-in system functions within a user-defined function, even ones that are nondeterministic (that is, functions that can return different data values on each call). For example, the getdate() function is considered nondeterministic because even though it is always invoked with the same argument, it returns a different value each time it is executed. However, the following nondeterministic built-in functions are still not allowed in user-defined functions:

▶ newid()

▶ newsequentialid()

▶ rand()

▶ textptr()

User-defined functions can also call other user-defined functions, with a limit of 32 levels of nesting. Nesting of functions can help improve the modularity and reusability of function code. For example, the following version of the getonlydate() function uses the striptime() function example shown earlier in this chapter:

```
CREATE FUNCTION dbo.getonlydate()
RETURNS datetime
as
BEGIN
DECLARE @date datetime
SET @date = dbo.striptime( getdate())
RETURN @date
end
```

Some additional restrictions and limitations of user-defined functions include:

▶ User-defined functions cannot contain an OUTPUT INTO clause that has a table as its target.

▶ User-defined functions cannot return multiple result sets.

▶ Error handling is restricted in a user-defined function—it does not support TRY . . . CATCH, @@ERROR, or RAISERROR

▶ User-defined functions cannot invoke stored procedures except extended stored procedures.

▶ User-defined functions cannot make use of dynamic SQL or temp tables (only table variables are allowed).

▶ SET statements are not allowed in a user-defined function.

▶ Use of the FOR XML clause is not allowed.

Using SSMS to Create Functions

To create a function by using SSMS, open the Object Explorer to the database in which you want to create the function. Then select the Programmability node, right-click the Functions node, select New, and then choose one of the three available options as shown in Figure 26.1:

▶ Inline Table-Valued Function

▶ Multistatement Table-Valued Function

▶ Scalar-Valued Function

SSMS opens a new query window populated with a template for that type of function. Listing 26.1 shows an example of the default template code for an inline table-valued function that would be opened into a new query window.

FIGURE 26.1   Creating a new function from the Object Browser in SSMS.

LISTING 26.1   An Example of a New Function Creation Script Generated by SSMS

```
-- ======================================================
-- Template generated from Template Browser using:
-- Create Scalar Function (New Menu).SQL
--
-- Use the Specify Values for Template Parameters
-- command (Ctrl-Shift-M) to fill in the parameter
```

```
-- values below.
--
-- This block of comments will not be included in
-- the definition of the function.
-- ================================================
SET ANSI_NULLS ON
GO
SET QUOTED_IDENTIFIER ON
GO
-- =============================================
-- Author:           <Author,,Name>
-- Create date: <Create Date, ,>
-- Description:      <Description, ,>
-- =============================================
CREATE FUNCTION <Scalar_Function_Name, sysname, FunctionName>
(
      -- Add the parameters for the function here
      <@Param1, sysname, @p1> <Data_Type_For_Param1, , int>
)
RETURNS <Function_Data_Type, ,int>
AS
BEGIN
      -- Declare the return variable here
      DECLARE <@ResultVar, sysname, @Result> <Function_Data_Type, ,int>

      -- Add the T-SQL statements to compute the return value here
      SELECT <@ResultVar, sysname, @Result> = <@Param1, sysname, @p1>

      -- Return the result of the function
      RETURN <@ResultVar, sysname, @Result>

END
GO
```

You can modify the template code as necessary to name the function and to specify the parameters, return value, and function body. When you are finished, you can execute the contents of the query window to create the function. After you create a function successfully, you should save the source code to a file by choosing File, Save or File, Save As. This way, you can re-create the function from the file if it is accidentally dropped from the database.

One thing you might notice about the function templates is that they contain template parameters for parameter names and function names, for example. These template parameters are in the format `<parameter_name, data_type, value>`:

▶ `parameter_name` is the name of the template parameter in the script.

▶ `data_type` is the optional data type of the template parameter.

▶ `value` is the default value to be used to replace every occurrence of the template parameter in the script.

You can automatically substitute values for template parameters by selecting Query, Specify Values for Template Parameters or by pressing Ctrl+Shift+M. The Specify Values for Template Parameters dialog, shown in Figure 26.2, appears.

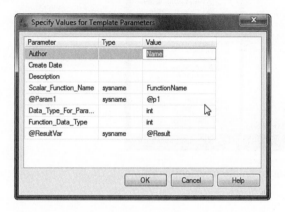

FIGURE 26.2   Using the Specify Values for Template Parameters dialog with functions in SSMS.

Enter the values for the template parameters in the Value column and then click OK. SSMS then substitutes any values you specified wherever the template parameter is defined within the template.

An alternative way to create a function from a template is to use the Template Browser in SSMS. You can open the Template Browser by selecting View, Template Browser in SSMS (see Figure 26.3) or by pressing Ctrl+Alt+T. The Template Browser window appears in SSMS (which is also shown in Figure 26.3).

You can double-click the template for the type of function you want to create or right-click the desired template and then select Open. SSMS opens a new query window populated with the template code.

NOTE

You are also able to edit the provided function templates available in the Template Browser by right-clicking them and selecting Edit. You can then customize the templates to include code fragments, comments, or a structure that is more to your preferences and save the changes to the template file. However, it is generally recommended that you not modify the Microsoft provided templates but instead create your own custom templates.

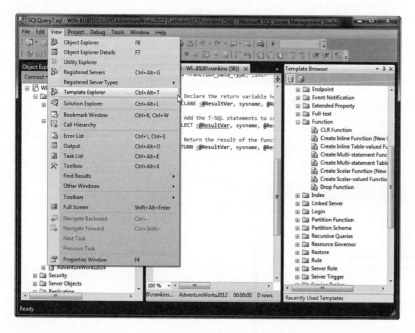

FIGURE 26.3   Opening the Template Browser to create functions in SSMS.

Creating Custom Function Templates

To create a custom function template, right-click the `Function` folder in the Template Browser and select New. SSMS then creates an entry in the Template Browser, and you can specify the name for the template, as shown in Figure 26.4.

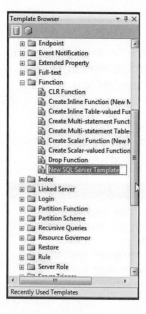

FIGURE 26.4   Creating a new function template in SSMS.

To begin adding code to the template, double-click it or right-click and select Open. A blank query window appears, and you can use it to enter the new template code. Probably the best way to get started is to copy the template code from one of the templates provided with SQL Server 2014.

Listing 26.2 shows an example of a new function template.

LISTING 26.2   An Example of a Custom Function Template

```
--===========================================
-- SQL Server 2014 Unleashed Sample
--   Create scalar-valued function template
--===========================================


USE <database_name, sysname, AdventurWorks2012>
GO


IF OBJECT_ID (N'<schema_nm, sysname, dbo>.<func_nm, sysname, fn_myfunc>')
      IS NOT NULL
    DROP FUNCTION <schema_nm, sysname, dbo>.<func_nm, sysname, fn_myfunc>
GO


CREATE FUNCTION <schema_nm, sysname, dbo>.<func_nm, sysname, fn_myfunc>
    (<parameter1, sysname, @param1> <parameter1_datatype,, int>,
      <parameter2, sysname, @param2> <parameter2_datatype,, int>,
      <parameter3, sysname, @param3> <parameter3_datatype,, int>)
RETURNS <return_value_datatype,,int>
WITH EXECUTE AS CALLER
AS
-- place the body of the function here
BEGIN
    DECLARE <variable1, sysname, @var1> <variable1_datatype,, int>,
            <variable2, sysname, @var2> <variable2_datatype,, int>

    select <variable1, sysname, @var1> = isnull(<parameter1, sysname, @param1> )
    <T-SQL_Body,,>

    RETURN <variable1, sysname, @var1>
END
GO
```

After you define a custom function template, you can use it as you do the built-in templates. You can double-click it or right-click and select Open, and SSMS opens a new query window with a new function creation script based on the custom template. If you use the default values for the template parameters, after the parameter substitution, your CREATE FUNCTION script should look like the one in Listing 26.3.

26

LISTING 26.3   An Example of a CREATE FUNCTION Script Generated from a Custom Function
Template

```
--==========================================
-- SQL Server 2014 Unleashed Sample
--   Create scalar-valued function template
--==========================================

USE AdventureWorks2012
GO


IF OBJECT_ID (N'dbo.fn_myfunction') IS NOT NULL
    DROP FUNCTION dbo.fn_myfunction
GO


CREATE FUNCTION dbo.fn_myfunction
    (@param1 int,
     @param2 int,
     @param3 int)
RETURNS int
WITH EXECUTE AS CALLER
AS
-- place the body of the function here
BEGIN
    DECLARE @var1 int,
            @var2 int

    select @var1 = isnull(@param1, @param2 )


    RETURN @var1
END
GO
```

Viewing and Modifying User-Defined Functions

Besides using T-SQL commands to create functions, you can also use them to view and
modify functions. You can get information by using the provided system procedures and
queries against system views. The following sections describe these methods.

Using T-SQL to View Functions

There are multiple methods to view the source code for a user-defined function. One way
is to use the sp_helptext procedure:

```
use AdventureWorks2012
go
exec sp_helptext getonlydate
```

```
go

/* result
Text
----------------------------------------------------------------
CREATE FUNCTION getonlydate ()
RETURNS datetime
AS
BEGIN    RETURN (select convert(datetime, convert(date, getdate()))))
END
*/
```

> **NOTE**
>
> To display the source code for the functions clearly, configure the SSMS query window to display results as text rather than in the grid by pressing Ctrl+T. You may also need to set the maximum number or characters displayed for Text results from the default of 256 characters which is likely too little to display the entire function. In SSMS, click on the Query menu and select Query Options. In the Query Options dialog, expand Results and click on Text. There you can set the maximum number of characters displayed in each column. The maximum value you can specify is 8192.

Another method to display the definition of a user defined function is to query the `definition` column of the `sys.sql_modules` system view:

```
SELECT definition FROM sys.sql_modules
WHERE object_id = object_id('AveragePayRate')
GO

/* result
definition
-----------------------------------------------------------
CREATE FUNCTION AveragePayRate(@jobtitle nvarchar(50) = '%')
RETURNS money
AS
BEGIN
    DECLARE @avg money
    SELECT @avg = avg(Rate)
    FROM HumanResources.EmployeePayHistory eph
        JOIN
        HumanResources.Employee e
        ON e.BusinessEntityID = eph.BusinessEntityID
        AND eph.RateChangeDate =
            (SELECT MAX(ratechangedate)
                FROM HumanResources.EmployeePayHistory ephmax
```

26

```
                        WHERE ephmax.BusinessEntityID = eph.BusinessEntityID)
        WHERE e.JobTitle like @jobtitle

        RETURN @avg
END
*/
```

A third method to view the definition of a user-defined function is to use the OBJECT_
DEFINITION system function:

```
SELECT OBJECT_DEFINITION(OBJECT_ID('striptime'))
GO

/* result
-------------------------------------------------------------------
CREATE FUNCTION striptime (@datetimeval datetime)
RETURNS datetime
AS
BEGIN
    DECLARE @dateval datetime
    SELECT @dateval = convert(date, isnull(@datetimeval, getdate()))
    RETURN @dateval
END
*/
```

If you want to display information about the input parameters for a function, you can
view the function parameters using the sys.parameters system view and join it to the
sys.types system view to display the parameter data type:

```
SELECT CONVERT(VARCHAR(15), p.name) AS parameter_name,
       CONVERT(VARCHAR(15), t.name) AS data_type,
       CASE p.is_output WHEN 1 THEN 'OUT' ELSE 'IN' END AS parameter_mode,
       p.parameter_id AS ordinal_position
FROM sys.parameters p
JOIN sys.types t
ON p.user_type_id = t.user_type_id
WHERE OBJECT_ID = OBJECT_ID('striptime')
GO

/* Result
parameter_name  data_type       parameter_mode ordinal_position
--------------- --------------- -------------- ----------------
                datetime        OUT                           0
@datetimeval    datetime        IN                            1
*/
```

To display information about the result columns returned by a table-valued function, you can view the columns returned by the function via the `sys.columns` system view:

```
SELECT convert(NVARCHAR(12), c.name) AS column_name,
       CONVERT(nvarchar(15), t.name
       + case when t.name LIKE '%char%'
             THEN '('   + CASE c.max_length
                             WHEN -1
                             THEN 'max'
                             ELSE cast(c.max_length as varchar(4))
                         END
                  + ')'
             ELSE ''
             END) AS datatype,
       c.precision,
       c.scale,
       c.column_id AS ordinal_position
FROM sys.columns c
INNER JOIN sys.types t
ON c.user_type_id = t.user_type_id
WHERE c.object_id = object_id('AveragePayRatebyJobTitle')
GO

/* Result
column_name   datatype          precision scale ordinal_position
------------  ----------------  --------- ----- ----------------
JobTitle      nvarchar(100)            0     0                1
avg_rate      money                   19     4                2
*/
```

SQL Server 2014 also provides the OBJECTPROPERTY function, which you can use to get more specific information about functions. One of the things you can find out is whether a function is a multistatement table function, an inline function, or a scalar function. The OBJECTPROPERTY function accepts an object ID and an object property parameter, and it returns the value 1 if the property is true, 0 if it is false, or NULL if an invalid function ID or property parameter is specified. The following property parameters are appropriate for functions:

▶ **IsTableFunction**—Returns 1 if the function is a table-valued function but not an inline function.

▶ **IsInlineFunction**—Returns 1 if the function is an inline table-valued function.

▶ **IsScalarFunction**—Returns 1 if the function is a scalar function.

▶ **IsSchemaBound**—Returns 1 if the function was created with the SCHEMABINDING option.

26

▶ **IsDeterministic**—Returns 1 if the function is deterministic (that is, it always returns the same result each time it is called with a specific set of input values).

The following example demonstrates a possible use of the OBJECTPROPERTY function with a query against the sys.objects system catalog (including a join to sys.schemas to get the schema name):

```
select convert(varchar(10), s.name) as 'schema',
  convert(varchar(20), o.name) as 'function',
  case objectproperty(o.object_id, 'IsScalarFunction')
      when 1 then 'Yes' else 'No' end as IsScalar,
  case objectproperty(o.object_id, 'IsTableFunction')
      when 1 then 'Yes' else 'No' end as IsTable,
  case objectproperty(o.object_id, 'IsInlineFunction')
      when 1 then 'Yes' else 'No' end as IsInline,
  case objectproperty(o.object_id, 'IsSchemaBound')
      when 1 then 'Yes' else 'No' end as IsSchemaBnd,
  case objectproperty(o.object_id, 'IsDeterministic')
      when 1 then 'Yes' else 'No' end as IsDtrmnstc
  from sys.objects o
  join sys.schemas s
  on o.schema_id = s.schema_id
where type_desc like '%FUNCTION%'
order by o.name
go

/* Result
schema      function             IsScalar IsTable IsInline IsSchemaBnd IsDtrmnstc
----------  -------------------- -------- ------- -------- ----------- ----------
dbo         AveragePayRate       Yes      No      No       No          No
dbo         AveragePayRate2      Yes      No      No       No          No
dbo         AveragePayRatebyJobT No       Yes     Yes      No          No
dbo         AveragePayRatebyJobT No       Yes     No       Yes         Yes
dbo         getonlydate          Yes      No      No       No          No
dbo         striptime            Yes      No      No       No          No
dbo         striptime2           Yes      No      No       No          No
dbo         ufnGetAccountingEndD Yes      No      No       No          No
dbo         ufnGetAccountingStar Yes      No      No       No          No
dbo         ufnGetContactInforma No       Yes     No       No          No
dbo         ufnGetDocumentStatus Yes      No      No       No          No
dbo         ufnGetProductDealerP Yes      No      No       No          No
dbo         ufnGetProductListPri Yes      No      No       No          No
dbo         ufnGetProductStandar Yes      No      No       No          No
dbo         ufnGetPurchaseOrderS Yes      No      No       No          No
dbo         ufnGetSalesOrderStat Yes      No      No       No          No
```

```
dbo          ufnGetStock           Yes    No    No    No    No
dbo          ufnLeadingZeros       Yes    No    No    Yes   Yes
dbo          valid_job_titles      No     Yes   Yes   No    No
*/
```

Using T-SQL to Modify Functions

You can use the ALTER FUNCTION command to change a function's definition without having to drop and re-create it. The syntax for the ALTER FUNCTION command is identical to the syntax for CREATE FUNCTION, except that you replace the CREATE keyword with the ALTER keyword. The following example modifies the AveragePricebyType2 function:

```
USE [AdventureWorks2012]
GO
ALTER FUNCTION [dbo].[AveragePayRatebyJobTitle2] (@rate money = 0.0)
RETURNS @table table (JobTitle nvarchar(30) null, avg_rate money null)
WITH SCHEMABINDING
AS
BEGIN
    INSERT @table
        SELECT CONVERT(VARCHAR(30), e.JobTitle), avg(Rate) as avg_rate
            FROM HumanResources.EmployeePayHistory eph
                JOIN
                HumanResources.Employee e
                ON e.BusinessEntityID = eph.BusinessEntityID
                AND eph.RateChangeDate =
                        (SELECT MAX(ratechangedate)
                            FROM HumanResources.EmployeePayHistory ephmax
                            WHERE ephmax.BusinessEntityID = eph.BusinessEntityID)
                group by e.JobTitle
                having avg(rate) > @rate
    RETURN
END
```

Using the ALTER FUNCTION command has a couple advantages over dropping and re-creating a function to modify it. The main advantage, as mentioned earlier, is that you don't have to drop the function first to make the change. The second advantage is that because you don't have to drop the function, you don't have to worry about reassigning permissions to the function. To determine whether a function has been altered since it was created, you can query the modify_date column in the sys.objects system view for that function.

```
select name, create_date, modify_date
 from sys.objects
where type_desc like '%FUNCTION%'
and name = 'AveragePayRatebyJobTitle2'
go
```

```
/* Result
name                      create_date            modify_date
-----------------------   --------------------   --------------------
AveragePayRatebyJobTitle2 2014-11-01 20:09:39.463 2014-11-01 23:57:23.110
*/
```

One limitation of the ALTER FUNCTION command is that you cannot use this command to change a table-valued function to a scalar function or to change an inline function to a multistatement function. You have to drop and re-create the function.

Using SSMS to View and Modify Functions

To view or edit a function within SSMS, open the Object Explorer to the database in which you want to create the function. Then select the Programmability node, right-click the Functions node, and then select either the Table-Valued Functions folder or the Scalar-Valued Functions folder. SSMS then displays a list of the functions of that type defined in that database within the Object Explorer.

> **NOTE**
>
> If the function you want to view or edit is not shown in the list, it was probably created after the list of functions in the Object Explorer was populated. You might need to refresh the function list in Object Explorer. To do this, you right-click the Functions folder and choose Refresh.

When you right-click a function name in the Object Explorer, you are presented with a number of options for viewing or modifying the function, as shown in Figure 26.5.

You can view or edit the function properties, view the function dependencies, delete the function, rename it, modify it, or script the function definition. If you choose to edit the function by clicking Modify, SSMS opens a new query window with the source code of the function extracted from the database as an ALTER FUNCTION command. You can edit the function as needed and execute the code in the query window to modify the function.

There are also options for scripting a function as a CREATE, ALTER, DROP, or SELECT command to either a new query window, a file, or the Clipboard, as shown in Figure 26.6.

You can also view the function properties by selecting the Properties option from the context menu. The Properties dialog appears, as shown in Figure 26.7. Unfortunately, except for the function permissions and extended properties, the properties shown are read-only.

For more information on the features and options for SSMS and for scripting objects, see Chapter 3, "SQL Server Management Studio."

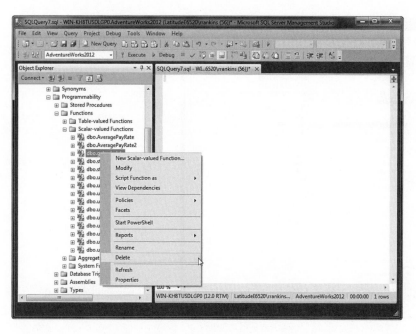

FIGURE 26.5   The Options menu for viewing and editing functions in SSMS.

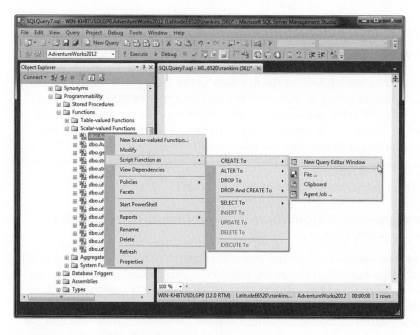

FIGURE 26.6   Options for scripting functions in SSMS.

FIGURE 26.7   The Function Properties dialog in SSMS.

Managing User-Defined Function Permissions

When a function is initially created, the only user who has permission to execute or query the function is the user who created it. To allow other users to execute a scalar function, you need to grant EXECUTE permission on the function to the appropriate user(s), group(s), or role(s). For a table-valued function, you need to grant SELECT permission to the user(s), group(s), or role(s) that will need to reference it. The following example grants EXECUTE permission on the getonlydate() function to everyone and SELECT permission on the AveragePriceByType function to the database user fred:

```
GRANT EXECUTE on dbo.getonlydate to public
GRANT SELECT on [HumanResources].[AveragePayRatebyJobTitle]to fred
```

For more detailed information on granting and revoking permissions, see Chapter 15, "Security and User Administration."

In SQL Server 2014, you can also specify the execution context of scalar-valued and multi-statement table-valued, user-defined functions. Essentially, this capability allows you to control which user account is used to validate permissions on objects referenced by the function, regardless of what user is actually executing the function. This provides additional flexibility and control in managing permissions for user-defined functions and the objects they reference. Only EXECUTE or SELECT permissions need to be granted to users on the function itself; you do not have to grant them explicit permissions on the referenced objects. Only the user account defined as the execution context for the function by the EXECUTE AS clause must have the necessary permissions on the objects the function accesses.

For example, in the following SQL script, the AverageBookPrice2 function is modified to run within the context of the dbo user. Any user who invokes this function essentially inherits the permissions of the dbo user on any objects accessed within the scope of the function temporarily within the execution of the function:

```
ALTER FUNCTION [dbo].[AveragePayRate2](@jobtitle nvarchar(50) = '%')
RETURNS MONEY
WITH EXECUTE AS 'dbo'
AS
BEGIN
    RETURN ( SELECT avg(eph.Rate)
    FROM HumanResources.EmployeePayHistory eph
        JOIN
        HumanResources.Employee e
        ON e.BusinessEntityID = eph.BusinessEntityID
        AND eph.RateChangeDate =
                (SELECT MAX(ratechangedate)
                FROM HumanResources.EmployeePayHistory ephmax
                WHERE ephmax.BusinessEntityID = eph.BusinessEntityID)
    WHERE e.JobTitle like @jobtitle)
END
```

Rewriting Stored Procedures as Functions

Before the advent of user-defined functions, if you wanted to do custom processing within SQL code, your only real option was to create stored procedures to do things that at times might work much better as functions. For example, you can't use the result set of a stored procedure in a WHERE clause or to return a value to be used as a column in a select list. Using a stored procedure to perform calculations on one or more columns in a result set often required using a cursor to step through each row in a result set and pass the column values fetched, one at a time, to the stored procedure as parameters. This procedure then typically returned the computed value via an output parameter, which had to be mapped to another local variable. Another alternative was to retrieve the initial result set into a temporary table and then perform additional queries or updates against the temporary table to modify the column values, which often required multiple passes. Neither of these methods was an efficient means of processing the data, but prior to SQL Server 2000, few other alternatives existed. If you needed to join against the result set of a stored procedure, you had to insert the result set into a temporary table first and then join against the temporary table, as shown in the following code fragment:

```
...
insert #results exec result_proc
select * from other_Table
   join #results on other_table.pkey = #results.keyfield
...
```

Now that SQL Server supports user-defined functions, you might want to consider rewriting some of your old stored procedures as functions. If the stored procedure returns a single result set and doesn't perform any of the actions listed previously that are not permitted in a function, it may be a candidate for being written as a table-valued function. If it returns a scalar value, usually via an output parameter, it is a candidate for being written as a scalar function. The following criteria also are indications that a procedure may be a good candidate for being rewritten as a function:

▶ The procedure logic is expressible in a single SELECT statement; however, it is written as a stored procedure, rather than a view, because of the need for it to be parameter-driven.

▶ The stored procedure does not perform update operations on tables, except against table variables.

▶ There are no dynamic SQL statements executed via the EXECUTE statement or sp_executesql.

▶ The stored procedure returns no more than a single result set.

▶ If the stored procedure returns a result set, its primary purpose is to build an intermediate result that is typically loaded into a temporary table, which is then queried in a SELECT statement.

The result_proc stored procedure, used earlier in this section, could possibly be rewritten as a table-valued function called fn_result(). The preceding code fragment could then be rewritten as follows:

```
SELECT *
    FROM fn_results() fn
    join other_table o.pkey = fn.keyfield
```

NOTE

While user-defined functions can help you modularize your code and simplify your code by avoiding having to repeat complex computations, you should try and avoid the urge to use user-defined functions just to simplify complex queries. This is especially true for scalar functions that reference tables or complex multistatement table-valued functions.

While inline table-valued functions can usually be incorporated into the outer query when SQL Server generates a query plan and optimized effectively as part of the entire query, scalar or complex multistatement table-valued functions are not.

When you use scalar UDFs with table access in a query, instead of performing an efficient JOIN with the tables referenced inside the function, it instead forces SQL Server to perform a separate table lookup per each row in the result set. Similarly, the multistatement table-valued function is treated like a "black box" and has to run to completion each time it is invoked within the query before its results can be incorporated into the final result set.

SQL Server's efficiency lies in the fact that it deals with data in SETS. Its power does not come in performing row-by-row operations, rather it wants to retrieve chunks of data and manipulate them as recordsets. With this in mind, you generally want to try and avoid certain operations that will cause more of a row-by-row operation and therefore impact performance. Unfortunately, the use of scalar functions within a set based operation results in this type of row-by-row operation so you should try and avoid using complex scalar UDFs with table access in large set-oriented queries.

Summary

User-defined functions in SQL Server 2014 allow you to create reusable routines that can help make your SQL code more straightforward and efficient.

In this chapter, you saw how to create and modify scalar functions and inline and multi-statement table-valued functions and how to invoke and use them in queries. Scalar functions can be used to perform more complex operations than those provided by the built-in scalar functions. Table-valued functions provide a way to create what are essentially parameterized views, and you can include them inline in your queries, just as you would in a table or view.

In the next chapter, you learn how to create and manage triggers in SQL Server 2014.

26

Creating and Managing Triggers

A *trigger* is a special type of database object executed automatically based on the occurrence of a database event. Prior to SQL Server 2005, the database events that fired triggers were based only on data manipulations, such as insertions, updates, or deletions. Starting with SQL Server 2005 triggers can also fire on events related to the definition of database objects. The two types of triggering events are referred to as Data Manipulation Language (DML) and Data Definition Language (DDL) events.

Most of the benefits derived from triggers are based on their event-driven nature. Once created, triggers automatically fire (without user intervention) based on an event in the database. This differs from other database code, which must be called explicitly in order to execute.

Say, for example, that you would like to keep track of historical changes to the data in several key tables in a database. Whenever a change is made to the data in the tables, you would like to put a copy of the data in a historical table before the change is made. You could accomplish this via the application code that is making the change to the data. The application code could copy the data to the history table before the change occurs and then execute the actual change. You could also manage this in other ways, such as by using stored procedures that are called by the application and subsequently insert records into the history tables.

These solutions work, but a trigger-based solution has some distinct advantages over them. With a trigger-based solution, a trigger can act on any modifications to the key tables. In the case of the history table example, triggers would automatically insert records into the history table whenever a modification was made to the data. This would all happen within the scope of the original transaction and would write history records for any changes made to these tables, including ad hoc changes that may have been made directly to the tables outside the application.

This is just one example of the benefits and uses of triggers. This chapter discusses the different types of triggers and further benefits they can provide.

What's New in Creating and Managing Triggers

The features and methods available for creating and managing triggers are essentially the same in SQL Server 2014 as all previous versions since SQL Server 2005. The upside to this is that you can take the knowledge and skills that you may already have with triggers and apply them directly to SQL Server 2014.

One notable addition to the list of deprecated features in 2014 is the ability to return result sets from triggers. The capability will be removed in the next version of SQL Server. Microsoft has indicated that there will be no replacement for this feature.

Using DML Triggers

DML triggers are invoked when a DML event occurs in the database. DML events manipulate or modify the data in a table or view. These events include insertions, updates, and deletions.

DML triggers are powerful objects for maintaining database integrity and consistency. They are able to evaluate data before it has been committed to the database. During this evaluation period, these triggers can perform a myriad of actions, including the following:

▶ Compare before and after versions of data.

▶ Roll back invalid modifications.

▶ Read from other tables, including those in other databases.

▶ Modify other tables, including those in other databases.

▶ Execute local and remote stored procedures.

Based on the nature of these actions, triggers were originally used in many cases to enforce referential integrity. Triggers were used when foreign key columns in one table had to be validated against primary keys or unique index values in another table. The triggers could fire when data was modified, and validations could be performed to ensure that referential integrity was maintained.

The advent of declarative referential integrity (DRI) diminished the need for referential integrity triggers. DRI is now generally implemented with database objects such as foreign key constraints that perform the referential integrity validation internally. Because of this, triggers generally handle more complex integrity concepts and enforce restrictions that cannot be handled through data types, constraints, defaults, or rules. Following are some examples of trigger uses:

▶ **Maintenance of duplicate and derived data**—A denormalized database generally introduces data duplications (that is, redundancy). Instead of exposing this redundancy to end users and programmers, you can keep the data in sync by using triggers. If the derived data is allowed to be out of sync, you might want to consider handling refreshes through batch processing or some other method instead.

▶ **Complex column constraints**—If a column constraint depends on other rows within the same table or rows in other tables, using a trigger is the best method for that column constraint.

▶ **Complex defaults**—You can use a trigger to generate default values based on data in other columns, rows, or tables.

▶ **Inter-database referential integrity**—When related tables are found in two different databases, you can use triggers to ensure referential integrity across the databases.

You can create stored procedures to perform these tasks, but the advantage of using triggers is that they fire automatically when defined for these tasks. You would have to remember to consistently execute the appropriate stored procedure code or SQL statements in your application code to perform the above tasks. With triggers, all associated data modifications are subject to the trigger code, except for bulk copy and a few other nonlogged actions. Even if a user utilizes an ad hoc tool, such as SQL Server Management Studio (SSMS) to make changes to the database, the integrity rules cannot be bypassed once the trigger is in place.

> **NOTE**
>
> Triggers and stored procedures are not mutually exclusive. You can have both triggers and stored procedures that perform modifications and validation on that same table. If desired, you can perform some tasks via triggers and other tasks via stored procedures.

Creating DML Triggers

You can create and manage triggers in SQL Server Management Studio or directly via Transact-SQL (T-SQL) statements. The Object Explorer in SSMS provides a simple means of creating triggers that you can use to generate the underlying T-SQL code. You expand the Object Explorer tree to the user table level and then right-click the `Triggers` node. When you select the New Trigger option, as shown in Figure 27.1, the trigger template shown in the right pane of Figure 27.1 appears.

You can populate the trigger template by manually editing it, or you can select the Query menu option Specify Values for Template Parameters. When you select Specify Values for Template Parameters, a screen appears, allowing you to fill in the basic values for the trigger, including the table that the trigger will be on and the events to respond to.

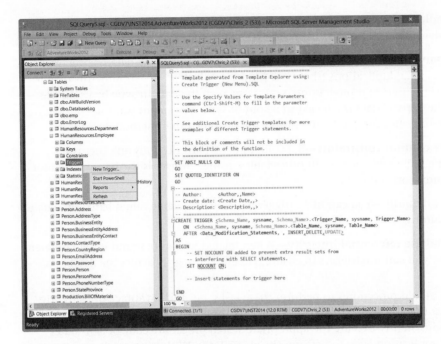

FIGURE 27.1   Using SSMS to create triggers.

You can launch the New Trigger template and other templates related to triggers via the Template Browser, which you open by selecting View, Template Browser in SSMS. Figure 27.2 shows a partial list of the available templates, including those related to triggers.

All the trigger templates provide a basic framework for you to create a trigger, but the core logic is up to you. Existing triggers or sample triggers are often good alternatives to the templates because they offer more of the core logic. You can right-click a trigger in the Object Explorer and select the Script Trigger As option. This option contains several different methods to script the trigger. After you script a trigger, you can modify it as necessary to meet your needs.

TIP

Using the `sys.triggers` catalog view is a good way to list all the triggers in a database. To use it, you simply open a new Query Editor window in SSMS and select all the rows from the view as shown in the following query:

```
SELECT * FROM sys.triggers.
```

FIGURE 27.2   The Template Browser.

After you have a basic trigger template, you can code the trigger, with limited restrictions. Almost every T-SQL statement you would use in a SQL batch or stored procedure is also available for use in the trigger code. However, you cannot use the following T-SQL commands in a DML trigger:

▶ ALTER DATABASE

▶ CREATE DATABASE

▶ DROP DATABASE

▶ RECONFIGURE

▶ RESTORE DATABASE and RESTORE LOG

The following sections describe the different types of DML triggers that can be coded and some of their common uses.

Using AFTER Triggers

An AFTER trigger is the original mechanism that SQL Server created to provide an automated response to data modifications. Prior to the release of SQL Server 2000, the AFTER trigger was the only type of trigger, and the word AFTER was rarely used in its name. Any trigger written for prior versions of SQL Server or documentation referring to these triggers is for AFTER triggers.

SQL Server 2000 introduced a new type of trigger called an INSTEAD OF trigger. This trigger is discussed later in the section titled "INSTEAD OF Triggers." The introduction of that new trigger and inclusion of the word AFTER in the name of the old trigger have helped accentuate the behavior of the AFTER trigger: The AFTER trigger executes *after* a data modification has taken place.

> **NOTE**
>
> Throughout the rest of this chapter, if the trigger type is not specified, you can assume that it is an AFTER trigger.

The fact that an AFTER trigger fires after a data modification might seem to be a simple concept, but it is critical to understanding how it works. The AFTER trigger fires after the data modification statement completes but before the statement's work is committed to the databases. The statement's work is captured in the transaction log but not committed to the database until the trigger has executed and performed its actions.

The trigger has the capability to roll back its actions as well as the actions of the modification statement that invoked it. This is possible because an implicit transaction exists that includes both the modification statement and trigger it fires. If the trigger does not issue a rollback, an implicit COMMIT of all the work is issued when the trigger completes.

The basic syntax for creating an AFTER trigger is as follows:

```
CREATE TRIGGER trigger_name
ON table_name
AFTER { INSERT | UPDATE | DELETE }
AS
SQL statements
```

The AFTER trigger is the default type of DML trigger, so the AFTER keyword is optional.

Listing 27.1 shows the code you use to create a trigger in the AdventureWorks2012 database. (You can find instructions for creating the AdventureWorks2012 database in the introduction chapter at the beginning of this book.) This new trigger prints a message, stating the number of rows updated by an UPDATE statement. You then execute a couple of UPDATE statements to see whether the trigger works.

LISTING 27.1   An Example of a Simple AFTER Trigger

```
CREATE TRIGGER tr_Person_upd ON Person.Person
AFTER UPDATE
AS
PRINT 'TRIGGER OUTPUT: ' +CONVERT(VARCHAR(5), @@ROWCOUNT)
+ ' rows were updated.'
GO
UPDATE Person.Person
SET FirstName = FirstName
```

```
WHERE Title = 'Mr.'
GO.
--TRIGGER OUTPUT: 577 rows were updated.
```

Even though you do not actually change the contents of the `FirstName` column (because you set it to itself), the trigger fires anyway. Listing 27.1 does not show a typical use of a trigger, but it gives you some insight into how and when a trigger fires. The fact that the trigger fires, regardless of what is updated, causes many developers to test the `@@rowcount` value at the beginning of the trigger code. If `@@rowcount` is equal to zero, the trigger can return without executing the remainder of the trigger code. This is a good tactic for optimizing the performance of triggers.

> **NOTE**
>
> Triggers are meant to guarantee the integrity of data. Although you can return messages in triggers (and result sets still for this release of SQL Server), doing so is not recommended. The programmers who write applications that perform modifications on a table are probably not prepared to get unexpected result sets or messages when they submit data modification statements.
>
> The ability to return result sets from triggers was added to the deprecated Database Engine features in SQL Server 2012. The next version of SQL Server will not support this capability, so be prepared to remove any code in triggers that may be doing this.
>
> The exception to not returning information for a trigger is returning an error with the `RAISERROR` command. If a trigger performs `ROLLBACK TRAN`, it should also execute `RAISERROR` to communicate the failure to the application.

Invoking AFTER Triggers

You know that the `AFTER` trigger fires when a data modification (such as an insertion, an update, or a deletion) takes place. What about the trigger's execution in relationship to other events, including the execution of constraints? The following events take place before an `AFTER` trigger executes:

- ▶ **Constraint processing**—This includes `CHECK` constraints, `UNIQUE` constraints, and `PRIMARY KEY` constraints.

- ▶ **Declarative referential actions**—These actions are defined by `FOREIGN KEY` constraints that ensure the proper relationships between tables. This includes cascading `FOREIGN KEY` constraints.

- ▶ **Triggering action**—This data modification caused the trigger to fire. The action occurs before the trigger fires, but the results are not committed to the database until the trigger completes.

You need to consider this execution carefully when you design triggers. For example, if you have a constraint and trigger defined on the same column, any violations to the constraint abort the statement, and the trigger execution does not occur. For example, if you have a foreign key constraint on a table that ensures referential integrity and a trigger that does some validation on that same foreign key column then the trigger validation will only execute if the foreign key validation is successful.

Specifying Trigger Firing Order

You can create more than one trigger on a table for each data modification action. In other words, you can have multiple triggers responding to an INSERT, an UPDATE, or a DELETE command. This can be useful in certain situations, but it can generate confusion because you cannot predict the order in which the triggers fire for the particular action.

Some of the confusion has been alleviated by the fact that SQL Server 2014 allows you to specify the first and last trigger that fire for a particular action. If you have four triggers responding to updates on a given table, you can set the order for two of the triggers (first and last), but the order of the remaining two triggers remains unknown.

The sp_settriggerorder procedure is the tool you use to set the trigger order. This procedure takes the trigger name, order value (FIRST, LAST, or NONE), and action (INSERT, UPDATE, or DELETE) as parameters. For example, you could use the following to set the firing order on the trigger used in this chapter's simple example:

```
sp_settriggerorder 'Person.tr_Person_upd' , FIRST, 'UPDATE'
```

The execution of this command sets the tr_Person_upd trigger as the first trigger to fire when an update happens to the table on which this trigger has been placed. If an ALTER statement is executed against the trigger after the trigger order has been defined, the firing order is lost. The sp_settriggerorder procedure must be run again to re-establish the firing order.

> **NOTE**
>
> It is recommended that you avoid defining multiple triggers for the same event on the same table when possible. Often, it is possible to include all the logic in one trigger defined for an action. This can simplify your database and you can avoid the uncertainty of the firing order.

Special Considerations with AFTER Triggers

Following are a few other considerations for AFTER triggers:

- ▶ AFTER triggers can be used on tables that also have cascading referential integrity constraints. The cascading feature, which was new to SQL Server 2000, allows you to define cascading actions when a user updates or deletes a primary key to which a foreign key points. This feature is discussed in more detail in Chapter 21, "Creating and Managing Tables."

- ▶ WRITETEXT and TRUNCATE TABLE do not fire triggers. BCP and Bulk Insert operations, by default, do not fire triggers either, but the FIRE_TRIGGERS hint can be specified to cause both AFTER and INSTEAD OF triggers to execute.

▶ Triggers are objects, so they must have unique names within the database. If you try to add a trigger with a name that already exists, you get an error message. You can, however, use ALTER on an existing trigger.

The following restrictions apply to AFTER triggers:

▶ AFTER triggers can be placed only on tables, not on views.

▶ A single AFTER trigger cannot be placed on more than one table.

▶ The text, ntext, and image columns cannot be referenced in the AFTER trigger logic.

Using inserted and deleted Tables

In most trigger situations, you need to know what changes were made as part of the data modification. You can find this information in the inserted and deleted tables. For the AFTER trigger, these temporary memory-resident tables contain the rows modified by the statement. With the INSTEAD OF trigger, the inserted and deleted tables are actually temporary tables created on-the-fly.

The inserted and deleted tables have identical column structures and names as the tables that were modified. Consider running the following statement against the AdventureWorks2012 database:

```
UPDATE [Production].[Product]
 SET [ListPrice] = '10'
 WHERE ProductSubcategoryID = 23
```

When this statement is executed, a copy of the rows to be modified is recorded, along with a copy of the rows after the modification. These copies are available to the trigger in the deleted and inserted tables.

If you want to be able to see the contents of the deleted and inserted tables for testing purposes, you can create a copy of the table and then create a trigger on that copy (see Listing 27.2). You can perform data modification statements and view the contents of these tables without the modification actually taking place.

LISTING 27.2   Viewing the Contents of the inserted and deleted Tables

```
--Create a copy of the Product table in the AdventureWorks2012 database
SELECT *
 INTO [Production].[Product_copy]
 FROM [Production].[Product]
GO
--add an AFTER trigger to this table for testing purposes
CREATE TRIGGER tr_Product ON [Production].[Product_copy]
 FOR INSERT, UPDATE, DELETE
 AS
 PRINT 'Inserted:'
```

27

```
select ProductNumber, ListPrice FROM inserted
PRINT 'Deleted:'
select ProductNumber, ListPrice FROM deleted
  ROLLBACK TRANSACTION
```

The `inserted` and `deleted` tables are available within the trigger after INSERT, UPDATE, and DELETE. Listing 27.3 shows the contents of `inserted` and `deleted`, as reported by the trigger when executing the preceding UPDATE statement.

LISTING 27.3   Viewing the Contents of the `inserted` and `deleted` Tables

```
UPDATE [Production].[Product_copy]
  SET [ListPrice] = '10'
  WHERE ProductSubcategoryID = 23


 Inserted:
ProductNumber                   ListPrice
------------------------        --------------------
SO-R809-L                       10.00
SO-R809-M                       10.00
SO-B909-L                       10.00
SO-B909-M                       10.00
Deleted:
ProductNumber                   ListPrice
------------------------        --------------------
SO-R809-L                       8.99
SO-R809-M                       8.99
SO-B909-L                       9.50
SO-B909-M                       9.50
```

> **NOTE**
>
> In SQL Server 2014, an error message is displayed when a rollback is initiated in a trigger. The error message indicates that the transaction ended in the trigger and that the batch has been aborted. Prior to SQL Server 2005, an error message was not displayed when a rollback was encountered in the trigger.

The nature of the `inserted` and `deleted` tables enables you to determine the action that fired the trigger. For example, when an INSERT occurs, the `deleted` table is empty because there were no previous values prior to the insertion. Table 27.1 shows the DML triggering events and the corresponding contents in the `deleted` and `inserted` tables.

TABLE 27.1   Determining the Action That Fired a Trigger

Statement	Contents of Inserted	Contents of Deleted
INSERT	Rows added	Empty
UPDATE	New rows	Old rows
DELETE	Empty	Rows deleted

NOTE

Triggers do not fire on a row-by-row basis. One common mistake in coding triggers is to assume that only one row is modified. However, triggers are set-based. If a single statement affects multiple rows in the table, the trigger needs to handle the processing of all the rows that were affected, not just one row at a time.

One common approach to dealing with the multiple rows in a trigger is to place the rows in a cursor and then process each row that was affected, one at a time. This approach works, but it can have an adverse effect on the performance of the trigger. To keep your trigger execution fast, you should try to use rowset-based logic instead of cursors in triggers when possible.

Rowset-based logic will typically join to the inserted or deleted table that is available to a trigger. You can join these tables to other tables that are being manipulated by the trigger. For example, a trigger on a Product table can update a related ProductCostHistory table with rowset-based logic such as the following:

```
Update Production.ProductCostHistory
set StandardCost = i.StandardCost
from inserted i
where i.ProductID = Production.ProductCostHistory.Productid
```

This kind of logic will allow the trigger update to work correctly if one ProductCostHistory record is changed or many ProductCostHistory rows are changed at once. This is much more efficient than loading all of the rows from the inserted table into a cursor that updates the ProductCostHistory records one at a time within the cursor loop.

Checking for Column Updates

The UPDATE() function is available inside INSERT and UPDATE triggers. UPDATE() allows a trigger to determine whether a column was affected by the INSERT or UPDATE statement that fired the trigger. By testing whether a column was actually updated, you can avoid performing unnecessary work.

For example, suppose a rule mandates that you cannot change the AddressLine2 for an address (a silly rule, but it demonstrates a few key concepts). Listing 27.4 creates a trigger for both INSERT and UPDATE that enforces this rule on the address table in the AdventureWorks2012 database.

LISTING 27.4   Using the UPDATE() Function in a Trigger

```
CREATE TRIGGER tr_Address_ins_upd ON [Person].[Address]
FOR INSERT, UPDATE
AS
IF UPDATE(AddressLine2)
 BEGIN
 RAISERROR ('You cannot change the AddressLine2.', 15, 1)
 ROLLBACK TRAN
 END
GO
UPDATE [Person].[Address]
SET AddressLine2 = AddressLine2
WHERE PostalCode = '98011'

Server: Msg 50000, Level 15, State 1, Procedure
 tr_Address_ins_upd, Line 6
 You cannot change the AddressLine2.
```

Listing 27.4 shows how you generally write triggers that verify the integrity of data. If the modification violates an integrity rule, an error message is returned to the client application, and the modification is rolled back.

The UPDATE() function evaluates to TRUE if you specify the column in the SET clause of the UPDATE statement. As shown in the preceding example, you do not have to change the value in the column for the UPDATE() function to evaluate to TRUE, but the column must be referenced in the UPDATE statement. For example, with the address update, the AddressLine2 column was set it to itself (the value does not change), but the UPDATE() function still evaluates to TRUE.

Now let see what happens with an INSERT statement on the address table:

```
INSERT [Person].[Address]
 (AddressLine1, AddressLine2, City, StateProvinceID
 , PostalCode, rowguid, ModifiedDate)
VALUES('mystreet', 'PO Box 999', 'Albany', 58,'97321'
    , NEWID(), GETDATE())

--Results from the previous insert
Server: Msg 50000, Level 15, State 1
You cannot change the  AddressLine2.
```

The UPDATE() function evaluates to TRUE and displays the error message. This outcome is expected because the trigger was created for INSERT as well, and the IF UPDATE condition is evaluated for both insertions and updates.

Now you can see what happens if you change the INSERT statement so that it does not include the AddressLine2 column in the INSERT:

```
INSERT [Person].[Address]
 (AddressLine1, City, StateProvinceID
 , PostalCode, rowguid, ModifiedDate)
VALUES('mystreet', 'Albany', 58,'97321'
     , NEWID(), GETDATE())
```

```
Server: Msg 50000, Level 15, State 1
You cannot change the AddressLine2.
```

The error message is still displayed, even though the insertion was performed without the AddressLine2 column. This process might seem counterintuitive, but the IF UPDATE condition always returns a TRUE value for INSERT actions. The reason is that the columns have either explicit default values or implicit (NULL) values inserted, even if they are not specified. The IF UPDATE conditions see this as a change and evaluate to TRUE.

If you change the tr_Address_ins_upd trigger to be for UPDATE only (not INSERT and UPDATE), the insertions can take place without error.

INSTEAD OF Triggers

An INSTEAD OF trigger, like its name implies, performs its actions *instead of* the action that fired it. This is much different from the AFTER trigger, which performs its actions after the statement that caused it to fire has completed. This means you can have an INSTEAD OF update trigger on a table that successfully completes but does NOT include the actual update to the table.

The basic syntax for creating an INSTEAD OF trigger is as follows:

```
CREATE TRIGGER trigger_name
ON table_name
INSTEAD OF { INSERT | UPDATE | DELETE }
AS
SQL statements
```

Listing 27.5 shows how to create a trigger that prints a message stating the number of rows to be updated by an UPDATE statement but it completes without performing the actual update. The script then executes an UPDATE against the table that has the trigger on it invoking the INSTEAD OF trigger. Finally, the script selects the rows from the table for review.

LISTING 27.5   A Simple INSTEAD OF Trigger

```
CREATE TRIGGER trI_Person_upd ON [Person].[Person]
INSTEAD OF UPDATE
AS
PRINT 'TRIGGER OUTPUT: '
```

27

```
+CONVERT(VARCHAR(5), @@ROWCOUNT) + ' rows were updated.'
GO


UPDATE [Person].[Person]
SET FirstName = 'Rachael'
WHERE BusinessEntityID = 1
GO
TRIGGER OUTPUT: 1 rows were updated.


SELECT FirstName, LastName
  FROM [Person].[Person]
WHERE BusinessEntityID = 1
GO
FirstName LastName
--------- --------
Ken       Sánchez
```

As you can see from the results of the SELECT statement, the first name (FirstName) column is not updated to 'Rachael'. The UPDATE statement is correct, but the INSTEAD OF trigger logic does not apply the update from the statement as part of the INSTEAD OF action. The only action the trigger carries out is to print the row update message.

The important point to realize is that after you define an INSTEAD OF trigger on a table, you need to include the logic in the trigger needed to perform the actual modification as well as any other actions that the trigger might need to carry out.

Invoking INSTEAD OF Triggers

To gain a complete understanding of the INSTEAD OF trigger, you must understand its execution in relationship to the other events that are occurring. The following key events are important when the INSTEAD OF trigger fires:

▶ **Triggering action**—The INSTEAD OF trigger fires instead of the triggering action. As shown earlier, the actions of the INSTEAD OF trigger replace the actions of the original data modification that fired the trigger.

▶ **Constraint processing**—Constraint processing—including CHECK constraints, UNIQUE constraints, and PRIMARY KEY constraints—happens after the INSTEAD OF trigger fires.

The trigger created in Listing 27.6 demonstrates the trigger execution order.

LISTING 27.6   INSTEAD OF Trigger Execution

```
CREATE TRIGGER Person_insInstead
ON Person.Person
INSTEAD OF insert
AS
```

```
--Insert the BusinessEntity record for the Person if it does not already exist
IF NOT EXISTS
(SELECT 1
    FROM [Person].[BusinessEntity] b
    JOIN inserted i ON i.BusinessEntityID = b.BusinessEntityID )
BEGIN
    SET IDENTITY_INSERT [Person].[BusinessEntity] ON
    INSERT [Person].[BusinessEntity]
        (BusinessEntityID, rowguid, ModifiedDate)
      SELECT I.BusinessEntityID, NEWID(), GETDATE()
        FROM inserted i
    SET IDENTITY_INSERT [Person].[BusinessEntity] OFF

    PRINT 'BusinessEntity was added before insert'

END


--Execute the original insert with the newly created BusinessEntityID
INSERT [Person].[Person]
        (BusinessEntityID, PersonType, NameStyle, Title, FirstName,
         MiddleName, LastName, Suffix, EmailPromotion,
         AdditionalContactInfo, Demographics, rowguid, ModifiedDate)
    SELECT BusinessEntityID, PersonType, NameStyle, Title, FirstName,
         MiddleName, LastName, Suffix, EmailPromotion,
         AdditionalContactInfo, Demographics, rowguid, ModifiedDate
      FROM Inserted
GO
```

The trigger in Listing 27.6 can be created in AdventureWorks2012. The key feature of this INSTEAD OF trigger is that it can satisfy a referential integrity constraint that was not satisfied before the INSERT was executed. Note the FOREIGN KEY constraint on the person table that references BusinessEntityID on the BusinessEntity table. The trigger first checks whether the BusinessEntity record associated with the BusinessEntityID of the person being inserted exists. If the BusinessEntity record does not exist for the inserted person's BusinessEntityID, the trigger inserts a new BusinessEntity record and uses it for the insertion of the person record.

If you execute the following INSERT statement, which has a BusinessEntityID that does not exist, it succeeds:

```
insert person.person
 (BusinessEntityID, PersonType, NameStyle, FirstName, LastName
  , EmailPromotion, rowguid, ModifiedDate)
  values (99999, 'EM', 0, 'John', 'Deer'
  , 0, NEWID (), getdate())
Go
```

This statement succeeds because the constraint processing happens after the INSTEAD OF trigger completes its actions. Conversely, if you were to create the same trigger as an AFTER trigger, the FOREIGN KEY constraint would execute before the AFTER trigger, and display a message indicating that a foreign key conflict had occurred.

Notice with the previous INSTEAD OF trigger example that the last action the trigger performs is the actual insertion of the employee record. The trigger was created to fire when an employee was inserted, so the trigger must perform the actual insertion. This insertion occurs in addition to any other actions that justify the trigger's creation.

Using AFTER Versus INSTEAD OF Triggers

Now that you have seen some of the key differences between AFTER and INSTEAD OF triggers, you need to decide which trigger to use. In the previous example (Listing 27.6), the INSTEAD OF trigger is the only trigger option for this kind of functionality. However, you can often use either trigger type to attain the same result.

Something you should consider when choosing one of these triggers is the efficiency of the overall modification. For example, if you have a modification that will cause a trigger to fire and often reject the modification, you might want to consider using the INSTEAD OF trigger. The rationale is that the INSTEAD OF trigger does not perform the actual modification until after the trigger completes, so you do not need to undo the modification. If you were to use an AFTER trigger in the same scenario, any modifications that were rejected would need to be rolled back because they have already been written to the transaction log by the time the AFTER trigger fires.

Conversely, if you have a situation in which the vast majority of the updates are not rejected, the AFTER trigger might be your best choice.

The particular situation dictates the preferred trigger, but you should keep in mind that INSTEAD OF triggers tend to be more involved than AFTER triggers because an INSTEAD OF trigger must perform the actual data modification that fired it.

Using AFTER and INSTEAD OF Triggers Together

An important consideration when coding an INSTEAD OF trigger is that it can exist on the same table as an AFTER trigger. INSTEAD OF triggers can also execute based on the same data modifications as AFTER triggers.

Consider, for example, the INSTEAD OF trigger from Listing 27.6 that you placed on the person table in the AdventureWorks2012 database. An AFTER trigger already existed on the person table. Listing 27.7 shows the code for the existing AFTER trigger on the person table.

LISTING 27.7   An AFTER Trigger Placed on the Same Table as an INSTEAD OF Trigger

```
ALTER TRIGGER Person.iuPerson ON Person.Person
AFTER INSERT, UPDATE NOT FOR REPLICATION AS
BEGIN
    DECLARE @Count int
```

```
    SET @Count = @@ROWCOUNT
    IF @Count = 0
        RETURN

    SET NOCOUNT ON

    IF UPDATE(BusinessEntityID) OR UPDATE(Demographics)
    BEGIN
        UPDATE Person.Person
        SET Person.Person.Demographics
        = N'<IndividualSurvey xmlns
        ="http://schemas.microsoft.com/sqlserver
        /2004/07/adventure-works/IndividualSurvey">
            <TotalPurchaseYTD>0.00</TotalPurchaseYTD>
            </IndividualSurvey>'
        FROM inserted
        WHERE Person.Person.BusinessEntityID = inserted.BusinessEntityID
            AND inserted.Demographics IS NULL

        UPDATE Person.Person
        SET Demographics.modify(N'declare default element namespace
         "http://schemas.microsoft.com/sqlserver
         /2004/07/adventure-works/IndividualSurvey"
            insert <TotalPurchaseYTD>0.00</TotalPurchaseYTD>
            as first
            into (/IndividualSurvey)1')
        FROM inserted
        WHERE Person.Person.BusinessEntityID = inserted.BusinessEntityID
            AND inserted.Demographics IS NOT NULL
            AND inserted.Demographics.exist
            (N'declare default element namespace
                "http://schemas.microsoft.com/sqlserver
                /2004/07/adventure-works/IndividualSurvey"
                /IndividualSurvey/TotalPurchaseYTD') <> 1
    END
END
go
```

This AFTER trigger fires for both insertions and updates, and it can exist on the same table as the Person_insInstead INSTEAD OF trigger described earlier. The combined effect on a person insertion with both the triggers on the person table is to have the following actions happen:

1. The INSERT statement is invoked.

2. The INSTEAD OF trigger fires, completes its validation, and ultimately does the person insertion that is written to the transaction log.

3. Constraint processing completes.

4. The AFTER trigger fires, performing its actions on the person record inserted by the INSTEAD OF trigger.

5. The AFTER trigger completes and commits the transaction to the database.

One of the key points in this example is that the AFTER trigger performs its actions on the row inserted by the INSTEAD OF trigger. It does not use the record from the original INSERT that started the trigger execution. Therefore, in this chapter's example, where the INSTEAD OF trigger generates a new BusinessEntityID, the new BusinessEntityID value is used in the AFTER trigger.

You need to consider rollback and recovery in this scenario as well, but they are beyond the scope of this discussion. This example simply shows that INSTEAD OF and AFTER triggers can be combined and that you need to consider the order of execution when designing a trigger solution.

Using Views with INSTEAD OF Triggers

One of the most powerful applications of an INSTEAD OF trigger is to a view. The INSTEAD OF trigger, unlike the AFTER trigger, can be applied to a view and triggered based on modifications to the view. For more information on views, see Chapter 24, "Creating and Managing Views."

The creation of INSTEAD OF triggers on views is important because data modifications against views have many restrictions. The list is extensive, but following are the primary restrictions:

▶ You cannot use data modification statements that apply to more than one table in the view in a single statement.

▶ All columns defined as NOT NULL in the underlying tables that are being inserted must have the column values specified in the INSERT statement.

▶ If the view was defined with the WITH CHECK OPTION clause, rows cannot be modified in a way that will cause them to disappear from the view.

You can use the INSTEAD OF trigger to overcome some of these restrictions. In particular, the first restriction (related to making a single table modification) can be addressed with the INSTEAD OF trigger. The INSTEAD OF trigger fires before the actual modification takes place, so it can resolve the modifications to the underlying tables associated with the view. It can then execute the modification directly against those base tables. The following example demonstrates this capability:

```
Use AdventureWorks2012
go
CREATE VIEW PersonEmails
as
select FirstName, LastName, EmailAddress
 from Person.Person p
  join person.EmailAddress e
   on p.BusinessEntityID  = E.BusinessEntityId
GO
```

This example creates a view in the AdventureWorks2012 database that joins data from the person and EmailAddress tables. It retrieves all person records and their related emails. Following is a sample set of rows from the view:

```
BusinessEntityID FirstName   LastName    EmailAddress
---------------- ---------   --------    ------------------------------
1                Ken         Sánchez     keneth@adventure-works.com
2                Terri       Duffy       terri0@adventure-works.com
3                Roberto     Tamburello  roberto0@adventure-works.com
4                Rob         Walters     rob0@adventure-works.com
5                Gail        Erickson    gail0@adventure-works.com
```

Let's say you want to update multiple columns via the view at one time. In particular, you want to update one column from one of the underlying tables in the view and one column from the other table in the view, as shown in the following example:

```
update PersonEmails
 set FirstName = 'Keneth'
 , EmailAddress = 'keneth@adventure-works.com'
 where BusinessEntityID = 1
GO
View or function ' PersonEmails' is not updateable
because the modification affects multiple base tables.
```

As you can see, an error message is generated indicating that multiple base tables cannot be updated. To get around this problem, you can use an INSTEAD OF trigger. The trigger can decipher the update to the view and apply the updates to the base table without causing the error. This functionality is demonstrated in the INSTEAD OF trigger shown in Listing 27.8.

LISTING 27.8   A Basic View with an INSTEAD OF Trigger

```
CREATE TRIGGER PersonEmails_updInstead
ON PersonEmails
INSTEAD OF UPDATE
AS
IF @@ROWCOUNT = 0 RETURN
```

```
--update the data related to the Person table
UPDATE Person.Person
   SET FirstName = i.FirstName,
       LastName = i.LastName
  FROM inserted i
 WHERE Person.Person.BusinessEntityID = i.BusinessEntityID

--update the data related to the EmailAddress table
UPDATE person.EmailAddress
   SET EmailAddress = i.EmailAddress
  FROM inserted i
 WHERE person.EmailAddress.BusinessEntityID  = i.BusinessEntityID
GO
```

The first update in Listing 27.8 deals with the updates to the `Person` table. A subsequent update in the trigger deals with the updates to the `EmailAddess` table. If you now execute the same UPDATE statement, you don't get an error message:

```
update PersonEmails
  set FirstName = 'Keneth'
  , EmailAddress = 'keneth@adventure-works.com'
  where BusinessEntityID = 1
GO
```

The following results show values selected from the `PersonEmails` view after the update is executed successfully:

```
BusinessEntityID FirstName  LastName   EmailAddress
---------------- ---------- ---------- ------------------------------
1                Keneth     Sánchez    keneth@adventure-works.com
2                Terri      Duffy      terri0@adventure-works.com
3                Roberto    Tamburello roberto0@adventure-works.com
4                Rob        Walters    rob0@adventure-works.com
5                Gail       Erickson   gail0@adventure-works.com
```

Notice that both the `FirstName` and `EmailAddress` for the first row (Mr. Sánchez) have been updated as expected.

NOTE

If you have been running all the examples in this chapter, you might have seen results from the previous `select` that showed the `FirstName` of Ken rather than Keneth. The reason for this is that another trigger named trI_Person_Upd exists on the `Person` table. This was an INSTEAD OF trigger table that simply printed out the number of rows affected but did not perform the actual update. This trigger would prevent the `FirstName` from being updated. This situation emphasizes the fact that care must be taken when multiple triggers exist on a given table.

You can see the added flexibility that you get by using the INSTEAD OF trigger on a basic view. This flexibility is also applicable to a more sophisticated view called a *distributed partitioned view*. With this type of view, data for the view can be partitioned across different servers. Partitioning this way enables you to scale a database solution and still have a single view of the data that appears as one table.

You can make data modifications via a distributed partitioned view, but some restrictions exist. If you do not meet the requirements for updating the view, you can use the INSTEAD OF trigger to bypass these restrictions; this is similar to adding an INSTEAD OF trigger on a nonpartitioned view.

INSTEAD OF Trigger Restrictions

INSTEAD OF triggers have many capabilities, but they also have limitations. Following are some of them:

▶ INSTEAD OF triggers do not support recursion. This means they cannot call themselves, regardless of the setting of the Recursive Triggers database option. For example, if an INSERT is executed on a table that has an INSTEAD OF trigger, and the INSTEAD OF trigger performs an INSERT on this same table, the INSTEAD OF trigger for this INSERT does not fire a second time. Any AFTER triggers defined on the same table for INSERT fire based on the INSTEAD OF trigger INSERT.

▶ You can define only one INSTEAD OF trigger for each action on a given table. Therefore, you can have a maximum of three INSTEAD OF triggers for each table: one for INSERT, one for UPDATE, and one for DELETE.

▶ A table cannot have an INSTEAD OF trigger and a FOREIGN KEY constraint with CASCADE defined for the same action. For example, you cannot have an INSTEAD OF trigger defined for DELETE on a given table as well as a foreign key with a CASCADE DELETE definition. You get an error if you attempt to do this. In this situation, you could have INSTEAD OF triggers defined on INSERT and UPDATE without receiving errors.

Using DDL Triggers

DDL triggers were introduced in SQL Server 2005. These triggers focus on changes to the definition of database objects as opposed to changes to the actual data. The definition of database objects is dictated by the DDL events that these triggers respond to.

The DDL events that these triggers fire on can be broken down into two main categories. The first category includes DDL events that are scoped at the database level and affect the definition of objects such as tables, indexes, and users. The second category of DDL triggers is scoped at the server level. These triggers apply to server objects, such as logins.

The number of DDL events at the database level far exceeds the number at the server level. Table 27.2 lists the DDL statements and system stored procedures that DDL triggers can fire on.

TABLE 27.2   DDL Statements and System Stored Procedures*

Statements and System Stored Procedures with Database-Level Scope

Create/Grant/Bind/Add	Alter/Update/Deny	Drop/Revoke/Unbind
CREATE_APPLICATION_ROLE	ALTER_APPLICATION_ROLE	DROP_APPLICATION_ ROLE
(sp_addapprole)	(sp_approlepassword)	(sp_dropapprole)
CREATE_ASSEMBLY	ALTER_ASSEMBLY	DROP_ASSEMBLY
CREATE_ASYMMETRIC_KEY	ALTER_ASYMMETRIC_KEY	DROP_ASYMMETRIC_KEY
ALTER_AUTHORIZATION	ALTER_AUTHORIZATION_ DATABASE	
	(sp_changedbowner)	
CREATE_BROKER_PRIORITY	CREATE_BROKER_PRIORITY	CREATE_BROKER_ PRIORITY
CREATE_CERTIFICATE	ALTER_CERTIFICATE	DROP_CERTIFICATE
CREATE_CONTRACT	DROP_CONTRACT	
CREATE_CREDENTIAL	ALTER_CREDENTIAL	DROP_CREDENTIAL
GRANT_DATABASE	DENY_DATABASE	REVOKE_DATABASE
CREATE_DATABASE_AUDIT_ SPEFICIATION	ALTER_DATABASE_AUDIT_ SPEFICIATION	DENY_DATABASE_AUDIT_ SPEFICIATION
CREATE_DATABASE_ENCRYPTION_ KEY	ALTER_DATABASE_ ENCRYPTION_KEY	DROP_DATABASE_ ENCRYPTION_KEY
CREATE_DEFAULT	DROP_DEFAULT	
BIND_DEFAULT	UNBIND_DEFAULT	
(sp_bindefault)	(sp_unbindefault)	
CREATE_EVENT_NOTIFICATION	DROP_EVENT_NOTIFICATION	
CREATE_EXTENDED_PROPERTY	ALTER_EXTENDED_PROPERTY	DROP_EXTENDED_ PROPERTY
(sp_addextendedproperty)	(sp_updateextended property)	(sp_dropextended-property)
CREATE_FULLTEXT_CATALOG	ALTER_FULLTEXT_CATALOG	DROP_FULLTEXT_ CATALOG
(sp_fulltextcatalog)	(sp_fulltextcatalog) and (sp_fulltext_database)	(sp_fulltextcatalog)
CREATE_FULLTEXT_INDEX	ALTER_FULLTEXT_INDEX	DROP_FULLTEXT_INDEX
(sp_fulltexttable)	(sp_fulltextcatalog), (sp_fulltext_column) and (sp_fulltext_column)	(sp_fulltexttable)
CREATE_FULLTEXT_STOPLIST	ALTER_FULLTEXT_STOPLIST	DROP_FULLTEXT_ STOPLIST
CREATE_FUNCTION	ALTER_FUNCTION	DROP_FUNCTION
CREATE_INDEX	ALTER_INDEX	DROP_INDEX

Create/Grant/Bind/Add	Alter/Update/Deny	Drop/Revoke/Unbind
	(sp_indexoption)	
CREATE_MASTER_KEY	ALTER_MASTER_KEY	DROP_MASTER_KEY
CREATE_MESSAGE_TYPE	ALTER_MESSAGE_TYPE	DROP_MESSAGE_TYPE
CREATE_PARTITION_FUNCTION	ALTER_PARTITION_FUNCTION	DROP_PARTITION_ FUNCTION
CREATE_PARTITION_SCHEME	ALTER_PARTITION_SCHEME	DROP_PARTITION_ SCHEME
CREATE_PLAN_GUIDE (sp_create_plan_guide)	ALTER_PLAN_GUIDE (sp_control_plan_guide)	DROP_PLAN_GUIDE (sp_control_plan_ guide)
CREATE_PROCEDURE	ALTER_PROCEDURE (sp_procoption)	DROP_PROCEDURE
CREATE_QUEUE	ALTER_QUEUE	DROP_QUEUE
CREATE_REMOTE_SERVICE_BINDING	ALTER_REMOTE_SERVICE_ BINDING	DROP_REMOTE_SERVICE_ BINDING
CREATE_SPATIAL_INDEX		
RENAME (sp_rename)		
CREATE_ROLE (sp_addrole), and (sp_addgroup)	ALTER_ROLE	DROP_ROLE (sp_droprole), and (sp_dropgroup)
ADD_ROLE_MEMBER	DROP_ROLE_MEMBER	
CREATE_ROUTE	ALTER_ROUTE	DROP_ROUTE
CREATE_RULE	DROP_RULE	
BIND_RULE (sp_bindrule)	UNBIND_RULE (sp_unbindrule)	
CREATE_SCHEMA (sp_addrole), (sp_adduser), (sp_addgroup), and (sp_grantdbaccess)	ALTER_SCHEMA (sp_changeobjectowner)	DROP_SCHEMA
CREATE_SEARCH_PROPERTY_LIST	ALTER_SEARCH_PROPERTY_LIST	DROP_SEARCH_ PROPERTY_LIST
CREATE_SEQUENCE_EVENTS	CREATE_SEQUENCE_EVENTS	CREATE_SEQUENCE_ EVENTS
CREATE_SERVER_ROLE	ALTER_SERVER_ROLE	DROP_SERVER_ROLE
CREATE_SERVICE	ALTER_SERVICE	DROP_SERVICE
ALTER_SERVICE_MASTER_KEY	BACKUP_SERVICE_MASTER_KEY	RESTORE_SERVICE_ MASTER_KEY

27

Create/Grant/Bind/Add	Alter/Update/Deny	Drop/Revoke/Unbind
ADD_SIGNATURE (for signature operations on non-schema scoped objects; database, assembly, trigger)	DROP_SIGNATURE	
ADD_SIGNATURE_SCHEMA_OBJECT (for schema scoped objects; stored procedures, functions)	DROP_SIGNATURE_SCHEMA_OBJECT	
CREATE_SPATIAL_INDEX	ALTER_INDEX can be used for spatial indexes.	DROP_INDEX can be used for spatial indexes.
CREATE_STATISTICS	DROP_STATISTICS	UPDATE_STATISTICS
CREATE_SYMMETRIC_KEY	ALTER_SYMMETRIC_KEY	DROP_SYMMETRIC_KEY
CREATE_SYNONYM	DROP_SYNONYM	
CREATE_TABLE	ALTER_TABLE (sp_tableoption)	DROP_TABLE
CREATE_TRIGGER	ALTER_TRIGGER (sp_settriggerorder)	DROP_TRIGGER
CREATE_TYPE (sp_addtype)	DROP_TYPE (sp_droptype)	
CREATE_USER (sp_adduser), and (sp_grantdbaccess)	ALTER_USER (sp_change_users_login)	DROP_USER (sp_dropuser), and (sp_revokedbaccess)
CREATE_VIEW	ALTER_VIEW	DROP_VIEW
CREATE_XML_INDEX	ALTER_INDEX can be used for XML indexes.	DROP_INDEX can be used for XML indexes.
CREATE_XML_SCHEMA_COLLECTION	ALTER_XML_SCHEMA_COLLECTION	DROP_XML_SCHEMA_COLLECTION

Statements and System Stored Procedures with Server-Level Scope

Create/Grant/Bind/Add	Alter/Update/Deny	Drop/Revoke/Unbind
ALTER_AUTHORIZATION_SERVER	ALTER_SERVER_CONFIGURATION	ALTER_INSTANCE (sp_configure) and (sp_addserver)
CREATE_AVAILABILITY_GROUP	ALTER_AVAILABILITY_GROUP	DROP_AVAILABILITY_GROUP
CREATE_CREDENTIAL	ALTER_CREDENTIAL	DROP_CREDENTIAL
CREATE_CRYPTOGRAPHIC_PROVIDER	ALTER_CRYPTOGRAPHIC_PROVIDER	DROP_CRYPTOGRAPHIC_PROVIDER
CREATE_DATABASE	ALTER_DATABASE	DROP_DATABASE

Create/Grant/Bind/Add	Alter/Update/Deny	Drop/Revoke/Unbind
	(sp_fulltext_database)	
CREATE_ENDPOINT	ALTER_ENDPOINT	DROP_ENDPOINT
CREATE_EVENT_SESSION	ALTER_EVENT_SESSION	DROP_EVENT_SESSION
CREATE_EXTENDED_PROCEDURE	DROP_EXTENDED_PROCEDURE	
(sp_addextendedproc)	(sp_dropextendedproc)	
CREATE_LINKED_SERVER	ALTER_LINKED_SERVER	DROP_LINKED_
(sp_addlinkedserver)	(sp_serveroption)	(sp_dropserver)
CREATE_LINKED_SERVER_LOGIN	DROP_LINKED_SERVER_LOGIN	
(sp_addlinkedsrvlogin)	(sp_droplinkedsrvlogin)	
CREATE_LOGIN	ALTER_LOGIN	DROP_LOGIN
(sp_addlogin), (sp_grant-login), (xp_grantlogin), and (sp_denylogin)	(sp_defaultdb), (sp_defaultlanguage), (sp_password), and (sp_change_users_login)	(sp_droplogin), (sp_revokelogin), and (xp_revokelogin)
CREATE_MESSAGE	ALTER_MESSAGE	DROP_MESSAGE
(sp_addmessage)	(sp_altermessage)	(sp_dropmessage)
CREATE_REMOTE_SERVER	ALTER_REMOTE_SERVER	DROP_REMOTE_SERVER
(sp_addserver)	(sp_setnetname)	(sp_dropserver)
CREATE_RESOURCE_POOL	ALTER_RESOURCE_POOL	DROP_RESOURCE_POOL
GRANT_SERVER	DENY_SERVER	REVOKE_SERVER
ADD_SERVER_ROLE_MEMBER	DROP_SERVER_ROLE_MEMBER	
CREATE_SERVER_AUDIT	ALTER_SERVER_AUDIT	DROP_SERVER_AUDIT
CREATE_SERVER_AUDIT_SPECIFICATION	ALTER_SERVER_AUDIT_SPECIFICATION	DROP_SERVER_AUDIT_SPECIFICATION
CREATE_WORKLOAD_GROUP	CREATE_WORKLOAD_GROUP	CREATE_WORKLOAD_GROUP

** *System stored procedures are enclosed in parentheses and are shown in the row below the related DDL event.*

27

Triggers created on the DDL events are particularly important for auditing purposes. In the past, it was very difficult to isolate changes to the definition of a database or to secure them from change. With DDL triggers, you have the tools necessary to manage these changes.

Creating DDL Triggers

The basic syntax for creating a DDL trigger follows:

```
CREATE TRIGGER trigger_name
ON { ALL SERVER | DATABASE }
[ WITH <ddl_trigger_option> [ ,...n ] ]
{ FOR | AFTER } { event_type | event_group } [ ,...n ]
AS { sql_statement  [ ; ] [ ...n ] | EXTERNAL NAME < method specifier >  [ ; ] }
```

The best way to illustrate the use of the DDL trigger syntax and power of these triggers is to look at a few examples. The example shown in Listing 27.9 illustrates the creation of a DDL trigger that is scoped at the database level and prevents table-level changes.

LISTING 27.9   A Database-Scoped DDL Trigger for Tables

```
CREATE TRIGGER tr_TableAudit
ON DATABASE
FOR CREATE_TABLE, ALTER_TABLE, DROP_TABLE
AS
    PRINT 'You must disable the TableAudit trigger in order
       to change any table in this database'
    ROLLBACK
GO
```

This trigger is fired whenever the CREATE, ALTER, or DROP TABLE statements are executed. Consider, for example, the following statements that can be run against the AdventureWorks2012 database:

```
SELECT *
INTO Person.Person_Copy
from Person.Person
```

```
You must disable the TableAudit trigger in order to change any table in this
database
Msg 3609, Level 16, State 2, Line 1
The transaction ended in the trigger. The batch has been aborted.
```

The SELECT INTO statement will ultimately create a new Person_Copy table. With the tr_TableAudit trigger in place on the AdventureWorks2012 database, an error message is displayed, and the execution is prevented.

This type of trigger is useful for controlling development and production database environments. It goes beyond the normal security measures and helps manage unwanted change. For development environments, this type of trigger enables the database administrator to lock down an environment and focus all changes through that person.

The previous examples include events scoped at the database level. Let's look at an example that applies to server-level events. The script in Listing 27.10 creates a trigger scoped at the server level. It prevents changes to the server logins. When this trigger is installed, it displays a message and rolls back any login changes that are attempted.

LISTING 27.10   A Server-Scoped DDL Trigger for Logins

```
CREATE TRIGGER tr_LoginAudit
ON ALL SERVER
FOR CREATE_LOGIN, ALTER_LOGIN, DROP_LOGIN
AS
    PRINT 'You must disable the tr_LoginAudit trigger before making login changes'
    ROLLBACK
```

The DDL trigger examples we have looked at thus far have targeted specific events listed in Table 27.2. These individual events can also be referenced via an event group. Event groups are hierarchical in nature and can be referenced in DDL triggers instead of the individual events. For example, the table-level trigger from Listing 27.9 can be changed as shown in Listing 27.11 to accomplish the same result. In Listing 27.11, the DDL_TABLE_EVENTS group reference replaces the individual event references to CREATE_TABLE, ALTER_TABLE, and DROP_TABLE.

LISTING 27.11   An Example of a DDL Trigger Referencing an Event Group

```
USE [AdventureWorks2012]
IF  EXISTS (SELECT * FROM sys.triggers
    WHERE name = N'tr_TableAudit' AND parent_class=0)
DROP TRIGGER [tr_TableAudit] ON DATABASE
go

CREATE TRIGGER tr_TableAudit
ON DATABASE
FOR DDL_TABLE_EVENTS
AS
    PRINT 'You must disable the TableAudit trigger in
        order to change any table in this database'
    ROLLBACK
GO
```

SQL Server Books Online has an excellent diagram listing all the event groups that can be used to fire DDL triggers. Refer to the "DDL Event Groups" topic in Books Online, which shows the event groups and related DDL events they contain. Event groups simplify administration and allow for auditing at a high level.

The DDL trigger examples we have looked at thus far have executed simple print statements. To further extend the functionality of DDL triggers, you can code them to capture event information related to the DDL trigger execution. You do this by using the EVENTDATA function. The EVENTDATA function returns an XML string that includes the time of the event, server process ID (SPID), and type of event that fired the trigger. For some events, additional information, such as the object name or T-SQL statement, is included in the XML string as well.

27

The EVENTDATA function is essentially the replacement for the inserted and deleted tables available with DML triggers but not available with DDL triggers. It gives you information you can use to implement an auditing solution that captures changes to a data definition. This function is particularly useful in situations in which you do not want to prevent changes to your definition, but you want a record of the changes that occur.

Listing 27.12 shows a DDL trigger that utilizes the EVENTDATA function to capture any changes to indexes in the AdventureWorks2012 database. Several event data elements are selected from the EVENTDATA XML string and displayed whenever a change is made to an index.

LISTING 27.12   An Example of a DDL Trigger That References an Event Group

```
CREATE TRIGGER tr_ddl_IndexAudit
ON DATABASE
FOR CREATE_INDEX, ALTER_INDEX, DROP_INDEX
AS
  DECLARE @EventData XML
-- Capture event data from the EVENTDATA function
  SET @EventData = EVENTDATA()
-- Select the auditing info from the XML stream
  SELECT   @EventData.query ('data(/EVENT_INSTANCE/PostTime)')
              AS [Event Time],
           @EventData.query ('data(/EVENT_INSTANCE/EventType)')
              AS [Event Type],
           @EventData.query ('data(/EVENT_INSTANCE/ServerName)')
              AS [Server Name],
           @EventData.query ('data(/EVENT_INSTANCE/TSQLCommand/CommandText)')
              AS [Command Text]
GO
```

To test the DDL trigger in Listing 27.12, you can run the following statement to create an index on the Employee table in the AdventureWorks2012 database:

```
CREATE NONCLUSTERED INDEX [NC_Employee_BirthDate]
    ON [HumanResources].[Employee]
(
    [BirthDate] ASC
)
```

The INDEX CREATE statement completes successfully, and the event-specific information appears in the Results pane.

You can further extend the auditing capabilities of this type of DDL trigger by writing the results to an audit table. This would give you a quick way of tracking changes to database objects. This type of approach dramatically improves change control and reporting on database changes.

Managing DDL Triggers

The administration of DDL triggers is similar to the administration of DML triggers, but DDL triggers are located in a different part of the Object Explorer tree. The reason is that DDL triggers are scoped at the server or database level, not at the table level. Figure 27.3 shows the Object Explorer tree and the nodes related to DDL triggers at the database level. The `tr_TableAudit` trigger you created earlier in this chapter is shown under the `Database Triggers` node. Figure 27.3 shows the options available when you right-click a database trigger in the Object Explorer tree.

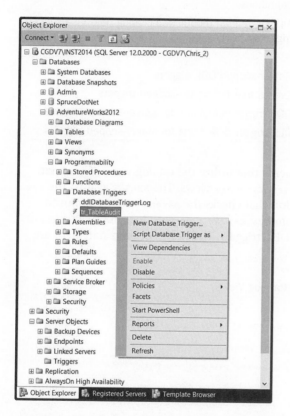

FIGURE 27.3   Using SSMS to manage DDL triggers.

The DDL triggers scoped at the server level are found in the `Triggers` node under the `Server Objects` node of the Object Explorer tree. (The `Server Objects` node is near the bottom of Figure 27.3.)

You can obtain information about DDL triggers by using catalog views. These views provide a convenient and flexible means for querying database objects, including DDL triggers. Table 27.3 lists the catalog views that relate to triggers. The table includes the scope of the trigger that the view reports on and a brief description of what it returns.

TABLE 27.3   Catalog Views for DDL Triggers

Catalog View	Description
Statements with Database-Level Scope	
sys.triggers	All triggers, including DDL database-scoped triggers
sys.trigger_events	All trigger events, including those that fire DDL database-scoped triggers
sys.sql_modules	All SQL-defined modules, including trigger definitions
sys.assembly_modules	All CLR-defined modules, including database-scoped triggers
Statements with Server-Level Scope	
sys.server_triggers	Server-scoped DDL triggers
sys.server_trigger_events	Events that fire server-scoped triggers
sys.sql_modules	DDL trigger definitions for server-scoped triggers
sys.server_assembly_modules	CLR trigger definitions for server-scoped triggers

Listing 27.13 shows sample SELECT statements that utilize the catalog views. These statements use the sys.triggers and sys.server_triggers views. The SELECT against the sys.triggers table uses a WHERE clause condition that checks the parent_class column to retrieve only DDL triggers. The SELECT from sys.server_triggers does not need a WHERE clause because it inherently returns only DDL triggers. The results of each statement are shown below each SELECT in the listing.

LISTING 27.13   Viewing DDL Triggers with Catalog Views

```
--DATABASE SCOPED DDL TRIGGERS
select left(name,20) 'Name', create_date, modify_date, is_disabled
 from sys.triggers
 where parent_class = 0


--Name                  create_date              modify_date              is_disabled
--------------------- ----------------------- ----------------------- -----------
--tr_TableAudit        2009-06-18 12:48:43.140 2009-06-18 12:48:43.140 0
--tr_ddl_IndexAudit    2009-06-22 06:35:10.233 2009-06-22 06:35:10.233 0


--SERVER SCOPED DDL TRIGGERS
select left(name,20) 'Name', create_date, modify_date, is_disabled
 from sys.server_triggers


--Name                  create_date              modify_date              is_disabled
--------------------- ----------------------- ----------------------- -----------
--tr_LoginAudit        2009-06-18 12:13:46.077 2005-06-18 12:13:46.077 0
```

Using Nested Triggers

Triggers can be nested up to 32 levels. If a trigger modifies records in a table on which another trigger exists, the trigger on the second table is fired. If the second trigger modifies data in another table that also has a trigger, the trigger on the third table will fire, and so on. If the nesting level is exceeded, the entire operation is canceled, and the transaction is rolled back.

The following error message is returned if the nesting level is exceeded:

```
Server: Msg 217, Level 16, State 1, Procedure ttt2, Line 2
Maximum stored procedure nesting level exceeded (limit 32).
```

By default, nested triggers in SQL Server are enabled. You can disable nested triggers by setting the nested triggers option of sp_configure to 0 (off):

```
EXEC sp_configure 'nested triggers', 0
GO
RECONFIGURE WITH OVERRIDE
GO
```

After the nested triggers option is turned off, the only triggers to fire are those that are part of the original data modification: the top-level triggers. If updates to other tables are made via the top-level triggers, those updates are completed, but the triggers on those tables do not fire. For example, say you have an UPDATE trigger on the Person table in the AdventureWorks2012 database and an UPDATE trigger on the EmailAddress table as well. In addition, let's say the trigger on the Person table also updates the EmailAddress table. If an update is made to the Person table, the Person trigger fires and completes the updates on the EmailAddress table. However, the trigger on the EmailAddress table does not fire.

While the default configuration is to allow nested triggers, there are reasons for turning off the nested triggers option. For example, you might want triggers to fire on direct data modifications but not on modifications that are made by another trigger. Say you have a trigger on every table that updates the audit time. You might want the audit time for a table to be updated by a trigger when that table is being updated directly, but you might not want the audit date updated on any of the other tables that are part of the nested trigger executions. This can be accomplished by turning off the nested triggers option.

Another reason to disable nested triggers is to simplify database operations and avoid excessive nesting. With nested triggers, a seemingly innocuous single row insert statement can turn into a complex multi-statement, multi-table transaction.

Using Recursive Triggers

Nested triggers allow an update on another table modified within a trigger to fire a trigger on that other table. However, if a trigger modifies records in the *same* table for which the trigger was created, the trigger does not fire again unless the recursive triggers option is turned on. recursive triggers is a database option that is turned off by default.

The first command in the following example checks the setting of `recursive triggers` for the `AdventureWorks2012` database, and the second sets `recursive triggers` to `TRUE`:

```
select DATABASEPROPERTYEX ('AdventureWorks2012', 'IsRecursiveTriggersEnabled')
ALTER DATABASE AdventureWorks2012 SET RECURSIVE_TRIGGERS ON
```

If you turn off nested triggers, recursive triggers are automatically disabled, regardless of how the database option is set. The maximum nesting level for recursive triggers is the same as for nested triggers: 32 levels.

You should use recursive triggers with care. It is easy to create an endless loop, as shown in Listing 27.14, which creates a recursive trigger on a new test table in the `AdventureWorks2012` database.

LISTING 27.14   The Error Message Returned for an Endless Loop with Recursive Triggers

```
--The first statement is used to disable the previously created
--DDL trigger which would prevent any changes.
DISABLE TRIGGER ALL ON DATABASE
EXEC sp_configure 'nested triggers', 1
RECONFIGURE WITH OVERRIDE
ALTER DATABASE AdventureWorks2012 SET RECURSIVE_TRIGGERS ON
CREATE TABLE rk_tr_test (id int IDENTITY)
GO
CREATE TRIGGER rk_tr ON rk_tr_test FOR INSERT
AS INSERT rk_tr_test DEFAULT VALUES
GO
INSERT rk_tr_test DEFAULT VALUES

Server: Msg 217, Level 16, State 1, Procedure rk_tr, Line 2
Maximum stored procedure nesting level exceeded (limit 32).
```

The recursion described thus far is known as *direct recursion*. Another type of recursion exists as well: indirect recursion. With *indirect recursion*, a table that has a trigger fires an update to another table, and that table, in turn, causes an update to happen to the original table on which the trigger fired. This action causes the trigger on the original table to fire again.

With indirect recursion, setting the `recursive triggers` database setting to `FALSE` does not prevent the recursion from happening. The only way to prevent this type of recursion is to set the `nested triggers` setting to `FALSE`, which, in turn, prevents all recursion.

Summary

Triggers are among the most powerful tools for ensuring the quality of data in a database. The range of commands that can be executed from within triggers and their capability to automatically fire give them a distinct role in defining sound database solutions.

Chapter 28, "Transaction Management and the Transaction Log," looks at the methods for defining and managing transactions within SQL Server 2014.

CHAPTER 28

Transaction Management and the Transaction Log

Transaction management is an important area in database programming. The transactions you construct and issue can have a huge impact on the performance of SQL Server and the consistency of your databases. This chapter looks at the methods for defining and managing transactions in SQL Server 2014.

What's New in Transaction Management

SQL Server 2014 introduces the ability to reduce transaction latency by designating some or all transactions as delayed durable. A delayed durable transaction (also known as lazy commit) returns control to the client before the transaction log record is written to disk. Fully durable transactions return control to the client only after the log records for the transaction are written to disk. This is the default transaction behavior in SQL Server. Transaction durability can be controlled at the database level, COMMIT level, or ATOMIC block level. This chapter will compare fully durable and delayed durable transactions and how they are managed, as well as when and how to implement delayed durability.

What Is a Transaction?

A *transaction* is one or more SQL statements that must be completed as a whole or, in other words, as a single logical unit of work. Transactions provide a way of collecting and associating multiple actions into a single all-or-nothing multiple-operation action. All operations within the transaction must be fully completed or not performed at all.

Consider a bank transaction in which you move $1,000 from your checking account to your savings account. This transaction is, in fact, two operations: a decrement of your checking account and an increment of your savings account. Consider the impact on your finances if the bank's server went down after it completed the first step and never got to the second! When the two operations are combined, as a transaction, they either both succeed or both fail as a single, complete unit of work.

A transaction is a logical unit of work that has four special characteristics, known as the ACID properties:

▶ **Atomicity**—Associated modifications are an all-or-nothing proposition; either all are done or none are done.

▶ **Consistency**—After a transaction finishes, all data is in the state it should be in, all internal structures are correct, and everything accurately reflects the transaction that has occurred.

▶ **Isolation**—One transaction cannot interfere with the processes of another transaction.

▶ **Durability**—After the transaction has finished, all changes made are permanent.

The responsibility for enforcing the ACID properties of a transaction is split between T-SQL developers and SQL Server. The developers are responsible for ensuring that the modifications are correctly collected together and that the data is going to be left in a consistent state that corresponds with the actions being taken. SQL Server ensures that the transaction is isolated and durable, undertakes the atomicity requested, and ensures the consistency of the final data structures. The transaction log of each database provides the durability for the transaction. As you see in this chapter, you have some control over how SQL Server handles some of these properties.

How SQL Server Manages Transactions

SQL Server uses the database's transaction log to record the modifications that occur within the database. Each log record is labeled with a unique log sequence number (LSN), and all log entries that are part of the same transaction are linked together so that they can be easily located if the transaction needs to be undone or redone. The primary responsibility of logging is to ensure transaction durability—either ensuring that the completed changes make it to the physical database files or ensuring that any unfinished transactions are rolled back in the event of an error or a server failure.

What is logged? Obviously, the start and end of a transaction are logged, but SQL Server also logs the actual data modification, page allocations and de-allocations, and changes to indexes. SQL Server keeps track of a number of pieces of information, all with the aim of ensuring the ACID properties of the transaction.

After a transaction has been committed, it cannot be rolled back. The only way to undo a committed transaction is to write another transaction to reverse the changes made. A transaction can be rolled back before it is committed, however.

SQL Server provides transaction management for all users, using the following components:

▶ Transaction-control statements to define the logical units of work

▶ A write-ahead transaction log

▶ An automatic recovery process

▶ Data-locking mechanisms to ensure consistency and transaction isolation

Defining Transactions

You can define transactions in SQL Server in three ways:

▶ **AutoCommit**—Every T-SQL statement is its own transaction and automatically commits when it finishes. This is the default mode in which SQL Server operates.

▶ **Explicit**—This approach provides programmatic control of the transaction, using the BEGIN TRAN and COMMIT/ROLLBACK TRAN/WORK commands.

▶ **Implicit**—In this mode, when you issue certain SQL commands, SQL Server automatically starts a transaction. You must finish the transaction by explicitly issuing the COMMIT/ROLLBACK TRAN/WORK commands.

Each of these methods is discussed in the following sections.

> **NOTE**
>
> The terms for explicit and implicit transactions can be somewhat confusing. The way to keep them straight is to think of how a multistatement transaction is initiated, not how it is completed. AutoCommit transactions are in a separate category because they are both implicitly started and committed.
>
> Implicit and explicit transactions have to be explicitly ended, but explicit transactions must also be explicitly started with the BEGIN TRAN statement, whereas no BEGIN TRAN is necessary to start a multistatement transaction when in implicit transaction mode.

28

AutoCommit Transactions

AutoCommit is the default transaction mode for SQL Server. Each individual T-SQL command automatically commits or rolls back its work at the end of its execution. Each SQL statement is considered to be its own transaction, with begin and end control points implied. Following is an example:

```
[implied begin transaction]
UPDATE account
   SET balance = balance + 1000
   WHERE account_no = "123456789"
[implied commit or rollback transaction]
```

If an error is present in the execution of the statement, the action is undone (that is, rolled back); if no errors occur, the action is completed, and the changes are saved.

Now let's consider the banking transaction mentioned at the beginning of this chapter that involved moving money from a savings account to a checking account. Assume that it is written as follows in T-SQL:

```
declare @checking_account char(10),
        @savings_account char(10)
select @checking_account = '0003456321',
       @savings_account = '0003456322'
update account
   set balance = balance - $1000
   where account_number = @checking_account
update savings_account
   set balance = balance + $1000
   where account_number = @savings_account
```

What would happen if an error occurred in updating the savings account? With AutoCommit, each statement is implicitly committed after it completes successfully, so the update for the checking account has already been committed. You would have no way of rolling it back except to write another separate update to add the $1,000 back into the account. If the system crashed during the updates, how would you know which updates, if any, completed, and whether you need to undo any of the changes because the subsequent commands were not executed? You would need some way to group the two commands together as a single logical unit of work so they can complete or fail as a whole. SQL Server provides transaction control statements that allow you to explicitly create multistatement user-defined transactions.

Explicit User-Defined Transactions

To have complete control of a transaction and define logical units of work that consist of multiple data modifications, you need to write explicit user-defined transactions. Any SQL Server user can make use of the transaction control statements; no special privileges are required.

To start a multistatement transaction, use the BEGIN TRAN command, which optionally takes a transaction name:

```
BEGIN TRAN[SACTION] [transaction_name [WITH MARK ['description']]]
```

The transaction name is essentially meaningless as far as transaction management is concerned, and if transactions are nested (which is discussed later in this chapter), the name is useful only for the outermost BEGIN TRAN statement. Rolling back to any other name, besides a savepoint name (savepoints are covered in the next section), generates an error message similar to the following error message and does not roll back the transaction:

```
Msg 6401, Level 16, State 1, Line 5
Cannot roll back t2. No transaction or savepoint of that name was found.
```

Naming transactions is really useful only when you use the WITH MARK option. If the WITH MARK option is specified, a transaction name must be specified. WITH MARK allows for restoring a transaction log backup to a named mark in the transaction log. (For more information on restoring database and log backups, see Chapter 11, "Database Backup and Restore.") This option allows you to restore a database to a known state or to recover a set of related databases to a consistent state. However, you need to be aware that BEGIN TRAN records are written to the log only if an actual data modification occurs within the transaction.

You complete an explicit transaction by issuing either a COMMIT TRAN or COMMIT [WORK] statement, and you can undo an explicit transaction by using either ROLLBACK TRAN or ROLLBACK [WORK]. The syntax of these commands is as follows:

```
COMMIT [TRAN[SACTION] [transaction_name]] | [WORK]


ROLLBACK [TRAN[SACTION] [transaction_name | savepointname]] | [WORK]
```

The COMMIT statement marks the successful conclusion of a transaction. This statement can be coded as COMMIT, COMMIT WORK, or COMMIT TRAN. The only difference is that the first two versions are SQL-92 ANSI-compliant.

The ROLLBACK statement unconditionally undoes all work done within the transaction. This statement can also be coded as ROLLBACK, ROLLBACK WORK, or ROLLBACK TRAN. The first two commands are ANSI-92 SQL-compliant and do not accept user-defined transaction names. ROLLBACK TRAN is required if you want to roll back to a savepoint within a transaction.

The following example shows how you could code the previously mentioned banking example as a single transaction in SQL Server:

```
declare @checking_account char(10),
        @savings_account char(10)
select @checking_account = '0003456321',
       @savings_account = '0003456322'
begin tran
update account
   set balance = balance - $1000
   where account_number = @checking_account
```

28

```
if @@error != 0
begin
    rollback tran
    return
end
update savings_account
   set balance = balance + $1000
   where account_number = @savings_account
if @@error != 0
begin
    rollback tran
    return
end
commit tran
```

Certain commands cannot be specified within a user-defined transaction, primarily because they cannot be effectively rolled back in the event of a failure. In most cases, because of their long-running nature, you would not want them to be specified within a transaction anyway. Following are the commands you cannot specify in a user-defined transaction:

ALTER DATABASE	DROP DATABASE
ALTER FULLTEXT CATALOG	DROP FULLTEXT CATALOG
ALTER FULLTEXT INDEX	DROP FULLTEXT INDEX
BACKUP DATABASE	RESTORE DATABASE
BACKUP LOG	RECONFIGURE
CREATE DATABASE	RESTORE LOG
CREATE FULLTEXT CATALOG	UPDATE STATISTICS
CREATE FULLTEXT INDEX	

Savepoints

A *savepoint* allows you to set a marker in a transaction that you can roll back to in order to undo a portion of the transaction but keep the remainder of the transaction still active, which you can subsequently commit or choose to roll back completely. The syntax is as follows:

```
SAVE TRAN[SACTION] savepointname
```

Savepoints are not ANSI-SQL 92-compliant, so you must use the SQL Server–specific transaction management commands that allow you to specify a named point within the transaction and then recover back to it.

The following code illustrates the differences between the two types of syntax when using the SAVE TRAN command:

```
SQL-92 Syntax SQL Server-Specific Syntax
BEGIN TRAN mywork
 UPDATE table1...
 SAVE TRAN savepoint1
  INSERT INTO table2...
  DELETE table3...
  IF @@error = -1
     ROLLBACK WORK
COMMIT WORK     BEGIN TRAN mywork
 UPDATE table1...
 SAVE TRAN savepoint1
  INSERT INTO table2...
  DELETE table3...
  IF @@error = -1
     ROLLBACK TRAN savepoint1
COMMIT TRAN
```

Note the difference between the SQL-92 syntax on the left and the SQL Server–specific syntax on the right. In the SQL-92 syntax, when you reach the ROLLBACK WORK command, the *entire* transaction is undone rather than undoing only to the point marked by the savepoint. You have to use the SQL Server–specific ROLLBACK TRAN command and specify the savepoint name to roll back the work to the savepoint and still be able to subsequently roll back or commit the rest of the transaction.

Nested Transactions

As a rule, you can't have more than one active transaction per user session within SQL Server. However, suppose you have a SQL batch that issues a BEGIN TRAN statement and then subsequently invokes a stored procedure, which also issues a BEGIN TRAN statement. Because you can have only one transaction active, what does the BEGIN TRAN inside the stored procedure accomplish? In SQL Server, this leads to non-ANSI standard transaction behavior referred to as *nested transactions*.

To determine whether transactions are open and how deep they are nested within a connection, you can use the global function @@trancount. If no transaction is active, the transaction nesting level is 0. For each BEGIN TRAN statement issued, the transaction nesting level is incremented by 1; for each COMMIT TRAN statement issued, the transaction nesting level is decremented. The overall transaction remains open and can be entirely rolled back until the transaction nesting level returns to 0.

You can use the @@trancount function to monitor the current status of a transaction. For example, what would SQL Server do when encountering the following transaction (which produces an error because of the reference constraint on the titles table)?

```
use AdventureWorks2012
go
BEGIN TRAN
    DELETE FROM Person.Person
```

28

```
    WHERE BusinessEntityID = 100
go
```

```
/* output
Msg 547, Level 16, State 0, Line 2
The DELETE statement conflicted with the REFERENCE constraint
"FK_EmailAddress_Person_BusinessEntityID". The conflict occurred in database
"AdventureWorks2012", table "Person.EmailAddress", column 'BusinessEntityID'.
The statement has been terminated.
*/
```

Is the transaction still active? You can find out by using the `@@trancount` function:

```
select @@trancount
go
```

```
-----------
          1
```

In this case, `@@trancount` returns a value of `1`, which indicates that the transaction is still open and in progress. This means that you can still issue commands within the transaction and commit the changes, or you can roll back the transaction. Also, if you were to log out of the user session from SQL Server before the transaction nesting level reached 0, SQL Server would automatically roll back the transaction.

Although nothing prevents you from coding a BEGIN TRAN within another BEGIN TRAN, doing so has no real benefit, even though such cases might occur. However, if you nest transactions in this manner, you must execute a COMMIT statement for each BEGIN TRAN statement issued. The reason is that SQL Server modifies the `@@trancount` with each transaction statement and considers the transaction finished only when the transaction nesting level returns to 0. Table 28.1 shows the effects that transaction control statements have on `@@trancount`.

TABLE 28.1   Transaction Statements' Effects on `@@trancount`

Statement	Effect on `@@trancount`
BEGIN TRAN	+1
COMMIT	−1
ROLLBACK	Sets to 0
SAVE TRAN savepoint	No effect
ROLLBACK TRAN savepoint	No effect

Following is a summary of how transactional control relates to the values reported by `@@trancount`:

▶ When you log in to SQL Server, the value of `@@trancount` for your session is initially `0`.

▶ Each time you execute `begin transaction`, SQL Server increments `@@trancount`.

▶ Each time you execute `commit transaction`, SQL Server decrements `@@trancount`.

▶ Actual work is committed only when `@@trancount` reaches `0` again.

▶ When you execute `ROLLBACK TRANSACTION`, the transaction is canceled, and `@@trancount` returns to `0`. Notice that `ROLLBACK TRANSACTION` cuts straight through any number of nested transactions, canceling the overall main transaction. This means that you need to be careful how you write code that contains a `ROLLBACK` statement. You need to be sure to check for the return status up through all levels and exit accordingly so you don't continue executing data modifications that were meant to be part of the larger overall transaction.

▶ Setting savepoints and rolling back to a savepoint do not affect `@@trancount` or transaction nesting in any way.

▶ If a user connection is lost for any reason when `@@trancount` is greater than `0`, any pending work for that connection is automatically rolled back. SQL Server requires that multistatement transactions be explicitly committed.

▶ Because the `BEGIN TRAN` statement increments `@@trancount`, each `BEGIN TRAN` statement must be paired with a `COMMIT` for the transaction to complete successfully.

Let's look at some sample SQL Statements to see the values of `@@trancount` as the transaction progresses. The example in Table 28.2 shows a simple explicit transaction with a nested `BEGIN TRAN`.

TABLE 28.2   `@@trancount` Value Changes with Explicit Transactions

SQL Statement	`@@trancount` Value
SELECT "Starting....."	0
BEGIN TRAN	1
DELETE FROM table1	1
BEGIN TRAN	2
INSERT INTO table2	2
COMMIT	1
UPDATE table3	1
COMMIT	0

It's important to understand that in SQL Server, transactions are nested *syntactically only*. The only `COMMIT TRAN` statement that has an impact on real data is the last one, the statement that returns `@@trancount` to `0`. That statement fully commits the work done by the initial and nested transactions. Until that final `COMMIT TRAN` is encountered, all the work can be rolled back with a `ROLLBACK` statement.

28

As a general rule of thumb, if a transaction is already active, you shouldn't issue another BEGIN TRAN statement. You should check the value of @@trancount to determine whether a transaction is already active. If you want to be able to roll back the work performed within a nested transaction without rolling back the entire transaction, you can set a save-point instead of issuing a BEGIN TRAN statement. Later in this chapter, you see an example showing how to check @@trancount within a stored procedure to determine whether the stored procedure is being invoked within a transaction and then issue a BEGIN TRAN or SAVE TRAN, as appropriate.

Implicit Transactions

AutoCommit transactions and explicit user-defined transactions, which are the default transaction mode in SQL Server 2014, are not ANSI-92 SQL-compliant. The ANSI-92 SQL standard states that any data retrieval or modification statement issued should implicitly begin a multistatement transaction that remains in effect until an explicit ROLLBACK or COMMIT statement is issued. Microsoft refers to this transaction mode as IMPLICIT_TRANSACTIONS.

To enable implicit transactions for a connection in SQL Server 2014, you need to enable the IMPLICIT_TRANSACTIONS session setting using the following command:

```
SET IMPLICIT_TRANSACTIONS ON
```

After this option is turned on, transactions are implicitly started, if they are not already in progress, whenever any of the following commands are executed:

ALTER TABLE	INSERT
CREATE	OPEN
DELETE	REVOKE
DROP	SELECT
FETCH	TRUNCATE TABLE
GRANT	UPDATE

Note that neither the ALTER VIEW nor ALTER PROCEDURE statement starts an implicit transaction.

You must explicitly complete implicit transactions by issuing a COMMIT or ROLLBACK; a new transaction is started again on the execution of any of the preceding commands. If you plan to use implicit transactions, the main issue to be aware of is that locks are held until you explicitly commit the transaction. This can cause problems with concurrency and the system's capability to truncate the transaction log.

Even when using implicit transactions, you can still issue the BEGIN TRAN statement and create transaction nesting. In Table 28.3, you can see the effect that the IMPLICIT_ TRANSACTIONS ON setting has on the value of @@trancount as various statements are executed.

TABLE 28.3   `@@trancount` Value Changes with Implicit Transactions

SQL Statements	@@trancount Value
SET IMPLICIT_TRANSACTIONS ON	0
go	0
INSERT INTO table1	1
UPDATE table2	1
COMMIT	0
go	0
SELECT * FROM table1	1
BEGIN TRAN	2
DELETE FROM table1	2
COMMIT	1
go	1
DROP TABLE table1	1
COMMIT	0

As you can see in this example, if a BEGIN TRAN is issued while a transaction is still active, transaction nesting occurs, and a second COMMIT is required to finish the transaction. The main difference between this example and the preceding one is that here, a BEGIN TRAN is not required to start the transaction. The first INSERT statement initiates the transaction. When you are running in implicit transaction mode, you don't need to issue a BEGIN TRAN statement; in fact, you should avoid doing so to prevent transaction nesting and the need for multiple commits.

The following example shows the previous banking transaction using implicit transactions:

```
set implicit_transactions on
go

declare @checking_account char(10),
        @savings_account char(10)
select @checking_account = '0003456321',
       @savings_account = '0003456322'
update account
    set balance = balance - $1000
    where account_number = @checking_account
if @@error != 0
begin
    rollback
    return
end
update savings_account
```

```
    set balance = balance + $1000
    where account_number = @savings_account
if @@error != 0
begin
    rollback
    return
end
commit
```

This example is nearly identical to the explicit transaction example except for the lack of a BEGIN TRAN statement. In addition, when in implicit transaction mode, you cannot roll back to a named transaction because no name is assigned when the transaction is invoked implicitly. You can, however, still set savepoints and roll back to savepoints to partially roll back work within an implicit transaction.

TIP

If you need to know within your SQL code whether implicit transactions are enabled so you can avoid issuing explicit BEGIN TRAN statements, you can check the @@options function. @@options returns a bitmap that indicates which session-level options are enabled for the current session. If bit 2 is on, implicit transactions are enabled. The following code snippet can be used in stored procedures or SQL batches to check this value and decide whether to issue a BEGIN TRAN statement:

```
if @@options & 2 != 2 -- bit 2 is not turned on
    BEGIN TRAN -- issue begin tran because implicit transactions are off
```

Implicit Transactions Versus Explicit Transactions

When would you want to use implicit transactions versus explicit transactions? If you are porting an application from another database environment, such as DB2 or Oracle, that uses implicit transactions, that application converts over to SQL Server more easily and with fewer code changes if you run in implicit transaction mode. Also, if the application you are developing needs to be ANSI-compliant and run across multiple database platforms with minimal code changes, you might want to use implicit transactions.

If you use implicit transactions in your applications, you need to be sure to issue explicit COMMIT statements as soon as possible for each logical unit of work to prevent leaving transactions open and holding locks for an extended period of time, which can have an adverse impact on concurrency and overall system performance.

If an application is going to be hosted only on SQL Server, it is recommended that you use AutoCommit and explicit transactions so that changes are committed as quickly as possible and so that only those logical units of work that are explicitly defined contain multiple commands within a transaction.

Transactions and T-SQL Batches

There is no inherent transactional quality to T-SQL batches. As you have seen already, unless you provide the syntax to define a single transaction made up of several statements, each individual statement in a batch is its own separate transaction, and each statement is carried to completion or fails individually.

The failure of a transaction within a batch typically does not cause the batch to stop processing (one exception is a rollback in a TRIGGER if you are not using TRY...CATCH logic). In other words, in most cases, transaction flow does not affect process flow. After a ROLLBACK TRAN statement, processing continues with the next statement in the batch or stored procedure. For this reason, you should be sure to check for error conditions after each data modification within a transaction and exit the batch or stored procedure, as appropriate.

Consider the banking transaction again, this time removing the RETURN statements:

```
/* This code is for example purposes only */

/*  DO NOT TRY THIS AT HOME!!!  */

declare @checking_account char(10),
        @savings_account char(10)
select @checking_account = '0003456321',
        @savings_account = '0003456322'
begin tran
update account
   set balance = balance - $1000
   where account_number = @checking_account
if @@error != 0
    rollback tran
update savings_account
   set balance = balance + $1000
   where account_number = @savings_account
if @@error != 0
    rollback tran
commit tran
```

Assume that a check constraint on the account prevents the balance from being set to a value less than 0. If the checking account has less than $1,000 in it, the first update fails, and the T-SQL code catches the error condition and rolls back the transaction. At this point, the transaction is no longer active, but the batch still contains additional statements to execute. Without a return after the rollback, SQL Server continues with the next statement in the batch, which in this case is the update to the savings account. However, this now executes as its own separate transaction, and it automatically commits if it completes successfully. This is not the result you want because now that second update is its own separate unit of work, so you have no way to roll it back.

28

The key concept to keep in mind here is that transaction flow does not affect program flow. In the event of an error within a transaction, you need to make sure you have the proper error checking and a means to exit the transaction in the event of an error. This prevents the batch from continuing with any remaining modifications that were meant to be a part of the original transaction. As a general rule, a RETURN statement should almost always follow a rollback.

In addition to being able to define multiple transactions within a batch, you can also have transactions that span multiple batches. For example, you could write an application that begins a transaction in one batch and then asks for user verification during a second batch. The SQL might look like this:

First batch:

```
use Adventureworks2012
go
begin TRANSACTION
insert HumanResources.Department (Name, GroupName, ModifiedDate)
    values ('Database Administration', 'Executive General and Administration',
GETDATE())
if @@error = 0
    print 'Department insert was successful. Please go on.'
else
    print 'Department insert failed. Please roll back'
go
```

Second batch:

```
UPDATE Person.PersonPhone
SET PhoneNumber = '808-555-0194',
ModifiedDate = GETDATE()
WHERE BusinessEntityID = 20771


commit transaction
```

Writing transactions that span multiple batches is almost always a bad idea. The locking and concurrency problems can become complicated, with awful performance implications. What if the application prompted for user input between batches, and the user went out to lunch? Locks would be held until the user got back and continued the transaction. In general, you want to enclose each transaction in a single batch, using conditional programming constructs to handle situations like the preceding example. Following is a better way to write that code:

```
begin TRANSACTION
insert HumanResources.Department (Name, GroupName, ModifiedDate)
OUTPUT INSERTED.DepartmentID
    values ('Database Administration', 'Executive General and Administration',
GETDATE())
```

```
if @@error = 0
begin
    print 'Department insert was successful. Please go on.'
    UPDATE Person.PersonPhone
        SET PhoneNumber = '808-555-0194',
        ModifiedDate = GETDATE()
        WHERE BusinessEntityID = 20771
    COMMIT transaction
end
ELSE
begin
    print 'Department insert failed. Please roll back'
    ROLLBACK TRANSACTION
end
go
```

The important point in this example is that the transaction now takes place within a single batch for better performance and consistency. As you see in the next section, it is usually best to encode transactions in stored procedures for even better performance and to avoid the possibility of unfinished transactions.

> **NOTE**
>
> It is also important to know that transactions can also be initiated from the application side using ADO.NET or JDBC methods that effectively issue BEGIN/COMMIT TRAN statements to SQL Server. These application initiated transactions can create the same phenomenon of cross-batch transactions, open transactions, locking, and so on. It is important for application developers to understand the implications of how they manage transactions. We've all seen cases where application based transactions were not coded efficiently and transactions were left open for too long (or indefinitely) with a significant impact on concurrency and application performance. This is why it's suggested that they keep all transaction activity limited to a single batch of commands or manage all transaction based activity within stored procedures.

Transactions and Stored Procedures

Because SQL code in stored procedures runs locally on the server, it is recommended that entire transactions be completely encapsulated within stored procedures to speed transaction processing. This way, the entire transaction executes within a single stored procedure call from the client application, rather than being executed across multiple requests. The less network traffic that occurs between the client application and SQL Server during transactions, the faster they can finish.

Another advantage of using stored procedures for transactions is that doing so helps you avoid the occurrence of partial transactions—that is, transactions that are started but not fully committed. Using stored procedures this way also avoids the possibility of user interaction within a transaction. The stored procedure keeps the transaction processing completely contained because it starts the transaction, carries out the data modifications, completes the transaction, and returns the status or data to the client.

Stored procedures also provide the additional benefit that if you need to fix, fine-tune, or expand the duties of the transaction, you can do all this at one time, in one central location. Your applications can share the same stored procedure, providing consistency for the logical unit of work across your applications.

Although stored procedures provide a useful solution to managing transactions, you need to know how transactions work within stored procedures and code for them appropriately. Consider what happens when one stored procedure calls another, and they both do their own transaction management. Obviously, they now need to work in concert with each other. If the called stored procedure has to roll back its work, how can it do so correctly without causing data integrity problems?

The issues you need to deal with go back to the earlier topics of transaction nesting and transaction flow versus program flow. Unlike a rollback in a trigger (see the next section), a rollback in a stored procedure does not abort the rest of the batch or the calling procedure.

For each BEGIN TRAN encountered in a nested procedure, the transaction nesting level is incremented by 1. For each COMMIT encountered, the transaction nesting level is decremented by 1. However, if a rollback other than to a named savepoint occurs in a nested procedure, it rolls back all statements to the outermost BEGIN TRAN, including any work performed inside the nested stored procedures that has not been fully committed. It then continues processing the remaining commands in the current procedure as well as the calling procedure(s).

To explore the issues involved, you can work with the sample stored procedure shown in Listing 28.1. The procedure takes a single integer argument, which it then attempts to insert into a table (test_table). All data entry attempts—whether successful or not—are logged to a second table (auditlog). Listing 28.1 contains the code for the stored procedure and the tables it uses.

LISTING 28.1   Sample Stored Procedure and Tables for Transaction Testing

```
CREATE TABLE test_table (col1 int)
go
CREATE TABLE auditlog (who varchar(128), valuentered int null)
go
CREATE PROCEDURE trantest @arg INT
AS
BEGIN TRAN
   IF EXISTS( SELECT * FROM test_table WHERE col1 = @arg )
   BEGIN
      RAISERROR ('Value %d already exists!', 16, -1, @arg)
      ROLLBACK TRANSACTION
   END
```

```
    ELSE
    BEGIN
        INSERT INTO test_table (col1) VALUES (@arg)
        COMMIT TRAN
    END

INSERT INTO auditlog (who, valuentered) VALUES (USER_NAME(), @arg)
 return
```

Now explore what happens if you call this stored procedure in the following way and check the values of the two tables:

```
set nocount on
EXEC trantest 1
EXEC trantest 2
SELECT * FROM test_table
SELECT valuentered FROM auditlog
go
```

The execution of this code gives the following results:

```
col1
-----------
1
2


valuentered
-----------
1
2
```

These would be the results you would expect because no errors would occur, and nothing would be rolled back.

Now, if you were to run the same code a second time, test_table would still have only two rows because the procedure would roll back the attempted insert of the duplicate rows. However, because the procedure and batch are not aborted, the code would continue processing, and the rows would still be added to the auditlog table. The result would be as follows:

```
set nocount on
EXEC trantest 1
EXEC trantest 2
SELECT * FROM test_table
SELECT valuentered FROM auditlog
go
```

28

```
/* output
Msg 50000, Level 16, State 1, Procedure trantest, Line 6
Value 1 already exists!

Msg 50000, Level 16, State 1, Procedure trantest, Line 6
Value 2 already exists!

col1
-----------
1
2


valuentered
-----------
1
2
1
2
*/
```

Now explore what happens when you execute the stored procedure from within a transaction:

```
set nocount on
BEGIN TRAN
EXEC trantest 3
EXEC trantest 1
EXEC trantest 4
COMMIT TRAN
SELECT * FROM test_table
SELECT valuentered FROM auditlog
go
```

The execution of this code gives the following results:

```
Msg 50000, Level 16, State 1, Procedure trantest, Line 6
Value 1 already exists!

Msg 266, Level 16, State 2, Procedure trantest, Line 0
Transaction count after EXECUTE indicates that a COMMIT or ROLLBACK TRANSACTION
 statement is missing. Previous count = 1, current count = 0.

Msg 3902, Level 16, State 1, Line 6
The COMMIT TRANSACTION request has no corresponding BEGIN TRANSACTION.
/* output
```

```
col1
-----------
1
2
4

valuentered
-----------
1
2
1
2
1
4
*/
```

A number of problems are occurring now. For starters, you get a message telling you that the transaction nesting level was messed up. More seriously, the results show that the value 4 made it into the test_table table anyway and that the auditlog table picked up the inserts of 1 and the 4 but lost the fact that you tried to insert a value of 3. What happened?

Let's examine this example one step at a time. First, you start the transaction and insert the value 3 into trantest. The stored procedure starts its own transaction, adds the value to test_table, commits that, and then adds a row to auditlog. Next, you execute the procedure with the value 1. This value already exists in the table, so the procedure raises an error and rolls back the transaction. Remember that a ROLLBACK undoes work to the outermost BEGIN TRAN—which means the start of this batch. This rolls back everything, including the insert of 3 into trantest and auditlog. The auditlog entry for the value 1 is inserted and not rolled back because it occurred after the transaction was rolled back and is a standalone, automatically committed statement now.

You then receive an error regarding the change in the transaction nesting level because a transaction should leave the state of a governing procedure in the same way it was entered; it should make no net change to the transaction nesting level. In other words, the value of @@trancount should be the same when the procedure exits as when it was entered. If it is not, the transaction control statements are not properly balanced.

Also, because the batch is not aborted, the value 4 is inserted into trantest, an operation that completes successfully and is automatically committed. Finally, when you try to commit the transaction, you receive the last error regarding a mismatch between BEGIN TRAN and COMMIT TRAN because no transaction is currently in operation.

The solution to this problem is to write the stored procedures so that transaction nesting doesn't occur and so the stored procedure rolls back only its own work. When a rollback occurs, it should return an error status so that the calling batch or procedure is aware of the error condition and can choose to continue or abort the work at that level. You can manage this by checking the current value of @@trancount and determining what needs to

28

be done. If a transaction is already active, the stored procedure should not issue a BEGIN TRAN and nest the transaction; rather, it should set a savepoint. This allows the procedure to perform a partial rollback of its work. If no transaction is active, the procedure can safely begin a new transaction. The following SQL code fragment is an example of using this approach:

```
DECLARE @trancount INT
/* Capture the value of the transaction nesting level at the start */
SELECT @trancount = @@trancount
IF (@trancount = 0)   -- no transaction is currently active, start one
   BEGIN TRAN mytran
ELSE                  -- a transaction is active, set a savepoint only
   SAVE TRAN mytran
.
.
.
/* This is how to trap an error. Roll back either to your
   own BEGIN TRAN or roll back to the savepoint. Return an
   error code to the caller to indicate an internal failure.
   How the caller handles the transaction is up to the caller.*/
IF (@@error <> 0)
BEGIN
   ROLLBACK TRAN mytran
   RETURN -1969
END
.
.
.
/* Once you reach the end of the code, you need to pair the BEGIN TRAN,
   if you issued it, with a COMMIT TRAN. If you executed the SAVE TRAN
   instead, you have nothing else to do...end of game! */
IF (@trancount = 0)
  COMMIT TRAN

RETURN 0
```

If you apply these concepts to all stored procedures that need to incorporate transaction processing as well as the code that calls the stored procedures, you should be able to avoid problems with transaction nesting and inconsistency in your transaction processing. You just need to be sure to check the return value of the stored procedure and determine whether the whole batch should be failed or whether that one call is of little importance to the overall outcome and the transaction can continue.

Transactions and Triggers

SQL Server 2014 provides two types of Data Manipulation Language (DML) triggers: AFTER and INSTEAD OF. INSTEAD OF triggers perform their actions before any modifications are made to the actual table or view the trigger is defined on.

Whenever a trigger is invoked, it is always invoked within another transaction, whether it's a single-statement AutoCommit transaction or a user-defined multistatement transaction. This is true for both AFTER triggers and INSTEAD OF triggers. Even though an INSTEAD OF trigger fires before, or "instead of," the data modification statement itself, if a transaction is not already active, an AutoCommit transaction is still automatically initiated as the data modification statement is invoked and prior to the invocation of the INSTEAD OF trigger. (For more information on AFTER and INSTEAD OF triggers, see Chapter 27, "Creating and Managing Triggers.")

> **NOTE**
>
> Although the information presented in this section applies to both AFTER and INSTEAD OF triggers, the examples presented pertain primarily to AFTER triggers.

Because the trigger is already operating within the context of a transaction, the only transaction control statements you should ever consider using in a trigger are ROLLBACK and SAVE TRAN. You don't need to issue a BEGIN TRAN because a transaction is already active; a BEGIN TRAN would only serve to increase the transaction nesting level, and that would complicate things further.

Triggers and Transaction Nesting

To demonstrate the relationship between a trigger and the transaction nesting level, you can use the following SQL code to create a trigger on the employee table:

```
use AdventureWorks2012
go
CREATE TRIGGER tD_auditlog ON employee
FOR DELETE
AS
    DECLARE @msg VARCHAR(255)

    SELECT @msg = 'Trancount in trigger = ' + CONVERT(VARCHAR(2), @@trancount)

    PRINT @msg

    RETURN
go
```

The purpose of this trigger is simply to show the state of the @@trancount within the trigger as the deletion is taking place.

If you now execute code for implied and explicit transactions, you can see the values of @@trancount and behavior of the batch. First, here's the implied transaction:

28

```
set nocount on
print 'Trancount before delete = ' + CONVERT(VARCHAR(2), @@trancount)
DELETE FROM auditlog  WHERE valuentered = 5
print 'Trancount after delete = ' + CONVERT( VARCHAR(2), @@trancount)
go
```

The results of this are as follows:

```
Trancount before delete = 0
Trancount in trigger = 1
Trancount after delete = 0
```

Because no transaction starts until the DELETE statement executes, the first value of @@trancount indicates this with a value of 0. Within the trigger, the transaction count has a value of 1; you are now inside the implied transaction caused by the DELETE. After the trigger returns, the DELETE is automatically committed, the transaction is finished, and @@trancount returns to 0 to indicate that no transaction is currently active.

Now explore what happens within an explicit transaction:

```
begin tran
print 'Trancount before delete = ' + CONVERT(VARCHAR(2), @@trancount)
DELETE FROM auditlog WHERE valuentered = 5
print 'Trancount after delete = ' + CONVERT( VARCHAR(2), @@trancount)
commit tran
print 'Trancount after commit = ' + CONVERT( VARCHAR(2), @@trancount)
go
```

This code gives the following results:

```
Trancount before delete = 1
Trancount in trigger = 1
Trancount after delete = 1
Trancount after commit = 0
```

In this example, a transaction is already active when the DELETE is executed. The BEGIN TRAN statement initiates the transaction, and @@trancount is 1 before the DELETE is executed. The trigger becomes a part of that transaction, which is not committed until the COMMIT TRAN statement is executed.

What would happen, however, if the trigger performed a rollback? You can find out by modifying the trigger to perform a rollback as follows:

```
ALTER TRIGGER tD_employee ON employee
FOR DELETE
AS
print 'Trancount in trigger = ' + CONVERT(VARCHAR(2), @@trancount)
```

```
ROLLBACK TRAN

return
```

Now rerun the previous batch. The outcome this time is as follows:

```
Trancount before delete = 1
Trancount in trigger = 1
Msg 3609, Level 16, State 1, Line 3
The transaction ended in the trigger. The batch has been aborted.
```

Notice in this example that the batch did not complete, as evidenced by the missing output from the last two print statements. When a rollback occurs within a trigger, SQL Server aborts the current transaction, continues processing the commands in the trigger, and after the trigger returns, aborts the rest of the batch and returns error message 3609 to indicate that the batch has been aborted because the transaction ended within the trigger. A ROLLBACK TRAN statement in a trigger rolls back all work to the first BEGIN TRAN statement. It is not possible to roll back to a specific named transaction, although you can roll back to a named savepoint, as discussed later in this section.

Again, the batch and transaction are aborted when the trigger rolls back; any subsequent statements in the batch are not executed. The key concept to remember is that the trigger becomes an integral part of the statement that fired it and of the transaction in which that statement occurs.

It is important to note, however, that although the batch is aborted immediately after the trigger that performed a rollback returns, any statements within the trigger that follow the ROLLBACK TRAN statement but before it returns are executed. For example, you can modify the previous trigger further to include a print statement after the ROLLBACK TRAN statement:

```
ALTER TRIGGER tD_employee ON employee
FOR DELETE
AS
print 'Trancount in trigger = ' + CONVERT(VARCHAR(2), @@trancount)

ROLLBACK TRAN

print 'Trancount in trigger after rollback = ' + CONVERT(VARCHAR(2), @@trancount)

return
```

Now, if you rerun the previous batch, you can see the print statement after the ROLLBACK TRAN but before the RETURN statement is executed:

28

```
Trancount before delete = 1
Trancount in trigger = 1
Trancount in trigger after rollback = 0
Msg 3609, Level 16, State 1, Line 3
The transaction ended in the trigger. The batch has been aborted.
```

Notice that the Trancount after the ROLLBACK TRAN in the trigger is now 0. If the trigger subsequently performed any data modifications following the ROLLBACK TRAN, they would now be running as AutoCommit transactions. For this reason, you must be sure to issue a RETURN statement to exit the trigger after a ROLLBACK TRAN is issued to avoid the trigger performing any operations that would then be automatically committing, leaving no opportunity to roll them back.

> **NOTE**
>
> The preceding behavior described in this section of T-SQL batches aborting when a roll-back occurs in a trigger only applies when you are not using TRY...CATCH logic in your SQL code. If a rollback occurs in a trigger invoked by a statement within a TRY...CATCH construct, the batch is NOT automatically aborted, but instead control is passed to the CATCH block. You then have the option of continuing or aborting the rest of the batch, but the transaction itself has entered a state in which it remains open but cannot be committed nor perform any action that would generate a write to the transaction log, such as modifying data or trying to roll back to a savepoint. The locks acquired by the transaction are maintained, and the connection is also kept open. You should explicitly issue a ROLLBACK statement in the CATCH block to reverse the effects of the transaction and release any locks, etc. If the transaction is not rolled back before the batch finishes, an error message will be sent to the client application that indicates an uncommittable trans-action was detected and rolled back.

Triggers and Multistatement Transactions

Now let's look at another example. First, you need to create a trigger to enforce referential integrity between the titles table and publishers table:

```
create trigger tr_auditlog_i on auditlog for insert as
declare @rows int  -- create variable to hold @@rowcount
select @rows = @@rowcount
if @rows = 0 return
if update(valuentered) and (select count(*)
        from inserted i, test_table tt
        where tt.col1 = i.valuentered ) != @rows
  begin
        rollback transaction
        raiserror ('Invalid value inserted', 16, 1)
  end
return
go
```

Now, run a multistatement transaction with an invalid `value` in the second `insert` statement:

```
/* transaction inserts rows into a table */
begin tran add_records
INSERT INTO auditlog (who, valuentered) VALUES (USER_NAME(), 2)
INSERT INTO auditlog (who, valuentered) VALUES (USER_NAME(), 5)
INSERT INTO auditlog (who, valuentered) VALUES (USER_NAME(), 4)
commit tran
go

/* output
Msg 50000, Level 16, State 1, Procedure tr_auditlog_i, Line 10
Invalid value inserted
Msg 3609, Level 16, State 1, Line 3
The transaction ended in the trigger. The batch has been aborted.
*/
```

How many rows are inserted if 5 is an invalid value? In this example, no rows are inserted because the ROLLBACK TRAN in the trigger rolls back all modifications made by the trigger, including the insert with the bad value and all statements preceding it within the transaction. After the RETURN statement is encountered in the trigger, the rest of the batch is aborted.

CAUTION

You should never issue a BEGIN TRAN statement in a trigger because a transaction is already active at the time the trigger is executed. Rolling back to a named transaction in a trigger is illegal and generates a runtime error, rolling back the transaction and immediately terminating processing of the trigger and batch. The only transaction control statements you should ever consider including in a trigger are ROLLBACK TRAN and SAVE TRAN.

28

Using Savepoints in Triggers

Although BEGIN TRAN statements are not recommended within a trigger, you can set a savepoint in a trigger and roll back to the savepoint. This technique rolls back only the operations within the trigger subsequent to the savepoint. The trigger and transaction it is a part of are still active until the transaction is subsequently committed or rolled back. The batch continues processing.

Savepoints can be used to avoid a trigger's arbitrarily rolling back an entire transaction. You can roll back to the named savepoint in the trigger and then issue a `raiserror` and return immediately to pass the error code back to the calling process. The calling process can then check the error status of the data modification statement and take appropriate action, either rolling back the transaction, rolling back to a savepoint in the transaction, or ignoring the error and committing the data modification.

The following example shows a trigger that uses a savepoint:

```
alter trigger tr_titles_i on titles for insert as
declare @rows int   -- create variable to hold @@rowcount
select @rows = @@rowcount
if @rows = 0 return
save tran titlestrig
if update(pub_id) and (select count(*)
        from inserted i, publishers p
        where p.pub_id = i.pub_id ) != @rows
  begin
      rollback transaction titlestrig
      raiserror ('Invalid pub_id inserted', 16, 1)
  end
return
```

This trigger rolls back all work since the savepoint and returns an error number of 50000. In the transaction, you can check for the error number and make the decision about whether to continue the transaction, roll back the transaction, or, if savepoints were set in the transaction, roll back to a savepoint and let the transaction continue. The following example rolls back the entire transaction if either of the first two inserts fail, but it rolls back to the named savepoint only if the third insert fails, allowing the first two to be committed:

```
begin tran add_records
INSERT INTO auditlog (who, valuentered) VALUES (USER_NAME(), 2)
if @@error = 50000 -- roll back entire transaction and abort batch
    begin
    rollback tran add_records
    return
    end
INSERT INTO auditlog (who, valuentered) VALUES (USER_NAME(), 5)
if @@error = 50000 -- roll back entire transaction and abort batch
    begin
    rollback tran add_records
    return
    end
INSERT INTO auditlog (who, valuentered) VALUES (USER_NAME(), 4)
if @@error = 50000 -- roll back entire transaction and abort batch
    begin
    rollback tran add_records
    return
    end
commit tran
go
```

> **TIP**
>
> When you use a savepoint inside a trigger, the trigger does not roll back the transaction. Therefore, the batch is not automatically aborted. You must explicitly return from the batch after rolling back the transaction to prevent subsequent statements from executing.

Transactions and Locking

SQL Server issues and holds on to locks for the duration of a transaction to ensure the isolation and consistency of the modifications. Data modifications that occur within a transaction acquire exclusive locks, which are then held until the completion of the transaction. Shared locks, or read locks, are held for only as long as the statement needs them; usually, a shared lock is released as soon as data has been read from the resource (for example, row, page, table). You can modify the length of time a shared lock is held by using keywords such as HOLDLOCK in a query or setting the REPEATABLE_READ or SERIALIZABLE lock isolation levels. If one of these options is specified, shared locks are held until the completion of the transaction.

What this means for you as a database application developer is that you should try to hold on to as few locks or as small a lock as possible for as short a time as possible to avoid locking contention between applications and to improve concurrency and application performance. The simple rule when working with transactions is to keep them short and keep them simple. In other words, you should do what you need to do in the most concise manner, in the shortest possible time. You should keep any extraneous commands that do not need to be part of the logical unit of work—such as SELECT statements, commands for dropping temporary tables, commands for setting up local variables, and so on—outside the transaction.

To modify the manner in which a transaction and its locks can be handled by a SELECT statement, you can issue the SET TRANSACTION ISOLATION LEVEL statement. This statement allows the query to choose how much it is protected against other transactions modifying the data being used. The SET TRANSACTION ISOLATION LEVEL statement has the following mutually exclusive options:

▶ READ COMMITTED—This setting is the default for SQL Server. Modifications made within a transaction are locked exclusively, and the changes cannot be viewed by other user processes until the transaction completes. Commands that read data only hold shared locks on the data for as long as they are reading it. Because other transactions are not blocked from modifying the data after you have read it within your transaction, subsequent reads of the data within the transaction might encounter *nonrepeatable reads* or *phantom data*.

▶ READ UNCOMMITTED—With this level of isolation, one transaction can read the modifications made by other transactions prior to being committed. This is, therefore, the least restrictive isolation level, but it is one that allows the reading of dirty and uncommitted data. This option has the same effect as issuing NOLOCK within SELECT

28

statements, but it has to be set only once for your connection. This option should never be used in an application in which accuracy of the query results is required.

▶ **REPEATABLE READ**—When this option is set, as data is read, locks are placed and held on the data for the duration of the transaction. These locks prevent other transactions from modifying the data you have read so that you can carry out multiple passes across the same information and get the same results each time. This isolation level is obviously more restrictive than READ COMMITTED and READ UNCOMMITTED, and it can block other transactions. However, although it prevents nonrepeatable reads, it does not prevent the addition of new rows or *phantom rows* because only *existing* data is locked.

▶ **SERIALIZABLE**—This option is the most restrictive isolation level because it places a range lock on the data. This prevents any modifications to the data being read from until the end of the transaction. It also avoids phantom reads by preventing rows from being added or removed from the data range set.

▶ **SNAPSHOT**—Snapshot isolation specifies that data read by any statement will see only data modifications that were committed before the start of the transaction. The effect is as if the statements in a transaction see a snapshot of the committed data as it existed at the start of the transaction. The ALLOW_SNAPSHOT_ISOLATION database option must be set to ON for a transaction to specify the SNAPSHOT isolation level.

READ_COMMITTED_SNAPSHOT Isolation

In addition to the SNAPSHOT isolation level, SQL Server also supports a special form of read-committed isolation, referred to as READ_COMMITTED_SNAPSHOT. This form of isolation is similar to snapshot isolation, but unlike snapshot isolation, which sees the version of the data at the start of the transaction, read committed snapshot queries see the version of the data at the start of the statement.

To enable the READ_COMMITTED_SNAPSHOT isolation level for queries, you need to enable the READ_COMMITTED_SNAPSHOT database option. Any queries that normally would run at the standard READ_COMMITTED isolation level automatically run at the READ_COMMITTED_SNAPSHOT isolation level without requiring any code changes.

For more information on transaction isolation levels and their effect on lock types, locking behavior, and performance, see Chapter 37, "Locking and Performance."

Coding Effective Transactions

Poorly written or inefficient transactions can have a detrimental effect on concurrency of access to data and overall application performance. SQL Server can hold locks on a number of resources while the transaction is open; modified rows acquire exclusive locks, and other locks might also be held, depending on the isolation level used. To reduce locking contention for resources, transactions should be kept as short and efficient as possible. During development, you might not even notice that a problem exists; the problem might become noticeable only after the system load is increased and multiple users are executing transactions simultaneously. Following are some guidelines to consider when coding transactions to minimize locking contention and improve application performance:

▶ Do not return result sets within a transaction. Doing so prolongs the transaction unnecessarily. Perform all data retrieval and analysis outside the transaction.

▶ Never prompt for user input during a transaction. If you do, you lose all control over the duration of the transaction. (Even the best programmers miss this one on occasion.) On the failure of a transaction, be sure to issue the rollback before putting up a message box telling the user that a problem occurred.

▶ Keep the start and end of a transaction together in the same batch or, better yet, use a stored procedure for the operation.

▶ Keep the transaction short. Start the transaction at the point where you need to do the modifications. Do any preliminary work beforehand.

▶ Make careful use of different locking schemes and transaction isolation levels.

▶ If user input is unavoidable between data retrieval and modification and you need to handle the possibility of another user modifying the data values read, use optimistic locking strategies or snapshot isolation rather than acquiring and holding locks by using HOLDLOCK or other locking options. Chapter 37 covers optimistic locking methods and snapshot isolation in more detail.

▶ Collect multiple transactions into one transaction or batch transactions together if appropriate. This advice might seem to go against some of the other suggestions, but it reduces the amount of overhead SQL Server will encounter to start, finish, and log the transactions.

▶ If you are updating a very large block of data in a table, consider breaking the single large transaction up into multiple chunks and reducing the size and scope of the single transaction into multiple smaller transactions. The downside of this approach is that it breaks a single atomic change across multiple transactions, but this may be necessary in an active system to prevent long-term blocking of the table being modified and also to prevent excessive log growth.

Transaction Logging and the Recovery Process

Every SQL Server database has its own transaction log that keeps a record of all data modifications in a database (for example, insert, update, delete) in the order in which they occur. This information is stored in one or more log files associated with the database. The information stored in these log files cannot be modified or viewed effectively by any user process.

SQL Server uses a write-ahead log. In full transaction durability mode, which is the default transaction mode, the buffer manager guarantees that changes are written to the transaction log before the changes are written to the database. The buffer manager also ensures that the log pages are written out in sequence so that transactions can be recovered properly in the event of a system crash.

The following is an overview of the sequence of events that occurs when a transaction modifies data in full transaction durability mode:

1. Writes a BEGIN TRAN record to the transaction log in the log buffer.

2. Writes data modification information to transaction log pages in the log buffer.

3. Writes data modifications to the database in buffer cache memory.

4. Writes a COMMIT TRAN record to the transaction log in the log buffer.

5. Flushes the transaction log records from the log buffer to the transaction log file(s) on disk.

6. Sends a COMMIT acknowledgment to the client process.

7. Any locks acquired during the processing of the transaction are released.

In the default transaction mode, durability of transactions is guaranteed on commit because the corresponding log records are persisted to disk before the transaction commit succeeds and returns control to the client. In delayed transaction durability mode, SQL Server uses asynchronous writes when writing the log to disk. The transaction commit processing does not wait for log I/O to finish before returning control to the client. Instead, transaction log records are kept in a buffer and written to disk when the buffer fills or a buffer flushing event takes place. This reduces contention for log I/O between concurrent transactions, which can increase transaction throughput.

The sequence of events performed by SQL Server when a transaction modifies data in delayed durability mode is as follows:

1. Writes a BEGIN TRAN record to the transaction log in the log buffer.

2. Writes data modification information to transaction log pages in the log buffer.

3. Writes data modifications to the database in buffer cache memory.

4. Writes a COMMIT TRAN record to the transaction log in the log buffer.

5. Sends a COMMIT acknowledgment to the client process.

6. Locks held by the transaction are released.

7. Writes transaction log records to the transaction log file(s) on disk when the log buffer is full or a log buffer flushing event takes place.

As you can see from this sequence, while delayed durability enables write transactions to continue running as if the log had been flushed to disk, the actual writes to disk are deferred and written to disk later by a background task. This is an optimistic handling of the transaction—the system assumes that the log flush will happen.

So what causes the log buffer to be flushed to disk? The log buffer is 60KB in size and will be flushed automatically to disk when the log buffer becomes full. Delayed durable transactions are also saved to disk whenever a fully durable transaction is executed against any table (durable memory-optimized or disk-based) in the database or the `sp_flush_log` stored procedure is explicitly invoked.

Notice that in either fully durable or delayed durability transactions, the data records are not written to disk when a COMMIT occurs. This is done to minimize overall database disk I/O. Also, whether using fully durable or delayed durability transactions, all log writes are performed sequentially to ensure that the log records are physically written to disk in the proper sequence. Because all modifications to the data can be recovered from the transaction log, it is not critical that data changes be written to disk right away. Even in the event of a system crash or power failure, the data can be recovered from the log if it hasn't been written to the database.

However, when using delayed durability, there is the chance of data loss under certain circumstances. For example, in the case of a catastrophic event, like a server crash, you will lose the data for all committed transactions for which the COMMIT record has not been saved to disk. Also, even during a planned shutdown/restart, some transactions that have not been written to disk may be lost. You should expect that a planned shutdown/restart may lose the same data as a catastrophic event and explicitly force the flush of transactions to disk with `sp_flush_log` before shutting down SQL Server. Also, any time that you want to ensure that all delayed durability transactions are written to disk you should invoke a durable transaction or run `sp_flush_log`. Either of these actions will force all current records in the log buffer to be flushed to disk.

WARNING

If you cannot tolerate any data loss in your system, you should not use delayed durability on your tables. For critical transactions, use fully durable transactions or run `sp_flush_log`.

Also, be aware that you can lose more than 60KB of transaction log activity. If the log buffer contains the COMMIT records for a long running transaction and the system crashes before the log buffer is written to disk, the entire transaction will be rolled back during the recovery process (discussed later in this chapter). The potential for work/data loss is greater than just 60KB.

Also, log backups only back up what is on disk, so a log backup will not contain any delayed durable transactions that are still in the log buffer at the time of the log backup.

So when might you want to consider using use delayed transaction durability? You could benefit from using delayed durability if you are experiencing a bottleneck on transaction log writes and can tolerate the potential for some data loss. If you detect that your performance issues are due to latency in transaction log writes, your applications will likely benefit from using delayed transaction durability. Also, if your system has workloads with a high contention level as a result waiting for locks to be released, delayed transaction durability can help reduce commit time and thus release locks faster, which can result in higher throughput. For more information on determining if your system is experiencing latency in transaction log writes or high lock contention, see Chapter 39, "Monitoring SQL Server Performance."

TIP

If your transaction log is not currently a bottleneck, it's probably best not to enable delayed durability transactions in your database. If you do consider implementing this option, you should test your specific workload to determine if any possible performance gain is worth the risk of data loss. If you run a system such as a banking application where data loss is unacceptable, you may want to look into other means of reducing log I/O contention, such as moving your transaction log to faster disks like solid state drives.

If you decide that delayed durability may provide a performance benefit for your application(s) and you can risk the potential for data loss, there are three ways to control transaction durability. First, you could set the default transaction durability mode at the database level with the ALTER DATBASE command:

```
ALTER DATABASE ... SET DELAYED_DURABILITY = { DISABLED | ALLOWED | FORCED }
```

The default setting is DISABLED, which prevents any transactions in the database from using delayed durability. The ALLOWED setting allows the transaction durability to be set at the individual transaction level. If you enable the FORCED setting, every transaction in the database that can use delayed durability will do so, even if the individual transaction specifies that it should be fully durable.

If you prefer to let individual transactions determine whether they should use delayed durability or not, configure the database DELAYED_DURABILITY setting to ALLOWED and explicitly specify the DELAYED_DURABILITY option in the COMMIT statement:

```
COMMIT [ TRAN  [ transaction_name | @tran_name_variable ]]
  [ WITH ( DELAYED_DURABILITY = { OFF | ON } ) ]
```

If the DELAYED_DURABILITY setting for the database is DISABLED and you specify DELAYED_DURABILITY = ON in a COMMIT statement, the database setting takes precedence and the DELAYED_DURABILITY option will be ignored without warning or error message.

You can also specify the transaction durability within the atomic block level of a natively compiled stored procedure with the DELAYED_DURABILITY = { OFF | ON } clause. For more information on using natively compiled stored procedures, see Chapter 33, "In-Memory Optimization and the Buffer Pool Extension."

NOTE

Regardless of the database setting or the delayed durability option specified for COMMIT, some transactions are always executed as fully durable. For example, system transactions, cross-database transactions, and operations involving FileTable, Change Tracking, and Change Data Capture are always executed as fully durable transactions.

Whether using fully durable or delayed durable transactions, SQL Server ensures that the log records are always written before the modifications are made to the affected data pages by recording the log sequence number (LSN) for the log record, which is making the change on the modified data page(s). Modified, or "dirty," data pages can be written to disk only when the LSN recorded on the data page is less than the LSN of the last log page written to the transaction log.

When and how are the data changes written to disk? Obviously, they must be written out at some time; otherwise, it could take an exceedingly long time for SQL Server to start up if it had to redo all the transactions contained in the transaction log. Also, how does SQL Server know during recovery which transactions to reapply, or roll forward, and which transactions to undo, or roll back? The following section looks at the mechanisms involved in the recovery process.

The Checkpoint Process

During recovery, SQL Server examines the transaction log for each database and verifies whether the changes reflected in the log are also reflected in the database. In addition, it examines the log to determine whether any data changes that were written to the data were caused by a transaction that didn't complete before the system failure.

As discussed earlier, a fully durable transaction COMMIT writes the log records for the transaction from the log buffer to the transaction log on disk (see Figure 28.1). Dirty data pages are written out either by the Lazy Writer or checkpoint process. The Lazy Writer process runs periodically to check whether the number of free buffers has fallen below a certain threshold, reclaims any unused pages, and writes out any dirty pages that haven't been referenced recently.

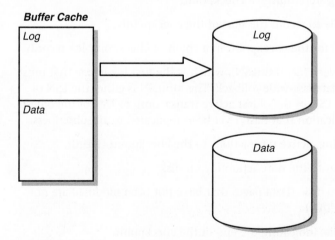

FIGURE 28.1   A fully durable transaction commit writes all "dirty" log pages from cache to disk.

28

The checkpoint process also scans the buffer cache periodically and writes all dirty log pages and dirty data pages (whether the changes in the dirty log and data pages have been committed or not) to disk (see Figure 28.2). The purpose of the checkpoint is to sync up the data stored on disk with the changes recorded in the transaction log. Typically, the checkpoint process finds little work to do because most dirty pages have been written out previously by the worker threads or Lazy Writer process.

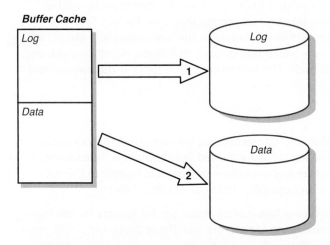

FIGURE 28.2   A checkpoint writes log pages from cache to disk and then writes all "dirty" data pages.

SQL Server performs the following steps during a checkpoint:

1. Writes a record to the log file to record the start of the checkpoint.

2. Stores information recorded for the checkpoint in a chain of checkpoint log records.

3. Records the minimum recovery LSN (MinLSN), which is the first log image that must be present for a successful database-wide rollback. The MinLSN is either the LSN of the start of the checkpoint, LSN of the oldest active transaction, or LSN of the oldest transaction marked for replication that hasn't yet been replicated to all subscribers.

4. Writes a list of all outstanding, active transactions to the checkpoint records.

5. Writes all modified log pages to the transaction log on disk.

6. Writes all dirty data pages to disk. (Data pages that have not been modified are not written back to disk to save I/O.)

7. Writes a record to the log file, indicating the end of the checkpoint.

8. Writes the LSN of the start of the checkpoint log records to the database boot page. (This is done so that SQL Server can find the last checkpoint in the log during recovery.)

Figure 28.3 shows a simplified version of the contents of a transaction log after a checkpoint. (For simplicity, the checkpoint records are reflected as a single log entry.)

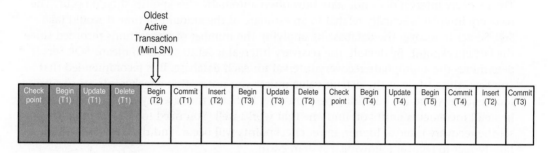

FIGURE 28.3   A simplified view of the end of the transaction log with various completed and active transactions, as well as the last checkpoint.

The primary purpose of a checkpoint is to reduce the amount of work the server needs to do at recovery time to redo or undo database changes. A checkpoint can occur under the following circumstances:

▶ When a checkpoint statement is executed explicitly for the current database.

▶ When ALTER DATABASE is used to change a database option. ALTER DATABASE automatically checkpoints the database when database options are changed.

▶ When an instance of SQL Server is shut down gracefully either due to the execution of the SHUTDOWN statement or because the SQL Server service was stopped.

▶ When SQL Server periodically generates automatic checkpoints in each database to reduce the amount of time the instance would take to recover the database.

NOTE

The SHUTDOWN WITH NOWAIT statement does not perform what is considered a graceful shutdown of SQL Server. This statement forces a shutdown of SQL Server without waiting for current transactions to complete and without executing a checkpoint of each database. This type of shutdown may cause the subsequent restart of SQL Server to take a longer time to recover the databases on the server.

Automatic Checkpoints

By default, the frequency of automatic checkpoints is determined by the setting of the recovery interval for SQL Server. However, the determination of when to perform a checkpoint is based on the number of records in the log, not a specific period of time. The time interval between the occurrences of automatic checkpoints can be highly variable. If few modifications are made to the database, the time interval between automatic checkpoints could be quite long. Conversely, automatic checkpoints can occur quite frequently if the update activity on a database is high.

The recovery interval does not state how often automatic checkpoints should occur. The recovery interval is actually related to an estimate of the amount of time it would take SQL Server to recover the database by applying the number of transactions recorded since the last checkpoint. By default, the recovery interval is set to 0, which means SQL Server determines the appropriate recovery interval for each database. It is recommended that you keep this setting at the default value unless you notice that checkpoints are occurring too frequently and are impairing performance. If that is the case, try to increase the value in small increments until you find one that works well. You need to be aware that if you set the recovery interval higher, fewer checkpoints will occur, and the database will likely take longer to recover following a system crash.

If the database is using either the full or bulk-logged recovery model, an automatic checkpoint occurs whenever the number of log records reaches the number that SQL Server estimates it can process within the time specified by the recovery interval option.

If the database is using the simple recovery model, an automatic checkpoint occurs whenever the number of log records reaches the number that SQL Server estimates it can process during the time specified by the recovery interval option or the log becomes 70% full and the database is in log truncate mode. A database is considered to be in log truncate mode when the database is using the simple recovery model and one of the following events has occurred since the last full backup of the database:

▶ A minimally logged operation is performed in the database, such as a minimally logged bulk copy operation or a minimally logged WRITETEXT statement.

▶ An ALTER DATABASE statement is executed that adds or deletes a file in the database.

When a database is configured to use the simple recovery model, the automatic checkpoint also truncates the unused portion of the transaction log prior to the oldest active transaction.

> **NOTE**
>
> If a long-running transaction was active at the time of the SQL Server crash, recovery may take significantly longer than the value specified for the recovery interval option. For example, if an update transaction was in process and had been processing for 2 hours before the server instance became disabled, the actual recovery of the database could take considerably longer than the recovery interval value to roll back the incomplete long-running transaction.

Indirect Checkpoints

Introduced in SQL Server 2014, *indirect checkpoints* provide a mechanism for configuring checkpoint intervals at the individual database level. Indirect checkpoints can provide potentially faster, more predictable recovery times for your critical databases than automatic checkpoints.

In addition to providing finer control over database recovery time for specific databases, indirect checkpoints can also help reduce checkpoint-related I/O spikes by continually writing dirty pages to disk in the background. However, an online transactional workload on a database that is configured for indirect checkpoints could experience performance degradation because the background writer used by the indirect checkpoint process may increase the total write load for a server instance.

When you set a specific target recovery time for a database, SQL Server internally calculates the Target Dirty Buffer threshold. This is a count of the number of buffers that have been modified by database transaction. This count is kept in a Dirty Page List as the transactions are logged in the transaction log. A new background process in SQL Server 2014, the Recovery Writer, periodically checks the Dirty Page List and when the number of dirty pages exceeds the Target Dirty Buffer threshold, it flushes the dirty buffers to disk and updates the Dirty Page List. This process helps ensure that no more than the target dirty buffers are in the buffer pool so that the database can be recovered within the target recovery time.

To override the automatic checkpointing for a specific database in SQL Server, you need to set the recovery interval value for a database to a value greater than zero. You can do so with the ALTER DATABASE command:

```
ALTER DATABASE dbname SET TARGET_RECOVERY_TIME =target_recovery_time { SECONDS |
MINUTES }
```

For example, to set the target recovery time for the AdventureWorks2012 database to 2 minutes (or 120 seconds), you run the following:

```
ALTER DATABASE AdventureWorks2012 SET TARGET_RECOVERY_TIME = 120 seconds
```

To view the target recovery time for a database, you run the following SQL statement:

```
Select target_recovery_time_in_seconds
from sys.databases where name = 'AdventureWorks2012'
GO


target_recovery_time_in_seconds
-------------------------------
                  120
```

You can also set and view the target_recovery_time setting for a database in SSMS. In the SSMS Object Explorer, right-click on the database name and select Properties. In the Properties dialog, select the Options page and scroll down to display the Recovery options, as shown in Figure 28.4.

28

NOTE

Indirect checkpoints can reduce the overall recovery time for a specific database, but you need to be aware that there could be a performance hit if you enable indirect checkpoints on a very busy OLTP database. If you set it too low, it can lead to increased IO load by the background writer operation. Be sure you test any changes to the target recovery time in a test environment before enabling in production.

FIGURE 28.4   Setting/viewing the Target Recovery Time in SSMS

Manual Checkpoints

In addition to automatic checkpoints, a checkpoint can be explicitly initiated by members of the sysadmin fixed server role or the db_owner or db_backupoperator fixed database roles. The syntax for the CHECKPOINT command is as follows:

```
CHECKPOINT [ checkpoint_duration ]
```

To minimize the performance impact on other applications, SQL Server 2014 by default adjusts the frequency of the writes that a checkpoint operation performs. SQL Server uses this strategy for automatic checkpoints and for any CHECKPOINT statement that does not specify the checkpoint_duration value.

You can use the checkpoint_duration option to request the amount of time, in seconds, for the checkpoint to complete. When checkpoint_duration is specified, SQL Server attempts to perform the checkpoint within the requested duration. The performance impact of using `checkpoint_duration` depends on the number of dirty pages, the activity on the system, and the actual duration specified. For example, if the checkpoint would normally complete in 120 seconds, specifying a `checkpoint_duration` of 60 seconds causes SQL Server to devote more resources to the checkpoint than would be assigned by default to be able to complete the checkpoint in half the time. In contrast, specifying a `checkpoint_duration` of 240 seconds causes SQL Server to assign fewer resources than would be assigned by default. In other words, a short `checkpoint_duration` increases the resources devoted to the checkpoint, and a longer `checkpoint_duration` reduces the resources devoted to the checkpoint.

Regardless of the checkpoint duration specified, SQL Server always attempts to complete a checkpoint when possible. In some cases, a checkpoint may complete sooner than the specified duration, and at times it may run longer than the specified duration.

The Recovery Process

When SQL Server is started, it verifies that completed transactions recorded in the log are reflected in the data and that incomplete transactions whose changes are reflected in the data are rolled back out of the database. This is the recovery process. Recovery is an automatic process performed on each database during SQL Server startup. Recovery must be completed before the database is made available for use.

The recovery process guarantees that all completed transactions recorded in the transaction log are reflected in the data and all incomplete transactions reflected in the data are rolled back. During recovery, SQL Server looks for the last checkpoint record in the log. Only the changes that occurred or were still open since the last checkpoint need to be examined to determine the need for any transactions to be redone (that is, rolled forward) or undone (that is, rolled back). After all the changes are rolled forward or rolled back, as necessary, the database is checkpointed, and recovery is complete.

The recovery algorithm has three phases centered around the last checkpoint record in the transaction log, as shown in Figure 28.5.

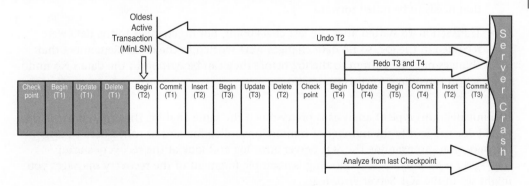

FIGURE 28.5   The phases of the recovery process.

These phases are as follows:

1. **Analysis phase**—SQL Server reads forward from the last checkpoint record in the transaction log. This pass identifies a list of pages (the dirty page table [DPT]) that might have been dirty at the time of the system crash or when SQL Server was shut down, as well as a list of the uncommitted transactions at the time of the crash.

2. **Redo (roll-forward) phase**—During this phase, SQL Server rolls forward all the committed transactions recorded in the log since the last checkpoint. This phase returns the database to the state it was in at the time of the crash. The starting point for the redo pass is the LSN of the oldest committed transaction within the DPT, so that only changes not previously checkpointed (only the committed dirty pages) are reapplied.

3. **Undo (rollback) phase**—This phase moves backward from the end of the log to the oldest active transaction at the time of the system crash or shutdown. All transactions that were not committed at the time of the crash but had pages written to the database are undone so that none of their changes are actually reflected in the database.

Now let's examine the transactions in the log in Figure 28.5 and determine how they will be handled during the recovery process:

▶ Transaction T1 is started and committed prior to the last checkpoint. No recovery is necessary.

▶ Transaction T2 started before the last checkpoint but had not completed at the time of the system crash. The changes written out by the checkpoint process for this transaction have to be rolled back.

▶ Transaction T3 started before the last checkpoint was issued and committed after that checkpoint but prior to the system crash. The changes made to the data after the checkpoint need to be rolled forward.

▶ Transaction T4 started and committed after the last checkpoint. This entire transaction needs to be rolled forward.

▶ Transaction T5 started after the last checkpoint, but no changes to the data were recorded in the log, so no data changes were written to the data. (Remember that changes must be written to the log before they can be written to the data.) No undo action is required for this transaction.

In a nutshell, this type of analysis is pretty much the same analysis the recovery process would do. To identify the number of transactions rolled forward or rolled back during recovery, you can examine the SQL Server error log and look at the recovery startup messages for each database. Following is a sample fragment of the recovery messages you might see in the SQL Server error log:

```
2015-02-01 21:42:13.410 spid8s      Server name is 'LATITUDEE6520\UNLEASHED2014'.
This is an informational message only. No user action is required.
```

```
2015-02-01 21:42:13.420 spid21s     Starting up database 'InMemory'.
2015-02-01 21:42:13.420 spid18s     Starting up database 'msdb'.
2015-02-01 21:42:13.420 spid19s     Starting up database 'AdventureWorks2012'.
2015-02-01 21:42:13.420 spid10s     Starting up database 'mssqlsystemresource'.
2015-02-01 21:42:13.420 spid20s     Starting up database 'pubs2'.
2015-02-01 21:42:13.420 spid22s     Starting up database 'mytest'.
2015-02-01 21:42:13.430 spid10s     The resource database build version is
12.00.2000. This is an informational message only. No user action is required.
2015-02-01 21:42:13.440 spid18s     1 transactions rolled forward in database
'msdb' (4:0). This is an informational message only. No user action is required.
2015-02-01 21:42:13.440 spid21s     1 transactions rolled forward in database
'InMemory' (6:0). This is an informational message only. No user action is required.
2015-02-01 21:42:13.440 spid19s     1 transactions rolled forward in database
'AdventureWorks2012' (5:0). This is an informational message only. No user action is
required.
2015-02-01 21:42:13.440 spid20s     4 transactions rolled forward in database
'pubs2' (7:0). This is an informational message only. No user action is required.
2015-02-01 21:42:13.450 spid10s     Starting up database 'model'.
2015-02-01 21:42:13.460 spid22s     37 transactions rolled forward in database
'mytest' (8:0). This is an informational message only. No user action is required.
2015-02-01 21:42:13.470 spid10s     Clearing tempdb database.
2015-02-01 21:42:13.510 spid10s     Starting up database 'tempdb'.
2015-02-01 21:42:13.520 spid8s      0 transactions rolled back in database 'msdb'
(4:0). This is an informational message only. No user action is required.
2015-02-01 21:42:13.620 spid8s      0 transactions rolled back in database
'AdventureWorks2012' (5:0). This is an informational message only. No user action is
required.
2015-02-01 21:42:13.620 spid24s     The Service Broker endpoint is in disabled or
stopped state.
2015-02-01 21:42:13.620 spid24s     The Database Mirroring endpoint is in disabled
or stopped state.
2015-02-01 21:42:13.620 spid18s     0 transactions rolled back in database 'pubs2'
(7:0). This is an informational message only. No user action is required.
2015-02-01 21:42:13.620 spid18s     Recovery is writing a checkpoint in database
'pubs2' (7). This is an informational message only. No user action is required.
2015-02-01 21:42:13.630 spid18s     1 transactions rolled back in database 'mytest'
(8:0). This is an informational message only. No user action is required.
2015-02-01 21:42:13.630 spid18s     Recovery is writing a checkpoint in database
'mytest' (8). This is an informational message only. No user action is required.
2015-02-01 21:42:13.630 spid24s     Service Broker manager has started.
```

Managing the Transaction Log

Each database in SQL Server has at least one transaction log file. The transaction log file contains the transaction log records for all changes made in that database. By default, transaction log files have the file extension .ldf.

A database can have several log files, and each log file can have a maximum size of 32TB. A log file cannot be part of a filegroup. No information other than transaction log records can be written to a log file.

Regardless of how many physical files have been defined for the transaction log, SQL Server treats it as one contiguous file. The transaction log for a database is actually managed as a set of virtual log files (VLFs). VLFs have no fixed size, and there is no fixed number of VLFs for a physical log file. The size and number of VLFs is not configurable. SQL Server determines the size of the VLFs dynamically based on the total size of all the log files and the growth increment specified for the log. Figure 28.6 shows an example of a physical log file divided into multiple virtual log files.

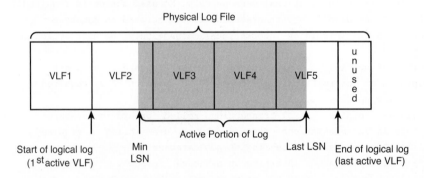

FIGURE 28.6   The structure of a physical log file showing VLFs.

The transaction log is essentially a wrap-around file. Initially, the logical log file begins at the start of the physical log file. As transactions are committed, new log records are added to the end of the logical log, and the logical log expands toward the end of the physical log. When the logical log reaches the end of the physical log file, SQL Server attempts to wrap around and start writing log records back at the beginning of the physical log file, as shown in Figure 28.7.

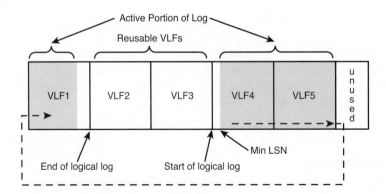

FIGURE 28.7   An example of the active portion of a log cycling around to reusable VLF at the beginning of a log file.

SQL Server, however, can reuse only the first VLF if it is no longer part of the logical log; that is, the VLF does not contain any active log records, and the contents of the inactive VLFs have been truncated. Log truncation frees any virtual logs whose records all appear before the MinLSN. The MinLSN is the log sequence number of the oldest log record required for a successful database recovery.

In environments where the log is not being maintained, SQL Server automatically truncates and reuses the space in the VLFs at the beginning of the log file as soon as it reaches the end of the log file. This can occur as long as the VLFs at the beginning of the log file do not contain the MinLSN. SQL Server assumes that the log is not being maintained when the database is in simple recovery mode or when you have never performed a full backup of the database.

If the database is configured to use the bulk-logged or full recovery models so that the log is being maintained, the reusable portion of the log prior to the MinLSN cannot be truncated or purged until the transaction log has actually been backed up.

If the first VLF cannot be reused because it contains the MinLSN or it hasn't been truncated yet, SQL Server needs to expand the log file. This is done by adding a new VLF to the end of the physical log (as long as the log file is still configured to grow automatically). SQL Server can then continue writing log records to the new VLF. However, if the log file is not configured to auto-grow, a 9002 error is generated, indicating that the log file is out of space.

Certain conditions can cause log records to remain active, preventing the MinLSN from moving out of the first VLF, which in turn prevents the VLFs at the beginning of the physical log file from being reused. Some of the conditions that can lead to the log space not being reused include, but are not limited to, the following:

- ▶ No checkpoint has taken place yet since the log was last truncated, and the log records are needed for database recovery.

- ▶ A database or log backup is in progress.

- ▶ A long-running transaction is still active.

- ▶ Database mirroring is paused.

- ▶ The database is the primary database for transactional replication, and transactions relevant to the publications have not yet been delivered to the distribution database. (For more information on replication, see Chapter 43, "Data Replication.")

- ▶ A database snapshot is being created (for more information, see Chapter 29, "Database Snapshots").

If something is preventing the log from being truncated, SQL Server 2014 provides information in the system catalogs to determine what is preventing log truncation. This information is available in the log_reuse_wait_desc column of the sys.databases catalog view, which you can display by using a query similar to the following:

```
select name, log_reuse_wait_desc
   from sys.databases
   where name = db_name()
```

When a log file is configured to auto-grow and there is significant update activity against the database and the inactive portion of the transaction log is not being truncated frequently enough (or at all) to allow for the reuse of VLFs, the log file size can become excessive. This can lead to insufficient disk space in the file system that contains the log file. This can subsequently also lead to a 9002 out-of-space error if the log file needs to grow and not enough disk space is available. At times, you might need to shrink the log file to reduce its size.

Shrinking the Log File

After the log has been backed up and the active portion of the log has wrapped around to the beginning of the log file, the VLFs at the end of the physical log can be deleted from the log file, and the log file can be reduced in size.

When you shrink a log file, the space freed can only come from the end of the log file. The unit of size reduction is the size of the virtual log file. For example, if you have a 1GB log file that has been divided into five 200MB virtual log files, the log file can only be shrunk in 200MB increments. The file size can be reduced to sizes such as 800MB or 400MB, but the file cannot be reduced to sizes such as 333MB or 750MB.

SQL Server 2014 provides the DBCC SHRINKFILE command for shrinking the transaction log file. Its syntax is as follows:

```
DBCC SHRINKFILE ( { 'file_name' } { [,EMPTYFILE] | [,target_size ] } )
   [ WITH NO_INFOMSGS ]
```

If no target size is specified for the DBCC SHRINKFILE command, SQL Server removes as many of the inactive virtual log files from the end of the physical log file as possible to restore the transaction log file to its default size. The default size of the transaction log file is the size specified when the log file was created or the last size set by using the ALTER DATABASE command.

If a target size is specified for DBCC SHRINKFILE, SQL Server attempts to remove as many VLFs from the end of the log file as possible to reduce the log file to as close to the target size as possible without making the log smaller than the specified target size. After shrinking, the log file is typically somewhat larger than the target size, especially if the target size is not a multiple of the VLF size.

If no VLFs beyond the target_size mark contain an active portion of the log, all the VLFs that come after the target_size mark are freed, and the DBCC SHRINKFILE statement completes successfully with no messages. However, if any VLF beyond the target_size mark does contain an active portion of the log, SQL Server frees from the end of the physical log file as many of the VLFs as possible that do not contain active portions of the log. When this occurs, the DBCC SHRINKFILE command returns an informational message indicating that not all the requested space was freed. When the active portion of the log moves off the VLF(s) at the end of the physical log file, you can reissue the DBCC SHRINKFILE statement again to free the remaining space.

You can also use SQL Server Management Studio (SSMS) to shrink the transaction log file. In the Object Browser, expand the Databases folder and right-click the target database. Then select Tasks, Shrink, and Files. The Shrink File dialog appears, as shown in Figure 28.8.

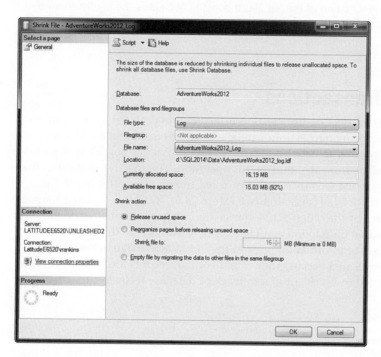

FIGURE 28.8   The SSMS Shrink File dialog.

In the File Type drop-down list, select Log. To shrink the log file to its default size, click the radio button next to Release Unused Space in the Shrink Action area of the dialog box. To shrink the log file to a desired size, click the radio button next to Reorganize Pages Before Releasing Unused Space and specify the desired target size. After you choose the desired shrink option, click OK.

In addition to manually shrinking the transaction log, SQL Server also provides a database option, AUTO_SHRINK, that can be enabled to shrink the log and database files automatically when space is available at the end of the file. If you are regularly backing up or truncating the log, the AUTO_SHRINK option keeps the size of the log file in check. The auto-shrink process runs periodically and determines whether the log file can be shrunk. The Log Manager keeps track of how much log space has been used since the auto-shrink process last ran. The auto-shrink process then shrinks the log either to 125% of the maximum log space used since auto-shrink last ran or the default size of the transaction log file, whichever is larger.

> **TIP**
>
> Repeated growing and shrinking of the log file can lead to excessive file fragmentation, which can have an adverse impact on the file I/O performance. It is recommended that instead of using `AUTO_SHRINK`, you set the transaction log to the size it is expected to grow to during normal processing and enable the auto-grow option so that it doesn't run out of space if something prevents the log from being truncated. By doing so, you help avoid the need for the log file to be constantly expanded during normal processing and also avoid excessive fragmentation of the log file. If something causes the log file to auto-grow and exceed the normal log file size, you can always manually shrink the file back to its normal size.

Long-Running Transactions

As you have already seen, transaction information is recorded in each database's transaction log. However, long-running transactions can be a cause of consternation to a system administrator who is attempting to back up and prune the transaction log. Only the inactive portion of the log can be truncated during this operation. The inactive portion of the log is the pages that contain log records for all completed transactions prior to the first log record of the oldest still-active transaction (see Figure 28.9). Even if completed transactions follow the first record of the oldest active transaction, they cannot be removed from the log until the oldest active transaction completes. The reason is that the log is pruned by clearing out entire pages of information prior to the oldest active transaction. Pages after that point cannot be cleared because they might contain records for the active transaction that would be needed in the event of a rollback or database recovery.

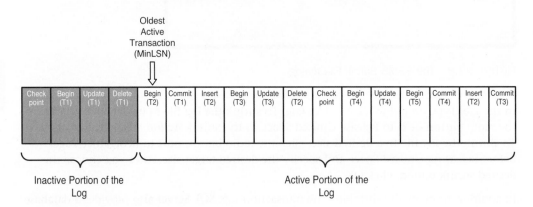

FIGURE 28.9   The inactive portion of the log is the pages in the log prior to the oldest active transaction.

In addition to preventing the log from being pruned, long-running transactions can degrade concurrency by holding locks for an extended period of time, preventing other users from accessing the locked data.

To get information about the oldest active transaction in a database, you can use the DBCC OPENTRAN command, whose syntax is as follows:

```
DBCC OPENTRAN [('DatabaseName' | DatabaseId)]
[WITH TABLERESULTS [, NO_INFOMSGS]]
```

The following example displays a sample of the oldest active transaction for the AdventureWorks2012 database:

```
DBCC OPENTRAN (AdventureWorks2012)
go


Transaction information for database 'AdventureWorks2012'.


Oldest active transaction:
    SPID (server process ID): 55
    UID (user ID) : -1
    Name           : user_transaction
    LSN            : (122:656:1)
    Start time     : Feb 24 2013 10:53:45:237AM
    SID            : 0x010500000000000515000000eb298cb70b71e039c84cff87e9030000
DBCC execution completed. If DBCC printed error messages, contact your system
administrator.
```

DBCC OPENTRAN returns the server process ID (SPID) of the process that initiated the transaction, user ID, name of the transaction (naming transactions are helpful here because the names might help you identify the SQL code that initiated the transaction), LSN of the page containing the initial BEGIN TRAN statement for the transaction, and, finally, time the transaction was started.

If you specify the TABLERESULTS option, this information is returned in two columns that you can load into a table for logging or comparison purposes. The NO_INFOMSGS option suppresses the display of the 'DBCC execution completed...' message. The following example runs DBCC OPENTRAN and inserts the results into a temp table:

```
CREATE TABLE #opentran_results
( result_label VARCHAR(30), result_value VARCHAR(46))

insert #opentran_results
    exec ('dbcc opentran (AdventureWorks2012) WITH TABLERESULTS,  no_infomsgs')

select * from #opentran_results
go
```

28

```
result_label                        result_value
--------------------------------    -------------------------------------------------
OLDACT_SPID                         55
OLDACT_UID                          -1
OLDACT_NAME                         user_transaction
OLDACT_RECOVERYUNITID               0
OLDACT_LSN                          (122:656:1)
OLDACT_STARTTIME                    Feb 24 2013 10:53:45:237AM
OLDACT_SID                          0x0105000000000000515000000eb298cb70b71e039c84c
```

If no open transactions exist for the database, you receive the following message from
DBCC OPENTRAN:

```
No active open transactions.
DBCC execution completed. If DBCC printed error messages, contact your system
administrator.
```

DBCC OPENTRAN provides a means for you to identify which transactions are potential problems, based on their longevity. If you capture the process information at the same time,
using sp_who, you can identify who or what application is causing the longest-running
transaction(s). Using this information, you can terminate the process, if necessary, or you
can just have a quiet word with the user if the query is ad hoc or with the application
developers if it is SQL code generated by a custom application.

Distributed Transactions

Typically, transaction management controls only the data modifications made within
a single SQL Server instance. However, the increasing interest and implementation of
distributed systems brings up the need to access and modify data distributed across multiple SQL Server instances within a single unit of work.

What if in the banking example, the checking accounts reside on one SQL Server instance
and the savings accounts on another? Moving money from one account to another would
require updates to two separate SQL Server instances. How do you modify data on two
different instances and still treat it as a single unit of work? You need some way to ensure
that the distributed transaction retains the same ACID properties as a local transaction.
To provide this capability, SQL Server ships with the MS DTC service, which provides the
capability to control and manage the integrity of multiserver transactions. MS DTC uses
the industry-standard two-phase commit protocol to ensure the consistency of all parts of
any distributed transaction passing through SQL Server and any referenced linked servers.

To specify that SQL Server should use the MS DTC service to manage a distributed transaction, simply use the BEGIN DISTRIBUTED TRANSACTION statement as follows:

```
BEGIN DISTRIBUTED TRANSACTION
-- One thousand dollars is subtracted from the savings account.
UPDATE savings_server.savings_db.dbo.account
  SET balance = balance - 1000
```

```
WHERE account_number = 12345;
-- One thousand dollars is added to the checking account.
UPDATE checking_server.checking_db.dbo.account
 SET balance = balance + 1000
WHERE account_number = 98765;
COMMIT TRANSACTION;
```

All other transaction control statements operate as if you were running the transaction on a single instance. The transaction will be either committed or rolled back on all instances involved. The SQL Server instance where the BEGIN DISTRIBUTED TRANSACTION statement is issued becomes the transaction originator and controls the completion of the transaction. When a subsequent COMMIT TRANSACTION or ROLLBACK TRANSACTION statement is issued within the session, the controlling instance requests that MS DTC manage the completion of the distributed transaction across all of the instances involved.

Chapter 17, "Managing Linked Servers," covers the process of configuring linked servers to support writing distributed transactions.

Summary

A transaction is a logical unit of work as well as a unit of recovery. The successful control of transactions is of the utmost importance to the correct modification of related information. In this chapter, you learned how to define and control transactions, examined different transaction-management schemes, learned how the recovery process works, and discovered how to correctly code transactions within triggers and stored procedures. You also learned methods for optimizing transactions to improve application performance, and you got an overview of locking as is relates to transactions. Locking is covered in more detail in Chapter 37. In addition, this chapter discussed the snapshot isolation options available in SQL Server 2014. Snapshot isolation provides the capability to keep versions of row data that existed prior to the start of a transaction.

Chapter 29 discusses the concept of database snapshots, which provide a way to keep a read-only, static view of a database.

28

CHAPTER 29

Database Snapshots

Database snapshots have been a feature of competing database products (Oracle and DB2) for years. Database snapshots are great for fulfilling point-in-time reporting requirements, reverting a database back to a point in time (recoverability and availability), and for potentially reducing the processing impact of querying against your primary transactional databases (by creating a database snapshot on a database mirror or a secondary replica in an AlwaysOn Availability Group).

Keep in mind that database snapshots are point-in-time and read-only. Database snapshots are not materialized views. Materialized views become part of the data object (table) that they are touching (that is, that are bound to them); when data changes in the base tables, materialized views change (that is, are updated). Database snapshots are point-in-time reflections of an entire database and are not bound to the underlying database objects from which they pull their data. They provide a full, read-only copy of the database at a specific point in time. Because of this point-in-time aspect, data latency must be well understood for all users of this feature: snapshot data is only as current as at the time the snapshot was made.

Database snapshots have solved many companies' reporting, data safeguarding, and performance issues and directly contributed to higher availability across the board. Be aware, though, that plenty of restrictions apply to using database snapshots. In fact, these restrictions may prohibit you from using snapshots at all. Database snapshot restrictions and when you can safely create database snapshots are covered later in this chapter.

What's New with Database Snapshots

With SQL Server 2014, there is little new to this feature beyond what was available in SQL Server 2012. One hundred percent of the SQL code you have set up for creating and managing snapshots should still work perfectly with SQL Server 2014. No upgrade pain here. However, database mirroring is a deprecated feature in SQL Server 2014 and may not be available in a future release of SQL Server. If you are considering using database snapshots with database mirroring, you may want to plan to switch to using readable secondary replicas with AlwaysOn Availability Groups instead.

> **NOTE**
>
> The examples in this chapter are based on the `AdventureWorks2012` database.

What Are Database Snapshots?

Microsoft has kept up its commitment of providing a database engine foundation that can be highly available 7 days a week, 365 days a year. Database snapshots contribute to this goal in several ways:

▶ They decrease recovery time of a database because you can restore a database to a point in time with a database snapshot—referred to as *reverting*.

▶ They create a security blanket (safeguard) prior to running mass updates on a critical database. If something goes wrong with the update, the database can be reverted in a shorter amount of time than recovering from a database backup.

▶ They can provide a read-only, point-in-time reporting database for ad hoc or canned reporting needs quickly (thus increasing reporting environment availability).

▶ They can provide a read-only, point-in-time reporting and off-loaded database for ad hoc or canned reporting needs quickly from a database mirror or secondary replica of an AlwaysOn Availability Group (again, increasing reporting environment availability and also offloading reporting impact away from your production server/principal database server).

▶ As a bonus, database snapshots can be used to create testing or QA synchronization points to enhance and improve all aspects of critical testing (thus decreasing bad code from going into production that directly affects the stability and availability of that production implementation).

The most common terms associated with database snapshots are

▶ **Source database**—This is the database on which the database snapshot is based. A database is a collection of data pages. It is the fundamental data storage mechanism that SQL Server uses.

▶ **Snapshot database**—There can be one or more database snapshots defined against any one source database. All snapshots must reside in the same SQL Server instance.

▶ **Database snapshot sparse file**—This new data page allocation contains the original source database data pages when updates occur to the source database data pages. One sparse file is associated with each database data file. If you have a source database allocated with one or more separate data files, you have corresponding sparse files for each of the snapshots.

▶ **Reverting to a database snapshot**—If you restore a source database based on a particular database snapshot that was done at a point in time, you are reverting. You are actually doing a database RESTORE operation with a FROM DATABASE_SNAPSHOT statement.

▶ **Copy-on-write technology**—As part of an update transaction in the source database, a copy of the source database data page is written to a sparse file so that the database snapshot can be served correctly (that is, can still see the data page as of the snapshot point in time).

A database snapshot is simply a point-in-time view of the entire database. It's not a copy of the database—at least not a full copy when it is originally created. What is actually done when a snapshot is created is covered shortly. Figure 29.1 shows conceptually how a database snapshot can be created from a source database on a single SQL Server instance.

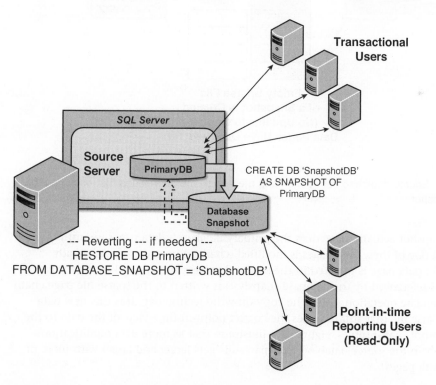

FIGURE 29.1   Basic database snapshot concept: a source database and its database snapshot, all on a single SQL Server instance.

This point-in-time view of a database's data never changes, even though the data (data pages) in the primary database (the source of the database snapshot) may change. It is truly a snapshot at a specific point in time. The snapshot simply references the data pages that were present at the time the snapshot was created. If a data page is updated in the source database after the snapshot is created, a copy of the original source data page is moved to a new page chain in the data file(s) allocated to the snapshot which are created as *sparse files*. This is done using copy-on-write technology. Figure 29.2 shows the sparse file that is created, alongside the source database itself.

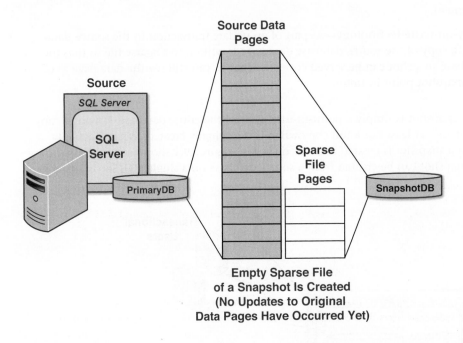

FIGURE 29.2   Source database data pages and the sparse file data pages that comprise the database snapshot.

A database snapshot actually references the primary database's data pages up until the point that one of these data pages is modified (changed in any way). As already mentioned, if a data page is updated in the source database, the original copy of the data page (which is referenced by the database snapshot) is written to the sparse file page chain as part of an update operation, using the copy-on-write technology. It is this new data page in the sparse file that still provides the correct point-in-time view of the data to the database snapshot that it serves. Figure 29.3 illustrates that as more data modifications (updates) occur in the source database, the sparse file gets larger and larger with more of the original data pages.

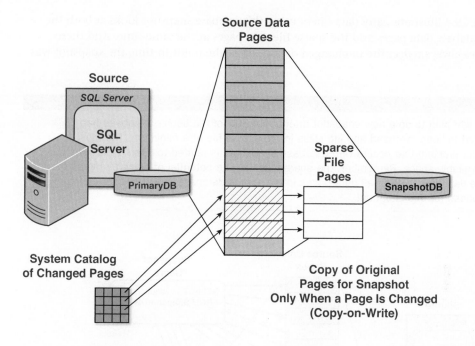

Source Data Pages

Source

SQL Server

SQL Server

PrimaryDB

Sparse File Pages

SnapshotDB

System Catalog of Changed Pages

Copy of Original Pages for Snapshot Only When a Page Is Changed (Copy-on-Write)

FIGURE 29.3   Data pages being copied to the sparse file for a database snapshot as pages are being updated in the source database.

Eventually a sparse file could contain the entire original database if all data pages in the primary database were changed. As you can also see in Figure 29.3, which data pages the database snapshot uses from the original (source) database and which data pages are used from the sparse file are all managed by references in the system catalog for the database snapshot. Because SQL Server is using the copy-on-write technology, a certain amount of overhead is incurred during write operations. This is one of the critical factors you must sort through if you plan on using database snapshots. Nothing is free. The overhead includes the copying of the original data page, the writing of this copied data page to the sparse file, and then the subsequent metadata updating to the system catalog that manages the database snapshot data page list. Because of this sharing of data pages, it should also be clear why database snapshots must be within the same instance of a SQL Server: Both the source database and snapshot start out using the same data pages and then diverge as data in the source data pages is modified. In addition, when a database snapshot is created, SQL Server rolls back any uncommitted data changes for that database snapshot; only committed transactions are part of a newly created database snapshot. And, as you might expect of something that shares data pages, database snapshots become unavailable if the source database becomes unavailable (for example, if it is damaged or goes offline).

29

As Figure 29.4 illustrates, any data query using the database snapshot looks at both the source database data pages and the sparse file data pages at the same time. And these data pages always reflect the unchanged data pages at the point in time the snapshot was created.

> **NOTE**
>
> You might plan to do a new snapshot after about 30% of the source database has changed to keep overhead and file sizes in the sparse file at a minimum. The most frequent problem that occurs with database snapshots is related to sparse file sizes and available space. Remember, the sparse file has the potential of being as big as the source database itself (if all data pages in the source database eventually get updated). Plan ahead for this situation!

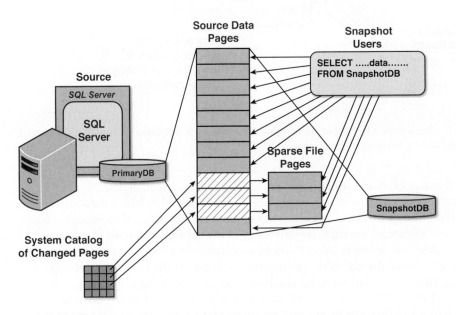

FIGURE 29.4   A query using the database snapshot touches both source database data pages and sparse file data pages to satisfy a query.

There are, of course, alternatives to database snapshots, such as data replication, log shipping, and even materialized views, but none are as easy to manage and use as database snapshots.

Limitations and Restrictions of Database Snapshots

Many restrictions or limitations are involved with using database snapshots in SQL Server. Some of them are pretty restrictive and may determine whether you can consider using snapshots. For example, even in SQL Server Management Studio 2014, you still cannot set up database snapshots or revert a database to a snapshot via the GUI or a wizard; it must all be done using T-SQL statements. The following are some of the other restrictions and limitations associated with database snapshots:

▶ You must drop all other database snapshots before you can revert a source database from a database snapshot.

▶ The more updates to pages in the source database, the bigger your database snapshot sparse files become.

▶ A database snapshot can be done only for an entire database, not for a subset of the database.

▶ No additional changes can be made to a database snapshot. It is read-only and can't even have additional indexes created for it to make queries run faster.

▶ Additional overhead is incurred on update operations on the source database due to the copy-on-write technique (not with SELECT statements).

▶ If you're using a database snapshot to revert (restore) a source database, neither the snapshot nor source database is available while the snapshot is being restored.

▶ The source database cannot be dropped, detached, or restored until all database snapshots are dropped first.

▶ Files of the source database or the snapshot cannot be dropped.

▶ For the database snapshot to be used, the source database must also be online and available (unless the source database is a mirrored database).

▶ The database snapshot must be on the same SQL Server instance as the source database.

▶ Database snapshot files must be on NTFS volumes only (not FAT 32 or RAW partitions).

▶ Full-text indexing is not supported in database snapshots.

▶ If a source database ever goes into a RECOVERY_PENDING status, the database snapshot also becomes unavailable.

▶ If a database snapshot ever runs out of disk space, it is marked as SUSPECT and must be dropped and recreated in order to access it.

29

This may seem like a lot of restrictions and limitations—and it is. It is hoped that Microsoft will address some of these restrictions in a future release, especially the requirement to drop all other database snapshots before reverting to a specific snapshot, but most of these restrictions/limitations have been in place since snapshots were introduced in SQL Server 2005, so it's not looking likely that they will be going away any time soon. These current restrictions may disqualify many folks from getting into the database snapshot business. Others may find database snapshots incredibly useful.

Copy-on-Write Technology

The copy-on-write technology that Microsoft first introduced with SQL Server 2005 is at the core of database snapshot capabilities. In this section, we walk through a typical transactional user's update of data in a source database to illustrate how the copy-on-write technology works.

As you can see in Figure 29.5, an update transaction is initiated against the SourceDB database (labeled A). Before the data is updated in the source database's data page, the change is written to the transaction log (labeled B). The copy-on-write technology also copies the original source database data page in its unchanged state to the sparse data file (also labeled B) and updates the metadata page references in the system catalog (also labeled B) with this movement. After the copy-on-write technology finishes its write on the sparse file, the original update transaction is properly committed, and an acknowledgment is sent back to the user (labeled C). As you can see, using database snapshots adds extra overhead to any transaction that updates, inserts, or deletes data from the source database.

> **NOTE**
>
> Database snapshots cannot be used for any of SQL Server's internal databases—tempdb, master, msdb, or model. Also, database snapshots are supported only in the Enterprise and Developer Editions of SQL Server 2014.

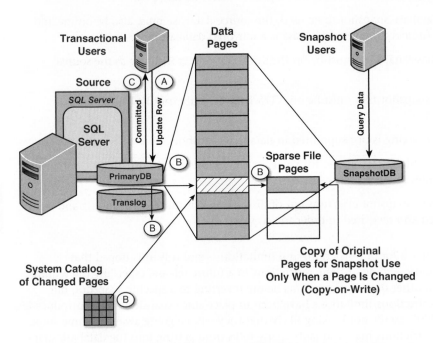

FIGURE 29.5   Using the copy-on-write technology with database snapshots.

When to Use Database Snapshots

As mentioned previously, there are a few basic ways you can use database snapshots effectively. Each use is for a particular purpose, and each has its own benefits. After you have factored in the limitations and restrictions mentioned earlier, you can consider these uses. Let's look at each of them separately.

Reverting to a Snapshot for Recovery Purposes

Probably the most basic usage of database snapshots is decreasing recovery time of a database by restoring a troubled database with a database snapshot—referred to as reverting. As Figure 29.6 shows, one or more regularly scheduled snapshots can be generated during a 24-hour period, effectively providing you with data recovery milestones that can be rapidly used. As you can see in this example, four database snapshots are six hours apart (6:00 a.m., 12:00 p.m., 6:00 p.m., and 12:00 a.m.). Each is dropped and re-created once per day, using the same snapshot name. Any one of these snapshots can be used to recover the source database rapidly in the event of a logical data error (such as rows deleted or a table being dropped). This technique is not supposed to take the place of a good maintenance plan that includes full database backups and incremental transaction log dumps. However, it can be extremely fast to get a database back to a particular milestone.

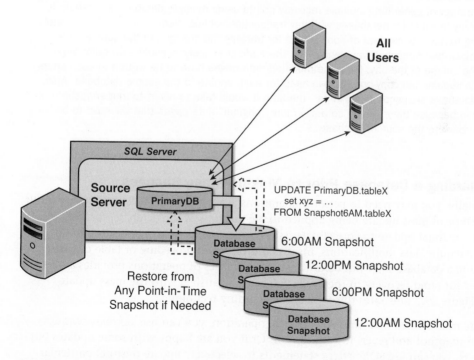

FIGURE 29.6   Basic database snapshot configuration: a source database and one or more database snapshots at different time intervals.

To revert to a particular snapshot interval, you simply use the RESTORE DATABASE command with the FROM DATABASE_SNAPSHOT statement. This is a complete database restore; you cannot limit it to just a single database object. In addition, you must drop all other database snapshots before you can use one of them to restore a database.

As you can also see in Figure 29.6, as an alternative to a complete database restore from a snapshot, a targeted SQL statement could be used instead if you knew exactly what you wanted to restore at the table and row level. You could simply use SQL statements (such as an UPDATE SQL statement or an INSERT SQL statement) from one of the snapshots to selectively apply only the fixes you are sure need to be recovered (reverted). In other words, you don't restore the entire database from the snapshot; you only retrieve some of the snapshot's data using SQL statements and bring the original data row values back into the source database from the snapshot. This is at the row and column level and usually requires quite a bit of detailed analysis before it can be applied to a production database.

It is also possible to use a snapshot to recover a table that someone accidentally dropped. There is a little data loss since the last snapshot, but it is a simple INSERT INTO statement from the latest snapshot before the table drop. So be careful here, but consider the value as well.

> **NOTE**
>
> This strategy of generating multiple recovery points using multiple database snapshots is really only feasible for databases with low transaction volume. Remember, each snapshot is going to have its own set of sparse files for tracking the changes to the source database since that snapshot was generated. The earliest snapshots could grow quite large over the course of the day. Plus, the modified data pages have to be written to each snapshot, increasing the copy-on-write overhead for each update to the source database. Also, as a database snapshot grows larger, the time it would take to revert to that snapshot will increase because there will be so many more "original" data pages that will have to be copied back to the source database.

Safeguarding a Database Prior to Making Mass Changes

Occasionally, you may need to perform operations against your database tables that result in some type of mass update being applied to big portions of the database, for example, running a manual update to correct data issues or deploying a new application build that may require data modifications, inserts, and/or stored procedure or table changes. Generating a database snapshot before any of these types of operations provides a nice safety net for rapid recovery in the event you are not satisfied with the mass update results. Figure 29.7 illustrates this type of safeguarding technique.

If you are not satisfied with the entire update operation, you can use RESTORE DATABASE from the snapshot and revert it to this point. Or if you are happy with some updates but not others, you can use SQL UPDATE statements to selectively update (restore) particular values back to their original values from the snapshot.

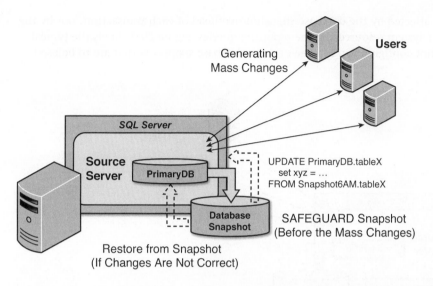

FIGURE 29.7   Creating a before database snapshot prior to scheduled mass updates to a database.

Providing a Testing (or Quality Assurance) Starting Point (Baseline)

In testing and the QA phases of your development life cycle, you often need to conduct tests over and over. These are either logic tests or even performance tests. To aid testing and QA, snapshots can be generated from a test database prior to full testing (create a testing baseline database snapshot) and then the test database can be reverted back to its original state at any point, using that baseline snapshot. This procedure can be done any number of times. Figure 29.8 shows how easy it is to simply create a testing reference point (or synchronization point) with a database snapshot.

You then just run your test scripts or do any manual testing—as much as you want—and then revert back to this starting point rapidly. Then you run more tests again with the same baseline data.

Providing a Point-in-Time Reporting Database

If what you really need is a true point-in-time reporting database from which you can run ad hoc or canned reports, often a database snapshot can serve this purpose much better than resorting to log shipping or data replication. One advantage of using a database snapshot for reporting purposes versus running reports against the primary database is that it avoids any locking contention issues between the report queries and the update transactions because the report queries are executed against a read-only, point-in-time copy of the source database.

However, key to determining when you can use this database snapshot technique is whether the database server instance can effectively support both the reporting workload and the transaction load. You wouldn't want the update transactions against this database to be adversely affected by the database snapshot overhead of each transaction, nor by the consumption of system resources by the reporting queries. Figure 29.9 shows the typical database snapshot configuration for one or more database snapshots that are to be used for reporting.

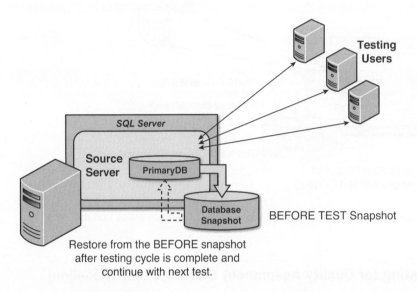

FIGURE 29.8   Establishing a baseline testing database snapshot before running tests and then reverting when finished.

Remember, this is a point-in-time snapshot of the source database. How frequently you need to create a new snapshot is dictated by your reporting requirements for data latency (how old the data can be in these reports).

Providing a Highly Available and Offloaded Reporting Database from a Database Mirror

If you are still using the now deprecated database mirroring feature to improve your system availability, you can also create a database snapshot against this mirrored database and expose the snapshot to your reporting users. Even though the mirrored database cannot be used for any access whatsoever (it is in constant restore mode), SQL Server allows a snapshot to be created against it (as shown in Figure 29.10). This is a very powerful configuration in that a database snapshot against a mirror does not impact the processing load of the principal server—guaranteeing high performance against the principal server. Also, when the database snapshot is isolated over to the mirror server, the performance of the reporting users is also more predictable because they are not competing with the transactional users for resources or locks on the principal server. The only real issues arise when the principal server fails over to the mirror database. You now have both transactional and reporting users using the same database server instance, and the performance of them all is affected.

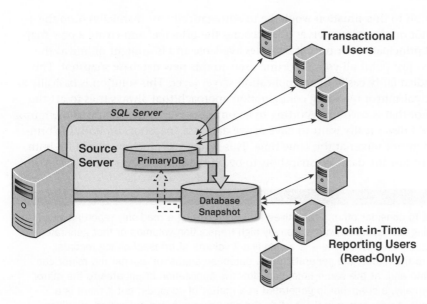

FIGURE 29.9 A point-in-time reporting database via a database snapshot.

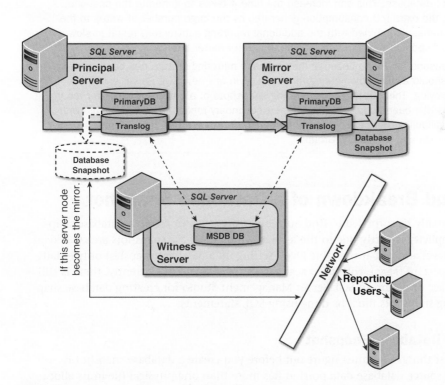

FIGURE 29.10 Creating a database snapshot for reporting against a mirrored database to offload the reporting impact on the principal server.

A possible solution to this situation would be to automatically (or manually) drop the database snapshot on the mirror server if it becomes the principal and create a new snapshot on the old principal server once it becomes available and is brought online as the mirror. You then just point all your reporting users to this new database snapshot. This task can be handled fairly easily in an application server layer. This solution is basically a reciprocal principal/mirror reporting configuration approach that always tries to get the database snapshot that is used for reporting to be on the server that is acting as the mirror server. You would never really want to have active database snapshots on both the principal server and mirror server at the same time. This is way too much overhead for both servers. You want just the database snapshots to be on the mirror server.

> **NOTE**
>
> You may want to consider other alternatives for implementing a read-only reporting environment dealing with systems with extremely high transaction volumes or that generate very large transactions. When there is a significant volume of transaction log records being copied to the mirror, the generation of a database snapshot against the mirror can take a long time and, at the same time, can slow the application of updates to the mirror database. Normally, a snapshot is generated in a matter of seconds, but if there is a large uncommitted transaction in flight when the snapshot is being generated, modifications copied to the snapshot that haven't been committed yet have to be rolled back from the snapshot database. This can increase the time it takes to generate the snapshot. Additionally, the extra I/O consumption generated by the large number of writes to the snapshot database combined with the additional reporting activity may result in slower application of updates to the mirror leading to greater mirror latency.
>
> For these reasons, and also because the database mirroring feature has been deprecated, you should avoid implementing this solution in any new SQL Server environment you are deploying. This strategy of generating snapshots of a database mirror for reporting purposes has been supplanted by the new secondary replica feature available with AlwaysOn Availability Groups. For more information on this feature, see Chapter 45, "SQL Server AlwaysOn and Availability Groups."

Setup and Breakdown of a Database Snapshot

You might actually be surprised to find out how easily you can set up a database snapshot. This simplicity is partly due to the level at which database snapshots are created: at the database level and not at the table level. Setting up a database snapshot only entails running a CREATE DATABASE with the AS SNAPSHOT OF statement. Currently, there is still no user interface or wizard in SQL Server Management Studio for creating database snapshots. Creating snapshots must be done using SQL statements.

Creating a Database Snapshot

One of the first things you must figure out before you create a database snapshot is whether your source database data portion has more than one physical file in its allocation. All of the data file references must be accounted for in the snapshot. To get a list of all of the data files for a database, you can run the following query within the source database:

```
use AdventureWorks2012
go
select name, physical_name from sys.database_files
where type_desc = 'ROWS'
go
```

The data file allocations for this database returned by this query are as follows:

```
name                        physical_name
------------------------    ------------------------------------------
AdventureWorks2012_Data   C:\MSSQL\Data\AdventureWorks2012_Data.mdf
```

When creating a snapshot, you need only specify information about the data files of the database for the snapshot:

```
CREATE DATABASE AdventureWorks2012_6AM_snapshot
ON
 ( NAME = AdventureWorks2012_Data,
    FILENAME= 'C:\mssql\data\Adventureworks2012_6AM.ss'
 )
AS SNAPSHOT OF AdventureWorks2012
go
```

Creating the database snapshot is really that easy. Now let's walk through a simple example showing how to create a series of four database snapshots against the AdventureWorks2012 source database that represent snapshots six hours apart (refer to Figure 29.6). Here is the next snapshot to be run at 12:00 p.m.:

```
CREATE DATABASE AdventureWorks2012_12PM_snapshot
ON
 ( NAME = AdventureWorks2012_Data,
    FILENAME= 'C:\mssql\data\Adventureworks2012_12PM.ss'
 )
AS SNAPSHOT OF AdventureWorks2012
go
```

These represent snapshots at equal time intervals and can be used for reporting or reverting.

NOTE

In the examples presented here, we use a simple naming convention for the database names for snapshots and for the snapshot files themselves. The database snapshot name is the source database name, followed by a qualifying description of what this snapshot represents, followed by the word *snapshot*, all separated with underscores.

For example, a database snapshot that represents a 6:00 a.m. snapshot of the `AdventureWorks2012` database would have this name:

```
"AdventureWorks2012_6AM_snapshot"
```

The snapshot file-naming convention is similar. The name would start with the database name that the snapshot is for (`AdventureWorks2012`, in our example), followed by the data portion indication (for example, data, data1), a short identification of what this snapshot represents (for example, 6AM), and then the filename extension `.ss` to distinguish it from `.mdf` and `.ldf` files. For example, the snapshot filename for the preceding database snapshot would look like this:

```
"AdventureWorks2012_data_6AM.ss"
```

To view these newly created snapshots from the SQL Server instance point of view, using a SQL query against the master.`sys.databases` system catalog, as follows:

```
SELECT name,
       database_id,
       source_database_id, -- source DB of the snapshot
       create_date,
       snapshot_isolation_state_desc
FROM master.sys.databases
WHERE name LIKE 'Adventureworks%'Go
```

This shows the existing source database and the existing database snapshots:

```
name                            database_id source_database_id create_date
snapshot_isolation_state_desc
------------------------------- ------- ---------------- ----------------------------
AdventureWorks2014              5       NULL             2014-10-27 02:28:17.820 OFF
AdventureWorks2012              6       NULL             2014-10-27 18:13:04.853 OFF
AdventureWorks2012_6AM_snapshot 7       6                2014-10-27 18:39:26.260 ON
AdventureWorks2012_12PM_snapshot 8      6                2014-10-27 18:39:36.870 ON
```

Note that `source_database_id` column for the database snapshots contains the database ID of the source database (6).

You can view information on the newly created physical file for the sparse file (for the database snapshot) by querying the `sys.master_files` system catalog:

```
SELECT database_id, file_id, name, physical_name
FROM sys.master_files
WHERE Name = 'AdventureWorks2012_data'
and is_sparse = 1
go
```

Note that we are focusing on only the sparse files for the newly created database snapshot (that is, the `is_sparse = 1` qualification). This query results in the following:

database_id	file_id	name	physical_name
7	1	AdventureWorks2012_Data	C:\mssql\data\Adventureworks2012_6AM.ss
8	1	AdventureWorks2012_Data	C:\mssql\data\Adventureworks2012_12PM.ss

To see the number of bytes that a snapshot sparse file is using, you can issue a series of SQL statements against system catalog views/tables by using `fn_virtualfilestats` and `sys.master_files`. However, the following is a quick-and-dirty stored procedure that should make this task much easier. Just create this stored procedure on your SQL Server instance (in the `master` database), and you can use it to see the size of any database snapshot sparse file on your server (also available in the downloadable SQL script file for this chapter):

```
CREATE PROCEDURE sp_SSU_SNAPSHOT_SIZE
      @DBDATA varchar(255) = NULL
AS
if @DBDATA is not null
   BEGIN
      SELECT B.name as 'Sparse files for Database Name',
             A.DbId, A.FileId, KBOnDisk = BytesOnDisk/1024.0
      FROM fn_virtualfilestats
 (NULL, NULL) A,
            sys.master_files B
      WHERE A.DbID = B.database_id
        and A.FileID = B.file_id
        and B.is_sparse = 1
        and B.name = @DBDATA
   END
ELSE
   BEGIN
      SELECT B.name as 'Sparse files for Database Name',
             A.DbId, A.FileId, KBOnDisk = BytesOnDisk/1024.0
      FROM fn_virtualfilestats (NULL, NULL) A,
            sys.master_files B
      WHERE A.DbID = B.database_id
        and A.FileID = B.file_id
        and B.is_sparse = 1
   END
Go
```

Once the `sp_SSU_SNAPSHOT_SIZE` stored procedure is created, you can run it with or without the name of the data portion of the database for which you have created a snapshot. If you do not supply the data portion name, you see all sparse files and their sizes on the SQL Server instance. The following example shows how to execute this stored procedure to see the sparse file current size for the `AdventureWorks2012_data` portion:

```
EXEC sp_SSU_SNAPSHOT_SIZE 'AdventureWorks2012_Data'
Go
```

29

This returns the number of bytes that the sparse file is using on disk:

```
Sparse files for Database Name DbId   FileId KBOnDisk
------------------------------ ------ ------ ----------
AdventureWorks2012_Data          7      1     2880.000000
AdventureWorks2012_Data          8      1     2880.000000
```

Currently, the sparse file is very small (2880KB) because it was recently created. Little to no source data pages have changed, so it is nearly empty right now. It will start growing as data is updated in the source database and data pages are copied to the sparse file (by the copy-on-write mechanism). You can use the sp_SSU_SNAPSHOT_SIZE stored procedure to keep an eye on the sparse file size.

Once created, the database snapshot is ready for you to use. The following SQL statement selects rows from this newly created database snapshot for a typical point-in-time–based query against the CreditCard table:

```
SELECT [CreditCardID]
     , [CardType]
     , [CardNumber]
     , [ExpMonth]
     , [ExpYear]
     , [ModifiedDate]
  FROM [AdventureWorks2012_6AM_snapshot].[Sales].[CreditCard]
WHERE CreditCardID = 1
Go
This statement delivers the correct point-in-time result rows from the database
snapshot:
CreditCardID CardType    CardNumber      ExpMonth ExpYear ModifiedDate
------------ ----------- --------------- -------- ------- -----------------------
1            SuperiorCard 33332664695310 11       2006    2007-08-30 00:00:00.000
```

You can take a look at how this all looks from SQL Server Management Studio. Figure 29.11 shows the database snapshot database snapshots AdventureWorks2012_6AM_snapshot and AdventureWorks2012_12PM_snapshot along with the source database AdventureWorks2012. It also shows the results of the system queries on these database object properties.

Removing a Database Snapshot

If you want to get rid of a snapshot or overlay a current snapshot with a more up-to-date snapshot, you simply use the DROP DATABASE command and then create it again. The DROP DATABASE command immediately removes the database snapshot entry and all sparse file allocations associated with the snapshot. The following example drops the database snapshot previously created:

```
Use [master]
go
DROP DATABASE AdventureWorks2012_6AM_snapshot
go
```

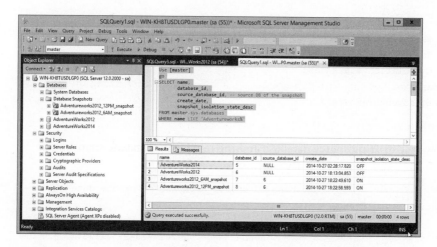

FIGURE 29.11   Viewing Database Snapshot information in SSMS.

If you want, you can also drop (delete) a database snapshot from SQL Server Management Studio by right-clicking the database snapshot entry and choosing the Delete option. However, it's best to do everything with scripts so that you can accurately reproduce the same action over and over.

Reverting to a Database Snapshot for Recovery

If you have a database snapshot defined for a source database, you can use that snapshot to revert the source database to that snapshot's point-in-time milestone. In other words, you consciously overlay a source database with the point-in-time representation of that database (which was generated when you created the snapshot). You must remember that you will lose all data changes that occurred from that point-in-time moment and the current state of the source database. However, this may be exactly what you intend.

Reverting a Source Database from a Database Snapshot

Reverting is just a logical term for using the DATABASE RESTORE command with the FROM DATABASE_SNAPSHOT statement. It effectively causes the point-in-time database snapshot to become the source database. Under the covers, much of this is managed from the system catalog metadata level. However, the results are that the source database will be in exactly the same state as the database snapshot. When you use a database snapshot as the basis of a database restore, all other database snapshots that have the same source database must

29

first be dropped. Again, to see what database snapshots may be defined for a particular
database, you can execute the following query:

```
Use [master]
go
SELECT name,
       database_id as dbid,
       source_database_id as src_dbid, -- source DB of the snapshot
       create_date,
       snapshot_isolation_state_desc
FROM sys.databases
where name like 'Adventureworks%'
Go
```

This query shows the existing source database and the remaining database snapshot, as
follows:

```
name                              database_id source_database_id create_date
snapshot_isolation_state_desc
--------------------------------- -------- -------------- ---------------------------
AdventureWorks2014                5           NULL               2014-10-27 02:28:17.820 OFF
AdventureWorks2012                6           NULL               2014-10-27 18:13:04.853 OFF
Adventureworks2012_12PM_snapshot 8           6                  2014-10-27 18:22:58.593 ON
```

In this example, there is one remaining snapshot against the AdventureWorks2012 database. If there were any other snapshots still present, they would need to be dropped first.
Then you can proceed to restore the source database with the remaining snapshot that
you want. These are the steps:

To revert to the remaining 12 PM snapshot, issue the following RESTORE DATABASE
command:

```
USE [master]
go
RESTORE DATABASE AdventureWorks2012
FROM DATABASE_SNAPSHOT = 'AdventureWorks2012_6AM_snapshot'
go
```

NOTE

Just as if you were restoring the source database from a database backup, the source
database cannot be in use when reverting from a snapshot.

When this restore process is complete, the modified pages in the source database are
overwritten with the snapshot copies so that the source database is reverted to essentially
the same point-in-time as the snapshot database until updates begin to be applied to the
source database again.

Database Snapshots Maintenance and Security Considerations

With regard to database snapshots, several things need to be highly managed: snapshot sparse file size, data latency that corresponds to your users' needs, the location of the sparse files within your physical deployment, the sheer number of database snapshots you are willing to support against a single database instance, and the security and access needs of users of database snapshots.

Security for Database Snapshots

By default, you get the security roles and definitions that you have created in the source database available to you within the database snapshot *except* for roles or individual permissions that you have in the source database used for updating data or objects. This is referred to as "inherited from the source database." These updating rights are not available to you in a database snapshot because a database snapshot is, by nature, read-only. If you have specialized roles or restrictions you want to be present in the database snapshot, you need to define them in the source database, and you get them automatically in the snapshot database. You manage security for the snapshot database from the source database.

Snapshot Sparse File Size Management

Sparse file size is probably the most critical aspect to deal with when managing database snapshots. It is imperative that you keep a close watch on the growing size of any (and all) database snapshot sparse files you create. If your snapshot runs out of space because you didn't manage file size well, it is marked suspect and is no longer available to use. The only path out of this scenario is to drop the snapshot and re-create it. Following are some issues to consider for sparse files:

▶ Monitor sparse files regularly. Make use of stored procedures such as the `sp_SSU_SNAPSHOTSIZE` stored procedure to help with this situation.

▶ Pay close attention to the volatility of the source database. The rate of data change directly translates to the size of the sparse file and how fast it grows. The rule of thumb is to drop and re-create a database snapshot when the sparse file is at around 30% of the size of the source database. Your data latency user requirements may demand a faster rate of drop/re-create.

▶ Isolate sparse files away from the source database data files. You do not want to compete with source database disk I/O if possible. Always try to spread your disk I/O across multiple devices as much as possible.

Number of Database Snapshots per Source Database

In general, you shouldn't have too many database snapshots defined on a database because of the copy-on-write overhead each snapshot requires. However, this all depends on the volatility of the source database and a server's capacity. If there is low volatility and the server is not using much CPU, memory, and disk capacity, your database could more readily support many separate database snapshots at once. If the volatility is high and CPU, memory, and perhaps disk capacity are saturated, you should try and minimize the number of database snapshots generated.

Summary

Database snapshots can be thought of as an enabling capability with many purposes. They are great for fulfilling point-in-time reporting requirements easily, reverting a database to a point in time (recoverability and availability), insulating a database from issues that may arise during mass adhoc updates, and potentially reducing the processing impact of querying against the primary transactional databases. You must remember that database snapshots are point-in-time and read-only. The only way to update a snapshot is to drop it and re-create it. Data latency of this point-in-time snapshot capability must always be made very clear to any of its users.

Database snapshots are snapshots of the entire database, not a subset. This clearly makes data snapshots very different from alternative data access capabilities such as data replication and materialized views. This is certainly a useful extension to SQL Server but should not to be used as a substitute for good old database backups and restores for recoverability purposes. The next chapter, Chapter 30, "Database Maintenance," provides a detailed explanation of the best practices surrounding maintaining a database.

Database Maintenance

Database maintenance is an essential part of database administration that is needed to keep databases healthy. It includes tasks performed after your database is created to ensure the integrity of the data in the database, provide performance improvements, and help keep your database safe.

This chapter examines some of the key tasks that should be included in your database maintenance plan. It discusses the means for creating these plans, including tools such as the Maintenance Plan Wizard that is part of SQL Server 2014. These tools make the creation of a solid database maintenance plan easier and provide a framework that allows you to create the plan once and let automation do the rest of the work.

> **NOTE**
>
> **What Needs to Be Maintained**
>
> The core tasks related to the maintenance of a SQL Server database are backing up the database and log, rebuilding indexes, updating statistics, and running integrity checks against the database. These ongoing, repetitive tasks are best run on a scheduled basis and are the backbone of the maintenance plan. Other tasks related to maintenance involve managing access by the users, maintaining data files, and monitoring performance. These tasks are more apt to be performed on an ad hoc basis when the need arises.

What's New in Database Maintenance

The required database maintenance tasks in SQL Server 2014 have remained the same as in earlier versions, and the tools to perform that maintenance are generally the same as they were in SQL Server 2005. Maintenance plans are still the core tool for performing database maintenance. These plans and the tools to create the plans (such as the Maintenance Plan Wizard) look and behave much like they did in SQL Server 2012.

There are, however, some subtle changes related to the creation of a maintenance plan in SQL Server 2014, including the following:

▶ You can now specify the account in the Maintenance Plan Wizard that the plan will run under.

▶ The screen where you define database backups now contains several tabs for defining your backups. This was all done on one screen in the past. New options that are available on this screen include database compression settings and an option to setup backup encryption.

▶ The Define Rebuild Index Task has new advanced options for handling index types that do not support online index rebuilds. You can now choose to exclude indexes that do not support online indexing or you can choose to rebuild the indexes offline.

One other important note in SQL Server 2014 is that the `sqlmaint` utility has been slotted for removal in the next version of Microsoft SQL Server. `sqlmaint` can be used to run maintenance plans that were created with previous versions of SQL Server. It could be run from the command prompt and was a handy way of scheduling database maintenance.

The Maintenance Plan Wizard

The Maintenance Plan Wizard is a tool that is available in SSMS. It provides an automated means for creating the basic tasks needed to maintain a database. It does not include all the tasks available for use in a maintenance plan but is a great starting point that allows you to quickly generate the basic elements of a good plan.

You launch the Maintenance Plan Wizard by expanding the `Management` node in SSMS and then right-clicking Maintenance Plans and selecting Maintenance Plan Wizard. The Maintenance Plan Wizard is like most other Microsoft wizards in that it presents sequential dialog boxes that allow you to incrementally provide the information needed to create the wizard's objective.

The Maintenance Plan Wizard first displays an introductory dialog box. When you click Next, it displays a dialog box (like the one shown in Figure 30.1) that allows you to specify the name and a description for your maintenance plan. You should choose a naming convention that will allow you to easily identify a maintenance plan and the type of maintenance it is performing. The name is displayed in the Object Explorer tree, and a good naming convention will make it easier to locate the plan you want.

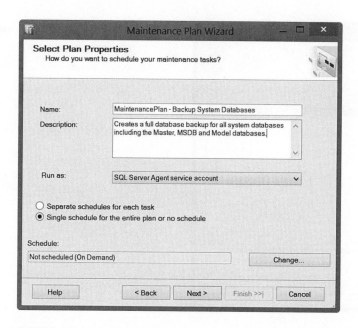

FIGURE 30.1   Setting the Maintenance Plan Properties using the Maintenance Plan Wizard.

The Select Plan Properties screen also allows you to specify the schedule for the maintenance plan. This schedule will be tied to the corresponding scheduled job that is created when the Maintenance Plan Wizard completes. You will find that the scheduling dialog that appears when you click on the Change button is very flexible and consistent with other places in SQL Server where a schedule can be defined.

After you name the maintenance plan and specify the schedule, you can click Next. The dialog box that appears next allows you to select the maintenance tasks you would like to perform on the server. Figure 30.2 shows the Select Maintenance Tasks dialog, with the tasks that are available from the wizard. You can select more than one task for a given plan. As mentioned earlier, the tasks listed in the wizard are not all the tasks available in a maintenance plan.

The dialog box that appears next, as shown in Figure 30.3, allows you to specify the order in which the tasks are executed. Obviously, the order of the tasks can be a critical factor and is dependent on the type of tasks you are running. You can click the Move Up and Move Down buttons to change the order of the tasks.

The dialog boxes discussed so far are consistent for all the maintenance plans. The dialog boxes that follow are dependent on the tasks selected for the plan. Each task has a relevant set of properties that are displayed for entry in a subsequent dialog box. The following sections cover some of the common maintenance tasks and the wizard screens that relate to them.

30

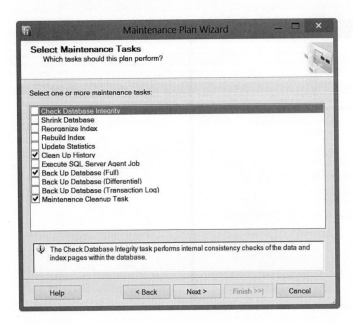

FIGURE 30.2   Selecting maintenance tasks in the Maintenance Plan Wizard.

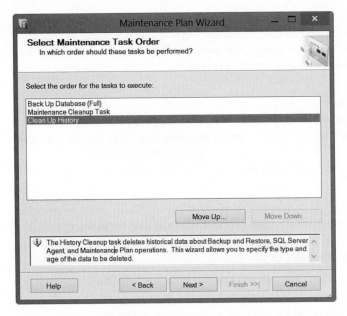

FIGURE 30.3   Selecting the order of the maintenance tasks in the Maintenance Plan Wizard.

Backing Up Databases

Backing up databases is the most basic element of a maintenance plan—and probably the most important part. The importance of backups and the role they play are discussed in detail in Chapter 11, "Database Backup and Restore," but basically, backups are needed to help limit the amount of data loss. For example, in the event of a disk drive failure, database backups can be used to restore the database data that was located on that drive.

The database backup options available via a maintenance plan include full, differential, and transaction log backups. The type of backup you select for a plan is heavily dependent on the type of environment you are maintaining and the type of database you are backing up. Databases that have very few changes may only need a nightly full backup and do not require transaction log or differential backups.

In most cases, it is a good idea to take a full backup of your system and user databases each night. Figure 30.4 shows the general backup options the wizard displays for a full backup. This is the first of 3 tabs that are available in SQL Server 2014. In prior versions all the information related to the full backups was displayed on one screen.

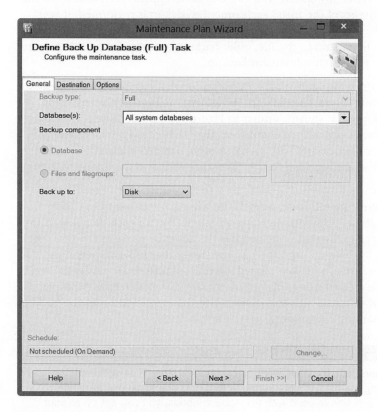

FIGURE 30.4   Full backup—General Tab.

To set the General properties for a full backup, you need to first define the databases you want to back up. You select the databases by using the Databases drop-down at the top of the screen. This drop-down is unique in that it gives you a variety of radio button options rather than just a simple list. You can choose to back up all databases, all system databases, or all user databases, or you can select specific databases.

After you select the database(s) you want to back up, you must select a destination for the backup files. The General properties tab includes a Back up to drop down which defines the type of destination for the backup. The options available in the drop down include Disk and Tape, which were available in prior versions. The third option is URL, which is new to SQL Server 2014 and allows Windows Azure Blob storage service to be used as a backup destination.

Click on the Destination tab to enter the rest of the information related to the backup destination as shown in Figure 30.5. The destination includes the type of media (that is, tape or disk) and the file or files on that medium. The option Back Up Databases Across One or More Files allows you to specify one or more fixed files that the database backup will always be written to. With this option, you can choose to append each backup to the file(s) or overwrite the contents of the file(s) each time the backup is performed. If you choose to overwrite the backup each time, you have only the latest backup available for restoration. If you choose to append to the file, older backups are retained on this file, and the file continues to grow with each subsequent backup.

Keep in mind that the options available on the Destination tab are driven by the `Back up to selection` that was made on the General tab. When Disk or Tape is selected as the destination, the Destination tab is shown, similar to Figure 30.5. If URL is selected as the Destination, then the relevant options are enabled on the Destination tab including SQL credential, Azure storage container, and URL prefix. A more detailed explanation of SQL Server Backup to URL is discussed in Chapter 19, "Working with and Deploying to Azure SQL Database."

The preferred option for creating full backups with the wizard is the option to Create a Backup File for Every Database. This option creates a separate file for each database in the maintenance plan. The backup file that is created has the database name as the first part of the filename, followed by `_backup_` and then a time stamp that indicates when the backup was created. For example, a backup named `master_FullDBBackup_201202100549.BAK` would be a backup file created using this option for the `Master` database. Multiple versions of backups can be retained with this option, and the identification of the backup is simple because of the naming convention.

CAUTION

You should use the option Back Up Databases Across One or More Files with caution. The pitfall with overwriting the file with this option is that only one backup is available for restoration. When this option is used with the Append option, you can eat up all your disk space if the file is not cleaned up. In addition, if multiple databases are backed up with the plan, all these backups will be spread across the file or files specified for the destination. A separate backup for each database is not created with this option. This can lead to confusion and complicate the restoration process.

Generally speaking, you should steer clear of backing up the database to a single file or set of files. Instead, you should choose the option Create a Backup File for Every Database. This option has fewer pitfalls and requires little attendance.

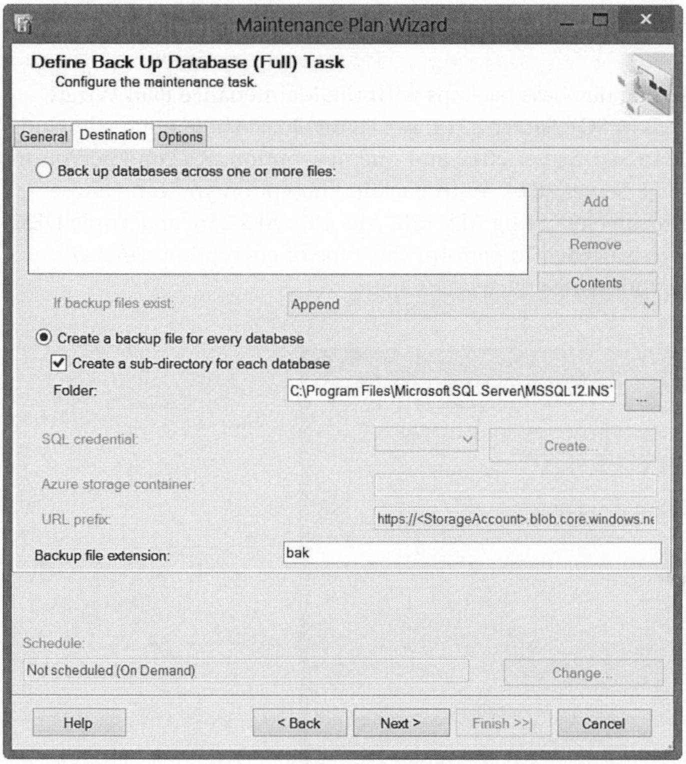

FIGURE 30.5   Full backup—Destination Tab.

When you use the Create a Backup File for Every Database option, you need to specify a folder for the database backups to be written to. You can use the default folder, or you can change it to a folder of your choice. It is a good practice to choose a folder on a drive that is different from the drive where your database files reside. Having backups on the same drive as your data could be a big problem if that drive fails and your only backups are on that drive. If you select the option Create a Sub-directory for Each Database, each database has a separate subfolder under the folder specified for the backup.

30

CAUTION

The main pitfall associated with the option Create a Backup File for Every Database is that many backup files can be created and are not automatically deleted by default. This point has been mentioned already, but it is a critical consideration. The good news is that you can add the deletion of the older backups to the maintenance plan using the Maintenance Plan Wizard. To accomplish this, you need to select the Maintenance Cleanup task and provide the desired retention information that determines when the older backups are removed.

The options available for creating database backups with the Maintenance Plan Wizard were moved to the Options tab in SQL Server 2014; see Figure 30.6. These options include a number that were available in SQL Server 2012 and one new option, Backup Encryption, which was introduced with SQL Server 2014. With Backup Encryption you can choose from several encryption algorithms including AES 128, AES 192, AES 256, and Triple DES. A certificate or asymmetric key is needed to perform this type of encryption. Further details related to Backup Encryption are covered in Chapter 11.

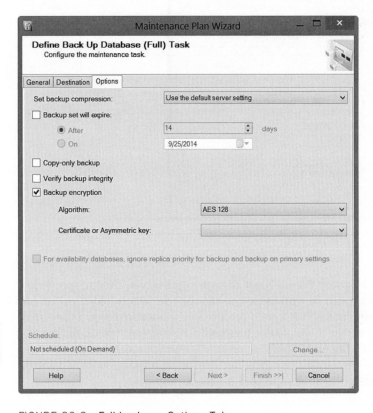

FIGURE 30.6   Full backup—Options Tab.

An option to define the compression for the database backup file was introduced in SQL Server 2008. The Set Backup Compression drop-down at the top of the screen determines whether compression will be used. If the default for the server is set to compress backup or the specific option Compress Backup is selected, the backup file is created in a compressed format that will reduce the size of the backup file and save disk space. The trade-off when using compressed backups is that the creation of these backups takes additional CPU resources during their creation. However, the additional CPU processing time is typically offset by the faster I/O as a result of the reduced size of the backup file.

NOTE

In SQL Server 2014, compressed backups can only be performed in the Enterprise, Developer, Business Intelligence, and Standard Edition. Every edition of SQL Server 2008 and later can restore compressed backups, however.

The next two options on the screen allow you to define an expiration on the backup set and/or create a copy-only backup. The Backup set will expire check box and related fields specify when the backup set can be overwritten. The copy-only backup option allows for a backup to be taken without disrupting the backup chain.

Another useful option on this screen is Verify Backup Integrity. If you select this option, SQL Server checks the integrity of the backup files that were written as part of the backup operation. Selecting this option extends the execution time for the backup plan but is generally a good idea to ensure that you have a viable backup for recovery. It is particularly useful when backups have been written across multiple files. Unfortunately, the backup task does not allow you to utilize the checksum options available with the SQL Server 2014 BACKUP command, but the basic VERIFY option suffices in most instances.

Checking Database Integrity

The Define Database Check Integrity Task screen of the Maintenance Plan Wizard, shown in Figure 30.7, allows you to schedule the database consistency command DBCC CHECKDB, which checks the data pages for inconsistencies and is a good tool for ensuring that a database is healthy. The integrity checks can be made before each backup or on an independent schedule.

The options available for checking database integrity via the wizard are limited.

Checking the Include Indexes check box causes integrity checks to be performed on the index pages as well. Checking the index pages for each table extends the amount of time the task runs, but it is the most thorough way to perform an integrity check. If problems are found, you can run the DBCC CHECKDB command manually with additional options to repair the problems. In some cases, the problems cannot be fixed without the possibility of data loss. You should consider contacting Microsoft support if you receive consistency errors in a critical database.

30

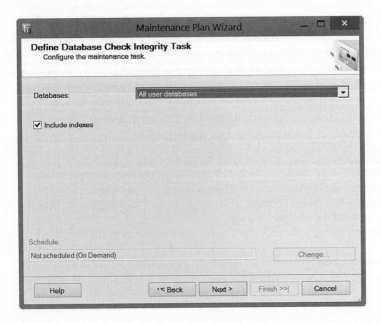

FIGURE 30.7   The Define Database Check Integrity Task screen of the Maintenance Plan Wizard.

Shrinking Databases

The Define Shrink Database Task page of the Maintenance Plan Wizard, shown in Figure 30.8, can be useful for keeping the size of your databases manageable. As its name implies, this task is used to reduce the overall size of a database. This task's execution is essentially the equivalent to running the DBCC SHRINKDATABASE command, and it contains task options that mirror the options available with the DBCC command.

The setting Shrink Database When It Grows Beyond specifies the overall database size that must be exceeded for the shrink operation to occur. You set the size in megabytes, and it must be a whole number. If the database, including data and log files, is smaller than this size, the shrink operation does not occur.

The remaining options determine how the shrink operation runs when the shrink threshold is exceeded. The Amount of Free Space to Remain After Shrink option determines how much space is left in the database files after the shrink operation is finished. This is a target percentage and may not be feasible if the amount of disk space is limited. SQL Server does its best to achieve the target percentage, but it is not guaranteed. Generally, in environments where you have abundant disk space, it is best to leave at least 10% free after the operation so that the database can grow without the need for expanding the size of the database files.

The last settings on the screen determine how free space beyond the target percentage is handled. For example, let's assume that a large number of rows were deleted from a database and the target free space percentage is set to 10%. The shrink operation is run and is able to shrink the database such that 40% is now free. You can choose to retain in the database files the 30% beyond the target that is free by selecting the Retain Freed Space in Database Files option. Choosing this option is the same as running the DBCC SHRINK DATABASE command with the NOTRUNCATE option. With this option, you do not see any changes to the size of the database files, and the free space on the disk remains unchanged.

FIGURE 30.8   The Define Shrink Database Task page of the Maintenance Plan Wizard.

The other option, Return Freed Space to Operating System, can reduce the size of the database files and return that space to the operating system. This option utilizes the TRUNCATEONLY option that comes with the DBCC SHRINK DATABASE command and is the option needed to free up disk space on a server.

TIP

Running the Shrink Database task for every database is generally not recommended. With the Shrink Database task, the database is condensed so that the data is located on contiguous pages in the database data file(s). This involves the movement of pages from one part of the file to another. This movement can cause fragmentation in tables and indexes. The fragmentation can, in turn, cause performance problems and undo work that may have been done with other tasks, such as rebuilding the indexes.

The other main problem with shrinking the database relates to the cost of expanding the database at a later time. For example, let's say you have a database that has grown to 1GB. You shrink the database so that it is now only 800MB, but normal use of the database causes it to expand again. The expansion of the database files can be expensive

30

and cause performance problems during the actual expansion, especially on high-volume production systems. In addition, the constant shrinking and expanding of the database files results in excessive fragmentation of the database files themselves within the file system.

The best solution is to purchase the appropriate amount of disk space and size the database appropriately so that the database files do not need to expand frequently and the shrink operation is not needed. This is easier said than done, but it is the right solution nonetheless.

Maintaining Indexes and Statistics

Maintaining indexes and statistics is essential in most database environments, especially those that have frequent changes to the data. These changes can cause tables and their indexes to become fragmented and inefficient. These types of environments can also lead to outdated statistics on indexes. Outdated statistics can cause the query engine to make less-than-optimal choices when determining the best access path to the data.

The maintenance of indexes and statistics is facilitated through the use of three different tasks in the Maintenance Plan Wizard: Reorganize Index, Rebuild Index, and Update Statistics. Using the Reorganize Index task is equivalent to running the ALTER INDEX REORGANIZE command. This task defragments and compacts clustered and nonclustered indexes on tables and views. This helps improve index-scanning performance and should improve overall response time. The operation is always done online and is also equivalent to running the ALTER INDEX REBUILD command.

Figure 30.9 shows the screen you use to define the Reorganize Index task. This screen allows you to select tables, views, or tables and views. You can also select specific tables or views that you want to reorganize. The Compact Large Objects option is equivalent to ALTER INDEX LOB_COMPACTION = ON. It causes data in large object (LOB) data types, such as image or text objects, to be compacted.

The Reorganize Index task migrates the rows in the leaf-level pages so that they match the logical ordering of the index. This behavior improves performance, but it is not as extensive as the Rebuild Index task, which is equivalent to the ALTER INDEX REBUILD command. It is also equivalent to the deprecated DBCC DBREINDEX command. When the Rebuild Index task is executed, it rebuilds the indexes from scratch. This rebuilding can achieve the best performance results, but it also has the most impact on users of the database.

Figure 30.10 shows the options available for rebuilding an index with the Maintenance Plan Wizard.

FIGURE 30.9   The Reorganize Index task options in the Maintenance Plan Wizard.

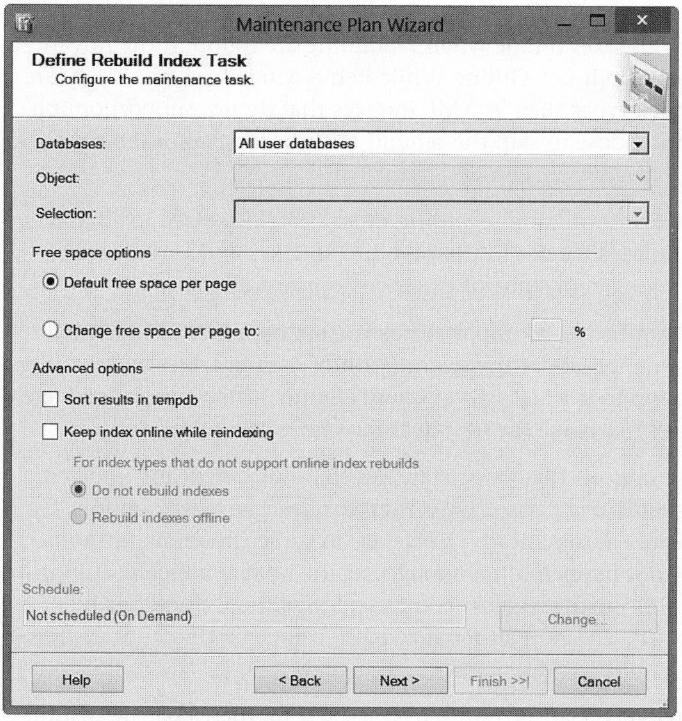

FIGURE 30.10   The Rebuild Index task options in the Maintenance Plan Wizard.

The options for rebuilding are separated into two sections: Free Space Options and Advanced Options. The Free Space Options section pertains to the amount of free space left in the index pages after the rebuild operation completes. This free space is defined by the fill factor for the index. When the Reorganize Pages with the Default Amount of Free Space option is used, the fill factor is reset to the value used when the index was created. The other option, Change Free Space per Page Percentage To, allows you to choose a new fill factor value to be used for all indexes that have been selected for the rebuild operation.

The following advanced Rebuild Index task options are available:

▶ **Sort Results in `tempdb`**—This option is equivalent to the `SORT_IN_TEMPDB` option for the index. It causes `tempdb` to be used to store intermediate results while rebuilding the index. If this option is not used, these intermediate results are stored in the database in which the index resides. Storing the results in `tempdb` can help prevent unnecessary growth of the user database in which the index is being rebuilt. It can also improve performance of the rebuild option by spreading I/O across disk devices if tempdb resides on separate physical drives from where the database files reside.

▶ **Keep Index Online While Reindexing**—This option, available only in the Enteprise and Developer editions of SQL Server, is equivalent to the `ONLINE` option for the index. It allows users to access the underlying table and associated indexes during the index rebuild operation. If this option is not used, the index rebuild is on offline operation, and a table lock is held on the table that is having its indexes rebuilt.

Two options related to keeping indexes online when rebuilding are found in the Advanced Options section just below the Keep Index Online While Reindexing check box. They are useful when a database has index types such as XML indexes that do not support online index operations. You can now choose to skip the rebuild of these indexes or rebuild them offline.

These index options and further information regarding indexes are discussed in Chapter 22, "Creating and Managing Indexes." Refer to Chapter 32, "Indexes and Performance," for details on the performance impact of some of the index options discussed.

The maintenance of statistics can be just as important as the maintenance of indexes on a table. Statistics contain information about the distribution of data in tables and indexes and provide valuable information to the SQL Server query engine. When the statistics are outdated, the query engine may not make the best decisions for getting the data.

Fortunately, there are database options that cause statistics to be automatically updated. The `AUTO UPDATE STATISTICS` and `AUTO UPDATE STATISTICS ASYNCHRONOUSLY` options cause index statistics to be created automatically. However, in some situations the automatic update of statistics does not happen often enough, or the update happens at inopportune times and can cause performance issues. You can address these situations by scheduling the updating of statistics via a maintenance plan, using the Update Statistics task.

Figure 30.11 shows the Maintenance Plan Wizard screen for setting the Update Statistics task options.

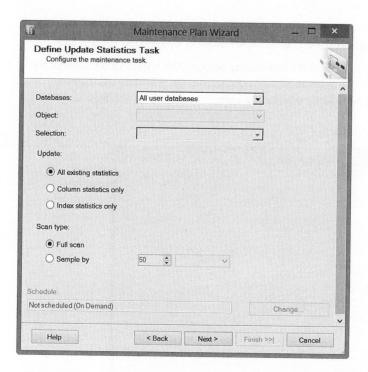

FIGURE 30.11   The Update Statistics task options in the Maintenance Plan Wizard.

The top portion of the Define Update Statistics Task screen is much like the option screens for maintaining indexes. You can choose the type of objects (tables or views) on which you want to update statistics, or you can focus on specific tables or views. The Update options at the bottom of the screen identify the types of statistics to be updated. If the All Existing Statistics option is selected, statistics for both indexes and columns are updated. Statistics on columns exist if the AUTO CREATE STATISTICS option has been set to ON or the statistics were manually created. The other two update options on the screen allow you to focus the update of statistics on columns only or indexes only.

Scheduling a Maintenance Plan

One of the greatest features of a maintenance plan is that you can schedule it. Scheduling takes manual work off your plate and provides consistency that might be missed if the plan had to be run manually. History is kept for each of the scheduled executions, which provides an audit trail, and notifications can be tied to the scheduled plans to allow a user to respond to failures or other results from the plan.

A schedule can be created for an entire maintenance plan, or individual schedules can be created for each task in the plan. The scheduling selection is available on the Select Plan Properties screen, which is one of the first screens displayed while using the Maintenance Plan Wizard (refer to Figure 30.1). Choose the Separate Schedules for Each Task option to create a schedule for each task. The default option is Single Schedule for the Entire Plan or

30

No Schedule. If you choose the option for separate schedules, the Schedule Change button is enabled on the task definition screen, and this schedule is tied to that specific task.

Both scheduling options utilize the same scheduling screen. The screen to set scheduling options, shown in Figure 30.12, appears when you click on the Schedule Change button. This screen contains the same flexible scheduling features available in the SQL Server Agent.

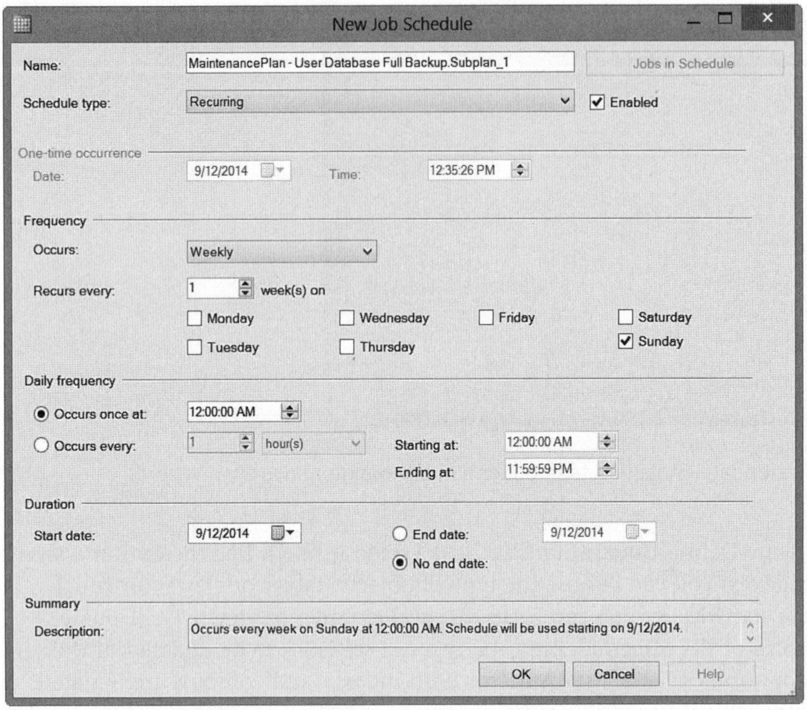

FIGURE 30.12   Scheduling options in the Maintenance Plan Wizard.

When a maintenance plan is saved, a scheduled SQL Server Agent job with the same name as the maintenance plan is created. The job schedule defined for the maintenance plan is applied to the scheduled job, and the SQL Server Agent manages the execution of the job, based on the schedule. Scheduling changes made to the maintenance plan are automatically reflected in the scheduled job. In addition, if the name of the maintenance plan is changed, the name of the scheduled job is changed as well. If an attempt is made to delete the scheduled job related to the maintenance plan, an error is returned, disallowing the deletion.

> **TIP**
>
> Scheduling in the Maintenance Plan Wizard is limited to one schedule per plan or task depending on which option you choose. You can surpass this limitation by adding additional schedules to the scheduled job associated with the maintenance plan. To do so, you simply open the associated scheduled job located in the `SQL Server Agent` node in SSMS and create the additional schedules. This capability is handy when you want a varied execution, such as a weekly schedule combined with daily executions of the same plan.

The scheduled job associated with a maintenance plan executes an SSIS package. Figure 30.13 shows an example of the scheduled job step for a SQL Server 2014 maintenance plan.

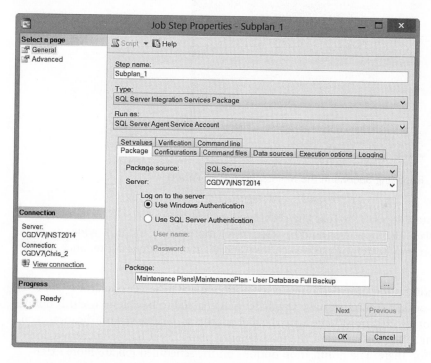

FIGURE 30.13   Scheduled job step for a maintenance plan.

The utilization of SSIS in the execution of maintenance plans was a significant change in SQL Server 2005. SSIS provides added workflow capabilities and extends the feature set for maintenance plans. The scheduled job step that executes an SSIS package for the maintenance plan shows some of the options and flexibility of SSIS, but the real power is in the maintenance plan editor and the Business Intelligence Design Studio (BIDS) used to manage all SSIS packages. Chapter 47, "SQL Server Integration Services," provides further details on SSIS. The maintenance plan editor is discussed in the following section.

30

An integral part of a scheduled maintenance plan is the notification and reporting capabilities. The Select Report Options screen is displayed at the end of the Maintenance Plan Wizard (see Figure 30.14).

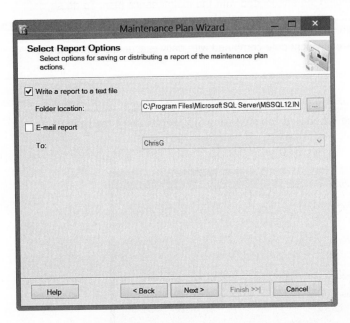

FIGURE 30.14   Reporting options in the Maintenance Plan Wizard.

The option Write a Report to a Text File provides details about the execution of each maintenance plan. This option should be selected for most plans, and it provides excellent information for researching past executions and diagnosing any maintenance plan failures.

The E-mail Report option provides a means for notifying a SQL Server operator when a task completes or fails. You must have Database Mail enabled to be able to use this option, and the operator selected must have a valid email address to receive the notification. You can also edit the job associated with the maintenance plan after it has been created and set up notification there. The notification options on the scheduled job are more extensive than those in the Maintenance Plan Wizard.

CAUTION

If you have a maintenance plan generate a report, you need to make sure you have a means for cleaning up the files. The wizard does not create a plan that deletes the older report files. You can address this situation by modifying the plan after the wizard has created it and adding a Maintenance Cleanup task. This same task can be used to delete old database backup files. The modification of a maintenance plan and addition of the Maintenance Cleanup task are discussed in the following section.

Managing Maintenance Plans Without the Wizard

You can create or modify maintenance plans in SQL Server 2014 without using the Maintenance Plan Wizard. To create a new maintenance plan without the wizard, right-click the `Maintenance Plan` node in the Object Explorer and select New Maintenance Plan. You are prompted for a maintenance plan name and then taken to the Design tab for the maintenance plan. The Design tab consists of a properties section at the top of the screen and a plan designer surface that is empty for a new maintenance plan.

Existing maintenance plans are displayed in the Design tab when you right-click the plan and select Modify. Figure 30.15 shows the Design tab for a maintenance plan that was created with the Maintenance Plan Wizard to back up the system databases.

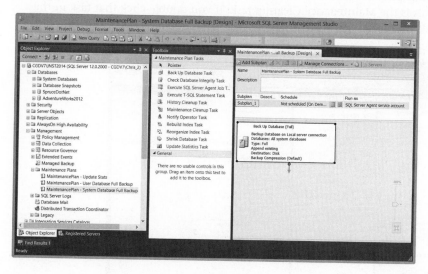

FIGURE 30.15   The maintenance plan Design tab.

The plan designer surface on the Design tab has drag-and-drop capabilities that allow you to add maintenance tasks to your plan. The available tasks are located in the Toolbox component. The Toolbox and the related tasks are shown in Figure 30.15 in the middle portion of the screen. To add a tool from the Toolbox, you drag the item from the Toolbox to the plan designer surface. Alternatively, you can double-click the task, and the task appears on the plan designer surface.

On the plan designer surface, you can move each of the tasks around, link them to other tasks, and edit them by double-clicking them. You can also right-click a task to edit it, group it with other tasks, autosize it, and gain access to other task options. You can right-click an empty section of the plan designer surface to add annotations or comments that provide additional information about the task or the overall plan.

30

> **NOTE**
>
> The dialog boxes displayed when you edit a task are unique for each task. The available maintenance plan tasks display an options screen like the one displayed during the execution of the Maintenance Plan Wizard. This provides consistency that is in place regardless of where the task is defined.

Adding a task to an existing maintenance plan is a good starting point to become familiar with the workings of the Design tab. Consider, for example, the maintenance plan shown in Figure 30.15. This plan, which was initially created with the Maintenance Plan Wizard, is used to create full database backups of all the system databases. One critical aspect that is missing from this plan is a task to remove older database backups. The task that can help you with this is the Maintenance Cleanup task. If you double-click that task in the Toolbox, the task is added to the plan designer surface, as shown in Figure 30.16.

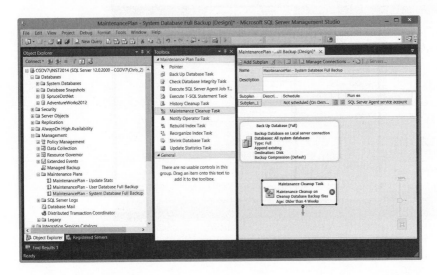

FIGURE 30.16   Adding a task to the plan designer surface.

After you add a task to the plan designer surface, you need to configure it. Note that a small red X icon appears on the right side of the task if the task has not yet been configured. To configure the Maintenance Cleanup task, double-click it on the plan designer surface. Figure 30.17 shows the screen that appears so you can configure the Maintenance Cleanup task.

You can use the Maintenance Cleanup task to clean up old backup files or maintenance plan text reports. The deletion of older backup files is particularly important because database backups tend to be large files and can use up a significant amount of disk space. The File Location section of the screen enables you to delete a specific file, or you can delete files in a folder based on search criteria. In most cases, you want to search the folder to delete older files.

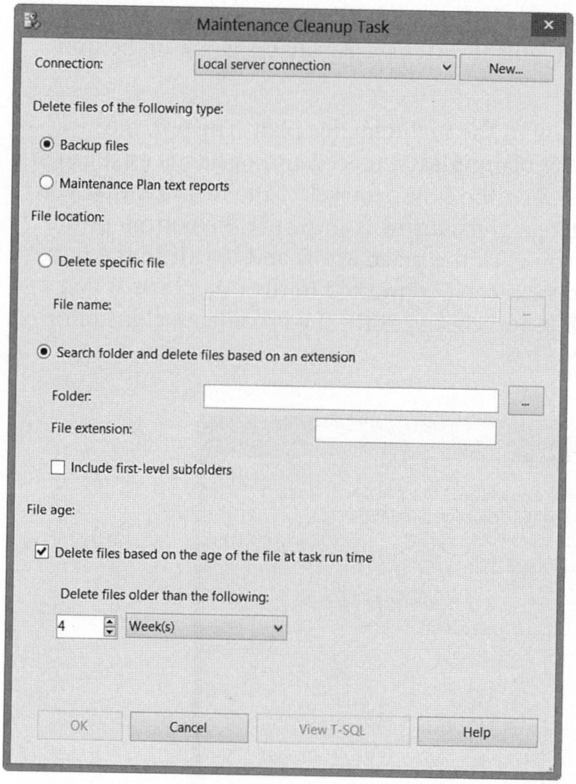

FIGURE 30.17   Configuring the Maintenance Cleanup task.

When cleaning up database backup files, you typically specify the file extension BAK. If you chose to write each database's backups to a separate folder, you should choose the Include First-Level Subfolders options, which allows you to search all first-level subfolders that exist under the folder specified. This simplifies the cleanup process and eliminates the need to have a separate cleanup task for each subfolder.

In the last section of the configuration screen for the Maintenance Cleanup task, you specify how old a file must be in order to be deleted. The default is four weeks, but you can adjust this setting to the desired time frame by using the related drop-downs. If you uncheck Delete Files Based on the Age of the File at Task Run Time, all files in the folder or subfolders are deleted, regardless of age.

NOTE

The deletion of database backup files is not based on the file dates or the name of the backup file. The Maintenance Cleanup task uses a procedure named `xp_delete_file` that examines the database backup and time the backup was created. Renaming the database backup file does not affect its inclusion in the deletion process.

30

After configuring the options for the Maintenance Cleanup task, you can click the View T-SQL button at the bottom of the screen. This feature reveals what is going on behind the scenes when the plan executes.

When you click OK, the task is ready to use in the maintenance plan. The task runs in parallel with the other tasks defined in the plan unless a precedence or link is established between the tasks. To establish a link between the tasks, you select the first task that you want to execute. When the task is selected, a green arrow is shown at the bottom of the task's box in the plan designer surface. You click the green arrow and drag it to the task that you want to run next. The green arrow is then connected to the other task. If you double-click the green arrow (or right-click and choose Edit), the Precedence Constraint Editor appears, as shown in Figure 30.18.

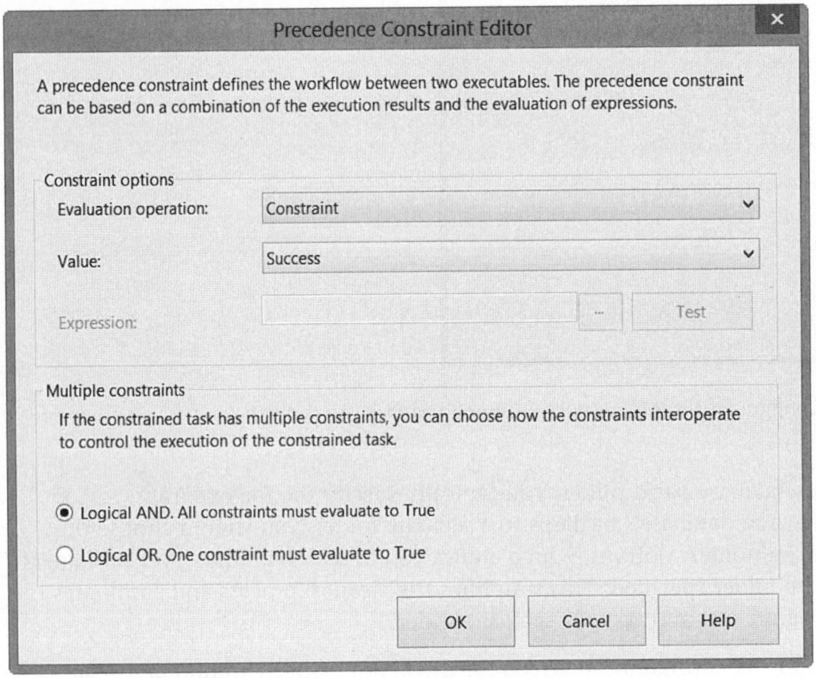

FIGURE 30.18   The Precedence Constraint Editor.

The paragraph at the top of the Precedence Constraint Editor gives a good description of what a precedence constraint is. In short, it can link tasks together based on the results of their execution. For example, if a backup database task succeeds, a Maintenance Cleanup task can be defined to run next. You can also set the constraint value so that the next task will run only if the first task fails, or you can have the next task run based on the prior task's completion, regardless of whether it succeeds or fails. In addition, you can link multiple tasks together with precedence. You define the logical relationship between tasks in the Multiple Constraints section of the Precedence Constraint Editor.

The workflow and relationships that can be defined between tasks for a maintenance plan are extensive and beyond the scope of this chapter. Many of the workflow concepts are similar to those of the SSIS designer in SQL Server 2014.

Executing a Maintenance Plan

Maintenance plans that have been scheduled run automatically according to the schedule defined. You can also run maintenance plans manually by right-clicking a maintenance plan and selecting Execute or by selecting the SQL Server Agent job associated with the maintenance plan and starting the job. The execution behavior is different, depending on the means you use. If you choose to run the maintenance plan from the Management node, the SSIS package is launched, and the Execute Maintenance Plan window displays the current status of the plan execution.

If you run the SQL Server Agent job to execute the maintenance plan, a dialog box indicating the execution status of the job appears. The dialog does not indicate success for the maintenance plan until the entire maintenance plan has completed. The dialog box for the job can be closed, and the job will still continue to run. The Execute Maintenance Plan window, on the other hand, does not have an option to close it, and it must stay open until the plan completes.

There are two other means for monitoring the execution of maintenance plans. The Job Activity Monitor shows a status of execution while a maintenance plan is executing. You can set the refresh settings on the Job Activity Monitor to auto-refresh for the desired increment. You can also monitor the execution by establishing a connection to the SSIS server in SSMS. To establish an SSIS connection in SSMS, you click the Connect drop-down in the Object Explorer and choose Integration Services. Figure 30.19 shows an example of the Object Explorer with an Integration Services connection.

The Integration Services connection in the Object Explorer shows the packages that are running in addition to the packages that have been created. If you expand the Stored Packages node and navigate to the MSDB node, you see a node named Maintenance Plans that shows all the SSIS packages that have been created. You can also edit the package with SQL Server Data Tools (SSDT). SSDT is the replacement for the SQL Server 2008 Business Intelligence Development Studio (BIDS). The details of SSDT are beyond the scope of this chapter. See Chapter 47 for more information on SSDT and other Integration Services features.

> **NOTE**
>
> SSIS does not need to be installed on the SQL Server machine to be able to create and execute maintenance plans. In the initial release of SQL Server 2005, this was a requirement but was changed with SQL Server 2005 SP2. This change carried over to later versions of SQL Server, and maintenance plans are now fully functional with the SQL Server Database Services installation.

30

FIGURE 30.19   The Object Explorer with an Integration Services connection.

Maintenance Without a Maintenance Plan

You can perform database maintenance without the use of the built-in maintenance plans that come with SQL Server. The additional complexity in SQL Server 2014 may steer some people away from the use of these plans. In addition, these plans cannot be easily scripted, so deployment to multiple environments is not straightforward.

Database maintenance that is performed without a maintenance plan is often performed using custom scripts or stored procedures that execute the T-SQL commands to perform the maintenance. Often these maintenance commands or custom scripts are then scheduled to run on a regular basis by manually setting up jobs within the SQL Server Agent job scheduler in SQL Server Management Studio. (For more information on setting up and scheduling jobs in SQL Server Agent, see Chapter 13, "SQL Server Agent.")

Setting up maintenance tasks manually is a viable option, especially for the more experienced DBA because it requires additional development work and familiarity with the maintenance commands and options. However, even the experienced DBA should consider using maintenance plans because maintenance tasks set up manually may lack the integration with other SQL Server components that is offered with the SQL Server 2014 maintenance plans.

Database Maintenance Policies

Policy-Based Management, a new management feature introduced in SQL Server 2008, allows you to manage your SQL Server instances through clearly defined policies, reducing the potential for administrative errors or oversight. The policy-based framework implements the policies you defined via a Policy Engine, SQL Server Agent jobs, SQLCLR, DDL triggers, and Service Broker. You can choose to have the policies you defined be applied or evaluated against a single server or a group of servers, thus improving the scalability of monitoring and administration.

Policy-Based Management allows you to prescribe the way you want your databases maintained, and the system will help ensure things stay that way. Essentially, Policy-Based Management allows you to define rules for one or more SQL Servers and evaluate them. The goal of this feature is to make it easier for you to manage one or more servers by notifying you when servers are out of compliance with the database maintenance policies you have defined.

For example, you could define a policy to ensure that transaction log backups are being performed on the appropriate intervals on your OLTP databases. Policy-Based Management allows you to determine when one of your databases is not in compliance with your log backup policy. You can set up this policy to be evaluated on demand or via a schedule.

For more information on defining and using policies, see Chapter 14, "SQL Server Policy-Based Management."

Summary

Establishing a database maintenance plan is important. Just like your car or your home, a database needs maintenance to keep working properly. The powerful features available with the SQL Server 2014 maintenance plans and Maintenance Plan Wizard make the creation of a robust maintenance plan relatively easy. If you establish your maintenance plans early in the life of your databases, you will save yourself time and aggravation in the long run.

Chapter 31, "Understanding SQL Server Data Structures," delves further into the importance of SQL Server Data Structures. The physical files associated with databases, how tables and indexes are placed in filegroups, and how rows in tables are stored in a database are just some of the topics covered in the next chapter.

30

PART V

SQL Server Performance and Optimization

IN THIS PART

Understanding SQL Server Data Structures

A number of factors affect SQL Server performance. One of the key factors is your table and index design; poor table and index design can result in excessive I/O and poor performance. To aid in developing a good table and index design in an effort to improve SQL Server performance by minimizing I/O, you need to have a good understanding of SQL Server data structures and indexes.

In this chapter, you learn about the underlying structures of databases, tables, rows, and indexes and how SQL Server maintains index and data structures because this information provides a basis for understanding the performance of your tables and indexes. This chapter discusses the storage structures in SQL Server and how these storage structures are maintained and managed. This information should help give you a better understanding of the issues and factors that influence good table and index design.

What's New for Data Structures

There are no significant changes to data structures in SQL Server 2014 except for the addition of updateable clustered columnstore indexes and memory-optimized tables and indexes. In SQL Server 2012, columnstore indexes were nonclustered only and were not updateable. In SQL Server 2014, clustered columnstore index is updateable, so your workloads can perform insert, update, and delete operations on clustered columnstore indexes. This chapter covers the changes to columnstore indexes available in SQL Server 2014.

memory-optimized tables are part of the new In-Memory OLTP feature in SQL Server 2014. In-Memory OLTP is a memory-optimized database engine integrated into the SQL Server engine and is designed as a means to significantly improve OLTP performance. There are differences in the storage structure of memory-optimized tables and disk based tables. These differences are covered in detail in Chapter 33, "In-Memory Optimization and the Buffer Pool Extension."

Understanding Data Structures

SQL Server DBAs and users do not see data and storage the same way SQL Server does. A DBA or end user sees a database more logically as the following:

- ▶ Databases, physically stored in files
- ▶ Tables and indexes, placed in filegroups within databases
- ▶ Rows, stored in tables

SQL Server internally sees these storage structures at a lower, physical level as

- ▶ Databases, physically stored in data and log files
- ▶ Pages within these files, allocated to tables and indexes
- ▶ Data and index rows, stored in slots on pages

Database Files and Filegroups

Databases in SQL Server 2014 span at least two, and optionally several, database files. There must always be at least one file for data and one file for the transaction log. These database files are normal operating system files created in a directory within the operating system. These files are created when the database is created or when a database is expanded.

Each database file has the following set of properties:

- ▶ **A logical filename**—This name is used for internal reference to the file.
- ▶ **A physical filename**—This name is the actual physical pathname of the file.
- ▶ **An initial size**—If no size is specified for primary data file, its initial size, by default, is the minimum size required to hold the contents of the model database.
- ▶ **An optional maximum size**—A maximum file size limit can be specified.
- ▶ **A file growth increment**—This amount is specified in megabytes or as a percentage.

The information and properties about each file for a database are stored in the database visible via the system catalog view called `sys.database_files`. This view exists in every database and contains information about each of the database files. The `master` database contains a similar view, `sys.master_files`, which contains file information for all databases within the SQL Server instance. Table 31.1 lists the most useful columns in the `sys.database_files` view.

TABLE 31.1   The `sys.database_files` View

Column Name	Description
file_id	A file identification number that is unique within each database
file_guid	GUID for the file
type	File type (0=rows [that is, data files], 1=log, 2=FILESTREAM, 4=Full-text catalogs prior to SQL Server 2014
type_desc	Description of the file type (ROWS, LOG, FILESTREAM, FULLTEXT)
data_space_id	0 represents a log file; values > 0 represent the ID of the filegroup the data file belongs to
name	The logical name of the file
filename	The physical name of the file, including path
state	File state (0 = OFFLINE, 1 = RESTORING, 2 = RECOVERING, 3 = RECOVERY_PENDING, 4 = SUSPECT, 6 = OFFLINE, 7=DEFUNCT)
state_desc	Description of the file state (OFFLINE, RESTORING, RECOVERING, RECOVERY_PENDING, SUSPECT, OFFLINE, DEFUNCT)
size	Current size of the file specified as number of 8KB pages
max_size	Maximum file size specified as number of 8KB pages
growth	File growth setting (0=fixed, >0=autogrow in units of 8KB pages or by percentage if is_percent_growth is set to 1)
is_media_read_only	1= file is on read-only media
is_read_only	1= file is marked read-only
is_sparse	1= file is a sparse file
is_percent_growth	1= growth of file value is percentage

NOTE

SQL Server uses the file location information visible in the `sys.master_files` catalog view most of the time. However, the Database Engine uses the file location information stored in the primary file to initialize the file location entries in the `master` database when attaching a database using the `CREATE DATABASE` statement with either the `FOR ATTACH` or `FOR ATTACH_REBUILD_LOG` options.

Every database can have three types of files:

▶ Primary data file

▶ Secondary data files

▶ Log files

In addition, databases can also have FILESTREAM data files and full-text data files.

Primary Data File

Every database has only one primary database file. The location of the primary database file is stored in the master database (visible via the filename column in the sys.master_files view). When SQL Server opens a database, it looks for this file and then reads from the file information on the other files defined for the database.

The file extension for the primary database file defaults to .mdf. The primary database file always belongs to the default filegroup. It is often sufficient to have only one database file for storing your tables and indexes (the primary database file). The file can, of course, be created on a RAID partition or SAN to help spread I/O across multiple physical drives. However, if you need finer control over placement of your tables across disks or disk arrays, or if you want to be able to back up only a portion of your database via filegroups, you can create additional, secondary data files for a database.

Secondary Data Files

A database can have any number of secondary files (in reality, the maximum number of files per database is 32,767, but that should be sufficient for most implementations). You can put a secondary file in the default filegroup or in another filegroup defined for the database. Secondary data files have the file extension ".ndf" by default.

Following are some situations in which the use of secondary database files might be beneficial:

▶ You want to perform a partial backup. A backup can be performed for the entire database or a subset of the database. The subset is specified as a set of files or filegroups. The partial backup feature is useful for large databases, where it is impractical to back up the entire database. When recovering with partial backups, a transaction log backup must also be available. For more information about backups, see Chapter 11, "Database Backup and Restore."

▶ You want more control over placement of database objects. When you create a table or index, you can specify the filegroup in which the object is created. This could help you spread I/O by placing your most active tables or indexes on separate filegroups defined on separate physical disks or disk arrays (although this isn't relevant in typical SAN environments).

▶ Creating multiple files on a single physical disk or logical volume provides no real performance benefit but could help in recovery. If you have a 1.5TB database in a single file and have to restore it, you need to have enough disk space available to create a new 1.5TB file. If you don't have 1.5TB of space available on a single drive, you cannot restore the database. On the other hand, if the database was created with three files each 500GB in size, you more likely will be able to find three 500GB chunks of space available in your disk array or SAN.

The Log File

Each database must have at least one log file. The log file contains the transaction log records of all changes made in a database (for more information on what is contained in the transaction log, see Chapter 28, "Transaction Management and the Transaction Log"). By default, log files have the file extension `.ldf`.

A database can have several log files, and each log file can have a maximum size of 32TB. A log file cannot be part of a filegroup. No information other than transaction log records can be written to a log file.

For more information on the log file and log file management, see Chapter 28.

File Management

When you create a database or add a file to an existing database, there are options available for specifying the initial size of the file(s), as well as whether they are allowed to auto grow and by how much. By default, database files are configured to grow automatically as space is needed. You can control whether to use this feature along with the increment by which the file is to be expanded. The increment can be specified as a fixed number of megabytes or as a percentage of the current size of the file. You can also set a limit on the maximum size of the file or allow it to grow until no more space is available on the disk.

Listing 31.1 provides an example of a database being created with a 10MB growth increment for the first database file, 20MB for the second, and 20% growth increment for the log file.

LISTING 31.1 Creating a Database with Autogrowth

```
CREATE DATABASE Customer
ON ( NAME='Customer_Data',
     FILENAME='D:\SQL_data\Customer_Data1.mdf',
     SIZE=50,
     MAXSIZE=100,
     FILEGROWTH=10),
   ( NAME='Customer_Data2',
     FILENAME='E:\SQL_data\Customer_Data2.ndf',
     SIZE=100,
     FILEGROWTH=20)
LOG ON ( NAME='Customer_Log',
     FILENAME='F:\SQL_data\Customer_Log.ldf',
     SIZE=50,
     FILEGROWTH=20%)
GO
```

The Customer_Data file has an initial size of 50MB, a maximum size of 100MB, and a file increment of 10MB.

The Customer_Data2 file has an initial size of 100MB, has a file growth increment of 20MB, and can grow until the E: disk partition is full.

The transaction log has an initial size of 50MB; the file increases by 20% with each file growth. The increment is based on the current file size, not the size originally specified.

When creating or expanding data files in SQL Server 2014, SQL Server uses fast file initialization. This allows for the fast execution of the file creation and growth. With fast file initialization, the space is added to the data file immediately, but without initializing the logical pages in the data file with zeros. The existing disk content in the data file is not overwritten until new data is written to the files. This provides a huge performance advantage when a data file autogrows while an application is attempting to write data to the database. The application does not need to wait until the space is initialized; it can begin writing to the database immediately.

SQL Server also provides an option to autoshrink databases as well as manually shrink databases. However, shrinking a database is a resource-intensive process and should be done only if it is absolutely imperative to reclaim disk space. Also, if a data file is constantly shrinking and growing, it can lead to excessive file fragmentation at the file system level as well as excessive logical fragmentation within the file, both of which can lead to poor I/O performance.

Using Filegroups

All databases have a primary filegroup that contains the primary data file. There can be only one primary filegroup. If you don't create any other filegroups or change the default filegroup to one other than the primary filegroup, all files will be in the primary unless specifically placed in another.

In addition to the primary filegroup, you can add one or more filegroups to the database, and a filegroup can contain one or more files. The main purpose of using filegroups is to provide more control over the placement of files and data on your server. When you create a table or index, you can map it to a specific filegroup, thus controlling the placement of data. A typical SQL Server database installation generally uses a single RAID array to spread I/O across disks and create all files in the primary filegroup; more advanced installations or installations with very large databases spread across multiple array sets can benefit from the finer level of control of file and data placement afforded by additional filegroups.

For example, for a simple database such as AdventureWorks2012, you can create just one primary file that contains all data and objects and a log file that contains the transaction log information. For a larger and more complex database, such as a securities trading system where large data volumes and strict performance criteria are the norm, you might create the database with one primary file and four additional secondary files. You can then set up filegroups so you can place the data and objects within the database across all five files. If you have a table that itself needs to be spread across multiple disk arrays for performance reasons, you can place multiple files in a filegroup, each of which resides on a different disk, and create the table on that filegroup. For example, you can create three files (Data1.ndf, Data2.ndf, and Data3.ndf) on three disk arrays, respectively, and then assign them to the filegroup called spread_group. Your table can then be created specifically on the filegroup spread_group. Queries for data from the table are spread across the three disk arrays, thereby improving I/O performance.

If a filegroup contains more than one file, when space is allocated to objects stored in that filegroup, the data is stored proportionally across the files. In other words, if you have one file in a filegroup with twice as much free space as another, the first file has two extents allocated from it for each extent allocated from the second file (extents and space allocation are discussed in more detail later in this chapter).

Listing 31.2 provides an example of using filegroups in a database to control the file placement of the customer_info table.

LISTING 31.2   Using a Filegroup to Control Placement for a Table

```
CREATE DATABASE Customer
ON ( NAME='Customer_Data',
     FILENAME='D:\SQLData\Customer_Data1.mdf',
     SIZE=50,
     MAXSIZE=100,
     FILEGROWTH=10)
LOG ON ( NAME='Customer_Log',
     FILENAME='D:\SQLData\Customer_Log.ldf',
     SIZE=50,
     FILEGROWTH=20%)
GO


ALTER DATABASE Customer
 ADD FILEGROUP Cust_table
GO


ALTER DATABASE Customer
 ADD FILE
   ( NAME='Customer_Data2',
     FILENAME='D:\SQLData\Customer_Data2.ndf',
     SIZE=100,
     FILEGROWTH=20)
 TO FILEGROUP Cust_Table
GO
```

```
USE Customer
CREATE TABLE customer_info
(cust_no INT, cust_address NCHAR(200), info NVARCHAR(3000))
 ON Cust_Table
GO
```

The CREATE DATABASE statement in Listing 31.2 creates a database with a primary data-base file and log file. The first ALTER DATABASE statement adds a filegroup. A secondary database file is added with the second ALTER DATABASE command. This file is added to the Cust_Table filegroup. The CREATE TABLE statement creates a table; the ON Cust_Table clause places the table in the Cust_Table filegroup (the Customer_Data2 file on the G: disk partition).

The sys.filegroups system catalog view contains information about the database file-groups defined within a database, as shown in Table 31.2.

TABLE 31.2   The sys.filegroups System Catalog View

Column Name	Description
name	Name of the data space, unique within the database.
data_space_id	Data space ID number, unique within the database.
type	FG = Filegroup.
type_desc	Description of data space type: ROWS_FILEGROUP.
is_default	1 = This is the default data space. The default data space is used when a filegroup or partition scheme is not specified in a CREATE TABLE or CREATE INDEX statement.
	0 = This is not the default data space.
filegroup_guid	GUID for the filegroup.
	NULL = PRIMARY filegroup.
log_filegroup_id	Not used; value is NULL.
is_read_only	1 = Filegroup is read-only.
	0 = Filegroup is read/write.

The following statement returns the filename, size in megabytes (not including autogrow), and the name of the filegroup to which each file belongs:

```
SELECT
    convert(varchar(30), sf.name) as filename,
    size/128 as size_in_MB,
    convert(varchar(30), sfg.name) as filegroupname
 FROM sys.database_files sf
 INNER JOIN sys.filegroups sfg
 ON sf.data_space_id = sfg.data_space_id
```

```
go

/* output
filename                              size_in_MB  filegroupname
-----------------------------------   ----------  -------------------------

Customer_Data                         50          PRIMARY
Customer_Data2                        100         Cust_table
*/
```

FILESTREAM Filegroups

FILESTREAM storage is a feature available in SQL Server 2014 for storing unstructured data, such as documents, images, and videos. FILESTREAM storage helps to solve the issues with using unstructured data by integrating the SQL Server Database Engine with the NTFS file system for storing the unstructured data, such as documents and images, on the file system with the database storing a pointer to the data. Although the actual data resides outside the database in the NTFS file system, you can still use Transact-SQL (T-SQL) statements to insert, update, query, and back up FILESTREAM data, while maintaining transactional consistency between the unstructured data and corresponding structured data with the same level of security.

NOTE

To use FILESTREAM storage, you must first enable FILESTREAM storage at the Windows level as well as at the SQL Server instance level. You can enable FILESTREAM at the Windows level during installation of SQL Server 2014 or at any time using SQL Server Configuration Manager. After you enable FILESTREAM at the Windows level, you next need to enable FILESTREAM for the SQL Server instance. You can do this either through SQL Server Management Studio (SSMS) or via T-SQL.

After you enable FILESTREAM for the SQL Server instance, you can enable it for a database by creating a FILESTREAM filegroup. You can do this when the database is created (or to an existing database) by adding a filegroup and including the CONTAINS FILESTREAM clause. Unlike regular filegroups, a FILESTREAM filegroup can contain only a single file reference, which is actually a file system folder rather than an actual file. The actual folder must not exist (although the path up to the folder must exist); SQL Server creates the filestream folder. For example, in Listing 31.3, the code adds a FILESTREAM filegroup called CustFSGroup and adds the folder D:\SQLData\custinfo_FS into the filegroup. This custinfo_FS folder is created by SQL Server in the D:\SQLData folder.

LISTING 31.3   Adding a FILESTREAM Filegroup to a Database

```
ALTER DATABASE Customer
 ADD FILEGROUP Cust_FSGroup CONTAINS FILESTREAM

ALTER DATABASE Customer
 ADD FILE
   ( NAME=custinfo_FS,
     FILENAME = 'D:\SQLData\custinfo_FS')
     to FILEGROUP Cust_FSGroup
GO
```

If you look in the D:\SQLData\custinfo_FS folder, you should see a Filestream.hdr file and an $FSLOG folder. The Filestream.hdr file is a FILESTREAM container header file that should not be moved or modified.

As you can see in the example in Listing 31.3, for FILESTREAM files or filegroups, unlike regular files, you do not specify size or growth information. No space is preallocated. The file and filegroup grow as data is added to tables that have been created with FILESTREAM columns.

As you create tables with FILESTREAM columns, a subfolder is created in the filegroup folder for each table. The filenames are GUIDs. Each FILESTREAM column created in the table results in another subfolder created under the table subfolder. The column subfolder name is also a GUID. At this point, there still are no actual files created. That happens after you start adding rows to the table. A file is created in the column subfolder for each row inserted into the table with a non-NULL value for the FILESTREAM column.

In SQL Server 2014, a FILESTREAM filegroup can contain more than one file. Being able to create multiple files in a FILESTREAM filegroup can improve I/O scalability for FILESTREAM data by placing the files on different volumes. This feature eliminates the need for complicated workarounds that used partitioning and multiple FILESTREAM filegroups in order to improve I/O scalability for FILESTREAM data. The following example adds a new FILESTREAM filegroup to the Customer database that contains two files:

```
ALTER DATABASE Customer
add
  FILEGROUP [FSGroup2] CONTAINS FILESTREAM

ALTER DATABASE Customer
ADD FILE
  (
     NAME = N'FS_1',
     FILENAME = N'D:\BlobStore\FS_1',
     MAXSIZE = UNLIMITED
  ),
```

```
(
    NAME = N'FS_2',
    FILENAME = N'd:\BlobStore\FS_2',
    MAXSIZE = 100MB
)
TO FILEGROUP [FSGroup2]
```

For more information on creating and using tables with FILESTREAM columns, see Chapter 21, "Creating and Managing Tables."

Database Pages

Except for memory-optimized tables (which are covered in Chapter 33), all information in SQL Server is stored at the page level. The page is the smallest level of I/O in SQL Server and is the fundamental storage unit. Pages contain the data itself or information about the physical layout of the data. The page size is the same for all page types: 8KB, or 8,192 bytes. The pages are arranged in two basic types of storage structures: linked data pages and index trees.

Databases are divided into logical 8KB pages. Within each file allocated to a database, the pages are numbered contiguously from 0 to n. The actual number of pages in the database file depends on the size of the file. Pages in a database are uniquely referenced by specifying the database ID, the file ID for the file the page resides in, and the page number within the file. When you expand a database with ALTER DATABASE, the new space is added at the end of the file, and the page numbers continue incrementing from the previous last page in the file. If you add a completely new file, its first page number is 0. When you shrink a database, pages are removed from the end of the file only, starting at the highest page in the database and moving toward lower-numbered pages until the database reaches the specified size or a used page that cannot be removed. This ensures that page numbers within a file are always contiguous.

Page Types

There are nine page types in SQL Server, as listed in Table 31.3.

TABLE 31.3   Page Types

Page Type	Stores
Data	Data rows for all data except text, ntext, image, nvarchar(max), varchar(max), varbinary(max), and xml data
Row Overflow	Data columns that cause a data row to exceed the 8060 bytes per page limit
LOB	Large object types (text, ntext, image, nvarchar(max), varchar(max), varbinary(max), xml data, as well as varchar, nvarchar, varbinary, and sqlvariant types when the data row size exceeds 8KB)

Page Type	Stores
Index	Index entries and pointers
Global Allocation Map	Information about allocated (used) extents
Page Free Space	Information about page allocation and free space on pages
Index Allocation Map	Information about extents used by a table or an index
Differential Changed Map	Information about which extents have been modified since the last full database backup
Bulk Changed Map	Information about which extents have been used in a minimally logged or bulk-logged operation since the last BACKUP LOG statement

All pages, regardless of type, have a similar layout. They all have a page header, which is 96 bytes, and a body, which consequently is 8,096 bytes. The page layout is shown in Figure 31.1.

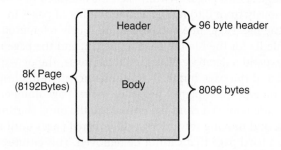

FIGURE 31.1   SQL Server page layout.

Data Pages

The actual data rows in tables are stored on data pages. Figure 31.2 shows the basic structure of a data page.

The following sections discuss and examine the contents of the data page.

The Page Header

The *page header* contains control information for the page. Some fields assist when SQL Server checks for consistency among its storage structures, and some fields are used when navigating among the pages that constitute a table. Table 31.4 describes the more useful fields contained in the page header.

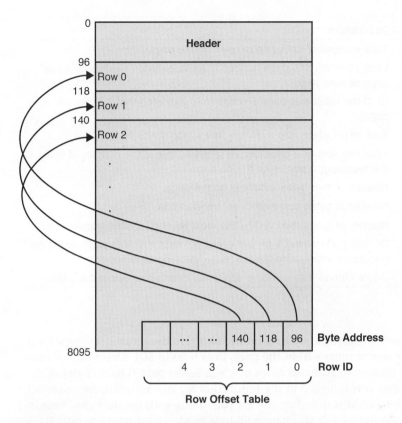

FIGURE 31.2   The structure of a SQL Server data page.

TABLE 31.4   Information Contained in the Page Header

Page Header Fields	Description
PageID	Unique identifier for the page. It consists of two parts: the file ID number and page number.
NextPage	File number and page number of the next page in the chain (0 if the page is the last or only page in the chain or if the page belongs to a heap table).
PrevPage	File number and page number of the previous page in the chain (0 if the page is the first or only page in the chain or if the page belongs to a heap table).
ObjectID	ID of the object to which this page belongs.
PartitionID	ID of the partition of which this page is a part.
AllocUnitID	ID of the allocation unit that contains this page.
LSN	Log sequence number (LSN) value used for changes and updates to this page.

Page Header Fields	Description
SlotCnt	Total number of rows (slots) used on the page.
Level	Level at which this page resides in an index tree (0 indicates a leaf page or data page).
IndexID	ID of the index this page belongs to (0 indicates that it is a data page).
freedata	Byte offset where the available free space starts on the page.
Pminlen	Minimum size of a data row. Essentially, this is the number of bytes in the fixed-length portion of the data rows.
FreeCnt	Number of free bytes available on the page.
reservedCnt	Number of bytes reserved by all transactions.
Xactreserved	Number of bytes reserved by the most recently started transaction.
tornBits	Bit string containing 1 bit per sector for detecting torn page writes (or checksum information if torn_page_detection is not on).
flagBits	2-byte bitmap that contains additional information about the page.

The Data Rows

Following the page header, starting at byte 96 on the page, are the actual data rows. Each data row has a unique row number within the page. Data rows in SQL Server cannot cross page boundaries. The maximum available space in a SQL Server page is 8,060 bytes of in-row data. When a data row is logged in the transaction log (for an insert, for example), additional logging information is stored on the log page along with the data row. Because log pages are 8,192 bytes in size and also have a 96-byte header, a log page has only 8,096 bytes of available space. If you want to store the data row and logging information on a single log page, the in-row data cannot be more than 8,060 bytes in size. This, in effect, limits the maximum in-row data row size for a table in SQL Server 2014 to 8,060 bytes as well.

> **NOTE**
>
> Although 8,060 bytes is the maximum size of in-row data, 8,060 bytes is not the maximum row size limit in SQL Server 2014. Data rows can also have row-overflow and large object (LOB) data stored on separate pages, as you see later in this chapter.

The number of rows stored on a page depends on the size of each row. For a table that has all fixed-length, non-nullable columns, the size of the row and the number of rows that can be stored on a page are always the same. If the table has any variable or nullable fields, the number of rows stored on the page depends on the size of each row. SQL Server attempts to fit as many rows as possible in a page. Smaller row sizes allow SQL Server to fit more rows on a page, which reduces page I/O and allows more data pages to fit in memory. This helps improve system performance by reducing the number of times SQL Server has to read data in from disk.

Because each data row also incurs some overhead bytes in addition to the actual data, the maximum amount of actual data that can be stored in a single row on a page is slightly less than 8,060 bytes. The actual amount of overhead required per row depends on whether the table contains any variable-length columns. If you attempt to create a table with a minimum row size including data and row overhead that exceeds 8,060 bytes, you receive an error message as shown in the following example (remember that a multibyte character set data type such as nchar or nvarchar requires 2 bytes per character, so an nchar(4000) column requires 8,000 bytes):

```
CREATE TABLE customer_info2
(cust_no INT, cust_address NCHAR(25), info NCHAR(4000))
go
/* output
Msg 1701, Level 16, State 1, Line 1
Creating or altering table 'customer_info2' failed because the
 minimum row size would be 8061, including 7 bytes of internal
overhead. This exceeds the maximum allowable table row size of 8060
bytes.
*/
```

If the table contains variable-length or nullable columns, you can create a table for which the minimum row size is less than 8,060 bytes, but the data rows could conceivably exceed 8,060 bytes. SQL Server allows the table to be created. If you then try to insert a row that exceeds 8,060 bytes of data and overhead, the data that exceeds the 8,060-byte limit for in-row data is stored in a row-overflow page.

The Structure of Data Rows The data for all fixed-length data fields in a table is stored at the beginning of the row. All variable-length data columns are stored after the fixed-length data. Figure 31.3 shows the structure of the data row in SQL Server.

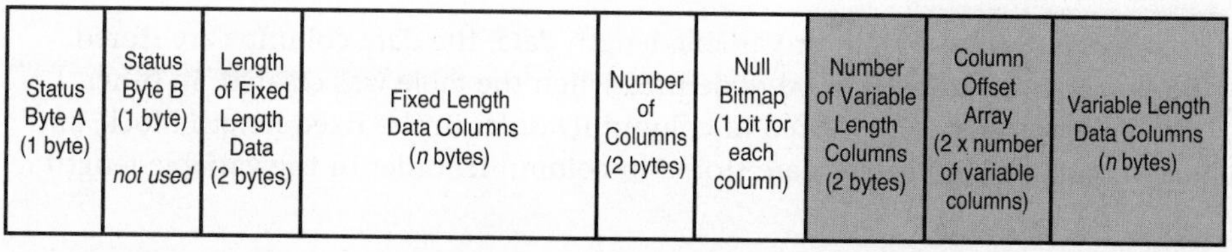

Status Byte A (1 byte)	Status Byte B (1 byte) not used	Length of Fixed Length Data (2 bytes)	Fixed Length Data Columns (n bytes)	Number of Columns (2 bytes)	Null Bitmap (1 bit for each column)	Number of Variable Length Columns (2 bytes)	Column Offset Array (2 x number of variable columns)	Variable Length Data Columns (n bytes)

FIGURE 31.3   The structure of a SQL Server data row.

The total size of each data row is a factor of the sum of the size of the columns plus the row overhead. Seven bytes of overhead is the minimum for any data row:

▶ 1 byte for status byte A.

▶ 1 byte for status byte B (currently, only 1 bit is used indicating that the record is a ghost-forwarded row).

▶ 2 bytes to store the length of the fixed-length columns.

- ▶ 2 bytes to store the number of columns in the row.

- ▶ 1 byte for every multiple of 8 columns (`ceiling(numcols / 8)`) in the table for the NULL bitmap. A 1 in the bitmap indicates that the column allows NULLs.

The values stored in status byte A are as follows:

- ▶ **Bit 0**—This bit provides version information. In SQL Server 2014, it's always 0.

- ▶ **Bits 1 through 3**—This 3-bit value indicates the nature of the row. 0 indicates that the row is a primary record, 1 indicates that the row has been forwarded, 2 indicates a forwarded stub, 3 indicates an index record, 4 indicates a blob fragment, 5 indicates a ghost index record, 6 indicates a ghost data record, and 7 indicates a ghost version record. (Many of these topics, such as forwarded and ghost records, are discussed in further detail later in this chapter.)

- ▶ **Bit 4**—This bit indicates that a NULL bitmap exists. This bit is somewhat unnecessary because a NULL bitmap is always present, even if no NULLs are allowed in the table.

- ▶ **Bit 5**—This bit indicates that one or more variable-length columns exists in the row.

- ▶ **Bit 6**—This bit indicates the row contains versioning information.

- ▶ **Bit 7**—This bit is not currently used.

If the table contains any variable-length columns, the following additional overhead bytes are included in each data row:

- ▶ 2 bytes to store the number of variable-length columns in the row.

- ▶ 2 bytes times the number of variable-length columns for the offset array. This is essentially a table in the row identifying where each variable-length column can be found within the variable-length column block.

Within each block of fixed-length or variable-length data, the data columns are stored in the column order in which they were defined when the table was created. In other words, all fixed-length fields are stored in column ID order in the fixed-length block, and all nullable or variable-length fields are stored in column ID order in the variable-length block.

Storage of the `sql_variant` Data Type   The `sql_variant` data type can contain a value of any column data type in SQL Server except for `text`, `ntext`, `image`, variable-length columns with the MAX qualifier, and `timestamp`. For example, a `sql_variant` in one row could contain character data; in another row, an integer value; and in yet another row, a float value. Because they can contain any type of value, `sql_variant` columns are always considered variable length. The format of a `sql_variant` column is as follows:

- ▶ Byte 1 indicates the actual data type being stored in the `sql_variant`.

- ▶ Byte 2 indicates the `sql_variant` version, which is always 1 in SQL Server 2014.

▶ The remainder of the `sql_variant` column contains the data value and, for some data types, information about the data value.

The data type value in byte 1 corresponds to the values in the `xtype` column in the `systypes` database system table. For example, if the first byte contains a hex 38, that corresponds to the `xtype` value of 56, which is the `int` data type.

Some data types stored in a `sql_variant` column require additional information bytes stored at the beginning of the data value (after the `sql_variant` version byte). The data types requiring additional information bytes and the values in these information bytes are as follows:

▶ Numeric and decimal data types require 1 byte for the precision and 1 byte for the scale.

▶ Character strings require 2 bytes to store the maximum length and 4 bytes for the collation ID.

▶ Binary and varbinary data values require 2 bytes to store the maximum length.

Storage of Sparse Columns   Sparse columns are ordinary columns that use an optimized storage format for NULL values. Sparse columns reduce the space requirements for NULL values at the cost of more overhead to retrieve non-NULL values. A rule of thumb is to consider using sparse columns when you expect at least 90% of the rows to contain NULL values. Prime candidates are tables that have many columns where most of the attributes are NULL for most rows—for example, when different attributes apply to different subsets of rows and, for each row, only a subset of columns are populated with values.

The sparse columns feature significantly increases the number of possible columns in a table from 1,024 to 30,000. However, not all 30,000 can contain values. The number of actual populated columns you can have depends on the number of bytes of data in the rows. With sparse columns, storage of NULL values is optimized, requiring no space at all for storing NULL values. This is unlike nonsparse columns, which, as you saw earlier, do need space even for NULL values (a fixed-length NULL value requires the full column width, and a variable-length NULL requires at least 2 bytes of storage in the column offset array).

Although sparse columns themselves require no space for NULL values, there is some fixed overhead space required to allow rows to contain sparse columns. This space is needed to add the sparse vector to the end of the data row. A sparse vector is added to the end of a data row only if at least one sparse column is defined on the table.

The sparse vector is used to keep track of the physical storage of sparse columns in the row. It is stored as the last variable-length column in the row. No bit is stored in the NULL bitmap for the sparse vector column, but it is included in the count of the variable columns (refer to Figure 31.3 for the general structure of a data row). The bytes stored in the sparse vector are shown in Table 31.5.

TABLE 31.5   Bytes Stored in the Sparse Vector

Name	Number of Bytes	Description
Complex column header	2	A value of 05 indicates the column is a sparse vector
Sparse column count	2	Number of sparse columns
Column ID set	2 × # of sparse columns	The column IDs of each column with a value stored in the sparse vector
Column offset table	2 × # of sparse columns	The offset of the ending position of each sparse column
Sparse data	Depends on actual values	The actual data values for each sparse column stored in column ID order

With the required overhead space for the sparse vector, the maximum size of all fixed-length non-NULL sparse columns is reduced to 8,019 bytes per row.

As you can see, the contents of a sparse vector are like a data row structure within a data row. If you refer to Figure 31.3, you can see that the structure of the sparse vector is similar to the shaded structure of a data row. One of the main differences is that the sparse vector stores no information for any sparse columns that contain NULL values. Also, fixed-length and variable-length columns are stored the same within the sparse vector. However, if you have any variable-length columns in the sparse vector that are too large to fit in the 8,019-byte limit of the data row, they are stored on row-overflow pages.

The Row Offset Table

The location of a row within a page is identified by the row offset table, which is located at the end of the page. To find a specific row within a page, SQL Server looks up the starting byte address for a given row ID in the row offset table, which contains the offset of the row from the beginning of the page (refer to Figure 31.2). Each entry in the row offset table is 2 bytes in size, so for each row in a table, an additional 2 bytes of space is added in from the end of the page for the row offset entry.

The row offset table keeps track of the logical order of rows on a data page. If a table has a clustered index defined on it, the data rows are stored in clustered index order. However, they may not be physically stored in clustered key order on the page itself. Instead, the row offset array indicates the logical clustered key order of the data rows. For example, row offset slot 0 refers to the first row in the clustered index key order, slot 1 refers to the second row, slot 2 refers to the third row, and so on. The physical location of the rows on the page may be in any order, depending on when rows on the page were inserted or deleted.

Row-Overflow Pages

While the maximum in-row size is 8,060 bytes per row, SQL Server 2014 allows actual rows to exceed this size for tables that contain varchar, nvarchar, varbinary, sql_variant, or common language runtime (CLR) user-defined type columns. Although the length of each one of these columns must still fall within the limit of 8,000 bytes (unless you are using the LOB version of these data types), the total combined width of the row is allowed to exceed the 8,060-byte limit.

When a combination of `varchar`, `nvarchar`, `varbinary`, `sql_variant`, or CLR user-defined type columns exceeds the 8,060-byte limit, SQL Server moves the record column with the largest width to another page in the `ROW_OVERFLOW_DATA` allocation unit, while maintaining a 24-byte pointer to the row-overflow page on the original page. Moving large records to another page occurs dynamically as records are lengthened based on update operations. Update operations that shorten records may cause records to be moved back to the original page in the `IN_ROW_DATA` allocation unit.

Row-overflow pages are used only under certain circumstances. For one, the row itself has to exceed 8,060 bytes; it does not matter how full the data page itself is. If a row is less than 8,060 bytes and there's not enough space in the data page, normal page splitting occurs to store the row. Also, each column in a row must be completely on the page or completely off it. A variable-length column cannot have some of its data on the regular data page and some of its data on the row-overflow page. One row can span multiple row-overflow pages depending on how many large variable-length columns there are.

Be aware that having data rows that require a row-overflow page increases the I/O cost of retrieving the data row. Querying and performing other select operations, such as sorts or joins on large records that contain row-overflow data, also slow processing time because these records are processed synchronously instead of asynchronously.

Therefore, when you design a table with multiple `varchar`, `nvarchar`, `varbinary`, `sql_variant`, or CLR user-defined type columns, you might want to consider the percentage of rows that are likely to require row overflow and the frequency with which this overflow data is likely to be queried. If there are likely to be frequent queries on many rows of row-overflow data, you should consider normalizing the table so that some columns are moved to another table, reducing the overall row size so that the rows fit within 8,060 bytes. The data can then be recombined in a query using an asynchronous `JOIN` operation.

> **TIP**
>
> Because of the performance implications, row-overflow pages are intended to be a solution for situations in which most of your data rows fit completely on your data pages and you only occasionally have rows that require a row-overflow page. Row-overflow pages allow SQL Server to handle the large data rows effectively without requiring a redesign of your table. However, if you find more than a few of your rows exceed the in-row size, you probably should look into using the LOB data types or redesigning your table.

LOB Data Pages

If you want to store large amounts of text or binary data, you can use the `varchar(max)`, `nvarchar(max)`, and `varbinary(max)` data types. (For information about how to use these data types, see Chapter 21, "Creating and Managing Tables," and Chapter 38, "Database Design and Performance.") Each column for a row of these data types can store up to 2GB (minus 2 bytes) of data. By default, the LOB values are not stored as part of the data row, but as a collection of pages on their own. For each LOB column, the data page contains a 16-byte pointer, which points to the location of the initial page of the LOB data. A row with several LOB columns has one pointer for each column.

> **NOTE**
>
> The other LOB data types, `text`, `ntext`, and `image`, have been deprecated and are scheduled to be removed in a future version of SQL Server, so you should avoid using them.

The pages that hold LOB data are 8KB in size, just like any other page in SQL Server. An individual LOB page can hold LOB data for multiple columns and also from multiple rows. A LOB data page can even contain a mix of LOB data. This helps reduce the storage requirements for the LOB data, especially when smaller amounts of data are stored in these columns. For example, if SQL Server could store data for only a single column for a single row on a single LOB data page and the data value consisted of only a single character, it would still use an entire 8KB data page to store that data! Definitely not an efficient use of space.

A LOB data page can hold LOB data for only a single table, however. A table with a LOB column has a single set of pages to hold all its LOB data.

LOB information is presented externally (to the user) as a long string of bytes. Internally, however, the information is stored within a set of pages. The pages are not necessarily organized sequentially but are logically organized as a B-tree structure. (B-tree structures are covered in more detail later in this chapter.) If an operation addresses some information in the middle of the data, SQL Server can navigate through the B-tree to find the data. In previous versions, SQL Server had to follow the entire page chain from the beginning to find the desired information.

If the amount of the data in the LOB field is less than 32KB, the 16-byte pointer in the data row points to an 84-byte root structure in the LOB B-tree. This root structure points to the pages and location where the actual LOB data is stored (see Figure 31.4). The data itself can be placed anywhere within the LOB pages for the table. The root structure keeps track of the location of the information in a logical manner. If the data is less than 64 bytes, it is stored in the root structure itself.

If the amount of LOB data exceeds 32KB, SQL Server allocates intermediate B-tree index nodes that point to the LOB pages. In this situation, the intermediate node pages are stored on pages not shared between different occurrences of LOB columns; the intermediate node pages store nodes for only one LOB column in a single data row.

Storing LOB Data in the Data Row

To further conserve space and help minimize I/O, SQL Server 2014 supports storing LOB data in the actual data row. When the LOB data is stored outside the data row pages, at a minimum, SQL Server needs to perform one additional page read per row to get the LOB data.

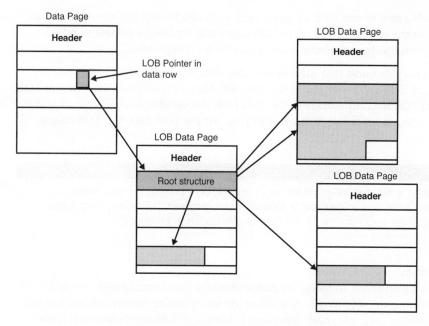

FIGURE 31.4   LOB data root structure pointing at the location of LOB data in the LOB B-tree.

Why would you want to store LOB data in the row? Why not just store the data in a varchar(8000)? Well, primarily because there is an upper limit of 8KB if the data is stored within the data row (not counting the other columns). Using a LOB data type, you can store more than 2 billion bytes of text or binary data. If you know most of your records will be small, but on occasion, some very large values will be stored, the text in row option provides optimum performance and better space efficiency for the majority of your LOB values, while providing the flexibility you need for the occasional large values. This option also provides the benefit of keeping the data all in a single column instead of having to design the table to split the data across multiple columns or rows when the data exceeds the size limit of a single row.

If you want to enable the text in row option for a table with a LOB column, use the sp_tableoption stored procedure:

```
exec sp_tableoption Production.Document, 'text in row', 512
```

This example enables up to 512 bytes of LOB data in the Document table to be stored in the data row. The maximum amount of LOB data that can be stored in a data row is 7,000 bytes. When a LOB value exceeds the specified size, rather than store the 16-byte pointer in the data row as it would normally, SQL Server stores the 24-byte root structure that contains the pointers to the separate chunks of LOB data for the row in the LOB column.

The second parameter to sp_tableoption can be just the option ON. If no size is specified, the option is enabled with a default size of 256 bytes. To disable the text in row option, you can set its value to 0 or OFF with sp_tableoption. When the option is turned off, all LOB data stored in the row is moved off to LOB pages and replaced with the standard 16-byte pointer. This can be a time-consuming process for a large table.

Also, you should keep in mind that just because this option is enabled it doesn't always mean that the LOB data will be stored in the row. All other data columns that are not LOB take priority over LOB data for storage in the data row. If a variable-length column grows and there is not enough space left in the row or page for the LOB data, the LOB data is moved off the page.

> **NOTE**
>
> Like the LOB data types it is intended for (text, ntext, and image), the text in row feature has also been deprecated and is planned to be removed in a future. Data types using the MAX length specification do not require this option to be enabled.

Storage of MAX Data

The recommended alternative to using the text and image data types in SQL Server 2014 is the option of defining variable-length data using the MAX specifier. When you use the MAX specifier with varchar, nvarchar, and varbinary columns, SQL Server determines automatically whether to store the data as a regular varchar, nvarchar, or varbinary value or as a LOB. Essentially, if the actual length is less than 8,000 bytes, SQL Server treats it as if it were one of the regular variable-length data types, including using row-overflow pages if necessary. If the MAX column exceeds 8,000 bytes, it is stored like LOB data.

Index Pages

Index information is stored on index pages. An index page has the same layout as a data page. The difference is the type of information stored on the page. Generally, a row in an index page contains the index key and a pointer to the page or row at the next (lower) level.

The actual information stored in an index page depends on the index type and whether it is a leaf-level page. A leaf-level clustered index page is the data page itself; you've already seen its structure. The information stored on other index pages is as follows:

▶ **Clustered indexes, nonleaf pages**—Each index row contains the index key and a pointer (the fileId and a page address) to a page in the index tree at the next lower level.

▶ **Nonclustered index, nonleaf pages**—Each index row contains the index key and a page-down pointer (the file ID and a page address) to a page in the index tree at the next lower level. For nonunique indexes, the nonleaf row also contains the row locator information for the corresponding data row.

▶ **Nonclustered index, leaf pages**—Rows on this level contain an index key and a reference to a data row. For heap tables, this is the Row ID; for clustered tables, this is the clustered key for the corresponding data row.

31

The actual structure and content of index rows, as well as the structure of the index tree, are discussed in more detail later in this chapter.

Space Allocation Structures

When a table or index needs more space in a database, SQL Server needs a way to determine where space is available in the database to be allocated. If the table or index is still fewer than eight pages in size, SQL Server must find a mixed extent with one or more pages available that can be allocated. If the table or index is eight pages or larger in size, SQL Server must find a free uniform extent that can be allocated to the table or index.

Extents

If SQL Server allocated space one page at a time as pages were needed for a table (or an index), SQL Server would be spending a good portion of its time just allocating pages, and the data would likely be scattered noncontiguously throughout the database. Scanning such a table would not be very efficient. For these reasons, pages for each object are grouped together and allocated in extents; an extent consists of eight logically contiguous pages.

When a table or index is created, it is initially allocated a page on a mixed extent. If no mixed extents are available in the database, a new mixed extent is allocated. A mixed extent can be shared by up to eight objects (each page in the extent can be assigned to a different table or index).

As the table grows to at least eight pages in size, all future allocations to the table are done as *uniform extents*.

Figure 31.5 shows the use of mixed and uniform extents.

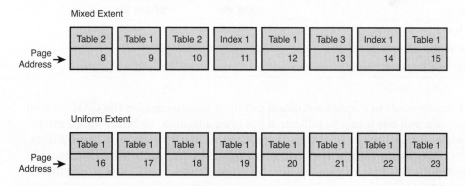

FIGURE 31.5   Mixed and uniform extents.

If SQL Server had to search throughout an entire database file to find free extents, it wouldn't be efficient. Instead, SQL Server uses two special types of pages to record which extents have been allocated to tables or indexes and whether it is a mixed or uniform extent:

▶ Global allocation map pages (GAMs)

▶ Shared global allocation map pages (SGAMs)

Global and Shared Global Allocation Map Pages

The allocation map pages track whether extents have been allocated to objects and indexes and whether the allocation is for mixed extents or uniform extents. As mentioned in the preceding section, there are two types of GAMs:

▶ **Global allocation map (GAM)**—The GAM keeps track of all allocated extents in a database, regardless of what the extents are allocated to. The structure of the GAM is straightforward: each bit in the page outside the page header represents one extent in the file, where 1 means that the extent is not allocated, and 0 means that the extent is allocated. Nearly 8,000 bytes (64,000 bits) are available in a GAM page after the header and other overhead bytes are taken into account. Therefore, a single GAM covers approximately 64,000 extents, or 4GB (64,000 * 64KB) of data.

▶ **Shared global allocation map (SGAM)**—The SGAM keeps track of mixed extents that have free space available. An SGAM has a structure similar to a GAM, with each bit representing an extent. A value of 1 means that the extent is a mixed extent and there is free space (at least one unused page) available on the extent. A value of 0 means that the extent is not currently allocated, that the extent is a uniform extent, or that the extent is a mixed extent with no free pages.

Table 31.6 summarizes the meaning of the bit in GAMs and SGAMs.

TABLE 31.6   Meaning of the GAM and SGAM Bits

Extent Usage	GAM Bit	SGAM Bit
Free, not used	1	0
Uniform or mixed with no free pages	0	0
Mixed, with free pages available	0	1

When SQL Server needs to allocate a uniform extent, it simply searches the GAM for a bit with a value of 1 and sets it to 0 to indicate it has been allocated. To find a mixed extent with free pages, it searches the SGAM for a bit set to 1. When all pages in a mixed extent are used, its corresponding bit is set to 0. When a mixed extent needs to be allocated, SQL Server searches the GAM for an extent whose bit set to 1 and sets the bit to 0, and the corresponding SGAM bit is set to 1. There is some more processing involved as well, such as spreading the data evenly across database files, but the allocation algorithms are still relatively simple.

SQL Server is able to easily locate GAM pages in a database because the first GAM page is located at the third page in the file (page number 2). There is another GAM every 511,230 pages after the first GAM. The fourth page (page number 3) in each database file is the SGAM page, and there is another SGAM each 511,230 pages after the first SGAM.

Page Free Space Pages

A *page free space (PFS)* page records whether each page is allocated and the amount of free space available on the page. Each PFS covers 8,088 contiguous pages in the file. For each of the 8,088 pages, the PFS has a 1-byte record that contains a bitmap for each page indicating whether the page is empty, 1 to 50% full, 51 to 80% full, 81 to 95% full, or more than 95% full. The first PFS page in a file is located at page number 1, the second PFS page is located at page 8088, and each additional PFS page is located every 8,088 pages after that. SQL Server uses PFS pages to find free pages on extents and to find pages with space available on extents when a new row needs to be added to a table or index.

Figure 31.6 shows the layout of GAM, SGAM, and PFS pages in a database file. Note that every file has a single file header located at page 0.

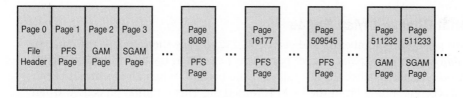

FIGURE 31.6   The layout of GAM, SGAM, and PFS pages in a database file.

Index Allocation Map Pages

Index allocation map (IAM) pages keep track of the extents used by a heap or index. Each heap table and index has at least one IAM page for each file where it has extents. An IAM cannot reference pages in other database files; if the heap or index spreads to a new database file, a new IAM for the heap or index is created in that file. IAM pages are allocated as needed and are spread randomly throughout the database files.

An IAM page contains a small header that has the address of the first extent in the range of pages being mapped by the IAM. It also contains eight page pointers that keep track of index or heap pages that are in mixed extents. These pointers might or might not contain any information, depending on whether any data has been deleted from the tables and the page(s) released. Remember, an index or heap will have no more than eight pages in mixed extents (after eight pages, it begins using uniform extents), so only the first IAM page stores this information. The remainder of the IAM page is for the allocation bitmap. The IAM bitmap works similarly to the GAM, indicating which extents over the range of extents covered by the IAM are used by the heap or index the IAM belongs to. If a bit is on, the corresponding extent is allocated to the table.

Each IAM covers a possible range of 63,903 extents (511,224 pages), covering a 4GB section of a file. Each bit represents an extent within that range, whether or not the extent is allocated to the object that the IAM belongs to. If the bit is set to 1, the relative extent in the range is allocated to the index or heap. If the bit is set to 0, the extent is either not allocated or might be allocated to another heap or index.

For example, assume that an IAM page resides at page 649 in the file. If the bit pattern in the first byte of the IAM is 1010 0100, the first, third, and sixth extents within the range of the IAM are allocated to the heap or index. The second, fourth, fifth, seventh, and eighth extents are not.

> **NOTE**
>
> For a heap table, the data pages and rows within them are not stored in any specific order. Unlike clustered tables, the pages in a heap structure are not linked together in a page chain. The only logical connection between data pages is the information recorded in the IAM pages, which are linked together. The structure of heap tables is examined in more detail later in this chapter.

Differential Changed Map Pages

The seventh page (page number 6), and every 511,232nd page thereafter, in the database file is the *differential changed map* (DCM) page. This page keeps track of which extents in a file have been modified since the last full database backup. When an extent has been modified, its corresponding bit in the DCM is turned on. This information is used when a differential backup is performed on the database. A differential backup copies only the extents changed since the last full backup was made. Using the DCM, SQL Server can quickly tell which extents need to be backed up by examining the bits on the DCM pages for each data file in the database. When a full backup is performed for the database, all the bits are set back to 0.

Bulk Changed Map Pages

The eighth page (page number 7), and every 511,232nd page thereafter, in the database file is the *bulk changed map* (BCM). When you perform a minimally or bulk-logged operation in SQL Server 2014 in BULK_LOGGED recovery mode, SQL Server logs only the fact that the operation occurred and doesn't log the actual data changes. The operation is still fully recoverable because SQL Server keeps track of what extents were actually modified by the bulk operation in the BCM page. Similar to the DCM page, each bit on a BCM page represents an extent within its range, and if the bit is set to 1, that indicates that the corresponding extent has been changed by a minimally logged bulk operation since the last full database backup. All the bits on the BCM page are reset to 0 whenever a full database backup or log backup occurs.

When you initiate a log backup for a database using the BULK_LOGGED recovery model, SQL Server scans the BCM pages and backs up all the modified extents along with the contents of the transaction log itself. You should be aware that the log file itself might be small, but the backup of the log can be many times larger if a large bulk operation has been performed since the last log backup.

Data Compression

Data compression, a feature available in the Enterprise and Developer Editions, helps to reduce both storage and memory requirements as the data is compressed both on disk and when brought into the SQL Server data cache.

When compression is enabled and data is written to disk, it is compressed and stored in the designated compressed format. When the data is read from disk into the buffer cache, it remains in its compressed format. This helps reduce both storage requirements and memory requirements. It also reduces I/O because more data can be stored on a data page when it's compressed. When the data is passed to another component of SQL Server, however, the Database Engine then has to uncompress the data on the fly. In other words, every time data has to be passed to or from the buffered cache, it has to be compressed or uncompressed. This requires extra CPU overhead to accomplish. However, in most cases, the amount of I/O and buffer cache saved by compression more than makes up for the CPU costs, boosting the overall performance of SQL Server.

Data compression can be applied on the following database objects:

▶ Tables (clustered or heap)

▶ Nonclustered indexes

▶ Indexed views

As the DBA, you need to evaluate which of the preceding objects in your database could benefit from compression and then decide whether you want to compress it using either row-level or page-level compression. Compression is enabled or disabled at the object level There is no single option you can enable that turns compression on or off for all objects in the database. Fortunately, other than turning compression on or off for the preceding objects, you don't have to do anything else to use data compression. SQL Server handles data compression transparently without your having to re-architect your database or your applications.

Row-Level Compression

Row-level compression isn't true data compression. Instead, space savings are achieved by using a more efficient storage format for fixed-length data to use the minimum amount of space required. For example, the int data type uses 4 bytes of storage regardless of the value stored, even NULL. However, only a single byte is required to store a value of 100. Row-level compression allows fixed-length values to use only the amount of storage space required.

Row-level compression saves space and reduces I/O by

▶ Reducing the amount of metadata required to store data rows

▶ Storing fixed-length numeric data types as if they were variable-length data types, using only as many bytes as necessary to store the actual value

- ▶ Storing CHAR data types as variable-length data types
- ▶ Not storing NULL or 0 values

Row-level data compression provides less compression than page-level data compression, but it also incurs less overhead, reducing the amount of CPU resources required to implement it.

Row-level compression can be enabled when creating a table or index or using the ALTER TABLE or ALTER INDEX commands by specifying the WITH (DATA_COMPRESSION = ROW) option. The following example enables row compression on the Document table in the AdventureWorks2012 database:

```
ALTER TABLE Production.Document REBUILD WITH (DATA_COMPRESSION=ROW)
```

Additionally, if a table or index is partitioned, you can apply compression at the partition level.

When row-level compression is applied to a table, a new row format is used that is unlike the standard data row format discussed previously, which has a fixed-length data section separate from a variable-length data section (see Figure 31.3). This new row format is referred to as column descriptor, or CD, format. The name of this row format refers to the fact that every column has description information contained in the row itself. Figure 31.7 illustrates a representative view of the CD format (a definitive view is difficult because, except for the header, the number of bytes in each region is completely dependent on the values in the data row).

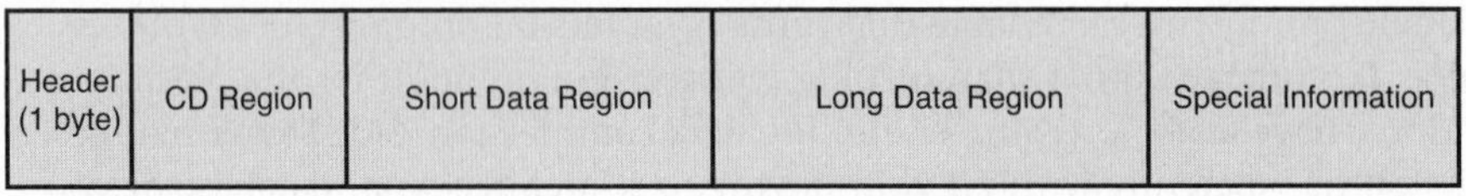

Header (1 byte)	CD Region	Short Data Region	Long Data Region	Special Information

FIGURE 31.7   A representative structure of a CD format row.

The row header is always 1 byte in length and contains information similar to Status Bits A in a normal data row:

- ▶ **Bit 0**—This bit indicates the type of record (1 = CD record format).
- ▶ **Bit 1**—This bit indicates whether the row contains versioning information.
- ▶ **Bits 2–4**—This three-bit value indicates what kind of information is stored in the row (such as primary record, ghost record, forwarding record, index record).
- ▶ **Bit 5**—This bit indicates whether the row contains a long data region (with values greater than 8 bytes in length).
- ▶ **Bits 6 and 7**—These bits are not used.

The CD region consists of two parts. The first is either a 1- or 2-byte value indicating the number of short columns (8 bytes or less). If the most significant bit of the first byte is set to 0, it's a 1-byte field representing up to 127 columns; if it's 1, it's a 2-byte field representing up to 32,767 columns. Following the first 1 or 2 bytes is the CD array. The CD array uses 4 bits for each column in the table to represent information about the length of the column. A bit representation of 0 indicates the column is NULL. A bit representation of the values 1 to 9 indicates the column is 0 to 8 bytes in length, respectively. A bit representation of 10 (0xa) indicates that the corresponding column value is a long data value and uses no space in the short data region. A bit representation of 11 (0xb) represents a bit column with a value of 1, and a bit representation of 12 (0xc) indicates that the corresponding value is a 1-byte symbol representing a value in the page compression dictionary (the page compression dictionary is discussed next in the page-level compression section).

The short data region contains each of the short data values. However, because accessing the last columns can be expensive if there are hundreds of columns in the table, columns are grouped into clusters of 30 columns. At the beginning of the short data region, there is an area called the *short data cluster array*. Each entry in the array is a single byte, which indicates the sum of the sizes of all the data in the previous cluster in the short data region; the value is essentially a pointer to the first column of the cluster (no row offset is needed for the first cluster because it starts immediately after the CD region).

Any data value in the row longer than 8 bytes is stored in the long data region. This can include LOB and row-overflow pointers. Long data needs an actual offset value to allow SQL Server to locate each value. This offset array looks similar to the offset array used in the standard data row structure. The long data region consists of three parts: an offset array, a long data cluster array, and the long data. The long data cluster array is similar to the short data cluster array; it has one entry for each 30-column cluster (except for the last one) and serves to limit the cost of locating columns near the end of a long list of columns.

The special information section at the end of the row contains three optional pieces of information. The existence of any or all of this information is indicated by bits in the first 1-byte header at the beginning of the row. The three special pieces of information are

- ▶ **Forwarding pointer**—This pointer is used in a heap when a row is forwarded due to an update (forward pointers are discussed later in this chapter).

- ▶ **Back pointer**—If the row is a forwarded row, it contains a pointer back to the original row location.

- ▶ **Versioning information**—If snapshot isolation is being used, 14 bytes of versioning information are appended to the row.

Page-Level Compression

Page-level compression is an implementation of true data compression, using both column prefix and dictionary-based compression. Data is compressed by storing repeating values or common prefixes only once and then referencing those values from other columns and rows. When you implement page compression for a table, row compression is applied as well. Page-level compression offers increased data compression over row-level compression alone but at the expense of greater CPU utilization. It works using these techniques:

▶ First, row-level data compression is applied to fit as many rows as it can on a single page.

▶ Next, column prefix compression is run. Essentially, repeating patterns of data at the beginning of the values of a given column are removed and substituted with an abbreviated reference, which is stored in the compression information (CI) structure stored after the page header.

▶ Finally, dictionary compression is applied on the page. Dictionary compression searches for repeated values anywhere on a page and stores them in the CI.

Page compression is applied only after a page is full and if SQL Server determines that compressing a page will save a meaningful amount of space.

The amount of compression provided by page-level data compression is highly dependent on the data stored in a table or index. If a lot of the data repeats itself, compression is more efficient. If the data is more randomly discrete values, fewer benefits are gained from using page-level compression.

Column prefix compression looks at the column values on a single page and chooses a common prefix that can be used to reduce the storage space required for values in that column. The longest value in the column that contains the prefix is chosen as the anchor value. A row that represents the prefix values for each column is created and stored in the CI structure that immediately follows the page header. Each column is then stored as a delta from the anchor value, where repeated prefix values in the column are replaced by a reference to the corresponding prefix. If the value in a row does not exactly match the selected prefix value, a partial match can still be indicated.

For example, consider a page that contains the following data rows before prefix compression as shown in Figure 31.8.

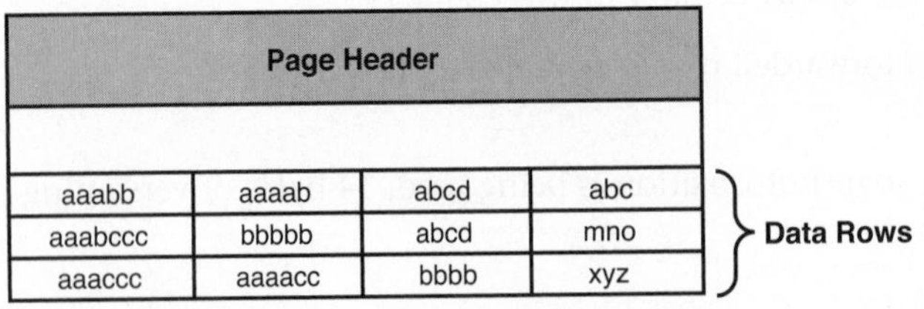

Page Header			
aaabb	aaaab	abcd	abc
aaabccc	bbbbb	abcd	mno
aaaccc	aaaacc	bbbb	xyz

Data Rows

FIGURE 31.8   Sample page of a table before prefix compression.

After you apply column prefix compression on the page, the CI structure is stored after the page header holding the prefix values for each column. The columns then are stored as the difference between the prefix and column value, as shown in Figure 31.9.

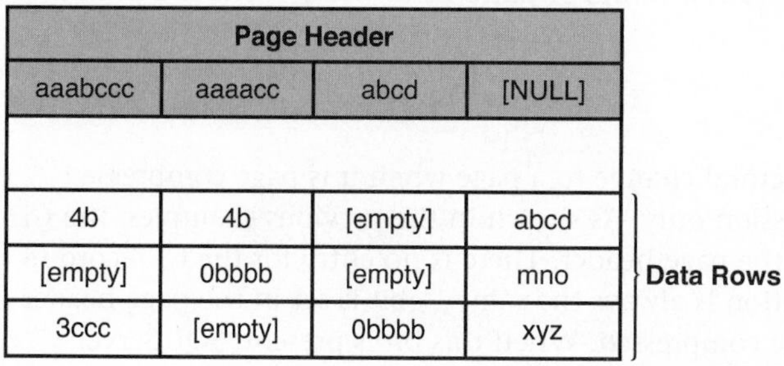

Page Header			
aaabccc	aaaacc	abcd	[NULL]
4b	4b	[empty]	abcd
[empty]	0bbbb	[empty]	mno
3ccc	[empty]	0bbbb	xyz

Data Rows

FIGURE 31.9   Sample page of a table after prefix compression.

In the first column in the first data row, the value 4b represents that the first four characters of the prefix (aaab) are present at the beginning of the column for that row and also the character b. If you append the character b to the first four values of the prefix, it rebuilds the original value of aaabb. For any columns values that are [empty], the column matches the prefix value exactly. Any column value that starts with 0 means that none of the first characters of the column match the prefix. For the fourth column, there is no common prefix value in the columns, so no prefix value is stored in the CI structure.

After column prefix compression is applied to every column individually on the page, SQL Server then looks to apply dictionary compression. Dictionary compression looks for repeated values anywhere on the page and also stores them in the CI structure after the column prefix values. Dictionary compression values replace repeated values anywhere on a page. Figure 31.10 illustrates the same page shown previously after dictionary compression has been applied.

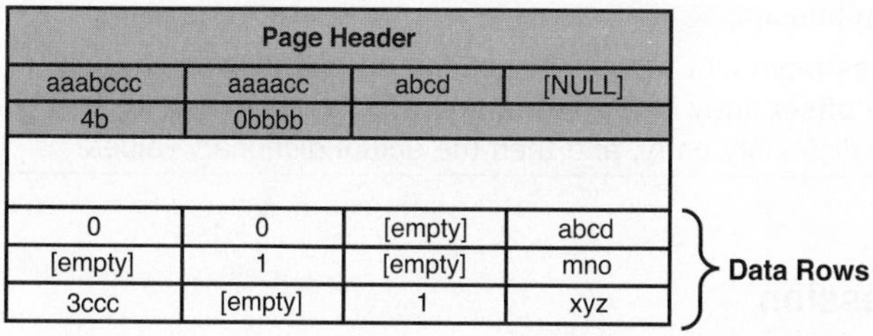

Page Header			
aaabccc	aaaacc	abcd	[NULL]
4b	0bbbb		
0	0	[empty]	abcd
[empty]	1	[empty]	mno
3ccc	[empty]	1	xyz

Data Rows

FIGURE 31.10   Sample page of a table after dictionary compression.

The dictionary is stored as a set of these duplicate values and a symbol to represent these values in the columns on the page. As you can see in this example, 4b is repeated in multiple columns in multiple rows, and the value is replaced by the symbol 0 throughout the page. The value 0bbbb is replaced by the symbol 1. SQL Server recognizes that the value stored in the column is a symbol and not a data value by examining the coding in the CD array, as discussed earlier.

Not all pages contain both the prefix record and a dictionary. Having them both depends on whether the data has enough repeating values or patterns to warrant either a prefix record or a dictionary.

The CI Record

The CI record is the only main structural change to a page when it is page compressed versus a page that uses row compression only. As shown in the previous examples, the CI record is located immediately after the page header. There is no entry for the CI record in the row offset table because its location is always the same. A bit is set in the page header to indicate whether the page is page compressed. When this bit is present, SQL Server knows to look for the CI record. The CI record contains the data elements shown in Table 31.7.

TABLE 31.7   Data Elements Within the CI Record

Name	Description
Header	This structure contains 1 byte to keep track of information about the CI. Bit 0 is the version (currently always 0), Bit 1 indicates the presence of a column prefix anchor record, and Bit 2 indicates the presence of a compression dictionary.
PageModCount	This value keeps track of the number of changes to the page to determine whether the compression on the page should be re-evaluated and the CI record rebuilt.
Offsets	This element contains values to help SQL Server find the dictionary. It contains the offset of the end of the Column prefix anchor record and offset of the end of the CI record itself.
Anchor Record	This record looks exactly like a regular CD record (see Figure 31.7). Values stored are the common prefix values for each column, some of which might be NULL.
Dictionary	The first 2 bytes represent the number of entries in the dictionary, followed by an offset array of 2-byte entries, which indicate the end offset of each dictionary entry, and then the actual dictionary values.

Implementing Page Compression

Page compression can be implemented for a table at the time it is created or by using the ALTER TABLE command, as in the following example:

```
ALTER TABLE Sales.SalesOrderDetail REBUILD WITH (DATA_COMPRESSION=PAGE)
```

Unlike row compression, which is applied immediately on the rows, page compression isn't applied until the page is full. The rows cannot be compressed until SQL Server can determine what encodings for prefix and dictionary substitution are going to be used to replace the actual data. When you enable page compression for a table or a partition, SQL Server examines every full page to determine the possible space savings. Any pages that are not full are not considered for compression. During the compression analysis, the prefix and dictionary values are created, and the column values are modified to reflect the prefix and dictionary values. Then row compression is applied. If the new compressed page can hold at least five additional rows, or 25% more rows than the page currently holds, the page is compressed. If neither one of these criteria is met, the compressed version of the page is discarded.

New rows inserted into a compressed page are compressed as they are inserted. However, new entries are not added to the prefix list or dictionary based on a single new row. The prefix values and dictionary symbols are rebuilt only on an all-or-nothing basis. After the page is changed a sufficient number of times, SQL Server evaluates whether to rebuild the CI record. The PageModCount field in the CI record is used to keep track of the number of changes to the page since the CI record was last built or rebuilt. This value is updated every time a row is updated, deleted, or inserted. If SQL Server encounters a full page during a data modification and the PageModCount is greater than 25 or the PageModCount divided by the number of rows on the page is greater than 25%, SQL Server reapplies the compression analysis on the page. Again, only if recompressing the page creates room for five additional rows, or 25% more rows than the page currently holds, the new compressed page replaces the existing page.

In B-tree structures (nonclustered indexes or a clustered table), only the leaf-level and data pages are considered for compression. When you insert a new row into a leaf or data page, if the compressed row fits, it is inserted, and nothing more is done. If it doesn't fit, SQL Server attempts to recompress the page and then recompress the row based on the new CI record. If the row fits after recompression, it is inserted, and nothing more is done. If the row still doesn't fit, the page needs to be split. When a compressed page is split, the CI record is copied to the new page exactly as it was, along with the rows moved to the new page. However, the PageModCount value is set to 25, so that when the new page gets full, it will be immediately analyzed for recompression. Leaf and data pages are also checked for recompression whenever you run an index rebuild or shrink operation.

If you enable compression on a heap table, pages are evaluated for compression only during rebuild and shrink operations. Also, if you drop a clustered index on a table, turning it into a heap, SQL Server runs compression analysis on any full pages. Compression is avoided during normal data modification operations on a heap to avoid changes to the Row IDs, which are used as the row locators for any indexes on the heap. (See the "Understanding Index Structures" section later in this chapter for a discussion of row locators.) Although the RowModCounter is still maintained, SQL Server essentially ignores it and never tries to recompress a page based on the RowModCounter value.

Evaluating Page Compression

Before choosing to implement page compression, you should determine if the overhead of page compression will provide sufficient benefit in space savings. To determine how changing the compression state will affect a table or an index, you can use the SQL Server

2014 `sp_estimate_data_compression_savings` stored procedure, which is available only in the editions of SQL Server that support data compression. This stored procedure evaluates the effects of compression by sampling up to 5,000 pages in the table and creating a copy of these 5,000 pages of the table in `tempdb`, performing the compression, and then using the sample to estimate the overall size for the table after compression. The syntax for `sp_estimate_data_compression_savings` is as follows:

```
sp_estimate_data_compression_savings
    [ @schema_name = ] 'schema_name'
  , [ @object_name = ] 'object_name'
  , [@index_id = ] index_id
  , [@partition_number = ] partition_number
  , [@data_compression = ] 'data_compression'
```

> **WARNING**
>
> Do not run `sp_estimate_data_compression_savings` in an active production database, as it can have a significant impact on performance while running.

You can estimate the data compression savings for a table for either row or page compression by specifying either `'ROW'` or `'PAGE'` as the value for the `@data_compression` parameter. You can also estimate the average size of the compressed table if compression is disabled by specifying NONE as the value for @data_compression. You can also use the `sp_estimate_data_compression_savings` procedure to estimate the space savings for compression on a specific index or partition. The following example estimates the space savings if page compression were applied to the `SalesOrderDetail` table in the `AdventureWorks2012` database versus using row compression:

```
sp_estimate_data_compression_savings 'Sales', 'SalesOrderDetail', NULL, NULL, 'PAGE'
GO

/* output
object_name       schema_name index_id partition_number size_with_current_
compression_setting(KB) size_with_requested_compression_setting(KB)
sample_size_with_current_compression_setting(KB) sample_size_with_requested_
compression_setting(KB)
----------------  ----------- -------- ---------------- ---------------------------
------------- ------------------------------------------------- --------------------------
----------------- --------------------------------------------------- ----------------

SalesOrderDetail  Sales          1        1               10          4912      10032      4912
SalesOrderDetail  Sales          2        1               378         3968      3784       3968
SalesOrderDetail  Sales          3        1               2336        1496      2336       1496
*/
```

```
sp_estimate_data_compression_savings 'Sales', 'SalesOrderDetail', NULL, NULL, 'ROW'
GO

/* output
object_name       schema_name index_id partition_number size_with_current_
compression_setting(KB) size_with_requested_compression_setting(KB)
sample_size_with_current_compression_setting(KB) sample_size_with_requested_
compression_setting(KB)
----------------- ----------- -------- ---------------- --------------------------
------------ ----------------------------------------- --------------------------
--------------------- -------------------------------------------------
SalesOrderDetail  Sales         1        1       10040     7080     10048    7080
SalesOrderDetail  Sales         2        1        3784     3968      3784    3968
SalesOrderDetail  Sales         3        1        2336     1696      2336    1696
*/
```

You can see in this example that the space savings from page compression would be significant, with an estimated reduction in the size of the table itself (index_id = 1) from 10,040KB to 4,920KB, a savings of more than 50%. Row compression would not provide nearly as significant a savings, with an estimated reduction in size from 10,040KB to only 7,080KB, only a 30% savings.

If you compress the table, you can compare the estimated space savings to the actual size. For example, let's look at the initial size of the SalesOrderDetail table:

```
select sum(page_count) as pages, sum(compressed_page_count) as compressed_pages
from sys.dm_db_index_physical_stats (DB_ID(),
OBJECT_ID('Sales.SalesOrderDetail'), 1, null, 'DETAILED')
where index_level = 0

SELECT SUM(used_page_count/ 128.0) AS size_in_MB
FROM sys.dm_db_partition_stats
WHERE object_id=OBJECT_ID('Sales.SalesOrderDetail') AND index_id=1
GO

/* output
pages compressed_pages
----- ----------------
1237              0

size_in_MB
----------
  9.804687
*/
```

Now, implement page compression on the `SalesOrderDetail` table:

```
ALTER TABLE sales. SalesOrderDetail   REBUILD WITH (DATA_COMPRESSION=PAGE)
```

Now, re-examine the size of the `sales_big` table:

```
select sum(page_count) as pages, sum(compressed_page_count) as compressed_pages
from sys.dm_db_index_physical_stats (DB_ID(),
OBJECT_ID('Sales.SalesOrderDetail'), 1, null, 'DETAILED')
where index_level = 0

SELECT SUM(used_page_count/ 128.0) AS size_in_MB
FROM sys.dm_db_partition_stats
WHERE object_id=OBJECT_ID('Sales.SalesOrderDetail') AND index_id=1
GO

/* output
pages compressed_pages
----- ----------------
  596             590


size_in_MB
----------
  4.796875
*/
```

In this example, you can see that the table was reduced in size from 1,237 pages to 596 pages (9.8MB to 4.8MB), pretty much right in line with the estimated space savings. You can also see that compression was reasonably effective, compressing 590 of 596 pages.

Be aware that you may not always receive the space savings predicted due to the effects of fill factor and the actual size of the rows. For example, if you have a row that is 8,000 bytes long and compression reduces its size by 40%, only one row can still fit on the data page, so there is no space savings for that page. If the results of running `sp_estimate_ data_compression_savings` indicate that the table will grow, this indicates that many of the rows in the table are using nearly the full precision of the data types, and the addition of the small overhead needed for the compressed format is more than the savings from compression. In this, it is obvious that there is no advantage to enabling compression.

Managing Data Compression with SSMS

The preceding examples show the T-SQL commands you can use to evaluate and manage row and page compression in SQL Server 2014. SSMS provides a Data Compression Wizard for evaluating and performing data compression activities. To invoke the Data Compression Wizard, right-click on the table in the Object Explorer and select Storage and then select Manage Compression. Click Next to move past the Welcome page to bring up the Select Compression Type page, as shown in Figure 31.11.

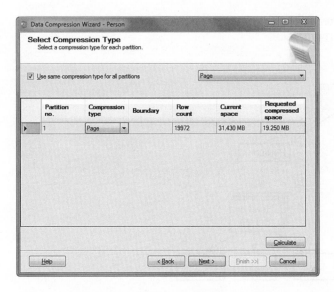

FIGURE 31.11   The Data Compression Wizard's Select Compression Type page.

On the Compression Type Page, you can choose the compression type to use at the partition level or to use the same compression type for all partitions. You can also see the estimated savings for selected compression type by clicking on the Calculate button. After you click on Calculate, the wizard displays the current partition size and requested compression size in the corresponding columns (note that it might take a few moments to do the calculation).

After making your selections, click on Next to display the Select and Output Option page. Here, you have the opportunity to have the wizard generate a script of commands you can run manually to implement the selected compression type. If you choose to generate a script, you have the option to save the script to a file, the Clipboard, or to a new query window in SSMS. You also have the option to run the compression changes immediately or schedule a SQL Agent job to run the changes at a specified time.

Understanding Table Structures

A table is logically defined as a set of columns with certain properties, such as the data type, nullability, constraints, and so on. Information about data types, column properties, constraints, and other information related to defining and creating tables can be found in Chapters 21 and 24, "Creating and Managing Views."

Internally, a table is contained in one or more partitions. A partition is a user-defined unit of data organization. By default, a table consists of a single partition that contains all the table pages. This partition resides in a single filegroup, as described earlier. When a table has multiple partitions, the data is partitioned horizontally so that groups of rows are mapped into individual partitions, based on a specified column. The partitions can be placed in one or more filegroups in the database. The table is treated as a single logical entity when queries or updates are performed on the data. Figure 31.12 shows the organization of a table in SQL Server 2014.

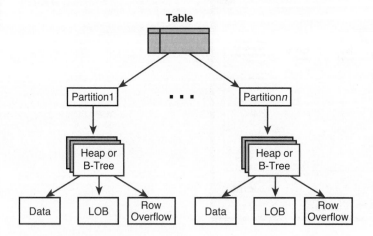

FIGURE 31.12   Table organization in SQL Server 2014.

Each table has one row in the `sys.objects` catalog view, and each table and index in a database is represented by a single row in the `sys.indexes` catalog view. Each partition of a table or index is represented by one or more rows in the `sys.partitions` catalog view. Each partition can have three types of data, each stored on its own set of pages: in-row data pages, row-overflow pages, and LOB data pages. Each of these types of pages has an allocation unit, which is contained in the `sys.allocation_units` view. There is always at least one allocation unit for the in-row data. The following sample query shows how to view the partition and allocation information for the `databaselog` and `currency` tables in the `AdventureWorks2012` database:

```
use AdventureWorks2012
go
SELECT convert(varchar(15), o.name) AS table_name,
     p.index_id as indid,
     convert(varchar(30), i.name) AS index_name,
      convert(varchar(18), au.type_desc) AS allocation_type,
      au.data_pages as d_pgs,
      partition_number as ptn
FROM sys.allocation_units AS au
    JOIN sys.partitions AS p ON au.container_id = p.partition_id
    JOIN sys.objects AS o ON p.object_id = o.object_id
    JOIN sys.indexes AS i ON p.index_id = i.index_id AND i.object_id = p.object_id
WHERE o.name = N'databaselog' OR o.name = N'currency'
ORDER BY o.name, p.index_id;
```

```
/* output
table_name    indid index_name                      allocation_type       d_pgs ptn
----------    ----- ------------------------------   ------------------    ----- ---
Currency          1 PK_Currency_CurrencyCode         IN_ROW_DATA               1   1
Currency          2 AK_Currency_Name                 IN_ROW_DATA               1   1
DatabaseLog       0 NULL                             IN_ROW_DATA             782   1
DatabaseLog       0 NULL                             LOB_DATA                  0   1
DatabaseLog       0 NULL                             ROW_OVERFLOW_DATA         0   1
DatabaseLog       2 PK_DatabaseLog_DatabaseLogID     IN_ROW_DATA               4   1
*/
```

In this example, you can see that the DatabaseLog table (which is a heap table) has three allocation units associated with the table—LOB, row-overflow, and in-row data—and one allocation unit for the nonclustered index PK_DatabaseLog_DatabaseLogID. The currency table (which is a clustered table) has a single in-row allocation unit for both the table (index_id = 1) and the nonclustered index (AK_Currency_Name).

In SQL Server 2014, there are three types of tables: heap tables, clustered tables, and memory-optimized tables. In this chapter, we'll look at how heap and clustered tables are stored. Memory-optimized tables will be looked at in Chapter 33.

Heap Tables

A table without a clustered index is a *heap table*. There is no imposed ordering of the data rows for a heap table. Additionally, there is no direct linkage between the data pages in a heap table.

By default, a heap has a single partition. Heaps have one row in sys.partitions, with an index ID of 0 for each partition used by the heap. When a heap has multiple partitions, each partition has a heap structure that contains the data for that specific partition. For example, if a heap has four partitions, there are four heap structures (one in each partition) and four rows in sys.partitions.

Depending on the data types in the heap, each heap structure has one or more allocation units to store and manage the data for each partition. At a minimum, each heap has one IN_ROW_DATA allocation unit per partition. The heap also has one LOB_DATA allocation unit per partition if it contains large object columns. It also has one ROW_OVERFLOW_DATA allocation unit per partition if it contains variable-length columns that exceed the 8,060-byte row size limit.

To access the contents of a heap, SQL Server uses the IAM pages. Each heap table has at least one IAM page. The address of the first IAM page is available in the undocumented sys.sytem_internals_allocation_units system view. The column first_iam_page points to the first IAM page in the chain of IAM pages that manage the space allocated to the heap in a specific partition. The following query returns the first IAM pages for each of the allocation units for the heap table DatabaseLog in AdventureWorks2012:

```
use AdventureWorks2012
go
select p.partition_number as ptn,
     type_desc,
     filegroup_id,
     first_iam_page
from sys.system_internals_allocation_units i
inner join
sys.partitions p
on p.hobt_id = i.container_id
where p.object_id = OBJECT_ID('DatabaseLog')
and index_id = 0
go

/* output
ptn type_desc             filegroup_id first_iam_page
--- ------------------    ------------ --------------
  1 IN_ROW_DATA                      1 0x120100000100
  1 LOB_DATA                         1 0x170100000100
  1 ROW_OVERFLOW_DATA                1 0x000000000000
*/
```

Note that the value 0x000000000000 for the first_iam_page for ROW_OVERFLOW_DATA indicates that no extents have yet been allocated for storing row-overflow data.

> **NOTE**
>
> The sys.system_internals_allocation_units system view is reserved for Microsoft SQL Server internal use only. Future compatibility and availability of this view is not guaranteed.

The data pages and rows in the heap are not sorted in any specific order and are not linked. The IAM page registers which extents are used by the table. SQL Server can then simply scan the allocated extents referenced by the IAM page, in physical order. This essentially avoids the problem of page chain fragmentation during reads because SQL Server always reads full extents in sequential order. Using the IAM pages to set the scan sequence also means that rows from the heap often are not returned in the order in which they were inserted.

As discussed earlier, each IAM can map a maximum of 63,903 extents for a table. As a table uses extents beyond the range of those 63,903 extents, more IAM pages are created for the heap table as needed. A heap table also has at least one IAM page for each file on which the heap table has extents allocated. Figure 31.13 illustrates the structure of a heap and how its contents are traversed using the IAM pages.

SYS.SYSTEM_INTERNALS_ALLOCATION_UNITS

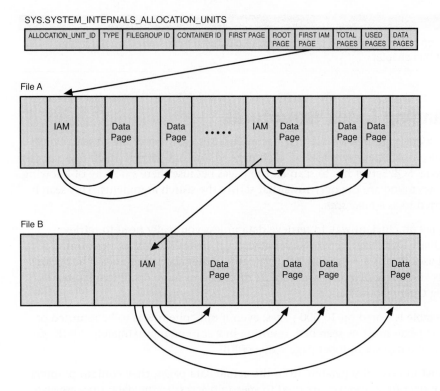

FIGURE 31.13   The structure of a heap table.

Clustered Tables

A *clustered table* is a table that has a clustered index defined on it. When you create a clustered index, the data rows in the table are physically sorted in the order of the columns in the index key. The data pages are chained together in a doubly linked list (each page points to the next page and to the previous page). In a nonclustered heap table, data pages are not linked. Only index pages within a level are linked in this manner to allow for ordered scans of the data in an index level. Because the data pages of a clustered table constitute the leaf level of the clustered index, they are chained as well. This allows for an ordered table scan. The page pointers are stored in the page header. Figure 31.14 shows a simplified example of the data pages of a clustered table. (Note that the figure shows only the data pages.)

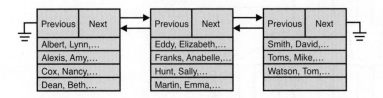

FIGURE 31.14   The data page structure of a clustered table.

> **TIP**
>
> More details on the structure and maintenance of clustered tables are provided in the remainder of this chapter.

Understanding Index Structures

When you run a query against a table that has no indexes, SQL Server has to read every page of the table, looking at every row on each page to find out whether each row satisfies the search criteria. SQL Server has to scan all the pages because there's no way of knowing whether any rows found are the only rows that satisfy the search arguments. This search method is referred to as a *table scan*.

A table scan is *not* an efficient way to retrieve data unless you really need to retrieve all rows. The Query Optimizer in SQL Server always calculates the cost of performing a table scan and uses that as a baseline when evaluating other access methods. The various access methods and query plan cost analysis are discussed in more detail in Chapter 34, "Understanding Query Optimization."

Suppose that a table is stored on 10,000 pages; even if only one row is to be returned or modified, all the pages must be searched, resulting in a scan of approximately 80MB of data (that is, 10,000 pages × 8KB per page = 80,000KB).

Indexes are structures stored separately from the actual data pages; they contain pointers to data pages or data rows. Indexes are used to speed up access to the data; they are also the mechanism used to enforce the uniqueness of key values.

Indexes in SQL Server are balanced trees (B-trees; see Figure 31.15). There is a single root page at the top of the tree, which branches out into N pages at each intermediate level until it reaches the bottom (leaf level) of the index. The leaf level has one row stored for each row in the table. The index tree is traversed by following pointers from the upper-level pages down through the lower-level pages. Each level of the index is linked as a doubly linked list.

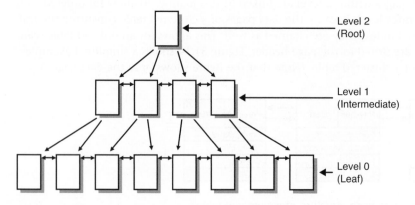

FIGURE 31.15   The basic structure of a B-tree index.

An index can have many intermediate levels, depending on the number of rows in the table, index type, and index key width. The maximum number of columns in an index is 16; the maximum width of an index row is 900 bytes.

To provide a more efficient mechanism to identify and locate specific rows within a table quickly and easily, SQL Server supports two types of B-tree indexes: clustered and nonclustered. SQL Server 2014 also supports columnstore indexes which are discussed later in this chapter.

Clustered Indexes

When you create a clustered index, all rows in the table are sorted and stored in the clustered index key order. Because the rows are physically sorted by the index key, you can have only one clustered index per table. You can think of the structure of a clustered index as being similar to a filing cabinet: The data pages are like folders in a file drawer in alphabetical order, and the data rows are like the records in the file folder, also in sorted order.

You can think of the intermediate levels of the index tree as the file drawers, also in alphabetical order, that assist you in finding the appropriate file folder. Figure 31.16 shows an example of a clustered index tree structure.

In Figure 31.16, note that the data page chain is in clustered index order. However, the rows on each page might not be physically sorted in clustered index order, depending on when rows were inserted or deleted in the page. SQL Server still keeps the proper sort order of the rows via the row IDs and the row offset table. A clustered index is useful for range-retrieval queries or searches against columns with duplicate values because the rows within the range are physically located in the same page or on adjacent pages.

The data pages of the table are also the leaf level of a clustered index. To find all clustered index key values, SQL Server must eventually scan all the data pages.

SQL Server performs the following steps when searching for a value using a clustered index:

1. Queries the system catalogs for the page address for the root page of the index. (For a clustered index, the `root_page` column in `sys.system_internals_allocation_units` points to the top of the clustered index for a specific partition.)

2. Compares the search value against the key values stored on the root page.

3. Finds the highest key value on the page where the key value is less than or equal to the search value.

4. Follows the page pointer stored with the key to the appropriate page at the next level down in the index.

5. Continues following page pointers (that is, repeats steps 3 and 4) until the data page is reached.

6. Searches the rows on the data page to locate any matches for the search value. If no matching row is found on that data page, the table contains no matching values.

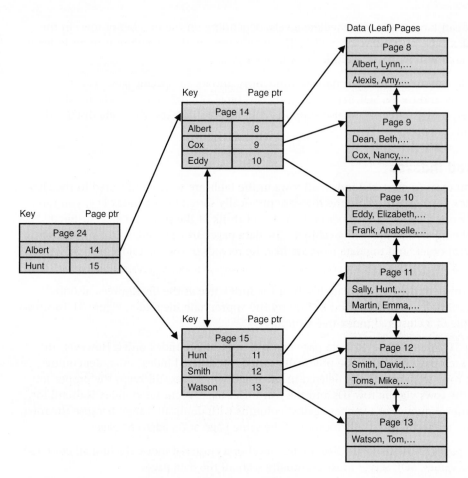

FIGURE 31.16   The structure of a clustered index.

By default, a clustered index has a single partition and thus has at least one row in sys. partitions with index_id = 1. When a clustered index has multiple partitions, a separate B-tree structure contains the data for that specific partition.

Depending on the data types in the clustered index, each clustered index structure has one or more allocation units in which to store and manage the data for a specific partition. At a minimum, each clustered index has one IN_ROW_DATA allocation unit per partition. If the table contains any LOB data, the clustered index also has one LOB_DATA allocation unit per partition and one ROW_OVERFLOW_DATA allocation unit per partition if the table contains any variable-length columns that exceed the 8,060-byte row size limit.

Clustered Index Row Structure

The structure of a clustered index row is similar to the structure of a data row except that it contains only key columns; this structure is detailed in Figure 31.17.

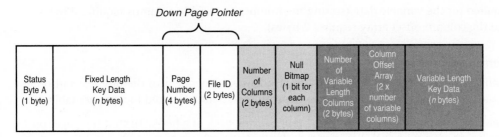

(Shaded Areas represent data present only when index contains nullable or variable length columns)

FIGURE 31.17   Clustered index row structure.

Notice that unlike a data row, index rows do not contain the status byte B or the 2 bytes to hold the length of fixed-length data fields. Instead of storing the length of the fixed-length data, which also indicates where the fixed-length portion of a row ends and the variable-length portion begins, the page header `pminlen` value is used to help describe an index row. The `pminlen` value is the minimum length of the index row, which is essentially the sum of the size of all fixed-width fields and overhead. Therefore, if no variable-length or nullable fields are in the index key, `pminlen` also indicates the width of each index row.

The null bitmap field and field for the number of columns in the index row are present only when an index key contains nullable columns. The number of columns value is only needed to determine how many bits are needed in the null bitmap and therefore how many bytes are required to store the null bitmap (1 byte per eight columns). The data contents of a clustered index row include the key values along with a 6-byte down-page pointer (the first 2 bytes are the file ID, and the last 4 bytes are the page number). The down-page pointer is the last value in the fixed-data portion of the row.

Nonunique Clustered Indexes

When a clustered index is defined on a table, the clustered index keys are used as row locators to identify the data rows being referenced by nonclustered indexes (more on this topic in the following section on nonclustered indexes). Because the clustered keys are used as unique row pointers, there needs to be a way to uniquely refer to each row in the table. If the clustered index is defined as a unique index, the key itself uniquely identifies every row. If the clustered index was not created as a unique index, SQL Server adds a 4-byte integer field, called a *uniqueifier*, to the data row to make each key unique when necessary. When is the uniqueifier necessary? SQL Server adds the uniqueifier to a row when the row is added to a table and that new row contains a key that is a duplicate of the key for an already-existing row.

The uniqueifier is added to the variable-length data area of the data row, which also results in the addition of the variable-length overhead bytes. Therefore, each duplicate row in a clustered index has a minimum of 4 bytes of overhead added for the additional uniqueifier. If the row had no variable-length keys previously, an additional 8 bytes of overhead are added to the row to store the uniqueifier (4 bytes) plus the overhead bytes required for the variable data (storing the number of variable columns requires 2 bytes, and the column offset array requires 2 bytes).

Nonclustered Indexes

A nonclustered index is a separate index structure, independent of the physical sort order of the data rows in the table. You can have up to 999 nonclustered indexes per table.

A nonclustered index is similar to the index in the back of a book. To find the pages on which a specific subject is discussed, you look up the subject in the index and then go to the pages referenced in the index. This method is efficient as long as the subject is discussed on only a few pages. If the subject is discussed on many pages, or if you want to read about many subjects, it can be more efficient to read the entire book.

A nonclustered index works similarly to the book index. From the index's perspective, the data rows are randomly spread throughout the table. The nonclustered index tree contains the index key values, in sorted order. There is a row at the leaf level of the index for each data row in the table. Each leaf-level row contains a data row locator to locate the actual data row in the table.

If no clustered index is created for the table, the data row locator for the leaf level of the index is an actual pointer to the data page and the row number within the page where the row is located (see Figure 31.18).

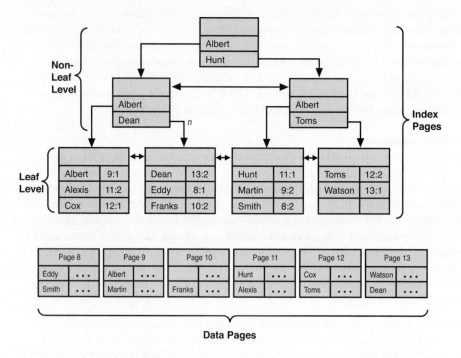

FIGURE 31.18   A nonclustered index on a heap table.

Nonclustered indexes on clustered tables use the associated clustered index key value for the record as the data row locator. When SQL Server reaches the leaf level of a nonclustered index, it uses the clustered index key to start searching through the clustered index to find the actual data row (see Figure 31.19). This adds some I/O to the search itself, but the benefit is that if a page split occurs in a clustered table, or if a data row is moved (for example, as a result of an update), the nonclustered index row locator stays the same. As long as the clustered index key value itself is not modified, no data row locators in the nonclustered index have to be updated.

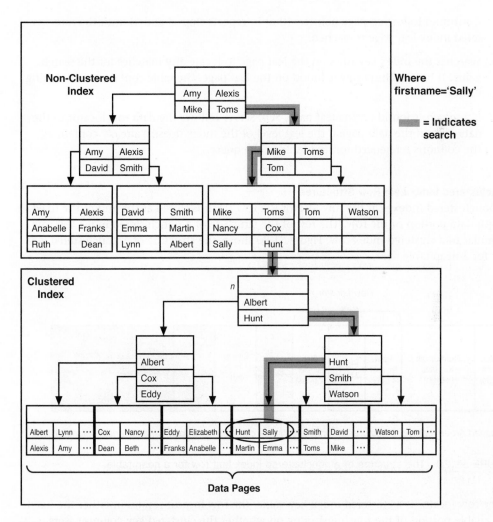

FIGURE 31.19   A nonclustered index on a clustered table.

SQL Server performs the following steps when searching for a value by using a nonclustered index:

1. Queries the system catalog to determine the page address for the root page of the index.

2. Compares the search value against the index key values on the root page.

3. Finds the highest key value on the page where the key value is less than or equal to the search value.

4. Follows the down-page pointer to the next level down in the nonclustered index tree.

5. Continues following page pointers (that is, repeats steps 3 and 4) until the nonclustered index leaf page is reached.

6. Searches the index key rows on the leaf page to locate any matches for the search value. If no matching row is found on the leaf page, the table contains no matching values.

7. If a match is found on the leaf page, SQL Server follows the data row locator to the data row on the data page if the leaf level of the index doesn't already contain all the columns referenced for that table in the query.

Nonclustered Index Leaf Row Structures

In nonclustered indexes, if the row locator is a row ID, it is stored at the end of the fixed-length data portion of the row. The rest of the structure of a nonclustered index leaf row is similar to a clustered index row. Figure 31.20 shows the structure of a nonclustered leaf row for a heap table.

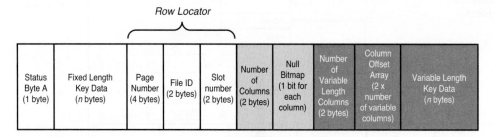

(Shaded Areas represent data present only when index contains nullable or variable length columns)

FIGURE 31.20   The structure of a nonclustered index leaf row for a heap table.

If the row locator is a clustered index key value, the row locator resides in either the fixed or variable portion of the row, depending on whether the clustered key columns were defined as fixed or variable length. Figure 31.21 shows the structure of a nonclustered leaf row for a clustered table.

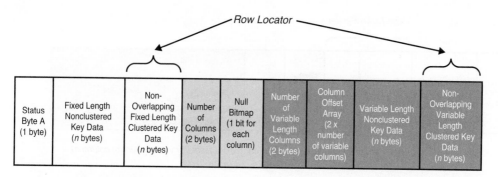

(Shaded Areas represent data present only when index contains nullable or variable length columns)

FIGURE 31.21   The structure of a nonclustered index leaf row for a clustered table.

When the row locator is a clustered key value and the clustered and nonclustered indexes share columns, the data value for the key is stored only once in the nonclustered index row. For example, if your clustered index key is on `lastname` and you have a nonclustered index defined on both `firstname` and `lastname`, the index rows do not store the value of `lastname` twice, but only once for both keys.

If the nonclustered index contains any included columns, the included columns are appended to the key data fields in the index leaf row only. Included column values are not included as part of the index key itself and not stored in the nonleaf rows. If the nonclustered index is defined as a filtered index, the structure of the index key rows is the same as for a non-filtered index, but rows are stored in the index for only the key values meeting the filter criteria. For more information on defining filtered indexes or adding included columns to an index, see Chapter 22, "Creating and Managing Indexes."

Nonclustered Index Nonleaf Row Structures

The nonclustered index nonleaf rows are similar in structure to clustered index nonleaf rows in that they contain a page-down pointer to a page at the next level down in the index tree. The nonleaf rows don't need to point to data rows; they only need to provide the path to traverse the index tree to a leaf row. If the nonclustered index is defined as unique, the nonleaf index key row contains only the index key value and page-down pointer. Figure 31.22 shows the structure of a nonleaf index row for a unique nonclustered index.

If the nonclustered index is not defined as a unique index, the nonleaf rows also contain the row locator information for the corresponding data row. Storing the row locator in the nonleaf index row ensures each index key row is unique (because the row locator, by its nature, must be unique). Ensuring each index key row is unique allows any corresponding nonleaf index rows to be located and deleted more easily when the data row is deleted. For a heap table, the row locator is the corresponding data row's page and row pointer, as shown in Figure 31.23.

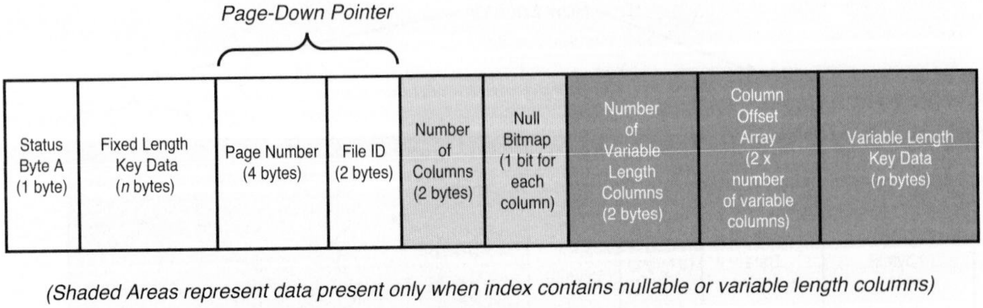

Page-Down Pointer
Status Byte A (1 byte)
Fixed Length Key Data (n bytes)
Page Number (4 bytes)
File ID (2 bytes)
Number of Columns (2 bytes)
Null Bitmap (1 bit for each column)
Number of Variable Length Columns (2 bytes)
Column Offset Array (2 x number of variable columns)
Variable Length Key Data (n bytes)
(Shaded Areas represent data present only when index contains nullable or variable length columns)

FIGURE 31.22 The structure of a nonclustered nonleaf index row for a unique index.

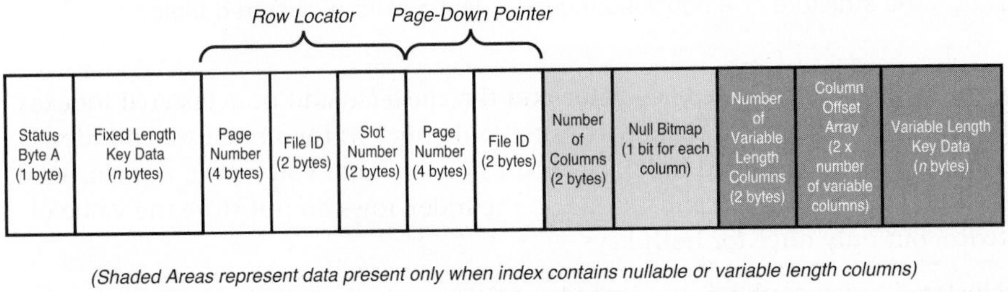

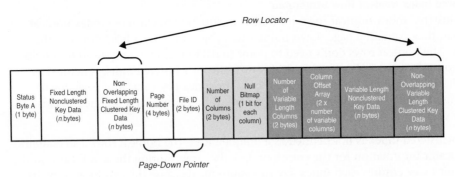

Row Locator
Page-Down Pointer
Status Byte A (1 byte)
Fixed Length Key Data (n bytes)
Page Number (4 bytes)
File ID (2 bytes)
Slot Number (2 bytes)
Page Number (4 bytes)
File ID (2 bytes)
Number of Columns (2 bytes)
Null Bitmap (1 bit for each column)
Number of Variable Length Columns (2 bytes)
Column Offset Array (2 x number of variable columns)
Variable Length Key Data (n bytes)
(Shaded Areas represent data present only when index contains nullable or variable length columns)

FIGURE 31.23 The structure of a nonclustered nonleaf index row for a nonunique index on a heap table.

If the table is clustered, the clustered key values are stored in the nonleaf index rows of the nonunique nonclustered index just as they are in the leaf rows, as shown in Figure 31.24.

Row Locator
Status Byte A (1 byte)
Fixed Length Nonclustered Key Data (n bytes)
Non-Overlapping Fixed Length Clustered Key Data (n bytes)
Page Number (4 bytes)
File ID (2 bytes)
Number of Columns (2 bytes)
Null Bitmap (1 bit for each column)
Number of Variable Length Columns (2 bytes)
Column Offset Array (2 x number of variable columns)
Variable Length Nonclustered Key Data (n bytes)
Non-Overlapping Variable Length Clustered Key Data (n bytes)
Page-Down Pointer
(Shaded Areas represent data present only when index contains nullable or variable length columns)

FIGURE 31.24 The structure of a nonclustered nonleaf index row for a nonunique index on a clustered table.

As you can see, it's possible for the index pointers and row overhead to exceed the size of the index key itself. This is why, for I/O and storage reasons, it is always recommended that you keep your index keys as small as possible.

Columnstore Indexes

SQL Server 2012 introduced a new query acceleration feature based on a type of index called a *columnstore index*. Columnstore indexes, combined with enhanced query processing features, can improve query performance for data warehouse applications significantly. Columnstore indexes can eliminate the need to rely on other data warehousing strategies such as prebuilt aggregates, summary tables, and indexed views.

In SQL Server 2012, columnstore indexes were limited to nonclustered columnstore indexes only and tables with a nonclustered columnstore index could not be updated. To update the data, you had to drop and rebuild the index or swap out partitions. In SQL Server 2014, this feature was enhanced to allow the creation of clustered columnstore indexes. The clustered columnstore index permits data modifications and bulk load operations.

Unlike typical row storage, which stores multiple columns of data in one or more rows per page, as you've seen in the previous sections of this chapter, a columnstore index stores the values for each column in their own separate set of disk pages. The advantage of columnar storage is the ability to read the values of a specific column of a table without having to read the values of all the other columns. In row-oriented storage this is impossible because the individual column values are physically stored grouped in rows on the pages. Reading a row in order to read a column value requires fetching the entire page in memory, thus automatically reading all the other columns in the row as well. Figure 31.25 illustrates the difference between column store and row store approaches.

As you can see in Figure 31.25, rather than storing the values for columns C1 through C10 together in rows on a data page, the values for columns C1 through C10 are stored in different groups of pages in the columnstore index. SQL Server columnstore indexes are "pure" column stores, not a hybrid, because they store all data for separate columns on separate pages. The benefits of columnstore indexes are as follows:

▶ Only the columns needed to satisfy a query are accessed (this is often fewer than 15% of the columns in a typical fact table), improving I/O scan performance.

▶ Better compression of the data can be achieved due to the redundancy of data within a column.

▶ Buffer hit rates are improved because data is highly compressed, and frequently accessed parts of commonly used columns can remain in memory more easily.

So if all the values of a column are stored separately, how does SQL Server re-create a row of data when you query a columnstore? For example, if the first column contains all the product IDs and the second column contains all the order dates, how does SQL Server keep track of which product was ordered on which date? The answer is that that the position of the value in the column indicates which row it belongs to. So, row 1 in the `ProductID` column correlates with row 1 in the `OrderDate` column, and row 2 in `ProductID` correlates with row 2 in `OrderDate`, and so on.

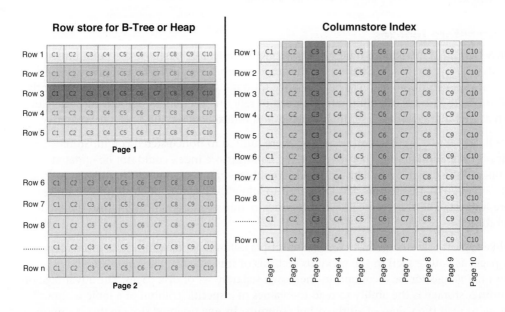

FIGURE 31.25   Comparison between row store and columnstore data storage.

The `COLUMNSTORE` index feature of SQL Server 2014 uses the same xVelocity columnar storage technology as that offered in PowerPivot and Microsoft SQL Server Analysis Server, but adapted to the SQL Server product, specifically to the SQL Server storage and memory model. Normally, in a multidimensional online analytical processing (MOLAP) system, the entire columnar database is treated as a single monolithic file and loaded entirely in memory. Such a use pattern would not work along with the complex memory management of the SQL Server buffer pool. Besides, the storage options of SQL Server are capped at the maximum of 2GB size of a `BLOB` value, which would make for a fairly small columnar storage database. To address this size limitation, `COLUMNSTORE` indexes in SQL Server use the xVelocity technology on smaller chunks of the data called *segments*, as shown in Figure 31.26.

A segment represents a group of consecutive rows in the columnstore index. For example segment 1 might contain rows from 0 to row number 1,000,000, segment 2 would have rows from 1,000,001 to 2,000,000, segment 3 from 2000001, and on. Each column segment is essentially like a `VARINARY(MAX)` column containing the actual segment data. The maximum amount of data that can be stored in segment is 2GB, which is the maximum size of a `VARBINARY(MAX)` column value. Each column will have an entry for each segment in the `sys.column_store_segments` system catalog. The rows in the `sys.column_store_segments` store base information on the segment, such as the min and max IDs for the segment and whether the segment has null values.

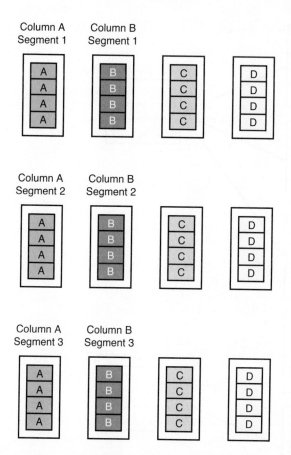

FIGURE 31.26   Use of segments in columnstore indexes in SQL Server 2014.

Besides column segments, a columnstore also stores dictionaries associated with the columnstore columns. Dictionaries provide a means of compressing the data stored in the columns, which leads to efficiently encoding large data types, like strings. The actual data values are stored once in the dictionary with a corresponding entry number. The values stored in the column segments will then just be the entry numbers in the dictionary that correspond to the data value. This technique can yield very good compression for repeated values because the value is stored just once in the dictionary and only the repeated entry number is stored in the actual columnstore index. However, this technique is not efficient if the values are all distinct and the required storage space actually increases. Large columns (strings) with distinct values would be poor candidates for columnstore indexes.

There is a separate dictionary stored for each column in a columnstore index, and any string columns will have two types of dictionaries: a primary dictionary and a secondary dictionary (see Figure 31.27).

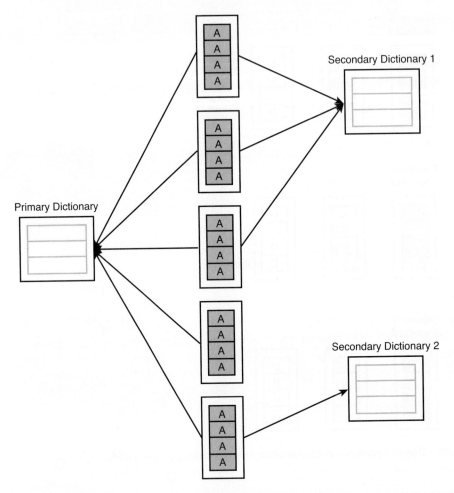

FIGURE 31.27   Primary and secondary dictionaries in a columnstore.

The primary dictionary is a global dictionary used by all segments of a column. The secondary dictionary is an overflow dictionary for entries that did not fit in the primary dictionaries. It can be shared by several segments of a column; the relation between dictionaries and column segments is one-to-many. Information on the dictionaries is stored in `sys.column_store_dictionaries`. This catalog view contains one row for each column in a columnstore index that describes the structure and type of dictionary built for the column.

When to Use Columnstore Indexes

Columnstore indexes are generally not ideal for highly selective queries, which access only a few rows or queries that lookup a single row or a small range of rows. In these situations, normal row store indexes will perform better.

Columnstore indexes have been designed to accelerate common data warehouse queries, typically those which require scanning, aggregation, and filtering of large amounts of data. You can create both row store indexes and a nonclustered columnstore index on the same table. The Query Optimizer will decide when to use the columnstore index and when to use standard clustered or nonclustered indexes. However, keep in mind that nonclustered columnstore indexes are not suited for OLTP environments because creating a nonclustered columnstore index on a table makes that table read-only. Updates are not allowed on tables with nonclustered columnstored indexes.

To load data into a table with nonclustered columnstore index, you first load the data into a normal table stored as a heap or with a clustered index and then create the nonclustered columnstore index. To add to, or modify data in, a nonclustered columnstore index, you'll need to do one of the following:

▶ Disable or drop the columnstore index, update/load the data in the table, and then rebuild the column store index.

▶ Load the data into a staging table without a nonclustered columnstore index, create a columnstore index on the staging table and switch the staging table into an empty partition of the main table.

▶ Switch a partition from the table with the nonclustered columnstore index into an empty staging table, add/modify the data, create the nonclustered columnstore index on the staging table, and switch the staging table back into the partition of the main table.

Clustered columnstore indexes are updateable, and you can load or modify data in a clustered columnstore index using the standard INSERT, UPDATE, and DELETE statements without having to drop it. A clustered columnstore index includes a rowstore table called the deltastore for temporarily storing new or modified rows. The deltastore stores rows until the number of rows is large enough to be moved into the columnstore. The minimum size of a deltastore rowgroup is 102,400 rows. When bulk loading a large number of rows that exceeds the minimum deltastore rowgroup size, most of the rows go directly to the clustered columnstore without passing through the deltastore. For small bulk loads with less than 102,400 rows, or when rows at the end of the bulk load might be too few in number to meet the minium rowgroup size, the rows go directly to the deltastore. When a delatastore reaches the maximum number of rows (which is 1,048,576 rows), it is closed and moved into the columnstore.

When you update a row in the clustered columnstore index, SQL Server marks the row as logically deleted and inserts the modified row into the deltastore. When you delete a row from a clustered column store index, if the row is in the columnstore, the row is marked as logically deleted but remains in the columnstored until the index is rebuilt. If the deleted row exists in the deltastore, SQL Server deletes the row from the deltastore.

All deltastore operations are handled automatically behind the scenes. When querying a clustered column store index, the index combines query results from both the columnstore and the deltastore.

In addition to clustered columnstore indexes being updateable, there are also some other differences between nonclustered columnstore and clustered columnstore indexes. Clustered columnstore indexes have no key columns. All columns in the table are included in the index and it is the primary storage method for the entire table. No other indexes can be defined on the table. In addition, a table with clustered columnstore indexes cannot be configured with any unique, primary key or foreign key constraints. You also cannot create a clustered columnstore index on a table that includes computed columns, sparse columns, or non-supported data types, such as `text`, `XML` or `varchar(max)`.

A nonclustered columnstore index can be created on a subset of columns in a table that can also have a clustered index as well as nonclustered indexes defined on it. The nonclustered columnstore index requires extra storage to store a copy of the columns in the index.

For more information on creating and using columnstore indexes, see Chapter 51, "Parallel Data Warehouse."

Data Modification and Performance

Now that you have a better understanding of the storage structures in SQL Server, it's time to look at how SQL Server maintains and manages those structures when data modifications are taking place in the database.

Inserting Data

When you add a data row to a heap table, SQL Server adds the row to the heap wherever space is available. SQL Server uses the IAM and PFS pages to identify whether any pages with free space are available in the extents already allocated to the table. If no free pages are found, SQL Server uses the information from the GAM and SGAM pages to locate a free extent and allocate it to the table.

For clustered tables, the new data row is inserted to the appropriate location on the appropriate data page relative to the clustered index key order. If no more room is available on the destination page, SQL Server needs to link a new page in the page chain to make room available and add the row. This is called a *page split*.

In addition to modifying the affected data pages when adding rows, SQL Server needs to update all nonclustered indexes to add a pointer to the new record. If a page split occurs, this incurs even more overhead because the clustered index needs to be updated to store the pointer for the new page added to the table. Fortunately, because the clustered key is used as the row locator in nonclustered indexes when a table is clustered, even though the page and row IDs have changed, the nonclustered index row locators for rows moved by a page split do not have to be updated as long as the clustered key column values remain the same.

Page Splits

When a page split occurs, SQL Server looks for an available page to link into the page chain. It first tries to find an available page in the same extent as the pages it will be linked to. If no free pages exist in the same extent, it looks at the IAM to determine whether there are any free pages in any other extents already allocated to the table or index. If no free pages are found, a new extent is allocated to the table.

When a new page is found or allocated to the table and linked into the page chain, the original page is "split." Approximately half the rows are moved to the new page, and the rest remain on the original page (see Figure 31.28). Whether the new page goes before or after the original page when the split is made depends on the amount of data to be moved. In an effort to minimize logging, SQL Server moves the smaller rows to the new page. If the smaller rows are at the beginning of the page, SQL Server places the new page before the original page and moves the smaller rows to it. If the larger rows are at the beginning of the page, SQL Server keeps them on the original page and moves the smaller rows to the new page after the original page.

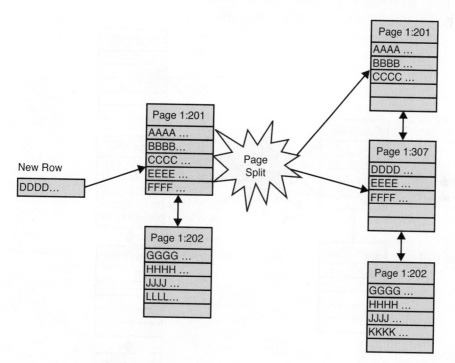

FIGURE 31.28   Page splitting due to inserts.

After determining where the new row goes between the existing rows and whether the new page is to be added before or after the original page, SQL Server has to move rows to the new page. The simplified algorithm for determining the split point is as follows:

1. Place first row (with the lowest clustered key value) at the beginning of first page.

2. Place the last row (with the highest clustered key value) on the second page.

3. Place the row with the next lowest clustered key value on the first page after the existing row(s).

4. Place the next-to-last row (with the second highest clustered key value) on the second page.

5. Continue alternating back and forth until the space between the two pages is balanced or one of the pages is full.

In some situations a double split can occur. If the new row has to go between two existing rows on a page, but the new row is too large to fit on either page with any of the existing rows, a new page is added after the original. The new row is added to the new page, a second new page is added after that, and the remaining original rows are inserted into the second new page. An example of a double split is shown in Figure 31.29.

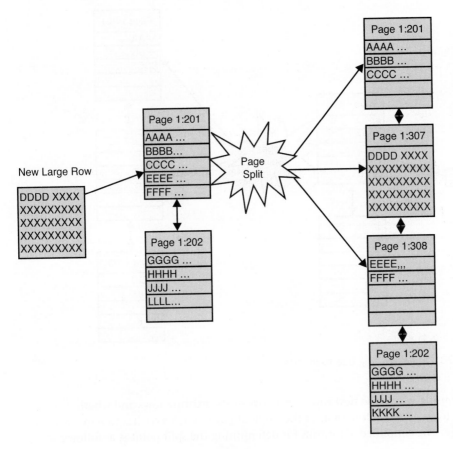

FIGURE 31.29   Double page split due to large row insert.

> **NOTE**
>
> Although page splits are expensive when they occur, they do generate free space in the split pages for future inserts into those pages. Page splits also help keep the index tree balanced as rows are added to the table. However, if you monitor the system with Performance Monitor and are seeing hundreds of page splits per second, you might want to consider rebuilding the clustered index on the table and applying a lower fill factor to provide more free space in the existing pages. This can help improve system performance until eventually the pages fill up and start splitting again. For this reason, some shops supporting high-volume online transaction processing (OLTP) environments with a lot of insert activity rebuild the indexes with a lower fill factor on a daily basis.

Deleting Rows

What happens when rows are deleted from a table? How, and when, does SQL Server reclaim the space when data is removed from a table?

Deleting Rows from a Heap

In a heap table, SQL Server does not automatically compress the space on a page when a row is removed; that is, the rows are not all moved up to the beginning of the page to keep all free space at the end. To optimize performance, SQL Server holds off on compacting the rows until the page needs contiguous space for storing a new row.

Deleting Rows from an Index

Because the data pages of a clustered table are actually the leaf pages of the clustered index, the behavior of data row deletes on a clustered table is the same as row deletions from an index page.

When rows are deleted from the leaf level of an index, they are not actually deleted but are marked as ghost records. Keeping the row as a ghost record makes it easier for SQL Server to perform key-range locking (key-range locking is discussed in Chapter 37, "Locking and Performance"). If ghost records were not used, SQL Server would have to lock the entire range surrounding the deleted record during the delete operation. With the ghost record still present and visible internally to SQL Server (it is not visible in query result sets), SQL Server can use the ghost record as an endpoint for the key-range lock to prevent "phantom" records with the same key value from being inserted, while allowing inserts of other values to proceed.

Ghost records do not stay around forever, though. SQL Server has a special internal housekeeping process that periodically examines the leaf level of B-trees for ghost records and removes them. This is the same thread that performs the autoshrink process for databases.

Whenever you delete a row, all nonclustered indexes need to be updated to remove the pointers to the deleted row. Nonleaf index rows are not ghosted when deleted. As with heap tables, however, the space is not compressed on the nonleaf index page until space is needed for a new row.

Reclaiming Space

Only when the last row is deleted from a data page is the page deallocated from the table. The only exception is if it is the last page remaining; all tables must have at least one page allocated, even if it's empty. When a deletion of an index row leaves only one row remaining on the page, the remaining row is moved to a neighboring page, and the now-empty index page is deallocated.

If the page to be deallocated is the last remaining used page in a uniform extent allocated to the table, the extent is deallocated from the table as well.

Updating Rows

SQL Server 2014 performs row updates by evaluating the number of rows affected, whether the rows are being accessed via a scan or index retrieval, and whether any index keys are being modified and automatically chooses the appropriate and most efficient update strategy for the rows affected. SQL Server can perform two types of update strategies:

▶ In-place updates

▶ Not-in-place updates

In-Place Updates

In SQL Server 2014, in-place updates are performed as often as possible to minimize the overhead of an update. An in-place update means that the row is modified where it is on the page, and only the affected bytes are changed.

When an in-place update is performed, in addition to the reduced overhead in the table itself, only a single modify record is written to the log. However, if the table has a trigger on it or is marked for replication, the update is still done in place but is recorded in the log as a delete followed by an insert (this provides the before-and-after image for the trigger that is referenced in the `inserted` and `deleted` tables and to provide complete row information for replication).

In-place updates are performed whenever a heap is being updated and the row still fits on the same page, or when a clustered table is updated and the clustered key itself is not changed. You can get an in-place update if the clustered key changes but the row does not have to move; that is, the sorting of the rows wouldn't change.

Not-In-Place Updates

If the change to a clustered key prevents an in-place update from being performed, or if the modification to a row increases its size such that it can no longer fit on its current page, the update is performed as a delete followed by an insert; this is referred to as a *not-in-place update.*

When performing an update that affects multiple index keys, SQL Server keeps a list of the rows that need to be updated in memory, if it's small enough; otherwise, it is stored in `tempdb`. SQL Server then sorts the list by index key and type of operation (delete or insert).

This list of operations, called the *input stream*, consists of both the old and new values for every column in the affected rows as well as the unique row identifier for each row.

SQL Server then examines the input stream to determine whether any of the updates conflict or would generate duplicate key values while processing (if they were to generate a duplicate key after processing, the update cannot proceed). It then rearranges the operations in the input stream in a manner to prevent any intermediate violations of the unique key.

For example, consider the following update to a table with a unique key on a sequential primary key:

```
update table1 set pkey = pkey + 1
```

Even though all values would still be unique when the update finished, if the update were performed internally one row at a time in sequential order, it would generate duplicates during the intermediate processing as the pkey value was incremented and matched the next pkey value. SQL Server would rearrange and rework the updates in the input stream to process them in a manner that would avoid the duplicates and then process them a row at a time. If possible, deletes and inserts on the same key value in the input stream are collapsed into a single update. In some cases, you might still get some rows that can be updated in place.

Forward Pointers

As mentioned earlier, when page splits on a clustered table occur, the nonclustered indexes do not need to be updated to reflect the new location of the rows because the row locator for the row is the clustered index key rather than the page and row ID. When an update operation on a heap table causes rows to move, the row locators in the nonclustered index would need to be updated to reflect the new location or the rows. This could be expensive if there were a larger number of nonclustered indexes on the heap.

SQL Server 2014 addresses this performance issue through the use of forward pointers. When a row in a heap moves, it leaves a forward pointer in the original location of the row. The forward pointer avoids having to update the nonclustered index row locator. When SQL Server is searching for the row via the nonclustered index, the index pointer directs it to the original location, where the forward pointer redirects it to the new row location.

A row never has more than one forward pointer. If the row moves again from its forwarded location, the forward pointer stored at the original row location is updated to the row's new location. There is never a forward pointer that points to another forward pointer. If the row ever shrinks enough to fit back into its original location, the forward pointer is removed, and the row is put back where it originated.

When a forward pointer is created, it remains unless the row moves back to its original location. The only other circumstance that results in forward pointers being deleted occurs when the entire database is shrunk. When a database file is shrunk and the data reorganized, all row locators are reassigned because the rows are moved to new pages.

Summary

One of the most important aspects of improving SQL Server performance is proper table and index design. Understanding how SQL Server stores and manages data and indexes will help you make more informed decisions when designing your tables in indexes. However, choosing the appropriate indexes for SQL Server to use to process queries involves thoroughly understanding the queries and transactions being run against the database, understanding the bias of the data, understanding how SQL Server uses indexes, and staying aware of the performance implications of over indexing tables in an OLTP environment. This information is covered in the next chapter.

Indexes and Performance

Proper table and index design is a key issue in achieving optimum SQL Server application performance. You can often realize substantial performance gains in your SQL Server applications by creating the proper indexes to support the queries and operations being performed. At the same time, it's important to keep in mind that although many indexes on a table can help improve response time for queries and reports, too many indexes can hurt the performance of inserts, updates, and deletes due to the overhead required to maintain the index and data rows. Additionally, other index design decisions, such as which column(s) to create a clustered index on, might be influenced as much by how the data is inserted and modified and what the possible locking implications might be as they are by the query response time alone.

The previous chapter described the underlying structures of databases, tables, rows, and indexes and how SQL Server maintains index and data structures as a basis for understanding the performance impact of indexes during INSERT, UPDATE, and DELETE operations. This chapter discusses how SQL Server evaluates and uses indexes to improve query response time. Using this information, you should have a better understanding of the issues and factors that influence good table and index design.

What's New for Indexes and Performance

SQL Server 2014 provides only a few enhancements related to indexes and performance. One new enhancement is clustered columnstore indexes, which was discussed in the previous chapter and also in Chapter 51, "Parallel Data Warehouse."

SQL Server 2014 also introduces new cardinality estimation logic. The cardinality estimator has been re-designed in SQL Server 2014 to improve the quality of query plans and ostensibly, query performance. The new cardinality estimator is based on in-depth cardinality estimation research on modern workloads and Microsoft learnings over the past 15 years. The new cardinality estimator incorporates assumptions and algorithms that work well on modern OLTP and data warehousing workloads. However, the cardinality estimator logic is complex and an exhaustive list of all changes has not been documented. Some of the changes are highlighted in this chapter as they pertain to index selection.

> **NOTE**
>
> This chapter assumes that you already have an understanding of the different types of indexes and how to define them. For more information on index types and how to create indexes, see Chapter 22, "Creating and Managing Indexes."

Index Utilization

Chapter 22 provided an understanding of table and index structures and the overhead required to maintain your data and indexes. Now it's time to put things into practice to actually come up with an index design for your database, defining the appropriate indexes to support your queries. To effectively determine the appropriate indexes that should be created, you need to determine whether they'll actually be used by the SQL Server Query Optimizer. If an index is not being used effectively, it's just wasting space and creating unnecessary overhead during updates.

The main criterion to remember is that SQL Server does not use an index for the more efficient row locator lookup if at least the first column of the index is not included in a valid search argument (SARG) or join clause. You should keep this point in mind when choosing the column order for composite indexes. For example, consider the following index on the `Person.Person` table in the `AdventureWorks2012` database:

```
create index IX_Person_LastName_FirstName_MiddleName on Person.Person (LastName,
FirstName, MiddleName)
```

Each of the following queries could use the index because they include the first column, `LastName`, of the index as part of the SARG:

```
select BusinessEntityID from Person.Person
    where LastName = 'Brown'
      and FirstName = 'Kevin'
      and MiddleName = 'F'


select BusinessEntityID from Person.Person
    where LastName = 'Brown'
      and FirstName = 'Kevin'
```

```
select BusinessEntityID from Person.Person
   where LastName = 'Brown'
      and MiddleName = 'F'
```

However, the following queries do not use the index for a row locator lookup because they don't specify the LastName column as a SARG:

```
select BusinessEntityID from Person.Person
   where FirstName = 'Kevin'
      and MiddleName = 'F'
```

```
select BusinessEntityID from Person.Person
   where MiddleName = 'F'
```

For the index IX_Person_LastName_FirstName_MiddleName to be used for a row locator lookup in the last query, you would have to reorder the columns so that MiddleName is first—but then the index wouldn't be useful for any queries specifying only LastName or LastName and FirstName. Satisfying all the preceding queries in this case would require additional indexes on the Person table.

> **NOTE**
>
> For the two preceding queries, if you were to display the execution plan information (as described in Chapter 36, "Query Analysis"), you might see that the queries actually use the IX_Person_LastName_FirstName_MiddleName index to retrieve the result set. However, if you look closely, you can see the queries are not using the index in the most efficient manner; the index is being used to perform an index scan rather than an index seek. An index seek is what we are really after. (Alternative query access methods are discussed in more detail in Chapter 34, "Understanding Query Optimization".) In an index seek, SQL Server searches for the specific SARG by walking the index tree from the root level down to the specific row(s) with matching index key values and then uses the row locator value stored in the index key to directly retrieve the matching row(s) from the data page(s); the row locator is either a specific row identifier or the clustered key value for the row.
>
> For an index *scan*, SQL Server searches all the rows in the leaf level of the index, looking for possible matches. If any are found, it then uses the row locator to retrieve the data row.
>
> Although both seeks and scans use an index, the index scan is still more expensive in terms of I/O than an index seek but slightly less expensive than a table scan, which is why it is used. However, in this chapter you learn to design indexes that result in index seeks, and when this chapter talks about queries using an index, index seeks are what it refers to (except for the section on index covering, but that's a horse of a slightly different color).

You might think that the easy solution to get row locator lookups on all possible columns is to index all the columns on a table so that any type of search criteria specified for a query can be helped by an index. This strategy might be somewhat appropriate in a read-only decision support system (DSS) environment that supports ad hoc queries, but it is not likely because many of the indexes probably still wouldn't even be used. As you see in the section "Index Selection," just because an index is defined on a column doesn't mean that the Query Optimizer is necessarily always going to use it if the search criteria are not selective enough. Also, creating that many indexes on a large table could take up a significant amount of space in the database, increasing the time required to back up and run DBCC checks on the database. As mentioned in the preceding chapter, too many indexes on a table in an OLTP environment can generate a significant amount of overhead during inserts, updates, and deletes and have a detrimental impact on performance.

TIP

A common design mistake often made is too many indexes defined on tables in OLTP environments. In many cases, some of the indexes are redundant or are never even considered by the SQL Server Query Optimizer to process the queries used by the applications. These indexes end up simply wasting space and adding unnecessary overhead to data updates.

A case in point was one client who had eight indexes defined on a table, four of which had the same column, which was a unique key, as the first column in the index. That column was included in the WHERE clauses for all queries and updates performed on the table. Only one of those four indexes was ever used.

It is hoped that by the end of this chapter, you understand why all these indexes were unnecessary and are able to recognize and determine which columns benefit from having indexes defined on them and which indexes to avoid.

Index Selection

To determine which indexes to define on a table, you need to perform a detailed query analysis. This process involves examining the search clauses to see what columns are referenced, knowing the bias of the data to determine the usefulness of the index, and ranking the queries in order of importance and frequency of execution. You have to be careful not to examine individual queries and develop indexes to support one query without considering the other queries that are executed on the table as well. You need to come up with a set of indexes that work for the best cross-section of your queries.

TIP

A useful tool to help you identify your frequently executed and critical queries is SQL Server Profiler. I've found SQL Server Profiler to be invaluable when going into a new client site and having to identify the problem queries that need tuning. SQL Server Profiler allows you to trace the procedures and queries being executed in SQL Server and capture the runtime, reads and writes, execution plans, and other processing information. This information can help you identify which queries are providing substandard performance, which ones are being executed most often, which indexes are being used by the queries, and so on.

You can analyze this information yourself manually or save a trace to analyze with the Database Engine Tuning Advisor. The features of SQL Server Profiler are covered in more detail in Chapter 5, "SQL Server Profiler." The Database Engine Tuning Advisor is discussed in more detail in Chapter 40, "SQL Server Database Engine Tuning Advisor."

Unfortunately, SQL Server Profiler is a deprecated feature and slated to be removed in a future version of SQL Server, so it's probably not a good idea to get too familiar with using this tool for analysis. Another method of capturing query activity is using Extended Events, but currently, the Database Engine Tuning Advisor is unable to process an Extended Events trace file. Still, you would be able to analyze the Extended Events trace to get query statistics. For more information on Extended Events, see Chapter 39, "Monitoring SQL Server Performance."

Additionally, SQL Server provides a number of dynamic management objects for capturing query and index statistics and index usage. Some of these include `sys.dm_exec_query_stats`, `sys.dm_exec_procedure_stats`, `sys.dm_exec_query_plan`, `sys.dm_db_index_usage_stats`, and the `sys.dm_db_missing_index_*` DMVs. The index related DMVs are discussed in this chapter. The sys.dm_exec_query_stats DMV is covered in Chapters 36 and 39, and sys.dm_exec_query_plan is covered in Chapter 36.

Because it's usually not possible to index for everything, you should index first for the queries most critical to your applications or those run frequently by many users. If you have a query that's run only once a month, is it worth creating an index to support only that query and having to maintain it throughout the rest of the month? The sum of the additional processing time throughout the month could conceivably exceed the time required to perform a table scan to satisfy that one query.

TIP

If, due to query response time requirements, you must have an index in place when an infrequently executed query is run, consider creating the index only when you run the query and then dropping the index for the remainder of the month. This approach is feasible as long as the time it takes to create the index and run the query that uses the index doesn't exceed the time it takes to simply run the query without the index in place.

Evaluating Index Usefulness

SQL Server provides indexes for two primary reasons: as a method to enforce the uniqueness of the data in the database tables and to provide faster access to data in the tables. Creating the appropriate indexes for a database is one of the most important aspects of physical database design. Because you can't have an unlimited number of indexes on a table, and it wouldn't be feasible anyway, you should create indexes on columns that have high selectivity so that your queries will use the indexes. The selectivity of an index can be defined as follows:

```
Selectivity ratio = Number of unique index values / Number of rows in table
```

If the selectivity ratio is high—that is, if a large number of rows can be uniquely identified by the key—the index is highly selective and useful to the Query Optimizer. The optimum selectivity would be 1, meaning that there is a unique value for each row. A low selectivity means that there are many duplicate values and the index would be less useful. The SQL Server Query Optimizer decides whether to use any indexes for a query based on the selectivity of the index. The higher the selectivity, the faster and more efficiently SQL Server can retrieve the result set.

For example, say that you are evaluating useful indexes on the `Person` table in the `AdventureWorks2012` database. Assume that most of the queries access the table either by last name and first name or by `PersonType`. Because a large number of concurrent users modify data in this table, you are allowed to create only one of the two possible indexes—an index on `LastName` and `FirstName` or an index on `PersonType`. Which one should you choose? Let's perform some analysis to see which one is a more useful, or selective, index.

First, you need to determine the selectivity based on the last name and first name with a query on the `Person` table in the `AdventureWorks2012` database:

```
select count(distinct LastName + FirstName) as '# unique',
    count(*) as '# rows',
    str(count(distinct LastName + FirstName)
        / cast (count(*) as real),6,4) as 'selectivity'
from Person.Person
GO

/* output
    # unique       # rows selectivity
----------- ----------- -----------
      19516       19972 0.9772
*/
```

The selectivity ratio calculated for the `LastName` and `FirstName` columns on the Person table, 0.9772, indicates that an index on `LastName` and `FirstName` would be highly selective and a good candidate for an index. All but 456 rows in the table contain a unique record for each combination of last name and first name.

Now, look at the selectivity of the `PersonType` column:

```
select count(distinct PersonType) as '# unique',
    count(*) as '# rows',
    str(count(distinct PersonType) / cast (count(*) as real),6,4) as 'selectivity'
from Person.Person
GO

/* output
    # unique       # rows selectivity
----------- ----------- -----------
          6       19972 0.0003
*/
```

As you can see, an index on the `PersonType` column would be much less selective (0.0003) than an index on the `LastName` and `FirstName` columns and definitely not as useful.

One of the questions to ask at this point is whether a few values in the `PersonType` column that have a high number of duplicates are skewing the selectivity or whether there are just a few unique values in the table. You can determine this with a query similar to the following:

```
select PersonType,
       count(*) as numrows,
       count(*)/b.totalrows * 100 as percentage
from Person.Person a,
     (select convert(numeric(8,2), count(*)) as totalrows from  Person.Person) as b
group by PersonType, b.totalrows
having count(*) > 1
order by 2 desc
go


/* output
PersonType     numrows                                         percentage
----------     -----------    ------------------------------------------

IN               18484                                       92.549569300
SC                 753                                        3.770278300
GC                 289                                        1.447025800
EM                 273                                        1.366913600
VC                 156                                        0.781093500
SP                  17                                        0.085119100
*/
```

As you can see, most of the `PersonType` values are relatively unique, except for one value, `'IN'`, which accounts for more than 92% of the values in the table. Therefore, `PersonType` is probably not a good candidate for an indexed column, especially if most of the time you are searching for `Person` records with a `PersonType` of `'IN'`. SQL Server would generally find it more efficient to scan the whole table rather than search via the index.

NOTE

When a single value skews the selectivity of an index, as in this example with the `PersonType` column, this type of column might be a candidate for a filtered index. See the section "Filtered Indexes and Statistics," later in this chapter.

As a general rule of thumb, if the selectivity ratio for a nonclustered index key is less than 0.85 (in other words, if the Query Optimizer cannot discard at least 85% of the rows based on the key value), the Query Optimizer generally chooses a table or index scan to process the rows for that table rather than a nonclustered index. In such cases, performing a scan to find all the qualifying rows is more efficient than seeking through the B-tree to locate a large number of data rows.

NOTE

You can relate the concept of selectivity to a hypothetical example. Say that you need to find every instance of the word SQL in this book. Would it be easier to do it by using the index and going back and forth from the index to all the pages that contain the word, or would it be easier just to scan each page from beginning to end to locate every occurrence? What if you had to find all references to the word *squonk*, if any? *Squonk* would definitely be easier to find via the index (actually, the index would help you determine that it doesn't even exist). Therefore, the selectivity for *Squonk* would be high, and the selectivity for SQL would be much lower.

How does SQL Server determine whether an index is selective and which index, if it has more than one to choose from, would be the most efficient to use? For example, how would SQL Server know how many rows the following query might return?

```
select * from table
    where key between 1000000 and 2000000
```

If the table contains 10,000,000 rows with values ranging between 0 and 20,000,000, how does the Query Optimizer know whether to use an index or a table scan? There could be 10 rows in the range, or 900,000. How does SQL Server estimate how many rows are between 1,000,000 and 2,000,000? The Query Optimizer gets this information from the index statistics, as described in the next section.

Index Statistics

As mentioned earlier, the selectivity of a key is an important factor that determines whether an index will be used to retrieve the data rows that satisfy a query. SQL Server stores the selectivity and a histogram of sample values of the key; based on the statistics stored for the key columns for the index and the SARGs specified for the query, the Query Optimizer decides which index to use.

To see the statistical information stored for an index, use the DBCC SHOW_STATISTICS command, which returns the following pieces of information:

▶ A histogram that contains an even sampling of the values for the first column in the index key. SQL Server stores up to 200 sample values in the histogram.

▶ Index densities for the combination of columns in the index. Index density indicates the uniqueness of the index key(s) and is discussed later in this section.

▶ The number of rows in the table at the time the statistics were computed.

▶ The number of rows sampled to generate the statistics.

▶ The number of sample values (steps) stored in the histogram.

▶ The average key length.

▶ Whether the index is defined on a string column.

▶ The date and time the statistics were generated.

The syntax for DBCC SHOW_STATISTICS is as follows:

```
DBCC SHOW_STATISTICS (tablename, index)
```

Listing 32.1 displays the abbreviated output from DBCC SHOW_STATISTICS, showing the statistical information for the IX_Person_LastName_FirstName_MiddleName nonclustered index on the LastName, FirstName, and MiddleName columns of the Person table.

LISTING 32.1 DBCC SHOW_STATISTICS Output for the IX_Person_LastName_FirstName_MiddleName Index on the Person Table

```
DBCC SHOW_STATISTICS ('Person.Person', IX_Person_LastName_FirstName_MiddleName)
Go


/* output
Name                                          Updated              Rows Rows Sampled Steps
Density Average key length String Index Filter Expression Unfiltered Rows
--------------------------------------------- -------------------- ----- ------------ -----
--------- ------------------ ------------ ----------------- ---------------
IX_Person_LastName_FirstName_MiddleName Dec  3 2014  1:06PM 19972        19972     199
0.5505741         28.23934 YES           NULL                 19972

  All density Average Length Columns
  ----------- -------------- ------------------------------------------------
  0.0008291874      11.2126 LastName
  5.124001E-05      23.02013 LastName, FirstName
  5.05025E-05       24.23934 LastName, FirstName, MiddleName
  5.00701E-05       28.23934 LastName, FirstName, MiddleName, BusinessEntityID

RANGE_HI_KEY RANGE_ROWS EQ_ROWS  DISTINCT_RANGE_ROWS AVG_RANGE_ROWS
------------ ---------- -------  -------------------- --------------
Abbas                 0       1                     0              1
Adams                10      86                     6       1.666667
Alexander            28     123                    15       1.866667
Allen                 0      82                     0              1
Alonso                1      93                     1              1
Alvarez               5      99                     4           1.25
Anand                 2      74                     2              1
Andersen              0      95                     0              1
Anderson              0      85                     0              1
Arthur                9      24                     8          1.125
Arun                  0      58                     0              1
Ashe                  0      30                     0              1
Bailey                9      95                     7       1.285714
...
Murphy               15      97                     2            7.5
Nara                  6      95                     3              2
```

Nath	4	88	4	1
Navarro	2	106	1	2
Nelson	6	72	3	2
Ortega	42	84	24	1.75
Pal	14	94	9	1.555556
Parker	2	80	2	1
Patel	2	86	1	2
Patterson	3	117	2	1.5
Perez	11	170	7	1.571429
Perry	1	122	1	1
Peterson	4	92	2	2
Phillips	4	80	2	2
Powell	21	116	16	1.3125
Prasad	0	88	0	1
Price	2	84	1	2
...				
Xie	1	95	1	1
Xu	0	166	0	1
Yang	3	99	3	1
Ye	2	68	2	1
Young	7	87	3	2.333333
Yuan	3	92	2	1.5
Zeng	8	71	6	1.333333
Zhang	0	98	0	1
Zhao	0	67	0	1
Zheng	0	68	0	1
Zhou	0	71	0	1
Zhu	0	67	0	1
Zwilling	20	2	6	3.333333

```
*/
```

Looking at the output, you can determine that the statistics were last updated on December 3, 2014. At the time the statistics were generated, the table had 19972 rows, and all 19972 rows were sampled to generate the statistics (no filtering was applied). The average key length is 28.23934 bytes. From the All density information, you can see that this index is highly selective. (A low density means high selectivity; index densities are covered shortly.)

After the general information and the index densities, the index histogram is displayed.

The Statistics Histogram

Up to 200 sample values can be stored in the statistics histogram. Each sample value is called a step. The sample value stored in each step in the RANGE_HI_KEY column is the endpoint of a range of values. Four values are stored for each step:

▶ **RANGE_ROWS**—This indicates how many other rows are inside the range between the current step and the step prior, not including the step values themselves.

▶ **EQ_ROWS**—This is the number of rows that have the same value as the sample value. In other words, it is the number of duplicate values for the step.

▶ **Range density**—This indicates the number of distinct values within the range. The range density information is actually displayed in two separate columns, DISTINCT_RANGE_ROWS and AVG_RANGE_ROWS:

> ▶ **DISTINCT_RANGE_ROWS**—The number of distinct values between the current step and the step prior, not including the step values.

> ▶ **AVG_RANGE_ROWS**—The average number of rows per distinct value within the range of the step.

In the output in Listing 32.1, key values in the first column of the index are stored as the sample values in the histogram. You can see that there are a number of duplicates in the index key for the last name of Andersen (EQ_ROWS is 95 and 85). For comparison purposes, Listing 32.2 shows the DBCC SHOW_STATISTICS output for the PK_Person_BusinessEntityID index on the Person table in AdventureWorks2012.

LISTING 32.2 DBCC SHOW_STATISTICS Output for the PK_Person_BusinessEntityID Index on the Person Table in the AdventureWorks2012 Database

```
DBCC SHOW_STATISTICS ('Person.Person', PK_Person_BusinessEntityID)
Go


/* output
Name                 Updated              Rows     Rows Sampled    Steps   Density
Average key length   String Index   Filter Expression    Unfiltered Rows
------------------------ -------------------- ------- --------------- -------
- ---------- -------------------- --------------- -------------------- ------
- -----------
PK_Person_BusinessEntityID  Mar 14 2012  1:14PM  19972    19972           8
1         4                    NO              (null)              19972


All density  Average Length    Columns
-----------  ----------------- ----------------
5.00701E-5   4                 BusinessEntityID


RANGE_HI_KEY   RANGE_ROWS   EQ_ROWS   DISTINCT_RANGE_ROWS   AVG_RANGE_ROWS
-------------  ----------   -------   --------------------  --------------
1              0            1         0                     1
264            262          1         262                   1
493            127          1         127                   1
1704           607          1         607                   1
```

1805	95	1	95	1
1933	63	1	63	1
2061	95	1	95	1
20777	18715	1	18715	1
*/				

As you can see in this example, there are a greater number of rows per range and a fewer number of duplicates for each step value (actually, the statistics show that all the values are distinct as you would expect for a primary key). Also, only 8 steps in the histogram are used, and the last bucket represents 18,715 rows. This imbalance of range rows across the step values is a good indication that the statistics are likely out of date and should be updated.

How the Statistics Histogram Is Used

The histogram steps are used for SARGs only when a constant expression is compared against an indexed column and the value of the constant expression can be determined at query compile time. The following SARG examples show where histogram steps can be used:

- ▶ where col_a = getdate()
- ▶ where cust_id = 12345
- ▶ where monthly_sales < 10000 / 12
- ▶ where LastName like "Smith" + "%"

Some constant expressions cannot be evaluated until query runtime. They include search arguments that contain local variables or subqueries and also join clauses, such as the following:

- ▶ where price = @avg_price
- ▶ where total_sales > (select sum(qty) from sales)
- ▶ where titles.pub_id = publishers.pub_id

For these types of statements, you need some other way of estimating the number of matching rows. In addition, because histogram steps are kept only on the first column of the index, SQL Server must use a different method for determining the number of matching rows for SARGs that specify multiple column values for a composite index, such as the following:

```
select * from Person.Person
   where LastName = 'Brown'
     and FirstName = 'Kevin'
```

When the histogram is not used or cannot be used, SQL Server uses the index density values to estimate the number of matching rows.

Index Densities

SQL Server stores the density values of each combination of columns (in key order) in the index for use in queries where the SARG value is not known until runtime or when the SARG is on multiple columns of the index. For composite keys, SQL Server stores the density for the first column of the composite key; for the first and second columns; for the first, second, and third columns; and so on. This information is shown in the All density section of the DBCC SHOW_STATISTICS output in Listings 32.4 and 32.5.

Index density essentially represents the inverse of all unique key values of the key. The density of each key is calculated by using the following formula:

Key density = 1.00 / Count of distinct key values in the table

Therefore, the density for the LastName column in the Persons table in the AdventureWorks2012 database is calculated as follows:

```
Select Density = 1.00/ (select count(distinct LastName) from Person.Person)

go
/* output
Density
---------------------------------------
0.0008291873963
*/
```

The density for the combination of the columns LastName and FirstName is as follows:

```
Select Density = 1.00/ (select count(distinct LastName+FirstName) from Person.
Person)
go

/* output
Density
---------------
0.0000512400081
*/
```

Notice that, unlike with the selectivity ratio, a smaller index density indicates a more selective index. As the density value approaches 1, the index becomes less selective and essentially useless. When the index selectivity is poor, the Query Optimizer might choose to do a table scan or a leaf-level index scan rather than perform an index seek because it is more cost-effective.

> **TIP**
>
> Watch out for database indexes that have poor selectivity. Such indexes are often more of a detriment to the performance of the system than they are a help. Not only are they usually not used for data retrieval, but they also slow down your data modification statements because of the additional index overhead. You should identify such indexes and consider dropping them.

Typically, the density value should become smaller (that is, more selective) as you add more columns to the key. For example, in Listing 32.2, the densities get progressively smaller (and thus, more selective) as additional columns are factored in, as shown in Table 32.1.

TABLE 32.1   Index Densities for the `IX_Person_LastName_FirstName_MiddleName` Index on the `Person` Table

Key Column	Index Density
LastName	0.0008291874
LastName, FirstName	5.124001E-05 (.00005124001)
LastName, FirstName, MiddleName	5.05025E-05 (.0000505025)

Estimating Rows Using Index Statistics

How does the Query Optimizer use the index statistics to estimate the number of rows that match the SARGs in a query?

SQL Server uses the histogram information when searching for a known value being compared to the leading column of the index key column, especially when the search spans a range or when there are duplicate values in the key. Consider this query on the `Person` table in the `AdventureWorks2012` database:

```
select * from Person
    where LastName = 'Alexander'
```

Because the `LastName` values in the table are not unique, SQL Server uses the histogram on `LastName` (refer to Listing 32.2) to estimate the number of matching rows. For the value of `'Alexander'`, it would look at the `EQ_ROWS` value, which is `123`. This indicates that there are approximately 123 rows in the table that have a `LastName` value of `'Alexander'`.

When an exact match for the search argument is not found as a step in the histogram, SQL Server uses the `AVG_RANGE_ROWS` value for the next step greater than the search value. For example, SQL Server would estimate that for a search value of `'Adamsley'`, on average, it would match approximately 1.86667 rows because that is the `AVG_RANGE_ROWS` value for the step value of `'Alexander'`, which is the next step value greater than `'Adamsley'`.

When the query is a range retrieval that spans multiple steps, SQL Server sums the `RANGE_ROWS` and `EQ_ROWS` values between the endpoints of the range retrieval. For example, when we use the histogram in Listing 32.2, if the search argument were `where LastName <= 'Alexander'`, the row estimate would be 0 + 1 + 10 + 86 + 28 + 123, or 248 rows.

As mentioned previously, when the histogram cannot be used, SQL Server uses just the index density to estimate the number of matching rows. The formula is straightforward for an equality search; it looks like this:

Row estimate = Number of rows in table × Index density

For example, to estimate the number of matching rows for any given `LastName` in the `Person` table, multiply the number of rows in the `Person` table by the index density for the `LastName` key (0.001862197), as follows:

```
select count(*) * 0.0008291874 as 'Row Estimate'
from Person.Person
go

/* output
Row Estimate
-------------------
16.5605307528
*/
```

If a query specifies both the `LastName` and `FirstName` as SARGs, and if the SARG for `LastName` is a constant expression that can be evaluated at optimization time, SQL Server uses both the index density on `LastName` and `FirstName` as well as the histogram on `LastName` to estimate the number of matching rows. For some data values, the estimated number of matching rows for `LastName` and `FirstName` calculated using the index density could be greater than the estimated number of rows that match the specific `LastName`, as determined by the histogram. SQL Server uses whichever is the smaller of the two to calculate the row estimate.

Multiplying the number of rows in the `Person` table by the index density for `LastName`, `FirstName` (5.124001E-05), you can see that it is nearly unique, essentially matching only a single row:

```
select count(*) * 5.124001E-05 as 'Row Estimate'
from Person.Person

/* output
Row Estimate
--------------
1.02336547972
*/
```

In this example, SQL Server would use the index density on `LastName` and `FirstName` to estimate the number of matching rows. In this case, it is estimated that the query will return, on average, one matching row. You can see these matching rowcount estimates being used when viewing the estimated execution plan in SSMS. (For details on how to view and interpret execution plans, see Chapter 36.) Figure 32.1 shows the Tooltip for the estimated execution plan for the following query:

```
SELECT * FROM Person.Person p
WHERE p.LastName = 'Smith'
AND p.FirstName = 'John'
```

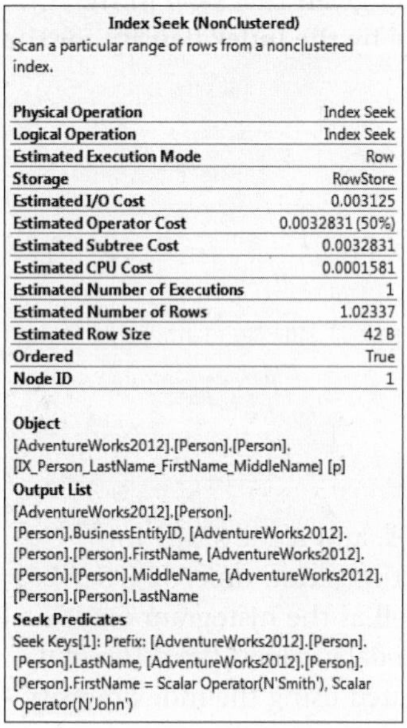

Index Seek (NonClustered)	
Scan a particular range of rows from a nonclustered index.	
Physical Operation	Index Seek
Logical Operation	Index Seek
Estimated Execution Mode	Row
Storage	RowStore
Estimated I/O Cost	0.003125
Estimated Operator Cost	0.0032831 (50%)
Estimated Subtree Cost	0.0032831
Estimated CPU Cost	0.0001581
Estimated Number of Executions	1
Estimated Number of Rows	1.02337
Estimated Row Size	42 B
Ordered	True
Node ID	1
Object	
[AdventureWorks2012].[Person].[Person]. [IX_Person_LastName_FirstName_MiddleName] [p]	
Output List	
[AdventureWorks2012].[Person]. [Person].BusinessEntityID, [AdventureWorks2012]. [Person].[Person].FirstName, [AdventureWorks2012]. [Person].[Person].MiddleName, [AdventureWorks2012]. [Person].[Person].LastName	
Seek Predicates	
Seek Keys[1]: Prefix: [AdventureWorks2012].[Person]. [Person].LastName, [AdventureWorks2012].[Person]. [Person].FirstName = Scalar Operator(N'Smith'), Scalar Operator(N'John')	

FIGURE 32.1   Setting and viewing index properties in SSMS.

If you look at the value for Estimated Number of Rows, you see it reports a value of 1.02337, which matches the calculated estimate for row counts above based upon the index density for the LastName and FirstName columns in the Person table.

What happens if the search value is outside the range of values in the histogram? Typically, SQL Server estimates that only a single row will match when a search value exceeds the maximum value for ascending data in the statistics histogram. Consider a hypothetical example with the Sales.SalesOrderHeader table with new rows added each day and an index on OrderDate. Consider the following query against this Sales table:

```
SELECT item, category, amount FROM Sales.SalesOrderHeader AS s
WHERE OrderDate = '2014-11-19';
```

The query is asking for orders that occurred on 11/19/2014, but assume that statistics were last updated on 11/15/2014. In prior versions of SQL Server, the cardinality estimator assumes the 11/19/2014 values do not exist since the date exceeds the maximum date in the histogram, so the estimated number of matching rows is only 1. This situation is known as the ascending key problem and could lead to improper index selection. Thinking there is at most 1 matching row, SQL Server will likely use the index on OrderDate. But what if 1 million rows had been added with a date of 2014-11-19?

This behavior has changed with the cardinality estimator in SQL Server 2014. Now, even if statistics have not been updated to include the most recently inserted since the last statistics update, the cardinality estimator assumes the values exist and uses the average cardinality for each value in the column to estimate the number of matching rows. While still not as accurate as matching against actual values in the histogram, it's a better estimate than assuming no rows exist.

Generating and Maintaining Index and Column Statistics

At this point, you might ask, "How do the index statistics get created?" and "How are they maintained?" The index statistics are first created when you create the index on a table that already contains data rows or when you run the UPDATE STATISTICS command. Index statistics can also be automatically updated by SQL Server. SQL Server can be configured to constantly monitor the update activity on the indexed key values in a database and update the statistics through an internal process, when appropriate.

Auto-Update Statistics

To automatically update statistics, an internal SQL Server process monitors the updates to a table's columns to determine when statistics should be updated. SQL Server internally keeps track of the number of modifications made to a column via column modification counters (colmodctrs). SQL Server uses information about the table and the colmodctrs to determine whether statistics are out of date and need to be updated. Statistics are considered out of date in the following situations:

▶ When the table size has gone from 0 to > 0 rows

▶ When the number of rows in the table at the time the statistics were gathered was 500 or fewer and the colmodctr of the leading column of the statistics object has changed by more than 500

▶ When the table had more than 500 rows at the time the statistics were gathered and the colmodctr of the leading column of the statistics object has changed by more than 500 + 20% of the number of rows in the table

If the statistics are defined on a temporary table, there is an additional threshold for updating statistics every six column modifications if the table contains fewer than 500 rows.

The colmodctrs are incremented in the following situations:

▶ When a row is inserted into the table

▶ When a row is deleted from the table

▶ When an indexed column is updated

Whenever the index statistics have been updated for a column, the `colmodctr` for that column is reset to 0.

When SQL Server generates an update of the column statistics, it generates the new statistics based on a sampling of the data values in the table. Sampling helps minimize the overhead of the AutoStats process. The sampling is random across the data pages, and the values are taken from the table or the smallest nonclustered index on the columns needed to generate the statistics. After a data page containing a sampled row has been read from disk, all the rows on the data page are used to update the statistical information.

CAUTION

Having up-to-date statistics on tables helps ensure that optimum execution plans are being generated for queries at all times. In most cases, you would want SQL Server to automatically keep the statistics updated. However, it is possible that Auto-Update Statistics can cause an update of the index statistics to run at inappropriate times in a production environment or run too often in a high-volume environment. If this problem is occurring, you might want to turn off the AutoStats feature and set up a scheduled job to update statistics during off-peak periods. If you choose to do this, do not forget to update statistics periodically; otherwise, the resulting performance problems might end up being much worse than the momentary ones caused by the AutoStats process.

To determine how often the AutoStats process is being run, you can use SQL Server Profiler to determine when an automatic update of index statistics is occurring by monitoring the `Auto Stats` event in the `Performance` event class or by setting up an Extended Events session to monitor the `auto_stats` event. (For more information on using SQL Server Profiler, see Chapter 5, and for more information on monitoring SQL Server using Extended Events, see Chapter 39.)

If necessary, it is possible to turn off the AutoStats behavior by using the `sp_autostats` system stored procedure. This stored procedure allows you to turn the automatic updating of statistics on or off for a specific index or all the indexes of a table. The following command turns off the automatic update of statistics for the index named `IX_Person_LastName_FirstName_MiddleName` on the `Person.Person` table:

```
Exec sp_autostats 'Person.Person', 'OFF', 'IX_Person_LastName_FirstName_MiddleName'
```

When you run `sp_autostats` and simply supply the table name, it displays the current setting for all the indexes on the table. Following are the settings for the `Person.Person` table:

```
Exec sp_autostats 'Person.Person'
go

/* output
```

```
Index Name                                AUTOSTATS  Last Updated
----------------------------------------  ---------  --------------------
[PK_Person_BusinessEntityID]              ON         6/19/2013 12:02:23 AM
[IX_Person_LastName_FirstName_MiddleName] OFF        3/14/2012 1:14:44 PM
[AK_Person_rowguid]                       ON         3/14/2012 1:14:44 PM
[_WA_Sys_00000006_693CA210]               ON         6/18/2013 10:46:46 PM
[_WA_Sys_00000005_693CA210]               ON         6/18/2013 10:46:46 PM
[_WA_Sys_00000002_693CA210]               ON         6/18/2013 11:11:36 PM
*/
```

There are three other ways to disable auto-updating of statistics for an index:

▶ Specify the STATISTICS_NORECOMPUTE clause when creating the index.

▶ Specify the NORECOMPUTE option when running the UPDATE STATISTICS command.

▶ Specify the NORECOMPUTE option when creating statistics with the CREATE STATISTICS command. (You learn more about this command in the "Creating Statistics" section, later in the chapter.)

You can also turn AutoStats on or off for the entire database by setting the database option in SQL Server Management Studio; to do this, right-click the database in Object Explorer to bring up the Database Properties dialog, select the Options page, and set the Auto Update Statistics option to False. You can also disable or enable the AutoStats option for a database by using the ALTER DATABASE command:

```
ALTER DATABASE dbname SET AUTO_UPDATE_STATISTICS { ON | OFF }
```

NOTE

What actually happens when you execute sp_autostats or use the NORECOMPUTE option in the UPDATE STATISTICS command to turn off Auto-Update Statistics for a specific index or table? SQL Server internally sets a flag in the system catalog to inform the internal SQL Server process not to update the index statistics for the table or index that has had the option turned off using any of these commands. To re-enable Auto Update Statistics, you either run UPDATE STATISTICS without the NORECOMPUTE option or execute the sp_autostats system stored procedure and specify the value 'ON' for the second parameter.

Asynchronous Statistics Updating

In versions prior to SQL Server 2005, when SQL Server determined that the statistics being examined to optimize a query were out of date, the query would wait for the statistics update to complete before compilation of the query plan would continue. This is still the default behavior in SQL Server 2014. However, the database option, AUTO_UPDATE_STATISTICS_ASYNC, can be enabled to support asynchronous statistics updating.

When the AUTO_UPDATE_STATISTICS_ASYNC option is enabled, queries do not have to wait for the statistics to be updated before generating the query plan. Instead, SQL Server puts the out-of-date statistics on a queue to be updated by a worker thread, which runs as a background process. The query and any other concurrent queries are optimized immediately using the existing out-of-date statistics. Because there is no delay for updated statistics, query response times are more predictable, even if the out-of-date statistics may cause the Query Optimizer to choose a less-efficient query plan. Queries that start after the updated statistics are ready use the updated statistics.

Manually Updating Statistics

Whether or not you've disabled AutoStats, you can still manually update index statistics by using the UPDATE STATISTICS T-SQL command, whose syntax is as follows:

```
UPDATE STATISTICS table | view
    [ { { index | statistics_name }
          | ( { index |statistics_name } [ ,...n ] ) } ]
    [ WITH [ [ FULLSCAN ]
             | SAMPLE number { PERCENT | ROWS } ]
             | RESAMPLE
        [ [ , ] [ ALL | COLUMNS | INDEX ]
        [ [ , ] NORECOMPUTE ] ]
```

If neither the FULLSCAN nor SAMPLE option is specified, the default behavior is to perform a sample scan to calculate the statistics, and SQL Server automatically computes the appropriate sample size.

The FULLSCAN option forces SQL Server to perform a full scan of the data in the table or index to calculate the statistics. This generates more accurate statistics than using sampling but is also the most time-consuming and I/O-intensive method. When you use the SAMPLE option, you can specify a fixed number of rows or a percentage of rows to sample to build or update the index statistics. If the sampling ratio specified ever results in too few rows being sampled, SQL Server automatically corrects the sampling, based on the number of existing rows in the table or view. At a minimum, approximately 1,000 data pages are sampled.

The RESAMPLE option specifies that the statistics be generated using the previously defined sampling ratio. This RESAMPLE option is useful for indexes or column statistics created with different sampling values. For example, if the index statistics were created using FULLSCAN, and the column statistics were created using a 50% sample, specifying the RESAMPLE option would update the statistics using FULLSCAN on the indexes and using the 50% sample for the others.

Specifying ALL, COLUMNS, or INDEX specifies whether the UPDATE STATISTICS command affects all existing statistics or only column or index statistics. By default, if no option is specified, the UPDATE STATISTICS statement affects all statistics.

As previously discussed, SQL Server automatically updates the index statistics by default. If you specify the NORECOMPUTE option with UPDATE STATISTICS, it disables AutoStats for the table or index.

When the automatic update statistics option is turned off, you should run the UPDATE STATISTICS command periodically, when appropriate. To determine the last time statistics were updated, you run the following command:

```
select STATS_DATE(tableid, indexid)
```

Following is an example:

```
select STATS_DATE(object_id('Sales.SalesOrderDetail'), 1)
go

/* output
----------------------
2013-06-17 01:33:40.357
*/
```

> **TIP**
>
> You can get the index ID from sys.indexes for each index on a table by using the following query:
>
> ```
> select name, index_id from sys.indexes
>     Where object_id = object_id('table_name')
>     and index_id > 0
> ```

If you want to update statistics on all eligible indexes of the tables in a database, you can use the sp_updatestats system procedure:

```
sp_updatestats [ [ @resample = ] 'resample']
```

Invoking sp_updatestats is the same as running UPDATE STATISTICS and specifying the ALL keyword for all user-defined tables in the database. If you don't specify a resample option, it will update statistics using the default sampling option for each table.

Column-Level Statistics

In addition to statistics on indexes, SQL Server can also store statistics on individual columns that are not part of any indexes. Knowing the likelihood of a particular value being found in a nonindexed column can help the Query Optimizer better estimate the number of matching rows for SARGs on the nonindexed columns. This helps it determine the optimal execution plan, whether or not SQL Server is using an index to actually locate the rows.

For example, consider the following query:

```
SELECT soh.SalesOrderID, OrderDate
    FROM Sales.SalesOrderHeader soh
    JOIN Sales.SalesOrderDetail sod
      ON soh.SalesOrderID = sod.SalesOrderID
    WHERE sod.OrderQty >= 25
```

SQL Server knows the density of the SalesOrderID column in both the SalesOrderHeader and SalesOrderDetail tables because of indexes on the column in those tables. There is no index on OrderQty. However, if the Query Optimizer were to know how many rows in the sales table had an OrderQty greater than or equal to 25, it would be better able to choose the most efficient query plan for joining between SalesOrderHeader and SalesOrderDetail. For example, assume that, on average, there are over 121,000 SalesOrderDetail records. However, there are only approximately 90 records where the OrderQty is greater than or equal to 25. With the statistics on OrderQty, SQL Server has the opportunity to determine this, and knowing there might be only about 90 matching rows SalesOrderDetail, it might choose a different, more efficient, join strategy between the two tables.

Being able to keep statistics on the OrderQty column without having to add it to an existing index with SalesOrderID or create a separate index on OrderQty provides SQL Server with the selectivity information it needs for optimization. By not having to create an index on OrderQty to generate statistics on the column, you avoid incurring the overhead of having to maintain the index key rows for each insert, update, and delete that occurs on the table. Only the index statistics on OrderQty need to be maintained, which is required only after many modifications to the data have occurred.

By default, SQL Server generates column statistics automatically when queries are optimized and the column is specified in a SARG or join clause. If no column statistics exist and the Query Optimizer needs to estimate the approximate density or distribution of column values, SQL Server automatically generates statistics for that column. This rule has two exceptions:

▶ Statistics are not automatically created for columns when the cost of creating the statistics exceeds the cost of the query plan itself.

▶ Statistics are not automatically created when SQL Server is too busy (that is, when there are too many outstanding query compilations in progress).

If you want to disable or re-enable the database option to autocreate statistics in the database, you use the ALTER DATABASE command:

```
ALTER DATABASE dbname SET AUTO_CREATE_STATISTICS { ON | OFF }
```

You can also turn the Auto Create Statistics option on or off for the entire database by setting the database option in SSMS. In Object Explorer, right-click the database to bring up the Database Properties dialog, select the Options page, and set the Auto Create Statistics option to True or False.

Column statistics are stored in the system catalogs. General information about them can be viewed in the sys.stats catalog view. Autogenerated statistics have a name in the format _WA_Sys_columnIDsystemgeneratednumber. You can retrieve a list of autogenerated column statistics with a query similar to the following:

```
SELECT cast(object_name(object_id) as varchar(30)) as 'table',
       cast (name as varchar(30)) as autostats
   FROM sys.stats
   WHERE auto_created = 1
     AND objectproperty (object_id, 'IsUserTable') = 1
ORDER BY 1
go


/* output
table                               autostats
-----------------------------       -------------------------
BillOfMaterials                     _WA_Sys_00000003_1DE57479
CurrencyRate                        _WA_Sys_00000004_398D8EEE
CurrencyRate                        _WA_Sys_00000003_398D8EEE
Customer                            _WA_Sys_00000005_3B75D760
Customer                            _WA_Sys_00000003_3B75D760
...
ShoppingCartItem                    _WA_Sys_00000004_0B5CAFEA
StateProvince                       _WA_Sys_00000006_1B9317B3
StateProvince                       _WA_Sys_00000003_1B9317B3
WorkOrderRouting                    _WA_Sys_00000004_373B3228
*/
```

Creating Statistics

If you want finer control over how the column statistics are generated, you can use the CREATE STATISTICS command. Its syntax is similar to that of UPDATE STATISTICS, with the exception that you specify a column or list of columns instead of an index on which to create statistics:

```
CREATE STATISTICS statistics_name ON table (column [,...n])
    [   WITH  [ [ FULLSCAN | SAMPLE number { PERCENT | ROWS } ] [,] ]
        [ NORECOMPUTE]       ]
```

Any column that can be specified as an index key can also be specified for statistics, except for XML columns or when the maximum allowable size of the combined column values exceeds the 900-byte limit on an index key. Statistics can also be created on computed columns if the ARITHABORT and QUOTED_IDENTIFIER database options are set to ON. In addition, statistics can be created on CLR user-defined type columns if the CLR type supports binary ordering.

If you want to create single-column statistics on all eligible columns in a database, you can use the `sp_createstats` system procedure:

```
sp_createstats [[@indexonly =] 'indexonly']
        [, [@fullscan =] 'fullscan']
        [, [@norecompute =] 'norecompute']
```

The created statistics have the same name as the column on which they are created. Statistics are not created on columns that already have statistics on them (for example, the first column of an index or a column that already has explicitly created statistics).

To display a list of all column statistics, whether autogenerated or manually created, you can use a query similar to the previous one, but include user-created statistics as well:

```
SELECT cast(object_name(object_id) as varchar(30)) as 'table',
       cast (name as varchar(30)) as name,
       stats_id
   FROM sys.stats
   WHERE objectproperty (object_id, 'IsUserTable') = 1
     and (auto_created = 1 or user_created = 1)
order by 1, 3
go


/* output
table                       name                            stats_id
--------------------------- ------------------------------- ----------
BillOfMaterials             _WA_Sys_00000003_1DE57479              4
CurrencyRate                _WA_Sys_00000004_398D8EEE              3
CurrencyRate                _WA_Sys_00000003_398D8EEE              4
Customer                    _WA_Sys_00000005_3B75D760              4
Customer                    _WA_Sys_00000003_3B75D760              6
Customer                    _WA_Sys_00000002_3B75D760              7
Document                    _WA_Sys_00000002_403A8C7D              4
Document                    _WA_Sys_00000004_403A8C7D              7
Employee                    _WA_Sys_00000005_49C3F6B7              4
...
SalesPerson                 _WA_Sys_00000002_5CA1C101              3
SalesPerson                 _WA_Sys_00000006_5CA1C101              4
SalesTerritory              _WA_Sys_00000003_72910220              4
SalesTerritoryHistory       _WA_Sys_00000002_7D0E9093              3
ShoppingCartItem            _WA_Sys_00000004_0B5CAFEA              3
StateProvince               _WA_Sys_00000006_1B9317B3              5
StateProvince               _WA_Sys_00000003_1B9317B3              6
WorkOrderRouting            _WA_Sys_00000004_373B3228              3
*/
```

To remove a collection of statistics on one or more columns for a table in the current database, you use the DROP STATISTICS command, which has the following syntax:

```
DROP STATISTICS {table | view}.statistics_name
```

Be aware that dropping the column statistics could affect how your queries are optimized, and less efficient query plans might be chosen. Also, if the Auto Create Statistics option is enabled for the database, SQL Server is likely to automatically create statistics on the columns the next time they are referenced in a SARG or join clause for a query.

String Summary Statistics

SQL Server 2014 supports string summary statistics for estimating the selectivity of LIKE conditions. String summary statistics are statistical summaries of substring frequency distribution for character columns. String summary statistics can be created on columns of type text, ntext, char, varchar, and nvarchar. String summary statistics allow SQL Server to estimate the selectivity of LIKE conditions, where the search string may have any number of wildcards in any combination, including LIKE conditions where the first character is a wildcard. In previous versions of SQL Server, row estimates could not be accurately obtained when the leading character of a search string was a wildcard character. String summary statistics allow SQL Server to estimate the selectivity of any of the following predicates:

▶ Column LIKE 'string%'

▶ Column LIKE '%string'

▶ Column LIKE '%string%'

▶ Column LIKE 'str[abc]ing'

▶ Column LIKE '%abc%xy'

String summary statistics include additional information beyond what is displayed by DBCC SHOW_STATISTICS for the histogram. You can determine whether string summary statistics have been created for a column or an index by examining the String Index column returned by DBCC SHOW_STATISTICS. If the value is YES, the statistics for that column or index also include a string summary. However, DBCC SHOW_STATISTICS does not display the actual contents of the string summary.

SQL Server Index Maintenance

SQL Server indexes are self-maintaining, which means that any time a data modification (such as an update, a delete, or an insert) takes place on a table, the index B-tree is automatically updated to reflect the correct data values and current rows. Generally, you do not have to do any maintenance of the indexes, but indexes and tables can become fragmented over time. There are two types of fragmentation: external fragmentation and internal fragmentation.

External fragmentation occurs when the logical order of pages does not match the physical order or the extents allocated to the table are not contiguous. These situations occur typically with clustered tables as a result of page splits and pages being allocated and linked into the page chain from other extents. External fragmentation is usually not much of an issue for most queries performing small result set retrievals via an index. It's more of a performance issue for ordered scans of all or large parts of a table or index. If the table is heavily fragmented and the pages are not contiguous, scanning the page chain is more expensive and can significantly impact performance when reading the data in from disk.

Internal fragmentation occurs when an index is not using up all the space within the pages in the table or index. Fragmentation within an index page can happen for the following reasons:

▶ As more records are added to a table, space is used on the data page and on the index page. As a result, the page eventually becomes completely full. If another insert takes place on that page and there is no more room for the new row, SQL Server splits the page into two, each page now being about 50% full. If the clustered key values being inserted are not evenly distributed throughout the table (as often happens with clustered indexes on sequential keys), this extra free space might not be used.

▶ Frequent `update` statements can cause fragmentation in the database at the data and index page levels because the updates cause rows to move to other pages. Again, if future clustered key values inserted into the table are not evenly distributed throughout the table, the empty slots left behind might not be used.

▶ As rows are deleted, space becomes freed up on data and index pages. If no new rows within the range of deleted values on the page are inserted, the page remains sparse.

NOTE

Internal fragmentation is not always a bad thing. Although pages that are not completely full use up more space and require more I/O during retrieval, free space within a page allows for rows to be added without having to perform an expensive page split. For some environments where the activity is more insert-intensive than query-intensive, you might want more free space in pages. This can be accomplished by applying the fill factor when creating the index on the table. Applying the fill factor is described in more detail in the next section.

Usually in a system, all these factors contribute to the fragmentation of data within the data pages and index pages. In an environment subject to a lot of data modification, you might see a lot of fragmentation on the data and index pages over a period of time. These sparse and fragmented pages remain allocated to the table or index even if they have only a single row or two, and the extent containing the page remains allocated to the table or index.

Data fragmentation can adversely affect performance for table or index scanning operations because the data is spread across more pages than necessary. More I/Os are required to retrieve the data. SQL Server provides a dynamic management view (DMV), `sys.dm_db_index_physical_stats`, which is a multistatement table-valued function that returns size and fragmentation information for the data and indexes of a specified table or view. The results from the function are returned by a normal SELECT statement and thus can be saved to a table for reporting purposes and historical analysis. The syntax of `dm_db_index_physical_stats` is as follows:

```
sys.dm_db_index_physical_stats (
    { database_id | NULL | 0 | DEFAULT }
  , { object_id | NULL | 0 | DEFAULT }
  , { index_id | NULL | 0 | -1 | DEFAULT }
  , { partition_number | NULL | 0 | DEFAULT }
  , { mode | NULL | DEFAULT } )
```

The parameters for `dm_db_index_physical_stats` are summarized in Table 32.2.

TABLE 32.2   `dm_db_index_physical_stats` Parameters

Parameter	Description
database_id	The ID of the database. The default is 0, which returns information for all databases. NULL, 0, and DEFAULT are equivalent values in this context. If you specify NULL or 0, for database_id, you must specify NULL for object_id, index_id, and partition_number.
object_id	The object ID of the table or view the index is on. Valid inputs are the ID number of a table or view, NULL, 0, or DEFAULT. The default is 0, which returns information for all tables and views in the specified database. NULL, 0, and DEFAULT are equivalent values in this context.
index_id	The ID of the index. Valid inputs are the ID number of an index, 0 if object_id is a heap, NULL, -1, or DEFAULT. The default is -1, which returns information for all indexes for a table or view. NULL, -1, and DEFAULT are equivalent values in this context. If you specify NULL for index_id, you must also specify NULL for partition_number.
partition_number	The partition number in the object. Valid inputs are the partition_number of an index or a heap, NULL, 0, or DEFAULT. The default is 0, which returns information for all partitions of the object. NULL, 0, and DEFAULT are equivalent values in this context. Use a partition_number of 1 for a nonpartitioned index or heap.
mode	The scan level used to obtain physical index statistics. Valid inputs are DEFAULT, NULL, LIMITED, SAMPLED, or DETAILED. The default mode is LIMITED. NULL and DEFAULT are equivalent values in this context.

The `sys.dm_db_index_physical_stats` function requires only an Intent-Shared table lock, regardless of the mode in which it runs. This provides for the capability to run the `sys.dm_db_index_physical_stats` function online without blocking update activity on a table.

The scan-level mode determines the level of scanning performed by the function to obtain the physical statistics for the index. The `LIMITED` mode is the fastest and scans the smallest number of pages. It scans all data pages for a heap but scans only leaf-level pages for an index. It also returns only a subset of the data columns, as shown in Table 32.3. The `SAMPLED` mode returns statistics based on a 1% sample of all the pages in the index or heap. If the index or heap has fewer than 10,000 pages, `DETAILED` mode is used instead of `SAMPLED`. The `SAMPLED` scan mode displays information for only data pages of a heap and leaf-level pages of an index. The `DETAILED` mode scans all pages and returns all statistics for all data and index levels.

TIP

The scan modes get progressively slower from `LIMITED` to `DETAILED` because more work is performed in each mode. To quickly gauge the size or fragmentation level of a table or an index, first use the `LIMITED` mode. It is the fastest and does not return a row for each nonleaf level in the `IN_ROW_DATA` allocation unit of the index.

Table 32.3 describes the result columns returned by the `dm_db_index_physical_stats` table-valued function.

TABLE 32.3   `dm_db_index_physical_stats` Result Columns

Column Name	Data Type	Description	Displayed in LIMITED Scan Mode
database_id	Smallint	A database ID of the database containing the table or view.	Yes
object_id	int	The object ID of the table or view where the index is located.	Yes
index_id	int	The index ID of the index. 0 indicates a heap.	Yes
partition_number	int	A partition number within the owning table, view, or index.	Yes
index_type_desc	nvarchar(60)	The index type. Values are HEAP, CLUSTERED INDEX, NONCLUSTERED INDEX, PRIMARY XML INDEX, and XML INDEX.	Yes
alloc_unit_type_desc	nvarchar(60)	A description of the allocation unit type. Values are IN_ROW_DATA, LOB_DATA, and ROW_OVERFLOW_DATA.	Yes
index_depth	tinyint	The number of index levels.	Yes

Column Name	Data Type	Description	Displayed in LIMITED Scan Mode
index_level	tinyint	The current level of the index. 0 indicates index leaf levels, heaps, and LOB_DATA or ROW_OVERFLOW_DATA allocation units.	Yes
avg_fragmentation_in_percent	float	The percentage of logical fragmentation (out-of-order pages in the index).	Yes
fragment_count	bigint	The number of fragments (physically consecutive leaf pages) in the index.	Yes
avg_fragment_size_in_pages	float	The average number of pages in one fragment in an index.	Yes
page_count	bigint	The total number of index or data pages at the current level.	Yes
avg_page_space_used_in_percent	Float	The average percentage of available data storage space used in all pages.	No
record_count	Bigint	The total number of records at the current level.	No
ghost_record_count	Bigint	The number of ghost records ready for removal by the ghost cleanup task.	No
version_ghost_record_count	Bigint	The number of ghost records retained by an outstanding snapshot isolation transaction in an allocation unit.	No
min_record_size_in_bytes	Int	The minimum record size, in bytes.	No
max_record_size_in_bytes	Int	The maximum record size, in bytes.	No
avg_record_size_in_bytes	Float	The average record size, in bytes.	No
forwarded_record_count	Bigint	The number of forwarded records in a heap.	No
compressed_page_count_	Bigint	The number of compressed pages in a heap.	No

Listing 32.3 shows examples of running sys.dm_db_index_physical_stats on the SaleOrderDetail table, using both LIMITED and DETAILED scan modes.

LISTING 32.3   `sys.dm_db_index_physical_stats` Examples

```
use AdventureWorks2012
go
select str(index_id,3,0) as indid,
      left(index_type_desc, 20) as index_type_desc,
      index_depth as idx_depth,
      index_level as idx_level,
      str(avg_fragmentation_in_percent, 5,2) as avg_frgmnt_pct,
      str(page_count, 10,0) as pg_cnt
  FROM sys.dm_db_index_physical_stats
      (db_id(), object_id('Sales.SalesOrderDetail'),null, 0, 'LIMITED')

select str(index_id,3,0) as indid,
      left(index_type_desc, 20) as index_type_desc,
      index_depth as idx_depth,
      index_level as idx_level,
      str(avg_fragmentation_in_percent, 5,2) as avg_frgmnt_pct,
      str(page_count, 10,0) as pg_cnt
  FROM sys.dm_db_index_physical_stats
    (db_id(), object_id('Sales.SalesOrderDetail'),null, 0, 'DETAILED')
go


/* output
indid index_type_desc      idx_depth idx_level avg_frgmnt_pct pg_cnt
----- -------------------- --------- --------- -------------- ----------
   1  CLUSTERED INDEX              3         0  1.17                 596
   2  NONCLUSTERED INDEX          3         0  2.64                 454
   3  NONCLUSTERED INDEX          2         0  2.92                 274


indid index_type_desc      idx_depth idx_level avg_frgmnt_pct pg_cnt
----- -------------------- --------- --------- -------------- ----------
   1  CLUSTERED INDEX             3         0  1.17                 596
   1  CLUSTERED INDEX             3         1 100.0                   3
   1  CLUSTERED INDEX             3         2  0.00                   1
   2  NONCLUSTERED INDEX          3         0  2.64                 454
   2  NONCLUSTERED INDEX          3         1 66.67                   3
   2  NONCLUSTERED INDEX          3         2  0.00                   1
   3  NONCLUSTERED INDEX          2         0  2.92                 274
   3  NONCLUSTERED INDEX          2         1  0.00                   1
*/
```

You can see from the output in Listing 32.3 that the logical fragmentation (`avg_frgmnt_pct`) is very low (less than 3%) for the leaf level (`idx_level` = 0) for all of the indexes on `SalesOrderDetail`. This indicates that this table is not yet heavily fragmented. However, as you monitor it over time and it does start to show fragmentation, you'll need to decide whether to rebuild the index or simply defragment the index if you want to improve the performance of table scans or clustered index scans for the SalesOrderDetail table.

The degree of fragmentation helps you decide which defragmentation method to use. A rough guideline to use to help decide is to examine the avg_fragmentation_in_percent value returned by the sys.dm_db_index_physical_stats function. If the avg_fragmentation_in_percent value is greater than 5% but less than 30%, that index is a candidate for reorganization. If the avg_fragmentation_in_percent value is greater than 30%, you should consider rebuilding the index. If you also have a dedicated maintenance window large enough to perform a rebuild instead of simply reorganizing the index, you may as well run a rebuild because it performs a more thorough defragmentation than reorganizing the index.

Another factor in determining whether an index needs to be defragmented is how the data is accessed. If your applications are performing primarily single-row lookups, randomly accessing individual rows of data, the internal or external fragmentation is not a factor when it comes to query performance. Accessing one row from a fragmented table is just as easy as from an unfragmented table. However, if your applications are performing ordered range scan operations and reading all or large numbers of the pages in a table, excessive fragmentation can greatly slow down the scan. The more contiguous and full the pages, the better the performance will be of the scanning operations.

> **TIP**
>
> If you have very low levels of fragmentation (less than 5%), it is recommended that you not bother with either a reorganization or a rebuild because the benefit of removing such a small amount of fragmentation is not enough to justify the cost of reorganizing or rebuilding the index.

In SQL Server 2014, the ALTER INDEX command provides options for defragmenting an index. Following is the syntax for the ALTER INDEX command:

```
ALTER INDEX { index_name | ALL }
    ON  [ database_name. [ schema_name ] . | schema_name. ]
        table_or_view_name
    { REBUILD
      [ [PARTITION = ALL]
                    [ WITH ( <rebuild_index_option> [ ,...n ] ) ]
        | [ PARTITION = partition_number
            [ WITH ( <single_partition_rebuild_index_option>
                    [ ,...n ] )
            ]
        ]
      ]
    | DISABLE
    | REORGANIZE
```

```
        [ PARTITION = partition_number ]
        [ WITH ( LOB_COMPACTION = { ON | OFF } ) ]
  | SET ( <set_index_option> [ ,...n ] )
        }
[ ; ]


<rebuild_index_option > ::=
{
    PAD_INDEX = { ON | OFF }
  | FILLFACTOR = fillfactor
  | SORT_IN_TEMPDB = { ON | OFF }
  | IGNORE_DUP_KEY = { ON | OFF }
  | STATISTICS_NORECOMPUTE = { ON | OFF }
  | ONLINE = { ON | OFF }
  | ALLOW_ROW_LOCKS = { ON | OFF }
  | ALLOW_PAGE_LOCKS = { ON | OFF }
  | MAXDOP = max_degree_of_parallelism
  | DATA_COMPRESSION = { NONE | ROW | PAGE }
    [ ON PARTITIONS ( { <partition_number_expression> | <range> }
    [ , ...n ] ) ]
}
<range> ::=
<partition_number_expression> TO <partition_number_expression>
}


<single_partition_rebuild_index_option> ::=
{
    SORT_IN_TEMPDB = { ON | OFF }
  | MAXDOP = max_degree_of_parallelism
  | DATA_COMPRESSION = { NONE | ROW | PAGE } }
}


<set_index_option>::=
{
    ALLOW_ROW_LOCKS = { ON | OFF }
  | ALLOW_PAGE_LOCKS = { ON | OFF }
  | IGNORE_DUP_KEY = { ON | OFF }
  | STATISTICS_NORECOMPUTE = { ON | OFF }
}
```

The REORGANIZE option is always performed online, regardless of which edition of SQL Server 2014 you are running, allowing for other users to continue to update and query the underlying data in the table while the REORGANIZE process is running. The REBUILD option can be executed online only if you are running SQL Server 2014 Enterprise or Developer Editions. In all other editions of SQL Server 2014, the REBUILD option is executed offline. When it is executed offline, SQL Server acquires locks on the underlying data and associated indexes so any data modifications to the table are blocked until the rebuild completes. Rebuilding a clustered index offline acquires a Schema modification lock on the table preventing and reads or writes to the table for the duration of the rebuild. An offline rebuild of a nonclustered index acquires a shared table lock preventing modifications to the table, but allowing reads during the duration of the rebuild.

Reorganizing an index uses minimal system resources to defragment only the leaf level of clustered and nonclustered indexes of tables and views. The first phase of the reorganization process compacts the rows on the leaf pages, reapplying the current fill factor value to reduce the internal fragmentation. To view the current fill factor setting, you can run a query such as the following against the sys.indexes system catalog view:

```
select cast(name as varchar(30)) as name, index_id, fill_factor
    from sys.indexes
    where object_id = object_id('Sales.SalesOrderDetail')
go


/* output
name                            index_id fill_factor
------------------------------- -------- -----------
PK_SalesOrderDetail_SalesOrder      1         0
AK_SalesOrderDetail_rowguid         2         0
IX_SalesOrderDetail_ProductID       3         0
*/
```

For more information on fill factor and how to set it, see the "Setting the Fill Factor" section, later in this chapter.

The second phase of the reorganization process involves the rearranging of the leaf-level pages so that the logical and physical order of the pages match, thereby reducing the external fragmentation of the leaf level of the index. SQL Server 2014 runs a REORGANIZATION of an index online because the second phase processes only two pages at a time, in an operation similar to a bubble sort. When defragmenting the index, SQL Server 2014 determines the first physical page belonging to the leaf level and the first logical page in the leaf level, and it swaps the data on those two pages. It then identifies the next logical and physical page and swaps them, and so on, until no more swaps need to be made. At this point, the logical page ordering matches the physical page ordering. While swapping the logical and physical pages, SQL Server uses an additional new page as a temporary storage area. After each page swap, SQL Server releases all locks and latches and saves the key of the last moved page.

The following example uses ALTER TABLE to reorganize the clustered index on the SalesOrderDetail table:

```
ALTER INDEX [PK_SalesOrderDetail_SalesOrderID_SalesOrderDetailID] on Sales.
SalesOrderDetail REORGANIZE
```

After running this command, you can run a query similar to the query in Listing 32.3 to display the fragmentation of the `ci_sales_big` index on the `sales_big` table:

```
select str(s.index_id,3,0) as indid,
      left(i.name, 20) as index_name,
      left(index_type_desc, 20) as index_type_desc,
      index_depth as idx_depth,
      index_level as level,
      str(avg_fragmentation_in_percent, 5,2) as avg_frgmnt_pct,
      str(page_count, 10,0) as pg_cnt
   FROM sys.dm_db_index_physical_stats
      (db_id('AdventureWorks2012'), object_id('Sales.SalesOrderDetail'),1, 0,
'DETAILED') s
    join sys.indexes i on s.object_id = i.object_id and s.index_id = i.index_id
go

/* output

                           index_type_      idx_depth      avg_frgmnt_pct indid
index_name                 desc             level          pg_cnt
-----  -------------------- ----- -------------- ----
   1   PK_SalesOrderDetail_ CLUSTERED INDEX    3       0  0.67  596
   1   PK_SalesOrderDetail_ CLUSTERED INDEX    3       1  100.0   3
   1   PK_SalesOrderDetail_ CLUSTERED INDEX    3       2  0.00    1
*/
```

As you can see, the average fragmentation percentage is down to .67% from 1.17%, indicating that the index is now further defragmented. However, if the average fragmentation percentage of the intermediate level of any index (level > 0) is still above the 30% threshold, that would indicate that the nonleaf levels are still heavily fragmented. To defragment the nonleaf levels of the index, you need to rebuild the index. The following example shows how to rebuild the index using the ALTER INDEX command:

```
ALTER INDEX [PK_SalesOrderDetail_SalesOrderID_SalesOrderDetailID] on
Sales.SalesOrderDetail REBUILD
```

After running this command, you can again run a query similar to the query in Listing 32.3 to display the fragmentation of the clustered index on the `SalesOrderDetail` table:

```
select str(s.index_id,3,0) as indid,
      left(i.name, 20) as index_name,
      left(index_type_desc, 20) as index_type_desc,
      index_depth as idx_depth,
      index_level as level,
      str(avg_fragmentation_in_percent, 5,2) as avg_frgmnt_pct,
      str(page_count, 10,0) as pg_cnt
   FROM sys.dm_db_index_physical_stats
      (db_id('AdventureWorks2012'), object_id('Sales.SalesOrderDetail'),1, 0,
```

```
'DETAILED') s
    join sys.indexes i on s.object_id = i.object_id and s.index_id = i.index_id
go

/* output
indid index_name              index_type_desc idx_depth level avg_frgmnt_pct pg_cnt
----- --------------------    --------------- --------- ----- -------------- ----------
    1  PK_SalesOrderDetail_   CLUSTERED INDEX         3     0  1.17              596
    1  PK_SalesOrderDetail_   CLUSTERED INDEX         3     1  66.67               3
    1  PK_SalesOrderDetail_   CLUSTERED INDEX         3     2  0.00                1
*/
```

You can see from these results that the REBUILD option performs a more thorough defrag-mentation of the PK_SalesOrderDetail_SalesOrderID_SalesOrderDetailID index than REORGANIZE. The average fragmentation percentage of both the leaf and intermediate levels is now less.

> **NOTE**
>
> When you rebuild a nonclustered index, the rebuild operation requires enough temporary disk space to store both the old and new indexes. However, if the index is disabled before being rebuilt, the disk space made available by disabling the index can be reused by the subsequent rebuild or any other operation. No additional space is required except for temporary disk space for sorting, which is typically only about 20% of the index size.
>
> Therefore, if disk space is limited, it may be helpful to disable a nonclustered index before rebuilding it. For more information on disabling indexes, see the "Disabling Indexes" section, later in this chapter.

One of the other options to the CREATE INDEX and ALTER INDEX commands is the FILLFACTOR option. The fill factor allows you to specify, as a percentage, the fullness of the pages at the data and leaf index page levels, essentially deciding how much free space to create in the index and data pages to make room for new rows and avoid page splits.

Setting the Fill Factor

Fill factor is a setting you can use when creating an index to specify, as a percentage, how full you want your data pages or leaf-level index pages to be when the index is created. A lower fill factor has the effect of spreading the data and leaf index rows across a greater number of pages by leaving more free space in the pages. This reduces page splitting and dynamic reorganization of index and data pages, which can improve performance in envi-ronments where there are a lot of inserts and updates to the data, while at the same time reducing performance for queries because an increased number of pages need to be read to retrieve multiple rows. A higher fill factor has the effect of packing more data and index rows per page by leaving less free space in the pages. Using a higher fill factor is useful in environments where the data is relatively static because it reduces the number of pages required for storing the data and its indexes, and it helps improve performance for queries by reducing the number of pages that need to be accessed.

By default, when you create an index on a table, if you don't specify a value for FILLFACTOR, the default value is 0. With a FILLFACTOR setting of 0, or 100, the data pages for a clustered index and the leaf pages for a nonclustered index are created completely full. However, space is left within the nonleaf nodes of the index for one or two more rows. The default fill factor to be used when creating indexes is a server-level configuration option. If you want to change the server-wide default for the fill factor, you use the sp_configure command:

```
sp_configure 'fill factor',N
```

It is generally recommended that you leave the server-wide default for fill factor as 0 and specify your FILLFACTOR settings on an index-by-index basis. You can specify a specific fill factor value for an index by including the FILLFACTOR option for the CREATE INDEX statement:

```
CREATE [UNIQUE] [CLUSTERED | NONCLUSTERED] INDEX index_name
    ON [ [database_name.][schema_name.]] table_or_view_name
    [ WITH ( <relational_index_option> [ ,...n ] ) ]
<relational_index_option> ::=
{ PAD_INDEX  = { ON | OFF }
  | FILLFACTOR = fillfactor
  | SORT_IN_TEMPDB = { ON | OFF }
  | IGNORE_DUP_KEY = { ON | OFF }
  | STATISTICS_NORECOMPUTE = { ON | OFF }
  | DROP_EXISTING = { ON | OFF }
  | ONLINE = { ON | OFF }
  | ALLOW_ROW_LOCKS = { ON | OFF }
  | ALLOW_PAGE_LOCKS = { ON | OFF }
  | MAXDOP = max_degree_of_parallelism }
```

The FILLFACTOR option for the CREATE INDEX command allows you to specify, as a percentage, how full the data or leaf-level index pages should be when you create an index on a table. The specified percentage can be from 1 to 100. Specifying a value of 80 would mean that each data or leaf page would be filled approximately 80% full at the time you create the index. It is important to note that as more data gets modified or added to a table, the fill factor is not maintained at the level specified during the CREATE INDEX command. Over a period of time, you will find that each page has a different percentage of fullness as rows are added and deleted.

TIP

A fill factor setting specified when creating a nonclustered index affects only the nonclustered index pages and doesn't affect the data pages. To apply a fill factor to the data pages in a table, you must provide a fill factor setting when creating a clustered index on the table. Also, it is important to remember that the fill factor is applied only at index creation time and is not maintained by SQL Server. When you begin updating and inserting data, the free space generated in the index pages by the fill factor setting is eventually lost. Therefore, specifying a fill factor when creating your indexes is useful only if the table already contains data or if you simply want to set a default fill factor for the index other than 0 that will be used when indexes are rebuilt or reorganized by ALTER INDEX.

If you specify only the FILLFACTOR option, only the data or leaf-level index pages are affected by the fill factor. To specify the level of fullness for nonleaf pages, use the PAD_INDEX option together with FILLFACTOR. This option allows you to specify how much space to leave open on each node of the index, which can help to reduce page splits within the nonleaf levels of the index. You don't specify a value for PAD_INDEX; it uses the same percentage value specified with the FILLFACTOR option. For example, to apply a 50% fill factor to the leaf and nonleaf pages in a nonclustered index on ProductNumber in the Product table, you would execute the following:

```
CREATE INDEX Product_Number_index on Production.Product (ProductNumber)
       with (FILLFACTOR = 50, PAD_INDEX = ON)
```

TIP

When you use PAD_INDEX, the value specified by FILLFACTOR cannot be such that the number of rows on each index node falls below two. If you do specify such a value, SQL Server internally overrides it so that the number of rows on an intermediate index page is never less than two.

Reapplying the Fill Factor

When might you need to re-establish the fill factor for your indexes or data? As data gets modified in a table, the value of FILLFACTOR is not maintained at the level specified in the CREATE INDEX statement. As a result, each page can reach a different level of fullness. Over a period of time, this can lead to heavy fragmentation in the database if insert/delete activity is not evenly spread throughout the table, and it could affect performance. In addition, if a table becomes very large and then very small, rows could become isolated within data pages. This space will likely not be recovered until the last row on the page is deleted and the page is marked as unused. To either spread out rows or to reclaim space by repacking more rows per page, you need to reapply the fill factor to your clustered and nonclustered indexes.

In environments where insert activity is heavy, reapplying a low fill factor might help performance by spreading out the data and leaving free space on the pages, which helps to minimize page splits and possible page-locking contention during heavy OLTP activity. You can use Performance Monitor to monitor your system and determine whether excessive page splits are occurring. (See Chapter 39 for more information on using Performance Monitor.)

A DBA must manually reapply the fill factor to improve the performance of the system. This can be done by using the ALTER INDEX command discussed earlier or by dropping and re-creating the index. ALTER INDEX is preferred because, by default, it applies the original fill factor specified when the index was created, or you can provide a new fill factor to override the default. The original fill factor for an index is stored in sys.indexes in the fill_factor column. In addition, if you use the ALTER INDEX command to reorganize or rebuild your table or index, it attempts to reapply the index's original fill factor when it reorganizes the pages.

Disabling Indexes

Another feature available in SQL Server 2014 is the capability to set an index as disabled. When an index is disabled, the definition of the index is maintained in the system catalogs, but the index itself contains no index key rows. Disabling an index prevents use of the index by any queries against the table. Disabling a clustered index also prevents access to the underlying table data.

You can manually disable an index at any time by using the ALTER INDEX DISABLE statement:

```
ALTER INDEX Product_number_index ON Production.Product DISABLE
```

The reasons you might want to disable an index include the following:

▶ Correcting a disk I/O or allocation error on an index page and then rebuilding the index later

▶ Temporarily removing the index for troubleshooting purposes

▶ Saving temporary disk space while rebuilding nonclustered indexes

When you disable an index, the index is not maintained while it is disabled, and the Query Optimizer does not consider it when creating query execution plans. However, statistics on a disabled nonclustered index remain in place and are updated automatically if the AutoStats option is in effect.

If you disable a clustered index, all nonclustered indexes on the table are automatically disabled as well. The nonclustered index cannot be re-enabled until the clustered index is either enabled or dropped. After you enable the clustered index, the nonclustered indexes must be explicitly enabled unless the clustered index was enabled by using the ALTER INDEX ALL REBUILD statement. Because the data rows of the table cannot be accessed while the clustered index is disabled, the following operations cannot be performed on the table:

▶ SELECT, UPDATE, DELETE, and INSERT

▶ CREATE INDEX

▶ CREATE STATISTICS

▶ UPDATE STATISTICS

▶ ALTER TABLE statements that modify table columns or constraints

After an index is disabled, it remains in a disabled state until it is rebuilt or dropped. You can enable a disabled index by rebuilding it by using one of the following methods:

▶ ALTER INDEX statement with the REBUILD clause

▶ CREATE INDEX with the DROP_EXISTING clause

▶ DBCC DBREINDEX

To determine whether an index is currently disabled, you can use the INDEXPROPERTY function (a value of 1 indicates the index is disabled):

```
select indexproperty(object_id('Production.Product'), 'Product_number_index',
'IsDisabled')

/* output
-----------
1
*/
```

Managing Indexes with SSMS

So far, you've seen the commands necessary for index management. In addition to these commands, SSMS provides tools for managing indexes.

To reorganize or rebuild an index using SSMS, in the Object Explorer, connect to an instance of the SQL Server 2014 Database Engine and then expand that instance. Then expand Databases, expand the database that contains the table with the specified index, and expand Tables. Next, expand the table in which the index belongs and then expand Indexes. Finally, right-click the index to rebuild and then click Rebuild or Reorganize. To rebuild or reorganize all indexes on a table, right-click Indexes and select Rebuild All or Reorganize All.

You can also disable indexes in SSMS. In the Object Explorer, right-click the index you want to disable and then select the Disable option. To disable all indexes on a table, right-click on Indexes and select Disable All.

You can also use SSMS to modify indexes. In the Object Explorer, right-click the index you want to modify and then click Properties. In the Properties dialog that appears (see Figure 32.2), you can add or remove columns from the index, change the uniqueness setting, set the index option, set the fill factor, rebuild the index, view the index fragmentation, reorganize the index, and so on.

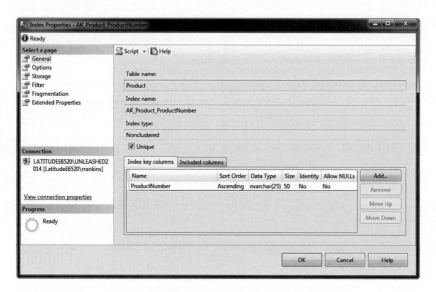

FIGURE 32.2   Setting and viewing index properties in SSMS.

Index Design Guidelines

SQL Server indexes are mostly transparent to end users and T-SQL developers and are typically not specified in queries unless you use table hints to force the Query Optimizer to use a particular index. (Although forcing indexes is generally not advised, using Query Optimizer table hints is covered in more detail in Chapter 40, "SQL Server Database Engine Tuning Adviser.") Normally, based on the index key histogram or density values, the SQL Server cost-based Query Optimizer automatically chooses the index that is least expensive from an I/O standpoint.

Chapter 34 goes into greater detail on how the Query Optimizer estimates I/O and determines the most efficient query plan. In the meantime, the following are some of the main guidelines to follow in creating useful indexes that the Query Optimizer can use effectively:

▶ For composite indexes, try to keep the more selective columns leftmost in the index. The first element in the index should be the most unique (if possible), and index column order in general should be from most to least unique. However, remember that selectivity doesn't help if the first ordered index column is not specified in your SARGs or join clauses. To ensure that the index is used for the largest number of queries, be sure the first ordered column is the column used most often in your queries.

▶ Be sure to index columns used in joins. Joins are processed inefficiently if no index on the column(s) is specified in a join. Remember that a PRIMARY KEY constraint automatically creates an index on a column, but a FOREIGN KEY constraint does not. You should create indexes on your foreign key columns if your queries commonly join between the primary key and foreign key tables.

▶ Tailor your indexes for your most critical queries and transactions. You cannot index for every possible query that might be run against your tables. However, your applications will perform better if you can identify your critical and most frequently executed queries and design indexes to support them. SQL Server Profiler, which is covered in Chapter 5, is a useful tool for identifying the most frequently executed queries. SQL Server Profiler can also help identify slow-running queries that might benefit from improved index design.

▶ Avoid indexes on columns that have poor selectivity. The Query Optimizer is not likely to use the indexes, so they would simply take up space and add unnecessary overhead during inserts, updates, and deletes. One possible exception occurs when the index can be used to cover a query. Index covering is discussed in more detail in the "Index Covering" section, later in this chapter.

▶ Choose your clustered and nonclustered indexes carefully. The next two sections discuss tips and guidelines for choosing between clustered or nonclustered indexes, based on the data contained in the columns and the types of queries executed against the columns.

Clustered Index Indications

Searching for rows via a clustered index is almost always faster than searching for rows via a nonclustered index—for two reasons. One reason is that a clustered index contains only pointers to pages rather than pointers to individual data rows; therefore, a clustered index is more compact than a nonclustered index. Because a clustered index is smaller and doesn't require an additional lookup via the row locator to find the matching rows, the rows can be found with fewer page reads than with a similarly defined nonclustered index. The second reason is that because the data in a table with a clustered index is physically sorted on the clustered key, searching for duplicate values or for a range of clustered key values is faster; the rows are adjacent to each other, and SQL Server can simply locate the first qualifying row and then search the rows in sequence until the last qualifying row is found. However, because you are allowed to create only one clustered index per table, you must judiciously choose the column or columns on which to define the clustered index.

If you require only a single index on a table, it's typically advantageous to make it a clustered index; the resulting overhead of maintaining clustered indexes during updates, inserts, and deletes can be considerably less than the overhead incurred by nonclustered indexes.

By default, the primary key on a table is defined as a clustered unique index. In most applications, the primary key column on a table is almost always retrieved in single-row lookups. For single-row lookups, a nonclustered index usually costs you only a few more I/Os than a similar clustered index. Are you or the users really going to notice a difference between three page reads to retrieve a single data row versus four- to six-page reads to retrieve a single data row? Not at all. However, if you have to perform a range retrieval, such as a lookup on last name, will you notice a difference between scanning 10% of the table versus having to find the rows using a full table scan? Most definitely. With this in mind, you might want to consider creating your primary key as a unique nonclustered index and choosing another candidate for your clustered index.

Following are guidelines to consider for other potential candidates for clustered indexes:

▶ **Columns with a number of duplicate values searched frequently (for example,** `WHERE last_name = 'Smith'`)—Because the data is physically sorted, all the duplicate values are kept together. Any query that tries to fetch records against such keys finds all the values, using a minimum of I/O. SQL Server locates the first row that matches the SARG and then scans the data rows in order until it finds the last row matching the SARG.

▶ **Columns often specified in the** ORDER BY **clause**—Because the data is already sorted, SQL Server can avoid having to re-sort the data if the ORDER BY is on the clustered index key and the data is retrieved in clustered key order. Remember that even for a table scan, the data is retrieved in clustered key order because the data in the table is in clustered key order. The only exception is if a parallel query operation is used to retrieve the data rows; in that case, the results need to be re-sorted when the result sets from each parallel thread are merged. (For more information on parallel query strategies, see Chapter 34.)

▶ **Columns often searched for within a range of values (for example,** WHERE **price between $10 and $20)**—A clustered index can be used to locate the first qualifying row in the range of values. Because the rows in the table are in sorted order, SQL Server can simply scan the data pages in order until it finds the last qualifying row within the range. When the result set within the range of values is large, a clustered index scan is significantly more efficient in terms of total logical I/O performed than repeated row locator lookups via a nonclustered index.

▶ **Columns, other than the primary key, frequently used in join clauses**—Clustered indexes tend to be smaller than nonclustered indexes; the amount of page I/O required per lookup is generally less for a clustered index than for a nonclustered index. It can be a significant difference when joining many records. An extra page read or two might not seem like much for a single-row retrieval, but add those additional page reads to 100,000 join iterations, and you're looking at a total of 100,000 to 200,000 additional page reads.

When you consider columns for a clustered index, you might want to try to keep your clustered indexes on relatively static columns to minimize the re-sorting of data rows when an indexed column is updated. Any time a clustered index key value changes, the entire data row has to be moved to keep the clustered data values in physical sort order. In addition, all nonclustered indexes using the clustered key as the row locator to that row also need to be updated.

You should also avoid creating clustered indexes on wide keys that are made up of several columns, especially several large-size columns. The reason is that the clustered key values are incorporated in all nonclustered indexes as the row locator. Because the nonclustered index entries contain the clustering key in addition to the key columns defined for that nonclustered index, the nonclustered indexes end up being significantly larger and less efficient in terms of I/O. In this situation, you may be better off leaving the clustered index on the primary key column(s) and creating a covering nonclustered index that includes the keys that you are considering for clustering.

Because you can physically sort the data in a table in only one way, you can have only one clustered index per table. Any other columns you want to index have to be defined with nonclustered indexes.

Nonclustered Index Indications

SQL Server allows you to create a maximum of 999 nonclustered indexes on a table. Until tables become extremely large, the actual space taken by a nonclustered index is a minor expense compared to the increased access performance. You need to keep in mind, however, that as you add more indexes to the system, performance of database modification statements is impacted due to the increased index maintenance overhead.

Also, when defining nonclustered indexes, you typically want to define indexes on columns that are more selective (that is, columns with low density values) so that they can be used effectively by the Query Optimizer. A high number of duplicate values in a nonclustered index can often make it more expensive (in terms of I/O) to process the query using the nonclustered index than a table scan. Let's look at a hypothetical example:

```
select Name from Production.Product
    where ListPrice between $5. and $10.
```

Assume that you have 1 million rows within the range; those 1 million rows could be randomly scattered throughout the table. Although the index leaf level has all the index rows in sorted order, reading all data rows one at a time would require a separate lookup via the row locator for each row in the worst-case scenario.

Thus, the worst-case I/O estimate for range retrievals using a nonclustered index is as follows:

> Number of levels in the nonclustered index
>
> + Number of index pages scanned to find all matching rows
>
> + (Number of matching rows × Number of pages per lookup via the row locator)

If you have no clustered index on the table, the row locator is simply a page and row pointer and requires one data page read to find the matching data row. If 1 million rows are in the range, the worst-case cost estimate to search via the nonclustered index with no clustered index on the table would be as follows:

> Number of index page reads to find all the row locators
>
> + (1 million matching rows × 1 data page read)
>
> = 1 million + I/O

If you have a clustered index on the table, the row locator is a clustered index key for the data row. Using the row locator to find the matching row requires searching the clustered index tree to locate the data row. Assuming that the clustered index has two nonleaf levels, it would cost three pages to find each qualifying row on a data page. If the range has 1 million rows, the worst-case cost estimate to search via the nonclustered index with a clustered index on the table would be as follows:

Number of index page reads to find all the row locators

+ (1 million matching rows × 3 pages per lookup via the row locator)

= 3 million + I/O

Contrast each of these scenarios with the cost of a table scan. If the entire table takes up 50,000 pages, a full table scan would cost only 50,000 in terms of I/O. Therefore, in this example, doing a table scan would actually be more efficient than using the nonclustered index.

The following guidelines help you identify potential candidates for nonclustered indexes for your environment:

In general, nonclustered indexes are useful for single-row lookups, joins, queries on columns that are highly selective, or queries with small range retrievals. Also, when considering your nonclustered index design, you should not overlook the benefits of index covering, as described in the following section.

Index Covering

Index covering is a situation in which all the information required by the query in the SELECT and WHERE clauses can be found entirely within the nonclustered index itself. Because the nonclustered index contains a leaf row corresponding to every data row in the table, SQL Server can satisfy the query from the leaf rows of the nonclustered index. This results in faster retrieval of data because all the information can come directly from the index page, and SQL Server avoids lookups of the data pages.

Because the leaf pages in a nonclustered index are linked together, the leaf level of the index can be scanned just like the data pages in a table. Because the leaf index rows are typically much smaller than the data rows, a nonclustered index that covers a query will be faster than a clustered index on the same columns because fewer pages would need to be read.

In the following example, a nonclustered index on the LastName and FirstName columns of the Person table would cover the query because the result columns and the SARGs can all be derived from the index itself:

```
SELECT LastName, FirstName FROM Person.Person
WHERE LastName LIKE 'A%'
ORDER BY LastName
```

Many other queries that use an aggregate function (such as MIN, MAX, AVG, SUM, and COUNT) or simply check for existence of criteria also benefit from index covering. The following aggregate query samples can take advantage of index covering:

```
select count(LastName) from Person.Person where LastName like 'M%'

select count(*) from Person.Person where LastName like 'M%'

select count(*) from Person.Person
```

You might wonder how the last query, which doesn't even specify a SARG, can use an index. SQL Server knows that by its nature, a nonclustered index contains a row for every data row in the table; it can simply count all the rows in any of the nonclustered indexes instead of scanning the whole table. For the last query, SQL Server chooses the smallest nonclustered index—that is, the one with the fewest number of leaf pages.

Index covering can sometimes occur when you are not expecting it. As discussed previously in this chapter, when you have a clustered index defined on a table, the clustered key is carried into all the nonclustered indexes to be used as the row locator to locate the actual data row. Having the additional clustered key column values in the nonclustered index provides more data values that can be used for index covering.

For example, assume that the Person table has a clustered index on LastName and FirstName and a nonclustered primary key defined on BusinessEntityID. Each row in the nonclustered index on BusinessEntityID would contain the clustered key values for LastName and FirstName for its corresponding data row. Because of this, the following query would actually be covered by the nonclustered index on BusinessEntityID:

```
select LastName, FirstName
   from Person.Persons
   where BusinessEntityID between 100 and 200
```

Explicitly adding additional columns to nonclustered indexes to promote the occurrence of index covering has historically been a common method of improving query response time. Consider the following query:

```
select StandardCost from Production.Product
   where ListPrice between $10 and $20
```

If you create an index on only the ListPrice column, SQL Server can find the rows in the index where ListPrice is between $10 and $20, but it has to access the data rows to retrieve StandardCost. With 100 rows in the range, the worst-case I/O cost to retrieve the data rows would be as follows:

> Number of index levels
>
> + Number of index pages to find the 100 matching rows
>
> + (100 × Number of pages per lookup via the row locator)

If the `StandardCost` column were added to the index on the `ListPrice` column, SQL Server could scan the index to retrieve the results instead of having to perform the lookups via the row locator against the table, resulting in faster query response. The I/O cost using index covering would be lower, as follows:

> Number of index levels
>
> + Number of index pages to scan to find the 100 matching rows

If you are considering padding your indexes to take advantage of index covering, beware of making an index too wide. As index row width approaches data row width, the benefits of covering are lost as the number of pages in the leaf level increases. As the number of leaf-level index pages approaches the number of pages in the table, the number of index levels also increases, increasing the I/O cost of using the index to locate data.

You should also avoid adding to the index columns that are frequently updated. Remember that any changes to the columns in the data rows cascade into the indexes as well. This increases the index maintenance overhead, which can adversely affect update performance.

As an alternative to adding columns to the nonclustered index key to encourage index covering, you might want to consider taking advantage of the included columns feature.

Included Columns

A feature available for nonclustered indexes in SQL Server 2014 is included columns. Included columns allow you to add nonkey columns to the leaf level of a nonclustered index for the purpose of index covering.

One advantage of included columns is that because the nonkey columns are stored only in the leaf level of the index, the nonleaf rows of the index are smaller, which helps reduce the overall size of the index, thereby helping reduce the I/O cost of using the index. Another advantage is that this feature allows you to exceed the SQL Server maximum limits of 16 index key columns and 900-byte index key size. The included nonkey columns are not factored in when calculating the number of index key columns or index key size. All data types are allowed as included columns except for the `text`, `ntext`, and `image` data types. To add included columns to an index, specify the `INCLUDE` clause to the `CREATE INDEX` statement:

```
CREATE INDEX NC_ListPrice on Production.Product (ListPrice) INCLUDE (StandardCost)
```

An additional advantage of included columns is that you can add columns to a unique index for index covering purposes without affecting the uniqueness of the actual index key(s) and without having to create a second index on the unique key column(s), which includes the additional covering columns. For example, consider that you have a large number of queries that search `Product` by `Name` to retrieve the `ListPrice` value. Creating a covering index on Name and `ListPrice` could improve performance of these queries. However, creating a unique index on `Name` and `ListPrice` would not enforce uniqueness on `Name` alone (it would allow the insertion of multiple rows with the same `Name` as long as they had different `ListPrice` values). Without using included columns, you would have to create a unique index on `Name` and an additional index on `Name` and `ListPrice` to enforce uniqueness on `Name` and also have a covering index on `Name` and `ListPrice`. However, with the included column feature, you can create just a single unique index on `Name` with `ListPrice` as an included column:

```
CREATE INDEX AK_Name_ListPrice on Production.Product (Name) INCLUDE (ListPrice)
```

TIP

If you have existing nonclustered indexes with a large index key size, you might want to consider redesigning them so that only columns used for searching and lookups are key columns. You should make all other columns that were added for index covering into included columns. This way, you still have all columns needed to cover your queries, but the index key itself is smaller and more efficient.

You still should be careful to avoid adding unnecessary columns as included columns of an index. Adding too many index columns, key or nonkey, can adversely affect performance for the following reasons:

▶ Fewer index leaf rows fit on a page, which results in more index pages at the leaf level and also can increase the number of levels in the index. This can increase I/O costs to search the leaf level of the index and also reduce data cache efficiency.

▶ Because of the increased leaf row size, more disk space is required to store the index, especially if you are adding `varchar(max)`, `nvarchar(max)`, `varbinary(max)`, or `xml` data types as nonkey index columns. Because the column values are also copied into the index leaf level, you are essentially storing the data values twice.

▶ Changes to the included columns in the data rows cascade into the leaf rows of the index as well. This increases the index maintenance overhead, which can adversely affect performance of data modifications.

Wide Indexes Versus Multiple Indexes

As an index key gets wider, the selectivity of the key generally becomes higher as well. It might seem that creating wide indexes would result in better performance. This is not necessarily true. The reason is that the wider the key, the fewer rows SQL Server stores on the index pages, requiring more pages at each level; this results in a higher number of levels in the index B-tree. To get to specific rows, SQL Server must perform more I/O.

To get better performance from queries, instead of creating a few wide indexes, you should consider creating multiple narrower indexes. The advantage here is that with smaller keys, the Query Optimizer can quickly scan through multiple indexes to determine the most efficient access plan. SQL Server has the option of performing multiple index lookups within a single query and merging the result sets together to generate an intersection of the indexes. Also, with more indexes, the Query Optimizer can choose from a wider variety of query plan alternatives.

If you are considering creating a wide key, you should individually check the distribution of values for each member of the composite key. If the selectivity on the individual columns is high, you might want to break up the index into multiple indexes. If the selectivity of individual columns is low but is high for combined columns, it makes sense to have wider keys on the table. To get to the right combination, you can populate your table with real-world data, experiment with creating multiple indexes, and check the distribution of values for each column. Based on the histogram steps and index density, you can make the decisions for an index design that works best for your environment.

Indexed Views

As discussed in Chapter 24, "Creating and Managing Views," SQL Server 2014 allows you to create indexed views. An indexed view is any view that has a unique clustered index defined on it. When a CREATE INDEX statement is executed on a view, the result set for the view is materialized and stored in the database with the same structure as a table with a unique clustered index. Changes made to the data in the underlying tables of the view are automatically reflected in the view the same way any changes to a table are reflected in its indexes. In addition to the unique clustered index, you can create additional nonclustered indexes on indexed views to provide additional query performance. Additional indexes on views might provide more options for the Query Optimizer to choose from during the optimization process.

In the Developer and Enterprise Editions of SQL Server 2014, when an indexed view exists on a table and you access the view directly within a query, the Query Optimizer automatically considers using the index on the view to improve query performance, just as an index on a table is used to improve performance. The Query Optimizer also considers using the indexed view, even for queries that do not directly name the view in the FROM clause. In other words, when a query might benefit from using the indexed view, the Query Optimizer can use the indexed view to satisfy the query in place of an existing index on the table itself. (For more information on how indexed views are used in query plans, see Chapter 34.)

It is important to note that although indexed views can be created in all editions of SQL Server 2014, only the Developer and Enterprise Editions automatically use indexed views to optimize queries. In the other editions, indexed views are not used to improve query performance unless the view is explicitly specified in the query and the NOEXPAND hint is specified as well. Without the NOEXPAND hint, SQL Server expands the view to its under-lying base tables and optimizes based on the table indexes. The following example shows the use of the NOEXPAND option to force SQL Server to use the indexed view specified in the query:

```
select * from my_indexed_view WITH (NOEXPAND)
    where ID between 'B914' and 'B999'
```

Indexed views add overhead and can be more complex for SQL Server to maintain over time than normal indexes. Each time an underlying table of a view is modified, SQL

Server has to update the view result set and potentially the index on that view. The scope of a view's index can be larger than that of any single table's index, especially if the view is defined on several large tables. The overhead associated with maintaining a view and its index during updates can negate any benefit that queries gain from the indexed view. Because of this additional maintenance overhead, you should create indexes only on views where the advantage provided by the improved speed in retrieving the results outweighs the increased maintenance overhead.

Following are some guidelines to consider when you design indexed views:

▶ Create indexes on views where the underlying table data is relatively static.

▶ Create indexed views that will be used by several queries.

▶ Keep the indexes narrow. As with table indexes, a smaller index allows SQL Server to access the data more efficiently.

▶ Create indexed views that will be significantly smaller than the underlying table(s). An indexed view might not provide significant performance gains if its size is similar to the size of the original table.

▶ You need to specify the NOEXPAND hint in editions of SQL Server other than the Developer and Enterprise Editions of SQL Server; otherwise, the indexed view is not used to optimize the query.

Indexes on Computed Columns

SQL Server 2014 allows you to build indexes on computed columns in your tables. Computed columns can participate at any position of an index, along with your other table columns, including in a PRIMARY KEY or UNIQUE constraint. To create an index on computed columns, you must set the following session options as shown:

▶ SET CONCAT_NULL_YIELDS_NULL ON

▶ SET QUOTED_IDENTIFIER ON

▶ SET ANSI_NULLS ON

▶ SET ANSI_PADDING ON

▶ SET ANSI_WARNINGS ON

▶ SET NUMERIC_ROUNDABORT OFF

If any of these six SET options were not in effect when you created the table, you get the following message when you try to create an index on the computed column:

```
Server: Msg 1934, Level 16, State 1, Line 2
CREATE INDEX failed because the following SET options
 have incorrect settings: '<OPTION NAME>'.
```

In addition, the functions in the computed column must be deterministic. A deterministic function is one that returns the same result every time it is called with the same set of input parameters.

When you create a clustered index on a computed column, it is no longer a virtual column in the table. The computed value for the column is stored in the data rows of the table. If you create a nonclustered index on a computed column, the computed value is stored in the nonclustered index rows but not in the data rows, unless you also have a clustered index on the computed column.

Be aware of the overhead involved with indexes on computed columns. Updates to the columns that the computed columns are based on result in updates to the index on the computed column as well.

Indexes on computed columns can be useful when you need an index on large character fields. As discussed earlier, the smaller an index, the more efficient it is. You could create a computed column on the large character field by using the CHECKSUM() function. CHECKSUM() generates a 4-byte integer that is relatively unique for character strings but not absolutely unique. (Different character strings can generate the same checksum, so when searching against the checksum, you need to include the character string as an additional search argument to ensure that you are matching the right row.) The benefit is that you can create an index on the 4-byte integer generated by the CHECKSUM() that can be used to search against the character string instead of having to create an index on the large character column itself. Listing 32.4 shows an example of applying this solution.

LISTING 32.4   Using an Index on a Computed Checksum Column

```
-- First add the computed column to the table
alter table HumanResources.Employee add title_checksum as CHECKSUM(JobTitle)
go


-- Next, create an index on the computed column
create index NC_Employee_titlechecksum on HumanResources.Employee(title_checksum)
go


-- In your queries, include both the checksum column and the Jobtitle column
--    in your search argument
select NationalIDNumber, HireDate
    from  HumanResources.Employee
    where title_checksum = checksum(N'Research and Development Engineer')
      and JobTitle = N'Research and Development Engineer'
```

SQL Server 2014 also supports persisted computed columns. With persisted computed columns, SQL Server stores the computed values in the table without requiring an index on the computed column. Like indexed computed columns, persisted computed columns are updated when any other columns on which the computed column depends are updated.

Persisted computed columns allow you to create an index on a computed column that is defined with a deterministic, but imprecise, expression. This option enables you to create an index on a computed column when SQL Server cannot determine with certainty whether a function that returns a computed column expression—for example, a CLR function that is created in the Microsoft .NET Framework—is both deterministic and precise.

Filtered Indexes and Statistics

As discussed earlier in this chapter, a nonclustered index contains a row for every row in the table, even rows with a large number of duplicate key values where the nonclustered index will not be an effective method for finding those rows. For these situations, SQL Server 2014 provides filtered indexes. Filtered indexes are an optimized form of nonclustered indexes, created by specifying a search predicate when defining the index. This search predicate acts as a filter to create the index on only the data rows that match the search predicate. This reduces the size of the index and essentially creates an index that covers your queries, which return only a small percentage of rows from a well-defined subset of data within your table.

Filtered indexes can provide the following advantages over full-table indexes:

▶ **Improved query performance and plan quality**—A well-designed filtered index improves query performance and execution plan quality because it is smaller than a full-table nonclustered index and has filtered statistics. Filtered statistics are more accurate than full-table statistics because they cover only the rows contained in the filtered index.

▶ **Reduced index maintenance costs**—Filtered indexes are maintained only when data modifications affect the data values contained in the index. Also, because a filtered index contains only the frequently accessed data, the smaller size of the index reduces the cost of updating the statistics.

▶ **Reduced index storage costs**—Filtered indexes can reduce disk storage for nonclustered indexes when a full-table index is not necessary. You can replace a full-table nonclustered index with multiple filtered indexes without significantly increasing the storage requirements.

Following are some of the situations in which filtered indexes can be useful:

▶ When a column contains mostly NULL values, but your queries search only for rows where data values are NOT NULL.

▶ When a column contains a large number of duplicate values, but your queries typically ignore those values and search only for the more unique values.

▶ When you want to enforce uniqueness on a subset of values—for example, a column on which you want to allow NULL values. A unique constraint allows only one NULL value; however, a filtered index can be defined as unique over only the rows that are NOT NULL.

▶ When queries retrieve only a particular range of data values and you want to index these values but not the entire table. For example, you have a table that contains a large number of historical values, but you want to search only values for the current year or quarter. You can create a filtered index on the desired range of values and possibly even use the INCLUDE option to add columns so your index fully covers your queries.

Now, you may be asking, "Can't some of the preceding solutions be accomplished using indexed views?" Yes, they can, but filtered indexes provide a better alternative. The most significant advantage is that filtered indexes can be used in any edition of SQL Server 2014, whereas indexed views are chosen by the optimizer only in the Developer and Enterprise editions unless you use the NOEXPAND hint in the other editions. In addition, filtered indexes have reduced index maintenance costs (the query processor uses fewer CPU resources to update a filtered index than an indexed view); the Query Optimizer considers using a filtered index in more situations than the equivalent indexed view; you can perform online rebuilds of filtered indexes (online index rebuilds are not supported for indexed views); and filtered indexes can be nonunique, whereas indexed views must be unique.

Based on these advantages, it is recommended that you use filtered indexes instead of indexed views when possible. Consider replacing indexed views with filtered indexes when the view references only one table, the view query doesn't return computed columns, and the view predicate uses simple comparison logic and doesn't contain a view.

Creating and Using Filtered Indexes

To define filtered indexes, you use the normal CREATE INDEX command but include a WHERE condition as a search predicate to specify which data rows the filtered index should include. In the current implementation, you can specify only simple search predicate such as IN; the comparison operators IS NULL, IS NOT NULL, =, <>, !=, >, >=, !>, <, <=, !<; and the logical operator AND. In addition, filtered indexes cannot be created on computed columns, user-defined data types, Hierarchyid, or spatial types.

For example, assume you need to search the SalesOrderHeader table in the AdventureWorks2012 database for sales since 6/1/2008. The majority of the rows in the SalesOrderHeader table have order dates prior to 6/1/2008. To create a filtered index on the OrderDate column, you would execute a command like the following:

```
create index OrderDate_Filt on sales.SalesOrderHeader (OrderDate)
    WHERE OrderDate >= '2008-07-01 00:00:00.000'
```

Now, let's look at a couple queries that may or may not use the new filtered index. First, let's consider the following query looking for any sales for 7/15/2008:

```
select SalesOrderID, ShipDate from sales.SalesOrderHeader
where OrderDate = '7/15/2008'
```

If you look at the execution plan in Figure 32.3, you can see that the filtered index, OrderDate_Filt, is used to locate the qualifying row values. The clustered index, PK_SalesOrderHeader_SalesOrderID, is used as the row locator to retrieve the data rows (as described earlier in the "Nonclustered Indexes" section).

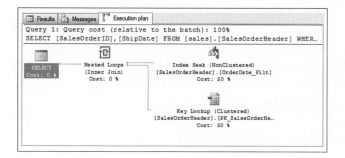

FIGURE 32.3   Query plan for a query that uses a filtered index.

> **NOTE**
>
> For more information on understanding and analyzing query plans, see Chapter 36, "Query Analysis."

If you run the following query using a data value that's outside the range of values stored in the filtered index, you see that the filtered index is not used (see Figure 32.4):

```
select SalesOrderID, ShipDate from sales.SalesOrderHeader
where OrderDate = '7/15/2006'
```

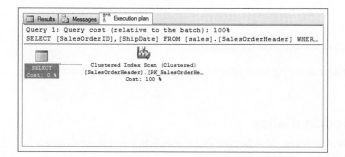

FIGURE 32.4   Query plan for a query using a value not in the filtered index.

Now let's consider a query that you might expect would use the filtered index but does not:

```
select SalesOrderID, ShipDate from sales.SalesOrderHeader
where OrderDate > '7/15/2008'
```

Now, you might expect that this query would use the filtered index because the data values are within the range of values for the filtered index, but due to the number of rows that match, SQL Server determines that the I/O cost of using the filtered nonclustered index to locate the matching rows and then retrieve the data rows using the clustered index row locators requires more I/Os than simply performing a clustered index scan of the entire table (the same query plan as shown in Figure 32.4).

In this case, you might want to use included columns on the filtered index so that the data values for the query can be retrieved using index covering without incurring the extra cost of using the row locators to retrieve the actual data rows. The following example creates a filtered index on `ord_date` that includes `ShipDate` and `SalesOrderID`:

```
create index OrderDate_Filt2 on sales.SalesOrderHeader (OrderDate)
INCLUDE (ShipDate, SalesOrderID)
WHERE OrderDate >= '2008-07-01 00:00:00.000'
```

If you rerun the same query and examine the query plan, you see that the filtered index is used this time, and SQL Server uses index covering (see Figure 32.5). You can tell that it's using index covering with the `OrderDate_filt2` index because there is no need for the clustered index to retrieve the data rows. Using the row locators is unnecessary because all the information requested by the query can be retrieved from the index leaf rows which also contain the values of the included columns.

FIGURE 32.5   Query plan using index covering on a filtered index with included columns.

Creating and Using Filtered Statistics

Similar to the way you use filtered indexes, SQL Server 2014 also lets you create filtered statistics. Like filtered indexes, filtered statistics are also created over a subset of rows in the table based on a specified filter predicate. Creating a filtered index on a column auto-creates the corresponding filtered statistics. In addition, filtered statistics can be created explicitly by including the WHERE clause with the CREATE STATISTICS statement.

Filtered statistics can be used to avoid a common issue with statistics where the cardinality estimation is skewed due to a large number of NULL or duplicate values or due to a data correlation between columns. For example, let's consider a hypothetical table called `book_titles` which contains 10,000 rows. All the cook books stored in the table (`book_type = 'trad_cook'` or `'mod_cook'`) are published by a single publisher (`pub_id = '0877'`). However, SQL Server stores column-level statistics on each of these columns independent of each other. Based on the statistics, SQL Server estimates there are 1,500 rows in the `book_titles` table where `pub_id = '0877'`, and 500 rows where the `book_type` is either `'trad_cook'` or `'mod_cook'`.

However, let's assume you were to execute the following query:

```
select * from book_titles where pub_id = '0877'
and book_type in ('trad_cook', 'mod_cook')
```

When the Query Optimizer estimates the selectivity of this query where each search predicate is part of an AND condition, it assumes the conditions are independent of one another and estimates the number of matching rows by taking the intersection of the two conditions. Essentially, it multiplies the selectivity of each of the two conditions together to determine the total selectivity. The selectivity of each is 0.15(1,500/10,000) and 0.05 (500/10,000), which, when multiplied together, comes out to approximately 0.0075, so the optimizer estimates 75 rows will match. However, because all 500 cook books are published by `publisher '0877'`, in actuality a total of 500 rows match. This disparity in estimated number of matching rows could lead the optimizer to possibly choose an inappropriate, and considerably more expensive, query plan to satisfy this query.

Filtered statistics can help solve this problem by letting you capture these types of data correlations in your column statistics. For example, to capture the fact that all cook books are also published by the same publisher, you could create the filtered statistics using the following statement:

```
create statistics pub_id_book_type on book_titles (pub_id, book_type)
where pub_id = '0877' and book_type in ('trad_cook', 'mod_cook')
```

When these filtered statistics are defined and the same query is run, SQL Server uses the filtered statistics to determine that the query will match five rows instead of only one.

Although using this solution could require having to define a number of filtered statistics, it can be effective to help fix your most critical queries where cardinality estimates due to data correlation or data skew issues are causing the Query Optimizer to choose poorly performing query plans.

Fortunately, the new cardinality estimator in SQL Server 2014 assumes filtered predicates on the same table have some correlation. For example, with the book_titles example, the previous query optimizer estimates there are 75 matching books:

```
.05 * .15 * 10,000 rows = 75 rows
```

The new cardinality estimates a higher cardinality by adding an exponential component to the estimation equation. The new formula used is the selectivity of the most selective filter * SQRT (selectivity of next most selective filter). Using this formula, the query optimizer now estimates that 193.64 rows match the predicate:

```
0.05 * SQRT(0.15) * 1000 rows = 193.64 rows
```

While still not a completely accurate estimate, for this scenario and specific data distribution, 193.64 rows is closer to the actual 500 rows that the query will return and should help lead to a more effective query plan for this query without having to create specific filtered statistics.

Choosing Indexes: Query versus Update Performance

I/O is the primary factor in determining query performance. The challenge for a database designer is to build a physical data model that provides efficient data access. Creating indexes on database tables allows SQL Server to access data with fewer I/Os. Defining useful indexes during the logical and physical data modeling step is crucial. The SQL Server Query Optimizer relies heavily on index key distribution and index density to determine which indexes to use for a query. The Query Optimizer in SQL Server can use multiple indexes in a query (through index intersection) to reduce the I/O required to retrieve information. In the absence of indexes, the Query Optimizer performs a table scan, which can be costly from an I/O standpoint.

Although indexes provide a means for faster access to data, they slow down data modification statements due to the extra overhead of having to maintain the index during inserts, updates, and deletes.

In a DSS environment, defining many indexes can help your queries and does not create much of a performance issue because the data is relatively static and doesn't get updated frequently. You typically load the data, create the indexes, and forget about it until the next data load. As long as you have the necessary indexes to support the user queries and they're getting decent response time, the penalties of having too many indexes in a DSS environment are the space wasted for indexes that possibly won't be used, the additional time required to create the excessive indexes, and the additional time required to back up and run DBCC checks on the data.

In an OLTP environment, on the other hand, too many indexes can lead to significant performance degradation, especially if the number of indexes on a table exceeds four or five. Think about it for a second. Every single-row insert is at least one data page write and one or more index page writes (depending on whether a page split occurs) for every index on the table. With eight nonclustered indexes, that would be a minimum of nine writes to the database for a single-row insert. Therefore, for an OLTP environment, you want as few indexes as possible—typically only the indexes required to support the update and delete operations and your critical queries, and to enforce your uniqueness constraints.

The natural solution, in a perfect world, would be to create a lot of indexes for a DSS environment and as few indexes as possible in an OLTP environment. Unfortunately, in the real world, you typically have an environment that must support both DSS and OLTP applications. How do you resolve the competing indexing requirements of the two environments? Meeting the indexing needs of DSS and OLTP applications requires a bit of a balancing act, with no easy solution. It often involves making hard decisions as to which DSS queries might have to live with table scans and which updates have to contend with additional overhead.

One solution is to have two separate databases: one for DSS applications and another for OLTP applications. Obviously, this method requires some method of keeping the databases in sync. The method chosen depends on how up-to-date the DSS database has to be. If you can afford some lag time, you could consider using a dump-and-load mechanism, such as Log Shipping or periodic full database restores. If the DSS system requires up-to-the-minute concurrency, you might want to consider using replication or database mirroring.

Another possible alternative is to have only the required indexes in place during normal processing periods to support the OLTP requirements. At the end of the business day, you can create the indexes necessary to support the DSS queries and reports, and they can run as batch jobs after normal processing hours. When the DSS reports are complete, you can drop the additional indexes, and you're ready for the next day's processing. Note that this solution assumes that the time required to create the additional indexes is offset by the time saved by the faster running of the DSS queries. If the additional indexes do not result in substantial time savings, they are probably not necessary and need not be created in the first place. The queries need to be more closely examined to select the appropriate indexes to best support your queries.

As you can see, it is important to choose indexes carefully to provide a good balance between data search and data modification performance. The application environment usually governs the choice of indexes. For example, if the application is mainly OLTP with transactions requiring fast response time, creating too many indexes might have an adverse impact on performance. On the other hand, the application might be a DSS with few transactions doing data modifications. In that case, it makes sense to create a number of indexes on the columns frequently used in queries.

Identifying Missing Indexes

When developing an index design for your database and applications, you should make sure you create appropriate indexes for the various queries that will be executed against your tables. However, it can be quite a chore to identify all the queries you may need to create indexes for. Fortunately, SQL Server 2014 provides a couple of tools to help you identify any indexes you may need in your database: The Database Engine Tuning Advisor and the missing index dynamic management objects.

The Database Engine Tuning Advisor

The Database Engine Tuning Advisor is a tool that can analyze a SQL Script file or a set of queries captured in a SQL Profiler trace and recommend changes to your indexing scheme. After performing its analysis, the Database Engine Tuning Advisor provides recommendations for new or more effective indexes, indexed views, and partitioning schemes, along with the estimated improvement in execution time should the recommendation be implemented. You can choose to implement the recommendations immediately or later, or you can save the SQL statements to a script file. For detailed information on using the Database Engine Tuning Advisor, see Chapter 40.

Although the Database Engine Tuning Advisor is a useful tool, and improvements have been made since it was introduced in SQL Server 2005 to improve its recommendations (such as running against the current plan cache contents versus a profiler trace), it does still have some limitations. For one, because the Database Engine Tuning Advisor gathers statistics by sampling the data, repeatedly running the tool on the same workload may produce different results as different samples are used. In addition, if you impose constraints, such as specifying maximum disk space for tuning recommendations, the Database Engine Tuning Advisor may be forced to drop certain existing indexes, and the resulting recommendation may produce a negative expected improvement. The Database Engine Tuning Advisor may also not make recommendations under the following circumstances:

▶ The table being tuned contains fewer than 10 data pages.

▶ The recommended indexes would not offer enough improvement in query performance over the current physical database design.

▶ The user who runs the Database Engine Tuning Advisor is not a member of the db_owner database role or the sysadmin fixed server role.

Missing Index Dynamic Management Objects

In addition to the Database Engine Tuning Advisor, SQL Server 2014 provides the missing index dynamic management objects to help identify potentially missing indexes in your database. The *missing index dynamic management objects* are a set of dynamic management objects:

▶ sys.dm_db_missing_index_group_stats—Returns summary information about missing index groups, such as the performance improvements that could be gained by implementing a specific group of missing indexes.

▶ sys.dm_db_missing_index_groups—Returns information about a specific group of missing indexes, such as the group identifier and identifiers of all missing indexes contained in that group.

▶ sys.dm_db_missing_index_columns—Returns detailed information about a missing index; for example, it returns the name and identifier of the table where the index is missing and the columns and column types that should make up the missing index.

▶ sys.dm_db_missing_index_details—Returns information about the database table columns missing an index.

After running a typical workload on SQL Server, you can query the dynamic management functions to retrieve information about possible missing indexes. Listing 32.5 provides a sample query that displays the missing index information for queries that were run in the AdventureWorks2012 database between 10:30 and 11:30 p.m. on 11/19/2014.

LISTING 32.5   Querying the Missing Index Dynamic Management Objects

```
SELECT
     mig.index_group_handle as handle,
     convert(varchar(50), statement) AS table_name,
          convert(varchar(12), column_name) AS Column_name,
          convert(varchar(10), column_usage) as ColumnUsage,
          avg_user_impact as avg_impact
FROM sys.dm_db_missing_index_details AS mid
CROSS APPLY sys.dm_db_missing_index_columns (mid.index_handle)
INNER JOIN sys.dm_db_missing_index_groups AS mig
ON mig.index_handle = mid.index_handle
inner join sys.dm_db_missing_index_group_stats AS migs
ON migs.group_handle = mig.index_group_handle
where mid.database_id = DB_ID('AdventureWorks2012')
and last_user_seek between '2014-11-19 22:30' and '2014-11-19 23:30'
ORDER BY mig.index_group_handle, mig.index_handle, column_id;
GO

/* output
handle table_name                                             Column_name  ColumnUsage avg_impact
------ -------------------------------------------------- ------------ ----------- ----
    24 [AdventureWorks2012].[Sales].[SalesOrderDetail] SalesOrderID INCLUDE        .89
    24 [AdventureWorks2012].[Sales].[SalesOrderDetail] OrderQty        INCLUDE     .89
    24 [AdventureWorks2012].[Sales].[SalesOrderDetail] SpecialOffer EQUALITY    80.89
*/
```

In this example, the optimizer recommends an index on the SpecialOffercolumn to support an equality operator. It is also recommending that the SalesOrderID and OrderQty columns be specified as an included column in the index. This index is estimated to improve performance by 80.89%.

Although the missing index feature provides some helpful information for identifying potentially missing indexes in your database, it too has a few limitations:

▶ It is not intended to fine-tune the existing indexes, only to recommend additional indexes when no useful index is found that can be used to satisfy a search or join condition.

▶ It reports only included columns for some queries. You need to determine whether the included columns should be specified as additional index key columns instead.

▶ It may return different costs for the same missing index group for different executions.

▶ It does not suggest filtered indexes.

▶ It is unable to provide recommendations for clustered indexes, indexed views, or table partitioning (you should use the Database Engine Tuning Advisor instead for these recommendations).

Probably the key limitation is that although the missing index feature is helpful for identifying indexes that may be useful for you to define, it's not a substitute for a well-thought-out index design.

Missing Index Feature Versus Database Engine Tuning Advisor

The missing indexes dynamic management objects are a lightweight, server-side, always-on feature for identifying and correcting potential indexing oversights. The Database Engine Tuning Advisor, on the other hand, is a comprehensive client-side tool that can be used to assess the physical database design and recommend new physical design structures for improving performance, including not only indexes, but also indexed views or partitioning schemes.

The Database Engine Tuning Advisor and missing indexes feature can possibly return different recommendations, even for a single-query workload. The reason is that the missing indexes dynamic management objects' index key column recommendations are not order-sensitive. On the other hand, the Database Engine Tuning Advisor recommendations include ordering of the key columns for indexes to optimize query performance.

Table 32.4 details some other differences between the missing indexes feature and Database Engine Tuning Advisor in greater detail.

TABLE 32.4   Differences Between Missing Index Features and Database Engine Tuning Advisor

Comparison Point	Missing Indexes Feature	Database Engine Tuning Advisor
Execution method	Server-side, always on	Client-side, standalone application
Scope of analysis	Quick, ad hoc analysis, providing limited information about missing indexes only	Thorough workload analysis, providing full recommendation report about the best physical database design configuration in the context of a submitted workload
Statements analyzed	SELECT statements only	SELECT, UPDATE, INSERT, and DELETE
Available disk storage space	Not factored into analysis	Factored into analysis; recommendations not provided if they would exceed available storage space
Columns ordering	Recommended index column order not provided	Optimal index column order determined based on query execution cost
Index type	Nonclustered only	Both clustered and nonclustered index recommendations provided
Indexed views recommendations	Not provided	Recommended in supported editions

Comparison Point	Missing Indexes Feature	Database Engine Tuning Advisor
Partitioning recommendations	Not provided	Recommended in supported editions
Impact analysis	An approximate impact of adding a missing index is reported via the `sys.dm_db_missing_index_group_stats` DMV	Up to 15 different analysis reports generated to provide information about the impact of implementing recommendations

Identifying Unused Indexes

As mentioned previously in this chapter, each index on a table adds additional overhead for data modifications because the indexes also need to be maintained as changes are made to index key columns. In an OLTP environment, excessive indexes on your tables can be almost as much of a performance issue as missing indexes. To improve OLTP performance, you should limit the number of indexes on your tables to only those absolutely needed; you definitely should eliminate any unnecessary and unused indexes that may be defined on your tables to eliminate the overhead they introduce.

Fortunately, SQL Server provides a DMV that you can use to identify which indexes in your database are not being used: `sys.dm_db_index_usage_stats`. The columns in the `sys.dm_db_index_usage_stats` are shown in Table 32.5.

TABLE 32.5   Columns in the `sys.dm_db_index_usage_stats` DMV

Column Name	Description
`database_id`	ID of the database on which the table or view is defined
`object_id`	ID of the table or view on which the index is defined
`index_id`	ID of the index
`user_seeks`	Number of seeks by user queries
`user_scans`	Number of scans by user queries
`user_lookups`	Number of bookmark lookups by user queries
`user_updates`	Number of updates by user queries
`last_user_seek`	Time of last user seek
`last_user_scan`	Time of last user scan
`last_user_lookup`	Time of last user lookup
`last_user_update`	Time of last user update
`system_seeks`	Number of seeks by system queries
`system_scans`	Number of scans by system queries
`system_lookups`	Number of lookups by system queries
`system_updates`	Number of updates by system queries
`last_system_seek`	Time of last system seek

Column Name	Description
last_system_scan	Time of last system scan
last_system_lookup	Time of last system lookup
last_system_update	Time of last system update

Every individual seek, scan, lookup, or update on an index by a query execution is counted as a use of that index, and the corresponding counter in the view is incremented. Thus, you can run a query against this DMV to see whether there are any indexes that your queries are not using; that is, indexes that either have no rows in the DMV or have 0 values in the user_seeks, user_scans, or user_lookups columns (or the time values of the last_user_* columns are significantly in the past). You especially need to focus on any indexes that don't show any user query activity but do have a high value in the last_user_update column. This indicates an index that's adding significant update over-head but not being used by any queries for locating data rows.

For example, the query shown in Listing 32.6 returns all indexes in the current database that have never been accessed; that is, they would have no records at all in the sys.dm_db_index_usage_stats table.

LISTING 32.6   A Query for Unused Indexes

```
SELECT  convert(varchar(12), OBJECT_SCHEMA_NAME(I.OBJECT_ID)) AS SchemaName,
        convert(varchar(20), OBJECT_NAME(I.OBJECT_ID)) AS ObjectName,
        convert(varchar(30), I.NAME) AS IndexName
FROM    sys.indexes I
WHERE   -- only get indexes for user created tables
        OBJECTPROPERTY(I.OBJECT_ID, 'IsUserTable') = 1
        -- ignore heaps
        and I.index_id > 0
        -- find all indexes that exist but are NOT used
        AND NOT EXISTS (
                SELECT  index_id
                FROM    sys.dm_db_index_usage_stats
                WHERE   OBJECT_ID = I.OBJECT_ID
                        AND I.index_id = index_id
                        AND database_id = DB_ID())
ORDER BY SchemaName, ObjectName, IndexName
```

Also, you should be aware that that the information is reported in the DMV both for oper-ations caused by user-submitted queries and for operations caused by internally generated queries, such as scans for gathering statistics. If you run UPDATE STATISTICS on a table, the sys.dm_db_index_usage_stats table will have a row for each index for the system scan performed by the UPDATE STATISTICS command. However, the index may still be unused by any queries in your applications. Consequently, you might want to modify the previous query to look for indexes with 0 values in the `last_user_*` columns instead of indexes with no row at all in the DMV. Listing 32.7 provides an alternative query.

LISTING 32.7   A Query for Indexes Unused by Application Queries

```
SELECT   convert(varchar(12), OBJECT_SCHEMA_NAME(I.OBJECT_ID)) AS SchemaName,
         convert(varchar(20), OBJECT_NAME(I.OBJECT_ID)) AS ObjectName,
         convert(varchar(30), I.NAME) AS IndexName
FROM     sys.indexes I
            LEFT OUTER JOIN
            sys.dm_db_index_usage_stats u
            on I.index_id = u.index_id
            and u.database_id = DB_ID()
WHERE    -- only get indexes for user created tables
         OBJECTPROPERTY(I.OBJECT_ID, 'IsUserTable') = 1
         -- ignore heaps
         and I.index_id > 0
         -- find all indexes that exist but are NOT used
            and isnull(u.last_user_seek, 0) = 0
            and isnull(u.last_user_scan, 0) = 0
            and isnull(u.last_user_lookup, 0) = 0
ORDER BY SchemaName, ObjectName, IndexName
```

Note that the information returned by `sys.dm_db_index_usage_stats` is useful only if your server has been running long enough and has processed a sufficient amount of your standard and peak workflows. Also, you should be aware that the data in the DMV is cleared each time SQL Server is restarted, or if a database is detached and reattached. To prevent losing useful information, you might want to create a scheduled job that periodically queries the DMVs and saves the information to your own tables so you can track the information over time for more thorough and complete analysis.

Summary

One of the most important aspects of improving SQL Server performance is proper table and index design. Choosing the appropriate indexes for SQL Server to use to process queries involves thoroughly understanding the queries and transactions being run against the database, understanding the bias of the data, understanding how SQL Server uses indexes, and staying aware of the performance implications of over indexing tables in an OLTP environment. In general, you should consider using clustered indexes to support range retrievals or when data needs to be sorted in clustered index order; you should use nonclustered indexes for single- or discrete-row retrievals or when you can take advantage of index covering.

Another feature for improving performance in SQL Server 2014 is In Memory Optimization and Memory-Optimized tables. To learn more about this exciting new feature, continue on to the next chapter.

In-Memory Optimization and the Buffer Pool Extension

With CPU speeds topping out and I/O rates maximized using solid state drives (SSDs), the next available strategy for increasing OLTP performance is through memory optimization. Databases, because of their size, typically reside on disk. Historically, main memory was significantly more expensive than disk, so typically the memory available for caching data was only a fraction of the size of the database. However, with the significantly reduced cost of system memory over the past 20 years, it's become more financially feasible to install large amounts of memory in the server. It is now possible for most OLTP databases, or at least the most critical tables, to fit entirely into memory which reduces the performance impact of disk-based I/O, which in turn increases transaction speed performance.

To take maximum advantage of the performance improvements that can be achieved from having your critical OLTP tables memory resident, Microsoft developed the In-Memory Optimization feature for SQL Server. In-Memory Optimization, more commonly referred to as In-Memory OLTP, is the primary and most important new feature introduced in SQL Server 2014. This new feature (which you may sometimes hear referred to by its project code name Hekaton) is fully integrated into the SQL Server database engine.

Another feature introduced in SQL Server 2014 to take advantage of the lower costs and increased sizes of SSDs, is the Buffer Pool Extension feature. The Buffer Pool Extension feature provides the ability for SQL Server to use solid-state drives (SSD) as a non-volatile random access memory (NvRAM) to extend the size of the buffer pool. By offloading buffer cache I/Os from mechanical disk to SSDs, the Buffer Pool Extension feature can significantly improve I/O throughput because of the lower latency and better random I/O performance of SSDs.

These exciting new features for SQL Server are discussed in this chapter.

Overview of In-Memory OLTP

In-Memory OLTP allows OLTP workloads to achieve significant improvements in performance, and reduction in processing time. The In-Memory OLTP engine is completely integrated with the SQL Server database engine and can be accessed transparently via your SQL Server applications. However, the In-Memory OLTP components' internal behavior and capabilities are different and distinct from the standard database engine components as shown in Figure 33.1

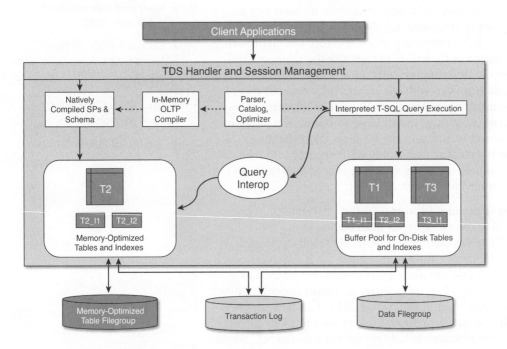

FIGURE 33.1   The SQL Server 2014 engine architecture with In-Memory OLTP.

Figure 33.1 shows that client applications connect to SQL Server the same way for memory-optimized tables or disk-based tables, whether it will be calling natively compiled stored procedures or interpreted Transact-SQL. Natively compiled stored procedures can only access memory-optimized tables, but interpreted T-SQL can access tables in either the buffer pool or memory-optimized tables using the interop capabilities. Notice also that memory-optimized tables do not share memory space with on-disk tables. Memory-optimized tables are stored completely differently than disk-based tables and these new data structures allow the data to be accessed and processed much more efficiently.

The main benefit of the SQL Server In-Memory OLTP architecture being integrated into the SQL Server engine is that you don't have to refactor your entire system to split data between in-memory and conventional on-disk database access, nor move the entire database into memory. You can specify what is stored in-memory or on-disk on a table by table basis. This way you can move only your more active operational tables into memory while keeping other tables and historical data on disk and in some cases, this can be done in a way that's transparent to your client applications.

In addition to integrating the In-Memory OLTP engine into the SQL Server engine, there were three other primary design goals:

▶ **Optimize data storage for main memory**—Data in in-memory tables is not stored on on-disk pages nor does it mimic the on-disk storage structure when loaded into memory, eliminating the complex buffer pool structure and code that manages it. Indexes also are not persisted on disk and instead are recreated on startup when the memory resident tables are loaded into memory.

▶ **Eliminate latches and locks**—All in-memory table and index structures are latch and lock free. Instead, SQL Server uses a new optimistic multiversion concurrency control mechanism to provide transaction consistency. The mechanism allows multiple sessions to work with the same data without locking/blocking and improves the stability of the system.

▶ **Compile requests to native code**—Standard T-SQL is an interpreter-based language that provides flexibility, but at the cost of increased CPU overhead. The In-Memory OLTP engine avoids this overhead by compiling statements and stored procedures into native machine code.

The new lock-free optimistic multiversion concurrency control mechanism, in conjunction with algorithms that have been optimized for memory-resident data, is one of the key points that differentiates the In-Memory OLTP engine from just pinning tables in memory with DBCC PINTABLE or from putting databases on SSDs. DBCC PINTABLE keeps a table in memory in SQL Server's buffer pool, but it still uses the same relational engine with locks and latches, so lock and latch contention can still occur, so it doesn't offer the scalability found in the In-Memory OLTP engine. The same is true for SSDs, which can provide higher I/O but also still use the same relational engine.

In contrast, the In-Memory OLTP engine makes an entirely new version of that row in memory and timestamps it when a row in a shared buffer is modified. The engine then analyzes and validates any updated rows before committing them. Since there are no locks or other wait states, the processing is faster and more scalable than when the traditional locking mechanism is used. However, this optimistic processing creates a lot of different row versions, leaving a number of discarded rows in memory. To handle the discarded row versions, SQL Server runs a new lock-free garbage collection process as part of the In-Memory OLTP engine which periodically cleans up all the unneeded rows.

In addition to the new lock-free design, the In-Memory OLTP engine includes a stored procedure compilation process that compiles T-SQL code into native Win64 code which reduces the number of instructions that the CPU must execute to process the query. The combination of the new query processing engine and the compiled stored procedures are the primary factors driving the high-performance of the In-Memory OLTP engine.

Despite all the promising capabilities of in-memory optimization, there are currently a number of limitations on the technology. This first release of In-Memory OLTP supports only a subset of SQL Server data types and features. Moving some of your tables into in-memory tables may require some changes to your SQL code and table schema. The features supported by In-Memory OLTP and the current limitations will be discussed in more detail later in this chapter.

In-Memory OLTP Concepts and Terminology

The concepts and terminology used to describe the components involved with In-Memory OLTP throughout this chapter include:

▶ **Memory-optimized tables**—Tables using the new data structures added as part of In-Memory OLTP. The primary store for memory-optimized tables is main memory, but a second copy in a different format is maintained on disk for durability purposes

▶ **Disk-based tables**—Tables that use the data structures that SQL Server has always used, with pages of 8K that need to be read from and written to disk as a unit. Each table also has its own data and index pages.

▶ **Natively compiled stored procedures**—The new object type supported by In-Memory OLTP that is compiled into native DLLs. Natively compiled stored procedures have the potential to increase performance even further than just using memory-optimized tables since there is no need for additional compilation and interpretation is reduced compared to standard interpreted Transact-SQL stored procedures. Natively compiled stored procedures can only reference memory-optimized tables.

▶ **Cross-container transactions**—Transactions that reference both memory-optimized tables and disk-based tables.

▶ **Durable and nondurable tables**—Memory-optimized tables by default are completely durable and offer full ACID support. Nondurable memory-optimized tables are supported by SQL Server but the contents of a nondurable table exist only in memory and are lost when the server restarts. The syntax DURABILITY=SCHEMA_ ONLY is used to create nondurable tables.

▶ **Interop**—This term refers to interpreted T-SQL statements that reference memory-optimized tables. Interop simplifies migration of your applications to In-Memory OLTP.

In-Memory Optimization Requirements

The In-Memory OLTP engine is supported only in the 64 bit Enterprise, Developer, or Evaluation editions of SQL Server 2014 running in a 64 bit version Windows Server 2012 R2, Windows Server 2012, or Windows Server 2008 R2 SP2. The In-Memory OLTP engine also requires an x64 server that supports the cmpxchg16b instruction, which all modern x64 processors do. You may run into a problem if you are implementing the In-Memory OLTP engine in a 64-bit virtual machine (VM) that's using an older virtual processor.

SQL Server will also require enough memory to store the tables and indexes of the tables you designate to be memory-optimized, plus additional memory for the row versions. The general recommendation is to allocated memory that is two times the on-disk size of the memory-optimized tables and indexes with a recommended maximum of 250GB. You also should have free disk space that's two times the size of your durable memory-optimized tables.

33

Limitations of In-Memory OLTP

Given its memory-intensive nature, and the fact that this is the first release of the feature, there are a number of restrictions for using the In-Memory OLTP engine. Primarily, a memory-optimized table can only have columns of these supported data types:

- ▶ bit
- ▶ tinyint, smallint, int, bigint
- ▶ money, smallmoney
- ▶ float, real
- ▶ datetime, smalldatetime, datetime2, date, time
- ▶ numeric, decimal
- ▶ char(n), varchar(n), nchar(n), nvarchar(n), sysname
- ▶ binary(n), varbinary(n)
- ▶ Uniqueidentifier

The following data types are not supported by memory-optimized tables:

- ▶ datetimeoffset
- ▶ geography
- ▶ hierarchyid
- ▶ image
- ▶ ntext, text
- ▶ sql_variant

▶ varchar(max), varbinary(max)

▶ xml

▶ User data types (UDTs)

In addition, the maximum row length of a memory-optimized table is limited to 8060 bytes. The 8060 byte limit is enforced at table-creation time, so unlike a disk-based table, a memory-optimized tables with two varchar(5000) columns could not be created.

In addition, there are a number of database features that aren't supported for memory-optimized databases or tables, including:

▶ Database mirroring

▶ Database snapshots

▶ Using DBCC CHECKDB and DBCC CHECKTABLE

▶ Computed columns

▶ Triggers

▶ FOREIGN KEY, CHECK, and UNIQUE constraints

▶ FILESTREAM storage

▶ ROWGUIDCOL

▶ Clustered indexes

▶ COLUMNSTORE indexes

▶ Data compression

▶ Multiple Active Result Sets (MARS)

▶ Change Data Capture (CDC)

Using In-Memory OLTP

In order to use in-memory-optimized tables, the database must first be configured to support In-Memory OLTP and then you need to create tables, specifying that they are to be memory-optimized.

Enabling a Database for In-Memory OLTP

Any database that will contain memory-optimized tables must have a MEMORY_OPTIMIZED_DATA filegroup defined which is used for storing the checkpoint files needed by SQL Server to recover the memory-optimized tables. The syntax for creating the filegroup is similar to creating a regular filestream filegroup, but must also specify the CONTAINS MEMORY_OPTIMIZED_DATA option. (For more information on creating and defining filegroups, see Chapter 20, "Creating and Managing Databases")

To create a new database with a MEMORY_OPTIMIZED_DATA filegroup, you would execute a command similar to the following:

```
CREATE DATABASE InMemory
  ON  PRIMARY ( NAME = N'InMemory_Data',
                FILENAME = N'D:\SQL2014\Data\InMemoryData.mdf' ,
                    SIZE = 2048MB),
  FILEGROUP [InMem_FG] CONTAINS MEMORY_OPTIMIZED_DATA
             ( NAME = N'InMemory_FG_dir',
                    FILENAME = N'D:\SQL2014\Data\InMemory_FG_dir')
  LOG ON ( NAME = N'InMemory_log',
           FILENAME = N'D:\SQL2014\Data\InMemory.ldf' ,
               SIZE = 1024MB)
  COLLATE Latin1_General_100_BIN2
GO
```

This command creates a database named InMemory with a memory-optimized filegroup container and filegroup named InMem_FG to the database. Notice that the MEMORY_OPTIMIZED_DATA filegroup specifies a directory, not a specific file name. Also notice the Latin1_General_100_BIN2 binary collation was specified. Currently, any indexes on memory-optimized tables can only be on columns using a Windows (non-SQL) BIN2 collation and natively compiled procedures only support comparisons, sorting, and grouping on those same collations. If you don't specify this as the default collation for the entire database, you'll need to specify the Latin1_General_100_BIN2 collation for any character columns within the CREATE TABLE statement of your memory-optimized tables.

> **NOTE**
>
> It is important to note that the Latin1_General_100_BIN2 is case- and accent-sensitive. This could introduce some side effects in your queries if you convert any existing tables to be memory-optimized.

It is also possible to add a MEMORY_OPTIMIZED_DATA filegroup to an existing database with the ALTER DATABASE command and then adding a directory to that filegroup:

```
ALTER DATABASE AdventureWorks2012
    ADD FILEGROUP AW_inmem_FG CONTAINS MEMORY_OPTIMIZED_DATA;
GO
ALTER DATABASE AdventureWorks2012
    ADD FILE (NAME='AW_inmem_FG_dir',
               FILENAME=N'D:\SQL2014\Data\AW_inmem_FG_dir')
      TO FILEGROUP AW_inmem_FG;
GO
```

SSMS also supports adding a memory-optimized filegroup to a database on the filegroup page, as shown in Figure 33.2

FIGURE 33.2   Configuring a `MEMORY_OPTIMIZED_DATA` filegroup in SSMS.

Once you have configured a `MEMORY_OPTIMIZED_DATA` filegroup for the database, you can create memory-optimized tables.

Creating Memory-Optimized Tables

Creating a memory-optimized table is similar to creating a regular table, with a few differences. The first is you need to specify the `MEMORY_OPTIMIZED = ON` option which tells SQL Server that the table is to be memory-optimized. This will create a table DLL which is loaded into memory.

A memory-optimized table can be defined with one of two `DURABILITY` values:

> ► `SCHEMA_AND_DATA`—When this option is specified, both the schema and the data will be persisted on disk. With this option, there are also two possible levels of durability which are controlled at the database level: full durability and delayed durability. The full durability option writes the transaction to disk upon commit, whereas the delayed durability option stores the transaction in memory and writes it to disk later. Delayed durability can improve performance but can also result in data loss in the event of a server crash or power outage. For more information on the delayed durability option, see Chapter 28, "Transaction Management and the Transaction Log."

▶ **SCHEMA_ONLY**—When this option is specified, only the table definition is persisted. The data is not. Only the empty table will be available after a server restart. Selecting this option provides the best performance but this option should only be used for transient data or in situations where data loss is acceptable.

Also, memory-optimized table must always have at least one index and all tables except for those created with the SCHEMA_ONLY option must have a declared primary key. Thus the single index requirement can be satisfied by defining a primary key constraint in the CREATE TABLE statement.

The following example shows the creation of a memory-optimized table with a nonclustered PRIMARY KEY index created on the ID column:

```
CREATE TABLE InMemTab
 ( [ID] int IDENTITY PRIMARY KEY NONCLUSTERED HASH WITH (BUCKET_COUNT = 1024),
   [Name] nvarchar(32) not null ,
   [City] nvarchar(50) null,
   [State] char(2) null,
   [LastModified] datetime2 not null
 )
WITH (MEMORY_OPTIMIZED = ON, DURABILITY = SCHEMA_AND_DATA);
```

As you can see, creating a memory-optimized table is similar to creating a regular table, with a few minor differences. Here, the first column, ID, is the primary key and is defined using the new hash index. The BUCKET_COUNT keyword specifies the size of the hash table. The general recommendation is that the BUCKET_COUNT value be set to between one and two times the maximum expected number of distinct values in the index (more on this in the "Indexes on Memory-Optimized Tables" section).

When a memory-optimized table is created, the In-Memory OLTP engine will generate and compile DML routines for accessing that table, and load the routines as DLLs. SQL Server itself does not perform the actual data manipulation on memory-optimized tables, instead it calls the appropriate DLL for the required operation when a memory-optimized table is accessed.

Currently, no schema changes are allowed once a memory-optimized table is created. If you need to make any changes to the table definition, including any index changes, you will need to drop and recreate the table. Indexes can only be specified as part of the CREATE TABLE syntax (inline specification of indexes is a new feature in SQL Server 2014). For example, if you wanted to create an additional nonclustered index on the Name column, you'd have to drop and recreate the table:

```
DROP TABLE InMemTab
go
CREATE TABLE InMemTab
 ( [ID] int IDENTITY PRIMARY KEY NONCLUSTERED HASH WITH (BUCKET_COUNT = 1024),
   [Name] nvarchar(32) COLLATE Latin1_General_100_BIN2 not null,
   [City] nvarchar(50) null,
```

```
[State] char(2) null,
[LastModified] datetime2 not null,
INDEX IDX_InMemTab_Name NONCLUSTERED (Name)
)
WITH (MEMORY_OPTIMIZED = ON, DURABILITY = SCHEMA_AND_DATA);
```

> **NOTE**
>
> If the default collation for the database is not `Latin1_General_100_BIN2`, you'll need to explicitly set the collation of any columns that contain character data to `Latin1_General_100_BIN2` in order to define an index that includes the column. Just to be safe, it's best to always specify the collation in the `CREATE TABLE` syntax.

Memory-Optimized Tables Row Structure

As mentioned previously, memory-optimized tables are not stored like disk-based tables. The main difference is that rows for memory-optimized tables are not stored on pages like disk-based tables, and space is not allocated from extents. The design principle behind the storage structure of memory-optimized tables is to optimize access for byte-addressable memory instead of block-addressable disk.

Rows for a single table are not stored in any specific order, and not necessarily near other rows from the same table. SQL Server knows which rows belong to the same table via the tables' indexes, which keep the rows linked together. This is why memory-optimized tables require at least one index be created on them. The index provides the structure for the tables.

The rows themselves also have a structure that is very different from the row structures used for disk-based tables. Each row consists of a header and a payload area containing the data values. Figure 33.3 provides a diagram of the memory-optimized table data row.

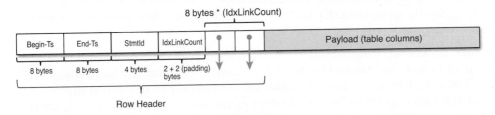

FIGURE 33.3   The SQL Server 2014 engine architecture with In-Memory OLTP.

The row header contains the following values:

▶ Two 8-byte fields holding In-Memory OLTP timestamps: a Begin-Ts and an End-Ts. The value of Begin-Ts is the timestamp of the transaction that inserted the row. The End-Ts value is the timestamp of the transaction that deleted the row. A special value (referred to as 'infinity') is used as the End-Ts value for rows that have not been deleted.

▶ A four-byte statement ID value—Every statement within a transaction has a unique StmtId value. When a row is created it stores the StmtId for the statement that created the row. It allows the statement to skip rows it has already inserted.

▶ A two-byte value (idxLinkCount) which is a reference count indicating how many indexes reference this row.

▶ An index pointer array—Contains a pointer for each index on the table. It is these pointers plus the index data structures that connect the rows of a table together. The number of pointers is equal to the number of indexes defined on the table.

Every database that supports memory-optimized tables manages two internal counters that are used to generate the Begin-Ts and End-Ts timestamps:

▶ **The Transaction-ID counter**—A global, unique value that is reset when the SQL Server instance is restarted and is incremented every time a new transaction starts.

▶ **The Global Transaction Timestamp**—A global, unique value that is not reset on a restart. It is incremented each time a transaction ends and begins validation processing and the new value is the timestamp for the current transaction.

When a row is first inserted into a memory-optimized table, before the insert transaction is completed, the transaction's timestamp is not known so the global Transaction_ID value is used for Begin-Ts until the transaction commits. Similarly, for a delete operation, the transaction timestamp is not known, so the End-Ts value for the deleted rows uses the global Transaction_ID value, which is replaced once the real Transaction Timestamp is known. The Begin-Ts and End-Ts values are the mechanism used to determine which other transactions are able to see this row.

The payload area contains the row data, including the key columns plus all the other columns in the row. With this structure, all indexes on a memory-optimized table are essentially covering indexes. The payload format varies depending on the table. When the table is created, the In-Memory OLTP compiler generates the DLLs for table operations. Based upon the payload format used initially when inserting rows into a table, it generates the appropriate commands for all row operations.

Indexes on Memory-Optimized Tables

As mentioned previously, each memory-optimized table must have at least one index because it is the indexes that connect the rows together (more on this later). The indexes on memory-optimized tables must be created as a part of the CREATE TABLE statement. You can't use the CREATE INDEX statement to create an index for a memory-optimized table after the table has already been created. Memory-optimized tables support a maximum of eight indexes, including the primary key index, and unique indexes are not allowed except for the primary key index.

Indexes on memory-optimized tables are never written to disk, not even to the transaction log. Only the data rows, and changes to the data, are written to the transaction log for durable tables defined with the SCHEMA_AND_DATA option. Instead, indexes on memory-optimized tables are populated based on the index definitions when SQL Server starts.

Memory-optimized indexes are also inherently covering indexes. Covering means that all memory-optimized table columns are virtually included in the index, so bookmark lookups are not needed to read the data. Rather than a reference to the primary key, memory-optimized indexes simply contain a memory pointer to the actual row in the table data structure. (If you are unfamiliar with these terms or concepts, you may want to review Chapters 31, "Understanding SQL Server Data Structures" and 32, "Indexes and Performance").

In addition, fragmentation and fillfactor do not apply to memory-optimized indexes. In disk-based indexes, fragmentation refers to pages in the B-tree being stored out-of-order on disk. This is not an issue for memory-optimized indexes since they are not written to or read from disk. Fillfactor in disk-based B-tree indexes refers to the degree to which the physical page structures are filled with index rows. Memory-optimized index structures do not have fixed-size pages so there's no degree of free space to consider.

There are two types of indexes available for memory-optimized tables:

▶ Nonclustered hash indexes which are designed for point lookups.

▶ Memory-optimized nonclustered indexes which are intended for range scans and ordered scans.

Hash Indexes

A hash index consists of an array of pointers with each element of the array referred to as a hash bucket. A hash function is applied against the index key column of each row and the result of the function determines which bucket it is stored in. All key values that hash to the same value are accessed from the same pointer in the hash index and are linked together in a chain. When a row is added to the table, the hash function is applied to the index key value in the row and inserted into a hash bucket if the hash key doesn't already exist. Figure 33.4 provides a simplified example of a hash index.

The figure has three buckets with 4 data rows. The top bucket contains one row. The second bucket from the top contains 2 rows. Notice how the rows are linked together. These rows have the same hash value and are linked together through the chain of index pointers in the data rows. The sixth bucket contains one row.

Figure 33.5 shows a diagram of a memory-optimized table with 2 hash indexes defined on it. The solid arrows represent pointers for Hash Index 1 while the dotted lines represent pointers for Hash Index 2. Notice how the linking of rows from Hash Index 2 is different from the linking for Hash Index 1.

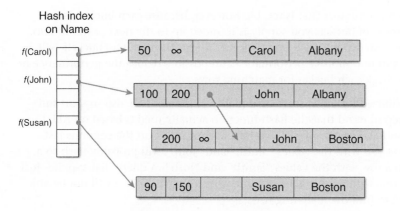

FIGURE 33.4   A simplified diagram of a hash index.

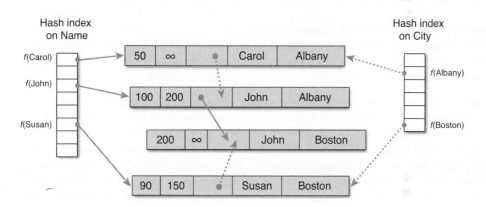

FIGURE 33.5   A diagram of a memory-optimized table with two hash indexes.

The performance of queries that scan an index chain greatly depends on the number of records in the chain. The greater the number of records, the slower the query. Two factors affect the size of the index chain. The first is the selectivity of the index key, essentially the number of distinct values in the table compared to the total number of rows. If there are a large number of duplicate values resulting in low selectivity, the less efficient the hash index will be.

The other factor is the number of hash buckets defined for the index. This also determines the size and amount of memory used by the hash index. The number of buckets is a fixed amount based upon the bucket count specified when the table is created. It is recommended that the number of buckets be set to a value equal to or greater than the estimated number of unique values to be stored in the index key column. This will allow for a greater likelihood that each bucket will only have rows with a single value in its chain.

Be careful not to choose a number that is too big however, because each bucket uses memory and the number of buckets you supply is rounded up to the next power of two. For example, a value of 50,000 will be rounded up to 65,536. Having extra buckets will only waste memory and not improve performance and possibly reduce the performance of scans which have to check each bucket for matching rows.

Hash indexes are optimized for index seeks on equality predicates and also support full index scans. Also, keep in mind that the hash function actually used is based on ALL the key columns, not a subset. For example, if you have a hash index on the columns last-name and firstname, a row with the values "Smith" and "John" will probably hash to a different bucket than a row with the values "Smith" and "Josh". A query that supplies just a lastname value, or one with an inexact firstname value (such as "Jo%") will not be able to use the hash index to find the matching rows.

If you have no idea of the number of buckets you'll need for a particular column, or for columns that will participate in searches over a range of values, you may want to consider creating a memory-optimized nonclustered index instead of a hash index.

Memory-Optimized Nonclustered Indexes

Memory-optimized nonclustered indexes are implemented using a new SQL Server data structure called a Bw-tree which is a lock- and latch-free variation of a B-tree index used for disk-based nonclustered indexes.

The general structure of Bw-tree nonclustered index is similar to SQL Server's regular B-trees, but the index pages are not a fixed size and once the index rows are built they cannot be modified. The maximum size of an index page is 8KB. Bw-tree pages are similar to a regular B-tree page in that each index page contains a set of ordered key values, and for each value there is a corresponding pointer. Unlike regular B-tree indexes where the index rows store the minimum value on the page it points to at the next level down, the key value stored in the Bw-tree index is the highest value possible on the page at the next level down. (For a refresher on nonclustered B-tree index structures in SQL Server, see Chapter 31.)

The upper levels of the index, the root and intermediate pages, are referred to as the internal pages and these pages contain pointers which point to an index page at the next level of the tree. However, unlike a SQL Server B-tree index, the page pointer is a logical page ID (PID) instead of a physical page number. The PID represents a position in a mapping table, which links each PID with a physical memory address where the index page resides. Also, unlike a B-tree index, the pages at the same level are not linked in a doubly linked list: each index page knows the PID of the next page at the same level but not the PID of the previous page. Linking to the next page at the same level is done by looking up the PID in the mapping table.

At the leaf level, the pointers point to the actual chain of data rows with the same index key values. Multiple data rows with the same index key are linked together like In-Memory OLTP hash indexes, via a pointer in the index pointer array. Figure 33.6 shows a simplified example of a memory-optimized nonclustered index.

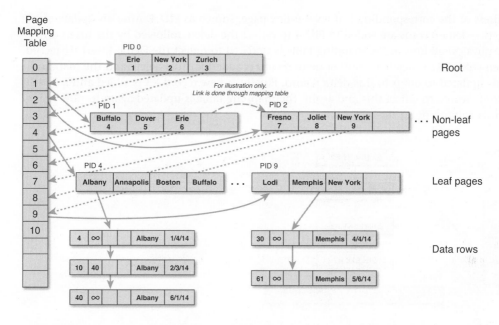

FIGURE 33.6   A diagram of memory-optimized nonclustered indexes.

Only a subset of the PID values are represented in Figure 33.6. The index pages are showing the key values that the index references. Each index row in the internal index pages contains a key value and the corresponding PID of the page at the next level down which contains that value as the highest ordered key value on that page. For example, the index key value "New York" on the root page has PID of 2, which maps to the index page with "New York" as the highest ordered key value. The leaf level index pages also contain index key values, but instead of a PID, they hold the memory address of a data row, which could be the first data row in a chain of data rows.

When modifications occur to an internal index page, rather than updating the index page, it is replaced with a new page and the mapping table is updated so that the PID now points to the new physical memory address of the index page. This avoids the need to change internal pages with references to obsolete pages.

At the leaf level, data changes are kept track of using a set of delta records. The leaf pages themselves are not replaced for every change. The delta records create a chain of memory pointers with the last pointer referencing the actual leaf index page. Each update to a page, which can be an insert or delete of a key value on that page, produces a page containing a delta record indicating the change that was made. An update is represented by two new delta records, one for the delete of the original value, and one for the insert of the new value. When each delta record is added, the mapping table is updated with the physical address of the page containing the newly added delta record.

Figure 33.7 illustrates this behavior. The mapping table is showing only a single page with logical address 4. The physical address in the mapping table originally was the memory address of the corresponding leaf level index page, shown as PID 4. After an update of R1, two delta records are added to PID 4 to reflect the delete followed by the insert and the physical address in the mapping table is updated to reflect the Delta: Insert R1 record. Then record R2 is deleted, another delta record is added for this delete and the mapping table updated to point to this delta record. Finally, a new record R3 is added and a delta record created to reflect this and again, the mapping table is updated again to now point to this delta record.

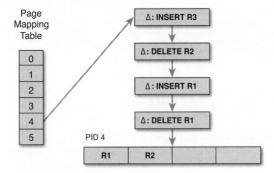

FIGURE 33.7   A single index leaf page and associated delta records.

When searching the nonclustered range index, the In-Memory OLTP engine must combine the delta records with the base index leaf page which makes the search operation a bit more expensive, but not having to completely replace the leaf page for every modification provides an overall performance savings. However, the delta pages are not kept around forever. Eventually, as discussed later in this chapter, the original page and the chain of delta records are consolidated into a new base page.

Memory-Optimized Nonclustered Index Page Structure

As mentioned previously, In-Memory OLTP nonclustered index pages are not a fixed size as they are for indexes on disk-based tables, although the maximum index page size is still 8KB. Memory-optimized nonclustered index pages all have a header area which contains the following information:

▶ **PID**—The pointer into the mapping table

▶ **Page Type**—leaf, internal, delta, or special

▶ **Right PID**—The PID of the next page to the right of the current page

▶ **Height**—The number of levels from the current page to the leaf

▶ The number of index key values stored on the page

▶ **Delta records statistics**—The number of delta records plus the space used by the delta key values

▶ **Max Key**—The upper limit of the index key values contained on the page

In addition, both leaf and internal pages contain two or three fixed length arrays:

▶ **Values**—A pointer array with entry that are each 8 bytes long. For internal pages the entry contains the PID of the page at the next level down. For a leaf page, the entry contains the memory address for the first row in a chain of rows having equal key values.

▶ **Keys**—This is the array of the key values. For internal pages, the key represents the first value on the page referenced by the PID. For leaf pages, the key is the value in the chain of rows.

▶ **Offsets**—This array exists only for indexes with variable length keys. Each entry is 2 bytes and contains the offset where the corresponding key starts in the key array on the page.

The smallest pages in a memory-optimized nonclustered index are typically the delta pages, which have a header which contains most of the same information as in an internal or leaf page, but the delta page headers don't include the arrays described for leaf or internal pages. A delta page only contains an operation code (insert or delete), a single key value, and the memory address of the first row in a chain of records.

Internal Maintenance of Memory-Optimized Nonclustered Indexes

As discussed in the previous section, a long chain of delta records can eventually degrade search performance. Eventually, the delta records need to be consolidated. When the In-Memory OLTP attempts to add a new delta record to a chain that already has 16 elements, the changes in the delta records will be consolidated into the referenced index page, and the page will then be rebuilt, including the changes indicated by the new delta record that triggered the consolidation. The newly rebuilt page will have the same PID but a new memory address and the page mapping table is updated with this new address. The old pages (index page plus delta pages) will be marked for garbage collection.

Two other type of index maintenance operations take place in addition to consolidation of delta records: split and merge.

Index pages grow as needed, starting from storing a single row to storing up to a maximum of 8K bytes. Once the index page grows to 8K bytes in size, an attempt to insert a new row into that index page will trigger a page split. For internal pages, this occurs when there is no more room to add another key value and pointer. For leaf pages, it occurs when SQL Server determines that there is insufficient space on the leaf index page to accommodate the new index value once the delta records are consolidated. The space needed is determined from the delta records statistics information in the page header of the leaf page, which is adjusted as each new delta record is added.

A split operation is done in two atomic steps. In the first step, SQL Server creates two new leaf-level pages (let's call them P1 and P2) and splits the old page values between them. It then adds an entry to the mapping table for the second newly created page (P2), adds the logical pointer to P2 to page P1, repoints the mapping table to the first newly created page (P1), and marks the old page and the delta records for garbage collection. This is all done as a single atomic operation and until complete, P1 and P2 are not accessible to any concurrent operations. Also, at this point, P2 is only accessible via the logical link form P1. It has no entry and is not accessible via a parent internal page.

In the second step, SQL Server creates a new internal page and populates it with key values that represent the new leaf-level pages. When the new internal page is built, the pointer in the mapping table is updated to point to the new page and the old internal page is marked for garbage collection.

Figure 33.8 illustrates both steps in a page split operation.

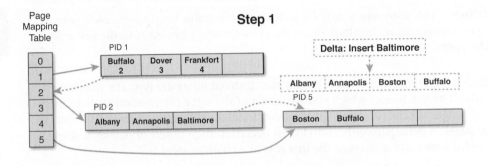

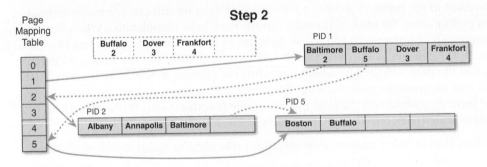

FIGURE 33.8   Page splitting of a memory-optimized nonclustered index.

The other process, page merging, occurs when a delete operation leaves an index page with records that use less than 10% of the maximum page size (currently 8K), or results in an index page with a single row on it. When either of these two conditions occurs, the page will be merged with its neighboring page. Like page splitting, this is also a multi-step operation. When a row is deleted from a page, a delta record for the delete is added and a check is made to determine if the page qualifies for merge (i.e. only one row remains or the remaining space after deleting the row will be less than 10% of maximum page size).

If the page qualifies for a merge, the merge is performed in three atomic steps. In the first step, a delta record is created and its pointer is set to point to the leaf index page, plus a special merge-delta record is created and points to the delete delta record. In one atomic step, the pointer in the page mapping table is updated to point to the merge delta page. The results of this step are illustrated in Figure 33.9.

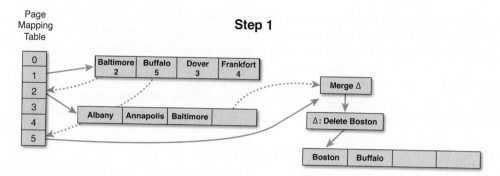

FIGURE 33.9   Step 1 of a page merge operation.

In the second step, a new internal page that does not reference the page to be merged is created and the mapping table is updated to point to the newly created internal page. The old internal page is marked for garbage collection. The results of step 2 are illustrated in Figure 33.10.

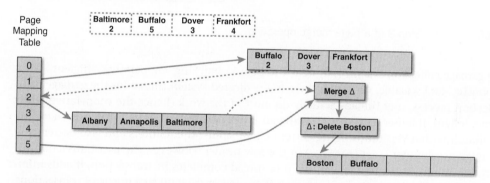

FIGURE 33.10   Step 2 of a page merge operation.

In the third and final step, a new leaf level page is created containing the merged contents of the two original leaf pages. The mapping table is updated to point to this new leaf page and the old pages and delta records are marked for garbage collection. The results of step 3 are illustrated in Figure 33.11.

Garbage Collection

Because SQL Server's In-Memory OLTP is a row-versioning system, data modifications generate versions of rows rather than updating row data. Eventually, older row versions will become stale. As described earlier, every row has a BeginTs and EndTs timestamp that indicate when the row was created and when it was deleted. Transactions only see the versions of rows that were valid at the time when the transaction started, that is, the Global Transaction Timestamp value at the time the transaction started is between the BeginTs and EndTs of the row. When the EndTs of a row is older than the Global Transaction Timestamp of the oldest active transaction in the system, the row is considered to be stale. Since stale rows are invisible to any active transactions, they serve no purpose anymore and will slow down scans of index structures and waste memory. Garbage collection is the process that cleans up these stale rows and reclaims memory.

Step 3

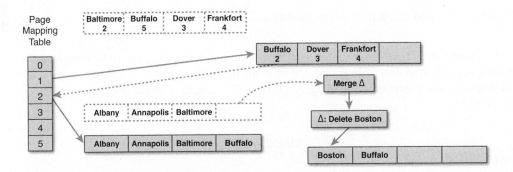

FIGURE 33.11   Step 3 of a page merge operation.

The garbage collection system is designed to be non-blocking, cooperative, efficient, responsive, and scalable. Although there is a dedicated system thread for the garbage collection process, user threads actually do most of the work (hence the cooperative aspect of the design). If a user thread is scanning an index and comes across a stale row version, it will unlink that version from the current chain, adjust the pointers and also decrement the reference counter (IdxLinkcount) in the row header. However, the user transaction does not deallocate the row. When the user thread completes its transaction, it adds information about the transaction (which rows it created or deleted) to a queue of transactions to be processed by the garbage collection process.

The garbage collector thread periodically (approximately once per minute) goes through the queue and analyzes stale rows to build work items, collections of rows that need to be deallocated. These work items are inserted into other queues partitioned on a logical CPU basis and user threads (and sometimes the system garbage collector) pick up one or more work items from a queue and deallocate the rows, freeing up the memory used by the rows.

The DMV sys.dm_db_xtp_index_stats returns a row for each index on each memory-optimized table, and the column rows_expired indicates how many rows have been detected as being stale during scans of that index. Another column, rows_expired_removed, indicates how many rows have been unlinked from the index. As mentioned previously, once rows have been unlinked from all indexes on a table, they can be removed by the garbage collection thread. The following is an example of a query using the `sys.dm_db_xtp_index_stats` DMV (the query joins the DMV to the sys.indexes catalog view to be able to return the index names):

```
SELECT name AS 'index_name',
       s.index_id,
       scans_started,
       rows_returned,
       rows_expired,
       rows_expired_removed
FROM sys.dm_db_xtp_index_stats s
JOIN sys.indexes i
       ON s.object_id=i.object_id
       and s.index_id=i.index_id
WHERE object_id('InMemTab') = s.object_id;
```

Maintaining Statistics on Memory-Optimized Tables

SQL Server creates index- and column-level statistics on memory-optimized tables, but in the current release, there is no mechanism in place to update the statistics automatically. The main reason is that SQL Server In-Memory OLTP does not keep any row modification counters so it has no mechanism to calculate when statistics should be auto-updated. Another reason is so that there will not be any chance of dependency failures due to waiting for statistics to be updated.

The problem with the lack of auto-updating of statistics is that indexes can only be created at the time the memory-optimized table is created, so the initial statistics are created when the table is empty. Since they are never updated automatically, is it up to you (or the database admins) to design and implement a statistics maintenance strategy for your system.

The general recommendation is to update the statistics after loading data into the table or whenever SQL Server or the database restarts. If the data in the memory-optimized table is volatile, you should develop a strategy that updates the statistics on a regular basis.

Statistics are updated on memory-optimized tables using the familiar UPDATE STATISTICS command, with one minor variation. When running UPDATE STATISTICS on memory-optimized tables, SQL Server always performs a full scan, unlike for disk-based tables where it samples the data by default.

You can also use the `sp_updatestats` stored procedure to update all statistics in the database. Unlike for disk-based tables, the `sp_updatestats` stored procedure always updates all statistics on memory-optimized tables. For disk-based tables, it will skip statistics that do not need to be updated.

NOTE

Before creating natively-compiled stored procedures on your memory-optimized tables, make sure your tables are loaded with data and you have updated all statistics on all of the tables to be accessed by the natively-compiled stored procedures. With natively-compiled stored procedures, the query plan is created at the time the procedure is created based upon the existing statistics. Natively compiled stored procedures are never recompiled on the fly. The only way to generate a new plan is to drop and recreate the stored procedure, or restart SQL Server.

Memory-Optimized Index Design Guidelines

The goal of optimization of natively compiled stored procedures is similar to the goal of optimization of interpreted procedures: to find query plans for each of the statements in the procedure so that they can be executed as efficiently as possible. The formula that the optimizer uses for assessing the relative cost of operations on memory-optimized tables is similar to the costing formula for operations on disk-based tables, with a few exceptions. Because of the differences in the way that memory-optimized tables are organized and managed and the different types of indexes available, the optimizer does need to be aware of different choices it may need to make, as well as various execution plan options that are not available when working with memory-optimized tables.

Some of the limitations pertain to the access paths available to the in-memory engine during query optimization with respect to its use of hash and range indexes. If the optimizer finds a not useful hash or range index, it will essentially perform a table scan, although the concept of a table scan is misleading since with memory-optimized tables, all data access is through indexes. The optimizer will choose one of the indexes to use through which all rows will be retrieved. Typically, the optimizer will choose a hash index over a range index if the cost estimations are the same.

If the query is performing a search of a range of values, or requires that rows be returned in a sorted order, a hash index will not be used as ordered scans cannot be performed against a hash index. Also, the optimizer cannot use a hash index unless the query provides search conditions for all columns contained in the index key. For example, if you have a hash index on two columns (city, state), a row for a customer from Albany, NY would hash to a completely different value than a row for a customer from Albany, GA. If a query only supplies a search condition on the city column, a hash value cannot be generated to search against the hash values stored in the index. For similar reasons, a hash index can only be used if the filter is based on an equality. If the query does not specify an exact value for one of the columns in the hash index key, the hash value cannot be determined. For a query with a condition of `city LIKE 'San%'`, which is essentially a range search, a hash lookup is not possible. A hash index will revert to a scan given an inequality predicate or if not all index keys are provided as search arguments.

Memory-optimized nonclustered indexes are better at retrieving ranges of values. However, they only support retrieving the table rows in the order that was specified when the index was created. Range indexes cannot be scanned in reverse order because, as shown previously, there is no concept of "previous pointers" in a range index on a memory-optimized table. For data to be searched or sorted in reverse order, the index would have to be created as a descending index. If reverse order scans or sorting of results in descending order are needed, it is possible to have two indexes on the same column, one defined as ascending and one defined as descending. It is also possible to have both a range and a hash index on the same column to support both equality and range searches.

When a column in a nonclustered index has the same value in many rows (i.e., there are a large number of duplicate values in the index key columns), performance can degrade for updates, inserts, and deletes. One way to improve performance in this situation is to add another column to the nonclustered index.

Do not create indexes on your memory-optimized tables that will be rarely used. Garbage collection works best if all indexes on the table are used frequently. Rarely-used indexes may cause the garbage collection system to not perform optimally for old row versions.

Determining the Optimal Bucket Count for Hash Indexes

You must specify a value for the BUCKET_COUNT parameter when you create the memory-optimized table. If you cannot determine the correct bucket count, use a nonclustered index instead. An incorrect BUCKET_COUNT value, especially one that is too low, can significantly impact workload performance, as well as recovery time of the database. It is better to overestimate the bucket count.

In most cases the bucket count should be between 1 and 2 times the number of distinct values in the index key. If the index key contains a lot of duplicate values (for example, if on average there are more than 10 rows for each index key value), use a nonclustered index instead.

You may not always be able to predict how many values a particular index key may have or will have. Performance should be acceptable if the BUCKET_COUNT value is within 5 times of the actual number of key values.

You can use the sys.dm_db_xtp_hash_index_stats DMV to obtain statistics about the number of empty buckets and the length of row chains in a hash index. The following example query can be used to obtain statistics about all the hash indexes in the current database (note, this query can take several minutes to run if there are large tables in the database):

```
SELECT
    object_name(hs.object_id) AS 'object name',
    i.name as 'index name',
    hs.total_bucket_count,
    hs.empty_bucket_count,
    floor((cast(empty_bucket_count as float)
                /total_bucket_count) * 100) AS 'empty_bucket_percent',
    hs.avg_chain_length,
    hs.max_chain_length
FROM sys.dm_db_xtp_hash_index_stats AS hs
    JOIN sys.indexes AS i
    ON hs.object_id=i.object_id AND hs.index_id=i.index_id
```

33

The key values to focus on to evaluate your hash bucket configuration are `empty_bucket_percent` and `avg_chain_length`.

The `empty_bucket_percent` column indicates the number of empty buckets in the hash index. If `empty_bucket_percent` is less than 10 percent, the bucket count is likely to be too low. Ideally, the `empty_bucket_percent` should be 33 percent or greater.

The `avg_chain_length` column indicates the average length of the row chains in the hash buckets. An average chain length of 1 is ideal. If `avg_chain_length` is greater than 10 and `empty_bucket_percent` is greater than 10 percent, there likely are many duplicate index key values. A nonclustered index on that index key would likely be more appropriate.

Using Memory-Optimized Tables

Now that we've discussed how to create memory-optimized tables and their indexes, you may be wondering how you use them. Memory-optimized tables can be accessed in two different ways: either using interpreted Transact-SQL through interop, or by creating and using natively compiled stored procedures.

Interpreted T-SQL Support for In-Memory OLTP

With just a handful of exceptions, you can access memory-optimized tables just like disk-based tables using interpreted T-SQL queries or DML operations (SELECT, INSERT, UPDATE, or DELETE), ad hoc batches, and SQL modules such as stored procedures, table-value functions, triggers, and views. Interpreted T-SQL refers to any T-SQL batches or stored procedures other than a natively compiled stored procedure.

Interpreted T-SQL access to memory-optimized tables is referred to as interop access. Interpreted T-SQL access is recommended for ad hoc queries and administrative tasks, reporting queries which typically use constructs not available in natively compiled stored procedures (such as windowing functions), or to migrate performance-critical parts of your application to memory-optimized tables, with minimal (or no) application code changes.

However, the following T-SQL constructs are not supported for interop access to data in memory-optimized tables:

▶ TRUNCATE TABLE

▶ MERGE with memory-optimized table as the target

▶ DYNAMIC and KEYSET cursors (they will automatically be downgraded to STATIC cursors)

▶ Access from CLR modules using context connection

▶ Referencing memory-optimized tables in an indexed view

▶ Locking hints: HOLDLOCK, PAGLOCK, ROWLOCK, TABLOCK, TABLOCKX, UPDLOCK, XLOCK, NOWAIT

▶ Isolation level hints: READCOMMITTED, READCOMMITTEDLOCK, READPAST, READUNCOMMITTED

▶ Cross-database queries and transactions

▶ Linked servers

As you can see, there are not a whole lot of restrictions on what you can do against memory-optimized tables from interpreted SQL and you may see performance improvements in certain types of applications just from migrating tables from disk-based to memory-optimized tables and reaping the benefits of the improved data access speed and elimination of latching and locking contention. However, if you then migrate your interpreted stored procedures to natively compiled stored procedures, you should see even further performance improvement.

Native Compilation

Native compilation allows faster data access and more efficient query execution than normal T-SQL stored procedures which are processed as interpreted Transact-SQL. Although you may see a 2X-3X performance improvement accessing memory-optimized tables using the interop engine, the overhead of using interpreted SQL is the limiting factor in the performance improvements that can be achieved with In-Memory OLTP. Even simple interpreted T-SQL statements may still require thousands, and possibly millions, of CPU instructions to execute. Significantly greater performance can be achieved utilizing native compilation.

The first step in native compilation is to convert the row-data manipulation and access logic into C code, which is then compiled into DLLs (one per each memory-optimized table) and loaded into SQL Server process memory. These DLLs consist of native CPU instructions which execute without any additional overhead of T-SQL code interpretation.

To see how performance benefits from native compilation, consider the simple operation where you need to read the value of a fixed-length column from a data row. For on-disk tables, SQL Server queries the system catalogs to obtain the starting offset and length of the column in the data row, and then performs the necessary operations to convert the sequence of bytes stored in the column to the required data type. With memory-optimized tables, the compiled DLL already knows the column offset and data type and the memory-optimized OLTP engine can read the data from the pre-defined offset in the row using a pointer of the proper data type without any further overhead required. This method significantly reduces the number of CPU instructions required for the operation.

> **NOTE**
>
> The downside to native compilation is that the DLLs are compiled at table creation time, so you cannot modify the table columns after the DLLs have been created. The pre-compiled code wouldn't know of the changes made. Recompiling the existing DLLs to reflect the new data row format would require exclusive access to the table for the duration, which violates one of the main design goals of the In-Memory OLTP engine by requiring locking. This is why any changes to the columns or index structures of a memory-optimized table require dropping and recreating the table.

To reduce the overhead of interpreted T-SQL even further, the In-Memory OLTP engine allows you to natively compile stored procedures. Natively compiled stored procedures are compiled to DLLs and loaded into SQL Server process memory in the same way as the table-related DLLs. The main difference between interpreted stored procedures and natively compiled stored procedures is that an interpreted stored procedure isn't compiled until its first execution whereas a natively compiled stored procedure is compiled when it is created. The compile process first translates the stored procedure T-SQL code into C code, and then into machine language. The code is stored as a DLL in a special folder on the SQL Server machine.

In addition to compiling memory-optimized tables and natively compiled stored procedures to native DLLs at create time, the table DLLs are recompiled after the database or server is restarted and natively compiled stored procedure DLLs are recompiled upon the first execution after restart. The information necessary to recreate the DLLs is stored in the database metadata. The binary DLLs are not stored in the database nor persisted in database backups. The binary DLLs and other native compilation-related files (which are kept for troubleshooting and supportability purposes) are stored in the XTP subfolder under the main SQL Server data directory. Files are grouped together in subfolders at the database level (the folder names match the database ID).

You do not need to maintain the files that are generated by native compilation. SQL Server automatically removes generated files that are no longer needed. However, if you are curious, you can view the name and location of the DLL files created for your memory-optimized tables and natively compiled procedures with the following query:

```
SELECT name, description
  FROM sys.dm_os_loaded_modules
  WHERE description = 'XTP Native DLL'
go

/* output
name                                            description
---------------------------------------------   ---------------
d:\SQL2014\Data\xtp\6\xtp_t_6_277576027.dll    XTP Native DLL
d:\SQL2014\Data\xtp\6\xtp_t_6_341576255.dll    XTP Native DLL
d:\SQL2014\Data\xtp\6\xtp_p_6_565577053.dll    XTP Native DLL
*/
```

To match the DLL files with the underlying table or stored procedure, the last bit of the file name is the object ID. You can identify the object ID of your memory-optimized tables and natively compiled stored procedures with the following query:

```
SELECT s.name + '.' + o.name as ObjectName, o.object_id
  FROM (
              SELECT schema_id, name, object_id
                FROM sys.tables
                WHERE is_memory_optimized = 1
              UNION ALL
```

```
          SELECT schema_id, name, object_id
            FROM sys.procedures
          ) as o
  JOIN sys.schemas s
  ON o.schema_id = s.schema_id
go

/* output
ObjectName      object_id
--------------- -----------
dbo.InMemTab    341576255
dbo.InMemInsert 565577053
*/
```

For example, you can see that memory-optimized table InMemTab has object ID 341576255, which corresponds to DLL xtp_t_6_341576255.dll.

Natively Compiled Stored Procedures

Natively compiled stored procedures can only access memory-optimized tables and currently support a smaller subset of T-SQL features as compared to the query interop engine.

The performance benefit of using natively compiled stored procedures increases with the number of rows and the complexity of the procedure code, or if the number of executions per second of the stored procedure is very high. If a procedure needs to process just a single row only occasionally, it's unlikely to benefit much from native compilation. A natively compiled stored procedure will likely exhibit much better performance improvement than an interpreted procedure if it uses aggregation, nested-loop joins, multi-statement SELECT, INSERT, UPDATE, and DELETE operations, complex expressions, or procedural logic, such as conditional statements and loops.

As stated previously, natively compiled stored procedures are compiled into a DLL when they are created, or are re-compiled upon first execution after a server or database restart. The query plan is generated during compilation based upon the data in the memory-optimized tables at the time the procedure is compiled into memory. If the table was empty at the time of compilation, or the data in the tables has changed significantly since the procedure was compiled, you can update the table and index statistics, but unlike interpreted procedures, you cannot simply recompile the natively compiled stored procedure. You will have to explicitly drop and recreate them after updating the table statistics. You'll want to be sure not to forget to script out the permissions on the natively compiled stored procedures before dropping them.

> **NOTE**
>
> Since the optimization of the query plan is dependent upon the data in the table at the time the natively compiled stored procedures are created, you may want to adjust your deployment strategy for databases with memory-optimized tables and natively compiled

stored procedures from the way it's done for disk-based and interpreted T-SQL procedures. You'll want to hold off creating the natively compiled procedures until after the memory-optimized tables are populated with data.

Creating Natively Compiled Stored Procedures

The following is an example of a natively compiled stored procedure that inserts a record into the InMemTab memory-optimized table:

```
create procedure dbo.InMemInsert(@Name nvarchar(32), @City nvarchar(50), @State
char(2))
with native_compilation, schemabinding, execute as owner
as
begin atomic with
(transaction isolation level = snapshot,
language = N'English')

  declare @OrdDate datetime = getdate();
  insert into dbo.InMemTab(Name, City, State, LastModified) values (@Name, @City, @
State, GETDATE());
end
go
```

The NATIVE_COMPILATION keyword in the WITH clause indicates that the Transact-SQL stored procedure is a natively compiled stored procedure. The SCHEMABINDING and EXECUTE AS clauses are required syntax, as well as the new BEGIN ATOMIC clause. Natively compiled stored procedures must run as a single all or nothing atomic block. Atomic blocks are blocks of T-SQL statements that are executed (atomically) within the transaction. Either all statements in the block succeed or the entire block will be rolled back.

In the current release, there are a number of restrictions on what sort of T-SQL operations can be performed in natively compiled stored procedures. A number of the restrictions are listed in Chapter 25, "Creating and Managing Stored Procedures." Still, there are so many restrictions, it's almost easier to list the supported features. A complete list can be found in SQL Server 2014 Books Online at this URL: http://msdn.microsoft.com/en-us/library/dn452279.aspx.

However, instead of trying to keep track of all of the supported features and restrictions, you can use the Native Compilation Advisor in SSMS. The Advisor provides a report of which features used in a stored procedure are not supported in natively compiled procedures. To invoke the Native Compilation Advisor, right click on the procedure name in the Object Explorer in SSMS and select Native Compilation Advisor (see Figure 33.12). This will bring up the Native Compilation Advisor. If the procedure contains elements that disqualify it from being natively compiled, you'll see a screen similar to the one shown in Figure 33.13 which provides a list of the elements within the procedure code that are not supported.

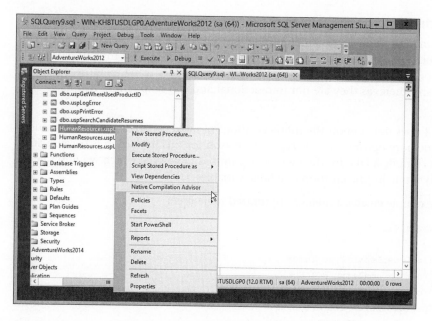

FIGURE 33.12   Invoking the Native Compilation Advisor in SSMS.

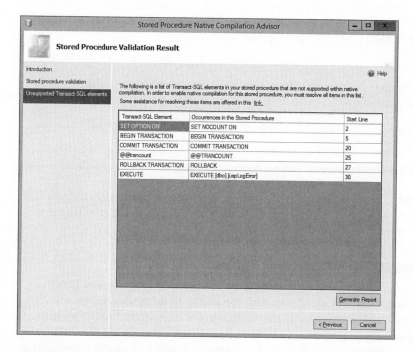

FIGURE 33.13   Native Compilation Advisor report for the `uspUpdateEmployeeHireInfo` Stored Procedure.

Memory-Optimized Table Variables

You can create memory-optimized table variables in SQL Server 2014. Memory-optimized table variables behave the same as regular table variables, but are stored in your database's memory space only and do not utilize tempdb. You can consider using memory-optimized table variables anywhere, as they are not transactional and can help relieve tempdb contention.

SQL Server 2014 does not support the inline creations of table variables however. It must be based on a memory-optimized table type. The reason for this limitation is because SQL Server needs to compile a DLL for the memory-optimized table type which wouldn't be possible with dynamic in-line creation of a table variable.

The following example creates a memory-optimized table type:

```
USE AdventureWorks2012
GO
CREATE TYPE SalesOrderDetailType_inmem
  AS TABLE ( OrderQty smallint NOT NULL,
             ProductID int NOT NULL,
             SpecialOfferID int NOT NULL,
             LocalID int NOT NULL,
             INDEX IX_ProductID NONCLUSTERED HASH (ProductID)
             WITH (BUCKET_COUNT = 131072),
             INDEX IX_SpecialOfferID NONCLUSTERED (SpecialOfferID)
             ) WITH (MEMORY_OPTIMIZED = ON );
GO
```

Note that, just like memory-optimized tables, memory-optimized table variables must be defined with at least one index.

Once you have defined the memory-optimized table type, you can create table variables based upon the type:

```
DECLARE @SalesDetail SalesOrderDetailType_inmem;
```

The memory-optimized table variables can be used as table valued parameters to both natively compiled and interpreted T-SQL stored procedures. They provide an efficient way of passing a bunch of rows to a stored procedure.

Transactions and Memory-Optimized Tables

As described previously in the sections describing the in-memory data row and index structures, SQL Server In-Memory OLTP uses row-versioning to determine which row versions are visible to which transactions. This is accomplished by maintaining an internal Transaction ID that serves the purpose of a timestamp. The timestamps are monotonically increasing every time a transaction commits. A transaction's start time is the timestamp in the database at the time the transaction starts. When the transaction commits, it generates a new timestamp, the Global Transaction Timestamp, which is used to uniquely identify that transaction. Timestamps are used to specify the following:

▶ **Commit/End Time**—The distinct point in time that represents the commit or end timestamp of the transaction. The commit time effectively identifies a transaction's location in the serialization history.

▶ **Validity Interval**—All rows in memory-optimized tables contain two timestamps: the begin timestamp (Begin-Ts) and the end timestamp (End-Ts). The validity interval for a record version denotes the range of timestamps where the version is visible to other transactions.

▶ **Logical Read Time**—This can be any value between the transaction's begin time and the current time. Only the row versions where the logical read time falls within the valid time interval are visible to the read.

The concepts of row versioning and version visibility are fundamental to providing proper concurrency control in In-Memory OLTP. A transaction executing at logical read time X must only see versions of rows where X is greater than the begin timestamp of the row and less than the end timestamp of a row.

> **NOTE**
>
> This section assumes a general understanding of transactions, transaction management, and isolation levels. If you are not familiar with these concepts, you may want to first review Chapter 28.

Row versioning on disk-based tables (using SNAPSHOT isolation or READ_COMMITTED_SNAPSHOT) provides a form of optimistic concurrency control. Reads are not blocked by writes, but a transaction that locks a row for update blocks other concurrent transactions attempting to update that row. With memory-optimized tables, there is no locking or blocking of writes—writers do not block writers. Instead, if two transactions attempt to update the same row, a write/write conflict (error 41302) will occur.

Additionally, memory-optimized tables allow optimistic concurrency control with the higher isolation levels, REPEATABLE READ and SERIALIZABLE. Locks are not taken to enforce the isolation levels. Instead, validation checks done at the end of the transaction ensure the repeatable read or serializability assumptions and if the assumptions were violated, the transaction is aborted.

Conflicts and failures tend to be rare and transactions on memory-optimized tables assume there will be no conflicts with concurrent transactions. Transactions proceed under the (optimistic) assumption that there will be no conflicts with other transactions. Not using locks and latches and not waiting for other transactions to finish processing the same rows is one of the factors that improves performance of memory-optimized tables. However, if any conflicts occur that may cause inconsistencies in the database or that may violate transaction isolation, SQL Server has a mechanism in place to detect and validate conflicts.

Conflict Detection and Validation

Prior to the final commit of transactions involving memory-optimized tables, SQL Server performs a validation step to determine if data changes could result in invalid data based on the requested isolation level. The validation phase of the commit processing makes sure that there is no invalid data.

Table 33.1 summarizes the error conditions that can occur during validation for memory-optimized table transactions.

TABLE 33.1   Error Conditions for Memory-Optimized Table Transactions

Error	Scenario
Write conflict. Attempting to update a record that has been updated since the transaction started.	Updating or deleting a row that has been updated or deleted by a concurrent transaction.
Repeatable read validation failure.	A row that was read by the transaction has changed (updated or deleted) since the transaction started.
Serializable validation failure.	A new (phantom) row has been inserted in one of the scan ranges in the transaction, since the transaction started.
Commit dependency failure.	The transaction took a dependency on another transaction that failed to commit, either due to one of the failures in this table, an out-of-memory condition, or due to failure to commit to the transaction log.

The failure conditions listed in Table 33.1 can occur at different points during a transaction. Figure 33.14 illustrates the phases of a transaction that accesses memory-optimized tables.

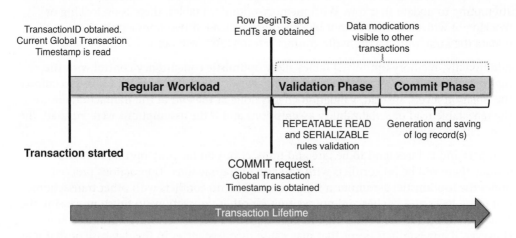

FIGURE 33.14   Lifetime of a transaction on memory-optimized tables.

As the start of the regular workload phase, the TransactionID and the Current Global Timestamp are obtained. The Current Global Timestamp value determines what row versions are visible to the transaction (i.e, those rows where the Global Timestamp is between the BeginTs and EndTs of the rows). Writes to tables during this phase are not visible to other transactions except for other row update and delete operations. If an update or delete operation sees that a row has been updated or deleted by another transaction, the operation will fail immediately with error 41302, "The current transaction attempted to update a record in table X that has been updated since this transaction started. The transaction was aborted."

Also during the regular workload phase, a transaction can read rows written by other transactions that are in the validation or commit phase, but have not yet committed. The rows are visible because the EndTs of the transaction is assigned at the start of the validation phase. When a transaction reads these as yet uncommitted rows, it takes a commit dependency on that transaction which has two main implications:

▶ The transaction cannot enter the commit phase until all commit dependencies have cleared.

▶ Result sets are not returned to the client until all dependencies have cleared which prevents the client from reading uncommitted data.

If any of the dependent transactions fails to commit, a commit dependency failure will be raised and the transaction will fail to commit with error 41301 ("A previous transaction that the current transaction took a dependency on has aborted, and the current transaction can no longer commit.").

While a memory-optimized table transaction will never be blocked waiting for a lock, commit dependency is technically a case of blocking in In-Memory OLTP. However, the time blocked should be very short and generally, blocking waits for commit dependencies will be minimal.

If no direct update conflicts occur and the transaction issues a commit, SQL Server generates the commit timestamp and the transaction enters the validation phase. It is during the validation phase that it will detect other potential violations of the properties specified by the transaction isolation level.

For example, assume a transaction, T1, was accessing a memory-optimized table using REPEATABLE READ isolation. Transaction T1 reads a row value and then another transaction, T2, updates that row value (which it can do because the row is not locked by T1). T2 then issues a commit before T1 commits. When T1 enters the validation phase, it will fail the validation check and SQL Server will abort the transaction.

The following are the steps performed during the validation phase:

▶ Check for isolation level violations.

▶ Wait for all commit dependencies to clear.

A SNAPSHOT isolation level validation error can occur if the current transaction inserted a row with the same primary key value as a row that was inserted by another transaction, and that transaction committed before the current transaction. If this is detected, it will raise error 41325, "The current transaction failed to commit due to a serializable validation failure" and the transaction will be aborted.

For REPEATABLE READ and SERIALIZABLE isolation transactions, SQL Server maintains a read-set for each transaction. The read-set is a set of pointers to the rows that have been read during the transaction. The read-set is used to check for non-repeatable reads. For SERIALIZABLE transactions, SQL Server also keeps a scan-set which is information about the predicate used to access a set of records. The scan-set is used to check for phantom rows.

If memory-optimized tables are accessed in REPEATABLE READ isolation, a validation error is possible when the current transaction has read any row that was subsequently updated by another transaction and that transaction was committed before the current transaction. This condition will raise error 41305, "The current transaction failed to commit due to a repeatable read validation failure" and the transaction will be aborted.

If memory-optimized tables are accessed in SERIALIZABLE isolation, validation can also encounter the REPEATABLE READ validation errors described in the preceding paragraph. In addition, if a transaction accesses memory-optimized tables in SERIALIZABLE isolation, SQL Server uses the transaction's scan-set to determine if any additional rows now meet the predicate's condition. If any rows in the scan-set can no longer be found, or if phantom rows inserted by other transactions that meet the specified filter conditions are encountered, the transaction will fail with error 41325 generated and the transaction will be aborted.

If the transaction gets through the isolation level validation, it then waits for any commit dependencies to clear. If any of the dependent transactions fails to commit, there is a commit dependency failure as described previously. If there are not commit dependency issues, the transaction moves on to the commit phase.

During the commit phase, if any of the modified tables were created with the SCHEMA_AND_DATA option, SQL Server must log the changes to harden them to disk. During transaction processing on durable tables, SQL Server generates a "write set" of changes, basically a list of DELETE/ INSERT operations with pointers to the version associated with each operation. Upon commit, this write set is written to the transaction log. Once the log record has been hardened to storage, the state of the transaction is changed to committed in the global transaction table. SQL Server then proceeds with any final post-processing, which is the final phase.

The main operations performed during post-processing are to update the timestamps of each of the rows inserted or deleted by the transaction. For a DELETE operation, the row's End-Ts value is set to the commit timestamp of the transaction. For an INSERT operation, the row's Begin-Ts value is set to the commit timestamp of the transaction. If the transaction failed or was explicitly rolled back, any inserted rows will be marked as garbage and deleted rows will have their end-timestamp changed back to infinity. The actual unlinking and deletion of old row versions is handled by the garbage collection system which was described previously in the "Garbage Collection" topic in this chapter.

In-Memory OLTP Transaction Isolation Levels

As discussed in the previous section, In-Memory OLTP supports three transaction isolation levels: SNAPSHOT, REPEATABLE READ, and SERIALIZABLE. SNAPSHOT isolation is the baseline isolation mode used for memory-optimized tables and is the one that should generally be used, especially for natively compiled stored procedures or when accessing memory-optimized tables using interpreted T-SQL.

The isolation level READ COMMITTED is also supported for accessing memory-optimized tables by interpreted T-SQL, but only for autocommit (single statement) transactions, as shown in the following example:

```
SET TRANSACTION ISOLATION LEVEL READ COMMITTED
go
insert into dbo.InMemTab(Name, City, State, LastModified)
    values ('Tom', 'Baltimore', 'MD', GETDATE());
go
```

Using the READ COMMITTED isolation level is not supported within multi-statement user transactions:

```
SET TRANSACTION ISOLATION LEVEL READ COMMITTED
go
BEGIN TRAN
   insert into dbo.InMemTab(Name, City, State, LastModified)
      values ('Sue', 'Buffalo', 'NY', GETDATE());
   SELECT * FROM InMemTab
COMMIT TRAN
GO
```

```
(1 row(s) affected)
Msg 41368, Level 16, State 0, Line 74
Accessing memory-optimized tables using the READ COMMITTED isolation level is
supported only for autocommit transactions. It is not supported for explicit
or implicit transactions. Provide a supported isolation level for the memory
optimized table using a table hint, such as WITH (SNAPSHOT).
```

Within interpreted T-SQL multi-statement transactions, you need to explicitly specify the isolation mode for memory-optimized tables via table hints:

```
SET TRANSACTION ISOLATION LEVEL READ COMMITTED
go
BEGIN TRAN
   insert into dbo.InMemTab WITH (SNAPSHOT)
      (Name, City, State, LastModified)
      values ('Sue', 'Buffalo', 'NY', GETDATE());
```

33

```
   SELECT * FROM InMemTab  WITH (SNAPSHOT)
COMMIT TRAN
GO


(1 row(s) affected)
ID     Name  City        State LastModified
-----  ----- ----------- ----- --------------------------
8      Tom   Baltimore   MD    2015-03-29 13:51:38.0170000
10     Sue   Buffalo     NY    2015-03-29 13:53:42.0430000

(2 row(s) affected)
```

If you are running in the default READ COMMITTED mode, a new database option, MEMORY_OPTIMIZED_ELEVATE_TO_SNAPSHOT, is available which transparently maps lower isolation levels (such as READ UNCOMMITTED and READ COMMITTED) to snapshot isolation when accessing memory-optimized tables from interpreted T-SQL transactions:

```
ALTER DATABASE CURRENT SET MEMORY_OPTIMIZED_ELEVATE_TO_SNAPSHOT = ON
GO
SET TRANSACTION ISOLATION LEVEL READ COMMITTED
go
BEGIN TRAN
   insert into dbo.InMemTab(Name, City, State, LastModified)
     values ('Mary', 'Boston', 'MA', GETDATE());
   SELECT * FROM InMemTab
COMMIT TRAN
GO


(1 row(s) affected)
ID     Name  City        State LastModified
-----  ----- ----------- ----- --------------------------
8      Tom   Baltimore   MD    2015-03-29 13:51:38.0170000
10     Sue   Buffalo     NY    2015-03-29 13:53:42.0430000
11     Mary  Boston      MA    2015-03-29 13:56:19.4000000
(3 row(s) affected)
```

This database option reduces the need to modify existing SQL code to explicitly specify a transaction isolation level for queries against memory-optimized tables.

> **NOTE**
>
> The MEMORY_OPTIMIZED_ELEVATE_TO_SNAPSHOT is not visible or settable within SSMS. It can only be set via the ALTER DATABASE command as shown in the preceding examples. To determine if the option is enabled for a specific database, you can run either of the following queries:

```
SELECT is_memory_optimized_elevate_to_snapshot_on
    FROM sys.databases
    WHERE name = 'AdventureWorks2012'

SELECT DATABASEPROPERTYEX('AdventureWorks2012',
                'IsMemoryOptimizedElevateToSnapshotEnabled');
```

Cross-Container Transactions

As you've seen in the preceding examples, when you execute interpreted T-SQL against memory-optimized tables, you need to specify the transaction isolation level either via a table hint or using the MEMORY_OPTIMIZED_ELEVATE_TO_SNAPSHOT hint. Any transactions you execute from interpreted T-SQL that access both disk-based and memory-optimized tables are referred to as cross-container transactions.

There are strict rules that govern which isolation level combinations are allowed when invoking cross-container transactions to assure that SQL Server can guarantee transactional consistency. The isolation levels that can be used with your memory-optimized tables in a cross-container transaction depend on what isolation level the transaction has defined for the SQL Server transaction. Most of the restrictions have to do with the fact that operations on disk-based tables and operations on memory-optimized tables each have their own transaction sequence number, even if they are accessed in the same T-SQL transaction. You can think of this behavior as having two sub-transactions within the larger transaction: one sub-transaction for the disk-based tables and one for the memory-optimized tables.

Table 33.2 lists the isolation levels that can be used together in cross-container transactions.

TABLE 33.2   Compatible Isolation Levels in Cross-Container Transactions

Disk-based Tables	Memory-Optimized Tables	Recommendations
READ COMMITTED	SNAPSHOT	This is the default combination and should be used for most situations
READ COMMITTED	REPEATABLE READ/ SERIALIZABLE	Use this combination during data migration and for memory-optimized table access in interop mode only
REPEATABLE READ/ SERIALIZABLE	SNAPSHOT	Use this combination during migration when no concurrent write operations are being performed on the memory-optimized tables
SNAPSHOT		Not supported
REPEATABLE READ/ SERIALIZABLE	REPEATABLE READ/ SERIALIZABLE	Not supported

Monitoring Transactions on Memory-Optimized Tables

Since transactions on memory-optimized tables are handled separately from transactions on disk-based tables, the standard DMVs for monitoring transactions don't provide information on memory-optimized table transactions. SQL Server 2014 provides the new `sys.dm_db_xtp_transactions` DMV for monitoring in-progress transactions on memory-optimized tables.

```
SELECT xtp_transaction_id ,
       transaction_id ,
       session_id ,
       begin_tsn ,
       end_tsn ,
       state_desc
   FROM sys.dm_db_xtp_transactions
   WHERE transaction_id > 0;
go


/* sample output
xtp_transaction_id transaction_id session_id begin_tsn end_tsn state_desc
------------------ -------------- ---------- --------- ------- ----------
85261              1730680        58         37        0       ACTIVE
85265              1731055        60         37        0       ACTIVE
*/
```

Let's examine some of the values in this output.

The `xtp_transaction_id` values are generated by the Transaction-ID counter and are consecutive. This is the value that SQL Server inserts into End-Ts for rows that an active transaction is deleting, and into Begin-Ts for rows that an active transaction is inserting. The `begin_tsn` value is the same for both. This is the current timestamp for the last committed transaction at the time the transaction started. The `end_tsn` timestamp is 0 for both transactions since they are both still active.

Logging, Checkpoint, and Recovery for In-Memory OLTP

Any data modifications on durable, memory-optimized tables (those created with `durability = schema_and_data`) are logged in the database transaction log to guarantee recovery of the tables to a known state after a system shutdown or failure. However, logging for memory-optimized tables is done differently than for disk-based tables.

In addition to writing log records for durable memory-optimized tables to disk, In-Memory OTLP also invokes a checkpoint process to write data for the tables to durable storage as well. SQL Server writes these pieces of information using log streams and checkpoint streams.

Log streams contain the changes made by committed transactions logged as insertion and deletion of row versions and are stored in the SQL Server transaction log.

Checkpoint streams come in two varieties, data streams and delta streams. Data streams contain all versions inserted during a timestamp interval. Delta streams are associated with a particular data stream and contain a list of integers indicating which versions in its corresponding data stream have been deleted. Checkpoint streams are stored in SQL Server filestream files which in essence are sequential files fully managed by SQL Server.

Transaction Logging

In-Memory OLTP's transaction logging is optimized for scalability and high performance through the use of reduced logging. Given the same workload, In-Memory OLTP will write significantly fewer log records for a memory-optimized table than for an equivalent disk-based table.

As described in the previous section, In-Memory OLTP does not use write-ahead logging as it does for disk-based tables. It only generates and saves log records at the time of the transaction commit rather than during each row operation. Since no "dirty data" from uncommitted transactions is ever written to disk, there's also no need to write any undo records to the transaction log since In-Memory OLTP won't ever need to rollback any uncommitted changes.

In addition, if you remember from the previous description of memory-optimized indexes, the indexes on memory-optimized tables are memory resident only. In-Memory OLTP doesn't write any index modifications to the transaction log either.

A third mechanism to reduce logging overhead for memory-optimized tables is to group multiple changes into one large log record (the max log records size in SQL Server 2014 is 24KB). Combining multiple log records into larger log records results in a fewer number of log records being written which minimizes the log-header overhead and helps reduce the contention for inserting into the log-buffer.

Checkpoint

If the transaction log was never truncated, all the changes that happened to your memory-optimized tables could be reconstructed from the transactions recorded in the log. However, this is not a feasible approach as the recovery time would be unacceptably long. Just as for operations on disk-based tables, one of the main reasons for checkpoint operations is to reduce recovery time. For In-Memory OLTP, the checkpoint process for memory-optimized tables is designed to satisfy two important requirements.

- ▶ **Continuous Checkpointing**—Checkpoint operations occur incrementally and continuously as transactional activity accumulates. A background process continuously scans transaction log records and writes to the data and delta files on disk.

- ▶ **Streaming I/O**—Writing to the data and delta files is done in an append-only manner by appending newly created rows to the end of the current data file and by appending the deleted rows to the corresponding delta file.

Checkpointing is the continuous background process of constructing data files and delta files and writing to them from the transaction log.

A checkpoint data file contains rows from one or more memory-optimized tables inserted by multiple transactions as part of INSERT or UPDATE operations. Multiple data files are created with each file covering a specific timestamp range. Each data file can be up to a maximum of 128MB in size (16MB for systems with 16GB or less of memory).

Once a data file is full, the rows inserted by new transactions are stored in another data file. Over time, the rows from durable memory-optimized tables are stored across one or more data files with each data file containing rows with a commit timestamp within the range of transaction timestamps contained in the file. For example a data file with transaction commit timestamps in the range of (100, 200) has all the rows inserted by transactions that have commit timestamps in this range.

Data files are append-only while they are open and are written to using sequential filestream I/O. Once data files are closed, they are strictly read-only. At recovery time the valid versions stored in the data files are reloaded into memory and reindexed.

When a row is deleted or updated by a future transaction, the row is not removed or changed in-place in the data file. Instead, the deleted rows are tracked in another type of 'delta' file. This eliminates random I/O on the data file. Each data file is paired with a corresponding delta file.

A delta file stores information about which rows contained in a data file have been subsequently deleted. There is a 1:1 correspondence between delta files and data files and the delta file has the same transaction range as its corresponding data file. Like data files, the delta file is written to using sequential filestream I/O. Delta files are append-only for the lifetime of the data file they correspond to. At recovery time, the delta file is used as a filter to avoid reloading deleted versions into memory. Because each data file is paired with exactly one delta file, the smallest unit of work for recovery is a single data/delta file pair. This allows the recovery process to be highly parallelizable.

A data and delta file pair is referred to as a Checkpoint File Pair (CFP). A maximum of 8192 CFPs are supported for each database.

Checkpoint Events

The data and delta files are written to continuously by the checkpoint background process. While the file is open, it has a state of UNDER CONSTRUCTION. When a checkpoint event occurs, the files UNDER CONSTRUCTION are closed and the state is set to ACTIVE. From this point, the new INSERTs will no longer be written to, but they are still ACTIVE since they are still subject to DELETE and UPDATE operations which will mark any corresponding rows in the data file as deleted in the associated delta file.

Checkpoint events for memory-optimized tables are independent of checkpoints for disk-based tables. Checkpoints for disk-based tables are generated based upon the configured recovery interval and involve flushing all "dirty pages" from the buffer pool to disk. A complete checkpoint of memory-optimized tables consists of multiple data and delta files, plus a checkpoint file inventory that contains references to all the data and delta files that make up a complete checkpoint.

The completion of a checkpoint involves flushing the latest content of data and delta files to disk and constructing the checkpoint inventory which is written to the transaction log. Checkpoint events are generated either automatically or manually.

An automatic checkpoint occurs when the overall size of the transaction log has grown by 512MB since the last checkpoint. This includes operations logged for disk-based tables as well. It is not dependent on the amount of work done on memory-optimized tables. It's conceivable that there may not have been any transactions on memory-optimized tables when an automatic checkpoint event occurs.

Manual checkpoints occur whenever an explicit CHECKPOINT command is initiated in the database and includes checkpoint operations for both disk-based tables and memory-optimized tables.

33

> **NOTE**
>
> Even though In-Memory OLTP checkpoints are a separate process from disk-based checkpoints, it still has its own log truncation LSN which can prevent the transaction log from being truncated if an In-Memory OLTP checkpoint hasn't occurred in a while.

Merging Checkpoint Files

The number of checkpoint files can continue to accumulate. As data modifications proceed, a "deleted" row remains in the data file but the delta file records the fact that it was deleted. Over time, the percentage of meaningful content in older data files falls, due to DELETES and UPDATES.

Since the recovery process reads the content of all data and delta files, recovery times will increase as it has to scan through a large number of files containing few relevant rows. To reduce the number of CFPs, SQL Server will eventually merge adjacent data files, so that rows marked as deleted actually get deleted from the checkpoint data file, and create a new CFP from the merged data files.

A background task runs periodically to examine all ACTIVE CFPs to determine if any adjacent sets of CFPs qualify to be merged. Files can be merged when the percentage of undeleted rows falls below a threshold. The main qualification must be that the merged files will result in a file of undeleted records that is 128MB or less in size (or 16MB for systems with 16GB of memory or less). Merging can also occur if two adjacent files are both less them 50% full (possibly as the result of a manual checkpoint having been run).

In most cases, automatic merging of checkpoint files will be sufficient to keep the number of files manageable. However, in rare situations or for testing purposes, you can manually initiate a checkpoint merge using the sp_xtp_merge_checkpoint_files stored procedure. To identify files that might be eligible for merge, you can examine the information returned by a query against the sys.dm_db_xtp_checkpoint_files DMV:

```
select file_type_desc,
       state_desc,
       lower_bound_tsn,
       upper_bound_tsn,
       file_size_in_bytes,
       file_size_used_in_bytes
 from sys.dm_db_xtp_checkpoint_files
 WHERE state_desc = 'ACTIVE'
```

Checkpoint Garbage Collection

At a certain point when the rows in a CFP are no longer needed (e.g., the oldest transaction still required by SQL Server is more recent than the time range covered by the CFP), the CFP will transition into a non-active state. This usually occurs when the log truncation point required for recovery is more recent than the largest transaction ID in the CFP transaction ID range.

Assuming a log backup has occurred, these CFPs are no longer required and can be removed by the checkpoint file garbage collection process which is a background process that runs automatically.

Recovery

The basic mechanism to recover or restore a database with memory-optimized tables is similar to the recovery process of databases with only disk-based tables. However, recovery of memory-optimized tables also includes the step of loading the memory-optimized tables into memory before the database is available for user access.

When SQL Server restarts, each database goes through a recovery process that consists of three phases:

1. The analysis phase.

2. The redo phase.

3. The undo phase.

During the analysis phase, the In-Memory OLTP engine identifies the checkpoint inventory to load and preloads its system table log entries. It will also process some file allocation log records.

During the redo phase, for memory-optimized tables, data from the data and delta file pairs are loaded into memory and then the data is updated from the active transaction log based on the last durable checkpoint and the in-memory tables are populated and indexes rebuilt. During the redo phase, disk-based and memory-optimized table recovery runs concurrently.

The undo phase is not needed for memory-optimized tables since In-Memory OLTP doesn't record any uncommitted transactions for memory-optimized tables.

When the above operations are completed for both disk-based and memory-optimized tables, the database is available for access.

Since loading memory-optimized tables into memory can increase recovery time, the In-Memory OLTP engine attempts to improve the load time of memory-optimized data from data and delta files by loading the data/delta files in parallel. It does this by first creating a Delta Map Filter. One thread per container reads the delta files and creates a delta map filter. Once the delta-map filter is created, data files are read using as many threads as there are logical CPUs. Each thread reading the data file reads the data rows and checks it against the associated delta map and only inserts the row into table if this row has not been marked deleted.

Managing Memory for In-Memory OLTP

When running In-Memory OLTP, SQL Server will need to be configured with sufficient memory to hold all your memory-optimized tables. If available memory is insufficient transactions will fail at run-time during any operations that require additional memory. Normally this would happen during INSERT or UPDATE operations, but could also happen for DELETE operations on a memory-optimized nonclustered index if the DELETE generates a page merge operation which, if you recall from the discussion previously in this chapter, requires allocating additional pages.

If the system runs out of memory during memory-optimized table transactions and you cannot add more memory to the SQL Server instance, you may have to drop some of your less critical memory-optimized tables to free up memory space.

A general rule of thumb is that you should have at least two times the amount of memory that you estimate the data itself will require. Beyond that, the total memory requirement depends on your workload profile. If there are a lot of data modifications generated by your OLTP operations, you'll need more memory for the row versions than if you're primarily performing reads of your memory-optimized tables. The current maximum amount of memory available for memory-optimized tables is 256GB.

To estimate the amount of memory for a memory-optimized table's rows, consider that the memory-optimized table is comprised of three components:

▶ The Row header/timestamps which is 24 bytes in size

▶ **Index pointers**—Each row includes one 8-byte pointer to the next row in the table for each index. The space required per row is the number of hash indexes times 8 bytes.

▶ **Data**—The size of the data portion of the row is determined by adding up the number of bytes for each data column. If any columns are variable length, use the max size in your calculations.

The total row size is the sum of the size of all three components. Assume that you'll be storing 1 million rows in your memory-optimized table and it has 2 hash indexes and the sum of the data column size is 200 bytes. The total space required for the data itself would be:

24 bytes

+ 16 bytes (2 index pointers @ 8 bytes each)

+ 200 bytes

= 240 bytes per row

From the above calculations, the size of each row in the memory-optimized table is 240 bytes. If the table held 1 million rows, the table will consume 1,000,000 * 240 bytes, or 240,000,000 bytes—approximately 240MB.

Estimating memory requirements for hash indexes is pretty straightforward. Each bucket requires 8 bytes, so you can just estimate the number of hash buckets you need and multiply it by 8 bytes.

The size for your memory-optimized nonclustered indexes depends on both the size of the index key and the number of rows in the table. You can assume each index row is 8 bytes plus the size of the index key (assume N bytes), so the maximum number of rows that fit on a page would be 8176/(N+8). Divide that result into the expected number of rows to get an initial estimate.

After calculating all of the above, multiply it by 2 to ensure you have enough space for data growth as well as for row versioning.

Monitoring Memory Usage

To keep an eye on your memory usage by memory-optimized tables and their indexes, SSMS provides a new report, Memory Usage by Memory-Optimized Objects. To bring up this report, right click on the database, select Reports, select Standard, and click on Memory Usage By Memory-Optimized Objects. This will bring up a report like that shown in Figure 33.15.

Alternatively, you can also get information on the memory usage of your memory-optimized tables by running a query against the sys.dm_db_xtp_table_memory_stats DMV:

```
SELECT CAST(OBJECT_NAME(object_id) AS varchar(24)) AS tablename,
       memory_allocated_for_table_kb AS table_alloc_kb,
       memory_used_by_table_kb AS table_used_kb,
       memory_allocated_for_indexes_kb AS idx_alloc_kb,
       memory_used_by_indexes_kb as idx_used_kb
FROM sys.dm_db_xtp_table_memory_stats
WHERE object_id > 0
GO

/*output
```

```
tablename                 table_alloc_kb table_used_kb idx_alloc_kb idx_used_kb
------------------------- -------------- ------------- ------------ -----------
salesorderdetail_newce    16945          15797         2048         2048
*/
```

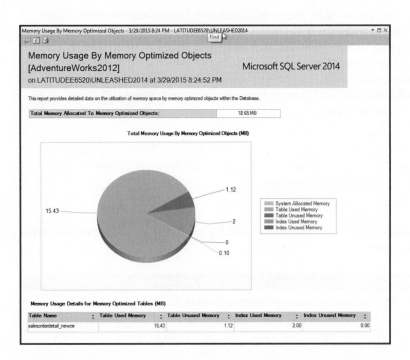

FIGURE 33.15   Memory Usage By Memory-Optimized Objects Report.

Managing Memory with the Resource Governor

In SQL Server 2014, you can use the Resource Governor to manage the amount of memory available for in-memory databases and objects. You can bind a database with memory-optimized table(s) databases to a resource pool, assign the desired amount of memory to the pool and that will be the maximum amount of memory available to memory-optimized objects in that database.

The first step is to create a resource pool for the In-Memory OLTP database, specifying a MIN_MEMORY_PERCENT and MAX_MEMORY_PERCENT of the same value. This will ensure that this fixed percentage of available memory is always available for the In-Memory OLTP database.

```
CREATE RESOURCE POOL InMemPool
    WITH (MIN_MEMORY_PERCENT = 50, MAX_MEMORY_PERCENT = 50);
ALTER RESOURCE GOVERNOR RECONFIGURE;
```

Next, bind the databases to the resource pool you just created, using the procedure sp_xtp_bind_db_resource_pool.

```
EXEC sp_xtp_bind_db_resource_pool 'AdventureWorks2012', 'InMemPool';
```

You should see a message returned by the above command to take the database offline and bring it back online in order for it to begin using the resource pool. SQL Server assigns memory to a resource pool as it is allocated, so simply associating a database with a pool will not transfer the assignment of any memory already allocated via the previous pool (which is probably the default pool). In order to activate the binding to the new pool, you need to take the database offline and bring it back online (after making sure there are not user sessions active in the database.

```
USE master
GO
ALTER DATABASE [AdventureWorks2012] SET OFFLINE WITH ROLLBACK IMMEDIATE;
ALTER DATABASE [AdventureWorks2012] SET ONLINE;
GO
```

As SQL Server reads data into the memory-optimized tables, it will associate the memory with the new resource pool.

> **NOTE**
>
> For more information on configuring resource pools and using Resource Governor, see Chapter 41, "Managing Workloads with the Resource Governor."

Backup and Recovery of Memory-Optimized Databases

Memory-optimized tables are backed up as part of regular database backups. A full backup of a database with one or more memory-optimized tables consists of the allocated storage for disk-based tables (if any), the active transaction log, and the data and delta file pairs (CPFs) for memory-optimized tables. It's important to keep in mind that the storage used by the CPFs for memory-optimized tables can be much larger than its size in memory, and it affects the size of the database backup.

For databases where the activity on the memory-optimized tables is primarily inserts, most of the memory-optimized tables data files will be in the Active state, fully loaded, and with very few deleted rows. The size of the database backup will be close to the size of data in memory.

For databases with frequent insert, delete, and update operations, each of the checkpoint file pairs in the worst case scenario could be only 50% loaded, after accounting for the deleted rows. The size of the database backup could be at least 2 times the size of data in memory. Additionally, there will likely be few checkpoint file pairs in states "Merge source" and "Required for backup/high availability" that will add to the size of database backup.

Differential backups are also allowed with databases containing memory-optimized tables. Differential backup of a database with memory-optimized tables contains the differential backup for filegroups storing disk-based tables plus the active transaction log. For a memory-optimized data filegroup, the differential backup uses the same algorithm as full database backup to identify the data and delta files for backup but it includes only memory-optimized table data files if they've been closed since the last full database backup. All delta files are still included since a delta file can be modified anytime in its lifetime.

If memory-optimized tables are a significant portion of your database size, the differential backup can be significantly smaller than a full backup.

Migrating to In-Memory OLTP

In-Memory OLTP is not necessarily a solution for every type of relational database performance problem. So when should you, or should you not, consider implementing In-Memory OLTP and what tables would make good candidates? The following scenarios are situations where you might be able to take advantage of the benefits of In-Memory OLTP.

▶ Applications that are incurring high lock/latch contention can alleviate this contention by converting the tables where the contention is occurring from disk-based tables to memory-optimized tables.

▶ Applications that are incurring high I/O and logging latency—In-Memory OLTP can help alleviate the excessive disk writes since most operations are in memory, index updates are not written to disk, and logging and checkpoint operations are streamlined to reduce I/O.

▶ Assuming that the business logic can be natively compiled, moving the data memory-optimized tables and the T-SQL code to natively compiled stored procedures may reduce the response times associated with poor performing procedures and reduce latency.

▶ Operations that require only read access to data that are suffering from CPU performance bottlenecks. Moving the data to In-Memory OLTP, it may be possible to significantly reduce CPU allowing you to achieve higher throughput.

▶ If you perform ETL with data-staging and load phases with numerous operations that need to be completed, including uploading data to staging tables in SQL Server, modifying the data, and then transferring the data to a target table, these types of operations can benefit significantly from using nondurable memory-optimized tables. The non-durable memory-optimized tables provide an efficient way to store staging data by completely eliminating physical storage cost as well as transactional logging.

Applications that would be unsuitable for migration to In-Memory OLTP include:

▶ Applications that require table features that are not supported by memory-optimized tables or if the application code for accessing and manipulating the table data uses constructs not supported for natively compiled procedures.

▶ When the size of the tables exceeds what SQL Server In-Memory OLTP or a particular machine supports, you would not be able to have all the required data in memory. You could try setting it up to have only some memory-optimized tables and some disk-based tables, but you'll need to analyze the workload carefully to identify those tables that will benefit most from migration to memory-optimized tables.

▶ Applications that are not primarily OLTP workload oriented. In-Memory OLTP, as the name implies, was designed to be of most benefit to OLTP operations. You may experience improvements for other types of processing, such as reporting and data warehousing, but those are not the design goals of this feature. You should carefully test all operations to verify that In-Memory OLTP provides measurable improvements.

▶ Applications that are highly dependent on the current locking behavior provided by pessimistic concurrency on disk-based tables. For example, an application might use the READPAST hint to manage work queues, which requires SQL Server to use locks in order to find the next row in the queue to process.

To help you determine the suitability of migrating your existing databases, tables, or store procedures to In-Memory OLTP, SQL Server provides a number of tools to aid in the assessment.

Using the AMR Tool

Before migrating any tables or stored procedures to use In-Memory OLTP, you ideally should perform a thorough analysis of your current workload to establish a baseline and identify if the system is a candidate for migration to In-Memory OLTP. SQL Server 2014 provides a tool called Analysis, Migration and Reporting (AMR), to assist with the performance analysis prior to migrating to In-Memory OLTP.

If you chose to install the complete set of management tools during the installation process, the AMR tool will be included. You can use this tool to analyze your workload and provide recommendations on the tables and procedures that may benefit most from migrating to In-Memory OLTP.

AMR uses information collected by the Transaction Performance Collection Sets in the Management Data Warehouse (MDW) to produce a Transaction Performance Analysis Overview. After running a representative workload, or using the data collector to gather performance statistics on your production system, you can review the Transaction Performance Analysis Overview reports. To bring up the AMR reports, right click on your

Management Data Warehouse database, select the "Report" item from the drop down menu, then select the "Management Data Warehouse" from the Report submenu, and then finally click on the "Transaction Performance Analysis Overview."

One of the reports available is the table usage analysis report which provides information on which tables are prime candidates for conversion to memory-optimized tables, as well as providing an estimate of the size of the effort required to perform the conversion, based on how many unsupported features the table concurrently uses. For example, it will point out unsupported data types and constraints used in the table. Another report will contain recommendations on which procedures might benefit from being converted to natively compiled procedures for use with memory-optimized tables.

Based on recommendations from the MDW reports, you can start looking into converting some of the recommended tables into memory-optimized tables. It is recommended that you start one at a time, starting with the ones indicated by the report that would benefit most from being converted to memory-optimized tables. If you start seeing benefits from the conversion, you can continue to convert more of your tables. Initially, it's recommended that you continue accessing the memory-optimized tables using your normal T-SQL interface to minimize application changes. Once the appropriate tables have been converted, you can then start planning a rewrite of the code into natively compiled stored procedures, again starting with the ones that the MDW reports indicate would provide the most benefit.

To assist in converting the tables and stored procedures, SQL Server 2014 provides two other tools, the Table Memory Optimization Advisor and the Native Compilation Advisor. The Native Compilation Advisor was discussed previously in the section on natively compiled stored procedures and provided some sample screen shots. Let's take a look at the Table Memory Optimization Advisor.

Using the Table Memory Optimization Advisor to Migrate Disk-Based Tables

After identifying one or more tables as candidates for conversion to memory-optimized tables, you can use the Table Memory Optimization Advisor to help migrate specific disk-based tables to memory-optimized tables.

The Memory Optimization Advisor can be launched by right-clicking the table in SSMS and then choosing the Memory Optimization Advisor option from the menu. The Memory Optimization Advisor is a wizard that walks you through various validation tests and provides migration warnings of potential issues with the table and/or indexes if you were to convert the table to a memory-optimized table. For example, Figure 33.16 shows the Migration Validation page for the SalesOrderDetail table in the AdventureWorks2012 database. As you can see, the SalesOrderDetail table contains a number of features which are not compatible with memory-optimized tables and the buttons to continue the process are grayed out.

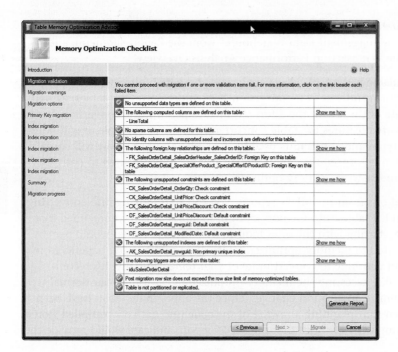

FIGURE 33.16   Memory Optimization Advisor Validation of `SalesOrderDetail` table.

If the table is a valid candidate for converting to a memory-optimized table, the wizard will walk you through the migration steps prompting for information to set up the memory-optimized table, such as selecting which memory-optimized filegroup to use, the logical file name and file path, the data durability option, the name to use to rename the original table, whether to copy the current table data to the new table, what column to define as the primary key, and whether to migrate any other existing indexes. When defining the indexes, if you are defining any as hash indexes, the wizard will recommend a hash bucket count based upon the table contents (you can override the hash bucket values if you disagree with the recommendation). The wizard also provides an estimate of the current memory cost of the table.

At the end of the wizard, you'll be presented with a summary screen to verify the migration options and actions (see Figure 33.17). You also have the option on this screen to generate a script of the actions to be performed if you prefer to save the script and run it yourself. Otherwise you can click the migrate button and let the Table Memory Optimization Advisor perform the migration which you can monitor in the Migration progress page.

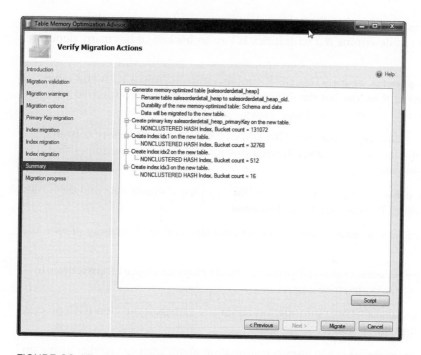

FIGURE 33.17   Memory Optimization Advisor Validation of `SalesOrderDetail` table.

Dynamic Management Views for In-Memory OLTP

The introduction of In-Memory OLTP in SQL Server 2014 brings with it a number of new DMVs that provide information about the In-Memory OLTP engine and memory-optimized tables and indexes. Each of these new DMVs and functions that contain "xtp" (an acronym of eXtreme Transaction Processing) in its name refers to the In-Memory OLTP Engine.

There are two types of In-Memory OLTP Dynamic Management Views. The Database specific DMVs provide information and statistics for the current database and start with "`sys.dm_db_xtp_`". Instance specific DMVs return information and statistics concerning the entire In-Memory OLTP Engine of the instance and start with "`sys.dm_xtp_`".

A number of the new DMVs have been presented previously in various sections in this chapter. The following is a complete list of the DMVs with a brief description of them:

- ▶ `sys.dm_db_xtp_checkpoint_stats`—Shows checkpoint statistics of the current database.

- ▶ `sys.dm_db_xtp_checkpoint_files`—This DMV shows information about checkpoint files, like the type of file (DATA or DELTA files), its size, and relative path.

- ▶ `sys.dm_db_xtp_gc_cycle_stats`—Shows garbage collection cycles for the current database.

▶ `sys.dm_db_xtp_hash_index_stats`—This DMV is very useful to deal with hash indexes. You can determine if a hash index is low on buckets or has many duplicate keys.

▶ `sys.dm_db_xtp_index_stats`—This DMV contains statistics about hash and range indexes collected since the last database restart. It is the memory-optimized tables equivalent to `sys.dm_db_index_usage_stats`.

▶ `sys.dm_db_xtp_memory_consumers`—This DMV reports stats for memory consumers of the current database. The view returns a row for each memory consumer that the database engine uses.

▶ `sys.dm_db_xtp_merge_requests`—Use this DMV to view status of data and delta files' merge operations, both automatic and manual.

▶ `sys.dm_db_xtp_table_memory_stats`—Shows allocated and used memory of user and system tables.

▶ `sys.dm_db_xtp_transactions`—Displays information about current transactions in the In-Memory OLTP database engine.

▶ `sys.dm_xtp_gc_stats`—Gives information about the garbage-collection (GC) process on memory-optimized tables.

▶ `sys.dm_xtp_gc_queue_stats`—Outputs information about each GC worker queue on the server, and various statistics about each.

▶ `sys.dm_xtp_system_memory_consumers`—Reports information on system level memory consumers for In-Memory OLTP.

▶ `sys.dm_xtp_transaction_stats`—Reports statistics about transactions that have run since the server started.

In addition to the above listed DMVs, there are also a few useful undocumented DMVs related to In-Memory OLTP:

▶ `sys.dm_db_xtp_nonclustered_index_stats`—Displays statistics on range indexes in memory-optimized tables.

▶ `sys.dm_db_xtp_object_stats`—Reports row insert, update, and delete attempts in memory-optimized tables.

▶ `sys.dm_xtp_threads`—Shows information about In-Memory OLTP threads like Base Address and thread type.

▶ `sys.dm_xtp_transaction_recent_rows`—As its name says, returns information of recent rows within transactions.

▶ `sys.fn_dblog_xtp`—Displays transaction log information similar to `sys.fn_dblog` but with additional In-Memory OLTP related columns.

▶ `sys.fn_dump_dblog_xtp`—Same as above, but also works with backup devices just like `sys.fn_dump_dblog`.

The Buffer Pool Extension

The Buffer Pool Extension feature in SQL Server 2014 is a form of memory optimization, but is separate and distinct from in-memory optimization. With the Buffer Pool Extension feature, SQL Server provides the SQL Server instance the ability to use locally attached solid-state drives (SSD) as non-volatile random access memory for buffering. This is a server-level configuration setting that allows a buffer pool to be extended beyond available physical RAM in the server to accommodate larger OLTP workloads. This helps to resolve I/O bottlenecks while improving overall I/O throughput, due to lower latency and better random I/O performance of SSDs. The larger hybrid buffer pool provides improved read performance.

The Buffer Pool Extension guarantees no risk of data loss, as it only holds clean pages (i.e., no pages with uncommitted modifications are stored in the Buffer Pool Extension).

With the Buffer Pool Extension, a file residing on SSD storage is used as an extension to the memory subsystem rather than the disk storage subsystem. When implementing the Buffer Pool Extension, it creates a multilevel caching hierarchy with level 1 (L1) as the DRAM and level 2 (L2) as the Buffer Pool Extension file on the SSD. Only clean pages are written to the L2 cache, which helps maintain data safety. The buffer manager automatically handles the movement of clean pages between the L1 and L2 caches.

The following is the syntax for enabling/disabling the Buffer Pool Extension feature in a SQL Server instance:

```
ALTER SERVER CONFIGURATION
 SET Buffer Pool Extension
 { ON ( FILENAME = 'os_file_path_and_name'
     ,SIZE = <size> [ KB | MB | GB ] )
 | OFF }
```

When running the ALTER SERVER CONFIGURATION command to create the Buffer Pool Extension, you specify the size and file path of the buffer pool caching file on the SSD. This file is a contiguous extent of storage on the SSD and is statically configured during startup of the instance of SQL Server. You also specify the size of the Buffer Pool Extension, which can be up to 32 times the value of max_server_memory.

> **NOTE**
>
> When implementing the Buffer Pool Extension feature, it's critical for performance reasons to make sure the file you are creating for the Buffer Pool Extension is on a **locally** attached SSD drive that is preferably dedicated for use only by the Buffer Pool Extension. You will likely not see much performance benefit from putting the Buffer Pool Extension file on a non-SSD drive or a drive residing in a SAN, nor if there is a lot of I/O activity on the SSD drive by other processes unrelated to use by the Buffer Pool Extension.

If you wish to modify any of the properties of the Buffer Pool Extension, you must first disable it. When the Buffer Pool Extension is disabled, all related configuration settings are removed from the registry. Additionally, the Buffer Pool Extension file is deleted upon shutdown of the instance of SQL Server.

To view the current Buffer Pool Extension configuration settings, you can query the `sys.dm_os_buffer_pool_extension_configuration` DMV.

> **NOTE**
>
> The Buffer Pool Extension feature is only supported on 64-bit Enterprise, Developer, or Evaluation editions of SQL Server 2014.

Summary

In-Memory OLTP and memory-optimized tables are exciting new features in SQL Server 2014. It is poised to be a game changer for OTLP based applications. However, it's important to understand it's not the solution for every OLTP application experiencing performance issues. The information in this chapter should help you understand what in-memory optimization is and how to implement it successfully to realize the significant performance gains it can provide.

This chapter also introduced the Buffer Pool Extension, a feature that you can implement to provide additional buffer pool space from attached SSD drives beyond the available physical RAM in SQL Server. This feature can help to resolve I/O bottlenecks while improving overall I/O throughput, due to lower latency and better random I/O performance of SSDs over standard disk drives.

The next chapter, "Understanding Query Optimization," takes a deeper dive into understanding SQL Server performance by providing an in-depth discussion on how SQL Server evaluates your queries to develop an optimal query plan for processing your queries.

Understanding Query Optimization

Query optimization is the process SQL Server goes through to analyze individual queries and determine the best way to process them. To achieve this end, SQL Server uses a cost-based Query Optimizer. As a cost-based Query Optimizer, its purpose is to determine the query plan that will access the data with the least amount of processing time in terms of CPU and logical and physical I/O. The Query Optimizer examines the parsed SQL queries and, based on information about the objects involved (for example, number of pages in the table, types of indexes defined, index statistics), generates a query plan. The query plan is the set of steps to be carried out to execute the query.

To allow the Query Optimizer to do its job properly, you need to have a good understanding of how the Query Optimizer determines query plans for queries. This knowledge will help you to understand what types of queries can be optimized effectively and to learn techniques to help the Query Optimizer choose the best query plan. This knowledge will help you write better queries, choose better indexes, and detect potential performance problems.

NOTE

To better understand the concepts presented in this chapter, you should have a reasonable understanding of how data structures and indexes affect performance. If you haven't already read Chapters 31, "Understanding SQL Server Data Structures" and 32, "Indexes and Performance," it is recommended that you review them now.

> **NOTE**
>
> Occasionally throughout this chapter, graphical execution plans are used to illustrate some of the principles discussed. Chapter 36, "Query Analysis," provides a more detailed discussion of the graphical execution plan output and describes the information contained in the execution plans and how to interpret it. In this chapter, the execution plans are provided primarily to give you an idea of what you can expect to see for the different types of queries presented when you are doing your own query analysis.

What's New in Query Optimization

New in SQL Server 2014 is the redesign of Cardinality Estimator. The Cardinality Estimator is the component that predicts the final row count and row counts of intermediate results (such as joins, filtering, and aggregation) for your queries. These estimates have a direct impact on the query plan choices made by the query optimizer such as join order, join type, etc. The updated Cardinality Estimator is designed to improve the quality of query plans and ostensibly, query performance. This is the first real update to the Cardinality Estimator since SQL Server 7.0.

The new Cardinality Estimator logic is based on in-depth cardinality estimation research on modern workloads and Microsoft learnings over the past 15 years and is the first, significant redesign of the SQL Server Query Optimizer cardinality estimation component since SQL Server 7.0. The new Cardinality Estimator incorporates assumptions and algorithms that work well on modern OLTP and data warehousing workloads. However, the Cardinality Estimator logic is complex and proprietary and an exhaustive list of all changes has not been documented. Some of the changes are highlighted in this chapter in the section "Row Estimation and Index Selection."

> **NOTE**
>
> Many of the internals of the Query Optimizer and its costing algorithms are considered proprietary and have not been made public. Much of the information provided here is based on analysis and observation of query plans generated for various queries and search values.
>
> The intent of this chapter is therefore not so much to describe the specific steps, algorithms, and calculations implemented by the Query Optimizer, but rather to provide a general overview of the query optimization process in SQL Server 2014 and what goes into estimating and determining an efficient query plan. Also, there are a number of possible ways SQL Server can optimize and process queries. The examples presented in this chapter focus on some of the more common optimization strategies.

What Is the Query Optimizer?

For any given SQL statement, the source tables can be accessed in many ways to return the desired result set. The Query Optimizer analyzes all the possible ways the result set can be generated and chooses the most appropriate method, called the *query plan* or *execution plan.* SQL Server uses a cost-based Query Optimizer. The Query Optimizer assigns a cost to every possible execution plan in terms of CPU resource usage and page I/O. The Query Optimizer then chooses the execution plan with the lowest associated cost.

Thus, the primary goal of the Query Optimizer is to find the least expensive execution plan that minimizes the total time required to process a query. Because I/O is the most significant factor in query processing time, the Query Optimizer analyzes the query and primarily searches for access paths and techniques to minimize the number of logical and physical page accesses as much as possible. The lower the number of logical and physical I/Os performed, the faster the query should run.

The process of query optimization in SQL Server is extremely complicated and is based on sophisticated costing models and data access algorithms. It is beyond the scope of a single chapter to explain in detail all the various costing algorithms that the Query Optimizer currently employs. This chapter is intended to help you better understand some of the concepts related to how the Query Optimizer chooses an execution strategy and provide an overview of the query optimization strategies employed to improve query processing performance.

Query Compilation and Optimization

Query compilation is the complete process from the submission of a query to its actual execution. There are many steps involved in query compilation—one of which is optimization. All T-SQL statements are compiled, but not all are optimized. Primarily, only the standard SQL Data Manipulation Language (DML) statements—SELECT, INSERT, UPDATE, and DELETE—require optimization. The other procedural constructs in T-SQL (IF, WHILE, local variables, and so on) are compiled as procedural logic but do not require optimization. DML statements are set-oriented requests that the Query Optimizer must translate into procedural code that can be executed efficiently to return the desired results.

> **NOTE**
>
> SQL Server also optimizes some Data Definition Language (DDL) statements, such as CREATE INDEX or ALTER TABLE, against the data tables. For example, a displayed query plan for the creation of an index shows optimization steps for accessing the table, sorting data, and inserting into the index tree. However, the focus in this chapter is on optimization of DML statements.

Compiling DML Statements

When SQL Server compiles an execution plan for a DML statement, it performs the following basic steps:

1. The query is parsed and checked for proper syntax, and the T-SQL statements are parsed into keywords, expressions, operators, and identifiers to generate a query tree. The query tree (sometimes referred to as the *sequence tree*) is an internal format of

the query that SQL Server can operate on. It is essentially the logical steps needed to transform the query into the desired result.

2. The query tree is then normalized and simplified. During normalization, the tables and columns are verified, and the metadata (data types, null properties, index statistics, and so on) about them is retrieved. In addition, any views are resolved to their underlying tables, and implicit conversions are performed (for example, an integer compared with a float value). Also during this phase, any redundant operations (for example, unnecessary or redundant joins) are removed, and the query tree is simplified.

3. The Query Optimizer analyzes the different ways the source tables can be accessed and selects the series of steps that return the results fastest while typically using the fewest resources. The query tree is updated with the optimized series of steps, and an execution plan (also referred to as query plan) is generated from the final, optimized version of the sequence tree.

4. After the optimized execution plan is generated, SQL Server stores the optimized plan in the plan cache.

5. SQL Server reads the execution plan from the plan cache and executes the query plan, returning the result set (if any) to the client.

The optimized execution plan is then left in the plan cache. If the same query or stored procedure is executed again and the plan is still available in the plan cache, the steps to optimize and generate the execution plan are skipped, and the stored query execution plan is reused to execute the query or stored procedure.

Optimization Steps

When the query tree is passed to the Query Optimizer, the Query Optimizer performs a series of steps to break down the query into its component pieces for analysis to generate an optimal execution plan:

1. **Query analysis**—The query is analyzed to determine search arguments and join clauses. A search argument is defined as a WHERE clause that compares a column to a constant. A join clause is a condition in the WHERE clause or JOIN clause that compares a column from one table to a column from another table.

2. **Row estimation and index selection**—Indexes are selected based on search arguments and join clauses (if any exist). Indexes are evaluated based on their distribution statistics and are assigned a cost.

3. **Join selection**—The join order is evaluated to determine the most appropriate order in which to access tables. In addition, the Query Optimizer evaluates the most appropriate join algorithm to match the data.

4. **Execution plan selection**—Execution costs are evaluated, and a query execution plan is created that represents the most efficient solution found by the optimizer.

The next four sections of this chapter examine each of these steps in more detail.

Query Analysis

The first step in query optimization is to analyze each table in the query to identify all search arguments (SARGs), OR clauses, and join clauses. The SARGs, OR clauses, and join clauses are used in the second step, index selection, to select useful indexes to satisfy a query.

Identifying Search Arguments

A SARG is defined as a WHERE clause that compares a column to a constant. The format of a SARG is as follows:

```
Column operator constant_expression [and...]
```

SARGs provide a way for the Query Optimizer to limit the rows searched to satisfy a query. The general goal is to match a SARG with an index to avoid a table scan. Valid operators for a SARG are =, >, <, >=, and <=, BETWEEN, and LIKE. Multiple SARGs can be combined with the AND clause. (A single index might match some or all of the SARGs ANDed together.) Following are examples of SARGs:

▶ flag = 7

▶ salary > 100000

▶ city = 'Saratoga' and state = 'NY'

▶ price between $10 and $20 (the same as price > = $10 and price <= $20)

▶ 100 between lo_val and hi_val (the same as lo_val <= 100 and hi_val >= 100)

▶ LastName like 'Sm%' (the same as LastName >= 'Sm' and LastName < 'Sn')

In some cases, the column in a SARG might be compared with a constant expression rather than a single constant value. The constant expression can be an arithmetic operation, a built-in function, a string concatenation, a local variable, or a subquery result. As long as the left side of the SARG contains a column, it's considered an optimizable SARG.

Identifying OR Clauses

The next statements the Query Optimizer looks for in the query are OR clauses. OR clauses are SARGable expressions combined with an OR condition rather than an AND condition and are treated differently than standard SARGs. The format of an OR clause is with all columns involved in the OR belonging to the same table.

```
SARG or SARG [or ...]
```

This IN statement

```
column in ( constant1, constant2, ...)
```

is also treated as an OR clause, becoming this:

```
column = constant1 or column = constant2 or ...
```

Some examples of OR clauses are as follows:

```
where LastName = 'Smith'  or FirstName = 'Fred'
where (Name like '%bearing%' and ListPrice > $25)
      or ProductSubcategoryID =  = "1234"
where LastName in ('Smith', 'Jones', 'N/A')
```

An OR clause is a disjunction; all rows matching either of the two criteria appear in the result set. Any row matching both criteria should appear only once.

The main issue is that an OR clause cannot be satisfied by a single index search. Consider the first example just presented:

```
where LastName = 'Smith'  or FirstName = 'Fred'
```

An index on LastName and FirstName helps SQL Server find all the rows where LastName = 'Smith' AND FirstName = 'Fred', but searching the index tree does not help SQL Server efficiently find all the rows where FirstName = 'Fred' and the last name is any value. Unless an index on FirstName exists as well, the only way to find all rows with FirstName = 'Fred' is to search every row in the table or scan every row in a nonclustered index that contains FirstName as a nonleading index key.

An OR clause can typically be resolved by either a table scan or by using the OR strategy. Using a table scan, SQL Server reads every row in the table and applies each OR criteria to each row. Any row that matches any one of the OR criteria is put into the result set.

A table scan is an expensive way to process a query, so the Query Optimizer looks for an alternative for resolving an OR. If an index can be matched against all SARGs involved in the OR clause, SQL Server evaluates the possibility of applying the index union strategy described later in this chapter, in the section, "Using Multiple Indexes."

Identifying Join Clauses

The next type of clause the Query Optimizer looks for during the query analysis phase is the join clause. A join condition is specified in the FROM clause using the JOIN keyword, as follows:

```
FROM table1 JOIN table2  on table1.column = table2.column
```

Alternatively, join conditions can be specified in the WHERE clause using the old-style join syntax, as shown in the following example:

```
Table1.Column Operator Table2.Column
```

A join clause always involves two tables, except in the case of a self-join, but even in a self-join, you must specify the table twice in the query. Here's an example:

```
select employee = e.LastName + ', ' + e.FirstName,
       manager = m.LastName + ', ' + m.FirstName
   from Employees e left outer join Employees m
   on e.ReportsTo = m.EmployeeID
   order by 2, 1
```

SQL Server treats a self-join just like a normal join between two different tables.

In addition to join clauses, the Query Optimizer also looks for subqueries, derived tables, and common table expressions and makes the determination whether they need to be flattened into joins or processed using a different strategy. Subquery optimization is discussed later in this chapter.

Row Estimation and Index Selection

When the query analysis phase of optimization is complete and all SARGs, OR clauses, and join clauses have been identified, the next step is to determine the selectivity of the expressions (that is, the estimated number of matching rows) and to determine the cost of finding the rows. Selectivity is the measure of how selective a predicate is. The Cardinality Estimator (CE) is the component that determines the selectivity of WHERE, JOIN, and HAVING clauses.

The cost of a query is measured primarily in terms of logical and physical I/O, with the goal of generating a query plan that results in the lowest estimated I/O and processing cost. Primarily, the Query Optimizer attempts to identify whether an index exists that can be used to locate the matching rows. If multiple indexes or search strategies can be considered, their costs are compared with each other and also against the cost of a table or clustered index scan to determine the least expensive access method.

An index is typically considered useful for optimizing an expression if the first column in the index is used in the expression and the search argument in the expression provides a means to effectively limit the search. If no useful indexes are found for an expression, typically a table or clustered index scan is performed on the table. A table or clustered index scan is the fallback tactic for the Query Optimizer to use if no lower-cost method exists for returning the matching rows from a table.

Evaluating SARG and Join Selectivity

To determine selectivity of a SARG, which helps in determining the most efficient query plan, the Cardinality Estimator uses the statistical information stored for the index or column, if any. If no statistics are available for a column or index, SQL Server will automatically create statistics on nonindexed columns specified in a SARG if the AUTO_CREATE_STATISTICS option is enabled for the database. SQL Server also automatically generates and updates the statistics for any indexed columns referenced in a SARG if the AUTO_UPDATE_STATISTICS option is enabled. In addition, you can explicitly create statistics for a column or set of columns in a table or an indexed view by using the CREATE STATISTICS command. Both index statistics and column statistics (whether created automatically or manually with the CREATE STATISTICS command) are maintained and kept up-to-date, as needed if the AUTO_UPDATE_STATISTICS option is enabled or if the UPDATE STATISTICS command is explicitly run for a table, index, or column. Available and up-to-date statistics allow the Cardinality Estimator to more accurately determine the selectivity used to assess different query plans and choose a high-quality plan.

If no statistics are available for a column or an index and the AUTO CREATE STATISTICS and AUTO UPDATE STATISTICS options have been disabled for the database or table, SQL Server cannot make an informed estimate of the number of matching rows for a SARG and resorts to using some built-in percentages for the number of matching rows for various types of expressions. The percentages used in SQL Server 2014 when no statistics are available are as follows:

Operator	Row Estimate (n = number of rows in table)
Equality (=)	$n^{.5}$
Closed Range Search (BETWEEN, > AND <, >= AND <=)	$n * .09$
Open Range Search (>, <, >=, <=)	$n * .3$

> **NOTE**
>
> In prior releases of SQL Server, the default row estimate for the equality operator (=) was $n^{.75}$.

Using these default percentages almost certainly results in inaccurate row estimates, which in turn usually results in inappropriate execution plans being chosen. You should always try to ensure that you have up-to-date statistics available for any columns referenced in your SARGs and join clauses.

When the value of a SARG can be determined at the time of query optimization, the Query Optimizer uses the statistics histogram to estimate the number of matching rows for the SARG. The histogram contains a sampling of the data values in the column and stores information on the number of matching rows for the sampled values, as well as for values that fall between the sampled values. If the statistics are up-to-date, this is the most accurate estimate of the number of matching rows for a SARG.

If the SARG contains an expression that cannot be evaluated until runtime but is an equality expression (such as a comparison to a local variable like name = @lastname), the Query Optimizer uses the density information from the statistics to estimate the number of matching rows. The density value reflects the overall uniqueness of the data values in the column or index. Density information does not estimate the number of matching rows as accurately as the histogram because its value is determined across the entire range of values in a column or an index key and can be skewed higher by one or more values that have a high number of duplicates. Expressions that cannot be evaluated until runtime include comparisons against local variables or function expressions that cannot be evaluated until query execution.

If an expression cannot be evaluated at the time of optimization and the SARG is not an equality search but a closed- or open-range search, the density information cannot be used. The same percentages are used for the row estimates as when no statistics are available (9% for a closed-range search and 30% for an open-range search).

As a special case, if a SARG contains the equality (=) operator and a unique index exists that matches the SARG, based on the nature of a unique index, the Query Optimizer knows, without having to analyze the index statistics, that at most one and only one row can match the SARG.

If the query contains a join clause, SQL Server determines whether any usable indexes or column statistics exist that match the column(s) in the join clause. Because the Query Optimizer has no way of determining what value(s) will join between rows in the table at optimization time, it can't use the statistics histogram on the join column to estimate the number of matching rows. Instead, it uses the density information, as it does for SARGs that are unknown during optimization.

A lower density value indicates a more selective index. As the density approaches 1, the join condition becomes less selective. For example, if a nonclustered index has a high density value, it will likely be more expensive in terms of I/O to retrieve the matching rows using the nonclustered index than to perform a table scan or clustered index scan, and the index likely will not be used.

NOTE

For a more thorough and detailed discussion of indexes and index and column statistics, see Chapter 32.

SARGs and Not Equal Operators

When a SARG contains a not equal operator (!= or <>), you might think that the selectivity of the SARG cannot be determined effectively for the simple reason that index or column statistics can only help you estimate the number of rows that match a specific value, not the number of nonmatching rows. However, for some SARGs with not equal operators, if index or column statistics are available, SQL Server 2014 is able to estimate the number of matching rows. For example, consider the following SARG:

```
WHERE qty <> 1000
```

Without any available index or column statistics on the qty column, SQL Server would treat the not equal SARG as a SARG with no available statistics. Potentially every row in the table could satisfy the search criteria, so it would estimate the number of matching rows as all rows in the table.

However, if index or column statistics were available for the `qty` column, the Query Optimizer would look up the search value (`1000`) in the statistics and estimate the number of rows that match that search value and then determine the number of qualifying rows for the query as the total number of rows in the table minus the estimated number of rows that match the search value. For example, if there are 150,000 rows in the table and the statistics indicate that 1,570 rows match, where `qty` = `1000`, the number of matching rows would be calculated as follows:

150,000	rows
– 1,570	rows (where `qty` = `1000`)
= 148,430	rows (where `qty` <> `1000`)

In this example, with the large number of estimated rows where `qty` <> `1000`, SQL Server would likely end up performing a table scan to resolve the query. However, if the Query Optimizer estimates that there is a very small number of rows where `qty` <> `1000`, the Query Optimizer might determine that it would be more efficient to use an index to find the nonmatching rows. You may be wondering how SQL Server efficiently searches the index for the rows where `qty` <> `1000` without having to look at every row. In this case, internally, it converts the inequality SARG into two range retrievals by using an OR condition:

```
WHERE qty < 1000 OR qty > 1000
```

NOTE

Even if a not equal SARG is optimizable, that doesn't necessarily mean an index will be used. It simply allows the Query Optimizer to make a more accurate estimate of the number of rows that will match a given SARG. More often than not, a not equal SARG will result in a table or clustered index scan. You should try to avoid using not equal SARGs whenever possible.

SARGs and LIKE Clauses

In legacy SQL Server versions prior to SQL Server 2005, the Query Optimizer would estimate the selectivity of a LIKE clause only if the first character in the string was a constant, treating it similar to a closed range search (`LastName LIKE 'S%'` is essentially the same as `Lastname >= 'S' and LastName < 'T'`). If the first character in the LIKE search value was a wildcard (for example, `LIKE '%Washer%'`), SQL Server had no statistics it could match the search argument against to estimate the number of rows that would match. SQL Server 2014 uses string summary statistics, which were introduced in SQL Server 2005, for estimating the selectivity of LIKE conditions.

String summary statistics provide a statistical summary of substring frequency distribution for character columns. String summary statistics can be created on columns of type `text`, `ntext`, `char`, `varchar`, and `nvarchar`. String summary statistics allow SQL Server to estimate the selectivity of `LIKE` conditions where the search string may have any number of wildcards in any combination, including when the first character is a wildcard. Using string summary statistics, SQL Server 2014 can estimate the selectivity of `LIKE` predicates similar to the following:

- ▶ `LastName LIKE 'Smith%'`

- ▶ `Sales.Store.Name LIKE '%Bikes'`

- ▶ `Production.Product.Name LIKE '%Washer%'`

- ▶ `title_id LIKE 'BU[1234567]001'`

- ▶ `Production.Product.Name LIKE '%Flat%Washer'`

The string summary statistics result in fairly accurate row estimates. However, if there is a user-specified escape character in a `LIKE` pattern (for example, `stor_name LIKE '%abc#_%'` `ESCAPE '#'`), SQL Server 2014 has to guess at the selectivity of the SARG.

The values generated for string summary statistics are not visible via `DBCC SHOW_STATISTICS`. However, `DBCC SHOW_STATISTICS` does indicate if string summary statistics have been calculated; if the value `YES` is specified in the `String Index` field in the first rowset returned by `DBCC SHOW_STATISTICS`, the statistics also include a string summary. Also, if the strings are more than 80 characters in length, only the first and last 40 characters are used for creating the string summary statistics. Accurate frequency estimates cannot be determined for substrings that do not appear in the first and last 40 characters of a string.

SARGS on Computed Columns

In versions of SQL Server prior to 2005, for a SARG to be optimizable, there had to be no computations on the column itself in the SARG. In SQL Server 2014, expressions involving computations on a column might be treated as SARGs during optimization if SQL Server can simplify the expression into an optimizable SARG for the purpose of row estimation. For example, the SARG in the following query

```
SELECT * FROM  sales.SalesOrderDetail WHERE UnitPrice*1000 = 5700
```

can be simplified to this for row estimation purposes:

```
SELECT * FROM  sales.SalesOrderDetail WHERE UnitPrice = 5.70
```

However, the simplification of the arithmetic operation to a simple scalar expression is used only during optimization to determine the estimate of the number of matching rows based upon available column or index statistics. During actual execution, SQL Server will still perform an evaluation of the arithmetic operation for each row and likely perform an index or table scan rather than an index seek to locate the matching rows as it would for a simple scalar equality search (such as `UnitPrice=5.70`). Still, doing the conversion during optimization and getting a row estimate from the statistics helps the Query Optimizer decide on other strategies to consider, such as index scanning versus table scanning, or it might help to determine the optimal join order if it's a multitable query.

SQL Server 2014 supports the creation, update, and use of statistics on computed columns, even when they are not persisted. The Query Optimizer can make use of the computed column statistics even when a query doesn't reference the computed column by name but rather contains an expression that matches the computed column expression. This feature avoids the need to rewrite the SARGs in queries with expressions that match a computed column expression to SARGs that explicitly contain the computed column itself.

When the SARG has a more complex operation performed on it, such as a function, it can potentially prevent effective optimization of the SARG. If you cannot avoid using a function or complex expression on a column in the search expression, you should consider creating a computed column on the table and creating an index on the computed column. This materializes the function result into an additional column on the table that can be indexed for faster searching, and the index statistics can be used to better estimate the number of matching rows for the SARG expression that references the function.

An example of using this approach would be for a query that has to find the number of orders placed in a certain month, regardless of the year. The following is a possible solution:

```
select distinct CustomerID
   from sales.SalesOrderHeader
   where datepart(month, OrderDate) = 6
```

This query gets the correct result set but ends up having to do so with a full table or index scan because the function on the `OrderDate` column prevents the Query Optimizer from using an index seek against any index that might exist on the `OrderDate` column.

If this query is used frequently in the system and quick response time is critical, you could create a computed column on the function and index it as follows:

```
alter table sales.SalesOrderHeader add OrderMonth as datepart(month,OrderDate)
create index nc_salesOrderHeader_ordermonth on SalesOrderHeader (OrderMonth)
```

Now, when you run the query on the table again, if you specify the computed column in the WHERE clause, the Query Optimizer can use the index on the computed column to accurately estimate the number of matching rows and possibly use the nonclustered index to find the matching rows and avoid a table scan, as it does for the following query:

```
select distinct CustomerID
   from sales.SalesOrderHeader
   where OrderMonth = 6
```

Even if the query still ends up using a table scan, it at least has statistics available to know how many rows it can expect to match where the month matches the value specified. In addition, if a computed column exists that exactly matches the SARG expression, SQL Server 2014 can still use the statistics and index on the computed column to optimize the query, even if the computed column is not specified in the query itself. For example, with the ord_month column defined on the sales table and an index created on it, the following query can also use the statistics and index to optimize the query:

```
select distinct CustomerID
   from sales.SalesOrderHeader
   where datepart(month, OrderDate) = 6
```

TIP

The automatic matching of computed columns in SQL Server 2014 enables you to create and exploit computed columns without having to change the queries in your application. Be aware, though, that computed column matching is based on identical comparison. For example, a computed column of the form A + B + C does not match an expression of the form A + C + B.

Estimating Access Path Cost

After the selectivity of each of the SARGs, OR clauses, and join conditions is determined, the next phase of optimization is estimating the access path cost of each search or join expression. The Query Optimizer attempts to identify the total cost of various access paths to the data and determine which path results in the lowest cost to return the matching rows for an expression.

The primary cost of an access path, especially for single-table queries, is the number of logical I/Os required to retrieve the data. Using the available statistics and the information stored in SQL Server regarding the average number of rows per page and the number of pages in the table, the Query Optimizer estimates the number of logical page reads necessary to retrieve the estimated number of rows using a table scan or any of the candidate indexes. It then ranks the candidate indexes to determine which access path would retrieve the matching data rows with the lowest cost, typically the access path that requires the fewest number of logical and physical I/Os.

NOTE

A logical I/O occurs every time a page is accessed. If the page is not in cache, a physical I/O is first performed to bring the page into cache memory, and then a logical I/O is performed against the page. Unless you are using the new In-Memory Optimization or Buffer Pool Extension features of SQL Server 2014, the Query Optimizer has no way of knowing whether a page will be in memory when the query is actually executed, so it always assumes a cold cache, that the first read of a page will be from disk. In a very few cases (for example, small OLTP queries), this assumption may result in a slightly slower plan being chosen that optimizes for the number of initial I/Os required to process the query. However, the cold cache assumption is a minor factor in the query plan costing, and it's actually the total number of logical I/Os that is the primary factor in determining the cost of the access path.

TIP

The following sections assume a general understanding of SQL Server index structures. If you haven't done so already, now is a good time to read through Chapter 32.

Estimating Clustered Index Cost

Clustered indexes are efficient for lookups because the rows that match the SARGs are clustered together on the same page or over a range of adjacent pages. SQL Server needs only to find its way to the first page and then read the rows from that page and any subsequent pages in the page chain until no more matching rows are found.

Therefore, the I/O cost estimate for a clustered index is calculated as follows:

Number of index levels in the clustered index

+

Number of pages to scan within the range of values

The number of pages to scan is based on the estimated number of matching rows divided by the number of rows per page. For example, if SQL Server can store 250 rows per page for a table, and 600 rows are within the range of values being searched, SQL Server would estimate that it would have to scan at least three pages to find the qualifying rows. If the index is three levels deep, the estimated logical I/O cost would be as follows:

	3	(index levels to find the first row)
+	3	(data pages: 600 rows divided by 250 rows per page)
=	6	logical page I/Os

For a unique clustered index and an equality operator, the logical I/O cost estimate is one data page plus the number of index levels that need to be traversed to access the data page.

When a clustered index seek is used to retrieve the data rows, you see a query plan similar to the one shown in Figure 34.1 generated for the following query:

```
SELECT * from Production.Product p WHERE p.ProductID = 965
```

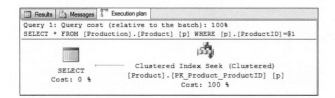

FIGURE 34.1   An execution plan for a clustered index seek.

Estimating Nonclustered Index Cost

When searching for values using a nonclustered index, SQL Server reads the index key values at the leaf level of the index and uses the bookmark to locate and read the data row. SQL Server has no way of knowing if matching search values will be on the same data page until it has read the bookmark. It is possible that while retrieving the rows, SQL Server might find all data rows on different data pages, or it might revisit the same data page multiple times. Either way, a separate logical I/O is required each time it visits the data page.

The I/O cost is therefore based on the depth of the index tree, the number of index leaf rows that need to be scanned to find the matching key values, and the number of matching rows. The cost of retrieving each matching row depends on whether the table is clustered or is a heap table (that is, a table with no clustered index defined on it). For a heap table, the nonclustered row bookmark is the page and row pointer (the row ID [RID]) to the actual data row. A single I/O is required to retrieve the data row. Therefore, the worst-case logical I/O cost for a heap table can be estimated as follows:

> Number of nonclustered index levels

+   Number of leaf pages to be scanned

+   Number of qualifying rows (each row represents a separate data page read)

> **NOTE**
>
> This estimate assumes that the data rows have not been forwarded. In a heap table, when a row has been forwarded, the original row location contains a pointer to the new location of the data row; therefore, an additional page read is required to retrieve the actual data row. The actual I/O cost would be one page greater per row than the estimated I/O cost for any rows that have been forwarded.

When a nonclustered index is used to retrieve the data rows from a heap table without a clustered index, you see a query plan similar to the one shown in Figure 34.2. Notice that in SQL Server 2014, the bookmark lookup operator is replaced by a RID lookup, essentially as a join with the RIDs returned by the nonclustered index seek.

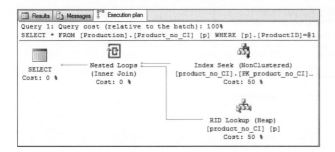

FIGURE 34.2   An execution plan for a nonclustered index seek against a heap table.

If the table is clustered, the row bookmark is the clustered key for the data row. The number of I/Os to retrieve the data row depends on the depth of the clustered index tree because SQL Server has to use the clustered index to find each row. The estimated logical I/O cost of finding a row using the nonclustered index on a clustered table is therefore as follows:

	Number of nonclustered index levels
+	Number of leaf pages to be scanned
+	Number of qualifying rows x Number of page reads to find a single row via the clustered index

For example, consider a heap table with a nonclustered index on last name. Assume that the index holds 800 rows per page (they're really big last names!), and 1,700 names are within the range you are looking for. If the index is three levels deep, the estimated logical I/O cost for the nonclustered index would be as follows:

3	(index levels)
+ 3	(leaf pages: 1,700 leaf rows/800 rows per page)
+ 1,700	(data page reads)
= 1,706	total logical I/Os

Now, assume that the table has a clustered index on it, and the size of the nonclustered index is the same. If the clustered index is three levels deep, including the data page, the estimated logical I/O cost of using the nonclustered index would be as follows:

3	(nonclustered index levels)
+ 3	(leaf pages: 1,700 leaf rows/800 rows per page)
+ 5,100	(1,700 rows x 3 clustered page reads per row)
= 5,106	(total logical I/Os)

> **NOTE**
>
> Although the I/O cost is greater for bookmark lookups in a nonclustered index when a clustered index exists on the table, the cost savings during row inserts, updates, and deletes using the clustered index as the bookmark are substantial, whereas the few extra logical I/Os per row during retrieval usually do not substantially impact query performance unless you are retrieving a substantially large number of rows.

For a unique nonclustered index using an equality operator, the I/O cost is estimated as the number of index levels traversed to access the bookmark plus the number of I/Os required to access the data page via the bookmark.

When a nonclustered index is used to retrieve the data rows on a table with a clustered index, you see a query plan similar to the one shown in Figure 34.3. Notice that in SQL Server 2014, the bookmark lookup operator is replaced by a clustered index Key Lookup, essentially as a join between the clustered index and the clustered index keys returned by the nonclustered index seek.

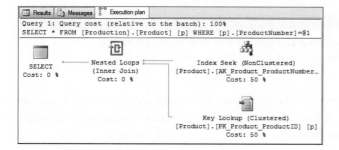

FIGURE 34.3   An execution plan for a nonclustered index seek against a table with a clustered index.

Covering Nonclustered Index Cost Estimation

When analyzing a query, the Query Optimizer considers any possibility to take advantage of index covering. *Index covering* is a method of using the leaf level of a nonclustered index to resolve a query when all the columns referenced in the query (in both the column list and WHERE clause, as well as any GROUP BY and ORDER BY columns) are included in the index leaf row as either index key columns or included columns.

Index covering can save a significant amount of I/O because the query doesn't have to access the data page to return the requested information. In most cases, a nonclustered index that covers a query is faster than a similarly defined clustered index on the table because the nonclustered index usually can store a greater number of rows per page in the index leaf level compared to the number of rows per page in the table itself because the size of an index leaf row is typically much smaller than the size of a data row. (As the nonclustered leaf row size approaches the data row size, however, the I/O cost savings are minimal, if any.)

If index covering can take place in a query, the Query Optimizer considers it and estimates the I/O cost of using the nonclustered index to cover the query. The estimated I/O cost of index covering is as follows:

Number of index levels

\+   Number of leaf-level index pages to scan

The number of leaf-level pages to scan is based on the estimated number of matching rows divided by the number of leaf index rows per page. For example, if index covering could be used on the nonclustered index on `title_id` for the query in the previous example, the estimated I/O cost would be the following:

3   (nonclustered index levels)

\+ 3   (leaf pages: 1,700 leaf rows/800 rows per page)

= 6   total logical I/Os

NOTE

For more information on index covering and when it can take place, as well as the included columns feature introduced in SQL Server 2014, see Chapter 32.

When index covering is used to retrieve the data rows, you might see a query plan similar to the one shown in Figure 34.4. If the entire leaf level of the index is searched, it displays as an index scan, as shown in this example.

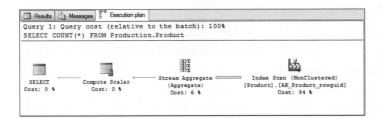

FIGURE 34.4   An execution plan for a covered index scan without limits on the search.

Other times, if the index keys can be searched to limit the range, you might see an index seek used, as shown in Figure 34.5. Note that the difference here from a normal index lookup is the lack of the RID or clustered index lookup because SQL Server does not need to go to the data row to find the requested information.

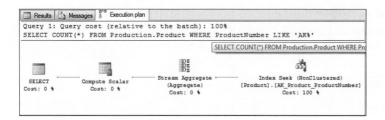

FIGURE 34.5   An execution plan for a covered index seek with limits on the search.

Estimating Table Scan Cost

If no usable index exists that can be matched with a SARG or a join clause, the Query Optimizer's only option is to perform a table scan or a covering nonclustered index scan. The estimate of the total I/O cost is simply the number of pages in the table, which is stored in the system catalogs and can be viewed by querying the used_page_count column of the sys.dm_db_partition_stats dynamic management view (DMV):

```
select used_page_count
    from sys.dm_db_partition_stats
    where object_id = object_id('Production.Product_noCI')
        and (index_id = 0       -- data pages for heap table
            or index_id = 1) -- data pages for clustered table


used_page_count
--------------------
15
```

Keep in mind that there are instances (for example, large range retrievals on a nonclustered index column) in which a table scan might be cheaper than a candidate index in terms of total logical I/O. For example, in the previous nonclustered index costing example, if the index does not cover the query, it costs between 1,706 and 5,106 logical I/Os to retrieve the matching rows using the nonclustered index, depending on whether a clustered index exists on the table or not. If the total number of pages in the table is less than either of these values, a table scan would be more efficient in terms of total logical I/Os than using a nonclustered index.

When a table scan is used to retrieve the data rows from a heap table, you see a query plan similar to the one shown in Figure 34.6.

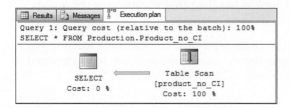

FIGURE 34.6   A table scan on a heap table.

When a table scan is used to retrieve the data rows from a clustered table, you see a query plan similar to the one shown in Figure 34.7. Notice that it displays as a clustered index scan because the table is the leaf level of the clustered index.

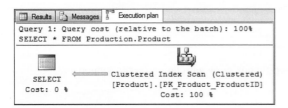

FIGURE 34.7   A table scan on a clustered table.

Using Multiple Indexes

SQL Server allows the creation of multiple indexes on a table. If a query has multiple SARGs that can each be efficiently searched using an available index, the Query Optimizer in SQL Server can make use of multiple indexes by intersecting the indexes or using the index union strategy.

Index Intersection

Index intersection is a mechanism that allows SQL Server to use multiple indexes on a table when you have two or more SARGs in a query and each can be efficiently satisfied using an index as the access path. Consider the following example:

```
SELECT SalesOrderID, OrderDate
    FROM Sales.SalesOrderHeader
    WHERE SalesPersonID = 276
      AND CustomerID = 30107
```

In this example, the Query Optimizer considers the option of searching the index leaf rows of both of the indexes on `SalesPersonID` and `CustomerID` to find the rows that meet each of the search conditions and joining on the matching bookmarks (either the clustered index key or RIDs if it's a heap table) for each result set. It then performs a merge join on the bookmarks and uses the output from that to retrieve the actual data rows for all the keys that are in both result sets.

The index intersection strategy is applied only when the cost of retrieving the keys for both indexes and then retrieving the data rows is less than that of retrieving the qualifying data rows using only one of the indexes or using a table scan.

You can go through the same analysis as the Query Optimizer to determine whether an index intersection makes sense. For example, the `SalesOrderHeader` table has a clustered index on `SalesOrderID`, and this clustered index is the bookmark used to retrieve the data rows for the matching data rows found via the nonclustered indexes. Assume the following statistics:

▶ There are 418 rows estimated to match where `SalesPersonID = 276`.

▶ There are approximately 552 index rows per leaf page for the index on `SalesPersonID`.

▶ There are 5.75 rows estimated to match where `CustomerID = 30107`.

▶ There are approximately 552 index rows per leaf page for the index on `CustomerID`.

▶ The Query Optimizer estimates that the overlap between the two result sets is 1 row.

▶ The number of levels in the index on `SalesPersonID` is 2.

▶ The number of levels in the index on `CustomerID` is 2.

▶ The number of levels in the clustered index on the `SalesOrderHeader` table is 3.

▶ The `SalesOrderHeader` table is 689 pages in size.

Using this information, you can calculate the I/O cost for the different strategies the Query Optimizer can consider.

A table scan would cost 689 pages.

A standard data row retrieval via the nonclustered index on `SalesPersonID` would have the following estimated cost:

1	Index page reads (root and intermediate pages to locate first leaf page)
+ 1	Leaf page reads (418 rows / 552 rows per page)
+ 1,254	(418 rows × 3 pages per bookmark lookup via the clustered index)
= 1,256	pages

A standard data row retrieval via the nonclustered index on `CustomerID` would have the following estimated cost:

1	Nonclustered index page reads (root and intermediate pages)
+ 1	Nonclustered leaf page reads (5.75 rows / 552 rows per dpage)
+ 18	(5.75 rows × 3 pages per bookmark lookup via clustered index)
= 20	Pages

The index intersection is estimated to have the following cost:

2	Pages (1 root page + 1 leaf page to find all the bookmarks for the 418 matching index rows on `SalesPersonID`)	
+ 2	Pages (1 root page + 1 leaf page to find all the bookmarks for the 5.75 matching index rows on `CustomerID`)	
+ 3	Page reads to find the 1 estimated overlapping row between the two indexes using the clustered index	
= 7	Pages	

As you can see from these examples, the index intersection strategy is definitely estimated to be the cheapest approach. If at any point the estimated intersection cost reaches 20 pages, SQL Server just uses the single index on `CustomerID` and checks both search criteria against the matching rows for `SalesPersonID`. If the estimated cost of using an index in any way ever exceeds 689 pages, a table scan is likely to be performed, with the criteria checked against all rows.

When an index intersection is used to retrieve the data rows from a table with a clustered index, you see a query plan similar to the one shown in Figure 34.8.

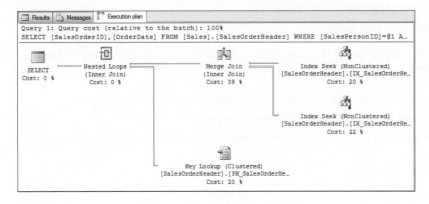

FIGURE 34.8   An execution plan for an index intersection on a clustered table.

If the table does not have a clustered index and has supporting nonclustered indexes for an index intersection, you see a query plan similar to the one shown in Figure 34.9.

Notice that in the example shown in Figure 34.9, the Query Optimizer performs a hash match join rather than a merge join on the RIDs returned by each nonclustered index seek and uses the results from the hash match join to perform an RID lookup to retrieve the matching data rows.

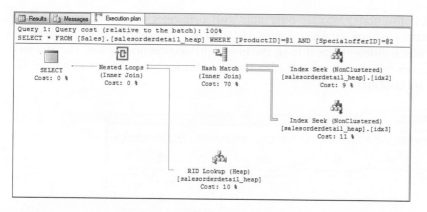

FIGURE 34.9   An execution plan for an index intersection on a heap table.

34

NOTE

To duplicate the query plan shown in Figure 34.9, you need to create a copy of the SalesOrderDetail table called SalesOrderDetail_heap using SELECT INTO and then create the following two indexes on the SalesOrderDetail_heap table:

```
SELECT * into Sales.SalesOrderdetail_heap from Sales.SalesOrderdetail
create index idx2 on Sales.SalesOrderdetail_heap (ProductID)
create index idx3
on Sales.SalesOrderdetail_heap (SpecialOfferID)
```

Then run a query similar to the following:

```
SELECT *
    FROM Sales.salesorderdetail_heap
    WHERE ProductID = 758
      AND SpecialofferID = 3
```

The Index Union Strategy

A strategy similar to the index intersection is applied when you have an OR condition between your SARGs, as in the following query:

```
SELECT SalesOrderID, OrderQty, ProductID
    from Sales.SalesOrderdetail
    where ProductID = 897
      or SalesOrderID  = 43877
```

The index union strategy (often referred to as the OR strategy) is similar to an index intersection, with one slight difference. With the index union strategy, SQL Server executes each part separately, using the most efficient index for each SARG and combining the results with a merge join, removing any duplicate bookmarks for rows that match both search arguments. It then uses the unique bookmarks to retrieve the result rows from the base table.

When the index union strategy is used on a table with a clustered index, you see a query plan similar to the one shown in Figure 34.10. Notice the addition of the Stream Aggregate step, which differentiates it from the index intersection query plan. The Stream Aggregate step performs a grouping on the bookmarks returned by the merge join to eliminate the duplicate bookmarks.

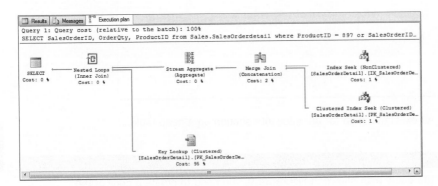

FIGURE 34.10   An execution plan for an index union strategy on a clustered table.

The following steps describe how SQL Server determines whether to use the index union strategy:

1. Estimate the cost of a table scan and the cost of using the index union strategy. If the cost of the index union strategy exceeds the cost of a table scan, stop here and simply perform a table scan. Otherwise, continue with the succeeding steps to perform the index union strategy.

2. Break the query into multiple parts, as in this example:

```
SELECT SalesOrderID, OrderQty, ProductID
    from Sales.SalesOrderdetail
    where ProductID = 897
SELECT SalesOrderID, OrderQty, ProductID
    from Sales.SalesOrderdetail
    where SalesOrderID   = 43877
```

3. Match each part with an available index.

4. Execute each piece and perform a join on the row bookmarks.

5. Remove any duplicate bookmarks.

6. Use the resulting list of unique bookmarks to retrieve all qualifying rows from the base table.

If any one of the OR clauses needs to be resolved via a table scan for any reason, SQL Server simply uses a table scan to resolve the whole query rather than applying the index union strategy.

When the index union strategy is used on a heap table (such as the `Sales.SalesOrder detail_heap` table), you see a query plan similar to the one shown in Figure 34.11.

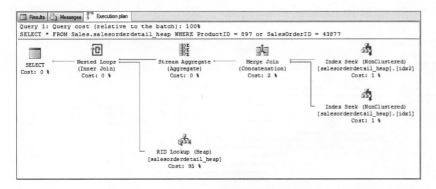

FIGURE 34.11   An execution plan for an index union strategy on a heap table.

When the OR in the query involves only a single column and a nonclustered index exists on the column, the Query Optimizer in SQL Server 2014 typically resolves the query with an index seek against the nonclustered index and then a bookmark lookup to retrieve the data rows. Consider the following query:

```
SELECT SalesOrderID, OrderQty, ProductID
    from Sales.SalesOrderdetail
    where ProductID in ( 897, 942, 744)
```

This query is the same as the following:

```
select SalesOrderID, OrderQty, ProductID
    from sales.
    where ProductID = 897
        or ProductID = 942
        or ProductID = 744
```

To process this query, SQL Server performs a single index seek that looks for each of the search values and then joins the list of bookmarks returned with either the clustered index or the RIDs of the target table. No removal of duplicates is necessary because each OR condition matches a distinct set of rows. Figure 34.12 shows an example of the query plan for multiple OR conditions against a single column.

Index Joins

Besides using the index intersection and index union strategies, another way of using multiple indexes on a single table is to join two or more indexes to create a covering index. This is similar to an index intersection, except that the final bookmark lookup is not required because the merged index rows contain all the necessary information. Consider the following example:

```
SELECT SalesOrderID
    FROM Sales.SalesOrderHeader
    WHERE SalesPersonID = 276
      AND CustomerID = 30107
```

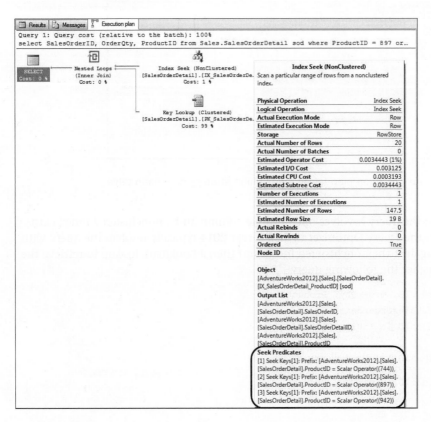

FIGURE 34.12   An execution plan using index seek to retrieve rows for an OR condition on a single column.

Again, the Sales.SalesOrderHeader table contains indexes on both the SalesPersonID and CustomerID columns. Each of these indexes contains the clustered index as a bookmark, and the clustered index contains the SalesOrderID column. In this instance, when the Query Optimizer merges the two indexes using a merge join, joining them on the matching clustered indexes, the index rows in the merge set have all the information needed to resolve the query because SalesOrderID is part of the nonclustered indexes. There is no need to perform a bookmark lookup on the data page. By joining the two index result sets, SQL Server creates the same effect as having one covering index on SalesPersonID, CustomerID, and SalesOrderID on the table. If you use the same numbers as in the "Index Intersection" section presented earlier, the estimated cost of the index join would be as follows:

2   Pages (1 root page + 1 leaf page to find all the bookmarks for the 418 matching
        index rows on `SalesPersonID`)

+ 2   Pages (1 root page + 1 leaf page to find all the bookmarks for the 5.75 matching
        index rows on `CustomerID`)

= 4   Pages

Figure 34.13 shows an example of the execution plan for an index join. Notice that it does
not include the bookmark lookup present in the index intersection execution plan (refer
to Figure 34.8).

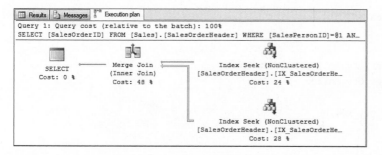

FIGURE 34.13   An execution plan for an index join.

Optimizing with Indexed Views

In SQL Server 2014, when you create a unique clustered index on a view, the result
set for the view is materialized and stored in the database with the same structure as a
table that has a clustered index. Changes made to the data in the underlying tables of
the view are automatically reflected in the view the same way as changes to a table are
reflected in its indexes. In the Developer and Enterprise Editions of SQL Server 2014, the
Query Optimizer automatically considers using the index on the view to speed up access
for queries run directly against the view. The Query Optimizer in the Developer and
Enterprise Editions of SQL Server 2014 also looks at and considers using the indexed view
for searches against the underlying base table, when appropriate.

> **NOTE**
>
> Although indexed views can be created in any edition of SQL Server 2014, they are
> considered for query optimization only in the Developer and Enterprise Editions of SQL
> Server 2014. In other editions of SQL Server 2014, indexed views are not used to opti-
> mize the query unless the view is explicitly referenced in the query and the NOEXPAND
> Query Optimizer hint is specified. For example, to force the Query Optimizer to consider
> using the sales_Qty_Rollup indexed view in the Standard Edition of SQL Server 2014,
> you execute the query as follows:

```
select * from SalesOrder_Qty_Rollup WITH (NOEXPAND)
    where ProductID between 817 and 830
```

The NOEXPAND hint is allowed only in SELECT statements, and the indexed view must be referenced directly in the query. (Only the Developer and Enterprise Editions consider using an indexed view that is not directly referenced in the query.) As always, you should use Query Optimizer hints with care. When the NOEXPAND hint is included in the query, the Query Optimizer cannot consider other alternatives for optimizing the query.

Consider the following example, which creates an indexed view on the SalesOrderDetail table, containing ProductID and sum(OrderQty) grouped by ProductID:

```
set quoted_identifier on
go

if object_id('SalesOrder_Qty_Rollup') is not null
    drop view SalesOrder_Qty_Rollup
go
create view SalesOrder_Qty_Rollup
with schemabinding
as
    select ProductID, sum(OrderQty) as total_qty, count_big(*) as NumOrders
        from Sales.SalesOrderDetail
        group by ProductID
go

create unique clustered index idx1 on SalesOrder_Qty_Rollup (ProductID)
go
```

The creation of the clustered index on the view essentially creates a clustered table in the database with the three columns ProductID, total_qty, and NumOrders. As you would expect, the following query on the view itself uses a clustered index seek on the view to retrieve the result rows from the view instead of having to scan or search the SalesOrderDetail table itself:

```
select * from SalesOrder_Qty_Rollup
    where ProductID between 817 and 830
```

However, the following query on the SalesOrderDetail table uses the indexed view SalesOrder_Qty_Rollup to retrieve the result set as well:

```
select ProductID,   sum(OrderQty)
    from Sales.SalesOrderDetail
    where ProductID between 817 and 830
    group by ProductID
```

Essentially, the Query Optimizer recognizes the indexed view essentially as another index on the `SalesOrderDetail` table that covers the query. The execution plan in Figure 34.14 shows the indexed view being searched in place of the table.

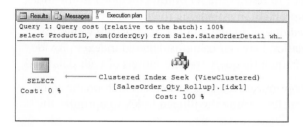

FIGURE 34.14   An execution plan showing an indexed view being searched to satisfy a query on a base table.

NOTE

In addition to the seven required SET options that need to be set appropriately when the indexed view is created, they must also be set the same way for a session to be able to use the indexed view in queries. The required SET option settings are as follows:

```
SET ARITHABORT ON
SET CONCAT_NULL_YIELDS_NULL ON
SET QUOTED_IDENTIFIER ON
SET ANSI_NULLS ON
SET ANSI_PADDING ON
SET ANSI_WARNINGS ON
SET NUMERIC_ROUNDABORT OFF
```

If these SET options are not set appropriately for the session running a query that could make use of an indexed view, the indexed view is not used, and the table is searched instead.

For more information on indexed views, see Chapters 24, "Creating and Managing Views," and 32, "Indexes and Performance."

You might find rare situations when using the indexed view in the Enterprise, Datacenter, or Developer Editions of SQL Server 2014 leads to poor query performance, and you might want to avoid having the Query Optimizer use the indexed view. To force the Query Optimizer to ignore the indexed view(s) and optimize the query using the indexes on the underlying base tables, you can specify the EXPAND VIEWS query option, as follows:

```
select * from SalesOrder_Qty_Rollup
   where ProductID between 817 and 830
   option (EXPAND VIEWS)
```

Optimizing with Filtered Indexes

SQL Server 2014 provides the ability to define filtered indexes and statistics on a subset of rows rather than on the entire rowset in a table. This is done by specifying simple predicates in the index create statement to restrict the set of rows included in the index. Filtered statistics help solve a common problem in estimating the number of matching rows when the estimates become skewed due to a large number of duplicate values (or NULLs) in an index or due to data correlation between columns. Filtered indexes provide query optimization benefits when you frequently query specific subsets of your data rows.

If a filtered index exists on a table, the optimizer recognizes when a search predicate is compatible with the filtered index; it considers using the filtered index to optimize the query if the selectivity is good.

For example, the SalesOrderDetail table in the AdventureWorks2012 database contains a large percentage of rows where UnitPriceDiscount is 0.00. A nonclustered index typically doesn't help for searches in which UnitPriceDiscount is 0.00 because the selectivity isn't adequate, and a table scan would be performed. An advantageous approach then is to create a filtered index on UnitPriceDiscount without including the values of 0.00 to reduce the size of the index and make it more efficient.

For example, first create an unfiltered index on UnitPriceDiscount is 0.00 on the SalesOrderDetail table:

```
create index unitPriceDiscount_unfiltered on Sales.SalesOrderDetail
(UnitPriceDiscount)
```

Then, execute the following two queries:

```
select SalesOrderID, ProductID, OrderQty
    from sales.salesOrderDetail where UnitPriceDiscount = 0.00
select SalesOrderID, ProductID, OrderQty
    from sales.salesOrderDetail where UnitPriceDiscount = 0.30
```

As you can see by the query plan displayed in Figure 34.15, a query where UnitPriceDiscount is 0.00 still uses a table scan instead of the index because the selectivity is poor, whereas it uses the index for UnitPriceDiscount = 0.30.

Now, drop the unfiltered index and re-create a filtered index that excludes values of 0:

```
drop index Sales.SalesOrderDetail.unitPriceDiscount_unfiltered
go
create index filt_unitPriceDiscount
   on Sales.SalesOrderDetail (UnitPriceDiscount)
   where UnitPriceDiscount <> 0.00
```

Re-run the queries and examine the query plan again. Figure 34.16 shows that the query where UnitPriceDiscount = 0.00 still uses a table scan as before, but the query where UnitPriceDiscount = 0.30 is able to use the filtered index instead of the unfiltered index on UnitPriceDiscount.

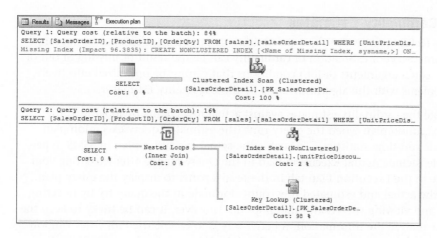

FIGURE 34.15   An execution plan showing index not being used due to poor selectivity.

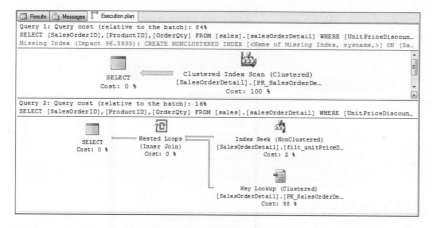

FIGURE 34.16   An execution plan showing the filtered index being used.

In this case, it may be more beneficial to define the filtered index instead of a normal index on UnitPriceDiscount because the filtered index will require less space and be a more efficient index by excluding all the rows with UnitPriceDiscount values of 0.00, especially if the majority of the queries against the table are searching for UnitPriceDiscount values that are nonzero.

NOTE

For more information on creating and using filtered indexes, see Chapter 32.

Evaluating Cardinality Estimates

One of the key factors that leads to the generation of a poor execution plan is inaccurate cardinality estimates. Poor estimation of cardinality can be the result of missing or out of date statistics, search arguments or join conditions that cannot be optimized effectively, or possibly problems with the algorithms used by the Cardinality Estimator.

You can validate the cardinality estimates against actual row counts by looking at the actual query execution plan when the query runs (the estimated query execution plan does not include run-time statistics). To enable the actual execution plan in SSMS, type ctrl-M or enable Include Actual Execution Plan in the Query menu. After executing your query, navigate to the Execution Plan tab in the results panel to display the query plan. You can view the actual and estimated row counts for node in the query try by hovering over the node and viewing the Tooltip that pops up. However, it can be tricky to keep the Tooltip up and analyze the information. A better way is to enable the Properties window by hitting F4 or selecting Properties Window form the View menu. Once the Properties window is displayed, simply click on the node in the execution plan you wish to examine, as shown in Figure 34.17.

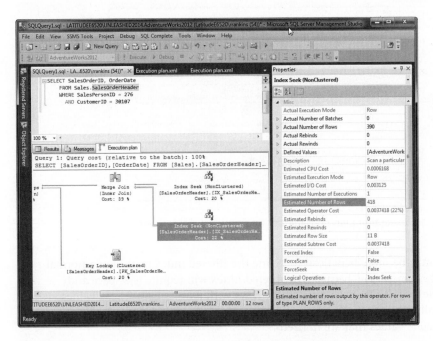

FIGURE 34.17   Validating the Actual versus Estimated number of rows in a query plan in SSMS.

In the Properties window, you'll see an entry for Actual Number of Rows and Estimated Number of Rows. If there is a significant discrepancy between the two, then something is skewing the row estimates, which probably needs to be investigated. Some potential items to look into are discussed at the end of this chapter.

Join Selection

The job of the Query Optimizer is incredibly complex. The Query Optimizer can consider literally thousands of options when determining the optimal execution plan. The statistics are simply one of the tools that the Query Optimizer can use to help in the decision-making process.

In addition to examining the statistics to estimate cardinality and determine the most efficient access paths for the SARGs and join conditions, the Query Optimizer must consider the optimum order in which to access the tables, the appropriate join algorithms to use, the appropriate sorting algorithms, and many other details too numerous to list here. The goal of the Query Optimizer during join selection is to determine the most efficient join strategy.

As mentioned at the beginning of this chapter, delving into the detailed specifics of the various join strategies and their costing algorithms is beyond the scope of a single chapter on optimization. In addition, some of these costing algorithms are proprietary and not publicly available. The goal of this section, then, is to present an overview of the most common query processing algorithms that the Query Optimizer uses to determine an efficient execution plan.

Join Processing Strategies

If you are familiar with SQL, you are probably very familiar with using joins between tables in creating SQL queries. A join occurs any time the SQL Server Query Optimizer has to compare two inputs to determine an output. The join can occur between one table and another table, between an index and a table, or between an index and another index (as described in the previous section).

The SQL Server Query Optimizer uses three primary types of join strategies when it must compare two inputs: nested loop joins, merge joins, and hash joins. The Query Optimizer must consider each one of these algorithms to determine the most appropriate and efficient algorithm for a given situation.

Each of the three supported join algorithms could be used for any join operation. The Query Optimizer examines all the possible alternatives, assigns costs to each, and chooses the least expensive join algorithm for a given situation. Merge and hash joins often greatly improve the query processing performance for very large data tables and data warehouses.

Nested Loop Joins

The nested loop join algorithm is by far the simplest of the three join algorithms. The nested loops join uses one input as the "outer" loop and the other input as the "inner" loop. As you might expect, SQL Server processes the outer input one row at a time. For each row in the outer input, the inner input is searched for matching rows.

Figure 34.18 illustrates a query that uses a nested loops join for the following query:

```
SELECT soh.SalesOrderID, OrderDate, Status, ProductID, OrderQty
  FROM Sales.SalesOrderDetail sod
  JOIN Sales.SalesOrderHeader soh
    ON sod.SalesOrderID = soh.SalesOrderID
  WHERE sod.SalesOrderID = 43918
```

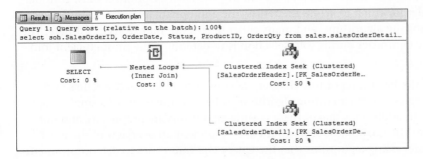

FIGURE 34.18   An execution plan for a nested loops join.

Note that in the graphical execution plan, the outer loop is represented as the top input table, and the inner loop is represented as the bottom input table. In most instances, the Query Optimizer chooses the input table with the fewest number of qualifying rows to be the outer loop to limit the number of iterative lookups against the inner table. However, the Query Optimizer may choose the input table with the greater number of qualifying rows as the outer table if the I/O cost of searching that table first and then performing the iterative loops on the other table is less than the alternative.

The nested loop join is the easiest join strategy for which to estimate the I/O cost. The cost of the nested loop join is calculated as follows:

>   Number of I/Os to read in outer input
> +   Number of matching rows × Number of I/Os per lookup oninner input
> =   Total logical I/O cost for query

The Query Optimizer evaluates the I/O costs for the various possible join orders as well as the various possible access paths and indexes available to determine the most efficient join order. The nested loops join is efficient for queries that typically affect only a small number of rows. As the number of rows in the outer loop increases, the effectiveness of the nested loops join strategy diminishes. The reason is the increased number of logical I/Os required as the number of qualifying rows increases.

Also, if there are no useful indexes on the join columns, the nested loop join is not an efficient join strategy because it requires a table scan lookup on the inner table for each row in the outer table. Lacking useful indexes to support an inner loop join, the Query Optimizer often opts to perform a merge or hash join.

Merge Joins

The merge join algorithm is more effective than the nested loops join for dealing with large data volumes or when the lack of limiting SARGs or useful indexes on SARGs leads to a table scan of one or both tables involved in the join. A merge join works by retrieving one row from each input and comparing them, matching on the join column(s). Figure 34.19 illustrates the following query that uses a merge join:

```
SELECT soh.SalesOrderID, OrderDate, Status, ProductID, OrderQty
   FROM Sales.SalesOrderDetail sod
   JOIN Sales.SalesOrderHeader soh
     ON sod.SalesOrderID = soh.SalesOrderID
```

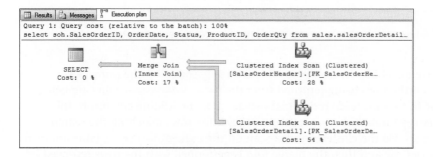

FIGURE 34.19   An execution plan for a merge join.

A merge join requires that both inputs be sorted on the merge columns—that is, the columns specified in the equality (ON) clauses of the join predicate. A merge join does not work if both inputs are not sorted. In the query shown in Figure 34.19, both tables have a clustered index on SalesOrderID, so the merge column (SalesOrderID) is already sorted for each table. If the merge columns are not already sorted, a separate sort operation may be required before the merge join operation. When the input is sorted, the merge join operation retrieves a row from each input and compares them, returning the rows if they are equal. If the inputs are not equal, the lower-value row is discarded, and another row is obtained from that input. This process repeats until all rows have been processed.

Usually, the Query Optimizer chooses a merge join strategy, as in this example, when the data volume is large and both columns are contained in an existing presorted index, such as a clustered primary key. If either of the inputs is not already sorted, the Query Optimizer has to perform an explicit sort before the join. Figure 34.20 shows an example of a sort being performed before the merge join is performed for the following query:

```
select soh.SalesOrderID, OrderDate, c.CustomerID, c.PersonID, c.StoreID
    from sales.SalesOrderHeader soh
        INNER JOIN Sales.Customer c
        ON soh.CustomerID = c.CustomerID
        WHERE soh.OrderDate = '2005-08-01'
```

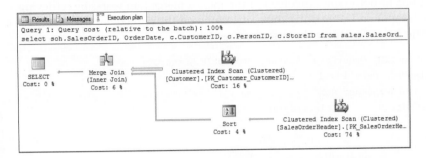

FIGURE 34.20   An execution plan for a merge join with a preliminary sort step.

In the query in Figure 34.20, the Customer table is already sorted on the primary key on CustomerID, but the rows being returned from the SalesOrderHeader table are being returned initially in SalesOrderID order. (SalesOrderID is the leading column in the clustered primary key on SalesOrderDetail.) The resulting rows matching the search criteria on OrderDate via the clustered index scan on the SalesOrderDetail table are then re-sorted by CustomerID, and then the merge join is performed with the rows retrieved from the Customer table.

If one or more of the inputs to the merge join is not sorted, and the additional sorting causes the merge join to be too expensive to perform, the Query Optimizer may consider using the hash join strategy instead.

Hash Joins

The final—and most complicated—join algorithm is the hash join. The hash join is an effective join strategy for dealing with large data volumes where the inputs might not be sorted and when no useful indexes exist on your tables for performing the join. Figure 34.21 illustrates the query plan for the following query that uses a hash join:

```
select soh.SalesOrderID, OrderDate, Status, ProductID, OrderQty
    from sales.SalesOrderHeader soh
        INNER JOIN Sales.salesorderdetail_heap sh
        ON soh.SalesOrderID = sh.SalesOrderID
```

The basic hash join algorithm involves separating the two inputs into a build input and probe input. The Query Optimizer usually attempts to assign the smaller input as the build input. The hash join scans the build input and creates a hash table. Each row from the build input is inserted into a hash bucket based on a hash key value, which is computed. The probe input is then scanned, one row at a time. A hash key value is computed for each row in the probe, and the hash bucket for that key is scanned for matches. The hash join is an effective join strategy when dealing with large data volumes and unsorted data inputs.

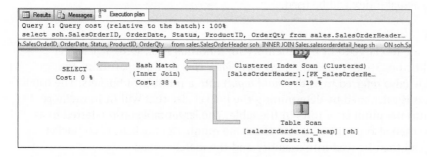

FIGURE 34.21   An execution plan for a hash join.

In a hash join, the keys that are common between the two tables are hashed into a hash bucket, using the same hash function. This bucket usually starts out in memory and then moves to disk, as needed. The type of hashing that occurs depends on the amount of memory required. Hashing is commonly used for inner and outer joins, intersections, unions, and differences. The Query Optimizer often uses hashing for intermediate processing.

Pseudocode for a simple hash join might look like this:

```
create an empty hash table
for each row in the input table
    read the row
    hash the key value
    insert the hashed key into the hash bucket
for each row in the larger table
    read the row
    hash the key value
    if hashed key value is found in the hash bucket
        output hash key and both row identifiers
drop the hash table
```

Although hashing is useful when no useful indexes are on the tables for a join, the Query Optimizer still might not choose it as the join strategy if it has a high cost in terms of memory required. If the entire hash table doesn't fit in memory, SQL Server has to split both the build and probe inputs into partitions, each containing a different set of hash keys, and write those partitions out to disk. As each partition is needed, it is brought into memory. This increases the amount of I/O and general processing time for the query.

To use the hashing strategy efficiently, it is best if the smaller input is used as the build input. If, during execution, SQL Server discovers that the build input is actually larger than the probe input, it might switch the roles of the build and probe input midstream. The Query Optimizer usually doesn't have a problem determining which input is smaller if the statistics on the columns involved in the query are current. Column-level statistics can also help the Query Optimizer determine the estimated number of rows matching a SARG, even if no actual index will be used.

Grace Hash Joins

If the two inputs are too large to fit into memory for a normal hash join, SQL Server might use a modified method, called the *grace hash join*. This method partitions the smaller input table (also referred to as the *build input*) into a number of buckets. The total number of buckets is calculated by determining the bucket size that will fit in memory and dividing it into the number of rows in the table. The larger table (also referred to as the *probe input*) is then also partitioned into the same number of buckets. Each bucket from each input can then be read into memory and the matches made.

A *hybrid join* is a join method that uses elements of both a simple in-memory hash and grace hash.

NOTE

Hash and merge join strategies can be applied only when the join is an equijoin—that is, when the join condition compares columns from two inputs with the equality (=) operator. If the join is not based on an equality (for example, using a BETWEEN clause), using nested loop joins is the only strategy that can be employed.

Determining the Optimal Join Order

In addition to determining the best join strategies, the Query Optimizer also evaluates and determines the optimal join order that would result in the most efficient query plan. In the query's execution plan, you might find that the order of the tables in the execution plan is a different order than specified in the query. Regardless of the join strategy used, the Query Optimizer needs to determine which table is the outer input and which is the inner input to the join strategy chosen. For example, consider the following query:

```
select soh.SalesOrderID, OrderDate, Status, ProductNumber, ListPrice
    from Sales.SalesOrderHeader soh
    join Sales.SalesOrderDetail sod
    on soh.SalesOrderID = sod.SalesOrderID
    join Production.Product p
    on p.ProductID = sod.ProductID
```

In addition to the possible access paths and join strategies available, the server can consider the following pool of possible join orders:

```
    SalesOrderHeader -> SalesOrderDetail -> Product

    Product -> SalesOrderDetail -> SalesOrderHeader

    SalesOrderDetail -> Product -> SalesOrderHeader
```

```
SalesOrderDetail -> SalesOrderHeader -> Product

SalesOrderHeader -> Product -> SalesOrderDetail

Product -> SalesOrderHeader -> SalesOrderDetail
```

For each of these join orders, the Query Optimizer considers the various access paths available for each table as well as the different join strategies available. For example, the Query Optimizer could consider the following possible join strategies:

▶ Perform a table scan on the `SalesOrderHeader` table and for each row perform an index seek against the `primary key` column on `SalesOrderDetail` to find the matching rows by `SalesOrderID`. And for each matching row in `SalesOrderDetail`, perform an index seek against the primary key of the `Product` table to find the matching rows in `Product` by `ProductID`.

▶ Perform a table scan on the `Product` table and for each row perform an index seek against the `ProductID` index on `SalesOrderDetail` to find the matching rows by `ProductID`. And for each matching row in `SalesOrderDetail`, perform an index seek against the primary key of the `SalesOrderHeader` table to find the matching rows in `SalesOrderHeader` by `SalesOrderID`.

▶ Perform a clustered index scan of the `primary key` index of the `Product` table and use a merge join to match it with an index scan of the `SalesOrderdetail` table on the `IX_SalesOrderDetail_ProductID` index. And for each of the qualifying rows from this merge join, perform a hash join with a clustered index scan of the primary key index of the `SalesOrderHeader` table.

▶ Perform an index scan of the `SalesOrderID` index of the `SalesOrderDetail` table and use a hash join to match it with a clustered index scan of the `Product` table. And for each of the qualifying rows from this hash join, perform another hash join with an index scan of the `SalesOrderID` index of the `SalesOrderHeader` table.

NOTE

If you run this query yourself and examine the query plan, you'll likely see that the third alternative is the one chosen by the Query Optimizer.

These are just four of the possibilities. There are many more options for the Query Optimizer to consider as execution plans for processing this join. For example, for each of the four options, there are other indexes to consider, and there are other possible join orders and strategies to consider as well.

As you can see, there can be a large number of execution plan options for the Query Optimizer to consider for processing a join, and this example is a relatively simple three-table join. The number of options increases exponentially as the number of tables involved in the query increases. The "Execution Plan Selection" section, later in this chapter, describes how the Query Optimizer deals with the large number of possible execution plan options.

34

Subquery Processing

SQL Server optimizes subqueries differently, depending on how they are written. For example, SQL Server attempts to flatten some subqueries into joins when possible, to allow the Query Optimizer to select the optimal join order rather than be forced to process the query inside-out. The following sections examine the different types of subqueries and how SQL Server optimizes them.

IN, ANY, and EXISTS Subqueries

In SQL Server, any query that contains a subquery introduced with an IN, = ANY, or EXISTS predicate is usually flattened into an existence join unless the outer query also contains an OR clause or unless the subquery is correlated or contains one or more aggregates.

An existence join is optimized the same way as a regular join, with one exception: With an existence join, as soon as a matching row is found in the inner table, the value TRUE is returned, and SQL Server stops looking for further matches for that row in the outer table and moves on to the next row. A normal join would continue processing to find all matching rows. The following query provides an example of an existence join and a quantified predicate subquery that will be converted to an existence join:

```
SELECT * FROM production.Product p
WHERE EXISTS (SELECT * FROM Sales.Salesorderdetail s
  WHERE s.productID = p.productID AND SellStartDate >= '2/1/2006')


SELECT * FROM production.Product p
WHERE p.ProductID IN (SELECT ProductID FROM sales.salesorderdetail
  WHERE SellStartDate >= '2/1/2006')
```

Figure 34.22 shows an example of the execution plan for both of these queries. You can see that the query plans are the same, providing evidence that the quantified predicate subquery is being flattened into an existence join.

Materialized Subqueries

If an outer query is comparing a column against the result of a subquery using any of the comparison operators (=, >, <, >=, <=, !=), and the subquery is not correlated, the results of the subquery are often resolved—that is, materialized—before comparison against the outer table column. For these types of queries, the Query Optimizer processes the query inside-out.

An example of this type of query is as follows:

```
SELECT ProductID FROM Sales.SalesOrderDetail
  WHERE OrderQty = (SELECT MAX(OrderQty) FROM sales.salesorderdetail)
```

In this example, the subquery is resolved first to find the maximum OrderQty value from the SalesOrderDetail table to compare against OrderQty in the outer query. Figure 34.23 shows an example of a query plan for this materialized subquery.

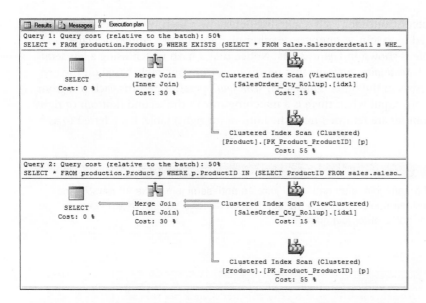

FIGURE 34.22   An execution plan for an existence join and a quantified predicate subquery flattened into an existence join.

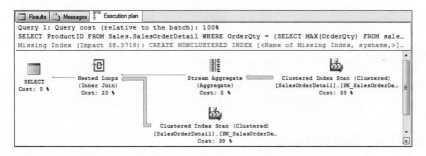

FIGURE 34.23   An execution plan for a materialized subquery.

Correlated Subqueries

A correlated subquery contains a reference to an outer table in a join clause in the subquery. Following is an example of a correlated subquery:

```
SELECT *
    FROM Production.ProductInventory  p
    WHERE Quantity IN (SELECT OrderQty
                    FROM sales.SalesOrderDetail sod
                    where sod.ProductID = p.ProductID)
```

Because correlated subqueries depend on values from the outer query for resolution, they cannot be processed independently. Instead, SQL Server usually processes correlated subqueries repeatedly, once for each qualifying outer row. Often, a correlated subquery looks like a nested loop join. A sample execution plan for the preceding correlated subquery example is shown in Figure 34.24. Notice that a hash match using a left semi join is performed. *Semi joins* are joins that return rows from one table based on the existence of related rows in the other table. A *left semi join* operation returns each row from the first (top or left) input when there is a matching row in the second (bottom or right) input. If the attributes are returned from the bottom (or right) table, it's referred to as a *right semi join*.

> **NOTE**
>
> The inverse of a semi join is an anti–semi join. An anti–semi join looks for rows in one table based on their non-existence in the other, such as for a NOT IN or NOT EXISTS type subquery, or for some outer join queries.

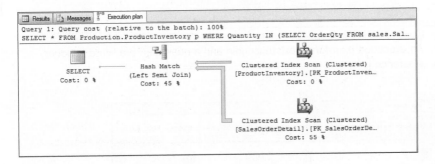

FIGURE 34.24   An execution plan for a correlated subquery.

Execution Plan Selection

At this point in the query optimization process, the Query Optimizer has examined the entire query and estimated the costs of all possible access paths for the SARGs and join clauses and also the various join orders and query-processing strategies. It now needs to choose which plan to pass on to SQL Server for execution.

For a single table query, choosing the best query plan typically involves choosing the access path and query processing strategy that results in the most efficient execution plan; usually, this is the plan that requires the fewest number of logical I/Os and typically requiring the least resources to process the query on that table. However, sometimes the Query Optimizer may choose a plan that returns rows faster to the user but with a greater, but reasonable, cost in resources (I/O plus CPU and memory). For example, processing a query in parallel (that is, using multiple CPUs simultaneously for the same query) typically requires more resources than processing it via a single CPU, but the query may complete much faster when processed in parallel. The Query Optimizer may choose to use such a parallel plan for execution if the load on the server is not adversely affected.

For a multitable query, choosing the best plan involves not only determining the cheapest access path and query processing strategy for each table individually, but also determining the best access paths in conjunction with the optimal join strategy that results in the lowest estimated query cost, as discussed in the earlier section "Join Selection."

In addition, if any UNION, ORDER BY, GROUP BY, or DISTINCT clauses are present, the Query Optimizer chooses the most efficient method to process them.

For all its options, the overriding factor in selecting a plan is primarily the overall I/O cost. The Query Optimizer usually selects a query plan that results in the least amount of I/O processing because I/O is often the most expensive aspect of a query. After the plan is selected, it's passed to the Database Engine for execution.

> **NOTE**
>
> As you can see in examples throughout this chapter, you can examine the query plan chosen by the Query Optimizer with the graphical execution plan feature of SSMS. You can also display a text representation of the execution plan by enabling the SHOWPLAN_TEXT, SHOWPLAN_ALL, SHOWPLAN_XML, STATISTICS PROFILE, or STATISTICS XML option in a user session. How to interpret the output from these tools is covered in Chapter 36, along with a discussion of other tools available for examining the query plan selection process.
>
> You also have the capability to influence or override the query plan selection process, using methods discussed in Chapter 35, "Managing the Query Optimizer."

34

The Query Optimizer can choose from many possible execution plans, especially when a large number of tables are involved in the query—and an even greater number of permutations of join strategies and index usage is possible. The number of permutations grows exponentially as the number of tables involved in the query grows. Some complex queries could potentially have millions of possible execution plans. In these cases, the Query Optimizer does not analyze all possible plan combinations. Instead, it tries to find an execution plan that has a cost reasonably close to the theoretical minimum.

Initially, SQL Server tries to determine whether only one viable plan for a query exists. This is called *trivial plan optimization*. For simple queries, this can save the Query Optimizer a lot of work. The idea behind trivial plan optimization is that cost-based optimization can be expensive to initialize and run. The Query Optimizer can try many possible variations in looking for the cheapest plan, and the time required to find the optimal query plan could potentially be longer than the time required to execute the query itself. If the Query Optimizer can determine by investigating the query and the relevant metadata that there is only one viable plan for a query, it can avoid a lot of the work required to initialize and perform cost-based optimization.

An example of a trivial query plan is a single table SELECT statement with a SARG on a unique key or a SELECT on a table with no indexes or GROUP BY clause. Another example is an INSERT statement using a VALUES clause into a table that doesn't participate in indexed views: There is only one way to insert this record. For each of these examples, the query plans are fairly obvious plans that are typically very inexpensive, so the Query Optimizer generates the plan without trying to find something better. If the Query Optimizer tried to consider every possible plan, the optimization cost could actually exceed the query processing time, outweighing any benefit provided by well-optimized queries.

If a trivial plan is not available, the Query Optimizer next performs some query simplifications, usually syntactic transformations of the query itself, such as commutative properties and operations that can be rearranged. An example of simplification is evaluation of simple single-table SARG filters before processing the joins. While the filters are logically evaluated after the joins, evaluating the filters before the joins still produces the correct result and is more efficient because it removes unqualified rows before the join operation is performed, resulting in fewer iterations and, subsequently, fewer I/Os.

After any attempts at query simplification, the Query Optimizer begins a more thorough optimization process. To avoid just running through all the possibilities that would cause the optimization process to take a long time, it breaks up the optimization into three phases. After each phase, the Query Optimizer applies a set of rules to evaluate the cost of any resulting plan. If, according to these rules, the plan is cheap enough, it chooses and submits that plan for execution. If, according to the rules, no plan is cheap enough, the Query Optimizer continues on to the next phase, with its own set of (usually more complex) rules to apply. In the vast majority of cases, the Query Optimizer finds a viable execution plan in the preliminary phases.

The first phase of optimization, Phase 0, contains a limited set of rules and is applied to queries with at least four tables. As you've seen previously, join reordering alone generates many potential plan candidates, so the Query Optimizer uses a limited number of join orders in Phase 0 and considers using only the hash or nested-loop join strategies. If, at the end of this phase, the Query Optimizer finds a plan with an estimated cost below the threshold for Phase 0, the optimization ends. Phase 0 is also referred to as the *transaction processing phase* because the final query plans produced by Phase 0 are typically found in transaction processing applications.

The next phase is Phase 1, or quick plan optimization. This phase applies additional transformation rules and examines different possible join orders than were considered in Phase 0. If, at the end of Phase 1, the Query Optimizer finds a best plan with a cost less than the threshold for Phase 1, optimization ends, and the best plan identified is returned.

Up to this point, the Query Optimizer has considered only nonparallel query plans. If more than one CPU is available to SQL Server and the cost of the least expensive plan produced by Phase 1 is greater than the Cost Threshold for Parallelism configuration setting, the Query Optimizer runs the Phase 1 optimization again, this time looking for the best parallel query plan. The costs of the nonparallel and parallel plans generated by Phase 1 are then compared and the Query Optimizer enters the last phase of optimization, Phase 2, for the cheaper of the two.

Phase 2 is also referred to as the full optimization phase. If the cost of the best nonparallel plan found so far is still below the parallelism threshold, or there is only a single CPU available, the full optimization phase continues using a brute-force method to find the best serial plan, checking additional combinations of indexes and processing strategies such as outer join reordering and automatic indexed view substitution for multitable views. In this phase, the Query Optimizer examines every possible execution plan and eventually chooses the cheapest one. The number of execution plans it considers during Phase 2 is restricted by a time limit. When the designated time limit for Phase 2 is reached, the Query Optimizer returns the cheapest plan found thus far.

Eventually, an execution plan is determined to be the most efficient. After this is determined, the execution plan is passed on to the SQL Server query processor to be executed.

Query Plan Caching

SQL Server 2014 has a pool of memory used to store both execution plans and data. The amount of memory allocated to execution plans or data changes dynamically, depending on the needs of the system. The portion of memory used to store execution plans is often referred to as the *plan cache*.

The first time a cacheable query is submitted to SQL Server, the query plan is compiled and put into the plan cache. Query plans are read-only re-entrant structures shared by multiple users. At most, there are two instances of a query plan at any time in the plan cache: a serial execution plan and parallel query execution plan. The same parallel execution plan is used for all parallel executions, regardless of the degree of parallelism.

When you execute subsequent SQL statements, the Database Engine first checks to see whether an existing execution plan for the same SQL statement already resides in the plan cache. If it finds one, SQL Server attempts to reuse the matching execution plan, thereby saving the overhead of having to recompile an execution plan for each ad hoc SQL statement issued. If no matching execution plan is found, SQL Server is forced to generate a new execution plan for the query.

The ability to reuse query plans for ad hoc queries in addition to caching query plans for stored procedures can help improve the performance for complex queries that are executed frequently because SQL Server can avoid having to compile a query plan every time it's executed if a matching query plan is found in memory first.

Query Plan Reuse

Query plan reuse for stored procedures is pretty straightforward. A main argument for using stored procedures is to promote plan reuse. For stored procedures and triggers, plan reuse is simply based on the procedure or trigger name. The first time a stored procedure is executed, the query plan is generated based on the initial parameters. On subsequent executions, SQL Server checks the plan cache to see whether a query plan exists for a procedure with the same name, and if one is found, it simply substitutes the new parameter values into the existing query plan for execution.

Another method that promotes query plan reuse is using the `sp_executesql` stored procedure for executing dynamic SQL statements. When using `sp_executesql`, typically you specify a dynamic query with explicitly identified parameters for SARGs. Here's an example:

```
sp_executesql N'select p.name, l.name, pi.quantity
from Adventureworks2012.Production.Product p
join Adventureworks2012.Production.ProductInventory pi
 on pi.ProductID = p.ProductID
join Adventureworks2012.Production.Location l
on pi.LocationID = l.LocationID
where l.name = @name', N'@name varchar(30)', 'Tool Crib'
```

When the same query is executed again via `sp_executesql`, SQL Server reuses the existing query plan (if it is still in the plan cache) and simply substitutes the different parameter values.

Although SQL Server can also match query plans for ad hoc SQL statements, there are some limitations as to when a plan can be reused. For SQL Server to match SQL statements to existing execution plans in the plan cache for ad hoc queries, all object references in the query must be qualified with at least the schema name, and fully qualified object names (database plus schema name) provide increased likelihood of plan reuse. In addition, plan caching for ad hoc queries requires an exact text match between the queries. The text match is both case sensitive and space sensitive. For example, the following two queries are logically identical, but because they are not textually identical, they would not share the same query plan:

```
select p.name,
       l.name,
       pi.quantity
from Adventureworks2012.Production.Product p
join Adventureworks2012.Production.ProductInventory pi
on pi.ProductID = p.ProductID
join Adventureworks2012.Production.Location l
on pi.LocationID = l.LocationID

select p.name, l.name, pi.quantity
from Adventureworks2012.Production.Product p
join
Adventureworks2012.Production.ProductInventory pi
on pi.ProductID = p.ProductID
join Adventureworks2012.Production.Location l
on pi.LocationID = l.LocationID
```

Another factor that can prevent query plan reuse by matching queries is differences in certain SET options, database options, or configuration options in effect for the user session when the query is invoked. For example, a query might optimize differently for one session if the ANSI_NULLS option is turned on than it would if it were turned off. The following list of SET options must match for a query plan to be reused by a session:

- ▶ ANSI_PADDING

- ▶ FORCEPLAN

- CONCAT_NULL_YIELDS_NULL

- ANSI_WARNINGS

- ANSI_NULLS

- QUOTED_IDENTIFIER

- ANSI_NULL_DFLT_ON

- ANSI_NULL_DFLT_OFF

If any one of these setting values does not match the setting options for a cached plan, the session generates a new query plan. Likewise, if the session is using a different language or DATEFORMAT setting than that used by a cached plan, it needs to generate a new execution plan. As you can see, sometimes fairly subtle differences can prevent plan reuse.

Simple Query Parameterization

For certain simple queries executed without parameters, SQL Server 2014 automatically replaces constant literal values with parameters and compiles the query plan. This simple parameterization of the query plan increases the possibility of query plan matching for subsequent queries. If a subsequent query differs in only the values of the constants, it matches with the parameterized query plan and reuses the query plan.

Consider this query:

```
SELECT * FROM AdventureWorks2012.Production.Product
  WHERE ProductNumber = 'AR-5381'
```

The search value 1 at the end of the statement can be treated like a parameter. When the query plan is generated for this query, the Query Optimizer replaces the search value with a placeholder parameter, such as @1. This process is called *simple parameterization*. Using the method of simple parameterization, SQL Server 2014 recognizes that following statement is identical to the first except for the search value of 9 and would generate essentially the same execution plan:

```
SELECT * FROM AdventureWorks2012.Production.Product
  WHERE ProductNumber = 'FW-9160'
```

This query will reuse the query plan generated by the first query.

NOTE

You can determine whether simple parameterization has been used for a query by examining the query plan information for the query. If the query plan information contains such placeholders as @1 and @2 in the search predicates when literal values were specified in the actual query, you know simple parameterization has been applied for the query. You can see an example of this back in Figure 34.13 where parameters were substituted in the query plan for the search arguments against SalesPersonID and CustomerID.

Query Plan Aging

A query plan is saved in cache along with a cost factor that reflects the cost of actually creating the plan when compiling the query. For ad hoc query plans, SQL Server sets its cost to 0, which indicates that the plan can be removed from the plan cache immediately if space is needed for other plans. For other query plans, such as for a stored procedure, the query plan cost is a measure of the amount of resources required to produce it. This cost is calculated in "number of ticks." The maximum plan cost is 31. The plan cost is determined as follows:

Every 2 I/Os required by the plan = 1 tick (with a maximum of 19 ticks)

Every 2 context switches in the plan = 1 tick (with a maximum of 8 ticks)

Every 16 pages (128KB) of memory required for the plan = 1 tick (with a maximum of 4 ticks)

All reusable query plans remain in cache until space is needed in the plan cache for a new plan. When space is needed, SQL Server removes the oldest unused execution plan from the plan cache that has the lowest plan cost.

As plans age in cache, the plan cost is not decremented until the size of the plan cache reaches 50% of the buffer pool size. When this occurs, the next access of the plan cache results in the plan cost for all query plans being decremented by 1. As plans reside in the plan cache over a period of time and are not reused, they eventually reach a plan cache cost of 0 and thus become eligible to be removed from cache the next time plan cache space is needed. However, when a query plan is reused, its plan cost is reset back to its initial value. This helps ensure that frequently accessed query plans remain in the plan cache.

Recompiling Query Plans

Certain changes in a database over time can cause existing execution plans to become either inefficient or invalid, based on the new state of the database. SQL Server detects the changes that invalidate an execution plan and marks the plan as not valid. A new plan is then automatically recompiled the next time the query that uses that query plan is invoked. Most query plan recompilations are required either for statement correctness or to obtain potentially faster query execution plans. The types of conditions that can invalidate a query plan include the following:

▶ Modifications made to the definition of a table or view referenced by the query using ALTER TABLE and ALTER VIEW

▶ Changes made to any indexes used by the execution plan

▶ Updates to the statistics used by the execution plan via either the UPDATE STATISTICS command or automatically

▶ Dropping of an index or indexed view used by the execution plan

▶ Execution of sp_recompile on a table referenced by the query plan

▶ Large numbers of changes to keys (generated by INSERT or DELETE statements from other users that modify a table referenced by the query)

▶ Adding or dropping a trigger on a table

▶ When the number of rows in the inserted or deleted tables grows significantly within a trigger defined on a table referenced in the query plan

▶ Execution of a stored procedure with the WITH RECOMPILE option specified

To avoid the unnecessary recompilation of statements that do not require it, SQL Server 2014 performs statement-level recompilation: Only the statement inside the batch or stored procedure that requires recompilation is recompiled. Statement-level recompilation helps improve query performance because, in most cases, only a small number of statements within a batch or stored procedure cause recompilations and their associated penalties, in terms of CPU time and locks. These penalties are therefore avoided for the other statements in the batch that do not have to be recompiled.

Forcing Query Plan Recompiles

If you suspect that a query plan that is being reused is not appropriate for the current execution of a query, you can also manually force the query plan to be recompiled for the query. This capability can be especially useful for parameterized queries. Query parameterization provides a performance benefit by minimizing compilation overhead, but a parameterized query often provides less specific costing information to the Query Optimizer and can result in the creation of a more general plan, which can be less efficient than a more specific plan created for a specific set of literal values.

If the initial parameterized query plan generated for the query was not based on a representative set of parameters, or if you are invoking an instance of the query with a nonrepresentative set of search values, you might find it necessary to force the Query Optimizer to generate a new query plan. You can force query recompilation for a specific execution of a query by specifying the RECOMPILE query hint. For more information on specifying the RECOMPILE query hint, see Chapter 35.

Monitoring the Plan Cache

You can view and get information about the query plans currently in plan cache memory by using some of the DMVs available in SQL Server 2014. Following are some of the useful ones related to monitoring the plan cache:

▶ **sys.dm_exec_cached_plans**—Returns general information about the query execution plans currently in the plan cache.

▶ **sys.dm_exec_query_stats**—Returns aggregate performance statistics for cached query plans.

▶ **sys.dm_exec_sql_text**—Returns the text of the SQL statement for a specified plan handle.

▶ `sys.dm_exec_cached_plan_dependent_objects`—Returns one row for every dependent object of a compiled plan.

▶ `sys.dm_exec_plan_attributes`—Returns one row per attribute associated with the plan for a specified plan handle.

sys.dm_exec_cached_plans

The `sys.dm_exec_cached_plans` DMV provides information on all the execution plans currently in the plan cache. Because the cache can have a large number of plans, you usually want to limit the results returned from `sys.dm_exec_cached_plans` by using a filter on the `cacheobjtype` column and also using the TOP clause. For example, the query shown in Listing 34.1 returns the top 10 compiled plans currently in the plan cache, sorted in descending order by the number of times the plan has been reused (`usecounts`).

LISTING 34.1   Returning the Top 10 Compiled Plans, by Usage Count

```
select top 10 objtype, usecounts, size_in_bytes, plan_handle
   from sys.dm_exec_cached_plans
   where cacheobjtype = 'Compiled Plan'
   order by usecounts desc
go

/* output
objtype    usecounts size_in_bytes plan_handle
---------  --------- ------------- ---------------------------------------------------
Prepared   127       65536         0x06000100962E9C11B820A2070000000000000000000000000
Adhoc      110       49152         0x06000100804AD300B8E02D0C0000000000000000000000000
Adhoc      40        16384         0x060001006CC40F18B860D80A0000000000000000000000000
Adhoc      26        8192          0x0600040023900901B820A1060000000000000000000000000
Adhoc      26        8192          0x060004003E77102CB8E0A3060000000000000000000000000
Proc       17        8192          0x05000400F578A275B8405F070000000000000000000000000
Adhoc      17        8192          0x06000400EBC44D2AB880A0060000000000000000000000000
Adhoc      15        8192          0x060001001AF2320BB8801A080000000000000000000000000
Proc       12        212992        0x05000400744F1F67B8604F0E0000000000000000000000000
Proc       12        49152         0x050004006A934A11B8C0550E0000000000000000000000000
*/
```

The types of plans in the plan cache are listed under the `cacheobjtype` column and can be any of the following:

▶ **Compiled Plan**—The actual compiled plan generated that can be shared by sessions running the same procedure or query.

▶ **Compiled Plan Stub**—A small, compiled plan stub generated when a batch is compiled for the first time and the Optimize for Ad Hoc Workloads option is enabled. It helps to relieve memory pressure by not allowing the plan cache to become filled with compiled plans that are not reused.

▶ **Parse Tree**—The internal parsed form of a query generated before compilation and optimization.

▶ **CLR Compiled Func**—Execution plan for a CLR-based function.

▶ **CLR Compiled Proc**—Execution plan for a CLR-based procedure.

▶ **Extended proc**—The cached information for an extended stored procedure.

The type of object or query for which a plan is cached is stored in the `objtype` column. This column can contain one of the following values:

▶ **Proc**—The cached plan is for a stored procedure or inline function.

▶ **Prepared**—The cached plan is for queries submitted using `sp_executesql` or for queries using the prepare and execute method.

▶ **Adhoc**—The cached plan is for queries that don't fall into any other category.

▶ **ReplProc**—The cached plan is for replication agents.

▶ **Trigger**—The cached plan is for a trigger.

▶ **View**—The cached plan is for a view or a noninline function. You typically see a parse tree only for a view or noninline function, not a compiled plan. The view or function typically does not have its own separate plan because it is expanded as part of another query.

▶ **UsrTab or SysTab**—The cached plan is for a user or system table that has computed columns. This is typically associated with a parse tree.

▶ **Default, Check, or Rule**—The cached plan is simply a parse tree for these types of objects because they are expanded as part of another query in which they are applied.

To determine how often a plan is being reused, you can examine the value in the `usecounts` columns. The `usecounts` value is incremented each time the cached plan is looked up and reused.

sys.dm_exec_sql_text

Overall, the information returned by `sys.dm_exec_cached_plans` is not overly useful unless you know what queries or stored procedures these plans refer to. You can view the SQL text of these query plans by writing a query that joins `sys.dm_exec_cached_plans` with the `sys.dm_exec_sql_text` DMV. For example, you can use the query shown in Listing 34.2 to return the SQL text for the top 10 largest ad hoc query plans currently in the plan cache.

LISTING 34.2   Returning the Top 10 Largest Ad Hoc Query Plans

```
select top 10 objtype, usecounts, size_in_bytes,  plan_handle,
     -- the following removes newline and carriage return from the sql text
     replace(replace( text, char(13), ' '), char(10), ' ') as sqltext
  from sys.dm_exec_cached_plans as p
  cross apply sys.dm_exec_sql_text (p.plan_handle)
  where cacheobjtype = 'Compiled Plan'
    and objtype = 'Adhoc'
  order by size_in_bytes desc, usecounts desc
```

sys.dm_exec_query_stats

The plan cache also keeps track of useful statistics about each cached plan, such as the amount of CPU or the number of reads and writes performed by the query plan since it was placed into the plan cache. This information can be examined using the sys.dm_exec_query_stats DMV, which returns statistics for each statement in a stored procedure or a SQL batch. To provide statistics for the procedure or batch as a whole, you need to summarize the data. Listing 34.3 provides a sample query that returns the I/O, CPU, and elapsed time statistics for the 10 most recently executed stored procedures.

LISTING 34.3   Returning Query Plan Stats for the 10 Most Recently Executed Procedures

```
select TOP 10 usecounts, size_in_bytes,
  max(last_execution_time) as last_execution_time,
  sum(total_logical_reads) as total_logical_reads,
  sum(total_physical_reads) as total_physical_reads,
  sum(total_worker_time/1000) as total_CPU_time,
  sum(total_elapsed_time/1000) as total_elapsed_time,
  replace(substring (text,
                     patindex('%create procedure%', text),
                     datalength(text)),
          'create procedure', '') as procname
  from sys.dm_exec_query_stats s
  join sys.dm_exec_cached_plans p on s.plan_handle = p.plan_handle
  CROSS APPLY sys.dm_exec_sql_text(p.plan_handle) as st
  where p.objtype = 'Proc' and p.cacheobjtype = 'Compiled Plan'
  group by usecounts, size_in_bytes, text
  order by max(last_execution_time) desc
```

Table 34.1 describes some of the most useful columns returned by the sys.dm_exec_query_stats DMV.

TABLE 34.1   Description of Columns for `sys.dm_exec_query_stats`

Column Name	Description
`sql_handle`	The token that refers to the batch or stored procedure that the query is part of. Can be used with `statement_start_offset` and `statement_end_offset` to retrieve the SQL text of the query using `sys.dm_exec_sql_text`.
`statement_start_offset`	The starting position of the query that the row describes within the text of its batch or stored procedure, indicated in bytes, beginning with `0`.
`statement_end_offset`	The ending position of the query that the row describes within the text of its batch or stored proc. A value of `-1` indicates the end of the batch.
`plan_generation_num`	The number of times the plan has been recompiled while it has remained in the cache.
`plan_handle`	A pointer to the plan. This value can be passed to the `dm_exec_query_plan` dynamic management function.
`creation_time`	The time the plan was compiled.
`last_execution_time`	The last time the plan was executed.
`execution_count`	The number of times the plan has been executed since it was last compiled.
`total_worker_time`	The total amount of CPU time, in microseconds, consumed by executions of this plan for the statement.
`last_worker_time`	The CPU time, in microseconds, consumed the last time the plan was executed.
`min_worker_time`	The minimum CPU time, in microseconds, this plan has ever consumed during a single execution.
`max_worker_time`	The maximum CPU time, in microseconds, this plan has ever consumed during a single execution.
`total_physical_reads`	The total number of physical reads performed by executions of this plan since it was compiled.
`last_physical_reads`	The number of physical reads performed the last time the plan was executed.
`min_physical_reads`	The minimum number of physical reads this plan has ever performed during a single execution.
`max_physical_reads`	The maximum number of physical reads this plan has ever performed during a single execution.
`total_logical_writes`	The total number of logical writes performed by executions of this plan since it was compiled.
`last_logical_writes`	The number of logical writes performed the last time the plan was executed.
`min_logical_writes`	The minimum number of logical writes this plan has ever performed during a single execution.

34

Column Name	Description
max_logical_writes	The maximum number of logical writes this plan has ever performed during a single execution.
total_logical_reads	The total number of logical reads performed by executions of this plan since it was compiled.
last_logical_reads	The number of logical reads performed the last time the plan was executed.
min_logical_reads	The minimum number of logical reads this plan has ever performed during a single execution.
max_logical_reads	The maximum number of logical reads this plan has ever performed during a single execution.
total_elapsed_time	The total elapsed time, in microseconds, for completed executions of this plan.
last_elapsed_time	The elapsed time, in microseconds, for the most recently completed execution of this plan.
min_elapsed_time	The minimum elapsed time, in microseconds, for any completed execution of this plan.
max_elapsed_time	The maximum elapsed time, in microseconds, for any completed execution of this plan.
query_hash	The binary hash value calculated on the query and used to identify queries with similar logic.
query_plan_hash	The binary hash value calculated on the query execution plan and used to identify similar query execution plans.
total_rows	Total number of rows returned by the query.
last_rows	Number of rows returned by the last execution of the query.
min_rows	Minimum number of rows returned by the query by any execution since it was loaded into the plan cache.
max_rows	Maximum number of rows returned by the query by any execution since it was loaded into the plan cache.

The query_hash and query_plan_hash values can be used to determine the aggregate resource usage for queries that differ only by literal values or with similar execution plans. You can use these values to write queries that you can use to help determine the aggregate resource usage for similar queries and similar query execution plans. For example, Listing 34.4 provides a query to find the query_hash and query_plan_hash values for queries that select from the Production.Product table searching by List_Price. Looking at the results, you can see that even with different search arguments, each of the matching queries generates the same query hash value as well as the same query plan hash values for queries that use similar query plans. However, each row indicates a separate instance of a cached plan for the query.

LISTING 34.4 Returning Query and Query Plan Hash Values for a Query

```
SELECT convert(varchar(54), substring(st.text, 1, 76)) AS 'Query Text',
       qs.query_hash AS 'Query Hash',
       qs.query_plan_hash as 'Query Plan Hash', st.text,
       qs.plan_handle
FROM sys.dm_exec_query_stats qs
CROSS APPLY sys.dm_exec_sql_text (qs.sql_handle) st
    WHERE st.text like 'select * from Production.Product where ListPrice%'
Go

/* output
Query Text                                          Query Hash          Query Plan Hash
--------------------------------------------------- ------------------- ----------
select * from Production.Product where ListPrice = 115 0x7DDEE2CD44F8584A
0xD05314ADE08D22B9
select * from Production.Product where ListPrice = 10  0x7DDEE2CD44F8584A
0xD05314ADE08D22B9
select * from Production.Product where ListPrice = 126 0x7DDEE2CD44F8584A
0xD05314ADE08D22B9
select * from Production.Product where ListPrice = 120 0x7DDEE2CD44F8584A
0xD05314ADE08D22B9
select * from Production.Product where ListPrice = 125 0x7DDEE2CD44F8584A
0xD05314ADE08D22B9
*/
```

This query hash or query plan hash value can be used in a query to aggregate performance statistics for similar queries. For example, the following query returns the average processing time and logical reads for the same queries that were returned in Listing 34.4:

```
SELECT
 SUM(total_worker_time) / SUM(execution_count)/1000. AS "Avg CPU Time(ms)",
 SUM(total_logical_reads) / SUM(execution_count) AS "Avg Reads"
FROM
sys.dm_exec_query_stats
where query_hash = 0x7DDEE2CD44F8584A
go

/* output
Avg CPU Time(ms)                          Avg Reads
----------------------------------------- --------------------
0.122000                                  15
*/
```

Listing 34.5 provides a sample query using the query hash value to return information about the top 25 queries ranked by average processing time.

LISTING 34.5   Returning Top 25 Queries Using Query Hash

```
SELECT TOP 25 query_stats.query_hash AS "Query Hash",
    SUM(query_stats.total_worker_time) / SUM(query_stats.execution_count) AS
 "Avg CPU Time",
    MIN(query_stats.statement_text) AS "Statement Text"
FROM
    (SELECT QS.*,
    SUBSTRING(ST.text, (QS.statement_start_offset/2) + 1,
    ((CASE statement_end_offset
        WHEN -1 THEN DATALENGTH(ST.text)
        ELSE QS.statement_end_offset END
            - QS.statement_start_offset)/2) + 1) AS statement_text
    FROM sys.dm_exec_query_stats AS QS
    CROSS APPLY sys.dm_exec_sql_text(QS.sql_handle) as ST) as query_stats
GROUP BY query_stats.query_hash
ORDER BY 2 DESC;
GO
```

sys.dm_exec_plan_attributes

If you want to get information about specific attributes of a specific query plan, you use
sys.dm_exec_plan_attributes. This DMV takes a plan_handle as an input parameter (see
Listing 34.1 for an example of a query that you can use to retrieve a query's plan handle)
and returns one row for each attribute associated with the query plan. These attributes
include information such as the ID of the database context in which the query plan was
generated, the ID of the user who generated the query plan, session SET options in effect
at the time the plan was generated, and so on. Many of these attributes are used as part of
the cache lookup key for the plan (indicated by the value 1 in the is_cache_key_column).
Following is an example of the output for sys.dm_exec_plan_attributes:

```
select convert(varchar(30), attribute) as attribute,
       convert(varchar(12), value) as value,
       is_cache_key
FROM
sys.dm_exec_plan_attributes (0x06000400EBC44D2AB880A00600000000000000000000000000)
where is_cache_key = 1
go

/* output
attribute                       value        is_cache_key
-----------------------------   -----------  ------------
set_options                     251          1
objectid                        690029420    1
dbid                            1            1
dbid_execute                    0            1
user_id                         -2           1
```

```
language_id                         0              1
date_format                         1              1
date_first                          7              1
compat_level                        120            1
status                              0              1
required_cursor_options             0              1
acceptable_cursor_options           0              1
merge_action_type                   0              1
is_replication_specific             0              1
optional_spid                       0              1
optional_clr_trigger_dbid           0              1
optional_clr_trigger_objid          0              1
parent_plan_handle                  NULL           1

*/
```

Note the attributes flagged as cache keys for the plan. If one of these properties does not match the state of the current user session, the plan cannot be reused for that session, and a new plan must be compiled and stored in the plan cache. If you see multiple plans in cache for what appears to be the same query, you can determine the key differences between them by comparing the columns associated with the plan's cache keys to see where the differences lie.

TIP

If SQL Server has been running for a while, with a lot of activity, the number of plans in the plan cache can become quite large, resulting in a large number of rows being returned by the plan cache DMVs. To run your own tests to determine which query plans get cached and when specific query plans are reused, you should clear out the cache occasionally. You can use the DBCC FREEPROCCACHE command to clear all cached plans from memory. If you want to clear only the cached plans for objects or queries in a specific database, you execute the following command:

```
DBCC FLUSHPROCINDB (dbid)
```

Keep in mind that you should run these commands only in a test environment. Running these commands in production servers could significantly impact the performance of the currently running applications.

Other Query Processing Strategies

In addition to the optimization strategies covered so far, SQL Server also has some additional strategies it can apply for special types of queries. These strategies are used to help further reduce the cost of executing various types of queries.

Predicate Transitivity

You might be familiar with the transitive property from algebra. The transitive property simply states that if A=B and B=C, then A=C. SQL Server supports the transitive property in its query predicates. Predicate transitivity enables SQL Server to infer a join equality from two given equalities. Consider the following example:

```
SELECT *
   FROM table1 t1
   join table2 t2 on t1.column1 = t2.column1
   join table3 t3 on t2.column1 = t3.column1
```

Using the principle of predicate transitivity, SQL Server is able to infer that `t1.column1` is equal to `t3.column1`. This capability provides the Query Optimizer with another join strategy to consider when optimizing this query. This might result in a more efficient execution plan.

The transitive property can also be applied to SARGs used on join columns. Consider the following query:

```
select OrderQty
from Sales.SalesOrderDetail sod
inner join Production.Product p
on sod.ProductID = p.ProductID
where p.ProductID = 777
```

Again, using transitive closure, it follows that `sod.ProductID` is also equal to 777. SQL Server recognizes this and can compare the search value against the statistics on both tables to more accurately estimate the number of matching rows from each table.

GROUP BY Optimization

One way SQL Server can process GROUP BY results is to retrieve the matching detailed data rows into a worktable and then sort the rows and calculate the aggregates on the groups formed. In SQL Server 2014, the Query Optimizer also may choose to use hashing to organize the data into groups and then compute the aggregates.

The hash aggregation strategy uses the same basic method for grouping and calculating aggregates as for a hash join. At the point where the probe input row is checked to determine whether it already exists in the hash bucket, the aggregate is computed if a hash match is found. The following pseudocode summarizes the hash aggregation strategy:

```
create a hash table
for each row in the input table
    read the row
    hash the key value
    search the hash table for matches
    if match found
        aggregate the value into the old record
```

```
    else
        insert the hashed key into the hash bucket
scan and output the hash table contents
drop the hash table
```

For some join queries that contain GROUP BY clauses, SQL Server might perform the grouping operation before processing the join. This could reduce the size of the input table to the join and lower the overall cost of executing the query.

> **NOTE**
>
> One important point to keep in mind is that regardless of the GROUP BY strategy employed, the rows are not guaranteed to be returned in sorted order by the grouping column(s). If the results must be returned in a specific sort order, you need to use the ORDER BY clause with GROUP BY to ensure ordered results.

Queries with DISTINCT

When the DISTINCT clause is specified in a query, SQL Server can eliminate duplicate rows by sorting the result set in a worktable to identify and remove the duplicates, similar to how a worktable is used for GROUP BY queries. In SQL Server 2014, the Query Optimizer can also employ a hashing strategy similar to that used for GROUP BY to return only the distinct rows before the final result set is determined.

In addition, if the Query Optimizer can determine at compile time that there will be no possibility of duplicate rows in the result set (for example, each row contains the table's primary key), the strategies for removing duplicate rows may be skipped altogether.

Queries with UNION

When you specify UNION in a query, SQL Server merges the result sets, applying one of the merge or concatenation operators with sorting strategies to remove any duplicate rows. Figure 34.25 shows an example of an execution plan for the following UNION query:

```
SELECT ProductID FROM Sales.SalesOrderDetail sod
  WHERE sod.OrderQty > 1000
UNION
SELECT productID FROM Production.Product p
  WHERE p.ProductID > 1000
```

You'll notice this execution plan is similar to the execution plan for the OR strategy where the rows are concatenated and then sorted to remove any duplicates.

If you specify UNION ALL in a query, SQL Server simply appends the result sets together. No intermediate sorting or merge step is needed to remove duplicates. Figure 34.26 shows the same query as in Figure 34.25, except that a UNION ALL is specified.

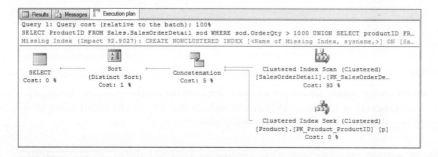

FIGURE 34.25   An execution plan for a UNION query.

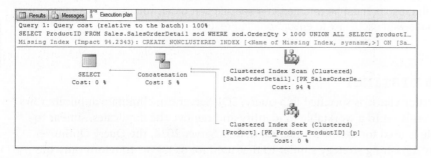

FIGURE 34.26   An execution plan for a UNION ALL query.

When you know that you do not need to worry about duplicate rows in a UNION result set, always specify UNION ALL to eliminate the extra overhead required for sorting.

When a UNION is used to merge large result sets together, SQL Server 2014 may opt to use a merge join or hash match operation to remove any duplicate rows. Figure 34.27 shows an example of the following UNION query where the rows are concatenated, and then a hash match operation is used to remove any duplicates:

```
SELECT ProductID FROM Sales.SalesOrderDetail sod
  WHERE sod.OrderQty > 1000
UNION
SELECT productID FROM Production.Product p
```

Queries Using Columnstore Indexes

xVelocity columnstore indexes, first introduced in SQL Server 2012, group and store data for each column in the table and then join all the columns to complete the whole index. This type of index differs from traditional indexes, which group and store data for each row of data and then join all the rows to complete the whole index. For certain types of queries, such as data warehousing types of queries that access large amounts of data, the SQL Server query processor can take advantage of the columnstore index to significantly improve query execution times.

When the optimizer identifies a columnstore index and generates a query plan that makes use of the columnstore index, you'll see the Columnstore Index Scan operator in the execution plan, as shown in Figure 34.28.

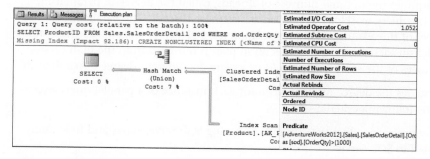

FIGURE 34.27   An execution plan for a UNION query, using a hash match to eliminate duplicate rows.

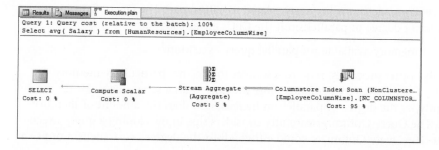

FIGURE 34.28   An execution plan for a query using a columnstore index.

For more information on the structure and creation of columnstore indexes, see Chapter 32.

Parallel Query Processing

The query processor in SQL Server 2014 includes parallel query processing—an execution strategy that can improve the performance of complex queries on computers with more than one processor.

SQL Server inserts exchange operators into each parallel query to build and manage the query execution plan. The exchange operator is responsible for providing process management, data redistribution, and flow control. The exchange operators are displayed in the query plans as the Distribute Streams, Repartition Streams, and Gather Streams logical operators. One or more of these operators can appear in the execution plan output of a query plan for a parallel query.

Whereas a parallel query execution plan can use more than one thread, a serial execution plan, used by a nonparallel query, uses only a single thread for its execution. Prior to query execution time, SQL Server determines whether the current system state and configuration allow for parallel query execution. If parallel query execution is justified, SQL Server determines the optimal number of threads, called the degree of parallelism, and distributes the query workload execution across those threads. The parallel query uses the same number of threads until the query completes. SQL Server reexamines the optimal degree of parallelism each time a query execution plan is retrieved from the plan cache. Individual instances of the same query could be assigned a different degree of parallelism.

SQL Server calculates the degree of parallelism for each instance of a parallel query execution by using the following criteria:

▶ How many processors does the computer running SQL Server have, and how many are allocated to SQL Server?

   If two or more processors are allocated to SQL Server, it can use parallel queries.

▶ What is the number of concurrent active users?

   The degree of parallelism is inversely related to CPU usage. The Query Optimizer assigns a lower degree of parallelism if the CPUs are already busy.

▶ Is sufficient memory available for parallel query execution?

   Queries, like other processes, require resources to execute, particularly memory. Obviously, a parallel query demands more memory than a serial query. More importantly, as the degree of parallelism increases, so does the amount of memory required. The Query Optimizer carefully considers this in developing a query execution plan. The Query Optimizer could either adjust the degree of parallelism or use a serial plan to complete the query.

▶ What is the type of query being executed?

   Queries that use several CPU cycles justify using a parallel execution plan. Some examples are joins of large tables, substantial aggregations, and sorting of large result sets. The Query Optimizer determines whether to use a parallel or serial plan by checking the value of the cost threshold for parallelism.

▶ Are a sufficient number of rows processed in the given stream?

   If the Query Optimizer determines that the number of rows in a stream is too low, it does not execute a parallel plan. This prevents scenarios where the parallel execution costs exceed the benefits of executing a parallel plan.

Regardless of the answers to the previous questions, the Query Optimizer does not use a parallel execution plan for a query if any one of the following conditions is true:

▶ The serial execution cost of the query is not high enough to consider an alternative parallel execution plan.

▶ A serial execution plan exists that is estimated to be faster than any possible parallel execution plan for the particular query.

▶ The query contains scalar or relational operators that cannot be run in parallel.

Parallel Query Configuration Options

Two server configuration options—maximum degree of parallelism and cost threshold for parallelism—affect the consideration for a parallel query. For single processor systems, these settings are ignored. On multi-processor systems, you may need to change the default settings for one or both of these options, but this should not be done arbitrarily. Proper settings depend on the number of available processors and the type and volume of activity the system will experience.

> **NOTE**
>
> Before making adjustments to these settings, you should first establish some baseline performance statistics as the system and query level. Then adjust the setting based upon typical recommendations provided in this section and compare the performance statistics against the baseline statistics to determine if performance has improved or degraded. For more information on performance monitoring and which performance metrics to evaluate that are related to these settings, see Chapter 39, "Monitoring SQL Server Performance."

The maximum degree of parallelism option limits the number of threads to use in a parallel plan execution. The range of possible values is 0 to 32. This value is configured to 0 by default, which allows the Query Optimizer to use up to the actual number of CPUs allocated to SQL Server. If you want to suppress parallel processing completely, set the value to 1.

> **TIP**
>
> Despite the advice you may see on the Internet, setting maximum degree of parallelism to 1 to disable parallel processing is not recommended. However, if the max degree of parallelism for a query is set to 0 on a 32-way server, SQL Server will try to use all 32 processors even if 7 processors might perform the job more efficiently. Because of this all-or-nothing behavior, if SQL Server uses the parallel plan, the time that is required by SQL Server to coordinate all the processors on a high-end server outweighs the advantages of using a parallel plan. If you have more than 8 processors allocated to SQL Server, a typical recommendation is to limit the maximum degree of parallelism option to 8.

The cost threshold for parallelism option establishes a ceiling value the Query Optimizer uses to consider parallel query execution plans. If the calculated value to execute a serial plan is greater than the value set for the cost threshold for parallelism, a parallel plan is generated. This value is defined by the estimated time, in seconds, to execute the serial plan. The range of values for this setting is 0 to 32767. The default value is 5. If the maximum degree of parallelism is set to 1, or if the computer has a single processor, the cost threshold for parallelism value is ignored.

TIP

The optimizer uses the cost threshold to figure out when it should start evaluating plans that can use multiple threads. Although there's no right or wrong number, 5 is a legacy setting and is rather low for today's modern systems. It's appropriate for purely OLTP applications, generally too low of a threshold for more complex queries, especially in mixed use environments. A general recommendation is to start with a setting of 50 and tuning up or down as appropriate, measuring the performance of the more critical queries in your application.

You can modify the settings for the maximum degree of parallelism and the cost threshold for parallelism server configuration options either by using the sp_configure system stored procedure or through SSMS. To set the values for these options, use the sp_configure system stored procedure via SSMS or via SQLCMD, as follows:

```
USE master
go
exec sp_configure 'show advanced options', 1
GO
RECONFIGURE
GO
exec sp_configure 'max degree of parallelism', 2
exec sp_configure 'cost threshold for parallelism', 15
RECONFIGURE
GO
```

To set these configuration options via SSMS, right-click the SQL Server instance in the Object Explorer and then click Properties. In the Server Properties dialog, select the Advanced page. The parallelism options are near the bottom, as shown in Figure 34.29.

Identifying Parallel Queries

You can identify when a parallel execution plan is being chosen by displaying the graphical execution plan in SSMS. The graphical execution plan uses icons to represent the execution of specific statements and queries in SQL Server. The execution plan output for every parallel query has at least one of these three logical operators:

▶ **Distribute Streams**—Receives a single input stream of records and distributes multiple output streams. The contents and form of the record are unchanged. All records enter through the same single input stream and appear in one of the output streams, preserving the relative order.

▶ **Gather Streams**—Assembles multiple input streams of records and yields a single output stream. The relative order of the records, contents, and form is maintained.

▶ **Repartition Streams**—Accepts multiple input streams and produces multiple streams of records. The record contents and format are unchanged.

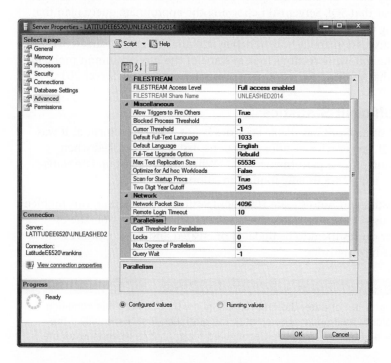

FIGURE 34.29   Setting SQL Server parallelism options.

Figure 34.30 shows an example of a query plan that uses parallel query techniques—both repartition streams and gather streams for the following query:

```
SELECT p.productID, sod.orderqty
  FROM Sales.SalesOrderDetail sod
  INNER JOIN Production.Product p
    ON sod.ProductID = p.ProductID
  ORDER BY Style
```

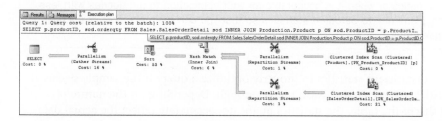

FIGURE 34.30   A graphical execution plan of a query using parallel query techniques.

Common Query Optimization Problems

So you've written a query and examined the query plan, and performance isn't what you expected. It might appear that SQL Server isn't choosing the appropriate query plan that you expect. Is something wrong with the query or with the Query Optimizer? Before delving into a detailed discussion about how to debug and analyze query plans (covered in detail in Chapter 36), the following sections look at some of the more common problems and SQL coding issues that can lead to poor query plan selection in SQL Server 2014.

Out-of-Date or Insufficient Statistics

Admittedly, having out-of-date or unavailable statistics is not as big a problem as it was "back in the day." In SQL Server releases prior to 7.0, the first question asked when someone was complaining of poor performance was, "When did you last update statistics?" If the answer was "Huh?" we usually found the culprit.

With Auto-Update Statistics and Auto-Create Statistics features in SQL Server, this problem is not as prevalent as it used to be. If a query detects that statistics are out of date or missing, it automatically causes them to be updated or created and then optimizes the query plan based on the new statistics.

NOTE

If statistics are missing or out of date, the first running query that detects this condition might run a bit more slowly as it updates or creates the statistics first, especially if the table is relatively large and also if it has been configured for FULLSCAN when indexes are updated.

However, SQL Server 2014 provides the AUTO_UPDATE_STATISTICS_ASYNC database option. When this option is set to ON, queries do not wait for the statistics to be updated before compiling. Instead, the out-of-date statistics are put on a queue for updating by a worker thread in a background process, and the query and any other concurrent queries compile immediately, using the existing out-of-date statistics. Although there is no wait for the statistics to be updated, the out-of-date statistics may cause the Query Optimizer to choose a less efficient query plan, but at least the response times will be more predictable. Any queries invoked after the updated statistics have been generated will use the updated statistics in generating a query plan. This may cause the recompilation of any cached plans that depend on the older statistics.

You should consider setting the AUTO_UPDATE_STATISTICS_ASYNC option to ON when any of your applications have experienced client request timeouts caused by queries waiting for updated statistics or when it is acceptable for your application to run queries with less efficient query plans due to outdated statistics so that you can maintain more predictable query response times.

You could have insufficient statistics to properly optimize a query if the sample size used when the statistics were generated wasn't large enough. Depending on the nature of your data and size of the table, the statistics might not accurately reflect the actual data distribution and cardinality. If you suspect that this is the case, you can update statistics by specifying the FULLSCAN option or a larger sample size, so SQL Server examines more records to derive the statistics.

Another common situation that results in out of data statistics is the "ascending key problem." This situation arises when search conditions reference newly inserted values that fall beyond the range of the values stored in the statistics histogram. For example, consider a sales order table that has a sales datetime data type column that is ever-increasing. Newly inserted rows will have a value greater than the last sampled histogram step. In OLTP systems, it is common for queries to use predicates against more recently inserted data, such as searching for all sales order records that were inserted in the last hour.

With very large tables, it may require the insertion of a significant number of rows before the threshold is reached to trigger an automatic update of the statistics. Typically, when a search value falls beyond the range of values stored in the statistics histogram, SQL Server estimates only 1 row will match the search condition. If there are a large number of newly added rows with values beyond the last value in the histogram, this underestimation can lead to the selection of a less than optimal execution plan.

Before SQL Server 2014, there were some one-off solutions available to address this issue, such as using trace flags 2389 and 2390 to enable automatic generation of statistics for ascending keys. However, the behavior was not on by default.

The new Cardinality Estimator addresses this ascending key problem by assuming that the queried values do exist in the table even if the value falls outside of the range of the histogram. If it detects that new rows have been added since the last time statistics were updates, instead of using the estimate of only 1 matching row, the CE now estimates the number of matching rows for values outside the histogram by multiplying the number of rows in the table by the alldensity value stored in the statistics for the search column.

For example, if the table contains 122,327 rows and the alldensity value for the saledate column is 0.0008880995, the row estimate for any search on a saledate that exceeds the maximum date stored in the statistics histogram for the saledate column would be 122,317 * 0.0008880995, or 109 rows.

> **NOTE**
>
> If the statistics used for the calculation were computed by scanning all rows in the table or indexed view rather than a sampling of the rows, the row estimate will be the lesser of the alldensity * the number of rows in the table or the estimated number of rows added since the last time the statistics were generated.

For more information on understanding and managing index statistics, see Chapter 32.

Poor Index Design

Poor index design is another reason—often a primary reason—why queries might not optimize as you expect them to. If no supporting indexes exist for a query, or if a query contains SARGs that cannot be optimized effectively to use the available indexes, SQL Server ends up performing either a table scan, an index scan, or a hash or merge join strategy that may be less efficient. If this appears to be the problem, you need to re-eval-uate your indexing decisions or rewrite the query so it can take advantage of an available index. For more information on designing useful indexes, see Chapter 32.

Search Argument Problems

It is a blessing as well as the curse of SQL that there are a number of ways to write a query and get the same result set. Some queries, however, might not be as efficient as others. A good understanding of the Query Optimizer can help you avoid writing search arguments that SQL Server can't optimize effectively. The following sections provide some tips to avoid some of the common "gotchas" encountered in SQL Server SARGs that can lead to poor or unexpected query performance.

Use Optimizable SARGs

As mentioned previously, in the section, "Identifying Search Arguments," the Query Optimizer uses search arguments to help it narrow down the set of rows to evaluate. The search argument is in the form of a WHERE clause that equates a column to a constant. The SARGs that optimize most effectively are those that compare a column with a constant value that is not an expression or a variable and with no operation performed against the column itself. The following is an example:

```
SELECT column1
    FROM table1
    WHERE column1 = 123
```

You should also try to avoid using any negative logic in your SARGs (for example, !=, <>, not in) or performing operations on, or applying functions to, the columns in the SARG.

Avoid Unknown Values in WHERE Clauses

You need to watch out for expressions in which the search value in the SARG cannot be evaluated until runtime. In these expressions, often the search value is a local variable or subquery that can be materialized to a single value.

SQL Server treats these expressions as SARGs but can't use the statistics histogram to esti-mate the number of matching rows because it doesn't have a value to compare against the histogram values during query optimization. The values for the expressions aren't known until the query is actually executed. In this situation, the Query Optimizer uses the index density information. The Query Optimizer is generally able to better estimate the number of rows affected by a query when it can compare a known value against the statis-tics histogram than when it has to use the index density to estimate the average number of rows that match an unknown value. This is especially true if the data in a table isn't distributed evenly. When you can, you should try to avoid using constant expressions that can't be evaluated until runtime so that the statistics histogram can be used rather than the density value.

To avoid using constant expressions in WHERE clauses that can't be evaluated until runtime, you should consider putting the queries into stored procedures and passing in the constant expression as a parameter. Because the Query Optimizer evaluates the value of a parameter prior to optimization, SQL Server evaluates the expression prior to optimizing the stored procedure.

For best results when writing queries inside stored procedures, you should use stored procedure parameters rather than local variables in your SARGs whenever possible. This strategy allows the Query Optimizer to optimize the query by using the statistics histogram, comparing the parameter value against the statistics histogram to estimate the number of matching rows. If you use local variables as SARGs in stored procedures, the Query Optimizer is restricted to using index density, even if the local variable is assigned the value of a parameter.

Other types of constructs for which it is difficult for the Query Optimizer to accurately estimate the number of qualifying rows or the data distribution using the statistics histogram include aggregations in subqueries, scalar expressions, user-defined functions, and non-inline table-valued functions.

Avoid Data Type Mismatches

Another common problem is data type mismatches. If you attempt to join tables on columns of different data types, the Query Optimizer might not be able to effectively use indexes to evaluate the join. This can result in a less efficient join strategy because SQL Server has to convert all values first before it can process the query. You should avoid this situation by maintaining data type consistency across the join key columns in your database.

Large Complex Queries

For complex queries with a large number of tables and join conditions, the number of possible execution plans can be enormous. The full optimization phase of the Query Optimizer has a time limit to restrict how long it spends analyzing all the possible query plans. There is no known general and effective shortcut to arrive at the optimal plan. To deal with such a large selection of plans, SQL Server 2014 implements a number of heuristics to deal with very large queries and attempt to come up with an efficient query plan within the time available. When it is not possible to analyze the entire set of plan alternatives and the heuristics are applied, it is not uncommon to encounter suboptimal query plans being chosen.

When is your query large enough to be a concern? Answering this question is difficult because the answer depends on the number of tables involved, the type and number of filter and join predicates, and the operations performed. If a query involves more than 12 tables, it is likely that the Query Optimizer is having to rely on heuristics and shortcuts to generate a query plan and may miss some optimal strategies.

In general, you get more optimal query plans if you can simplify your queries as much as possible. If that's not possible, you may need to consider breaking large complex queries up into smaller, more manageable queries using temporary tables or table variables to hold intermediate results that you'll combine back together at the end into a single result set.

Triggers

If you are using triggers on INSERT, UPDATE, or DELETE, it is possible that your triggers can cause performance problems. You might think that the INSERT, UPDATE, or DELETE is performing poorly when actually it is the trigger that needs to be tuned. In addition, you might have triggers that invoke data modifications that in turn fire other triggers. If you suspect that you are having performance problems with the triggers, you can monitor the SQL they are executing and the response time, as well as execution plans generated for statements within triggers using SQL Server Profiler. For more information on monitoring performance with SQL Server Profiler, see Chapter 5, "SQL Server Profiler." You can also see the query plans for statements executed in triggers by using SSMS if you enable the Include Actual Execution Plan option. For more information on using SSMS to view and analyze query plans, see Chapter 36.

The New Cardinality Estimator Changes

If you've upgraded to SQL Server 2014 and find that your queries are running more slowly than previously, it could actually be the new Cardinality Estimator. Changes in the cardinality estimates can result in a different query plan being chosen and it could end up being less efficient than the plan generated in a prior release.

If you suspect that the cause of the poor query optimization may be the result of the new Cardinality Estimator, the first step is to verify that it's using the new Cardinality Estimator. Just because you are running SQL Server 2014 doesn't mean that the new Cardinality Estimator is being used to optimize your queries. The database compatibility setting for the database context of your SQL Server session determines whether the new CE is being used or not for your queries. The database compatibility has to be set to SQL Server 2014 (version 120) to use the new CE. This will be the default for a new database created in SQL Server 2014, unless it's been changed.

If a database was upgraded from a previous version of SQL Server using an in-place upgrade or by restoring/attaching a database from a prior version of SQL Server, by default the database will retain the earlier compatibility level. If the database compatibility level is less than 120, then the legacy CE will be used to optimizer your queries.

Verifying the CE Version

You can determine which CE version was used for a specific query by viewing the query execution plan XML. This can be done by using the SET STATISTICS XML ON option to display the actual execution plan in addition to the query execution results. Near the top of the execution plan XML, look for the "CardinalityEstimationModelVersion" attribute:

```
<StmtSimple StatementCompId="0" StatementEstRows="100" StatementId="1"
StatementOptmLevel="FULL"
  StatementOptmEarlyAbortReason="GoodEnoughPlanFound"
CardinalityEstimationModelVersion="120" StatementSubTreeCost="0.319167"
StatementText="SELECT * FROM [salesorderdetail_newce] WHERE
[modifiedDate]=@1" StatementType="SELECT" QueryHash="0x37FE61D45CE3502A"
QueryPlanHash="0xF27C13066568D3F7" RetrievedFromCache="false">
```

If the value shown for the `CardinalityEstimationModelVersion` is 120, it's using the new CE. If the value is 70, it's using the legacy CE functionality.

You can also verify the CE version used by viewing the estimated or actual execution plan in SSMS and right clicking on the root node in the query plan and selecting the Properties option (see Figure 34.31). In the Properties panel that comes up, look for the `CardinalityEstimationModelVersion` value.

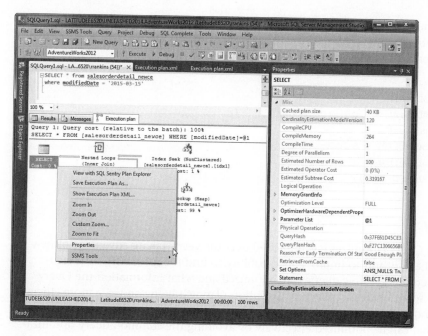

FIGURE 34.31   Verifying the CE version in SSMS.

Enabling or Disabling the New CE

If you determine that the problems with your query plan are a result of the new CE, or that your queries are not being optimized using the new CE, there are a few ways to enable/disable use of the new CE. As mentioned previously, setting the database compatibility level controls which CE is used by default for all queries in the database. If you are experiencing widespread issues with query performance using the new CE, you can set the database compatibility level to a level lower than 120. For example:

```
ALTER DATABASE [AdventureWorks2012] SET COMPATIBILITY_LEVEL = 110;
```

If you don't wish to disable the new CE for all queries, you can leave the database compatibility level set to 120 and force the use of the legacy CE at the individual query level using trace flag 9481 with the `QUERYTRACEON` query hint, as shown in the following example:

```
SELECT [AddressID],
       [AddressLine1],
       [AddressLine2]
FROM Person.[Address]
WHERE [StateProvinceID] = 9 AND
       [City] = 'Burbank'
OPTION (QUERYTRACEON 9481);
```

If you need to run your SQL Server database at a lower compatibility level than 120, but would like to force specific queries to use the new CE, you can specify trace flag 2312 with the QUERYTRACEON query hint:

```
SELECT [AddressID],
       [AddressLine1],
       [AddressLine2]
FROM Person.[Address]
WHERE [StateProvinceID] = 9 AND
       [City] = 'Burbank'
OPTION (QUERYTRACEON 2312);
```

Summary

The SQL Server Query Optimizer has improved over the years, taking advantage of new techniques and algorithms to improve its capability to find the most efficient execution plan. Understanding how queries are optimized and what information the Query Optimizer uses to generate and select an execution plan will help you write more efficient queries and choose better indexes. To help the Query Optimizer, you should at least try to write queries that can be optimized effectively by avoiding the common query optimization problems discussed in this chapter.

Most of the time, the Query Optimizer chooses the most efficient query plan. When it doesn't, the reason might be problems with the way the query itself is written, out-of-date or unavailable statistics, poor index design, or other common query performance problems, as discussed in this chapter. Still, on occasion, the Query Optimizer may make the wrong choice for an execution plan. When you suspect that the Query Optimizer is making the wrong decision, you can use SQL Server's table and Query Optimizer hints and the plan guide feature to override the Query Optimizer's decisions. However, before arbitrarily applying these hints, you should analyze the queries fully to try to determine why the Query Optimizer is choosing a particular plan. To aid you in this effort, SQL Server provides a number of tools to analyze the query plans generated and determine the source of the problem. These tools are described in Chapter 35.

Managing the Query Optimizer

The previous chapter covered how the Query Optimizer analyzes queries and determines the most efficient query plan to use to process the query. Considering the overwhelming number of query types and circumstances in which those queries are run, SQL Server does a surprisingly effective job of query optimization in most instances. Experience has shown that SQL Server's Query Optimizer is quite clever—and very, very good at wringing the best performance out of any hardware platform, especially with the latest enhancements to the cardinality estimator, which is based on in-depth cardinality estimation research on modern workloads and Microsoft learnings over the past 15 years. Still, because at times the Query Optimizer might sometimes make poor decisions as to how to best process a query, you need to know how and when you may need to override the Query Optimizer and force SQL Server to process a query in a specific manner.

What's New in Managing the Query Optimizer

There are no significant changes or enhancements to the options in SQL Server 2014 related to overriding or managing the query optimizer.

Should You Override the Query Optimizer?

You might be wondering, how often does SQL Server require manual intervention to execute a query optimally and should I try and override the Query Optimizer when it seems to be making a bad choice? The vast majority of the time, if index statistics are up to date and queries are well written with optimizable search arguments (SARGS) and join clauses, the query optimizer generates and selects an effective and efficient query plan. A lot of research and effort over the years has gone into developing the algorithms that the optimizer uses, and it's a rare occasion when you'll find that it "gets it wrong" and you have to "coerce" it into generating a different query plan. For this reason, you should treat the material covered in this chapter as a collection of techniques to be used only when other methods of getting optimal query performance have already failed.

Before indiscriminately applying the techniques discussed in this chapter, remember one very important point: Use of these features can effectively hide serious fundamental design or coding flaws in your database, application, or queries. In fact, if you're tempted to use these features (with a few moderate exceptions), it should serve as an indicator that the problems might lie elsewhere in the application or queries.

If you are satisfied that no such flaws exist and that SQL Server is choosing the wrong plan to optimize your query, you can use the methods discussed in this chapter to override two of the three most important decisions the Query Optimizer makes:

▶ Choosing which index, if any, to resolve the query

▶ Choosing the join strategy to apply in a multitable query

The other decision made by the Query Optimizer is the locking strategy to apply. Using table hints to override locking strategies is discussed in Chapter 37, "Locking and Performance."

Throughout this chapter, one point must remain clear in your mind: These options should be used only in exception cases to cope with specific optimization problems in specific queries in specific applications. There are therefore no standard or global rules of thumb to follow because the application of these features, by definition, means that normal SQL Server behavior isn't taking place.

The practical result of this idea is that you should test every option in your environment, with your data and your queries, and use the techniques and methods discussed in this chapter and the other performance-related chapters to optimize and fine-tune the performance of your queries. The fastest-performing query wins, so you shouldn't be afraid to experiment with different alternatives—but you shouldn't think that these statements and features are globally applicable or fit general categories of problems, either! There are, in fact, only three rules: Test, test, and test!

TIP

As a general rule, Query Optimizer and table hints should be used only as a last resort, when all other methods to get the Query Optimizer to generate a more efficient query plan have failed. Always try to find other ways to rewrite the queries to encourage the Query Optimizer to choose a better plan. This includes adding additional SARGs, substituting unknown values for known values in SARGS or trying to replace unknown values with known values, breaking up queries, converting subqueries to joins or joins to subqueries, and so on. Essentially, you should try other coding variations on the query itself to get the same result in a different way and try to see if one of the variations ends up using the more efficient query plan that you expect it to.

In reality, about the only time you should use these hints is when you're testing the performance of a query and want to see if the Query Optimizer is actually choosing the best execution plan. You can enable the various query analysis options, such as STATISTICS PROFILE and STATISTICS IO, and then see how the query plan and statistics change as you apply various hints to the query. You can examine the output to determine whether the I/O cost and/or runtime improves or gets worse if you force one index over another or if you force a specific join strategy or join order.

The problem with hard-coding table and Query Optimizer hints into application queries is that the hints prevent the Query Optimizer from modifying the query plan as the data in the tables changes over time. Also, if subsequent service packs or releases of SQL Server incorporate improved optimization algorithms or strategies, the queries with hard-coded hints may not be able to take advantage of them. Also, hard coding a query hint that addresses poor performance for specific parameter values could result in poorer performance overall for general use. Be sure to test the use of query hints with a wide variety of search values.

If you find that you must incorporate any of these hints to solve query performance problems, you should be sure to document which queries and stored procedures contain Query Optimizer and table hints. It's a good idea to periodically go back and test the queries to determine whether the hints are still appropriate. You might find that, over time, as the data values in the table change, the forced query plan generated because of the hints is no longer the most efficient query plan, and the Query Optimizer now generates a more efficient query plan on its own.

35

Using Optimizer Hints

You can specify three types of hints in a query to override the decisions made by the Query Optimizer:

▶ Table hints

▶ Join hints

▶ Query hints

The following sections examine and describe each type of table hint.

Forcing Index Selection with Table Hints

In addition to locking hints that can be specified for each table in a query, SQL Server 2014 allows you to provide table-level hints that enable you to specify the index SQL Server should use for accessing the table. The syntax for specifying an index hint is as follows:

```
SELECT column_list FROM tablename WITH (INDEX (indid | index_name [, ...]) )
```

This syntax allows you to specify multiple indexes. You can specify an index by name or by ID. It is recommended that you specify indexes by name as the IDs for nonclustered indexes can change if they are dropped and re-created in a different order than that in which they were created originally. You can specify an index ID of 0, or the table name itself, to force a table scan.

When you specify multiple indexes in the hint list, all the indexes listed are used to retrieve the rows from the table, forcing an index intersection or index covering via an index join. If the collection of indexes listed does not cover the query, a regular row fetch is performed after all the indexed columns are retrieved.

To get a list of all user-defined tables and the names of the indexes defined on them, you can execute a query against the sys.indexes catalog view similar to the one shown in Listing 35.1.

LISTING 35.1   Query Against sys.indexes Catalog View to Get Index Names and IDs

```
select 'Table name' = convert(char(20), object_name(object_id)),
       'Index name' = convert(char(30), name),
       'Index ID' = index_id,
       'Index Type' = convert(char(15), type_desc)
  from sys.indexes where object_id > 99 /*only system tables have id less than 99 */
   and index_id between 1 and 254    /* do not include rows for text columns
                              or tables without a clustered index*/
   /* do not include auto statistics */
   and is_hypothetical = 0
   and objectproperty(object_id, 'IsUserTable') = 1
order by 1, 3
```

The FORCESEEK table hint provides an additional query optimization option. This hint specifies that the Query Optimizer use only an index seek operation as the access path to the data in the table or view referenced in the query rather than an index scan or table scan. If a query plan contains table or index scan operators, forcing an index seek operation may yield better query performance. This is especially true when inaccurate cardinality or cost estimations cause the Optimizer to favor scan operations at plan compilation time.

You can further control the index seek options by specifying an index or column name to further control how the Optimizer should perform the index seek operation. By default, when you specify the FORCESEEK option, the Query Optimizer will determine which index to use to perform the index seek. To force the Optimizer to use an index seek using a specific index or column, the syntax is as follows:

```
WITH FORCESEEK [( index_value ( index_column_name  [ ,... ] ) )
```

For example, the following query forces the optimizer to use an index seek on the SalesOrderID column of the SalesOrderDetail_SalesOrderID_SalesOrderDetailID index:

```
SELECT h.SalesOrderID, h.TotalDue, d.OrderQty
   FROM Sales.SalesOrderHeader AS h
       INNER JOIN Sales.SalesOrderDetail AS d
       WITH (FORCESEEK
               (PK_SalesOrderDetail_SalesOrderID_SalesOrderDetailID
                 (SalesOrderID)))
       ON h.SalesOrderID = d.SalesOrderID
   WHERE h.TotalDue > 100
   AND (d.OrderQty > 5 OR d.LineTotal < 1000.00);
```

Before using the FORCESEEK table hint, you should make sure that statistics on the table are current and accurate. Also, you should evaluate the query for items that can cause poor cardinality or cost estimates and remove these items if possible. For example, replace local variables with parameters or literals and limit the use of multi-statement table-valued functions and table variables in the query.

Also, be aware that if you specify the FORCESEEK hint in addition to an index hint, the FORCESEEK hint can cause the Optimizer to use an index other than one specified in the index hint.

Specifying the FORCESCAN hint can be useful for queries in which the optimizer underestimates the number of affected rows and chooses a seek operation rather than a scan operation. The FORCESCAN hint specifies that the Query Optimizer use only an index scan or table scan operation as the access path to the referenced table or view. FORCESCAN can be specified with or without an INDEX hint. When combined with an INDEX hint, the Query Optimizer considers only scan access paths through the specified index when accessing the referenced table. To force a table scan, specify the INDEX hint INDEX(0) along with the FORCESCAN hint. For example, the following query forces a table scan on the SalesOrderDetail table:

```
SELECT h.SalesOrderID, h.TotalDue, d.OrderQty
   FROM Sales.SalesOrderHeader AS h
       INNER JOIN Sales.SalesOrderDetail AS d
       WITH (FORCESCAN, INDEX(0))
       ON h.SalesOrderID = d.SalesOrderID
   WHERE h.TotalDue > 100
   AND (d.OrderQty > 5 OR d.LineTotal < 1000.00);
```

Forcing Join Strategies with Join Hints

Join hints let you force the type of join that should be used between two tables. The join hints correspond with the three types of join strategies:

▶ LOOP

▶ MERGE

▶ HASH

You can specify join hints only when you use the ANSI-style join syntax—that is, when you actually use the keyword JOIN in the query. The hint is specified between the type of join and the keyword JOIN, which means you can't leave out the keyword INNER for an inner join. Thus, the syntax for the FROM clause when using join hints is as follows:

```
FROM table1 {INNER | OUTER} [LOOP | MERGE | HASH} JOIN table2
```

The following example forces SQL Server to use a hash join:

```
SELECT h.SalesOrderID, h.TotalDue, d.OrderQty
  FROM Sales.SalesOrderHeader AS h
      INNER HASH JOIN Sales.SalesOrderDetail AS d
      ON h.SalesOrderID = d.SalesOrderID
  WHERE h.TotalDue > 100
  AND (d.OrderQty > 5 OR d.LineTotal < 1000.00);
```

You can also specify a global join hint for all joins in a query by using a query processing hint.

Specifying Query Processing Hints

SQL Server 2014 enables you to specify additional query hints to control how your queries are optimized and processed. You specify query hints at the end of a query by using the OPTION keyword. There can be only one OPTION clause per query, but you can specify multiple hints in an OPTION clause, as shown in the following syntax:

```
OPTION (hint1 [, ...hintn])
```

Query hints are grouped into four categories: GROUP BY, UNION, JOIN, and miscellaneous.

GROUP BY Hints

GROUP BY hints specify how GROUP BY or COMPUTE operations should be performed. The following GROUP BY hints can be specified:

▶ **HASH GROUP**—This option forces the Query Optimizer to use a hashing function to perform the GROUP BY operation.

▶ **ORDER GROUP**—This option forces the Query Optimizer to use a sorting operation to perform the GROUP BY operation. This may help improve query performance if the data rows being returned are indexed and can be returned in GROUP BY sort order.

Only one GROUP BY hint can be specified at a time.

UNION Hints

The UNION hints specify how UNION operations should be performed. The following UNION hints can be specified:

▶ **MERGE UNION**—This option forces the Query Optimizer to use a merge operation to perform the UNION operation.

▶ **HASH UNION**—This option forces the Query Optimizer to use a hash operation to perform the UNION operation.

▶ **CONCAT UNION**—This option forces the Query Optimizer to use the concatenation method to perform the UNION operation.

Only one UNION hint can be specified at a time, and it must come after the last query in the UNION. The following is an example of forcing concatenation for a UNION:

```
select ProductID from Sales.SalesOrderDetail
    where OrderQty > 10
union
select ProductID from Production.Product
    where ListPrice > 1000
OPTION (CONCAT UNION)
```

JOIN Hints

The JOIN hint specified in the OPTION clause specifies that all join operations in the query are performed as the type of join specified in the hint. The JOIN hints that can be specified in the query hints are the same as the table hints:

▶ LOOP JOIN

▶ MERGE JOIN

▶ HASH JOIN

If you also specify a JOIN hint for a specific pair of tables, the table-level hints specified must be compatible with the query-level JOIN hint.

Miscellaneous Hints

The following miscellaneous hints can be used to override various query operations:

▶ **FORCE ORDER**—This option tells the Query Optimizer to join the tables in the order in which they are listed in the FROM clause and not to determine the optimal join order.

▶ **FAST n**—This hint instructs SQL Server to optimize the query to return the first n rows as quickly as possible, even if the overall throughput is reduced. In other words, it improves response time at the expense of total query execution time. This option generally influences the Query Optimizer to retrieve data using a nonclustered index that matches the ORDER BY clause of a query instead of using a different access method that would require a sort operation first to return rows in the specified order. After n number of rows have been returned, the query continues execution normally to produce its full result set.

▶ **ROBUST PLAN**—This option forces the Query Optimizer to attempt a plan that works for the maximum potential row size, even if it means degrading performance. If you have very wide VARCHAR columns, some types of query plans might create intermediate tables, and if any of the internal operations need to store and process rows in these intermediate tables, some rows might exceed SQL Server's row size limit. If this happens, SQL Server generates an error during query execution. When the ROBUST PLAN hint is specified, the Query Optimizer does not consider any plans that might encounter this problem.

▶ **MAXDOP** *number*—This hint overrides the server-level configuration setting for max degree of parallelism for the current query in which the hint is specified.

▶ **KEEP PLAN**—When this hint is specified, it forces the Query Optimizer to relax the estimated recompile threshold for a query. The estimated recompile threshold is the point at which a query is automatically recompiled when the estimated number of indexed column changes have been made to a table by updates, inserts, or deletes. Specifying KEEP PLAN ensures that the query is not recompiled as frequently when there are multiple updates to a table. This option is useful primarily for queries whose execution plan stays in memory, such as for stored procedures. You might want to specify this option for a stored procedure that does a lot of work with temporary tables, which can lead to frequent recompilations of the execution plan for the stored procedure.

▶ **KEEPFIXED PLAN**—This query hint tells the Query Optimizer not to recompile the query plan when there are changes in statistics or modifications to indexed columns used by the query via updates, deletes, or inserts. When this option is specified, the query is recompiled only if the schema of the underlying tables is changed or sp_recompile is executed against those tables.

▶ **EXPAND VIEWS**—This hint tells the Query Optimizer not to consider any indexed view as a substitute for any part of the query and to force the view to be expanded into its underlying query. This hint essentially prevents direct use of indexed views in the query plan.

▶ **MAXRECURSION** *number*—This hint specifies the maximum number of recursions allowed for the common table expression query, where number is an integer between 0 and 32767. When 0 is specified, no limit is applied. If this option is not specified, the default limit for the server is 100.

▶ **RECOMPILE**—This hint forces SQL Server not to keep the execution plan generated for the query in the plan cache after it executes. This forces a new plan to be generated the next time the same or a similar query plan is executed. RECOMPILE is useful for queries with variable values that vary widely each time they are compiled and executed. This hint can be used for individual statements within a stored procedure in place of the global WITH RECOMPILE option when you want only a subset of queries inside the stored procedure to be recompiled rather than all of them.

▶ **OPTIMIZE FOR** (*@variable_name = literal_constant* [, ...n])—This hint instructs SQL Server to use a specified value to optimize the SARGs for a local variable that is otherwise unknown when the query is compiled and optimized. The value is used only during query optimization and not during query execution. OPTIMIZE FOR can help improve optimization by allowing the Query Optimizer to use the statistics histogram rather than index densities to estimate the rows that match the local variable or can be used when you create plan guides.

▶ `OPTIMIZE FOR UNKNOWN`—This hint instructs the query optimizer to use statistical data instead of the initial values for local variables when the query is compiled and optimized, including parameters created with forced parameterization.

▶ `TABLE HINT (object_name [ , table_hint [ [, ]...n ] ] )`—Introduced in SQL Server 2012, you can also specify table hints in the Query Hint `OPTION` clause. It is recommended that the `TABLE HINT` clause be used only in the context of a plan guide. For all other ad hoc queries, it is recommend that normal table hints be used.

▶ `USE PLAN N'xml_plan'`—This hint instructs SQL Server to use an existing query plan for a query as specified by the designated `xml_plan`. The `USE PLAN` query hint can be used for queries whose plans result in slow execution times but for which you know better plans exist.

> **NOTE**
>
> Optimizer hints are not always executed. For example, the Query Optimizer is likely to ignore a `HASH UNION` hint for a query using the `UNION ALL` statement. Because `UNION ALL` means to return all rows whether or not there are duplicates, you don't need to hash these values to determine uniqueness and remove duplicates, so the normal concatenation is likely to still take place.

35

Using Forced Parameterization

In SQL Server 2014, if a SQL statement is executed without parameters, the Query Optimizer parameterizes the statement internally to increase the possibility of matching it against an existing execution plan. This process is called *simple parameterization*, sometimes referred to as auto-parameterization. Simple parameterization is somewhat limited in that it can parameterize only a relatively small number of queries that match a small number of very simple and strictly defined query templates. For example, simple parameterization is not possible for queries that contain any of the following query elements:

▶ References to more than one table

▶ `IN` clauses or `OR` expressions

▶ `UNION`

▶ Any query hints

▶ `DISTINCT`

▶ `TOP`

▶ Subqueries

▶ `GROUP BY`

▶ Not equal (`<>` or `!=`) comparisons

▶ References to functions

SQL Server 2014 enables you to override the default simple parameterization behavior of SQL Server and provide parameterization for more complex queries by specifying that all `SELECT`, `INSERT`, `UPDATE`, and `DELETE` statements in a database be implicitly parameterized when they are compiled by the Query Optimizer. You enable this by setting the `PARAMETERIZATION` option to `FORCED` in the `ALTER DATABASE` statement:

```
ALTER DATABASE dbname SET PARAMETERIZATION {FORCED | SIMPLE}
```

Setting the `PARAMETERIZATION` option is an online operation that can be issued at any time and requires no database-level exclusive locks.

Forced parameterization may improve the performance of queries for certain databases by reducing the frequency of query compilations and recompilations. Essentially, forced parameterization provides the query plan reuse benefits of parameterized queries without requiring you to rewrite a single line of application code. The databases that may benefit from forced parameterization generally support OLTP-type applications that experience high volumes of concurrent queries, such as point-of-sale applications.

When the `PARAMETERIZATION FORCED` option is enabled, any literal value that appears in a `SELECT`, `INSERT`, `UPDATE`, or `DELETE` statement, submitted in any form, is converted to a parameter during query compilation. The exceptions are literals that appear in the following query constructs:

▶ `INSERT...EXECUTE` statements

▶ Statements inside the bodies of stored procedures, triggers, or user-defined functions. SQL Server already reuses query plans for these routines.

▶ Prepared statements that have already been parameterized by the client-side application.

▶ Statements inside a T-SQL cursor.

▶ Any statement run in a context where `ANSI_PADDING` or `ANSI_NULLS` is set to `OFF`.

▶ Statements that contain more than 2,097 literals eligible for parameterization.

▶ Statements that reference variables, such as `WHERE st.state = @state`.

▶ Statements that contain the `RECOMPILE` or `OPTIMIZE FOR` query hints.

▶ Statements that contain a `COMPUTE` clause.

▶ Statements that contain a `WHERE CURRENT OF` clause.

If an execution plan for a query is cached, you can determine whether the query is parameterized by referencing the `sql` column of the `sys.syscacheobjects` DMV. If a query is parameterized, the names and data types of parameters are listed in this column before the text of the submitted SQL (for example, `@1 tinyint`).

Guidelines for Using Forced Parameterization

Consider the following guidelines when determining whether to enable forced parameterization for a database:

- ▶ Forced parameterization, in effect, changes the literal constants in a query to parameters when the query is compiled, and thus, the Query Optimizer might choose suboptimal plans for queries. For example, the Query Optimizer may be less likely to match the query to an indexed view or an index on a computed column. It may also choose suboptimal plans for queries posed on partitioned tables and distributed partitioned views. Forced parameterization should not be used for environments that rely heavily on indexed views and indexes on computed columns.

- ▶ Enabling the PARAMETERIZATION FORCED option causes all query plans for the database to be flushed from the plan cache.

- ▶ Generally, the PARAMETERIZATION FORCED option should be used only by experienced database administrators after determining that doing this does not adversely affect performance.

If forced parameterization is enabled and you want to override this behavior and have simple parameterization used for a single query and any others that are syntactically equivalent but differ only in their parameter values, you can use plan guides and specify PARAMETERIZATION SIMPLE when creating the plan guides. Conversely, rather than enabling PARAMETERIZATION FORCED for an entire database, you can use plan guides and specify the PARAMETERIZATION FORCED query option only for a specific set of syntactically equivalent queries that you have determined would benefit from forced parameterization.

Using the USE PLAN Query Hint

The USE PLAN query hint in SQL Server 2014 can be used to encourage the Query Optimizer to use the specified XML query plan for processing the query. This option provides more control over influencing the execution of a query than is possible with the other available query hints, such as FORCE ORDER, LOOP JOIN, and KEEP PLAN. None of these options individually are powerful enough to influence the Query Optimizer to consistently choose a particular query plan, especially when the referenced table row counts, statistics, indexes, and other attributes of the environment change.

The USE PLAN query hint is specified in the OPTION clause, and you provide it with a query plan in XML format. Listing 35.2 provides an example of the USE PLAN hint being specified for a merge join for a simple query that consists of a join between two tables. (Note: For the sake of space, the full XML plan has been truncated.)

LISTING 35.2   Specifying the USE PLAN Query Option

```
SELECT h.SalesOrderID, d.OrderQty
  FROM Sales.SalesOrderHeader AS h
       INNER HASH JOIN Sales.SalesOrderDetail AS d
       ON h.SalesOrderID = d.SalesOrderID
option (use plan N' <?xml version="1.0" encoding="utf-16"?>
<ShowPlanXML xmlns:xsi="http://www.w3.org/2001/XMLSchema-instance"
xmlns:xsd="http://www.w3.org/2001/XMLSchema" Version="1.2" Build="12.0.2000.8"
xmlns="http://schemas.microsoft.com/sqlserver/2004/07/showplan">
  <BatchSequence>
    <Batch>
      <Statements>
        <StmtSimple StatementCompId="1" StatementEstRows="121125"
        StatementId="1" StatementOptmLevel="FULL"
        CardinalityEstimationModelVersion="70" StatementSubTreeCost="2.10252"
        StatementText="SELECT h.SalesOrderID, d.OrderQty&#xD;&#xA;
        FROM Sales.SalesOrderHeader AS h&#xD;&#xA;
        INNER HASH JOIN Sales.SalesOrderDetail AS d&#xD;&#xA;
        ON h.SalesOrderID = d.SalesOrderID"
        StatementType="SELECT" QueryHash="0xE8464BC4D944F9C5"
        QueryPlanHash="0x794145525AFFF95A" RetrievedFromCache="true">
          <StatementSetOptions ANSI_NULLS="true" ANSI_PADDING="true"
          ANSI_WARNINGS="true" ARITHABORT="true" CONCAT_NULL_YIELDS_NULL="true"
          NUMERIC_ROUNDABORT="false" QUOTED_IDENTIFIER="true" />
        <QueryPlan DegreeOfParallelism="1" MemoryGrant="9184" CachedPlanSize="32"
                   CompileTime="2" CompileCPU="2" CompileMemory="336">...
          </QueryPlan>
        </StmtSimple>
      </Statements>
    </Batch>
  </BatchSequence>
</ShowPlanXML>')
```

To obtain an XML-formatted query plan, which you can provide to the USE PLAN query hint, SQL Server 2014 provides the following methods:

▶ Use the SET SHOWPLAN_XML or SET STATISTICS XML session options.

▶ Query the plan column of the sys.dm_exec_query_plan dynamic management view for a cached query plan.

▶ Enable the Include Actual Execution Plan option in SSMS and on the Execution Plan tab, right-click, and select the Show Execution Plan XML option.

▶ Use SQL Server Profiler and capture either the Showplan XML, Showplan XML Statistics Profile, or Showplan XML For Query Compile event classes.

> **NOTE**
>
> When the XML query plan contains a character string in single quotation marks ('), the quotation marks must be escaped by a second quotation mark before using the plan with the USE PLAN query hint. For example, a plan that contains WHERE A.varchar = 'This is a string' must be escaped by modifying the code to WHERE A.varchar = ''This is a string''; otherwise, it will generate a syntax error when submitted for execution.

You may choose to use the USE PLAN hint for queries where the execution plan chosen leads to slow execution times but for which you know a better plan exists. This scenario may commonly occur for queries that might have executed well in an earlier version of SQL Server but that perform poorly under an upgraded version. Another scenario could be a complex query that involves multiple tables where the compiled or recompiled query plan generated is occasionally not optimal, possibly as a result of out-of-date or missing statistics in any of the underlying tables or because of complex constructs in the query that cause the Query Optimizer to inaccurately estimate the size of the intermediate query results.

The USE PLAN query hint can be specified only for SELECT and SELECT INTO statements. Also, you can force only query plans that can be produced by the Query Optimizer's normal optimization strategy.

Because the USE PLAN option requires that the XML execution plan be hard-coded in the SQL statement itself, it is not a viable solution for deployed or third-party applications where it may not be possible or feasible to modify the queries directly. It's really useful only as a tool for troubleshooting poorly running queries. To force query plans to apply query hints to queries when you cannot or do not want to directly change the application or SQL code, you might consider using plan guides.

Using Plan Guides

At times, you might find it necessary to use query hints to improve the performance of queries for a particular query or a small set of queries. Although this may be easy to do when you have access to the application code, often the particular queries to be modified are embedded within a third-party application, and alteration of the queries themselves is virtually impossible. Also, if you start hard-coding query hints in your application code, changing them as necessary when data volumes change or when upgrading to a new version of SQL Server can be a difficult undertaking.

The plan guides feature in SQL Server 2014 provides an ideal solution for such scenarios by offering another mechanism for injecting query hints into the original query without having to modify the query itself. The plan guides mechanism uses an internal lookup system table, based on information in the sys.plan_guides catalog view, to map the original query to a substitute query or query template.

As described in the preceding chapter, when a SQL statement is submitted, it is first compared against the cached plans to check for a match. If a match exists, the cached query plan is used to execute the query. If no cached plan exists for the query, the Query

Optimizer next looks for a match against the set of existing plan guides, if any, stored in the current database for a match. If an active plan guide that matches the SQL statement is found, the original matching statement is substituted with the one from the plan guide, the query plan is compiled and cached, and the query is executed using the plan generated from the plan guide.

Queries that can benefit from plan guides are generally those that are parameter-based and those that are likely performing poorly because they use cached query plans whose parameter values do not represent a more representative scenario.

The plan guides feature essentially consists of two stored procedures to create, drop, enable, and disable plan guides and the `sys.plan_guides` metadata view that describes the stored plan guides. Plan guides are created and administered by using three system stored procedures:

▶ `sp_create_plan_guide`

▶ `sp_create_plan_guide_from_handle`

▶ `sp_control_plan_guide`

The syntax for these procedures is as follows:

```
sp_create_plan_guide [ @name = ] N'plan_guide_name'
    , [ @stmt = ] N'statement_text'
    , [ @type = ] N'{ OBJECT | SQL | TEMPLATE }'
    , [ @module_or_batch = ]
    {
                    N'[ schema_name. ] object_name'
        | N'batch_text'
        | NULL
    }
    , [ @params = ] { N'@parameter_name data_type [ ,...n ]' | NULL }
    , [ @hints = ] { N'OPTION ( query_hint [ ,...n ] )'
                | N'XML_execution plan'
                  | NULL }


sp_control_plan_guide [ @operation = ] N'<control_option>'
  [ , [ @name = ] N'plan_guide_name' ]

<control_option>::=
{
    DROP
  | DROP ALL
  | DISABLE
  | DISABLE ALL
  | ENABLE
  | ENABLE ALL
}
```

Note that the `sp_create_plan_guide` stored procedure enables you to pass an XML execution plan directly in the @hints parameter instead of embedding the output in a USE PLAN hint. This capability simplifies the process of applying a fixed query plan as a plan guide hint.

An additional stored procedure, `sp_create_plan_guide_from_handle`, allows you to create one or more plan guides from a query plan in the plan cache. The syntax for `sp_create_plan_guide_from_handle` is as follows:

```
sp_create_plan_guide_from_handle [ @name = ] N'plan_guide_name'
    , [ @plan_handle = ] plan_handle
    , [ [ @statement_start_offset = ] { statement_start_offset | NULL } ]
```

Instead of specifying an actual XML execution plan, you pass the handle for a query plan currently in the plan cache to the @plan_handle parameter. As shown in the preceding chapter, a plan_handle can be obtained from the sys.dm_exec_query_stats DMV. If the cached plan contains multiple queries in a SQL batch, you can specify the starting position of the statement within the batch via the @statement_start_offset parameter. The statement offset corresponds to the statement_start_offset column in the sys.dm_exec_query_stats dynamic management view. If no statement offset is specified, a plan guide is created for each statement in the batch using the query plan for the specified plan handle. The resulting plan guides are equivalent to plan guides that use the USE PLAN query hint to force the use of a specific plan.

Creating Plan Guides

Plan guides can be created to match queries executed in the following contexts:

▶ An OBJECT plan guide matches queries that execute in the context of T-SQL stored procedures, scalar functions, or multistatement table-valued functions.

▶ A SQL plan guide matches queries that execute in the context of ad hoc T-SQL statements and batches that are not part of a stored procedure or other compiled database object.

▶ A TEMPLATE plan guide matches ad hoc queries that parameterize to a specified form. These plan guides are used to override the current SET PARAMETERIZATION database option.

In the `sp_create_plan_guide` statement, you specify the query that you want optimized and provide the OPTION clause with the query hints necessary to optimize the query in the manner desired or an XML execution plan for the query plan you want the query to use. When the query executes, SQL Server matches the query to the plan guide and applies the forced query plan to the query at runtime.

The plan guide can specify any of the following query hints individually or combined with others, when applicable:

- ▶ {HASH | ORDER} GROUP

- ▶ {CONCAT | HASH | MERGE} UNION

- ▶ {LOOP | MERGE | HASH} JOIN

- ▶ FAST n

- ▶ FORCE ORDER

- ▶ MAXDOP *number_of_processors*

- ▶ OPTIMIZE FOR (*@variable_name* = *literal_constant*) [,...n]

- ▶ OPTIMIZE FOR UNKNOWN

- ▶ RECOMPILE

- ▶ ROBUST PLAN

- ▶ KEEP PLAN

- ▶ KEEPFIXED PLAN

- ▶ EXPAND VIEWS

- ▶ MAXRECURSION *number*

- ▶ TABLE HINT (*object_name* [, *table_hint* [[,]...n]])

- ▶ USE PLAN *<xmlplan>*

- ▶ PARAMETERIZATION { SIMPLE | FORCED }

The PARAMETERIZATION { SIMPLE | FORCED } query hint can be used only within a plan guide, and it specifies whether a query is parameterized as part of compiling a query plan. This option overrides the current setting of the PARAMETERIZATION option set at the database level.

Listing 35.3 provides a sample plan guide created for a simple SQL statement.

LISTING 35.3   Creating a Plan Guide for a Simple SQL Statement

```
sp_create_plan_guide @name = N'PlanGuide1',
@stmt = N'SELECT h.SalesOrderID, d.OrderQty
  FROM Sales.SalesOrderHeader AS h
      INNER HASH JOIN Sales.SalesOrderDetail AS d
      ON h.SalesOrderID = d.SalesOrderID ',
@type = N'SQL',
@module_or_batch = NULL,
@params = NULL,
@hints = N'OPTION (HASH JOIN)'
```

For plan guides of type `'SQL'` or `'TEMPLATE'` to match a query successfully, the values for `batch_text` and `@parameter_name data_type [,...n]` must be provided in exactly the same format as their counterparts submitted by the application. Specifically, they must match character for character, including comments and whitespaces.

> **TIP**
>
> When you are creating plan guides, be careful to specify the query in the `@stmt` parameter and any parameter names and values in the `@params` parameter exactly as they are received from the application. The best way to ensure this is to capture the batch or statement text from SQL Server Profiler. (See Chapter 5, "SQL Server Profiler," for more information on using SQL Server Profiler to capture SQL queries.) Also, as with the XML query plans passed to the USE PLAN query hint, single-quoted literal values, such as `'1/1/2000'`, need to be delimited with single quotation marks escaped by additional single quotation marks, as shown in Listing 35.1.

Managing Plan Guides

You use the `sp_control_plan_guide` stored procedure to enable, disable, or drop a plan guide. The following example drops the plan guide created in Listing 35.3:

```
sp_control_plan_guide N'DROP', N'PlanGuide1'
```

To execute `sp_control_plan_guide` on a plan guide of type OBJECT (for example, a plan guide created for a stored procedure), you must have at least ALTER permission on the object that is referenced by the plan guide. For all other plan guides, you must have at least ALTER DATABASE permission. Attempting to drop or alter a function or stored procedure that is referenced by a plan guide results in an error.

In SQL Server 2014, it is possible to define multiple plan guides for the same query. However, only one plan guide can be active at a time. You can use `sp_control_plan_guide` to enable and disable plan guides.

Validating Plan Guides

The new system function `sys.fn_validate_plan_guide` can be used to validate a plan guide. Plan guides can become invalid after changes such as dropping an index are made to the database. By validating a plan guide, you can determine whether the plan guide can be used unmodified by the query optimizer. The `sys.fn_validate_plan_guide` function returns the first error message encountered when the plan guide is applied to its query. If the plan guide is valid, an empty rowset is returned.

The `sys.plan_guides` Catalog View

All plan guides are stored in the `sys.plan_guides` database system catalog view. You can get information about the plan guides defined in a database by running a query against the `sys.plan_guides` catalog view, as in the following example:

35

```
select name, is_disabled, scope_type_desc, scope_object_id,
      parameters, hints, query_text from sys.plan_guides
```

Table 35.1 describes the columns in the `sys.plan_guides` catalog view.

TABLE 35.1   `sys.plan_guides` Columns

Column Name	Description
plan_guide_id	Unique identifier of the plan guide.
Name	Name of the plan guide.
create_date	Date and time the plan guide was created.
modify_date	Date the plan guide was last modified.
is_disabled	1 = disabled and 0 = enabled.
query_text	Text of the query on which the plan guide is created.
scope_type	Scope of the plan guide: 1 = OBJECT, 2 = SQL, and 3 = TEMPLATE.
scope_type_desc	Description of scope of the plan guide: OBJECT, SQL, or TEMPLATE.
scope_object_id	If scope_type is OBJECT, the object_id of the object defining the scope of the plan guide; otherwise, NULL.
scope_batch	If scope_type is SQL, the text of the SQL batch. If NULL, either the batch type is not SQL or scope_type is SQL, and the value of query_text applies.
parameters	The string defining the list of parameters associated with the plan guide. If NULL, no parameter list is associated with the plan guide.
hints	The query OPTION hints associated with the plan guide.

Plan Guide Best Practices

Following are some of the recommended best practices for using the USE PLAN query hint and the plan guides feature:

▶ The USE PLAN query hint and plan guides should be used only when other standard query tuning options, such as tuning indexes and ensuring the table has current statistics, have been extensively tried and have failed to produce the necessary results. When a query plan is forced by using either the USE PLAN query hint or a plan guide, it prevents the Query Optimizer from adapting to changing data distributions, new indexes, or improved query execution algorithms in successive SQL Server releases or service packs.

▶ You need to be sure to have a full understanding of query optimization and of the implications and long-term ramifications of forcing query plans.

▶ You should try to force only a small fraction of the workload. If you find you are forcing more than a few dozen queries, you should check whether other issues with the configuration could be limiting performance, including insufficient system resources, incorrect database configuration settings, missing indexes, poorly written queries, and other factors.

▶ It is not advisable to attempt to code by hand or modify the XML execution plan that is specified in the USE PLAN query hint. You should capture and use a plan produced by SQL Server itself. The XML execution plan is a lengthy and complex listing, and improper changes could prevent it from identically matching one of the Query Optimizer–generated plans, which would result in the USE PLAN hint being ignored.

▶ The USE PLAN query hint should not be directly embedded into the application code because that would make the maintenance of the application across query plan and SQL Server version changes difficult to manage. Also, embedding USE PLAN directly into the query generally prevents the plan for the query from being cacheable. The USE PLAN hint is intended primarily for ad hoc performance tuning and test purposes, and for use with the plan guides feature.

▶ The plan guides created for an application should be well documented and regularly backed up because they constitute an integral part of the application's performance tuning. You should also retain the scripts that you used to create plan guides and treat them as you would other source code for an application.

▶ After creating a plan guide, you should test to make sure that it is being applied to the intended queries.

Verifying That a Plan Guide Is Being Applied

When you have a plan guide defined, you might want to verify that the application query is making use of the plan guide. You can follow these steps to confirm whether a plan guide is being used:

1. After creating the plan guide, run SQL Server Profiler and configure it to capture the query text and XML execution plan for the application and the query in question and start the Profiler trace.

2. Run your application and cause it to invoke the query in question.

3. Stop the Profiler trace and collect the query plan by right-clicking the Showplan XML Statistics Profile event that corresponds to the query and then selecting the Extract Event Data option.

4. Save the event data to a file.

5. Open the Showplan.xml file in any text file viewer or Internet Explorer to examine the XML code.

6. If the plan guide was used to generate the query plan, the XML execution plan output contains the PlanGuideDB and PlanGuideName tags, as shown in the following example:

35

```
    <ShowPlanXML xmlns:xsi="http://www.w3.org/2001/XMLSchema-instance"
xmlns:xsd="http://www.w3.org/2001/XMLSchema" Version="1.2" Build="12.0.2000.8"
xmlns="http://schemas.microsoft.com/sqlserver/2004/07/showplan">
  <BatchSequence>
    <Batch>
      <Statements>
        <StmtSimple StatementCompId="1" StatementEstRows="121125"
StatementId="1" StatementOptmLevel="FULL" StatementSubTreeCost="2.10252"
CardinalityEstimationModelVersion="70" StatementSubTreeCost="2.10252"
StatementText="SELECT h.SalesOrderID, d.OrderQty&#xD;&#xA;
  FROM Sales.SalesOrderHeader AS h&#xD;&#xA;
      INNER HASH JOIN Sales.SalesOrderDetail AS d &#xD;&#xA;
ON h.SalesOrderID = d.SalesOrderID " StatementType="SELECT"
PlanGuideDB="AdventureWorks2012" PlanGuideName="PlanGuide1"
QueryHash="0xE8464BC4D944F9C QueryPlanHash="0x794145525AFFF95A"
RetrievedFromCache="true">
...
        </StmtSimple>
      </Statements>
    </Batch>
  </BatchSequence>
</ShowPlanXML>
```

Another way to view the XML execution plan is to enable the Include Actual Execution Plan option in SSMS and on the Execution Plan tab that displays after executing the query, right-click, and select the Show Execution Plan XML option.

As yet another option to help determine whether or not plan guides are being used, you can use two event classes available in the SQL Server 2014 Profiler: Plan Guide Successful and Plan Guide Unsuccessful. These event classes make it easier to verify whether plan guides are being used by the Query Optimizer. For example, if SQL Server cannot produce an execution plan for a query that contains a plan guide when the initial plan guide compilation is performed, the query is automatically compiled without using the plan guide, and the Plan Guide Unsuccessful event is raised. For more information on monitoring SQL Server using SQL Profiler, see Chapter 5.

NOTE

Note that the plan guide events are raised only during the initial compilation of a query that contains a plan guide when the query plan gets loaded into the plan cache. If you do not see either of these events, you may need to flush the plan cache using DBCC FREEPROCCACHE. However, do NOT do this in a production environment. Flushing the plan cache in a production environment can have a significantly detrimental effect on application performance.

There are two other additional Performance Monitor counters: Guided Plan Executions/ sec and Misguided Plan Executions/sec. These counters are available in the SQL Server, SQL Statistics Object. They report the number of plan executions in which the query plan has been successfully or unsuccessfully generated using a plan guide. For more information on monitoring SQL Server performance using Performance Monitor, see Chapter 39, "Monitoring SQL Server Performance."

Creating and Managing Plan Guides in SSMS

SQL Server 2014 enables you to create, delete, enable, disable, or script plan guides within SSMS. The plan guides options are available in the `Programmability` folder in Object Explorer. To create a new plan guide in SSMS, right-click on Plan Guides and select the New Plan Guide option. This brings up the dialog shown in Figure 35.1.

FIGURE 35.1   Creating a plan guide in SSMS.

To manage existing plan guides in SSMS, you can right-click on the plan guide name to bring up the context menu that allows you to enable, disable, delete, script, or view the properties of the plan guide, as shown in Figure 35.2.

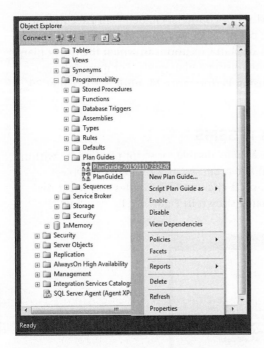

FIGURE 35.2   Managing a plan guide in SSMS.

Limiting Query Plan Execution with the Query Governor

Another tool for managing query plans in SQL Server 2014 is the query governor. Because SQL Server uses a cost-based Query Optimizer, the cost of executing a given query is always estimated before the query is actually executed. The query governor enables you to set a cost threshold to prevent certain long-running queries from being executed. This is not so much an optimization tuning tool as it is a performance problem prevention tool.

For example, if you have an application with an ad hoc reporting front end, you have no way of controlling what the user is going to request from the database and the type of query generated. The query governor allows you to prevent a runaway query from executing and using up valuable CPU and memory resources by processing a poorly formed query. You can set the query governor cost limit for the current user session by setting the session-level property QUERY_GOVERNOR_COST_LIMIT:

```
SET QUERY_GOVERNOR_COST_LIMIT value
```

The value specified is the maximum length of time, in seconds, a query is allowed to run. If the Query Optimizer estimates the query would take longer than the specified value, SQL Server does not execute it and displays an error message similar to the following:

```
Msg 8649, Level 17, State 1, Line 1
The query has been canceled because the estimated cost of this query (205317)
exceeds the configured threshold of 300. Contact the system administrator.
```

Although the option is specified in seconds, it is a relative value that corresponds to the estimated subtree cost, as calculated by the Query Optimizer. In other words, if you set the query governor cost limit to 100, it prevents the execution of any queries whose estimated subtree cost is greater than 100 seconds. The estimated subtree cost time is based on the query cost algorithm in SQL Server and might not map exactly to how long the query actually takes to run on your own system. The actual runtime depends on a number of factors: CPU speed, I/O speed, network speed, the number of rows returned over the network, and so on. You need to correlate the Query Optimizer runtime estimate to how long the query actually takes to run on your system to set the query governor cost limit to a value related to actual query runtime.

The best way to figure out how to set the query governor is to run your queries with the STATISTICS PROFILE and STATISTICS TIME session settings enabled. (These settings are discussed in more detail in Chapter 36, "Query Analysis.") You then can compare the values in the TotalSubtree Cost column for the first row of the STATISTICS PROFILE output with the elapsed time displayed by STATISTICS TIME for your query. If you do this for a number of your queries, you might be able to come up with an average correlation of the actual runtimes with the Query Optimizer's estimated query cost. For example, if the average cost estimate is 30 seconds and the actual runtimes are 15 seconds, you may need to double the setting for query governor cost limit to correspond to the actual execution time threshold; in other words, if you want the threshold to be 60 seconds for this example, you would want to set the query governor threshold to 120.

To configure a query governor threshold for all user connections, you can also set it at the server level. In SSMS, right-click the server in the Object Browser and choose Properties from the menu. In the Server Properties dialog, select the Connections page. Enable the Use Query Governor to Prevent Long-Running Queries check box and specify the desired cost threshold (see Figure 35.3). The cost threshold is specified in the same units as specified for the QUERY_GOVERNOR_COST_LIMIT session setting.

Alternatively, you can configure the server-wide query governor setting by using sp_configure:

```
sp_configure query governor cost limit, 300
```

35

FIGURE 35.3   Configuring the query governor settings in the SQL Server Properties dialog.

Summary

The SQL Server Query Optimizer continues to improve and most of the time, chooses the most efficient query plan. When it doesn't, the reason might be problems with the way the query itself is written, out-of-date or unavailable statistics, poor index design, or other common query performance problems. Still, on occasion, the Query Optimizer may make the wrong choice for an execution plan. When you suspect that the Query Optimizer is making the wrong decision, you can consider using the Query Optimizer hints and the plan guide features described in this chapter to override the Query Optimizer's decisions. However, before arbitrarily applying these hints, you should analyze the queries fully to try to determine why the Query Optimizer may be choosing a particular plan. To aid you in this effort, SQL Server provides a number of tools to analyze the query plans generated and determine the source of the problem. These tools are described in Chapter 36, "What's New in SSMS."

CHAPTER 36

Query Analysis

SQL Server's cost-based Query Optimizer typically does a good job of determining the best query plan for processing a query (note that query plans are also referred to as execution plans). At times, however, you might be a little bit skeptical about the plan the Query Optimizer generates or want to understand why it is choosing a specific plan. At the least, you will want to know the specifics about the query plans the Query Optimizer is generating, such as the following:

▶ Is the Query Optimizer performing seeks against the indexes you have defined, or is it performing table or index scans?

▶ Are work tables being used to process the query?

▶ What join strategy is being applied?

▶ What join order is the Query Optimizer using?

▶ What statistics and cost estimates is the Query Optimizer using to make its decisions?

▶ How do the Query Optimizer's estimates compare to actual I/O costs and row counts?

Fortunately, SQL Server provides some tools to help you answer these questions. The primary tool is SQL Server Management Studio (SSMS). SSMS provides a number of features for monitoring the estimated or actual execution plan as well as viewing the actual runtime statistics for your queries. This chapter describes how to display the graphical execution plan as well as client statistics within SSMS.

Although SSMS is a powerful and useful tool for query analysis, SQL Server also provides some text-based query analysis utilities as well. These tools are also described in this chapter, along with tips on how to use them most effectively.

What's New in Query Analysis

There are not many significant changes or new features related to Query Analysis provided in SQL Server 2014. The tools and commands are mostly unchanged from SQL Server 2012.

Query Analysis in SSMS

The main tool for query analysis in SQL Server 2014 is the Query Editor available in SSMS. The SSMS Query Editor can produce a graphical execution plan that provides analysis information in an intuitive and easy-to-view manner. You can display the execution plan in one of two ways: the estimated execution plan or the actual execution plan.

You can display an estimated execution plan for the entire contents of the query window or for any highlighted SQL code in the query window by choosing Display Estimated Execution Plan from the Query menu. You can also invoke it by using the Ctrl+L keyboard shortcut. This feature is useful for displaying and analyzing execution plans for long-running queries or queries with large result sets without having to actually run the query and wait for the results to be returned.

You can also display the actual execution plans for queries when they are executed by selecting the Include Actual Execution Plan option from the Query menu or by using the Ctrl+M keyboard shortcut. This option is a toggle that remains on until you select it again to disable it. When this option is enabled, your query results are displayed, along with an Execution Plan tab in the Results panel. Click the Execution Plan tab to display the execution plan for the query or queries that are executed. This option is especially useful when you want to execute commands and compare the actual runtime and I/O statistics with the execution plan estimates. (These statistics can be displayed with the SET STATISTICS options described in the "Query Statistics" section, later in this chapter.)

The graphical execution plans display a series of nodes connected by lines. Each node is represented by an icon, which indicates the logical and physical operator executed for that node. The execution plan flows from right to left and top to bottom, eventually ending at a statement icon, which indicates the type of query that generated the execution plan. This query might be a SELECT, INSERT, UPDATE, TABCREATE, and so on. The arrows between the icons indicate the movement of rows between operators. If the query window contains multiple statements, multiple query execution plans are displayed in the Execution Plan tab. For each query in the batch that is analyzed and displayed, the relative cost of the query is displayed as a percentage of the total cost of the batch.

To interpret and analyze the execution plan output, you start with the farthest icon on the right and read each ToolTip as you move left and down through the tree. Each icon in the query tree is called a node, and icons displayed under each other participate in the same level of the execution tree.

> **NOTE**
>
> The displayed width of each of the arrowhead lines in the graphical execution plan can indicate the relative cost, in estimated number of rows, and the row and data size of the data moving through the query. The smaller the width of the arrow, the smaller the estimated row count or row size. Moving the cursor over the line displays a ToolTip that indicates the estimated row count and row and data size.

Figure 36.1 shows a sample SSMS graphical execution plan window.

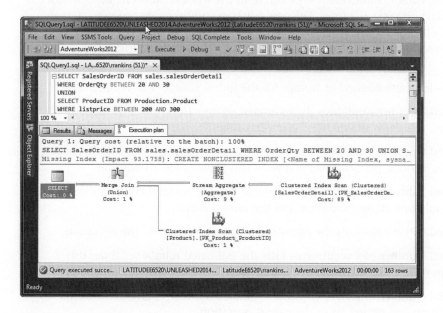

FIGURE 36.1   SSMS graphical execution plan.

The following sections describe the icons and information provided in the graphical execution plan.

Execution Plan ToolTips

When a graphical execution plan is presented in the Query Analyzer, you can get more information about each node in the execution plan by moving the mouse cursor over one of the icons. ToolTips for estimated execution plans are slightly different from the ToolTips displayed for an execution plan that is generated when a query is actually executed. The ToolTip displayed for an estimated execution plan provides the following information:

  ▶ **Physical Operation**—Lists the physical operation being performed for the node, such as a Clustered Index Scan, Index Seek, Aggregate, Hash or Nested Loop Join, and so on.

▶ **Logical Operation**—Lists the logical operation that corresponds with the physical operation, such as the logical operation of a union being physically performed as a merge join. The logical operator, if different from the physical operator, is listed in parentheses below the physical operator in the icon text in the graphical execution plan. Essentially, the logical operators describe the relational operation used to process a statement, while the physical operation describes how it is being performed.

▶ **Estimated Execution Mode**—Lists the expected execution mode to process the query. The current values are row or batch. In the row execution mode, operators process data one row at a time. The new batch execution mode processes data in batches, which is more efficient for large amounts of data, like the workloads present on data warehouse queries, or by some operators when columnstore indexes are available.

▶ **Storage**—Indicates method of storage for the index: RowStore or ColumnStore.

▶ **Estimated I/O Cost**—Indicates the estimated relative I/O cost for the operation. Preferably, this value should be as low as possible.

▶ **Estimated Operator Cost**—Indicates the estimated cost to execute the physical operation. For best performance, you want this value as low as possible.

▶ **Estimated Subtree Cost**—Lists the estimated cumulative total cost of this operation and all child operations preceding it in the same subtree.

▶ **Estimated CPU Cost**—Lists the estimated relative CPU cost for the operation.

▶ **Estimated Number of Executions**—Lists the estimated number of times this operation will be executed.

▶ **Estimated Number of Rows**—Lists the estimated number of rows to be output by the operation and passed on to the parent operation.

▶ **Estimated Row Size**—Indicates the estimated average row size of the rows being passed through the operator.

▶ **Ordered**—Indicates whether the rows are being retrieved via an index in sorted order.

▶ **Node ID**—Lists a unique identifier of the node within the execution plan.

▶ **Predicate**—Indicates the search predicate specified for the object in the original query.

▶ **Object**—Indicates which database object is being accessed by the operation being performed by the current node.

▶ **Seek Predicates**—Indicates the search predicate being used in the seek against the index when an index seek is being performed.

▶ **Output List**—Indicates which columns of data are being returned by the operation.

Some operators may also include the Actual Rebinds and Actual Rewinds counts. When an operator is on the outer side of a loop join, Actual Rebinds equals 1, and Actual Rewinds equals 0. If an operator is on the inner side of a loop join, the sum of the number of rebinds and rewinds should equal the number of rows returned by the table on the outer side of the join. A rebind means that one or more of the correlated parameters of the join changed and the inner side must be re-evaluated. A rewind means that none of the correlated parameters changed and the prior inner result set may be reused.

> **NOTE**
>
> Depending on the type of operator and other query characteristics, not all the preceding items are displayed in the ToolTip.

The ToolTips for an execution plan generated when the query is actually executed display the same information as the estimated execution plan, but the ToolTip also displays the actual number of rows returned by the operation and the actual number of executions. This information is useful in determining the effectiveness of the statistics on the column or index because it helps you compare how closely the estimated row count matches the actual row count. If a significant difference exists (significant being a relative term), you might need to update the statistics and possibly increase the sample size used when the statistics are updated to generate more accurate statistics. Significant differences in estimated and actual number of rows returned may also indicate issues with search values used to generate the row estimates such as unknown variable values, parameter sniffing, or search predicates that cannot be optimized effectively.

Figure 36.2 displays a sample ToolTip. Notice the difference between the Estimated Number of Rows value (36395.1) and the Actual Number of Rows value (1551). This indicates an obvious issue with missing or out-of-date statistics.

> **NOTE**
>
> To achieve the large difference between the actual row count and estimated row count shown in Figure 36.2, we disabled the AUTO-CREATE STATISTICS option for the database. If this option is not disabled, SQL Server automatically generates the missing statistics on the UnitPrice column before generating the execution plan. With the column statistics generated, it would likely come up with a better row estimate.

In this example, the ToolTip displays the information for a Table Scan physical operation. The Estimated I/O Cost and Estimated CPU Cost provide critical information about the relative performance of this query. You want these numbers to be as low as possible.

The Estimated Subtree Cost displays cumulated costs for this node and any previous nodes that feed into it. This number increases as you move from right to left in the execution plan diagram. For the next-to-last icon for a query execution path (the icon leading into the statement icon), the ToolTip displays the Total Estimated Subtree Cost for the entire query.

Clustered Index Scan (Clustered)	
Scanning a clustered index, entirely or only a range.	
Physical Operation	Clustered Index Scan
Logical Operation	Clustered Index Scan
Actual Execution Mode	Row
Estimated Execution Mode	Row
Storage	RowStore
Actual Number of Rows	1551
Actual Number of Batches	0
Estimated Operator Cost	1.05229 (60%)
Estimated I/O Cost	0.918681
Estimated CPU Cost	0.133606
Estimated Subtree Cost	1.05229
Number of Executions	1
Estimated Number of Executions	1
Estimated Number of Rows	1636.6
Estimated Row Size	95 B
Actual Rebinds	0
Actual Rewinds	0
Ordered	True
Node ID	16

Predicate
[AdventureWorks2012].[Sales].[SalesOrderDetail].[UnitPrice]
as [sod].[UnitPrice]>($3500.0000)
Object
[AdventureWorks2012].[Sales].[SalesOrderDetail].
[PK_SalesOrderDetail_SalesOrderID_SalesOrderDetailID]
[sod]

FIGURE 36.2   A ToolTip example.

> **NOTE**
>
> The total Estimated Subtree Cost displayed for the statement icon is the cost compared against the query governor cost limit setting, if enabled, to determine whether the query will be allowed to run. For more information on configuring and setting the query governor cost limit, see Chapter 34, "Understanding Query Optimization."

The Predicate section outlines the predicates and parameters the query uses. This information is useful in determining how the Query Optimizer is interpreting your search arguments (SARGs) and if they are being interpreted as SARGs that can be optimized effectively.

Putting all the ToolTip information together provides the key to understanding each operation and its potential cost. You can use this information to compare various incarnations of a query to determine whether changes to the query result in improved query plans and whether the estimated values are consistent with actual values.

> **NOTE**
>
> If the Query Optimizer has issued a warning about one of the execution plan operators, such as missing column statistics or missing join predicates, the icon is displayed with a yellow warning triangle (see Figure 36.3). These warnings indicate a condition that can cause the Query Optimizer to choose a less efficient query plan than otherwise expected. The ToolTip for the operation with the warning icon includes a Warnings item that indicates why the warning was generated.

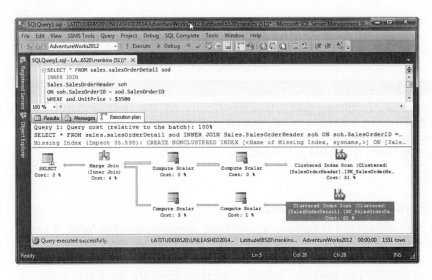

FIGURE 36.3   An example of an execution plan with warnings.

If you prefer to view the information about a node in an execution tree in more detail and with something more stable than a ToolTip, you can right-click the node and select Properties. This brings up the Properties window, as shown in Figure 36.4.

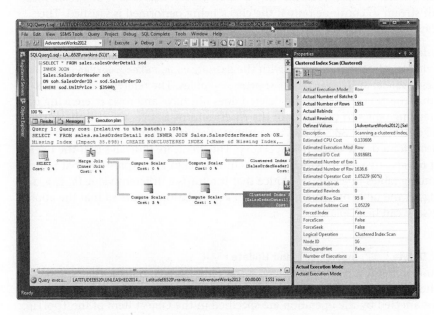

FIGURE 36.4   The query execution plan node properties.

The Properties window provides all the same information available in the ToolTip and also provides some more detailed information, along with descriptions of the types of information provided.

Logical and Physical Operator Icons

If you want to better understand the graphical execution plans displayed in SSMS, it helps to be able to recognize what each of the displayed icons represents. Recognizing them is especially valuable when you need to quickly locate operations that appear out of place for the type of query being executed. The following sections cover the more common logical and physical operators displayed in the Query Analyzer execution plans.

Assert

Assert is used to verify a condition, such as referential integrity (RI) or check constraint, or to ensure that a scalar subquery returns only a single row. It acts as sort of a roadblock, allowing a result stream to continue only if the check being performed is satisfied. The argument displayed in the Assert ToolTip spells out each check being performed.

For example, a deletion from the `Sales.SalesTerritory` table has to be verified to ensure that it doesn't violate referential integrity with the `SalesPerson`, `SalesOrderHeader`, `Customer`, `StateProvince`, and `SalesTerritoryHistory` tables. The reference constraints need to check that the `TerritoryID` being deleted does not have any rows referencing it in any of the referencing tables. If the result of the Assert returns a `NULL`, the stream continues through the query. Figure 36.5 shows the estimated execution plan and ToolTip of the Assert that appears for a delete on `SalesTerritory`. The Predicate indicates that the reference constraint rejects any case in which the matching foreign key expression that returns from the referencing tables is `NOT NULL`. Notice that it returns a different value (0, 1, 2, 3, or 4), depending on the table on which the foreign key violation occurs so that the appropriate error message can be displayed.

Clustered Index Delete, Insert, and Update

The Clustered Index physical operators Delete, Insert, and Update indicate that one or more rows in the specified clustered index are being deleted, inserted, or updated. The index or indexes affected by the operation are specified in the Object item of the ToolTip. The Predicate indicates which rows are being deleted or which columns are being updated.

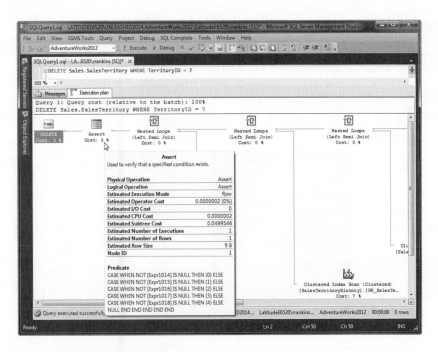

FIGURE 36.5   An `Assert` example.

Nonclustered Index Delete , Insert , and Update

Similar to the Clustered Index physical operators Delete, Insert, and Update, the
Nonclustered Index physical operators Delete, Insert, and Update indicate that one or
more rows in the specified nonclustered index are being deleted, inserted, or updated.

Clustered Index Scan and Seek

A Clustered Index Seek is a logical and physical operator that indicates the Query
Optimizer is using the clustered index to find the data rows via the index pointers. A
Clustered Index Scan (also a logical and physical operator) indicates whether the Query
Optimizer is scanning all or a subset of the table or index rows. Note that a table scan
against a table with a clustered index displays as a Clustered Index Scan; the Query
Optimizer is performing a full scan against all data rows in the table, which are in clus-
tered key order.

Figure 36.6 shows a Clustered Index Seek ToolTip. The ToolTip indicates that the seek is
being performed against the `PK_SalesOrderDetail_SalesOrderID_SalesOrderDetailID`
`index on the SalesOrderDetail` table. The Seek Predicates item indicates the search
predicate being used for the lookup against the clustered index, and the Query Optimizer
determines that the results will be output in clustered index order, as indicated by the
Ordered item indicating `true`.

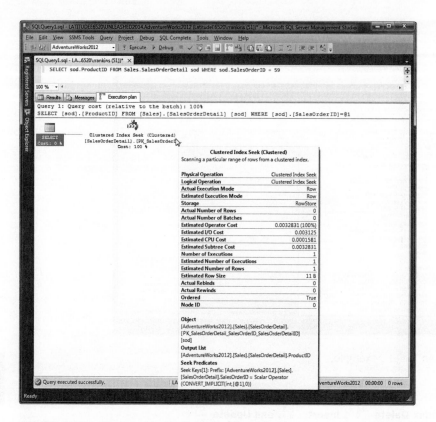

FIGURE 36.6   Clustered Index Seek ToolTip example.

Nonclustered Index Scan and Seek

A Nonclustered Index Seek is a logical and physical operator that indicates the Query Optimizer is using the nonclustered index to find the data rows via the index pointers. A Nonclustered Index Scan (also a logical and physical operator) indicates whether the Query Optimizer is scanning all or a subset of the nonclustered index rows. The Seek Predicates item in a Nonclustered Index Seek operator identifies the search predicate being used for the lookup against the nonclustered index. The Ordered item in the ToolTip indicates `true` if the rows will be returned in nonclustered index key order.

Columnstore Index Scan

The Columnstore Index Scan operator indicates that the Query Optimizer is scanning the specified columnstore index.

Collapse  and Split

A Split physical and logical operator indicates that the Query Optimizer has decided to break the rows' input from the previous update optimization step into a separate delete and insert operation. The Estimated Number of Rows in the Split icon ToolTips is normally double the input row count, reflecting this two-step operation. If possible, the Query Optimizer might choose later in the plan to collapse those rows, grouping by a key value. The collapse typically occurs if the query processor encounters adjacent rows that delete and insert the same key values.

Compute Scalar

The Query Optimizer uses the Compute Scalar operator to output a computed scalar value. This value might be returned in the result set or used as input to another operation in the query, such as a Filter operator. You might see this operator when data values that are feeding an input need to be converted to a different data type first.

Concatenation

The Concatenation operator indicates that the result sets from two or more input sources are being concatenated into a single output. You often see this when a UNION ALL is being used. You can force a concatenation union strategy by using the OPTION clause in the query and specifying a CONCAT UNION. Optimization of UNION queries, with examples of the execution plan outputs, is covered in Chapter 34.

Constant Scan

The Constant Scan operator introduces one or more constant rows into a query. A Compute Scalar operation sometimes is used to provide input to the Constant Scan operator. A Compute Scalar operator often follows a Constant Scan operator to add columns to any rows produced by the Constant Scan operator.

Deleted Scan and Inserted Scan

The Deleted Scan and Inserted Scan icons in the execution plan indicate that a trigger is being fired and that within that trigger, the Query Optimizer needs to scan either the deleted or inserted tables.

Filter

The Filter icon indicates that the input rows are being filtered according to the predicate indicated in the ToolTip. This operator is used primarily for intermediate operations that the Query Optimizer needs to perform.

Hash Match

Hash joins are covered in more detail in Chapter 34, but to understand the Hash Match physical operator, you must understand the basic concept of hash joins to some degree.

In a hash join, the keys common between the two tables are hashed into a hash bucket, using the same hash function. This bucket usually starts out in memory and then moves to disk as needed, which can have an adverse effect on performance. The type of hashing that occurs depends on the amount of memory required. Hashing is commonly used for inner and outer joins, intersections, unions, and differences. The Query Optimizer often uses hashing for intermediate processing.

A hash join requires at least one equality clause in the predicate, which includes the clauses used to relate a primary key to a foreign key. Usually, the Query Optimizer selects a hash join when the input tables are unsorted or are different in size, when no appropriate indexes exist, or when specific ordering of the result is not required. Hash joins help provide better query performance for large databases, complex queries, and distributed tables.

A hash match operator uses the hash join strategy and might also include other criteria to be considered a match. The other criteria are indicated in the `Probe Residual` clause shown in the Hash Match ToolTip.

Nonclustered Index Spool , Row Count Spool , and Table Spool

An Index Spool, Row Count Spool, or Table Spool icon indicates that the rows are being stored in a hidden spool table in the `tempdb` database, which exists only for the duration of the query. Generally, this spool is created to support a nested iteration operation because the Query Optimizer might need to use the rows again. If the operator is rewound (for example, by a Nested Loops operator) but no rebinding is needed, the spooled data is used instead of rescanning the input data.

Often, you see a Spool icon under a Nested Loops icon in the execution plan. A Table Spool ToolTip does not show a predicate because no index is used. An Index Spool ToolTip shows a `SEEK` predicate. A temporary work table is created for an index spool, and then a temporary index is created on that table. These temporary work tables are local to the connection and live only as long as the query.

The Row Count Spool operator counts how many rows are present in the input and returns just the number of rows. This operator is used when checking for the existence of rows, rather than the actual data contained in the rows (for example, an existence subquery or an outer join when the actual data from the inner side is not needed).

Eager Spool or Lazy Spool

The Query Optimizer selects to use either an Eager or Lazy method of filling the spool, depending on the query. The Eager method means that the spool table is built all at once upon the first request for a row from the parent operator. The Lazy method builds the spool table as a row is requested by its parent operator.

Log Row Scan

The Log Row Scan icon indicates that the transaction log is being scanned.

Merge Join

The merge join is a strategy requiring that both the inputs be sorted on the common columns, defined by the predicate. The Merge Join operator may be preceded by an explicit sort operation in the query plan. A merge join performs one pass through each input table, matching the columns defined in the WHERE or JOIN clause as it steps through each input. A merge join looks similar to a simple nested loop but uses only a single pass of each table. Occasionally, you might see an additional sort operation prior to the merge join operation when the initial inputs are not sorted properly. Merge joins are often used to perform inner joins, left outer joins, left semi-joins, left anti-semi-joins, right outer joins, right semi-joins, right anti-semi-joins, and union logical operations.

Nested Loops

Nested loop joins are also known as nested iteration. Basically, in a nested iteration, every qualifying row in the outer table is compared to every qualifying row in the inner table. This is why you may at times see a Spool icon of some sort providing input to a Nested Loop icon. This allows the inner table rows to be reused (that is, rewound). When every row in each table is being compared, it is called a naïve nested loops join. If an index is used to find the qualifying rows, it is referred to as an index nested loops join. Nested loops can be used to perform inner joins, left outer joins, left semi-joins, and left anti-semi-joins.

The number of comparisons performed for a nested loop join is the calculation of the number of outer rows times the estimated number of matching inner rows for each lookup. This can become expensive. Generally, a nested loop join is considered to be most effective when both input tables are relatively small.

Parameter Table Scan

The Parameter Table Scan icon indicates that a table is acting as a parameter in the current query. Typically, this icon is displayed when INSERT queries exist in a stored procedure.

Remote Delete , Remote Insert , Remote Query , Remote Scan , and Remote Update

The Remote Delete, Remote Insert, Remote Query, Remote Scan, and Remote Update operators indicate that the operation is being performed against a remote object such as a linked table.

RID Lookup

The RID Lookup operator indicates that a bookmark lookup is being performed on a heap table using a row identifier (RID). The ToolTip indicates the bookmark label used to look up the row and the name of the table in which the row is being looked up. The RID Lookup operator is always accompanied by a Nested Loop join operator.

Sequence

The Sequence operator executes each operation in its child node, moving from top to bottom in sequence, and returns only the end result from the bottom operator. You see this most often in the updates of multiple objects.

Sort

The Sort operator indicates that the input is being sorted. The sort order is displayed in the ToolTip's Order By item.

Stream Aggregate

You most often see the Stream Aggregate operation when you are aggregating a single input, such as a DISTINCT clause or a SUM, COUNT, MAX, MIN, or AVG operator. The output of this operator may be referenced by later operators in the query, returned to the client, or both.

Because the Stream Aggregate operator requires input ordered by the columns within its groups, a Sort operator often precedes the Stream Aggregate operator unless the data is already sorted due to a prior Sort operator or due to an ordered index seek or scan.

Table Delete , Table Insert , Table Scan , Table Update , and

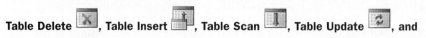

Table Merge

You see the Table Delete, Table Insert, Table Scan, and Table Update operators when the indicated operation is being performed against that table as a whole. The presence of these operators does not always mean a problem exists, although a table scan can be an indicator that you might need some indexes to support the query. A table scan may be performed on small tables even if appropriate indexes exist, especially when the table is only a single page or two in size.

Table-valued Function

The Table-valued Function operator is displayed for queries with calls to table-valued functions that cannot be optimized inline with the rest of the query. The Table-valued Function operator evaluates the table-valued function, and the resulting rows are stored in the tempdb database. When the parent operators request the rows, the Table-valued Function operator returns the rows from tempdb.

Top

The Top operator indicates a limit that is set, either by number of rows or a percentage, on the number of results to be returned from the input. The ToolTip may also contain a list of the columns being checked for ties if the WITH TIES option has been specified.

Parallelism Operators

The Parallelism operators indicate that parallel query processing is being performed. The associated logical operator displayed is one of the Distribute Streams, Gather Streams, or Repartition Streams logical operators.

▶ **Distribute Streams**   The Distribute Streams operator takes a single input stream of records and produces multiple output streams. Each record from the input stream appears in one of the output streams. Hashing is typically used to decide to which output stream a particular input record belongs.

▶ **Gather Streams**   The Gather Streams operator consumes several input streams and produces a single output stream of records by combining the input streams. If the output is ordered, the ToolTip will contain an Order By item indicating the columns being ordered.

▶ **Repartition Streams**   The Repartition Streams operator consumes multiple streams and produces multiple streams of records. Each record from an input stream is placed into one output stream. If the output is ordered, the ToolTip contains an Order By item indicating the columns being ordered.

> **NOTE**
>
> Parallel query processing strategies are covered in more detail in Chapter 34.

Analyzing Stored Procedures

When displaying the estimated execution plan for a stored procedure, you see multiple statement operators as inputs to the Stored Procedure operator, especially if you have any conditional branching in the stored procedure. One operator exists for each statement defined in the stored procedure. When conditional branching occurs in the stored procedure, SQL Server does not know at query optimization time which statements in the stored procedure will actually be executed, so it has to estimate a query plan for each individual statement. An example is shown in Figure 36.7.

When you execute the stored procedure with the Show Execution Plan option enabled, SSMS displays only the execution plans for the path or statements that are actually executed, as shown in Figure 36.8.

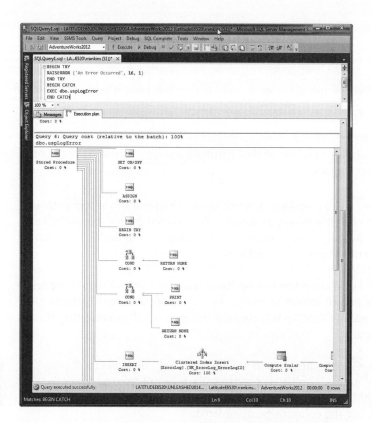

FIGURE 36.7   Estimated execution plan for a stored procedure.

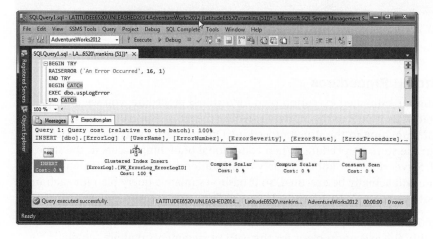

FIGURE 36.8   Actual execution plan used for a stored procedure.

In addition, because stored procedures can become quite complex, with multiple SQL statements, seeing the graphical execution plan in the SSMS Execution Plan window can be difficult. You might find it easier to break up the stored procedure into smaller batches or individual queries and analyze it a bit at a time.

Saving and Viewing Graphical Execution Plans

SQL Server Management Studio enables you to save an execution plan as an XML file. To save a graphical execution plan in SSMS, right-click anywhere on the graphical execution plan and choose Save Execution Plan As to bring up the Save As dialog (alternatively, you can choose the Save Execution Plan As option from the File menu).

When you save the execution plan to a file, the graphical execution plan is saved as an XML file with the .sqlplan file extension. To view a saved execution plan, click on the File menu; select Open and then File. In the Open File dialog, select Execution Plan files in the file type drop-down to limit the files displayed to just Execution Plan Files (see Figure 36.9). After you identify the file you want to load, click the Open button, and SSMS opens a new window with the selected execution plan displayed, providing a more complete view than is available in the results pane. Just as when the execution plan was originally generated, you can mouse over the operators and display the detailed information contained in the ToolTips.

FIGURE 36.9   Loading an execution plan into SSMS.

Displaying Execution Plan XML

In addition to viewing the graphical execution plan in SSMS, you can also display the XML generated by the Query Optimizer that is used to represent the graphical execution plan. Right-click on the execution plan and select the Show Execution Plan XML option (see Figure 36.10).

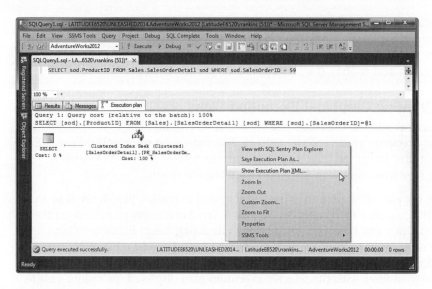

FIGURE 36.10   Generating execution plan XML in SSMS.

Selecting this option opens a new XML editor window with the SHOWPLAN_XML output generated by the query optimizer.

Missing Index Hints

One helpful feature in SQL Server Management Studio is Missing Index Hints when displaying the execution plan of a query. You can use the Missing Index Hints feature to help identify columns on which adding an index might help the query execute faster and more efficiently. Missing Index Hints is a lightweight, server-side, always-on feature using dynamic management objects and execution plans to provide information about missing indexes that could enhance query performance.

> **NOTE**
>
> The Missing Index Hints feature is separate from the Database Engine Tuning Advisor available in SQL Server 2014. The Database Engine Tuning Advisor is a more comprehensive tool that assesses the physical database design and recommends new physical design structures for performance improvement. In addition to index recommendations, it also considers whether indexed views or partitioning could be used to improve query performance.

When the Query Optimizer generates an execution plan, it analyzes what are the best available indexes for the specified search and join conditions. If a useful index is not found, the Query Optimizer generates a suboptimal query plan but still stores information about the missing indexes. The Missing Index Hints feature enables you to view information about these indexes so you can decide whether they should be implemented.

If any missing indexes are identified by the Query Optimizer, the Execution Plan tab in SSMS displays information related to all the missing indexes. If you put the mouse pointer over the missing index text, it displays a ToolTip showing the T-SQL code required to create the suggested missing index as suggested, as shown in Figure 36.11.

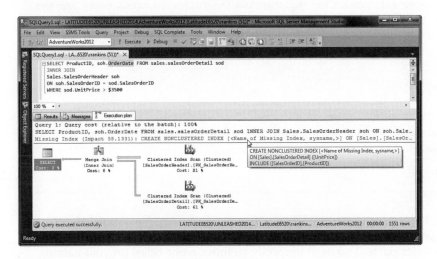

FIGURE 36.11   Displaying missing indexes in SSMS.

In addition to displaying a ToolTip with the T-SQL code, you can also generate the SQL code to create the recommended index by right-clicking on the missing index text and then selecting the Missing Index Details option from the drop-down list (see Figure 36.12). SSMS generates the T-SQL code in a new query window. An example of the T-SQL code generated is shown in Listing 36.1.

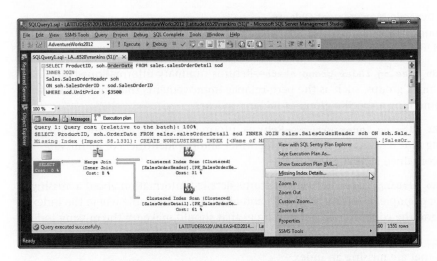

FIGURE 36.12   Generating T-SQL code to create a missing index.

LISTING 36.1   SQL Generated by SSMS Missing Index Hints Feature

```
/*
Missing Index Details from SQLQuery1.sql - LATITUDEE6520\UNLEASHED2014.
AdventureWorks2012 (LatitudeE6520\rrankins (51))
The Query Processor estimates that implementing the following index could improve
the query cost by 58.1331%.
*/


/*
USE [AdventureWorks2012]
GO
CREATE NONCLUSTERED INDEX [<Name of Missing Index, sysname,>]
ON [Sales].[SalesOrderDetail] ([UnitPrice])
INCLUDE ([SalesOrderID],[ProductID])
GO
*/
```

If you examine the SQL generated by SSMS, notice that it displays the estimated associated cost benefit expected by adding the recommended index. Also note that the script does not include an index name. You need to specify an index name based on your naming standards.

> **NOTE**
>
> If you decide to create a recommended index, be sure to review the subsequent query plan to determine if the query is using the index and that it provides the expected performance benefit.

Missing Index Dynamic Management Objects

The Missing Index Hints feature in SSMS draws information regarding missing indexes from a set of dynamic management objects available in SQL Server 2014:

▶ `sys.dm_db_missing_index_group_stats`—Returns summary information about missing index groups, such as the performance improvements that could be gained by implementing a specific group of missing indexes.

▶ `sys.dm_db_missing_index_groups`—Returns information about a specific group of missing indexes, such as the group identifier and the identifiers of all missing indexes contained in that group.

▶ `sys.dm_db_missing_index_columns`—Returns detailed information about a missing index; for example, it returns the name and identifier of the table where the index is missing and the columns and column types that should make up the missing index.

▶ `sys.dm_db_missing_index_details`—Returns information about the database table columns that are missing an index.

Although the missing indexes feature in SSMS is useful when analyzing individual queries, it's not convenient for analyzing missing indexes for a large set of SQL queries, like the set of queries executed by an application. This is where the dynamic management objects come in handy. After running a typical workload on SQL Server, you can retrieve information about missing indexes by querying the dynamic management functions directly. You can use the information returned by these dynamic management objects in scripts and use the information to generate CREATE INDEX statements to create the missing indexes. Listing 36.2 provides a sample query that displays the missing index information for the most recent query on the SalesOrderDetail table.

LISTING 36.2   Querying the Missing Index Dynamic Management Objects

```
SELECT TOP 1 WITH TIES
    mig.index_group_handle as handle,
    convert(varchar(30), replace(statement, '[AdventureWorks2012].', '')) AS table_
name,
    convert(varchar(12), column_name) AS Column_name,
    convert(varchar(10), column_usage) as ColumnUsage,
    avg_user_impact as avg_impact
FROM sys.dm_db_missing_index_details AS mid
CROSS APPLY sys.dm_db_missing_index_columns (mid.index_handle)
INNER JOIN sys.dm_db_missing_index_groups AS mig
    ON mig.index_handle = mid.index_handle
inner join sys.dm_db_missing_index_group_stats AS migs
    ON migs.group_handle = mig.index_group_handle
where mid.object_id = object_id('sales.SalesOrderDetail')
ORDER BY mig.index_group_handle desc
GO


/* output
handle        table_name                      Column_name   ColumnUsage avg_impact
----------    ------------------------------  -----------   ----------- ----------------
8             [Sales].[SalesOrderDetail]      UnitPrice     INEQUALITY  58.13
8             [Sales].[SalesOrderDetail]      SalesOrderID  INCLUDE     58.13
8             [Sales].[SalesOrderDetail]      ProductID     INCLUDE     58.13
*/
```

If you view the output of this query, you see that the optimizer is recommending an index on the UnitPrice column to support an inequality operator. It is also recommended that the SalesOrderID and ProductID columns be specified as included columns in the index. This index is estimated to improve performance by 58.13%. When you use this information, the CREATE INDEX statement for the recommended index would be the following:

```
CREATE NONCLUSTERED INDEX [UnitPrice_idx] ON [Sales].[SalesOrderDetail]
([UnitPrice]) INCLUDE ([SalesOrderID],[ProductID])
```

Missing Index Hints Feature Limitations

The Missing Index Hints feature provides some helpful information for identifying potentially missing indexes in your database, but it does have a few limitations:

▶ It is not intended to fine-tune the existing indexes, only to recommend additional indexes when no useful index is found that can be used to satisfy a search or join condition.

▶ It does not specify the order for columns to be specified in the index.

▶ For queries involving only inequality predicates, the cost information returned is less accurate than for equality operators.

▶ It only recommends adding included columns to indexes for some queries instead of creating composite indexes. You need to determine whether the included columns should be specified as additional index key columns instead.

▶ It returns only raw information about columns on which indexes might be missing.

▶ It may return different costs for the same missing index group for different executions.

▶ It does not suggest filtered indexes.

▶ The dynamic management objects can store information from a maximum of 500 missing indexes.

▶ It is unable to provide recommendations for clustered indexes, indexed views, or table partitioning. (Use the Database Engine Tuning Advisor instead for these recommendations.)

▶ After the SQL Server is restarted, all the information related to missing indexes is lost. To keep the information for later use, the DBA needs to back up all the data available within all the missing index dynamic management objects prior to restarting SQL Server.

NOTE

Although the Missing Index Hints feature is helpful for identifying indexes that may be useful for you to define, it's not a substitute for a well-thought-out index design. For more information on index design, see Chapter 32, "Indexes and Performance."

SSMS Client Statistics

You can use SSMS to get some additional information related to the client-side performance of the query by toggling the Include Client Statistics option in the Query menu. When turned on, the Client Statistics tab is added to the Results panel. This tab displays useful performance statistics in a tabular format that is related to how much work the client had to do to submit the query and process the results, including statistics about the network packets and elapsed time of the query.

SSMS keeps track of the statistics for previous executions within a session so that you can compare the statistics between different query executions. It also keeps track of the overall average statistics across all executions. Figure 36.13 shows an example of the client statistics displayed after three separate query executions.

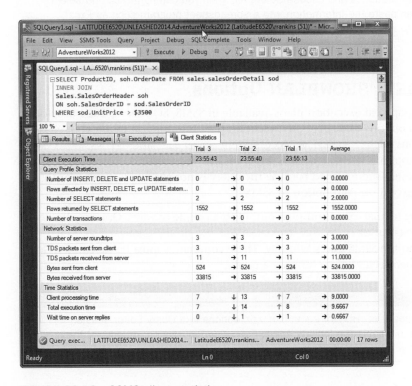

FIGURE 36.13   SSMS client statistics.

The first line in the Client Statistics tab displays the actual time the query was executed. The Time Statistics values are specified in number of milliseconds. Some of the most useful pieces of information include the number of rows returned by SELECT statements, total client processing time, total execution time, and number of bytes sent and received across the network.

The Average column contains the cumulative average since the Include Client Statistics option was enabled. Turning the option off and back on clears out all the historical statistics and resets the averages. Alternatively, you can also reset the client statistics by selecting the Reset Client Statistics option from the Query menu.

One of the most helpful features of the client statistics is the arrow indicators provided for the different executions, which makes it easy to identify which values increased, decreased, or stayed the same. This feature makes it easy to compare the runtime statistics between different queries or different executions of the same query.

TIP

Unlike the graphical execution plans, SSMS does not provide a way to save the client statistics. Fortunately, the statistics are displayed using a standard grid control. You can right-click the client statistics and choose Select All. Then you can right-click and select Copy. You can then paste the information into a spreadsheet program such as Excel, which allows you to save the information or perform further statistical analysis on it.

Using the SET SHOWPLAN Options

In addition to the graphical execution plans available in SSMS, SQL Server 2014 provides three SET SHOWPLAN options to display the execution plan information in a text or XML format. These options are SET SHOWPLAN_TEXT, SET SHOWPLAN_ALL, and SET SHOWPLAN_XML. When one of these options is enabled, SQL Server returns the execution plan generated for the query, but no results are returned because the query is not executed. It's similar to the Display Estimated Execution Plan option in SSMS.

You can turn on the textual execution plan output in a couple of ways. One way is to issue the SET SHOWPLAN_TEXT ON, SET SHOWPLAN_ALL ON, or SET SHOWPLAN_XML ON command directly in the SSMS query window. These commands must be executed in a separate batch by themselves before running a query.

TIP

Before enabling SHOWPLAN_TEXT or SHOWPLAN_ALL options in a Query Editor session in SSMS, be sure to disable the Include Actual Execution Plan option; otherwise, the SHOWPLAN options will have no effect.

SHOWPLAN_TEXT

Typing the following command in an SSMS query window turns on the SHOWPLAN_TEXT option:

```
SET SHOWPLAN_TEXT ON
GO
```

Setting this option causes the textual execution plan output to be displayed in the results panel but does not execute the query. You can also enable the SHOWPLAN_TEXT option by choosing the Query Options item from the Query menu. In the Query Options dialog, click the Advanced item and check the SET SHOWPLAN_TEXT option.

The SHOWPLAN_TEXT option displays a textual representation of the execution plan. Listing 36.3 shows an example for a simple inner join query.

> **TIP**
>
> When you are displaying the SHOWPLAN_TEXT information in SSMS, it is usually easiest to view if you configure SSMS to return results to text rather than as a grid.

LISTING 36.3   An Example of SHOWPLAN_TEXT Output

```
SET SHOWPLAN_TEXT ON
GO
SELECT ProductID, soh.OrderDate
from Sales.SalesOrderDetail sod
INNER JOIN
Sales.SalesOrderHeader soh
ON soh.SalesOrderID = sod.SalesOrderID
WHERE ProductID = 59
GO

/* output
StmtText
---------------------------------------------------------------------------------
---------------------------------------------------------------------------------
SELECT ProductID, soh.OrderDate FROM sales.salesOrderDetail sod
INNER JOIN
Sales.SalesOrderHeader soh
ON soh.SalesOrderID = sod.SalesOrderID
WHERE sod.ProductID = 59

(1 row(s) affected)

StmtText
---------------------------------------------------------------------------------
---------------------------------------------------------------------------------
---------------------------------------------------------------------------------
  |--Nested Loops(Inner Join, OUTER REFERENCES:([sod].[SalesOrderID]))
     |--Index Seek(OBJECT:([AdventureWorks2012].[Sales].[SalesOrderDetail].
[IX_SalesOrderDetail_ProductID] AS [sod]), SEEK:([sod].[ProductID]=(59)) ORDERED
FORWARD)
     |--Clustered Index Seek(OBJECT:([AdventureWorks2012].[Sales].
[SalesOrderHeader].[PK_SalesOrderHeader_SalesOrderID] AS [soh]), SEEK:([soh].[Sale
sOrderID]=[AdventureWorks2012].[Sales].[SalesOrderDetail].[SalesOrderID] as [sod].
[SalesOrderID]) ORDERED
*/
```

The output is read from right to left, similarly to the graphical execution plan. Each line represents a physical/logical operator. The text displayed matches the logical and physical operator names displayed in the graphical execution plan. If you can read the graphical query plan, you should have no trouble reading the SHOWPLAN_TEXT output.

In the example in Listing 36.3, SQL Server performs a clustered index seek on the SalesOrderHeader table, using the PK_SalesOrderHeader_SalesOrderID index, and a nonclustered index seek on SalesOrderDetail, using index IX_SalesOrderDetail_ ProductID. The inputs are combined using a nested loop join.

When the SHOWPLAN_TEXT option is set to ON, execution plan information about all subsequent SQL Server 2014 statements is returned until the option is set to OFF. Also, all subsequent commands are optimized but not executed. To turn off the textual execution plan output and allow execution of commands again, type the following command:

```
SET SHOWPLAN_TEXT OFF
GO
```

> **TIP**
>
> To switch from one SET SHOWPLAN option to another, remember that no commands are executed until the SET SHOWPLAN option is turned off. This includes setting the SET SHOWPLAN options. For example, to switch from SHOWPLAN_TEXT to either SHOWPLAN_ALL or SHOWPLAN_XML, you have to turn off SHOWPLAN_TEXT first with the SET SHOWPLAN_TEXT OFF command.

SHOWPLAN_ALL

The SHOWPLAN_ALL option displays the same textual execution plan information as the SHOWPLAN_TEXT option, and it also provides additional columns of output for each row of execution plan output. These columns provide much of the same information available in the graphical execution ToolTips, and the column headings correspond to the ToolTip items listed in the "Execution Plan ToolTips" section, earlier in this chapter. Table 36.1 describes the information provided in the data columns returned by the SHOWPLAN_ALL option.

TABLE 36.1   Data Columns Returned by SHOWPLAN_ALL

Column Name	Description
StmtText	The text of the T-SQL statement and also each of the physical operators in the execution plan. (It may optionally also contain the logical operators.)
StmtId	The number of the statement in the current batch.
NodeId	The ID of the node in the current query.
Parent	The node ID of the parent operator for the current operator.
PhysicalOp	Physical operator description for the current node.
LogicalOp	Logical operator description for the current node.

Column Name	Description
Argument	Supplemental information about the operation being performed.
DefinedValues	A comma-separated list of values introduced by this operator. These may be either computed expressions present in the current query or internal values introduced by the query processor to be able to process this query.
EstimateRows	Estimated number of rows of output produced by the operator.
EstimateIO	Estimated I/O cost for the operator.
EstimateCPU	Estimated CPU cost for the operator.
AvgRowSize	Estimated average row size (in bytes) of the row being passed through the operator.
TotalSubtreeCost	Estimated (cumulative) cost of this operation and all child operations.
OutputList	A comma-separated list of columns being projected by the current operation.
Warnings	A comma-separated list of warning messages relating to the current operation (for example, missing statistics).
Type	The type of node (either PLAN_ROW or the type of T-SQL statement).
Parallel	Whether the operator is running in parallel (1) or not (0).
EstimateExecutions	Estimated number of times this operator will be executed while running the current query.

36

TIP

When you are displaying the SHOWPLAN_ALL information in SSMS, it is usually easiest to view if you configure SSMS to return results to grid rather than as text.

SHOWPLAN_XML

When SET SHOWPLAN_XML is set to ON, SQL Server does not execute the query but returns execution information for each T-SQL batch as an XML document. The execution plan information for each T-SQL batch is contained in a single XML document. Each XML document contains the text of the statements in the batch, followed by the details of the execution steps and operators. The document includes the estimated costs, numbers of rows, indexes used, join order, and types of operators performed.

The SHOWPLAN_XML option generates the same XML output as the Show Estimated Execution Plan option in SSMS. In essence, you are looking at the same information, just without the pretty pictures. As a matter of fact, you can save the output from the SHOWPLAN_XML option to a file and open it back into SSMS as a SQL plan file. The recommended approach is to configure the query window to return results to a grid. If you return the results as text or to a file, the maximum output size you can configure in SSMS for displaying the values in a character column is 8,192 bytes. If the XML document exceeds this length, it is truncated and does not load correctly. In the grid results, the maximum size of XML data is 2MB.

After you run the query and generate the grid results, you can right-click on the result row and choose the Save Results As option to specify the file to save the results to. If all goes well, you end up with a .sqlplan file that you can then load back into SSMS for further analysis at a later date.

> **NOTE**
>
> The document containing the XML schema for the SET SHOWPLAN_XML output is available in the same directory as the SQL Server installation, which by default is c:\Program Files (x86)\Microsoft SQL Server\120\Tools\Binn\schemas\sqlserver\2004\07\ showplan\showplanxml.xsd.

Using sys.dm_exec_query_plan

Dynamic management views (DMVs) can return server state information that can be used to monitor and diagnose database engine issues and help tune performance. The sys.dm_exec_query_plan DMV returns the execution plan information for a T-SQL batch whose query execution plan resides in the plan cache. This can be any SQL batch, not just the batch executed by the current user session. The sys.dm_exec_query_plan DMV also provides the capability to retrieve the execution plan for currently long-running processes to help diagnose why they may be running slowly.

The execution plan information provided by sys.dm_exec_query_plan is returned in a column called query_plan, which is of the xml data type. This column provides the same information as SET SHOWPLAN XML. The syntax of sys.dm_exec_query_plan is

```
sys.dm_exec_query_plan ( plan_handle )
```

In SQL Server 2014, the query plans for various types of T-SQL batches are cached in an area of memory called the *plan cache*. Each cached query plan is identified by a unique identifier called a *plan handle*. To view the execution plan for one of these batches, you need to provide the plan handle for the batch to the sys.dm_exec_query_plan DMV.

The tricky part about using sys.dm_exec_query_plan is determining the plan handle to use. First, you need to determine the SPID for the process with the long-running query. This is usually accomplished using sp_who2 or via the SSMS Activity Monitor.

When you have the SPID, you can use the sys.dm_exec_requests DMV to obtain the plan handle (assume in this case that the SPID is 58):

```
select plan_handle from sys.dm_exec_requests where session_id = 58
go

/* output
```

```
plan_handle
-----------------------------------------------------------------------------
0x06000A00E96E6D2CB8A1F5050000000000000000000000000000
*/
```

When you have the plan handle, you can pass it on to the `sys.dm_exec_query_plan` DMV to return the query plan:

```
SELECT query_plan
FROM sys.dm_exec_query_plan (0x06000A00E96E6D2CB8A1F5050000000000000000000000000000)
```

Alternatively, to prevent having to copy and paste the plan handle from the `sys.dm_exec_requests` query into the query against `sys.dm_exec_query_plan`, you can use the CROSS APPLY clause, as in the following query:

```
SELECT query_plan FROM sys.dm_exec_requests cp
    CROSS APPLY sys.dm_exec_query_plan(cp.plan_handle)qp
    where cp.session_id = 58
```

If you return the results to grid, you can right-click the data in the `query_plan` column and save it to a file for archival. You can then load that file into SSMS to view the graphical execution plan, just like the output from the SET SHOWPLAN_XML option. Alternatively, in SSMS, you can also simply click on the XML hyperlink in the `query_plan` column to automatically open a new execution plan window in SSMS and display the selected execution plan.

To return the query plan for all currently running T-SQL batches, you can run the following:

```
SELECT query_plan FROM sys.dm_exec_requests cp
    CROSS APPLY sys.dm_exec_query_plan(cp.plan_handle)
```

In addition to returning the query plans for the currently running T-SQL batches, SQL Server 2014 also provides the `sys.dm_exec_query_stats` and `sys.dm_exec_cached_plans` DMVs. The `sys.dm_exec_cached_plans` DMV can be used to return information about all query plans currently residing in the plan cache. For example, to retrieve a snapshot of all query plans residing in the plan cache, you use the CROSS APPLY operator to pass the plan handles from `sys.dm_exec_cached_plans` to `sys.dm_exec_query_plan`, as follows:

```
SELECT * FROM sys.dm_exec_cached_plans cp
    CROSS APPLY sys.dm_exec_query_plan(cp.plan_handle)
```

To retrieve a snapshot of all query plans that currently reside in the plan cache for which the server has gathered statistics, use the CROSS APPLY operator to pass the plan handles from `sys.dm_exec_query_stats` to `sys.dm_exec_query_plan` as follows:

```
SELECT * FROM sys.dm_exec_query_stats qs
    CROSS APPLY sys.dm_exec_query_plan(qs.plan_handle)
```

36

Because `sys.dm_exec_query_plan` provides the capability to view the query plan for any session, a user must be a member of the sysadmin fixed server role or have the VIEW SERVER STATE permission on the server to invoke it.

NOTE

The SET SHOWPLAN_ALL and SET SHOWPLAN_TEXT options are deprecated features and may be removed in a future version of SQL Server. It is recommended that you switch to using the SET SHOWPLAN_XML option instead.

Query Statistics

In addition to the new dynamic management objects, SQL Server 2014 still provides the SET STATISTICS IO and SET STATISTICS TIME options, which display the logical and physical page reads incurred by a query and the CPU and elapsed time, respectively. These two SET options return statistics only from the actual execution of a query, as opposed to the estimates returned by SSMS and the SHOWPLAN options discussed previously. These two tools can be very useful in determining the actual cost of a query.

In addition to the IO and TIME statistics, SQL Server also provides the SET STATISTICS PROFILE and SET STATISTICS XML options. These options are provided to display execution plan information while also allowing the query to be executed.

STATISTICS IO

You can enable the STATISTICS IO option for individual user sessions, and you can turn it on in an SSMS query window by typing the following:

```
SET STATISTICS IO ON
GO
```

You can also set this option for the query session in SSMS by choosing the Options item in the Query menu. In the Query Options dialog, click the Advanced item and check the SET STATISTICS IO check box, as shown in Figure 36.14.

The STATISTICS IO option displays the scan count (that is, the number of iterations), the logical reads (from cached data), the physical reads (from physical storage), and the read-ahead reads.

Listing 36.4 displays the STATISTICS IO output for the same query executed in Listing 36.3. (Note that the result set has been deleted to save space.)

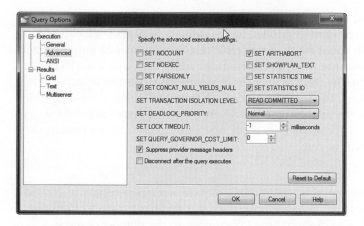

FIGURE 36.14   Enabling the STATISTICS IO option in SSMS.

LISTING 36.4   An Example of STATISTICS IO Output

```
set statistics io on
go
SELECT p.Name, sod.SalesOrderID
  FROM Production.Product AS p
  INNER JOIN Sales.SalesOrderDetail AS sod
  ON p.ProductID = sod.ProductID
  ORDER BY p.Name ;
Go

-- output deleted


(121317 row(s) affected)
Table 'SalesOrderDetail'. Scan count 504, logical reads 1403, physical reads 40,
read-ahead reads 3, lob logical reads 0, lob physical reads 0, lob read-ahead reads
0.
Table 'Product'. Scan count 1, logical reads 6, physical reads 1, read-ahead reads
2, lob logical reads 0, lob physical reads 0, lob read-ahead reads 0.
  .
```

Scan Count

The scan count value indicates the number of times the corresponding table was accessed during query execution. The outer table of a nested loop join typically has a scan count of 1. The scan count for the inner tables typically reflects the number of times the inner table is searched, which is usually the same as the number of qualifying rows in the outer table if the query is processed using nested loops. The number of logical reads for the inner table is equal to the scan count multiplied by the number of pages per lookup for each scan. Note that the scan count for the inner table might sometimes be only 1 for a nested join if SQL Server copies the needed rows from the inner table into a work table in cache memory and reads from the work table for subsequent iterations (for example, if it uses the Table Spool operation). The scan count for hash joins and merge joins is typically 1 for both tables involved in the join, but the logical reads for these types of joins are usually substantially higher. If the server uses a seek operation to find unique rows in the inner table, the scan count will be zero.

Logical Reads

The `logical reads` value indicates the total number of page accesses necessary to process the query. Every page is read from cache memory, even if it first has to be read from disk. Every physical read always has a corresponding logical read, so the number of physical reads will never exceed the number of logical reads. Because the same page might be accessed multiple times, the number of logical reads for a table could exceed the total number of pages in the table.

Physical Reads

The `physical reads` value indicates the actual number of pages read from disk. The value for physical reads can vary greatly and should decrease, or drop to zero, with subsequent executions of the query because the data will be loaded into the data cache by the first execution. The number of physical reads will also be lowered by pages brought into memory by the read-ahead mechanism.

Read-Ahead Reads

The `read-ahead reads` value indicates the number of pages read into cache memory using the read-ahead mechanism while the query was processed. Pages read by the read-ahead mechanism will not necessarily be used by the query. When a page read by the read-ahead mechanism is accessed by the query, it counts as a logical read, but not as a physical read.

The read-ahead mechanism can be thought of as an optimistic form of physical I/O, reading the pages into cache memory that it expects the query will need before the query needs them. When you are scanning a table or index, the table's index allocation map pages (IAMs) are looked at to determine which extents belong to the object. An extent consists of eight data pages. The eight pages in the extent are read with a single read, and the extents are read in the order that they are stored on disk. If the table is spread across multiple files, the read-ahead mechanism attempts parallel reads from up to eight files at a time instead of sequentially reading from the files.

LOB Reads

If the query retrieves `text`, `ntext`, `image`, or `large value` type (`varchar(max)`, `nvarchar(max)`, `varbinary(max)`) data, the `lob logical reads`, `lob physical reads`, and `lob read-ahead reads` values provide the logical, physical, and read-ahead read statistics for the large object (LOB) I/Os.

Analyzing STATISTICS IO Output

The output shown in Listing 36.4 indicates that the SalesOrderdetail table was scanned 504 times, with 40 physical reads (that is, 40 physical I/Os were performed) and 3 read-ahead reads. The Product table was scanned once, with only one physical read and 2 read-ahead read operations.

You can use the STATISTICS IO option to help evaluate the effectiveness of the amount of memory available for the data cache and to evaluate, over time, how long a table will stay in cache for a specific query. The lack of physical reads is a good sign, indicating that memory is sufficient to keep the data in cache. If you keep seeing many physical reads when you are analyzing and testing your queries, you might want to consider adding more memory to the server to improve the cache hit ratio. You can estimate the cache hit ratio for a query by using the following formula:

```
Cache hit ratio = (Logical reads - Physical reads) / Logical reads
```

The number of physical reads appears lower than it actually is if pages are preloaded by read-ahead activity. Because read-ahead reads lower the physical read count, they give the indication of a good cache hit ratio, when in actuality, the data is still being physically read from disk. The system could still benefit from more memory so that the data remains in cache and the number of read-ahead reads is reduced. STATISTICS IO is generally more useful for evaluating individual query performance than for evaluating overall cache hit ratio. The pages that reside and remain in memory for subsequent executions are determined by the data pages being accessed by other queries executing at the same time and the number of data pages being accessed by the other queries. If no other activity is occurring, you are likely to see no physical reads for subsequent executions of the query if the amount of data being accessed fits in the available cache memory. Likewise, if the same data is being accessed by multiple queries, the data tends to stay in cache, and the number of physical reads for subsequent executions tends to be low. However, if other queries executing at the same time are accessing large volumes of data from different tables or ranges of values, the data needed for the query you are testing might end up being flushed from cache, and the physical I/Os will increase. Depending on the other ongoing SQL Server activity, the physical reads you see displayed by STATISTICS IO can be inconsistent.

When you are evaluating individual query performance, examining the logical reads value is usually more helpful because the information is consistent across all executions, regardless of other SQL Server activity. Generally speaking, the queries with the fewest logical reads are the fastest queries. If you want to monitor the overall cache hit ratio for all SQL Server activity to evaluate the SQL Server memory configuration, use the Performance Monitor, which is discussed in Chapter 39, "Monitoring SQL Server Performance."

STATISTICS TIME

You can enable the STATISTICS TIME option for individual user sessions. In an SSMS query window, you type the following:

```
SET STATISTICS TIME ON
```

36

You can also set this option for the query session in SSMS by choosing the Options item in the Query menu. In the Query Options dialog, you click the Advanced item and check the SET STATISTICS TIME check box.

The STATISTICS TIME option displays the total CPU and elapsed time that it takes to actually execute a query. The STATISTICS TIME output for the query in Listing 36.4 returns the output shown in Listing 36.5. (Again, the data rows returned have been deleted to save space.)

LISTING 36.5   An Example of STATISTICS TIME Output

```
set statistics io on
set statistics time on
go

SELECT p.Name, sod.SalesOrderID
  FROM Production.Product AS p
  INNER JOIN Sales.SalesOrderDetail AS sod
  ON p.ProductID = sod.ProductID
  ORDER BY p.Name ;
Go

--output deleted

SQL Server parse and compile time:
   CPU time = 0 ms, elapsed time = 4 ms.

(121317 row(s) affected)
Table 'SalesOrderDetail'. Scan count 504, logical reads 1419, physical reads 0,
read-ahead reads 0, lob logical reads 0, lob physical reads 0, lob read-ahead reads
0.
Table 'Product'. Scan count 1, logical reads 6, physical reads 0, read-ahead reads
0, lob logical reads 0, lob physical reads 0, lob read-ahead reads 0.

 SQL Server Execution Times:
   CPU time = 62 ms,   elapsed time = 678 ms.
```

Here, you can see that the total execution time (678 ms), denoted by the elapsed time, was relatively low but more than 10 times higher than the CPU time. This is most likely due to the amount of time it took to buffer and return the results to the client. Network and physical I/O are activities that factor into the elapsed time but are not part of the actual CPU cycles required to process the query itself.

NOTE

In some situations, you might notice that the parse and compile time for a query is displayed twice. This happens when the query plan is added to the plan cache for possible reuse. The first set of information output is the actual parse and compile before placing the plan in cache, and the second set of information output appears when SQL Server retrieves the plan from cache. Subsequent executions still show the same two sets of output, but the parse and compile time is 0 when the plan is reused because a query plan is not being compiled.

If elapsed time is much higher than CPU time, the query had to wait for something, either I/O or locks. If you want to see the effect of physical versus logical I/Os on the performance of a query, you need to flush the pages accessed by the query from memory. You can use the DBCC DROPCLEANBUFFERS command to clear all clean buffer pages out of memory. Listing 36.6 shows an example of clearing the pages from cache and rerunning the query with the STATISTICS IO and STATISTICS TIME options enabled.

TIP

To ensure that none of the table is left in cache, make sure all pages are marked as clean before running the DBCC DROPCLEANBUFFERS command. A buffer is dirty if it contains a data row modification that has either not been committed yet or has not been written out to disk yet. To clear the greatest number of buffer pages from cache memory, make sure all work is committed, checkpoint the database to force all modified pages to be written out to disk, and then execute the DBCC DROPCLEANBUFFERS command.

CAUTION

The DBCC DROPCLEANBUFFERS command should be executed in a test or development environment only. Flushing all data pages from cache memory in a production environment can have a significantly adverse impact on system performance.

LISTING 36.6   An Example of Clearing the Clean Pages from Cache to Generate Physical I/Os

```
CHECKPOINT
go
DBCC DROPCLEANBUFFERS
go

SET STATISTICS IO ON
SET STATISTICS TIME ON
go

SELECT p.Name, sod.SalesOrderID
  FROM Production.Product AS p
```

36

```
   INNER JOIN Sales.SalesOrderDetail AS sod
   ON p.ProductID = sod.ProductID
   ORDER BY p.Name ;
Go

--output deleted

SQL Server parse and compile time:
   CPU time = 0 ms, elapsed time = 0 ms.

(121317 row(s) affected)
Table 'SalesOrderDetail'. Scan count 504, logical reads 1401, physical reads 40,
read-ahead reads 3, lob logical reads 0, lob physical reads 0, lob read-ahead reads
0.
Table 'Product'. Scan count 1, logical reads 6, physical reads 1, read-ahead reads
2, lob logical reads 0, lob physical reads 0, lob read-ahead reads 0.

 SQL Server Execution Times:
   CPU time = 62 ms,   elapsed time = 690 ms.
 .
```

Notice that even with the increased physical I/Os, the CPU and elapsed times do not significantly differ from the execution of the same query in Listing 36.5. This is likely because the number of physical I/Os is not significant enough to affect the overall performance and because nearly all the elapsed time is the result of the network I/O required to return 121,317 rows to the client.

You can use the STATISTICS TIME and STATISTICS IO options together in this way as a useful tool for benchmarking and comparing performance when modifying queries or indexes.

Using `datediff()` to Measure Runtime

Although the STATISTICS TIME option works fine for displaying the runtime of a single query, it is not as useful for displaying the total elapsed time for a stored procedure. The STATISTICS TIME option generates time statistics for every command executed within the stored procedure. This makes it difficult to read the output, and you would have to add them all up to determine the total elapsed time for the entire stored procedure.

Another way to display runtime for a stored procedure is to capture the current system time right before it starts, capture the current system time as it completes, and display the difference between the two, specifying the appropriate-sized `datepart` parameter to the `datediff()` function, depending on how long your procedures typically run. For example, if a procedure takes minutes to complete, you probably want to display the difference in seconds or minutes, rather than milliseconds. If the time to complete is in seconds, you likely want to specify a `datepart` of seconds or milliseconds. Listing 36.7 displays an example of using this approach.

LISTING 36.7   Using `datediff()` to Determine Stored Procedure Runtime

```
set statistics time off
set statistics io off
go
declare @start datetime2
select @start = getdate()
exec sp_help
select datediff(ms, @start, getdate()) as 'runtime(ms)'
go


-- output deleted

runtime(ms)
-----------
        213
```

STATISTICS PROFILE

The SET STATISTICS PROFILE option is similar to the SET SHOWPLAN_ALL option but allows the query to actually execute. It returns the same execution plan information displayed with the SET SHOWPLAN_ALL statement, with the addition of two columns that display actual execution information. The Rows column displays the actual number of rows returned in the execution step, and the Executions column shows the actual number of executions for the step. The Rows column can be compared to the EstimatedRows column, and the Execution column can be compared to the EstimatedExecution column to determine the accuracy of the execution plan estimates.

You can set the STATISTICS PROFILE option for individual query sessions. In an SSMS query window, you type the following statement:

```
SET STATISTICS PROFILE ON
GO
```

> **NOTE**
>
> The SET STATISTICS PROFILE option has been deprecated and may be removed in a future version of SQL Server. It is recommended that you switch to using the SET STATISTICS XML option instead.

STATISTICS XML

Similar to the STATISTICS PROFILE option, the SET STATISTICS XML option allows a query to execute while also returning the execution plan information. The execution plan information returned is similar to the XML document displayed with the SET SHOWPLAN_XML statement.

36

To set the STATISTICS XML option for individual query sessions in SSMS or another query tool, you type the following statement:

```
SET STATISTICS XML ON
GO
```

> **NOTE**
>
> With all the fancy graphical tools available, why would you want to use the text-based analysis tools? Although the graphical tools are useful for analyzing individual queries one at a time, they can be a bit tedious if you have to perform analysis on a number of queries. As an alternative, you can put all the queries you want to analyze in a script file and set the appropriate options to get the query plan and statistics output you want to see. You can then run the script through a tool such as `sqlcmd` and route the output to a file. You can then quickly scan the file or use an editor's Find utility to look for the obvious potential performance issues, such as table scans or long-running queries. Next, you can copy the individual problem queries you identify from the output file into SSMS, where you can perform a more thorough analysis on them.
>
> You could also set up a job to run this SQL script periodically to constantly capture and save performance statistics. This gives you a means to keep a history of the query performance and execution plans over time. This information can be used to compare performance differences as the data volumes and SQL Server activity levels change over time.
>
> Another advantage of the textual query plan output over the graphical query plans is that for very complex queries, the graphical plan tends to get very big and spread out so much that it's difficult to read and follow. The textual output is somewhat more compact and easier to see all at once.

Query Analysis with SQL Server Profiler

SQL Server Profiler serves as another powerful tool available for query analysis. When you must monitor a broad range of queries and database activity and analyze the performance, it is difficult to analyze all those queries individually. For example, if you have a number of stored procedures to analyze, how would you know which ones to focus on as problem procedures? You would have to identify sample parameters for all of them and manually execute them individually to see which ones were running too slowly and then, after they were identified, do some query analysis on them.

With SQL Server Profiler, you can simply define a trace to capture performance-related statistics on the fly while the system is being used normally. This way, you can capture a representative sample of the type of activity your database will receive and capture statistics for the stored procedures as they are being executed with real data values. Also, to avoid having to look at everything, you can set a filter on the Duration column so that it displays only items with a runtime longer than the specified threshold.

The events you want to capture to analyze query performance are listed under the Performance events. They include Showplan All, Showplan Statistics Profile, Showplan

Text, Showplan Text (Unencoded), Showplan XML, Showplan XML for Query Compile, and Showplan XML Statistics Profile. The data columns that you want to be sure to include when capturing the execution plan events are TextData, CPU, StartTime, Duration, and Reads and Writes. Also, for the Showplan Statistics and Showplan All events, you must also select the BinaryData data column.

Capturing the execution plan performance information with SQL Server Profiler provides you with all the same information you can capture with all the other individual tools discussed in this chapter. You can easily save the trace information to a file or table for replaying the sequence to test index or configuration changes or simply for historical analysis. If you choose any of the Showplan XML options, you have the option of saving the XML Showplan events separately from the overall trace file. You can choose to save all XML Showplan events in a single file or have separate files for each event (see Figure 36.15). You can then load the Showplan XML file into SSMS to view the graphical execution plans and perform your query analysis.

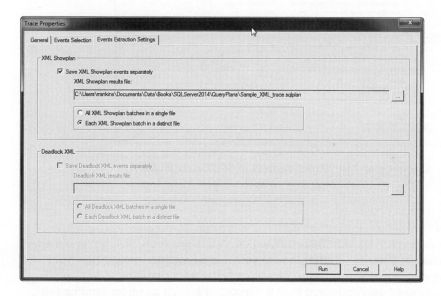

FIGURE 36.15   Saving XML Showplan events to a single file.

When you run a SQL Server Profiler trace with the Showplan XML event enabled, SQL Server Profiler displays the graphical execution plans captured in the bottom display panel of the Profiler window when you select a record with a Showplan XML EventClass. The graphical execution plans displayed in SQL Server Profiler are just like the ones displayed in SSMS, and they also include the same detailed information available via the ToolTips. Figure 36.16 shows an example of a graphical execution plan being displayed in SQL Server Profiler.

For more information on using SQL Server Profiler, see Chapter 5, "SQL Server Profiler."

> **NOTE**
>
> Because of the capability to view the graphical execution plans in SQL Server Profiler as well as the capability to save the XML Showplan events to a separate file, which you can bring into SSMS for analysis, the XML Showplan events provide a significant benefit over the other, older-style execution plan events provided. As a matter of fact, these other execution plan events are provided primarily for backward-compatibility purposes. In a future version of SQL Server, the Showplan All, Showplan Statistics Profile, Showplan Text, and Showplan Text (Unencoded) event classes will be deprecated. It is recommended that you switch to using the newer XML event classes instead.

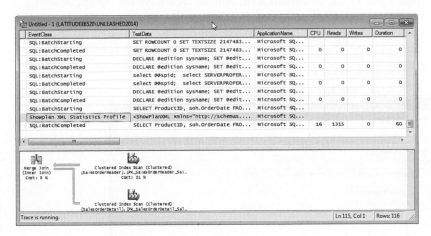

FIGURE 36.16   Displaying an XML Showplan event in SQL Server Profiler.

Summary

Between the features of SSMS and the text-based query analysis tools, SQL Server 2014 provides a number of powerful utilities to help you analyze and understand how your queries are performing and also help you develop a better understanding of how queries in general are processed and optimized in SQL Server 2014. Such an understanding can help ensure that the queries you develop will be optimized more effectively by SQL Server.

The tools discussed in this chapter are useful for analyzing individual query performance. However, in a multiuser environment, query performance is often affected by more than just how a single query is optimized. One of those factors is locking contention. Chapter 37, "Locking and Performance," delves into locking in SQL Server, its impact on query and application performance, and ways to minimize locking performance issues in SQL Server systems.

CHAPTER 37

Locking and Performance

This chapter examines locking and its impact on transactions and performance in SQL Server. It also reviews locking hints that you can specify in queries to override SQL Server's default locking behavior.

What's New in Locking and Performance

SQL Server 2014 doesn't provide any significant changes in locking behavior or features over what was provided in previous versions of SQL Server. There is, however, a new feature named *memory-optimized tables* that is related to locking. Memory-optimized tables (as the name indicates) reside in memory and do not use the same locking mechanisms as disk-based tables. Memory-optimized tables are not covered in this chapter but are covered in detail in Chapter 33, "In-Memory Optimization and the Buffer Pool Extension."

The Need for Locking

In any multiuser database, there must be a consistent set of rules for making changes to the data. For a true transaction-processing database, the database management system (DBMS) is responsible for resolving potential conflicts between two different processes that are attempting to change the same piece of information at the same time. Such a situation cannot occur because the consistency of a transaction cannot be guaranteed. For example, if two users were to change the same data at approximately the same time, whose change would be propagated? Theoretically, the results would be unpredictable because the answer is dependent on whose transaction completed last. Because most applications try to avoid "unpredictability" with data wherever possible (imagine a banking system returning "unpredictable" results, and you get the idea), some method must be available to guarantee sequential and consistent data changes.

Any relational database must support the ACID properties for transactions, as discussed in Chapter 28, "Transaction Management and the Transaction Log":

▶ Atomicity

▶ Consistency

▶ Isolation

▶ Durability

These ACID properties ensure that data changes in a database are correctly collected together and that the data is going to be left in a consistent state that corresponds with the actions being taken.

The main role of locking is to provide the isolation that transactions need. Isolation ensures that individual transactions don't interfere with one another, that a given transaction does not read or modify the data being modified by another transaction. In addition, the isolation that locking provides helps ensure consistency within transactions. Without locking, consistent transaction processing is impossible. Transactions are logical units of work that rely on a constant state of data, almost a "snapshot in time" of what they are modifying, to guarantee their successful completion.

Although locking provides isolation for transactions and helps ensure their integrity, it can also have a significant impact on the performance of the system. To keep your system performing well, you want to keep transactions as short, concise, and noninterfering as possible. This chapter explores the locking features of SQL Server that provide isolation for transactions. You'll come to understand the performance impact of the various levels and types of locks in SQL Server and how to define transactions to minimize locking performance problems.

Transaction Isolation Levels in SQL Server

Isolation levels determine the extent to which data being accessed or modified in one transaction is protected from changes to the data by other transactions. In theory, each transaction should be fully isolated from other transactions. However, in practice, for practical and performance reasons, this might not always be the case. In a concurrent environment in the absence of locking and isolation, the following four scenarios can happen:

▶ **Lost update**—In this scenario, no isolation is provided to a transaction from other transactions. Multiple transactions can read the same copy of data and modify it. The last transaction to modify the data set prevails, and the changes by all other transactions are lost.

- ▶ **Dirty reads**—In this scenario, one transaction can read data that is being modified by other transactions. The data read by the first transaction is inconsistent because the other transaction might choose to roll back the changes.

- ▶ **Nonrepeatable reads**—In this scenario, which is somewhat similar to zero isolation, a transaction reads the data twice, but before the second read occurs, another transaction modifies the data; therefore, the values read by the first read are different from those of the second read. Because the reads are not guaranteed to be repeatable each time, this scenario is called nonrepeatable reads.

- ▶ **Phantom reads**—This scenario is similar to nonrepeatable reads. However, instead of the actual rows that were read changing before the transaction is complete, additional rows are added to the table, resulting in a different set of rows being read the second time. Consider a scenario in which Transaction A reads rows with key values within the range of 1 through 5 and returns three rows with key values 1, 3, and 5. Before Transaction A reads the data again within the transaction, Transaction B adds two more rows with the key values 2 and 4 and commits the changes. Assuming that Transaction A and Transaction B both can run independently without blocking each other, when Transaction A runs the query a second time, it now gets five rows with key values 1, 2, 3, 4, and 5. This phenomenon is called phantom reads because in the second pass, you get records you did not expect to retrieve.

Ideally, a DBMS must provide levels of isolation to prevent these types of scenarios. Sometimes, for practical and performance reasons, databases relax some of the rules. The American National Standards Institute (ANSI) has defined four transaction isolation levels, each providing a different degree of isolation to cover the previous scenarios. ANSI SQL-92 defines the following four standards for transaction isolation:

- ▶ Read Uncommitted (Level 0)
- ▶ Read Committed (Level 1)
- ▶ Repeatable Read (Level 2)
- ▶ Serializable (Level 3)

SQL Server 2014 supports all the ANSI isolation levels; in addition, SQL Server 2014 also supports two additional transaction isolation levels that use row versioning. One is an alternative implementation of Read Committed isolation called Read Committed Snapshot, and the other is the Snapshot transaction isolation level.

You can set the default transaction isolation for a user session by using the SET TRANSACTION ISOLATION LEVEL T-SQL command, or for individual SQL statements, you can specify table-level isolation hints within the query. Using table-level hints is covered later in this chapter, in the section, "Table Hints for Locking."

37

Read Uncommitted Isolation

If you set the Read Uncommitted mode for a session, no isolation is provided to the SELECT queries in that session. A transaction that is running with this isolation level is not immune to dirty reads, nonrepeatable reads, or phantom reads.

To set the Read Uncommitted mode for a session, you run the following statements from the client:

▶ **T-SQL**—Use SET TRANSACTION ISOLATION LEVEL READ UNCOMMITTED.

▶ **ODBC**—Use the function call SQLSetConnectAttr with Attribute set to SQL_ATTR_TXN_ISOLATION and ValuePtr set to SQL_TXN_READ_UNCOMMITTED.

▶ **OLE DB**—Use the function call ITransactionLocal::StartTransaction with the isoLevel set to ISOLATIONLEVEL_READUNCOMMITTED.

▶ **ADO**—Set the IsolationLevel property of the Connection object to adXactReadUncommitted.

▶ **ADO.NET**—For applications using the System.Data.SqlClient managed namespace, call the SqlConnection.BeginTransaction method and set the IsolationLevel option to ReadUncommitted.

You need to be careful when running queries at Read Uncommitted isolation; it is possible to read changes that have been made to data that are subsequently rolled back. In essence, the accuracy of the results cannot be guaranteed. You should use this mode only when you need to get information quickly from an online transaction processing (OLTP) database, without affecting or being affected by the ongoing updates and when the accuracy of the results is not critical.

Read Committed Isolation

The Read Committed mode is the default locking-isolation mode for SQL Server. With Read Committed as the transaction isolation level, read operations can read pages only for transactions that have already been committed. No "dirty reads" are allowed. Locks acquired by update transactions are held for the duration of the transaction. However, in this mode, read requests within the transaction release locks as soon as the query finishes reading the data. Although this improves concurrent access to the data for updates, it does not prevent nonrepeatable reads or phantom reads. For example, within a transaction, a process could read one set of rows early in the transaction and then, before reading the information again, another process could modify the result set, resulting in a different result set being read the second time.

Because Read Committed is the default isolation level for SQL Server, you do not need to do anything to set this mode. If you need to set the isolation level back to Read Committed mode for a session, you run the following statements from the client:

▶ **T-SQL**—Use SET TRANSACTION ISOLATION LEVEL READ COMMITTED.

▶ **ODBC**—Use the function call SQLSetConnectAttr with Attribute set to SQL_ATTR_TXN_ISOLATION and ValuePtr set to SQL_TXN_READ_COMMITTED.

▶ **OLE DB**—Use the function call `ITransactionLocal::StartTransaction` with `isoLevel` set to `ISOLATIONLEVEL_READCOMMITTED`.

▶ **ADO**—Set the `IsolationLevel` property of the `Connection` object to `adXactReadcommitted`.

▶ **ADO.NET**—For applications using the `System.Data.SqlClient` managed namespace, call the `SqlConnection.BeginTransaction` method and set the `IsolationLevel` option to `ReadCommitted`.

Read Committed Snapshot Isolation

When the `READ_COMMITTED_SNAPSHOT` database option is set to `ON`, sessions running with the Read Committed isolation mode use row versioning to provide statement-level read consistency. When this database option is enabled and a transaction runs at the Read Committed isolation level, all statements within the transaction see a snapshot of the data as it exists at the start of the statement.

When the `READ_COMMITTED_SNAPSHOT` option is enabled for a database, SQL Server maintains versions of each row that is modified. Whenever a transaction modifies a row, an image of the row before modification is copied into a page in the version store, which is a collection of data pages in `tempdb`. If multiple transactions modify a row, multiple versions of the row are linked in a version chain. Queries running with Read Committed Snapshot isolation retrieve the last version of each row that had been committed when the statement started, providing a statement-level snapshot of the data.

In the Read Committed Snapshot isolation mode, read operations do not acquire shared page or row locks on the data. Therefore, readers using row versioning do not block other processes modifying the same data, and, similarly, processes modifying the data do not block the readers. In addition, because the read operations do not acquire locks, locking overhead is reduced. However, processes modifying data still block other processes modifying data because two operations cannot modify the same data at the same time. Exclusive locks on modified data are still acquired and held until the end of the transaction.

> **NOTE**
>
> Whereas normal read operations do not acquire shared locks when Read Committed Snapshot is enabled, SQL Server does still acquire shared locks when validating foreign keys, even if the transaction is using Read Committed Snapshot or Snapshot Isolation level. Be mindful of this if you see shared locks leading to blocking or deadlocks when using either method of snapshot isolation. You should check to see whether the shared locks being acquired are on an object that is referenced by a foreign key.

While locking overhead is reduced for read operations when using Read Committed Snapshot isolation, it does introduce overhead to maintain the row versions in `tempdb`. In addition, `tempdb` must have sufficient space to hold the row versions in addition to the space required for normal `tempdb` operations.

You might want to consider enabling the READ_COMMITTED_SNAPSHOT database option when blocking that occurs between read and write operations affects performance to the point that the overhead of creating and managing row versions is offset by the concurrency benefits. You may also consider using Read Committed Snapshot isolation when an application requires absolute accuracy for long-running aggregations or queries where data values must be consistent to the point in time that the query starts.

> **NOTE**
>
> You can use Read Committed Snapshot isolation mode with most existing SQL Server applications without making any change to the application code itself if the applications are written to use the default Read Committed isolation level. The behavior of Read Committed, whether to use row versioning or not, is determined by the database option setting, and this can be enabled or disabled without requiring any changes to the application code.

Repeatable Read Isolation

In Repeatable Read mode, SQL Server provides the same level of isolation for updates as in Read Committed mode, but it also allows the data to be read many times within the same transaction and guarantees that the same values will be read each time. Repeatable Read isolation mode prevents other users from updating data that has been read within the transaction until the transaction in which it was read is committed or rolled back. This way, the reading transaction does not pick up changes to the rows it read previously within the transaction. However, this isolation mode does not prevent additional rows (that is, phantom reads) from appearing in the subsequent reads.

Although preventing nonrepeatable reads is desirable for certain transactions, it requires holding locks on the data that has been read until the transaction is completed. This reduces concurrent access for multiple update operations and causes performance degradation due to lock waits and locking contention between transactions. It can also potentially lead to deadlocks. (Deadlocking is discussed in more detail in the "Deadlocks" section, later in this chapter.)

To set Repeatable Read mode for a session, you run the following statements from the client:

- ▶ **T-SQL**—Use SET TRANSACTION ISOLATION LEVEL REPEATABLE READ.

- ▶ **ODBC**—Use the function call SQLSetConnectAttr with Attribute set to SQL_ATTR_TXN_ISOLATION and ValuePtr set to SQL_TXN_REPEATABLEREAD.

- ▶ **OLE DB**—Use the function call ITransactionLocal::StartTransaction with isoLevel set to ISOLATIONLEVEL_REPEATABLEREAD.

- ▶ **ADO**—Set the IsolationLevel property of the Connection object to adXact REPEATABLEREAD.

▶ **ADO.NET**—For applications using the `System.Data.SqlClient` managed namespace, call the `SqlConnection.BeginTransaction` method and set the `IsolationLevel` option to `RepeatableRead`.

Serializable Read Isolation

Serializable Read mode is similar to repeatable reads but adds to it the restriction that rows cannot be added to a result set that was read previously within a transaction. This prevents phantom reads. In other words, Serializable Read locks the existing data being read as well as rows that do not yet exist. It accomplishes this by locking the data being read as well as locking across the range of values being read so that additional rows cannot be added to the range.

For example, say you run a query in a transaction that retrieves all records from the `Sales.SalesOrderHeader` table in the `AdventureWorks2012` database for a `Customer` with the `CustomerID` of `11300`. To prevent additional records from being added to the `SalesOrderHeader` table for this customer, SQL Server locks the entire range of values with `CustomerID` of `11300`. It accomplishes this by using key-range locks, which are discussed in the "Serialization and Key-Range Locking" section, later in this chapter.

Although preventing phantom reads is desirable for certain transactions, Serializable Read mode, like Repeatable Read, reduces concurrent access for multiple update operations and can cause performance degradation due to lock waits and locking contention between transactions and it can potentially lead to deadlocks.

To set Serializable Read mode for a session, you run the following statements from the client:

▶ **T-SQL**—Use `SET TRANSACTION ISOLATION LEVEL SERIALIZABLE`.

▶ **ODBC**—Use the function call `SQLSetConnectAttr` with `Attribute` set to `SQL_ATTR_TXN_ISOLATION` and `ValuePtr` set to `SQL_TXN_SERIALIZABLE`.

▶ **OLE DB**—Use the function call `ITransactionLocal::StartTransaction` with `isoLevel` set to `ISOLATIONLEVEL_SERIALIZABLE`.

▶ **ADO**—Set the `IsolationLevel` property of the `Connection` object to `adXact SERIALIZABLE`.

▶ **ADO.NET**—For applications using the `System.Data.SqlClient` managed namespace, call the `SqlConnection.BeginTransaction` method and set the `IsolationLevel` option to `Serializable`.

Snapshot Isolation

Snapshot Isolation is an additional isolation level available in SQL Server 2014. Similar to Read Committed Snapshot, Snapshot Isolation mode uses row versioning to take a point-in-time snapshot of the data. However, unlike Read Committed Snapshot isolation, which provides a statement-level snapshot of the data, Snapshot Isolation maintains a snapshot

37

of the data for the duration of the entire transaction. A data snapshot is taken when the transaction starts and the snapshot remains consistent for the duration of the transaction.

Snapshot Isolation mode provides the benefit of repeatable reads without acquiring and holding shared locks on the data that is read. This can help minimize locking and blocking problems between read operations and update operations. Read operations do not have to wait for write operations, and writes don't have to wait for reads.

To set the Snapshot Isolation mode for a session, you run the following statement:

```
SET TRANSACTION ISOLATION LEVEL SNAPSHOT
```

In addition, to be able to request the Snapshot Isolation mode in a session, you must enable the database option ALLOW_SNAPSHOT_ISOLATION with the ALTER DATABASE command:

```
ALTER DATABASE dbname SET ALLOW_SNAPSHOT_ISOLATION ON
```

When Snapshot Isolation mode is enabled, SQL Server assigns a transaction sequence number to each transaction that manipulates data using row versioning. When either the READ_COMMITTED_SNAPSHOT or ALLOW_SNAPSHOT_ISOLATION database option is set to ON, SQL Server stores a version of the previously committed image of the data row in tempdb whenever the row is modified by a transaction. Each of these versions is marked with the transaction sequence number of the transaction that made the change. The versions of the modified rows are linked together in a chain, with the most recent version of the row always stored in the current database and the versioned rows stored in tempdb.

When a transaction requests a read of data, it searches the version chain to locate the last committed version of the data row with a lower transaction sequence number than the current transaction. Row versions are kept in tempdb only long enough to satisfy the requirements of any transactions running under row versioning–based isolation levels. SQL Server keeps track of the sequence number of the oldest outstanding transaction and periodically deletes all row versions stamped with transaction sequence numbers lower than that.

You might consider using snapshot isolation in the following instances:

▶ When you want optimistic concurrency control

▶ When it is unlikely that your transaction would have to be rolled back because of an update conflict

▶ When an application generates reports based on long-running, multistatement queries that must have point-in-time consistency

▶ With systems that are incurring a high number of deadlocks because of read/write contention

There is a risk to using snapshot isolation, however. If two client applications both retrieve the same data and then both attempt to write changes to the data back to the database, then a conflict can occur. Fortunately, SQL Server 2014 resolves this problem by accepting the first transaction's writes and blocking the second transaction's writes. So, although snapshot isolation provides benefits for resolving conflicts between read and write operations, there can still be conflicts between multiple write operations. For systems with heavy read and insert activity and with little concurrent updating of the same resource, snapshot isolation can provide a solution for concurrency issues.

Another cost of snapshot isolation is that it can make heavy use of `tempdb`. For this reason, you should locate `tempdb` on its own high-performance drive system.

NOTE

Only one of the transaction isolation levels can be active at any given time for a user session. The isolation level you set within an application is active for the duration of the connection or until it is manually reset. To check the current transaction isolation level settings, you run the DBCC USEROPTIONS command and examine the value for isolation level, as in the following example:

```
DBCC USEROPTIONS
go


/* output
Set Option                         Value
---------------------------------- --------------
textsize                           2147483647
language                           us_english
dateformat                         mdy
datefirst                          7
lock_timeout                       -1
quoted_identifier                  SET
arithabort                         SET
ansi_null_dflt_on                  SET
ansi_warnings                      SET
ansi_padding                       SET
ansi_nulls                         SET
concat_null_yields_null            SET
isolation level                    snapshot
*/
```

Be aware that DBCC USEROPTIONS reports an isolation level of Read Committed Snapshot when the database option READ_COMMITTED_SNAPSHOT is set to ON but the current transaction isolation level for the session is explicitly set to Read Committed. The actual isolation level in effect for the user session is Read Committed.

Alternatively, you can also query the `transaction_isolation_level` column of the `sys.dm_exec_sessions` dynamic management view to determine the isolation level in effect for the current session, as in the following example:

37

```
SELECT transaction_isolation_level
    FROM sys.dm_exec_sessions
    WHERE session_id = @@spid
GO

/* output
transaction_isolation_level
---------------------------
                          2
*/
```

The transaction isolation level values returned can be interpreted as follows:

```
0 = Unspecified
1 = ReadUncomitted
2 = ReadCommitted
3 = Repeatable
4 = Serializable
5 = Snapshot
```

The Lock Manager

The responsibility for ensuring lock conflict resolution between user processes falls on the SQL Server Lock Manager. SQL Server automatically assigns locks to processes to guarantee that the current user of a resource (for example, a data row or page, an index row or page, a table, an index, or a database) has a consistent view of that resource, from the beginning to the end of a particular operation. In other words, what you start with is what you work with throughout your transaction. Nobody can change what you are working on in midstate, thereby ensuring the consistency of your transaction.

The Lock Manager is responsible for deciding the appropriate lock type (for example, shared, exclusive, update) and the appropriate granularity of locks (for example, row, page, table), according to the type of operation being performed and the amount of data being affected. Based on the type of transaction, the SQL Server Lock Manager chooses different types of lock resources. For example, a CREATE INDEX statement might lock the entire table, whereas an UPDATE statement might lock only a specific row.

The Lock Manager also manages compatibility between lock types attempting to access the same resources, resolves deadlocks, and escalates locks to a higher level, if necessary.

The Lock Manager manages locks for both shared data and internal system resources. For shared data, the Lock Manager manages row locks, page locks, and table locks on tables, as well as data pages, text pages, and leaf-level index pages. Internally, the Lock Manager uses latches to manage locking on index rows and pages, controlling access to internal data structures and, in some cases, for retrieving individual rows of data. Latches provide better system performance because they are less resource intensive than locks. Latches also provide greater concurrency than locks. Latches are typically used for operations such as page splits, deletion of index rows, movement of rows in an index, and so on. The main difference between a lock and a latch is that a lock is held for the duration of the transaction, and a latch is held only for the duration of the operation for which it is required. Locks are used to ensure the logical consistency of data, whereas latches are used to ensure the physical consistency of the data and data structures.

The remainder of this chapter examines how the Lock Manager determines the type and level of lock to assign, based on the type of command being executed, number of rows affected, and lock isolation level in effect.

Monitoring Lock Activity in SQL Server

To monitor the performance of a system, you need to keep track of locking activity in SQL Server. The following are the most commonly used methods to do so:

- ▶ Querying the `sys.dm_tran_locks` dynamic management view directly
- ▶ Viewing locking activity with SQL Server Profiler
- ▶ Monitoring locks with Performance Monitor

As you read through the rest of this chapter, you might want to examine or monitor the locking activity for the examples presented. To assist you in that effort, the following sections describe the methods of examining lock activity in SQL Server 2014.

> **NOTE**
>
> The `sp_lock` system stored procedure is another useful tool for gathering lock information. When run without any parameters, this stored procedure will return all of the locks currently held on the server. The `sp_lock` system stored procedure is not covered in detail in this chapter because it has been deprecated and will be removed in a future version of Microsoft SQL Server. Microsoft recommends that you query `sys.dm_tran_locks` dynamic management view instead of using `sp_lock`.

37

Querying the `sys.dm_tran_locks` View

The `sys.dm_tran_locks` dynamic management view returns information about all the locks currently granted or waiting to be granted in SQL Server. (The information is populated from the internal lock management structures in SQL Server 2014.) This view provides no historical information; rather, the data in this view corresponds to live Lock Manager information. This data can change at any time for subsequent queries of the view as locks are acquired and released.

The information returned by the view can be divided into two main groups: resource information and lock request information. The resource information describes the resource on which the lock request is being made, and the request information provides details on the lock request itself. Table 37.1 describes the most useful data columns returned by the `sys.dm_tran_locks` view.

TABLE 37.1   Useful Columns Returned by the `sys.dm_tran_locks` View

Column Name	Description
resource_type	Indicates the type of resource the lock is being held or requested on.
resource_subtype	Indicates a subtype of the `resource_type`, if any.
resource_database_id	Indicates the database ID of the database where the resource resides.
resource_description	Provides information about the resource that is not available from other resource columns.
resource_associated_entity_id	Indicates the ID of the entity in a database that the resource is associated with.
resource_lock_partition	Indicates the ID of the associated partition for a resource that is partitioned.
request_mode	Indicates the lock mode of the request that has been granted or is being waited on.
request_type	Indicates the request type. (The only current value is LOCK.)
request_status	Indicates the current status of this request (GRANT, CONVERT, or WAIT).
request_reference_count	Returns an approximate number of times the same requestor has requested this resource.
request_lifetime	Specifies a code indicating when the lock on the resource is released.
request_session_id	Indicates the ID of the session that generated the corresponding request.
request_exec_context_id	Indicates the ID of the execution context of the process that generated the lock request.
request_request_id	Indicates the batch ID of the process that generated the request.
request_owner_type	Indicates the type of entity that owns the request. Possible values include, but are not limited to, TRANSACTION, CURSOR, and SESSION.
request_owner_id	Specifies the ID of the specific owner of this request. This value is used for transactions for which this is the transaction ID.
request_owner_guid	Indicates the GUID of the specific owner of the lock request. This value is used only by a distributed transaction where the value corresponds to the MS DTC GUID for that transaction

Column Name	Description
request_owner_lockspace_id	Represents the lockspace ID of the requestor. The lockspace ID determines whether two requestors are compatible with each other and can be granted locks in modes that would otherwise conflict with one another.
lock_owner_address	Indicates the memory address of the internal data structure used to track the request.

Table 37.2 lists the possible lock request modes that can be displayed in the request_mode column of the sys.dm_tran_locks view.

TABLE 37.2   Lock Request Modes

Value	Lock Type	Description	Request Mode
1	N/A	No access provided to the requestor	NULL
2	Schema	Schema stability lock	Sch-S
3	Schema	Schema modification lock	Sch-M
4	Shared	Acquisition of a shared lock on the resource	S
5	Update	Acquisition of an update lock on the resource	U
6	Exclusive	Exclusive lock granted on the resource	X
7	Intent	Intent for a shared lock	IS
8	Intent	Intent for an update lock	IU
9	Intent	Intent for an exclusive lock	IX
10	Intent	Shared lock with intent for an update lock on subordinate resources	SIU
11	Intent	Shared lock with intent for an exclusive lock	SIX on subordinate resources
12	Intent	Update lock with an intent for an exclusive lock on subordinate resources	UIX
13	Bulk	BULK UPDATE lock used for bulk copy operations	BU
14	Key-Range	Shared lock on the range between keys and shared lock on the key at the end of the range; used for serializable range scan	Range_S_S
15	Key-Range	Shared lock on the range between keys, with an update lock on the key at the end of the range	Range_S_U
16	Key-Range	Exclusive lock used to prevent inserts into a range between keys	RangeIn-N
17	Key-Range	Key-range conversion lock created by overlap of RangeIn-N and shared (S) locks	RangeIn-S

37

Value	Lock Type	Description	Request Mode
18	Key-Range	Key-range conversion lock created by overlap of `RangeIn-N` and update (`U`) locks	`RangeIn-U`
19	Key-Range	Key-range conversion lock created by overlap of `RangeIn-N` and exclusive (`X`) locks	`RangeIn-X`
20	Key-Range	Key-range conversion lock created by overlap of `RangeIn-N` and `RangeS_S` locks	`RangeX-S`
21	Key-Range	Key-Range conversion lock created by overlap of `RangeIn-N` and `RangeS_U` locks	`RangeX-U`
22	Key-Range	Exclusive lock on range between keys, with an exclusive lock on the key at the end of the range	`RangeX-X`

Listing 37.1 provides an example of a query against the `sys.dm_tran_locks` view.

LISTING 37.1   An Example of a Query Against the `sys.dm_tran_locks` View

```
select request_session_id as spid,
        convert (varchar(20), db_name(resource_database_id))
            As db_name,
        convert(varchar(12), resource_type) as resrc_type,
        case when resource_type = 'OBJECT'
            then convert(varchar(20),
                            object_name(resource_associated_entity_id,
                                    resource_database_id))
            when resource_type = 'DATABASE'
            then ''
            when resource_type  IN ( 'FILE', 'METADATA' )
            then convert(varchar(20), resource_type)
            WHEN resource_type IN ( 'KEY', 'PAGE', 'RID' )
                and resource_database_id = db_id()
            THEN CONVERT(varchar(35),
                            ( SELECT OBJECT_NAME([object_id])
                                FROM sys.partitions
                                WHERE sys.partitions.hobt_id =
                                DTL.resource_associated_entity_id)
                                + ' - ' + DTL.resource_description)
            WHEN resource_type IN ( 'KEY', 'PAGE', 'RID' )
                and resource_database_id <> db_id()
            THEN convert(varchar(20), resource_description)
            else convert(varchar(20), resource_associated_entity_id)
            end as object,
        convert(varchar(12), request_type) as req_type,
        convert(varchar(6), request_mode) as mode,
        convert(varchar(8), request_status) as status
```

```
   from sys.dm_tran_locks dtl
order by request_session_id, object
go


/* output
spid db_name         resrc_type object                              req_type mode status
---- -------------   ---------- --------------------------------    -------- ---- ------
53   AdventureWorks2012 DATABASE                                    LOCK     S    GRANT
54   AdventureWorks2012 DATABASE                                    LOCK     S    GRANT
54   AdventureWorks2012 OBJECT   ProductCategory                    LOCK     IX   GRANT
54   AdventureWorks2012 KEY      ProductCategory - (61a06abd401c)   LOCK     X    GRANT
54   AdventureWorks2012 KEY      ProductCategory - (980d51a65019)   LOCK     X    GRANT
54   AdventureWorks2012 KEY      ProductCategory - (ab299e046963)   LOCK     X    GRANT
54   AdventureWorks2012 PAGE     ProductCategory - 1:1109           LOCK     IX   GRANT
54   AdventureWorks2012 PAGE     ProductCategory - 1:777            LOCK     IX   GRANT
*/
```

Note that the query in Listing 37.1 contains a CASE expression for displaying the locked object. If the resource type is KEY, PAGE, or RID and the database ID of the locked resource is the same as the current database context, it returns the name of the object associated with the KEY, PAGE, or RID lock along with the description of the locked resource obtained from the sys.partitions table in that database; otherwise, it returns just the locked resource description.

> **TIP**
>
> To save yourself the trouble of having to type in the query listed in Listing 37.1 or having to read it in from a file each time you want to run it, you might want to consider creating your own stored procedure or view that invokes this query.

> **NOTE**
>
> For some odd reason, there is no GUI-based lock monitoring tool provided with SQL Server 2014 to display the specific locks being held by processes or the locks being held on objects. The only locking information provided by the SSMS Activity Monitor in SQL Server 2014 is the indication of lock blocking and wait time provided by the Process Monitor and the Lock Waits information provided by the Resource Waits Monitor.

Viewing Locking Activity with SQL Server Profiler

Another tool to help you monitor locking activity in SQL Server 2014 is SQL Server Profiler. SQL Server Profiler provides a number of lock events that you can capture in a trace. The trace information can be viewed in real-time or saved to a file or database table for further analysis at a later date. Saving the information to a table allows you to run different reports on the information to help in the analysis.

> **NOTE**
>
> This chapter provides only a brief overview of how to capture and view locking information using SQL Server Profiler. For more information on the features and capabilities of SQL Server Profiler and how to use it, see Chapter 5, "SQL Server Profiler."

SQL Profiler provides the following lock events that can be captured in a trace:

- `Lock:Acquired`—Indicates when a lock on a resource, such as a data page or row, has been acquired.

- `Lock:Cancel`—Indicates when the acquisition of a lock on a resource has been canceled (for example, as the result of a deadlock).

- `Lock:Deadlock`—Indicates when two or more concurrent processes have deadlocked with each other.

- `Lock:Deadlock Chain`—Provides the information for each of the events leading up to a deadlock. This information is similar to that provided by the 1204 trace flag, which is covered in the "Deadlocks" section, later in this chapter.

- `Lock:Escalation`—Indicates when a lower-level lock has been converted to a higher-level lock (for example, when page-level locks are escalated to table-level locks).

- `Lock:Released`—Indicates that a process has released a previously acquired lock on a resource.

- `Lock:Timeout`—Indicates that a lock request that is waiting on a resource has timed out due to another transaction holding a blocking lock.

- `Lock:Timeout (timeout >0)`—Is similar to `Lock:Timeout` but does not include any events where the lock timeout is 0 seconds.

- `Deadlock Graph`—Generates an XML description of a deadlock.

Figure 37.1 shows an example of choosing a set of locking events to monitor with SQL Server Profiler.

SQL Server Profiler also provides a number of data values to display for the events being monitored. You might find the following data columns useful when monitoring locking activity:

- `spid`—The process ID of the process that generated the event.

- `EventClass`—The type of event being captured.

- `Mode`—For lock monitoring, the type of lock involved in the captured event.

- `ObjectID`—The ID of the object involved in the locking event—that is, the object that the lock is associated with.

- `DatabaseID`—The ID of the database involved in the locking event

- `TextData`—The query that generated the lock event.

▶ **LoginName**—The login name associated with the process.

▶ **ApplicationName**—The name of the application generating the lock event.

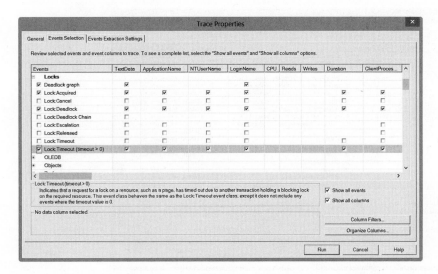

FIGURE 37.1   Choosing lock events in SQL Server Profiler.

Keep in mind that many internal system processes also acquire locks in SQL Server. If you want to filter out those processes and focus on specific processes, users, or applications, use the filters in SQL Server Profiler to include the information you want to trace or exclude the information you don't want to trace (see Figure 37.2).

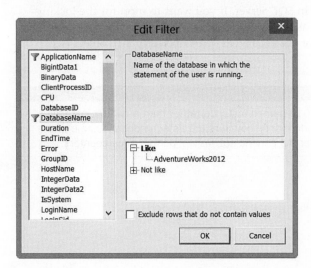

FIGURE 37.2   Filtering out unwanted information in SQL Server Profiler.

After you set up your events, data columns, and filters, you can begin the trace. Figure 37.3 shows an example of the type of information captured.

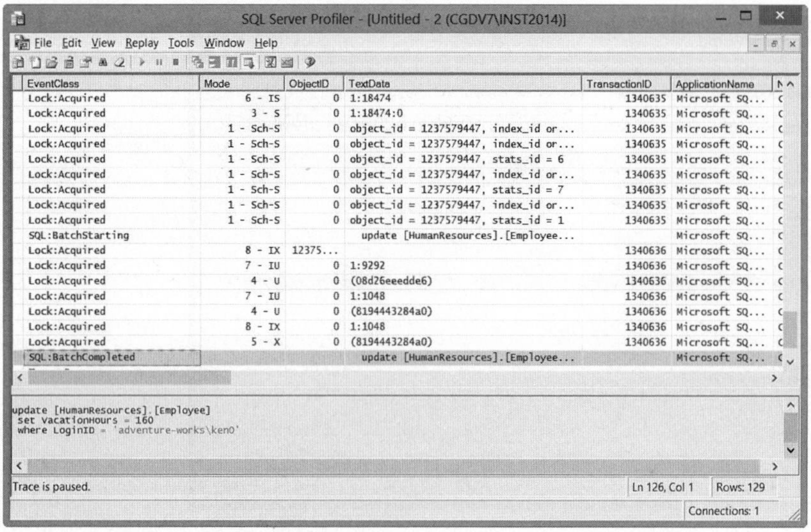

FIGURE 37.3   Locking information captured in a SQL Server Profiler trace.

Monitoring Locks with Performance Monitor

Another method of monitoring locking in SQL Server is through the Performance Monitor. The sys.dm_tran_locks view and SSMS Activity Monitor provide a snapshot of the actual locks currently in effect in SQL Server. If you want to monitor the locking activity as a whole on a continuous basis, you can use the Windows Performance Monitor and monitor the counters available for the SQLServer:Locks performance object (see Figure 37.4).

> **NOTE**
>
> If you are monitoring a SQL Server 2014 named instance rather than a default instance of SQL Server 2014, the SQL Server performance counters are listed under the name of the SQL Server instance rather than under the generic SQLServer performance counters.

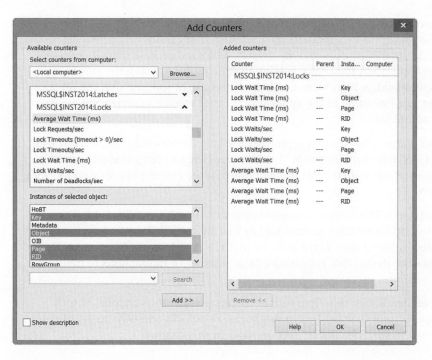

FIGURE 37.4   Choosing counters for the `SQLServer:Locks` performance object in Performance Monitor.

You can use the `SQLServer:Locks` object to help detect locking bottlenecks and contention points in the system as well as to provide a summary of the overall locking activity in SQL Server. You can use the information that Performance Monitor provides to identify whether locking problems are the cause of any performance problems. You can then take appropriate corrective actions to improve concurrency and the overall performance of the system. The counters that belong to the `SQLServer:Locks` object are as follows:

▶ **Average Wait Time**—This counter represents the average wait time (in milliseconds) for each lock request. A high value is an indication of locking contention that could be affecting performance of concurrent processes.

▶ **Lock Requests/sec**—This counter represents the total number of new locks and lock conversion requests made per second. A high value for this counter is not necessarily a cause for alarm; it might simply indicate a system with a high number of concurrent users.

▶ **Lock Timeouts (timeout > 0)/sec**—This counter is similar to the LockTimeouts/sec counter but does not include NOWAIT lock requests that time out immediately.

▶ **Lock Timeouts/sec**—This counter represents the total number of lock timeouts per second that occur for lock requests on a resource that cannot be granted before the lock timeout interval is exceeded. By default, a blocked process waits indefinitely unless the application specifies a maximum timeout limit, using the SET LOCK_TIMEOUT command. A high value for this counter might indicate that the timeout limit is set to a low value in the application or that you are experiencing excessive locking contention.

▶ **Lock Wait Time**—This counter represents the cumulative wait time for each lock request. It is given in milliseconds. A high value here indicates that you might have long-running or inefficient transactions that are causing blocking and locking contention.

▶ **Lock Waits/sec**—This counter represents the total number of lock requests generated per second for which a process had to wait before a lock request on a resource was granted. A high value might indicate inefficient or long-running transactions or a poor database design that is causing a large number of transactions to block one another.

▶ **Number of Deadlocks/sec**—This number represents the total number of lock requests per second that resulted in deadlocks. Deadlocks and ways to avoid them are discussed in the "Deadlocks" section, later in this chapter.

For more information on using Windows Performance Monitor for monitoring SQL Server performance, see Chapter 39, "Monitoring SQL Server Performance."

SQL Server Lock Types

Locking is handled automatically in SQL Server. The Lock Manager chooses the type of lock, based on the type of transaction (such as SELECT, INSERT, UPDATE, or DELETE). Lock Manager uses the following types of locks:

▶ Shared locks

▶ Update locks

▶ Exclusive locks

▶ Intent locks

▶ Schema locks

▶ Bulk update locks

In addition to choosing the type of lock, the Lock Manager in SQL Server 2014 automatically adjusts the granularity of the locks (for example, row, page, table), based on the nature of the statement that is executed and the number of rows that are affected.

Shared Locks

By default, SQL Server uses shared locks for all read operations. A shared lock is, by definition, not exclusive. Theoretically, an unlimited number of shared locks can be held on
a resource at any given time. In addition, shared locks are unique in that, by default, a
process locks a resource only for the duration of the read on the resource (row, page, or
table). For example, the query SELECT * from authors locks the first row in the authors
table when the query starts. After the first row is read, the lock on that row is released,
and a lock on the second row is acquired. After the second row is read, its lock is released,
and a lock on the third row is acquired, and so on. In this fashion, a SELECT query allows
other data rows that are not being read to be modified during the read operation. This
increases concurrent access to the data.

Shared locks are compatible with other shared locks as well as with update locks. A shared
lock does not prevent the acquisition of additional shared locks or an update lock by other
processes on a given row or page. Multiple shared locks can be held at any given time, for
a number of transactions or processes. These transactions do not affect the consistency of
the data. However, shared locks do prevent the acquisition of exclusive locks. Any transaction attempting to modify data on a page or a row on which a shared lock is placed is
blocked until all the shared locks are released.

> **NOTE**
>
> It is important to note that within a transaction running at the default isolation level of
> Read Committed, shared locks are not held for the duration of the transaction or even
> the duration of the statement that acquires the shared locks. Shared lock resources
> (row, page, table, and so on) are normally released as soon as the read operation on the
> resource is completed. SQL Server provides the HOLDLOCK clause for the SELECT state-
> ment, which you can use if you want to continue holding the shared lock for the duration
> of the transaction. HOLDLOCK is explained later in this chapter, in the section "Table Hints
> for Locking." Another way to hold shared locks for the duration of a transaction is to set
> the isolation level for the session or the query to Repeatable Read or Serializable Reads.
> There are also SERIALIZABLE and REPEATABLEREAD table hints that can be used in a
> SELECT statement to hold the shared locks.

37

Update Locks

Update locks are used to lock rows or pages that a user process intends to modify. When
a transaction tries to update a row, it must first read the row to ensure that it is modifying the appropriate record. If the transaction were to put a shared lock on the resource
initially, it would eventually need to get an exclusive lock on the resource to modify the
record and prevent any other transaction from modifying the same record. The problem
is that this could lead to deadlocks in an environment in which multiple transactions are
trying to modify data on the same resource at the same time. Figure 37.5 demonstrates
how deadlocks can occur if lock conversion takes place from shared locks to exclusive
locks. When both processes attempt to escalate the shared lock they both hold on a
resource to an exclusive lock, it results in a deadlock situation.

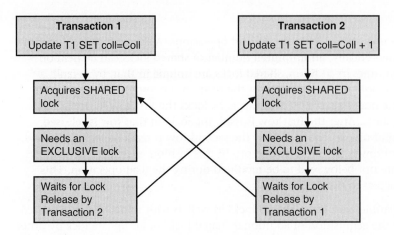

FIGURE 37.5   A deadlock scenario with shared and exclusive locks.

Update locks in SQL Server are provided to prevent this kind of deadlock scenario. Update locks are partially exclusive in that only one update lock can be acquired at a time on any resource. However, an update lock is compatible with shared locks, in that both can be acquired on the same resource simultaneously. In effect, an update lock signifies that a process wants to change a record, and it keeps out other processes that also want to change that record. However, an update lock allows other processes to acquire shared locks to read the data until the UPDATE or DELETE statement is finished locating the records to be affected. The process then attempts to escalate each update lock to an exclusive lock. At this time, the process waits until all currently held shared locks on the same records are released. After the shared locks are released, the update lock is escalated to an exclusive lock. The data change is then carried out, and the exclusive lock is held for the remainder of the transaction.

> **NOTE**
>
> Update locks are not used just for update operations. SQL Server uses update locks any time a search for data is required prior to performing the actual modification, such as with qualified updates and deletes (that is, when a WHERE clause is specified). Update locks are also used for insertions into a table because SQL Server must first search the data and related index to identify the correct position at which to insert the new row to maintain the sort order. After SQL Server has found the correct location and begins inserting the record, it escalates the update lock to an exclusive lock.

Exclusive Locks

As mentioned earlier, an exclusive lock is granted to a transaction when it is ready to perform data modifications. An exclusive lock on a resource makes sure no other transaction can interfere with the data locked by the transaction that is holding the exclusive lock. SQL Server releases the exclusive lock at the end of the transaction.

Exclusive locks are incompatible with other lock types. If an exclusive lock is held on a resource, any other read or data modification request for the same resource by other processes is forced to wait until the exclusive lock is released. Likewise, if a resource currently has read locks held on it by other processes, the exclusive lock request is forced to wait in a queue for the resource to become available.

Intent Locks

Intent locks do not really constitute a locking mode; rather, they act as a mechanism to indicate at a higher level of granularity the types of locks held at a lower level. The types of intent locks mirror the lock types previously discussed: shared intent locks, exclusive intent locks, and update intent locks. SQL Server Lock Manager uses intent locks as a mechanism to indicate that a shared, update, or exclusive lock is held at a lower level. For example, a shared intent lock on a table by a process signifies that the process currently holds a shared lock on a row or page within the table. The presence of the intent lock prevents other transactions from attempting to acquire a table-level lock that would be incompatible with the existing row or page locks.

Intent locks improve locking performance by allowing SQL Server to examine locks at the table level to determine the types of locks held on the table at the row or page level rather than searching through the multiple locks at the page or row level within the table. Intent locks also prevent two transactions that are both holding locks at a lower level on a resource from attempting to escalate those locks to a higher level while the other transaction still holds the intent lock. This prevents deadlocks during lock escalation.

You typically see three types of intent locks when monitoring locking activity: intent shared (IS) locks, intent exclusive (IX) locks, and shared with intent exclusive (SIX) locks. An IS lock indicates that the process currently holds, or has the intention of holding, shared locks on lower-level resources (row or page). An IX lock indicates that the process currently holds, or has the intention of holding, exclusive locks on lower-level resources. An SIX (pronounced as the letters S-I-X, not like the number six) lock occurs under special circumstances when a transaction is holding a shared lock on a resource and later in the transaction an IX lock is needed. At that point, the IS lock is converted to an SIX lock.

In the following example, the SELECT statement running at the serializable level acquires a shared table lock. It then needs an exclusive lock to update the row in the Sales. SalesOrderDetail table:

```
SET TRANSACTION ISOLATION LEVEL serializable
go
BEGIN TRAN
 select sum(OrderQty)
 FROM Sales.SalesOrderDetail
UPDATE Sales.SalesOrderDetail
    SET UnitPrice = $2004.99
    WHERE SalesOrderID = 43659
COMMIT TRAN
```

37

Because the transaction initially acquired a shared (s) table lock and then needed an exclusive row lock, which requires an intent exclusive (ix) lock on the table within the same transaction, the s lock is converted to an six lock.

> **NOTE**
>
> If only a few rows were in `Sales.SalesOrderDetail`, SQL Server might acquire only individual row or key locks rather than a table-level lock. SQL Server would then have an intent shared (is) lock on the table rather than a full shared (s) lock. In that instance, the UPDATE statement would then acquire a single exclusive lock to apply the update to a single row, and the x lock at the key level would result in the is locks at the page and table levels being converted to an ix lock at the page and table level for the remainder of the transaction.

Schema Locks

SQL Server uses schema locks to maintain structural integrity of SQL Server tables. Unlike other types of locks that provide isolation for the data, schema locks provide isolation for the schema of database objects, such as tables, views, and indexes within a transaction. The Lock Manager uses two types of schema locks:

▶ **Schema stability locks**—When a transaction is referencing either an index or a data page, SQL Server places a schema stability lock on the object. This ensures that no other process can modify the schema of an object—such as dropping an index or dropping or altering a stored procedure or table—while other processes are still referencing the object.

▶ **Schema modification locks**—When a process needs to modify the structure of an object (for example, alter the table, recompile a stored procedure), the Lock Manager places a schema modification lock on the object. For the duration of this lock, no other transaction can reference the object until the changes are complete and committed.

Bulk Update Locks

A bulk update lock is a special type of lock used only when bulk copying data into a table using the bcp utility or the BULK INSERT command. This special lock is used for these operations only when either the TABLOCK hint is specified to bcp or the BULK INSERT command or when the table lock on bulk load table option has been set for the table. Bulk update locks allow multiple bulk copy processes to bulk copy data into the same table in parallel, while preventing other processes that are not bulk copying data from accessing the table. If there are any indexes on the table, or any other processes already holding locks on the table, a bulk update lock cannot be granted.

SQL Server Lock Granularity

Lock granularity is essentially the amount of data locked as part of a query or update to provide complete isolation and serialization for the transaction. The Lock Manager needs to balance the concurrent access to resources versus the overhead of maintaining a large number of lower-level locks. For example, the smaller the lock size, the greater the number of concurrent users who can access the same table at the same time but the greater the overhead in maintaining those locks. The greater the lock size, the less overhead required to manage the locks, but concurrency is also less. Figure 37.6 demonstrates the trade-offs between lock size and concurrency.

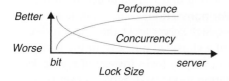

FIGURE 37.6   Trade-offs between performance and concurrency, depending on lock granularity.

Currently, SQL Server balances performance and concurrency by locking at the row level or higher. Based on a number of factors, such as key distribution, number of rows, row density, search arguments (SARGs), and so on, the Query Optimizer makes lock granularity decisions internally, and the programmer does not have to worry about such issues. SQL Server provides a number of T-SQL extensions that give you better control over query behavior from a locking standpoint. These Query Optimizer overrides are discussed in the "Table Hints for Locking" section, later in this chapter.

SQL Server provides the following locking levels:

▶ DATABASE—Whenever a SQL Server process is using a database other than `master`, the Lock Manager grants a database lock to the process. These are always shared locks, and they are used to keep track of when a database is in use to prevent another process from dropping the database, setting the database offline, or restoring the database. Note that because `master` and `tempdb` cannot be dropped or set offline, database locks are not required on those databases.

▶ FILE—A file lock is a lock acquired on a database file.

▶ EXTENT—Extent locks are used for locking extents, usually only during space allocation and deallocation. An extent consists of eight contiguous data or index pages. Extent locks can be shared extent or exclusive extent locks.

▶ ALLOCATION_UNIT—This type of lock is acquired on a database allocation unit.

▶ TABLE—With this type of lock, the entire table, inclusive of data and indexes, is locked. Examples of when table-level locks may be acquired include selecting all rows from a large table at the serializable level and performing unqualified updates or deletes on a table.

37

▶ **Heap or B-Tree (HOBT)**—This type of lock is acquired on a heap of data pages or on the B-Tree structure of an index.

▶ **PAGE**—With a page lock, the entire page, consisting of 8KB of data or index information, is locked. Page-level locks might be acquired when all rows on a page need to be read or when page-level maintenance needs to be performed, such as updating page pointers after a page split.

▶ **Row ID (RID)**—With an RID lock, a single row within a page is locked. RID locks are acquired whenever efficient and possible to do so in an effort to provide maximum concurrent access to the resource.

▶ **KEY**—SQL Server uses two types of key locks. The one that is used depends on the locking isolation level of the current session. For transactions that run in Read Committed or Repeatable Read isolation modes, SQL Server locks the actual index keys associated with the rows being accessed. (If a clustered index is on the table, the data rows are the leaf level of the index. You see key locks instead of row locks on those rows.) When in Serializable Read isolation mode, SQL Server prevents phantom rows by locking a range of key values so that no new rows can be inserted into the range. These are referred to as *key-range lo*cks. Key-range locks associated with a particular key value lock that key and the previous one in the index to indicate that all values between them are locked. Key-range locks are covered in more detail in the next section.

▶ **METADATA**—This type of lock is acquired on system catalog information

▶ **APPLICATION**—An application lock allows users to essentially define their own locks by specifying a name for the resource, a lock mode, an owner, and a timeout interval. Using application locks is discussed later in this chapter, in the section, "Using Application Locks."

Serialization and Key-Range Locking

As mentioned in the previous section, SQL Server provides serialization (Isolation Level 3) through the SET TRANSACTION ISOLATION SERIALIZABLE command. One of the isolations provided by this isolation level is the prevention against phantom reads. Preventing phantom reads means that the recordset that a query obtains within a transaction must return the same result set when it is run multiple times within the same transaction. That is, while a transaction is active, another transaction should not be allowed to insert new rows that would appear in the recordset of a query that were not in the original recordset retrieved by the transaction. SQL Server provides this capability though key-range locking.

As described earlier in this chapter, key-range locking in SQL Server provides isolation for a transaction from data modifications made by other transactions. This means that a transaction should return the same recordset each time. The following sections show how key-range locking works with various lock modes. Key-range locking covers the scenarios of a range search that returns a result set as well as searches against non-existent rows.

Key-Range Locking for a Range Search

In a scenario that involves key-range locking for a range search, SQL Server places locks on the index pages for the range of data covered in the WHERE clause of the query. (For a clustered index, the rows would be the actual data rows in the table.) Because the range is locked, no other transaction can insert new rows that fall within the range. In Figure 37.7, for example, transaction A has issued the following SELECT statement:

```
SET TRANSACTION ISOLATION LEVEL serializable
go
BEGIN TRAN
select * from Sales.SalesOrderDetail
where ProductID between 810 and 812
```

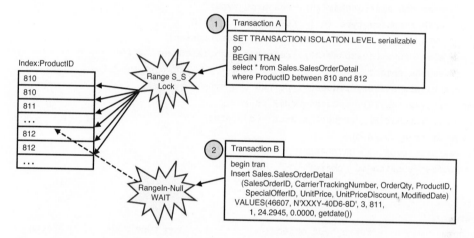

FIGURE 37.7   Key-range locking with a range search.

Transaction B is performing the following INSERT statement, attempting to insert a row that falls within the range being retrieved by transaction A (ProductID between 810 and 812):

```
begin tran
Insert Sales.SalesOrderDetail
    (SalesOrderID, CarrierTrackingNumber, OrderQty, ProductID,
SpecialOfferID, UnitPrice, UnitPriceDiscount, ModifiedDate)
  VALUES(46607, N'XXXY-40D6-8D', 3, 811,
        1, 24.2945, 0.0000, getdate())
```

Listing 37.2 shows a subset of the locks acquired when using the sys.dm_tran_locks catalog view. (In this sample output, SPID 54 is executing the SELECT statement, and SPID 58 is attempting the INSERT.)

LISTING 37.2   Viewing Key-Range Locks Using the `sys.dm_tran_locks` View

```
select request_session_id as spid,
       convert (varchar(20), db_name(resource_database_id))
             As db_name,
       convert(varchar(12), resource_type) as resrc_type,
       case when resource_type = 'OBJECT'
            then convert(varchar(20),
                         object_name(resource_associated_entity_id,
                                     resource_database_id))
            when resource_type = 'DATABASE'
            then ''
            when resource_type  IN ( 'FILE', 'METADATA' )
            then convert(varchar(20), resource_type)
            WHEN resource_type IN ( 'KEY', 'PAGE', 'RID' )
            THEN convert(varchar(20), resource_description)
            else convert(varchar(20), resource_associated_entity_id)
            end as object,
       convert(varchar(12), request_type) as req_type,
       convert(varchar(10), request_mode) as mode,
       convert(varchar(8), request_status) as status
   from sys.dm_tran_locks dtl
   where resource_type <> 'DATABASE'
order by request_session_id, object
go


/* output
spid db_name             resrc_type object                req_type mode        status
---- ------------------- ---------- -------------------   -------- ----------  ------
  54 AdventureWorks2012 KEY        (004878b8579f)        LOCK     S           GRANT
  54 AdventureWorks2012 KEY        (00a24beac3d1)        LOCK     RangeS-S    GRANT
  54 AdventureWorks2012 KEY        (00f842712257)        LOCK     S           GRANT
  54 AdventureWorks2012 KEY        (01fbd7bf8e71)        LOCK     RangeS-S    GRANT
  54 AdventureWorks2012 KEY        (020409c59dc0)        LOCK     RangeS-S    GRANT
  54 AdventureWorks2012 KEY        (02492a57e6ac)        LOCK     RangeS-S    GRANT
  54 AdventureWorks2012 KEY        (0271169f6c83)        LOCK     RangeS-S    GRANT
  54 AdventureWorks2012 KEY        (02c9562c994b)        LOCK     RangeS-S    GRANT
  54 AdventureWorks2012 KEY        (02ebe1f5109b)        LOCK     RangeS-S    GRANT
...
  54 AdventureWorks2012 PAGE       1:5205                LOCK     IS          GRANT
  54 AdventureWorks2012 PAGE       1:5206                LOCK     IS          GRANT
  54 AdventureWorks2012 OBJECT     SalesOrderDetail      LOCK     IS          GRANT
  58 AdventureWorks2012 KEY        (489e0991ff55)        LOCK     X           GRANT
  58 AdventureWorks2012 KEY        (7677809d799a)        LOCK     X           GRANT
  58 AdventureWorks2012 KEY        (da5c70c16e04)        LOCK     RangeI-N    WAIT
  58 AdventureWorks2012 PAGE       1:11168               LOCK     IX          GRANT
```

```
  58 AdventureWorks2012 PAGE      1:19854            LOCK   IX   GRANT
  58 AdventureWorks2012 PAGE      1:27237            LOCK   IX   GRANT
  58 AdventureWorks2012 PAGE      1:27256            LOCK   IX   GRANT
  58 AdventureWorks2012 PAGE      1:27258            LOCK   IX   GRANT
  58 AdventureWorks2012 OBJECT    SalesOrderDetail   LOCK   IX   GRANT
  58 AdventureWorks2012 OBJECT    SalesOrderHeader   LOCK   IS   GRANT
  58 AdventureWorks2012 OBJECT    SpecialOfferProduct LOCK  IS   GRANT
*/
```

To provide key-range isolation, SQL Server places RangeS-s locks (that is, a shared lock on the key range and a shared lock on the key at the end of the range) on the index keys for the rows with the matching values. It also places intent share (IS) locks on the page(s) and the table that contain the rows. The insert process acquires intent exclusive (IX) locks on the destination page(s) and the table. In this case, the insert process is waiting for a RangeIn-Null lock on the key range until the RangeS-s locks in the key range are released. The RangeIn-Null lock is an exclusive lock on the range between keys, with no lock on the key. This lock is acquired because the insert process is attempting to insert a new store ID that has no associated key value.

Key-Range Locking When Searching Non-existent Rows

In a scenario that involves key-range locking when searching non-existent rows, if a transaction is trying to delete or retrieve a row that does not exist in the database, it still should not find any rows at a later stage in the same transaction with the same query. For example, in Figure 37.8, Transaction A is trying to fetch a nonexistent row with the key value 20 using the following query:

```
SET TRANSACTION ISOLATION LEVEL serializable
go
BEGIN TRAN
select * from HumanResources.Department
where DepartmentID = 20
```

In another concurrent transaction, Transaction B is executing the following statement to insert a record with the same key value (DepartmentID = 20):

```
begin tran
set identity_insert HumanResources.Department on
Insert HumanResources.Department
    (DepartmentID, Name, GroupName, ModifiedDate)
  VALUES(20, 'Unleashed', 'Publishing', getdate())
```

In this mode, SQL Server prevents Transaction B (SPID 58) from inserting a new row by using a RangeS-S lock for Transaction A (SPID 54). This lock is placed on the index key rows for the rows in the range where DepartmentID equals 20. Transaction B holds a RangeIn-Null lock and waits for the RangeS-S lock to be released.

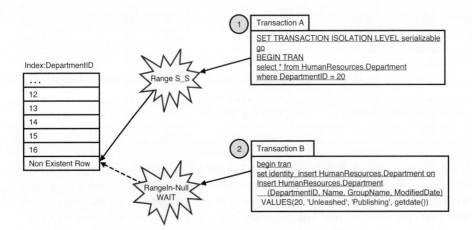

FIGURE 37.8   Key-range locking with a non-existent data set.

Listing 37.3 provides an example of the query against the `sys.dm_tran_locks` catalog view for these two transactions.

LISTING 37.3   Viewing Key-Range Locks on Non-existent Row

```
select request_session_id as spid,
      convert (varchar(20), db_name(resource_database_id)) As db_name,
      convert(varchar(12), resource_type) as resrc_type,
      case when resource_type = 'OBJECT'
          then convert(varchar(20), object_name(resource_associated_entity_id,
resource_database_id))
          when resource_type = 'DATABASE'
          then ''
          when resource_type  IN ( 'FILE', 'METADATA' )
          then convert(varchar(20), resource_type)
          WHEN resource_type IN ( 'KEY', 'PAGE', 'RID' )
          THEN convert(varchar(20), resource_description)
          else convert(varchar(20), resource_associated_entity_id)
          end as object,
      convert(varchar(12), request_type) as req_type,
      convert(varchar(16), request_mode) as mode,
      convert(varchar(8), request_status) as status
   from sys.dm_tran_locks dtl
   where resource_type <> 'DATABASE'
   and db_name(resource_database_id) = 'AdventureWorks2012'
order by request_session_id, object
go

/* output
```

spid	db_name	resrc_type	object	req_type	mode	status
54	AdventureWorks2012	KEY	(ffffffffffff)	LOCK	RangeS-S	GRANT
54	AdventureWorks2012	PAGE	1:409	LOCK	IS	GRANT
54	AdventureWorks2012	OBJECT	Department	LOCK	IS	GRANT
58	AdventureWorks2012	KEY	(ffffffffffff)	LOCK	RangeI-N	WAIT
58	AdventureWorks2012	PAGE	1:409	LOCK	IX	GRANT
58	AdventureWorks2012	OBJECT	Department	LOCK	IX	GRANT
58	AdventureWorks2012	OBJECT	syscolpars	LOCK	IX	GRANT

```
*/
```

Using Application Locks

SQL Server allows you to extend the resources that can be locked beyond the ones automatically provided. You can define your own custom locking resources and let the Lock Manager control the access to those resources as it would for any resource in a database. This essentially allows you to choose to lock anything you want. These user-defined lock resources are called *application locks*. To define an application lock, you use the sp_getapplock stored procedure and specify a name for the resource you are locking, a mode, an optional lock owner, and an optional lock timeout interval. The syntax for sp_getapplock is as follows:

```
sp_getapplock [ @Resource = ] 'resource_name',
    [ @LockMode = ] 'lock_mode'
    [ , [ @LockOwner = ] { 'transaction'  | 'session' } ]
    [ , [ @LockTimeout = ] 'value' ]
    [ , [ @DbPrincipal = ] 'database_principal' ]
```

Two resources are considered to be the same resource and are subject to lock contention if they have the same resource name and the same lock owner in the same database. The resource name used in these procedures can be any identifier up to 255 characters long. The lock owner can be specified as either transaction or session. Multiple requests for locks on the same resource can be granted only if the locking modes of the requests are compatible. (See the "Lock Compatibility" section, later in this chapter, for a lock compatibility matrix.) The possible modes of the lock allowed are shared, update, exclusive, intent exclusive, and intent shared. The database principal is the user, role, or application role that has permissions on an object in a database. The default is public.

For what purpose can you use application locks, and how do you use them? Suppose you have a table that contains a queue of items to be processed by the system. You need a way to serialize the retrieval of the next item from the queue so that the multiple concurrent processes do not grab the same item at the same time. In the past, one way this could be accomplished was by forcing an exclusive lock on the table. (The use of table hints to override default locking behavior is covered in the "Table Hints for Locking" section, later in this chapter.) Only the first process to acquire the exclusive lock would be able to retrieve the next item from the queue. The other processes would have to wait until

37

the exclusive lock was released. The problem with this approach is that the exclusive lock would also block other processes that might need to simply retrieve data from the table.

You can use application locks to avoid having to place an exclusive lock on the entire table. By using sp_getapplock, you can define and lock a custom lock resource for a transaction or session. Locks that are owned by the current transaction are released when the transaction commits or rolls back. Locks that are owned by the session are released when the session is closed. Locks can also be explicitly released at any time, with the sp_releaseapplock stored procedure. The syntax for sp_releaseapplock is as follows:

```
sp_releaseapplock [ @Resource = ] 'resource_name'
    [ , [ @LockOwner = ] { 'transaction' | 'session' }]
    [ , [ @DbPrincipal = ] 'database_principal' ]
```

> **NOTE**
>
> If a process calls sp_getapplock multiple times for the same lock resource, sp_releaseapplock must be called the same number of times to fully release the lock. In addition, if sp_getapplock is called multiple times on the same lock resource but specifies different lock modes each time, the resulting lock on the resource is a union of the different lock modes. Generally, the lock mode ends up being promoted to the more restrictive level of the existing lock mode and the newly requested mode. The resulting lock mode is held until the last lock release call is made to fully release the lock. For example, assume that a process initially called sp_getapplock and requested a shared lock. If it subsequently called sp_getapplock again and requested an exclusive lock, an exclusive lock would be held on the resource until sp_releaseapplock was executed twice.

In the following example, you first request an exclusive lock on an application lock called 'QueueLock' by using sp_getapplock. You then invoke the procedure to get the next item in the queue. After the procedure returns, you call sp_releaseapplock to release the application lock called 'QueueLock' to let another session acquire the application lock:

```
exec sp_getapplock 'QueueLock', 'Exclusive', 'session'
exec get_next_item_from_queue
exec sp_releaseapplock 'QueueLock', 'session'
```

As long as all processes that need to retrieve items from the queue execute this same sequence of statements, no other process can execute the get_next_item_from_queue procedure until the application lock is released. The other processes block attempts to acquire the exclusive lock on the resource 'QueueLock'. For example, Listing 37.4 shows an example of a query against the sys.dm_tran_locks view, showing one process (SPID 54) holding an exclusive lock on QueueLock, while another process (SPID 56) is waiting for an exclusive lock on QueueLock. (The hash value generated internally for QueueLock is shown as 18fb067e in the Resource_Desc field.)

LISTING 37.4   Viewing Application Locks Using sys.dm_tran_locks

```
select request_session_id as spid,
        convert (varchar(20), db_name(resource_database_id))
            As db_name,
        convert(varchar(12), resource_type) as resrc_type,
        case when resource_type = 'OBJECT'
            then convert(varchar(24), object_name(
                        resource_associated_entity_id,
                        resource_database_id))
            when resource_type = 'DATABASE'
            then ''
            when resource_type IN ( 'FILE', 'METADATA' )
            then convert(varchar(24), resource_type)
            WHEN resource_type IN ('KEY','PAGE','RID','APPLICATION')
            THEN convert(varchar(24), resource_description)
            else convert(varchar(24), resource_associated_entity_id)
            end as object,
        convert(varchar(12), request_type) as reqtype,
        convert(varchar(16), request_mode) as mode,
        convert(varchar(8), request_status) as status
    from sys.dm_tran_locks dtl
    where resource_type <> 'DATABASE'
order by request_session_id, object
go


/* output
spid db_name              resrc_type  object                       reqtype mode status
---- -------------------- ----------- ------------------------     ------- ---- ------
  54 AdventureWorks2012   APPLICATION 0:[QueueLock]:(18fb067e)LOCK    X   GRANT
  56 AdventureWorks2012   APPLICATION 0:[QueueLock]:(18fb067e) LOCK   X   WAIT
*/
```

Index Locking

As with locks on data pages, SQL Server manages locks on index pages internally. There is the opportunity for greater locking contention in index pages than in data pages. Contention at the root page of the index is the highest because the root is the starting point for all searches via the index. Contention usually decreases as you move down the various levels of the B-tree, but it is still higher than contention at the data page level due to the typically greater number of index rows per index page than data rows per data page.

If locking contention in the index becomes an issue, you can use ALTER INDEX to manage the locking behavior at the index level. The syntax of this command is as follows:

```
ALTER INDEX { index_name | ALL } ON object
{    ALLOW_ROW_LOCKS = { ON | OFF }
 |  ALLOW_PAGE_LOCKS = { ON | OFF }
```

The default for both ALLOW_ROW_LOCKS and ALLOW_PAGE_LOCKS is ON. When both of these options are enabled, SQL Server automatically makes the decision whether to apply row or page locks on the indexes and can escalate locks from the row or page level to the table level. When ALLOW_ROW_LOCKS is set to OFF, row locks on indexes are not used. Only page- or table-level locks are applied. When ALLOW_PAGE_LOCKS is set to OFF, no page locks are used on indexes, and only row- or table-level locks are applied. When ALLOW_ROW_LOCKS and ALLOW_PAGE_LOCK are both set to OFF, only a table-level lock is applied when the index is accessed.

> **NOTE**
>
> When ALLOW_PAGE_LOCKS is set to OFF for an index, the index cannot be reorganized.

SQL Server usually makes good choices for the index locks, but based on the distribution of data and nature of the application, you might want to force a specific locking option on a selective basis. For example, if you are experiencing a high level of locking contention at the page level of an index, you might want to force SQL Server to use row-level locks by turning off page locks.

As another example, if you have a lookup table that is primarily read-only (for example, one that is only refreshed by a weekly or monthly batch process), it may be more efficient to turn off page and row locking so that all readers simply acquire shared table-level locks, thereby reducing locking overhead. When the weekly or monthly batch update runs, the update process acquires an exclusive table-level lock when refreshing the table.

To display the current locking option for a given index, use the INDEXPROPERTY function:

```
select INDEXPROPERTY(object_ID , index_name,
            { 'IsPageLockDisallowed' | 'IsRowLockDisallowed' } )
```

> **CAUTION**
>
> SQL Server generally makes the correct decision in choosing the appropriate locking granularity for a query. It is generally not recommended that you override the locking granularity choices that the Query Optimizer makes unless you have good reason to do so and have evaluated all options first. Setting the inappropriate locking level can adversely affect the concurrency for a table or index.

Row-Level Versus Page-Level Locking

For years, it was often debated whether row-level locking was better than page-level locking. That debate still goes on in some circles. Many people argue that if databases and applications are well designed and tuned, row-level locking is unnecessary. This is borne out somewhat by the number of large and high-volume applications that were developed when row-level locking wasn't even an option. (Prior to SQL Server version 7, the smallest unit of data that SQL Server could lock was the page.) However, at that time, the page size in SQL Server was only 2KB. With page sizes expanded to 8KB, a greater number of rows (four times as many) can be contained on a single page. Page-level locks on 8KB pages could lead to greater page-level contention because the likelihood of the data rows being requested by different processes residing on the same page is greater. Using row-level locking increases the concurrent access to the data.

On the other hand, row-level locking consumes more resources (memory and CPU) than page-level locks simply because there are more rows than pages in a table. If a process needed to access all rows on a page, it would be more efficient to lock the entire page than acquire a lock for each individual row. This would result in a reduction in the number of lock structures in memory that the Lock Manager would have to manage.

Which is better—greater concurrency or lower overhead? As shown earlier, in Figure 37.6, it's a trade-off. As lock size decreases, concurrency improves, but performance degrades due to the extra overhead. As the lock size increases, performance improves due to less overhead, but concurrency degrades. Depending on the application, the database design, and the data, either page-level or row-level locking can be shown to be better than the other in different circumstances.

SQL Server makes the determination automatically at runtime—based on the nature of the query, the size of the table, and the estimated number of rows affected—of whether to initially lock rows, pages, or the entire table. In general, SQL Server attempts to first lock at the row level more often than the page level, in an effort to provide the best concurrency. With the speed of today's CPUs and the large memory support, the overhead of managing row locks is not as expensive as in the past. However, as the query processes and the actual number of resources locked exceed certain thresholds, SQL Server might attempt to escalate locks from a lower level to a higher level, as appropriate.

At times, SQL Server might choose to do both row and page locking for the same query. For example, if a query returns multiple rows, and if enough contiguous keys in a nonclustered index page are selected to satisfy the query, SQL Server might place page locks on the index while using row locks on the data. This reduces the need for lock escalation.

37

Lock Escalation

When SQL Server detects that the locks acquired by a query are using too much memory and consuming too many system resources for the Lock Manager to manage the locks efficiently, it automatically attempts to escalate row, key, or page locks to table-level locks. For example, because a query on a table continues to acquire row locks and every row in the table will eventually be accessed, it makes sense for SQL Server to escalate the row locks to a table-level lock. After the table-level lock is acquired, the row-level locks are released. This helps reduce locking overhead and keeps the system from running out of available lock structures. Recall from earlier sections in this chapter that the potential need for lock escalation is reflected in the intent locks that are acquired on the table by the process locking at the row or page level. While the default behavior in SQL Server is to escalate to table-level locks, SQL Server 2014 has the capability to escalate row or page locks to a single partition via the LOCK_ESCALATION setting in ALTER TABLE. This option allows you to specify whether escalation is always to the table or partition level. The LOCK_ESCALATION setting can also be used to prevent lock escalation entirely.

> **NOTE**
>
> SQL Server never escalates row locks to page locks, only to table or partition-level locks. Also, multiple partition-level locks are never escalated to a single table-level lock.

What are the lock escalation thresholds in SQL Server? Currently, SQL Server attempts lock escalation under the following conditions:

▶ Whenever a single T-SQL statement acquires at least 5,000 locks on a single reference of a table, table partition, or index (this value is subject to change in subsequent service packs or releases). Note that lock escalation does not occur if the locks are spread across multiple objects in the same statement—for example, 4,000 locks on one table and 2,500 locks on another.

▶ When the amount of memory required by lock resources exceeds 40% of the available Database Engine memory pool.

> **NOTE**
>
> Generally, if more memory is required for lock resources than is currently available in the Database Engine memory pool, the Database Engine allocates additional memory dynamically to satisfy the request for locks as long as more computer memory is available and the max server memory threshold has not been reached. However, if allocating additional memory would cause paging at the operating system level, more lock space is not allocated. If no more memory is available, or the amount of memory allocated to lock resources reaches 60% of the memory acquired by an instance of the Database Engine, further requests for locks generate an out-of-lock memory error.

If locks cannot be escalated because of lock conflicts, SQL Server reattempts lock escalation when every 1,250 additional locks are acquired. For example, if another process is also holding locks at the page or row level on the same table (indicated by the presence of that process's intent lock on the table), lock escalation cannot take place if the lock types are not compatible until the lower-level locks are released by the other processes. In this case, SQL Server continues acquiring locks at the row or page level until the table lock becomes available.

Controlling Lock Escalation

Escalating locks to the table or partition level can lead to locking contention or blocking for other transactions attempting to access a row or page in the same table. Under certain circumstances, you might want to disable lock escalation.

As mentioned previously, lock escalation can be enabled or disabled at the table level using the ALTER TABLE command:

```
ALTER TABLE tablename set (LOCK_ESCALATION ={ AUTO | TABLE | DISABLE } )
```

Setting the option to AUTO allows SQL Server to escalate to the table or partition level. Setting the option to DISABLE prevents escalation to the table or partition level.

SQL Server 2014 also supports disabling lock escalation for all tables in all databases within a SQL Server instance using either the 1211 or 1224 trace flags. Trace flag 1211 completely disables lock escalation, regardless of the memory required for lock resources. However, when the amount of memory required for lock resources exceeds 60% of the maximum available Database Engine memory, an out-of-lock memory error is generated. Alternatively, trace flag 1224 disables the built-in lock escalation based on the number of locks acquired, but lock escalation is still possible when the 40% of available Database Engine memory threshold is reached. However, as noted previously, if the locks cannot be escalated, SQL Server could still run out of available memory for locks.

NOTE

You should be extremely careful when considering disabling lock escalation via the trace flags. A poorly designed application could potentially exhaust the available SQL Server memory with excessive lock structures and seriously degrade SQL Server performance. It is usually preferable to control lock escalation at the object level via the ALTER TABLE command.

Lock Compatibility

If a process has already locked a resource, the granting of lock requests by other transactions on the same resource is governed by the lock compatibility matrix within SQL Server. Table 37.3 shows the lock compatibility matrix for the locks most commonly acquired by the SQL Server Lock Manager, indicating which lock types are compatible and which lock types are incompatible when requested on the same resource.

TABLE 37.3   SQL Server Lock Compatibility Matrix

	Requested Lock Type						Existing Lock Type		
	IS	S	U	IX	SIX	X	Sch-S	SCH-M	BU
Intent shared	Yes	Yes	Yes	Yes	Yes	No	Yes	No	No
Shared	Yes	Yes	Yes	No	No	No	Yes	No	No
Update	Yes	Yes	No	No	No	No	Yes	No	No
Intent exclusive	Yes	No	No	Yes	No	No	Yes	No	No
Shared with intent exclusive	Yes	No	No	No	No	No	Yes	No	No
Exclusive	No	No	No	No	No	No	Yes	No	No
Schema stability	Yes	Yes	Yes	Yes	Yes	Yes	Yes	No	Yes
Schema modify	No	No	No	No	No	No	No	No	No
Bulk update	No	No	No	No	No	No	Yes	No	Yes

For example, if a transaction has acquired a shared lock on a resource, the possible lock types that can be acquired on the resource by other transactions are intent shared, shared, update, and schema stability locks. Intent exclusive, SIX, exclusive, schema modification, and bulk update locks are incompatible with a shared lock and cannot be acquired on the resource until the shared lock is released.

Locking Contention and Deadlocks

In the grand scheme of things, the most likely culprits of SQL Server application performance problems are typically poorly written queries, poor database and index design, and locking contention. Whereas the first two problems result in poor application performance, regardless of the number of users on the system, locking contention becomes more of a performance problem as the number of users increases. It is further compounded by increasingly complex or long-running transactions.

Locking contention occurs when a transaction requests a lock type on a resource that is incompatible with an existing lock type on the resource. By default, the process waits indefinitely for the lock resource to become available. Locking contention is noticed in the client application through the apparent lack of response from SQL Server.

Figure 37.9 demonstrates an example of locking contention. Process 1 has initiated a transaction and acquired an exclusive lock on page 1:325. Before Process 1 can acquire the lock that it needs on page 1:341 to complete its transaction, Process 2 acquires an exclusive lock on page 1:341. Until Process 2 commits or rolls back its transaction and releases the lock on Page 1:341, the lock continues to be held. Because this is not a deadlock scenario (which is covered in the "Deadlocks" section, later in this chapter), by default, SQL Server takes no action. Process 1 simply waits indefinitely.

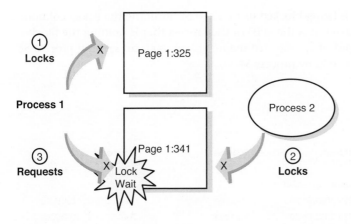

FIGURE 37.9   Locking contention between two processes.

Identifying Locking Contention

When a client application appears to freeze after submitting a query, this is often due to locking contention. To identify locking contention between processes, you can use the SSMS Activity Monitor, as discussed earlier in this chapter, in the "Monitoring Lock Activity in SQL Server" section; use the `sp_who2` stored procedure or query the `sys.dm_tran_locks` system catalog view. Figure 37.10 shows an example of a blocking lock as viewed in the SSMS Activity Monitor.

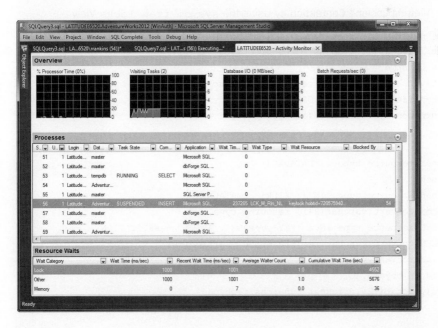

FIGURE 37.10   Examining locking contention between two processes in SSMS Activity Monitor.

To identify whether a process is being blocked using `sp_who2`, examine the `BlkBy` column. If any value besides '-' is displayed, it is the SPID of the process that is holding the blocking lock. In the following output of `sp_who2` (edited for space), you can see that process 56 is SUSPENDED, waiting on a lock held by process 54:

```
exec sp_who2
go


/* output
SPID Status      Login      HostName        BlkBy DBName             Command
---- ---------   ---------  -------------   ----- ------------------ ----------------
*** info for internal processes deleted ***
51   sleeping    rrankins   LATITUDEE6520     .   master             AWAITING COMMAND
52   sleeping    rrankins   LATITUDEE6520     .   master             AWAITING COMMAND
53   sleeping    rrankins   LATITUDEE6520     .   tempdb             AWAITING COMMAND
54   sleeping    rrankins   LATITUDEE6520     .   AdventureWorks2012 AWAITING COMMAND
55   sleeping    rrankins   LATITUDEE6520     .   master             AWAITING COMMAND
56   SUSPENDED   rrankins   LATITUDEE6520 54      AdventureWorks2012 INSERT
57   RUNNABLE    rrankins   LATITUDEE6520     .   AdventureWorks2012 SELECT INTO
*/
```

To determine what table, page, or rows are involved in blocking and at what level the blocking is occurring, you can query the `sys.dm_tran_locks` catalog view, as shown in Listing 37.5.

LISTING 37.5   Viewing Locking Contention by Using the `sys.dm_tran_locks` View

```
select request_session_id as spid,
       convert (varchar(20), db_name(resource_database_id))
           As db_name,
       convert(varchar(12), resource_type) as resrc_type,
       case when resource_type = 'OBJECT'
           then convert(varchar(24), object_name(
                       resource_associated_entity_id,
                       resource_database_id))
           when resource_type = 'DATABASE'
           then ''
           when resource_type IN ( 'FILE', 'METADATA' )
           then convert(varchar(24), resource_type)
           WHEN resource_type IN ( 'KEY', 'PAGE', 'RID', 'APPLICATION')
           THEN convert(varchar(24), resource_description)
           else convert(varchar(24), resource_associated_entity_id)
           end as object,
       convert(varchar(12), request_type) as reqtype,
       convert(varchar(16), request_mode) as mode,
```

```
        convert(varchar(8), request_status) as status
    from sys.dm_tran_locks dtl
    where resource_type <> 'DATABASE'
order by request_session_id, object
go


/* output
spid db_name              resrc_type object          reqtype mode status
---- ------------------   ---------- --------------  ------- ---- ------
  54 AdventureWorks2012 KEY          (cd8dc191aafa) LOCK    S    WAIT
  54 AdventureWorks2012 PAGE         1:409          LOCK    IS   GRANT
  54 AdventureWorks2012 OBJECT       Department     LOCK    IS   GRANT
  56 AdventureWorks2012 KEY          (52d6e7e34708) LOCK    X    GRANT
  56 AdventureWorks2012 KEY          (955f83aa836f) LOCK    X    GRANT
  56 AdventureWorks2012 KEY          (cd8dc191aafa) LOCK    X    GRANT
  56 AdventureWorks2012 PAGE         1:409          LOCK    IX   GRANT
  56 AdventureWorks2012 PAGE         1:9276         LOCK    IX   GRANT
  56 AdventureWorks2012 OBJECT       Department     LOCK    IX   GRANT
*/
```

From this output, you can see that Process 54 is waiting for a shared (S) lock on key cd8dc191aafa of page 1:409 of the Department table. Process 56 has an intent exclusive (IX) lock on that page because it has an exclusive (X) lock on the same key on that page. (Both have the same resource_Associated_Entity_id of cd8dc191aafa.)

As an alternative to sp_who2 and the sys.dm_tran_locks view, you can also get specific information on any blocked processes by querying the sys.dm_os_waiting_tasks system catalog view, as shown in Listing 37.6.

LISTING 37.6   Viewing Blocked Processes by Using the sys.dm_os_waiting_tasks View

```
select convert(char(4), session_id) as spid,
       convert(char(8), wait_duration_ms) as duration,
       convert(char(8), wait_type) as wait_type,
       convert(char(3), blocking_session_id) as blk,
       resource_description
from sys.dm_os_waiting_tasks
where blocking_session_id is not null
go


spid duration wait_type blk  resource_description
---- -------- --------- ---- ----------------------------------------------------
54   322034   LCK_M_S   56   keylock hobtid=72057594044874752 dbid=6
id=lock2f8427180 mode=X associatedObjectId=72057594044874752
```

Setting the Lock Timeout Interval

If you do not want a process to wait indefinitely for a lock to become available, SQL Server allows you to set a lock timeout interval by using the SET LOCK_TIMEOUT command. You specify the timeout interval in milliseconds. For example, if you want your processes to wait only 5 seconds (that is, 5,000 milliseconds) for a lock to become available, you execute the following command in the session:

```
SET LOCK_TIMEOUT 5000
```

If your process requests a lock resource that cannot be granted within 5 seconds, the statement is aborted, and you get the following error message:

```
Server: Msg 1222, Level 16, State 52, Line 1
Lock request time out period exceeded.
```

To examine the current LOCK_TIMEOUT setting, you can query the system function @@lock_timeout:

```
select @@lock_timeout
go

/* output
-----------
      5000
*/
```

If you want processes to abort immediately if the lock cannot be granted (in other words, no waiting at all), you set the timeout interval to 0. If you want to set the timeout interval back to infinity, execute the SET LOCK_TIMEOUT command and specify a timeout interval of –1.

Minimizing Locking Contention

Although setting the lock timeout prevents a process from waiting indefinitely for a lock request to be granted, it doesn't address the cause of the locking contention. In an effort to maximize concurrency and application performance, you should minimize locking contention between processes as much as possible. Some general guidelines to follow to minimize locking contention include the following:

▶ Keep transactions as short and concise as possible. The shorter the period of time locks are held, the less chance for lock contention. Keep commands that are not essential to the unit of work being managed by the transaction (for example, assignment selects, retrieval of updated or inserted rows) outside the transaction.

▶ Keep statements that comprise a transaction in a single batch to eliminate unnecessary delays caused by network input/output (I/O) between the initial BEGIN TRAN statement and the subsequent COMMIT TRAN commands.

▶ Consider coding transactions entirely within stored procedures. Stored procedures typically run faster than commands executed from a batch. In addition, because they are server resident, stored procedures reduce the amount of network I/O that occurs during execution of the transaction, resulting in faster completion of the transaction.

▶ Commit updates in cursors frequently and as soon as possible. Cursor processing is much slower than set-oriented processing and causes locks to be held longer.

NOTE

Even though cursors might run more slowly than set-oriented processing, cursors can sometimes be used to minimize locking contention for updates and deletions of a large number of rows from a table, which might result in a table lock being acquired. The UPDATE or DELETE statement itself might complete faster; however, if it is running with an exclusive lock on the table, then no other process can access the table until it completes. By using a cursor to update a large number of rows one row at a time and committing the changes frequently, the cursor uses page- or row-level locks rather than a table-level lock. It might take longer for the cursor to complete the actual update or delete, but while the cursor is running, other processes are still able to access other rows or pages in the table that the cursor doesn't currently have locked.

You can also use other looping constructs to produce the same type of result as a cursor. For example, a WHILE loop can be used that processes updates or deletions in batches as shown in the following script where 1000 rows are updated at a time:

```
declare @date datetime; set @date = getdate()
declare @rows int; set @rows = 1
declare @err int; set @err = 0
WHILE @rows > 0 AND @err = 0
BEGIN
 update TOP (1000) [AdventureWorks2012].[Person].[Person]
  set ModifiedDate = @date
  WHERE ModifiedDate <> @date
  select @rows = @@ROWCOUNT, @err = @@ERROR
END
```

▶ Use the lowest level of locking isolation required by each process. For example, if dirty reads are acceptable and accurate results are not imperative, consider using transaction Isolation Level 0. Use the Repeatable Read or Serializable Read isolation levels only if absolutely necessary.

▶ Never allow user interaction between a BEGIN TRAN statement and a COMMIT TRAN statement because doing so may cause locks to be held for an indefinite period of time. If a process needs to return rows for user interaction and then update one or more rows, consider using optimistic locking or Snapshot Isolation in your application. (Optimistic locking is covered in the "Optimistic Locking" section, later in this chapter.)

37

▶ Minimize "hot spots" in a table. Hot spots occur when the majority of the update activity on a table occurs within a small number of pages. For example, hot spots occur for concurrent insertions to the last page of a heap table or the last pages of a table with a clustered index on a sequential key. You can often eliminate hot spots by creating a clustered index in a table on a column or columns to order the rows in the table in such a way that insert and update activity is spread out more evenly across the pages in the table.

Deadlocks

A *deadlock* occurs when two processes are each waiting for a locked resource that the other process currently holds. Neither process can move forward until it receives the requested lock on the resource, and neither process can release the lock it is currently holding until it can receive the requested lock. Essentially, neither process can move forward until the other one completes, and neither one can complete until it can move forward.

Two primary types of deadlocks can occur in SQL Server:

▶ **Cycle deadlocks**—A cycle deadlock occurs when two processes acquire locks on different resources, and then each needs to acquire a lock on the resource that the other process has. Figure 37.11 demonstrates an example of a cycle deadlock.

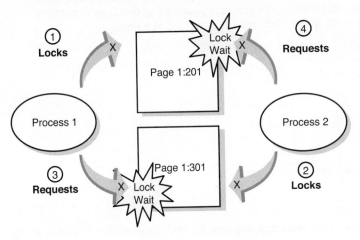

FIGURE 37.11   An example of a cycle deadlock.

In Figure 37.11, Process 1 acquires an exclusive lock on page 1:201 in a transaction. At the same time, Process 2 acquires an exclusive lock on page 1:301 in a transaction. Process 1 then attempts to acquire a lock on page 1:301 and begins waiting for the lock to become available. Simultaneously, Process 2 requests an exclusive lock on page 1:201, and a deadlock, or "deadly embrace," occurs.

▶ **Conversion deadlocks**—A conversion deadlock occurs when two or more processes each hold a shared lock on the same resource within a transaction and each wants to promote the shared lock to an exclusive lock, but neither can do so until the other releases the shared lock. An example of a conversion deadlock is shown in Figure 37.12.

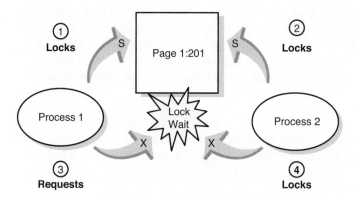

FIGURE 37.12   An example of a conversion deadlock.

In SQL Server 2014, in addition to deadlocks on lock resources, deadlocks can also occur on other resources such as memory, worker threads, parallel query execution related resources, and multiple active result sets (MARS) resources. For example, if Process 1 is holding a lock on the Product table and is waiting for memory to become available in order to continue, but Process 2 is holding some memory and cannot release it until it can acquire the lock on the Product table that Process 1 is holding, the processes can deadlock.

SQL Server automatically detects when a deadlock situation occurs. A separate process in SQL Server, called LOCK_MONITOR, checks the system for deadlocks roughly every 5 seconds. In the first pass, this process detects all the processes that are waiting on a lock resource. The LOCK_MONITOR thread checks for deadlocks by examining the list of waiting lock requests to see if any circular lock requests exist between the processes holding locks and the processes waiting for locks. When the LOCK_MONITOR detects a deadlock, SQL Server rolls back the transaction of one of the involved processes (the Victim), terminates the associated batch, and returns a 1205 error to the application. How does SQL Server determine which process to abort? It attempts to choose as the deadlock victim the transaction that it estimates would be least expensive to roll back. If both processes involved in the deadlock have the same rollback cost and the same deadlock priority, the deadlock victim is chosen randomly.

NOTE

As deadlocks occur, SQL Server begins reducing the deadlock detection interval and can potentially go as low as 100ms. In addition, the first few lock requests that cannot be satisfied after a deadlock is detected immediately trigger a deadlock search instead of waiting for the next deadlock detection interval. When deadlock frequency declines, the deadlock detection interval begins to increase back to 5 seconds.

37

You can influence which process will be the deadlock victim by using the SET DEADLOCK_PRIORITY statement. DEADLOCK_PRIORITY can be set to LOW, NORMAL, or HIGH. Alternatively, DEADLOCK_PRIORITY can also be set to any integer value from -10 to 10. The default deadlock priority is NORMAL. When two sessions deadlock, and the deadlock priority has been set to something other than the default, the session with the lower priority is chosen as the deadlock victim. If you have lower-priority processes that you would prefer always be chosen as the deadlock victims, you might want to set the process's deadlock priority to LOW. Alternatively, for critical processes, you might want to set the deadlock priority to HIGH to specify processes that should always come out as the winners in a deadlock scenario.

Avoiding Deadlocks

Although SQL Server automatically detects and handles deadlocks, you should try to avoid deadlocks in your applications. When a process is chosen as a deadlock victim, it has to resubmit its work because it has been rolled back. Frequent deadlocks create performance problems if you have to keep repeating work.

You can follow a number of guidelines to minimize, if not completely eliminate, the number of deadlocks that occur in your application(s). Following the guidelines presented earlier to minimize locking contention and speed up your transactions also helps to eliminate deadlocks. The less time for which a transaction is holding locks, the less likely the transition will be around long enough for a conflicting lock request to be requested at the same time. In addition, you might want to follow this list of additional guidelines when designing applications:

▶ Be consistent about the order in which you access the data from tables to avoid cycle deadlocks.

▶ Minimize the use of HOLDLOCK or queries that are running using Repeatable Read or Serializable Read isolation levels. This helps avoid conversion deadlocks. If possible, perform UPDATE statements before SELECT statements so that your transaction acquires an update or exclusive lock first. This eliminates the possibility of a conversion deadlock. (Later, in the "Table Hints for Locking" section in this chapter, you see how to use table-locking hints to force SELECT statements to use update or exclusive locks as another strategy to avoid conversion deadlocks.)

▶ Choose the transaction isolation level judiciously. You might be able to reduce deadlocks by choosing lower isolation levels.

Handling and Examining Deadlocks

SQL Server returns error number 1205 to the client when it aborts a transaction as a result of deadlock. The following is an example of a 1205 error message:

```
Msg 1205, Level 13, State 51, Line 1
Transaction (Process ID 53) was deadlocked on lock resources with another process
  and has been chosen as the deadlock victim. Rerun the transaction.
```

Because a deadlock is not a logical error but merely a resource contention issue, the client can resubmit the entire transaction. To handle deadlocks in applications, be sure to trap for message 1205 in the error handler. When a 1205 error occurs, the application can simply resubmit the transaction automatically. It is considered bad form to allow end users of an application to see the deadlock error message returned from SQL Server.

Earlier in this chapter, you learned how to use `sp_who2` and the `sys.dm_tran_locks` and `sys.dm_os_waiting_tasks` system catalog views to monitor locking contention between processes. However, when a deadlock occurs, one transaction is rolled back, and one is allowed to continue. If you examine the output from `sp_who2` or the system catalog views after a deadlock occurs, the information likely will not be useful because the locks on the resources involved will have since been released.

Fortunately, SQL Server provides a few different methods to identify and troubleshoot deadlocks that occur in SQL Server: deadlock trace flags, SQL Profiler, and Extended Events.

Monitoring Deadlocks with Trace Flags

Trace flags are a long-standing method to monitor deadlocks within SQL Server. They are trace flag 1204 and trace flag 1222. When enabled, they print deadlock information to the SQL Server error log. Trace flag 1204 provides deadlock information generated by each process involved in the deadlock. Trace flag 1222 provides deadlock information by processes and by resources. Both trace flags can be enabled to capture a complete representation of a deadlock event.

You use the DBCC TRACEON command to turn on the trace flags and DBCC TRACEOFF to turn them off. The 1204 and 1222 trace flags are global trace flags. Global trace flags are set at the server level and affect every connection on the server. They cannot be set for a specific session only. To enable or disable a global trace flag, the `-1` option must be specified as the second argument to the DBCC TRACEON and DBCC TRACEOFF commands. The following example shows how to globally enable the 1204 trace flag:

```
dbcc traceon(1204, -1)
```

If possible, it is best to set global trace flags whenever SQL Server is started up by adding the `-T` option with the appropriate trace flag value to the SQL Server startup parameters. For example, to have SQL Server turn on the 1204 trace flag automatically on startup, use the SQL Server Configuration Manager. In the SQL Server Configuration Manager window, click on SQL Server Services; in the right pane, right-click the SQL Server service for the appropriate SQL Server instance name and then select Properties. On the Startup Parameters tab type -T1204 in the Specify as startup parameter box and click the Add button (see Figure 37.13); then click OK to save the changes. You then need to stop and restart SQL Server for the trace flag to take effect.

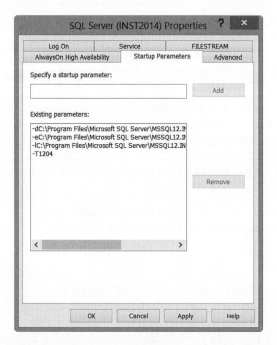

FIGURE 37.13   Setting the 1204 trace flag to be enabled on SQL Server startup.

> **CAUTION**
>
> The 1204 and 1222 trace flags may incur some additional processing overhead in SQL Server. They should be used only when you are debugging and tuning SQL Server performance, and they should not be left on indefinitely in a production environment. You should turn them off after you have diagnosed and fixed the problems.

The 1204 Trace Flag

Trace flag 1204 prints useful information to the SQL Server error log when a deadlock is detected. The following output is from the error log for this trace flag:

```
2014-06-07 00:38:04.44 spid5s      Deadlock encountered .... Printing deadlock
information
2014-06-07 00:38:04.44 spid5s      Wait-for graph
2014-06-07 00:38:04.44 spid5s
2014-06-07 00:38:04.44 spid5s      Node:1

2014-06-07 00:38:04.45 spid5s      KEY: 6:72057594044874752 (cd8dc191aafa)
CleanCnt:3 Mode:U Flags: 0x1
2014-06-07 00:38:04.45 spid5s       Grant List 0:
2014-06-07 00:38:04.45 spid5s          Owner:0x00000002F3433E00 Mode: U
```

```
Flg:0x40 Ref:0 Life:02000000 SPID:54 ECID:0 XactLockInfo: 0x00000002EA750C00
2014-06-07 00:38:04.45 spid5s          SPID: 54 ECID: 0 Statement Type: UPDATE Line
#: 1
2014-06-07 00:38:04.45 spid5s          Input Buf: Language Event: Update
HumanResources.Department
set Name = 'R&D'
where DepartmentID = 6

2014-06-07 00:38:04.45 spid5s       Grant List 1:
2014-06-07 00:38:04.45 spid5s       Requested by:
2014-06-07 00:38:04.45 spid5s          ResType:LockOwner
Stype:'OR'Xdes:0x00000002F8665900 Mode: U SPID:52 BatchID:0 ECID:0
TaskProxy:(0x00000002EB78C608) Value:0xf85bcb40 Cost:(0/0)
2014-06-07 00:38:04.45 spid5s
2014-06-07 00:38:04.45 spid5s       Node:2

2014-06-07 00:38:04.45 spid5s       KEY: 6:72057594044874752 (cd8dc191aafa)
CleanCnt:3 Mode:U Flags: 0x1
2014-06-07 00:38:04.45 spid5s        Grant List 0:
2014-06-07 00:38:04.45 spid5s        Grant List 1:
2014-06-07 00:38:04.45 spid5s          Owner:0x00000002F85BCA80 Mode: S
Flg:0x40 Ref:0 Life:02000000 SPID:52 ECID:0 XactLockInfo: 0x00000002F8665940
2014-06-07 00:38:04.45 spid5s          SPID: 52 ECID: 0 Statement Type: UPDATE Line
#: 1
2014-06-07 00:38:04.45 spid5s          Input Buf: Language Event: Update
HumanResources.Department
set Name = 'R&D'
where DepartmentID = 6

2014-06-07 00:38:04.45 spid5s       Requested by:
2014-06-07 00:38:04.45 spid5s          ResType:LockOwner Stype:'OR'Xdes:0x00000002EA75
0BC0 Mode: X SPID:54 BatchID:0 ECID:0
TaskProxy:(0x00000002EA5FA608) Value:0xf34340c0 Cost:(0/0)
2014-06-07 00:38:04.45 spid5s
2014-06-07 00:38:04.45 spid5s       Victim Resource Owner:
2014-06-07 00:38:04.45 spid5s          ResType:LockOwner
Stype:'OR'Xdes:0x00000002F8665900 Mode: U SPID:52 BatchID:0 ECID:0
TaskProxy:(0x00000002EB78C608) Value:0xf85bcb40 Cost:(0/0)
```

Although the 1204 output is somewhat cryptic, it is not too difficult to read if you know what to look for. If you look through the output, you can see where it lists the SPIDs of the processes involved in the deadlock (in this example, SPIDs 52 and 54) and indicates which process was chosen as the deadlock victim (Victim Resource Owner SPID:52). The type of statement involved is indicated by Statement Type. In this example, both processes were attempting an UPDATE statement. You can also examine the actual text of the query (Input Buf) that each process was executing at the time the deadlock occurred. The output also displays the locks granted to each process (Grant List), the lock types (Mode:) of the locks held, and the lock resources requested by the deadlock victim.

The 1222 Trace Flag

Trace flag 1222 provides deadlock information, first by processes and then by resources. The information is returned in an XML-like format that does not conform to an XML schema definition. The output has three major sections:

▶ The first section declares the deadlock victim.

▶ The second section describes each process involved in the deadlock.

▶ The third section describes the resources involved.

The following example shows the 1222 trace flag output for the same deadlock scenario displayed by the 1204 trace flag output in the previous section:

```
2014-06-07 00:48:21.97 spid29s      deadlock-list
2014-06-07 00:48:21.97 spid29s       deadlock victim=process2ea722558
2014-06-07 00:48:21.97 spid29s        process-list
2014-06-07 00:48:21.97 spid29s         process id=process2ea722558 taskpriority=0
logused=0 waitresource=KEY: 6:72057594044874752 (cd8dc191aafa) waittime=3605
ownerId=787537 transactionname=user_transaction lasttranstarted=2014-06-
07T00:48:08.537 XDES=0x2ed0171d8 lockMode=U schedulerid=4 kpid=219936
status=suspended spid=52 sbid=0 ecid=0 priority=0 trancount=2 lastbatchstarted=
2014-06-07T00:48:18.363 lastbatchcompleted=2014-06-07T00:48:08.537
lastattention=1900-01-01T00:00:00.537 clientapp=Microsoft SQL Server Management
Studio - Query hostname=LATITUDEE6520 hostpid=104064
loginname=LatitudeE6520\rrankins isolationlevel=serializable (4) xactid=787537
currentdb=6 lockTimeout=4294967295 clientoption1=671090784 clientoption2=390200
2014-06-07 00:48:21.97 spid29s          executionStack
2014-06-07 00:48:21.97 spid29s           frame procname=adhoc line=1 stmtstart=58
sqlhandle=0x0200000062b7a032ee772860d8f4c5d37248e61f2ed0c4140000000000000000000000000
0000000000000000
2014-06-07 00:48:21.97 spid29s      UPDATE [HumanResources].[Department] set [Name] =
@1  WHERE [DepartmentID]=@2
2014-06-07 00:48:21.97 spid29s           frame procname=adhoc line=1
sqlhandle=0x0200000072e6680355bcebda62bed71d3c8be583dfae55fa0000000000000000000000000
0000000000000000
2014-06-07 00:48:21.97 spid29s      Update HumanResources.Department
2014-06-07 00:48:21.97 spid29s      set Name = 'R&D'
2014-06-07 00:48:21.97 spid29s      where DepartmentID = 6
2014-06-07 00:48:21.97 spid29s          inputbuf
2014-06-07 00:48:21.97 spid29s      Update HumanResources.Department
2014-06-07 00:48:21.97 spid29s      set Name = 'R&D'
2014-06-07 00:48:21.97 spid29s      where DepartmentID = 6
```

2014-06-07 00:48:21.97 spid29s   process id=process2ed923498 taskpriority=0
logused=0 waitresource=KEY: 6:72057594044874752 (cd8dc191aafa) waittime=7748
ownerId=787539 transactionname=user_transaction lasttranstarted=2014-06-
07T00:48:11.427 XDES=0x2f85cd6a8 lockMode=X schedulerid=2 kpid=182448
status=suspended spid=54 sbid=0 ecid=0 priority=0 trancount=2
lastbatchstarted=2014-06-07T00:48:14.217 lastbatchcompleted=2014-06-07T00:48:11.427
lastattention=1900-01-01T00:00:00.427 clientapp=Microsoft SQL Server Management
Studio - Query hostname=LATITUDEE6520 hostpid=104064
loginname=LatitudeE6520\rrankins isolationlevel=serializable (4) xactid=787539
currentdb=6 lockTimeout=4294967295 clientoption1=671090784 clientoption2=390200
2014-06-07 00:48:21.97 spid29s   executionStack
2014-06-07 00:48:21.97 spid29s   frame procname=adhoc line=1 stmtstart=58
sqlhandle=0x0200000062b7a032ee772860d8f4c5d37248e61f2ed0c41400000000000000000000000000
0000000000000000
2014-06-07 00:48:21.97 spid29s   UPDATE [HumanResources].[Department] set [Name] =
@1 WHERE [DepartmentID]=@2
2014-06-07 00:48:21.97 spid29s   frame procname=adhoc line=1
sqlhandle=0x0200000072e6680355bcebda62bed71d3c8be583dfae55fa00000000000000000000000000
0000000000000000
2014-06-07 00:48:21.97 spid29s   Update HumanResources.Department
2014-06-07 00:48:21.97 spid29s   set Name = 'R&D'
2014-06-07 00:48:21.97 spid29s   where DepartmentID = 6
2014-06-07 00:48:21.97 spid29s   inputbuf
2014-06-07 00:48:21.97 spid29s   Update HumanResources.Department
2014-06-07 00:48:21.97 spid29s   set Name = 'R&D'
2014-06-07 00:48:21.97 spid29s   where DepartmentID = 6
2014-06-07 00:48:21.97 spid29s   resource-list
2014-06-07 00:48:21.97 spid29s   keylock hobtid=72057594044874752 dbid=6
objectname=AdventureWorks2012.HumanResources.Department
indexname=PK_Department_DepartmentID id=lock2f86e5b80 mode=U
associatedObjectId=72057594044874752
2014-06-07 00:48:21.97 spid29s   owner-list
2014-06-07 00:48:21.97 spid29s   owner id=process2ed923498 mode=U
2014-06-07 00:48:21.97 spid29s   owner id=process2ed923498 mode=X
requestType=convert
2014-06-07 00:48:21.97 spid29s   waiter-list
2014-06-07 00:48:21.97 spid29s   waiter id=process2ea722558 mode=U
requestType=convert
2014-06-07 00:48:21.97 spid29s   keylock hobtid=72057594044874752 dbid=6
objectname=AdventureWorks2012.HumanResources.Department
indexname=PK_Department_DepartmentID id=lock2f86e5b80 mode=U
associatedObjectId=72057594044874752
2014-06-07 00:48:21.97 spid29s   owner-list
2014-06-07 00:48:21.97 spid29s   owner id=process2ea722558 mode=S

37

```
2014-06-07 00:48:21.97 spid29s            owner id=process2ea722558 mode=U
requestType=convert
2014-06-07 00:48:21.97 spid29s            waiter-list
2014-06-07 00:48:21.97 spid29s              waiter id=process2ed923498 mode=X
requestType=convert
```

Monitoring Deadlocks with SQL Server Profiler

If you still find the 1204 and 1222 trace flag outputs too difficult to interpret, you'll be pleased to know that SQL Server Profiler provides a much more user-friendly way of capturing and examining deadlock information. As discussed in the "Monitoring Lock Activity in SQL Server" section, earlier in this chapter, SQL Profiler provides three deadlock events that can be monitored:

▶ Lock:Deadlock

▶ Lock:Deadlock Chain

▶ Deadlock Graph

The Lock:Deadlock and Lock:Deadlock Chain events aren't really very useful in SQL Server 2014. The Lock:Deadlock event generates a simple trace record that indicates when a deadlock occurs between two processes. The SPID column indicates what process was chosen as the deadlock victim. The Lock:Deadlock Chain event generates a trace record for each process involved in the deadlock. Unfortunately, neither of these trace events provides any detailed information, such as the queries involved in the deadlock. (You would need to also trace the T-SQL commands executed to capture this information, but you would then be capturing all SQL statements, not just those involved in the deadlock.)

Fortunately, SQL Server Profiler provides the Deadlock Graph event. When this event is enabled, SQL Server Profiler populates the TextData data column in the trace with XML data about the processes and objects involved in the deadlock. This XML data can then be used to display a Deadlock Graph in SQL Server Profiler itself, or the XML can be extracted to a file, which can be read in and viewed in SSMS. Figure 37.14 shows an example of a Deadlock Graph being displayed in SQL Server Profiler.

The Deadlock Graph displays the processes, resources, and relationships between the processes and resources. The following components make up a Deadlock Graph:

▶ **Process node**—An oval containing information about each thread that performs a task involved in the deadlock (for example, INSERT, UPDATE, or DELETE).

▶ **Resource node**—A rectangle containing information about each database object being referenced (for example, a table, an index, a page, a row, or a key).

▶ **Edge**—A line representing a relationship between a process and resource. A request edge occurs when a process waits for a resource. An owner edge occurs when a resource waits for a process. The lock mode is included in the edge description.

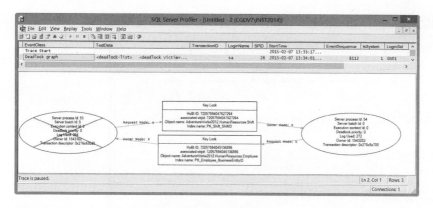

FIGURE 37.14   Displaying a Deadlock Graph in SQL Server Profiler.

Figure 37.14 displays the deadlock information for the processes involved in the deadlocks displayed by the 1204 and 1222 trace flag output listed in the previous sections. You can see that it displays the resource(s) involved in the deadlock in the Resource node (Key Lock), the lock type held on the resource by each process (Owner Mode: U), the lock type being requested by each process (Request Mode: X and Request Mode: U), and general information about each process (for example, SPID, deadlock priority) displayed in each process node. The process node of the process chosen as the deadlock victim has an X through it. If you place the mouse pointer over a process node, a ToolTip displays the SQL statement for that process involved in the deadlock. If the graph appears too large or too small for the profiler window, you can right-click anywhere within the graph to bring up a context menu that allows you to increase or decrease the size of the graph.

To save a Deadlock Graph to a file for further analysis at a later date, you can right-click the Deadlock Graph event in the top panel and choose the Extract Event Data option. To save all Deadlock Graph events contained in a SQL Server trace to one or more files, you select File, Export, Extract SQL Server Events and then choose the Extract Deadlock Events option. In the dialog that appears, you have the option to save all Deadlock Graphs contained in the trace to a single file or to save each to a separate file.

SQL Server Profiler can also save all Deadlock Graphs to a file automatically. When you are configuring a trace with the Deadlock Graph event selected, go to the Events Extraction Settings tab and click Save Deadlock XML Events Separately. There you can specify the file where you want the deadlock events to be saved. You can select to save all Deadlock Graph events in a single XML file or to create a new XML file for each Deadlock Graph. If you choose to create a new XML file for each Deadlock Graph, SQL Server Profiler automatically appends a sequential number to the filename for each deadlock captured. Figure 37.15 shows an example of the Events Extraction Settings tab to have a Profiler trace automatically generate a separate file for each deadlock trace.

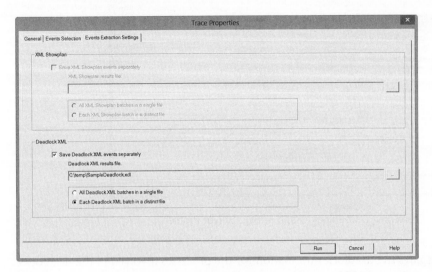

FIGURE 37.15 Configuring SQL Server Profiler to export Deadlock Graphs to individual files.

You can use SSMS to open and analyze any SQL Server Profiler Deadlock Graphs that you have saved to a file. To do so, in SSMS select File, Open and then click File. In the Open File dialog box, select the SQL Deadlock Files (*.xdl) file type. You now have a filtered list of only deadlock files (see Figure 37.16). After you select the file or files, you are able to view them in SSMS.

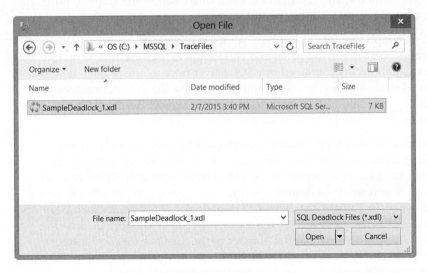

FIGURE 37.16 Opening a Deadlock Graph file in SSMS.

Monitoring Deadlocks with Extended Events

While trace flags and SQL Server Profiler provides mechanisms to identify and trouble-shoot deadlocks, this is SQL Server 2014. There must be a better, more efficient way to monitor deadlocks. Trace flags seem rather archaic and cryptic, and you won't always have SQL Server Profiler running on a production system (plus SQL Server Profiler is being deprecated). Fortunately, there are Extended Events. Extended Events are positioned to replace SQL Profiler, and Extended Events are more powerful with less performance impact on SQL Server than SQL Profiler. Extended Events were introduced in SQL Server 2008. In SQL Server 2014, Extended Events are integrated into SQL Server Management Studio, which makes it much easier to set up and monitor Extended Events. (For more information on configuring and using Extended Events, see Chapter 39.)

Fortunately, however, for monitoring deadlocks with Extended Events, there is nothing special that you have to set up or configure. The built-in `system_health` extended events session runs automatically on SQL Server startup and can be thought of like a "black box recorder" for SQL Server. One of the events that it is configured to capture are any deadlock events that occur. With the `system_health` extended events session, you can now get deadlock information after the fact without having to enable any trace flags or have a profiler trace running.

In SSMS for SQL Server 2014, there is an interface to view the events captured by any extended event sessions defined, including the `system_health` session. If a deadlock has occurred in a SQL Server instance, expand the SQL Server instance in the SSMS Object Explorer, expand the Management Folder, expand Extended Events, expand Sessions, and finally, expand `system_health`. Right-click `package0.event_file` and select View Target Data. This will open a new window in SSMS listing the events captured in the `system_health` event file. If the SQL Server instance has been running for a while, this file will likely contain a large number of events because the `system_health` session is capturing a number of other events in addition to deadlocks. Fortunately, however, you can filter the events by clicking on the Extended Events menu item and selecting the Filters option. In the Filters dialog (shown in Figure 37.17), select Name in the Field column, Contains as the Operator, and type `xml` as the Value. If you want to narrow it down even further to a specific time frame, you can click the Set Time Filter check box and specify the time range to use. In the Find in Extended Events dialog that comes up, type in the value `deadlock` to locate the first deadlock event captured in the file. Click on OK to apply the filter, and you should see all the deadlock events captured, as shown in Figure 37.18.

To view the details of a deadlock event, select the desired event in the list and the details will be displayed in the Details tab, which shows the values for the fields captured. For deadlock events, this will simply be the `xml_report` field, and the value is the XML data. However, for deadlock events, there will also be a Deadlock tab. If you click on the Deadlock tab, SSMS will display the XML graph like that displayed in SQL Server Profiler (see Figure 37.19).

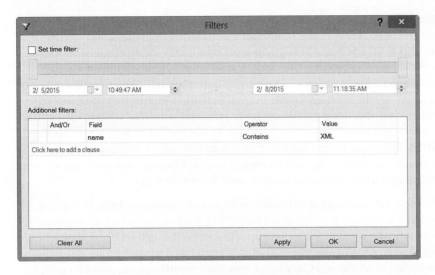

FIGURE 37.17   Filtering `system_health` Extended Events to show only deadlock events.

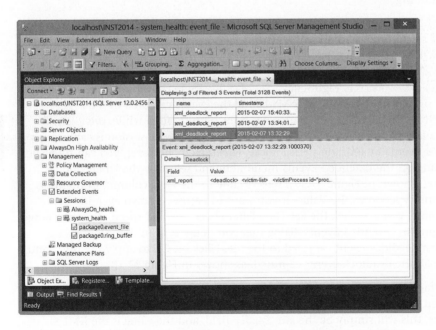

FIGURE 37.18   Displaying the filtered deadlock Extended Events in SSMS.

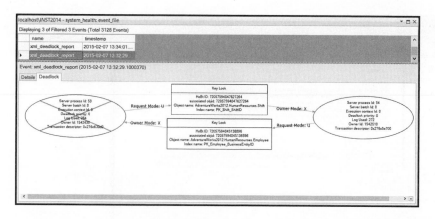

FIGURE 37.19   Displaying the Deadlock Graph for a deadlock extended event.

If you'd prefer to capture deadlock events separately from the other `system_health` extended events, you can create your extended event session and set it up to only capture deadlock events. This can be done quite easily using the Extended Events New Session Wizard. Using the New Session Wizard is covered in detail in Chapter 39, so we won't go into the specific steps here. However, you can also create an extended event session using T-SQL statements like the one shown in Listing 37.7. This script will create an extended event session called Deadlocks that will automatically run on SQL Server startup. The contents will be saved to a file in the SQL Server Log directory. (You can modify this path to specify a different location.) The default maximum file size is 1GB, with a maximum of five rollover files.

LISTING 37.7   Creating a Deadlock Extended Event Session Using T-SQL

```
Use master
go
CREATE EVENT SESSION [Deadlocks] ON SERVER
ADD EVENT sqlos.scheduler_monitor_deadlock_ring_buffer_recorded(
    ACTION(sqlserver.database_id,sqlserver.database_name)),
ADD EVENT sqlserver.xml_deadlock_report(
    ACTION(sqlserver.database_id,sqlserver.database_name))
ADD TARGET package0.event_file
        (SET filename=N'C:\MSSQL\ExtendedEvents\Deadlocks.xel')
WITH (STARTUP_STATE=ON)
GO
```

After you've created this session, you can start it immediately by right-clicking on it in the SSMS Object Explorer and selecting Start Session, as shown in Figure 37.20.

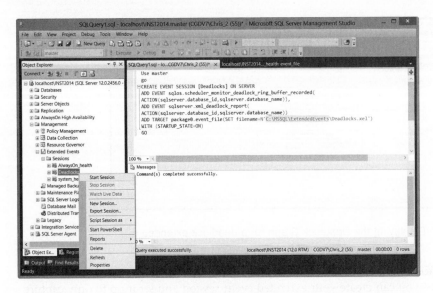

FIGURE 37.20   Starting the Deadlocks extended event session.

Table Hints for Locking

As mentioned previously in this chapter, in the "Transaction Isolation Levels in SQL Server" section, you can set an isolation level for your connection by using the SET TRANSACTION ISOLATION LEVEL command. This command sets a global isolation level for an entire session, which is useful if you want to provide a consistent isolation level for an application. However, sometimes you might want to specify different isolation levels for specific queries or for different tables within a single query. SQL Server allows you to do this by supporting table hints in the SELECT, MERGE, UPDATE, INSERT, and DELETE statements. In this way, you can override the isolation level currently set at the session level.

In this chapter, you have seen that locking is dynamic and automatic in SQL Server. Based on certain factors (for example, SARGs, key distribution, data volume), the Query Optimizer chooses the granularity of the lock (that is, row, page, or table level) on a resource. Although it is usually best to leave such decisions to the Query Optimizer, you might encounter certain situations in which you want to force a different lock granularity on a resource than what the optimizer has chosen. SQL Server provides additional table hints that you can use in the query to force lock granularity for various tables participating in a join.

SQL Server also automatically determines the lock type (SHARED, UPDATE, EXCLUSIVE) to use on a resource, depending on the type of command being executed on the resource. For example, a SELECT statement uses a shared lock. SQL Server also provides additional table hints to override the default lock type.

The table hints to override the lock isolation, granularity, or lock type for a table can be provided using the WITH operator of the SELECT, UPDATE, INSERT, and DELETE statements.

The following sections discuss the various locking hints that can be passed to an optimizer to manage isolation levels and the lock granularity of a query.

> **NOTE**
>
> Although many of the table-locking hints can be combined, you cannot combine more than one isolation level or lock granularity hint at a time on a single table. Also, the NOLOCK and READUNCOMMITTED hints described in the following sections cannot be used on tables that are the target of INSERT, UPDATE, MERGE, or DELETE queries.

Transaction Isolation-Level Hints

SQL Server provides a number of hints that you can use in a query to override the default transaction isolation level:

▶ **HOLDLOCK**—HOLDLOCK maintains shared locks for the duration of the entire state-ment or for the entire transaction, if the statement is in a transaction. This option is equivalent to the Serializable Read isolation level. The following hypothetical example demonstrates the usage of the HOLDLOCK statement within a transaction:

```
declare @seqno int
begin transaction
-- get a UNIQUE sequence number from sequence table
SELECT @seqno = isnull(seq#,0) + 1
from sequence WITH (HOLDLOCK)

-- in the absence of HOLDLOCK, shared lock will be released
-- and if some other concurrent transaction could
-- update the sequence number before the following statement
-- is run

UPDATE sequence
set    seq# = @seqno

commit tran
```

> **NOTE**
>
> As discussed earlier in this chapter, in the "Deadlocks" section, using HOLDLOCK in this manner leads to potential deadlocks between processes executing the transaction at the same time. For this reason, the HOLDLOCK hint, as well as the REPEATABLEREAD and SERIALIZABLE hints, should be used sparingly, if at all. In this example, it might be better for the SELECT statement to use an update or an exclusive lock on the sequence table, using the hints discussed later in this chapter, in the section, "Lock Type Hints." Another option would be to use an application lock, as discussed previously in this chapter, in the section, "Using Application Locks."

37

▶ **NOLOCK**—You can use this option to specify that no shared lock be placed on the resource. This option is similar to running a query at Isolation Level 0 (Read Uncommitted), which allows the query to ignore exclusive locks and read possibly uncommitted changes. The NOLOCK option is a useful feature in reporting environments, where the accuracy of the results is not critical.

▶ **READUNCOMMITTED**—This is the same as specifying the Read Uncommitted mode when using the SET TRANSACTION ISOLATION LEVEL command, and it is the same as the NOLOCK table hint.

▶ **READCOMMITTED**—This is the same as specifying the Read Committed mode when you use the SET TRANSACTION ISOLATION LEVEL command. The query waits for exclusive locks to be released before reading the data. This is the default locking isolation mode for SQL Server. However, if the database option READ_COMMITTED_SNAPSHOT is ON, SQL Server does not acquire shared locks on the data and uses row versioning.

▶ **READCOMMITTEDLOCK**—This option specifies that read operations acquire shared locks as data is read and release those locks when the read operation is completed, regardless of the setting of the READ_COMMITTED_SNAPSHOT database option.

▶ **REPEATABLEREAD**—This is the same as specifying Repeatable Read mode with the SET TRANSACTION ISOLATION LEVEL command. It prevents nonrepeatable reads within a transaction and behaves similarly to the HOLDLOCK hint.

▶ **SERIALIZABLE**—This is the same as specifying Serializable Read mode with the SET TRANSACTION ISOLATION LEVEL command. It prevents phantom reads within a transaction and is equivalent to using the HOLDLOCK hint.

▶ **READPAST**—This hint specifies that the query skip over the rows or pages locked by other transactions, returning only the data that can be read. Read operations specifying READPAST are not blocked. When specified in an UPDATE or DELETE statement, READPAST is applied only when reading data to identify which records to update. READPAST can be specified only in transactions operating at the Read Committed or Repeatable Read isolation levels. This lock hint is useful when reading information from a SQL Server table used as a work queue. A query using READPAST skips past queue entries locked by other transactions to the next available queue entry, without having to wait for the other transactions to release their locks.

Lock Granularity Hints

You can use lock granularity hints to override the lock granularity selected by the Query Optimizer:

▶ **ROWLOCK**—You can use this option to force the Lock Manager to place a row-level lock on a resource instead of a page-level or a table-level lock. You can use this option in conjunction with the XLOCK lock type hint to force exclusive row locks.

▶ **PAGLOCK**—You can use this option to force a page-level lock on a resource instead of a row-level or table-level lock. You can use this option in conjunction with the XLOCK lock type hint to force exclusive page locks.

▶ **TABLOCK**—You can use this option to force a table-level lock instead of a row-level or page-level lock. You can use this option in conjunction with the HOLDLOCK table hint to hold the table lock until the end of the transaction.

▶ **TABLOCKX**—You can use this option to force a table-level exclusive lock instead of a row-level or page-level lock. No shared or update locks are granted to other transactions as long as this option is in effect. If you are performing large-scale data maintenance on a SQL Server table and you don't want interference from other transactions, using this option is one of the ways to essentially put a table into a single-user mode.

Lock Type Hints

You can use the following optimizer hints to override the lock type that SQL Server chooses to use:

▶ **UPDLOCK**—This option is similar to HOLDLOCK except that whereas HOLDLOCK uses a shared lock on the resource, UPDLOCK places an update lock on the resource for the duration of the transaction. This allows other processes to read the information but not acquire update or exclusive locks on the resource. This option provides read repeatability within the transaction while preventing potential deadlocks that can result when using HOLDLOCK.

▶ **XLOCK**—This option places an exclusive lock on the resource for the duration of the transaction. This prevents other processes from acquiring locks on the resource.

Optimistic Locking

With many applications, clients need to fetch the data to browse through it, make modifications to one or more rows, and then post the changes back to the database in SQL Server. These human-speed operations are slow in comparison to machine-speed operations, and the time lag between the fetch and post might be significant. (Consider a user who goes to lunch after retrieving the data.)

For these applications, you would not want to use normal locking schemes such as SERIALIZABLE or HOLDLOCK to lock the data so it can't be changed from the time the user retrieves it to the time he or she applies any updates. This would violate one of the key rules for minimizing locking contention and deadlocks: Do not allow user interaction within transactions! You would also lose all control over the duration of the transaction. In a multiuser OLTP environment, the indefinite holding of the shared locks could significantly affect concurrency and overall application performance due to blocking on locks and locking contention.

On the other hand, if the locks are not held on the rows being read, another process could update a row between the time it was initially read and when the update is posted. When the first process applies the update, it would overwrite the changes made by the other process, resulting in a lost update.

So how do you implement such an application? How do you allow users to retrieve information without holding locks on the data and still ensure that lost updates do not occur?

Optimistic locking is a technique used in situations in which reading and modifying data processes are widely separated in time. Optimistic locking helps a client avoid overwriting another client's changes to a row without holding locks in the database.

One approach for implementing optimistic locking is to use the `rowversion` data type. Another approach is to take advantage of the optimistic concurrency features of snapshot isolation.

Optimistic Locking Using the `rowversion` Data Type

SQL Server 2014 provides a special data type called `rowversion` that can be used for optimistic locking purposes within applications. The purpose of the `rowversion` data type is to serve as a version number in optimistic locking schemes. SQL Server automatically generates the value for a `rowversion` column whenever a row that contains a column of this type is inserted or updated. The `rowversion` data type is an 8-byte binary data type, and other than guaranteeing that the value is unique and monotonically increasing, the value is not meaningful; you cannot look at the individual bytes and make any sense of them.

> **NOTE**
>
> In previous versions of SQL Server, the `rowversion` data type was also referred to as the `timestamp` data type. While this data type synonym still exists in SQL Server 2014, it has been deprecated, and the `rowversion` data type name should be used instead to ensure future compatibility.

In an application that uses optimistic locking, the client reads one or more records from the table, being sure to retrieve the primary key and current value of the `rowversion` column for each row, along with any other desired data columns. Because the query is not run within a transaction, any locks acquired for the `SELECT` are released after the data has been read. At some later time, when the client wants to update a row, it must ensure that no other client has changed the same row in the intervening time. The `UPDATE` statement must include a `WHERE` clause that compares the `rowversion` value retrieved with the original query, with the current `rowversion` value for the record in the database. If the `rowversion` values match—that is, if the value that was read is the same as the value currently in the database—no changes to that row have occurred since it was originally retrieved. Therefore, the change attempted by the application can proceed. If the `rowversion` value in the client application *does not* match the value in the database, that particular row has been changed since the original retrieval of the record. As a result, the state of the row that the application is attempting to modify is not the same as the row that currently exists in the database. As a result, the transaction should not be allowed to take place, to avoid the lost update problem.

To ensure that the client application does not overwrite the changes made by another process, the client needs to prepare the T-SQL UPDATE statement in a special way, using the rowversion column as a versioning marker. The following pseudocode represents the general structure of such an update:

```
UPDATE theTable
   SET theChangedColumns = theirNewValues
   WHERE primaryKeyColumns = theirOldValues
     AND rowversion = itsOldValue
```

Because the WHERE clause includes the primary key, the UPDATE can apply only to exactly one row or to no rows; it cannot apply to more than one row because the primary key is unique. The second part of the WHERE clause provides the optimistic "locking." If another client has updated the row, the rowversion no longer has its old value (remember that the server changes the rowversion value automatically with each update), and the WHERE clause does not match any rows. The client needs to check whether any rows were updated. If the number of rows affected by the update statement is zero, the row has been modified since it was originally retrieved. The application can then choose to reread the data or do whatever recovery it deems appropriate. This approach has one problem: How does the application know whether it didn't match the row because the rowversion was changed, because the primary key had changed, or because the row had been deleted altogether?

In SQL Server 2000, there was an undocumented tsequal() function (which was documented in prior releases) that could be used in a WHERE clause to compare the rowversion value retrieved by the client application with the rowversion value in the database. If the rowversion values matched, the update would proceed. If not, the update would fail, with error message 532, to indicate that the row had been modified. Unfortunately, this function is no longer provided in SQL Server 2005 and later releases. Any attempt to use it now results in a syntax error. As an alternative, you can programmatically check whether the update modified any rows, and if not, you can check whether the row still exists and return the appropriate message. Listing 37.8 provides an example of a stored procedure that implements this strategy.

LISTING 37.8   An Example of a Procedure for Optimistic Locking

```
create proc optimistic_update
        @id int, -- provide the primary key for the record
        @data_field_1 varchar(10), -- provide the data value to be updated
        @rowversion rowversion -- pass in the rowversion value retrieved with
                        -- the initial data retrieval
as
-- Attempt to modify the record
update data_table
  set data_field_1 = @data_field_1
```

```
where id = @id
  and versioncol = @rowversion
-- Check to see if no rows updated
IF @@ROWCOUNT=0
BEGIN
  if exists (SELECT * FROM data_table WHERE id=@id)
  -- The row exists but the rowversions don't match
  begin
    raiserror ('The row with id "%d" has been updated since it was read',
               10, 1, @id)
    return -101
  end
  else -- the row has been deleted
  begin
    raiserror ('The row with id "%d" has been deleted since it was read',
               10, 2, @id)
    return -102
  end
end
ELSE
  PRINT 'Data Updated'
return 0
```

Using this approach, if the update doesn't modify any rows, the application receives an error message and knows for sure that the reason the update didn't take place is that either the rowversion value didn't match or the row was deleted. If the row is found and the rowversion values match, the update proceeds normally.

Optimistic Locking with Snapshot Isolation

SQL Server 2014's Snapshot Isolation mode provides another mechanism for implementing optimistic locking through its automatic row versioning. If a process reads data within a transaction when Snapshot Isolation mode is enabled, no locks are acquired or held on the current version of the data row. The process reads the version of the data at the time of the query. Because no locks are held, it doesn't lead to blocking, and another process can modify the data after it has been read. If another process does modify a data row read by the first process, a new version of the row is generated. If the original process then attempts to update that data row, SQL Server automatically prevents the lost update problem by checking the row version. In this case, because the row version is different, SQL Server prevents the original process from modifying the data row. When it attempts to modify the data row, the following error message appears:

```
Msg 3960, Level 16, State 4, Line 2
Snapshot isolation transaction aborted due to update conflict. You cannot use
 snapshot isolation to access table 'dbo.data_table' directly or indirectly in
```

database 'AdventureWorks2012' to update, delete, or insert the row that has been modified or deleted by another transaction. Retry the transaction or change the isolation level for the update/delete statement.

To see how this works, you can create the following table:

```
use AdventureWorks2012
go
create table data_table
    (id int identity,
     data_field_1 varchar(10),
     rowver rowversion)
go
insert data_table (data_field_1) values ('foo')
go
```

Next, you need to ensure that AdventureWorks2012 is configured to allow snapshot isolation:

```
use master
go
ALTER DATABASE AdventureWorks2012 SET SINGLE_USER WITH ROLLBACK IMMEDIATE
ALTER DATABASE AdventureWorks2012 SET ALLOW_SNAPSHOT_ISOLATION ON
ALTER DATABASE AdventureWorks2012 SET MULTI_USER
```

In one user session, you execute the following SQL statements:

```
Use AdventureWorks2012
Go
SET TRANSACTION ISOLATION LEVEL SNAPSHOT
go
begin tran
select * from data_table
go
/* output
id          data_field_1 timestamp
----------  ------------ ----------------
1           foo          0x0000000000000BC4
*/
```

Now, in another user session, you execute the following UPDATE statement:

```
update data_table set data_field_1 = 'bar'
  where id = 1
```

Then you go back to the original session and attempt the following update:

```
update data_table set data_field_1 = 'fubar'
  where id = 1
go

/* output
Msg 3960, Level 16, State 6, Line 1
Snapshot isolation transaction aborted due to update conflict. You cannot use
snapshot isolation to access table 'dbo.data_table' directly or indirectly in
database 'AdventureWorks2012' to update, delete, or insert the row that has been
modified or deleted by another transaction. Retry the transaction or change the
isolation level for the update/delete statement.
*/
```

Note that for the first process to hold on to the row version, the SELECT and UPDATE statements must be run in the same transaction. When the transaction is committed or rolled back, the row version acquired by the SELECT statement is released. However, because the SELECT statement run at the Snapshot Isolation level does not hold any locks, there are no locks being acquired or held by that SELECT statement within the transaction, so it avoids the problems that would normally be encountered by using HOLDLOCK or the Serializable Read isolation level. Because no locks were held on the data row, the other process was allowed to update the row after it was retrieved, generating a new version of the row. The automatic row versioning provided by SQL Server's Snapshot Isolation mode prevented the first process from overwriting the update performed by the second process, thereby preventing a lost update.

CAUTION

Locking contention is prevented in the preceding example only because the transaction performed only a SELECT before attempting the UPDATE. A SELECT run with Snapshot Isolation mode enabled reads the current version of the row and does not acquire or hold locks on the actual data row. However, if the process were to perform any modification on the data row, the update or exclusive locks acquired would be held until the end of the transaction, which could lead to locking contention, especially if user interaction is allowed within the transaction after the update or exclusive locks are acquired.

Also, be aware of the overhead generated in `tempdb` when Snapshot Isolation mode is enabled for a database, as described in the section, "Transaction Isolation Levels in SQL Server," earlier in this chapter.

Because of the overhead incurred by snapshot isolation and the cost of having to roll back update conflicts, you should consider using Snapshot Isolation mode only to provide optimistic locking for systems where there is little concurrent updating of the same resource so that it is unlikely that your transactions have to be rolled back because of an update conflict.

Summary

Locking is critical in a multiuser environment for providing transaction isolation. SQL Server supports all ANSI-defined transaction isolation levels, including the Snapshot Isolation level for applications that can benefit from optimistic concurrency. The Lock Manager in SQL Server automatically locks data at the row level or higher, as necessary, to provide the appropriate isolation while balancing the locking overhead with concurrent access to the data. It is important to understand how locking works and what its effect is on application performance to develop efficient queries and applications.

SQL Server provides a number of tools for monitoring and identifying locking problems and behavior. In addition, SQL Server provides a number of table-locking hints that give the developer better control over the default lock types and granularity used for certain queries.

Although following the guidelines to minimize locking contention in applications is important, another factor that affects locking behavior and query performance is the actual database design. Chapter 38, "Database Design and Performance," discusses database design and its effect on database performance and provides guidelines to help ensure that transactions and T-SQL code run efficiently.

37

Database Design and Performance

Various factors contribute to the optimal performance of a database application. Some of these factors include logical database design (rules of normalization), physical database design (denormalization, indexes, data placement), choice of hardware (SMP servers/multiprocessor servers), network bandwidth (LAN versus WAN), client and server configuration (memory, CPU), data access techniques (ODBC, ADO, OLEDB), and application architecture (two-tier versus n-tier). This chapter helps you understand some of the key database design issues to ensure that you have a reliable high-performance application.

> **NOTE**
>
> Index design is often considered part of physical database design. Because index design guidelines and the impact of indexes on query and update performance are covered in detail in Chapter 32, "Indexes and Performance," this chapter does not discuss index design. It focuses instead on other aspects of database design and performance.

What's New in Database Design and Performance

Many of the database design and performance considerations that applied to previous versions of SQL Server still apply to SQL Server 2014. These principles are basic in nature and are not affected by the version of the database management system. This chapter focuses on those relatively unchanged principles.

There is, however, a new section in this chapter that focuses on running SQL Server in a virtual environment. Running SQL Server in a Virtual Machine (VM) has been an option for some time but was generally frowned upon because it was difficult to get acceptable performance in this type of environment. Advancements in the VM Software, the underlying Operating System (OS), and improved hardware now make virtualizing SQL Server a viable option.

Basic Tenets of Designing for Performance

Designing for performance requires making trade-offs. For example, to get the best write performance out of a database, you must sacrifice read performance. Before you tackle database design issues for an application, it is critical to understand your goals. Do you want faster read performance? Faster write performance? A more understandable design?

Following are some basic truths about physical database design for SQL Server 2014 and the performance implications of each:

▶ It's important to keep table row sizes as small as possible. Doing so is not about saving disk space. Having smaller rows means more rows fit on a single 8KB page, which means fewer physical disk reads are required to read a given number of rows.

▶ You should use indexes to speed up read access. However, the more indexes a table has, the more overhead there is to insert, update, and delete rows from the table due to index maintenance.

▶ Using triggers to perform any kind of work during an insert, an update, or a delete exacts a performance toll and decreases concurrency by lengthening transaction duration.

▶ Implementing declarative referential integrity (via primary and foreign keys) helps maintain data integrity, but enforcing foreign key constraints during inserts, updates, and deletes requires extra lookups of the related data rows.

▶ Using ON DELETE CASCADE referential integrity constraints helps maintain data integrity but requires extra work on the server's part to apply the deletes on the related child records.

Keeping tables as narrow as possible—that is, ensuring that the row size is as small as possible—is one of the most important things you can do to ensure that a database performs well. To keep your tables narrow, you should choose column data types with size in mind. You shouldn't use the bigint data type if the int will do. If you have zero-to-one relationships in tables, you should consider vertically partitioning the tables. (See the "Vertical Data Partitioning" section, later in this chapter, for details on this scenario.)

Cascading deletes (and updates) cause extra lookups to be done whenever a delete runs against the parent table. In many cases, the optimizer uses worktables to resolve delete and update queries. Enforcing these constraints manually, from within stored procedures, for example, can give better performance. This is not a wholehearted endorsement against referential integrity constraints. In most cases, the extra performance hit is worth the saved aggravation of coding everything by hand. However, you should be aware of the cost of this convenience.

Logical Database Design Issues

A good database design is fundamental to the success of any application. Logical database design for relational databases follows rules of normalization. As a result of normalization, you create a data model that is usually, but not necessarily, translated into a physical data model. A logical database design does not depend on the relational database you intend to use. The same data model can be applied to Oracle, Sybase, SQL Server, or any other relational database. On the other hand, a physical data model makes extensive use of the features of the underlying Database Engine to yield optimal performance for the application. Physical models are much less portable than logical models.

> **TIP**
>
> If portability is a big concern to you, consider using a third-party data modeling tool, such as ERwin or ERStudio. These tools have features that make it easier to migrate your logical data models to physical data models on different database platforms. Of course, using these tools just gets you started; to get the best performance out of your design, you need to tweak the physical design for the platform you have chosen.

Normalization Conditions

Any database designer must address two fundamental issues:

▶ Designing the database in a simple, understandable way that is maintainable and makes sense to its developers and users

▶ Designing the database such that data is fetched and saved with the fastest response time, resulting in high performance

Normalization is a technique used on relational databases to organize data across many tables so that related data is kept together based on certain guidelines. Normalization results in controlled redundancy of data; therefore, it provides a good balance between disk space usage and performance. Normalization helps people understand the relationships between data and enforces rules to ensure that the data is meaningful.

> **TIP**
>
> Normalization rules exist, among other reasons, to make it easier for people to understand the relationships between data. But a perfectly normalized database sometimes doesn't perform well under certain circumstances, and it may be difficult to understand. There are good reasons to deviate from a perfectly normalized database.

Normalization Forms

Five normalization forms exist, represented by the symbol 1NF for first normal form, 2NF for second normal form, and so on. If you follow the rules for the first rule of normalization, your database can be described as "in first normal form."

Each rule of normalization depends on the previous rule for successful implementation, so to be in second normal form (2NF), your database must also follow the rules for first normal form.

A typical relational database used in a business environment falls somewhere between second and third normal forms. It is rare to progress past the third normal form because fourth and fifth normal forms are more academic than practical in real-world environments.

Following is a brief description of the first three rules of normalization.

First Normal Form

The first rule of normalization requires removing repeating data values and specifies that no two rows in a table can be identical. This means that each table must have a logical primary key that uniquely identifies a row in the table.

Consider a table that has four columns—`PublisherName`, `Title1`, `Title2`, and `Title3`—for storing up to three titles for each publisher. This table is not in first normal form due to the repeating `Title` columns. The main problem with this design is that it limits the number of titles associated with a publisher to three.

Removing the repeating columns so there is just a `PublisherName` column and a single `Title` column puts the table in first normal form. A separate data row is stored in the table for each title published by each publisher. The combination of `PublisherName` and `Title` becomes the primary key that uniquely identifies each row and prevents duplicates.

Second Normal Form

A table is considered to be in second normal form if it conforms to the first normal form and all nonkey attributes of the table are fully dependent on the entire primary key. If the primary key consists of multiple columns, nonkey columns should depend on the entire key and not just on a part of the key. A table with a single column as the primary key is automatically in second normal form if it satisfies first normal form as well.

Assume that you need to add the publisher address to the database. Adding it to the table with the `PublisherName` and `Title` column would violate second normal form. The primary key consists of both `PublisherName` and `Title`, but the `PublisherAddress` attribute is an attribute of the publisher only. It does not depend on the entire primary key.

To put the database in second normal form requires adding an additional table for storing publisher information. One table consists of the `PublisherName` column and `PublisherAddress`. The second table contains the `PublisherName` and `Title` columns. To retrieve the `PublisherName`, `Title`, and `PublisherAddress` information in a single result would require a join between the two tables on the `PublisherName` column.

Third Normal Form

A table is considered to be in third normal form if it already conforms to the first two normal forms and if none of the nonkey columns are dependent on any other nonkey columns. All such attributes should be removed from the table.

Let's look at an example that comes up often during database architecture. Suppose that an employee table has four columns: EmployeeID (the primary key), salary, bonus, and total_salary, where total_salary = salary + bonus. Existence of the total_salary column in the table violates the third normal form because a nonkey column (total_salary) is dependent on two other nonkey columns (salary and bonus). Therefore, for the table to conform to the third rule of normalization, you must remove the total_salary column from the employee table.

Benefits of Normalization

Following are the major advantages of normalization:

▶ Because information is logically kept together, normalization provides improved overall understanding of the system.

▶ Because of controlled redundancy of data, normalization can result in fast table scans and searches (because less physical data has to be processed).

▶ Because tables are smaller with normalization, index creation and data sorts are much faster.

▶ With less redundant data, it is easier to maintain referential integrity for the system.

▶ Normalization results in narrower tables. Because you can store more rows per page, more rows can be read and cached for each I/O performed on the table. This results in better I/O performance.

Drawbacks of Normalization

One result of normalization is that data is stored in multiple tables. To retrieve or modify information, you usually have to establish joins across multiple tables. Joins are expensive from an I/O standpoint. Multitable joins can have an adverse impact on the performance of the system. The following sections discuss some of the denormalization techniques you can use to improve the performance of a system.

TIP

An adage for normalization is, "Normalize 'til it hurts; denormalize 'til it works." To put this maxim into use, try to put your database in third normal form initially. Then, when you're ready to implement the physical structure, drop back from third normal form, where excessive table joins are hurting performance. A common mistake is that developers make too many assumptions and over-denormalize the database design before even a single line of code has been written to even begin to assess the database performance.

Denormalizing a Database

After a database has been normalized to the third form, database designers intentionally backtrack from normalization to improve the performance of the system. This technique of rolling back from normalization is called *denormalization*. Denormalization allows you to keep redundant data in the system, reducing the number of tables in the schema and reducing the number of joins to retrieve data.

> **TIP**
>
> Duplicate data is more helpful when the data does not change very much, such as in data warehouses. If the data changes often, keeping all "copies" of the data in sync can create significant performance overhead, including long transactions and excessive write operations.

Denormalization Guidelines

When should you denormalize a database? Consider the following points:

▶ Be sure you have a good overall understanding of the logical design of the system. This knowledge helps in determining how other parts of the application are going to be affected when you change one part of the system.

▶ Don't attempt to denormalize the entire database at once. Instead, focus on the specific areas and queries that are accessed most frequently and are suffering from performance problems.

▶ Understand the types of transactions and the volume of data associated with specific areas of the application that are having performance problems. You can resolve many such issues by tuning the queries without denormalizing the tables.

▶ Determine whether you need virtual (computed) columns. Virtual columns can be computed from other columns of the table. Although this violates third normal form, computed columns can provide a decent compromise because they do not actually store another exact copy of the data in the same table.

▶ Understand data integrity issues. With more redundant data in the system, maintaining data integrity is more difficult, and data modifications are slower.

▶ Understand storage techniques for the data. You may be able to improve performance without denormalization by using RAID, SQL Server filegroups, and table partitioning.

▶ Determine the frequency with which data changes. If data is changing too often, the cost of maintaining data and referential integrity might outweigh the benefits provided by redundant data.

▶ Use the performance tools that come with SQL Server (such as SQL Server Profiler) to assess performance. These tools can help isolate performance issues and give you possible targets for denormalization.

> **TIP**
>
> If you are experiencing severe performance problems, denormalization should *not* be the first step you take to rectify the problem. You need to identify specific issues that are causing performance problems. Usually, you discover factors such as poorly written queries, poor index design, inefficient application code, or poorly configured hardware. You should try to fix these types of issues before taking steps to denormalize database tables.

Essential Denormalization Techniques

You can use various methods to denormalize a database table and achieve desired performance goals. Some of the useful techniques used for denormalization include the following:

- ▶ Keeping redundant data and summary data

- ▶ Using virtual columns

- ▶ Performing horizontal data partitioning using multiple tables rather than table partitioning

- ▶ Performing vertical data partitioning

Redundant Data

From an I/O standpoint, joins in a relational database are inherently expensive. To avoid common joins, you can add redundancy to a table by keeping exact copies of the data in multiple tables. The following example uses the AdventureWorks2012 database and demonstrates this point. It shows a three-table join to get a person's LoginID and their related email address:

```
select e.LoginID, a.EmailAddress
from  HumanResources.Employee e
 join  Person.Person p
  on e.BusinessEntityID = p.BusinessEntityId
 join Person.EmailAddress a
  on e.BusinessEntityID = a.BusinessEntityID
 where e.BusinessEntityID = 1
```

You could improve the performance of this query by adding the EmailAddress column to the HumanResources.Employee table. This would eliminate the joins altogether. Here is what the revised query would look like if this denormalization technique were implemented:

```
select e.LoginID, e.EmailAddress
from  HumanResources.Employee e
 where e.BusinessEntityID = 1
```

38

As you can see, the `EmailAddress` column is now redundantly stored in two places: the `HumanResources.Employee` table and the `Person.EmailAddress` table. It is obvious that with more redundant data in the system, maintaining referential integrity and data integrity is more difficult. For example, if the person's email address changes in the `Person.EmailAddress` table, to preserve data integrity, you would also have to change the corresponding `EmailAddress` column value in the `HumanResources.Employee` table to reflect the correct value. You could use SQL Server triggers to maintain data integrity, but you should recognize that update performance could suffer dramatically. For this reason, it is best if redundant data is limited to data columns whose values are relatively static and are not modified often.

Computed Columns

A number of queries calculate aggregate values derived from one or more columns of a table. Such computations can be CPU-intensive and can have an adverse impact on performance if they are performed frequently. One of the techniques to handle such situations is to create an additional column that stores the computed value. Such columns are called *virtual columns*, or *computed columns*. Since SQL Server 7.0, computed columns have been natively supported. You can specify such columns in `create table` or `alter table` commands. The following example demonstrates the use of computed columns:

```
create table emp (
        empid int not null primary key,
        salary money not null,
        bonus money not null default 0,
        total_salary as ( salary+bonus )
        )
go
insert emp (empid, salary, bonus) values (100, $150000.00, $15000)
go
select * from emp
go
empid       salary          bonus                 total_salary
----------- -------------   --------------------- ----------------

100             150000.0000    15000.0000           165000.0000
```

By default, virtual columns are not physically stored in SQL Server tables. SQL Server internally maintains a column property named `is_computed` that can be viewed from the `sys.columns` system view. It uses this column to determine whether a column is computed. The value of the virtual column is calculated at the time the query is run. All columns referenced in the computed column expression must come from the table on which the computed column is created. You can, however, reference a column from another table by using a function as part of the computed column's expression. The function can contain a reference to another table, and the computed column calls this function.

Since SQL Server 2000, computed columns have been able to participate in joins to other tables, and they can be indexed. Creating an index that contains a computed column creates a physical copy of the computed column in the index tree. Whenever a base column participating in the computed column changes, the index must also be updated This adds some overhead and may possibly slow down update performance.

In SQL Server 2014, you also have the option of defining a computed column so that its value is physically stored. You accomplish this with the ADD PERSISTED option, as shown in the following example:

```
--Alter the computed SetRate column to be PERSISTED
ALTER TABLE emp
 alter column total_salary ADD PERSISTED
```

SQL Server automatically updates the persisted column values whenever one of the columns that the computed column references is changed. Indexes can be created on these columns, and they can be used just like nonpersisted columns. One advantage of using a computed column that is persisted is that it has fewer restrictions than a nonpersisted column. In particular, a persisted column can contain an imprecise expression, which is not possible with a nonpersisted column. Any float or real expressions are considered imprecise. To ensure that you have a precise column you can use the COLUMNPROPERTY function and review the IsPrecise property to determine whether the computed column expression is precise.

Summary Data

Summary data is most helpful in a decision support environment, to satisfy reporting requirements and calculate sums, row counts, or other summary information that is stored in a separate table. You can create summary data in a number of ways:

- ▶ **Real-time**—Every time your base data is modified, you can recalculate the summary data, using the base data as a source. This is typically done using stored procedures or triggers.

- ▶ **Real-time incremental**—Every time your base data is modified, you can recalculate the summary data, using the old summary value and the new data. This approach is more complex than the real-time option, but it could save time if the increments are relatively small compared to the entire dataset. This, too, is typically done using stored procedures or triggers.

- ▶ **Delayed**—You can use a scheduled job or custom service application to recalculate summary data on a regular basis. This is the recommended method to use in an OLTP system to keep update performance optimal.

Horizontal Data Partitioning

As tables grow larger, data access time also tends to increase. For queries that need to perform table scans, the query time is proportional to the number of rows in the table. Even when you have proper indexes on such tables, access time slows as the depth of the index trees increases. The solution is splitting the table into multiple tables such that each table has the same table structure as the original one but stores a different set of data. Figure 38.1 shows a billing table with 90 million records. You can split this table into

12 monthly tables (all with the identical table structure) to store billing records for each month.

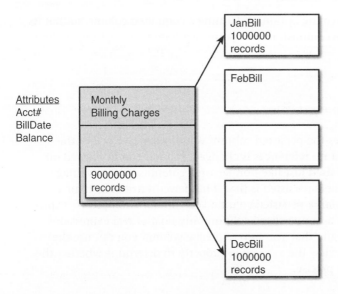

Attributes
Acct#
BillDate
Balance

Monthly
Billing Charges

90000000
records

JanBill
1000000
records

FebBill

DecBill
1000000
records

FIGURE 38.1   Horizontal partitioning of data.

You should carefully weigh the options when performing horizontal splitting. Although a query that needs data from only a single month gets much faster, other queries that need a full year's worth of data become more complex. Also, queries that are self-referencing do not benefit much from horizontal partitioning. For example, the business logic might dictate that each time you add a new billing record to the billing table, you need to check any outstanding account balance for previous billing dates. In such cases, before you do an insert in the current monthly billing table, you must check the data for all the other months to find any outstanding balance.

TIP

Horizontal splitting of data is useful where a subset of data might see more activity than the rest of the data. For example, say that in a healthcare provider setting, 98% of the patients are inpatients, and only 2% are outpatients. In spite of the small percentage involved, the system for outpatient records sees a lot of activity. In this scenario, it makes sense to split the patient table into two tables—one for the inpatients and one for the outpatients.

When splitting tables horizontally, you must perform some analysis to determine the optimal way to split the table. You need to find a logical dimension along which to split the data. The best choice takes into account the way your users use your data. In the example that involves splitting the data among 12 tables, date was mentioned as the optimal split candidate. However, if the users often did ad hoc queries against the billing table for a full year's worth of data, they would be unhappy with the choice to split that data among 12 different tables. Perhaps splitting based on a customer type or another attribute would be more useful.

NOTE

You can use partitioned views to hide the horizontal splitting of tables. The benefit of using partitioned views is that multiple horizontally split tables appear to the end users and applications as a single large table. When this is properly defined, the optimizer automatically determines which tables in the partitioned view need to be accessed, and it avoids searching all tables in the view. The query runs as quickly as if it were run only against the necessary tables directly. For more information on defining and using partitioned views, see Chapter 24, "Creating and Managing Views."

In SQL Server 2014, you also have the option of physically splitting the rows in a single table over more than one partition. This feature, called *partitioned tables*, utilizes a partitioning function that splits the data horizontally and a partitioning scheme that assigns the horizontally partitioned data to different filegroups. When a table is created, it references the partitioned schema, which causes the rows of data to be physically stored on different filegroups. No additional tables are needed, and the table is still referenced with the original table name. The horizontal partitioning happens at the physical storage level and is transparent to the user. *Partitioned tables* are discussed in more detail in Chapter 21 "Creating and Managing Tables."

Vertical Data Partitioning

As you know, a database in SQL Server consists of 8KB pages, and a row cannot span multiple pages. Therefore, the total number of rows on a page depends on the width of the table. This means the wider the table, the smaller the number of rows per page. You can achieve significant performance gains by increasing the number of rows per page, which in turn reduces the number of I/Os on the table. Vertical splitting is a method of reducing the width of a table by splitting the columns of the table into multiple tables. Usually, all frequently used columns are kept in one table, and others are kept in the other table. This way, more records can be accommodated per page, fewer I/Os are generated, and more data can be cached into SQL Server memory. Figure 38.2 illustrates a vertically partitioned table. The frequently accessed columns of the `authors` table are stored in the `author_primary` table, whereas less frequently used columns are stored in the `author_secondary` table.

TIP

Make the decision to split data very carefully, especially when the system is already in production. Changing the data structure might have a system-wide impact on a large number of queries that reference the old definition of the object. In such cases, to minimize risks, you might want to use SQL Server views to hide the vertical partitioning of data. Also, if you find that users and developers are frequently joining between the vertically split tables because they need to pull data together from the two tables, you might want to reconsider the split point or the splitting of the table itself. Doing frequent joins between split tables with smaller rows requires more I/Os to retrieve the same data than if the data resided in a single table with wider rows.

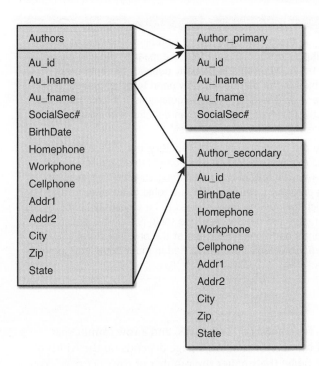

FIGURE 38.2   Vertical partitioning of data.

Performance Implications of Zero-to-One Relationships

Suppose that one of the development managers in your company, Bob, approaches you to discuss some database schema changes. He is one of several managers whose groups all use the central User table in your database. Bob's application makes use of about 5% of the users in the User table. Bob has a requirement to track five yes/no/undecided flags associated with those users. He would like you to add five one-character columns to the User table to track this information. What do you tell Bob?

Bob has a classic zero-to-one problem. He has some data he needs to track, but it applies to only a small subset of the data in the table. You can approach this problem in one of three ways:

▶ **Option 1: Add the columns to the User table**—In this case, 95% of your users will have NULL values in those columns, and the table will become wider for everybody.

> **NOTE**
>
> You can reduce the space requirements for the NULL values in the additional columns if you define them as sparse columns. However, sparse columns require a bit more overhead to retrieve the non-NULL values. The rule of thumb is to consider using sparse columns when the space saved is at least 20% to 40%, which would likely be the case in this example when the columns will only be populated for 5% of the records in the table. For more information on sparse columns and how to define them, see Chapter 21, "Creating and Managing Tables."

▶ **Option 2: Create a new table with a vertical partition of the User table**—The new table will contain the User primary key and Bob's five flags. In this case, 95% of your users will still have NULL data in the new table, but the User table is protected against these effects. Because other groups don't need to use the new partition table, this is a nice compromise.

▶ **Option 3: Create a new vertically partitioned table as in Option 2 but populate it only with rows that have at least one non-NULL value for the columns in the new partition**—This option is great for database performance, and searches in the new table will be wonderfully fast. The only drawback to this approach is that Bob's developers will have to add additional logic to their applications to determine whether a row exists during updates. Bob's folks will need to use an outer join to the table to cover the possibility that a row doesn't exist.

Depending on the goals of the project, any one of these options can be appropriate. Option 1 is simple and is the easiest to code for and understand. Option 2 is a good compromise between performance and simplicity. Option 3 gives the best performance in certain circumstances but impacts performance in certain other situations and definitely requires more coding work to be done.

Database Filegroups and Performance

Filegroups allow you to decide where on disk a particular object should be placed. You can do this by defining a filegroup within a database, extending the database onto a different drive or set of drives, and then placing a database object on the new filegroup.

Every database, by default, has a primary filegroup that contains the primary data file. There can be only one primary filegroup. This primary filegroup contains all the pages assigned to system tables. It also contains any additional database files created without specifying a filegroup. Initially, the primary filegroup is also the default filegroup. There can be only one default filegroup, and indexes and tables that are created without specifying a filegroup are placed in the default filegroup. You can change the default filegroup to another filegroup after it has been created for a database.

In addition to the primary filegroup, you can add one or more additional filegroups to the database that are named user-defined filegroups. Each of those filegroups can contain one or more files. The main purpose of using filegroups is to provide more control over

38

the placement of files and data on the server. When you create a table or an index, you can map it to a specific filegroup, thus controlling the placement of data. A typical SQL Server database installation generally uses a single RAID array to spread I/O across disks and create all files in the primary filegroup; more advanced installations or installations with very large databases spread across multiple array sets can benefit from the finer level of control of file and data placement afforded by additional filegroups.

For example, for a simple database such as AdventureWorks2012, you can create just one primary file that contains all data and objects and a log file that contains the transaction log information. For a larger and more complex database, such as a securities trading system, where large data volumes and strict performance criteria are the norm, you might create the database with one primary file and four secondary files. You can then set up filegroups so you can place the data and objects within the database across all five files. If you have a table that itself needs to be spread across multiple disk arrays for performance reasons, you can place multiple files in a filegroup, each of which resides on a different disk, and create the table on that filegroup. For example, you can create three files (Data1.ndf, Data2.ndf, and Data3.ndf) on three disk arrays and then assign them to the filegroup called spread_group. Your table can then be created specifically on the spread_group filegroup. Queries for data from the table are then spread across the three disk arrays, thereby improving I/O performance.

Filegroups are most often used in high-performance environments to isolate key tables or indexes on their own set of disks, which are in turn typically part of a high-performance RAID array. Assuming that you start with a database that has just a PRIMARY filegroup (the default), the following example shows how you would add an index filegroup on a new drive and move some nonclustered indexes to it:

```
-- add the filegroup
alter database Grocer
        add filegroup FG_INDEX

-- Create a new database file and add it to the FG_INDEX filegroup
alter database Grocer
add file(
    NAME = Grocer_Index,
        FILENAME = 'g:\Grocer_Index.ndf',
        SIZE = 2048MB,
        MAXSIZE = 8192MB,
        FILEGROWTH = 10%
) to filegroup FG_INDEX

create nonclustered index xOrderDetail_ScanDT
    on OrderDetail(ScanDT)
    on FG_INDEX
```

Moving the indexes to a separate RAID array minimizes I/O contention by spreading out the I/O generated by updates to the data that affect data rows and require changes to index rows as well.

> **NOTE**
>
> Because the leaf level of a clustered index is the data page, if you create a clustered index on a filegroup, the entire table moves from the existing filegroup to the new filegroup. If you want to put indexes on a separate filegroup, you should reserve that space for nonclustered indexes only.

Having your indexes on a separate filegroup gives you the following advantages:

- ▶ Index scans and index page reads come from a separate disk, so they need not compete with other database processes for disk time.

- ▶ Inserts, updates, and deletes on the table are spread across two separate disk arrays. The clustered index, including all the table data, is on a separate array from the nonclustered indexes.

- ▶ You can target your budget dollars more precisely because the faster disks improve system performance more if they are given to the index filegroup rather than the database as a whole.

The next section gives specific recommendations on how to architect a hardware solution based on using separate filegroups for data and indexes.

RAID Technology

Redundant array of inexpensive disks (RAID) is used to configure a disk subsystem to provide better performance and fault tolerance for an application. The basic idea behind using RAID is that you spread data across multiple disk drives so that I/Os are spread across these drives. RAID has special significance for database-related applications, where you want to spread random I/Os (data changes) and sequential I/Os (for the transaction log) across different disk subsystems to minimize disk head movement and maximize I/O performance.

The four significant levels of RAID implementation that are most common in database implementations are as follows:

- ▶ RAID 0 is data striping with no redundancy or fault tolerance.

- ▶ RAID 1 is mirroring, where every disk in the array has a mirror (copy).

- ▶ RAID 5 is striping with parity, where parity information for data on one disk is spread across the other disks in the array. The contents of a single disk can be re-created from the parity information stored on the other disks in the array.

▶ RAID 10, or 1+0, is a combination of RAID 1 and RAID 0. Data is striped across all drives in the array, and each disk has a mirrored duplicate, offering the fault tolerance of RAID 1 with the performance advantages of RAID 0.

RAID Level 0

RAID Level 0 provides the best I/O performance among all other RAID levels. A file has sequential segments striped across each drive in the array. Data is written in a round-robin fashion to ensure that data is evenly balanced across all drives in the array. However, if a media failure occurs, no fault tolerance is provided, and all data stored in the array is lost. RAID 0 should not be used for a production database where data loss or loss of system availability is not acceptable. RAID 0 is occasionally used for `tempdb` to provide the best possible read and (especially) write performance. RAID 0 is helpful for random read requirements, such as those that occur on `tempdb` and in data segments.

TIP

Although the data stored in `tempdb` is temporary and noncritical data, failure of a RAID 0 striped set containing `tempdb` results in loss of system availability because SQL Server requires a functioning `tempdb` to carry out many of its activities. If loss of system availability is not an option, you should not put `tempdb` on a RAID 0 array. You should use one of the RAID technologies that provides redundancy.

If momentary loss of system availability is acceptable in exchange for the improved I/O and reduced cost of RAID 0, recovery of `tempdb` is relatively simple. The `tempdb` database is re-created each time the SQL Server instance is restarted. If the disk that contained your `tempdb` was lost, you could replace the failed disk, restart SQL Server, and the files would automatically be re-created. This scenario is complicated if the failed disk with the `tempdb` file also contains your `master` database or other system databases. See Chapter 11, "Database Backup and Restore," for a more detailed discussion of restoring system databases.

RAID 0 is the least expensive of the RAID configurations because 100% of the disks in the array are available for data, and none are used to provide fault tolerance. Performance is also the best of the RAID configurations because there is no overhead required to maintain redundant data.

Figure 38.3 depicts a RAID 0 disk array configuration.

RAID Level 1

With RAID 1, known as disk mirroring, every write to the primary disk is written to the mirror set. Either member of the set can satisfy a read request. RAID 1 devices provide excellent fault tolerance because in the event of a media failure, either on the primary disk or mirrored disk, the system can still continue to run. Writes are much faster than with RAID 5 arrays because no parity information needs to be calculated first. The data is simply written twice.

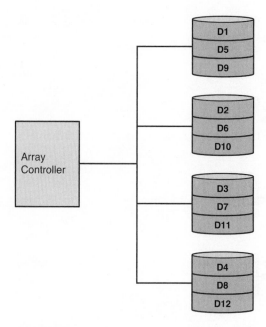

FIGURE 38.3   RAID Level 0.

RAID 1 arrays are best for transaction logs and index filegroups. RAID 1 provides the best fault tolerance and best write performance, which is critical to log and index performance. Because log writes are sequential write operations and not random access operations, they are best supported by a RAID 1 configuration.

RAID 1 arrays are more expensive RAID configurations because only 50% of total disk space is available for actual storage. The rest is used to provide fault tolerance. Figure 38.4 shows a RAID 1 configuration.

Because RAID 1 requires that the same data be written to two drives at the same time, write performance is slightly less than when writing data to a single drive because the write is not considered complete until both writes have been done. Using a disk controller with a battery-backed write cache can mitigate this write penalty because the write is considered complete when it occurs to the battery-backed cache. The actual writes to the disks occur in the background.

RAID 1 read performance is often better than that of a single disk drive because most controllers now support split seeks. Split seeks allow each disk in the mirror set to be read independently of each other, thereby supporting concurrent reads.

RAID Level 10

RAID 10, or RAID 1+0, is a combination of mirroring and striping. It is implemented as a stripe of mirrored drives. The drives are mirrored first, and then a stripe is created across the mirrors to improve performance. This should not be confused with RAID 0+1, which is different and is implemented by first striping the disks and then mirroring.

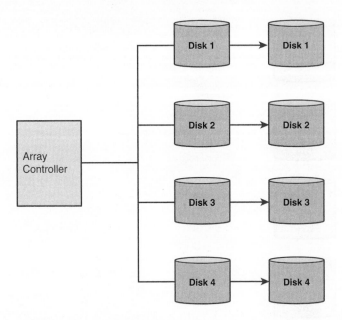

FIGURE 38.4   RAID Level 1.

Many businesses with high-volume OLTP applications opt for RAID 10 configurations. The shrinking cost of disk drives and the heavy database demands of today's business applications are making this a much more viable option. If you find that your transaction log or index segment is pegging your RAID 1 array at 100% usage, you can implement a RAID 10 array to get better performance. This type of RAID carries with it all the fault tolerance (and cost!) of a RAID 1 array, with all the performance benefits of RAID 0 striping.

RAID Level 5

RAID 5 is most commonly known as striping with parity. In this configuration, data is striped across multiple disks in large blocks. At the same time, parity bits are written across all the disks for a given block. Information is always stored in such a way that any one disk can be lost without any information in the array being lost. In the event of a disk failure, the system can still continue to run (at a reduced performance level) without downtime by using the parity information to reconstruct the data lost on the missing drive.

Some arrays provide "hot-standby" disks. The RAID controller uses the standby disk to rebuild a failed drive automatically, using the parity information stored on all the other drives in the array. During the rebuild process, performance is markedly worse.

The fault tolerance of RAID 5 is usually sufficient, but if more than one drive in the array fails, you lose the entire array. It is recommended that a spare drive be kept on hand in the event of a drive failure, so the failed drive can be replaced quickly before any other drives fail.

Many of the RAID solutions available today support "hot-spare" drives. A hot-spare drive is connected to the array but doesn't store any data. When the RAID system detects a drive failure, the contents of the failed drive are re-created on the hot-spare drive, and it is automatically swapped into the array in place of the failed drive. The failed drive can then be manually removed from the array and replaced with a working drive, which becomes the new hot spare.

RAID 5 provides excellent read performance but expensive write performance. A write operation on a RAID 5 array requires two writes: one to the data drive and one to the parity drive. After the writes are complete, the controller reads the data to ensure that the information matches (that is, that no hardware failure has occurred). A single write operation causes four I/Os on a RAID 5 array. For this reason, putting log files or tempdb on a RAID 5 array is not recommended. Index filegroups, which suffer worse than data filegroups from bad write performance, are also poor candidates for RAID 5 arrays. Data filegroups where more than 10% of the I/Os are writes are also not good candidates for RAID 5 arrays.

Note that if write performance is not an issue in your environment—for example, in a DSS/data warehousing environment—you should, by all means, use RAID 5 for your data and index segments.

In any environment, you should avoid putting tempdb on a RAID 5 array. tempdb typically receives heavy write activity, and it performs better on a RAID 1 or RAID 0 array.

RAID 5 is a relatively economical means of providing fault tolerance. No matter how many drives are in the array, only the space equivalent to a single drive is used to support fault tolerance. This method becomes more economical with more drives in the array. You must have at least three drives in a RAID 5 array. Three drives would require that 33% of available disk space be used for fault tolerance, four would require 25%, five would require 20%, and so on.

Figure 38.5 shows a RAID 5 configuration.

Although the recommendations for using the various RAID levels presented here can help ensure that your database performance will be optimal, reality often dictates that your optimum disk configuration might not be available. You may be given a server with a single RAID 5 array and told to make it work. Although RAID 5 is not optimal for tempdb or transaction logs, the write performance can be mitigated by using a controller with a battery-backed write cache.

If possible, you should also try to stripe database activity across multiple RAID 5 arrays rather than a single large RAID 5 array to avoid I/O saturation of the disks in the array.

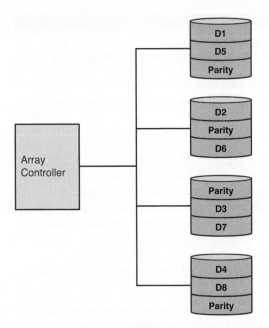

FIGURE 38.5   RAID Level 5.

SQL Server and SAN Technology

With the increased use of storage area networks (SANs) in SQL Server environments, it is important to understand the design and performance implications of implementing SQL Server databases on SANs. SANs are becoming increasingly more common in SQL Server environments these days for a number of reasons:

▶ Increasing database sizes

▶ The increasing prevalence of clustered environments

▶ The performance advantages and storage efficiencies and flexibilities of SANs

▶ The increasing needs of recoverability and disaster recovery

▶ Simplified disk administration

In large enterprises, a storage area network (SAN) can be used to connect multiple servers to a centralized pool of disk storage. Compared to managing hundreds of servers, each with its own separate disk arrays, SANs help simplify disk administration by treating all the company's storage as a single resource. Disk allocation, maintenance, and routine backups are easier to manage, schedule, and control. In some SANs, the disks themselves can copy data to other disks for backup without any processing overhead at the host computers.

What Is a SAN?

A SAN contains multiple high-performance hard drives coupled with high-performance caching controllers. The hard drives are often configured into various RAID configurations. These drive configurations are virtualized so that the consumer does not know which hard drives a SQL Server or other device connected to the SAN will access. Essentially, the SAN presents blocks of storage to servers that can consist of a single hard drive, multiple hard drives, or portions of hard drives in a logical unit called a logical unit number (LUN). Connection to a SAN is typically through Fibre Channel, a high-speed optical network.

SANS can provide advantages over locally attached storage. Most SANs provide features that allow you to clone, snapshot, or rapidly move data (replicate) from one location to another, much faster than file copies or data transfers over your network. This increases the usefulness of SANs for disaster recovery. SANs also provide a shared disk resource for building server clusters, even allowing a cluster or server to boot off a SAN.

Another reason for the increased use of SANs is that they offer increased utilization of storage. With locally attached storage, large amounts of disk space can end up being wasted. With a SAN, you can expand or contract the amount of disk space allocated to a server or cluster as needed.

Due to their cost and complexity, however, SANs are not for everybody. They only really make sense in large enterprises. They are not a good choice for small environments with relatively small databases, for companies with limited budgets (SANs are expensive), or for companies that require disaster recovery on only one or a few SQL Servers.

SAN Considerations for SQL Server

Before you rush out and purchase a SAN or two for your SQL Server environments, there are some considerations to keep in mind when using SANs with SQL Server.

Cache Performance

One of the reasons SANs can offer superior performance to locally attached storage is they typically are configured with a significant amount of cache space. This is normally a good thing. However, because the SAN provides storage services to multiple servers, the available cache space is shared as well. If there is significant activity against the SAN, there can be extensive cache turnover. This means that the large cache space may not always be available to SQL Server, so some of the performance gains provided by the large cache are not realized.

38

> **NOTE**
>
> Cache turnover in a SAN can lead to widely varying physical I/O response times. When SQL Server performs I/O against the SAN, it's considered a physical I/O whether or not the data resides in the SAN cache. When the physical I/O performance for SQL Server is measured, the performance can be orders of magnitude faster when the data is residing in the SAN cache than when the data has to be physically read from the disks in the SAN. It is important that you perform benchmarking with your SAN vendor to ensure that your SAN cache will be adequate to provide optimal database performance.

Avoid Disk Drive Contention

SAN storage is divided into LUNs. Servers attached to the SAN recognize one or more of these units as a disk partition or drive. However, these LUNs may share the same disk drives. For example, consider six 100GB drives in the SAN. Theoretically, this could be divided into two LUNs of 300GB each. Although each LUN may be allocated to different SQL Servers, some of the drives shared between the two LUNs could experience twice the I/O from both servers than if the drives were dedicated to a single server. To avoid this situation, most SANs support *zoning*, which allows the SAN administrator to dedicate entire disks in the SAN to your LUN to isolate the I/O on the drives in the LUN to your SQL Server.

In addition, you should try to ensure that your database log files are on a LUN consisting of dedicated drives separate from the LUN (or LUNs) used for your SQL Server data files. Log files typically are written sequentially, unlike data files where data access tends to consist more of random reads and writes. Sharing a LUN between data files and log files generally does not provide optimal IO performance. Unfortunately, your SAN administrator may not permit you to dedicate a separate disk or set of disks to your log files. An alternative may be to place your log files on a local RAID 1 or RAID 10 array. However, you might want to benchmark to determine which solution provides better performance because the caching capabilities of the SAN may offset the potential drive contention in the SAN.

Additional SAN Performance Considerations

Some SAN administrators may attempt to convince you to use RAID 5 for all data and log files. Before following their advice, you should benchmark the system using a representative load to ensure that RAID 5 will offer the best performance for your log files, `tempdb`, and any write-intensive filegroups.

You should also ensure that the hardware your SQL Server system uses to connect to the SAN provides optimal performance. Make sure that you have the correct and most up-to-date drivers for your SAN components. If you can, consider using multiple high-speed host bus adapters (HBAs) to connect your servers to your SAN to avoid the I/O contention that can occur with a single HBA. If you do use multiple HBAs, try to ensure they are on different buses to prevent bus saturation and that the HBAs are plugged into the PCI slots offering the highest speed.

SANs are complex, and delivering optimal performance for a SQL Server solution using a SAN is challenging. Benchmark your SQL Server to determine if bottlenecks exist with your SAN. Be willing to work with your SAN administrator or vendor to fine-tune your SAN configuration and carefully consider and benchmark any recommendations they may make to ensure optimal performance.

SQL Server and VM Technology

A VM or Virtual Machine is an emulation of a particular computer system. The VM allows for a program or operating system to be created within another host environment.

The host environment is typically the physical server that contains more than one VM instance. The VMs that are running on the host are referred to as guests.

This technology has become very popular because it does have some distinct advantages. These advantages include lower energy costs because there are less physical machines running. Fewer physical servers mean that there is less space taken in data centers and less hardware to maintain. There are also benefits related to rapid deployment of new environments, simplified hardware migration, and additional options for disaster recovery.

In the past, SQL Server was not considered the best candidate for VM technology because of the resource intensive nature of the SQL Server application. Past VM environments were not well suited for high volume production loads. Virtualization has come a long way in the past few years and it is now feasible to virtualize SQL Server and obtain acceptable levels of performance. There are, however, a number of implementation pitfalls you want to avoid when virtualizing SQL Server. These pitfalls can lead to poor performance. Given the resource-intensive nature of SQL Server it is imperative that the host, virtual machine (VM) and SQL Server are configured properly in order for SQL Server to achieve the same levels of performance you expect in a non-virtualized environment.

The sections that follow provide virtualization recommendations for three layers that are involved in the virtualization of SQL Server. These layers include the underlying server that is hosting the VMs, the VM itself, and finally the SQL Server instance that is running within the VM. All three of these areas play a critical role in achieving optimal performance. The VM and SQL Server licensing is a fourth area that deserves attention too but it is beyond the scope of this chapter (an overview of SQL Server licensing in a virtual environment is provided in Chapter 1, "SQL Server 2014 Overview").

> **NOTE**
>
> The tips provided in this section are focused on SQL Server, are general in nature, and apply to virtual environments regardless of the underlying VM software. Optimization tips for specific VM software such as VMWare or Hyper-V are beyond the scope of this section. There are, however, several white papers available (including the following) that you may want to refer to for your specific VM implementation:
>
> ▶ http://www.vmware.com/files/pdf/solutions/SQL_Server_on_VMware-Best_Practices_Guide.pdf
>
> ▶ http://download.microsoft.com/download/6/1/D/61DDE9B6-AB46-48CA-8380-D7714C9CB1AB/Best_Practices_for_Virtualizing_and_Managing_SQL_Server_2012.pdf.

VM Host Recommendations

The VM Host is the underlying server where the VM instances are installed. The VM Host must be configured properly in order to achieve optimal performance for the host, the VM guests running on the host and the SQL Server Instance(s) running within the VM guests. The following list contains some of the more useful tips for configuring the host for best performance:

1. Use the most current version of the OS running on the VM Host. OS improvements in virtualization are advancing with each OS release and can vastly improve the performance and flexibility within the VM environment.

2. Provide sufficient resources (especially CPU, memory and disk) on the host machine so that the host can handle the peak load of all VM machines that may be running on the host at any given time. The same guidelines for allocating server resources for a non-virtualized environments apply here as well

3. Do not oversubscribe the host CPUs/cores. If the host becomes CPU saturated with the VMs and host demanding all CPU resources, SQL Server performance will degrade. Maintain a 1:1 ratio of physical cores to virtual CPUs.

4. Ensure that the "High Performance" power plan has been enabled on the server. SQL Server can incur intense loads and must have peak performance at all times. The balanced power plan or custom plan can pull resources from SQL Server and lead to SQL Server performance degradation.

5. Be careful not to overcommit memory in the VM and avoid using Memory ballooning on the host. Memory ballooning allows a physical host to allocate unused memory from its guest VMs to other VMs requiring additional memory. SQL Server is a memory intensive application and you do not want the VM host stealing memory from any VMs that are running SQL Server.

6. Monitor the performance of the VM Host to ensure that you are getting acceptable results. Use the same proven Performance Monitor counters that you would use for a non-virtualized SQL Server. This may include Physical Disk - Avg. Disk Sec Read, Physical Disk - Avg. Disk Sec Write, Processor - % Processor Time and Memory - Available Mbytes.

VM Guest Recommendations

The VM guest is the instance of the VM software that is running on the VM Host. There can be one or more of these VM guests on a given host. The ability to run more than one VM instance on a given host is a very powerful feature but careful consideration needs to be given to the number of VM guests that are run on a host, the resources that these VM guests will need and the configuration of those VM guests to achieve optimal performance for SQL Server. The following list contains tips for configuring the VM guest to achieve the best performance for a virtualized SQL Server:

1. Segregate the SQL Server workload to different Virtual Hard Drives (VHDs). This involves placing different types of SQL Server files on different VHDs. For example, the database files should be on one VHD, the log files should be on another. The database backups, OS and tempdb files should each have their own VHD as well. This helps segregate the IO and reduce bottleneck on the disk. If possible, the VHDs should not share physical disks to further segregate the IO.

2. Do not share the disks that relate to the SQL Server VHDs with other VM guests and their VHDs. The underlying storage for the SQL Server should be dedicated to SQL Server and no other VM.

3. Configure your VHDs to be a fixed size. VMs offer dynamic or differencing disks as an option but the fixed VHD is almost always the best choice for SQL Server implementations.

4. Ensure that the VM guest OS is also set to use the "High Performance" power plan.

5. Enable the Lock Pages in Memory Option in Windows. This setting, granted to the service account that SQL Server runs under, allows the SQL Server process to keep the memory allocated to it in physical memory. It prevents the system from paging the SQL Server buffer pool pages to virtual memory on disk, which can be very detrimental to SQL Server performance.

6. Do not over allocate the available Host memory and CPU to the VM guests. The host has a limited amount of resources and you want to make sure that each VM guest that is running SQL Server has adequate resources. If resources are over allocated to VM guests then the performance of those VMs is not predictable. There are allocation limits that vary depending on the OS and version of VM software that you are running so be sure to review the related documentation.

7. Monitor the performance of the VM quest to ensure that you are getting acceptable results. Use the same proven Performance Monitor counters that you would use for a non-virtualized SQL Server. This may include Physical Disk - Avg. Disk Sec Read, Physical Disk - Avg. Disk Sec Write, Processor - % Processor Time and Memory - Available Mbytes.

SQL Server in a VM

The SQL Server instance is installed within a VM guest. For the most part SQL Server does not know that it is running in a virtual environment. It expects to get resources in much the same way that it does in a non-virtualized environment. With that in mind, SQL Server should be installed and configured much like you would do in a non-virtual environment using standard SQL Server best practices. Two best practices that are particularly important in a virtual environment are:

1. Set the Maximum Server Memory in SQL Server. The memory that has been allocated to the VM and the memory needed by the VM guest OS need to be considered with this setting. SQL Server is capable of consuming all memory in a virtual machine and setting Maximum Server Memory to a value less than the total memory allocated to the VM guest allows you to reserve sufficient memory for the OS and other applications that may be running in the VM guest. A Maximum Server Memory value should always be provided if the Lock Pages in Memory option is utilized.

38

2. Monitor the performance of your SQL Server instance. Use the same proven Performance Monitor counters that you would use for a non-virtualized SQL Server. This is the only way to prove that your instance is performing properly and that you have not run into one of those virtualization pitfalls that were mentioned earlier.

The creation, maintenance, and optimization of a virtual environment can be complicated. In many work places today there are individuals that specialize in virtualization and the underlying hardware. If you are fortunate enough to have a VM expert, then seek their advice before you attempt to virtualize your SQL Server environment.

Summary

A good database design is the best place to start to ensure that your database application runs smoothly. This chapter outlined some of the fundamental aspects a database design that you should consider. If you have the luxury of designing the database system from the ground up, be sure to use what you learned in this chapter in the early stages of developing your database system. If you inherit a database with an inadequate design, the design principles described in this chapter still apply, but they may be a bit harder to implement.

The next chapter, "Monitoring SQL Server Performance," delves into the tools and techniques you can use to evaluate the performance of your SQL Server instance. Monitoring is tightly linked to database design and is essential in achieving optimal database performance.

Monitoring SQL Server Performance

No SQL Server implementation is perfect out of the box. As you build and add SQL Server–based applications to your server, you should take an active approach to monitoring performance. You also need to keep re-evaluating as more and more load is placed on your servers and data volume grows. This chapter focuses on SQL Server monitoring and leaves monitoring of the other types of servers (including application servers, backup servers, domain controllers, file and print servers, mail/messaging servers, and web servers) for the specialists in those areas.

You can monitor many things on your SQL Server platform, ranging from physical and logical I/O to the network packets passing between the server and your client applications. To make this monitoring task a little cleaner, this chapter classifies the key monitoring elements into network, processors, memory/cache, and disk systems. Figure 39.1 shows how these key elements interrelate with SQL Server 2014 and Windows. The aspect of utilization— whether CPU utilization, memory utilization, or something else—is at the center of most of the discussions in this chapter. The important concept to remember is how to monitor or measure utilization and how to make changes to improve this utilization because you are still not in a perfect world of infinite CPU power, infinite disk space, infinite network load capability, and infinite memory.

It is essential that you know which tools you can use to get this valuable information. These tools include SQL Server Management Studio (SSMS) Activity Monitor, Data Collector, Extended Events, Windows Performance Monitor and its various counters, a few SQL Server DBCC options (not covered here), SQL Server Profiler (see Chapter 5, "SQL

Server Profiler"), System Center Monitoring Pack for MS SQL Server 2014, and a variety of SQL Server dynamic management views (DMVs). Although many other third-party products are available for performance monitoring, some of which do a fantastic job of gathering and aggregating performance data from a number of sources, there is just not enough space in this chapter to cover all the various third-party tools and their features. Instead, this chapter focuses on the performance monitoring tools provided out of the box with SQL Server 2014.

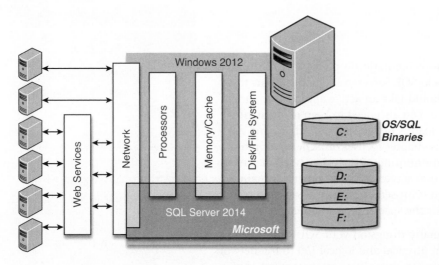

FIGURE 39.1   Key elements of SQL Server 2014 performance monitoring: network, processors, memory/cache, and disks.

What's New in Monitoring SQL Server Performance

Performance tuning and troubleshooting are time-consuming tasks for the administrator. To help provide insights quickly into performance issues, SQL Server 2014 provides some new and enhanced features for monitoring SQL Server performance. If you also install the System Center Monitoring Pack for MS SQL Server 2014, you will have a more enterprise visualization capability across multiple versions of SQL Server engines and other Service engines.

Extended Events were introduced in SQL Server 2008 as a lightweight mechanism that supports capturing, filtering, and acting on events generated by the server process. Extended Events provide a flexible and powerful way to provide a low granular level of information about the server system. Unfortunately, as powerful as they were, there was no interface for creating, managing, and viewing Extended Events; it was all done using T-SQL commands, making them somewhat difficult to define and use. Fortunately, SQL Server 2014 now provides a graphic user interface (GUI) within SQL Server Management Studio (SSMS) to create, manage, and view Extended Events. In addition, some new Extended Events have been added to SQL Server 2014, and all the events and fields available in SQL Profiler are now available in Extended Events. SQL Server 2014 also changed several extended event variables to be more friendly such as changing `synchronous_bucketizer` to just `histogram`.

SQL Server 2014 also introduces a few new dynamic management views (DMVs) and enhancements to existing DMVs as described later in this chapter. These have mostly been in support of Availability Groups and managing the lock priority of online operations but have also added some additional columns to several other DMVs (such as `sys.dm_exec_query_profiles`).

Performance Monitoring Tools

In versions of SQL Server prior to SQL Server 2008, the tools available for monitoring SQL Server performance were somewhat limited. Yes, you had the Windows Performance Monitor, Activity Monitor, SQL Server Profiler, and SQL Trace, but performing in-depth performance monitoring usually required the purchase of third-party tools to collect, monitor, and view performance information in a useful way.

SQL Server 2014 provides a number of tools you can use to collect, analyze, monitor, and report performance-related data. The usual old-timers such as SQL Server Profiler and Database Engine Tuning Advisor still exist and are available to you, but SQL Server 2014 also includes the Activity Monitor, the Data Collector and management data warehouse, SQL Server Utility, and SQL Server Extended Events. Also, with System Center Monitoring Pack for MS SQL Server 2014, you will have a more enterprise visualization capability across multiple versions of SQL Server engines and other Service engines (such as Analysis Services, Integration Service, Reporting Services, and so on).

> **NOTE**
>
> For a discussion on using SQL Server Profiler for monitoring and analyzing performance, see Chapter 5, "SQL Server Profiler." For more information on the Database Engine Tuning Advisor, see Chapter 40, "SQL Server Database Engine Tuning Advisor." In addition, the Activity Monitor is already covered in detail in Chapter 3, "SQL Server Management Studio," so detailed information on Activity Monitor is not provided in this chapter.

The Data Collector and the MDW

SQL Server 2014 includes a performance monitoring tool called the Data Collector. The Data Collector is designed to collect performance-related data from multiple sources from one or more SQL Servers, store it in a central data warehouse, and present the data through reports in SQL Server Management Studio. The main purpose of the Data Collector is to provide an easy way to automate the collection of critical performance data. The Data Collector gathers information from Windows performance counters, snapshots of data grabbed from dynamic management objects, and details on disk utilization.

Data collection can be configured to run continuously or on a user-defined schedule. You can adjust the scope of data collection to suit the needs of your test and production environments. The Data Collector provides a single central point for data collection across your database servers and applications and, unlike SQL Trace, is not limited to collecting performance data only.

The Data Collector feature consists of the following components:

▶ **Data collection sets**—These are the definitions and scheduled jobs for collecting performance data. They are stored in the `msdb` system database.

▶ **The Data Collector runtime component**—This standalone process, called `Dcexec.exe`, is responsible for loading and executing the SSIS packages that are part of a collection set.

▶ **SQL Server Integration Services (SSIS) packages**—These packages are used to collect and upload the data.

▶ **The management data warehouse database**—This is a relational database where the collected data is stored. It also contains the views and stored procedures needed for collection management.

▶ **MDW Reports**—These reports are built in to SSMS for viewing the collected performance data.

Figure 39.2 provides an overview of the Data Collector architecture and how the various components interact.

> **NOTE**
>
> The Data Collector is not a zero-impact monitoring solution. It incurs approximately a 2% to 5% performance hit on the servers where it's collecting data. This performance hit is mainly on the CPU.

Data Collection Sets

A *data collection set* is group of collection items. A *collection set* is the unit of data collection that a user can interact with through the user interface. Data collection sets are defined and deployed on a SQL Server 2014 instance and can be run independently of each other. Each collection set is run by a SQL Server Agent job or jobs, and data is uploaded to the management data warehouse on a predefined schedule.

Out of the box, SQL Server 2014 provides the following built-in System Data Collection Sets and reports:

▶ **Disk Usage**—Collects local disk usage information for all the databases of the SQL Server instance. This information can help you determine current space utilization and future disk space requirements for disk capacity planning.

▶ **Server Activity**—Collects SQL Server instance-level resource usage information like CPU, memory, and I/O. This information can help you monitor short-term to long-term resource usage trends and identify potential resource bottlenecks on the system. It can also be used for resource capacity planning.

▶ **Query Statistics**—Collects individual statement-level query statistics, including query text and query plans. This information can help you identify the top resource-consuming queries that may need performance tuning.

The definition of the system collection sets cannot be modified. However, you can define your own collection sets or define your own custom reports for this data.

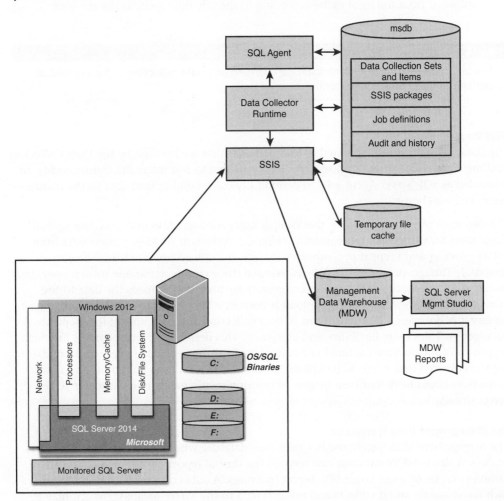

FIGURE 39.2   Data Collector architecture.

Data Collector Runtime Component

The Data Collector runtime component is invoked by a standalone process called `Dcexec.exe`. This component manages data collection based on the definitions provided in a collection set. The Data Collector runtime component is responsible for loading and executing the SSIS packages that are part of a collection set.

A collection set can be run in one of the following collection and upload modes:

▶ **Noncached mode**—Data collection and upload are executed on the same schedule. The packages collect data as scheduled and then immediately upload data.

▶ **Cached mode**—Data collection and upload are performed on different schedules. The collection package continues to collect and cache data until stopped. Data is uploaded from the local cache according to the schedule specified by the user.

> **NOTE**
>
> The Data Collector runtime component can perform only data collection or data upload. It cannot run these tasks concurrently.

SSIS Packages

The Data Collector is implemented as SSIS packages that are invoked by the Data Collector runtime component. These packages can be configured to run manually, continuously, or scheduled as SQL Server Agent jobs to periodically collect and upload data to the management data warehouse.

The two most important tasks for the SSIS packages are data collection and data upload. These tasks are carried out by separate packages. A collection package gathers data from a data provider and keeps it in temporary storage. An upload package reads the data in temporary storage, processes the data as required (for example, removing unnecessary data points, normalizing the data, and data aggregation), and then uploads the data to the management data warehouse. The upload is done as a bulk insert to minimize the impact on server performance. The separation of data collection and data upload into separate packages provides more flexibility and efficiency. This design supports scenarios in which snapshots of the data are captured at frequent intervals (for example, every 15 seconds), but the collected data needs to be uploaded only every hour. Data collection and upload frequency should be determined by the monitoring requirements of a particular SQL Server installation.

The Management Data Warehouse

The management data warehouse is a relational database where the Data Collector stores its data. A single MDW database can serve as the central repository for data collectors running on one or more target SQL Server instances. A data collector is configured on each target server, and it collects and uploads data to the MDW database, which may be on a remote server. Between the time the data is captured and the time it is uploaded, the Data Collector may write temporary data into cache files on the target server.

> **NOTE**
>
> You can install the MDW on the same instance of SQL Server that is running the Data Collector. However, if server resources or performance are an issue on the server that is being monitored, you might want to install the management data warehouse on a different computer to avoid additional CPU and I/O contention.

The MDW can become quite large, growing at approximately 250–500MB per day. This is roughly around 2GB of database storage per server each week. You need to decide how long you want to retain the data based on your performance monitoring needs and your storage availability. For the most part, you can probably stick with the default retention settings, which are 14 days for Query Statistics and Server Activity History data collections and two years for Disk Usage Summary collections.

The required schemas and the objects to support the predefined system collection sets are created when you run the wizard to create the MDW. Two schemas are created: `core` and `snapshots`. The `core` schema describes the tables, stored procedures, and views used to organize and identify collected data. These tables are shared among all the data tables created for individual collector types. The `snapshots` schema describes the objects needed to store and maintain the data collected by the collector types that are provided.

A third schema, `custom_snapshots`, is created if you create your own user-defined collection sets that include collection items that use the Generic T-SQL Query collector type.

> **CAUTION**
>
> You should not directly modify any data stored in the management data warehouse. Changing the data that you have collected invalidates the legitimacy of the collected data. Also, instead of directly accessing the MDW tables, you should always use the documented stored procedures and functions provided with the Data Collector to access instance and application data.

MDW Reports

The MDW reports included in SSMS present the information gathered by the Data Collector in the following areas:

▶ Query performance statistics and use of indexes

▶ Server activity information, including waiting processes, memory usage, CPU/scheduler usage, and disk I/O

▶ Disk usage information

Each of the reports presents a summary of the data at a high level, with the capability to drill down into the details. Sometimes the reports can provide information to help direct you to a solution for a performance problem. For example, if the query performance statistics report shows an extremely slow-running query, you can drill down through the report to expose more details on the query, right down to the query plan. The query plan could indicate that there is a missing index on that table, and creating that index could make a major difference in the query performance.

39

Installing and Configuring the Data Collector

Before you can use the Data Collector, you must complete the following tasks:

▶ Create logins and map them to Data Collector roles.

▶ Configure the management data warehouse.

NOTE

The management data warehouse can be installed on a server running SQL Server 2008 or later.

The Data Collector has specific roles for data collection and management data warehouse tasks. The logins and roles required for data collection need to be created on the server that performs the data collection. Logins and roles for the MDW need to be created in the server that hosts the MDW. These logins and the MDW are created using the Configure Management Data Warehouse Wizard, which performs the following tasks:

▶ Creates the management data warehouse

▶ Installs the predefined System Data Collection Sets

▶ Maps logins to management data warehouse roles

▶ Enables data collection

▶ Starts the System Data Collection Sets

To invoke the Configure Management Data Warehouse Wizard, perform the following tasks on the SQL Server instance where you want to host the MDW:

1. Ensure that SQL Server Agent is running (for information on starting SQL Server Agent, see Chapter 13, "SQL Server Agent").

2. In Object Explorer in SSMS, expand the server instance that will host the MDW and expand the Management node for that server.

3. Right-click Data Collection and then click Configure Management Data Warehouse. This starts the Configure Management Data Warehouse Wizard.

TIP

If you've already created a repository database for the SQL Server Utility (see the "SQL Server Utility" section later in this chapter), you must use this same database as the MDW for the Data Collector. And, you can skip the process of creating the MDW and jump right to the configuration of the Data Collector. On the Configure Management Data Warehouse Storage screen (look ahead to Figure 39.4), you specify the name of the server that was set up as the utility control point (UCP) and specify the name of the utility data warehouse database that was set up to collect the SQL Server Utility performance statistics.

---

4. Specify the name of the server instance that will host the MDW and click on New to create the MDW database as shown in Figure 39.3.

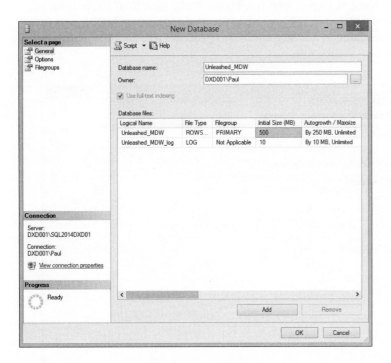

FIGURE 39.3   The New Database screen.

This brings up the standard New Database dialog. Enter the name you want to use for the MDW database (like in our example: "Unleashed_MDW") and specify the location of the database files if you want the database created in a different drive or directory than the default data file directory.

TIP

If you are creating the MDW on a server that you will also be monitoring with the Data Collector, it's a good idea to put the MDW on drives separate from where your production databases reside to avoid the potential for any I/O contention between the MDW and your production databases.

Also, because of the anticipated growth of the MDW, you might want to change the default autogrow size of the MDW from 100MB to possibly 250 or 500MB and set the initial size to at least 500MB or 1GB.

Before saving your settings and creating the MDW database, display the Options page and make sure that the database is configured for Simple recovery model. For the current release of the Data Collector, the management data warehouse should be created using the Simple recovery model, to minimize logging.

When you are satisfied with the database configuration, click on OK to create the MDW database. After the database is created and you are brought back to the Configure Management Data Warehouse Storage screen (see Figure 39.4), click Next to continue to the Map Logins and Users screen. On this screen, assign the appropriate MDW roles to your SQL Server users (see Figure 39.5). Any users who need to view the Data Collector reports need at least the `mdw_reader` role.

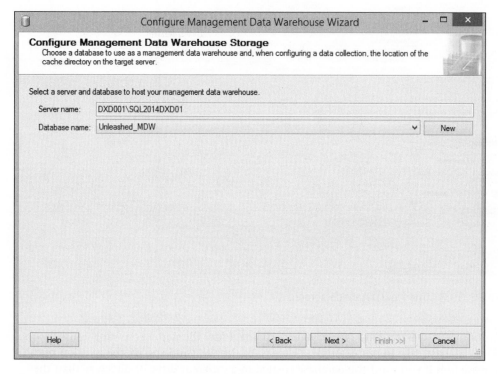

FIGURE 39.4   The Configure Management Data Warehouse Storage screen.

By default, no user is a member of the MDW database roles. User membership in these roles must be granted explicitly. Members of the `mdw_admin` role have Read, Write, Update, and Delete access to the management data warehouse. Members of this role can change the management data warehouse schema when required (for example, adding a new table when a new collection type is installed) and run maintenance jobs on the management data warehouse, such as archive or cleanup. Members of the `mdw_writer` role can upload and write data to the management data warehouse; any Data Collector that stores data in the management data warehouse has to be a member of this role. Members of the `mdw_reader` role have Read access to the management data warehouse primarily for the purpose of supporting troubleshooting by providing access to historical data.

It is recommended that you create a new login for data collection and map it as shown in Figure 39.5 (SQL login of "DataCollector").

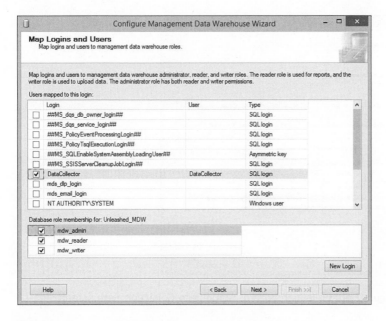

FIGURE 39.5   The Map Logins and Users screen.

After you map the users, click on Next to bring up the Complete the Wizard screen, which provides a summary of the tasks to be performed. If everything looks okay, click Finish to perform the configuration of the MDW, which includes running the installation script to install the required schema objects in the MDW.

After you have created the MDW and made it available, the next step is to begin data collection for one or more of your SQL Server instances. Right-click on the `Data Collection` node in Object Explorer and select the Configure Data Collection option this time. On the Setup Data Collection Sets screen (see Figure 39.6), specify the name of the server that hosts the MDW and the name of the MDW database created previously. When specifying the server, you can also specify which directory you want the Data Collector to use for its local file cache (again, if possible, this should be on a different drive than where your database data files reside to minimize I/O contention). If you leave the value blank, it uses the default SQL Agent `TEMP` directory.

It is also here that you must specify what type of Data Collector Sets you want to enable— either a System Data Collection Set and/or a Transaction Performance Collection Set:

▶ **System Data Collection Sets**—Collects performance statistics for general purpose troubleshooting.

▶ **Transaction Performance Collection Sets**—Collects statistics for transaction performance issues.

We'll choose to enable a System Data Collection Set. If everything looks okay, click Finish to have the wizard perform the configuration of the data collection sets and enable data collection.

39

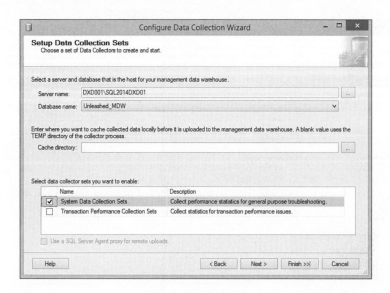

FIGURE 39.6   The Configure Data Collection Wizard: Setup Data Collection Sets screen.

The System Data Collectors

When the Configure Data Collection Wizard is finished, you should see four additional nodes under the `Data Collector` node: `Disk Usage`, `Query Statistics`, `Server Activity`, and `Utility Information`. You can double-click each node, or right-click and select Properties, to open the Properties window. The Properties window for the Disk Usage Data Collector is shown in Figure 39.7.

The main item you may want to change in the Data Collection Set Properties window is the data collection and upload schedule. By default, the wizard configures the Disk Usage Collection set to run in noncached mode every six hours. Depending on how active your server is, you might want to increase or decrease the frequency that it runs. You can also configure how long it should retain data in the MDW. By default, it is configured to retain data for two years (730 days). This is probably fine for keeping track of disk usage, but for more active Data Collector Sets, you might want to reduce the retention period to reduce the size of the MDW. For example, the default retention period for the Query Statistics and Server Activity Data Collectors is 14 days.

Both the Query Statistics and Server Activity Data Collectors are configured to cache data and upload to the MDW on a separate schedule. If you look in the General page of the Data Collection Set Properties window for these Data Collectors, you see that the schedule Query Statistics Data Collector is to gather information every 10 seconds, and the Server Activity collector gathers information every 60 seconds. To view the upload schedule, click on the Uploads page (see Figure 39.8). Both Data Collectors, by default, are configured to upload the cached data to the MDW every 15 minutes. To change the upload schedule, you can either pick from an existing schedule or create a new one (Figure 39.8 shows the Pick Schedule list). The Upload Properties page also displays the last time the cached data was uploaded to the MDW.

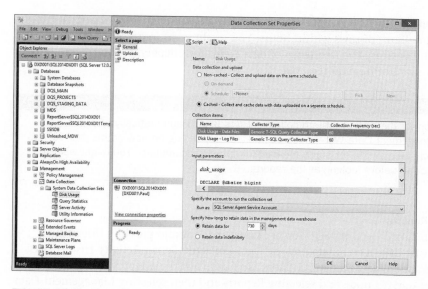

FIGURE 39.7   Data Collection Set Properties window for the Disk Usage Data Collector.

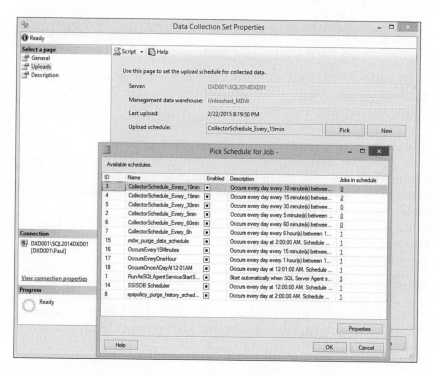

FIGURE 39.8   Data Collection Set upload schedule.

In very active servers, the Data Collector can generate a lot of data, and its storage tables can fill up with millions of rows within hours. You might want to modify the collector job schedules and decrease the frequency of data collections depending on the use of each server and your monitoring requirements.

> **NOTE**
>
> Data collection for the built-in system collection sets begins automatically after the Configure Management Data Warehouse completes. Depending on how active your servers are, it likely will take awhile for some meaningful data to accumulate. You might want to wait an hour or so before looking at the reports.

Data Collector Reports

After you set up data collection, SQL Server Management Studio provides three new reports for viewing data accumulated by the Data Collector: Server Activity History, Disk Usage Summary, and Query Statistics History. You can view these reports by right-clicking on the `Data Collection` node and selecting Reports and then selecting Management Data Warehouse. From there, you can choose one of the three built-in reports:

- ▶ **Disk Usage Summary**—Displays data and log file sizes (starting size and current size) and average daily growth

- ▶ **Query Statistics History**—Displays query execution statistics including the top 10 queries by CPU, Duration, Total I/O, Physical Reads, and Logical Writes

- ▶ **Server Activity History**—Displays performance statistics in four general areas: CPU %, Disk I/O Usage, Memory Usage, and Network Usage, plus SQL Server Wait statistics by wait type and SQL Server activity

Figure 39.9 displays an example of the Disk Usage Summary Report. All the data collection reports provide drill-down capabilities on just about every data element and widget displayed in the main report. For example, in the Disk Usage Summary report, you can click on the database name to display a more detailed breakdown of the disk usage for that specific database. Figure 39.10 shows the Disk Usage details for the DQL_MAIN database. If you click on the Data/Log Files Autogrowth/Autoshrink Events or the Disk Space Used by Data files +/- options, these show more detailed accounts of what has been happening for this disk usage for the database.

If you want to run reports for any of the monitored servers without having to navigate to the `Data Collection` node for each server instance, you can open the server instance that hosts the MDW. Browse to the MDW database in the SSMS Object Browser and right-click on that database. Then select Reports and select the Management Data Warehouse Overview report (see Figure 39.11).

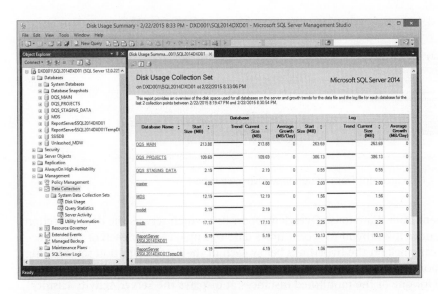

FIGURE 39.9   Disk Usage Summary report.

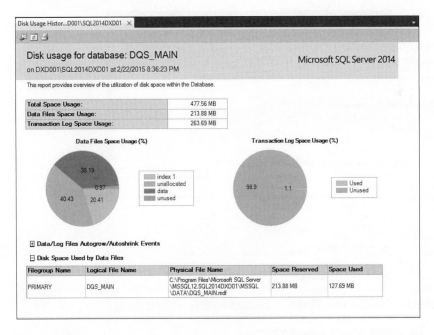

FIGURE 39.10   Disk Usage report for DQS_MAIN database.

39

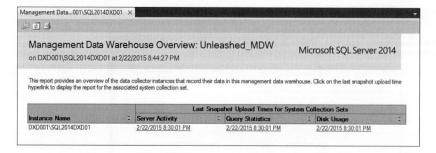

FIGURE 39.11   Management Data Warehouse Overview report.

The Management Data Warehouse Overview report lists which servers the data collection is running on and shows the most recent times data was uploaded for each of the collection sets. You can click on the hyperlinks below each of the listed collection sets to bring up that corresponding report for that server. For example, if you click on the link below Server Activity for one of the monitored instances, it displays the Server Activity History report, as shown in Figure 39.12.

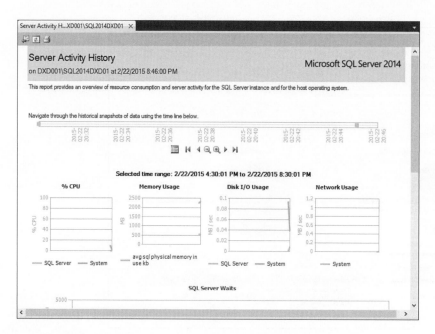

FIGURE 39.12   The Server Activity History report.

Like the Disk Usage report, most of the data elements in the Server Activity History report are hyperlinks that let you drill down into more detail. For example, you can click in the line in the Disk I/O Usage graph to bring up additional detail by disk of the Disk Response Time, Average Disk Queue Length, Disk Transfer Rate, as well as the average, minimum, and maximum I/O reads and writes for the processes running during the data collection session.

If you want to narrow down the report to a specific time frame, you can click on a point in the timeline shown on the report to set the end time of the data displayed. You can click on the magnifying glass to increase or decrease the size of the interval displayed and click the arrow buttons to move to the next or previous interval. For finer control over the time period displayed, click on the calendar icon to bring up the dialog shown in Figure 39.13. Here, you can set the specific start time and choose an interval (15 minutes or 1, 4, 12, or 24 hours) to display from that start time.

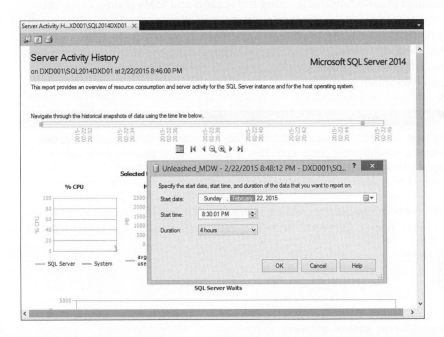

FIGURE 39.13   Defining the time frame to display in a Data Collection report.

The Data Collector reports contain a lot of data, especially if you drill down into the details. There are more details than we have space to get into in this chapter. You should plan to spend some time examining each of these reports by drilling down into the various details and selecting different time frames and so on to get familiar with what they have to offer. For example, you can drill from the Query Statistics History report to the individual query details, including the graphical execution plan.

Managing the Data Collector

To stop collecting performance data for a SQL Server instance, right-click on Data Collection in the Management node and click Disable Data Collection. If you want to stop a specific data collection set, expand the Data Collection node and then expand the System Data Collection Sets folder. Right-click on the data collection set you want to stop and select Stop Data Collection Set.

You can also force a collection set to gather data and upload statistics manually by right-clicking on the data collection set and selecting Collect and Upload Now.

To check on the status and history of the Data Collectors, you can right click on the Data Collection node and select View Logs. This launches the log viewer that displays the activity that has occurred for each of the data collection sets, such as which collection sets are active and the collection and upload history of each of the collection sets.

Managing the Data Collector in T-SQL

Much of the Data Collector can be managed effectively within SSMS. However, if you have to perform a number of tasks repeatedly, using the wizards and SSMS dialogs can some-times become tedious. Fortunately, the Data Collector provides an extensive collection of stored procedures that you can use to perform any data collection task. In addition, you can use functions and views to retrieve configuration data from the msdb and management data warehouse databases, execution log data, as well as the performance data stored in the management data warehouse.

> **TIP**
>
> As with most tools in SSMS, when using the GUI, you can click the Script button to gener-ate a script for the actions being performed. This is a great way to become more familiar with the T-SQL commands and procedures for managing the Data Collector.

For example, to enable or disable the Data Collector in a SQL Server instance, you can use the sp_syscollector_enable_collector and sp_syscollector_disable_collector stored procedures:

```
USE msdb;
GO
EXEC dbo.sp_syscollector_disable_collector;
GO
EXEC dbo.sp_syscollector_enable_collector;
GO
```

To force the running of a noncached collection set and have it upload to the MDW for collection sets configured in noncached collection mode, use the sp_syscollector_run_collection_set system procedure:

```
sp_syscollector_run_collection_set
        [[ @collection_set_id = ] collection_set_id]
        , [[ @name = ] 'name' ]
```

You can pass either the collection set ID or the collection name. When you are passing one, the other parameter can be NULL:

```
USE msdb;
GO
EXEC sp_syscollector_run_collection_set @name = 'Disk Usage'
go
```

To force a manual update of a cached mode Data Collector, you can use the `sp_syscollector_upload_collection_set` procedure:

```
USE msdb;
GO
EXEC sp_syscollector_upload_collection_set @name = 'Server Activity'
go
```

To stop or start a specific collector set, you can use the `sp_syscollector_start_collection_set` and `sp_syscollector_stop_collection` set stored procedures:

```
USE msdb;
GO
EXEC dbo.sp_syscollector_stop_collection_set @name = 'Disk Usage'
GO
EXEC dbo.sp_syscollector_start_collection_set @name = 'Disk Usage'
GO
```

To modify a collection set, you can use the `sp_syscollector_update_collection_set` procedure. The syntax is as follows:

```
sp_syscollector_update_collection_set
    [ [ @collection_set_id = ] collection_set_id ]
    , [ [ @name = ] 'name' ]
    , [ [ @new_name = ] 'new_name' ]
    , [ [ @target = ] 'target' ]
    , [ [ @collection_mode = ] collection_mode ]
    , [ [ @days_until_expiration = ] days_until_expiration ]
    , [ [ @proxy_id = ] proxy_id ]
    , [ [ @proxy_name = ] 'proxy_name' ]
    , [ [ @schedule_uid = ] 'schedule_uid' ]
    , [ [ @schedule_name = ] 'schedule_name' ]
    , [ [ @logging_level = ] logging_level ]
    , [ [ @description = ] 'description' ]
```

If the collection set is running, the only options you can modify are the `schedule_uid` and `description`. You need to stop the collection set with `sp_syscollector_stop_collection_set` first to change other options like the `collection-mode` or `days_until_expiration`. For example, the following code changes the number of days to retain collection set data to seven days for the Server Activity collection set:

```
USE msdb;
GO
EXEC dbo.sp_syscollector_stop_collection_set @name = 'Disk Usage'
GO
EXEC dbo.sp_syscollector_update_collection_set
@name = N'Server Activity',
@days_until_expiration = 7;
```

39

```
GO
EXEC dbo.sp_syscollector_start_collection_set @name = 'Disk Usage'
GO
```

To view information about the configured collection sets, you can run a query on the syscollector_collection_sets table similar to the following:

```
use msdb
go
select collection_set_id as ID,
       cast (scs.name as varchar(20)) as name,
       is_running as 'running',
       case collection_mode when 0 then 'cached'
            else 'noncached' end as coll_mode,
       days_until_expiration as retntn,
       cast (s.name as varchar(30)) as schedule
 from syscollector_collection_sets scs
        inner join
      sysschedules s
        on scs.schedule_uid = s.schedule_uid
go


/* output
ID name               running coll_mode retntn schedule
-- ----------------- ------- --------- ------ -------------------------------
 1 Disk Usage         1       noncached    730 CollectorSchedule_Every_15min
 2 Server Activity    1       cached         7 CollectorSchedule_Every_15min
 3 Query Statistics   1       cached        14 CollectorSchedule_Every_15min
*/
```

You can also use other informational views to view the data collection configuration. To display the location of the temporary cache and the MDW, for instance, you use the following:

```
use msdb
go
select * From syscollector_config_store
go


/* output
parameter_name    parameter_value
----------------  ------------------
CacheDirectory    NULL
CacheWindow       1
CollectorEnabled  1
MDWDatabase       Unleashed_MDW
MDWInstance       DXD001\SQL2014DXD01
*/
```

To display the data collection capture and upload information from the execution log, use this:

```
select top 10 csc.name as collection_set, start_time
 From syscollector_execution_log sel
       inner join
     syscollector_collection_sets csc
       on sel.collection_set_id = csc.collection_set_id
order by start_time desc
go



/* output
collection_set       start_time
------------------   -----------------------

Disk Usage           2015-02-22 14:30:04.313
Query Statistics     2015-02-22 14:30:03.313
Server Activity      2015-02-22 14:30:02.757
Disk Usage           2015-02-22 14:30:01.993
Server Activity      2015-02-22 14:30:01.800
Query Statistics     2015-02-22 14:30:01.377
*/
```

You can also use the stored procedures, functions, and views that are provided to create your own end-to-end data collection scenarios.

Creating a Customized Data Collection Set

Although you cannot change or delete the built-in system Data Collectors, you can define your own custom data collection sets. However, currently, you can define them only in T-SQL. There are four different collector types that you can use to build a collector set:

▶ **T-SQL query**—Executes a user-provided T-SQL statement as an input parameter, saves the output from the query, and then uploads the output to the management data warehouse.

▶ **SQL Trace**—Uses SQL Trace to monitor the SQL Server Relational Engine with trace data coming from the system default trace or from one or more custom traces.

▶ **Performance counters**—Collects specific performance counter information from Windows Performance Monitor on the computer running SQL Server 2014.

▶ **Query activity**—Collects query statistics and query activity information along with the query plan and query text for queries that meet predefined criteria. Essentially, this collector type collects the same information as the Query Statistics collection set, so it is recommended that you simply use the predefined Query Statistics collection set.

39

One of the reasons you might create a customized data collection set is that the default system Data Collector for Query Statistics does not store all the statements. It captures only the worst performing queries based on the algorithms specified in the collection set. You might want to collect more queries than the top three worst performing ones. However, if you create your own data collection for query statistics, you should probably disable the default system collector to reduce data collection overhead.

This chapter shows how to create a custom collection set to monitor a few Performance Monitor counters.

Assuming you've already set up your MDW, you can begin by creating the data collection set and adding the collection items you want it to contain. To create the data collection set, use the `sp_syscollector_create_collection_set` procedure. Next, you need to create the `collection_items` to indicate what information you want the collection set to collect. If you are creating collection items for Performance Monitor counters, The Performance Counter collector type takes three input parameters:

▶ **Objects**—The SQL Server objects running in an instance of SQL Server

▶ **Counters**—The counters associated with a SQL Server object

▶ **Instances**—The instances of the specified object

Some input parameters support wildcard characters, which enable you to include multiple counters in a single statement. However, you can use wildcards only at the Counters and Instances levels and, even then, only at the beginning of the string (for example, `'* Processor'`) or at the end of the string (for example, `'Memory *'`).

An example of the creation of a custom collection set for capturing information for the `Logical Disk` and `Process` Performance Monitor counters is shown in Listing 39.1.

LISTING 39.1   Creating a Custom Collection Set

```
Use msdb
go


Declare @collection_set_id_1 int
```

```
Declare @collection_set_uid_2 uniqueidentifier
EXEC [dbo].[sp_syscollector_create_collection_set]
    @name=N'Disk I/O Perf and SQL CPU',
    @collection_mode=1, -- non-cached
    @description=
  N'Collects logical disk performance counters and SQL Process CPU',
    @target=N'',
    @logging_level=0,
    @days_until_expiration=7,
    @proxy_name=N'',
    @schedule_name=N'CollectorSchedule_Every_5min',
    @collection_set_id=@collection_set_id_1 OUTPUT,
    @collection_set_uid=@collection_set_uid_2 OUTPUT
Select collection_set_id_1=@collection_set_id_1,
       collection_set_uid_2=@collection_set_uid_2


/***********************************************
**  Now, create the desired collection items
***********************************************/

Declare @collector_type_uid_3 uniqueidentifier
Select @collector_type_uid_3 = collector_type_uid
   From [dbo].[syscollector_collector_types]
   Where name = N'Performance Counters Collector Type';
Declare @collection_item_id_4 int
EXEC [dbo].[sp_syscollector_create_collection_item]
@name=N'Logical Disk Collection and SQL Server CPU',
@parameters=N'<ns:PerformanceCountersCollector xmlns:ns="DataCollectorType">
    <PerformanceCounters Objects="LogicalDisk"
        Counters="Avg. Disk Bytes/Read"
        Instances="*" />
    <PerformanceCounters Objects="LogicalDisk"
        Counters="Avg. Disk Bytes/Write"
        Instances="*" />
    <PerformanceCounters Objects="LogicalDisk"
        Counters="Avg. Disk sec/Read"
        Instances="*" />
    <PerformanceCounters Objects="LogicalDisk"
        Counters="Avg. Disk sec/Write"
        Instances="*" />
    <PerformanceCounters Objects="LogicalDisk"
        Counters="Disk Read Bytes/sec"
        Instances="*" />
    <PerformanceCounters Objects="LogicalDisk"
        Counters="Disk Write Bytes/sec"
        Instances="*" />
```

39

```
        <PerformanceCounters Objects="Process"
            Counters="% Privileged Time"
            Instances="sqlservr" />
        <PerformanceCounters Objects="Process"
            Counters="% Processor Time"
            Instances="sqlservr" />
</ns:PerformanceCountersCollector>',
@collection_item_id=@collection_item_id_4 OUTPUT,
@frequency=5,
@collection_set_id=@collection_set_id_1,
@collector_type_uid=@collector_type_uid_3
Select @collection_item_id_4
Go
```

After you create the collection set, you can start this data collection, either through SSMS (your user-defined collection sets will be listed directly within the Data Collection node) or with the following stored procedure call:

```
Declare @collection_set_id int
select @collection_set_id = collection_set_id
from syscollector_collection_sets
where name = 'Disk I/O Perf and SQL CPU'

EXEC sp_syscollector_start_collection_set
        @collection_set_id = @collection_set_id
go
```

Because there aren't any custom reports available for displaying the results of the custom collection set just defined, you need to run a query in the MDW database to view the collected Performance Monitor counter values. A sample query (which could serve as the basis for a custom report) is provided in Listing 39.2.

LISTING 39.2   Querying the MDW for Custom Data Collection Values

```
Use Unleashed_MDW
Go
select spci.path as 'Counter Path', spci.object_name as 'Object Name',
spci.counter_name as 'counter Name', spci.instance_name,
spcv.formatted_value as 'Formatted Value',
spcv.collection_time as 'Collection Time',
sii.instance_name as 'SQL Server Instance',*
from snapshots.performance_counter_values spcv
        inner join
    snapshots.performance_counter_instances spci
        on spcv.performance_counter_instance_id = spci.performance_counter_id
        inner join
```

```
    core.snapshots_internal si
        on si.snapshot_id = spcv.snapshot_id
        inner join
    core.source_info_internal sii
        on sii.source_id = si.source_id
        inner join
    msdb..syscollector_collection_sets scs
        on scs.collection_set_uid = sii.collection_set_uid
where
    scs.name = 'Disk I/O Perf and SQL CPU'
order by spcv.collection_time desc
```

It is possible to create your own custom reports using SQL Server Reporting Services that query the information for your custom collection sets in the MDW database. For more information on creating custom reports, see Chapter 48, "SQL Server 2014 Reporting Services."

Data Collector Limitations and Recommendations

Although the Data Collector is a great start to a built-in performance monitoring tool, it does have some limitations. One key limitation is the limited number of built-in data providers and the reports available. It is hoped that future versions will make it easier to extend the Data Collector to add additional collection sets and reports.

If you are defining your own custom Data Collectors, consider these recommendations:

▶ Combine multiple performance counter or query collection items into a single collection item wherever possible.

▶ Combine collection items into a single collection set whenever possible unless you need separate data retention periods or different collection schedules for the collection items.

▶ If you collect data frequently, it is more efficient to run the collection set in cached collection mode than starting and stopping a new process every time new data must be collected. In cached collection mode, the collection process runs continuously. As a general rule, if you will be capturing data every five minutes or less, consider using a collection set that runs in cached collection mode.

▶ If you are collecting data less frequently than every five minutes, using noncached mode is more efficient than leaving a generally idle process running all the time.

▶ Although the collection frequency for cached collection sets can be set to run as frequently as every five seconds, be aware that more frequent collection has correspondingly high overhead. Always choose the lowest collection frequency that will meet your needs.

Currently, removing a data collection after it has been configured is not supported. You can disable data collections but cannot remove them or the SSIS packages and jobs associated with them after they have been defined. Attempting to manually remove a data collection may lead to errors if you try to reimplement the data collection in the future. In addition, you should not drop or change the name of the MDW database because all the jobs are based on the original database name.

Another key limitation in the Data Collector is the lack of built-in alerting in the event that certain performance thresholds are crossed while monitoring the system. In contrast, the SQL Server Utility, which performs more limited monitoring and data capture than the Data Collector, does provide a threshold and alerting mechanism.

SQL Server Utility

SQL Server 2014 includes a new multiserver management tool named the SQL Server Utility. This new tool takes performance monitoring in SQL Server to the next level by providing the capability to monitor specific performance metrics for one or more SQL Server instances in a single view from a single SQL Server instance. The performance information is captured in a database, and you can view this information in one convenient place from within the SSMS environment.

Some basic setup is required to start using the SQL Server Utility. You accomplish this basic setup by using the new Utility Explorer available in SSMS. You click View on the SSMS menu bar and then select Utility Explorer. This Utility Explorer has a tree-like structure similar to the Object Explorer, and it integrates into the SSMS environment in much the same way.

The first page displayed when you launch the Utility Explorer is shown in Figure 39.14. This screen outlines all the utility configuration steps and is a handy launch point into wizards that guide you through the setup process. You can also click on the Video link next to each step to obtain further help on configuring that step.

This chapter focuses on the performance monitoring capabilities of the SQL Server Utility and the specific metrics available for collection. To enable these capabilities, you only need to do the following:

1. Create a utility control point.

2. Connect to an existing UCP.

3. Enroll instances of SQL Server into the UCP.

The UCP is a central repository for storing configuration information and performance data for all the instances that have been enrolled in the SQL Server Utility. Each SQL Server Utility has only one UCP that you define by clicking on the first link listed in the Utility Configurations Steps. A wizard guides you through the creation.

> **NOTE**
>
> The SQL Server Utility collection set can work side by side with non–SQL Server Utility collection sets, such as those set up for data collection in the MDW. In other words, a managed instance of SQL Server can be monitored by other collection sets while it is

a member of a SQL Server Utility. However, you must disable data collection while the instance of SQL Server is being enrolled into the SQL Server Utility.

In addition, after the instance is enrolled with the UCP, when you restart the non–SQL Server Utility collection sets, all collection sets on the managed instance upload their data to the utility management data warehouse (UMDW), `sysutility_mdw`.

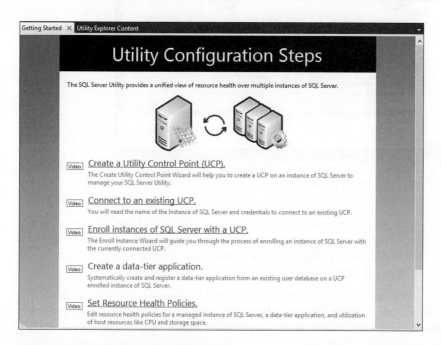

FIGURE 39.14   Utility Configuration Steps.

After you create the UCP, a new tab named Utility Explorer Content is displayed within the Utility Explorer (see Figure 39.15). This Utility Explorer window is also called the SQL Server Utility *dashboard*. This dashboard is the main window for viewing performance metrics captured by the SQL Server Utility. The information displayed on this screen immediately after creating the UCP is the performance information for the UCP itself. Each UCP is automatically a managed instance and thus has performance data collected for it.

The following four performance utilization metrics are captured by the SQL Server Utility and displayed on the Utility Explorer Content screen:

▶ CPU utilized by the SQL Server instance

▶ Database file utilization

▶ Storage volume utilization

▶ CPU utilized by the computer running the instance

39

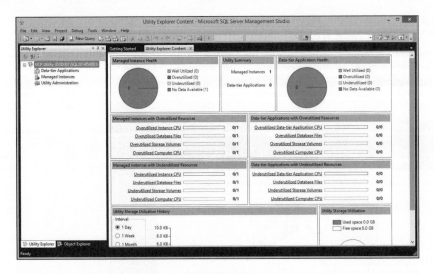

FIGURE 39.15   SQL Server Utility dashboard.

This performance data is broken down based on utilization thresholds and displayed in the dashboard window based on whether the specific metric is overutilized, underutilized, or well utilized. This breakdown is created for each managed instance as well as data-tier applications, a discussion of which is beyond the scope of this chapter.

The key to making this performance information valuable for you is defining the thresholds for each one of these metrics. Overutilization or underutilization, to some degree, is a matter of personal preference. A CPU that is at 70% utilization may be considered overutilized for some but not for others. The thresholds for these metrics can be defined using the Utility Administration node in the Utility Explorer. Figure 39.16 shows the policy screen where the global policies for the managed instances can be defined. These policies are essentially the thresholds for each of the four performance categories displayed in the SQL Server Utility dashboard.

The real power of the SQL Server Utility lies in its capability to collect the kind of performance data that we have been talking about for other SQL Server instances. This multi-server management capability is easy to implement and simply requires that you enroll the other SQL Server instances with the UCP. As mentioned earlier, you can do this by using the third link on the Utility Configuration Steps page. You can also right-click on the Managed Instances node in the Utility Explorer and select Enroll Instance. The Enroll Instance Wizard guides you through the enrollment steps. Upon completion of the wizard, the new instance appears in the Utility Explorer Content tab, as shown in Figure 39.17.

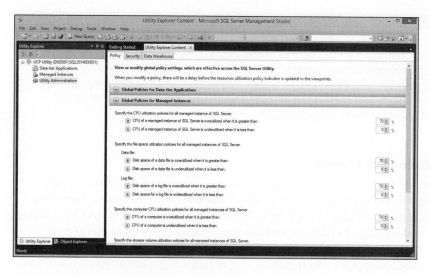

FIGURE 39.16   Global policies for managed instances.

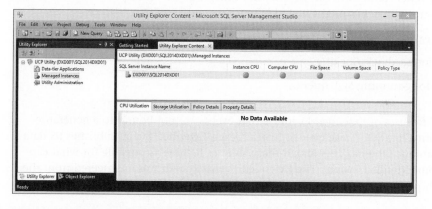

FIGURE 39.17   Managed instances.

The performance data collected by the SQL Server Utility is stored in the utility management data warehouse. The UMDW is a database named `sysutility_mdw` that is automatically created on the UCP instance when the UCP is created. It can be viewed in the list of databases in Object Explorer. By default, each managed instance enrolled in the UCP sends configuration and performance data to the UCP database every 15 minutes. The frequency of data collections provides for a comprehensive set of historical information. This data can be viewed in the Utility Explorer across different intervals, including daily, weekly, monthly, and yearly views. These views provide a sound foundation for identifying problems or identifying trends that can lead to problems in the enrolled SQL Server instances.

> **CAUTION**
>
> The frequency of collection of data in the UMDW database can also lead to a large database. Make sure that you monitor the size of the `sysutility_mdw` database over time. You can manage the data retention period through the SQL Server Utility Explorer. Click on Utility Administration and then select the Data Warehouse tab. You can drag the slider to change the retention period from the default value of one year to one, three, or six months if the UMDW database is becoming too large.

SQL Server Extended Events

SQL Server Extended Events are truly the future event-oriented framework that all SQL Server–based systems and applications will be using going forward. Extended Events are highly flexible to define, are able to capture almost any action or event within your reach, are lightweight in their implementation, and are flexible enough to create simple or complex monitoring across multiple systems and environments. In other words, Extended Events provide a unified approach to handling events across SQL Server systems, while at the same time enabling users to isolate specific events for troubleshooting purposes.

The Extended Events Framework can be utilized to help SQL Server implementations in many ways. Some approaches might include the following:

▶ Isolating excessive CPU utilization

▶ Looking for deadlocks/locking

▶ Locating long-running SQL queries

One of the key features of Extended Events is that events are not bound to a general set of output columns like SQL Trace events. Instead, each Extended Event publishes its data using its own unique schema. This makes the system as flexible as possible for what can be returned from Extended Events. The Extended Events system was engineered from the ground up with performance in mind, so events should have minimal impact on system performance.

Figure 39.18 shows the overall makeup of the SSEE Framework. There is basically an Extended Events engine that runs within SQL Server and drives the event gathering for active sessions. This capability essentially provides a standard and powerful way to dynamically monitor active processes, while at the same time having minimal effect on those processes.

Looking a little closer at Figure 39.18, you can see the concept of Extended Events packages (a package), which contain one or more Extended Events objects. The Extended Events engine allows any event to be bound to any target. In other words, events can push their results to any location for consumption, such as Event Tracing for Windows (ETW), or can be exposed via Views in SMSS, and so on. Predicates are used to filter what events (that are firing) get pushed to the target (consumer). This capability greatly adds to the flexibility of the Extended Events infrastructure.

The next sections examine the main elements of Extended Events.

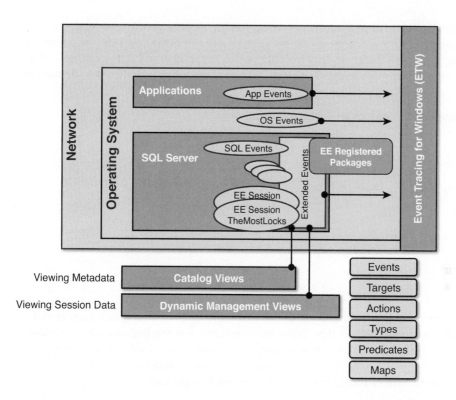

FIGURE 39.18   SQL Server Extended Events Framework.

Packages

A *package* is a container for SQL Server Extended Events objects. It is the basic unit within which all other Extended Events objects ship. Four kinds of Extended Events packages are included in SQL Server 2014:

▶ `package0`—Extended Events system objects. This is the default package.

▶ `sqlserver`—SQL Server-related objects.

▶ `sqlos`—SQL Server Operating System (SQLOS)-related objects.

▶ `SecAudit`—Security Audit events.

> **NOTE**
>
> The `SecAudit` package is used by SQL Server audit. None of the objects in the `SecAudit` package are available through the Extend Events data definition language.

You can see these four packages by running the following query:

```
select * from sys.dm_xe_packages
```

39

Packages can interact with one another to avoid having to provide the same code in multiple contexts. In other words, if one package exposes an action that can be bound to an event, any number of other events in other packages can also use it. For example, the package0 package that ships with SQL Server 2014 contains objects designed to be used by all the other packages.

A package can contain any or all of the following objects:

- ▶ Events
- ▶ Targets
- ▶ Actions
- ▶ Types
- ▶ Predicates
- ▶ Maps

Events

Events are monitoring points of interest in the execution path of a program, such as SQL Server. An event firing indicates that the point of interest was reached and provides state information from the time the event was fired. Events can be used solely for tracing purposes or for triggering actions. These actions can either be synchronous or asynchronous. There can be one or more events in an event session package.

To see a list of the events provided with SQL Server, you can run the following query:

```
select * from sys.dm_xe_objects where object_type = 'event'
```

As stated previously, events have a schema that defines their contents. This schema is composed of event columns with well-defined types. You can view the event schema by querying sys.dm_xe_object_columns, as in the following example:

```
select name, column_id, type_name, column_type
from sys.dm_xe_object_columns
where object_name = 'page_split'
go
```

```
/* output
name                 column_id type_name                  column_type
------------------   --------- -------------------------- -----------
UUID                         0 guid_ptr                   readonly
VERSION                      1 uint8                      readonly
CHANNEL                      2 etw_channel                readonly
KEYWORD                      3 keyword_map                readonly
file_id                      0 uint16                     data
page_id                      1 uint32                     data
database_id                  2 uint32                     data
```

```
rowset_id                      3 uint64                       data
splitOperation                 4 page_split_operation_state   data
new_page_file_id               5 uint16                       data
new_page_page_id               6 uint32                       data
*/
```

Columns marked with `column_type` data are the values that will be filled in at runtime. The read-only columns provide metadata about the event. Notice that one of the columns in the output is the channel for the event; this indicates the category of the event. The available event channels in SQL Server 2014 are as follows:

▶ **Admin**—Admin events are primarily targeted to the end users, administrators, and support. They include events such as error reports and deprecation announcements.

▶ **Operational**—Operational events are used for analyzing and diagnosing a problem or occurrence. They can be used to trigger tools or tasks based on the problem or occurrence. An example of an operational event is one in which a database is attached or detached.

▶ **Analytic**—Analytic events are those that fire on a regular basis, often in high volume. They describe program operation such as lock acquisition and SQL Server statement execution. They are typically aggregated to support performance analysis.

▶ **Debug**—Debug events are used solely by support engineers to help diagnose and solve engine-related problems.

Targets
Targets are event session consumers and indicate where output is located, such as a file, ring buffer, or a bucket with aggregation. Targets can process events synchronously or asynchronously. Extended Events provides several predefined targets you can use as appropriate for directing event output. An example of one of our favorites is provided later in this chapter.

You can find a list of available targets in SQL Server 2014 by running the following query:

```
select * from sys.dm_xe_objects where object_type ='target'
```

Predicates
Predicates are a set of logical evaluation rules for events when they are processed that serve to filter events. They help reduce the volume of captured data and tailor down the output for analysis. In effect, they enable the Extended Events user to selectively capture event data based on specific criteria.

There are two different types of predicates in SQL Server 2014: `pred_compare` and `pred_source`. The `pred_compare` predicates are comparison functions, such as `>=`.

To view a list of the `pred_compare` predicates available in SQL Server 2014, you can run the following query:

```
select * from sys.dm_xe_objects where object_type = 'pred_compare'
```

39

If you run this query, you'll notice that there are a number of similar `pred_compare` predicates with the same comparison function but for different data types (for example, `greater_than_int64` and `greater_than_float64`).

The `pred_source` predicates are extended attributes that can be used within predicates to filter on attributes not carried by the event's own schema (such as `transaction_id` or `database_id`). The available `pred_source` predicates can be listed by using the following query:

```
select * from sys.dm_xe_objects where object_type = 'pred_source'
```

Actions

Actions are programmatic responses or series of responses to an event. Actions are bound to an event, and each event may have a unique set of actions. Actions are performed synchronously in association with bound events. They can be used to accomplish certain tasks or simply provide more information relevant to the events.

There are many types of actions, and they have a wide range of capabilities:

▶ Receive a stack dump and inspect data.

▶ Store state information in a variable.

▶ Bring event data from multiple places together.

▶ Append new data to existing event data.

To view a list of the actions available in SQL Server 2014, you can run the following query:

```
select * from sys.dm_xe_objects where object_type = 'action'
```

Types and Maps

Two kinds of data types can be defined in an event: scalar types and maps. Scalar types are single values, like integers. Maps are tables that map internal object values to static, predefined, user-friendly descriptions. They help you see what the internal values stand for (making them human consumable) but allow the event to more efficiently store the integer map value rather than the actual text.

Like all the other elements discussed thus far, types and maps can also be viewed by querying the `sys.dm_xe_objects` catalog view:

```
select * from sys.dm_xe_objects
where object_type in ('type', 'map')
```

Although types are relatively self-explanatory, maps require a lookup to expose the associated human-readable text when appropriate. The map values are stored in the DMV called `sys.dm_xe_map_values`. To list the `map_keys` and `map_values` for lock types, for example, you can run the following query:

```
select * from sys.dm_xe_map_values where name = 'lock_mode'
```

Extended Events Catalog Views and DMVs

To get metadata information about what events, actions, fields, and targets have been defined, you can use the catalog views supplied with SQL Server.

For catalog views, the following short list shows the SELECT statements and their purposes (that use the predefined Extended Events catalog views).

To list the defined event sessions, you use the following:

```
SELECT * FROM sys.server_event_sessions;
```

To list the actions on each event (of an event session), run this:

```
SELECT * FROM sys.server_event_session_actions;
```

To list the events in an event session, run the following:

```
SELECT * FROM sys.server_event_session_events;
```

To list the defined columns of events and targets in the event sessions, use this statement:

```
SELECT * FROM sys.server_event_session_fields;
```

And, to list the event targets for an event session, you use the following:

```
SELECT * FROM sys.server_event_session_targets;
```

You use the dynamic management objects to obtain session metadata and session data itself (as it is being gathered during execution). The metadata is obtained from the catalog views, and the session data is created when you start and run an event session.

To list the session dispatcher pools, you use the following statement:

```
SELECT * FROM sys.dm_os_dispatcher_pools;
```

To list the event package objects, use this:

```
SELECT * FROM sys.dm_xe_objects;
```

To list the schema for all objects, run this statement:

```
SELECT * FROM sys.dm_xe_object_columns;
```

To list the registered packages in the Extended Events engine, use this:

```
SELECT * FROM sys.dm_xe_packages;
```

To list the active Extended Events sessions, run the following:

```
SELECT * FROM sys.dm_xe_sessions;
```

To list the session targets, run this statement:

```
SELECT * FROM sys.dm_xe_session_targets;
```

To list the defined session events, use this:

```
SELECT * FROM sys.dm_xe_session_events;
```

To list the defined event session actions, use this:

```
SELECT * FROM sys.dm_xe_session_event_actions;
```

To view the mapping of internal keys to readable text, use the following:

```
SELECT * FROM sys.dm_xe_map_values;
```

Specific variations might be as follows:

```
SELECT map_value Keyword from sys.dm_xe_map_values
where name = 'keyword_map';
```

```
SELECT map_key, map_value from sys.dm_xe_map_values
where name = 'lock_mode';
```

And finally, to list the configuration values for objects bound to a session, you use the following:

```
SELECT * FROM sys.dm_xe_session_object_columns;
```

Creating and Managing Extended Events Sessions in SSMS

In SQL Server 2008, setup and management of Extended Events was entirely T-SQL based. (There was no GUI tool available for Extended Events.) In addition, viewing the information captured by Extended Events was possible only through T-SQL queries. Fortunately, SQL Server 2014 has remedied this situation by incorporating a GUI into SSMS for creating and managing Extended Events sessions as well as viewing the information captured.

To view or create Extended Events sessions in SSMS, expand the SQL Server instance in the Object Explorer, then expand the Management folder, and then expand Extended Events and expand the Sessions folder. Within the Sessions folder, you will see a list of the defined Extended Events sessions (see Figure 39.19).

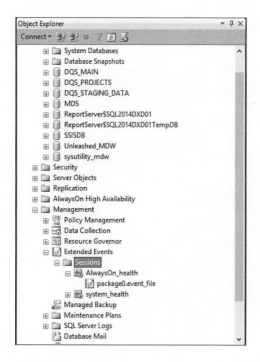

FIGURE 39.19   Viewing Extended Events sessions in SSMS.

As you can see in Figure 39.19, SQL Server 2014 ships with two Extended Events sessions already defined: the `AlwaysOn_health` session and the `system_health` session.

The `AlwaysOn_health` session is a preconfigured Extended Events session for monitoring and troubleshooting AlwaysOn Availability Groups. For more information on AlwaysOn Availability Groups, see Chapter 45, "SQL Server AlwaysOn and Availability Groups."

The `system_health` session is included by default with SQL Server and starts automatically when the SQL Server Database Engine starts. The `system_health` session collects system data that you can use to help troubleshoot performance issues in the Database Engine. The `system_health` session runs with little to no noticeable performance impact on SQL Server, and it is recommended that you do not stop or delete the session. The information captured by the `system_health` session and how you can use it is covered later in this section.

There are two ways to create Extended Events sessions in SSMS: the New Session Wizard or the New Session dialog. If you are new to Extended Events, it's probably best to start with the wizard, so that's what we'll take a look at first.

Using the New Extended Events Session Wizard

To launch the New Session Wizard, right-click on the Sessions folder and select New Session Wizard. This will initially bring up the Introduction page. Click Next on the Introduction page to bring up the Set Session Properties page, as shown in Figure 39.20.

39

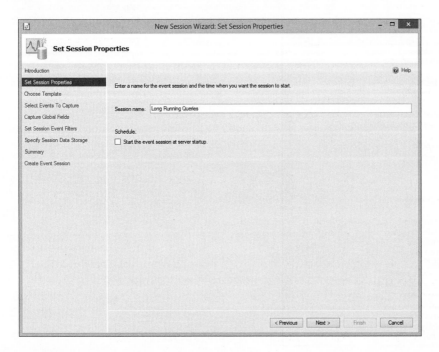

FIGURE 39.20   The Set Session Properties page.

On this page, you enter the name of the session and whether you want this Extended Events session to start automatically whenever SQL Server starts. After entering a name for the session, click Next to bring up the Choose Template page, as shown in Figure 39.21.

On the Choose Template page, you can choose to use one of the provided event session templates or to start without a template. The templates are preconfigured sessions designed for common problems. Selecting a template will prepopulate your session with the typical events and fields normally used for that type of session. The following is a list of the templates currently provided:

- **Count Query Locks**—Captures the number of locks acquired by each query, which can be useful to identify the most lock intensive queries.

- **Query Batch Sampling**—Collects detailed information on a sampling of the batch and RPC level statements as well as error information. By default, events are only collected from 20% of the active sessions on the server at any given time.

- **Query Batch Tracking**—Collects all batch and RPC level statements as well as error information. (Collection size may be very large.) To reduce the collection size, consider applying a filter.

- **Query Detail Sampling**—Collects detailed information on a sampling of each statement executing on your system as a result of query batches or stored procedures and tracks any errors back to the specific statement that caused them. By default, events are captured on 20% of the active sessions on the server at any given time.

▶ **Query Detail Tracking**—Collects detailed information on all statements executing on your system as a result of query batches or stored procedures as well as any error. Without filtering, collection size can be extremely large, especially on very busy systems.

▶ **Query Wait Statistic**—Collects internal and external wait statistics for a sampling of the individual query statements, batches, and RPCs. Events are only collected from 20% of the active sessions on the server at any given time.

▶ **Activity Tracking**—Collects general activity on the system, similar to the Default Trace that exists in the SQL Trace system, but without including security audit events. (Audit events should be tracked using the SQL Server Audit feature.)

▶ **Connection Tracking**—Collects connection activity for a server by tracking the login and logout events. Problems are recorded using the `connectivity_ring_buffer_recorded` event.

▶ **Database Log File IO Tracking**—Collects I/O monitoring information for database logs by capturing asynchronous I/O, database log flushes, file writes, spinlock back-offs of type `LOGFLUSHQ` and waits of type `WRITELOG`.

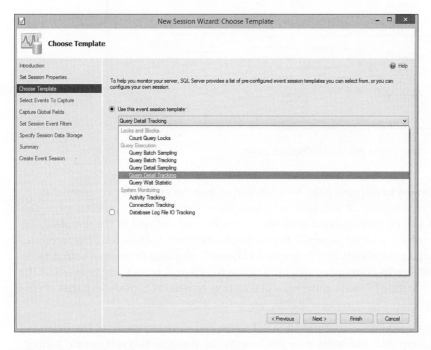

FIGURE 39.21   The Choose Template page.

You can add your own templates to SSMS, as well, if you've built out event sessions that you'd like to use as a basis for creating future sessions. In the SSMS Object Explorer, right-click on the template you want to use as a template and select Export Session. By default, it saves the session template in the `Documents\SQL Server Management Studio\Templates\XEventTemplates` folder for the current user.

Once you've decided on a template to use, click Next to bring up the Select Events to Capture page (we've selected the Query Detail Tracking template), as shown in Figure 39.22.

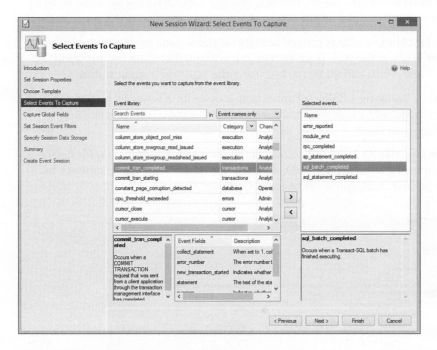

FIGURE 39.22   The Select Events to Capture page.

On the Select Events to Capture page, you can add or remove events to be captured in the Extended Event Session. If you selected a template on the Choose Template page, the Selected Events will be prepopulated with the events that are defined in the template. As you can see, you have a lot of potential events to choose from. Fortunately, the interface enables you to filter the events by category and channel, and also provides a search facility to help locate events containing specific keywords. When you click on an event in the Event Library or Selected Events window, a description of what is captured by that event is displayed.

If you have any experience working with SQL Profiler trace events, many of the Extended Events may look familiar, but some may not be quite as obvious. You can use the following query to list the Extended Events, which are equivalent to SQL trace events:

```
SELECT DISTINCT
    tb.trace_event_id,
    te.name AS 'Event Class',
    em.package_name AS 'Package',
```

```
    em.xe_event_name AS 'XEvent Name',
    tb.trace_column_id,
    tc.name AS 'SQL Trace Column',
    am.xe_action_name as 'Extended Events action'
 FROM (sys.trace_events te
    LEFT OUTER JOIN sys.trace_xe_event_map em
    ON te.trace_event_id = em.trace_event_id)
    LEFT OUTER JOIN sys.trace_event_bindings tb
    ON em.trace_event_id = tb.trace_event_id
    LEFT OUTER JOIN sys.trace_columns tc
    ON tb.trace_column_id = tc.trace_column_id
    LEFT OUTER JOIN sys.trace_xe_action_map am
    ON tc.trace_column_id = am.trace_column_id
 ORDER BY te.name, tc.name
```

Once you have selected the events you want to capture, click on Next to bring up the Capture Global Fields screen, as shown in Figure 39.23.

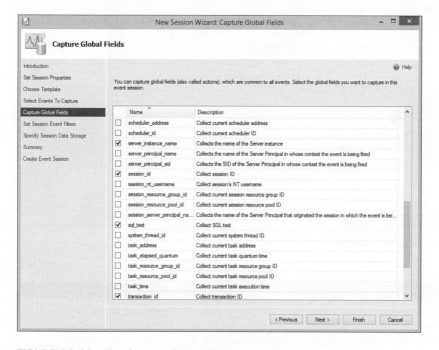

FIGURE 39.23   The Capture Global Fields page.

On the Capture Global Fields page, you specify which fields (that is, columns) of information you want to capture for the events in your session. Again, if you started with a template, the fields defined in the template are preselected. You can select or remove any fields as desired. By default, the fields are sorted by name. However, you can click on the top of the check box column to sort the events by selected/deselected. After making your selections, click Next to move on to specifying any filters for the event session.

Filters (also referred to as predicates) are used to limit the events you want to capture. It's important to specify filters if you are not sampling events to limit the number of events being captured. If you specified a template to create the event session, the Filters from template box will be prepopulated and you cannot modify or remove these filters (see Figure 39.24). You can add additional filters if you want. For example, if you want to capture only long-running queries, you might want to set a filter on Duration to limit the session to capturing only events that exceed the specified duration threshold.

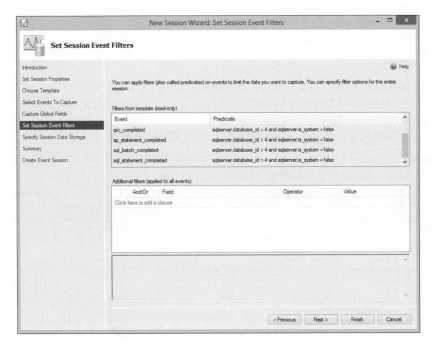

FIGURE 39.24   Specifying session event filters.

> **NOTE**
>
> Unfortunately, the New Session Wizard currently only supports specifying filters that apply to all events. The New Session Wizard does not support configuring event-specific filters. To set an event-specific filter, such as Duration for `sql_batch_completed` or `rpc_completed` events, you'll need to modify the Extended Events session after you've created it via the wizard. You will learn how to modify Extended Events sessions later in this section.

Once you have added any additional filters you want to apply, click Next to move to specify where you want the captured events stored on the Specify Session Data Storage page (see Figure 39.25) The two options available are to save to a file and/or to save to a `ring_buffer`. The `ring_buffer` is an in-memory structure that uses one of two FIFO modes of holding the captured events in memory. The first mode is the simple FIFO mode where the oldest event is discarded when the memory allocated to the ring buffer is exhausted. The other mode is a per-event FIFO method where a specified number of events of each type are kept and only the oldest events of each type are discarded when the limit on each event has been reached.

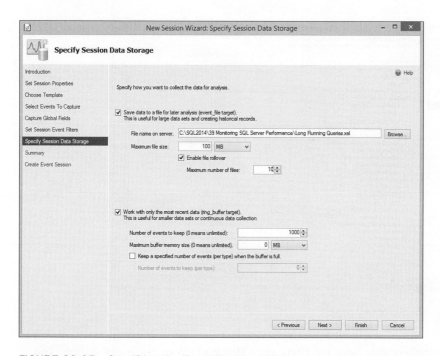

FIGURE 39.25   Specifying the Event Session target.

The `ring_buffer` target is useful typically for live monitoring or when you only want to examine the recent activity that has been captured. If you want to keep a history of the events captured, you will want to specify a file as the event target. To save to a file, select the Save Data to a File for Later Analysis check box and then specify the path and filename of a file and the server where you want to save the data. You can specify the maximum size of the file and optionally specify whether you want to enable file rollover when the maximum file size is reached and the maximum number of rollover files you want it to create.

When an event file target is created, the filename you specify is appended with `_0_` and a long integer value that is calculated as the number of milliseconds between January 1, 1600, and the date and time the file is created.

After you finish setting up your event session targets, click Next to bring up the Summary page (see Figure 39.26). On the Summary page, you can review the selections you made to verify they are correct before you create the session. You can also click the Script button to create a T-SQL Script to create the Extended Events session. Creating a script is useful if you want to re-create the session in the future without having to go through all the steps in the wizard again.

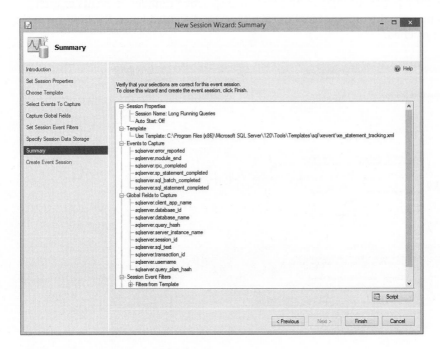

FIGURE 39.26   The Summary page.

Once you are satisfied with your selections, click Finish to Create the event session. You should then be presented with the Create Event Session page, as shown in Figure 39.27.

You have two options available on the Summary page to specify if you want to have SQL Server start the event session when you close the wizard and whether to have SSMS open up a window to view the events live on the screen as they are captured.

Using the New Session Dialog

Once you are more familiar with creating Extended Events sessions or want more flexibility in defining them (especially setting more advanced event filters), you may want to skip the New Session Wizard and just jump right into the New Session dialog. You can invoke the New Session dialog by right-clicking on the Sessions folder in SSMS and selecting New Session. The New Session dialog consists of four property pages (General, Events, Data Storage, and Advanced), starting with the General page shown in Figure 39.28.

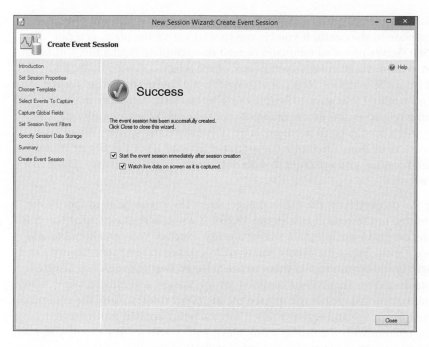

FIGURE 39.27   The Create Event Session page.

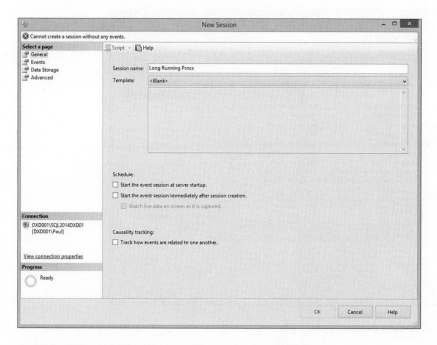

FIGURE 39.28   The New Session General Properties page.

On the General Properties page, you can specify the Event Session name and option-ally specify a template to start with. If you choose to start with a template, you can use one of the SQL Server-provided templates or read in a template from a file. Unlike the New Session Wizard, you can fully modify any of the selected events, fields, and filters imported from the template. You can also specify the startup properties for the Event Session and whether you want to enable causality tracking. Causality tracking enables correlating related events across different user sessions. When causality tracking is enabled, each event fired is given a unique activity ID across the system. When one session causes work to be done on another session, the activity ID of the parent session is sent to the child session, and the child session outputs the parent's activity ID the first time it fires an event.

After specifying the properties on the General page, select the Events page to specify the events to be captured in the session (see Figure 39.29). If you specified a template on the General page, the events in the template will be already selected. You can choose to add events or remove events. Select the events you want to capture in the Event Library panel and click the right arrow button to add them to the Selected Events panel. The Selected Events panel lists the events that will be captured for the session and indicates how many global fields (that is, actions) are being captured for the event (indicated by the column with the lightning bolt icon) and whether any filters are being applied for that event (indicated by the column with the funnel icon). Once you've selected the events you want to capture in the session, the next step is to configure each of the events.

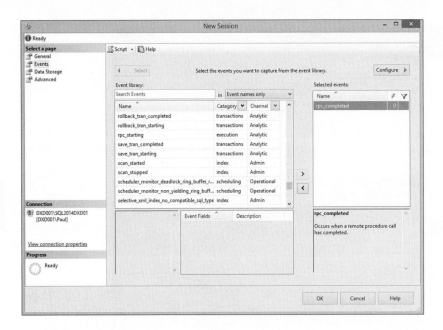

FIGURE 39.29 The New Session Events Properties page.

To configure the events, select the event in the Selected Events panel and click on the Configure button. This changes the Events Page to the view shown in Figure 39.30. In the Event Fields tab, you can select any additional event field you want to capture for the selected event. Any fields that are displayed on the Event Fields tab without check boxes represent fields that are always collected for that event. Other optional fields may also be checked by default. To select or deselect any of the optional fields, set or clear the check box in front of the optional field.

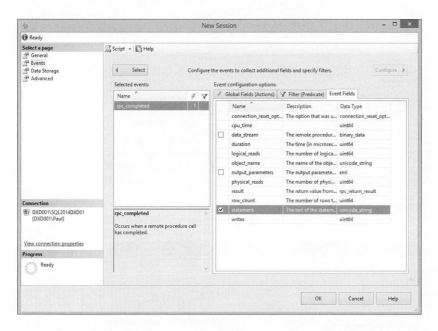

FIGURE 39.30   The Configure Event page.

On the Filter (Predicate) tab, you can specify any optional filters for the selected event (see Figure 39.31). Note that all event filters are available in this dialog, unlike the New Session Wizard, which only allows you to set filters on global fields.

On the Global Fields (Actions) tab (see Figure 39.32), you can select which Extended Events global fields you want to include in the event session. Note that you can sort the global fields by any of the three columns by clicking on the column header, to make it easier to identify the fields you want to filter on. For example, in Figure 39.32, the fields have been sorted by whether they have been selected.

After configuring the selected event, select another event in the Selected Events panel to specify the fields and any filters for that event. If you want to add additional events to the session, click on the Select button to go back to the Select Events page. If you are finished specifying the events you want to include in the session, click on Data Storage to bring up the Data Storage page, where you can specify the target(s) for storing the event data (see Figure 39.33).

39

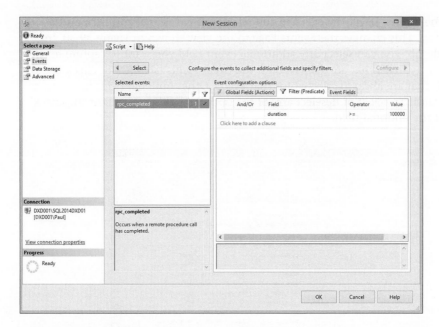

FIGURE 39.31   Specifying filters for an event.

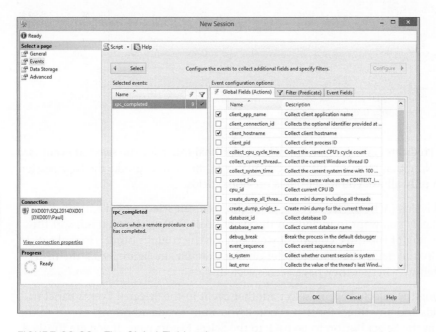

FIGURE 39.32   The Global Fields tab.

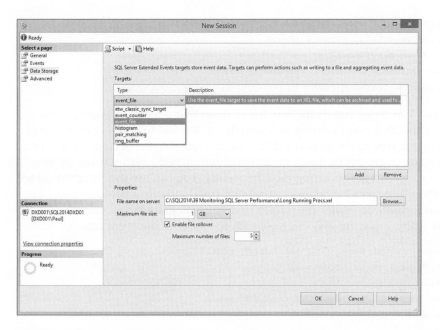

FIGURE 39.33   Selecting targets on the Data Storage page.

NOTE

While tempting, resist the urge to click the OK button to save the changes you've made for your event fields or event filters. Clicking OK does not take you to the Data Storage page but instead saves the event session and closes the dialog without giving you the opportunity to specify additional settings. If you do accidentally click on OK, you can always go back in and modify/add additional settings by right-clicking on the session in SSMS and selecting the Properties option.

On the Data Storage page, you can choose to save the events to file or a ring buffer as discussed previously. In addition, there are four other targets you can choose from for the event session:

▶ **etw_classic_sync_target**—This target is used to correlate SQL Server events with Windows operating system or application event data. Data is stored in an Event Tracking for Windows (ETW) event log.

▶ **event_counter**—This target simply counts all specified events that occur after an Extended Events session is started. This is useful for obtaining information about workload characteristics (that is, how many times certain events are triggered) without adding the overhead of full event collection. This counter has no configurable options. To view the output from the event counter target, you can use the following query (replace session_name with the name of the event session):

```
SELECT name, target_name, CAST(xet.target_data AS xml)
FROM sys.dm_xe_session_targets AS xet
JOIN sys.dm_xe_sessions AS xe
    ON (xe.address = xet.event_session_address)
WHERE xe.name = 'session_name'
```

▶ **histogram**—This target counts the number of times that a specified event occurs, based on a specified event column or action. It can be used to group occurrences of a specific event type based on event data such as a specified event column or action. The histogram target can be useful for troubleshooting performance issues by identifying which events are occurring most frequently. You can use this information to help identify "hot spots" or "chokepoints" that could indicate a potential cause of performance issues. To review the output from the histogram target, you can use the following query, replacing session_name with the name of the event session:

```
SELECT name, target_name, CAST(xet.target_data AS xml)
FROM sys.dm_xe_session_targets AS xet
JOIN sys.dm_xe_sessions AS xe
    ON (xe.address = xet.event_session_address)
WHERE xe.name = 'session_name'
```

▶ **pair_matching**—Use to determine when a specified paired event does not occur in a matched set. Many events come in pairs (for example, lock acquisition and lock release). Event pairing matches paired events using one or more columns of data that are present in each event, and if an event sequence is paired, both events are discarded. By discarding matched sets, the event session includes only unpaired events, such as lock acquisitions that have not been released.

NOTE

For more detailed information on the etw_classic_sync_target, histogram, and pair_matching Extended Events targets and the available options for them, refer to the Extended Events Targets topic in the SQL Server Help Library.

Once you have specified the target(s) for your Extended Events session, the last step is to specify any advanced options on the Advanced page (see Figure 39.34). On this page, you can specify the event retention mode, maximum dispatch latency, max memory and event size, and the memory partition mode.

Event retention mode (EVENT_RETENTION_MODE) specifies how the event session should handle event loss. The recommended setting, Single Event Loss, allows a single event to be dropped if the event buffers are full. Allowing a single event to be lost when event buffers are full provides for acceptable SQL Server performance characteristics, while minimizing the loss of data in the processed event stream. If you select Multiple Event Loss, full event buffers containing multiple events can be lost from the session. The number of events lost depends on the memory size allocated to the session, the partitioning of the memory, and the size of the events in the buffer. This option ensures minimal performance impact on the server under circumstances where event buffers are filling too quickly (for example, capturing too many events on a very busy system), but it could result in large numbers of events being lost from the session. Selecting No Event Loss ensures that all events raised will be retained. This option is not recommended because it forces all tasks that fire events to wait until space is available in an event buffer. As you can surmise, this can lead to noticeable performance issues while the event session is active and user sessions are forced to wait for events to be flushed from the buffer.

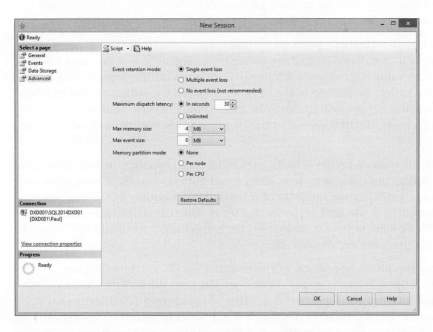

FIGURE 39.34   Specifying advanced event session options.

NOTE

You can determine whether events are being dropped from a session by querying the `dm_xe_sessions` DMV and looking at the `dropped_event_count` field. Dropping of events usually isn't a huge problem especially if you are collecting query performance statistics over thousands of query executions. However, if you find the number of events lost is excessive, you may want to consider either decreasing the number of events being captured or increasing the size of the event buffer via the `MAX_MEMORY` option.

The Max memory size option (`MAX_MEMORY`) specifies the maximum amount of memory to allocate to the session for event buffering. (Note that this is only the amount of memory to allocate for the event buffer, not for the entire event session. That is determined by the ring buffer size.) The default setting for `MAX_MEMORY` is 4MB. By default, this memory is divided up into three buffers of equal size so that a session can be publishing events to one buffer while other buffers are being processed. By default, each buffer will be approximately 1.3MB in size (4MB divided by 3).

39

At times, certain single events may be too large to fit in the event buffer. You can determine if your session is dropping large events by looking at the `dm_xe_sessions` DMV and checking the `largest_event_dropped_size` value. If this value is larger than one third the size of your event buffer (`MAX_MEMORY`), you may want to configure Max Event Size. The Max Event Size option (`MAX_EVENT_SIZE`) specifies the maximum allowable size for events. The `MAX_EVENT_SIZE` option should be set to a value larger than max memory. When max event size is set to a value other than zero, two buffers of the specified size are created in addition to max memory. The total memory used for event buffering will then be max memory plus two times the max event size.

The Maximum Dispatch Latency option (`MAX_DISPATCH_LATENCY`) specifies the amount of time that events will be buffered in memory before being dispatched to the event session targets. The default value is 30 seconds. A value of 0 indicates infinite latency, which indicates that the buffers are flushed to the targets only when the buffers are full or when the event session closes. If you will primarily be monitoring the event session "live," you may want to set a lower dispatch latency so the events are presented more closely in "real time."

The memory partition mode option (`MEMORY_PARTITION_MODE`) specifies the location of the internal event buffers and determines how many event buffers to create. A value of `NONE` is the default and creates just the single set of three buffers within the SQL Server instance as discussed previously. If `PER_NODE` is specified, a set of buffers is created for each NUMA node (3 times the number of nodes), and if `PER_CPU` is specified, a set of buffers is created for each CPU (2.5 times the number of CPUs).

After configuring the advanced options, before you click on OK to create the event session, you can script out your configured event session from the user interface by clicking on the Script button at the top of the page. This will generate a T-SQL script that you can use to create the event session. Generating a T-SQL script to create the session can be useful to re-create the session on another SQL Server instance without having to go through all the pages and options of the New Session dialog. Once you click on OK to create the session, the commands to create the session will be executed. The session will then be visible in the Sessions folder in the Object Explorer in SSMS. From there, you can manage and work with the defined event sessions.

Managing and Working with Sessions in SSMS

Within SSMS 2014, for the event sessions that have been defined, you can view and modify session properties, start and stop event sessions, export event sessions as templates, generate a script containing the T-SQL commands to create the event session, and one of the more useful capabilities of SSMS 2012 is the ability to view the target data of the event session or view the live data being captured by an actively running session.

You can change the configuration of an event session by right-clicking the session name in Object Explorer and clicking Properties. The same user interface will be presented as in the New Session dialog, but showing the currently configured settings. Most settings can be changed on a running session, but changes to any of the advanced options will require the session to be stopped. Also, you cannot change the settings (such as the file location) of a target configuration (Data Storage option) for an event session. You will have to delete the target and re-add it to change that. Be aware that deleting an event file target from the session properties will also delete any target data, so be sure you've saved the target file(s) in another location first.

Most of the event session actions available within SSMS are accessible by right-clicking on the session name in the Sessions folder (see Figure 39.35). From the context menu that comes up, you can open the session Properties dialog, start and stop the session, export the session to a template, script the session, or delete the session definition.

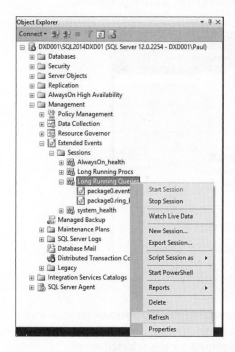

FIGURE 39.35   Event session context menu.

Viewing Event Session Data in SSMS

To view the events captured by an event session, expand the session in the Sessions folder to list the event package targets (as shown in Figure 39.35). There are essentially two types of event session data displays: in-memory targets and event stream and event file targets.

In-memory targets include the ring buffer, event counter, histogram, and event paring targets. The data from these will be displayed in SSMS in a simple grid format showing a point in time view of the data at the time you opened the data target. To refresh the view, you can right-click in the table to manually refresh the data, or you can set an automatic refresh interval. However, the ring buffer is an exception. Viewing the ring buffer in SSMS shows just a single row containing the XML output of the ring buffer. Double-clicking the row opens the document in the XML viewer in SSMS, but it's not nearly as readable as a grid view of the events.

What you will most likely end up viewing in SSMS is the event file or the event session live view. You can open the live view of a running session by right-clicking on the session name and choosing the Watch Live Data menu item. This will open a page in SSMS that provides you with a scrolling display of the events as they come from the event session (see Figure 39.36). Viewing the live data is very similar to viewing a live trace in SQL Profiler. The main difference with viewing Extended Events live data is that Extended Events does not cause the performance degradation associated with SQL Profiler.

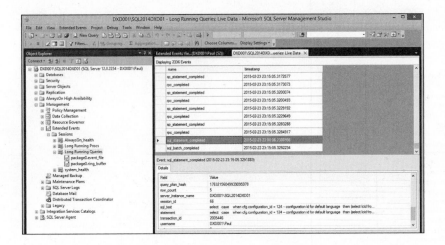

FIGURE 39.36   Viewing a live event session in SSMS.

By default, the Live Event Stream shows the list of events in the top window pane. If you select one of the events, the details for the captured event are displayed in the bottom window pane. The details pane displays the fields captured for the selected event.

Within SSMS, you can also open an event file target to view the events captured by an event session. You can right-click on the `Package0.event_file` item and select View Target Data, or you can open an XEL file directly into SSMS via the File menu in SSMS or by double-clicking or simply dragging an XEL file onto the SSMS window. You can also open multiple files into a single view by selecting Open on the File menu and choosing Merge Extended Events Files and using the dialog to collect multiple files to be merged into a single view.

Event files are displayed in the same user interface in SSMS as the Live Event Stream.

When you are viewing an event file or event stream, SSMS displays a new toolbar. The tools available in this toolbar include the following:

▶ **Start Data Feed/Stop Data Feed**—Applies only when viewing live data to start or stop the live data feed.

▶ **Clear Data from Table**—Applies only when viewing live data to clear the current contents of the display.

▶ **Enable Auto Scroll**—Like the same feature in SQL Profiler, applies only when viewing live data to keep moving the point of focus to the last event captured.

▶ **Show Details Pane**—Opens or closes the details pane.

▶ **Filters**—Provides a way to specify time or value filters on the event fields to limit the events that are displayed.

▶ **Grouping and Aggregation**—Provides a way to do some basic analysis of the event data directly in the UI.

▶ **Bookmarks**—Provides a way to mark selected events so that you can find them again quickly with the Bookmark navigation buttons.

▶ **Find in Extended Events Window**—A standard SSMS Find dialog to locate items in all or selected table columns.

▶ **Choose Columns**—Lets you specify additional columns to display in the grid.

▶ **Display Settings**—Provides a way to save the configuration of the display (columns, filter, sorting, and group/aggregation).

All of these toolbar items are also available under the Extended Events menu item, plus an additional Export option. This option lets you export the list of events currently displayed to an XEL file, a SQL Server table, or a CSV file. This option is not available when viewing live data.

One of the more useful of the tools is Choose Columns. By default, SSMS only displays the event name and the event timestamp. Most likely, you'll want to display more columns in the tabular format. Click the Choose Columns option in the toolbar or right-click on a column heading and select Choose Columns. This brings up the Choose Columns dialog shown in Figure 39.37. Select the columns you want to display by double-clicking a column in the Available Columns panel or select one or more columns and click the right arrow to move them over to the Selected Columns pane. Click OK to save the changes.

The Filter tool is also very useful and a significant improvement over SQL Profiler. You can limit the events viewed to a specified time period and add a number of additional filters on the fields captured in the event trace. An example of the Filters tool is shown in Figure 39.38. You can also quickly add filters by right-clicking on a cell in the grid and selecting Filter by This Value.

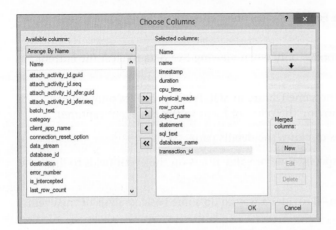

FIGURE 39.37   Choosing session event columns to display.

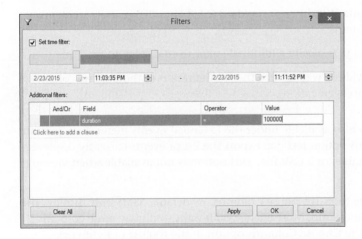

FIGURE 39.38   Specifying session event display filters.

The Grouping and Aggregation tools are also an enticing feature in SSMS for analyzing session event data. You can group results similar to using the GROUP BY clause in Transact-SQL. The data grouped together in the grid is based upon the column or columns you choose to group on, and you can expand and collapse the data. After grouping the data, you can then aggregate it (as shown in Figure 39.39).

Creating and Managing Extended Events Sessions in T-SQL
The new interface in SSMS makes it much easier to create and manage Extended Events sessions, as well as script them out, but you might sometimes have to create an Extended Events session from scratch without the GUI—for example, if you are working in a SQL Server 2008 environment where the GUI tools are not available.

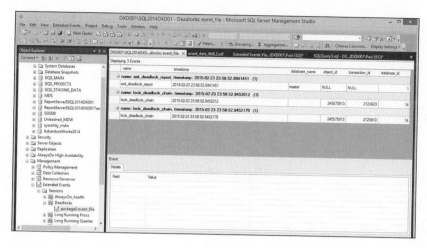

FIGURE 39.39   Using grouping and aggregation for viewing Extended Events session data.

Creating events (event sessions) is performed using the CREATE, ALTER and DROP EVENT statements. These Data Definition Language (DDL) statements completely control the creation and activation of Extended Events. All the Extended Events objects are created in the msdb database. Only those users with CONTROL SERVER permissions can create, alter, or drop Extended Events objects. To use the catalog and dynamic management views, you need at least VIEW SERVER STATE permission.

The example shown in Listing 39.3 creates an Extended Events session to capture deadlock events. As you examine the CREATE EVENT SESSION T-SQL code in Listing 39.3, notice that two events are being added with the ADD EVENT statements. One will gather the standard deadlock chain information, and the other will retrieve the XML based deadlock report. Also, notice the TARGET statement specifies a filename where the deadlock events will be captured.

The CREATE EVENT SESSION T-SQL code is as follows:

LISTING 39.3   Creating an Event Session Named Deadlocks Using T-SQL

```
IF EXISTS(SELECT * FROM sys.server_event_sessions WHERE name='Deadlocks')
DROP EVENT session Deadlocks ON SERVER;

CREATE EVENT SESSION [Deadlocks] ON SERVER
    ADD EVENT sqlserver.xml_deadlock_report (
        ACTION (sqlserver.database_id, sqlserver.database_name)),
    ADD EVENT sqlserver.lock_deadlock_chain (
        ACTION (sqlserver.database_id, sqlserver.database_name))
    ADD TARGET package0.event_file
        (SET filename = N'C:\SQL2014\\Deadlocks.xel')
```

39

```
WITH (MAX_MEMORY = 4096 KB,
       EVENT_RETENTION_MODE = ALLOW_SINGLE_EVENT_LOSS,
       MAX_DISPATCH_LATENCY = 30 SECONDS,
       MAX_EVENT_SIZE = 0 KB,
       MEMORY_PARTITION_MODE = NONE,
       TRACK_CAUSALITY = OFF,
       STARTUP_STATE = ON)
GO
```

After the event session is created, you can start it by using the ALTER EVENT SESSION command:

```
-- START EVENT SESSION
ALTER EVENT SESSION Deadlocks ON SERVER STATE=start;
:
```

Now, let's generate some activity on the server that will be captured by the event session. To do this, you need to set up two sessions within SSMS to create a deadlock between them. Using the AdventureWorks2014 database, you can enter the following transactions into each of the two sessions, but don't execute them just yet:

```
--- Step 1 - run in each session first
USE AdventureWorks2014;
BEGIN TRAN
SELECT * FROM DatabaseLog dl WITH (HOLDLOCK)

--- Step 2
DELETE DATABASELog

-- Step 3
ROLLBACK
```

Okay, now in each of the two sessions, highlight and run the commands listed in step 1 to begin a transaction and have each session acquire and hold shared locks on the DatabaseLog table. Once the step 1 statements have been executed in each session, execute the DELETE statement in each session separately. You should see both sessions "suspended" as they are waiting to acquire the exclusive lock. Eventually, one of the sessions should generate a deadlock error. At this point, execute step 3 in the session that wasn't chosen as the deadlock victim.

Now, at this point, we should have a deadlock event captured in the Deadlocks Extended Events session target. You probably now want to examine the deadlock information captured. If you've captured the events to a target file (as we've done in this example), you can view the events captured in the file using the sys.fn_xe_file_target_read_file function. The syntax of this function is as follows:

```
sys.fn_xe_file_target_read_file ( path, mdpath, initial_file_name, initial_offset )
```

The `path` argument is the pathname to the target file including the file name. The path can also contain wildcards so that you only need to specify the root filename without having to know the full filename with the system-generated timestamp. The `mdpath` argument is not required in SQL Server 2014 and is maintained for backward compatibility. `initial_file_name` is an `nvarchar(260)` and specifies the first file to read from the path. If null is specified, all the files found in the path are read. `initial_offset` is used to specify the number of events to skip when reading from the file. If null is specified as the argument, the entire file is read.

Before you can read the file, you need to know the path and filename of the file, which you can get from the system catalogs with a query similar to the following (replacing the value for `session_name` with the name of the event session you want to get the filename for):

```
SELECT CONVERT(nvarchar(260),field.value)
FROM
    sys.server_event_sessions AS SESSION
        INNER join
    sys.server_event_session_targets AS TARGET
        ON session.event_session_id = target.event_session_id
        INNER JOIN
    sys.dm_xe_object_columns AS col
        ON target.name = col.object_name
        AND col.column_type = 'customizable'
        LEFT OUTER JOIN
    sys.server_event_session_fields AS field
        ON target.event_session_id = field.event_session_id
        AND target.target_id = field.object_id
        AND col.name = field.name
WHERE
    target.package + '.' + target.name='package0.event_file'
    AND session.name='event_session_name'
    AND col.name = 'filename'
```

Listing 39.4 incorporates the preceding query to retrieve the contents from the target file for the Deadlocks Extended Events session. The results of the query when run in SSMS as grid results are shown in Figure 39.40.

LISTING 39.4   Reading Events from a Session Target File

```
DECLARE @filename nvarchar(1024) =
(SELECT
    -- @filename = CONVERT(nvarchar(1024), field.value)
    REPLACE( CONVERT(nvarchar(1024), field.value), '.xel', '*.xel')
FROM
    sys.server_event_sessions AS SESSION
        INNER join
```

```
    sys.server_event_session_targets AS TARGET
        ON session.event_session_id = target.event_session_id
        INNER JOIN
    sys.dm_xe_object_columns AS col
        ON target.name = col.object_name
        AND col.column_type = 'customizable'
        LEFT OUTER JOIN
    sys.server_event_session_fields AS field
        ON target.event_session_id = field.event_session_id
        AND target.target_id = field.object_id
        AND col.name = field.name
WHERE
    target.package + '.' + target.name='package0.event_file'
    AND session.name='Deadlocks'
    AND col.name = 'filename'
)
SELECT FILE_NAME, OBJECT_NAME, CAST(event_data AS XML) AS 'event_data_XML'
FROM sys.fn_xe_file_target_read_file(@filename, NULL, null, null)
```

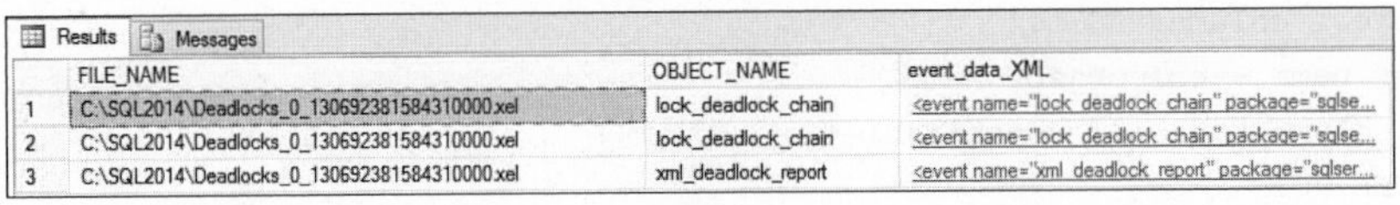

	FILE_NAME	OBJECT_NAME	event_data_XML
1	C:\SQL2014\Deadlocks_0_130692381584310000.xel	lock_deadlock_chain	<event name="lock_deadlock_chain" package="sqlse...
2	C:\SQL2014\Deadlocks_0_130692381584310000.xel	lock_deadlock_chain	<event name="lock_deadlock_chain" package="sqlse...
3	C:\SQL2014\Deadlocks_0_130692381584310000.xel	xml_deadlock_report	<event name="xml_deadlock_report" package="sqlser...

FIGURE 39.40   Events captured by the Deadlocks Extended Events session.

When you return a column of XML data type in SSMS to grid results, the XML data is converted to a hyperlink. Clicking on the data value in the grid results will open it in an XML window in SSMS. Figure 39.41 shows an example of the event_data_XML value for the xml_deadlock_report report as displayed in the SSMS XML Editor.

If you'd like to view the graphical XML report like that shown in SQL Profiler when you capture XML deadlock trace events, you can save the XML document as a *.xdl file. When you reopen it in SSMS, it will display the graphical XML report.

> **NOTE**
>
> Before SSMS can correctly display the Deadlock Graph, you may need to edit the XML document before you save it to remove the Extended Events tags. Delete the lines up to the <deadlock> tag at the beginning of the file and delete all lines after the </deadlock> line at the end of the file.

However, there is a much easier way to view the graphical XML report in SSMS. For this example, expand the Deadlocks session in the Object Explorer and right-click on package0.event_file and select View Target Data. When you select the `xml_deadlock_report` event in the Event Viewer window, a new Deadlock tab is displayed. Click on this tab to view the Deadlock Graph, as shown in Figure 39.42.

```
event_data_XML1.xml  X  Extended Events Vie...(DXD001\Paul (52))*    SQLQuery5.sql - DX...(DXD001\Paul (61))*    DXD001\SQL2014DXD...dlocks: Live Data
   <event name="xml_deadlock_report" package="sqlserver" timestamp="2015-02-24T07:58:52.894Z">
      <data name="xml_report">
         <value>
            <deadlock>
               <victim-list>
                  <victimProcess id="processfa5e9468" />
               </victim-list>
               <process-list>
                  <process id="processfa5e9468" taskpriority="0" logused="0" waitresource="OBJECT: 14:245575913:0 " waittime="2346" owne
                     <executionStack>
                        <frame procname="adhoc" line="1" stmtend="34" sqlhandle="0x02000000e73766164a4236aef3d00891e1fef477821e1c0d0000000
   unknown   </frame>
                     </executionStack>
                     <inputbuf>
   DELETE DATABASELog
                     </inputbuf>
                  </process>
                  <process id="process116254108" taskpriority="0" logused="0" waitresource="OBJECT: 14:245575913:0 " waittime="9224" own
                     <executionStack>
                        <frame procname="adhoc" line="1" stmtend="34" sqlhandle="0x02000000e73766164a4236aef3d00891e1fef477821e1c0d0000000
   unknown   </frame>
                     </executionStack>
                     <inputbuf>
   DELETE DATABASELog
                     </inputbuf>
                  </process>
               </process-list>
               <resource-list>
                  <objectlock lockPartition="0" objid="245575913" subresource="FULL" dbid="14" objectname="AdventureWorks2014.dbo.Databa
                     <owner-list>
                        <owner id="process116254108" mode="S" />
                        <owner id="process116254108" mode="IX" requestType="convert" />
100 %   ◄  <
```

FIGURE 39.41   Viewing an `xml_deadlock_report` in the SSMS XML Editor.

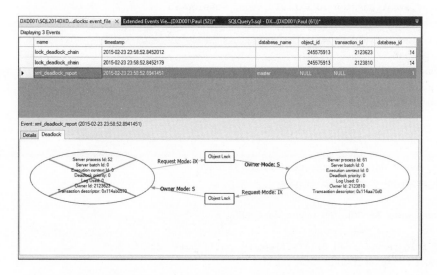

FIGURE 39.42   Viewing a Deadlock graph in the SSMS Extended Events session viewer.

With the deadlock events discussed thus far, we are interested in viewing the XML data generated as a single XML document. However, while event data for all Extended Events are returned as XML, for other types of events, you'll probably want to parse the XML into its individual values for display and filtering. Listing 39.5 provides a sample query that retrieves the name of the target file from Long Running Queries Extended Events session, reads the event records for all `sp_statement_completed` events into a `temp` table, and then returns the top 10 longest-running statements from the `#events` `temp` table.

LISTING 39.5   Reading Events from a Session Target File

```
/****
** Get the filename for the Session Target File
****/
DECLARE @filename nvarchar(260) =
(SELECT
    REPLACE( CONVERT(nvarchar(260), field.value), '.xel', '*.xel')
FROM
    sys.server_event_sessions AS SESSION
        INNER join
    sys.server_event_session_targets AS TARGET
        ON session.event_session_id = target.event_session_id
        INNER JOIN
    sys.dm_xe_object_columns AS col
        ON target.name = col.object_name
        AND col.column_type = 'customizable'
        LEFT OUTER JOIN
    sys.server_event_session_fields AS field
        ON target.event_session_id = field.event_session_id
        AND target.target_id = field.object_id
        AND col.name = field.name
WHERE
    target.package + '.' + target.name='package0.event_file'
    AND session.name='Long Running Queries'
    AND col.name = 'filename'
)


/****
-- copy the XML event data into the temp table #Events
--  for all sp_statment_completed events
****/
SELECT CAST(event_data AS XML) AS event_data_XML, *
INTO #events
FROM sys.fn_xe_file_target_read_file(@filename, null, null, null)
WHERE OBJECT_NAME = 'sp_statement_completed'
;


/****
-- Return the top ten queries with the longest duration
****/
SELECT TOP 10
  event_data_XML.value ('(/event/data  [@name=''duration'']/value)[1]', 'BIGINT')
```

```
    AS duration,
  event_data_XML.value ('(/event/data [@name=''cpu_time'']/value)[1]', 'BIGINT')
    AS cpu_time,
  event_data_XML.value ('(/event/data [@name=''physical_reads'']/value)[1]',
'BIGINT')
    AS physical_reads,
  event_data_XML.value ('(/event/data [@name=''logical_reads'' ]/value)[1]',
'BIGINT')
    AS logical_reads,
  event_data_XML.value ('(/event/data [@name=''writes'']/value)[1]', 'BIGINT')
    AS writes,
  event_data_XML.value ('(/event/data [@name=''row_count'']/value)[1]', 'BIGINT')
    AS row_count,
  event_data_XML.value ('(/event/data [@name=''statement'']/value)[1]',
'NVARCHAR(4000)')
    AS statement
FROM #Events
WHERE event_data_XML.value ('(/event/data [@name=''duration'']/value)[1]',
'BIGINT') > 1000
ORDER BY event_data_XML.value ('(/event/data [@name=''duration'']/value)[1]',
'BIGINT') DESC;


DROP TABLE #events
```

To stop an Extended Events session, issue the ALTER EVENT SESSION command with the STATE equal to stop, as shown here:

```
-- STOP EVENT SESSION
ALTER EVENT SESSION Deadlocks
ON SERVER STATE=stop;
```

Various Extended Events sessions can be defined for monitoring purposes within the SQL Server environment, your application environment, and at the operating system level. You will likely build up a complete library of Extended Events sessions that represent what you are most interested in monitoring about your environment. They will then become valuable tools for years to come. You may want to check online in the various SQL Server forums and Microsoft resource sites to locate additional user-defined Extended Events session templates to aid you in creating an extensive library of Extended Events sessions to extend your monitoring capability.

The system_health Extended Events Session
The previous sections have discussed how to set up and manage your own Extended Events sessions, but there is also an Extended Events session that is included with SQL Server that captures some useful information that you can use without having to even set up your own Extended Events session. The session is the system_health session, and it is configured to start automatically when SQL Server starts. The event data is captured to

39

two targets, a `ring_buffer` and an `event_file`. The event file is called `system_health.` `xel` and is located in the SQL Server log directory (the same location where the SQL Server error log files are stored).

The `system_health session` collects the following information:

▶ The `sql_text` and `session_id` for any sessions that encounter an error that has a `severity >= 20`.

▶ The `sql_text` and `session_id` for any sessions that encounter a memory-related error (error numbers 17803, 701, 802, 8645, 8651, 8657, and 8902).

▶ A record of any nonyielding scheduler problems (error number 17883).

▶ Any deadlocks that are detected.

▶ The `callstack`, `sql_text`, and `session_id` for any sessions that have waited on latches (or other interesting resources) for > 15 seconds.

▶ The `callstack`, `sql_text`, and `session_id` for any sessions that have waited on locks for > 30 seconds.

▶ The `callstack`, `sql_text`, and `session_id` for any sessions that have waited for a long time for preemptive waits.

▶ The callstack and `session_id` for CLR allocation and virtual allocation failures.

▶ The `ring_buffer` events for the memory broker, scheduler monitor, memory node OOM, security, and connectivity.

▶ System component results from `sp_server_diagnostics`.

▶ Instance health collected by `scheduler_monitor_system_health_ring_buffer_recorded`.

▶ CLR allocation failures.

▶ Connectivity errors using `connectivity_ring_buffer_recorded`.

▶ Security errors using `security_error_ring_buffer_recorded`.

As you can see, a lot of interesting and useful events are already being captured, many of the basic sort of events that you would want to capture to monitor overall system performance. You can view the `system_health` events in SSMS just like user-defined event sessions: by either viewing the live stream or by viewing the event file.

Windows Performance Monitor

Windows Performance Monitor is a graphical tool that provides a visual display of built-in Windows performance counters, either in real time or as a way to review historical data. It is supplied as part of the installation of any Windows server or workstation (in Windows Server 2008 it is called *Reliability and Performance Monitor*). Hundreds of performance counters are available. These counters can be monitored on the local machine or remotely over the network, and they can be set up to monitor any object and counter on multiple systems at once from one session. A small subset of performance information is also available via the Windows Task Manager Performance tab. However, all this information and more is available using the Performance Monitor facility.

> **NOTE**
>
> This chapter covers the version of Performance Monitor available in Windows Server 2012, Windows Server 2008, Windows Server 2008 R2, Windows Vista, Windows 7 and Windows 8. If you are running on Windows XP, Windows Server 2003, or earlier versions of Windows, the interface and functionality of Performance Monitor are a bit more limited than the version presented here. However, many of the concepts of using Performance Monitor and performance counters are still similar.

Performance Monitor features multiple graph views that enable you to visually review performance log data. You can add performance counters to Performance Monitor individually or by creating custom Data Collector Sets. The recent version of Windows Performance Monitor combines the functionality of previous standalone tools including Performance Logs and Alerts (PLA), Server Performance Advisor (SPA), and System Monitor.

You can use Windows Performance Monitor to examine how programs you run affect your computer's performance, both in real time and by collecting log data for later analysis. When you install SQL Server, additional performance counters are installed that you can use to monitor SQL Server performance elements such as cache utilization, locking, wait states, and I/O performance. Performance Monitor can be launched from many different points. From SQL Profiler, choose the Tools menu option and choose the Performance Monitor item. Figure 39.43 shows this menu option from SQL Profiler. You can also launch it from the `Administrative Tools` folder in the Windows Start menu.

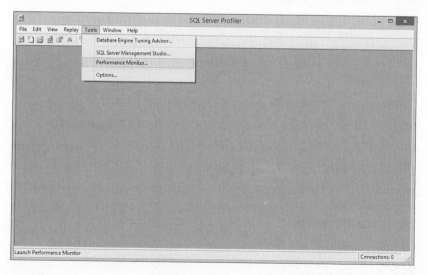

FIGURE 39.43   Launching Performance Monitor from SQL Profiler.

Performance Monitor Views

When you first launch Performance Monitor, you are presented with the Welcome screen (in Windows 2008, the Welcome screen is the Resource Overview). Click on Performance Monitor in the `Monitoring Tools` folder to bring up the Performance Monitor main display. In the Performance Monitor main display, you can view the performance information in one of three different modes:

▶ **Graphic chart**—This view, the default, shows the selected counters as colored lines over a timeline with the y-axis representing the value and the x-axis representing time. You can also add gridlines (horizontal and vertical). This view lets you view performance trends over time.

▶ **Histogram chart**—This view shows the selected counters as colored horizontal bars (as in a histogram). These histogram bars change dynamically to reflect the data sampling values. With this view, you see a current snapshot of the performance counters rather than the trend of activity over time.

▶ **Report display**—In this mode, you see the current values for counters collected under their parent object in a textual display format. Like the histogram view, this view does not show you the activity trends, just the current sampling value, but it is great for showing what counters you are collecting data with.

Figure 39.44 shows the basic graphic chart view interface for Performance Monitor displaying several useful system counters that are explained later in this chapter. These counters are added to Performance Monitor through the creation of Performance Monitor Data Collector Sets.

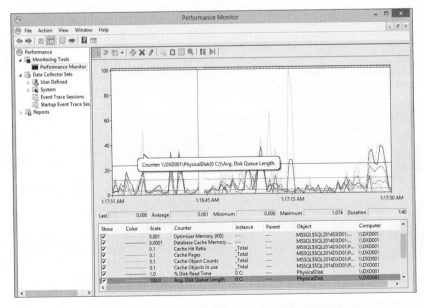

FIGURE 39.44   Performance Monitor chart view, with various counters.

When you open the Performance Monitor view, depending on the OS version you are running, you see up to three default performance counters: Memory: Pages/sec, PhysicalDisk:Avg.Disk Queue Length, and Processor:% Processor Time. These counters provide a good start, but you really want to see many other counters that reflect the complete picture of how your server is behaving. This chapter explains the recommended ones to use for SQL Server in the "SQL Server Performance Counters" section.

You add a counter by clicking the large plus sign toolbar button near the top. The Add Counters dialog that appears (see Figure 39.45) allows you to select the computer to monitor (this can be a remote server), a performance object, any specific counters, and an instance of the counter, if applicable. You can select the Show Description check box to get a simple explanation of the currently selected counter. When you are done making your selections of counters to add, click OK to return to the Performance Monitor screen.

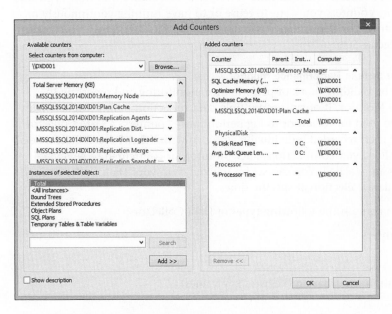

FIGURE 39.45   Adding a counter in Performance Monitor.

You can customize the look of the lines in the chart view by right-clicking and selecting Properties. On the Data tab of the System Monitor Properties dialog, you can specify the color, width, and style of line for each of your counters. You can also change the scale of a counter's value so that the line appears within the graph's scale of 1 to 100.

TIP

To quickly rescale all the counters, select all the counters in the bottom panel of the Chart view window, right-click, and select Scale Selected Counters. Performance Monitor automatically selects a scale for each counter such that all lines appear within the display.

To remove a counter, you simply highlight the line in the bottom area of the Chart view window and press the Delete key or click on the red X button in the toolbar. If you just want to temporarily hide a counter to make the display a little less busy, you can right-click a counter in the bottom area of the Chart view and select Hide Selected Counters.

The Chart view also provides a way to make a specific counter or set of counters stand out in the display by making the line or lines black and bold. This capability can help you focus on the trend of a specific counter. To turn on highlighting, select one or more counters in the bottom area of the Chart view and click on the Highlight button on the toolbar (the one that looks like highlighter pen just to the right of the big red X).

Adding counters like this in an ad hoc manner is fine for a quick monitoring session. However, after you close the Performance Monitor tool, you lose the counters you have selected, so they are not available the next time you open Performance Monitor. Typically, you need to set up those counters you want to reuse or to have running continuously or on a schedule that captures the performance counters to a log file. To do this, you create one or more Data Collector Sets.

Creating Data Collector Sets in Performance Monitor

A *Data Collector Set* is the building block of performance monitoring and reporting in Windows Performance Monitor. It organizes multiple data collection points into a single component that can be used for review or to log performance counters. A Data Collector Set can be created and then recorded individually, grouped with other Data Collector Sets and incorporated into logs, viewed in Performance Monitor, or configured to generate alerts when thresholds are reached. You can set up schedules on your Data Collector Sets to have them run the data collection at specific times.

Data Collector Sets can contain the following types of Data Collectors:

▶ Performance counters

▶ Event trace data

▶ System configuration information (Registry key values)

Performance counters are measurements of system state or activity. They can be included in the operating system or can be part of individual applications. When you install SQL Server, a number of SQL Server–specific performance counters are installed (a number of the more useful ones are described later in this chapter). Windows Performance Monitor requests the current value of performance counters at specified time intervals.

Event trace data is collected from trace providers, which are components of the operating system or of individual applications that report actions or events. Output from multiple trace providers can be combined into a trace session.

Configuration information is collected from key values in the Windows Registry. Windows Performance Monitor can record the value of a Registry key at a specified time or interval as part of a log file.

The easiest way to create a Data Collector Set is to create a custom view of counters in Performance Monitor (similar to what was shown in the previous section). When you are satisfied with the counters and settings you have configured, right-click on the Performance Monitor node in the Monitoring Tools folder, select New, and then select Data Collector Set. This starts the Create Data Collector Set Wizard, which walks you through the following steps:

1. The wizard prompts for a name for the Data Collector Set. Enter a name and click Next.

2. Specify the root directory where the Performance Monitor log files will be written and click Next.

3. Specify if you want the Data Collector to run under a different user ID and if you want to start the Data Collector immediately or to just save the Data Collector Set. Click Finish to return to Performance Monitor.

The newly created Data Collector Set is listed under the User Defined folder in the Data Collector Sets node in Performance Monitor.

You can also create a Data Collector Set manually or from a template by right-clicking on the User Defined folder in the Data Collector Sets node and selecting New, Data Collector Set. This launches a modified version of the Create New Data Collector Set Wizard, as shown in Figure 39.46.

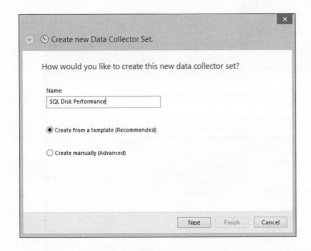

FIGURE 39.46   The Create New Data Collector Set Wizard.

You first specify a name for the collector set and then choose whether to create it from a template or manually. Then you click Next.

If you choose to create from a template, the next screen displays the built-in templates provided with Windows; these standard templates focus on general system performance or diagnostics. You can also choose to import your own templates by clicking on the Browse button.

NOTE

Creating your own Data Collector Set templates in Performance Monitor is relatively easy. If you have a Data Collector Set that you've set up with the performance counters and settings that you would like to reuse, simply right-click the Data Collector Set you want to export and click Save Template. Select a directory in which to store the collector set as an XML file and click Save. You can now copy this template for use on other computers.

After selecting the template, navigate to the next screen to specify the root directory for the log files. On the final screen, you have the option again to start the collector immediately, save it, or open the properties for the Data Collector Set so you can make further modifications to it, such as specifying a schedule, setting a stop condition based on duration or file size limit or specifying a scheduled task to run when the Data Collector stops.

If you choose to create a new Data Collector Set manually instead of using a template, you are presented with the screen shown in Figure 39.47. You have the option to create a Data Collector Set that generates data logs or to create a Performance Counter Alert. If you are creating data logs, you can specify what sort of information you want to include in the collector set (in this example, we're logging performance counters only).

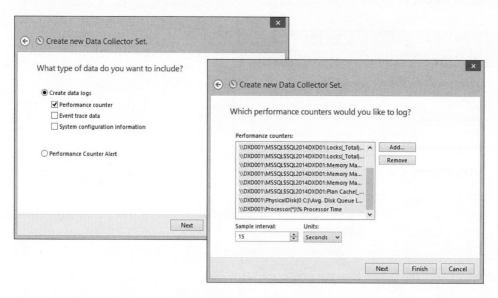

FIGURE 39.47   Creating a new Data Collector Set manually to capture performance counters.

Depending on the Data Collector types you select, you are presented with dialogs to add Data Collectors to your Data Collector Set. In this example, you are presented with the dialog to add performance counters, as shown in Figure 39.47.

After defining the counters, you are presented with the familiar options to specify the root directory and whether to save, run, or edit the properties of the Data Collector Set.

After you create a Data Collector Set, you can add additional Data Collectors to it as desired. They can be additional performance counter event traces, configuration Data Collectors, or performance counter alerts.

Running a Data Collector Set in Performance Monitor

The easiest way to run a Data Collector Set is to right-click on it and choose Start. When you are done capturing, right-click again and choose Stop. However, this is probably not the most effective way to execute your Data Collector Sets. A more effective approach is to set up a schedule for data collection.

During Data Collector Set creation, you can configure the schedule by selecting Open Properties for this Data Collector Set at the end of the Create New Data Collector Set Wizard. After a Data Collector Set is created, you can access the schedule options by right-clicking the Data Collector Set name in the Microsoft Management Console (MMC) navigation pane and selecting Properties. When the Properties dialog is displayed, click the Schedule tab to specify the schedule when you want the Data Collector to run. You can specify the start date, time, or day for data collection. If you do not want to collect new data after a certain date, select Expiration Date and choose a date from the calendar. You can create multiple schedules for a single Data Collector Set.

The Data Collector runs continuously unless you specify a Stop condition for a Data Collector Set. The Stop condition can be set in the Stop Condition tab. To stop collecting data after a period of time, select Overall Duration and choose the quantity and units. On the Stop Condition tab, you can also specify limits to segment data collection into separate logs. Select the Restart the Data Collector Set at Limits option to continue running the Data Collector after the limit is reached. You can select Duration to configure a time period for data collection to write to a single log file, or select Maximum Size to restart the Data Collector Set or to stop collecting data when the log file reaches a specific size. If you select both limits, data collection stops or restarts when the first limit is reached.

TIP

If you are running a Data Collector continuously, you should set a limit so that the Data Collector breaks the log file into multiple segments. In addition to preventing the file from becoming exceedingly large, breaking up the log file also enables you to view the log file segments prior to the current one while the Data Collector Set is running. Unfortunately, you cannot directly open the currently active log file for a Data Collector Set to view the live data collection. However, if you have a previous report available, you can open the report in the Performance Monitor window. When this report is open, click the View Current Activity button (or press Ctrl+T), and you can view the current activity in real time as it's being captured.

39

Viewing Data Collector Set Results in Performance Monitor

To view a Data Collector Set report in Windows Performance Monitor, expand Reports and click User Defined or System. Then expand the Data Collector Set that you want to view as a report. Simply click the report that you want to view from the list of available reports. The report opens in the console pane.

If you want to open one or more log files in Performance Monitor (perhaps you have a set of log files copied from another server), in the Windows Performance Monitor navigation pane, expand Monitoring Tools and click Performance Monitor. In the console pane toolbar, click the Add Log Data button (or press Ctrl+L). The Performance Monitor Properties page opens with the Source tab active (see Figure 39.48). In the Data Source section, follow these steps:

1. Select Log Files and click Add.

2. Browse to the log file you want to view and click Open.

3. To add multiple log files to the Performance Monitor view, click Add again.

4. Click Time Range to see times included in the log or logs you selected.

5. When you are finished selecting log files, click OK.

6. Right-click in the Performance Monitor display and click Add Counters to select the counters you want to display in Performance Monitor. Only the counters included in the log file or files you selected in step 4 are made available.

FIGURE 39.48   Importing log files into Performance Monitor.

For a single log file, you can move the beginning and ending time sliders to view only a portion of the log file in Performance Monitor.

For multiple log files, you can move the beginning and ending time sliders to choose the time period (from all the selected log files) to view in Performance Monitor. If a log has data from the time period you select, it is available in the display.

Why Use Performance Monitor?

You might be asking, "With all the new performance monitoring tools provided with SQL Server, is there a need to continue to use Performance Monitor?"

Even though many of the performance counters and relevant information are now available in the SQL Server Data Collector, as mentioned previously, the Data Collector does incur some overhead on SQL Server. Performance Monitor, on the other hand, incurs significantly less impact on SQL Server performance.

In addition, the SQL Server Data Collector currently doesn't have a built-in alerting capability. As mentioned previously, you can set up performance counter alerts in Performance Monitor. In addition, Performance Monitor enables you to monitor more than what is provided with SQL Server Data Collector, including all aspects of the operating system as well as other applications.

One other feature that's very useful with Performance Monitor logs is the capability to import performance counter logs into SQL Server Profiler for correlation of performance counters with SQL Profiler trace events.

> **NOTE**
>
> For more information on importing and viewing performance counter logs in SQL Server Profiler, see Chapter 5.

SQL Server Performance Counters

For each SQL Server instance installed, Performance Monitor has a number of SQL Server–specific performance objects added to it, each with a number of associated counters. Each SQL Server instance has its own set of monitoring objects because you certainly wouldn't want to mix monitoring values across multiple instances. Performance counters for named instances use the naming convention MSSQL$ followed by the instance name (for example, MSSQL$SQL2014DEV:General Statistics). Performance counters for the default instance of SQL Server use the naming convention of SQLSERVER followed by the counter name (for example, SQLServer:General Statistics).

Table 39.1 provides a list of the SQL Server performance counters available for SQL Server 2014.

39

TABLE 39.1   SQL Server Performance Objects

Performance Object	Description
SQLServer:Access Methods	Information on searches and allocations of SQL Server database objects (for example, the number of index searches or number of pages allocated to indexes and data)
SQLServer:Backup Device	Information about backup devices, such as the throughput of the backup device
SQLServer:Buffer Manager	Information about the memory buffers used by SQL Server
SQLServer:Buffer Node	Information about buffer free page accesses
SQLServer:CLR	Information about common language runtime (CLR) objects
SQLServer:Cursor Manager by Type	Information about cursors
SQLServer:Cursor Manager Total	Information about cursors
SQLServer:Database Mirroring	Information about database mirroring
SQLServer:Databases	Database-specific information such as the amount of free log space available or the number of active transactions in the database
SQL Server:Deprecated Features	Information on the number of times deprecated features are used
SQLServer:Exec Statistics	Execution statistics information
SQLServer:General Statistics	General server-wide activity, such as the number of logins per second
SQL Server:HADR Availability Replica	Information about SQL Server AlwaysOn Availability Groups availability replicas
SQL Server:HADR Database Replica	Information about SQL Server AlwaysOn Availability Groups database replicas
SQLServer:Latches	Information about the latches on internal resources, such as database pages
SQLServer:Locks	Information about the individual lock requests made by SQL Server, such as lock timeouts and deadlocks
SQLServer:Memory Manager	Information about SQL Server memory usage, such as the total number of lock structures currently allocated
SQLServer:Plan Cache	Information about the SQL Server cache used to store objects such as stored procedures, triggers, and query plans
SQLServer: Resource Pool Stats	Information about Resource Governor resource pool statistics
SQLServer:SQL Errors	Information about SQL Server errors

Performance Object	Description
SQLServer:SQL Statistics	Query statistics, such as the number of batches of T-SQL statements received by SQL Server
SQLServer:Transactions	Transaction statistics, such as the overall number of transactions and the number of snapshot transactions
SQLServer:User Settable	Custom counters that can be a custom stored procedure or any T-SQL statement that returns a value to be monitored
SQLServer: Wait Statistics	Information about waits
SQLServer: Workload Group Stats	Information about Resource Governor workload group statistics
SQLAgent:Alerts	Information about SQL Server Agent alerts
SQLAgent:Jobs	Information about SQL Server Agent jobs
SQLAgent:JobSteps	Information about SQL Server Agent job steps
SQLAgent:Statistics	General information about SQL Server Agent
SQLServer:Replication Agents	Information about replication agent activity
SQLServer:Replication Snapshot	Information about replication agent activity
SQLServer:Replication Logreader	Information about replication agent activity
SQLServer:Replication Dist.	Information about replication agent activity
SQLServer:Replication Merge	Information about replication agent activity
SQLServer:Broker Activation	Information about Service Broker-activated tasks
SQLServer:Broker Statistics	General Service Broker information
SQLServer:Broker Transport	Information on Service Broker networking

User-Defined Counters

You can extend the range of information that Performance Monitor displays by creating up to 10 of your own counters. These user-defined counters appear under the SQLServer:User Settable:Query object, which contains the 10 counters as instances, starting with User Counter 1. You define your own counters by calling stored procedures with the names sp_user_counter1 through sp_user_counter10, which are located in the master database.

These counters work differently than they did under previous versions of SQL Server and require you to call the stored procedures to update the information they return to Performance Monitor. To make any real use of these stored procedures, you now need to call them within a loop or as part of a job that is scheduled on some recurring basis.

Using these counters allows you to monitor any information you want, whether it is system, database, or even object-specific. The only restriction is that the stored procedure can take only a single integer value argument.

39

The following sample user-defined counter procedure sets the counter value to the average connection time for all user connections. Processes that have a `session_id` less than 50 are internal system processes (checkpoint, Lazy Writer, and so on):

```
DECLARE @value INT

SELECT @value = AVG( DATEDIFF( mi, login_time, GETDATE()))
FROM sys.dm_exec_sessions
WHERE session_id > 50


EXEC sp_user_counter1 @value
```

You could further extend this information by creating additional user procedures for returning the minimum and maximum times connected, as well as database usage. Your only limitation is that you can monitor only a maximum of 10 pieces of information at one time.

Accessing Performance Counters via T-SQL

Most of the SQL Server–oriented performance counter values can also be seen at any point in time via the dynamic management view `sys.dm_os_performance_counters`:

```
SELECT * from sys.dm_os_performance_counters
```

This view shows the performance counter category (referred to as the object name), the counter name, the name of the specific instance of the counter (often a database name), the current counter value as of the time the DMV is queried, and the counter data type.

The following query uses `sys.dm_os_performance_counters` to return the performance counters and current values for the `SQL:Server Buffer Manager` category:

```
SELECT [object_name], [counter_name], [cntr_value]
FROM sys.[dm_os_performance_counters]
WHERE [object_name] = 'SQLServer:Buffer Manager';


/* output
object_name                 counter_name                    cntr_value
-------------------------   -----------------------------   ----------
SQLServer:Buffer Manager    Buffer cache hit ratio                 933
SQLServer:Buffer Manager    Buffer cache hit ratio base            933
SQLServer:Buffer Manager    Page lookups/sec                  71378580
SQLServer:Buffer Manager    Free list stalls/sec                     8
SQLServer:Buffer Manager    Database pages                      128330
SQLServer:Buffer Manager    Target pages                      16138240
SQLServer:Buffer Manager    Integral Controller Slope                1
SQLServer:Buffer Manager    Lazy writes/sec                      36356
SQLServer:Buffer Manager    Readahead pages/sec                 618849
SQLServer:Buffer Manager    Page reads/sec                      654170
SQLServer:Buffer Manager    Page writes/sec                     802333
```

```
SQLServer:Buffer Manager   Checkpoint pages/sec           108378
SQLServer:Buffer Manager   Background writer pages/sec         0
SQLServer:Buffer Manager   Page life expectancy             5092

*/
```

You should keep in mind that many of the performance counters are accumulation counters, and you have to run them at intervals and determine the difference (change) from one interval to the next. Others are current values of aspects such as transaction rates, memory usage, and hit ratios.

Summary

Attacking SQL Server performance is not a simple task because so many variables are involved. Tuning queries and a proper database design are a huge part of this, but dealing with SQL Server as an engine that consumes resources and the physical machine is equally important. This is why it is so critical to take an orderly, methodical approach when undertaking this task. As pointed out in this chapter, you need to basically peel apart the box on which SQL Server has been installed, one component at a time (network, CPU, memory, and disk). This way, you can explore the individual layer or component in a clear and concise manner. Within a short amount of time, you will be able to identify the biggest performance offenders and resolve them.

The next chapter, "SQL Server Database Engine Tuning Advisor," discusses the utility available in SQL Server 2014 that analyzes your databases and query activity and makes indexing and table partitioning recommendations that you can use to optimize query performance without having to have an expert understanding of the database structure or the internals of SQL Server (although if you've been reading the chapters up to this point, you are on your way to becoming such an expert).

SQL Server Database Engine Tuning Advisor

This chapter covers one of Microsoft's hidden capabilities, the Database Engine Tuning Advisor (DTA). This tool can make table, partitioning, and index tuning recommendations to support certain workloads. This can also include doing what-if scenarios on physical database changes *before* they are finalized or put into production. In addition, you can also do things like troubleshoot the performance of a specific query or set of queries (your problem children). But what Database Engine Tuning Advisor really offers is a proven database utility that has years of performance and tuning rules embedded, integration with the query optimizer, and it makes even the most novice database developer look like a seasoned veteran when it comes to database tuning.

What's New in SQL Server Database Engine Tuning Advisor

One of the most useful features added back in SQL Server 2012 is the ability to use SQL Server's query plan cache as the source of the workload you want to use as the basis of tuning. This is really useful because you have a great mix of queries that have been hitting the database that represent the typical variety of queries you want to optimize on and that you want to leverage for all around tuning results. There is also an ability to utilize production metadata, statistics, and hardware information to help tune your database but still be executing on a test server. (This feature is only available via the command line DTA utility, though.) This allows you to get tuning recommendations that have a "production system" basis without running DTA on the production server and impacting your application. More on this cool feature later. All of the DTA features have not changed for SQL Server 2014.

SQL Server Instance Architecture

Figure 40.1 illustrates the address space architecture of an instance of SQL Server 2014. When you fire up a SQL Server instance, two main areas are allocated: the code area and memory pool area. The code area is mostly static executable code of the SQL Server kernel; SQL Server .NET Library DLLs; Open Data Services code; the stack space; and a variable code area that contains distributed query OLE DB providers, OLE automation objects, and extended stored procedures as they are needed by user requests.

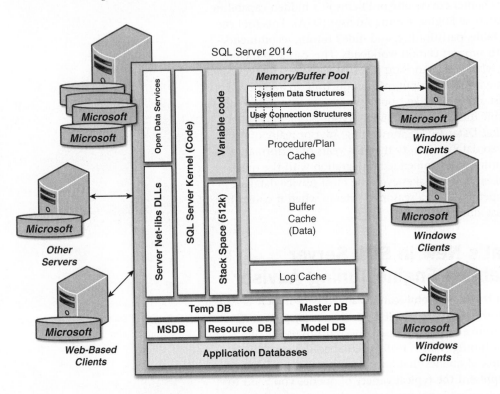

FIGURE 40.1   The SQL Server 2014 instance architecture.

The memory pool area of SQL Server is the most dynamically changing part of an instance. Even now, the once-static system data structures and user connection structures (connection context) are controlled by user requests and dynamically allocate structures as they are needed. Then, there are the primary SQL Server databases master, tempdb, msdb, and model. Of these system-wide databases, tempdb has the most significance for performance because it is the heart of all internal tables, indexing, sorting, grouping, and other worktable activity for the entire SQL Server instance.

The unknown portion of the problem occurs when you add application databases to the instance. How can you tune your database to meet the user's requirements? How do you optimize your indexing strategy? How do you know what partitions are best, if any? Figure 40.1 highlights this Application Database portion of the SQL Server instance. But in tuning your database, you must consider *all* portions of the SQL Server 2014 instance and how they work together. Database Engine Tuning Advisor is the one way to cover most of the most critical aspects of database tuning that will consider this entire picture. Make running it a habit regardless of your tuning experience. You want nothing to slip through the cracks.

The following shows a generalization of the types of applications you might find in the real world that would be implemented using SQL Server 2014 and the general behavior they elicit:

▶ **Online transaction processing (OLTP)**—Mix of reads, writes, updates, and deletes. Large number of concurrent users.

▶ **Data warehouse**—Incremental loads (deltas), aggregation/transformation processing, then primarily read-only. Medium number of users.

▶ **Online analytical processing (OLAP)**—Big loads, then primarily read-only. Medium to large number of simultaneous users.

▶ **Mixed server**—Mix of reads, writes, updates, deletes, big loads, and big extracts. Large number of users. Web-based ecommerce transaction mix.

This is not a complete list, just a generalized one. It is important to know the combined behavior of all application processing when you are tuning.

Database Engine Tuning Advisor

The Database Engine Tuning Advisor (DTA) has been a decent supplement for helping with SQL Server performance. It is not the hottest offering from Microsoft, but it can be valuable in enforcing some basic design options in regard to partitioning, indexing, and basic table structures. You can use either the GUI version of the DTA or the batch command-line version to achieve the same results. With DTA, you can run an analysis against an entire database or just focus on as little as one table within a database. Say that you have one problem child table that is at the heart of all your misery. In this case, you would probably just want to tune that one table for optimal database access.

To tune and analyze anything, DTA must base its analysis on something. That something is usually a set of SQL queries that represent the "workload" of data accesses you want the database to support well. These data accesses (that is, the workload) can be attained in many ways. One way is to create a SQL script that contains any or all of the data accesses (SQL statements) you want considered in the tuning effort; you can also direct DTA to use the query plans in the cache to represent the source of the tuning exercise and, finally, you can simply capture real SQL transactions by using SQL Profiler traces. You can easily retain these traces in .trc file form or keep the captured SQL traces in a SQL table.

40

In the example you are about to run, you use a series of SQL statements in a file named TRAFFIC_4TUNING.sql that will generate a pretty healthy workload of mixed transactions (updates, inserts, and selects) and is used as the basis of our database tuning exercise. This will be run against the AdventureWorks2014 database. Okay, let's start by using the GUI version of DTA in SQL Server Management Studio (SSMS) to see how DTA does its magic.

The Database Engine Tuning Advisor GUI

From the Tools menu in SSMS, you can select the Database Engine Tuning Advisor option to invoke the GUI for DTA. Or you can invoke this GUI by selecting Start, All Programs, Microsoft SQL Server 2014, Performance Tools, Database Engine Tuning Adviser Program from your desktop (see Figure 40.2).

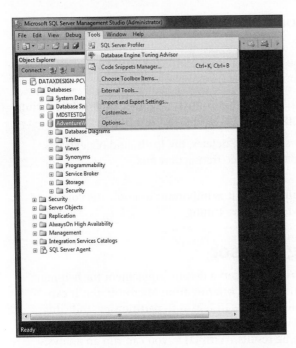

FIGURE 40.2   Database Engine Tuning Advisor from the SSMS toolbar.

> **NOTE**
>
> It's best not to run the DTA against a live production database. You should make a copy of the database in a safe place for this type of detailed analysis. You should use a copy of the production database, though, because you want all decisions to be based on reality, and your workload should also reflect true production data accesses. There is also an option, with SQL 2014, that allows you to use your production database's metadata, statistics, and hardware information as the basis of tuning recommendations in conjunction with your test server. This option is great if you have limited space or servers available in your test environments.

As part of getting started you must connect to a SQL Server instance that you want to use for your DTA session. (Specify the SQL Server instance in the connection dialog box and connect.) When you are connected to the target SQL Server platform, a default for a session name appears; it is the user's name and the date on which the analysis is being done. Figure 40.3 shows this new session start and the specification of what workload (File) to use for the analysis. As you can see, there is also a Table option as well as a Plan Cache option. We have identified the .sql file named TRAFFIC_4TUNING.sql as the workload file to use for this analysis.

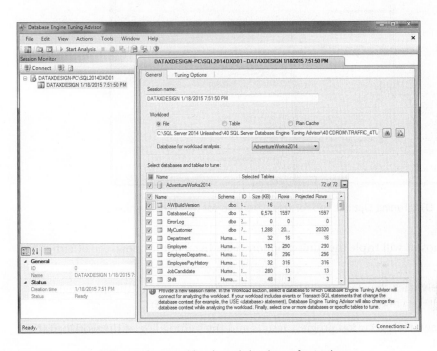

FIGURE 40.3   DTA session, workload, and database for tuning.

We will target the AdventureWorks2014 database for our tuning. As you can see in Figure 40.3, it is also possible to narrow the tuning to just specific tables within a database. However, the workload you use in DTA will mostly drive what tables get all of the attention for tuning recommendations. Once you specify the workload information and the target of your tuning, you can choose specific tuning options by clicking on the Tuning Options tab. As you can see in Figure 40.4, there are a number of tuning options such as having a limit on the tuning time, the type of physical design structures to consider, any partitioning strategy to align with, and what to do with existing physical design structures. As you can also see in Figure 40.4, if you take a look at the Advanced Options dialog, you can specify some maximum space parameters to stay within, adjust the maximum columns per index not to exceed, and the online index recommendations approach. We'll keep these to be offline recommendations.

40

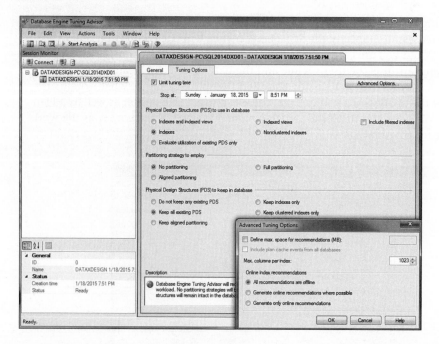

FIGURE 40.4   DTA Tuning Options tab for this database for this tuning analysis.

Someday, Microsoft will triple the tuning option types here, but for now, the offerings are limited.

Now, you simply click the Start Analysis menu item (the one with a little green right arrow next to it) or choose Actions, Start Analysis (see Figure 40.5).

Figure 40.6 shows the execution progress results and the Tuning Log of the workload that was being used.

Also, as you can see in Figure 40.6, when the progress is complete, a Recommendations tab and a Reports tab appear for this session.

When you click on the Recommendations tab (as shown in Figure 40.7), you can see that the tuning analysis is estimating that it can improve things by about 57%. Because we only wanted index recommendations, you don't see any partitioning recommendations. However, as shown by the Index Recommendations portion of this section, a series of index recommendations are being identified that can likely help out quite a bit.

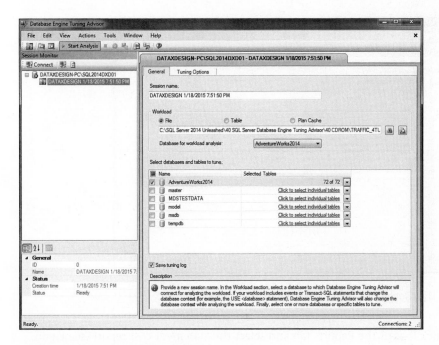

FIGURE 40.5   Starting DTA analysis.

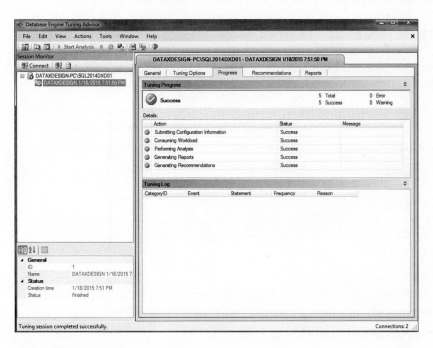

FIGURE 40.6   DTA Tuning progress completed successfully.

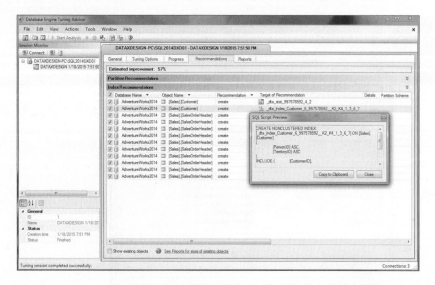

FIGURE 40.7   DTA Recommendations tab, Index Recommendations.

If we take a quick look at the Reports tab and select the Statement cost report (see Figure 40.8), we can also see that the most improvement can come from changes directed at the Select statement against the `Customer` table. This has all of our attention now!

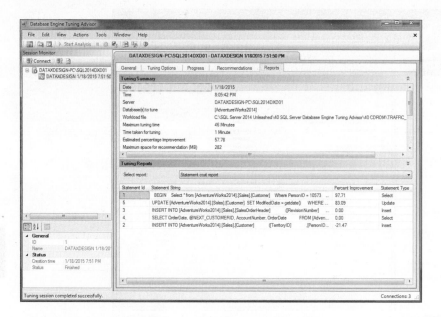

FIGURE 40.8   Tuning reports; Statement cost report.

If you also take a quick look at the Statement-index relations report (recommended), you will see specific index name references that are matched to the SQL Statement they will benefit (shown in Figure 40.9). This is now *very* clear that we need to add this index.

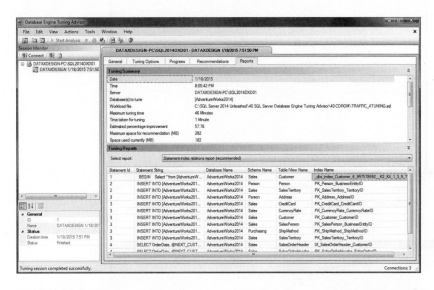

FIGURE 40.9   Tuning reports, Statement-index relations report (recommended).

Now, looking back at the Index Recommendations tab (as shown back in Figure 40.7), the second index recommendation is a new, nonclustered index on the Customer table that looks to have the most impact on that Select statement. We have also opened up the definition of that index recommendation with the SQL Script Preview by clicking on the Definition to the right of the index recommendation.

This is very promising, so let's actually create this new index and then rerun DTA to see whether it had the desired effect. Figure 40.10 shows the creation of the recommended new index on the Customer table.

We'll now set up the same workload and run a new analysis session to see how things have changed. Figure 40.11 shows the second analysis session being run (and completed successfully). A new set of recommendations and reports has been generated.

40

FIGURE 40.10　Create the new index to tune the database with SSMS.

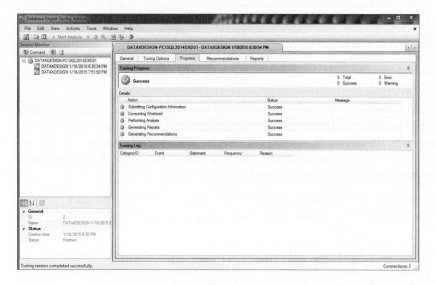

FIGURE 40.11　Running a new tuning analysis session with the index changes.

Once this completes, we jump to the Recommendations tab (as shown in Figure 40.12) and can see that there is a 0% estimated improvement recommendation now. This means that the changes we just made have resolved any poor-running SQL and that now the necessity of new index changes has been determined.

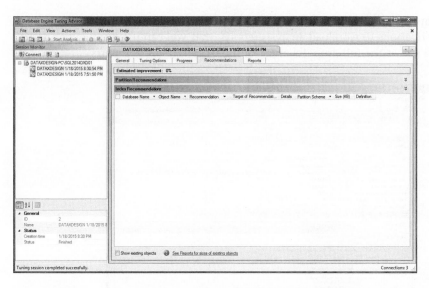

FIGURE 40.12   DTA Recommendations tab, second analysis session.

As you can see by opening the Statement cost report for this recommendation session (Figure 40.13), the SQL statements that are in our workload have been completely satisfied by the current physical schema. No more improvements are to be had (0% improvements for each SQL statement). By the way, this is how you know you are done.

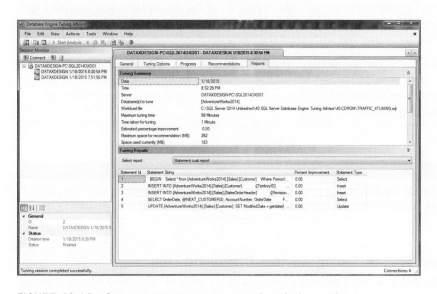

FIGURE 40.13   Statement cost report, second analysis session.

40

Okay. Great sequence of tuning. There are also several other reports, ranging from detailed index recommendations to workload analysis reports, that you can use during your analysis. Figure 40.14 shows the full drop-down list of the various analysis reports.

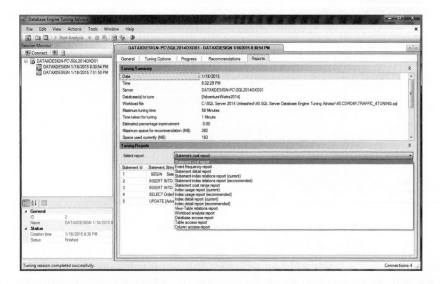

FIGURE 40.14   Reports, all options.

At any time, you can choose to preview the workload of the file or table you specified for the analysis. You simply choose View, Preview Workload Table or View, Preview Workload File, and SQL Profiler is invoked with your SQL trace.

If you are satisfied with the recommendations of any one of your tuning sessions, you can choose to have them saved to a .sql file and scheduled to be applied at some later time, or you can apply them immediately by selecting Actions, Apply Recommendations or Actions, Save Recommendations.

It's that simple.

TIP

If you regularly run the DTA with a good sampling of your typical transaction workload, you can proactively identify potential changes that will keep your application humming.

The Database Engine Tuning Advisor Command Line

DTA is also available in a batch mode so that you don't have to be around to run it online (because doing so can often take hours if you have a large workload to analyze). In addition, this mode enables you to run the same tests over and over, with varying options.

You can easily view DTA command-line options by using the help option of the command itself (that is, the -? option). You simply run this option at the command line and have its output piped into a file for viewing in Notepad (or another editor):

```
C:> DTA -? > dta.out
Microsoft (R) SQL Server Microsoft SQL Server Database Engine Tuning Advisor command
line utility
Version 12.0.2000.8 ((SQL14_RTM).140220-1832 )
Copyright (c) 2014 Microsoft. All rights reserved.
Usage:
DTA.EXE  [-S ServerName[\Instance]]
    [-U LoginId]
    [-P Password]
    [-E]
    [-d DatabaseName]
    [-D DatabaseName[, DatabaseName]]
    [-Tl TableName[, TableName]]
    [-Tf TableListFileName]
    [-if WorkloadFileName]
    [-it WorkloadTableName]
    [-ip]
    [-ipf]
    [-s SessionName]
    [-of [ScriptFileName]]
    [-or [ReportFileName]]
    [-rl Report[, Report]]
    [-ox [OutputXmlFileName]]
    [-F]
    [-ID SessionID]
    [-ix InputXmlFileName]
    [-A TuningTime]
    [-n NumberOfEvents]
    [-m MinimumImprovement]
    [-fa PhysicalDesignStructure]
    [-fp PartitionStrategy]
    [-fk PhysicalDesignStructure]
    [-fx]
    [-fi]
    [-B StorageSize]
    [-c MaxKeyColumnsInIndex]
    [-C MaxColumnsInIndex]
    [-e TuningLogTable]
    [-N OnlineOption]
    [-q]
```

40

```
[-u]
[-x]
[-a]
[-?]
```

This output has the following components:

▶ **-S ServerName[\Instance]**—Indicates the name of the SQL Server instance with which to connect. This is the server against which all tuning analysis and supporting table updates will be made.

▶ **-U LoginId**—Indicates the login ID to use in establishing a connection to SQL Server (specified via the -s option).

▶ **-P Password**—Specifies the password for the specified login ID.

▶ **-E**—Uses a trusted connection to connect to the server.

▶ **-d DatabaseName**—Identifies the database to connect to when tuning.

▶ **-D DatabaseName**—Provides a list of database names for tuning. Names are separated by commas.

▶ **-Tl TableName**—Provides a list of table names that should be tuned. Names are separated by commas. If only one database is specified through the -D option, table names do not need to be qualified with the database name. Otherwise, the fully qualified name, in the form [Database].[Schema].[Table], is required for each table.

▶ **-Tf TableListFileName**—Indicates the name of a file containing the list of tables to be tuned. Tables listed within the file must appear on separate lines, and the names must be qualified by database name and, optionally, by schema name. The optional table-scaling feature may be invoked by following the name of a table with a number that indicates the projected number of rows in that table (for example, '[myDatabase].[dbo].[myTable] 500').

▶ **-if WorkloadFileName**—Specifies the path and filename of the workload file to use as input for tuning. These are the accepted formats:

  ▶ ***.trc**—SQL Server Profiler trace file

  ▶ ***.xml**—SQL Server Profiler XML trace file

  ▶ ***.sql**—SQL Server script

▶ **-it WorkloadTableName**—Indicates the name of the table containing the workload trace for tuning. The name is specified as [Database].[Schema].[Table].

▶ **-ip**—Indicates that the workload should be taken from the plan cache.

▶ **-ipf**—Specifies that the query should be filtered on the basis of database ID. The default value is false.

▶ **-s SessionName**—Specifies the name of the new tuning session.

▶ **-of** `ScriptFileName`—Indicates that T-SQL script with recommendations should be written to a file. If a filename is supplied, the recommendations are written to that destination; otherwise, the filename is generated based on the session name.

▶ **-or** `ReportFileName`—Indicates that the report should be written to a file. If a filename is supplied, the report is written to that destination; otherwise, the filename is generated based on the session name.

▶ **-rl** `Report`—Specifies the list of analysis reports to generate. You select one or more of the following:

   ▶ `ALL`—Generate all reports

   ▶ `NONE`—Do not generate any reports

   ▶ `STMT_COST`—Statement cost report

   ▶ `EVT_FREQ`—Event frequency report

   ▶ `STMT_DET`—Statement detail report

   ▶ `CUR_STMT_IDX`—Statement-index relations report (current)

   ▶ `REC_STMT_IDX`—Statement-index relations report (recommended)

   ▶ `STMT_COSTRANGE`—Statement cost range report

   ▶ `CUR_IDX_USAGE`—Index usage report (current)

   ▶ `REC_IDX_USAGE`—Index usage report (recommended)

   ▶ `CUR_IDX_DET`—Index detail report (current)

   ▶ `REC_IDX_DET`—Index detail report (recommended)

   ▶ `VIW_TAB`—View-table relations report

   ▶ `WKLD_ANL`—Workload analysis report

   ▶ `DB_ACCESS`—Database access report

   ▶ `TAB_ACCESS`—Table access report

   ▶ `COL_ACCESS`—Column access report

By default, all reports are generated.

▶ **-ox** `OutputXmlFileName`—Indicates the name of the XML file to which the application writes output.

▶ **-F**—Permits Database Engine Tuning Advisor to overwrite existing output files (specified using any of the `o?` options).

▶ **-ID** `SessionID`—Specifies the ID of a session for which Database Engine Tuning Advisor should generate results.

40

▶ **-ix InputXmlFileName**—Indicates the name of the XML file that specifies a user configuration (that is, a user-specified configuration). Note that command-line options take precedence in the event that duplicate parameters are found in the file.

▶ **-A TuningTime**—Indicates the maximum amount of time, in minutes, that Database Engine Tuning Advisor will spend tuning. In general, longer times produce higher-quality recommendations. When 0 is specified as a value, the tuning time is unlimited. When a value is not specified, the tuning time is limited to 8 hours.

▶ **-n NumberOfEvents**—Specifies the number of events to tune.

▶ **-m MinimumImprovement**—Specifies that Database Engine Tuning Advisor should offer only recommendations for which the estimated improvement meets or exceeds the supplied value (in percentages). If no value is specified, recommendations are provided regardless of the degree of improvement.

▶ **-fa PhysicalDesignStructure**—Specifies the physical design structures for which Database Engine Tuning Advisor should consider proposing new recommendations. You select one of the available options:

 ▶ **IDX_IV**—Clustered and nonclustered indexes and indexed views

 ▶ **IDX**—Clustered and nonclustered indexes

 ▶ **IV**—Indexed views

 ▶ **NCL_IDX**—Nonclustered indexes

When no option is specified, IDX is used.

▶ **-fp PartitionStrategy**—Specifies the partitioning support requested that Database Engine Tuning Advisor should consider adding. You select one of the available options:

 ▶ **NONE**—No partitioning strategies

 ▶ **FULL**—Full partitioning (best performance)

 ▶ **ALIGNED**—Aligned partitioning (best manageability)

When no option is specified, NONE is used.

▶ **-fk PhysicalDesignStructure**—Specifies the physical design structures that Database Engine Tuning Advisor cannot remove from the existing database scheme. You select one of the available options:

 ▶ **ALL**—Keep all existing physical design structures

 ▶ **NONE**—Do not keep any existing physical design structures

 ▶ **CL_IDX**—Keep clustered indexes

 ▶ **IDX**—Keep clustered and nonclustered indexes

 ▶ **ALIGNED**—Keep aligned partitioning

When no option is specified, ALL is used.

▶ -fx—Specifies that Database Engine Tuning Advisor will evaluate the usefulness of existing physical design structures and will follow up with recommendations to drop low-use structures. This option cannot be used with the -fa and -fp options.

▶ -fi—Specifies that filtered indexes be considered for new recommendations.

▶ -B StorageSize—Specifies the maximum space, in megabytes, that can be consumed by the total size of all recommendations.

▶ -c MaxKeyColumnsInIndex—The maximum number of key columns in indexes proposed by the application.

▶ -C MaxColumnsInIndex—The maximum number of columns in indexes proposed by the application.

▶ -e TuningLogTable—The name of a table or file where Database Engine Tuning Advisor writes log messages that occurred during tuning. The table name should be supplied in the form [Database].[Schema].[Table]. That table is created on the server against which tuning is conducted. The filename must have the .xml extension. If no table or filename is passed, the default table is used.

▶ -N OnlineOption—Specifies whether objects should be created online, offline, or online where possible. If online indices are to be created, the tag "ONLINE=ON" is appended to the DDL script for all objects that can or should be created online. Select one of the available options:

    ▶ OFF—Offline only

    ▶ MIXED—Online where possible

    ▶ ON—Online only

OFF is the default.

▶ -q—Sets quiet mode. No information is written to the console, including progress and header information.

▶ -u—Launches the Database Engine Tuning Advisor GUI and passes all supplied command-line arguments as the initial configuration settings.

▶ -x—Starts the session and exits. All results are written to a database only. The output may be generated later by supplying the -ID parameter.

▶ -a—Tunes and applies recommendations without prompting.

▶ -?—Displays usage information.

Typical DTA command-line execution would look like this:

```
C:> DTA -S DATAXDESIGN-PC\SQL2014DXD01 -E -D AdventureWorks2014 -if
traffic_4tuning.sql -s MySession3 -of MySession3OutputScript.sql -ox
MySession3Output.xml -fa IDX_IV -fp NONE -fk NONE
```

This is the same tuning we did from the GUI. Figure 40.15 shows the command-line execution results.

FIGURE 40.15   DTA command-line utility execution.

If you want to utilize your production server's characteristics (hardware, index statistics, and metadata information) to come up with a more realistic set of recommendations, you can use the TestServer option in your XML input file (see XML below):

```xml
<?xml version="1.0" encoding="utf-16" ?>
<DTAXML xmlns:xsi="http://www.w3.org/2001/XMLSchema-instance"
xmlns="http://schemas.microsoft.com/sqlserver/2004/07/dta">
  <DTAInput>
    <Server>
      <Name>[DATAXDESIGN-PC\SQL2014DXD01]</Name>
      <Database>
        <Name>AdventureWorks2014</Name>
      </Database>
    </Server>
    <Workload>
      <File>c:\TRAFFIC_4TUNING.sql</File>
    </Workload>
    <TuningOptions>
      <TestServer>[DATAXDESIGN-PC\SQL2014DXD01]</TestServer>
      <TuningTimeInMin>60</TuningTimeInMin>
      <FeatureSet>IDX_IV</FeatureSet>
      <Partitioning>NONE</Partitioning>
      <KeepExisting>NONE</KeepExisting>
      <OnlineIndexOperation>OFF</OnlineIndexOperation>
    </TuningOptions>
  </DTAInput>
</DTAXML>
```

This will instruct DTA to pull the physical server information (SQL Server metadata, index statistics, and the physical hardware information of the indicated production server [Server element in the XML]). Then, a database shell will get created on a test server that is used to report out all the DTA recommendations but will be based on the production server's information. Figure 40.16 illustrates how this DTA variation would work. End results are likely more indicative of the real production changes that will need to be made to tune based on the workload provided.

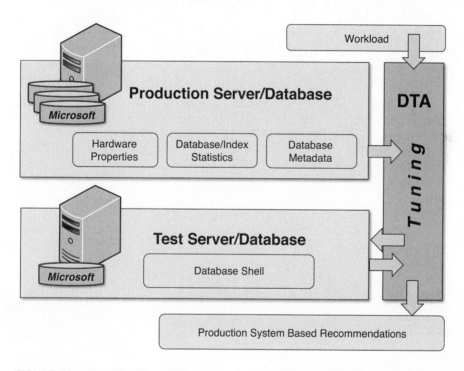

FIGURE 40.16   DTA utility utilizing production metadata, statistics, and hardware via the TestServer option.

Summary

To proactively identify needed enhancements to the indexing, partitioning, or physical table design, you should be running the DTA utility with a good representation of the production workload on a fairly regular basis. Don't wait until the database application is having major performance issues. DTA has matured enough where most of the recommendations are going to be fairly accurate if you have provided a good workload that represents what must be tuned for. Using DTA is not an excuse to blame others, though. (Don't blame Microsoft if the recommendations don't help much.) Use DTA results for what they are and test your application as much as possible with any changes that are being suggested. This is *your* responsibility. You will then have well-tested, well-documented, and well-formulated recommendations that you can take confidently into a production environment.

Chapter 41, "Managing Workloads with the Resource Governor," describes how to successfully manage and control SQL processing and not put your SQL Server environment in jeopardy.

Managing Workloads with the Resource Governor

If you have ever had a user kick off a runaway report that brought the system to its knees, effectively halting your production online transaction processing (OLTP) activity, you might have wished for a mechanism in SQL Server that would limit the amount of hardware resources allocated to ad hoc reporting requests so that normal production activity was not affected. Such a mechanism could prevent certain processes from consuming too many of the available SQL Server resources, ensuring that your more critical, higher-priority processes would consistently have access to the resources they need.

Fortunately, SQL Server 2014 provides such a mechanism: Resource Governor. Resource Governor allows you to classify different types of sessions on your server, which in turn allows you to control how server resources are assigned to a given activity. In SQL Server 2005 and earlier, queries fought among themselves to decide which one would grab the necessary resources first, and it was hard to predict who would win out. By using Resource Governor, you are able to instruct SQL Server to limit the resources a particular session can access. This capability can help ensure that your OLTP processes continue to provide predictable performance that isn't adversely affected by unpredictable activity. For example, with Resource Governor, you can specify that no more than 20% of CPU and/or memory resources should be allocated to processes that run reports. When this feature is enabled, no matter how many reports are run, they can never exceed their designated resource allocation. Of course, this reduces the performance of the reports, but at least your production OLTP performance isn't as negatively affected by runaway reports anymore.

> **NOTE**
>
> Resource Governor is available only in the Enterprise and Developer Editions of SQL Server 2014.

What's New for Resource Governor

Resource Governor was first introduced in SQL Server 2008. SQL Server 2014 provides enhancements to the Resource Governor that enables you to more effectively govern performance. In previous versions of SQL Server, the Resource Governor was limited to managing workloads based on CPU and memory resources. SQL Server 2014 added the ability to manage workloads based on physical I/O. This is a significant enhancement because physical I/O is often times the main resource bottleneck in a SQL Server environment. This can be especially important when running your SQL Server instance in a private cloud or in a hosted environment where shared I/O resources can be a point of contention.

Overview of Resource Governor

Resource Governor works by controlling the allocation of resources according to workloads. When a connection request is submitted to the Database Engine, the request is classified based on a classifier function. The classifier function is a scalar function that you define via T-SQL. The classifier function evaluates information about the connection (for example, login ID, application name, hostname, server role) to determine how it should be classified. After the connection request is classified, it is routed to a workload group defined for that classification (or if the connection cannot be classified, it is routed to the default workload group). Each workload group is associated with a resource pool. A resource pool represents the physical resources of SQL Server. In SQL Server 2014, the physical resources available for configuration are CPU, memory, and physical I/O, which is new to SQL Server 2014. The resource pool specifies the maximum amount of CPU, memory, and/or physical I/O resources that are to be allocated to a specific type of workload. When a connection is classified and put into the correct workload group, the connection is allocated the resources assigned to it, and then the query is passed on to the query optimizer for execution. This process is illustrated in Figure 41.1.

Resource Governor is designed to address the following types of resource issues, which are commonly found in a database environment:

► **Runaway queries**—These resource-intensive queries can take up most or all of the server resources.

► **Unpredictable workload execution**—This situation occurs when you have concurrent applications on the same server that are not isolated from each other, and the resulting resource contention causes unpredictable performance.

▶ **Workload prioritization**—You might want to ensure that a critical workload is given priority to the system resources so it can process faster than other workloads or is guaranteed to complete if there is resource contention.

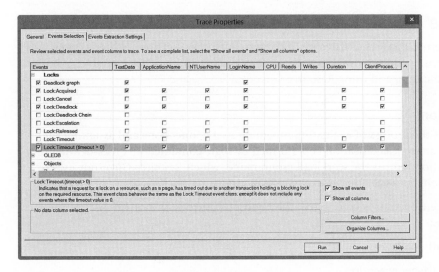

FIGURE 41.1   Overview of the Resource Governor.

In addition to enabling you to classify incoming connections and route their workloads to a specific group, Resource Governor also enables you to do the following:

▶ Monitor resource usage for each workload in a group

▶ Pool resources and set pool-specific limits on CPU, memory, and physical I/O allocation, which can prevent or minimize the probability of runaway queries

▶ Associate grouped workloads with a specific pool of resources

▶ Identify and set priorities for workloads

The current release of Resource Governor has the following limitations:

▶ Resource allocation is available for CPU, memory, or physical I/O usage. There is no support for managing network resource utilization.

▶ There is no workload monitoring or management between SQL Server instances.

▶ Physical I/O governance is limited to user operations. System tasks such as write operations to the transaction log and Lazy Writer I/O operations cannot be managed by the Resource Governor.

▶ You cannot set an I/O threshold on the internal resource pool.

▶ Resource Governor manages only resource consumption of the Database Engine. You cannot use Resource Governor to manage workloads within SSAS, SSIS, or SSRS.

In the following sections, you learn how to set up and configure Resource Governor for use, how Resource Governor works under the hood, and how you can use Resource Governor to better prioritize and manage a SQL Server's workload.

Resource Governor Components

Resource Governor consists of three main components: classification, resource pools, and workload groups. Understanding these three components and how they interact is important to understanding and using Resource Governor.

Classification

Classification is the process of evaluating incoming user connections and assigning them to a workload group. Classification is performed by logic contained in a user-defined function. The function returns the workload group name, which Resource Governor uses to route the sessions into the appropriate workload groups.

When Resource Governor is configured, the login process for a session consists of the following steps:

1. Login authentication

2. LOGON trigger execution

3. Classification

Resource Pools

A *resource pool*, or *pool*, represents the allocation of physical resources of the SQL Server. A resource pool has two parts:

▶ The first part specifies the minimum resource reservation. This part of the resource pool does not overlap with other pools.

▶ The other part specifies the maximum possible resource reservation for the pool. The resource allocation is shared with other pools.

In SQL Server 2014, the pool resources are set by specifying a MIN or MAX allocation for CPU, memory, or physical I/O. The MIN setting specifies the minimum guaranteed resource availability of the pool. The MAX setting sets the maximum size of the pool for each of the resources.

Because there cannot be any overlap in the minimum resource reservation, the sum of the MIN values across all pools cannot exceed 100% of the total server resources. This ensures that each pool is guaranteed the specified resource allocation.

The MAX value can be set anywhere in the range between the MIN value and 100% inclusive. The MAX setting represents the maximum amount of resources a session can consume, as long as the resources are available and not in use by another pool that is configured with a nonzero MIN value. When a pool has a nonzero MIN percentage defined, the effective MAX value of other pools is readjusted down, as necessary, to the existing MAX value minus the sum total of the MIN values of other pools.

For example, consider you have two user-defined pools. One pool, Pool1, is defined with a MIN setting of 20% and a MAX setting of 100%. The other pool, Pool2, is defined with a MIN setting of 50% and a MAX setting of 70%. The resulting effective MAX setting for Pool1 is 50% (100% minus the MIN 50% of Pool2). The effective MAX setting of Pool2, however, remains at 70% rather than 80% because 70% is the configured MAX value of Pool2.

The shared part of the pool (the amount between the MIN and effective MAX values) is used to determine the amount of resources that can be consumed by the pool if the resources are available and not being consumed by another pool. When resources are consumed by a pool, they are assigned to the specified pool and are not shared until processing completes in that pool.

To illustrate this further, consider a scenario in which there are three user-defined resource pools:

▶ PoolA is defined with a MIN % of 10 and MAX % of 100.

▶ PoolB is defined with a MIN % of 35 and a MAX % of 90.

▶ PoolC is defined with a MIN % of 30 and a MAX % of 80.

The effective MAX of PoolA would be calculated as follows:

MAX % of PoolA	100
minus MIN % of PoolB	35
minus MIN % of PoolC	30
equals EFF MAX of PoolA	35

The total Shared % of resources of PoolA would then be calculated as follows:

Effective MAX % of PoolA	35
minus MIN % of PoolA	10
equals Shared % of PoolA	25

Table 41.1 illustrates the calculated effective MAX and Shared % values for all pools in this configuration.

TABLE 41.1   Effective MAX and Shared % Values for Multiple Pools

Resource Pool	MIN %	MAX %	Effective MAX %	Shared %
Internal	0	100	100	100
Default	0	100	25	25
PoolA	10	100	35	25
PoolB	35	90	50	15
PoolC	30	80	35	5

To coincide with the predefined workload groups, Resource Governor also has two predefined resource pools: the internal pool and default pool.

The internal pool represents the resources consumed by the internal processes of the Database Engine. This pool always contains only the internal group, and the pool is not alterable in any way. The Internal Pool has a fixed MIN % of 0 and a MAX % of 100, and resource consumption by the internal pool is not restricted or reduced by any settings in other pools. In other words, the effective MAX of the Internal Pool is always 100%. Any workloads in the internal pool are considered critical for server function, and Resource Governor allows the internal pool to consume 100% of available resources if necessary, even if it means the violation of the resource requirements of the other pools.

The default pool is the first predefined user pool. Prior to any configuration, the default pool contains only the default group. The default pool cannot be created or dropped, but it can be altered. The default pool can contain user-defined groups in addition to the default group.

Resource Governor in SQL Server 2014 now supports a total of 64 resource pools. Because two of them are reserved for the internal and default pools, a total of 62 user-definable resource pools can be configured.

Workload Groups

Workload groups are the logical containers for similar connections, which are grouped together as similar according to the classification criteria applied to each connection. A workload group also provides the mechanism for aggregate monitoring of resource consumption.

Resource Governor has two predefined workload groups: the internal group and default group. The internal workload group is used solely by internal Database Engine processes. You cannot change the classification criteria for the internal group, and you also cannot classify any user requests for assignment to the internal group. You can, however, monitor the internal group.

Connection requests are automatically classified into the default group when the following conditions exist:

▶ There are no criteria to classify a request.

▶ There is an attempt to classify the request into a non-existent group.

▶ There is a general classification failure.

Now that you have an understanding of the Resource Governor components, let's put them into use by enabling and setting up some resource groups.

Configuring Resource Governor

To begin using Resource Governor for managing the resources of your workloads, follow these steps:

1. Enable Resource Governor.

2. Create your user-defined resource pools.

3. Define your workload groups and assign them to pools.

4. Create the classifier function.

5. Register the classifier function with the Resource Governor.

NOTE

Resource Governor can be set up and managed using either SQL Server Management Studio (SSMS) or via T-SQL commands. In the following sections, we first show you how to perform the tasks in SSMS and how the same actions can be implemented using T-SQL. Unfortunately, configuring Physical I/O resource pools has not yet been implemented in SSMS and currently can only be configured via T-SQL commands.

Enabling Resource Governor

Before you can begin creating your resource pools, you need to first enable the Resource Governor. To enable Resource Governor in SSMS, in Object Explorer, expand the `Management` node, right-click on the `Resource Governor` node, and select Enable (see Figure 41.2).

Alternatively, you can also enable Resource Governor by using the `ALTER RESOURCE GOVERNOR` command in T-SQL:

```
ALTER RESOURCE GOVERNOR RECONFIGURE
```

When Resource Governor is not enabled, the `RECONFIGURE` option enables Resource Governor. Enabling Resource Governor has the following results:

▶ The classifier function, if defined, is executed for new connections so that their workload can be assigned to workload groups.

▶ The resource limits specified in the Resource Governor configuration are honored and enforced.

▶ Any connections that existed before Resource Governor was enabled are now affected by any configuration changes made when Resource Governor was disabled.

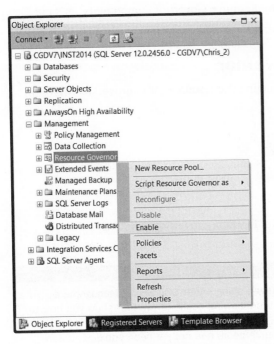

FIGURE 41.2   Enabling Resource Governor in SSMS.

When Resource Governor is already enabled, the RECONFIGURE option must be executed to apply any configuration changes made using the CREATE|ALTER|DROP WORKLOAD GROUP or CREATE|ALTER|DROP RESOURCE POOL statements.

To determine whether Resource Governor is currently enabled, you can run a SELECT statement against the sys.resource_governor_configuration system catalog table to view the is_enabled column:

```
select is_enabled from sys.resource_governor_configuration
go

/* output
is_enabled
----------
1
*/
```

To determine whether any Resource Governor configuration changes are pending, you can use the `sys.dm_resource_governor_configuration` dynamic management view (DMV):

```
select is_reconfiguration_pending
    from sys.dm_resource_governor_configuration
go

/* output
is_reconfiguration_pending
----------------------------
0
*/
```

To disable Resource Governor, right-click on the Resource Governor node and select Disable or execute the following command in T-SQL:

```
ALTER RESOURCE GOVERNOR DISABLE
```

Defining Resource Pools

When setting up a Resource Pool, you have to specify a name for the pool and set its properties. The properties available for a resource pool within SSMS are as follows:

▶ **Name**—The name used to refer to the resource pool

▶ **Minimum CPU %**—The guaranteed average CPU bandwidth for all requests to the resource pool when there is CPU contention

▶ **Maximum CPU %**—The maximum average CPU bandwidth for all requests to the resource pool when there is CPU contention

▶ **Min Memory %**—The guaranteed minimum amount of memory reserved for the resource pool that cannot be shared with other resource pools

▶ **Max Memory %**—The total server memory that can be used by requests to the resource pool

Creating a Resource Pool in SSMS

The following steps walk you through using SSMS to create a resource pool named `ReportPool` that you'll configure for handling report query workloads:

1. In Object Explorer, expand the `Management` node for a SQL Server Instance and expand the `Resource Governor` node.

2. Right-click on Resource Pools and select New Resource Pool to open the Resource Governor Properties page (see Figure 41.3).

3. In the Resource Pools grid, click the first column in the empty row. This row is labeled with an asterisk (*).

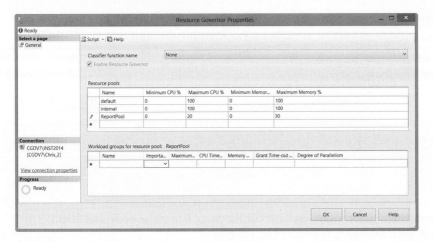

FIGURE 41.3   Creating a resource pool in SSMS.

> **NOTE**
>
> If the Resource Pools grid does not have a row labeled with an asterisk, Resource Governor has not been enabled yet. You can enable Resource Governor without leaving the Resource Governor Properties page by putting a checkmark in the Enable Resource Governor check box.

4. Double-click the empty cell in the Name column. Type in the name that you want to use for the resource pool. For this example, use the name ReportPool.

5. Set the CPU and Memory resource values (again, Physical I/O resource pools cannot yet be configured in SSMS). In this example, leave the Min CPU % and Min Memory % values at 0 and configure the Max CPU % and Max Memory % values at 20 and 30, respectively.

6. To create the pool and exit the dialog, click OK.

To verify that the new pool was created, expand the Resource Pools folder under the Resource Governor node and look for a node named ReportPool. Alternatively, you can run a query against the sys.resource_governor_resource_pools dynamic management view, similar to the following, which also displays the resource pool configuration:

```
select name,
       min_cpu_percent as MinCPU,
       max_cpu_percent as MaxCPU,
       min_memory_percent as 'MinMEM%' ,
       max_memory_percent as 'MaxMEM%'
from sys.resource_governor_resource_pools
go
```

```
/* output
name        MinCPU MaxCPU MinMEM% MaxMEM%
----------  ------ ------ ------- -------
internal    0      100    0       100
default     0      100    0       100
ReportPool  0      20     0       30
*/
```

> **NOTE**
>
> Missing from the SQL Server 2004 Resource Pools grid are properties related to the new I/O oriented resources. Fortunately, you can configure these new resources using T-SQL. This is discussed in the next section.

Creating a Resource Pool in T-SQL

Now that you've set up the ReportPool resource pool in SSMS, you are able to set up a second resource pool, OLTPPool, using T-SQL. The command to create a resource pool, CREATE RESOURCE POOL, takes up to eight arguments: MIN_CPU_PERCENT, MAX_CPU_PERCENT, MIN_MEMORY_PERCENT, MAX_MEMORY_PERCENT, CAP_CPU_PERCENT, AFFINITY, MIN_IOPS_PER_VOLUME and MAX_IOPS_PER_VOLUME. The MIN_IOPS_PER_VOLUME and MAX_IOPS_PER_VOLUME arguments are new to SQL Server 2014 and are used to create resource pools based on physical I/O. The I/O arguments specify the minimum and maximum reads or writes per second. The memory and CPU arguments specify a percentage value. The following example shows the creation of a resource pool based on memory, CPU, and I/O. After creating the resource pool, you need to run ALTER RESOURCE GOVERNOR RECONFIGURE to apply the new resource pool:

```
CREATE RESOURCE POOL OLTPPool
    WITH
        (min_cpu_percent=80,
         max_cpu_percent=100,
         min_memory_percent=75,
         max_memory_percent=100,
         MIN_IOPS_PER_VOLUME = 20,
         MAX_IOPS_PER_VOLUME = 100)
GO
ALTER RESOURCE GOVERNOR RECONFIGURE;
GO
```

Now that you've defined the resource pools needed, the next step is to define your workload groups and associate them with a resource pool.

Defining Workload Groups

After you define your resource pools, the next step is to create the workload groups and associate them with the appropriate resource pools. Multiple workgroups can be assigned to that same pool, but a workgroup cannot be assigned to multiple resource pools.

Creating Workload Groups in SSMS

To create a workload group in SSMS, perform the following steps:

1. In Object Explorer, expand the `Management` node, right-click the `Resource Governor` node, and then click Properties to bring up the Resource Governor Properties page.

2. In the Resource Pools grid, click the row for the resource pool you want to create a `workload group` for (in this example, the `ReportPool` resource pool). This creates a new empty row in the Workload Groups for Resource Pool grid for that pool.

3. Double-click the empty cell in the `Name` column for the empty workload group row and type in the name you want to use for the workload group (for this example, `ReportWG1`) and any other properties you want to specify (see Figure 41.4).

4. Click OK to exit the Properties page and create the workload group.

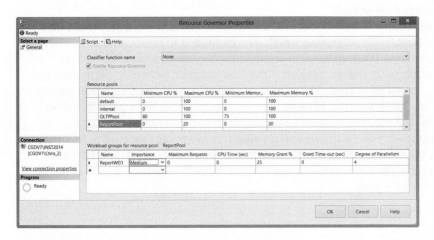

FIGURE 41.4   Creating a workload group in SSMS.

The additional, optional properties available for workload groups let you set a finer level of control over the execution of queries within a workload group. The options available are

▶ **Importance**—Specifies the relative importance (`LOW`, `MEDIUM`, or `HIGH`) of the workload group within the resource pool. If you define multiple workload groups in a resource pool, this setting determines whether requests within one workload group run at a higher or lower priority than other workload groups within the same resource pool. `MEDIUM` is the default setting. Currently, the weighting factor for each setting is `LOW=1`, `MEDIUM=3`, and `HIGH=9`. This means that the scheduler will attempt to execute sessions in workgroups with importance of `HIGH` three times more often than workgroups with `MEDIUM` importance, and nine times more often workgroups with `LOW` importance.

> **NOTE**
>
> Try to avoid having too many sessions in groups with high importance or assigning high importance to too many groups because the sessions will likely end up getting only equal time on the scheduler as your medium and low priority sessions.

▶ **Maximum Requests**—Specifies the maximum number of simultaneous requests allowed to execute in the workload group. The default setting, 0, allows unlimited requests.

▶ **CPU Time**—Specifies the maximum amount of CPU time, in seconds, that a request within the workload group can use. The default setting is 0, which means unlimited.

▶ **Memory Grant %**—Specifies, as a percentage, the maximum amount of execution grant memory that a single request can take from the resource pool. This percentage is relative to the amount of memory allocated to the resource pool. The allowed range of values is from 0 through 100. The default setting is 25. *Execution grant memory* is the amount of memory used for query execution, not for data buffers or cached plans, which can be shared by many sessions, regardless of resource pool or workload group. Note that setting this value to 0 prevents queries with SORT and HASH JOIN operations in user-defined workload groups from running. It is also not recommended that this value be set greater than 70 because the server may be unable to set aside enough free memory if other concurrent queries are running.

▶ **Grant Timeout**—Specifies the maximum time, in seconds, that a query waits for a resource to become available. If the resource does not become available, the process may fail with a timeout error. Note that a query does not always fail when the grant timeout is reached. A query fails only if there are too many concurrent queries running. Otherwise, the query may run with reduced resources, resulting in reduced query performance. The default setting is 0, which means the server calculates the timeout using an internal calculation based on query cost to determine the maximum time.

▶ **Degree of Parallelism**—Specifies the maximum degree of parallelism (DOP) for parallel queries. This values takes precedence over the global max degree of parallelism configuration setting, as well as any query hints. The allowed range of values is from 0 through 64. The default setting is 0, which means that processes use the global setting. Be aware that MAX_DOP specifies an upper limit only. The actual degree of parallelism is determined by the server based on the actual number of schedulers and available number of parallel threads, which may be less than the specified MAX_DOP. To better understand how the MAX_DOP setting is handled, consider the following:

   ▶ MAX_DOP as a query hint is considered only if it does not exceed the workload group MAX_DOP setting.

   ▶ MAX_DOP as a query hint always overrides the max degree of parallelism server configuration option.

► Workload group MAX_DOP always overrides the max degree of parallelism server configuration option.

► If a query is marked as serial at compile time, it cannot be changed back to parallel at runtime regardless of the workload group or server configuration setting.

► When the degree of parallelism is decided, it can be lowered only when memory pressure occurs. Workload group reconfiguration is not seen for tasks already waiting in the grant memory queue.

To verify that the new workload group was created, in SSMS Object Explorer, expand the Resource Governor node, expand the Resource Pools folder, expand the ReportPool node, and finally, expand the Workload Groups folder. You should then see a folder named ReportWG1.

Creating Workload Groups in T-SQL

Now that you've set up the ReportWG1 workload group in SSMS, you are able to set up a second workload group, OLTPWG1, using T-SQL. The command to create a resource pool, CREATE RESOURCE POOL, takes six optional arguments: IMPORTANCE, REQUEST_MAX_MEMORY_GRANT_PERCENT, REQUEST_MAX_CPU_TIME_SEC, GROUP_MAX_REQUESTS, REQUEST_MEMORY_GRANT_TIMEOUT_SEC, and MAX_DOP, which were described in the preceding section. The following example creates the OLTPWG1 workload group using only one of the optional arguments which sets the importance:

```
CREATE WORKLOAD GROUP OLTPWG1
    WITH ( IMPORTANCE = HIGH )
    USING OLTPPool
ALTER RESOURCE GOVERNOR RECONFIGURE
GO
```

To view the workload groups in T-SQL, you can run a query against the sys.resource_governor_workload_groups system catalog view, similar to the following, which also displays the workload group settings:

```
select wg.name,
       p.name as 'pool',
       group_max_requests as max_req,
       request_max_cpu_time_sec as max_cpu,
       request_max_memory_grant_percent as max_mem,
       request_memory_grant_timeout_sec as grant_timeout,
       max_dop
 from sys.resource_governor_workload_groups wg
      inner join
      sys.resource_governor_resource_pools p
      on wg.pool_id = p.pool_id
go
```

```
/* output
name        pool        max_req max_cpu max_mem grant_timeout max_dop
---------   ----------  ------- ------- ------- ------------- -------
internal    internal    0       0       25      0             0
default     default     0       0       25      0             0
ReportWG1   ReportPool  0       0       25      0             4
OLTPWG1     OLTPPool    0       0       25      0             0
*/
```

Creating a Classifier Function

After you define your resource pools and workload groups, you need to create a classification function that contains the logic to evaluate the connections and assign them to the appropriate workload group. The classifier function applies to each new session connection to SQL Server. Each session stays in the assigned workload group until it terminates, unless is it reassigned explicitly to a different group. There can be only one classifier function active at any given time. If no classifier function is defined or active, all connections are assigned to the default workload group.

The classifier function is a scalar function created with the CREATE FUNCTION statement, which must return a workgroup name as value of type SYSNAME (SYSNAME is a data type alias for nvarchar(128)). If the user-defined function returns NULL, 'default', or the name of a non-existent group, the session is assigned to the default workload group. The session is also assigned to the default context if the function fails for any reason.

The logic of the classifier function is typically based on connection properties and often determines the workload_group the connection should be assigned to based on values returned by system functions such as SUSER_NAME(), SUSER_SNAME(), IS_SRVROLEMEMBER(), IS_MEMBER(), HOST_NAME(), or APP_NAME(). In addition to these functions, you can use other available property functions when making classification decisions. The LOGINPROPERTY() function includes two properties (DefaultDatabase and DefaultLanguage) that can be used in classifier functions. In addition, the CONNECTIONPROPERTY() function provides access to the network transport and protocol being used for the connection, as well as details of the authentication scheme, the local IP address and TCP port, and the client's IP address. For example, you could assign a connection to a workload group based on which subnet a connection is coming in from.

> **TIP**
>
> If you decide to use either HOST_NAME() or APP_NAME() in your classifier function, be aware that it's possible for the values returned by these functions to be altered by users. In general, however, the APP_NAME() function tends to work very well for classifying connections.

> **TIP**
>
> A client session may time out if the classifier function does not complete within the speci-
> fied timeout for the client session. The timeout value is a client property, and as such,
> the server is unaware of the timeout value. A long-running classifier function can leave the
> server with orphaned connections for long periods. It is important that you create efficient
> classifier functions that finish execution before the client session timeout is exceeded.
>
> If you are using the Resource Governor, it is recommended that you enable the dedi-
> cated administrator connection (DAC) on the server. The DAC is not subject to Resource
> Governor classification and can be used to monitor and troubleshoot a classifier function.

For simplicity, the example presented in this chapter uses the SUSER_NAME() function.
Listing 41.1 first creates a couple of SQL Server logins (report_user and oltp_user),
which will be used within the classifier function to identify which workload group
session connections should be assigned to. After adding the logins as users in the
AdventureWorks2012 database, it then creates the classifier function in the master
database.

LISTING 41.1   Classifier Function Example

```
use master;
create login report_user with password='Rep0rter1'
create login oltp_user with password='01tPus3r1'
go


use AdventureWorks2012;
create user report_user
create user oltp_user
EXEC sp_addrolemember N'db_datawriter', N'report_user'
EXEC sp_addrolemember N'db_datareader', N'report_user'
EXEC sp_addrolemember N'db_datawriter', N'oltp_user'
EXEC sp_addrolemember N'db_datareader', N'oltp_user'
go


use master
go
CREATE FUNCTION dbo.WorkgroupClassifier ()
  RETURNS SYSNAME WITH SCHEMABINDING
AS
BEGIN
  DECLARE @WorkloadGroup SYSNAME = N'Unidentified';
  SET @WorkloadGroup = CASE suser_name()
    WHEN N'report_user' THEN
      N'ReportWG1'
    WHEN N'oltp_user' THEN
      N'OLTPWG1'
    ELSE N'Unidentified'
```

```
  END;
  RETURN @WorkloadGroup;
END;
Go
GRANT EXECUTE on dbo.WorkgroupClassifier to public
go
```

Before you put the classifier function into use, it's a good idea to test it. A poorly written classifier function could cause your system to become unresponsive. For example, you can test the `WorkgroupClassifier()` function in SSMS by executing the following commands under different login IDs:

```
-- Executed logged in as report_user
select dbo.WorkgroupClassifier()
go

/* output
---------
ReportWG1
*/


-- Executed logged in as oltp_user
select dbo.WorkgroupClassifier()
go

/* output
---------
OLTPWG1
*/


-- Executed Logged in as another user
select dbo.WorkgroupClassifier()
go

/* output
-----------------------
Unidentified
*/
```

After you verify the classifier function works as expected, you can then configure it as the classifier function using the `ALTER RESOURCE GOVERNOR` command:

```
ALTER RESOURCE GOVERNOR
  WITH (CLASSIFIER_FUNCTION = dbo.WorkgroupClassifier);
ALTER RESOURCE GOVERNOR RECONFIGURE;
```

After you create the function and apply the configuration changes, the Resource Governor classifier will use the workload group name returned by the function to send new requests to the appropriate workload group.

You can verify which classifier function Resource Governor is currently using by running the following query against the sys.resource_governor_configuration system catalog view:

```
select object_name(classifier_function_id) AS 'Classifier UDF name',
    is_enabled
from sys.resource_governor_configuration
go

/* output
Classifier UDF name   is_enabled
-------------------- ----------
WorkgroupClassifier   1
*/ At this point, your Resource Governor configuration is complete. You then should
monitor the system to make sure it's working as it should.
```

Monitoring Resource Usage

SQL Server provides three dynamic management views you can use to view and monitor your Resource Governor configuration:

▶ **sys.dm_resource_governor_workload_groups**—Returns workload group statistics along with the current in-memory configuration of the workload groups.

41

- ▶ **sys.dm_resource_governor_resource_pools**—Returns information about current state of your resource pools and resource pool statistics.

- ▶ **sys.dm_resource_governor_configuration**—Returns the in-memory configuration state of the Resource Governor. Output is the same as the sys.resource_governor_configuration system catalog view.

For example, the following query against the sys.dm_resource_governor_resource_pools DMV returns the configuration settings for each of the pools along with the actual memory allocated:

```
select name,
       min_cpu_percent as MinCPU,
       max_cpu_percent as MaxCPU,
       min_memory_percent as 'MinMEM%' ,
       max_memory_percent as 'MaxMEM%',
       max_memory_kb as 'MaxMemKB',
       used_memory_kb as 'UsedMemKB',
       target_memory_kb as 'TgtMemKB'
  from sys.dm_resource_governor_resource_pools
GO


/* output
name       MinCPU MaxCPU MinMEM% MaxMEM% MaxMemKB UsedMemKB TgtMemKB
---------- ------ ------ ------- ------- -------- --------- --------
internal   0      100    0       100     697584   162144    697584
default    0      100    0       100     174400   2960      174400
ReportPool 0      20     0       30      174400   0         174400
OLTPPool   80     100    75      100     697584   0         697584
*/
```

The following example displays statistics on the requests received within the defined workgroups:

```
select
    cast(g.name as nvarchar(10)) as wg_name,
    cast(p.name as nvarchar(10)) as pool_name,
    total_request_count as totreqcnt,
    active_request_count as actreqcnt,
    g.total_cpu_usage_ms as tot_cpu_use,
    total_cpu_limit_violation_count as tot_clvc,
    g.request_max_cpu_time_sec as req_mcts,
    g.total_reduced_memgrant_count as tot_rmc
```

```
from sys.dm_resource_governor_workload_groups g
    inner join
    sys.dm_resource_governor_resource_pools p
    on p.pool_id = g.pool_id
go

/* output
wg_name     pool_name   totreqcnt actreqcnt tot_cpu_use tot_clvc req_mcts tot_rmc
---------   ----------  --------- --------- ----------- -------- -------- -------
internal    internal    0         0         473462      0        0        0
default     default     880       1         6969        0        0        1
ReportWG1   ReportPool  0         0         0           0        0        0
OLTPWG1     OLTPPool    0         0         0           0        0        0
*/
```

Six other DMVs in SQL Server 2014 contain information related to Resource Governor:

▶ **sys.dm_exec_query_memory_grants**—Returns information about the queries that have acquired a memory grant or that still require a memory grant to execute. Resource Governor–related columns in this table are the group_id, pool_id, is_small, and ideal_memory_kb columns.

▶ **sys.dm_exec_query_resource_semaphores**—Returns information about the current query_resource semaphore status, providing general query-execution memory status information. The pool_id column provides a link to Resource Governor information.

▶ **sys.dm_exec_session**—Returns one row per session on SQL Server. The group_id column relates the information to Resource Governor workload groups.

▶ **sys.dm_exec_requests**—Returns information about each request currently executing within SQL Server. The group_id column relates the information to Resource Governor workload groups.

▶ **sys.dm_exec_cached_plans**—Returns a row for each query plan cached by SQL Server in the plan cache. The pool_id column relates the information to Resource Governor resource pools.

▶ **sys.dm_os_memory_brokers**—Returns information about internal allocations within SQL Server that use the Memory Manager. This information includes the following columns for the Resource Governor: pool_id, allocations_db_per_sec, predicted_allocations_kb, and overall_limit_kb.

The following query joins between `sys.dm_exec_session` and `sys.dm_resource_governor_workload_groups` to display which sessions are in which workload group:

```
SELECT
    CAST(g.name as nvarchar(10)) as poolname,
    s.session_id as 'session',
    s.login_time,
    CAST(s.host_name as nvarchar(15)) as host_name,
    CAST(s.program_name AS nvarchar(20)) as program_name
        FROM sys.dm_exec_sessions s
    INNER JOIN sys.dm_resource_governor_workload_groups g
        ON g.group_id = s.group_id
where g.name in ('default', 'ReportWG1', 'OLTPWG1')
go


/* output
poolname    session login_time              host_name        program_name
---------   ------- ---------------------   ---------------  --------------------
default          53 2015-02-26 21:55:49.630 LATITUDEE6520    Microsoft SQL Server
default          54 2015-02-26 23:30:22.170 LATITUDEE6520    Microsoft SQL Server
default          55 2015-02-26 23:30:22.163 LATITUDEE6520    Microsoft SQL Server
default          61 2015-02-26 23:34:26.123 LATITUDEE6520    Microsoft SQL Server
ReportWG1        56 2015-02-26 23:33:37.140 LATITUDEE6520    Microsoft SQL Server
OLTPWG1          60 2015-02-26 23:33:00.310 LATITUDEE6520    Microsoft SQL Server
*/
```

You can also monitor CPU, memory, and I/O resources allocated by the Resource Governor through the Windows Performance Monitor via a couple of performance counters:

▶ SQLServer: Resource Pool Stats

▶ SQLServer: Workload Group Stats

An instance of the SQLServer: Resource Pool Stats counter is available for each of the configured resource pools. Likewise, an instance of the SQLServer: Workload Group Stats counter is available for each of the configured workload groups (see Figure 41.5). These performance counters return the same information as that returned by the sys.dm_resource_governor_workload_groups and sys.dm_resource_governor_resource_pools DMVs but enable you to monitor these statistics over time.

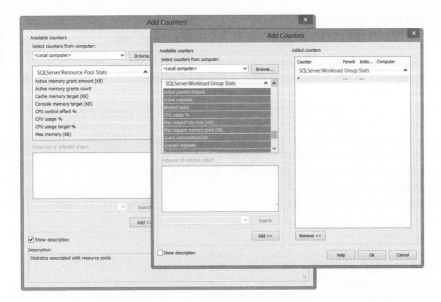

FIGURE 41.5   Monitoring resource pool and workload group statistics in Performance Monitor.

Modifying Your Resource Governor Configuration

You can modify settings for resource pools or workload groups in SQL Server Management Studio via the Resource Governor Properties page, as shown previously in Figure 41.4. You simply make the changes desired (for example, a Resource Pool Maximum CPU% or Workload Group Importance) and click OK to save the changes.

Alternatively, you can modify the resource pool using the ALTER RESOURCE POOL command. With this command, you can modify the minimum and maximum CPU and memory percentages for a resource pool. You can also modify the I/O oriented thresholds, which cannot be done via SSMS. The syntax is as follows:

```
ALTER RESOURCE POOL { pool_name | "default" }
[WITH
          ( [ MIN_CPU_PERCENT = value ]
    [ [ , ] MAX_CPU_PERCENT = value ]
    [ [ , ] CAP_CPU_PERCENT = value ]
    [ [ , ] AFFINITY {SCHEDULER = AUTO | (Scheduler_range_spec)
            | NUMANODE = (NUMA_node_range_spec)}]
    [ [ , ] MIN_MEMORY_PERCENT = value ]
    [ [ , ] MAX_MEMORY_PERCENT = value ]
    [ [ , ] MIN_IOPS_PER_VOLUME = value ]
    [ [ , ] MAX_IOPS_PER_VOLUME = value ]
)
]
```

You can modify workload group settings using the ALTER WORKLOAD GROUP command. You can change the workload group settings as well as move the workload group to another resource pool. The syntax is as follows:

```
ALTER WORKLOAD GROUP { group_name | "default" }
[ WITH
    ([ IMPORTANCE = { LOW | MEDIUM | HIGH } ]
            [ [ , ] REQUEST_MAX_MEMORY_GRANT_PERCENT = value ]
            [ [ , ] REQUEST_MAX_CPU_TIME_SEC = value ]
            [ [ , ] REQUEST_MEMORY_GRANT_TIMEOUT_SEC = value ]
            [ [ , ] MAX_DOP = value ]
            [ [ , ] GROUP_MAX_REQUESTS = value ] )
]
[ USING { pool_name | "default" } ]
```

> **NOTE**
>
> After executing your ALTER WORKLOAD GROUP or ALTER RESOURCE POOL commands, you need to run the ALTER RESOURCE GOVERNOR RECONFIGURE command to apply the changes.

The following example moves the ReportWG1 workload group from the ReportPool resource pool to the default resource pool:

```
ALTER WORKLOAD GROUP ReportWG1
USING [default];
GO
ALTER RESOURCE GOVERNOR RECONFIGURE
GO
```

You can also move a workload group to another resource pool in SSMS using the Resource Governor Properties page. Click the Resource Pool name in the Resource Pools grid; then right-click on Workload Group in the Workload Groups grid and select Move To (see Figure 41.6). This brings up the Move Workload Group dialog, which lists the available resource pools the workload group can be moved to. Select the desired resource pool and click OK.

Why move a workload group to a different resource pool? You might decide that a workload group should be in a resource pool that has different configuration settings, or you might want to move workload groups out of a resource pool so that you can drop the resource pool.

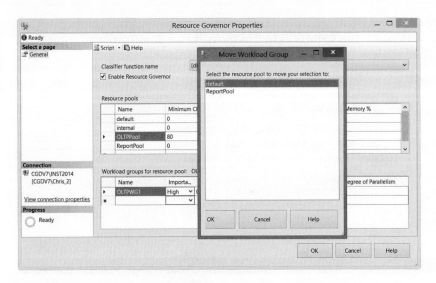

FIGURE 41.6   Moving a workload group in SSMS.

Deleting Workload Groups

You can delete a workload group or resource pool by using SQL Server Management Studio or T-SQL. To drop a workload group in SSMS, follow these steps:

1. Expand the `Management` node in Object Explorer and expand the `Resource Governor` node to display the `Resource Pools` folder.

2. Expand the node of the resource pool where the workload group is defined to display the `Workload Groups` folder.

3. Expand the `Workload Groups` folder to list the workload groups.

4. Right-click the workload group you want to drop and select Delete.

5. In the Delete Object window, the Workload Group is listed in the Object to Be Deleted list. Click OK to confirm the deletion.

To drop a workload group using T-SQL, use the `DROP WORKLOAD GROUP` command:

```
DROP WORKLOAD GROUP OLTPWG1
ALTER RESOURCE GOVERNOR RECONFIGURE
go
```

You cannot drop a workload group if there are any active sessions assigned to it. If a workload group contains active sessions, deleting the workload group or moving it to a different resource pool will fail when the `ALTER RESOURCE GOVERNOR RECONFIGURE` statement is called to apply the change. The following options provide a way to work around this problem:

▶ Wait until all the sessions from the affected group have disconnected and then rerun the ALTER RESOURCE GOVERNOR RECONFIGURE statement.

▶ Explicitly stop sessions in the affected group by using the KILL command and then rerun the ALTER RESOURCE GOVERNOR RECONFIGURE statement.

▶ Restart SQL Server. When the restart process is complete, the deleted group will not be created, and a moved group will automatically use the new resource pool assignment.

NOTE

If an attempt to reconfigure Resource Governor fails after dropping a workload group because of active sessions and you change your mind about dropping the workload group, you can restore it by rerunning the CREATE WORKLOAD GROUP command for that workgroup. After re-creating the workload group, run the ALTER RESOURCE GROUP RECONFIGURE command again, and the workload group is restored.

Deleting Resource Pools

To drop a resource pool in SSMS, follow these steps:

1. Expand the Management node in Object Explorer and expand the Resource Governor node to display the Resource Pools folder.

2. Expand the Resource Pools folder to list the resource pools defined.

3. Right-click the resource pool you want to drop and select Delete.

4. In the Delete Object window, the resource pool is listed in the Object to Be Deleted list. Click OK to confirm the deletion.

To drop a resource pool using T-SQL, use the DROP RESOURCE POOL command:

```
DROP RESOURCE POOL OLTPPOOL
ALTER RESOURCE GOVERNOR RECONFIGURE
go
```

You cannot drop a resource pool if any workload groups are still assigned to the resource pool. You need to drop the workload group or move it to another resource pool first.

Modifying a Classifier Function

If you need to make a change to the classifier function, it's important to note that the function cannot be dropped or altered while it is marked as the classifier function for the Resource Governor. Before you can modify or drop the classifier function, you first need to disable Resource Governor. Alternatively, you can replace the classifier function with another by running the ALTER RESOURCE GOVERNOR command and passing it a different

CLASSIFIER_FUNCTION name. You can also simply disable the current classifier function by executing the following command:

```
ALTER RESOURCE GOVERNOR
  WITH (CLASSIFIER_FUNCTION = NULL);
ALTER RESOURCE GOVERNOR RECONFIGURE;
```

The sample classifier function shown in Listing 41.1 uses a simple case expression to determine the workload group based on only two login IDs. If you have a more complex set of rules to apply or want to be able to make changes more dynamically than having to replace the classifier function each time you need to make a change, you can define your classifier function to look up the workload group names from a database table, rather than hard-coding the workload group names and matching criteria into the function. Performance should not be greatly affected when accessing the table to look up the workload group. The reason is that the table likely won't be very large and should remain cached in the buffer pool because it's being accessed repeatedly every time a connection is made to SQL Server.

Summary

Resource Governor offers many potential benefits, primarily the capability to prioritize SQL Server resources for critical applications and users and preventing "runaway" or unexpected queries from adversely impacting SQL Server performance significantly. It fits in with Microsoft's goal of providing predictable performance for your SQL Server applications.

Resource Governor also offers some potential pitfalls, however. For example, a misconfigured Resource Governor can not only hurt a server's overall performance, but can potentially lock up your server, requiring you to use the dedicated administrator connection to attach to the locked-up SQL Server to troubleshoot and fix the problem. Therefore, it is recommended that you implement Resource Governor only if you are an experienced DBA and have a good understanding of, and familiarity with, the workloads executed against your SQL Server databases. Even then, it's imperative that you test your configuration on a test server before rolling it out into production.

Also, after implementing a Resource Governor configuration, you should monitor your SQL Server performance to make sure the configuration has the desired effect. The next chapter, "SQL Server High Availability Fundamentals," provides guidelines for delivering High Availability to your SQL Server environment.

PART VI

SQL Server High Availability

IN THIS PART

CHAPTER 42

SQL Server High Availability Fundamentals

With SQL Server 2014, Microsoft continues to push the high availability (HA) bar higher and higher. Extensive HA options such as AlwaysOn Availability Groups and AlwaysOn Failover Cluster Instances, coupled with a variety of Windows Server family enhancements, provide almost everyone with a chance at achieving the mythical "five nines" (that is, 99.999% uptime).

Understanding your HA requirements is only the first step in implementing a successful HA application. Knowing what technical options exist is equally as important. Then, by following a few basic design guidelines, you can match your requirements to the best high-availability technical solution.

This chapter introduces a variety of fundamental HA options—such as redundant hardware configurations, RAID, and MSCS clustering—as well as more high-level options—such as SQL clustering, data replication, and change data capture—that should lead you to a solid high-availability foundation. Microsoft has slowly been moving in the direction of trying to make SQL Server (and the Windows operating systems) as continuously available as possible for as many of its options as possible. Remember that Microsoft is competing with the UNIX/Linux-based worlds that have offered (and achieved) much higher uptime levels for years. The SQL Server RDBMS engine itself and the surrounding services, such as Analysis Services, Integration Services, Notification Services, and Reporting Services, have all taken big steps toward higher availability.

What's New in High Availability

In a word, *AlwaysOn* (we think this can be considered a single word) has changed the face of HA for SQL Server platforms. These new options and several other tried-and-true options offer a very strong database engine foundation that can be highly available (7 days a week, 365 days a year). Microsoft's sights are set on being able to achieve five-nines reliability with almost everything it builds. Their SQL Server internal breakthrough introduced with SQL Server 2005 called "copy-on-write" technology has enabled Microsoft to greatly enhance several of its database high availability options. And with the combination of clustering and availability groups together, HA is easier to achieve than ever.

Here are a few of the most significant enhancements and new features that have direct or indirect effects on increasing high availability for a SQL Server 2014-based implementation:

▶ **SQL Server 2014 AlwaysOn Failover Cluster**—Builds a SQL Server instance level failover configuration on top of the Windows Server Failover clustering feature and Availability Groups.

▶ **SQL Server 2014 AlwaysOn Availability Groups**—Creates a database-level failover configuration with Primary and Secondary database replicas.

▶ **All SQL Server 2014 services as cluster managed resources**—All SQL Server 2014 services are cluster aware.

▶ **SQL Server 2014 peer-to-peer replication**—This option of data replication uses a publisher-to-publisher model (hence peer-to-peer).

▶ **SQL Server 2014 automatic page corruption recovery**—This enhancement in AlwaysOn configurations recognizes and corrects corrupt pages.

▶ **SQL Server 2014 transaction record compression**—This feature allows for compression of the transaction log records used in database mirroring and AlwaysOn configurations to increase the speed of transmission to the mirror or replica(s).

▶ **SQL Server 2014 fast recovery**—Administrators can reconnect to a recovering database after the transaction log has been rolled forward (and before the rollback processing has finished).

▶ **Online restore**—Database administrators can perform a restore operation while the database is still online.

▶ **Online indexing**—The online index option allows concurrent modifications (updates, deletes, and inserts) to the underlying table or clustered index data and any associated indexes during index creation time.

▶ **Online index builds**—Ability to create, rebuild, or drop indexes even when tables contain large objects (LOB data types). Some restrictions apply.

▶ **Indirect checkpoints**—Option for a database to automatically checkpoint using a new checkpointing algorithm that provides more accuracy around database recovery times.

▶ **Adding table columns that contain defaults**—Can now add table columns that contain default values via a metadata-only operation.

▶ **Database snapshot**—SQL Server 2014 allows for the generation and use of a read-only, stable view of a database. The database snapshot is created without the overhead of creating a complete copy of the database or having completely redundant storage.

▶ **Addition of a snapshot isolation level**—A new snapshot isolation (SI) level is being provided at the database level. With SI, users can access the last committed row, using a transactionally consistent view of the database.

▶ **Dedicated administrator connection**—SQL Server 2014 supports a dedicated administrator connection that administrators can use to access a running server even if the server is locked or otherwise unavailable. This capability enables administrators to troubleshoot problems on a server by executing diagnostic functions or Transact-SQL statements without having to take down the server.

At the operating system (OS) level, Windows 2008 and 2012 have greatly advanced the virtualization capabilities with hypervisor (Hyper-V) for both cloud and on-premise platforms for SQL Server. This has outperformed many competing virtual platforms (such as VMware). This has also firmly established virtualization for both development and production environments and allows entire application and database stacks to run on a completely virtual operating system footprint that will never bring down the physical server.

> **NOTE**
>
> Microsoft has announced that log shipping will stay in SQL Server for a while longer and will instead be deprecating database mirroring.

Keep in mind that Microsoft already has an extensive capability in support of high availability. The new HA features add significant gains to the already feature-rich offering.

What Is High Availability?

The availability continuum depicted in Figure 42.1 shows a general classification of availability based on the amount of downtime an application can tolerate without impacting the business. You would write your service-level agreements (SLAs) to support and try to achieve one of these continuum categories.

Topping the chart is the extreme availability category, so named to indicate that this is the least tolerant category and is essentially a zero (or near zero) downtime requirement (that is, sustained 99.5% to 100% availability). The mythical five-nines falls at the high end of this category. Next is the high availability category, which has a minimal tolerance for downtime (that is, sustained 95% to 99.4% availability). Most "critical" applications would fit into this category of availability need. Then comes the standard availability category, with a more normal type of operation (that is, sustained 83% to 94% availability). The acceptable availability category is for applications that are deemed noncritical to a company's business, such as online employee benefit package self-service applications. These applications can tolerate much lower availability ranges (sustained 70% to 82% availability) than the more critical services. Finally, the marginal availability category is for nonproduction custom applications, such as marketing mailing label applications that can tolerate significant downtime (that is, sustained 0% to 69% availability). Again, remember that availability is measured by the planned operation times of the application.

Availability Continuum

	Characteristic	Availability Range
Extreme Availability	Near zero downtime!	(99.5% – 100%) 1.8 days/yr – 5.26 min/yr
High Availability	Minimal downtime	(95% – 99.4%) 18 days/yr – 2.0 days/yr
Standard Availability	With some downtime tolerance	(83% – 94%)
Acceptable Availability	Non-critical Applications	(70% – 82%)
Marginal Availability	Non-production Applications	(up to 69%)

Availability Range **describes the percentage of time relative to the "planned" hours of operations**

8,760 hours/year | 168 hours/week | 24 hours/day
525,600 minutes/year | 7,200 minutes/week | 1,440 minutes/day

FIGURE 42.1   Availability continuum.

> **NOTE**
>
> Another featured book from Sams Publishing, called *Microsoft SQL Server High Availability*, can take you to the depths of high availability from every angle. This landmark offering provides a complete guide to high availability, beginning with ways to gather and understand your HA requirements, assess your HA needs, and completely build out high-availability implementations for the most common business scenarios in the industry. Pick up this book if you are serious about achieving five-nines of reliability.

Achieving the mythical five-nines (that is, a sustained 99.999% availability) falls into the extreme availability category (which tolerates between 5.26 minutes and 1.8 days of down time per year). In general, the computer industry calls this high availability, but we push this type of near-zero downtime requirement into its own extreme category, all by itself. Most applications can only dream about this level of availability because of the costs involved, the high level of operational support required, the specialized hardware that must be in place, and many other extreme factors.

The Fundamentals of HA

Every minute of downtime you have today translates into losses that you cannot well afford. You must fully understand how the hardware and software components work together and how, if one component fails, the others will be affected. High availability of an application is a function of all the components together, not just one by itself. Therefore, the best approach for moving into supporting high availability is to work on shoring up the basic foundation components of hardware, backup/recovery, operating system upgrading, ample vendor agreements, sufficient training, extensive quality assurance/testing, rigorous standards and procedures, and some overall risk-mitigating strategies, such as spreading out critical applications over multiple servers. By addressing these first, you add a significant amount of stability and high-availability capability across your hardware/system stack. In other words, you are moving up to a necessary level before you completely jump into a particular high-availability solution. If you do nothing further from this point, you have already achieved a portion of your high-availability goals.

Hardware Factors

You need to start by addressing your basic hardware issues for high availability and fault tolerance. This includes redundant power supplies, UPS systems, redundant network connections, and ECC memory (error correcting). Also available are "hot-swappable" components, such as disks, CPUs, and memory. In addition, most servers are now using multiple CPUs, fault-tolerant disk systems such as RAID, mirrored disks, storage area networks (SANs), Network Attached Storage (NAS), redundant fans, and so on.

Cost may drive the full extent of what you choose to build out. However, you should start with the following:

▶ Redundant power supplies (and UPSs)

▶ Redundant fan systems

▶ Fault-tolerant disks, such as RAID (1 through 10), preferably "hot swappable"

▶ ECC memory

▶ Redundant Ethernet connections

Backup Considerations

After you consider hardware, you need to look at the basic techniques and frequency of your disk backups and database backups. For many companies, the backup plan isn't what it needs to be to guarantee recoverability and even the basic level of high availability. At many sites, database backups are not being run, are corrupted, or aren't even considered necessary. You would be shocked by the list of Fortune 1000 companies where this occurs.

Operating System Upgrades

You need to make sure that all upgrades to your OS are applied and also that the configuration of all options is correct. This includes making sure you have antivirus software installed (if applicable), along with the appropriate firewalls for external-facing systems.

Vendor Agreements Followed

Vendor agreements come in the form of software licenses, software support agreements, hardware service agreements, and both hardware and software service-level agreements. Essentially, you are trying to make sure you can get all software upgrades and patches for your OS and for your application software at any time, as well as get software support, hardware support agreements, and both software and hardware SLAs in place to guarantee a level of service within a defined period of time.

Training Kept Up-to-Date

Training is multifaceted in that it can be for software developers to guarantee that the code they write is optimal, for system administrators who need to administer applications, and even for end users themselves to make sure they use the system correctly. All these types of training play into the ultimate goal of achieving high availability.

Quality Assurance Done Well

Testing as much as possible—and doing it in a very formal way—is a great way to guarantee a system's availability. Dozens of studies over the years have clearly shown that the more thoroughly you test (and the more formal your QA procedures), the fewer software problems you will have. Many companies foolishly skimp on testing, which has a huge impact on system reliability and availability.

Standards/Procedures Followed

Standards and procedures are interlaced tightly with training and QA. Coding standards, code walkthroughs, naming standards, formal system development life cycles, protection of tables from being dropped, use of governors, and so on all contribute to more stable and potentially more highly available systems.

Server Instance Isolation

By design, you may want to isolate applications (such as SQL Server's applications and their databases) away from each other to mitigate the risk of such an application causing another to fail.

Plain and simple, you should never put applications in each other's way if you don't have to. The only things that might force you to load up a single server with all your applications would be expensive licensing costs for each server's software and perhaps hardware scarcity (strict limitations to the number of servers available for all applications). A classic example occurs when a company loads up a single SQL Server instance with between two and eight applications and their associated databases. The problem is that the applications are sharing memory, CPUs, and internal work areas, such as `tempdb`. Figure 42.2 shows an overloaded SQL Server instance that is being asked to service seven major applications (Appl 1 DB through Appl 7 DB).

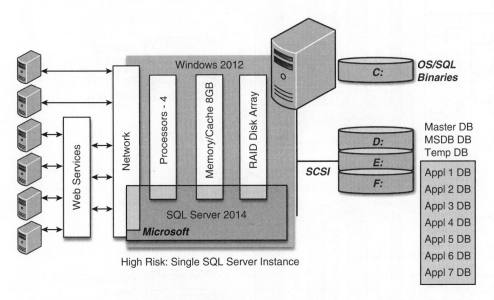

FIGURE 42.2   High risk: Many applications sharing a single SQL Server 2014 instance.

The single SQL Server instance in Figure 42.2 is sharing memory (cache) and critical internal working areas, such as `tempdb`, with all seven major applications. Everything runs fine until one of these applications submits a runaway query, and all other applications being serviced by that SQL Server instance come to a grinding halt. Most of this built-in risk could be avoided by simply putting each application (or perhaps two applications) onto their own SQL Server instance, as shown in Figure 42.3. This fundamental design approach greatly reduces the risk of one application affecting another.

Many companies make this fundamental error. The trouble is that they keep adding new applications to their existing server instance without a full understanding of the shared resources that underpin the environment. It is often too late when they finally realize that they are hurting themselves "by design." You have now been given proper warning of the risks. If other factors, such as cost or hardware availability, dictate otherwise, then at least it is a calculated risk that is entered into knowingly (and is properly documented as well).

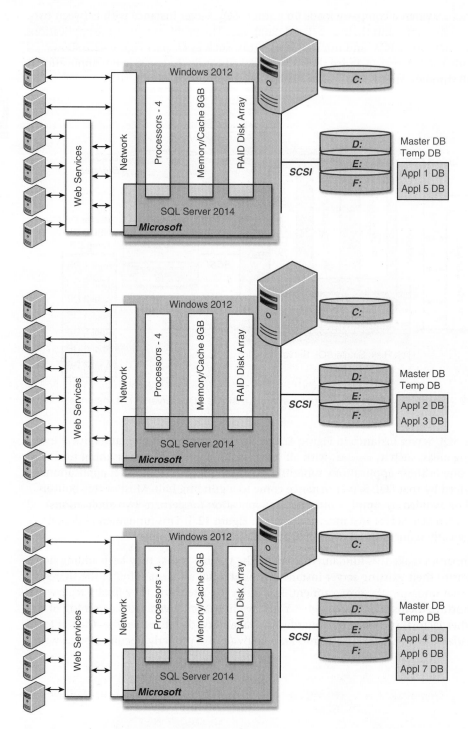

FIGURE 42.3   Mitigated risk: Isolating critical applications away from each other.

Building Solutions with One or More HA Options

When you have the fundamental foundation in place, as described in the preceding section, you can move on to building a tailored software-driven high-availability solution. Which HA option(s) you should be using really depends on your HA requirements. The following high-availability options are used both individually and, very often, together to achieve different levels of HA:

▶ AlwaysOn Failover Clustering Instance (FCI)

▶ AlwaysOn Availability Groups

▶ Failover Cluster Services

▶ SQL clustering

▶ Data replication (including peer-to-peer configurations)

▶ Change Data Capture

▶ Log shipping

All these options are readily available "out of the box" from Microsoft, from the Windows Server family of products and from Microsoft SQL Server 2014.

It is important to understand that some of these options can be used together, but not all go together. For example, you might use Failover Cluster Services (FCS) along with Microsoft SQL Server 2014's SQL Clustering to implement the SQL clustering database configuration.

Failover Cluster Services (FCS)

FCS could actually be considered a part of the basic HA foundation components described earlier, except that it's possible to build a high-availability system without it (for example, a system that uses numerous redundant hardware components and disk mirroring or RAID for its disk subsystem). Microsoft has made FCS the cornerstone of its clustering capabilities, and FCS is utilized by applications that are cluster-enabled. A prime example of a cluster-enabled technology is Microsoft SQL Server 2014.

FCS is the advanced Windows operating system configuration that defines and manages between 2 and 16 servers as "nodes" in a cluster. These nodes are aware of each other and can be set up to take over cluster-aware applications from any node that fails (for example, a failed server). This cluster configuration also shares and controls one or more disk subsystems as part of its high-availability capability. Figure 42.4 illustrates a basic two-node FCS configuration (configuring Failover Cluster Instances).

FCS can be set up in an active/passive or active/active mode. Essentially, in an active/passive mode, one server sits idle (that is, is passive) while the other is doing the work (that is, is active). If the active server fails, the passive one takes over the shared disk and the cluster-aware applications instantaneously.

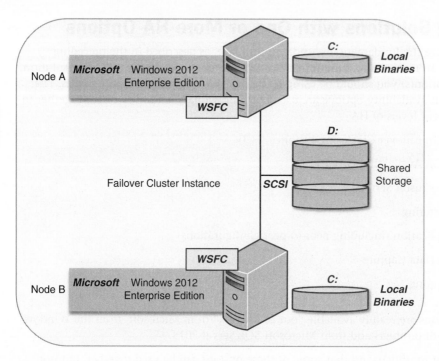

FIGURE 42.4   Basic two-node FCS configuration.

SQL Clustering

If you want a SQL Server instance to be clustered for high availability, you are essentially asking that this SQL Server instance (and the database) be completely resilient to a server failure and completely available to the application without the end user ever even noticing that there was a failure (or at least with minimal interruption). Microsoft provides this capability through the SQL Clustering option. SQL Clustering is built on top of FCS for its underlying detection of a failed server and for its availability of the databases on the shared disk (which is controlled by FCS). SQL Server is said to be a "cluster-aware/enabled" technology.

A SQL Server instance that is clustered can be created by actually creating a virtual SQL Server instance that is known to the application (the constant in the equation) and then two physical SQL Server instances that share one set of databases (shared storage). In an active/passive configuration, only one SQL Server instance is active at a time and just goes along and does its work. If that active server fails (and with it, the physical SQL Server instance), the passive server (and the physical SQL Server instance on that server) simply takes over instantaneously. This is possible because FCS also controls the shared storage where the databases are. The end user and application never really know which physical SQL Server instance they are on or whether one failed. Figure 42.5 illustrates a typical SQL Clustering configuration built on top of FCS (and Failover Cluster Instances).

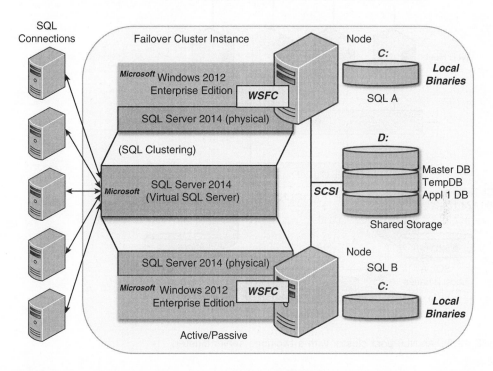

FIGURE 42.5   Basic SQL Clustering two-node configuration (active/passive).

Setup and management of this type of configuration are much easier than you might think. More and more often, SQL Clustering is the method chosen for most high-availability solutions. Later in this chapter, you see that other methods may also be viable for achieving high availability (based on the application's HA requirements). Chapter 44, "SQL Server Failover Clustering," covers this topic in more detail.

Extending the clustering model to include Network Load Balancing (NLB) pushes this particular solution even further into higher availability—from client traffic high availability to back-end SQL Server high availability. Figure 42.6 shows a four-host NLB cluster architecture acting as a virtual server to handle the network traffic coupled with a two-node SQL cluster on the back end. This setup is resilient from top to bottom.

The four NLB hosts work together, distributing the work efficiently. NLB automatically detects the failure of a server and repartitions client traffic among the remaining servers.

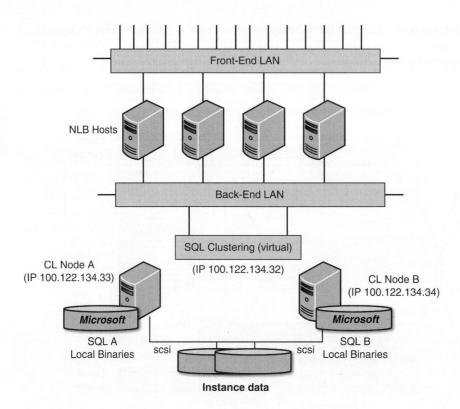

FIGURE 42.6   An NLB host cluster with a two-node server cluster.

The following apply to SQL Clustering in SQL Server 2014:

▶ **Full SQL Server 2014 Services as cluster-managed resources**—All SQL Server 2014 services, including the following, are cluster-aware:

  ▶ SQL Server DBMS engine

  ▶ SQL Server Agent

  ▶ SQL Server Full-Text Search

  ▶ Analysis Services

  ▶ Integration Services

  ▶ Notification Services

  ▶ Reporting Services

  ▶ Service Broker

Now, you can extend this fault-tolerant solution to embrace more SQL Server instances and all of SQL Server's related services. This is a big deal because things like Analysis Services previously had to be handled with separate techniques to achieve near high availability levels. Not anymore; each SQL Server service is now cluster-aware.

AlwaysOn Failover Clustering Instance (FCI)

New in SQL Server 2014 is the AlwaysOn capability. Being "always on" is a pretty powerful statement and commitment. It is now possible to mostly achieve this commitment with infrastructure, instance, database, and client connectivity level HA. Built on Windows Server Failover Clustering (WSFC or FCS as it is also known), the SQL Server AlwaysOn configuration leverages the tried-and-true experience and technology components of SQL clustering and database mirroring under the covers (and repackaged). This new packaging and enhancement has allowed Microsoft to deprecate database mirroring in favor of these new AlwaysOn options (FCI and Availability Groups). AlwaysOn Failover Cluster Instances (FCI) is the server-level instance portion of the AlwaysOn HA capability. (For more information, see Chapter 45, "SQL Server AlwaysOn and Availability Groups.") As you can see on the left side of Figure 42.7, the FCI is a two-node SQL cluster that is also utilizing the Availability Group capability. You'll learn more about the Availability Group (database-level availability) in the next section. The FCI becomes fault tolerant at the server instance level for maximum availability of SQL Server itself (just as you know and love SQL clustering from the past) and is utilizing a single storage location that is shared (owned) by the two underlying SQL instances for the clustered instances database storage. As you will see later, when coupled with Availability Groups (and even virtualization), a very high level of availability can be achieved.

AlwaysOn Availability Groups

Also new in SQL Server 2014 is the Availability Group capability. This is focused on database-level failover and availability by utilizing a data redundancy approach. Again, borrowing on the database mirroring experience (and underlying technologies), a transactionally consistent secondary replica is made that can be used for both read-only access (it is active for use at all times) as well as for failover if the primary database (primary replica) fails for any reason. In Figure 42.8, you can see a SQL Server AlwaysOn Availability Group being utilized for HA and even for distributing the read-only workload off of the primary SQL Server instance to the secondary replica. You can have up to four secondary replicas in an Availability Group, with the first secondary replica being used for automatic failover (using the synchronous-commit mode), and then other secondary replicas available for workload distribution and manual failover use. Remember, this is storing data redundantly, and you can sure burn up a lot of disk storage fast. When in synchronous-commit mode, that secondary replica can also be used to make database backups because it is completely consistent with the primary replica. Outstanding! You can find more on this subject in Chapter 45.

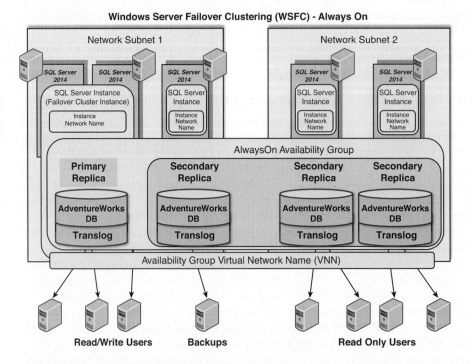

FIGURE 42.7   AlwaysOn SQL Failover Cluster Instance (FCI); two-node server cluster.

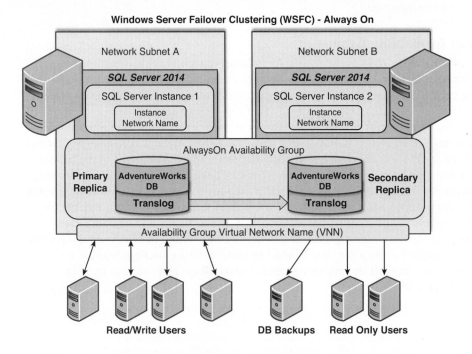

FIGURE 42.8   AlwaysOn Availability Group providing HA at the database level.

Data Replication

The next technology option that can be utilized to achieve high availability is data repli-cation. Originally, data replication was created to offload processing from a very busy server (such as an OLTP application that must also support a big reporting workload) or to geographically distribute data for different, very distinct user bases (such as worldwide product ordering applications). As data replication (transactional replication) became more stable and reliable, it started to be used to create "warm" (almost "hot") standby SQL Servers that could also be used to fulfill basic reporting needs. If the primary server ever failed, the reporting users would still be able to work (hence a higher degree of availability achieved for them), and the replicated reporting database could be used as a substitute for the primary server, if needed (hence a warm-standby SQL Server). When doing transactional replication in the "instantaneous replication" mode, all data changes were replicated to the replicate servers extremely quickly. With SQL Server 2000, updating subscribers allowed for even greater distribution of the workload and, overall, increased the availability of the primary data server and distributed the update load across the repli-cation topology. There are plenty of issues and complications involved in using the updat-ing subscribers approach (for example, conflict handlers, queues).

With SQL Server 2005, Microsoft introduced peer-to-peer replication, which is not a publisher/subscription model, but a publisher-to-publisher model (hence peer-to-peer). It is a lot easier to configure and manage than other replication topologies, but it still has its nuances to deal with. This peer-to-peer model allows excellent availability for this data and great distribution of workload along geographic (or other) lines. This may fit some companies' availability requirements and also fulfill their distributed reporting require-ments as well.

The top of Figure 42.9 shows a typical SQL data replication configuration of a central publisher/subscriber using continuous transactional replication. This can serve as a basis for high availability and also fulfills a reporting server requirement at the same time. The bottom of Figure 42.9 shows a typical peer-to-peer continuous transactional replication model that is also viable.

The downside of peer-to-peer replication comes into play if ever the subscriber (or the other peer) needs to become the primary server (that is, take over the work from the original server). This takes a bit of administration that is *not* transparent to the end user. Connection strings have to be changed, ODBC data sources need to be updated, and so on. But this process may take minutes as opposed to hours of database recovery time, and it may well be tolerable to end users. Peer-to-peer configurations handle recovery a bit better in that much of the workload is already distributed to either of the nodes. So, at most, only part of the user base will be affected if one node goes down. Those users can easily be redirected to the other node (peer), with the same type of connection changes described earlier.

With either the publisher/subscriber or peer-to-peer replication approach, there is a risk of not having all the transactions from the publishing server. However, often, a company is willing to live with this small risk in favor of availability. Remember that a replicated data-base is an approximate image of the primary database (up to the point of the last update that was successfully distributed), which makes it very attractive as a warm standby. For publishing databases that are primarily read-only, using a warm standby is a great way to distribute the load and mitigate the risk of any one server failing. Chapter 43, "Data Replication," covers data replication and all the various implementation scenarios that you might ever need to use.

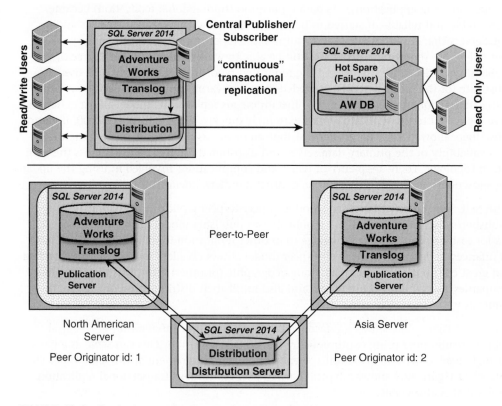

FIGURE 42.9   Basic data replication configurations for HA.

Change Data Capture

Recently, the Change Data Capture (CDC) capabilities have become much more stable and more tightly integrated into SQL Server. As illustrated in Figure 42.10, a change process is running that reads any change transactions from the transaction log and pushes them to a series of change tables. CDC does require that table objects and some CDC stored procedures be added to your SQL Server instance that is a source of data to be replicated. The CDC process and change table activity also adds overhead to the source SQL Server. Another CDC process (invoked via the SQL Agent) reads, transforms, and writes the table changes to another SQL Server database (target). This target can then be used for reporting or as a warm standby. The data in that target (replica) will be as recent as the last transaction set written from the change tables (usually quite current). Potential exists for some data loss, but CDC is yet another way to replicate data for both distributed workload and to achieve HA.

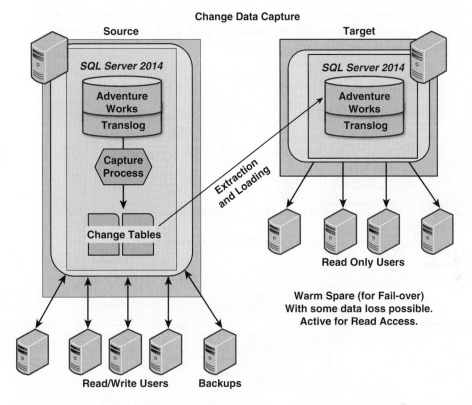

FIGURE 42.10   Utilizing CDC to provide distributed workload and HA at the database level.

Log Shipping

Another, more direct, method of creating a completely redundant database image is to utilize log shipping. Microsoft "certifies" log shipping as a method of creating an "almost hot" spare. Some folks even use log shipping as an alternative to data replication (it has been referred to as "the poor man's data replication"). Microsoft has announced that log shipping will stay in SQL Server and that they will instead be deprecating database mirroring (even though they had, at one time, announced that log shipping would be deprecated). So, if you still want to use log shipping, it is perfectly viable—for now.

Log shipping does three primary things:

▶ Makes an exact image copy of a database on one server from a database dump

▶ Creates a copy of that database on one or more other servers from that dump

▶ Continuously applies transaction log dumps from the original database to the copy

In other words, log shipping effectively replicates the data of one server to one or more other servers via transaction log dumps. Figure 42.11 shows a source/destination SQL Server pair that has been configured for log shipping.

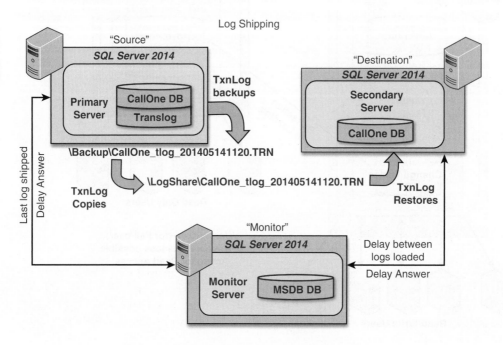

FIGURE 42.11   Log shipping in support of high availability.

Log shipping is a great solution when you have to create one or more failover servers. It turns out that, to some degree, log shipping fits the requirement of creating a read-only subscriber as well. The following are the gating factors for using log shipping as a method of creating and maintaining a redundant database image:

▶ Data latency lag is the time that exists between the transaction log dumps on the source database and when these dumps are applied to the destination databases.

▶ Sources and destinations must be the same SQL Server version.

▶ Data is read-only on the destination SQL Server until the log shipping pairing is broken (as it should be to guarantee that the transaction logs can be applied to the destination SQL Server).

The data latency restriction might quickly disqualify log shipping as an instantaneous high-availability solution (if you need rapid availability of the failover server). However, log shipping might be adequate for certain situations. If a failure ever occurs on the primary SQL Server, a destination SQL Server that was created and maintained via log shipping can be swapped into use fairly quickly. The destination SQL Server would contain exactly what was on the source SQL Server (right down to every user ID, table, index, and file allocation map, except for any changes to the source database that occurred after the last log dump was applied). This directly achieves a level of high availability. It is still not completely transparent, though, because the SQL Server instance names are different, and the end user may be required to log in again to the new server instance.

Database Mirroring

Microsoft has announced that database mirroring will be deprecated in all future SQL Server releases and advises not to plan on using this feature but to use AlwaysOn Availability Groups (first choice) or log shipping (last resort) instead.

Combining Failover with Scale-Out Options

SQL Server 2014 pushes combinations of options to achieve HA levels. Building up an AlwaysOn FCI configuration, with AlwaysOn Availability Groups with two or more replicas, launches you into distributed workload scalability and maximum HA.

Other HA Techniques That Yield Great Results

Microsoft has been revisiting (and architecting) several operations that previously required a table or whole database to be offline. For several critical database operations (such as recovery operations, restores, indexing, and others), Microsoft has either made the data in the database available earlier in the execution of the operation or made the data in the database completely available simultaneously with the operation. The following primary areas are now addressed:

▶ **Fast recovery**—This faster recovery option directly improves the availability of SQL Server databases. Administrators can reconnect to a recovering database after the transaction log has been rolled forward (and before the rollback processing has finished). Figure 42.12 illustrates how Microsoft makes a SQL Server 2014 database available earlier than many past Server versions and many other competing database engines.

In particular, a database in SQL Server 2014 becomes available when committed transaction log entries are rolled forward (termed redo) and no longer have to wait for the "in flight" transactions to be rolled back (termed undo).

▶ **Online restore**—Database administrators can perform a restore operation while the database is still online. Online restore improves the availability of SQL Server because only the data being restored is unavailable; the rest of the database remains online and available to users. In addition, the granularity of the restore has changed to be at the filegroup level and even at the page level, if needed. The remainder of the database remains available.

▶ **Online indexing**—Concurrent modifications (updates, deletes, and inserts) to the underlying table or clustered index data and any associated indexes can now be done during index creation time. For example, while a clustered index is being rebuilt, you can continue to make updates to the underlying data and perform queries against the data.

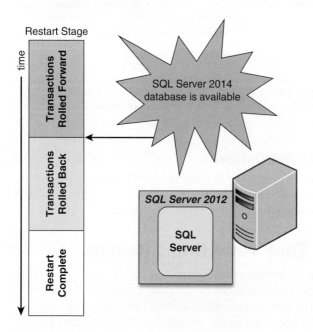

FIGURE 42.12 SQL Server 2014 databases become available earlier than older SQL Server releases (fast recovery).

▶ **Database snapshots**—You can now create a read-only, stable view of a database. A database snapshot is created without the overhead of creating a complete copy of the database or having completely redundant storage. A database snapshot is simply a reference point of the pages used in the database (that is defined in the system catalog). When pages are updated, a new page chain is started that contains the data pages changed since the database snapshot was taken, as illustrated in Figure 42.13.

As the original database diverges from the snapshot, the snapshot gets its own copy of original pages when they are modified. The snapshot can even be used to recover an accidental change to a database by simply reapplying the pages from the snapshot back to the original database.

The copy-on-write technology used for database mirroring also enables database snapshots. When a database snapshot is created on a database, all writes check the system catalog of "changed pages" first; if not there, the original page is copied (using the copy-on-write technique) and is put in a place for reference by the database snapshot (because this snapshot must be kept intact). In this way, the database snapshot and the original database share the data pages that have not changed.

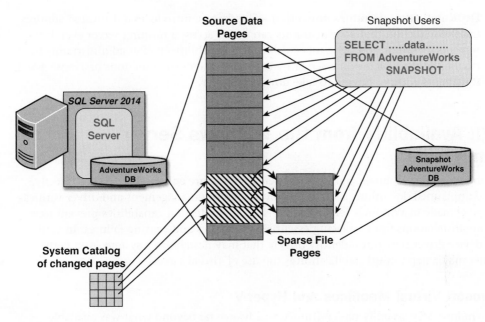

FIGURE 42.13   Database snapshots and the original database share pages are managed within the system catalog of SQL Server 2014.

▶ **Data partitioning improvements**—Data partitioning has been enhanced with native table and index partitioning. It essentially allows you to manage large tables and indexes at a lower level of granularity. In other words, a table can be defined to identify distinct partitions (such as by date or by a range of key values). This approach effectively defines a group of data rows that are unique to a partition.

These partitions can be taken offline, restored, or loaded independently while the rest of the table is available.

▶ **Addition of a snapshot isolation level**—This snapshot isolation (SI) level is a database-level capability that allows users to access the last committed row, using a transactionally consistent view of the database. This capability provides improved scalability and availability by not blocking data access of this previously unavailable data state. This new isolation level essentially allows data reading requests to see the last committed version of data rows, even if they are currently being updated as part of a transaction (for example, they see the rows as they were at the start of the transaction without being blocked by the writers, and the writers are not blocked by readers because the readers do not lock the data). This isolation level is probably best used for databases that are read-mostly (with few writes/updates) due to the potential overhead in maintaining this isolation level.

▶ **Dedicated administrator connection**—This feature introduces a dedicated administrator connection that administrators can use to access a running server even if the server is locked or otherwise unavailable. This capability enables administrators to troubleshoot problems on a server by executing diagnostic functions or Transact-SQL statements without having to take down the server.

High Availability from the Windows Server Family Side

To enhance system uptimes, numerous system architecture enhancements that directly reduce unplanned downtime, such as improved memory management and driver verification, were made in Windows Server family. New file protection capabilities prevent new software installations from replacing essential system files and causing failures. In addition, device driver signatures identify drivers that may destabilize a system. And perhaps another major step toward stabilization is the use of virtual servers.

Microsoft Virtual Machines and Hyper-V

The Windows Server family has continued to advance far beyond what was available just a few years back. Hyper-V has now outperformed many competing virtual platforms (such as VMware). This has also firmly established virtualization for both development and production environments and allows entire application and database stacks to run on a completely virtual operating system footprint that will never bring down the physical server. As shown in Figure 42.14, the host operating system—Windows Server 2012 in this case—manages the host system (at the bottom of the stack).

Windows provides a virtualization layer that manages virtual machines known as hypervisors (or Hyper-V for short) and provides the software infrastructure for hardware emulation. As you move up the stack, each virtual machine consists of a set of virtualized devices, the virtual hardware for each virtual machine.

A guest operating system and applications run in the virtual machine—unaware, for example, that the network adapter they interact with through the virtualization layer is only a software simulation of a physical Ethernet device. When a guest operating system is running, the special-purpose kernel takes mediated control over the CPU and hardware during virtual machine operations, creating an isolated environment in which the guest operating system and applications run close to the hardware at the highest possible performance.

This multithreaded capability runs as a system service, with each virtual machine running in its own thread of execution; I/O occurs in child threads. Hyper-V derives two core functions from the host operating system: The underlying host operating system kernel schedules CPU resources, and the device drivers of the host operating system provide access to system devices. This virtualization layer provides the software infrastructure to create virtual machines, manage instances, dynamically scale out (add more compute power, memory, and storage) and interact with guest operating systems transparently.

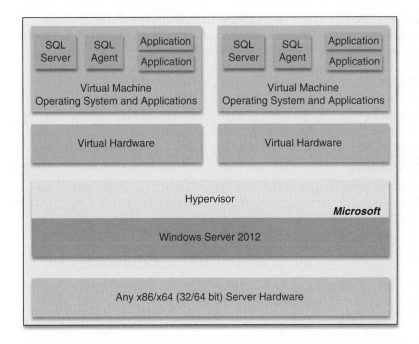

FIGURE 42.14   Microsoft Virtual Machines and Hyper-V server architecture.

Summary

As you come to completely understand and assess your application's high-availability requirements, you can create a matching high-availability solution that will serve you well for years to come. The crux of high availability is laying a fundamentally sound foundation that you can count on when failures occur and then, when failures do occur, determining how much data loss you can tolerate, how much downtime is possible, and what the downtime is costing you.

The overall future seems to be improving greatly in all the basic areas of your Microsoft platform footprint, including

▶ Cheaper and more reliable hardware components that are highly swappable

▶ The advent of virtual server/machine capabilities (with the Windows Server family) to insulate software failures from affecting hardware and vice-versa

▶ Enhancements that Microsoft is making to SQL Server 2014 that address availability such as the AlwaysOn capabilities

So, with SQL Server 2014, it's all about AlwaysOn features. We've devoted another whole chapter to explore these great capabilities fully. But as you have also seen in this chapter, you have several other HA options available depending on what your needs are. You have infrastructure options for HA, SQL Server instance level options for HA, SQL Server database level options for HA, SQL Server client connectivity features for HA, and some great administration and online maintenance options such as online indexing to get your entire SQL Server operational platform as near to 100% uptime as is currently possible. And last but not least, you can run your production SQL Server instances on one or more virtual server machines that will not bring down a physical server that houses them (which is very UNIX-like) nor affect the application that is running on it. More and more, we are being asked to get to that "extreme availability" level (virtually zero downtime). Microsoft embraces this direction and commitment and is trying to provide us the tools that we need to get there. Now, what availability do you need? Chances are that the tools are there for you to get it!

Chapter 43 delves into the complexities of the various data replication options available with SQL Server 2014.

CHAPTER 43

Data Replication

There is no such thing as a typical configuration or application anymore. Companies now have to support numerous hardware and software configurations in multi-tiered, distributed environments. These diverse configurations and applications (and users of the applications) come in all sizes and shapes. And, of course, you need a way to deal with varied data access requirements for these different physical locations; these remote or mobile users over a local area network, wide area network, wireless connections, and dial-up connections; and any needs over the Internet. Microsoft's data replication facility allows for a great breadth of capability to deal with many of these demands. However, to build a proper data replication implementation that meets many of these user requirements, you must have a thorough understanding of the business requirements and technical capabilities of data replication. Data replication is a set of technologies for storing and forwarding data and database objects from one database to another and then synchronizing this data between databases to maintain consistency. With SQL Server 2014, the data replication feature set offers broad capabilities in manageability, availability, programmability, mobility, scalability, and performance.

This chapter does the following:

▶ Helps you understand what data replication is

▶ Shows you how to understand and analyze user requirements of data

▶ Allows you to choose which replication configuration best meets these requirements (if any)

▶ Demonstrates how to implement a replication configuration

▶ Describes how to administer and monitor a data replication implementation

What's New in Data Replication

No new significant changes for this release of SQL Server replication other than firming up the high availability portions of the architecture and monitoring of replication operationally. This includes AlwaysOn Availability Groups and some Extended Events additions (to help Microsoft customer support engineers collect information in troubleshooting replication issues). The overall data replication approach that Microsoft has developed (since replication's inception back in SQL Server 6.5 days) has been so solid that competitors, such as Oracle (with its Oracle Streams technology), have tried to mimic this architectural approach.

The following are some of the new replication features and enhancements that make SQL Server 2014 data replication one of the best complete sets of data distribution tools on the market:

▶ **Highly availability and resilience with AlwaysOn Availability Groups**—Publication databases are supported with all replication types.

▶ **Extended Events**—Some much needed Extended Events have been added to help Microsoft customer support engineers troubleshoot replication issues.

▶ **Support for 15,000 partitions**—Replication topologies can now support up to 15,000 partitions for tables and indexes.

▶ **New system stored procedures for AlwaysOn support**—Locating and redirecting publication within an AlwaysOn configuration called for the addition of four new system stored procedures.

▶ **Change Tracking and Availability Groups**—Any database that has been enabled for Change Tracking (CT) can also be a part of an AlwaysOn Availability Group.

▶ **Change Data Capture and Availability Groups**—Same for Change Data Capture, this data replication configuration is also enabled to take advantage of AlwaysOn Availability Groups.

▶ **Peer-to-peer transactional replication is not available for all editions**—Peer-to-peer replication is still only available under SQL Server Enterprise Edition. We are not happy about that!

▶ SQL Server 2014 does not support replication to or from SQL Server 2005 or SQL Server Compact!

Many of these terms and references that we've just mentioned might be new or foreign to you now, but they are all explained in this chapter. At the end of this chapter, when you review these new features, you'll be able to appreciate much more readily their significance.

What Is Replication?

Long before you ever start setting up and using SQL Server data replication, you need to have a solid grasp of what data replication is and how it can be used to meet your company's needs. In its classic definition, data replication is based on the "store-and-forward" data distribution model, as shown in Figure 43.1. In other words, data that is inserted, updated, or deleted in one location (stored) is automatically distributed (forwarded) to one or more locations.

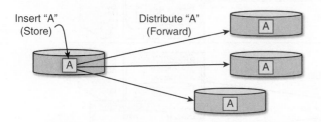

FIGURE 43.1   The store-and-forward data distribution model.

Of course, the data distribution model addresses all the other complexities of updates, deletes, data latency, autonomy, and so on. It is this data distribution model that Microsoft's data replication facility serves to implement. It has come a long way since the early days of Microsoft SQL Server replication (earlier than 6.5) and is now easily categorized as "production worthy." Numerous worldwide data replication scenarios have been implemented for some of the biggest companies in the world without a hitch. These scenarios fall into five major types:

▶ **Offloading**—You might need to deliver data to different locations to eliminate network traffic and unnecessary load on a single server (for example, when you need to isolate reporting activity away from your online transaction processing). The industry trend is to create an operational data store (ODS) data architecture that replicates core transactional data to a separate platform in real-time and delivers the data to the reporting systems, web services, and other data consumers without impacting the transactional systems in any way.

▶ **Enabling**—You might need to enable a group of users with a copy of data or a subset of data (vertically or horizontally) for their private use.

▶ **Partitioning**—You might need to move data off a single server onto several other servers to provide for high availability and decentralization of data (or partitioning of data). This might be the basis of serving customer call centers around the globe that must service "active" support calls (partitioned on active versus closed service requests).

▶ **Regionalization**—You might have regional ownership of data (for example, regional customers and their orders). In this case, it is possible to set up data replication to replicate data bi-directionally from two or more publishers of the same data.

▶ **Failover**—You could be replicating all data on a server to another server (that is, a failover server) so that if the primary server crashes, users can switch to the failover server quickly and continue to work with little downtime or data loss.

Figure 43.2 illustrates the topology of some of these replication variations.

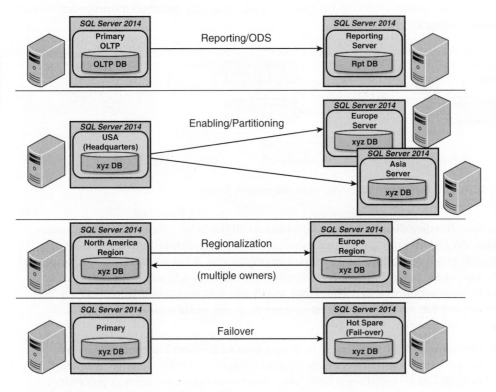

FIGURE 43.2   Some typical data replication scenarios.

As you may notice, you can use data replication for many reasons. Many of these reasons are discussed later in this chapter. First, however, you need to understand some of the common terms and metaphors Microsoft uses in relationship to data replication. They started with the "magazine" concept as the basis of the metaphor. A magazine is created by a publisher, distributed via the mail, and delivered to only those who have a subscription to the magazine. The frequency of the magazine publication can vary, as can the frequency of the subscription (depending on how often the subscriber wants to receive a new magazine). The publication (magazine) can also consist of one or more articles. One or more articles can be subscribed to.

The Publisher, Distributor, and Subscriber Magazine Metaphor

Any SQL Server can play up to three distinct roles in a data replication environment:

▶ **Publication server**—The publication server (or publisher) contains the database or databases that will be published (the magazine!). This is the source of the data that is to be replicated to other servers. In Figure 43.3, the Customer table (an article in the magazine) in the AdventureWorks2014 database is the data to be published. To publish data, the database that contains the data that will be published must first be enabled for publishing. Full publishing configuration requirements are discussed later in this chapter, in the section, "Setting Up Replication."

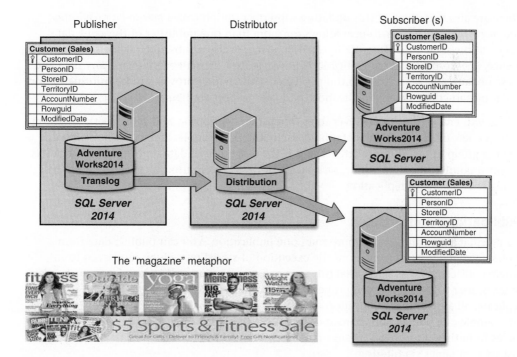

FIGURE 43.3   The publisher, distributor, and one or more subscribers.

▶ **Distribution server**—The distribution server (or distributor) can either be on the same server as the publication server or on a different server (in which case it is a remote distribution server). This server contains the distribution database. This database, also called the store-and-forward database, holds all the data changes that are to be forwarded from the published database to any subscription servers that subscribe to the data. A single distribution server can support several publication servers. The distribution server is truly the workhorse of data replication;

it is essentially the mail system that picks up the magazine and delivers it to the subscription holder.

▶ **Subscription server**—The subscription server (or subscriber) contains a copy of the database or portions of the database being published (for example, the `Customer` table in the `AdventureWorks2014` database). The distribution server sends any changes made to this table (in the published database) to the subscription server's copy of the `Customer` table. This is known as *store-and-forward*. Some data replication configurations send the data to the subscription server, and then the data is read-only. It is also possible for subscribers (known as updating subscribers) to make updates, which are sent back to the publisher. More on this in the "The Updating Subscribers Replication Model" and "Merge Replication" sections.

There are also variations of this updating subscriber option called *peer-to-peer replication* and *merge replication*. Peer-to-peer allows for more than one publisher of the same data (table) at the same time! Essentially, each publisher is also a subscriber at the same time (hence, peer-to-peer). Merge replication allows for each subscriber to update any data and these updates are passed back to the publisher. This chapter provides more information on updating subscribers, merge replication, and peer-to-peer configurations later.

Along with enabling distinct server roles (publisher, distributor, and subscriber), Microsoft utilizes a few more magazine metaphors, including publications and articles. A *publication* is a group of one or more articles and is the basic unit of data replication. An *article* is simply a pointer to a single table, or a subset of rows or columns out of a table, that will be made available for replication.

Publications and Articles

A single database can contain more than one publication. You can publish data from tables, from database objects, from the execution of stored procedures, and even from schema objects, such as referential integrity constraints, clustered indexes, nonclustered indexes, user triggers, extended properties, and collation. Regardless of what you plan to replicate, all articles in a publication are synchronized at the same time. Figure 43.4 shows an example of a publication (named `Cust_Orders` publication) with three articles (three tables from the `AdventureWorks2014` database). You can choose to replicate whole tables or just parts of tables via filtering.

Filtering Articles

You can create articles within a publication in several different ways. The basic way to create an article is to publish all the columns and rows contained in a table. Although this is the easiest way to create articles, your business needs might require that you publish only specific columns or certain rows of a table. This is referred to as *filtering vertically* or *horizontally*. When you filter vertically, you filter only specific columns, whereas with horizontal filtering, you filter only specific rows. In addition, SQL Server 2014 provides the added functionality of join filters and dynamic filters.

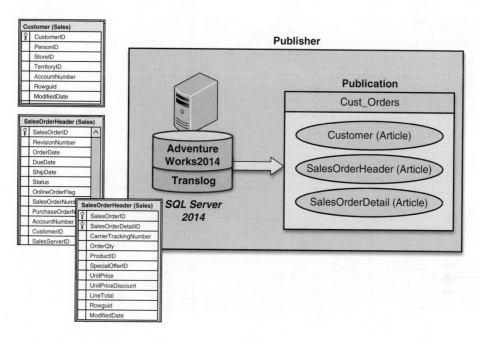

FIGURE 43.4 The `Cust_Orders` publication (in the `AdventureWorks2014` database).

As Figure 43.5 shows, you might need to replicate only a customer's `CustomerID`, `TerritoryID`, and `AccountNumber` to various subscribing servers around your company. In your company, the other data, such as `PersonIDAccountNumber`, may be restricted information that should not be replicated for general use. For that reason, you simply create an article for data replication that contains a subset of the `Customer` table that will be replicated to these other locations and excludes `PersonID` and `StoreID` (and `rowguid` and `ModifiedDate` as well).

As another example, you might need to publish only the `Customer` table data for a specific territory, such as for `TerritoryID = '1'`). This process, as shown in Figure 43.6, is known as horizontal filtering.

It is possible to combine horizontal and vertical filtering, as shown in Figure 43.7. This way, you can weed out unneeded columns and rows that aren't required for replication (that is, are not needed by the subscribers). For example, you might need only the customers that are in territory `'1'` and need only `CustomerID`, `TerritoryID`, and `AccountNumber` data to be published.

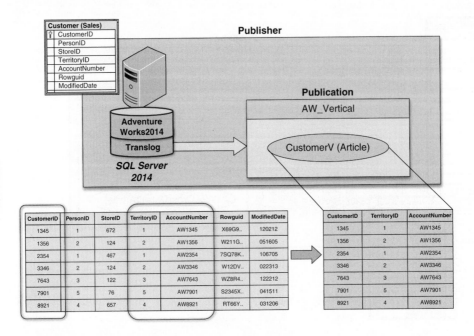

FIGURE 43.5   Vertical filtering creates a subset of columns from a table to be replicated to subscribers.

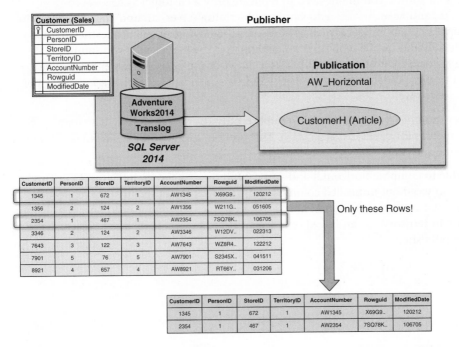

FIGURE 43.6   Horizontal filtering creates a subset of rows from a table to be replicated to subscribers.

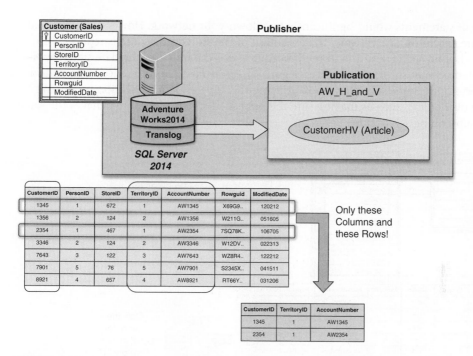

FIGURE 43.7   Combining horizontal and vertical filtering allows you to pare down the information in an article to only the important information needed by the subscribers.

As mentioned earlier, it is now possible to use join filters. Join filters enable you to use the values of one article (that is, values from a table) to determine what gets replicated from another article (that is, what values can be associated with another table) via a join. In other words, if you are publishing the Customer table data based on the customers that are in territory '1', you can extend filtering (that is, a join filter) to replicate only those orders for these customers (as shown in Figure 43.8). This way, you replicate only orders for customers that are needed by a subscriber (that needs to see only this filtered data). This type of replication can be efficient if it is done well.

You also can publish stored procedure executions, along with their parameters, as articles. This can be either a standard procedure execution article or a serializable procedure execution article. The difference is that the latter is executed as a serializable transaction; the serializable option is recommended because it replicates the procedure execution only if the procedure is executed within the context of a serializable transaction. If that same stored procedure is executed from outside a serializable transaction, changes to data in published tables are replicated as a series of DML statements. In general, replicating stored procedure executions gives you a major reduction in the number of SQL statements being replicated across the network versus standard DML statements.

For instance, if you wanted to update the Customer table for every customer via an UPDATE SQL statement, the resulting Customer table updates would be replicated as a large multi-step transaction involving at least 5,000 separate UPDATE statements at a minimum. This number of statements would significantly bog down your network. However, with stored procedure execution articles, only the execution of the stored procedure is replicated to the subscription server, and the stored procedure—not the numerous update statements—is executed on that subscription server. Figure 43.9 illustrates the difference in execution described earlier. Some subtleties when utilizing this type of data replication processing can't be overlooked, such as making sure the published stored procedure behaves the same on the subscribing server side.

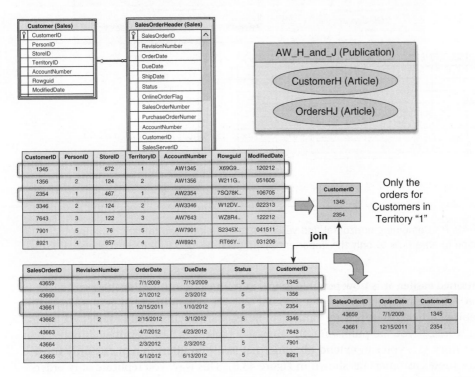

FIGURE 43.8   Horizontal and Join publication: Joining customers that are in territory '1' and their corresponding `SalesOrderHeader` rows.

Many more data replication terms are presented in this chapter, but it is essential that you first learn about the different types of replication scenarios that can be built and the reasons any of them would be desired over the others. It is also worth noting that Microsoft SQL Server 2014 supports replication to and from many different "heterogeneous" data sources. In other words, OLE DB and ODBC data sources can subscribe to SQL Server publications, and they can receive data replicated from a number of data sources, including Microsoft Exchange, Microsoft Access, Oracle, and DB2.

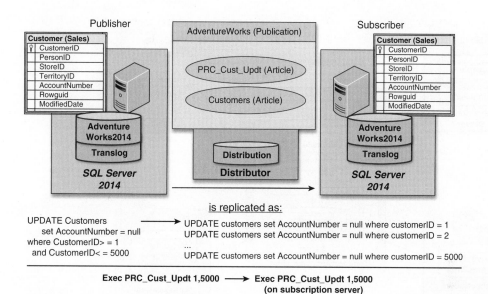

FIGURE 43.9   Comparison of stored procedure execution and standard SQL statement replication.

Replication Scenarios

In general, depending on your business requirements and hardware or network constraints, one of several different data replication models can be implemented, including the following:

- ▶ Central publisher
- ▶ Central publisher with a remote distributor
- ▶ Publishing subscriber
- ▶ Central subscriber
- ▶ Multiple publishers with multiple subscribers
- ▶ Updating subscribers and merge replication
- ▶ Peer-to-peer

The Central Publisher Replication Model

The central publisher replication model, shown in Figure 43.10, is Microsoft's default scenario and a common model used if your primary server has plenty of spare CPU cycles and you want a simple replication model. In this scenario, one SQL Server performs the function of both publisher and distributor. The publisher/distributor can have any number of subscribers. These subscribers can come in many different varieties, such as SQL Server 2014, SQL Server 2008/R2, and Oracle.

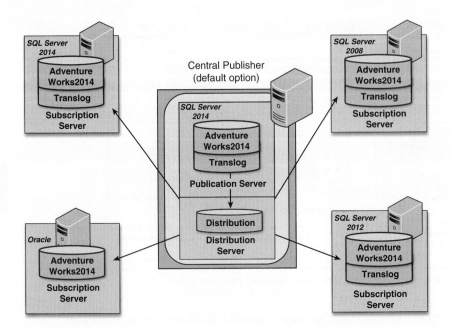

FIGURE 43.10   The central publisher scenario is fairly simple and is the replication model used most often.

The central publisher scenario can be used in the following situations:

▶ Creation of a copy of a database for ad hoc queries and report generation (classic use)

▶ Publication of master lists to remote locations, such as master customer lists or master price lists

▶ Maintenance of a remote copy of an online transaction processing (OLTP) database that could be used by the remote sites during communication outages

▶ Maintenance of a spare copy of an OLTP database that could be used as a "hot spare" in case of server failure

The Central Publisher with Remote Distributor Replication Model

The central publisher with remote distributor scenario, as shown in Figure 43.11, is mostly the same as the central publisher scenario and would be used in the same general situations. The major difference between the two is that in the central publisher with remote distributor scenario, a second server is used to perform the role of distributor. This is highly desirable when you need to free the publishing server from having to perform the distribution task from a CPU, disk, and memory point of view. This is also the best scenario from which to expand the number of publishers and subscribers. Remember that a single distribution server can distribute changes for several publishers. The publisher and distributor must be connected to each other via a reliable, high-speed data link. This remote distributor scenario is proving to be one of the best data replication configurations due to its minimal impact on the publication server and maximum distribution capability to any number of subscribers.

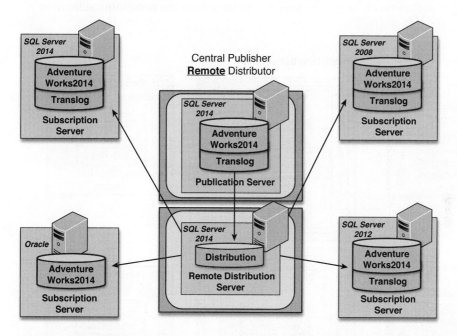

FIGURE 43.11   You use the central publisher with remote distributor scenario when you need to offload the distribution work to another server (to minimize the impact to the publishing server).

As mentioned previously, the central publisher/remote distributor approach can be used for all the same purposes as the central publisher scenario, and it also provides the added benefit of having minimal resource impact on the publication servers. If your OLTP server's activity affects more than 10% of your total data per day, this scenario can usually handle it without much issue. If your OLTP server has overburdened CPU, memory, and disk utilization, implementing this model easily solves these issues as well. The central publisher/remote distribution model is useful for the vast majority of all the data replication configurations due to its optimal characteristics. Nine out of ten replication scenarios that this author has implemented used the remote distributor replication model.

The Publishing Subscriber Replication Model

In the publishing subscriber scenario, as shown in Figure 43.12, the publication server also has to act as a distribution server to one subscriber. This subscriber, in turn, immediately publishes the data to any number of other subscribers. The configuration depicted here does not use a remote distribution configuration option but serves the same distribution model purpose. This scenario is best used when a slow or expensive network link exists between the original publishing server and all the other potential subscribers. This allows the initial (critical) publication of the data to be distributed from the original publishing server to that single subscriber across the slow, unpredictable, or expensive network line. Then, each of the many other subscribers can subscribe to the data, using faster, more predictable, "local" network lines than they would have with the publishing subscriber server.

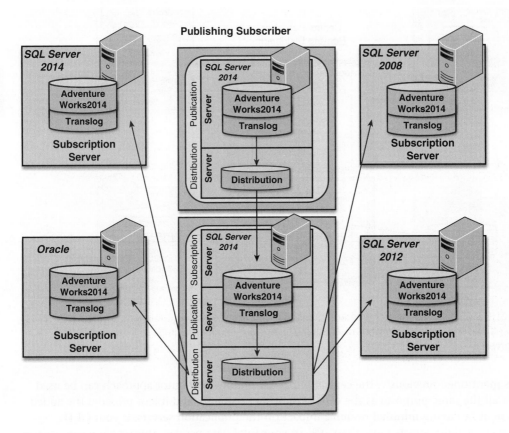

FIGURE 43.12   The publishing subscriber scenario works well when you have to deal with slow, unpredictable, or expensive network links in diverse geographic situations.

A classic example of this model is a company whose main office is in San Francisco and has several branch offices in Europe. Instead of replicating changes to all the branch offices in Europe, it replicates the updates to a single publishing subscriber server in Paris. This publishing subscriber server in Paris then replicates the updates to all other subscriber servers around Europe.

The Central Subscriber Replication Model

In the central subscriber scenario, as shown in Figure 43.13, several publishers replicate data to a single, central subscriber. Basically, this supports the concept of consolidating data at a central site. An example of this might be consolidating all new orders from regional sales offices to company headquarters. In such a situation, you now have several publishers of the Orders table, and you need to take some form of precaution, such as filtering by region. This would guarantee that no one publisher could update another region's orders.

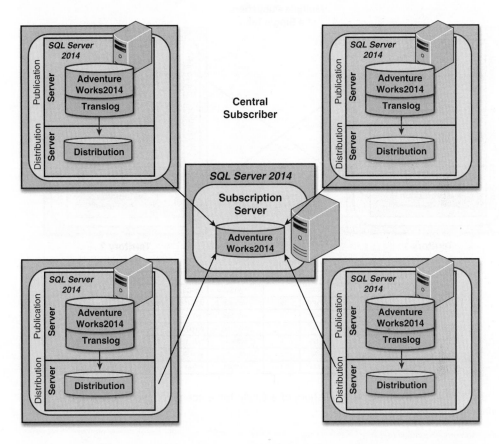

FIGURE 43.13   With the central subscriber scenario, several publishers send data to a single, central subscriber.

The Multiple Publishers with Multiple Subscribers Replication Model

In the multiple publishers with multiple subscribers scenario, as shown in Figure 43.14, a common table (such as the Customer table) is maintained on every server participating in the scenario. Each server publishes a particular set of rows (for example, the customer rows in a customer's own territory) that pertain to it—usually via filtering on something that identifies that site to the data rows it owns—and subscribes to the rows that all the other servers are publishing. The result is that each server has all the data at all times and can make changes to its data only. You must be careful when implementing this scenario to ensure that all sites remain synchronized. The most frequently used applications of this system are regional order processing systems and reservation tracking systems. When setting up this type of system, you need to make sure that only local users update local data. This check can be implemented through the use of stored procedures, restrictive views, or a check constraint.

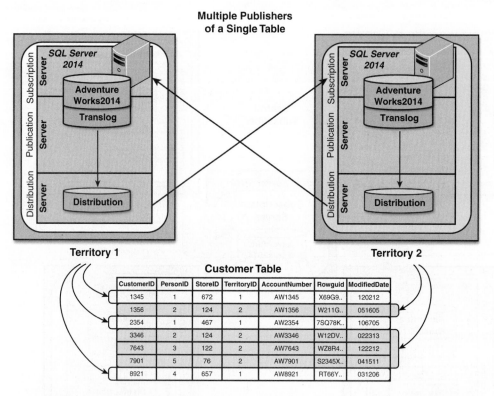

FIGURE 43.14   In the multiple publishers of a single table scenario, every server in the scenario maintains a common table.

The Updating Subscribers Replication Model

SQL Server 2014 has built-in functionality that allows the subscriber to update data in a table to which it subscribes and have those updates automatically made back to the publisher through either immediate or queued updates. This model, called the updating subscribers model, utilizes a two-phase commit process to update the publishing server as the changes are made on the subscribing server. These updates are then replicated to any other subscribers, but not to the subscriber that made the update.

Immediate updating allows subscribers to update data only if the publisher will accept these updates immediately. If the changes are accepted at the publisher, they are propagated to the other subscribers. The subscribers must be continuously and reliably connected to the publisher to make changes at the subscriber.

Queued updating allows subscribers to update data and then store those updates in a queue while disconnected from the publisher. When the subscriber reconnects to the publisher, the updates are propagated to the publisher. This functionality utilizes SQL Server 2014 queues and the queue reader agent or Microsoft Message Queuing (MSMQ).

A combination of immediate updating with queued updating allows the subscriber to use immediate updating but switch to queued updating if a connection cannot be maintained between the publisher and subscribers. After switching to queued updating, reconnecting to the publisher, and emptying the queue, the subscriber can switch back to immediate updating mode. An updating subscriber is shown in Figure 43.15.

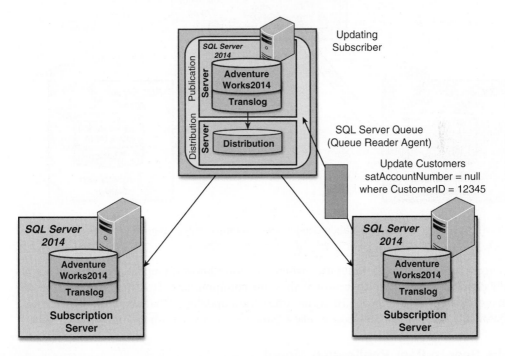

FIGURE 43.15   An updating subscriber updating its copy of a customer table and queuing the changes back to the publisher.

The updating subscriber model is also used in merge replication and allows for data to be updated at any subscriber and then resynchronized with the publisher and all other subscribers. This can be thought of as "updateable data from any location in the replication topology." Merge replication is predominately implemented by both the Snapshot Agent and Merge Agent, as shown in Figure 43.16. The Snapshot Agent carries out much of the work for merge replication, initiates most of the snapshot files containing schema and data of published tables, stores the files in the snapshot folder, and inserts synchronization jobs in the publication database. It will also create stored procedures, triggers, and system tables needed with merge replication.

Replication will begin only after merge replication ensures that the subscriber has the most recent snapshot of the table schema and the data that has been generated. The initial snapshot can also be an attached subscription database.

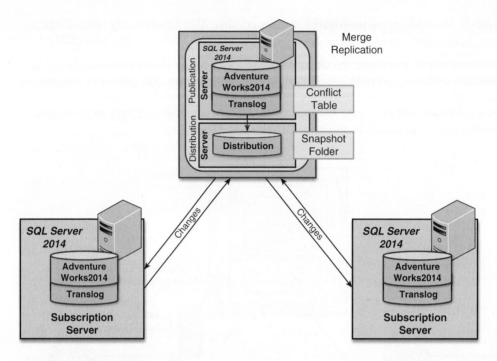

FIGURE 43.16   A merge replication scenario with multiple subscribers.

Merger replication is sometimes used when you don't know the update behavior of a globally distributed capability that must share some common data. This approach guarantees
that each subscriber (and publisher) has everyone's updates of that common data within a
reasonable amount of time—sort of like a "share all" approach for commonly used data.

The Peer-to-Peer Replication Model

In SQL Server 2014, the peer-to-peer replication model can provide a simpler way for all
nodes to have the same data and also gives them the capability to update this data independently. Peer-to-peer replication is different from subscriber updating in that there is no
publisher/subscriber hierarchical relationship. Each peer is equal in level. They establish
peer originator IDs so that each can keep track of where updates are coming from and can
be utilized if conflicts arise. Peers do not subscribe to each other's data; they share each
other's data. There are several limitations with peer-to-peer replication, most of which are
to protect this peer-to-peer relationship from being corrupted or from having major data
conflicts arise. There are no queues or immediate updating mechanisms involved, thus
making this approach very useful when you need to have the same data in more than one
place and need to update your local data to your heart's content. If your peers typically
do not update the same rows (as in regional data peer-to-peers), this replication model can
be very reliable with minimal issues. This type of replication model also allows for any
number of peers and provides a separate, very graphic wizard to configure each node in
the topology.

> **NOTE**
>
> New peer nodes can also be added to the topology without having to quiesce the topology, thus increasing the availability of the entire replication model.

Figure 43.17 illustrates a typical peer-to-peer configuration with each peer using a remote distribution server. Also note that with peer-to-peer replication, you might decide to prohibit updates to the other nodes' data by putting into place some type of stored procedure or view restrictions that allow the local node to update only its own local data. The example in Figure 43.17 shows that North American users can update customers with customer IDs between 1 and 3000, whereas Asian users can update customers with customer IDs between 3001 and 9000.

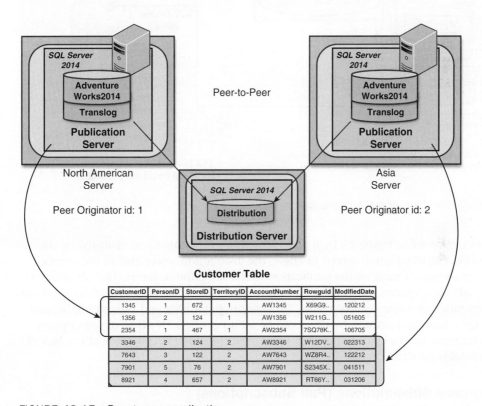

FIGURE 43.17   Peer-to-peer replication.

Subscriptions

A *subscription* is essentially a formal request and registration of that request for data that is being published. By definition, you subscribe to all articles of a publication.

When a subscription is being set up, you have the option of either having the data "pushed" to the subscriber server or "pulling" the data to the subscription server when it is needed. This is referred to as either a *push subscription* or *pull subscription*.

As shown in Figure 43.18, a pull subscription is set up and managed by the subscription server. The biggest advantage here is that pull subscriptions allow the system administrators of the subscription servers to choose what publications they will receive and when they receive them. With pull subscriptions, publishing and subscribing are separate acts and are not necessarily performed by the same user. In general, pull subscriptions are best when the publication does not require high security or if subscribing is done intermittently when the subscriber's data needs to be periodically brought up-to-date.

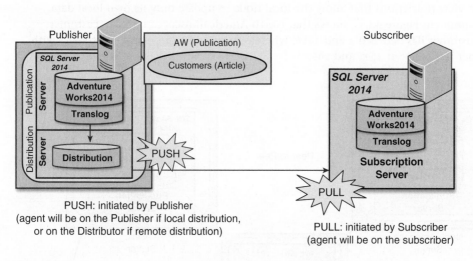

FIGURE 43.18   Push or pull subscriptions.

As you can also see in Figure 43.18, a push subscription is created and managed by the publication and distribution server. In effect, the distribution server and all the agents that do the work are pushing the publication to the subscription server. The advantage of using push subscriptions is that all the administration takes place in a central location (on the publication/distribution server side). In addition, publishing and subscribing happen at the same time, and many subscribers can be set up at once. This type of subscription is also recommended when dealing with heterogeneous subscribers because of the lack of pull capability on the subscription server side.

Anonymous Subscriptions (Pull Subscriptions)

It is possible to have "anonymous" subscriptions. An anonymous subscription is a special type of pull subscription that can be used in the following circumstances:

▶ When you are publishing data to the Internet

▶ When you have a huge number of subscribers

▶ When you don't want the overhead of maintaining extra information at the publisher or distributor

▶ When all the rules of your pull subscriptions apply to all your anonymous subscribers

Normally, information about all the subscribers, including performance data, is stored on the distribution server. Therefore, if you have a large number of subscribers or you do not want to track detailed information about the subscribers, you might want to allow anonymous subscriptions to a publication. Then little is kept at the distribution server, but it then becomes the responsibility of the subscriber to initiate the subscription and to keep synchronized.

The Distribution Database

The distribution database is a special type of database installed on the distribution server. This database, which is as a store-and-forward database, holds all transactions waiting to be distributed to any subscribers. This database receives transactions from any published databases that have designated it as their distributor. The transactions are held here until they are sent to the subscribers successfully. After a period of time, these transactions are purged from the distribution database. In some special situations, the transactions might not be purged for a longer period, enabling anonymous subscribers ample time to synchronize. The distribution database is the heart of the data replication facility. As you can see in Figure 43.19, the distribution database has several MS tables, such as MSarticles. These tables contain all the necessary information for the distribution server to fulfill the distribution role. Following are some of these tables:

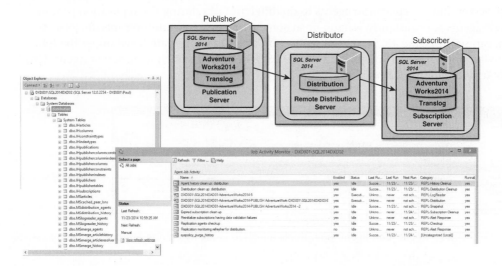

FIGURE 43.19   Tables of the distribution database and the distribution agents.

▶ **All the different publishers who will use this distribution server**—Stored in the MSpublisher_databases and MSpublication_access tables.

▶ **The publications and articles that will be distributed**—Stored in the MSpublications and MSarticles tables.

▶ **The complete information for all the Distribution Agents to perform their tasks**—Stored in the `MSdistribution_agents` table.

▶ **The complete information of the executions of these agents**—Stored in the `MSdistribution_history` table.

▶ **The subscribers**—Stored in `MSsubscriber_info`, `MSsubscriptions`, and other related tables.

▶ **Any errors that occur during replication and synchronization states**—Stored in `MSrepl_errors`, `MSsync_state`, and related tables.

▶ **The actual commands and transactions that are to be replicated**—Stored in the `MSrepl_commands` and `MSrepl_transactions` tables.

▶ **Heterogeneous (non-SQL Server) publishers' or subscribers' information**—Kept in the tables whose names begin with `IH`, such as `IHpublishers`, that will contain one row for each non-SQL Server publisher for which this distribution server distributes information.

Replication Agents

SQL Server utilizes replication agents to do different tasks during the replication process. These agents are constantly waking up at some frequency and fulfilling specific jobs. As you can see in Figure 43.20, several replication agent categories are listed under the Job Activity Monitor when you expand the SQL Server Agents branch (SQL Server Agent, Jobs, Job Activity Monitor branch).

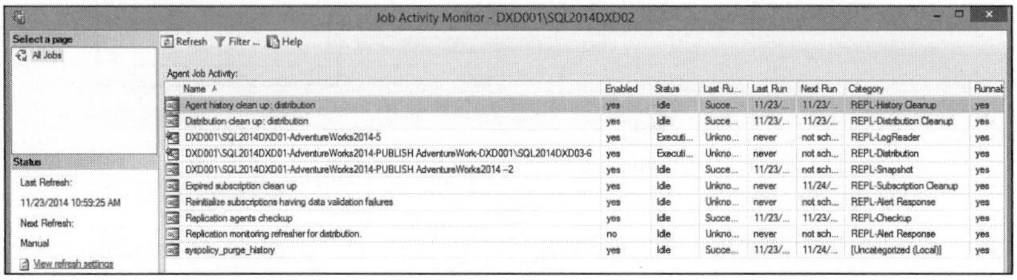

FIGURE 43.20   Replication agent jobs. Replication job category entries are prefixed with `REPL-`.

Here are the main replication agent categories:

▶ Snapshot Agent

▶ Log Reader Agent

▶ Distribution Agent

▶ Merge Agent (for updating subscribers)

▶ History Cleanup Agent

▶ Distribution Cleanup Agent

▶ Expired Subscription Cleanup Agent

▶ Reinitialize Subscriptions Having Data Validation Failures Agent

▶ Replication Monitoring Refresher for Distribution Agent

▶ Replication Agent Cleanup Agent

The Snapshot Agent

The Snapshot Agent is responsible for preparing the schema and initial data files of published tables and stored procedures, storing the snapshot on the distribution server, and recording information about the synchronization status in the distribution database. Each publication has its own Snapshot Agent that runs on the distribution server. It takes on the name of the publication within the publishing database within the machine on which it executes (that is, [Machine][Publishing database][Publication Name]).

Figure 43.20 also shows what this Snapshot Agent looks like under the SQL Server Agent, Job Activity Monitor branch in SQL Server Management Studio (SSMS). The Snapshot Agent (REPL-Snapshot category name) is named DXD01\SQL2014DXD01-AdventureWorks2014-PUBLISH AdventureWorks2014-2. In addition, these agents can be referenced from the Replication Monitor option (when you launch the Replication Monitor by right-clicking from the Replication branch in SQL Server Management Studio). Most often you are likely to use the SQL Server Agent path to these agents though.

It's worth noting that the Snapshot Agent might not even be used if the initialization of the subscriber's schema and data is done manually.

The Snapshot Agent Synchronization

The Snapshot Agent is the process that ensures both databases start on an even playing field. This process is known as *synchronization*. The synchronization process is performed whenever a publication has a new subscriber. Synchronization happens only one time for each new subscriber. It ensures that database schema and data are exact replicas on both servers. After the initial synchronization, all updates are made via replication.

When a new server subscribes to a publication, synchronization is performed. When synchronization begins, a copy of the table schema is copied to a file with the .sch extension. This file contains all the information necessary to create the table and any indexes on the tables, if they are requested. Next, a copy is made of the data in the table to be synchronized and written to a file (or several files) with the .bcp extension. The data file is a BCP, or bulk copy file. Both files are stored in the temporary working directory on the distribution server.

After the synchronization process has started and the data files have been created, any inserts, updates, and deletes are stored in the distribution database. These changes are not replicated to the subscription database until the synchronization process is complete.

When the synchronization process starts, only new subscribers are affected. Any subscriber that has been synchronized already and has been receiving modifications is unaffected. The synchronization set is applied to all servers waiting for initial synchronization. After the schema and data have been re-created, all transactions that have been stored in the distribution server are sent to the subscriber.

When you set up a subscription, it is possible to manually load the initial snapshot onto the server. This is known as *manual synchronization*. For extremely large databases, it is frequently easier to dump the database and then reload it on the subscription server. If you load the snapshot this way, SQL Server assumes that the databases are already synchronized and automatically begins sending data modifications.

Snapshot Agent Processing

Figure 43.21 shows the details of the Snapshot Agent execution for a typical push subscription. You can see the execution history by simply right-clicking the snapshot job and choosing View History.

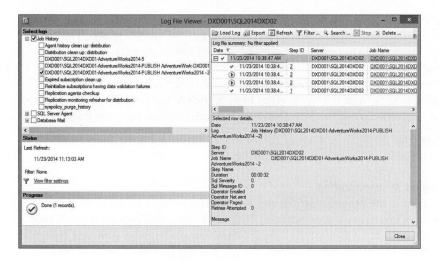

FIGURE 43.21 Snapshot agent execution job history.

The following sequence of tasks occurs with the Snapshot Agent:

1. The Snapshot Agent is initialized. This initialization can be immediate or at a designated time in the company's nightly processing window.

2. The agent connects to the publisher.

3. The agent generates schema files with the `.sch` file extension for each article in the publication. These schema files are written to a temporary working directory on the distribution server. These are the `create table` statements and such that will be used to create all objects needed on the subscription server side. They exist only for the duration of the snapshot processing.

4. All the tables in the publication are locked (held). The lock is required to ensure that no data modifications are made during the snapshot process.

5. The agent extracts a copy of the data in the publication and writes it to the temporary working directory on the distribution server. If all the subscribers are SQL Server machines, the data is written using a SQL Server native format, with the .bcp file extension. If you are replicating to databases other than SQL Server, the data is stored in standard text files with the .txt file extension. The .sch file and .txt files/.bmp files are known as a *synchronization set*. Every table or article has a synchronization set.

> **CAUTION**
>
> It's important to make sure you have enough disk space on the drive that contains the temporary working directory. The snapshot data files will potentially be huge, and this size is the most common reason for snapshot failure.

6. As you can see in Figure 43.22, the agent executes the object creations and bulk copy processing at the subscription server side in the order in which they were generated (or it skips the object creation part if the objects have already been created on the subscription server side and you have indicated this during setup). This process takes awhile, so it is best to do this in an off time so as not to impact the normal processing day. Network connectivity is critical here. Snapshots often fail at this point.

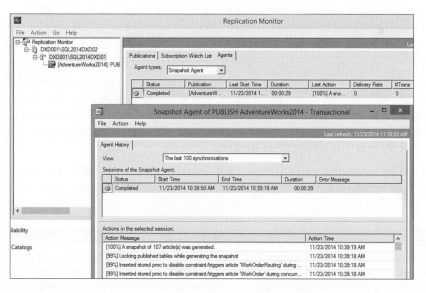

FIGURE 43.22 Snapshot agent delivering the snapshot to the subscriber (most recent operation on the top).

7. The Snapshot Agent posts the fact that a snapshot has occurred and what articles/ publications were part of the snapshot to the distribution database. This is the only information sent to the distribution database.

8. When all the synchronization sets are finished being executed, the agent releases the locks on all the tables of this publication. The snapshot is now considered finished.

The Log Reader Agent

The Log Reader Agent is responsible for moving transactions marked for replication from the transaction log of the published database to the distribution database. Each database published using transactional replication has its own Log Reader Agent that runs on the distribution server. It is easy to find because it takes on the name of the publishing database whose transaction log it is reading (`[Machine name] [Publishing DB name]`) and the `REPL-LogReader` category. Figure 43.20 shows the Log Reader Agent (`REPL-LogReader` category name) for the `AdventureWorks2014` database. It is named `DXD01\SQL2014DXD01-AdventureWorks2014-2`.

After initial synchronization has taken place, the Log Reader Agent begins to move transactions from the publication server to the distribution server. All actions that modify data in a database are logged to the transaction log in that database. This log is used not only in the automatic recovery process, but also in the replication process. When an article is created for publication and the subscription is activated, all entries about that article are marked in the transaction log. For each publication in a database, a Log Reader Agent reads the transaction log and looks for any marked transactions. When the Log Reader Agent finds a change in the log, it reads the changes and converts them to SQL statements that correspond to the action taken in the article. The SQL statements are then stored in a table on the distribution server, waiting to be distributed to subscribers.

Because replication is based on the transaction log, several changes are made in the way the transaction log works. During normal processing, any transaction that has either been successfully completed or rolled back is marked inactive. When you are performing replication, completed transactions are not marked inactive until the log reader process has read them and sent them to the distribution server.

Truncating and fast bulk-copying into a table are non-logged processes. In tables marked for publication, you cannot perform non-logged operations unless you temporarily turn off replication.

NOTE

One of the major changes in the transaction log comes when you have the Truncate Log on Checkpoint option turned on. When this option is on, SQL Server truncates the transaction log every time a checkpoint is performed, which can be as often as every several seconds. With replication, the inactive portion of the log is not truncated until the log reader process has read the transaction.

The Distribution Agent

A Distribution Agent moves transactions and snapshot jobs held in the distribution database out to the subscribers. This agent isn't created until a push subscription is defined for a subscriber. The Distribution Agent takes on the name of the publication database along with the subscriber information ([Machine name] [Publication DB name] [Subscriber machine name]). If you look back at Figure 43.20, you see a Distribution Agent (the REPL-Distribution category name) for the AdventureWorks2014 database to a subscriber. It is named DXD01\SQL2014DXD01--AdventureWorks2014 - PUBLISH AdventureWork - DXD01\SQL2014DXD03-6, where SQL2014DXD01 is the publisher and SQL2014DXD03 is the subscriber.

Those not set up for immediate synchronization share a Distribution Agent that runs on the distribution server. Pull subscriptions, to either snapshot or transactional publications, have a Distribution Agent that runs on the subscriber. Merge publications do not have a Distribution Agent at all. Rather, they rely on the Merge Agent, discussed next.

In transactional replication, the transactions have been moved into the distribution database, and the Distribution Agent either pushes out the changes to the subscribers or pulls them from the distributor, depending on how the servers are set up. All actions that change data on the publishing server are applied to the subscribing servers in the same order they were incurred. Figure 43.23 shows the latest history of the Distribution Agent and the total duration of the current subscription (02:00:23 hours, minutes, seconds, milliseconds in this example).

FIGURE 43.23   Distribution to Subscriber History.

The Merge Agent

When you are dealing with merge publications, the Merge Agent moves and reconciles incremental data changes that occur after the initial snapshot was created. Each merge publication has a Merge Agent that connects to the publishing server and the subscribing server and updates both as changes are made. In a full merge scenario, the agent first uploads all changes from the subscriber where the generation is 0 or greater than the last generation sent to the publisher. The agent gathers the rows in which changes were made, and the rows without conflicts are applied to the publishing database.

A conflict can arise when changes are made at both the publishing server and subscription server to a particular row(s) of data. A conflict resolver handles these conflicts. Conflict resolvers are associated with an article in the publication definition. These conflict resolvers are sets of rules or custom scripts that can handle any complex conflict situation that might occur. The agent then reverses the process by downloading any changes from the publisher to the subscriber. Push subscriptions have Merge Agents that run on the publication server, whereas pull subscriptions have Merge Agents that run on the subscription server. Snapshot and transactional publications do not use Merge Agents.

Other Specialized Agents

In Figure 43.20, you can see that several other agents have been set up to do house cleaning around the replication configuration:

▶ **Agent history clean up: Distribution**—This agent clears out agent history from the distribution database every 10 minutes (by default). Depending on the size of the distribution, you might want to vary the frequency of this agent.

▶ **Distribution clean up: Distribution**—This agent clears out replicated transactions from the distribution database every 72 hours by default. This agent is used for snapshot and transactional publications only. If the volume of transactions is high, the frequency of this agent should be adjusted downward so you don't have too large of a distribution database. However, the frequency of synchronization with subscribers drives this frequency adjustment.

▶ **Expired subscription clean up**—This agent detects and removes expired subscriptions from the published databases. As part of the subscription setup, an expiration date is set. This agent usually runs once per day by default. You don't need to change this frequency.

▶ **Reinitialize subscriptions having data validation failures**—This agent is manually invoked. It is not on a schedule, but it could be. It automatically detects the subscriptions that failed data validation and marks them for reinitialization. This can then potentially lead to a new snapshot being applied to a subscriber that had data validation failures.

▶ **Replication monitoring refresher for distribution**—Microsoft SQL Server Replication Monitor is designed to efficiently monitor a large number of computers. The queries that Replication Monitor uses to perform calculations and gather data are cached and refreshed on a periodic basis. Caching reduces the number of queries and calculations required as you view different pages in Replication Monitor and allows monitoring to scale well for multiple users. Cache refresh is handled by the Replication monitoring refresher for Distribution Agent. This job runs continuously, but the cache refresh schedule is based on waiting a certain amount of time after the previous refresh:

If there were agent history changes since the cache was last created, the wait time is a minimum of 4 seconds or the amount of time taken to create the previous cache.

If there were no agent history changes since the cache was last created, the wait time is a maximum of 30 seconds or the amount of time taken to create the previous cache. You don't need to change this frequency.

▶ **Replication agents checkup**—This agent detects replication agents that are not actively logging history. This checkup is critical because debugging replication errors is often dependent on an agent's history that has been logged.

Planning for SQL Server Data Replication

You must consider many factors when choosing a method to distribute data. Your business requirements determine which is the right method for you. In general, you need to understand the timing and latency of your data, its independence at each site, and your specific need to filter or partition the data.

Autonomy, Timing, and Latency of Data

Distributed data implementations can be accomplished using a few different facilities in Microsoft: Integration Services (IS), Distributed Transaction Coordinator (DTC), and Data Replication. The trick is to match the right facility to the type of data distribution you need to get done.

In some applications, such as online transaction processing and inventory control systems, data must be synchronized at all times. This requirement, called *immediate transactional consistency*, was known as tight consistency in previous versions of SQL Server.

SQL Server implements immediate transactional consistency data distribution in the form of two-phase commit processing. A *two-phase commit*, sometimes known as 2PC, ensures that transactions are committed on all servers, or the transaction is rolled back on all servers. This ensures that all data on all servers is 100% in sync at all times. One of the main drawbacks of immediate transactional consistency is that it requires a high-speed LAN to work. This type of solution might not be feasible for large environments with many servers because occasional network outages can occur. These types of implementations can be built with DTC and IS.

In other applications, such as decision support and report generation systems, 100% data synchronization all the time is not terribly important. This requirement, called *latent transactional consistency*, was known as loose consistency in previous versions of SQL Server.

Latent transactional consistency is implemented in SQL Server via data replication. Replication allows data to be updated on all servers, but the process is not a simultaneous one. The result is "real-enough-time" data. This is known as latent transactional consistency because a lag exists between the data updated on the main server and the replicated data. In this scenario, if you could stop all data modifications from occurring on all servers, all the servers would eventually have the same data. Unlike the two-phase consistency model, replication works over both LANs and WANs, as well as slow or fast links.

When planning a distributed application, you must consider the effect of one site's operation on another. This is known as *site autonomy*. A site with complete autonomy can continue to function without being connected to any other site. A site with no autonomy cannot function without being connected to all other sites. For example, applications that utilize two-phase commits rely on all other sites being able to immediately accept changes sent to them. In the event that any one site is unavailable, no transactions on any server can be committed. In contrast, sites using merge replication can be completely disconnected from all other sites and continue to work effectively, not guaranteeing data consistency. Luckily, some solutions combine both high data consistency and site autonomy.

Methods of Data Distribution

After you have determined the amount of transactional latency and site autonomy needed, based on your business requirements, you need to select the data distribution method that corresponds. Each different type of data distribution has a different amount of site autonomy and latency. With these distributed data systems, you can choose from several methods:

▶ **Distributed transactions**—Distributed transactions ensure that all sites have the same data at all times. You pay a certain amount of overhead cost to maintain this consistency. (We do not discuss this non-data replication method here.)

▶ **Transactional replication with updating subscribers**—Users can change data at the local location, and those changes are applied to the source database at the same time. The changes are then eventually replicated to other sites. This type of data distribution combines replication and distributed transactions because data is changed at both the local site and source database.

▶ **Peer-to-peer replication**—A variation on the transactional replication with updating subscribers theme is peer-to-peer replication, which is essentially full transactional replication between two (or more) sites, but is publisher-to-publisher (not update subscriber). There is no hierarchy—publisher (parent) and subscriber (child).

▶ **Transactional replication**—With transactional replication, data is changed only at the source location and is sent out to the subscribers. Because data is changed at only a single location, conflicts cannot occur.

▶ **Snapshot replication with updating subscribers**—This method is much like transactional replication with updating subscribers; users can change data at the local location, and those changes are applied to the source database at the same time. The entire changed publication is then replicated to all subscribers. This type of replication provides higher autonomy than transactional replication.

▶ **Snapshot replication**—A complete copy of the publication is sent out to all subscribers. This includes both changed and unchanged data.

▶ **Merge replication**—All sites make changes to local data independently and then update the publisher. It is possible for conflicts to occur, but they can be resolved.

SQL Server Replication Types

Microsoft has narrowed the field to three major types of data replication approaches within SQL Server: snapshot, transactional, and merge. Each replication type applies to only a single publication. However, it is possible to have multiple replication types per database.

Snapshot Replication

Snapshot replication makes an image of all the tables in a publication at a single moment in time and then moves that entire image to the subscribers. Little overhead on the server is incurred because snapshot replication does not track data modifications as the other forms of replication do. It is possible, however, for snapshot replication to require large amounts of network bandwidth, especially if the articles being replicated are large. Snapshot replication is the easiest form of replication to set up and is used primarily with smaller tables for which subscribers do not have to perform updates. An example of this might be a phone list that is to be replicated to many subscribers. This phone list is not considered to be critical data, and the frequency of it being refreshed is more than enough to satisfy all its users.

The primary agents used for snapshot replication are the Snapshot Agent and Distribution Agent.

▶ The Snapshot Agent creates files that contain the schema of the publication and the data. The files are temporarily stored in the snapshot folder of the distribution server, and then the distribution jobs are recorded in the distribution database.

▶ The Distribution Agent is responsible for moving the schema and data from the distributor to the subscribers.

A few other agents are also used; they deal with other needed tasks for replication, such as cleanup of files and history. In snapshot replication, after the snapshot has been delivered to all the subscribers, these agents delete the associated `.bcp` and `.sch` files from the distributor's working directory.

Transactional Replication

Transactional replication is the process of capturing transactions from the transaction log of the published database and applying them to the subscription databases. With SQL Server transactional replication, you can publish all or part of a table, views, or one or more stored procedures as an article. All data updates are then stored in the distribution database and sent and applied to any number of subscribing servers. Obtaining these updates from the publishing database's transaction log is extremely efficient. No direct reading of tables is required except during initial snapshot, and only the minimal amount of traffic is generated over the network. This has made transactional replication the most often used method.

As data changes are made, they are propagated to the other sites at nearly real-time; you determine the frequency of this propagation. Because changes are usually made only at the publishing server, data conflicts are avoided for the most part. As an example, push subscribers usually receive updates from the publisher in a minute or less, depending on the speed and availability of the network. Subscribers also can be set up for pull subscriptions. This capability is useful for disconnected users who are not connected to the network at all times.

The primary agents used for transactional replication are the Snapshot Agent, Log Reader Agent, and Distribution Agent:

▶ The Snapshot Agent creates files that contain the schema of the publication and the data. The files are stored in the snapshot folder of the distribution server, and the distribution jobs are recorded in the distribution database.

▶ The Log Reader Agent monitors the transaction log of the database that it is set up to service. Each database published has its own Log Reader Agent set up for replication, and it will copy the transactions from the transaction log of that published database into the distribution database.

▶ The Distribution Agent is responsible for moving the schema and data from the distributor to the subscribers for the initial synchronization and then moving all the subsequent transactions from the published database to each subscriber as they come in. These transactions are stored in the distribution database for a certain length of time and are eventually purged.

A few other agents deal with the other housekeeping issues surrounding data replication, such as schema files cleanup, history cleanup, and transaction cleanup.

Merge Replication

Merge replication involves getting the publisher and all subscribers initialized and then allowing data to be changed at all sites involved in the merge replication at the publisher and at all subscribers. All these changes to the data are subsequently merged at certain intervals so that, again, all copies of the database have identical data.

Occasionally, data conflicts have to be resolved. The publisher does not always win in a conflict resolution. Instead, the winner is determined by whatever criteria you establish.

The primary agents used for merge replication are the Snapshot Agent and Merge Agent:

▶ The Snapshot Agent creates files that contain the schema of the publication and the data. The files are stored in the snapshot folder of the distribution server, and the distribution jobs are recorded in the distribution database. This is essentially the same behavior as with all other types of replication methods.

▶ The Merge Agent takes the initial snapshot and applies it to all the subscribers. It then reconciles all changes made on all the servers, based on the rules you configure.

Preparing for Merge Replication

When you set up a table for merge replication, SQL Server performs three schema changes to the database. First, it must either identify or create a unique column for each row that will be replicated. This column is used to identify the different rows across all the different copies of the table. If the table already contains a column with the ROWGUIDCOL property set (and is a uniqueidentifier data type), SQL Server automatically uses that column for the row identifier. If not, SQL Server adds a column called rowguid to the table. SQL Server also places an index on this rowguid column.

Next, SQL Server adds triggers to the table to track changes that occur to the data in the table and record them in the merge system tables. The triggers can track changes at either the row or column level, depending on how you set it up. SQL Server supports multiple triggers of the same type on a table, so merge triggers do not interfere with user-defined triggers on the table.

Finally, SQL Server adds new system tables to the database that contains the replicated tables. The MSMerge_contents and MSMerge_tombstone tables track the updates, inserts, and deletes. These tables rely on rowguid to track which rows have actually been changed.

The Merge Agent is responsible for moving changed data from the site where it was changed to all other sites in the replication scenario. When a row is updated, the triggers added by SQL Server fire off and update the new system tables, setting the generation column equal to 0 for the corresponding rowguid. When the Merge Agent runs, it collects the data from the rows where the generation column is 0 and then resets the generation values to values higher than the previous generation numbers. This allows the Merge Agent to look for data that has already been shared with other sites without having to look through all the data. The Merge Agent then sends the changed data to the other sites.

When the data reaches the other sites, the data is merged with existing data according to rules you have defined. These rules are flexible and highly extensible. The Merge Agent evaluates existing and new data and resolves conflicts based on priorities or which data was changed first. Another available option is that you can create custom resolution strategies using the Component Object Model (COM) and custom stored procedures. After conflicts have been handled, synchronization occurs to ensure that all sites have the same data.

The Merge Agent identifies conflicts using the MSMerge_contents table. In this table, a column called lineage is used to track the history of changes to a row. The agent updates the lineage value whenever a user makes changes to the data in a row. The entry into this column is a combination of a site identifier and the last version of the row created at the site. As the Merge Agent is merging all the changes that have occurred, it examines each site's information to see whether a conflict has occurred. If a conflict has occurred, the agent initiates conflict resolution based on the criteria mentioned earlier.

Basing the Replication Design on User Requirements

As mentioned earlier, business requirements drive your replication configuration and method. In addition, nailing down all the details of the business requirements is the hardest part of a data replication design process. After you have completed the requirements gathering, the replication design usually just falls into place from it easily. The requirements gathering is highly recommended to get a prototype up and running as quickly as possible to measure the effectiveness of one approach over the other. You must understand several key aspects to make the right design decisions, including the following:

▶ What is the number of sites, and what is the site autonomy in the scope (location)?

▶ Which sites have the master data (data ownership)?

▶ What is the data latency requirement (by site)?

▶ What types of data accesses are being made (by site)?

  ▶ Reads

  ▶ Writes

  ▶ Updates

  ▶ Deletes

  This information needs to include exactly what data and data subsets that drive filtering are needed for the data accesses (by site).

▶ What is the volume of activity/transactions, including the number of users (by site)?

▶ How many machines do you have to work with (by site)?

▶ What are the available processing power (CPU and memory) and disk space on each of these machines (by site)?

▶ What are the stability, speed, and saturation level of the network connections between machines (by site)?

▶ What is the dial-in, Internet, or other access mechanism requirement for the data?

▶ What potential subscriber or publisher database engines are involved?

Figure 43.24 shows the factors that contribute to replication designs and the possible data replication configuration that would best be used. It is only a partial table because of the numerous factors and many replication configuration options available. However, it gives a good idea of the general design approach described here. Perhaps 95% of user requirements can be classified fairly easily. The other 5% might take some imagination in determining the best overall solution. Depending on the requirements that need to be supported, you might even end up with a solution using something like database mirroring or other distribution techniques.

Data Access scenario	Latency	Autonomy	Sites (locations)	Frequency	Network	Machines	Owner	Other	REPLICATION TYPE
Read Only Reporting	short	high	many	high	fast/ stable	1 server/site	1 OLTP site	Each site only needs regional data	CentralPublisher Transactionalrepl filter by region CDC Availability Groups
Read Only Reporting	long	high	many	low	fast/ stable	1 server/site	1 OLTP site	Each site only needs regional data	CentralPublisher Snapshotrepl filter by region CDC Availability Groups
Read Mostly A few updates	short	high	< 10	medium	fast/ stable	n server/site	1 OLTP site	Regional updates on one table	CentralPublisher Transactionalrepl Updating Subs Peer-to-Peer
Read Mostly A few updates	medium	high	< 10	medium	Slow/ unreliable	n server/site	All update	Regional update all tables	CentralPublisher Updating Subs Mergerepl
Read equal Equal updates	short	high	< 10	medium	fast/ stable	n server/site	All update	Regional update all tables	Peer-to-Peer Transactionalrepl
Inserts (new orders)	short	high	many	high	fast/ stable	1 server/site	All update sites	Each site only needs regional data	CentralSubscriber Transactionalrepl
Hot/Warm Spare	Very short	high	< 2	high	fast/ stable	1 server/site	1 OLTP site	Fail-over	CentralPublisher Transactionalrepl Availability Groups

FIGURE 43.24 Replication design factors.

Data Characteristics

You need to analyze the underlying data types and characteristics thoroughly. Issues such as collation or character set and data sorting come into play. You must be aware of what they are set to on all nodes of your replication configuration. SQL Server 2014 does not convert the replicated data and might even mistranslate the data as it is replicated because it is impossible to map all characters between character sets. It is best to look up the character set "mapping chart" for SQL Server replication to all other data target environments. Most are covered well, but problems arise with certain data types, such as `image`, `timestamp`, and `identity`. Sometimes, using the Unicode data types at all sites is best for consistency. Following is a general list of issues to watch out for in this regard:

▶ Collation consistency across all nodes of replication.

▶ Timestamp column data in replication. It might not be what you think.

▶ `identity`, `uniqueidentifier`, and `guid` column behavior with data replication.

▶ `text` or `image` data types to heterogeneous subscribers.

▶ Missing or unsupported data types because of prior versions of SQL Server or heterogeneous subscribers as part of the replication configuration.

▶ Maximum row size limitations between merge replication and transactional replication.

Figure 43.25 lists further SQL Server 2014 replication object limitations.

Microsoft SQL Server 2014 Replication object	Maximum sizes/numbers (32-bit)	Maximum sizes/numbers (64-bit)
Articles (merge publication)	256	256
Articles (snapshot or transactional publication)	32,767	32,767
Columns in a table (merge publication)	246	246
Columns in a table (SQL Server snapshot or transactional publication)	1000	1000
Columns in a table (Oracle snapshot or transactional publication)	995	995
Bytes for column used in a row filter (merge publication)	1024	1024
Bytes for a column used in a row filter (snapshot or transactional publication)	8000	8000

FIGURE 43.25 SQL Server 2014 replication object limitations.

> **NOTE**
>
> If you have triggers on your tables and you want them to be replicated along with your table, you should add the line of code NOT FOR REPLICATION so that the trigger code isn't executed redundantly on the subscriber side.

Setting Up Replication

In general, SQL Server 2014 data replication is exceptionally easy to set up via SQL Server Management Studio wizards. However, if you use the wizards, you need to be sure to generate SQL scripts for every phase of replication configuration. In a production environment, you are likely to rely heavily on scripts and not have the luxury of having much time to set up and break down production replication configurations via wizards. Generating SQL scripts also eases the setup/breakdown process in development, test, and user acceptance environments.

You always have to define any data replication configuration in the following order:

1. Create or enable a distributor to enable publishing.

2. Enable publishing (a distributor must be designated for a publisher).

3. Create a publication and define articles within the publication.

4. Define subscribers and subscribe to a publication.

Figure 43.26 shows SQL Server Management Studio Object Explorer with three separate server connections. These three servers represent a possible replication topology.

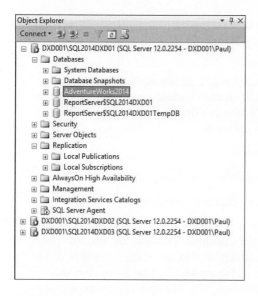

FIGURE 43.26   Three servers to be used in the replication topology (central publisher, remote distributor, and subscriber).

The following section takes you through the process of building up a typical central publisher/remote distribution data replication configuration. The following SQL Server named instances are used for different purposes (as shown in Figure 43.26):

▶ **Publisher**—A SQL2014DXD01 named instance

▶ **Distributor**—A SQL2014DXD02 named instance (REMOTE distributor)

▶ **Subscriber**—A SQL2014DXD03 named instance

The following section highlights the different areas in SQL Server Management Studio that are needed to create this replication configuration.

Creating a Distributor and Enabling Publishing

Before setting up a publisher, you have to designate a distribution server to be used by that publisher. As discussed earlier, you can either configure the local server as the distribution server or choose a remote server as the distributor (not on the same machine as the publication server). You can configure the server as a distributor and publisher at the same time, or you can configure the server as a dedicated distributor on the remote server separately. In the sample topology described here, you start by creating a remote distributor separately so you can orient yourself to what is happening on each server in the topology as it is being built up. You are also able to enable a specific SQL Server instance as the publisher that will use this distributor (all in one wizard sequence). This method is very efficient.

Before you can configure replication, you must be a member of the `sysadmin` server role, so you should ensure that now. Then you use the following steps to configure a server as a distributor (remote distributor):

1. In SQL Server Management Studio, locate the `Replication` node under the server that will be the distributor (under the `SQL2014DXD02` named instance node). Right-click the `Replication` node and choose Configure Distribution. This starts you through the wizard, which provides three options:

    ▶ Configure this server to be a distributor.

    ▶ Configure this server to be both a publisher and distributor.

    ▶ Configure this server to be a publisher that uses another server as its distributor.

2. When the wizard starts, click past the initial Configure Distribution Wizard splash page. Then choose the first radio button, which should say `'DXD01\SQL2014DXD02'` Will Act as Its Own Distributor (as shown in Figure 43.27). This designates this server as a distributor for one or more publishers. The distribution database and log are created here as well (and not on the publication server).

3. You are then asked how you want the replication agents to be started. Select the agents to be started automatically (the Yes option).

4. Next comes the location for the snapshot folder. Give it the proper network full pathname. Remember that potentially a large amount of data will be coming here, and it should be on a drive that can support the snapshot concept without filling up the drive.

5. When you are asked to configure the distribution database, select the default settings. Figure 43.28 shows all the distribution database name and location information.

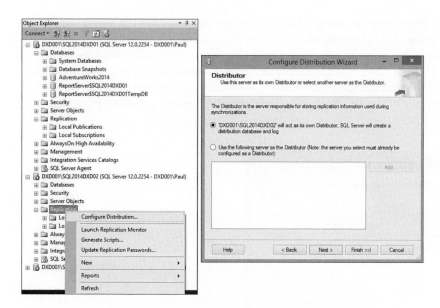

FIGURE 43.27   Configuring a separate distributor (REMOTE) wizard.

FIGURE 43.28   Specification of the distribution database name and location.

6. Identify the publisher if you know which SQL Server instance will be publishing the data that this distributor will distribute for. To do this, click the Add button at the bottom-right corner of the Publishers page to enable servers to use this distributor when they become publishers. You are prompted for the server name and authentication method for the distributor to reach this publisher. Specify DXD01\ SQL2014DXD01 as a publisher that will use this distributor. The end result, as shown in Figure 43.29, is DXD01\SQL2014DXD01 designated (checked) as a publisher that will use this distribution database (distributor). Remember to uncheck the SQL Server named instance of the distribution server if you don't want to publish from that server (the SQL2014DXD02 named instance).

FIGURE 43.29   Designate the publisher that will use this remote distributor.

7. Specify a distributor password. This is the password that will be used by publishers to connect to the distributor. You will be able to administer this password through SQL Server Management Studio directly. The wizard then summarizes what actions you want to take place, such as configure the distribution server or generate a script file with steps to configure distribution. Choose both. It's always good to have the scripts created now so you can start script-based configurations immediately. You'll be prompted for the script file location and action to follow when creating this script.

A Complete the Wizard page is displayed, describing all the tasks that are about to happen, along with their configuration specifications. Figure 43.30 shows this summary.

When you click Finish, several things begin to occur. First, a configuring dialog page comes up and spins its wheels through each step you have requested (as shown in Figure 43.31). A summary of steps, errors, and warnings is displayed on this page. When it completes, you can explore any issues (errors or warnings) by drilling down in the Report option (lower-right side of this dialog). Make sure that you see Success after each step of this configuration.

FIGURE 43.30   Completing the configuration of the distributor and enabling the publisher.

FIGURE 43.31   Configuring the distributor and enabling a publisher in progress.

Now is probably a good time to locate that distributor setup and enabling publication script and drop it into your replication administrator folder that you keep in a safe place. Figure 43.32 shows what this script looks like. Notice that the password is not displayed. The details of these scripts are described later in this chapter, in the "Scripting Replication" section.

43

```
ConfigureDistributi...(DXD001\Paul (57))  ×
/****** Scripting replication configuration. Script Date: 11/22/2014 9:27:18 PM ******/
  /****** Please Note: For security reasons, all password parameters were scripted with either NULL or an empt

  /****** Installing the server as a Distributor. Script Date: 11/22/2014 9:27:18 PM ******/
use master
exec sp_adddistributor @distributor = N'DXD001\SQL2014DXD02', @password = N''
  GO
exec sp_adddistributiondb @database = N'distribution', @data_folder = N'C:\Program Files\Microsoft SQL Serve
  GO

use [distribution]
if (not exists (select * from sysobjects where name = 'UIProperties' and type = 'U '))
    create table UIProperties(id int)
if (exists (select * from ::fn_listextendedproperty('SnapshotFolder', 'user', 'dbo', 'table', 'UIProperties'
    EXEC sp_updateextendedproperty N'SnapshotFolder', N'C:\Program Files\Microsoft SQL Server\MSSQL12.SQL201
else
    EXEC sp_addextendedproperty N'SnapshotFolder', N'C:\Program Files\Microsoft SQL Server\MSSQL12.SQL2014DX
  GO

exec sp_adddistpublisher @publisher = N'DXD001\SQL2014DXD01', @distribution_db = N'distribution', @security_
  GO
```

FIGURE 43.32   The script generated for creating the distributor and enabling a publisher.

When the distributor is configured and the distribution database is created (under System Databases), a series of replication agents (managed by SQL Server Agent) are created, with various duties, as described earlier in this chapter. Figure 43.33 shows the initial set of agents created on the distribution server (as seen from the Job Activity Monitor under the SQL Server Agent). No agents exist yet that actually publish data or distribute data. Those agents are created later, as you start publishing and subscribing.

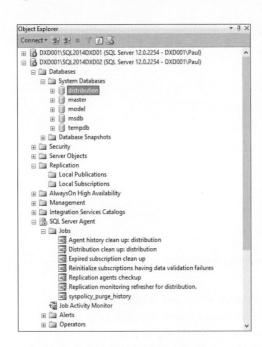

FIGURE 43.33   Initial replication agents on the distributor.

Creating a Publication

When the distribution database has been created and publishing has been enabled on the server, you can create and configure a publication. In SQL Server Management Studio, you start by locating the Replication node under the publication server from which you want to publish data (the DXD01\SQL2014DXD01 named instance in this example). Figure 43.34 shows the program item option when you right-click the Replication node under what will be the publication server. As you can see, there are three options; one to create a new publication, one to create a new Oracle publication, and one to create a new subscription.

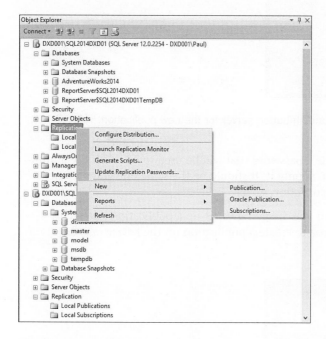

FIGURE 43.34   The New Publication item option on the server that will be the publisher.

You should choose to create a new publication (the first option). When you do, the New Publication Wizard is launched.

Here's how you create a new publication:

1. The first New Publication Wizard page outlines the two things that can be done with this wizard. The options are "Select the data and database objects you want to replicate" and "Filter the published data so that subscribers receive only the data they need." After this splash page, you need to specify how you want to distribute the data for this new publication. As you can see in Figure 43.35, you should use a remote distributor (the DXD01\SQL2014DXD02 named instance) to distribute data for this new publication you are defining.

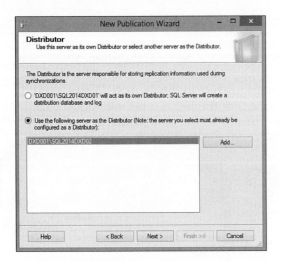

FIGURE 43.35   Specifying the remote distribution server for the new publication.

2. When you are asked to provide a password that will be used to establish the administrative link to the distributor, supply it. It should be the same one you specified earlier when setting up the distribution server.

3. Identify the database on which you are going to set up a publication (see Figure 43.36). For this example, choose to create a publication on the AdventureWorks2014 database.

FIGURE 43.36   Choosing the database that contains the data or objects you want to publish.

4. Choose the type of replication method for this publication: Snapshot Publication, Transactional Publication, Transactional Publication with Updateable Subscriptions, or Merge Publication Method of Replication. For this example, select Transactional Publication (as shown in Figure 43.37).

FIGURE 43.37   Specifying the publication type for replication (transactional publication in our example).

5. Next, you are presented with the place where you specify what tables and other objects to publish. These will become your articles. To keep this simple, just choose the primary stored procedures, views, indexed views, user-defined functions, and tables of the `AdventureWorks2014` database for this publication. (You do not select any filtering at this time.) Figure 43.38 shows the Articles specification page. Also in Figure 43.38, you can view the article properties that dictate how all article objects should be handled by replication (via the Article Properties button in the upper-right corner of this wizard screen). An example of this is specifying the delete statement delivery format behavior for this publication (for all tables) to be Do Not Replication DELETE Statements or Call <stored procedure> to do the deletes instead of individual delete statements.

The next wizard screen carefully analyzes what you are asking to become articles and highlights any dependencies that must be considered as part of replication. A good example of an article issue is that indexed views require the tables to which they are bound to be part of the replication.

6. Next comes the dialog for specifying filters. It is here where you can add SQL statements to horizontally or vertically filter what gets published via this article. We will not filter any data at this time. Simply click Next.

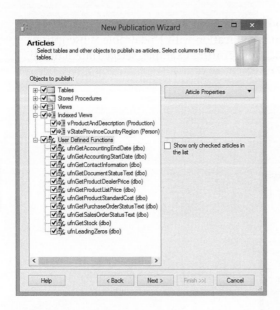

FIGURE 43.38   Choosing the tables and other objects that determine the articles to publish.

7. When the Snapshot Agent Wizard configuration screen prompts you to either create a snapshot immediately or at some scheduled time and to keep the snapshot available to initialize subscriptions, select to create a snapshot immediately and keep it available to initialize the subscription. As part of this Snapshot Agent creation, you have to specify under what security credentials you want the agent security to run. In addition, you can specify if you want the Log Reader Agent to use the same security settings as the Snapshot Agent. The rule of thumb here is to keep it simple and let these agents use the same security settings (as shown in Figure 43.39).

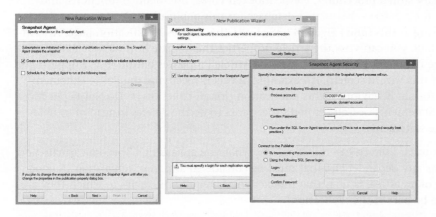

FIGURE 43.39   Agent security for Snapshot Agent and Log Reader Agent.

8. The wizard now has enough information to create the publication. When the wizard actions are summarized for you, choose to create the publication and generate a script file with all the steps to create the publication in it. Again, this script generation part is highly recommended. You certainly don't want to have to go through this wizard over and over. Once is enough.

9. When the summary of all choices made in the creation of a new publication is listed in the Complete the Wizard screen, name the publication appropriately. Your publication names should contain the type of publication method being used (for example, Snapshot, Transactional, Merge) and any other identifying qualifier that seems appropriate (usually reflecting the scope of the publication). Figure 43.40 shows this summary of actions and the publication name PUBLISH AdventureWorks2014 - Transactional.

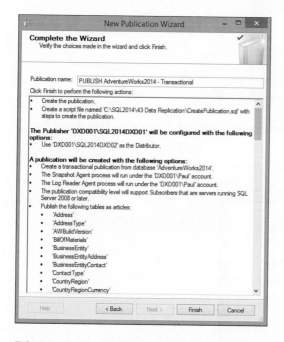

FIGURE 43.40   Publication action summary and naming the publication before it is created.

The actual creation of the publication is next. An action progress screen appears, showing each step (action) and indicating any errors or warnings occurring in the publication creation process. To view any errors or warnings, you simply click the Report button in the lower-right side after the processing completes. As you can see in Figure 43.41, this report lists, by name, all articles created.

As part of this process, several new agents (jobs) are added; they implement this publication using the designated distributor. There are no subscribers yet; they come later. Figure 43.42 shows the new jobs (agents) and publication entries. You are now ready to create subscriptions against this publication.

FIGURE 43.41   The publication steps and status, along with the report generated during this process.

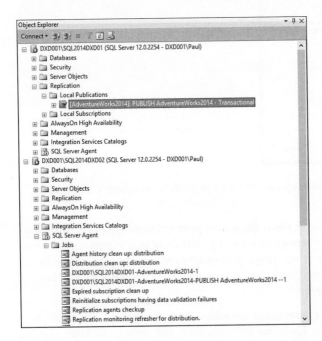

FIGURE 43.42   SQL Server Management Studio and the new publication agents (Snapshot Agent, Distribution Agent, and so on) and the new local publication.

As you can see in Figure 43.43, if you launch Replication Monitor (from the `Replication` node under the publication server), you can see the newly created publication and its status, and you have access to any servers subscribing to it (none yet), along with the common replication jobs that are servicing this publication.

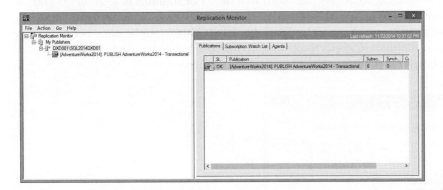

FIGURE 43.43   Replication Monitor, viewing the status of the newly created publication (from the publisher).

Because you chose to execute the snapshot immediately, the snapshot executes and utilizes the snapshot folder to generate the schema files (.sch files), data snapshot files (.bcp), and so on to fully enable a subscription when one is created. Figure 43.44 shows the contents of the snapshot folder being used for the publication of the `AdventureWorks2014` publication. Remember that this folder must be located in a place that is big enough to contain all the data that will be extracted and used for the snapshot; plan ahead.

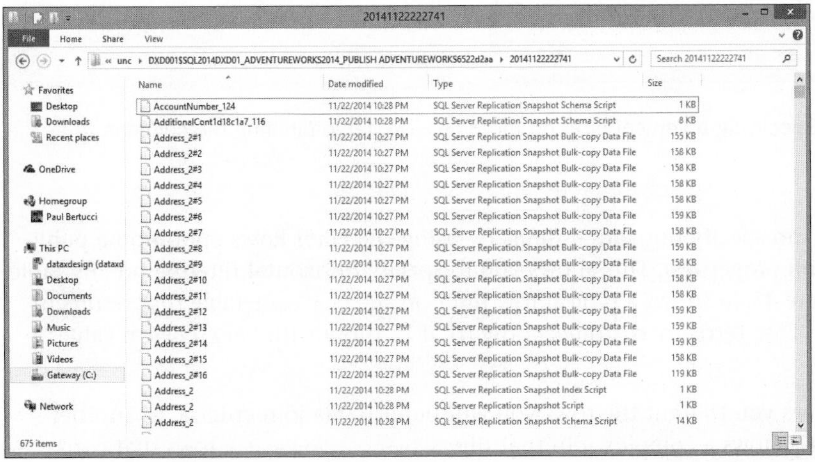

FIGURE 43.44   Contents of the snapshot folder produced for the publication.

Horizontal and Vertical Filtering

During the publication creation process, you could have done some filtering of the data, either horizontally or vertically (or both at the same time). The concept of filtering was covered earlier in this chapter. Figure 43.45 illustrates all you need to do to vertically filter (in terms of limiting what gets published to a subset of columns of a table). As you can see, you uncheck the AccountNumber column for the Customer table so that it isn't included in the article for that object in this publication. This might be done because account number information needs to be more tightly controlled within your company and shouldn't be part of what is viewed by any subscribing systems.

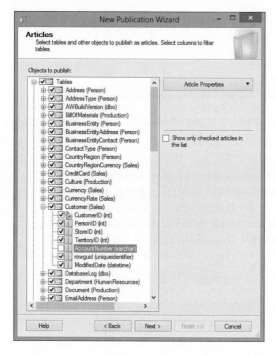

FIGURE 43.45   Specifying a vertical filter on the Customer table (limiting the columns to be published).

In addition, you can specify horizontal filters by using the Filter Rows option on a publication (publication properties). This allows you to specify horizontal filtering on any table you publish. Figure 43.46 shows a typical row filter on the Customer table that results in publishing North East Territory customers only (that is, those with TerritoryID values of 1 or 2).

Join filtering allows you to limit the rows you will publish, via join criteria, to another table. Figure 43.47 shows a complex join that filters SalesOrderHeader rows that correspond to North East Territory customers only (that is, those with TerritoryID values of 1 or 2).

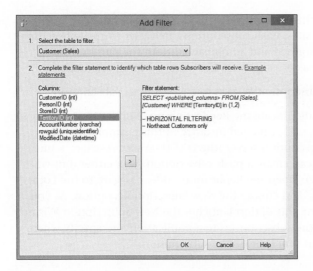

FIGURE 43.46   Specifying a horizontal filter on the `Customer` table (limiting the rows to be published).

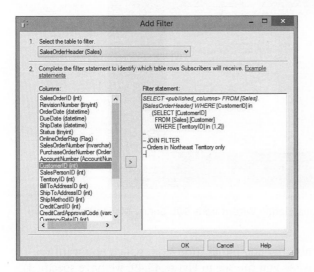

FIGURE 43.47   Specifying a join filter on the `SalesOrderHeader` table (limiting the sales rows that will be published by joining for the North East customers only).

Creating Subscriptions

Now that you have installed and configured the distributor, enabled publishing, and created a publication, you can create subscriptions.

Remember that two types of subscriptions can be created: push or pull. Pull subscriptions allow remote sites to subscribe to any publication that they are allowed to, but for this to work, you must be confident that the administrators at the other sites have properly configured the subscriptions at their sites. Push subscriptions are easier to create because all the subscription processes are performed and administered from the publication/distributor point of view. This also makes using them the most common approach.

For this example, we use the New Subscription Wizard to create a push subscription:

1. In SQL Server Management Studio, locate the Replication node under the publication server (the DXD01\SQL2014DXD01 named instance in this example) or the Replication node under the subscription server (the DXD001\SQL2014DXD03 named instance in this example). You can create a push subscription from either (but we use the subscription server here). Open the Replication node, navigate to the Local Subscription branch, right-click, and choose the New Subscriptions option. As you can see in Figure 43.48, choosing this option launches the New Subscription Wizard, where you can create one or more subscriptions to a publication and specify where and when to run the agents that synchronize the subscription.

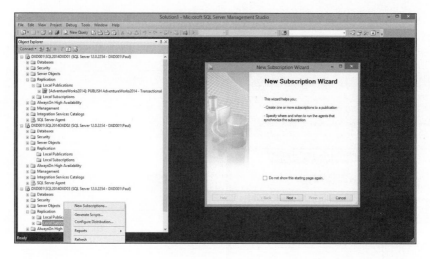

FIGURE 43.48   Launching the New Subscription Wizard from SQL Server Management Studio.

2. You first need to identify the publisher and publication from which you want to create one or more subscriptions. As you can see in Figure 43.49, we have specified the publisher (DXD01\SQL2014DXD01) and the publication that has been created for the AdventureWorks2014 database.

3. When you are presented with the option of where the replication agents will be run for the subscription, choose the first option—having the agents run at the distributor. This makes it a push subscription, which is much easier to control and manage centrally than a pull subscription (as shown in Figure 43.50).

FIGURE 43.49   Identifying the publication from which to subscribe.

FIGURE 43.50   Run all agents at the Distributor (push subscriptions).

4. Next, the New Database dialog appears, asking you to identify the database target for the subscription and the physical database files for its allocation (assuming that you want to create this from scratch using this wizard process). Figure 43.51 shows this New Database dialog, with the target database named AdventureWorks2014ODS. Essentially, we have decided to create a subscription that will continuously flow data from the publisher to the subscriber for all tables in the publication. This continuous replication at the transactional level effectively creates a mirror image of the data for operational usage. That's why we have used the suffix ODS, for Operational Data

Store, for the new database. This is a typical industry usage of replication that takes all read-only access to OLTP data and offloads it to the ODS copy of the same data (which is as close to up-to-date as the last transaction that was replicated to it).

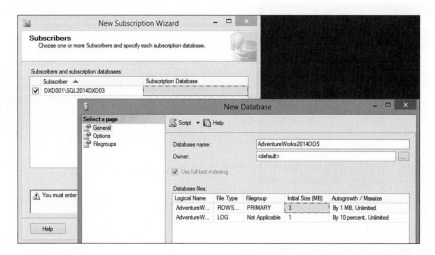

FIGURE 43.51   The New Database dialog specifying the target database (`AdventureWorks2014ODS`).

5. In the Subscribers screen, with the new entry for the target subscriber server (the `DXD01\SQL2014DXD03` named instance in this example), check the box for the target subscription server. Figure 43.52 shows this subscriber server and the subscription database target.

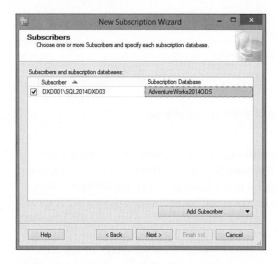

FIGURE 43.52   Specifying the subscription server target database.

6. Specify the process account and connection options for the Distribution Agent (to connect to the subscription server). Typically, you choose the option to use a domain account or choose to impersonate the process account (shown in Figure 43.53).

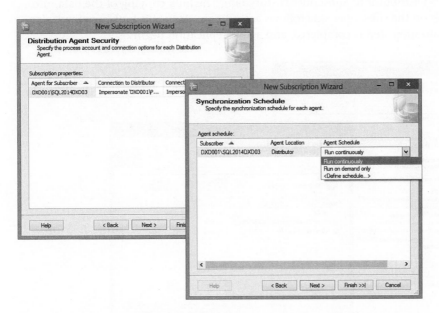

FIGURE 43.53   Distribution Agent security and synchronization schedule for the subscription (run continuously).

7. Specify the synchronization schedule for each agent. You want the Distribution Agent to run continuously, but you also have the options to run on a schedule and on demand (as also shown in Figure 43.53).

8. Specify the initialization of the subscription. You want the subscription to be initialized immediately, but, depending on the size of the database, this might be accomplished manually with a database backup of the publication database.

9. On the next screen, which lists the New Subscription Wizard actions, choose to create the subscription and generate a script file with all the steps to create the subscription for use later.

10. On the next wizard dialog, identify the location of the script to be generated. Click Next. Then you are presented with the final wizard summary screen. Click Finish to create your subscription, initialize the subscription database, and enjoy a full transactional replication implementation, as shown in Figure 43.54

   After you click Finish, the create subscription process starts and goes through each step, also shown in Figure 43.54. Remember to check for errors or warnings if any errors occur. When this process completes, you wait for the agents to initialize the target database and start replication to the subscriber. If you have specified that the schema and data be created immediately, things start happening quickly. The Distribution Agent finishes the job. As you can see in Figure 43.55, the Distribution Agent applies the schemas to the subscriber (as viewed from the Replication Monitor's Distributor to Subscriber History tab). The bulk copying of the data into the tables on the subscriber side follows accordingly. After this bulk copying is done, the initialization step is completed, and active replication begins.

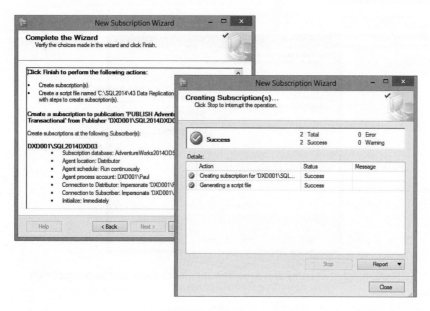

FIGURE 43.54   The New Subscription Wizard summary.

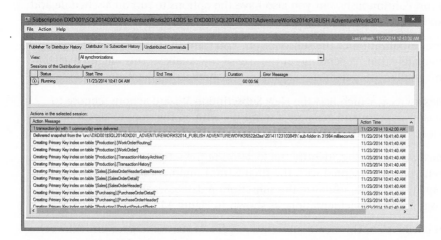

FIGURE 43.55   Delivering schemas and data to the subscriber.

The complete replication buildup is finished, and you should be fully functional for replicating transactions to the subscriber.

Figure 43.56 shows what the replication buildup looks like from the Replication Monitor as transactions flow through the replication topology. This screenshot shows the transaction counts and commands being delivered on the last leg in the journey (from the distributor to a subscriber). Figure 43.57 shows the full replication topology that was built (publisher, distributor, and subscriber).

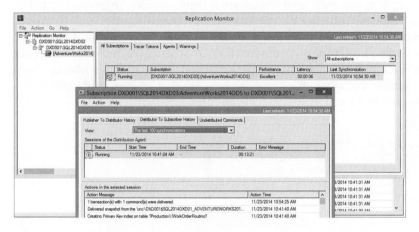

FIGURE 43.56   Transactions replicating to the subscriber (pushed).

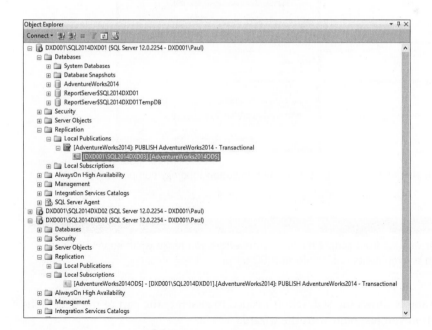

FIGURE 43.57   Full replication topology that was built (publisher, distributor, subscriber).

Your replication topology is now completely functional and will replicate flawlessly for as long as you require.

Scripting Replication

Earlier, it was strongly suggested that you generate SQL scripts for all that you do because going through wizards every time you have to configure replication is a difficult way to run a production environment. In the example in the preceding section, you always chose to generate these scripts as you built up the replication configuration. This was only half the scripts needed, however. You must also generate the breakdown scripts (that is, those that drop and remove replication components) to remove each component of the replication topology in case you need to start from scratch or, as an example, rebuild a subscriber that is completely nonfunctional. As you can see in Figure 43.58, SQL Server Management Studio has a great feature that allows the complete generation of all aspects of replication topology (including disabling and removing replication).

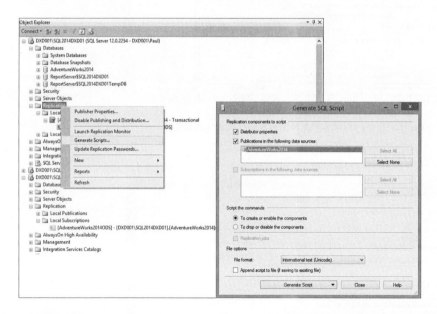

FIGURE 43.58 A script-generation feature for all replication topology components.

> **NOTE**
>
> Remember that working from scripts minimizes the errors you make while supporting your data replication environments (especially at 3:00 a.m.).

The following example shows the SQL scripts needed to generate the part of the data replication configuration you just built with the wizard:

```
-- Begin: Script to be run at PUBLISHER --
-----------------------------------------
-- Enabling the distribution database --
-----------------------------------------
use master
exec sp_adddistributor @distributor = N'DXD01\SQL2014DXD02', @password = N''
GO
exec sp_addsubscriber @subscriber = N'DXD01\SQL2014DXD03', @type = 0, @description =
➡N''
GO
-- End: Script to be run at Publisher --
-----------------------------------------
-- Enabling the replication database --
-----------------------------------------
use master
exec sp_replicationdboption @dbname = N'AdventureWorks2014', @optname = N'publish',
➡@value = N'true'
GO
exec [AdventureWorks2014].sys.sp_addlogreader_agent @job_login = N'DXD01\PAUL',
@job_password = null, @publisher_security_mode = 1
GO
exec [AdventureWorks2014].sys.sp_addqreader_agent @job_login = null, @job_password =
➡null, @frompublisher = 1
Go
-----------------------------------------
-- Adding the transactional publication --
-----------------------------------------
use [AdventureWorks2014]
exec sp_addpublication @publication = N'PUBLISH AdventureWorks2014 - Transactional',
@description = N'Transactional publication of database ''AdventureWorks2014''
from Publisher ''DXD01\SQL2014DXD01''.', @sync_method = N'concurrent', @retention =
0,
@allow_push = N'true', @allow_pull = N'true', @allow_anonymous = N'true', @enabled_
➡for_internet = N'false',
@snapshot_in_defaultfolder = N'true', @compress_snapshot = N'false', @ftp_port = 21,
➡ @ftp_login = N'anonymous',
@allow_subscription_copy = N'false', @add_to_active_directory = N'false', @repl_freq
➡= N'continuous',
@status = N'active', @independent_agent = N'true', @immediate_sync = N'true', @
allow_sync_tran = N'false',
@autogen_sync_procs = N'false', @allow_queued_tran = N'false', @allow_dts =
➡N'false', @replicate_ddl = 1,
@allow_initialize_from_backup = N'false', @enabled_for_p2p = N'false',
@enabled_for_het_sub = N'false'
GO
```

43

```
exec sp_addpublication_snapshot @publication = N'PUBLISH AdventureWorks2014 -
➡Transactional', @frequency_type = 1,
@frequency_interval = 0, @frequency_relative_interval = 0,
➡@frequency_recurrence_factor = 0, @frequency_subday = 0,
@frequency_subday_interval = 0, @active_start_time_of_day = 0,
➡@active_end_time_of_day = 235959,
@active_start_date = 0, @active_end_date = 0, @job_login = N'DXD01\PAUL',
➡@job_password = null,
@publisher_security_mode = 1
exec sp_grant_publication_access @publication = N'PUBLISH AdventureWorks2014 -
➡Transactional',
@login = N'sa'
GO
exec sp_grant_publication_access @publication = N'PUBLISH AdventureWorks2014 -
➡Transactional',
@login = N'DXD01\PAUL'
GO
exec sp_grant_publication_access @publication = N'PUBLISH AdventureWorks2014 -
➡Transactional',
@login = N'NT Service\MSSQL$SQL2014DXD01'
GO
exec sp_grant_publication_access @publication = N'PUBLISH AdventureWorks2014 -
➡Transactional',
@login = N'NT SERVICE\SQLAgent$SQL2014DXD01'
GO
exec sp_grant_publication_access @publication = N'PUBLISH AdventureWorks2014 -
➡Transactional',
@login = N'NT SERVICE\Winmgmt'
GO
exec sp_grant_publication_access @publication = N'PUBLISH AdventureWorks2014 -
➡Transactional',
@login = N'NT SERVICE\SQLWriter'
GO
----------------------------------------
-- Adding the transactional articles --
----------------------------------------
use [AdventureWorks2014]
exec sp_addarticle @publication = N'PUBLISH AdventureWorks2014 - Transactional',
@article = N'Address', @source_owner = N'Person', @source_object = N'Address',
@type = N'logbased', @description = N'', @creation_script = N'',
@pre_creation_cmd = N'drop', @schema_option = 0x000000000803509F,
@identityrangemanagementoption = N'manual', @destination_table = N'Address',
@destination_owner = N'Person', @status = 24, @vertical_partition = N'false',
@ins_cmd = N'CALL [sp_MSins_PersonAddress]', @del_cmd = N'CALL [sp_MSdel_
PersonAddress]',
@upd_cmd = N'SCALL [sp_MSupd_PersonAddress]'
```

```
GO
use [AdventureWorks2014]
exec sp_addarticle @publication = N'PUBLISH AdventureWorks2014 - Transactional',
. . .

-- all other articles in the publication removed


--------------------------------------------
-- Adding the transactional subscriptions --
--------------------------------------------
use [AdventureWorks2014]
exec sp_addsubscription @publication = N'PUBLISH AdventureWorks2014 -
➥Transactional',
@subscriber = N'DXD01\SQL2014DXD03', @destination_db = N'AdventureWorks2014ODS',
@subscription_type = N'Push', @sync_type = N'automatic', @article = N'all',
@update_mode = N'read only', @subscriber_type = 0

exec sp_addpushsubscription_agent @publication = N'PUBLISH AdventureWorks2014 -
➥Transactional',
 @subscriber = N'DXD01\SQL2014DXD03', @subscriber_db = N'AdventureWorks2014ODS',
 @job_login = N'DXD01\PAUL', @job_password = null, @subscriber_security_mode = 1,
 @frequency_type = 64, @frequency_interval = 1, @frequency_relative_interval = 1,
 @frequency_recurrence_factor = 0, @frequency_subday = 4, @frequency_subday_interval
= 5,
 @active_start_time_of_day = 0, @active_end_time_of_day = 235959, @active_start_date
= 0,
 @active_end_date = 0, @dts_package_location = N'Distributor'
GO
```

The complete set of buildup and breakdown scripts for the example used here are available on the website for this book in the code listings and sample databases folder. They are labeled CreatingXXX.sql for the buildup scripts and RemoveXXX.sql for the breakdown scripts; where XXX will be Publication, Distribution, and Subscription.

Monitoring Replication

After replication is up and running, it is important for you to monitor it and see how things are running. You can do this in several ways, including using SQL statements, SQL Server Management Studio, and Windows Performance Monitor. You are interested in the agent's successes and failures, the speed at which replication is done, and the synchronization state of tables involved in replication. Other issues to watch for are the sizes of the distribution database, growth of the subscriber databases, and available space on the distribution server's snapshot working directory.

Replication Monitoring SQL Statements

One way to look at the replication configuration and validate row counts, for example, is to use various replication stored procedures, including the following:

▶ `sp_helppublication`—Information on the publication server

▶ `sp_helparticle`—Article definition information

▶ `sp_helpdistributor`—Distributor information

▶ `sp_helpsubscriberinfo`—Subscriber server information

▶ `sp_helpsubscription`—Subscription information

These stored procedures are all extremely useful for verifying exactly how the replication configuration is really configured. If you execute these stored procedures (from the publication database), you get a great documentation of your complete replication topology that can be included in run books or other system documentation. Here's what you might do to see how the current replication configuration has been built out:

```
use AdventureWorks2014
go
exec sp_helppublication
exec sp_helparticle @publication='PUBLISH AdventureWorks2014 - Transactional'
exec sp_helpdistributor
exec sp_helpsubscriberinfo
exec sp_helpsubscription
go
```

It yields this result:

```
1 PUBLISH AdventureWorks2014 - Transactional        0    1    1    0
----------------------------------------------------------------------
1  Address          [Person].[Address]            Address
2  AddressType      [Person].[AddressType]        AddressType
3  AWBuildVersion   [dbo].[AWBuildVersion]        AWBuildVersion
4  BillOfMaterials  [Production].[BillOfMaterials] BillOfMaterials
5  Contact          [Person].[Contact]            Contact
6  ContactCreditCard [Sales].[ContactCreditCard]  ContactCreditCard
7  ContactType      [Person].[ContactType]        ContactType
...
```

In addition, `sp_replcounters` shows the activity of this replication session. You can see the volume of traffic and the throughput here:

```
exec sp_replcounters
go
```

It yields this result:

```
database repl_trans rate trans/sec latency (sec) etc.
AdventureWorks2014    0        1562.5    1.243
```

For actual row count validation, you can use `sp_publication_validation`, which goes through and checks the row counts of the publication and subscribers:

```
exec sp_publication_validation @publication
    = 'PUBLISH AdventureWorks2014 - Transactional'
go
```

It yields this result:

```
Generated expected rowcount value of 19614 for Address.
Generated expected rowcount value of 6 for AddressType.
Generated expected rowcount value of 1 for AWBuildVersion.
Generated expected rowcount value of 2679 for BillOfMaterials.
Generated expected rowcount value of 19972 for Contact.
Generated expected rowcount value of 19118 for ContactCreditCard.
Generated expected rowcount value of 20 for ContactType.
Generated expected rowcount value of 238 for CountryRegion.
Generated expected rowcount value of 109 for CountryRegionCurrency.
Generated expected rowcount value of 19118 for CreditCard.
Generated expected rowcount value of 8 for Culture.
```

Another way to monitor replication is to look at the actual data being replicated. To do this, you first run the SELECT count (*) FROM tblname statement against the table where data is being replicated. Then you verify directly whether the most current data available is in the database. If you make a change to the data in the published table, do the changes show up in the replicated tables? If not, you might need to investigate how replication was configured on the server.

If you are allowing updatable subscriptions, the replication queue comes into play. You need to learn all about the queueread command prompt utility. This utility configures and begins the queue reader agent, which reads messages stored in the SQL Server queue or a Microsoft message queue and applies those messages to the publisher.

To help you visualize how replication works and to help you monitor replication, the following sample stored procedure, called TRAFFIC_GENERATOR, takes one parameter (the number of rows [new customers in the Customer table] you want to have inserted at a time) and generates new rows in the Customer table that can reflect different data activity that will be published (this stored procedure has been included on the website for this book in the code listings and sample databases folder):

```
Use AdventureWorks2014
Go
------------------------------------------------------------
-- generate 500 new customers for replication testing --
------------------------------------------------------------
exec TRAFFIC_GENERATOR 500
go
```

This example shows how to execute this stored procedure to insert 500 new customers. If you don't supply any parameter, the default is 100 new customers. Try it out.

The following messages appear after you execute the TRAFFIC_GENERATOR stored procedure:

```
INSERTING ROW: 1
INSERTING ROW: 2
INSERTING ROW: 3
INSERTING ROW: 4
INSERTING ROW: 5
INSERTING ROW: 6
INSERTING ROW: 7
INSERTING ROW: 8
INSERTING ROW: 9
INSERTING ROW: 10
...
INSERTING ROW: 500
```

Figure 43.59 shows this stored procedure, which is included on the website for this book in the code listings and sample databases folder and also shows the load it is generating across the replication topology.

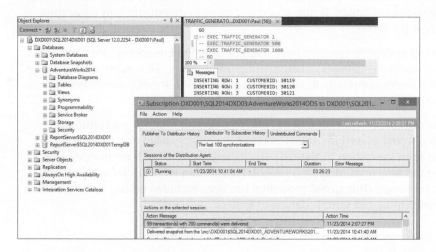

FIGURE 43.59   The executing TRAFFIC_GENERATOR stored procedure for testing data replication and replication monitor.

Monitoring Replication within SQL Server Management Studio

As you can imagine, SQL Server Management Studio provides considerable information about the status of replication. Most of this information is available via Replication Monitor. In Replication Monitor, you can see the activity for publishers, distributors, and subscribers; you can see all agent details; and you can configure alerts.

Through Replication Monitor, you also can invoke validation subscriptions processing to see if replication is in sync. You just navigate to the publication whose subscription you want to validate, right-click, and choose Validate Subscription option. This allows you to verify that the subscriber has the same number of rows of replicated data as the publisher. You can validate all subscriptions or just a particular one. Validation options are extensive and include using fast row count methods, actual row count methods, and even checksum comparisons of row data. This is a huge feature for SQL Server 2014. Figure 43.60 shows the results of running a complete subscription validation.

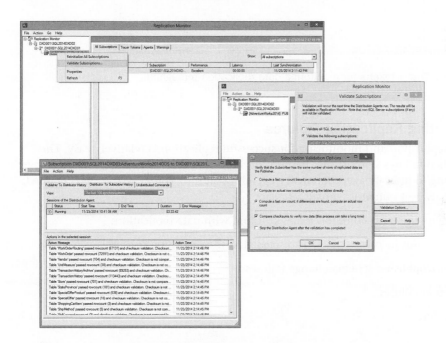

FIGURE 43.60   Validation of subscriptions via Replication Monitor.

Another great feature to help monitor replication is tracer tokens. Essentially, you create a marker (called a token) that flows through the full replication topology (from publisher to distributor to subscriber). It does not affect data tables! This flow is monitored and measured, down to the millisecond, and is for a specific publisher-to-subscriber path.

Figure 43.61 shows the Tracer Tokens tab of the Replication Monitor and the Insert Tracer button that you can click to fire off the token through the topology. You can click this button to quickly see where bottlenecks exist (for example, from publisher to distributor, from distributor to subscriber) and the latency of the data flow along the way. In this example, it took the tracer token 2 seconds in total to traverse from the publisher to the distributor and to the subscriber. This is also called a "synthetic transaction."

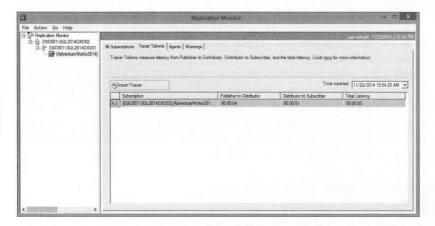

FIGURE 43.61   Tracer tokens for monitoring data replication throughput.

Troubleshooting Replication Failures

Configuring replication and monitoring for successful replication is relatively easy. The fun begins when failures start arising. Replication Monitor pays for itself quickly. Red flags begin appearing to indicate agent failures. Depending on how you have the alerts defined, you probably also get numerous emails or pages.

The following are the most common issues you find with data replication:

▶ Data row count inconsistencies, as discussed in the preceding section

▶ Subscriber/publisher schema change failures

▶ Connection failures

▶ Agent failures

For the conventional replication situations, if the problem is with the validation of subscriptions processing, it is usually best to resynchronize the subscription by dropping it and resubscribing or by reinitializing the subscription.

Another common issue is that the SQL Server Agent service doesn't start. Manually attempting to restart this service usually shakes things loose. Sometimes an object on the subscriber becomes messed up. The solution is usually to create that object again and reload its data via BCP or SSIS. Then you can resynchronize the subscription. In such a case, the subscription included this object originally, but it has become invalid in some way. With a heterogeneous subscriber, you often see connection errors due to invalid login IDs used in the ODBC connection. The quick fix is usually to just redefine the ODBC data source connection information.

A much more complex failure can arise when the replication queue is stopped due to some type of SQL language failure in the command being replicated. This situation is extremely serious because it stops all replication from continuing, and the distribution database starts growing rapidly. Replication keeps trying to execute, but it fails each time. This situation is essentially a permanent roadblock. The solution is to locate the exact transaction in the distribution database and delete it physically from the transaction queue. This action is highly unusual, but it is necessary when the circumstance presents itself. First, by looking at the error detail information in the Distribution Agent history, you can isolate the SQL statement on which it is choking. Then you have to find it in the distribution database. You start by executing the sp_browsereplcmds stored procedure from the distribution database. This gives you all the replication transactions (that is, each xact_seqno) along with the associated SQL command. You have to pump this to a text file for searching. You then search this data for the matching SQL command. When you locate it, you look for its associated transaction number (xact_seqno). You use this xact_seqno value to delete it from the Msrepl_commands table in the distribution database. This frees up the roadblock. You see this type of issue only about once every six months, if at all (it is hoped).

Peer-to-Peer Replication

For data distribution requirements that must have updates in multiple nodes, peer-to-peer replication is ideal. You must worry about conflicts, but typically they are rare and very easily handled by a simple conflict handler. Peer-to-peer replication is transactional replication based and can have any number of peers. A separate wizard is used to set up peer-to-peer replication because of its unique characteristics. Remember, there are essentially no subscribers, just publishers. All peers are handled by one or more distributors and are assigned a unique peer originator ID value to help in transactional consistency and conflict resolution. If you have been doing replication since the SQL Server 6.5 days, the peer-to-peer configuration topology viewer is much like that old user interface. To do peer-to-peer, you must first set up distribution and a publication from which to start from. Once a valid publication has been identified on the first node of your peer-to-peer topology, you can invoke the Peer-to-Peer Configuration Wizard. To make things easy, we have included a test script called REPLTEST.sql on the website for this book that contains a create database for a small database with the same name (REPLTEST) that we will use for our peer-to-peer example. Go grab this script right now and create the database on two SQL Server instances (SQL2014DXD01 and SQL2014DXD03 in our example). We will also use a third SQL Server instance to be a remote distributor (SQL2014DXD02). As you can also see in this script, there is a table create and an insert statement to populate rows in the table. Let's also create this table in both SQL Server instances but not populate any data yet. We'll let peer-to-peer replication distribute data later for us (from one peer to the other).

Now, set up your remote distributor as we did before and enable this distributor to publish for both DXD001\SQL2014DXD01 and DXD001\SQL2014DXD03. For DXD001\SQL2014DXD03 instance, set up DXD001\SQL2014DXD02 to be its distributor as well. Then, on DXD001\

SQL2014DXD01 instance, create a Peer-to-Peer publication (not the Transactional publication we did before) on the REPLTEST database that contains only one table (employee table), as shown in Figure 43.62.

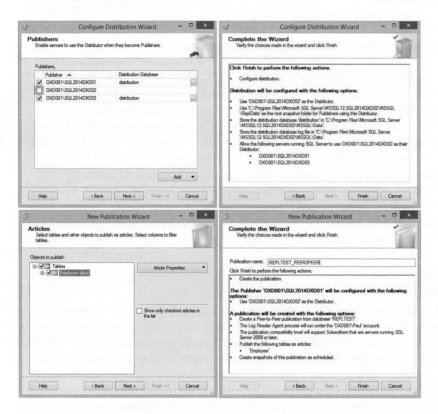

FIGURE 43.62   Creating the REPLTEST Peer-to-Peer replication for the Employee table.

Figure 43.63 shows the special invocation of peer-to-peer creation from SQL Server Management Studio.

You basically create publications that will become shared in the peer-to-peer topology. You add "nodes" on an equal hierarchical level that participate in the publication equally. You can add any number of peers (nodes), and in SQL Server 2014, this can be done without interrupting the existing replication topology. Figures 43.64 through 43.67 show the eight-step setup of a publication named REPLTEST_PEER2PEER for the database named REPLTEST and the addition of two nodes to the topology.

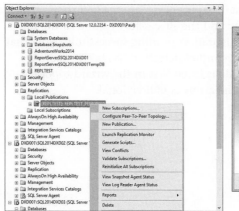 

FIGURE 43.63   Peer-to-Peer Wizard launch.

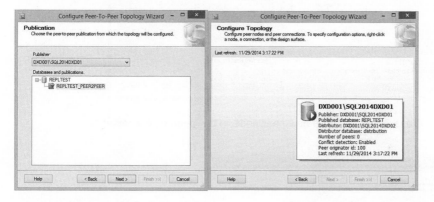

FIGURE 43.64   Steps 1 and 2: Setup of the publication that becomes the first node in a peer-to-peer topology.

You basically (1) identity the publication to use for peer-to-peer replication, (2) have that first node available in the viewer (SQL2014DXD01 node; right-click on the node for details), (3) add a new peer node, (4) identity how distribution will occur (both use the same distribution database), (5) add a new peer connection (drag and drop connection), (6) set up the Log Reader Agent security, (7) then the Distribution Agent security, and finally (8) how the data was initialized (we have empty tables so just say we did it manually). Once the summary dialog appears go ahead and click Finish.

Peers are typically initialized manually for consistency purposes. Figure 43.68 shows the Configure Peer-to-Peer Topology Wizard summary and the successful creation of the full (two-node) topology. Figure 43.69 shows the configuration running successfully. Note that each node is assigned a unique originator ID, and conflict detection has been enabled. Notice also that it really doesn't matter which node is listed first in the wizard topology because they are equal (no hierarchy exists) and the arrow is bidirectional.

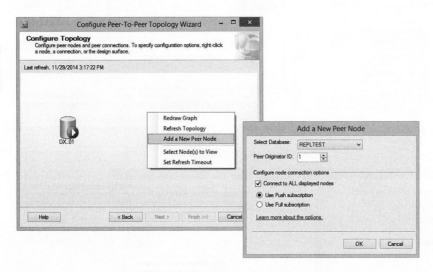

FIGURE 43.65   Steps 3 and 4: Add a new peer node in the peer-to-peer topology.

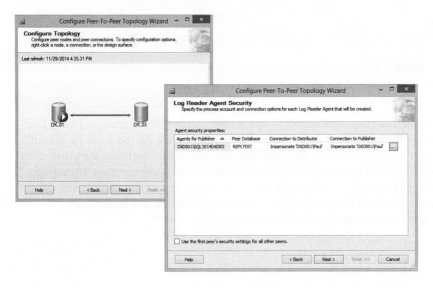

FIGURE 43.66   Steps 5 and 6: Two nodes and log reader agent security setup.

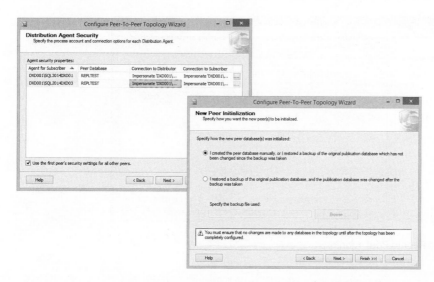

FIGURE 43.67   Steps 7 and 8: Distribution Agent Security and initialization option setup.

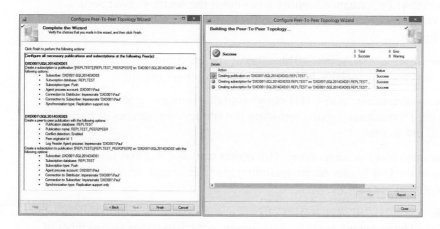

FIGURE 43.68   Configure Peer-to-Peer Topology Wizard summary and complete topology.

43

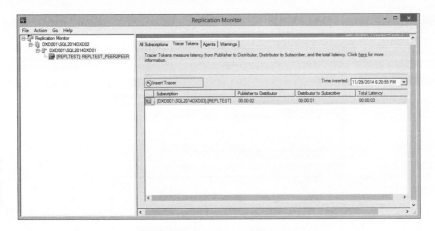

FIGURE 43.69   Peer-to-Peer running.

The Performance Monitor

You can use Windows Performance Monitor to monitor the health of your replication scenario. When you install SQL Server, you get several new objects and counters in Performance Monitor:

▶ `SQLServer:Replication Agents`—This object contains counters used to monitor the status of all replication agents, including the total number running.

▶ `SQLServer:Replication Dist`—This object contains counters used to monitor the status of the Distribution Agents, including the latency and number of transactions transferred per second.

▶ `SQLServer:Replication Logreader`—This object contains counters used to monitor the status of the Log Reader Agent, including the latency and number of transactions transferred per second.

▶ `SQLServer:Replication Merge`—This object contains counters used to monitor the status of the Merge Agents, including the number of transactions and number of conflicts per second.

▶ `SQLServer:Replication Snapshot`—This object contains counters used to monitor the status of the Snapshot Agents, including the number of transactions per second.

As you can see in Figure 43.70, we chose to monitor the typical things critical for replication: the LogReader counters, the distribution server counters, and some default processor times to keep an eye on load at the publisher.

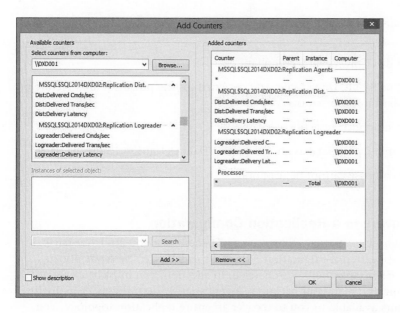

FIGURE 43.70 Performance Monitor counters for replication monitoring.

The Replication Monitor also provides an option called Subscription Watch List that enables you to set some monitoring thresholds on how quickly and reliably data is being replicated to the subscribers. The monitor can send alerts and also expose these visually with status values such as critical, excellent, so on.

Replication in Heterogeneous Environments

SQL Server 2014 allows for transactional and snapshot replication of data into and out of environments other than SQL Server. This is termed heterogeneous replication. The easiest way to set up this replication is to use ODBC or OLE DB and create a push subscription to the subscriber. This is much easier to make work than you might imagine. SQL Server can publish to the following database types:

- ▶ Microsoft Access

- ▶ Oracle

- ▶ Sybase

- ▶ IBM DB2/AS400

- ▶ IBM DB2/MVS

SQL Server can replicate data to any other type of database, provided that the following are true:

► The driver must be ODBC Level 1 compliant.

► The driver must be 32-bit, thread safe, and designed for the processor architecture on which the distribution process runs.

► The driver must support transactions.

► The driver and underlying database must support Data Definition Language (DDL).

► The underlying database cannot be read-only.

Backup and Recovery in a Replication Configuration

A replication-oriented backup strategy will reap major benefits for you after you have implemented a data replication configuration. You must realize that the scope of data and what you must back up together have changed. In addition, you must be aware of the recovery time frame and plan your backup/recovery strategy accordingly. You might not have multiple hours available to you to recover an entire replication topology. You now have databases that are conceptually joined, and you might need to back them up together in one synchronized backup. Figure 43.71 shows overall backup strategies for the most common recovery needs.

Recovery Need	Backup Strategy
100% data, All sites, Small Recovery Window	Coordinated DB backups at all sites involved in the replication configuration (publisher, distributor & all subscribers). Somewhat complex to do and backups must be done at same time (some data loss can occur).
100% data, All sites, Medium Recovery Window	Backup Publication DB and Distribution DB together. Replication can be recovered from this point very easily without reconfiguring anything. Just have to re-initialize the subscribers. This is the most common approach being used.
100% data, All sites, Big Recovery Window	Backup of Publication DB only. Can then reconfigure replication via scripts and reinitialize distribution, and all subscribers fairly easily.

FIGURE 43.71   Common backup strategies for different recovery needs.

When backing up environments, you need to back up the following at each site:

► Publisher (published database, `msdb`, and `master`)

► Distributor (distribution database, `msdb`, and `master`)

► Subscribers (subscriber database, optionally `msdb`, and `master` when pull subscriptions are being done)

You should always make copies of your replication scripts and keep them handy. At a minimum, you need to keep copies at the publisher and distributor and one more location, such as at one of your subscribers. You will use them for recovery someday.

You shouldn't forget to back up `master` and `msdb` when any new replication object is created, updated, or deleted.

If you have allowed updating of subscribers using queued updates, you need to expand your backup capability to include these queues.

When using the AlwaysOn features (like Availability Groups), you must consider what you have on a failover replica before applying backups anywhere. It gets a bit more complicated than without Availability Groups and replicas. Remember, you can make backups of your primary from your replica in an AlwaysOn configuration.

In general, you will find that even when you walk up and pull the plug on your distribution server, publication server, or any subscribers, automatic recovery works well to get you back online and replicating quickly, without human intervention.

Some Thoughts on Performance

From a performance point of view, the replication configuration defaults err on the side of optimal throughput. That's the good news. The bad news is that everybody is different in some way, so you have to consider a bit of tuning of your replication configuration. In general, you can get your replication configuration working well by doing the following:

▶ Keeping the amount of data to be replicated at any one point small by running agents continuously, instead of at long, scheduled intervals.

▶ Setting a minimum amount of memory allocated to SQL Server by using the Min Server Memory option to guarantee ample memory across the board.

▶ Using good disk drive physical separation rules, such as keeping the transaction log on a separate disk drive from the data portion. Your transaction log is much more heavily used when you opt for transactional replication.

▶ Putting your snapshot working directory on a separate disk drive to minimize disk drive arm contention. You should use a separate snapshot folder for each publication.

▶ Publishing only what you need. By selectively publishing only the minimum amount of data required, you implement a much more efficient replication configuration, which is faster overall.

▶ Trying to run snapshots in nonpeak times so your network and production environments aren't bogged down.

▶ Minimizing transformation of data involved with replication.

Log Shipping

If you have a small need to create a read-only (ad hoc query/reporting) database environment that can tolerate a high degree of data latency, you might be a candidate for using log shipping. Log shipping is still a feature for SQL Server 2014. We no longer describe full setup and deployment of this feature, but you can find this in earlier editions of this book. (It is described in detail in *SQL Server 2000 Unleashed*, though.) For those who have current log shipping configurations, it is time to move to AlwaysOn Availability groups. This transition will be easy because the two capabilities are so much alike. (Actually, many aspects of new AlwaysOn features came from log shipping.)

Change Data Capture

Microsoft introduced a new feature called Change Data Capture (CDC) in the last release which is designed to make it much easier and less resource intensive to identify and retrieve changed data from tables in an online transaction processing (OLTP) database. In a nutshell, CDC captures and records INSERT, UPDATE, and DELETE activity in an OLTP database and stores it in a form that is easily consumed by an application, such as a SQL Server Integration Services (SSIS) package. This enables another option for developers to move (replicate) data to other targets that is extremely effective (because it deals with the delta's changes, not the entire data sets all at once). Other software providers such as IBM have developed a whole line of very expensive replication capabilities around change data capture principles. You can get the same (and more) capability very easily with SQL Server for fractions of the cost.

In the past, capturing data changes for your tables for auditing or extract, transform, and load (ETL) purposes required using replication, timestamp columns, triggers, complex queries, or expensive third-party tools. None of these other methods are easy to implement, and many of them use a lot of server resources, negatively affecting the performance of the OLTP server.

Change Data Capture provides for a more efficient mechanism for capturing the data changes in a table.

> **NOTE**
>
> Change Data Capture is available only in the SQL Server 2014 Developer, Enterprise, and Datacenter Editions. Change Tracking is available on all SQL Server 2014 editions.

The source of change data for Change Data Capture is the SQL Server transaction log. As inserts, updates, and deletes are applied to tables, entries that describe those changes are added to the transaction log. When Change Data Capture is enabled for a database, a SQL Server Agent capture job is created to invoke the sp_replcmds system procedure. This procedure is an internal server function and is the same mechanism used by transactional replication to harvest changes from the transaction log.

> **NOTE**
>
> If replication is already enabled for the database, the transactional log reader used for replication is also used for CDC. This strategy significantly reduces log contention when both replication and Change Data Capture are enabled for the same database.

The principal task of the Change Data Capture process is to scan the log and identify changes to data rows in any tables configured for Change Data Capture. As these changes are identified, the process writes column data and transaction-related information to the Change Data Capture tables. The changes can then be read from these change tables to be applied as needed.

The Change Data Capture Tables

When CDC is enabled for a database and one or more tables, an associated Change Data Capture table is created for each table being monitored. The Change Data Capture tables are used to store the changes made to the data in corresponding source tables, along with some metadata used to track the changes. By default, the name of the CDC change table is schemaname_tablename_CT and is based on the name of the source table.

The first five columns of a Change Data Capture change table are metadata columns and contain additional information relevant to the recorded change:

▶ _$start_lsn—Identifies the commit log sequence number (LSN) assigned to the change. This value can be used to determine the order of the transactions.

▶ _$end_lsn—Is currently not used and in SQL Server 2014 is always NULL.

▶ _$seqval—Can be used to order changes that occur within the same transaction.

▶ _$operation—Records the operation associated with the change: 1 = delete, 2 = insert, 3 = update before image (delete), and 4 = update after image (insert)

▶ _$update_mask—Is a variable bit mask with one defined bit for each captured column to identify what columns were changed. For insert and delete entries, the update mask always has all bits set. Update rows have the bits set only for the columns that were modified.

The remaining columns in the Change Data Capture change table are identical to the columns from the source table in name and type and are used to store the column data gathered from the source table when an insert, update, or delete operation is performed on the table.

For every row inserted into the source table, a single row is inserted into the change table, and this row contains the column values inserted into the source table. Every row deleted from the source table is also inserted as a single row into the change table but contains the column values in the row before the delete operation. An update operation is captured as a delete followed by an insert, so two rows are captured for each update: one row entry to capture the column values before the update and a second row entry to capture the column values after the update.

In addition to the Change Data Capture tables, the following Change Data Capture metadata tables are also created:

▶ `cdc.change_tables`—Contains one row for each change table when Change Data Capture is enabled on a source table.

▶ `cdc.index_columns`—Contains one row for each index column used by Change Data Capture to uniquely identify rows in the source table. By default, this is the column of the primary key of the source table, but a different unique index on the source table can be specified when Change Data Capture is enabled on the source table. A primary key or unique index is required on the source table only if Net Change Tracking is enabled.

▶ `cdc.captured_columns`—Contains one row for each column tracked in each source table. By default, all columns of the source table are captured, but you can include or exclude columns when enabling Change Data Capture for a table by specifying a column list.

▶ `cdc.ddl_history`—Contains a row for each Data Definition Language (DDL) change made to any table enabled for Change Data Capture. You can use this table to determine when a DDL change occurred on a source table and what the change was.

▶ `cdc.lsn_time_mapping`—Contains a row for each transaction stored in a change table and is used to map between log sequence number (LSN) commit values and the actual time the transaction was committed.

Although you can query the Change Data Capture tables directly, it is not recommended. Instead, you should use the Change Data Capture functions, which are discussed later.

All these objects associated with a CDC instance are created in the special schema called `cdc` when Change Data Capture is enabled for a database.

Enabling CDC for a Database

Before you can begin capturing data changes for a table, you must first enable the database for Change Data Capture. You do this by running the stored procedure `sys.sp_cdc_enable_db` within the desired database context. When a database is enabled for Change Data Capture, the CDC schema, CDC user, and metadata tables, as well as the system functions, are used to query for change data.

> **NOTE**
>
> To determine whether a database is already enabled for CDC, you can check the value in the `is_cdc_enabled` column in the `sys.databases` catalog view. A value of `1` indicates that CDC is enabled for the specified database.

The following SQL code enables CDC for the `AdventureWorks2014` database and then checks that CDC is enabled by querying the `sys.databases` catalog view:

```
use AdventureWorks2014
go
exec  sys.sp_cdc_enable_db
go
select name, database_id, is_cdc_enabled
from sys.databases
where name = 'AdventureWorks2014'
go


name                 database_id      is_cdc_enabled
------------------------------------------------------
AdventureWorks2014    7               1
```

43

> **NOTE**
>
> The examples presented here are run against the AdventureWorks2014 database, but you can also run them against the AdventureWorks2008 database. However, be aware that some of the column values displayed may not be exactly the same.

Enabling CDC for a Table

When the database is enabled for Change Data Capture, you can use the sys.sp_cdc_ enable_table stored procedure to enable a Change Data Capture instance for any tables in that database. The sp_cdc_enable_table stored procedure supports the following parameters:

▶ **@source_schema**—Specifies the name of the schema in which the source table resides.

▶ **@source_name**—Specifies the name of the source table.

▶ **@role_name**—Indicates the name of the database role used to control access to Change Data Capture tables. If this parameter is set to NULL, no role is used to limit access to the change data. If the specified role does not exist, SQL Server creates a database role with the specified name.

▶ **@capture_instance**—Specifies the name of the capture instance used to name the instance-specific Change Data Capture objects. By default, this is the source schema name plus the source table name in the format schemaname_sourcename. A source table can have a maximum of two capture instances.

▶ **@supports_net_changes**—Is set to 1 or 0 to indicate whether support for querying for net changes is to be enabled for this capture instance. If this parameter is set to 1, the source table must have a defined primary key, or an alternate unique index must be specified for the @index_name parameter.

▶ **@index_name**—Specifies the name of a unique index to use to uniquely identify rows in the source table.

▶ **@captured_column_list**—Specifies the source table columns to be included in the change table. By default, all columns are included in the change table.

▶ **@filegroup_name**—Specifies the filegroup to be used for the change table created for the capture instance. If this parameter is NULL or not specified, the default filegroup is used. If possible, it is recommended you create a separate filegroup from your source tables for the Change Data Capture change tables.

▶ **@allow_partition_switch**—Indicates whether the SWITCH PARTITION command of ALTER TABLE can be executed against a table that is enabled for Change Data Capture. The default is 1 (enabled). If any partition switches occur, Change Data Capture does not track the changes resulting from the switch. This causes data inconsistencies when the change data is consumed.

The @source_schema, @source_name, and @role_name parameters are the only required parameters. All the others are optional and apply default values if not specified.

To implement basic change data tracking for a table, let's first create a copy of the Customer table to play around with:

```
select * into MyCustomer from Sales.Customer
alter table MyCustomer add Primary key (CustomerID)
```

Now, to enable CDC on the MyCustomer table, you can execute the following:

```
EXEC sys.sp_cdc_enable_table
@source_schema = N'dbo',
@source_name   = N'MyCustomer',
@role_name     = NULL
```

> **NOTE**
>
> If this is the first time you are enabling CDC for a table in the database, you may see the following messages, which indicate that SQL Server is enabling the SQL Agent jobs to begin capturing the data changes in the database:
>
> ```
> Job 'cdc.AdventureWorks2014_capture' started successfully.
> Job 'cdc.AdventureWorks2014_cleanup' started successfully.
> ```
>
> The Capture job that is created generally runs continuously and is used to move changed data to the CDC tables from the transaction log. The Cleanup job runs on a scheduled basis to remove older data from the CDC tables so that they don't grow too large. By default, it automatically removes data that is more than three days old. The properties of these jobs can be viewed and modified using the sys.sp_cdc_help_jobs and sys.sp_cdc_change_job procedures, respectively.

To determine whether or not a source table has been enabled for Change Data Capture, you can query the is_tracked_by_cdc column in the sys.tables catalog view for that table:

```
select is_tracked_by_cdc
from sys.tables
where name = 'MyCustomer'
go

is_tracked_by_cdc
-----------------
1
```

43

> **TIP**
>
> To get information on which tables are configured for CDC and what the settings for each are, you can execute the `sys.sp_cdc_help_change_data_capture` stored procedure. It reports the name and ID of the source and Change Tracking tables, the CDC table properties, the columns included in the capture, and the date the CDC was enabled/created for the source table.

Querying the CDC Tables

After you enable change data tracking for a table, SQL Server begins capturing any data changes for the table in the Change Data Capture tables. To identify the data changes, you need to query the Change Data Capture tables. Although you can query the Change Data Capture tables directly, it is recommended that you use the CDC functions instead. The main CDC table-valued functions (TVFs) are

▶ `cdc.fn_cdc_get_all_changes_capture_instance`

▶ `cdc.fn_cdc_get_net_changes_capture_instance`

> **NOTE**
>
> The Change Data Capture change table and associated CDC table-valued functions created along with it constitute what is referred to as a *capture instance*. A capture instance is created for every source table that is enabled for CDC.
>
> Each capture instance is given a unique name based on the schema and table names. For example, if the table named `sales.products` is CDC enabled, the capture instance created is named `sales_products`. The name of the CDC change table within the capture instance is `sales_products_CT`, and the names of the two associated CDC query functions are:
> `cdc.fn_cdc_get_all_changes_sales_products` and
> `cdc.fn_cdc_get_net_changes_sales_products`.

Figure 43.72 shows the table-valued functions that are created for the `MyCustomer` table that we enabled for CDC.

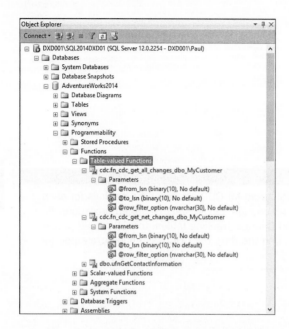

FIGURE 43.72   Table-valued functions created for `MyCustomer` table that has been enabled for CDC.

Both of the CDC table-valued functions require two parameters to define the range of log sequence numbers to use as the upper and lower bounds to determine which records are to be included in the returned result set. A third required parameter, the `row_filter_option`, specifies the content of the metadata columns as well as the rows to be returned in the result set. Two values can be specified for the `row_filter` for the `cdc.fn_cdc_get_all_changes_capture_instance` function: `"all"` and `"all update old"`.

If `"all"` is specified, the function returns all changes within the specified LSN range. For changes due to an update operation, only the row containing the new values after the update are returned. If `"all update old"` is specified, the function returns all changes within the specified LSN range. For changes due to an update operation, this option returns both the before and after update copies of the row.

For the `cdc.fn_cdc_get_net_changes_capture_instance` function, three values can be specified for the `row_filter` parameter: `"all"`, `"all with mask"`, and `"all with merge"`. If `"all"` is specified, the function returns the LSN of the final change to the row, and the operation needed to apply the change to the row is returned in the `_$start_lsn` and `_$operation` metadata columns. The `_$update_mask` column is always NULL. If `"all with mask"` is specified, the function returns the LSN of the final change to the row and the operation needed to apply the change to the row. Plus, if the `_$operation` equals 4 (that is, it contains the after update row values), the columns actually modified in the update are identified by the bit mask returned in the `_$update_mask` column.

If the "all with merge" option is passed, the function returns the LSN of the final change to the row and the operation needed to apply the change to the row. The _$operation column will have one of two values: 1 for delete and 5 to indicate that the operation needed to apply the change is either an insert or update. The column _$update_mask is always NULL.

So how do you determine what LSNs to specify to return the rows you need? Fortunately, SQL Server provides several functions to help determine the appropriate LSN values for use in querying the TVFs:

▶ **sys.fn_cdc_get_min_lsn**—Returns the smallest LSN associated with a capture instance validity interval. The validity interval is the time interval for which change data is currently available for its capture instances.

▶ **sys.fn_cdc_get_max_lsn**—Returns the largest LSN in the validity *interval*.

▶ **sys.fn_cdc_map_time_to_lsn** and **sys.fn_cdc_map_lsn_to_time**—Are used to correlate LSN values with a standard time value.

▶ **sys.fn_cdc_increment_lsn** and **sys.fn_cdc_decrement_lsn**—Can be used to make an incremental adjustment to an LSN value. This adjustment is sometimes necessary to ensure that changes are not duplicated in consecutive query windows.

So before you can start querying the CDC tables, you need to generate some records in them by running some data modifications against the source tables. First, you need to run the statements in Listing 43.1 against the MyCustomer table to generate some records in the dbo_MyCustomer_CT Change Data Capture change table.

LISTING 43.1   Some Data Modifications to Populate the MyCustomer CDC Capture Table

```
delete MyCustomer where CustomerID = 22

Insert MyCustomer (PersonID, StoreID, TerritoryID,
                   AccountNumber, rowguid, ModifiedDate)
Values (20778, null, 9,
        'AW' + RIGHT('00000000'
        + convert(varchar(8), IDENT_Current('MyCustomer')), 8),
        NEWID(),
        GETDATE())

declare @ident int
select @ident = SCOPE_IDENTITY()

update MyCustomer
set TerritoryID = 3,
    ModifiedDate = GETDATE()
where CustomerID = @ident
```

Now that you have some rows in the CDC capture table, you can start retrieving them. First, you need to identify the min and max LSN values to pass to the `cdc.fn_cdc_get_all_changes_dbo_MyCustomer` function. This can be done using the `sys.fn_cdc_get_min_lsn` and `sys.fn_cdc_get_max_lsn` functions. Listing 43.2 puts all these pieces together to return the records stored in the CDC capture table.

LISTING 43.2   Querying the `MyCustomer` CDC Capture Table

```
USE AdventureWorks2014
GO


--declare variables to represent beginning and ending lsn
DECLARE @from_lsn BINARY(10), @to_lsn BINARY(10)

-- get the first LSN for table changes
SELECT @from_lsn = sys.fn_cdc_get_min_lsn('dbo_MyCustomer')

-- get the last LSN for table changes
SELECT @to_lsn = sys.fn_cdc_get_max_lsn()

-- get all changes in the range using "all update old" parameter
SELECT *
FROM cdc.fn_cdc_get_all_changes_dbo_MyCustomer
        (@from_lsn, @to_lsn, 'all update old');

GO
```

| $start_lsn | $seqval | $operation | $update_mask | CustomerID | PersonID |
StoreID	TerritoryID	AccountNumber	rowguid	ModifiedDate	
0x000000BF000001780005 0x000000BF000001780002 1			0x7F	22	NULL	494
3 AW00000022 9774AED6-D673-412D-B481-2573E470B478 2008-10-13 11:15:07.263					
0x000000BF000001C80004 0x000000BF000001C80003 2			0x7F	31220	20778	NULL
9 AW00031220 750656B6-0CFC-488D-B50B-0AF60C984D47 2014-07-07 12:47:08.050					
0x000000BF000001D00003 0x000000BF000001D00002 3			0x48	31220	20778	NULL
9 AW00031220 750656B6-0CFC-488D-B50B-0AF60C984D47 2014-07-07 12:47:08.050					
0x000000BF000001D00003 0x000000BF000001D00002 4			0x48	31220	20778	NULL
3 AW00031220 750656B6-0CFC-488D-B5v0B-0AF60C984D47 2014-07-07 12:47:08.057					

Because the option `"all update old"` is specified in Listing 43.2, all the rows in the `dbo_MyCustomer_CT` capture table are returned, including the deleted row, inserted row, and both the before and after copies of the row updated.

If you want to return only the final version of each row within the LSN range (and the `@supports_net_changes` was set to `1` when CDC was enabled for the table), you can use the `cdc.fn_cdc_get_net_changes_capture_instance` function, as shown in Listing 43.3.

LISTING 43.3   Querying the `MyCustomer` CDC Capture Table for Net Changes

```
USE AdventureWorks2014
GO


--declare variables to represent beginning and ending lsn
DECLARE @from_lsn BINARY(10), @to_lsn BINARY(10)

-- get the first LSN for table changes
SELECT @from_lsn = sys.fn_cdc_get_min_lsn('dbo_MyCustomer')

-- get the last LSN for table changes
SELECT @to_lsn = sys.fn_cdc_get_max_lsn()

-- get all changes in the range using "all with_merge" parameter
SELECT *
FROM cdc.fn_cdc_get_net_changes_dbo_MyCustomer
        (@from_lsn, @to_lsn, 'all with merge');

GO


__$start_lsn           __$operation __$update_mask CustomerID
PersonID     StoreID      TerritoryID AccountNumber
rowguid                          ModifiedDate
---------------------- ------------ -------------- -----------
----------- ----------- ----------- -------------
-------------------------------------- ----------------------
0x000000BF000001780005 1     NULL    22    NULL    494    3      AW00000022
        9774AED6-D673-412D-B481-2573E470B478 2008-10-13 11:15:07.263
0x000000BF000001D00003 5     NULL    31220  20778 NULL    3      AW00031220
        750656B6-0CFC-488D-B50B-0AF60C984D47 2014-07-07 12:47:08.057
```

For typical ETL-type applications, querying for change data is an ongoing process, making periodic requests for all the changes that occurred since the last request which need to be applied to the target. For these types of queries, you can use the `sys.fn_cdc_increment_lsn` function to determine the next lowest LSN boundary that is greater than the max LSN boundary of the previous query. To demonstrate this, let's first execute some additional data modifications against the `MyCustomer` table:

```
Insert MyCustomer (PersonID, StoreID, TerritoryID,
                    AccountNumber, rowguid, ModifiedDate)
Values (20779, null, 12,
        'AW' + RIGHT('00000000'
        + convert(varchar(8), IDENT_Current('MyCustomer')), 8),
        NEWID(),
        GETDATE())


delete MyCustomer where CustomerID = 30119
```

The max LSN from the previous examples is 0x000000390000144C0004. We want to increment from this LSN to find the next set of changes. In Listing 43.4, you pass this value to the sys.fn_cdc_increment_lsn to set the min LSN value you'll use with the cdc.fn_cdc_get_net_changes_dbo_MyCustomer function as the lower bound.

LISTING 43.4   Using sys.fn_cdc_increment_lsn to Return the Net Changes to the MyCustomer CDC Capture Table Since the Last Retrieval

```
--declare variables to represent beginning and ending lsn
DECLARE @from_lsn BINARY(10), @to_lsn BINARY(10)

-- get the Next lowest LSN after the previous Max LSN
SELECT @from_lsn = sys.fn_cdc_increment_lsn(0x000000390000144C0004)

-- get the last LSN for table changes
SELECT @to_lsn = sys.fn_cdc_get_max_lsn()

-- get all changes in the range using "all with_merge" parameter
SELECT *
FROM cdc.fn_cdc_get_net_changes_dbo_MyCustomer
        (@from_lsn, @to_lsn, 'all with merge');

GO


__$start_lsn          __$operation __$update_mask CustomerID
PersonID     StoreID       TerritoryID AccountNumber
rowguid                       ModifiedDate
---------------------- ------------ -------------- -----------
----------- ----------- ----------- ------------- ----------------------------------
-- ----------------------
0x000000C1000000680003 5    NULL   31221 20779 NULL   12    AW00031221
      B17916B6-D8A5-458C-BA79-0CD6A063B4D8 2014-07-07 12:54:33.840
0x000000C1000000700005 1    NULL   30119 10573 NULL   1    AW00030119
      0A3463AB-162E-4804-93E6-A2EC3703F26A 2014-07-06 21:36:56.233
```

If you want to retrieve the changes captured during a specific time period, you can use the `sys.fn_cdc_map_time_to_lsn` function, as shown in Listing 43.5.

LISTING 43.5 Retrieving All Changes to `MyCustomer` During a Specific Time Period

```
DECLARE @begin_time datetime,
        @end_time datetime,
        @begin_lsn binary(10),
        @end_lsn binary(10);

SET @begin_time = '2014-07-06 21:36:56.200'
SET @end_time = '2014-07-06 21:54:59.999'

SELECT @begin_lsn = sys.fn_cdc_map_time_to_lsn
                    ('smallest greater than', @begin_time);

SELECT @end_lsn = sys.fn_cdc_map_time_to_lsn
                    ('largest less than or equal', @end_time);

SELECT *
FROM cdc.fn_cdc_get_net_changes_dbo_MyCustomer
        (@begin_lsn, @end_lsn, 'all');
Go
```

__$start_lsn	__$operation	__$update_mask	CustomerID
PersonID StoreID	TerritoryID	AccountNumber	
rowguid		ModifiedDate	
---------------------- ------------ -------------- -----------			
----------- ----------- ----------- -------------			
------------------------------------ ----------------------			
0x000000C1000000700005 1 NULL 30119 10573 NULL 1 AW00030119			
0A3463AB-162E-4804-93E6-A2EC3703F26A 2014-07-06			

CDC and DDL Changes to Source Tables

One of the common challenges when capturing data changes from your source tables is how to handle DDL changes to the source tables. This can be an issue if the downstream consumer of the changes has not reflected the same DDL changes for its destination tables.

Enabling Change Data Capture on a source table in SQL Server 2014 does not prevent DDL changes from occurring. However, Change Data Capture does help to mitigate the effect on the downstream consumers by allowing the delivered result sets that are returned from the CDC capture tables to remain unchanged even as the column structure of the underlying source table changes. Essentially, the capture process responsible for populating the change table ignores any new columns not present when the source table was enabled for Change Data Capture. If a tracked column is dropped, NULL values are supplied for the column in the subsequent change entries.

However, if the data type of a tracked column is modified, the data type change is also propagated to the change table to ensure that the capture mechanism does not introduce data loss in tracked columns as a result of mismatched data types. When a column is modified, the capture process posts any detected changes to the cdc.ddl_history table. Downstream consumers of the change data from the source tables that may need to be alerted of the column changes (and make similar adjustments to the destination tables) can use the stored procedure sys.sp_cdc_get_ddl_history to identify any modifications to the source table columns.

So how do you modify the capture instance to recognize any added or dropped columns in the source table? Unfortunately, the only way to do this is to disable CDC on the table and re-enable it. However, in an active source environment where it's not possible to suspend processing while CDC is being disabled and re-enabled, there is the possibility of data loss between when CDC is disabled and re-enabled.

Fortunately, CDC allows two capture instances to be associated with a single source table. This makes it possible to create a second capture instance for the table that reflects the new column structure. The capture process then captures changes to the same source table into two distinct change tables having two different column structures. While the original change table continues to feed current operational programs, the new change table feeds environments that have been modified to incorporate the new column data. Allowing the capture mechanism to populate both change tables in tandem provides a mechanism for smoothly transitioning from one table structure to the other without any loss of change data. When the transition to the new table structure has been fully effected, the obsolete capture instance can be removed.

CDC and AlwaysOn Availability Groups

CDC is fully interoperable with the new AlwaysOn features of SQL Server 2014. Additional complications arise when failover scenarios occur (from primary to replica). For these reasons, a few additional stored procedures have been provided that help this all out. In particular, If CDC is enabled for a database, but replication is not, the capture process used to harvest changes from the log and push them through CDC change tables runs at the CDC host as its own SQL Agent job. To resume the harvesting of changes after failover, you must run the sp_cdc_add_job at the new primary to create the new local capture job:

```
EXEC sys.sp_cdc_add_job @job_type = 'capture';
```

If you have both CDC and replication running at the same time, replication will handle the harvesting job coordination in the failover scenario.

In addition, to ensure that the new harvesting is "clean" after a failover, you should also run the CDC add job stored procedure with the 'cleanup' option:

```
EXEC sys.sp_cdc_add_job @job_type = 'cleanup';
```

When within an AlwaysOn configuration, best practice dictates that you have actually created this job ahead of time on the replica node but have it disabled. Then, when you need it quickly, it can be simply enabled, and away you go.

Change Tracking

In addition to Change Data Capture, SQL Server 2008 version also introduced Change Tracking. Change Tracking is a lightweight solution that provides an efficient change tracking mechanism for applications. Although they are similar in name, the purposes of Change Tracking and Change Data Capture differ.

Change Data Capture is an asynchronous mechanism that uses the transaction log to record all the changes to a data row and store them in change tables. All intermediate versions of a row are available in the change tables. The information captured is stored in a relational format that can be queried by client applications such as ETL processes.

Change Tracking, in contrast, is a synchronous mechanism that tracks modifications to a table but stores only the fact that a row has been modified and when. It does not keep track of how many times the row has changed or the values of any of the intermediate changes. However, having a mechanism that records that a row has changed, you can check to see whether data has changed and obtain the latest version of the row directly from the table itself rather than querying a change capture table.

> **NOTE**
>
> Unlike Change Data Capture, which is available only in the Enterprise, Datacenter, and Developer Editions of SQL Server, Change Tracking is available in all editions.

Change Tracking operates by using tracking tables that store a primary key and version number for each row in a table that has been enabled for Change Tracking. Applications can then check to see whether a row has changed by looking up the row in the tracking table by its primary key and see if the version number is different from when the row was first retrieved.

One of the common uses of Change Tracking is for applications that have to synchronize data with SQL Server. Change Tracking can be used as a foundation for both one-way and two-way synchronization applications.

One-way synchronization applications, such as a client or mid-tier caching application, can be built to use Change Tracking. The caching application, which requires data from a SQL Server database to be cached in other data stores, can use Change Tracking to determine when changes have been made to the database tables and refresh the cache store by retrieving data from the modified rows only to keep the cache up-to-date.

Two-way synchronization applications can also be built to use Change Tracking. A typical example of a two-way synchronization application is the occasionally connected application—for example, a sales application that runs on a laptop and is disconnected from the central SQL Server database while the salesperson is out in the field. Initially, the client application queries and updates its local data store from the SQL Server database. When it reconnects with the database later, the application synchronizes with the database, and data changes will flow from the laptop to the database and from the database to the laptop. Because data changes happen in both locations while the client application is disconnected, the two-way synchronization application must be able to detect conflicts. A conflict occurs if the same data is changed in both data stores in the time between synchronizations. The client application can use Change Tracking to detect conflicts by identifying rows whose version number has changed since the last synchronization. The application can implement a mechanism to resolve the conflicts so that the data changes are not lost.

Implementing Change Tracking

To use Change Tracking, you must first enable it for the database and then enable it at the table level for any tables for which you want to track changes. Change Tracking can be enabled via T-SQL statements or through SQL Server Management Studio.

To enable Change Tracking for a database in SSMS, right-click on the database in Object Explorer to bring up the Properties dialog and select the Change Tracking page. To enable Change Tracking, set the Change Tracking option to True (see Figure 43.73). Also on this page, you can configure the retention period for how long SQL Server retains the Change Tracking information for each data row and whether to automatically clean up the Change Tracking information when the retention period has been exceeded.

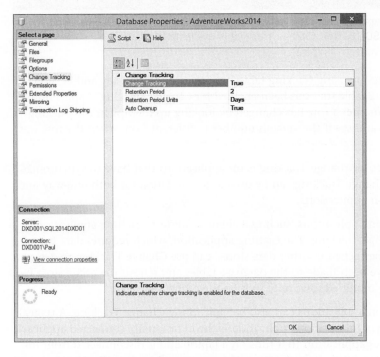

FIGURE 43.73   Enabling Change Tracking for a database.

You can also enable Change Tracking with the ALTER DATABASE command:

```
ALTER DATABASE AdventureWorks2014
SET CHANGE_TRACKING = ON
(CHANGE_RETENTION = 2 DAYS, AUTO_CLEANUP = ON)
```

After enabling Change Tracking at the database level, you can then enable Change Tracking for the tables for which you want to track changes. To enable Change Tracking for a table in SSMS, right-click on the table in Object Explorer to bring up the Properties dialog and select the Change Tracking page. Set the Change Tracking option to True to enable Change Tracking (see Figure 43.74).

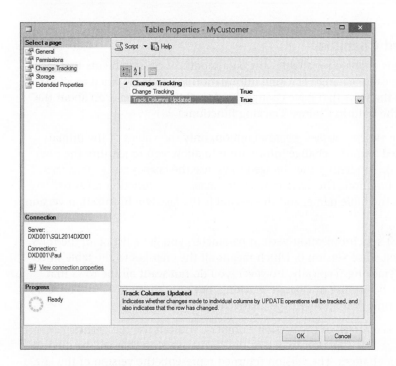

FIGURE 43.74   Enabling Change Tracking for a table.

The TRACK_COLUMNS_UPDATED option specifies whether SQL Server should store in the internal Change Tracking table any extra information about which specific columns were updated. Column tracking allows an application to synchronize only when specific columns are updated. This capability can improve the efficiency and performance of the synchronization process, but at the cost of additional storage overhead. This option is set to OFF by default.

Change Tracking can also be enabled via T-SQL with the ALTER TABLE command:

```
USE [AdventureWorks2014]
GO
ALTER TABLE [dbo].[MyCustomer]
    ENABLE CHANGE_TRACKING WITH(TRACK_COLUMNS_UPDATED = ON)
```

> **TIP**
>
> To determine which tables and databases have Change Tracking enabled, you can use the sys.change_tracking_databases and sys.change_tracking_tables catalog views.

Identifying Tracked Changes

After Change Tracking is enabled for a table, any data modification statements that affect rows in the table cause Change Tracking information for each modified row to be recorded. To query for the rows that have changed and to obtain information about the changes, you can use the built-in Change Tracking functions.

Unless you enabled the TRACK_COLUMNS_UPDATED option, only the values of the primary key column are recorded with the change information to allow you to identify the rows that have been changed. To identify the changed rows, use the CHANGETABLE (CHANGES ...) Change Tracking function. The CHANGETABLE (CHANGES ...) function takes two parameters: The first is the table name, and the second is the last synchronization version number.

If you pass 0 for the last synchronization version parameter, you get a list of all the rows that have been modified since version 0, which means all the changes to the table since first enabling Change Tracking. Typically, however, you do not want all the rows that have changed from the beginning of Change Tracking, but only those rows that have changed since the last time you retrieved the changed rows.

Rather than having to keep track of the version numbers, you can use the CHANGE_TRACKING_CURRENT_VERSION() function to obtain the current version that will be used the next time you query for changes. The version returned represents the version of the last committed transaction.

Before an application can obtain changes for the first time, the application must first execute a query to obtain the initial data from the table and a query to retrieve the initial synchronization version using CHANGE_TRACKING_CURRENT_VERSION() function. The version number that is retrieved is passed to the CHANGETABLE(CHANGES ...) function the next time it is invoked.

The following example illustrates how to obtain the initial synchronization version and initial data set:

```
USE AdventureWorks2014
Go
declare @synchronization_version bigint
```

```
Select change_tracking_version =  CHANGE_TRACKING_CURRENT_VERSION();

-- Obtain initial data set.

select CustomerID, TerritoryID, @synchronization_version as version
 from MyCustomer
where CustomerID <= 5
go

change_tracking_version
-----------------------
0


CustomerID  TerritoryID   version
----------- ----------- ---------
1           1             NULL
2           1             NULL
3           4             NULL
4           4             NULL
5           4             NULL
```

As you can see, because no updates have been performed since Change Tracking was enabled, the initial version is 0.

Now let's perform some updates on these rows to effect some changes:

```
update MyCustomer
    set TerritoryID = 5
    where CustomerID = 4

update MyCustomer
    set TerritoryID = 4
    where CustomerID = 5
```

Now you can use the CHANGETABLE(CHANGES ...) function to find the rows that have changed since the last version (0):

```
declare @last_synchronization_version bigint
set @last_synchronization_version = 0
SELECT
    CT.CustomerID as CustID, CT.SYS_CHANGE_OPERATION,
    CT.SYS_CHANGE_COLUMNS, CT.SYS_CHANGE_CONTEXT
FROM
    CHANGETABLE(CHANGES MyCustomer, @last_synchronization_version) AS CT
Go
```

```
CustID SYS_CHANGE_OPERATION SYS_CHANGE_COLUMNS SYS_CHANGE_CONTEXT
------ -------------------- ------------------ ------------------
4      U                    0x0000000004000000 NULL
5      U                    0x0000000004000000 NULL
```

You can see in these results that this query returns the customer IDs of the two rows that were changed. However, most applications also want the data from these rows as well. To return the data, you can join the results from CHANGETABLE(CHANGES ...) with the data in the user table. For example, the following query joins with the MyCustomer table to obtain the values for the PersonID, StoredID, and TerritoryID columns. Note that the query uses an OUTER JOIN to make sure that the change information is returned for any rows that may have been deleted from the user table. Also, at the same time you are retrieving the data rows, you also want to retrieve the current version as well to use the next time the application comes back to retrieve the latest changes:

```
declare @last_synchronization_version bigint
set @last_synchronization_version = 0
select current_version = CHANGE_TRACKING_CURRENT_VERSION()

SELECT
    CT.CustomerID as CustID,
    C.PersonID,
    C.StoreID,
    C.TerritoryID,
    CT.SYS_CHANGE_OPERATION,
    CT.SYS_CHANGE_COLUMNS, CT.SYS_CHANGE_CONTEXT
FROM
    MyCustomer C
        RIGHT OUTER JOIN
    CHANGETABLE(CHANGES MyCustomer, @last_synchronization_version) AS CT
        on C.CustomerID = CT.CustomerID
go


current_version
--------------------
2


CustID      PersonID    StoreID     TerritoryID
SYS_CHANGE_OPERATION SYS_CHANGE_COLUMNS SYS_CHANGE_CONTEXT
----------- ----------- ----------- -----------
-------------------- ------------------ --------------------
4           NULL        932         5
U                        0x0000000004000000 NULL
5           NULL        1026        4
U                        0x0000000004000000 NULL
```

You can see in the output from this query that the current version is now 2. The next time the application issues a query to identify the rows that have been changed since this query, it will pass the value of 2 as the `@last_synchronization_version` to the `CHANGETABLE(CHANGES ...)` function.

CAUTION

The version number is *not* specific to a table or user session. The Change Tracking version number is maintained across the entire database for all users and change tracked tables. Whenever a data modification is performed by any user on any table that has Change Tracking enabled, the version number is incremented.

For example, immediately after running an update on change tracked table A in the current application and incrementing the version to 3, another application could run an update on change tracked table B and increment the version to 4, and so on. This is why you should always capture the current version number whenever you are retrieving the latest set of changes from the change tracked tables.

If an application has not synchronized with the database in a while, the stored version number could no longer be valid if the Change Tracking retention period has expired for any row modifications that have occurred since that version. To validate the version number, you can use the `CHANGE_TRACKING_MIN_VALID_VERSION()` function. This function returns the minimum valid version that a client can have and still obtain valid results from `CHANGETABLE()`. Your client applications should check the last synchronization version obtained against the value returned by this function, and if the last synchronization version is less than the version returned by this function, that version is invalid. The client application has to reinitialize all the data rows from the table. The following T-SQL code snippet can be used to validate the `last_synchronization_version`:

```
-- Check individual table.
IF (@last_synchronization_version <
    CHANGE_TRACKING_MIN_VALID_VERSION(OBJECT_ID('MyCustomer')))
    BEGIN
        -- Handle invalid version and do not enumerate changes.
        -- Client must be reinitialized.
    END
```

Identifying Changed Columns

In addition to information about which rows were changed and the operation that caused the change (insert, update, or delete—reported as I, U, or D in the SYS_CHANGE_OPERATION), the `CHANGETABLE(CHANGES ...)` function also provides information on which columns were modified if you enabled the `TRACK_COLUMNS_UPDATED` option. You can use this information to determine whether any action is needed in your client application based on which columns changed.

To identify whether a specific column has changed, you can use the `CHANGE_TRACKING_IS_COLUMN_IN_MASK` (column_id, change_columns) function. This function interprets the

`SYS_CHANGE_COLUMNS` bitmap value returned by the `CHANGETABLE(CHANGES ...)` function and returns a 1 if the column was modified or `0` if it was not:

```
declare @last_synchronization_version bigint
set @last_synchronization_version = 0

SELECT
    CT.CustomerID as CustID,
    TerritoryChanged = CHANGE_TRACKING_IS_COLUMN_IN_MASK
                        (COLUMNPROPERTY(OBJECT_ID('MyCustomer'),
                        'TerritoryID', 'ColumnId'),
                        CT.SYS_CHANGE_COLUMNS),
    CT.SYS_CHANGE_OPERATION,
    CT.SYS_CHANGE_COLUMNS
FROM
    CHANGETABLE(CHANGES MyCustomer, @last_synchronization_version) AS CT
go


CustID      TerritoryChanged SYS_CHANGE_OPERATION SYS_CHANGE_COLUMNS
----------- ---------------- -------------------- ------------------
4           1                U                    0x0000000004000000
5           1                U                    0x0000000004000000
```

In the query results, you can see that both update operations (`SYS_CHANGE_OPERATION = 'U'`) modified the `TerritoryID` column (`TerritoryChanged = 1`).

Change Tracking Overhead

Although Change Tracking has been optimized to minimize the performance overhead on DML operations, it is important to know that there are some performance overhead and space requirements within the application databases when implementing Change Tracking.

The performance overhead associated with using Change Tracking on a table is similar to the index maintenance overhead incurred for insert, update, and delete operations. For each row changed by a DML operation, a row is added to the internal Change Tracking table. The amount of overhead incurred depends on various factors, such as

► The number of primary key columns

► The amount of data being changed in the user table row

► The number of operations being performed in a transaction

► Whether column Change Tracking is enabled

Change Tracking also consumes some space in the databases where it is enabled as well. Change Tracking data is stored in the following types of internal tables:

▶ **Internal change tables**—There is one internal change table for each user table that has Change Tracking enabled.

▶ **Internal transaction table**—There is one internal transaction table for the database.

These internal tables affect storage requirements in the following ways:

▶ For each change to each row in the user table, a row is added to the internal change table. This row has a small fixed overhead plus a variable overhead equal to the size of the primary key columns. The row can contain optional context information set by an application. In addition, if column tracking is enabled, each changed column requires an additional 4 bytes per row in the tracking table.

▶ For each committed transaction, a row is added to an internal transaction table.

If you are concerned about the space usage requirements of the internal Change Tracking tables, you can determine the space they use by executing the sp_spaceused stored procedure. The internal transaction table is called sys.syscommittab. The names of the internal change tables for each table are in the form change_tracking_object_id. The following example returns the size of the internal transaction table and internal change table for the MyCustomer table:

```
exec sp_spaceused 'sys.syscommittab'
declare @tablename varchar(128)
set @tablename = 'sys.change_tracking_'
                + CONVERT(varchar(16), object_id('MyCustomer'))
exec sp_spaceused @tablename
------------------------------------------------------
syscommittab    0                   0 KB   0 KB   0 KB   0 KB
change_tracking_941246408    2                16 KB  8 KB  8 KB  0 KB
```

Summary

Replication is a powerful feature of SQL Server that can be used in many business situations. Companies can use replication for anything from roll-up reporting to relieving the main server from ad hoc queries and reporting. It is critical to let your company's requirements drive the type of replication technique to use. Determining the replication option and configuration to use is difficult, but actually setting it up is reasonably easy. Microsoft has come a long way in this regard. Peer-to-peer replication seems to have the most promise of delivering multimaster symmetric replication in a production environment. Microsoft's overall architectural approach and implementation is the model for the industry. With the addition of Change Data Capture and Change Tracking, it has never been easier to distribute data and to detect deltas (changes) for any number of application purposes. And the biggest addition to replication and change data capture has been to make it interoperable with the AlwaysOn features so you can have highly available replication and CDC topologies for your critical applications.

You should not be afraid to use these capabilities. They are more than production-worthy, and the flexibility they offer and the overall performance are just short of incredible, incredible, incredible (replication humor for you).

SQL Server Failover Clustering

Enterprise computing requires that the entire set of technologies you use to develop, deploy, and manage mission-critical business applications be highly reliable, scalable, and resilient. These technologies include the network, the entire technology stack, the operating systems on the servers, the applications you deploy, the database management systems, and everything in between.

An enterprise must now be able to provide a complete solution with regard to the following:

▶ **Scalability**—As organizations grow, so does the need for more computing power. The systems in place must enable an organization to leverage existing hardware and to quickly and easily add computing power as needs demand.

▶ **Availability**—As organizations rely more on information, it is critical that the information be available at all times and under all circumstances. Downtime is not acceptable. Moving to five-nines reliability (which means 99.999% uptime) is a must, not a dream.

▶ **Interoperability**—As organizations grow and evolve, so do their information systems. It is impractical to think that an organization will not have many heterogeneous sources of information. It is becoming increasingly important for applications to get to all the information, regardless of its location.

▶ **Reliability**—An organization is only as good as its data and information. It is critical that the systems providing that information be bulletproof.

It is assumed that you will provide a certain level of foundational capabilities with regard to network, hardware, and operating system resilience. As a part of the SQL Server AlwaysOn offering, AlwaysOn Failover Cluster Instances leverage Windows Server Failover Clustering (WSFC) functionality to provide local high availability through redundancy at the server-instance level—a failover cluster instance (FCI). An FCI is a single instance of SQL Server that is installed across Windows Server Failover clustering (WSFC) nodes and, possibly, across multiple subnets. On the network, an FCI appears to be an instance of SQL Server running on a single computer, however, the FCI provides failover from one WSFC node to another if the current (active) node becomes unavailable. The good news is that you can achieve many of your enterprise's demands easily and inexpensively by using Windows Server Failover Clustering (WSFC), Network Load Balancing (NLB), and SQL Server failover clustering (or combinations of them).

What's New in SQL Server AlwaysOn Failover Clustering

Not really much new in this area for SQL Server 2014. The biggest changes came in SQL Server 2012. Much of what's new for WSFC and SQL Server failover clustering simplifies providing SQL instance-level resilience and is an important part of the high-availability options of AlwaysOn Failover Cluster Instances and participating in AlwaysOn Availability Groups (when also including database-level failover). Chapter 45, "SQL Server AlwaysOn and Availability Groups," covers the core SQL AlwaysOn and Availability Group features. Other items worth noting include the following:

▶ **Multisite failover clustering**—With Windows 2008 and later, a multisite failover cluster configuration can be created that includes nodes that are dispersed across multiple physical sites or data centers. Multisite failover clusters are referred to as geographically dispersed failover clusters, stretch clusters, or multisubnet clusters. This enables you to create a SQL Server multisite failover cluster.

▶ **WSFC requirement for SQL clustering and AlwaysOn**—When you want to configure SQL Server failover clustering (without AlwaysOn), AlwaysOn Failover Cluster Instances (FCIs), and AlwaysOn Availability Groups, you must first create a WSFC cluster that embraces these servers. The good news is that it is simpler than ever via the Create Cluster Wizard in the Failover Cluster Manager.

▶ **Reduction in the hardware limitations and constraints**—Previously, you had to know what hardware and software limitations you had to deal with when configuring SQL clustering configurations. With WSFC and SQL Server 2014, many of these limitations have been eliminated, such as nodes not having to be exactly the same anymore. You must still check compatibility lists, but the list is really short now.

▶ **No need to have a dedicated network interface card (NIC) between nodes**—With WSFC improvements, a dedicated network connection between the nodes in the cluster is no longer needed. You only need to have a valid network path from each node that is used to monitor the nodes in the cluster; it doesn't have to be dedicated, thus simplifying the hardware needed and the configuration process.

▶ There are some slight changes to the SQL installation and options in the SQL installer to more clearly address SQL Clustering setup and completion steps (configure SQL clustering setup for each nodes first, followed by an Advanced wizard to complete the SQL Server clustering configuration).

These features and enhancements combine to make setting up SQL Server failover clustering and SQL Server FCIs an easy high-availability proposition. They take much of the implementation risk out of the equation and make this type of installation available to a broader installation base.

How Microsoft SQL Server Failover Clustering Works

Put simply, SQL Server 2014 allows failover and failback to or from another node in a cluster at the server-instance level. This is an immensely powerful tool for achieving higher availability virtually transparently.

There are two approaches to implementing SQL Server failover clustering: active/passive or active/active modes.

In an active/passive configuration, an instance of SQL Server actively services database requests from one of the nodes in a SQL Server failover cluster (that is, the active node). Another node is idle until, for whatever reason, a failover occurs (to the passive node). With a failover situation, the secondary node (the passive node) takes over all SQL Server resources without the end user ever knowing that a failover has occurred. The only exception to this is that the end user (a SQL client) might experience a brief transactional interruption because SQL Server failover clustering cannot take over in-flight transactions. However, the end user (client) still just points at a single (virtual) SQL Server and truly doesn't care which node is fulfilling requests. Figure 44.1 shows a typical two-node failover clustering configuration in an active/passive mode, in which Node 2 is idle (that is, passive). This type of configuration is perfect for creating the SQL Server instance-level failover needed. SQL Server is just an application that will run within this type of clustering configuration.

In an active/active configuration, you can have both nodes active at the same time and put separate SQL Server instances doing different jobs on each. This really isn't a true Oracle RAC-like capability, but rather, it is simply using both nodes for processing power of different workloads. This does give organizations with more constrained hardware availability a chance to use a clustering configuration that can fail over to or from any node, without having to set aside idle hardware, but introduces a load issue on each node individually if failovers occur. So, be careful with this idea.

As previously mentioned, SQL Server failover clustering is actually created within (on top of) WSFC. WSFC, not SQL Server, is capable of detecting hardware or software failures and automatically shifting control of the managed resources to a healthy node. SQL Server 2014 implements failover clustering based on the clustering features of the WSFC. In other words, SQL Server is a fully "cluster-aware" application and becomes a set of resources managed by WSFC. The failover cluster shares a common set of cluster resources such as clustered (that is, shared) disk drives.

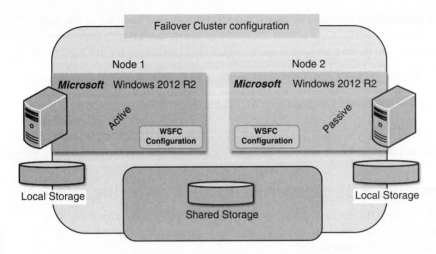

FIGURE 44.1   A typical two-node active/passive SQL Server clustering configuration.

NOTE

You can install SQL Server on as many servers as you want; the number is limited only by the operating system license and SQL Server edition you have purchased. However, WSFC should not be overloaded with more than 10 or so SQL Servers to manage if you can help it.

Understanding WSFC

A *server failover cluster* is a group of two or more physically separate servers running WSFC and working collectively as a single system. The server failover cluster, in turn, provides high availability, scalability, and manageability for resources and applications. In other words, a group of servers is physically connected via communication hardware (network), shares storage (via SCSI or Fibre Channel connectors), and uses WSFC software to tie them all together into managed resources.

Server failover clusters can preserve client access to applications and resources during failures and planned outages. It is server instance-level failover. If one of the servers in a cluster is unavailable due to failure or maintenance, resources and applications move (fail over) to another available cluster node.

NOTE

Prior to Windows Server 2008 R2, clustering was done with Microsoft Cluster Services (MSCS). If you are running on these older versions of operating systems, refer to *SQL Server 2008 R2 Unleashed* to see how to set up SQL clustering on older operating systems.

Clusters use an algorithm to detect a failure, and they use failover policies to determine how to handle the work from a failed server. These policies also specify how a server is to be restored to the cluster when it becomes available again.

Although clustering doesn't guarantee continuous operation, it does provide availability sufficient for most mission-critical applications and is the building block of numerous high-availability solutions. WSFC can monitor applications and resources, automatically recognizing and recovering from many failure conditions. This capability provides great flexibility in managing the workload within a cluster, and it improves the overall availability of the system. Technologies that are "cluster-aware"—such as SQL Server, Microsoft Message Queuing (MSMQ), Distributed Transaction Coordinator (DTC), and file shares—have already been programmed to work within (under the control of) WSFC.

WSFC still has some hardware and software compatibility to worry about but now has a Cluster Validation Wizard built in to see whether your configuration will work. You can also still refer to Microsoft's support site for server clustering (Microsoft support policy for server clusters at http://support.microsoft.com/kb/309395). In addition, SQL Server FCIs are not supported where the cluster nodes are also domain controllers.

Let's look a little closer at a two-node active/passive cluster configuration. At regular intervals, known as *time slices*, the failover cluster nodes look to see if they are still alive. If the active node is determined to be failed (not functioning), a failover is initiated, and another node in the cluster takes over for the failed node. Each physical server (node) uses separate network adapters for their own network connection. (Therefore, there is always at least one network communication capability working for the cluster at all times, as shown in Figure 44.2.)

The *shared disk* array is a collection of physical disks (SCSI RAID or Fibre Channel-connected disks) that the cluster accesses and controls as resources. WSFC supports *shared nothing* disk arrays, in which only one node can own a given resource at any given moment. All other nodes are denied access until they own the resource. This protects the data from being overwritten when two computers have access to the same drives concurrently.

The *quorum drive* is a logical drive designated on the shared disk array for WSFC. This continuously updated drive contains information about the state of the cluster. If this drive becomes corrupt or damaged, the cluster installation also becomes corrupt or damaged.

NOTE

In general (and as part of a high-availability disk configuration), the quorum drive should be isolated to a drive all by itself and be mirrored to guarantee that it is available to the cluster at all times. Without it, the cluster doesn't come up at all, and you cannot access your SQL databases.

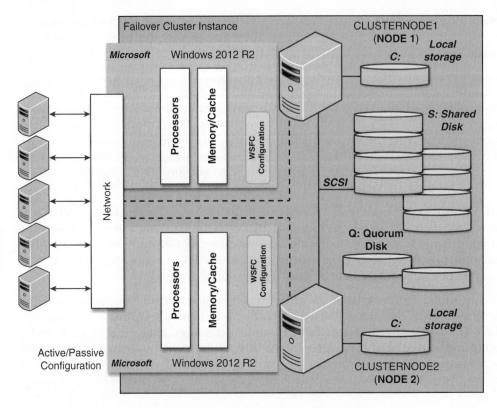

FIGURE 44.2   A two-node active/passive WSFC cluster configuration.

The WSFC architecture requires there to be a single quorum resource in the cluster that is used as the tie-breaker to avoid split-brain scenarios. A split-brain scenario happens when all the network communication links between two or more cluster nodes fail. In these cases, the cluster may be split into two or more partitions that cannot communicate with each other. WSFC guarantees that even in these cases, a resource is brought online on only one node. If the different partitions of the cluster each brought a given resource online, this would violate what a cluster guarantees and potentially cause data corruption. When the cluster is partitioned, the quorum resource is used as an arbiter. The partition that owns the quorum resource is allowed to continue. The other partitions of the cluster are said to have "lost quorum," and WSFC and any resources hosted on nodes that are not part of the partition that has quorum are terminated.

The quorum resource is a storage-class resource and, in addition to being the arbiter in a split-brain scenario, is used to store the definitive version of the cluster configuration. To ensure that the cluster always has an up-to-date copy of the latest configuration information, you should deploy the quorum resource on a highly available disk configuration (using mirroring, triple-mirroring, or RAID 10, at the very least).

The notion of quorum as a single shared disk resource means that the storage subsystem has to interact with the cluster infrastructure to provide the illusion of a single storage device with very strict semantics. Although the quorum disk itself can be made highly available via RAID or mirroring, the controller port may be a single point of failure. In addition, if an application inadvertently corrupts the quorum disk or an operator takes down the quorum disk, the cluster becomes unavailable.

This situation can be resolved by using a majority node set option as a single quorum resource from an WSFC perspective. In this set, the cluster log and configuration information are stored on multiple disks across the cluster. A new majority node set resource ensures that the cluster configuration data stored on the majority node set is kept consistent across the different disks.

The disks that make up the majority node set could, in principle, be local disks physically attached to the nodes themselves or disks on a shared storage fabric (that is, a collection of centralized shared storage area network [SAN] devices connected over a switched-fabric or Fibre Channel–arbitrated loop SAN). In the majority node set implementation that is provided as part of WSFC in Windows Server 2008 and above, every node in the cluster uses a directory on its own local system disk to store the quorum data, as shown in Figure 44.3.

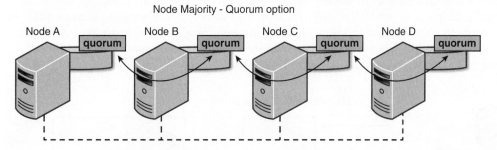

FIGURE 44.3   A node majority.

If the configuration of the cluster changes, that change is reflected across the different disks. The change is considered to have been committed (that is, made persistent) only if that change is made to a majority of the nodes (that is, [Number of nodes configured in the cluster]/2) + 1). In this way, a majority of the nodes have an up-to-date copy of the quorum data. WSFC itself starts up only if a majority of the nodes currently configured as part of the cluster are up and running.

If there are fewer nodes, the cluster is said not to have quorum, and therefore WSFC waits (trying to restart) until more nodes try to join. Only when a majority (or quorum) of nodes are available does WSFC start up and bring the resources online. This way, because the up-to-date configuration is written to a majority of the nodes, regardless of node failures, the cluster always guarantees that it starts up with the most up-to-date configuration.

With Windows 2008 and above, a few more quorum drive configurations are possible that address various voting strategies and also support geographically separated cluster nodes, as follows:

▶ **Node Majority**—More than one-half of the voting nodes in the cluster must vote affirmatively for the cluster to be healthy.

▶ **Node and File Share Majority**—Like Node Majority, but a remote file share is also configured as a voting witness, and connectivity from any node to that share is also counted as an affirmative vote. More than one-half of the possible votes must be affirmative for the cluster to be healthy.

▶ **Node and Disk Majority**—Again, like Node Majority quorum mode, except that a shared disk cluster resource is also designated as a voting witness, and connectivity from any node to that shared disk is also counted as an affirmative vote.

▶ **Disk Only**—Where a shared disk cluster resource is designated as a witness and connectivity by any node to that shared disk is counted as an affirmative vote.

Extending WSFC with NLB

You can also use a critical technology called Network Load Balancing (NLB) to ensure that a server is always available to handle requests. NLB works by spreading incoming client requests among a number of servers linked together to support a particular application. A typical example is to use NLB to process incoming visitors to your website. As more visitors come to your site, you can incrementally increase capacity by adding servers. This type of expansion is often referred to as *software scaling*, or *scaling out*. Figure 44.4 illustrates this extended clustering architecture with NLB.

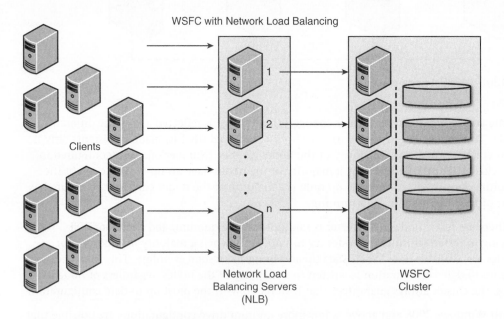

FIGURE 44.4   An NLB configuration.

By using both WSFC and NLB clustering technologies together, you can create an *n*-tier infrastructure. For instance, you can create an n-tiered e-commerce application by deploying NLB across a front-end web server farm and use WSFC clustering on the back end for your line-of-business applications, such as clustering your SQL Server databases. This approach gives you the benefits of near-linear scalability without server or application-based single points of failure. This, combined with industry-standard best practices for designing high-availability networking infrastructures, can ensure that your Windows-based, Internet-enabled business will be online all the time and can quickly scale to meet demand. You also have AlwaysOn options now (with SQL Server 2014). Other tiers could be added to the topology, such as an application-center tier that uses component load balancing. This further extends the clustering and scalability reach for candidate applications that can benefit from this type of architecture.

How WSFC Sets the Stage for SQL Server Clustering

Good setup practices are to document all the needed Internet Protocol (IP) addresses, network names, domain definitions, and SQL Server references to set up a two-node SQL Server failover clustering configuration (configured in an active/passive mode) before you actually physically set up your clustering configuration.

You would first identity the servers (nodes), such as SQLFOUR (the first node) and SQLFIVE (the second node), and the cluster group name of E2A3CLUSTER.

The cluster controls the following resources:

▶ Physical disks (Cluster Disk 1 is for the quorum disk, Cluster Disk 2 is for the shared disks, and so on)

▶ The cluster IP address (e.g., IP: 192.168.1.214)

▶ The cluster name (network name) (e.g., E2A3CLUSTER)

▶ The Distributed Transaction Coordinator (DTC)

▶ The SQL Server virtual IP address (e.g., IP: 192.168.1.211)

▶ The SQL Server virtual name (network name) (e.g., SQLProdFCI)

▶ SQL Server (e.g., MSSQLSERVER)

▶ SQL Server Agent

▶ The SQL Server full-text search service instance (if installed)

After you successfully install, configure, and test your failover cluster (WSFC), you are ready to add the SQL Server components as resources to be managed by WSFC. This is where the magic happens. Figure 44.5 shows how the Failover Cluster Manager should look after you install and configure a two-node failover cluster. It doesn't have SQL Server 2014 installed yet!

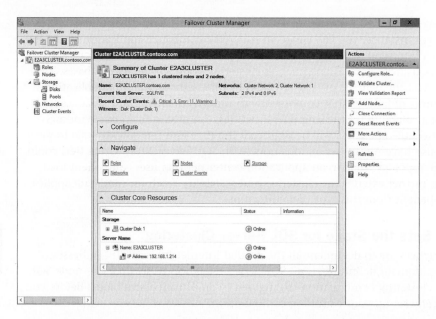

FIGURE 44.5   Windows 2012 Failover Cluster Manager, showing the failover cluster prior to installing SQL Server.

Installing SQL Server Failover Clustering

When you install SQL Server in a failover clustered server configuration, you create it as a virtual SQL Server. A virtual SQL Server is not tied to a specific physical server; it is associated with a virtualized SQL Server name that is assigned a separate IP address (not the IP address or name of the physical servers on which it runs). Handling matters this way allows for your applications to be completely abstracted away from the physical server level.

Failover clustering has a new workflow for all Setup scenarios in SQL Server 2014. The two options for installation are

▶ **Integrated installation**—This option creates and configures a single-node SQL Server failover cluster instance. Additional nodes are added by using the Add Node functionality in Setup. For example, for Integrated installation, you run Setup to create a single-node failover cluster. Then you run Setup again for each node you want to add to the cluster.

▶ **Advanced/Enterprise installation**—This option consists of two steps; the prepare step prepares all nodes of the failover cluster to be operational. Nodes are defined and prepared during this initial step. After you prepare the nodes, the Complete step is run on the active node—the node that owns the shared disk—to complete the failover cluster instance and make it operational.

Figure 44.6 shows the same two-node cluster configuration as Figure 44.1, with all the SQL Server and WSFC components identified. This virtual SQL Server is the only thing the end user will ever see. As you can also see in Figure 44.6, the virtual server name is SQLProdFCI, and the SQL Server instance name defaults to blank (you can, of course, give your instance a name). Figure 44.6 also shows the other cluster group resources that will be part of the SQL Server Clustering configuration: MSDTC (now optional), SQL Agent, SQL Server Full-Text Search, and the shared disk where the databases and the quorum will live. Starting with Windows Server 2008, SQL Server does not require that the DTC be clustered, and we've shown it outside of the cluster configuration in Figure 44.6. You can find more information about this at http://technet.microsoft.com/en-us/library/cc730992(WS.10).aspx.

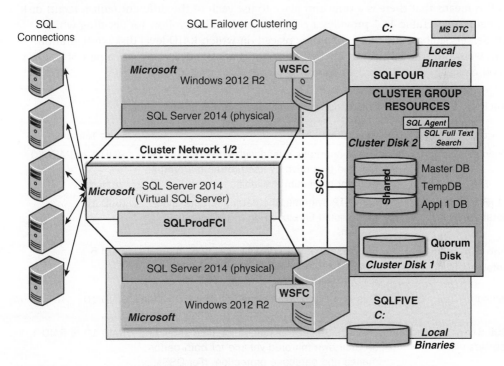

FIGURE 44.6   A basic SQL Server failover clustering configuration.

Yes, earlier OS versions required DTC to be clustered.

SQL Server Agent will be installed as part of the SQL Server installation process, and it is associated with the SQL Server instance it is installed for. The same is true for SQL Server Full-Text Search; it is associated with the particular SQL Server instance that it is installed to work with. The SQL Server installation process completely installs all software on all nodes you designate.

Configuring SQL Server Database Disks

Before we go too much further, we need to talk about how you should lay out a SQL Server implementation on the shared disks managed by the failover cluster. The overall usage intent of a particular SQL Server instance dictates how you might choose to configure your shared disk and how it might be best configured for scalability and availability.

In general, RAID 0 is great for storage that doesn't need fault tolerance; RAID 1 or RAID 10 is great for storage that needs fault tolerance but doesn't have to sacrifice too much performance (as with most online transaction processing [OLTP] systems); and RAID 5 is great for storage that needs fault tolerance but whose data doesn't change that much (that is, low data volatility, as in many decision support systems [DSSs]/read-only systems).

All this means that there is a time and place to use each of the different fault-tolerant disk configurations. Table 44.1 provides a good rule of thumb to follow for deciding which SQL Server database file types should be placed on which RAID level disk configuration. (This would be true regardless of whether or not the RAID disk array was a part of a SQL Server cluster.)

TABLE 44.1   SQL Server Clustering Disk Fault-Tolerance Recommendations

Device	Description	Fault Tolerance
Quorum drive	The quorum drive used with WSFC should be isolated to a drive by itself (often mirrored as well, for maximum availability).	RAID 1 or RAID 10
OLTP SQL Server database files	For OLTP systems, the database data/index files should be placed on a RAID 10 disk system.	RAID 10
DSS SQL Server database files	For DSSs that are primarily read-only, the database data/index files should be placed on a RAID 5 disk system.	RAID 5
tempdb	This is a highly volatile form of disk I/O (when not able to do all its work in the cache).	RAID 10
SQL Server transaction log files	The SQL Server transaction log files should be on their own mirrored volume for both performance and database protection. (For DSSs, this could be RAID 5 also.)	RAID 10 or RAID 1

TIP

A good practice is to balance database files across disk arrays (that is, controllers). In other words, if you have two (or more) separate shared disk arrays (both RAID 10) available within a cluster group's resources, you should put the data file of Database 1 on the first cluster group disk resource (for example, DiskRAID10-A) and its transaction log on the second cluster group disk resource (for example, DiskRaid10-B). Then you should put the data file of Database 2 on the second cluster group disk resource of DiskRAID10-B and its transaction log on the first cluster group disk resource of `DiskRAID10-A`. In this way, you can stagger these allocations and in general balance the overall RAID controller usage, minimizing any potential bottlenecks that might occur on one disk controller. In addition, FILESTREAM filegroups must be put on a shared disk, and FILESTREAM must be enabled on each node in the cluster that will host the FILESTREAM instance. You can also use geographically dispersed cluster nodes, but additional items such as network latency and shared disk support must be verified before you get started. On Windows 2008, most hardware and iSCSI supported hardware can be used, without the need to use "certified hardware." When you are creating a cluster on Windows 2008 or above, you can use the cluster validation tool to validate the Windows cluster; it also blocks SQL Server Setup when problems are detected with the Windows 2008 or above cluster.

Installing Network Interfaces

You might want to take a final glance at Failover Cluster Manager so that you can verify that both SQLFOUR and SQLFIVE nodes and their cluster network interfaces are completely specified and their state (status) is up. If you like, you should also double-check the IP addresses and network names against the Excel spreadsheet created for this failover cluster specification.

Installing WSFC

First of all, make sure the cluster service is up and running (via Services in the Server Manager). Also, as you can see in Figure 44.7, the two nodes and the cluster are in the "UP" state.

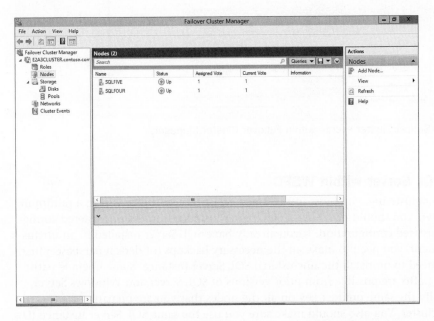

FIGURE 44.7   Cluster and two nodes are "UP" via the Cluster Manager.

> **NOTE**
>
> If the cluster service is not started and won't start, you cannot install SQL Server failover clustering. You have to remove and then reinstall WSFC from scratch. You should browse the Event Viewer to familiarize yourself with the types of warnings and errors that can appear with WSFC.

Cluster Events

Finding out what is happening with your failover cluster via the Cluster Events option within Failover Cluster Manager is pretty easy and offers ample filtering so that you can focus on critical issues (as you can see in Figure 44.8).

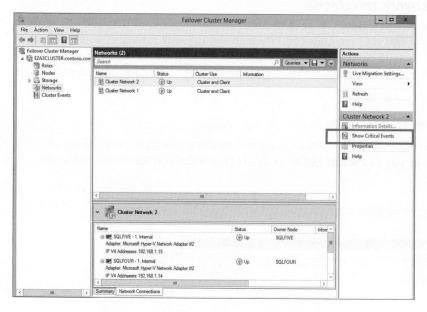

FIGURE 44.8   Critical Cluster events within Failover Cluster Manager.

Installing SQL Server within WSFC

For SQL failover clustering, you must install a new SQL Server instance within a minimum two-node cluster. You should not move a SQL Server instance from an unclustered configuration to a clustered configuration. If you already have SQL Server installed in an unclustered environment, you need to make all the necessary backups (or detach databases) first, and then you need to uninstall the unclustered SQL Server instance. Some upgrade paths and migration paths are possible from prior versions of SQL Server and Windows Server. You must specify the same product key on all the nodes that you are preparing for the same failover cluster. You also should make sure you use the same SQL Server instance ID for all the nodes that are prepared for the failover cluster.

With all WSFC resources running and in the online state, you run the SQL Server 2014 Setup program from the node that is online (for example, USPETSDSQLTST01). You are asked to install all software components required prior to installing SQL Server (.NET Framework 3.5 or 4.0, Microsoft SQL Native Client, Microsoft Visual Studio 2010 Shell, and the Microsoft SQL Server 2014 Setup support files). Make sure that you have the proper permissions to do a SQL Server install!

SQL Server integrated failover cluster installation consists of the following steps:

1. Advanced cluster preparation—Create and configure an initial SQL Server failover cluster instance to be used in the SQL Server failover cluster.

2. Advanced cluster completion—Add additional nodes to the SQL Server failover cluster and complete the High Availability configuration.

Okay, let's launch the Advanced cluster preparation Wizard from the SQL Server Installation Center Installation Advanced option for SQLFOUR node. The standard Welcome to SQL Server Installation Center Wizard begins. It starts with a rule check of the node in the cluster (SQLFOUR). Figure 44.9 shows the SQL Server Installation Center launch dialog and the results of a successful initial Failover Cluster Rules check for the SQLFOUR node.

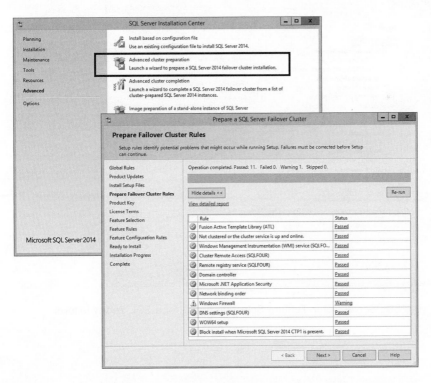

FIGURE 44.9   A Microsoft SQL Server Setup Support Rules check.

> **NOTE**
>
> SQL Server failover clustering is available with SQL Server 2014 Standard Edition, Enterprise Edition, and Developer Edition. However, Standard Edition supports only a two-node cluster. If you want to configure a cluster with more than two nodes, you need to upgrade to SQL Server 2014 Enterprise Edition.

If this check fails (warnings are acceptable), you must resolve any errors before you continue. After product key and licensing terms dialogs are completed, the install setup files are loaded.

Once completed, you are then prompted to proceed to the SQL Server feature installation portion of setup. You are presented with a checklist of features you want to install. Figure 44.10 shows the Feature Selection dialog. Following the Feature Selection dialog is a set of feature rules validation checks that must be passed for things like Cluster Supported for This Edition, Product Update Language Compatibility, and others.

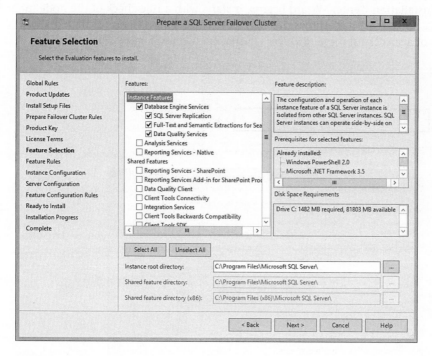

FIGURE 44.10   The SQL Server Setup Feature Selection dialog for a SQL Server failover cluster install.

You then see the Instance Configuration dialog, as shown in Figure 44.11, where we identity the default instance name of MSSQLSERVER (the default).

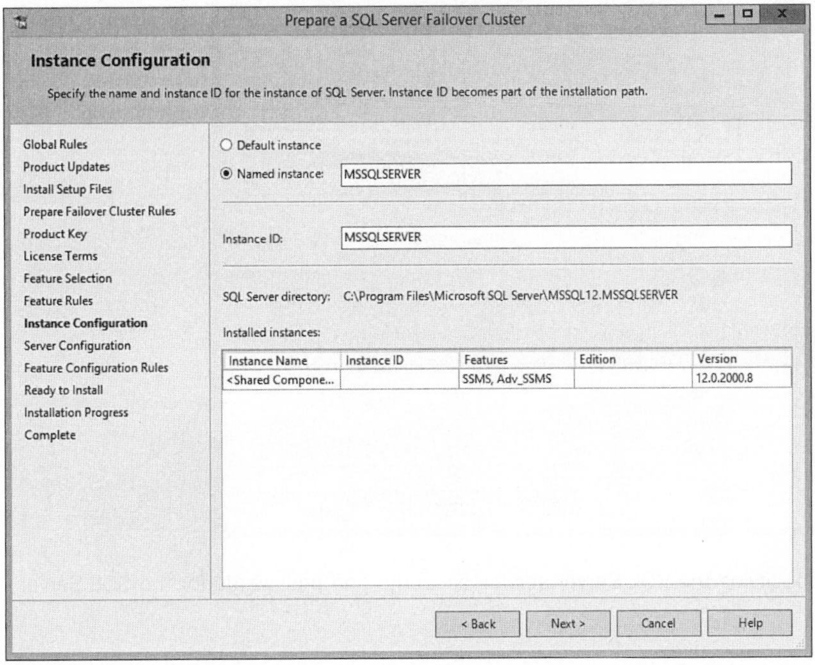

FIGURE 44.11   Specifying the SQL Server name (MSSQLSERVER) default instance name.

You will then need to specify the Server configuration service accounts for the SQL Server Agent and so on. These should be the same for both nodes you will be including in the SQL Server Cluster configuration (as you can see in Figure 44.12, sqlserveragent account name and sqlservice account name).

Now, complete the SQL Server Installation for this node as shown in Figure 44.13.

Now, you must repeat the same steps for the second node that is to be in your SQL Server Cluster (SQLFIVE in our example).

Once completed, we can move on to complete the SQL Server Cluster (which we'll do from the first node (SQLFOUR)).

Back to the SQL Server Installation Center and the Advanced option. We'll now start the Advanced cluster completion wizard to finish off the SQL Clustering configuration (as shown in Figure 44.14).

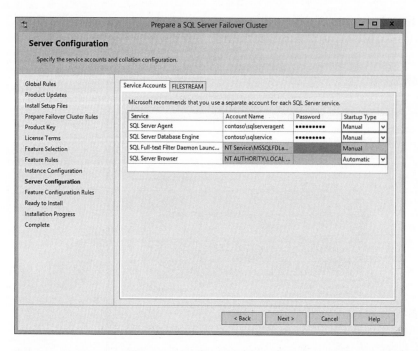

FIGURE 44.12   Specifying the SQL Server service accounts and passwords for the SQL Server (MSSQLSERVER).

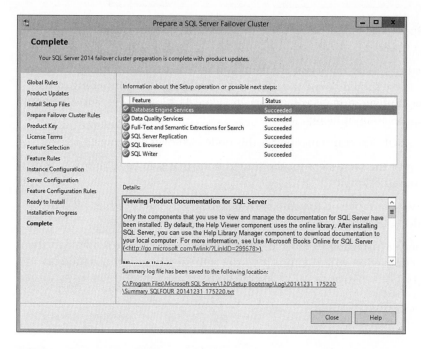

FIGURE 44.13   The SQL Server 2014 failover cluster preparation and install is complete for this node.

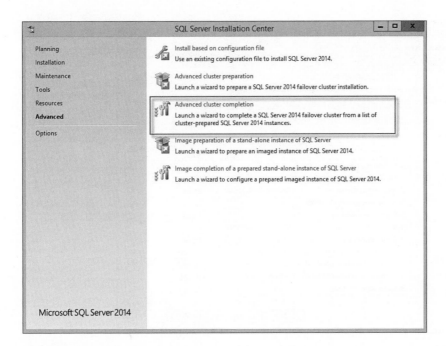

FIGURE 44.14   The SQL Server 2014 Advanced cluster completion wizard: SQL Server Installation Center.

Initially, this will take you through a set of rules checks to make sure you can successfully install the SQL Server Failover Cluster. Figure 44.15 shows the results of the rules check. Some warnings are acceptable. Any errors (not warnings) must be corrected immediately before proceeding.

Next comes the Cluster Node Configuration. We must specify an existing SQL Server instance (MSSQLSERVER), the node it is on (SQLFOUR), and specify a virtual SQL Server name (SQL Server Network Name); this will be the name the client applications will see (and to which they will connect). When an application attempts to connect to an instance of SQL Server 2014 that is running on a failover cluster, the application must specify both the virtual server name and instance name (if an instance name was used), such as SQLProdFCI\VSQLSRV1 (virtual server name\SQL Server instance name other than the default) or SQLProdFCI (just the virtual SQL Server name without the default SQL Server instance name). The virtual server name must be unique on the network. As you can see in Figure 44.16, the nodes also appear (SQLFOUR, SQLFIVE) since they are both configured for clustering and share the instance name (MSSQLSERVER).

> **NOTE**
>
> A good naming convention to follow is to preface all virtual SQL Server names and virtual SQL Server instance names with a V. This way, you can easily identify which SQL Server machines on your network are clustered. For example, you could use VSQL2012DXD as a virtual SQL Server name and VSQLSRV1 as an instance name.

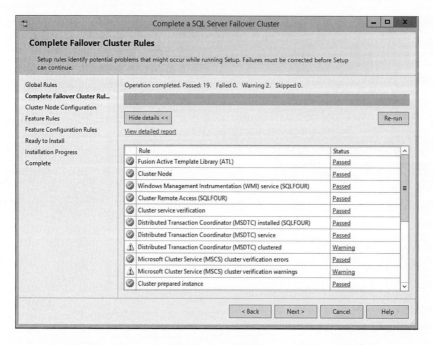

FIGURE 44.15   Complete Failover Cluster Rules.

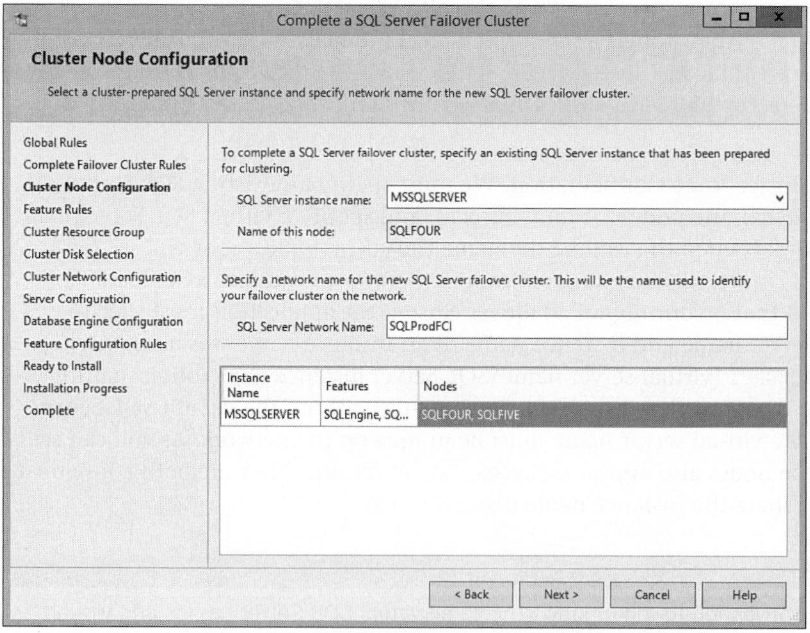

FIGURE 44.16   Cluster Node Configuration.

Next comes the Cluster Resource Group specification for your SQL Cluster followed by the selection of the disks to be clustered. This is where the SQL Server resources are placed within WSFC. We will just use the SQL Server (MSSQLSERVER) resource group name (the default) and click Next, as you can see in Figure 44.17. Immediately following the resource group assignment comes the identification of which clustered disks are to be used via the Cluster Disk Selection dialog, also shown in Figure 44.17. It contains a Cluster Disk 2 disk option (that was our shared drive volume), and a Cluster Disk 1 disk option (that was the Quorum drive location). You simply select the available drive(s) where you want to put your SQL database files (the Cluster Disk 2 disk drive option in this example). As you can also see, the only "qualified" disk is this Cluster Disk 2 drive. If the quorum resource is in the cluster group you have selected, a warning message is issued, informing you of this fact. A general rule of thumb is to isolate the quorum resource to a separate cluster group.

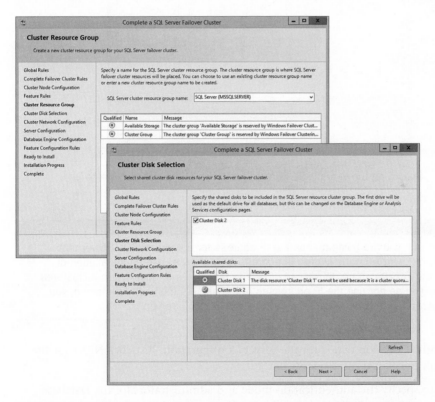

FIGURE 44.17   Cluster resource group specification and cluster disk selection.

The next thing you need to do for this new virtual server specification is to identify an IP address and which network it should use. As you can see in the Cluster Network Configuration dialog, shown in Figure 44.18, you simply type in the IP address (in our example, 192.168.1.211) that is to be the IP address for this virtual SQL Server for the available networks known to this cluster configuration (in this example, it is for the

`Cluster Network 2` network). If the IP address being specified is already in use, an error occurs.

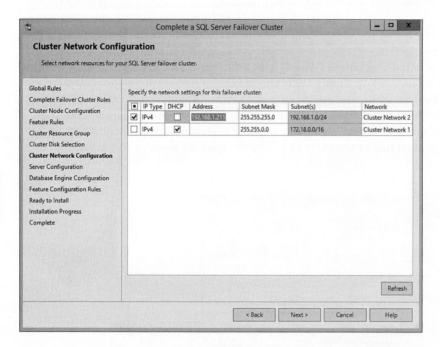

FIGURE 44.18   Specifying the virtual SQL Server IP address and which network to use.

> **NOTE**
>
> Keep in mind that you are using a separate IP address for the virtual SQL Server that is completely different from the cluster IP addresses. In an unclustered installation of SQL Server, the server can be referenced using the machine's IP address. In a clustered configuration, you do not use the IP addresses of the servers themselves; instead, you use this separately assigned IP address for the "virtual" SQL Server.

We'll then see the Collation dialog for the Server Configuration: Just click NEXT for the collation default of `SQL_Latin1_General_CP1_CI_AS`.

You will have to specify the authentication mode and administrators for the Database engine next (your choice of Windows Authentication mode or Mixed mode) and then any SQL Server administrators.

At this point, you have worked your way down to the Feature Configuration Rules check to determine if everything specified to this point is correct. The next dialog shows a summary of what is about to be done in this install and the location of the configuration file (and path) that can be used later if you are doing command-line installs of new nodes in the cluster. We've drawn a box around this configuration file path location at the bottom right of the Ready to Install dialog to show you where it is being created (if needed) as you can see in Figure 44.19.

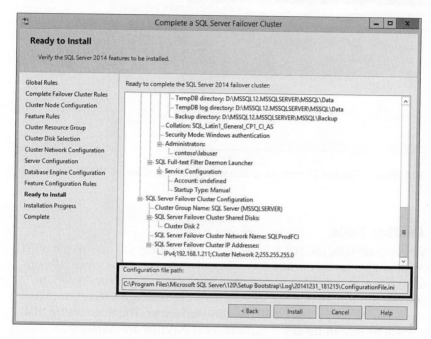

FIGURE 44.19   Ready to install the full SQL Server cluster.

The next step is to click on the Install button.

The setup process installs SQL Server binaries locally on this node (that is, in `C:\Program Files\Microsoft SQL Server`). The database files for the `master`, `model`, `tempdb`, and `msdb` databases are placed on the `shared` drive in this example (Cluster Disk 2). This is the shared disk location that must be available to all nodes in the SQL Server failover cluster.

When the process is complete, you can pop over into the Failover Cluster Manager and see how SQL Server was just installed within the failover cluster. As you can see in Figure 44.20, SQL Server resource has been successfully installed and is usable within the cluster (visible via the Roles node in the Failover cluster). As you can also see, the owner Node is the `SQLFOUR` node.

When you right-click the SQL Server resource entry in the Failover Cluster Manager, you have an option to take the resource offline, to initiate a move to another node, and many other items. You sometimes need to do this when you're trying to fix or test a SQL Server clustering configuration. However, when you're initiating full SQL Server failover to another node (for example, from `SQLFOUR` to `SQLFIVE`), you typically use the Move Service or Application to Another Node technique because you want all the resources for the cluster group to fail over—not just one specific resource.

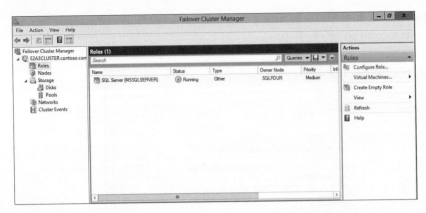

FIGURE 44.20   SQL Server Failover Cluster Node install complete and within the Failover Cluster Manager.

Fail Over to Another Node

If the current "active" node fails, the SQL Cluster will automatically fail over to the other node providing high availability at the SQL Server Instance level (as we wanted). We can also manually fail over a node or evict a node from a SQL Server cluster configuration. In the next section, we will simply stop the SQLFOUR Server to simulate a server crash and show you the effects of a client connection to our clustered server. You must realize that client connections will be broken for any inflight transactions that are currently processing. Be careful here.

In addition, the failure, move, and taking offline of a node is also written to the System event log.

Congratulations! You are now up and running, with your SQL Server Failover Cluster intact and should now be able to start achieving significantly higher availability for your end users. You can easily register this new virtual SQL Server (SQLProdFCI) within SQL Server Management Studio (SSMS) and completely manage and access it as you would any other SQL Server instance.

The Client Connection Impact of a Failover

To help in visualizing exactly what effect a SQL Server failure and subsequent failover may have on an end-user application, we'll go ahead and install a small test database on this SQL Server failover cluster called CompSales2014. (See the Introduction chapter for information on how to download and install the CompSales2014 sample database.) This shouldn't take you more than about 10 minutes to do. Use SSMS to do this install but start by connecting to the virtual SQL Server (SQLProdFCI in our example) that we just created (as shown in Figure 44.21).

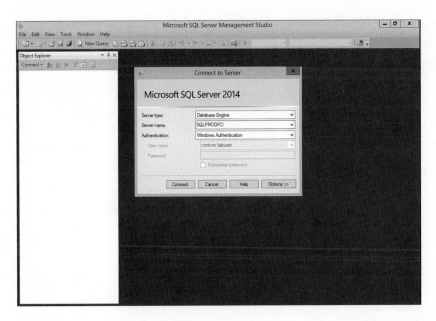

FIGURE 44.21   Connect to the virtual SQL Server (SQLProdFCI) and CompSales2014 database installed via SSMS.

We'll now do a simple SELECT query with an extra system variable column thrown in that provides us some additional execution insight as to where this query is getting executed from. In particular, we'll add @@SERVERNAMEto a Top 100 Select against the Product table of CompSales2014.

From a query window within SSMS, execute the following SQL statement:

```
SELECT TOP 100 *
       @@SERVERNAME AS SERVERNAME

 FROM [CompSales2014].[Product]
```

As you can see in Figure 44.22, this yields a result set that not only shows the first 100 products in that table but also the server name from which the query is targeting execution against (SQLProdFCI in our case).

We then crash (power down) the SQLFOUR node in the SQL Cluster (you can see the result of the node being down from the Failover Cluster Manager in Figure 44.23).

We then simply re-executed the same SQL statement we just did without reconnecting or changing anything from our client connection point of view. As you can see in Figure 44.24, the result set is exactly the same as we saw before. But, from the client's point of view, everything is completely transparent and highly available.

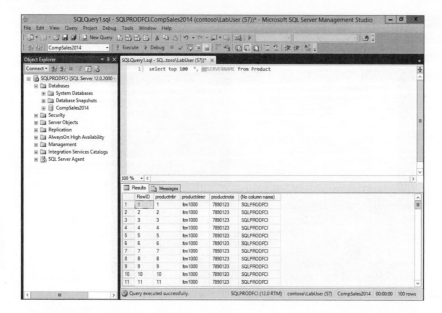

FIGURE 44.22   Execute the SELECT statement against our virtual SQL Server and
CompSales2014 database.

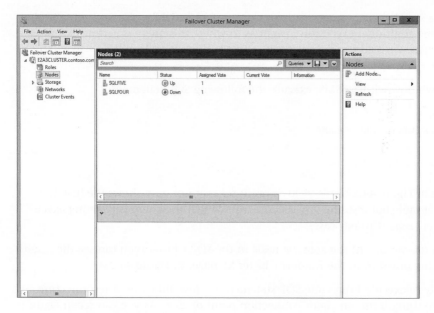

FIGURE 44.23   SQLFOUR node is down as shown via the Failover Cluster Manager.

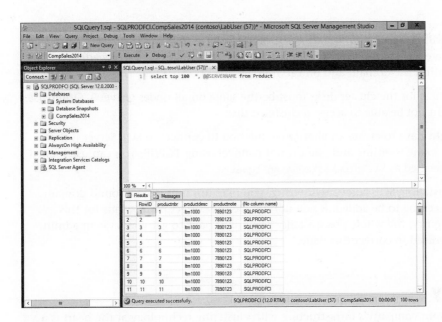

FIGURE 44.24   Re-execute the SELECT statement against our virtual SQL Server and
CompSales2014 database.

As you can see here, the reference to the SQL Server instance in the client connection
string info in any App.config XML file is very straightforward and completely shields the
client from having to make any adjustments should there be a failure. Simply specify the
virtual SQL Server name (SQLProdFCI in our case) in the connection string element:

```xml
<?xml version="1.0" encoding="utf-8" ?>
<configuration>
    <configSections>
    </configSections>
    <connectionStrings>
        <add name="WindowsApplication4.Properties.Settings.
        CompSales2014ConnectionString"
        connectionString="Data Source=SQLProdFCI;Initial
Catalog=CompSales2014;
Integrated Security=True"
            providerName="System.Data.SqlClient" />
    </connectionStrings>
</configuration>
```

Potential Problems to Watch Out for with SQL Server Failover Clustering

Many potential problems can arise during setup and configuration of SQL Server
Clustering. Following are some items you should watch out for:

▶ SQL Server service accounts and passwords should be kept the same on all nodes, or a node will not be able to restart a SQL Server service. You can use `administrator` or a designated account (for example, `Cluster` or `ClusterAdmin`) that has administrator rights within the domain and on each server.

▶ Drive letters for the cluster disks must be the same on all nodes (servers). Otherwise, you might not be able to access a clustered disk.

▶ You might have to create an alternative method to connect to SQL Server if the network name is offline and you cannot connect using TCP/IP. You can use named pipes, specified as `\\.\pipe\$$\SQLA\sql\query`.

▶ When installing SQL failover clustering, you may run into issues around domain entries needing to be added. If you don't have the correct permissions for this domain entry, the whole process fails. You might have to get your system admin folks involved to correct this issue.

Summary

Building out your company's infrastructure with clustering technology at the heart is a huge step toward achieving five-nines reliability. If you do this, every application, system component, or database you deploy on this architecture has that added element of resilience. WSFC and SQL failover clustering are high-availability approaches at the instance level. As you will see with the AlwaysOn features, expanding this resilience to the database tier will add even more high availability and scalability to your implementations. And, in many cases, the application or system component changes needed to take advantage of these clustering technologies are completely transparent. Utilizing a combination of NLB and WSFC allows you not only to fail over applications but also to scale for increasing network capacity as well.

The two-node active/passive node is one of the most common SQL Server failover clustering configurations used.

Remember that SQL Server 2014 supports other concepts related to high availability, such as the new AlwaysOn features, data replication, log shipping, and others. You might use these solutions rather than SQL Server failover clustering, depending on your requirements or some in combination.

Clustering is a complex subject. The information contained in this chapter is sufficient to start you in this area, but for a much more complete and thorough understanding of how to assess your high-availability needs, to evaluate what you should build for high availability, and to implement a high-availability platform that uses WSFC and SQL Server failover clustering, find a copy of *Microsoft SQL Server High Availability* by Paul Bertucci (Sams Publishing). This book is loaded with full explanations, a formal approach to achieving five-nines reliability, and numerous real-life examples.

Chapter 45 explains how to take advantage of the new AlwaysOn capability that is taking the database world by storm.

SQL Server AlwaysOn and Availability Groups

With SQL Server 2014, Microsoft continues to push the high-availability (HA) and performance (scale-out) bar higher and higher. Extensive HA options such as AlwaysOn Availability Groups and AlwaysOn Failover Cluster Instances, coupled with a variety of Windows Server family enhancements, provide almost everyone with a chance at achieving the mythical *five-nines* (that is, 99.999% uptime). We'll dive into the AlwaysOn new features in this chapter. This capability is taking the database world by storm. It is truly the next generation of HA and scale-out for existing and new database tiers of any kind. Some of the concepts and technical approaches in AlwaysOn and availability groups might seem a bit reminiscent of SQL clustering and database mirroring because they are. Both of these earlier features paved the way for what we now know as AlwaysOn and availability groups.

What's New in SQL Server AlwaysOn and Availability Groups

Now, with a couple of years under their belt with these features, Microsoft is starting to open up several of the previously tight limitations such as the number of secondaries allowed.

▶ You can use AlwaysOn and availability groups with complex data managed through FILESTREAM, even when using Remote Blog Storage and FileTable.

▶ Up to 8 secondary replicas can be defined for any one availability group. This used to be 4 secondary replicas max.

▶ There can be up to 3 Synchronous Commit replicas.

▶ And, client applications can achieve failover across multiple subnets (as many as 64) almost as fast as they can achieve failover within a single subnet.

SQL Server AlwaysOn and Availability Groups

Typical use cases (scenarios) for AlwaysOn and availability groups include the following:

▶ Need for High Availability nearing five-nines (99.999% available). This means that your database layer must be super resilient to failure and have nearly no data loss in the case of failure.

▶ You have disaster recovery (DR) needs that need to replicate data to another site (perhaps on the other side of the country or planet), but you can tolerate a little bit of data loss (and data latency).

▶ You have a performance need to offload some operational functions such as database backups away from your primary database. These must be completely accurate and have the highest integrity for recovery purposes.

▶ You have a performance and availability need to offload read-only processing/ access away from your primary transactional database, and you can tolerate a bit of latency. Even when the primary is down, you still provide read-only access to your applications.

All of the these can be addressed by this new AlwaysOn Availability Groups feature, and it's easier to do than you think.

Windows Failover Cluster Services

Windows Failover Cluster Services (WFCS) is actually considered a part of the basic HA foundation components described earlier, except that it's possible to build an HA system without it (for example, a system that uses numerous redundant hardware components and disk mirroring or RAID for its disk subsystem). Microsoft has made WFCS the cornerstone of its clustering capabilities, and WFCS is used by applications that are cluster enabled. A prime example of a cluster-enabled technology is Microsoft SQL Server 2014 (and most of its components). For more on clustering or SQL clustering, see Chapter 44, "SQL Server Failover Clustering."

WFCS can be set up in an active/passive or active/active mode. Essentially, in an active/ passive mode, one server sits idle (passive) while the other is doing the work (active). If the active server fails, the passive one takes over the shared disk and the cluster-aware applications instantaneously.

AlwaysOn Failover Clustering Instances

Being "always on" is a pretty powerful statement and commitment. It is now possible to mostly achieve this commitment with infrastructure, instance, database, and client-connectivity-level HA. Built on WSFC (or Failover Cluster Server (FCS) as it is also known), the SQL Server AlwaysOn configuration leverages the tried-and-true experience and technology components of SQL clustering and database mirroring under the covers (and repackaged). This new packaging and enhancement has allowed Microsoft to deprecate database mirroring in favor of these new AlwaysOn options (FCI and availability groups). AlwaysOn Failover Cluster Instances (FCI) is the server-level instance portion of the AlwaysOn HA capability. As you can see on the left side of Figure 45.1, the FCI is a two-server (node) SQL cluster that will also be utilized in an availability group configuration to give the primary (the application database that your application uses) the highest level of resilience possible. We didn't have to make the primary have SQL instance-level availability, but are showing you that you can do more than just simple AlwaysOn configurations. This SQL Server clustered instance shares the database as a part of its clustering configuration for the instance. Server A and Server B form the SQL cluster and are configured as an active/passive cluster. The entire SQL cluster will be Node 1 in our availability group configuration. More on the availability group (database-level availability) in the next section.

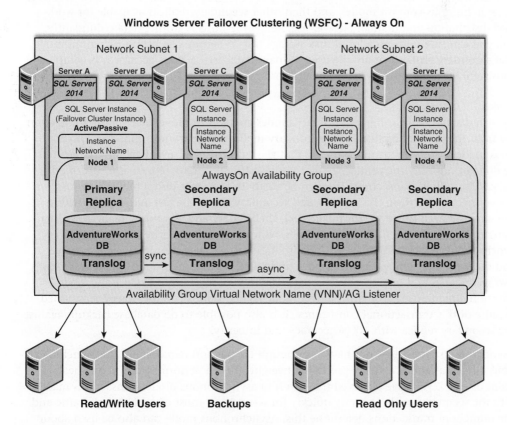

FIGURE 45.1   AlwaysOn and availability group components.

The FCI becomes fault tolerant at the server instance level for maximum availability of SQL Server itself (just as you know and love SQL clustering from the past) and is using a single storage location that is shared (owned) by the two underlying SQL instances for the clustered instances' database storage. Okay, let's continue exploring the concepts with AlwaysOn Availability Groups.

AlwaysOn Availability Groups

Figure 45.1 also shows the availability group capability. Availability groups are focused on database-level failover and availability by utilizing a data redundancy approach. Again, borrowing from the database mirroring experience (and underlying technologies), a transactionally consistent secondary replica is made that can be used for both read-only access (active for use at all times) and for failover if the primary database (primary replica) fails for any reason. In Figure 45.1, you can see a SQL Server AlwaysOn Availability Group being used for HA and even for distributing the read-only workload off of the primary SQL Server instance to the secondary replica. You can have up to four secondary replicas in an availability group with the first secondary replica being used for automatic failover (using the synchronous-commit mode), and then other secondary replicas available for workload distribution and manual failover use. Remember, this is storing data redundantly, and you can sure burn up a lot of disk storage fast. When in synchronous-commit mode, that secondary replica can also be used to make database backups because it is completely consistent with the primary replica. Outstanding!

Modes

As with database mirroring, two primary modes are used to move data via the transaction log from the primary replica to the secondary replicas; synchronous mode and asynchronous mode. Synchronous mode means that the data writes of any database change must be done in not only the primary replica but also the secondary replica as a part of one logical committed transaction. This can be costly in the sense of doubling the writes, so the connection between the primary and secondary should be fast and nearby (within the same subnet). However, for this reason, the primary and secondary replicas are in a transactionally consistent state at all times, which makes failover nearly instantaneous. Synchronous mode is what is used for automatic failover between the primary replica and the secondary replica. You can have up to 3 nodes in Synchronous mode (essentially two secondaries and one primary at once). Figure 45.1 shows that Node 1 and Node 2 are configured to use automatic failover mode (synchronous). As previously mentioned, because of this transactional consistency, it is also possible to do database backups against the secondary replica with 100% accuracy and integrity.

Asynchronous mode does not have the commit transaction requirement that synchronous mode has and is actually pretty lightweight (from a performance and overhead point of view). We have observed that, even in asynchronous mode, transactions made it to the secondary replicas pretty quickly (in seconds) in most cases. Network traffic and the number of transactions determine this. Asynchronous mode can also be used about anywhere you need within your stable network (across the country or even to another continent if you have decent network speeds).

The AlwaysOn Availability Groups feature also takes advantage of transaction record compression, which allows for compression of the transaction log records used in database mirroring and AlwaysOn configurations to increase the speed of transmission to the mirror or replicas.

In addition, as with database mirroring, during the data replication of the transaction, if data page errors are detected, the data pages on the secondary replica are repaired as a part of the transaction writes to the replica and raise the overall database stability even further (if you had not been replicating). Nice feature.

Read-Only Replicas

As you can also see in Figure 45.1, creating more secondary replicas is possible (up to eight). However, these must be asynchronous replicas. You can easily add these to the availability group and provide distribution of workload and significant mitigation to your performance. Figure 45.1 shows two additional secondary replicas used to handle all the read-only data accesses that would normally be hitting the primary database. These read-only replicas will have near-real-time data and can be pretty much anywhere you want (from a stable network point of view).

For Disaster Recovery

Figure 45.2 shows a typical AlwaysOn with availability groups configuration for DR purposes. It has a primary replica in Data Center 1, and its secondary replica is in Data Center 2. We use the asynchronous mode because of the distance and network speeds.

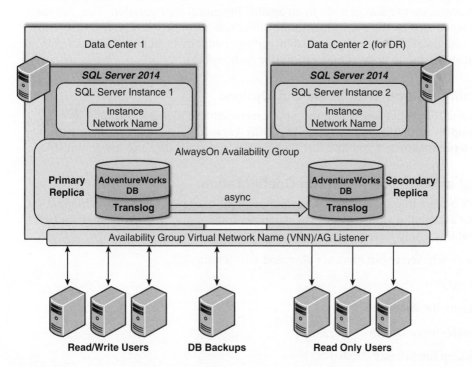

FIGURE 45.2   An AlwaysOn and availability group configuration for disaster recovery.

This means that the secondary replica at the DR site is only as good as the most recent transaction that was written asynchronously. Some data loss may happen in this mode, but for the DR purposes, this is easily meeting the DR requirements and service levels needed. As a bonus (almost free actually), the DR site (secondary replica) can also be used for read-only data access (as also shown in Figure 45.2). You are essentially leveraging a copy of the primary database that would normally not have been considered available if other DR technologies were being used. Most are in continuous update mode and do not support read-only modes at all.

Availability Group Listeners

Looking back at Figure 45.1, we also see that the virtual network names (VNNs) that are created for the WSFCs will be used when the availability group is created. In particular, the availability group must know the virtual network names (that reference the individual instances) of all nodes in the availability group. These can be used directly to reference the primary or the secondary replicas. But for more stability (and consistency), you can create an availability group listener as part of the availability group that abstracts these VNNs away from the application that must use the databases. In this way, the application sees only one connection name at all times, and the underlying failover state is completely insulated away from the application, yielding even higher consistency and availability from the application point of view.

Endpoints

Availability groups also leverage the endpoint concept for all communication (and visibility) from one node to another node in an availability group configuration. They are the exposed point used by the availability group communication between nodes. This is also the case with database mirroring. Availability group endpoints will be created as a part of each availability group node configuration (for each replica).

Combining Failover with Scale-Out Options

SQL Server 2014 pushes combinations of options to achieve higher availability levels. Building up an AlwaysOn FCI configuration with AlwaysOn Availability Groups with two or more replicas launches you into distributed workload scalability and maximum HA.

Building a Multinode AlwaysOn Configuration

Now, let's build a multinode AlwaysOn configuration, create the clustering configuration, define the availability group, specify the databases roles, replicate the databases, and get our availability group listener up and running, as follows:

1. Verify SQL Server instances are alive and well (exist).

2. Set up WSFC.

3. Prepare the database.

4. Enable AlwaysOn HA.

5. Back up the primary databases.

6. Create the availability group.

7. Select the databases for the availability group.

8. Identify the primary and secondary replicas.

9. Synchronize the data (primary to replica).

10. Set up the listener (availability group listener).

11. Connect using the listener.

12. Fail over to a secondary.

Figure 45.3 shows the basic configuration that we will build. We have three nodes to work with but will focus on getting the primary and one secondary up and running in this example. The failover cluster will be named sqlproduction, the availability group will be named DXD-AG1, and the listener will be named DXD-AG1Listener. We'll create and use a database named CompSales2014. The third node can be used to create another secondary replica for read-only accesses if you want.

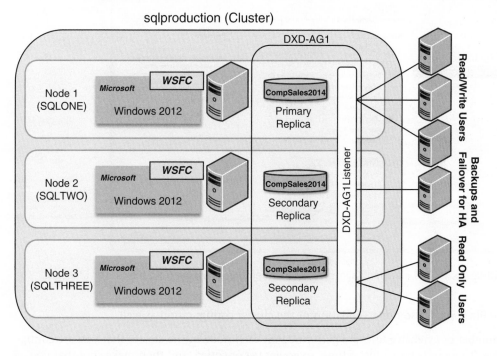

FIGURE 45.3   The DXD AlwaysOn configuration details.

We've also indicated how the availability group will be used: primary (Node 1) for both read/write operations, secondary (Node 2) for backup and failover. The other secondary (Node 3, if you add it) can be used for read-only access. Okay, let's get going.

Verify SQL Server Instances

We will assume that you have installed and have running at least two SQL Server instances on separate nodes that can be clustered for this configuration. These don't have to be mirror images of each other, just viable SQL Server instances that can be enabled for AlwaysOn (Enterprise or Developer Editions). Verify that the SQL Server instances are alive and well.

Set Up Failover Clustering

For each of the servers (nodes), you need to configure WSFC.

Chapter 44 showed you how to do this via the Server Manager of each node. We'll not cover this here except to show you what the configured feature should look like before you begin creating your AlwaysOn and Availability Group configuration.

As you can see in Figure 45.4, the Failover Cluster feature must be installed for each node.

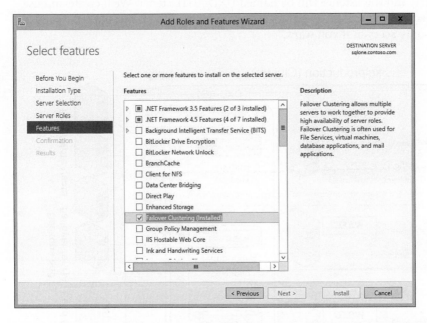

FIGURE 45.4   The installed Failover Clustering feature as shown from the Server Manager.

You likely have also run a validation of the cluster configuration as well.

A number of extensive tests are performed on each node in the cluster that you are configuring. These tests take a bit of time, so go get tea or coffee, and then make sure that you look through the summary report for any true errors. You'll likely see a few warnings that refer to items that were not essential to the configuration (some TCP/IP or network-related things are usually here). Figure 45.5 shows this cluster configuration validation running for the newly created cluster configuration. You are now ready to get into the AlwaysOn business.

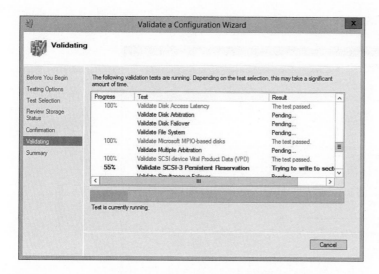

FIGURE 45.5   Validation test for the cluster configuration.

We've already created the cluster group access point (named sqlproduction) as you can see in Figure 45.6. The IP address for this access point is: 192.168.1.120.

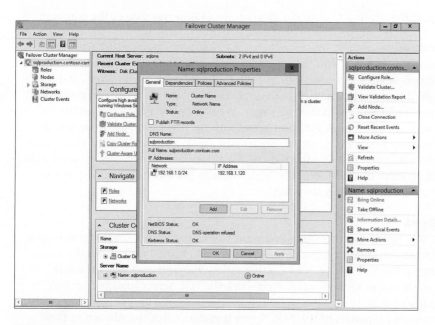

FIGURE 45.6   Access point for administering the cluster and cluster name.

This cluster will contain three nodes; SQLONE, SQLTWO, and SQLTHREE, as shown in the Failover Cluster Manager in Figure 45.7.

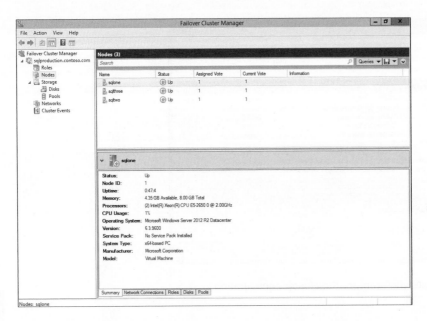

FIGURE 45.7   Failover Cluster Manager with the sqlproduction cluster and three nodes.

Okay, time to start the AlwaysOn configuration on the SQL Server side of the equation.

Prepare the Database

We first want to make sure that you have a primary database that can be used for this example. In the sample files and code listings folder for this book on the Web (and for this chapter), you'll find a script named `CreateDB4AlwaysOn.sql` that you can pull into SQL Server Management Studio (SSMS) right now. We will create a database on the SQLONE node and add a test table for you to play with for this example. If you already have another database you want to use, go ahead and use it. Figure 45.8 shows our script in a query window that was just executed. It created a database named `CompSales2014` (as mentioned earlier), created a `Product` table, added data to the table for testing purposes, and did an initial database backup (to `NULL`).

Enable AlwaysOn HA

For each of the SQL Server instances that you want to include in the AlwaysOn configuration, you need to enable their instances for AlwaysOn (if is turned off by default). From each node, bring up the SQL Server 2014 Configuration Manager and select the SQL Server Services node in the Services pane. Right-click the SQL Server instance for this node (a default instance name of MSSQLSERVER in this example) and choose Properties. Figure 45.9 shows the properties of this SQL Server instance. Click the AlwaysOn High Availability tab and choose Enable. Notice that the cluster name appears in this dialog box because this server was identified already in the cluster configuration step. Now, click OK (or apply) and you'll receive a note about having to restart the service for this option to be used. After you have closed the Properties dialog, go ahead and right-click the SQL Server instance service again, but this time choose the Restart option. This will enable the AlwaysOn HA feature. For each of the other nodes (SQLTWO and SQLTHREE), do the same for their SQL Server configuration and the SQL Server instance that is to be included in the AlwaysOn configuration.

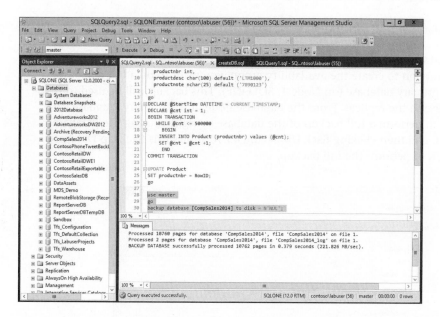

FIGURE 45.8   SSMS execution of create db, create table, and initial database backup (to NULL).

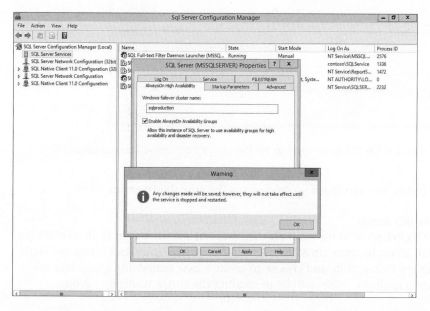

FIGURE 45.9   Enabling AlwaysOn HA via SQL Server Configuration Manager.

You could have also done this from PowerShell. At the prompt, just type in **SQLPS** and press Enter. You then enter the following:

```
Enable -SqlAlwaysOn -PATH SQLSERVER:\SQL\EMU-SQL1\Default -FORCE
```

It will even restart the SQL Server service for you.

Back Up the Database

Before we venture on to create the availability group, you want to do a full database backup of the primary database (on Node 1: SQLONE). This backup will be used to replicate the database to the replicas. From the database node of the primary database (in SSMS), choose to perform a full backup of the database by right-clicking the database, choosing Tasks, and then clicking Back Up. Figure 45.10 shows this Back Up Database dialog. Click OK to perform the full backup.

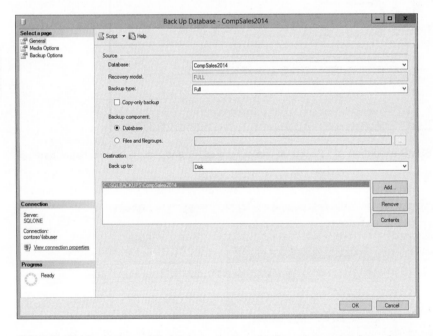

FIGURE 45.10   Doing a full database backup for the primary database (CompSales2014).

When you finish this, you can move on to creating the availability group.

Create the Availability Group

From Node 1 (SQLONE node in the example), expand out the AlwaysOn High Availability node for this SQL Server instance (in SSMS). As you can see in Figure 45.11, you can right-click the Availability Group node and choose to create a new availability group (via the wizard). This is where all the action will be in creating the entire availability group.

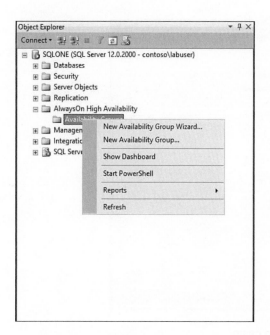

FIGURE 45.11   Invoking the New Availability Group Wizard from SSMS.

This starts the New Availability Group Wizard, which will select the databases, specify the replicas, select the data synchronization, and then do validation. Initially, there is a splash page for the wizard on which you'll just click Next. This brings you to the Specify Availability Group Name dialog. Figure 45.12 shows this dialog and the availability group name of DXD-AG1 being specified. Click Next.

Select the Databases for the Availability Group

Next you are asked to identify which application databases you want to include in this availability group. Figure 45.13 shows our list of databases and the one we've selected (CompSales2014). Click Next.

Identify the Primary and Secondary Replicas

Specifying the replicas and how they will be used is next. Initially, there will only be one server instance (the primary). Click the Add Replicas button in the lower left (below the Server Instances list) and choose the secondary replication instance you want (SQLTWO in this example, Node 2). Now, both the primary and secondary instances should be listed. You also want to specify that each of these should be using automatic failover (up to two) by checking the check boxes. We also want the synchronous commits (up to three) option for both to get this HA feature. Figure 45.14 shows each failover and commit option specified for each server instance.

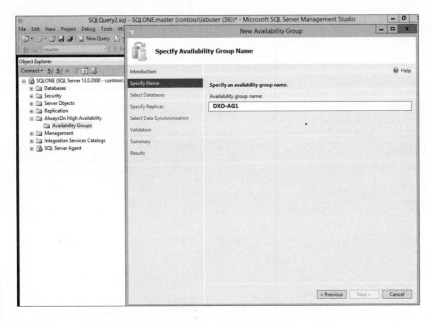

FIGURE 45.12   Specifying the availability group name.

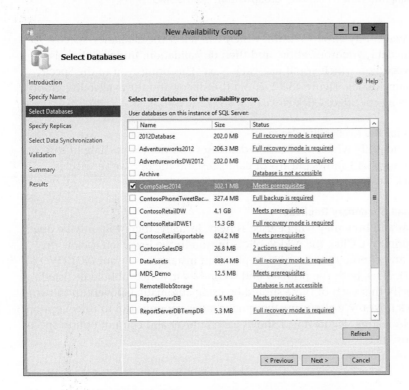

FIGURE 45.13   Specifying the databases for the availability group.

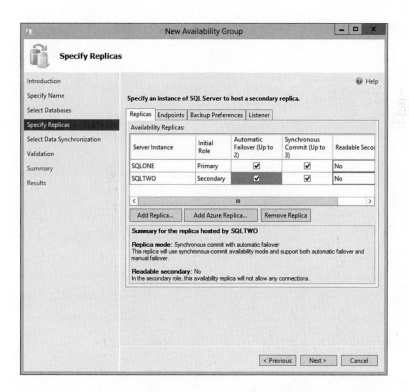

FIGURE 45.14   Specifying the instance of SQL Server to host a secondary replica and failover options.

If you click on the Endpoints tab, you will see the endpoints that are getting generated for use by the instances to communicate with each other (`hadr_endpoint` for each SQL Server instance). We'll make no changes to these (take the default).

If you also click the Backup Preferences tab, you can indicate how (and where) you want database backups to be performed once the availability group is formed and the replicas are active. As you can see in Figure 45.15, we'll keep the Prefer Secondary as our option for doing database backups, thus relieving the primary from this overhead task. If the secondary isn't available for doing a backup, the primary is used (with this option).

If you click on the Listener tab, you can see that you have two options here: not to set up the availability group listener at this time or to create one now. We'll actually do this a bit later, so skip this for now (specify Do Not Create an Availability Group Listener Now) and click Next.

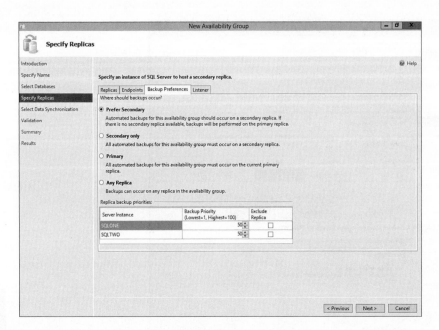

FIGURE 45.15   Specifying database backup preferences: Prefer Secondary option.

Synchronize the Data

Now you set up your data synchronization preferences. Figure 45.16 shows your various options. You can use the Full option, which will do full database and log backups for each selected database. Then these databases get restored to each secondary and joined to the availability group. The Join Only option starts data synchronization up where you have already restored a database and log backup. (In other words, you already restored a database at a secondary, and you just want to have that secondary join the availability group.) The Skip Initial Data Synchronization option simply says you will do the full backups for the primary databases. We've chosen the Full option and must specify a shared network location accessible by all replicas.

It is important that this shared location be fully accessible by the service accounts from all nodes in the availability group (the service account being used by the SQL Server services on each node). After choosing your option, click Next. This finishes the availability group creation, and you'll now see the new group under the Availability Group node in SSMS. The availability group is functional now. You will see the primary and secondary replicas, the databases within the availability group, and an indication at the database node level as to whether the database is synchronized. If so, you are in business. However, to complete the abstraction of instance names away from the applications, you want to create the availability group listener to complete this configuration.

FIGURE 45.16   Specifying the initial data synchronization options for the replicas in the availability group.

Set Up the Listener

The cluster's VNN gets bound to the availability group listener name in this process. It is also the name exposed to the applications to connect to the availability group. As long as at least one node is functioning in the availability group, the applications never know that any node has failed.

Right-click the availability group we created and choose to create a new listener (Add Listener). You can now specify the listener DNS name (DXD-AG1Listener in this example), a port (use 1444), and specify to use a static IP address for this listener. A small dialog box will appear (as you can see in Figure 45.17) that indicates the IPv4 address of this listener (192.168.1.213 in this example). Click OK.

Figure 45.18 shows the availability group and the new availability group listener we just configured.

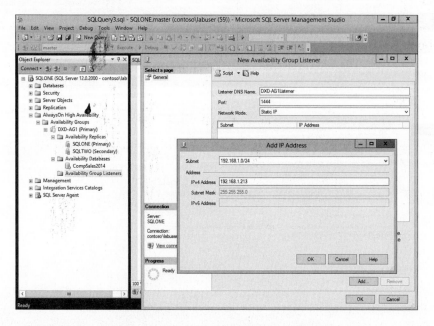

FIGURE 45.17   Specifying the new availability group listener.

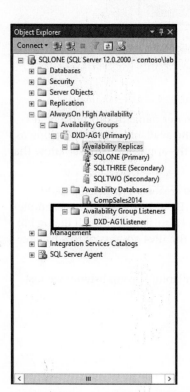

FIGURE 45.18   The new availability group listener (ready to use).

Connect Using the Listener

Let's do a quick test with SSMS to connect to this new availability group listener as if it were its own SQL Server instance. As shown in Figure 45.19, we've started a new connection dialog that specifies the availability group listener name we just created. Go ahead and connect.

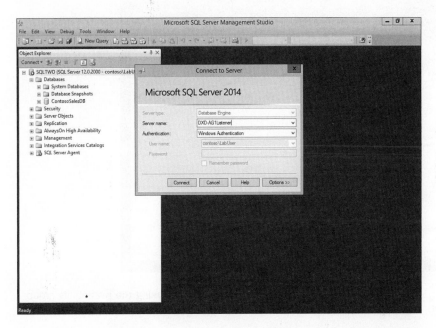

FIGURE 45.19   Connection using the availability group listener (DXD-AG1Listener).

Then, after we connect, we open up a new query window (as shown in Figure 45.20) so that we can do a simple SELECT statement to query for the server name (SELECT @@servername;) and the first 1000 rows from the Product table in CompSales2014. As you can see, it returns the underlying SQL Server node name of SQLONE, which is the current primary node. In Figure 45.20, you can also see that the database is in a synchronized state and is fully functional within the availability group configuration. We are in business!

Fail Over to a Secondary

You can fail over from within SQL Server by right-clicking the primary replica of the Availability Group node and selecting Failover. Or, you can do this from the Failover Manager. Let's jump back over to the Failover Manager for Node 1 and see what things look like from there. Figure 45.21 shows the option to move this clustered role to another node (which is just another way of saying fail it over to another node). It also shows your failover options of Best Possible (the normal secondary replica) or to a specific replica (Move to Node SQLTWO or Move to Node SQLTHREE). When you select one of these (like Best Possible), you'll get a Please Confirm Action warning. Remember, when you fail over, client connections will be broken and re-established to the new node and may have to rerun any changes that were not committed yet. Figure 45.22 shows the execution of the same query (via the listener) and the different node (SQLTWO) that is satisfying the client connection successfully. That is High Availability at work.

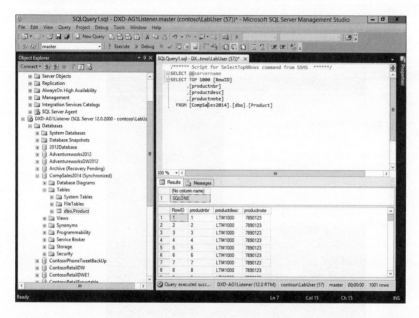

FIGURE 45.20   Select @@servername and a Product table select using the availability group listener connect.

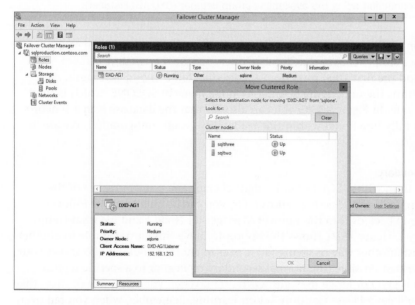

FIGURE 45.21   Failover Cluster Manager moving (failover) from one node to another.

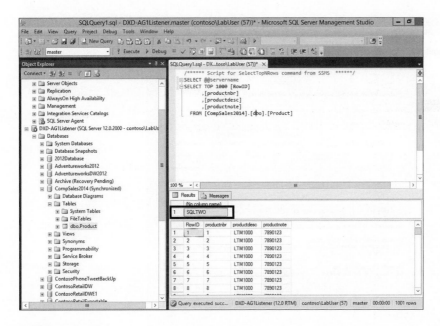

FIGURE 45.22 `Select @@servername` and a Product table select using the availability group listener connection.

Adding Replicas

To add another replica to the configuration, you simply right-click the Availability Replicas node within the availability group you want to add it to and choose Add Replica. You'll have to connect to existing replicas first and then identify (connect) to the new replica you want to add.

Then, as you can see in Figure 45.23, you identify how you want this replica to be used in the availability group (read-only Yes for this example). We also want this to be updated asynchronously, so *do not* check the Automatic Failover or Synchronous Commit boxes. Finish the wizard the same way we did for the first replica (data synchronization, shared network location for backups, and so on).

Then, after this is finished, you'll have another replica available to use for read-only access (as was originally outlined in our three-node cluster in Figure 45.3). AlwaysOn and availability groups turn out to be pretty easy to configure and leverage. No reason for you to wait.

As you can see in Figure 45.24, it is now super easy to just query the Product table from the secondary (read-only) replica of SQLTHREE directly without impacting any other node in the configuration.

45

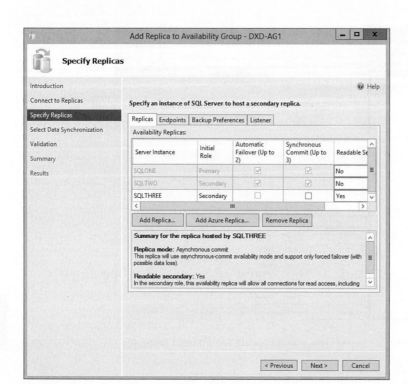

FIGURE 45.23   Adding secondary replicas to your existing availability group.

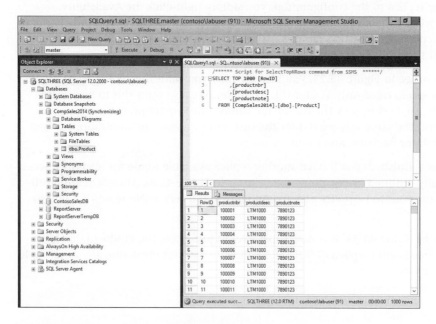

FIGURE 45.24   Querying the Product table via the Read-Only Secondary (SQLTHREE).

Dashboard and Monitoring

Various system views, a dashboard, and dynamic management views have been added for monitoring (and debugging) the AlwaysOn Availability Groups feature. The AlwaysOn dashboard (right-click the availability group and select Show Dashboard) is used to obtain an at-a-glance view of the health of an AlwaysOn availability group, its availability replicas, and databases.

You can use this dashboard to do the following:

▶ Choose a replica for a manual failover.

▶ Estimate data loss if you force failover.

▶ Evaluate data-synchronization performance.

▶ Evaluate the performance impact of a synchronous-commit secondary replica.

The dashboard also provides key availability group states and performance indicators, including the following:

▶ Replica roll-up state

▶ Synchronization mode and state

▶ Estimated data loss

▶ Estimated recovery time (redo catch-up)

▶ Database replica details

▶ Synchronization mode and state

▶ Time to restore log

SQL Server AlwaysOn and availability groups dynamic management views are also available with SQL Server 2014, including the following:

▶ sys.dm_hadr_auto_page_repair

▶ sys.dm_hadr_cluster_networks

▶ sys.dm_hadr_availability_group_states

▶ sys.dm_hadr_database_replica_cluster_states

▶ sys.dm_hadr_availability_replica_cluster_nodes

▶ sys.dm_hadr_database_replica_states

▶ sys.dm_hadr_availability_replica_cluster_states

▶ sys.dm_hadr_instance_node_map

▶ sys.dm_hadr_availability_replica_states

▶ sys.dm_hadr_name_id_map

45

▶ `sys.dm_hadr_cluster`

▶ `sys.dm_tcp_listener_states`

▶ `sys.dm_hadr_cluster_members`

And finally, SQL Server AlwaysOn and Availability Groups catalog views make it easy to see key components of the configuration. These include the following:

▶ `sys.availability_databases_cluster`

▶ `sys.availability_groups_cluster`

▶ `sys.availability_group_listener_ip_addresses`

▶ `sys.availability_read_only_routing_lists`

▶ `sys.availability_group_listeners`

▶ `sys.availability_replicas`

▶ `sys.availability_groups`

Summary

With SQL Server 2014, it's all about the AlwaysOn features. The update (adoption) of the AlwaysOn and availability group capabilities has already been nothing short of astonishing. Older, more complex HA solutions are being cast aside left and right in favor of this clean, highly scalable method to achieve five-nines and high performance. It is truly the next generation of HA and scale-out for existing and new database tiers of any kind. As mentioned earlier, some of the concepts and technical approaches in AlwaysOn and availability groups might seem a bit reminiscent of SQL clustering and database mirroring because they are. But both of these earlier features have paved the way for what we now know as AlwaysOn and availability groups. Microsoft publicly advises all of its customers that have implemented log shipping, database mirroring, and even SQL clustering to get to AlwaysOn and availability groups as soon as possible.

The next chapter describes "SQL Server 2014 Analysis Services." This is a comprehensive coverage of SSAS and how to build up a star-schema based OLAP cube.

PART VII

SQL Server Business Intelligence Features

IN THIS PART

NOTE

Chapters 48-51 are available online for readers of the printed edition of this book. You can register your book and access those chapters here: informit.com/title/9780672337291.

SQL Server 2014 Analysis Services

SQL Server 2014 Analysis Services (SSAS) continues to expand with numerous data warehousing, data mining, and online analytical processing (OLAP)–rich tools and technologies. And Microsoft continues to attack the data warehousing/business intelligence (BI) market by pouring millions and millions of dollars into this area. Microsoft knows that the world is hungry for analytics and is betting the farm on it. As a part of its internal project named Madison, a few years back, Microsoft has been acquiring other complementary BI technologies to accelerate its plans (such as acquiring the MPP data warehousing appliance company DATAllegro and rolling it under its BI offering; see Chapter 51, "Parallel Data Warehouse"). Other more traditional (and much more expensive) OLAP and BI platforms such as Cognos, Hyperion, Business Objects, and Micro Strategies are being challenged, if not completely replaced, by SSAS in many organizations.

A chief data architect from a prominent Silicon Valley company said recently, "I can build [using SSAS] sound, extremely usable, highly scalable, OLAP cubes myself, faster and smarter than the entire data warehouse team could do only a few years ago. And, now I also have an in-memory option as well." This is what Microsoft has been trying to bring to the forefront for years—"BI for the masses."

What's New in SSAS

As some of you may recall, SQL Server 2005 was the big jump into completely redeploying Analysis Services—from the architecture, to the development environment, to the multidimensional languages supported, and even to the wizard-driven deployments. SQL Server 2014 continues to raise this core work up a few more notches with various enhancements such as Power View Reports against Multidimensional models. Following are some of the top features:

▶ **BI features with SharePoint 2013**—An architecture for SQL Server 2014 PowerPivot that supports a PowerPivot server outside of a SharePoint 2013 farm. This architecture leverages Excel Services for querying, loading, refreshing, and saving data.

▶ **Excel 2013 and PowerPivot**—PowerPivot (in Microsoft Excel 2013) supports deep integration with data exploration workflows.

▶ **Tabular model**—The now proven feature of Analysis Services of running in Tabular mode, including optimized storage for measures and key performance indicators (KPIs), extended data categorizations, extended characters, hierarchy annotation, and improved support when importing from Data Market (external data) data feeds.

▶ **Tabular model designer diagram view**—The diagram view for Tabular models displays tables, with relationships between them, in a graphical format. Columns, measures, hierarchies, and KPIs can be filtered, and you can choose to view the model using a defined perspective.

▶ **xVelocity in-memory analytics engine for tabular models**—This Analysis Services engine services tabular model databases. The xVelocity engine uses in-memory storage and performs calculations that aggregate and manipulate data in real time. Previously, the xVelocity engine was available only via PowerPivot for SharePoint; you can use the xVelocity engine on a standalone Analysis Services instance with no dependency on SharePoint whatsoever.

▶ **Using trace events in multidimensional databases**—To help troubleshoot lock-related query or processing problems. This includes new events that show you Locks Acquired, Locks Released, Locks Waiting (that further complement existing lock events), `Deadlock`, and `LockTimeOut` events.

▶ **Resource usage event classes**—Event class that can also be used as an additional column on the `Command End` event or `Query End` event. In the `TextData` column for this event, you can capture the number of reads or writes, reads, or writes as measured in kilobytes, CPU time in milliseconds, rows scanned, and rows returned.

▶ **Power View Reports-Added functionality supporting Power View Reports against Multidimensional Models**—This functionality helps organizations maximize existing BI Investments by leveraging their OLAP cubes to be used with most other client reporting tools including the support for queries using Data Analysis Expressions (DAX).

▶ **Unified BI semantic modeling schema (BISM)**—Both multidimensional models and tabular models are based on a unified BISM, which is a superset of the schema provided in previous releases as the Unified Dimensional Model (UDM). You can easily work with both types of models by using common application programming interfaces (APIs) (AMO and XMLA) and connect to servers and instances running in either tabular or multidimensional mode by using both ADOMD.NET and OLEDB providers.

▶ **Languages supported**—Analysis Services language support includes MDX, DMX, DAX, XML/A, and ASSL. Support for these languages varies slightly by model type, as follows:

  ▶ PowerPivot workbooks use DAX for calculations and queries.

  ▶ Tabular model databases support DAX calculations, DAX queries, and MDX queries.

  ▶ Multidimensional model databases support MDX calculations and MDX queries as well as ASSL.

  ▶ Data mining models support DMX and ASSL.

  ▶ Analysis Services PowerShell is supported for tabular, multidimensional, and data mining models.

  ▶ All databases support XML/A.

Understanding SSAS and OLAP

Because OLAP is at the heart of SSAS, you need to understand what it is and how it solves the requirements of decision makers in a business. As you might already know, data warehousing requirements typically include all the capability needed to report on a business's transactional history, such as sales history. This transactional history is often organized into subject areas and tiers of aggregated information that can support some online querying and usually much more batch reporting. Data warehouses and data marts typically extract data from online transaction processing (OLTP) systems and serve data up to these business users and reporting systems. In general, these are all called decision support systems (DSS), or BI systems, and the latency of this data is determined by the business requirements it must support. Typically, this latency is daily or weekly, depending on the business needs, but more and more, we are seeing more real-time (or near-real-time) reporting requirements.

OLAP falls squarely into the realm of BI. The purpose of OLAP is to provide for a mostly online reporting environment that can support various end user reporting requirements. Typically, OLAP representations are of OLAP cubes. A cube is a multidimensional representation of basic business facts that can be accessed easily and quickly to provide you with the specific information you need to make a critical decision. It is useful to note that a cube can be composed of from 1 to N dimensions. However, remember that the business facts represented in a cube must exist for all the dimensions being defined for the fact. In other words, all dimensional values (that is, intersections) have to be present for a fact value to be stored in the cube.

Figure 46.1 illustrates the `Sales_Units` historical business fact, which is the intersection of time, product, and geography dimensional data. For a particular point in time (February 2014), for a particular product (IBM laptop model 451D), and in a particular country (France), the sales units were 996 units. With an OLAP cube, you can easily see how many of these laptop computers were sold in France in February 2014.

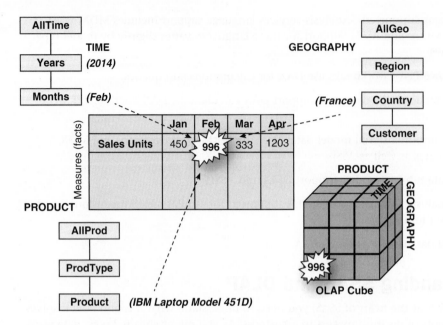

FIGURE 46.1   Multidimensional representation of business facts.

Basically, cubes enable you to look at business facts via well-defined and organized dimensions (time, product, and geography dimensions, in this example). Note that each of these dimensions is further organized into hierarchical representations that correspond to the way data is looked at from the business point of view. This provides for the capability to drill down into the next level from a higher, broader level (like drilling down into a specific country's data within a geographic region, such as France's data within the European geographic region).

SSAS directly supports this and other data warehousing capabilities. In addition, SSAS allows a designer to implement OLAP cubes using a variety of physical storage techniques that are directly tied to data aggregation requirements and other performance considerations. You can easily access any OLAP cube built with SSAS via the PowerPivot capabilities, you can write custom client applications by using MDX with OLE DB for OLAP or ActiveX Data Objects Multidimensional (ADO MD), and you can use a number of third-party "OLE DB for OLAP" compliant tools.

Microsoft found that bridging many platforms and tools required a much more robust data model that spanned all BI concepts and could be shared between them all. As you can see in Figure 46.2, this has given birth to the BI Semantic Model (BISM), which is a superset of the old Unified Dimensional Model (UDM) that has driven SSAS for many years. This BISM enables you to conceptualize all multidimensional and tabular model representations in SSAS. It is also worth noting that many of the leading OLAP and statistical analysis software vendors have joined the Microsoft Data Warehousing Alliance and are continuing to build front-end analysis and presentation tools for SSAS. The data mining capabilities that are also a part of SSAS provide a rich avenue for organized data discovery. This includes using SQL Server DMX (data mining expressions).

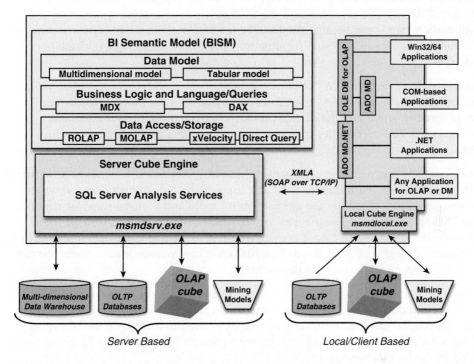

FIGURE 46.2   SQL Server Analysis Services environment.

This chapter takes you through the major components of SSAS, discusses a mini-methodology for OLAP cube design, and leads you through creating and managing a robust OLAP cube that can easily be used to meet a company's BI needs.

Understanding the SSAS Environment Wizards

Welcome to the "land of wizards." This implementation of SSAS, as with older versions of SSAS, is heavily wizard-oriented. SSAS has a Cube Wizard, a Dimension Wizard, a Partition Wizard, a Storage Design Wizard, a Usage Analysis Wizard, a Usage-Based Optimization Wizard, an Aggregation Wizard, a Calculated Cells Wizard, a Mining Model Wizard, and a few other wizards. All of them are useful, and many of their capabilities are also available through editors and designers. Using a wizard is helpful for those who need to have a little structure in the definition process and who want to rely on defaults for much of what they need. The wizards are also plug-and-play oriented and have been made available in all SQL Server and .NET development environments. In other words, you can access these wizards from wherever you need to, when you need to. All the wizard-based capabilities can also be coded in MDX, DMX, and ASSL.

Figure 46.2 shows how SSAS fits into the overall scheme of the SQL Server 2014 environment. SSAS has become completely integrated into the SQL Server platform. Utilizing many different mechanisms, such as SSIS and direct data source access capabilities, a vast amount of data can be funneled into the SSAS environment. Most of the cubes you build will likely be read-only because they will be for BI. However, a write-enabled capability (WriteBack) is available in SSAS for situations that meet certain data updatability requirements.

As you can also see in Figure 46.2, the basic components in SSAS are all focused on building and managing data cubes. SSAS consists of the analysis server, processing services, integration services, and a number of data providers. SSAS has both server-based and client-/local-based SSAS capabilities. This essentially provides a complete platform for OLAP/BI.

You create cubes by preprocessing aggregations (that is, pre-calculated summary data) that reflect the desired levels within dimensions and support the type of querying that will be done. These aggregations provide the mechanism for rapid and uniform response times to queries. You create them *before* the user uses the cube. All queries utilize either these aggregations, the cube's source data, a copy of this data in a client cube, data in cache, or a combination of these sources. A single Analysis Server can manage many cubes. You can have multiple SSAS instances on a single machine.

By orienting around the BSIM, SSAS allows for the definition of a cube that contains data measures and dimensions. Each cube dimension can contain a hierarchy of levels to specify the natural categorical breakdown that users need to drill down into for more details. Look back at Figure 46.1, and you can see a product hierarchy, time hierarchy, and geography hierarchy representation.

The data values within a cube are represented by measures (the facts). Each measure of data might utilize different aggregation options, depending on the type of data. Unit data might require the SUM (summarization) function, Date of Receipt data might require the MAX function, and so on. Members of a dimension are the actual level values, such as the particular product number, the particular month, and the particular country. Microsoft has solved most of the limitations within SSAS. SSAS addresses up to 2,147,483,647 of most anything within its environment (for example, dimensions in a database, attributes in a dimension, databases in an instance, levels in a hierarchy, cubes in a database, measures in a cube). In reality, you will probably not have more than a handful of dimensions. Remember that dimensions are the paths to the interesting facts. Dimension members should be textual and are used as criteria for queries and as row and column headers in query results.

Every cube has a schema from which the cube draws its source data. The central table in a schema is the fact table that yields the cube's data measures. The other tables in the schema are the dimension tables that are the source of the cube dimensions. A classic star-schema data warehouse design has this central fact table along with multiple dimension tables. This is a great starting point for OLAP cube creation, as you can see in Figure 46.3. Here, we show you a high-tech company's computer sales star-schema data warehouse that can be used as the source of building up an OLAP cube within SSAS.

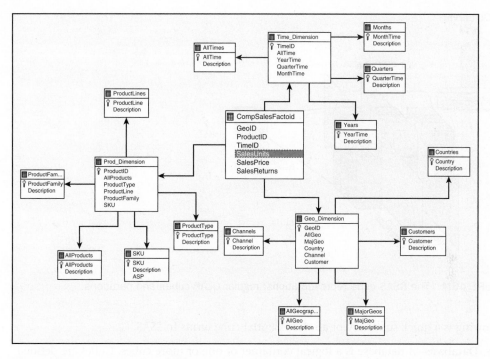

FIGURE 46.3   A star-schema data warehouse design with a central fact table and multiple dimensions of these facts as the source for an OLAP cube in SSAS.

SSAS allows you to build dimensions and cubes from heterogeneous data sources. It can access relational OLTP databases, multidimensional data databases, text data, and any other source that has an OLE DB provider available. You don't have to move all your data first; you just connect to its source. In SSAS, you can also design OLAP cubes from scratch. Then you can have SSAS create the relational schema of tables in SQL Server that you want to populate with the transactional data that will drive the OLAP cube.

Essentially, cubes can be regular or local cubes. Regular cubes are based on real tables as the data source, have aggregations, and occupy physical storage space of some kind. If a data source that contributes to this cube changes, the cube must be reprocessed. Figure 46.4 shows this cube representation and that it may also consist of something called partitions.

Local cubes are entirely contained in portable SSAS files (that is, tables) and can be browsed without a connection to an SSAS instance. This is really like being in "disconnected" mode.

Write-enabled dimensions within a cube enable updates (that is, writes) of data that can be shared back (that is, written back) with the data sources.

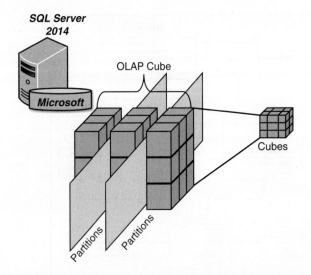

FIGURE 46.4 The SSAS cube representations: regular OLAP cubes and partitions.

Following is a quick summary of all the essential cube terms in SSAS:

▶ **Database**—A database is a logical container of one or more cubes. Cubes are defined within Analysis Server databases.

▶ **Cube**—A cube is a multidimensional representation of the business facts. Types of cubes are regular and local.

▶ **Data source**—The data source is the origin of a cube's data.

▶ **Measure group**—This group is a collection (or grouping) of one or more measures into some type of logical unit for business purposes. A measure group does not occupy any physical space. It is metadata only.

▶ **Measure**—A measure is a data fact representation. A measure is typically a data value fact, such as price, unit, or quantity.

▶ **Cell**—A cell is the part of a data measure that is at the intersection of the dimensions. The cell contains the data value. If an intersection (that is, cell) has no value yet, it does not physically exist until it is populated.

▶ **Dimension**—A cube's dimension is defined by the aggregation levels of the data that are needed to support the data requirements. A dimension can be shared with other cubes, or it can be private to a cube. The structure of a dimension is directly related to the dimension table columns, member properties, or structure of OLAP data mining models. This structure becomes the hierarchy and should be organized accordingly. You can also have strict parent/child dimensions in which two columns are identified as being parent and child, and the dimension is organized according to them. In a regular dimension, each column in the dimension contributes a hierarchy level.

▶ **Level**—A level includes the nodes of the hierarchy or data mining model. Each level contains the members. Millions of members are possible for each level.

▶ **Partition**—One or more partitions comprise a cube. Using a partition is a way to physically separate parts of a cube. This separation essentially lets you deal with individual slices of a data cube separately, querying only the relevant data sources. If you partition by dimension, you can perform incremental updates to change that dimension independently of the rest of the cube. Consequently, you have to reprocess only the aggregations that are affected by those changes. This is an excellent feature for scalability.

▶ **Hierarchy**—A hierarchy is a set of members in a dimension and their position relative to each other. Hierarchies can either be balanced or unbalanced. Being balanced simply means that all branches of the hierarchy descend to the same level. An unbalanced hierarchy allows for branches to descend to different levels. It is also possible to define more than one hierarchy for a single dimension. A great example of this is "fiscal calendar time" and "Gregorian calendar time" being defined in one dimension—a Time dimension that contains both `time.gregorian` and `time.fiscal`.

As mentioned previously, SSAS has many wizards. Which wizards you use depends on what you need to create. The "Creating an OLAP Database" section, later in this chapter, outlines the order and path through this maze of wizards.

OLAP Versus OLTP

One of the primary goals of OLAP is to increase data retrieval speed for business-related queries that are critical to decisions. Very often, there is a need to broaden the scope of a business query or to drill down into more granular details of the query. OLAP was created to facilitate this type of capability. A multidimensional schema is not a typical normalized relational database; redundant data is stored to facilitate quick retrieval. The data in a multidimensional database should be relatively static; in fact, data is not useful for decision support if it changes constantly. The information in a data warehouse is built out of carefully chosen snapshots of business data from OLTP systems. If you capture data at the right times for transfer to the data warehouse, you can quickly make accurate comparisons of important business activities over time.

In an OLTP system, transaction speed is paramount. Data modification operations must be quick, deal with concurrency (locking/holding of resources), and provide transactional consistency. An OLTP system is constantly changing; snapshots of the OLTP system, even if taken only a few seconds apart, are all different. Although historical information is certainly available in an OLTP system, using it for BI-type analysis might be impractical. Storing old data in an OLTP system becomes expensive, and you might need to reconstruct history dynamically from a series of transactions. In addition, OLTP designs and indexes usually don't support large-scale decision support querying.

SSAS supports three OLAP storage methods—MOLAP, ROLAP, and HOLAP—providing flexibility to the data warehousing solution and enabling powerful partitioning and aggregation optimization capabilities.

46

Figure 46.5 shows the MOLAP, HOLAP, and ROLAP storage continuum. MOLAP stores all data locally (to SSAS), and ROLAP is the opposite (storing all data in the relational database). MOLAP is by far the most often used storage approach. The following sections take a closer look at these storage methods.

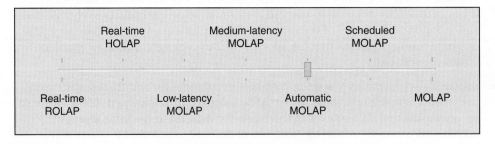

FIGURE 46.5   MOLAP, HOLAP, and ROLAP storage continuum.

MOLAP

Multidimensional OLAP (MOLAP) is an approach in which cubes are built directly from OLTP data sources or from dimensional databases and downloaded to a persistent store.

In SSAS, data is downloaded to the server, and the details and aggregations are stored in a native Microsoft OLAP format. No zero-activity records are stored.

The dimension keys in the fact tables are compressed, and bitmap indexing is used. A high-speed MOLAP query processor retrieves the data.

ROLAP

Relational OLAP (ROLAP) uses fact data in summary tables in the OLTP data source to make data much more current (real-time). The summary tables are populated by processes in the OLTP system and are not downloaded to SSAS. The summary tables are known as materialized views and contain various levels of aggregation, depending on the options you select when building data cubes with SSAS. SSAS builds the summary tables with a column for each dimension and each measure. It indexes each dimension column and creates an additional index on all the dimension columns.

HOLAP

SSAS implements a combination of MOLAP and ROLAP called hybrid OLAP (HOLAP). Here, the facts are left in the OLTP data source, and aggregations are stored in the SSAS server. You use SSAS to boost query performance. This approach helps avoid data duplication, but performance suffers a bit when you query fact data in the OLTP summary tables. The amount of performance degradation depends on the level of aggregation selected.

ROLAP and HOLAP are useful in situations in which an organization wants to leverage its investment in relational database technology and existing infrastructure. The summary tables of facts are also accessible in the OLTP system via normal data access methods.

However, when you are using SSAS, both ROLAP and HOLAP require more storage space because they don't use the storage optimizations of the pure MOLAP-compressed implementation.

An Analytics Design Methodology

A data warehouse can be built from the top down or from the bottom up. To build a top-down warehouse, you need to form a complete picture or logical data model for the entire organization (or all the subsystems within the scope of the project, such as all financial systems). In contrast, building a warehouse from the bottom up takes a much more departmental or specific business-area focus (for example, a sales order system only). This breaks the task of modeling the data into more manageable chunks. Such a departmental approach produces data marts that are potentially subsets of the overall data warehouse. The bottom-up approach can simplify implementation. It helps get departmental or business-area information to the people who need it, makes it easier to protect sensitive data, and results in better query response times because data marts deal with less data than a voluminous transactional system. The potential risk in the data mart approach is that disparity in data mart implementation can result in a logically disjointed enterprise data warehouse if efforts aren't carefully coordinated across the organization.

Before you embark on an OLAP database creation effort, the time you spend understanding the underlying requirements is the best time you can give your effort. If scope is set correctly, you will be able to achieve an industrial-strength OLAP design without much difficulty.

First, you need to take care of some design groundwork as follows:

1. Carefully assess the scope of what you want to represent in the BI environment. Start small, as the bottom-up approach suggests. For instance, just tackle the sales data facts.

2. Coordinate your efforts with other related BI efforts. Let people know that you are carving out a specific subject area or departmental data and, when you finish, publish your design to everyone.

3. Seek out any shared dimensions that might have already been created for other cubes. You want to leverage these as much as possible for the sake of data consistency and nonredundant processing.

4. Understand your data sources. The OLAP cube you create will be only as good as the data you put into it. It's best to understand the dirty data issues of what you are about to touch long before you try to build an OLAP cube with it.

An Analytics Mini-Methodology

To successfully build OLAP solutions, you are advised to carefully assess the requirements of your end users in as detailed fashion as is possible. A mini-methodology that focuses on the essential usages and characteristics of an analytic solution can prove invaluable.

46

The following sections outline a solid approach to nailing down your BI requirements and yielding optimal OLAP designs that solve your end users' needs.

Assumption: You are building a business area–focused OLAP cube.

Requirements Phase

1. Identify the processing requirements for this DSS. What analysis do you need to do? Are trend reporting, forecasting, and so on necessary? These can often be represented in use case form (via UML).

    a. Ask each user what business decision questions he or she needs to have answered.

    b. Ask each user how often he or she needs these questions answered and exactly when the questions must be answered.

    c. Ask each user how current the data must be to get accurate answers. (This speaks to data latency.)

2. Identify the data needed to fulfill these requirements. What data must be touched to provide answers? The best way to capture this type of information is a logical data model. Even a rough model is better than none at all. This is the point where you focus on the facts that need to be analyzed.

3. Identify all possible hierarchies and level representations (that is, aggregations). This is how the data is used. Most users are likely to tell you that they want to see product data in the product hierarchy structure that has already been set up (for example, product family, product groups).

4. Identify the time hierarchies that the users need. Because time is usually implicit, it just needs to be clarified in terms of levels of aggregation (for example, years, quarters, months, weeks, days) and whether it needs to be fiscal versus Gregorian calendar, both, or something else.

5. Understand the data that each user can view from a security point of view.

Design Phase

1. Analyze which data sources are needed to fulfill the requirements. See whether dimensions or OLAP cubes that already exist can be shared.

2. Understand what data transformations need to be done to the source data to provide it to the OLAP world. This might include pre-aggregation, reformatting, data integrity verifications, and so on.

3. Translate these requirements into an OLAP model design:

    a. Translate to MOLAP if your data sources are not going to be leveraged at all and you will be taking full advantage of OLAP storage.

    b. Translate to ROLAP if you are going to leverage an existing relational design and storage.

c. Translate to HOLAP if you are going to partially utilize the source data storage and partially utilize OLAP storage. This is the most frequently used approach.

Construction Phase

1. Implement data extraction, transformation, and loading (ETL) logic (via T-SQL, SSIS, or other methods).

2. Create the data sources to be used.

3. Create the dimensions.

4. Create the cube.

5. Select data measures (that is, the data facts) for the cube.

6. Design the storage and aggregations.

7. Process the cube. This brings the data into the OLAP environment.

8. Verify data integrity.

Implementation Phase

1. Define the security roles in the cube.

2. Train the user to use the system.

3. Process the data into the OLAP environment (from production data sources).

4. Verify data integrity.

5. Allow users to use the OLAP cube.

Maintenance Phase

1. Evaluate access optimization in the OLAP cube via usage analysis.

2. Do data mining discovery, if desired.

3. Make schema changes/enhancements, as necessary.

An OLAP Requirements Example: CompSales International

Following is an abbreviated requirement that reflects an actual implementation that was done for a large Silicon Valley company. We follow the mini-methodology as closely as possible to implement this requirement in SSAS, pointing out which facilities of SSAS should be used for which purpose along the way.

CompSales International Requirements

A large computer manufacturer named CompSales International needs to do basic analytical processing of its product data in a new BI environment. The main business issues at hand are related to minimizing channel inventory and better understanding market demand for the company's most popular products. The detailed data processing requirements are as follows:

1. You want to view sales unit actuals and sales returns for system and non-system products for the past two years via the product hierarchy (All Products, Product Types, Product Lines, Product Families, SKUs), geography hierarchy (All Geos, Major Geos, Countries, Channels, Customers), and different time levels (All Time, Years, Quarters, Months).

2. You want to view data primarily at the yearly and monthly levels, although the finance department also uses it a little bit at quarterly levels.

3. You want to view net sales (sales minus returns) at all levels of the hierarchy.

4. The fiscal and Gregorian calendar are the same for CompSales International.

5. One day past month-end processing, all "actuals" data from the prior month is available (sales units and returns).

You need to implement some general design decisions using SSAS, including the following:

▶ **Hierarchies (dimensions)**—This includes product, geography, and time.

▶ **Facts (measures)**—This includes sales units, sales returns, and net sales (units minus returns) calculated.

▶ **OLAP storage**—This will be MOLAP or HOLAP (if you want to use the star-schema data mart that already contains most of what you are after).

▶ **Physical tables that exist**—This includes `Geo_Dimension`, `Prod_Dimension`, `Time_Dimension`, and `CompSalesFactoid` (the fact table that will become your measures in the OLAP cube). This data is updated weekly. Each of these tables uses an artificial key into the main facts table for performance reasons (`GeoID`, `ProductID`, `TimeID`). In addition, several member/value description tables are associated with each dimension table. Basically, there is one table for each level in a dimension. These description tables can be leveraged to make the result rows from OLAP queries much more user friendly (look back at Figure 46.3 and you can see all tables included in `CompSales` and how they are related via primary/foreign key references).

Figure 46.6 illustrates the desired hierarchies and facts for CompSales International's requirements.

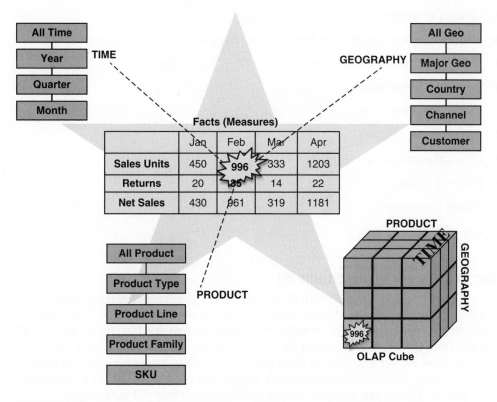

FIGURE 46.6   CompSales International's multidimensional OLAP requirements.

OLAP Cube Creation

A star-schema data mart/warehouse named CompSales2014 is used as the basis of creating the OLAP cube example in this chapter. You can download this data mart, CompsSales2014.zip, from the Sams Publishing website for this book title at www.informit.com/title/9780672337291 in the code listings and sample databases folder. You can easily unzip and attach this database to any SQL Server 2014 database instance. This is not an SSAS database; it is a SQL Server database of a star-schema data warehouse/mart. We use this SQL Server database as the source for the exercises in this chapter. You will build the SSAS OLAP cube yourself (by following the steps outlined here).

You'll spend most of the construction phase using SQL Server BI capabilities within Visual Studio and Microsoft SQL Server Management Studio (SSMS). All wizards and editors are invoked from either Visual Studio BI or SSMS. As mentioned earlier, Microsoft has moved to a project orientation. You must have already installed SSAS and any BI features (often downloaded from Microsoft separately). In general, here's what you'll be doing in this example:

1. Create a BI project.

2. Identify data sources and data source views that you want to use for a new cube.

3. Define the basic dimensions for the cube (Time, Geography, Product).

4. Define the hierarchies.

5. Process the dimensions.

6. Create a cube structure.

7. Define the measure groups/measures.

8. Process the cube.

9. Deploy the solution.

10. Use the cube.

Using SQL Server Visual Studio BI

The SQL Server Visual Studio (VS) with BI capabilities is a project option from within Visual Studio when you install the BI features as a part of the BI/Analysis Services install process. We will assume you have installed SQL Server Analysis Services, the BI features, BI templates, and SQL Server 2014. When VS is open, you choose File, New Project (or just click on the New Project icon item in the left pane). You now choose what type of project this will be: either an Analysis Service project, Integration Services project, or a Reporting Services project. Within the Analysis Services project options you will now choose either Analysis Services Tabular Project, Analysis Services Multidimensional and Data Mining Project, Import From Server (Multidimensional and Data Mining), Import from PowerPivot, or Import from Server (Tabular). Figure 46.7 shows the New Project dialog from which you should highlight the Analysis Services Project option, choose the Analysis Services Multidimensional and Data Mining Project template, and specify a project name, project location, and solution name for this new BI project. In our example, the solution name will be CompSalesUnleashed.

> **NOTE**
>
> You can also start a new project by leveraging any other existing SSAS database project. You can easily clone an existing project and tweak it a bit to fit your new needs. To do this, you use the Import from Server (multidimensional and data mining) option or Import from PowerPivot option. Tabular projects can also be leveraged separately now.

After you create a new project, a set of objects is presented to you in the upper-left pane, which is the Solution Explorer. On the right pane is the Server Explorer. Figure 46.8 shows the Solution Explorer and Server Explorer for the new project. All OLAP project objects will show here, including data sources, dimensions, cubes, mining structures, and roles.

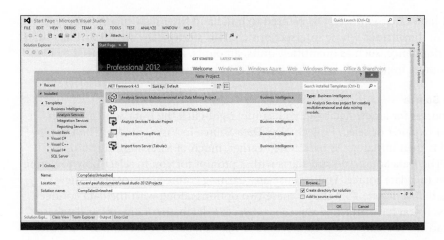

FIGURE 46.7   The SQL Server Visual Studio 2012 New BI Project dialog.

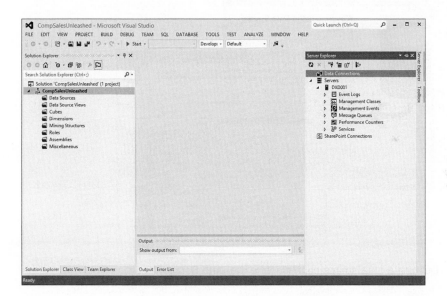

FIGURE 46.8   The VS Solution Explorer and Server Explorer view for the new
CompSalesUnleashed project.

Creating an OLAP Database

Remember that an OLAP database is made up of data sources, dimensions, and cubes. A data source is simply a pointer to data somewhere, such as via a Jet OLE DB provider, an OLE DB provider, SQL Native Client, Microsoft Directory Services, or even SSIS packages. You populate the data in your cube from the data source. Dimensions are constructed of columns from tables that you select to be used to build and filter data cubes. Cubes are combinations of dimensions whose intersections contain strategically significant measures of business performance, such as quantities, units, amounts, and so on. You need to identify the data sources from which your OLAP cube is to be based.

Adding a Data Source

To add data sources for a new database, you simply right-click the Data Sources object in the Solution Explorer or select Project, New Data Source in Visual Studio. The Data Source Wizard is then initiated. As mentioned earlier, much of SSAS administration is wizard based. The Data Source Wizard starts with a prompt for you to select how to define the connection to a data source. You can use any existing connections or create new ones from this dialog. Figure 46.9 shows these two options, along with the data connection properties. If you have attached the CompSales2014 database (or any other database) already, you can easily create a new connection to this database for use in this example.

FIGURE 46.9   Defining a data source connection in the Data Source Wizard.

Figure 46.10 shows the Connection Manager dialog, where you specify the provider to use (for example, Native OLE DB\SQL Native Client 11.0), the name of the database to connect to, and the authentication method to use for the connection. You should go ahead and establish a connection to the CompSales2014 database you just attached and click the Test Connection button in the lower-left corner to verify that it is valid. If you have referenced the CompSales2014 database from VS before, it may already appear in the Data Connections list.

FIGURE 46.10   Connection Manager specification for a new data source.

As part of this connection specification wizard sequence, you must specify the imper-sonation information. That is, you must define what credentials SSAS should use to connect to the data source. You can specify a specific username and password, use the service account, use the credentials of the current user, or use default authentication. You can also create a specialized domain account to use for all SSAS connections. We recommend using the service account approach, which is easily leveraged for most cube administration.

To finish, you must name the data source Comp Sales2014 and then click the Finish button. Your data source then appears in the Solution Explorer, under Data Sources. As part of this process, an XML file is created, from which you can easily manage all connec-tion properties for this data source (Comp Sales2014.ds in this example). Remember that you have just established connection information only—nothing more.

If you right-click the Comp Sales2014.ds entry under the Data Sources object, you can view the complete XML code of this entry by selecting the View Code option.

The following XML code represents this data source connection:

```
<DataSourcexmlns:xsd="http://www.w3.org/2001/XMLSchema"
xmlns:xsi="http://www.w3.org/2001/XMLSchema-instance"
xmlns:ddl2="http://schemas.microsoft.com/analysisservices/2003/engine/2"
xmlns:ddl2_2="http://schemas.microsoft.com/analysisservices/2003/engine/2/2"
xmlns:ddl100_100="http://schemas.microsoft.com/analysisservices/2008/engine/100/100"
```

46

```
xmlns:ddl200="http://schemas.microsoft.com/analysisservices/2010/engine/200"
xmlns:ddl200_200="http://schemas.microsoft.com/analysisservices/2010/engine/200/200"
xmlns:ddl300="http://schemas.microsoft.com/analysisservices/2011/engine/300"
xmlns:ddl300_300="http://schemas.microsoft.com/analysisservices/2011/engine/300/300"
xmlns:dwd="http://schemas.microsoft.com/DataWarehouse/Designer/1.0"
xsi:type="RelationalDataSource" dwd:design-time-name="bfc68784-f6e1-4691-b0ac-
71396dd28510" xmlns="http://schemas.microsoft.com/analysisservices/2003/engine">

<ID>Comp Sales2014</ID>
<Name>Comp Sales2014</Name>
<CreatedTimestamp>0001-01-01T00:00:00Z</CreatedTimestamp>
<LastSchemaUpdate>0001-01-01T00:00:00Z</LastSchemaUpdate>
<ConnectionString>Provider=SQLNCLI11.1;Data Source=
DXD001\SQL2014DXD01;Integrated Security=SSPI;
Initial Catalog=CompSales2014</ConnectionString>
<ConnectionStringSecurity>Unchanged</ConnectionStringSecurity>
<ImpersonationInfo>
<ImpersonationMode>ImpersonateAccount</ImpersonationMode>
<Account>DXD001\Paul</Account>
<ImpersonationInfoSecurity>PasswordRemoved</ImpersonationInfoSecurity>
</ImpersonationInfo>
<Timeout>PT0S</Timeout>
</DataSource>
```

You can also choose the View Designer option on this data source entry (a right mouse click of the data source you just created: Comp Sales2014.ds), which allows you to view and modify the properties of the data source entry.

Creating Data Source Views

Because you will be basing your cube on a data warehouse/data mart star schema you already have available, you need to further define exactly what you need to have access to within that data source. Creating a data source view essentially allows you to look more deeply into the metadata of the data source and add additional relationships, create things like calculations, and set logical keys on the metadata of the data source. You start by right-clicking the Data Source View object in the Solution Explorer and selecting New Data Source View (or choosing Project, New Data Source View). This starts the Data Source View Wizard, which you use to define what view of data to use for the cube. The first dialog box allows you to select a data source to use as the basis of the data source view. Figure 46.11 shows the data source Comp Sales2014 that you defined earlier. Choose it and click Next.

If you need to limit the data source to a particular schema within the database, you can click the Advanced button and specify a schema (or schemas) to be restricted to and retrieve any foreign key and primary key relationships that may exist (see Figure 46.12).

FIGURE 46.11   Identifying which data source to use for the view in the Data Source View Wizard.

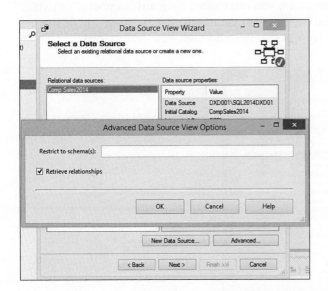

FIGURE 46.12   Advanced schema restriction and Retrieve Relationships in the Data Source View Wizard.

If your schema doesn't include foreign key specifications, you can use this wizard to try to discover foreign key relationships, using a few different types of column name matching. Use a simple primary key column name matching technique to identify any foreign key relationships with other tables in your schema. If you have used some type of common naming convention on your source tables, you can easily leverage this name-matching dialog.

You essentially can identify the following:

▶ Matches based on the exact column name match (as compared to the primary key column):

```
Order.CustomerID (foreign key) Ø Customer.CustomerID (primary key)
```

▶ Matches based on the column name being the primary key table name:

```
Order.Customer Ø Customer.CustomerID (primary key)
```

▶ Matches based on similar column name by comparing the table name concatenated with its primary key column name and then loosely comparing it to other column names of other tables:

```
Order.CustomerID Ø CustomerID (concatenated to Customer+ID=CustomerID)
Order.Customer ID Ø CustomerID
Order.Customer_ID Ø CustomerID
```

Next, you must select the tables (and/or views) you want to be included from your data source view. As you can see in Figure 46.13, you can choose from any number of objects. You should select the base tables you need in your data source views. These will be the CompSalesFactoid, Geo_Dimension, Prod_Dimension, and Time_Dimension tables.

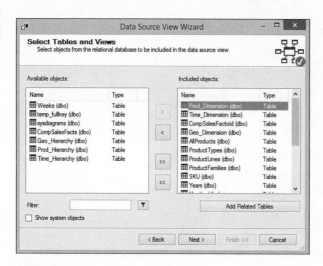

FIGURE 46.13   Available and included objects for your data source views in the Data Source View Wizard.

However, you should also click the Add Related Tables button to add all related tables. Using the Add Related Tables button will actually follow the Primary Key to Foreign Key relationships in the source schema. We've seen a little inconsistency of the wizard not adding all related tables properly. Please double-check the list of tables with our figures list (Figure 46.13). This completes the set of tables that comprise the data source views for your cube.

You now complete this wizard by naming the data source views (`Comp Sales2014 DSV`) and clicking Finish.

When you exit the wizard, you end up in the designer view in Visual Studio, with a graphical representation of the data source views that will be the basis of the cube you are building (see Figure 46.14). This figure highlights the primary fact table (`CompSalesFactoid`), the primary dimension tables (`Time_Dimension`, `Prod_Dimension`, `Geo_Dimension`), and all tables related to these dimensions (that contain the values/descriptions of the member entries for the hierarchies of the dimensions).

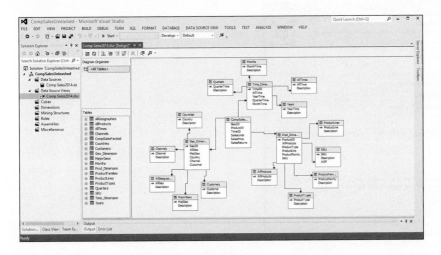

FIGURE 46.14   A designer graphical representation of the data source views.

Now, because you have fully specified data source views, you can easily define a cube via the Cube Wizard. Or you can start defining your cube's dimensions and then use these dimensions in the Cube Wizard later. Because we have provided you with a ready-made source database, you can go ahead and create your dimensions and hierarchies first.

Defining Dimensions and Hierarchies

You are now ready to start defining dimensions and hierarchies to your database. Dimensions are the building blocks for cubes in SSAS. You start by right-clicking the Dimensions object in the Solution Explorer (or choosing Project, New Dimension). You can create a new (standard) dimension or define a dimension that is linked to another SSAS cube or database.

For this example, you will be creating three new cube dimensions, based on the dimension tables you have in your data source views (`Time_Dimension`, `Prod_Dimension`, `Geo_Dimension`). When you choose the New Dimension option, you are welcomed to the Dimension Wizard. You need to build the new dimensions by using your data source views. As you can see in Figure 46.15, the first wizard dialog prompts you to specify whether you will be using a data source to create a dimension. This is the wizard build method. If you haven't defined any data sources (and perhaps don't have them yet), you can use a template approach to define dimensions. This is the bottom-most option on this dialog. If you want a time dimension but do not have a previously defined set of tables that represent your time dimension (in your data source), you can choose the second or third options to generate a well-formed time representation via this wizard. We discuss this option later. You do have a valid data source to use, so you will use the first option to create your first dimension (which is a Time Dimension based on the Comp Sales 2014 data warehouse/mart Time_Dimension table).

FIGURE 46.15   Creating a dimension by using a data source in the Dimension Wizard.

When you choose the first option (Use an Existing Table), you are prompted to identify the data source view you want to use to provide data to the new dimension. Because you have already defined the data source view in a previous step (the Comp Sales2014DSV data source view), it should be available for you to use. Figure 46.16 shows the Comp Sales2014 DSV data source views and all the tables available for your use. You should highlight this data source view along with the main table the dimension will be based on (Time_Dimension table in this case). As you can see in Figure 46.17, the key columns show up automatically. The fact table's time is keyed by a pseudo-key called TimeID, with no other key columns needed. You have a chance to identify any other columns you might also want to include in this dimension (do not do so in this example though) and click Next.

You have probably noticed that the time dimension table has all the other levels of the time dimension hierarchy as separate columns in it. A few related tables to this time dimension table hold the member value descriptions that correspond to each level in the hierarchy. It is really nice to have the member-level descriptions available in the cube for ease of use by the end user. It is pretty easy to include these related tables in the next step of generating this dimension. Figure 46.18 shows the list of related tables identified earlier in the data source views. You need to check all the related tables for inclusion in the time dimension and click Next (they are likely already checked automatically).

FIGURE 46.16   Identifying which data source views to use for a dimension in the Dimension Wizard.

FIGURE 46.17   The key column of the table the dimension is based on.

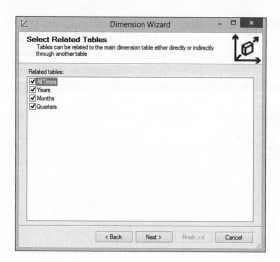

FIGURE 46.18   Including the related member description tables in the dimension in the Dimension Wizard.

It is now time to select the attributes you want to include in the dimension. As shown in Figure 46.19, the Dimension Wizard presents a Dimension Attributes list, along with the attribute key column and attribute name column correspondences. You need to identify the correct key column value from your data source views for Attribute Key Column. You also should enable these attributes for browsing for your dimension; this essentially makes them available (surfaces them) in your dimension hierarchy. Notice also that you identify the types of attribute characteristics. The default is the Regular attribute for general use. Several other attribute types correspond to the anticipated behavior or characteristics of the attribute itself. They might follow date-based behavior, currency type behavior, or other variations such as slowly changing attributes (and hence slowly changing dimensions). For this example, you check the check box for each dimension attribute you need: All Time, Year Time, Quarter Time, and Month Time, along with the dimension key itself (TimeID). Then, for the selected dimension attributes, you specify the attribute type Regular, check the box for enabling these attributes for browsing, and click Next.

As you can see in Figure 46.20, the last step of the dimension generation process shows you the summary of what you have defined and prompts you to name the dimension you are about to create (Time_Dimension in this case).

FIGURE 46.19   Selecting dimension attributes and attribute types for the dimension in the Dimension Wizard.

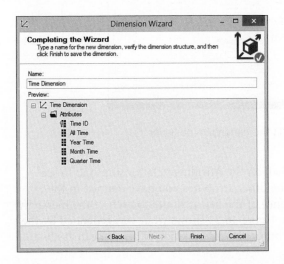

FIGURE 46.20   Finishing the generation of the time dimension.

After you click Next, you are placed in the dimension designer for the dimension you just created. In addition, a dimension entry is added to the Solution Explorer, and now you can easily create the hierarchical view for this dimension. This task is quite easy because all the attributes that represent a level in a hierarchy are visible (because you enabled them), and you can simply drag them into a hierarchy from within this designer. As you can see in Figure 46.21, you can click and drag any attribute listed in this dimension from the Attributes pane (on the far left) to the Hierarchies pane. A new hierarchy is created automatically when you pull your first attribute into this work area. Your goal is to create the following hierarchy for the time dimension (in this order, from top to bottom):

1. All Time

2. Year Time

3. Quarter Time

4. Month Time

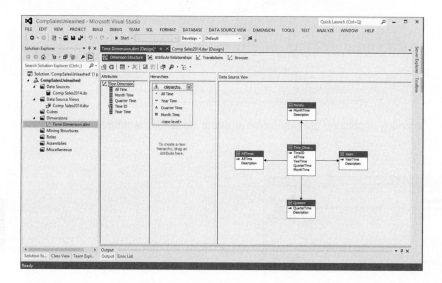

FIGURE 46.21   Creating the time hierarchy in the dimension designer.

In addition, from this designer, you can click on the Attribute Relationships tab to see how the dimension key relates to any of the other attributes you have defined in the dimension. Usually, there is a correspondence of the key attribute to each of the hierarchy levels (which show how they can be used). Figure 46.22 shows what was generated by the Dimension Wizard. If you need to specify other attribute relationships, you can easily do so here.

If you want to browse the data that will make up your dimension that is coming from the data source, you must first process your dimension (populate the values that represent the dimension and hierarchy). Oh, by the way, don't forget to identity the Analysis Services server you want to be using. You do this by updating the properties of the project: Server configuration. In our example, this should be set from LocalHost to DXD001\ SQL2014DXD001. Now, you can use the process icon (the second icon) in the upper-left corner of the dimension structure designer, which takes you through a two-step process sequence. Step one is to deploy the definitions and see whether any errors might exist. Step two is to populate the values (run the processing). If you like, you can do this now.

When this sequence is done, you should be able to open the Dimension Browser and navigate around in your fully populated dimension hierarchy (as shown in Figure 46.23).

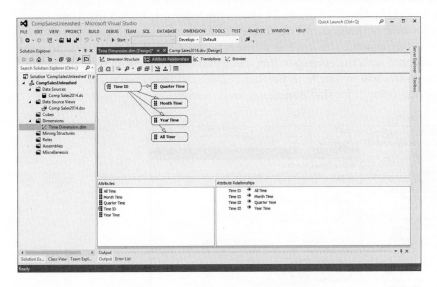

FIGURE 46.22   Attribute relationships in your dimension.

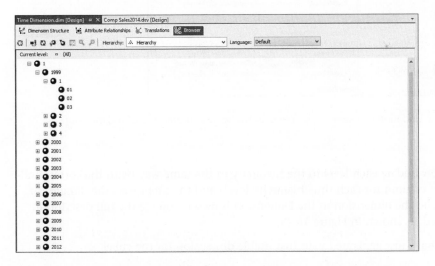

FIGURE 46.23   Browsing the time dimension hierarchy.

You will probably notice that the data values being displayed in the time hierarchy are numeric. These are the key values of each level in the hierarchy. If you want to see the full description of the hierarchy values instead of just the key values, you can easily modify the properties of each hierarchy level column's NameColumn and ValueColumn properties to have them pull the descriptive (more natural) values from the related table entries. You simply browse down into the Property window of any level of the hierarchy and update the values with the corresponding column names of the related table's description column name. The window at the top of Figure 46.24 shows the top-level column (All Times) column properties with nothing identified in its `NameColumn` or `ValueColumn` properties (actually (none) is the default). The window at the bottom of Figure 46.24 shows the properties partially updated with the corresponding description columns from the corresponding reference table. You will update both the `NameColumn` and the `ValueColumn` properties with the Description column for that dimension level description.

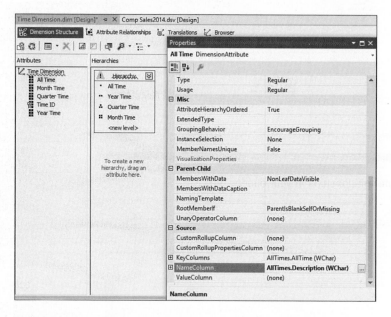

FIGURE 46.24   Updating the `NameColumn` and `ValueColumn` properties of a dimension hierarchy.

You should now update each level in the hierarchy in the same way (with the corresponding description column for each time hierarchy level) and then reprocess the dimension. When you reload the dimension in the Dimension Browser, you see the full description values displayed, as shown in Figure 46.25.

That's it! You have just generated your first usable dimension for the cube!

If you didn't have such a well-defined data source set of tables to base your time dimension on, you could use either of the other two kinds of time dimension options within this wizard. As you can see in Figure 46.26, you need to specify the date periods that will be used when generating the hierarchies, along with the corresponding attributes (time table columns). Setting these attributes is relatively standard.

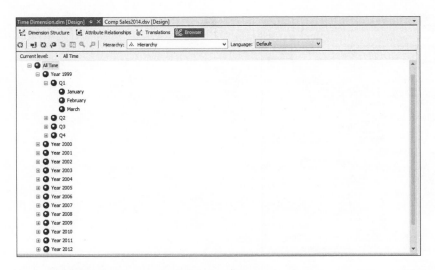

FIGURE 46.25   Full descriptions of hierarchy levels.

FIGURE 46.26   Specifying the time period and hierarchy attributes when not using a data source table.

Figure 46.27 shows the different server time dimension options that Microsoft provides for your convenience. Microsoft has tried to cover the primary variations of time dimensions and calendars in the market: Fiscal, Reporting (for example, for Marketing, which also includes week-by-month patterns such as 4-4-5 calendars), Manufacturing, and even ISO 8601 calendars. The process is to first identify a time period and then select the calendar type to use. The wizard then creates a server time dimension that meets your needs.

FIGURE 46.27   Calendaring options for server time dimensions in the Dimension Wizard.

> **NOTE**
>
> You might want to have multiple time dimensions in your cube to fulfill multiple business unit group needs. You can create as many as you need and then provide perspectives of the cube for each group that include only each group's specific time dimension for its needs.

Creating the Other Dimensions

Now you essentially need to go through the whole process of creating a dimension and a hierarchy for the other dimensions (Product and Geography). The process is as follows:

1. Invoke the Dimension Wizard (by right-clicking the Dimensions object in the Solution Explorer).

2. Choose the creation method for the dimension to use the existing table from a data source approach.

3. Specify the `Comp Sales2014 DSV` data source view.

4. Select the main dimension table to use (`Prod_Dimension` for the Product dimension and `Geo_Dimension` for the Geography dimension).

5. Identify the key column of each new dimension (`ProductID` for the Product dimension and `GeoID` for the Geography dimension).

6. Select the related tables.

7. Specify the dimension attributes and the attribute types (regular).

8. Name the dimension (`Product_Dimension` and `Geography_Dimension`) and finish the Dimension Wizard (which places you in the dimension designer).

9. Drag the dimension attributes to the Hierarchies pane to create the dimension hierarchy view.

Use the following product hierarchy, in this order (see Figure 46.28):

1. All Products

2. Product Type

3. Product Line

4. Product Family

5. SKU

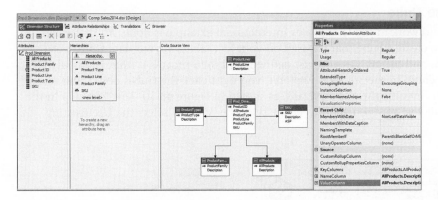

FIGURE 46.28   Creating the product hierarchy in the dimension designer.

Use the following geography hierarchy, in this order (see Figure 46.29):

1. All Geo

2. Maj Geo

3. Country

4. Channel

5. Customer

6. Update the `NameColumn` and `ValueColumn` properties of each dimension hierarchy level.

7. Process the dimension and browse the dimension.

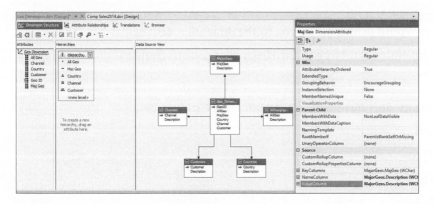

FIGURE 46.29   Creating the geography hierarchy in the dimension designer.

Creating the Cube

Most of the hard work in the CompSales International example is done. All that is left to do now is to create a cube that is based on your fact tables in your data source, use the dimensions and hierarchies you just defined, and then process it (that is, populate the cube with data). In the Solution Explorer, you right-click the Cubes object and select New Cube. This invokes the Cube Wizard, as shown in Figure 46.30. This first step in the wizard is asking you how you want to create the cube. We will select the Use Existing Tables option.

FIGURE 46.30   Selecting the build method for the cube in the Cube Wizard.

Next, you identify the measure group tables from the data source view that will be used to provide data to the cube. Available data source views are listed in this dialog. Because you have already defined a data source view (Comp Sales2014 DSV), you simply highlight it and check the primary fact table (use `CompSalesFactoid` as your measure group table) that will provide your data, as shown in Figure 46.31, and click Next.

FIGURE 46.31   Selecting the data source view and measure group table to use for the cube.

The wizard detects the possible data measures (facts) from the measure group table you just identified. In this measure group table, there are Sales Units, Sales Prices, Sales Returns, and a Count measure to choose from. Select all of them, as shown in Figure 46.32.

FIGURE 46.32   Selecting the measures (facts) that will be in the cube.

If you have dimensions defined already (as you chose to do earlier), you want the new cube to use these definitions. The next wizard dialog lists any shared dimensions that have been created already. Your dimensions are listed there, and you need to check all the ones to be used for your cube (Time_Dimension, Product_Dimension, and Geography_ Dimension), as shown in Figure 46.33. Then you click Next.

FIGURE 46.33   Selecting the existing dimensions for your cube.

As you can see in Figure 46.34, the last dialog in this wizard shows a preview of your complete cube definition and provides a place to name the cube (for this example, name it Comp Sales2014). Now you click Finish.

FIGURE 46.34   Naming the cube and previewing the cube definition in the Cube Wizard.

You are now put in the cube designer, which shows the completed cube design for Comp Sales. The cube designer provides all related cube information within the single IDE (Visual Studio). Figure 46.35 shows the cube designer and all related tabs that can be invoked from here (Dimension Usage, Calculations, KPIs, Actions, Partitions, Aggregations, Perspectives, Translations, and the Cube Data Browser).

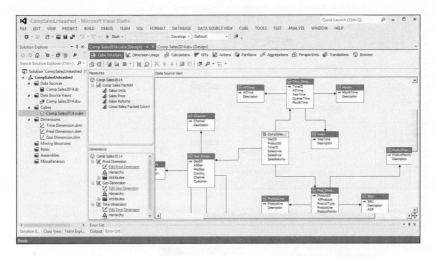

FIGURE 46.35   The Comp Sales2014 cube definition in the cube designer.

Building and Deploying the Cube

You basically have a cube definition now, but it is just an empty shell. You need to process it and then deploy it so that it is instantiated and populated with data (via the data source view). Remember that this cube definition is a solution project, just like a C# code project. It must be deployed before it can be used. First, you need to verify that the properties of the cube you are building are set correctly. You must have these properties correct before the cube can be processed. (Process, in this case, means build the cube structure and populate the measures and their associated dimensions.) You can assume that the properties will not be set correctly, so you should take a quick look and update them accordingly. You start by going to the Project menu item in Visual Studio and locating the Properties item entry (see Figure 46.36).

After you select this option, you navigate to the Deployment entry (the configuration property on the bottom). You need to focus on the Target (the target of the deployment) properties. As you can see in Figure 46.37, the `Server` property should be pointing to the location where you want this cube to be deployed. The `Database` property is simply the name under which you will deploy the database. For this example, you should make sure to specify a valid Server value; the default is `(localhost)`. The default in this property usually is not what you want to happen and usually results in an error during the deployment step. Therefore, you should specify this value explicitly (such as `DXD001\ SQL2012DXD01`, which is the Analysis Services server, and `CompSalesUnleashed` as the

`Database` entry). After the cube is deployed, you will be able to connect to this server (SSAS engine) with SSMS and administer the cube accordingly.

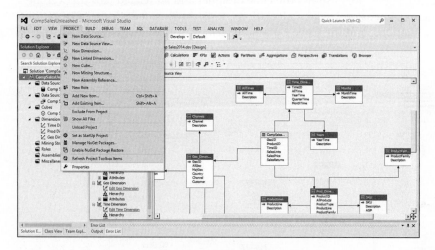

FIGURE 46.36   Selecting the cube properties for Comp Sales from the Project menu.

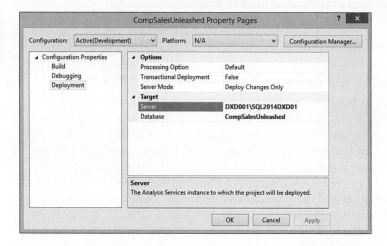

FIGURE 46.37   Deployment properties for the Comp Sales cube.

After you apply these property changes, you are ready to first do a build and then deploy your SSAS cube. You start by making sure you have a successful build by using the Build menu item on the toolbar or using the specific build option for the current SSAS solution: Build CompSalesUnleashed. They both do the same thing. If you have no errors (and you have received a Build Succeeded message in the lower-left message bar of Visual Studio), you can deploy this SSAS solution.

Again, you should choose the Build menu item in the toolbar and click the Deploy Solution option to deploy this cube. Immediately, a Deployment Progress dialog box appears in the lower-right corner of Visual Studio. When the deployment has progressed, you receive a Deployment Completed Successfully message.

Populating the Cube with Data

Now you can process actual data into your cube from the data source view. To do so, you right-click the Comp Sales cube entry in the Solution Explorer and choose the Process item or choose the Process icon for the cube in the cube designer (second icon from the left in the cube designer). A Process Cube dialog appears, with the object list of available cubes to process. You select the Comp Sales2014 cube (by highlighting it) and then click the Run button to start the processing of data (see Figure 46.38). You can also see in Figure 46.38 that the Process Option defaults to Process Full. Other options here vary depending on what part of the cube needs to be reprocessed (such as when you have structure changes, data refreshes, incremental data changes, so on).

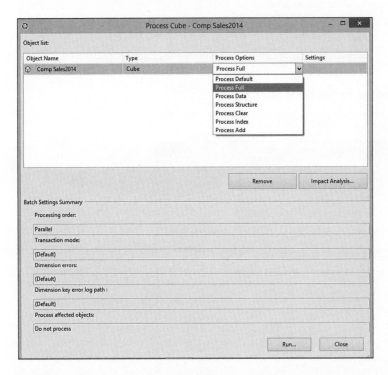

FIGURE 46.38   Process Cube dialog for Comp Sales2014.

A Process Progress dialog appears as the processing begins. Remember that this data is the dimension member values and the measure data values and has not been aggregated up through a complete cube representation (at all levels in the hierarchies). That will be done shortly, via the Aggregation Design Wizard. You can actually use your cube right now, but browsing would be challenging from a performance point of view.

Aggregating Data Within the Cube

The last step of creating your OLAP cube is running through the Aggregation Design Wizard and determining how best to represent and aggregate the data for your users. This is the point at which you must determine the optimal aggregation levels and storage method for these aggregations (MOLAP, HOLAP, or ROLAP) for the optimal performance of queries against the cube.

You double-click the cube entry in the Solution Explorer (`Comp Sales2014.cube`) to bring up the cube designer for your newly created cube. Then you click the Partitions tab to see the current partition for Comp Sales. Figure 46.39 shows the default storage mode is MOLAP and that there is no Aggregation Design for this cube yet. Just to the lower right of this tab is the Storage Settings option, which shows the different storage options possible for your partition, as shown in Figure 46.40.

FIGURE 46.39   The Partitions for the Comp Sales cube.

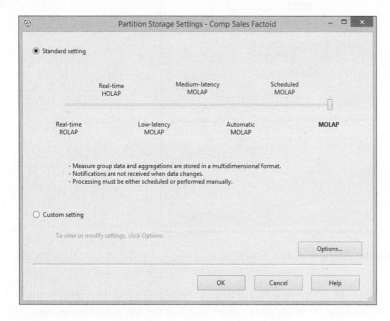

FIGURE 46.40   Specifying MOLAP storage mode for your cube in the Storage Settings dialog.

You need to indicate what type of storage mode and caching options you want for the partition that will contain your aggregations (these storage modes are discussed earlier in this chapter). You want to optimize performance and don't need real-time refreshes of the data. For these reasons, you specify the MOLAP (native SSAS storage) mode. Figure 46.40 shows this MOLAP specification in the Storage Settings dialog. This dialog works as a sliding scale. You just need to make sure the slider is positioned at the MOLAP storage option.

You also want to take advantage of the proactive caching capabilities that come with SSAS. You can activate this feature by clicking the Options button of this dialog and then checking the Enable Proactive Caching check box at the top of the Storage Options dialog that appears (see Figure 46.41). In addition, you use the option Update the Cache When Data Changes, as indicated in Figure 46.41, along with interval times for these refreshes. Enabling proactive caching will also change the overall storage option on the continuum from MOLAP to Automatic MOLAP.

FIGURE 46.41   Enabling proactive caching for the cube.

A good rule of thumb is to refresh the cache interval based on response requirements and the volatility of the data from the data source views and whether the changes will have a dramatic effect on the BI query results.

Now you can run through the Aggregation Design Wizard to see whether you can optimize your partition for querying. You simply go to the Aggregations Design tab for this cube (from the cube designer) and choose the Design Aggregations option (click the first icon in the Design Aggregations tab or right-click within the Aggregations Design tab and choose Design Aggregations). This launches the Design Aggregation Wizard.

First up is the dialog you use to review the aggregation usage you want for each dimension. We'll choose Unrestricted, as shown in Figure 46.42. The next wizard dialog allows you to specify object counts of the total population of facts and the number of values at each hierarchical level within each dimension. If you know what the full extent of counts will be for your cube, you can manually supply these count values in the Estimated Count column (see Figure 46.43). You typically do this when you have been able to load only a partial amount of data or the data will grow quite rapidly over time. If you are building a statically sized cube and have populated the data already, you just click the Count button to tell the wizard to use the actual data as the basis of the aggregation.

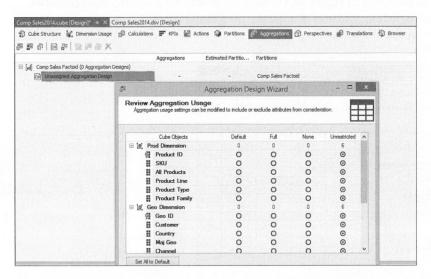

FIGURE 46.42   Specifying the aggregation usage options for each dimension's attributes in the Aggregation Design Wizard.

The next dialog optimizes the storage, based on the level of aggregation. You can specify a maximum storage approach (you create optimized storage based on the amount of disk space you can allocate to the cube), tell the wizard to simply optimize to achieve a certain percentage of performance gain (for example, 50%, 80%), specify to start the aggregation design process dynamically, and stop when you feel the cube is optimized enough, or do no design aggregation at all. You really want to see the design aggregation process happen. Remember that the higher the performance you want, the more storage it will require (and the longer it will take to reprocess the aggregations). As you can see in Figure 46.44, you should select the I Click Stop option and stop the design aggregation when the optimization level starts to level off (somewhere between 75% to 88% optimization level). Any further optimization would really just waste storage space.

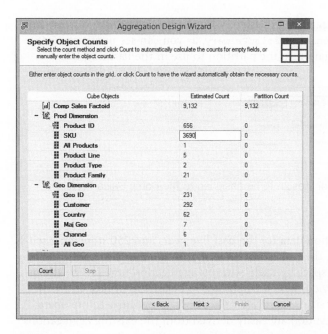

FIGURE 46.43   Specifying cube object counts for aggregation in the Aggregation Design Wizard.

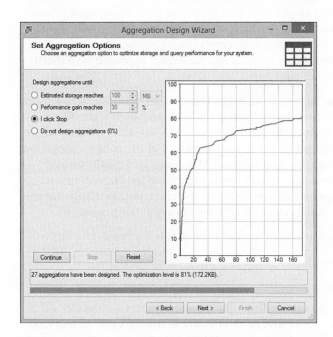

FIGURE 46.44   Setting the optimal storage and query performance level in the Aggregation Design Wizard.

When you are satisfied with the aggregation design, you simply click Next and name this design (the sample is named `AggregationDesignPrimary`, as you can see in Figure 46.45). You then assign this design aggregation to the partition to use in the Partition tab.

FIGURE 46.45 Resulting aggregation design to be assigned to the Comp Sales Factoid partition.

If your company has sales transaction data for the past five years and 250 stores that sell an average of 1,000 items per day, the fact table will have 456,500,000 rows. This is obviously a challenge in terms of disk space by itself, without aggregation tables to go along with it. The control that SSAS provides here is important in balancing storage and retrieval speed (that is, performance versus size). Aggregations are built to optimize rollup operations so that higher levels of aggregation are easily derived from the existing aggregations to satisfy broader queries. If a high degree of query optimization weren't possible due to limitations in storage space, SSAS might choose to build aggregates of monthly or quarterly data only. If a user queried the cube for yearly or multiyear data, those aggregations would be created dynamically from the highest level of pre-aggregated data. With disk storage becoming more and more inexpensive and servers becoming more powerful, the tendency is to opt for meeting performance gains. A recommended approach is to specify between an 80% and 90% performance gain here.

You are now ready to complete the Aggregation Design Wizard. The final step is to either process this aggregation or save your results and process it later. You should choose to process this aggregation now and then click Finish (see Figure 46.46). The Process Progress dialog appears immediately, and you get to watch the full extent of the cube's aggregation partitions being built (that is, populated). Aggregation SQL queries are actually created under the covers to populate all these aggregation levels (which are implementing your design levels). It's nice to have Microsoft dynamically create these complex queries for this critical performance optimization step so you don't have to worry about it yourself.

When this step completes, you have a fully optimized cube that is ready for data browsing. Congratulations!

Browsing Data in the Cube

You're ready to browse some cube data now. There are several ways to view data in a multidimensional cube. OLE DB for OLAP and ADO MD expose interfaces to do this kind of data browsing, and many leading vendors have used these interfaces to build front-end analysis tools and ActiveX controls. These tools should prove useful for developers of user interfaces in data warehousing and data mart projects. You can also easily browse a cube's data from either Visual Studio or SSMS or via any tool or facility that uses the multidimensional extensions of SQL (that is, SQL with DMX and MDX extensions).

FIGURE 46.46   Deploy and process the aggregation now to complete your cube.

To browse your newly created cube from SSMS, you fire up SSMS and connect to the SSAS server (Analysis Services server type) on which you deployed your cube. You should not connect to the SQL Server Database Engine. These are two completely different servers. When you are connected, you expand the Databases tree on the left until you can see the cube you created (Comp Sales, in this example).

> **NOTE**
>
> In Visual Studio, you can simply click the Browse tab when you are in the cube designer. All browse functionality uses the same plug-ins, whether you are in Visual Studio or SSMS. In either Visual Studio or SSMS, you can browse the cube (the entire cube with all dimensions) or just a dimension (using the dimension browser).

In SSMS (and if you have connected to Analysis Services), you just right-click the Comp Sales cube entry and choose the Browse option. As you can see in Figure 46.47, a multi-paned, drag-and-drop interface is your view into the data in your cube.

The middle pane lists all cube objects that you can drag into the data browsing pane (on the right). You can expand any of the cube hierarchy objects and see the actual member entries that are in your cube for each level. This capability is helpful when you want to further filter data in the browser (for example, focus on a particular SKU value or a particular geography, such as United States or France).

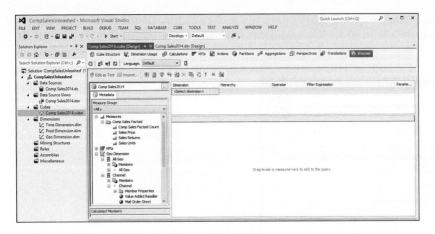

FIGURE 46.47   Browsing data in your cube in the SMSS data browser.

The data browsing pane is easy to use. For example, say that you simply want to see all product sales and product returns for SKUs across all geographies, for each year in the cube. To do this, you expand the measures object until you see all the measures in the Comp Sales cube. Then you drag Sales Units to the center of the lower portion of the data browsing pane (into the Drag levels or measures here to add to the query section in the lower right). You do the same for the Sales Returns measure. Data values (totals) for these measures are already displayed immediately. These are the total (aggregated) values for sales returns and sales units across all products, all geographies, and all times. To see the product breakdown of these data measures, you drag the SKU object within the product dimension object to this section. You immediately see the data measure values being broken out by each product SKU value. Now, you drag the Year Time object within the time dimension to this same area, just in front of the other dimensions and measures. You now see the data broken out by the years as shown in Figure 46.48.

Now, let's drag the SKU attribute in the Prod dimension into the top Select Dimension section above the data browser. This is the dimension-level filtering capability within the data browser. You now just select (via the drop-downs of each section within a filter specification) the level and type of filtering you want to do for the dimension you are working with. You can specify any number of filters within any number of dimensions. To just filter on a particular SKU (product), simply select it from the filter expression drop-down. In our example, we choose to filter on a SKU value Equal to (=) 'LT Slimline 1000' within the prod dimension. Figure 46.49 shows the fully specified Prod Dimension filter.

The data values you now see are only those for this particular product (SKU). You can also just add a dimension or dimension level to the filter portion within the data browser or just drag off dimensions, measures, or filters from the data browser if you don't want to use them anymore. This is very easy indeed. The cube browser shows you what your cube has in it and also illustrates the utility of a dimensional database. Users can easily analyze data in meaningful ways.

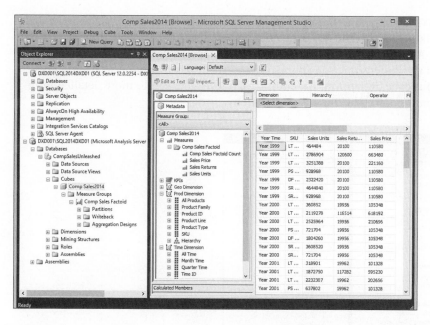

FIGURE 46.48   Sales units and sales returns for all SKUs by years in the SMSS data browser.

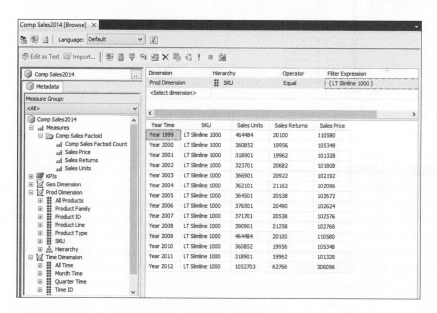

FIGURE 46.49   Complex data browsing with full dimensions and filtering in the SMSS data browser.

Both VS and SSMS allow you to browse individual dimension member data. You just right-click any dimension in the left pane of SSMS (for example, the time dimension) and choose Browse. As you can see in Figure 46.50, the dimension browser opens with All as the top node in the dimension. You simply expand the levels to see the actual member values within this cube dimension. Expanding each level gets you to more detailed information as you move down the dimension hierarchy.

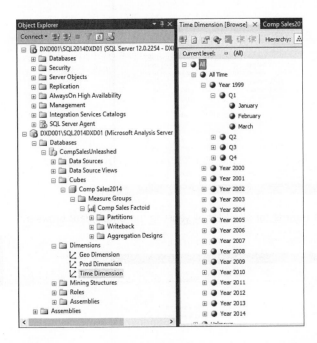

FIGURE 46.50   Browsing the Time dimension using SSMS.

Delivering Data to Users

SSAS provides a great deal of flexibility for building scalable OLAP solutions, but how do you present the data to users? The client-side components deliver much of the functionality of SSAS, using the same code base for the dimensional calculation engine, caching, and query processing. You can use the Pivot Table Service to manage client/server connections, and this is the layer for user interfaces to access SSAS cubes through the OLE DB for OLAP interface. ADO MD provides an application-level programming interface for development of OLAP applications. Third-party tools and Microsoft Excel and other Microsoft Office products will use the Pivot Table Service and PowerPivot to access cubes.

Slices of data that are retrieved to the client computer can also be saved locally for analysis when the client computer is disconnected from the network. Users can download the data in which they are interested and analyze it offline. The Pivot Table Service and PowerPivot can also create simple OLAP databases by accessing OLE DB–compliant data sources.

With the ADO MD interface, developers will be able to access and manipulate objects in an SSAS database, enabling web-based OLAP application development.

Many independent software vendors, such as Brio, Cognos, Business Objects, Micro Strategies, and Hyperion, work with Microsoft to leverage the rich features of these OLAP services. They offer robust user interfaces that can access SSAS's cubes. It is getting easier and easier to bring OLAP to the masses.

Multidimensional Expressions

The OLE DB for OLAP specification contains MDX syntax that is used to build datasets from cubes and is used to define cubes themselves. Developers of OLE DB OLAP providers can map MDX syntax to SQL statements or native query languages of other OLAP servers, depending on the storage techniques.

MDX statements build datasets by using information about cubes from which the data will be read. This includes the number of axes to include, the dimensions on each axis and the level of nesting, the members or member tuples and sort order of each dimension, and the dimension members used to filter, or slice, the data. (*Tuples* are combinations of dimensions such as time and product that present multidimensional data in a two-dimensional dataset.)

An MDX statement has four basic parts:

▶ Member scope information, using the WITH MEMBER clause

▶ Dimension, measure, and axis information in the SELECT clause

▶ The source cube in the FROM clause

▶ Dimension slicing in the WHERE clause

Expressions in an MDX statement operate on numbers, strings, members, tuples, and sets. *Numbers* and *strings* mean the same thing here as they do in other programming contexts. *Members* are the values in a dimension, and *levels* are groups of members. *Sets* are collections of tuple elements to further combine facts. If the dimension were time, a particular year, quarter, or month would be a member, and month values would belong to the month level. You use the dimension browser in SSAS to view members of a dimension.

The following example shows an MDX SQL expression:

```
WITH MEMBER [Measures].[Total Sales Units]
        AS 'Sum([Measures].[Sales Units])'
SELECT
    {[Measures].[Total Sales Units]} ON COLUMNS,
    {Topcount([ProdDimension].[SKU].members,100,
                    [Measures].[Total Sales Units])}
    ON ROWS
FROM [Comp Sales2014]
WHERE ([Time_Dimension].[All Time])
```

46

You can download this simple query against the Comp Sales cube from the code listings and sample databases folder at www.informit.com/title/9780672337291 (`TotalSalesQuery.mdx`). This query returns the sums of the sales units for products for all time periods. Figure 46.51 shows the full execution of this query within a query window of SSMS. Notice that the metadata for the cube is also made available in the center pane of SSMS, along with an MDX Functions tab that provides all the MDX functions that can be used. This feature is very helpful for building valid MDX queries within this environment. Also notice that the result set display area is very specialized in order to display multidimensional results.

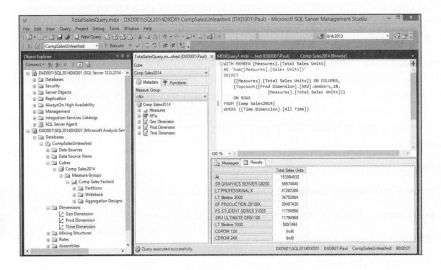

FIGURE 46.51   Comp Sales MDX query execution in SSMS.

This simple MDX statement shows the basic parts of a working query. In this case, measures are displayed in columns, and the product dimension members make up the axes of this multidimensional query and are displayed in rows. The display of multiple dimensions in rows like this is how the term tuple is used in the context of SSAS.

Much more could be said about MDX syntax, and a complete discussion of MDX could fill its own chapter. For more information, see the *Multidimensional Expressions (MDX) Reference*, which is available on the Microsoft website at http://msdn.microsoft.com/en-us/library/ms145506.aspx. It contains detailed information about MDX expressions and grammar.

ADO MD

ADO MD is an easy-to-use access method for dimensional data via an OLE DB for OLAP provider. You can use ADO MD in Visual Basic, Visual C++, C#, and Visual J++.

Like ADO, ADO MD offers a rich application development environment that can be used for multitier client/server and web application development.

You can retrieve information about a cube, or metadata, and execute MDX statements by using ADO MD to create cellsets to return interesting data to a user. ADO MD is another subject too broad to cover in detail in this chapter. Specifications for OLE DB for OLAP and ADO MD are available on the Microsoft website at http://msdn2.microsoft.com/en-us/library/ms126037.aspx and show these and other multidimensional data access capabilities.

Calculated Members (Calculations)

Remember from the Comp Sales requirements that there was an additional user need to see the difference between sales units and sales returns (sales units minus sales returns) to yield net sales. One approach is to use the SSAS calculated members (calculations) capability. This creates an expression against existing measures that will be treated the same as a measure. Basically, you need to complete the requirements for the Comp Sales cube by adding a calculation measure to this cube for net sales units.

To create a calculation, you go back to Visual Studio and the cube designer. Then you click the Calculations tab and create a new calculation measure called Sales Units NET with the calculation expression of (Sales Units - Sales Returns), as shown in Figure 46.52. Many functions are available for use that should meet your individual calculation needs.

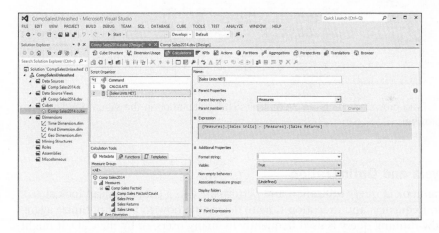

FIGURE 46.52   A new calculated measure of Sales Units NET in the Visual Studio cube designer.

This calculation fulfills the data measure requirements of Comp Sales. All that is left to do is to process the cube so others can use it. The following sample MDX query uses the newly created calculation measure:

```
WITH MEMBER [Measures].[Total Sales Units NET]
        AS 'Sum([Measures].[Sales Units NET])'
SELECT
     {[Measures].[Total Sales Units NET]} ON COLUMNS,
     {Topcount([ProdDimension].[SKU].members,100,
```

```
                        [Measures].[Total Sales Units NET])}
    ON ROWS
FROM [Comp Sales2014]
WHERE ([Time_Dimension].[All Time])
```

Figure 46.53 shows this new calculated measure listed in the cube's metadata pane. You can see how easy it is to use in the cube data browser. You might want to check the math, however, to make sure the calculation is correct. You can download this simple query against the Comp Sales2014 cube from the code listings and sample databases folder at www.informit.com/title/9780672337291(`TotalSalesNETquery.mdx`).

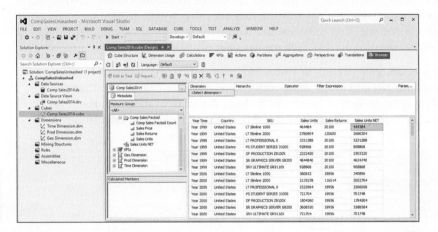

FIGURE 46.53   Data browsing using the Sales Units NET calculation in the Visual Studio cube designer data browser.

Query Analysis and Optimization

In SSAS, you can look at query utilization and performance in a cube. You can look at queries by user, frequency, and execution time to determine how to better optimize aggregations. If a slow-running query is used frequently by many users, or by the CEO, it might be a good candidate for individual tuning. A usage-based analysis capability can be used to change aggregations based on actual live queries that the cube must service. This adjusts aggregations based on a query to reduce response time. You start this wizard by right-clicking the cube's assigned aggregation within Aggregations and choosing the Usage-Based Optimization option. Figure 46.54 shows the Usage-Based Optimization Wizard splash page.

The Usage-Based Optimization Wizard allows you to filter queries by user, frequency of execution, time frame, and execution time. You see a record for each query you have run since the date you began, the number of times it was executed, and the average execution time, in seconds. This is like a SQL trace analysis of your OLAP queries.

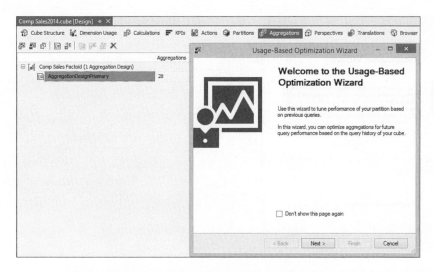

FIGURE 46.54   The Usage-Based Optimization Wizard.

Because aggregations already exist, the wizard asks whether you want to replace them or add new ones. If you replace the existing aggregations, the cube is reprocessed with this particular query in mind.

Generating a Relational Database

The examples you have worked with up to this point have been from a dimensional database that uses a star or snowflake schema (the CompSales2014 database). Very often, however, you create cubes based on requirements only and do not have an existing data source (or sources) to draw on at design time. After you complete your cube design, you can choose to generate a relational schema that can be used to retain (that is, stage) the cube's source data or that can be a data warehouse/data mart unto itself. Figure 46.55 shows the start of the Schema Generation Wizard for building a data warehouse/staging database from the top down.

> **NOTE**
>
> Designing dimensional databases is an art form and requires not only sound dimensional modeling knowledge, but also knowledge of the business processes with which you are dealing. Data warehousing has several design approaches. Regardless of which approach you take, having a good understanding of the approach's design techniques is critical to the success of a data warehouse project. Although Microsoft provides a powerful set of tools to implement data marts, astute execution of design methods is critical to getting the correct data—the truly business-significant business data—to the end users.

FIGURE 46.55   Generating a relational schema from the cube and dimension definitions.

Limitations of a Relational Database

Even using a tool such as SSAS, you face limitations when dealing with a normalized database. Using a view can often solve (or mask) these issues. In some cases, however, more complicated facts and dimensions might require denormalized tables or a dimensional database in the storage component of the data warehouse to bring information together. Data cleansing and transformation are also major considerations before you attempt to present decision makers with data from OLTP systems.

Cube Perspectives

A great feature in SSAS is cube perspectives. This is essentially a way to create working views of a complex cube that is focused on just what a particular user or group of users need. They don't need all the dimensions, calculations, levels, and key performance indicators (KPIs) that would otherwise be visible as part of a complex SSAS cube. Therefore, you need a method to tailor or limit a larger cube environment to be just what the users need and nothing more—hence, the cube perspective. Figure 46.56 shows the Perspectives tab in the cube designer. It allows you to easily customize a view (perspective), which is what will be deployed and referenced by a target user group. In this example, you are creating a new perspective called Comp Sales WITHOUT Sales Price, which excludes the extremely sensitive Sales Price data measure from any user given access to this perspective.

You can have any number of perspectives on a cube. Figure 46.57 shows what a cube user sees when trying to browse (or access) cube data via a perspective.

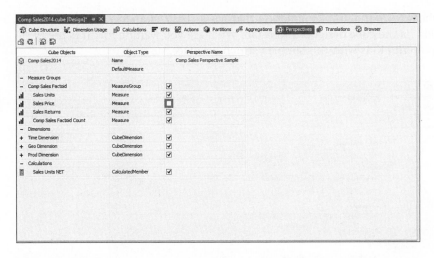

FIGURE 46.56   Creating cube perspectives within SSAS in the cube designer.

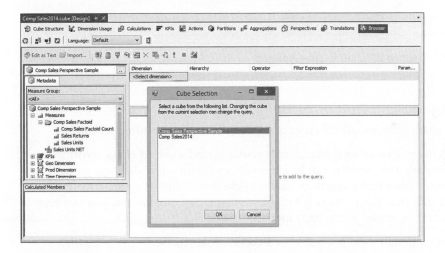

FIGURE 46.57   Browsing cube data via a perspective in the cube designer.

Using perspectives is a great way to simplify the user's life in an already-complicated OLAP world.

KPIs

Figure 46.58 shows another great capability in SSAS: creating embedded KPIs. Just like calculated members (regular calculations), KPIs allow you to define thresholds, goals, status indications, and trend expressions that become part of an OLAP cube. Each can then be graphically displayed in a variety of ways (for example, gauges, thermometers, traffic lights, trend indications such as up arrows, smiling faces). This is perfect for an executive dashboard or portal implementation that has its basis in an SSAS cube. You can easily access KPIs via the cube designer's KPIs tab. What are you waiting for? It is pretty easy to create powerful KPIs with this simple yet rich interface.

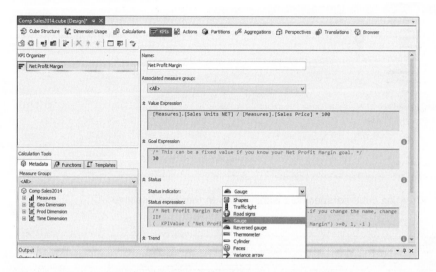

FIGURE 46.58   Creating KPIs in the cube designer.

Data Mining

With SSAS, a much more robust selection of capabilities for data mining is available.

Data mining is the process of understanding potentially undiscovered characteristics or distributions of data. Data mining can be extremely useful for OLAP database design in finding and recognizing that patterns or values might define different hierarchy levels or dimensions that were not previously known. As you create dimensions, you can even choose a data mining model as the basis for a dimension.

Basically, a data mining model is a reference structure that represents the grouping and predictive analysis of relational or multidimensional data. It is composed of rules, patterns, and other statistical information of the data that it was analyzing. These are called *cases*. A *case set* is simply a means for viewing the physical data. Different case sets can be constructed from the same physical data. Basically, a case is defined from a particular point of view. If the algorithm you are using supports the view, you can use mining models to make predictions based on these findings.

Another aspect of a data mining model is using training data. This process determines the relative importance of each attribute in a data mining model. It does this by recursively partitioning data into smaller groups until no more splitting can occur. During this partitioning process, information is gathered from the attributes used to determine the split. Probability can be established for each categorization of data in these splits. This type of data can be used to help determine factors about other data utilizing these probabilities.

This training data, in the form of dimensions, levels, member properties, and measures, is used to process the OLAP data mining model and further define the data mining column structure for the case set.

In SSAS, Microsoft provides several data mining algorithms (or techniques):

▶ **Association Rules**—This algorithm builds rules that describe which items are most likely to appear together in a transaction. The rules help predict when the presence of one item is likely with another item (which has appeared in the same type of transaction before).

▶ **Clustering**—This algorithm uses iterative techniques to group records from a dataset into clusters that contain similar characteristics. This is one of the best algorithms, and it can be used to find general groupings in data.

▶ **Sequence Clustering**—This algorithm is a combination of sequence analysis and clustering, and it identifies clusters of similarly ordered events in a sequence. The clusters can be used to predict the likely ordering of events in a sequence, based on known characteristics.

▶ **Decision Trees**—This classification algorithm works well for predictive modeling. It supports the prediction of both discrete and continuous attributes.

▶ **Linear Regression**—This regression algorithm works well for regression modeling. It is a configuration variation of the Decision Trees algorithm, obtained by disabling splits. (The whole regression formula is built in a single root node.) The algorithm supports the prediction of continuous attributes.

▶ **Logistic Regression**—This regression algorithm works well for regression modeling. It is a configuration variation of the Neural Network algorithm, obtained by eliminating the hidden layer. This algorithm supports the prediction of both discrete and continuous attributes.

▶ **Naïve Bayes**—This classification algorithm is quick to build, and it works well for predictive modeling. It supports only discrete attributes, and it considers all the input attributes to be independent, given the predictable attribute.

▶ **Neural Network**—This algorithm uses a gradient method to optimize parameters of multilayer networks to predict multiple attributes. It can be used for classification of discrete attributes as well as regression of continuous attributes.

▶ **Time Series**—This algorithm uses a linear regression decision tree approach to analyze time-related data, such as monthly sales data or yearly profits. The patterns it discovers can be used to predict values for future time steps across a time horizon.

To create an OLAP data mining model, SSAS uses either an existing source OLAP cube or an existing relational database/data warehouse, a particular data mining technique/ algorithm, case dimension and level, predicted entity, or, optionally, training data. The source OLAP cube provides the information needed to create a case set for the data mining model. You then select the data mining technique (decision tree, clustering, or one of the

46

others). It uses the dimension and level that you choose to establish key columns for the case sets. The case dimension and level provide a certain orientation for the data mining model into the cube for creating a case set. The predicted entity can be either a measure from the source OLAP cube, a member property of the case dimension and level, or any member of another dimension in the source OLAP cube.

> **NOTE**
>
> The Data Mining Wizard can also create a new dimension for a source cube and enables users to query the data mining data model data just as they would query OLAP data (using the SQL DMX extension or the mining structures browser).

In Visual Studio, you simply initiate the Data Mining Wizard by right-clicking the `Mining Structures` entry in the Solution Explorer. You cannot create new mining structures from SSMS. When you are past the wizard's splash screen, you have the option of creating your mining model from either an existing relational database (or data warehouse) or an existing OLAP cube (as shown in Figure 46.59).

FIGURE 46.59   Selecting the definition method to use for the mining structure in the Data Mining Wizard.

You want to define a data mining model that can shed light on product (SKU) sales characteristics and that will be based on the data and structure you have created so far in your Comp Sales Unleashed cube. For this example, you choose to use the existing OLAP cube you already have (from the existing cube method).

You must now select the data mining technique you think will help you find value in your cube's data. Clustering is probably the best one to start from because it finds natural groupings of data in a multidimensional space. It is useful when you want to see general groupings in your data, such as hot spots. You are trying to find these types of things with sales of products (for example, things that sell together or belong together). Figure 46.60 shows the data mining technique Microsoft Clustering being selected.

FIGURE 46.60   Using clustering to identify natural groups in the Data Mining Wizard.

Now you have to identify the source cube dimension to use to build the mining structure. As you can see in Figure 46.61, you choose Product Dimension to fit the mining intentions stated earlier.

FIGURE 46.61   Identifying the product dimension as the basis for the mining structure in the Data Mining Wizard.

46

You then select the case key or point of view for the mining analysis. Figure 46.62 illustrates the case to be based on the product dimension and at the SKU level (that is, the individual product level).

FIGURE 46.62   Identifying the basic unit of analysis for the mining model in the Data Mining Wizard.

You now specify the attributes and measures as case-level columns of the new mining structure. Figure 46.63 shows the possible selections. You can simply choose all the data measures for this mining structure. Then you click the Next button.

FIGURE 46.63   Specifying the measure for the mining model in the Data Mining Wizard.

As you can see in Figure 46.64, the next few wizard dialogs allow you to specify the mining model column usage (choose all but the count measure), the mining structure column's content and data types (use the defaults that were detected for most items unless we specifically describe something different), identify a filtered slice to use for the model training (you don't need to use this now because you want the whole cube), and finally identify the number of cases to be reserved for model testing or the percentage of data to be used for testing (we have specified a percentage of data for testing to be about 33%—this should be enough to get a good test going).

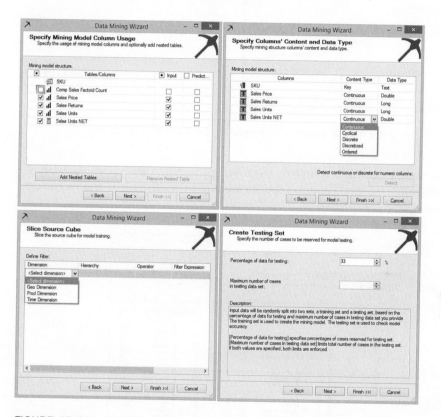

FIGURE 46.64   Specifying a column's content, slice filters, and model data training percentages.

The mining model is now specified and must be named and processed. Figure 46.65 shows what you have named the mining structure (Product Dimension MS) and the mining model name itself (Product Dimension MM). Also, you select the Allow Drill Through option so you can look further into the data in the mining model after it is processed. Then you click the Finish button.

FIGURE 46.65   Naming the mining model and completing the Data Mining Wizard.

When the Data Mining Wizard is complete, the mining structure viewer pops up, with your mining structure case-level column's specification (on the center left) and its correlation to your cube (see Figure 46.66).

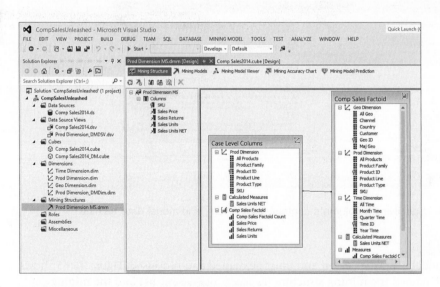

FIGURE 46.66   Your new mining structure in the mining structure viewer.

You must now process the mining structure to see what you come up with. You do this by selecting the Mining Model toolbar option and selecting the Process option. You then see the usual Process dialog, and you have to choose to run this (process the mining structure). After the mining structure processing completes, a quick click on the Cluster Diagram tab shows the results of the clustering analysis (see Figure 46.67). Notice that because you selected to allow drill through, you can simply right-click any of the clusters identified and see the data that is part of the cluster (and choose Drill Through). This viewer clearly shows that there is some clustering of SKU values that might indicate products that sell together or belong together.

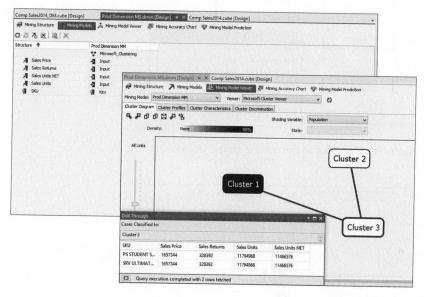

FIGURE 46.67   Clustering results and drilling through to the data in the mining model viewer.

If you click the Cluster Profiles tab of this viewer, you see the data value profile characteristics that were processed (see Figure 46.68).

Figure 46.69 shows the clusters of data values of each data measure in the data mining model. This characteristic information gives you a good idea of what the actual data values are and how they cluster together.

Finally, you can see the cluster node contents at the detail level by changing the mining model viewer type to Microsoft Generic Content Tree Viewer, which is just below the Mining Model Viewer tab on top. Figure 46.70 shows the detail contents of each model node and its technical specification of a report format.

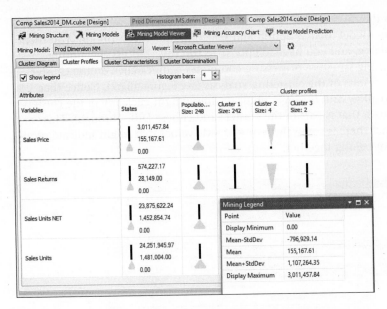

FIGURE 46.68 Cluster data profiles in the mining model viewer.

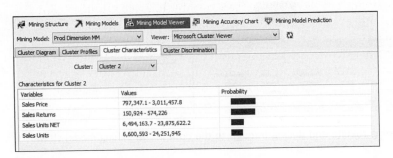

FIGURE 46.69 Cluster characteristics of the data values for each measure in the mining model viewer.

If you want, you can now build new cube dimensions that can help you do predictive modeling based on the findings of the data mining structures you just processed. In this way, you could predict sales units of one SKU and the number of naturally clustered SKUs quite easily (based on the past data mining analysis). This type of predictive modeling is very powerful.

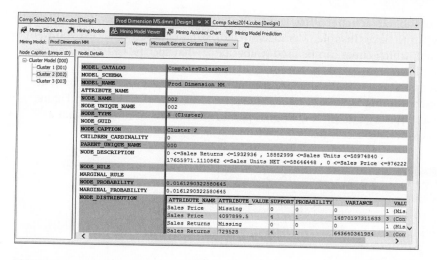

FIGURE 46.70   The Microsoft Generic Content Tree Viewer of the cluster nodes in the mining model viewer.

Security and Roles

Security is straightforward in SSAS. For each database or cube, roles are identified with varying levels of granularity for users. Roles are used when accessing the data in cubes. The process works like this: A role is defined, and then an individual user or group who is a member of that role is assigned that role. To create the roles you need for this data, you right-click on the `Roles` entry in the Solution Explorer and select New Role. Figure 46.71 shows the creation of a database role with process database and read definition permissions.

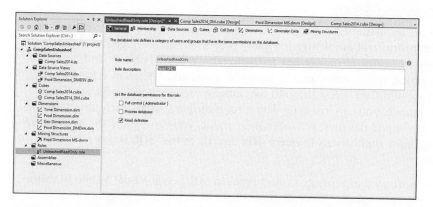

FIGURE 46.71   Creating a database role and permissions in the role designer.

46

The other tabs of the role designer allow you to further specify the controls, such as which members you want to have this role (Membership tab), what data source access you want (Data Sources tab), which cubes can be used (Cubes tab), what specific cell data the role has access to (Cell Data tab), what dimensions can be accessed (Dimensions tab), what dimensional data can be accessed (Dimension Data tab), and what mining structures are allowed to be used (Mining Structures tab). These are additive. As you can see in Figure 46.72, you can also specify full MDX queries as part of the process of filtering what a member and role can have access to.

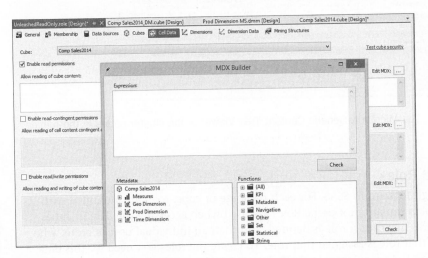

FIGURE 46.72   Specifying MDX-based filtering, using the role designer.

Tabular Models and SSAS

Tabular models are in-memory databases in Analysis Services. They use state-of-the-art compression algorithms and multithreaded query processor and leverage the xVelocity in-memory analytics engine to deliver fast access to tabular model objects and data by many client reporting applications such as Microsoft Excel and Microsoft Power View. Tabular models support data access through two modes: cached mode and DirectQuery mode. In cached mode, you can integrate data from multiple sources, including relational databases, data feeds, and flat files. In DirectQuery mode, you can bypass the in-memory model, allowing client applications to query data directly at the (SQL Server relational) source.

Tabular models are created as separate project types in SQL Server Visual Studio BI using tabular model project templates. You can import data from multiple sources and then enrich the model by adding relationships, calculated columns, measures, KPIs, and hierarchies. These tabular models can then be deployed to a tabular instance of Analysis Services where client reporting applications can leverage them easily. These tabular models can be managed in SQL Server Management Studio just like multidimensional models. They can also be partitioned for optimized processing and secured to the row level by using role-based security. OLAP and tabular are very different, though, and therefore require separate SSAS instance installations. At installation time, you have to pick one or the other.

SSIS

SSIS provides a robust means to move data between sources and targets. Data can be exported, validated, cleaned up, consolidated, transformed, and then imported into a destination of any kind. With any OLAP/SSAS implementation, you will undoubtedly have to transform, clean, or preprocess data in some way.

You can combine multiple column values into a single calculated destination column or divide column values from a single source column into multiple destination columns. You might need to translate values in operational systems. For example, many OLTP systems use product codes stored as numeric data. Few people are willing to memorize an entire collection of product codes. An entry of 100235 for a type of shampoo in a product dimension table is useless to a vice president of marketing who is interested in how much of that shampoo was sold in California in the past quarter.

Cleanup and validation of data are critical to the data's value in the data warehouse. The old saying "garbage in, garbage out" applies. If data is missing, redundant, or inconsistent, high-level aggregations can be inaccurate, so you should at least know that these conditions exist. Perhaps data should be rejected for use in the warehouse until the source data can be reconciled. If the shampoo of interest to the vice president is called Shamp in one database and Shampoo in another, aggregations on either value would not produce complete information about the product.

The SSIS packages define the steps in a transformation workflow. You can execute the steps serially and in combinations of serially, in parallel, or conditionally. For more information on SSIS, see Chapter 47, "SQL Server Integration Services."

OLAP Performance

Performance is a big emphasis of SSAS. Usage-based aggregation is at the heart of much of what you can do to help in this area. In addition, the proactive caching mechanism in SSAS has allowed much of what was previously a bottleneck (and a slowdown) to be circumvented.

When designing cubes for deployment, you should consider the data scope of all the data accesses (that is, all the OLAP queries that will ever touch the cube). You should only build a cube that is big enough to handle these known data scopes. If you don't have requirements for something, you shouldn't build it. This helps keep things a smaller, more manageable size (that is, smaller cubes), which translates into faster overall performance for those who use the cube.

You can also take caching to the extreme by relocating the OLAP physical storage components on a solid-state disk device (that is, a persistent memory device). This can give you tenfold performance gains. The price of this type of technology has been dramatically reduced within the past year or so, and the ease of transparently applying this type of solution to OLAP is a natural fit. It affects both the OLAP data population process and the day-to-day what-if usage by the end users. You should keep these types of surgical incisions in mind when you face OLAP performance issues in this platform. They are easy to apply, the gains are huge, and you quickly get a return on your investment.

Summary

This chapter discusses the OLAP approach, SSAS terms, and the tools Microsoft provides to enable OLAP cubes. It presents a mini-methodology to follow that should help you get an OLAP project off the ground and running smoothly. These efforts are typically not simple, and a well-trained data warehouse analyst, BI specialist, or data architect is usually worth his or her weight in gold because of the results (and value) that can be achieved through good OLAP cube design.

Sometimes it is difficult to engage end users and get them to use an OLAP cube successfully. Easy-to-use third-party tools can greatly help with this problem.

From an SSAS point of view, the ease of control of storage methods, dimension creation, degrees of aggregation, cube partitioning, and usage-based optimization are features that make this product a serious data warehousing tool. It is getting easier and easier to publish OLAP data via websites or other means. SSAS is truly the land of the wizards, but having a wizard lead you through a good OLAP cube design is critical. The wizards significantly reduce the expense and complexity of a data warehouse or data mart OLAP solution, enabling you to build many more much-needed solutions for your end users.

The next chapter, "SQL Server Integration Services," ventures into the very robust offering from Microsoft in regards to data enablement, manipulation, and aggregation for not only Analysis Services, but most other production platforms that require complex data transformations.

SQL Server Integration Services

Microsoft Integration Services is a platform for building enterprise-level data integration and data transformations. You use Integration Services to solve complex business problems by copying or downloading files, sending email messages in response to events, updating data warehouses, cleaning and mining data, and managing SQL Server objects and data. The packages can work alone or with other packages to address most of your complex business needs that involve data transformation. Integration Services can extract and transform data from a wide variety of sources, such as XML data files, flat files, and relational data sources, and then load the data into one or more destinations at the same time.

Integration Services includes a rich set of built-in tasks and transformations, tools for constructing packages, and the Integration Services service for running and managing packages. You can also use these Integration Services tools without writing a single line of code, or you can program the extensive Integration Services object model to create packages programmatically and code custom tasks and other package objects.

As you may be aware, SQL Server 2000's Data Transformation Services (DTS) was completely redeployed into and integrated with the Business Intelligence Development Studio (BIDS), Visual Studio environments, and SQL Server Management Studio (SSMS). This chapter describes the SQL Server Integration Services (SSIS) environment and how SSIS addresses complex data movement and integration needs.

SSIS focuses on importing, exporting, and transforming data from one or more data sources to one or more data targets. This is Microsoft's version of extraction, transformation, and loading (ETL) on steroids. Competing ETL products include Informatica, Talend, and many others, but Microsoft has simply bundled this functionality together with SQL Server, thus providing more reasons to purchase SQL Server and not have to buy any expensive competing products. Other Microsoft solutions exist for importing and exporting data (such as the Bulk Copy Program, bcp), but SSIS can be used for a larger variety of data transformation, workflow, FTP, notifications, and other purposes, and its strength is in direct data access and with complex data transformations.

Support for migrating or running Data Transformation Services (DTS) packages has been discontinued in this release. The following DTS functionality has been discontinued including using the DTS runtime, the Package Migration Wizard, nonsupport of DTS packages maintenance in SSMS, the Execute DTS 2000 Package task, and the Upgrade Advisor scan of DTS packages. Best to get off of DTS now!

If you still use the Bulk Copy Program (bcp), a section at the end of this chapter describes this legacy SQL Server capability. bcp is still the workhorse of many production environments and cannot just be discarded every time a new version of SQL Server comes along. We estimate that bcp will be around for years to come.

The alternatives to SSIS and bcp in the Microsoft SQL Server 2014 environment include replication, change data capture, distributed queries, BULK INSERT, and SELECT INTO/INSERT. This chapter helps you determine how and when to use both SSIS and bcp as opposed to these other alternatives.

What's New with SSIS

In SQL Server 2014, Microsoft hasn't changed much other than continuing to make SSIS into a much more comprehensive and robust data integration platform—with the emphasis on the word *platform*. The following are some of the highlights of SSIS 2014:

▶ A deployment model of deploying projects to the Integration Services server.

▶ Can now use server environments to specify runtime values for packages contained in a project.

▶ For SSIS projects, SSISDB catalog database is now the container for those deployments.

▶ Views, stored procedures, and stored functions to help in troubleshooting performance and data problems.

▶ Flat File connection manager now supports parsing of flat files with embedded qualifiers.

▶ The SSIS Designer is now smarter about re-mapping columns when a new data source is connected. Columns are re-mapped based on their name and data type rather than by lineage ID.

▶ You can install SQL Server Data Tools - Business Intelligence for Visual Studio 2014 side-by-side with SQL Server Data Tools (SSDT)

▶ Microsoft has made the Integration Services Merge and Merge Join transformations more robust and reliable.

▶ Integration Services now includes the DQS Cleansing transformation that enables you to more easily and accurately improve the quality of data.

▶ The ability to use SQL Server 2014's Change Data Capture technology from within Integration Services.

SSIS Basics

As the world becomes ever more data-oriented, much greater emphasis is being placed on getting data from one place to another. To complicate matters, data can be stored in many different formats, contexts, filesystems, and locations. In addition, the data often requires significant transformation and conversion processing as it is being moved around. Whether you are trying to move data from Excel to SQL Server, create a data mart (or data warehouse), or distribute data to heterogeneous databases, you are essentially enabling someone with data.

This section describes the SSIS environment and how it is addressing these needs. As mentioned earlier, the focus is on importing, exporting, and transforming data from one or more data sources to one or more data targets.

Common requirements for SSIS might include the following:

▶ Exporting data out of SQL Server tables to other applications and environments (for example, ODBC or OLE DB data sources or via flat files)

▶ Importing data into SQL Server tables from other applications and environments (for example, ODBC or OLE DB data sources or via flat files)

▶ Initializing data in some data replication situations, such as initial snapshots

▶ Aggregating data (that is, data transformation) for distribution to/from data marts or data warehouses

▶ Changing the data's context or format before importing or exporting it (that is, data conversion)

Some typical business scenarios for SSIS might include the following:

▶ Enabling data marts to receive data from a master data warehouse through periodic updates (see Figure 47.1)

47

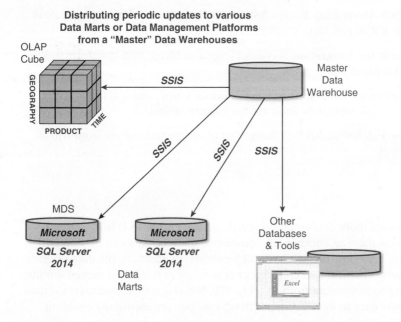

FIGURE 47.1   Distributing periodic updates to various data marts or master data management platforms.

- ⟶ Enabling Master Data Services (MDS) to receive data from an Enterprise data warehouse through periodic updates (also see Figure 47.1)

- ▶ Populating an Enterprise data warehouse from legacy systems (see Figure 47.2)

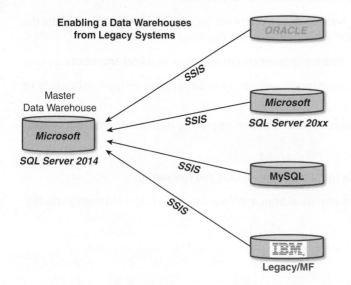

FIGURE 47.2   Populating a data warehouse from one or more data sources.

▶ Initializing heterogeneous replication subscriber tables on Oracle from a SQL Server 2014 Publisher (see Figure 47.3)

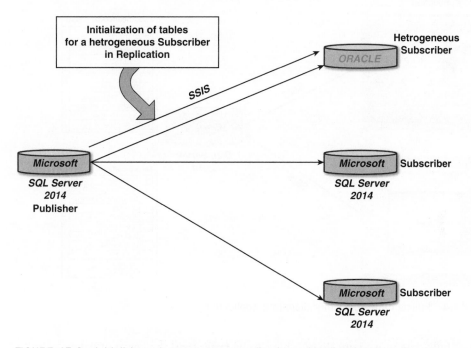

FIGURE 47.3   Initializing a heterogeneous replication subscriber (such as Oracle).

▶ Pulling sales data directly into SQL Server 2014 from an Access or Excel application (see Figure 47.4)

▶ Exporting static time-reporting data files (that is, flat files) for distribution to remote consultants

▶ Importing new orders directly or indirectly from a sales force automation or distributed sales systems

In general, you need SSIS if any of the following conditions exist:

▶ You need to import data directly into SQL Server from one or more ODBC data sources, .NET and OLE DB data providers, or via flat files.

▶ You need to export data directly out of SQL Server to one or more ODBC data sources, .NET and OLE DB data providers, or via flat files.

▶ You need to perform data conversions, data cleansing/data standardization, master data management, transformations, merges, or aggregations on data from one or more data sources for distribution to one or more data targets. You also need SSIS if you need to access the data directly via any ODBC data source, .NET or OLE DB data providers, or via flat files.

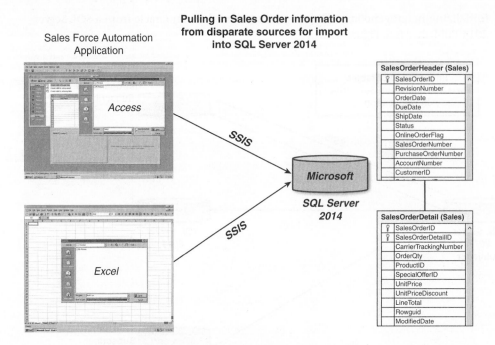

FIGURE 47.4   Pulling data from other disparate applications.

▶ Your bulk data movement doesn't have to be faster than the speed of light. Unfortunately, SSIS must utilize conventional connection techniques to these data sources. It must also create intermediate buffers to hold data during the transformation steps. This usually disqualifies SSIS on the high-performance side of requirements (at least for large, bulk data movements with any type of data transformations defined). However, many performance enhancements are present in SSIS and the data providers that are now supported, which has resulted in about a 50% increase in bulk data movement speeds. Alternative importing/exporting facilities such as bcp offer better performance but lack the flexibility of SSIS.

The following additional SSIS data sources and destinations are supported:

▶ An XML source for extracting data from XML documents directly

▶ Full insert and updating support for SQL Server Mobile destinations

▶ Reading and writing to Raw data files (sources and destinations)

▶ Creating an in-memory ADO DB recordset via a destination

▶ Direct access to a number of Analysis Services object destinations (for example, mining models, cubes, and dimensions)

▶ The ADO.NET DataReader source and destination for reading and writing to any .NET Framework data provider

SQL Server 2014 supports the following additional SSIS data transformations:

▶ Data warehousing operations, such as the Aggregate, Pivot, Un-pivot, and Slowly Changing Dimension transformations

▶ Enhanced text data mining via the Term Extraction and Term Lookup transformations

▶ Caching for Lookup transformations

▶ Enhancing data values from a lookup table via the Data Lookup and Fuzzy Lookup transformations

▶ The identification of similar data rows via the Fuzzy Grouping transformation

▶ Multiple downstream data flow component data distribution via the Conditional Split and Multicast transformations

▶ The merging and combining of data rows from multiple upstream data flow components via the Union All, Merge, and Merge Join transformations

▶ Extensive copying and modifying of column data values, using the Copy Column, Data Conversion, and Derived Column transformations

▶ Sample rowset extractions, using the Percentage Sampling and Row Sampling transformations

▶ Sorting of data and identification of duplicate data rows via the Sort transformation

Don't forget to convert to the project deployment model using the Project Conversion Wizard, edit your package configuration and data sources after upgrading, and potentially update execute package tasks to use project referencing and use parameters to pass data from parent packages to child packages. We recommend migration as rapidly as is feasible.

47

SSIS Architecture and Concepts

You can think of SSIS as a data import/export/transformation layer in the overall system architecture that you are deploying for at least most of your Microsoft-based applications and a few non-Microsoft applications (see Figure 47.5). SSIS allows you to "data enable" almost all the individual applications or systems that are part of your overall implementation, such as OLTP databases, multidimensional cubes, data warehouses, Excel files, Access databases, flat files, other heterogeneous database sources, and even XML and web services. The Integration Services object model includes both native and managed APIs for doing most SSIS work. This includes APIs for any of the SSIS tools, the command-line utilities, and even custom applications. SSIS Designer and the Integration Services Wizard both use the Integration Services object model. SSIS includes the integration service itself (that is, the service that manages all SSIS packages), the Integration Services object model, the SSIS runtime and runtime executables, and the data flow task (which has a data flow engine, source, transformation, and destination components).

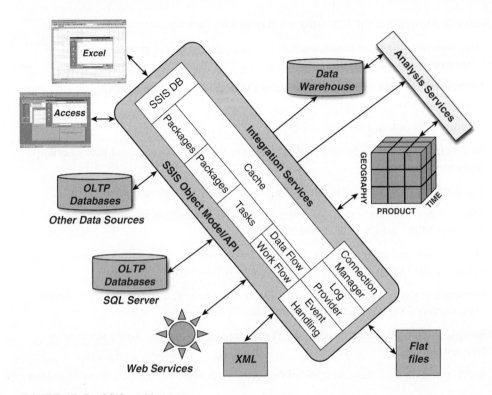

FIGURE 47.5   SSIS architecture.

Microsoft uses SSIS packages to implement any data movement/transformation. Basically, Microsoft treats SSIS packages as if they are managed code and requires that you create Integration Services projects and deployment utilities as part of managing these SSIS packages. In addition, separate Integration Services Connection projects can now be created to aid in connection and provider services. All in all, this is a very good approach that significantly reduces errors and allows you to go through a reasonably formal release to production (that is, development and deployment) cycle.

SSIS packages contain a collection of connections, control flow elements, data flow elements, event handlers, variables, and configurations. They take the form of tasks, containers, transformations, and workflows. SSIS packages go through one or more steps that are either executed sequentially or in parallel at package execution time. In a nutshell, when an SSIS package is executed, it does the following:

1. Connects to any identified data source

2. Copies data (and database objects, if needed)

3. Transforms data

4. Disconnects from the data sources

5. Notifies users, processes, and even other packages of events (such as sending an email when something is done or has errors)

The basic SSIS package consists of the following:

▶ **SSIS packages**—A package is a discrete, named collection of connections, control flow, and data flows that implement data movement/data transformation.

▶ **SSIS control flow and tasks**—One or more tasks and containers drive what the package does. You organize control flow based on what you want the package to do. Tasks are the actions taken to accomplish the desired data transformation and movement. A task can execute any SQL statement, send mail, bulk insert data, run a Visual Studio Tool for Application script (VSTA), or launch another package or an external program.

▶ **SSIS containers**—A container groups one or more related tasks that you want to manage together (and reuse together).

▶ **Workflows**—Workflows are definable precedence constraints that allow you to link two tasks, based on whether the first task executes, executes successfully, or executes unsuccessfully. Workflow containers are the wrappers for the tasks and are the means for the flow of control. A task can run alone, parallel to another task, or sequentially, according to precedence constraints. Precedence constraints are of three types:

   ▶ `Unconditional`—It does not matter whether the preceding step failed or succeeded.

   ▶ `On success`—The preceding step must have been successful for the execution of the next step.

   ▶ `On failure`—This constraint returns the appropriate error.

▶ **SSIS data flow**—The data flow identifies the sources and destinations that extract and load data; identifies the transformations that manipulate or enhance the data; and provides the paths that link sources, transformations, and destinations.

▶ **SSIS data flow task**—A data flow task creates, orders, and runs the data flows themselves, using a data flow engine.

▶ **SSIS transformations**—Transformations are one or more functions or operations applied against a piece of data before the data arrives at the destination.

In SSIS, everything is pretty much a task or a collection of tasks (one or more containers, tasks in containers), as you can see in Figure 47.6. Control flow determines the overall execution of the package and data flows that access the data, transform it, and write it. Precedence constraints determine the overall control flow—connecting the executables, containers, and tasks into an ordered control flow.

47

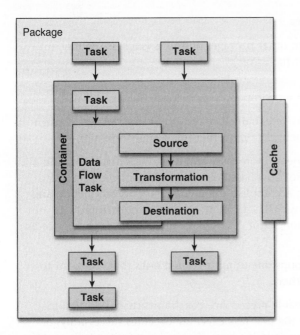

FIGURE 47.6   SSIS package elements.

SSIS also has several objects that extend package functionality:

▶ **SSIS event handlers**—These workflow tasks run in response to events raised by a package, task, or container. This is much the same as most programming languages, such as Java or C#. If a task (or package or container) has some issue (that is, raises an event), the event handler can be used to handle the issue appropriately. Typical events in data transformation processing that need to be handled with event handlers might include connections not being established, disk space issues, and so on. You can even have the event handlers write out emails or initiate other workflows.

▶ **SSIS configurations**—These objects are used to help parameterize many of the previously hard-bound characteristics of packages at runtime. When a package is run, the configuration information is loaded (updating the values of the package's properties), and then the package is run using the new configuration values (all without having to modify the package). SSIS configurations use the classic property/value pair paradigm to represent the properties that are to be configurable. Following are the varied methods of representing configuration files:

  ▶ **Configuration table in SQL Server**—This table stores configuration entries for use by the packages.

  ▶ **Environment variables (VARs)**—These can be referenced by the package.

  ▶ **Parent package VARs**—These can be used by child packages.

  ▶ **Entry in Registry**—The Registry can also contain the configuration values.

▶ **SSIS Logging**—Logging can be done from any task or package to write out any type of logging information desired. When a supplied logging provider is used, a package can provide a rich runtime history. Logs are associated with packages (that is, the reference point), but any task (or container) can write to any package's log. In this way, it is possible to have consolidated logs of a driver package with the full execution history of all child packages. The log providers (out of the box) write to a flat file (text file) or to SQL Server tables. Other custom logging providers can be used, though. You can log what you need to log—start date/time, end date/time, records transformed, errors, and so on.

▶ **SSIS variables**—SSIS has both system variables and user-defined variables. System variables provide runtime package object information to tasks or other packages. This information is helpful when you want to reference these system variables to help decide what to do next. (They can be used in expressions, scripts, and configurations.) User-defined variables are really for specialized variables that are not found as system variables and only have to be used within a package's scope. Again, these variables can be used in expressions, scripts, and configurations within a package.

SSIS packages can run other packages. This capability is very helpful when you want to granularly break out common data transformations for reuse by many different higher-level solutions (that is, higher-level packages that execute common-detail-level transformation packages).

> **NOTE**
>
> When an SSIS package is first created, it is given a globally unique identifier (GUID) that is added to the package's ID property and a name that is added to its NAME property. After these are created, they become part of the reference mechanism for the package itself. If you simply want to give an existing package a new NAME or ID value, you can do so directly or with the dtutil command-line utility.

You can also create packages that can be restarted at a point of failure, including restarting specific tasks within a package (and not all the tasks in a package). If a package had more than one data flow task and one completed but the others didn't, you could restart just the data flow tasks that had not completed without rerunning the ones that had worked fine. Long-running packages can also create checkpoints to provide milestones from which to restart. This capability will save many sleepless nights for the folks doing production support for data transformation processing.

SSIS Tools and Utilities

SSIS includes several tools that simplify package creation, execution, and management. These tools are available within the Visual Studio/Integration Services Project IDE (as shown in the drop-down list in Figure 47.7) or integrated into other component-based tools (such as SSMS, as shown in Figure 47.8).

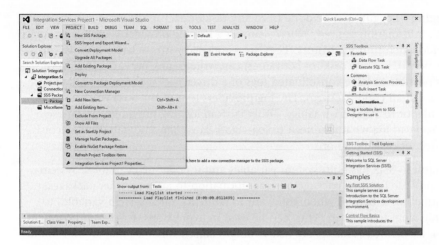

FIGURE 47.7   Package creation options within Visual Studio – Integration Services Projects:
New SSIS Package.

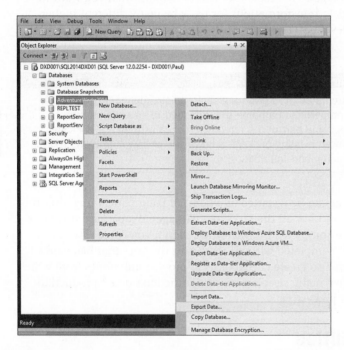

FIGURE 47.8   Invoking SSIS import/export data (package creation) capability from
within SSMS.

Also, within SSMS, you can organize packages; execute packages (via the Execute Package utility); import and export packages to and from the SQL Server `ssis catalog` database (SSISDB), the SSIS package store, and the filesystem (`.dtsx` files).

Following are the primary working environments for creating, managing, and deploying SSIS packages:

▶ **Import and Export Wizard**—You can use this wizard, available within Visual Studio/BI Development Studio, SSDT, or from SSMS, to build packages to import, export, and transform data or to copy database objects (see Figure 47.9). This is an easy way to create the basic SSIS packages that you need quickly and deploy them with great ease.

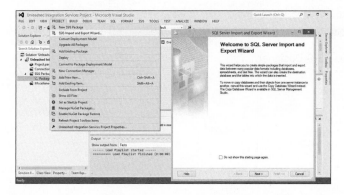

FIGURE 47.9   The Import and Export Wizard from Visual Studio – Integration Services Projects.

▶ **SSIS Designer**—This standard GUI is available in the Visual Studio/BI Development Studio, as part of an SSIS project. It lets you construct/manipulate packages containing complex workflows, multiple connections to heterogeneous data sources, and even event-driven logic (see Figure 47.10). This is the same IDE that all code development uses in the .NET platform, making it extremely easy to start developing right away.

▶ **SSIS command-line utilities**—A number of utilities are available within SSMS to aid you in running and managing SSIS packages (see Figure 47.11). One example is the Execute Package utility (which uses `dtexec` and `dtutil` command-line utilities). If the utility accesses a package that is stored in `ssis catalog` database (SSISDB), the command prompt may require a username and password.

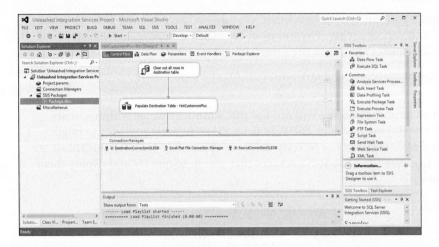

FIGURE 47.10   The Visual Studio SSIS Designer.

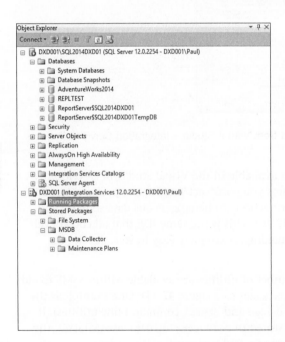

FIGURE 47.11   The Integration Services branch in SSMS.

▶ **SSIS Query Builder**—Query Builder provides an easy-to-use GUI for quickly developing SQL queries, testing the queries, and embedding them into the SSIS packages that you are developing. It is sort of like a mini SQL Query Profiler. It is entirely point-and-click oriented. Figure 47.12 shows the point at which you can invoke the

Query Builder as you add Execute SQL Task as part of an SSIS package to the SQL Task Editor.

Figure 47.13 shows the full Query Builder interface, along with a SQL statement that is being developed that retrieves employee information.

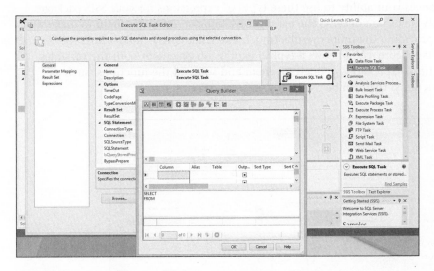

FIGURE 47.12   Invoking the Query Builder interface from the SQL Task Editor.

FIGURE 47.13   The Query Builder GUI for developing SQL queries.

47

▶ **SSIS Expression Builder**—You can use Expression Builder to develop the simple or complex expressions that get used by a package (the expression property of the package configuration). These expressions are things like validating working directories on a local machine where an SSIS package has been deployed and other complex evaluations that you want to have used by an SSIS package property. This graphical tool enhances your ability to use these types of expressions for your SSIS packages. It not only helps you develop the expressions, but also evaluates them to make sure they are providing the proper results (much like what Query Builder does for SQL statements). Figure 47.14 shows a typical expression palette of both the variables that can have expressions defined for them and some of the functions (such as string functions) that can be used with the expression.

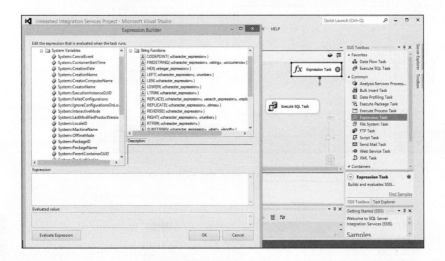

FIGURE 47.14   The SSIS Expression Builder GUI for developing expressions.

Finally, after you have created SSIS packages, you need to execute them via command-line execution, within SQL programs, or via other .NET–supported programming languages. You can easily do this by using the `dtexec` package execution utility. You manage packages by using the `dtutil` utility.

A Data Transformation Requirement

Let's consider a true-life data export requirement that is best served by using SSIS. The requirement is for a small business intelligence data mart (on SQL Server 2014) to be spun off each week from the main OLTP database (also on SQL Server 2014) that addresses a product sales manager's needs to see the total year-to-date business that a customer has generated. This data mart is merely a standard SQL Server database and tables that have been transformed (that is, aggregated) for a targeted purpose. As an option, the manager would also like to spin off an Excel version of this (or at least a comma-delimited .csv file for Excel), which will be distributed via email to all salespeople in the region. This overall requirement has been named "Hot Customers Plus" to indicate the emphasis on customers who are generating significant business for the company (and they will be customers who have made greater than $5,000 worth of orders). The offloaded data mart is on a separate machine from the critical OLTP system for all the right reasons; no reporting or ad hoc queries are done against the OLTP system. This process must be repeated on a weekly basis as a total refresh (see Figure 47.15). We use the `AdventureWorks2014` database for this example.

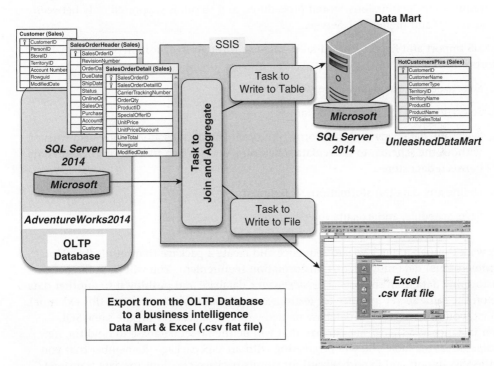

FIGURE 47.15   Creating a data mart and a comma-delimited flat file from an OLTP database using SSIS.

Essentially, order data from the OLTP database (contained in the `Customer`, `Product`, `Store`, `SalesTerritory`, `SalesOrderHeader`, and `SalesOrderDetails` tables) must be aggregated for every order for each customer. In addition, the total amount to be stored in the `YTDTotalSales` column in the data mart has to be extended out to reflect the summary of each product for each customer. The manager is also interested only in customers who are ordering products that total $5,000 or more. Although the requirements are many, SSIS should be able to handle all this with no problem.

So that you can get a good feel for the two main SSIS tool capabilities, this chapter takes you through generating the solution to this requirement using the SSIS Import and Export Wizard first, and then we walk through the same solution using SSIS Designer.

Running the Import and Export Wizard

The SSIS Import and Export Wizard is a streamlined interface solely used to generate SSIS packages for importing or exporting data. It is really quite powerful and provides an easy but sophisticated way to move data from or to any OLE DB, ODBC, or text source to another OLE DB, ODBC, or text source. You can also define simple or complex data transformations using the many options provided by the wizard. The wizard can also copy database schema, but the transfer of all other database objects, such as indexes, constraints, users, permissions, stored procedures, and so on, is supported only between SQL Server 7.0 and higher SQL Servers.

The SSIS Import and Export Wizard takes the user through five basic steps for both imports and exports:

1. Select/identify the data source (source).

2. Select/identify the destination (target).

3. Select the data copy and transformation type. The options are to copy data with or without the schema, to move data based on a query, or to transfer objects and data between data stores.

4. Define any data transformations, if required.

5. Save, schedule, and execute the package.

Let's walk through a quick wizard sequence and create a package that fulfills the "Hot Customers Plus" data movement/transformation requirement. You will be pulling and transforming data from the AdventureWorks2014 database and pushing it to another database on the same server instance for testing convenience (SQL2014DXD01 in this example). So, first, you need to create a database named UnleashedDataMart on the same SQL Server instance as AdventureWorks2014 that will be the target database to hold the new HotCustomersPlus table you will be creating with an SSIS package. Remember that you use the SSIS Import and Export Wizard for simple package creations (or data transfers). Nothing fancy here. To get started, here's what you do:

1. Fire up the SSIS Import and Export Wizard from within SSMS by right-clicking the database branch for the database from which you will be exporting data (as shown in Figure 47.16). If you select the Tasks option, you are given the option of either importing or exporting data. Actually, you end up invoking the same wizard in both cases, but we want to export data from this database, so choose the Export Data option.

2. Work through the steps of the SSIS Wizard. The initial step is identifying the source for the data. In this example, you need to choose a valid SQL Server and source database (in this example, DXD001\SQL2014DXD01 for the server and AdventureWorks2014 for the database). In addition, you must provide the appropriate access credentials (Windows authentication or SQL Server authentication) for this source SQL Server. You have a few options of exactly what access mechanism to use (to this data source). Choose the SQL Native Client connection method (see Figure 47.17).

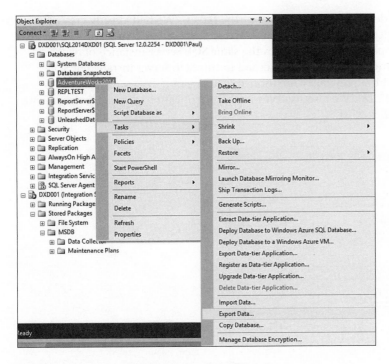

FIGURE 47.16   Invoking the Export Data Wizard.

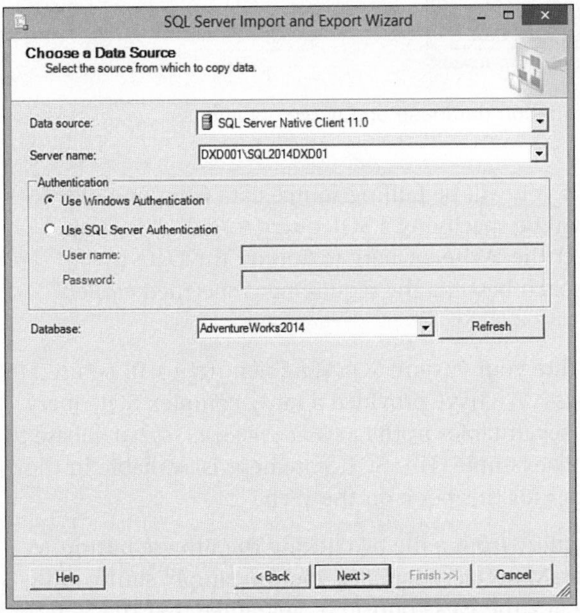

FIGURE 47.17   Identifying the SSIS source database and server locations.

3. Next is the data "destination" specification (the target). We had already created a new database (called `UnleashedDataMart`) for this purpose before we started and use that for this example. Our example uses the same SQL Server instance of DXD001\ SQL2014DXD01, using the connection method to this SQL Server instance of SQL Native Client, and the previously mentioned database of `UnleashedDataMart` (as shown in Figure 47.18). We also use Windows authentication. You are finished with this window, so click Next.

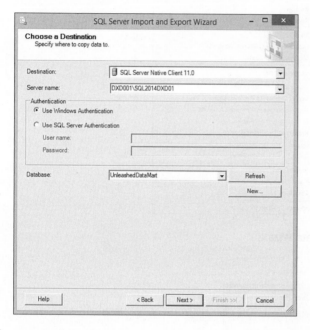

FIGURE 47.18   Identifying the SSIS destination database and server locations.

4. The next step in the wizard asks if you will be pulling source data from one or more tables (or views) or if you will be specifying a SQL query to pull data from the source. For this example, select the Write a Query to Specify the Data to Transfer option because this approach best fits the requirement specified earlier (see Figure 47.19).

5. In the next step in the wizard, create your custom SQL statement that will be used to select data from the source database. We have provided a fairly complex SQL query that selects (and joins) data from seven tables in the AdventureWorks2014 database to fulfill the data requirement for this example. This SQL Statement is available in the sample files and code listings folder for this book on the Web.

In this window, you can select a query from a file by clicking the Browse button to search for this file ("UnleashedDataMartQuery.sql"), or you can simply start coding directly in the window. You can click the Parse button to guarantee that the SQL statement has valid syntax and form (see Figure 47.20). You can test it (preview the data) in the next wizard step.

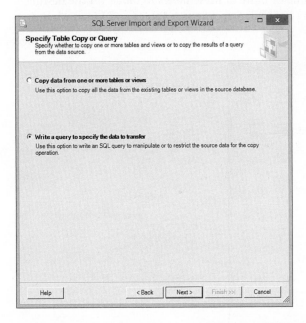

FIGURE 47.19   Specifying to use tables or a query for data transfer from the data source.

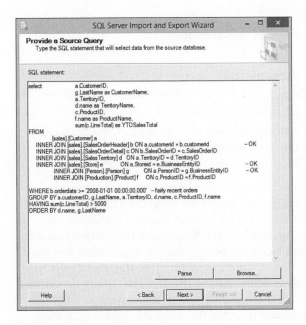

FIGURE 47.20   Providing a SQL query to select data from a data source.

However, if you chose to copy data directly from the database tables (and not use a SQL query), you would be provided a list of tables and views from the source database and would be able to map one or more of these tables to tables on the destination database. Figure 47.21 shows how this Select Source Tables and Views window would look.

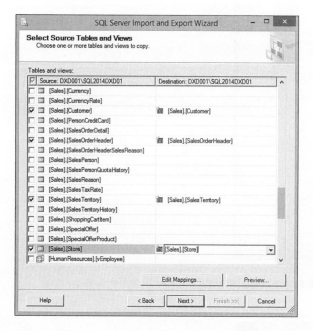

FIGURE 47.21   Mapping source tables and views to a destination.

6. Rename the destination table by changing [dbo].[Query] to [dbo]. [HotCustomersPlus] (see Figure 47.22). All subsequent references to this destination target will be what you want.

7. Click the Preview button on this dialog to actually execute the SQL query specified in step 5. Figure 47.23 shows the Preview Data results of the custom SQL query. Close this data preview window when you are finished reviewing the data results.

8. Click the Edit Mappings button to see the details of the column-level mappings being defined. At this point, you can further subset the columns, change data types, use precision or scale change, and/or not have a column mapped during the data transformation. As you can see in Figure 47.24, the Source and Destination columns are side-by-side, and when you click a column name, you can adjust what you want to occur (such as ignore or map to the column). In addition, at the object level, you can have the table created at the destination, have it truncate the data in an existing table at the destination, or append data to existing data at the destination. For this example, choose to completely drop and re-create the destination table each time. You are basically done creating the logic and data mappings for this simple data

transformation. It's not fulfilling the whole requirement, but it is doing the biggest part of the extract and transformation. We'll do the Excel part later from SSIS Designer.

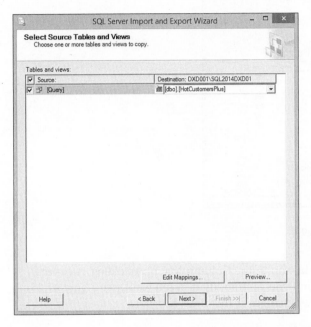

FIGURE 47.22   Source query mapping to a destination

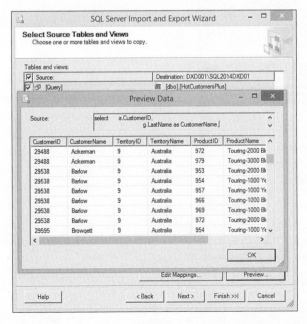

FIGURE 47.23   Previewing the data from a SQL query.

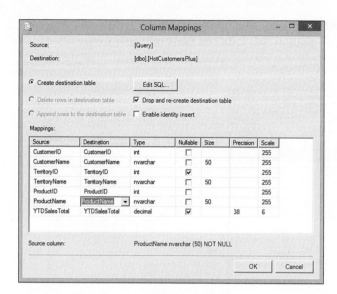

FIGURE 47.24   Column Mappings options.

9. If you want, click the Edit SQL button in the Column Mappings dialog. A CREATE TABLE SQL statement appears, and you can modify it if you want (see Figure 47.25). You don't need to do any further changes at this time, however.

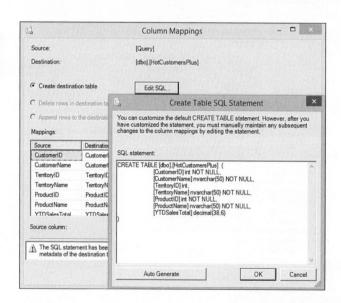

FIGURE 47.25   Manually customizing the default CREATE TABLE statement.

10. In the Save and Run Package dialog that appears, choose Run Immediately and Save SSIS Package. Save the SSIS package in SQL Server in the `msdb` SQL Server database (see Figure 47.26). It is also possible to save the SSIS package in a structured storage file at the filesystem level (in a `.dtsx` file).

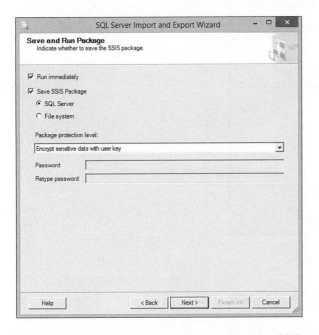

FIGURE 47.26   Options for executing and saving SSIS packages.

11. In the Save SSIS Package dialog, you specify the name of the package, description of the package, and location where the package is to be stored. For this example, specify the name "HotCustomersPlus" for the SSIS package, as shown in Figure 47.27.

12. When the SSIS Wizard displays the Complete the Wizard dialog, summarizing all the actions to be taken, carefully review the list and then click Finish when you are ready to proceed. After you click Finish, the wizard's execution console appears, as shown in Figure 47.28. This console shows all the steps taken, the status of these steps, and informational detail, as required. In Figure 47.28, note the `Copying to` `[dbo].[HotCustomersPlus]` table message that 4431 rows were transferred. There is an error in the step above the row copy that refers to the drop of the target table not being found. This was expected since the table never existed before; this was the first time it would have been created. Subsequent runs will not have this error. Following this particular "Copying" step are the simple post execute and cleanup actions for the package.

FIGURE 47.27   Saving a package for reuse.

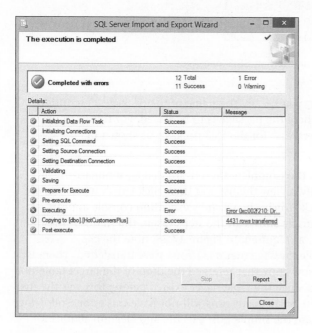

FIGURE 47.28   SSIS package initialization, saving, and execution.

If you would like, you can also query the system catalog table that contains the metadata for packages. In this case, the system table [msdb].[dbo].[sysssispackages] contains this metadata for SSIS packages starting with SQL Server 2005, and going forward. The following simple SQL query shows the metadata entry for the package you just created:

```
SELECT * FROM [msdb].[dbo].[sysssispackages]
```

The results look like this:

```
name              id          description           createdate
HotCustomersPlus  025EBC25... Weekly Data Mart updates...  2013-07-18 ...
```

Figure 47.29 shows the execution tasks for doing straight table copying (transferring) using SSIS packages of the tables to create a quick-and-dirty (refreshable) data mart. This method of spinning off data quickly is very useful, and it fits our requirements.

FIGURE 47.29   An SSIS package straight table copy/transfer example.

The SSIS Designer

The SSIS Designer is extremely easy to use and gives a user the flexibility of editing and manipulating any of the package properties in any order needed, as opposed to the strict sequential order of the SSIS Wizard. After you have mastered all the package concepts, you will find that you will be spending most of your time using the Visual Studio SSIS Designer instead of the wizard.

Because you have already created an SSIS package using the wizard, you can just open a version of this package (which you could have optionally stored in the filesystem as a .dtsx file when we were creating it within the wizard) with the SSIS Designer to see some of the SSIS Designer's capabilities (see Figure 47.30). So, create a new Integration Services project with a name like HotCustomersPlusProject. You then simply locate an existing .dtsx package file (such as HotCustomersPlus.dtsx) using the File Open option within SSIS Designer (as shown in Figure 47.31). We have supplied the filesystem version of this package (HotCustomersPlus.dtsx) for you in the sample files and code listings folder for this book on the Web if you want to use this one. Otherwise, you'd have to run through the wizard again but choose the store at the filesystem options for the package.

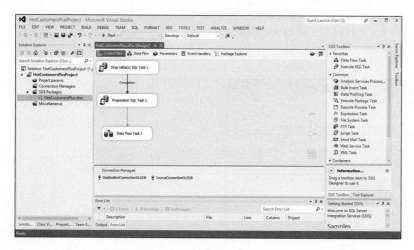

FIGURE 47.30   The SSIS Designer: opening the HotCustomersPlus.dtsx package.

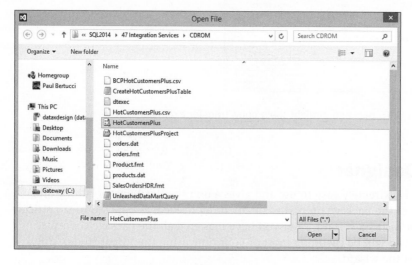

FIGURE 47.31   Opening the HotCustomersPlus.dtsx package.

As you can also see with the SSIS Designer, you are within the common Visual Studio IDE environment, which is used for any type of managed code. SSIS package creation is now just another option of a code development project. The SSIS Designer includes a main designer pane, a palette of toolbox icons to the left, an error pane on the bottom, the Solution Explorer to the right, and Properties pane in the bottom right. The Connection Manager sits directly below the designer pane, and there are four basic tabs in the designer pane for different purposes: the Control Flow pane is for overall task, control of flow, and constraint specification; the Data Flow pane is for generating and manipulating the data mapping and transformation itself; the Event Handlers pane is for defining what error handling needs to be part of this package; and the Package Explorer pane is for an overall view of the elements of the package.

The SSIS Designer is truly a point, click, and drag working environment. For anything in the workspace, you simply click the icon, such as DestinationConnectionOLEDB (in the Connection Managers pane) or the Preparation SQL Task icon in the Control Flow pane to see its properties, or you click the solid line between the Preparation SQL Task and Data Flow Task boxes to see the task constraints and workflow defined for the package.

You are about to modify this SSIS package to more fully support the HotCustomersPlus data mart and Excel comma-delimited flat file creation requirements because the wizard could not completely do that.

You will be using the SSIS Toolbox to the left to add functionality to this small SSIS package so that it will completely fulfill the data mart requirements outlined earlier. If you look back at Figure 47.30, you see this simple SSIS package within the SSIS Designer. Now, you can modify any existing tasks or add others to this SSIS package. If you recall, you originally set up this package to create a new destination table (on the other SQL Server instance) as the first step. Because you already executed this once, that table now exists (HotCustomersPlus on the destination SQL Server instance). Therefore, you need to change this first step to truncate the destination table instead of re-creating it each time. In addition, you need to add another task to this package that will spin off newly populated data (from the destination table) into an Excel comma-delimited flat file that can be easily distributed to the sales team. As you change this package, you also relabel the tasks to be more reflective of what they are doing (and not use the default task naming that the wizard used).

The sales team is waiting, so follow these steps:

1. You don't need the Drop Table(s) SQL Task 1 step because you will be utilizing the existing table created from the wizard. So, first just delete this step. You can use a truncate table approach to clear the existing table out before repopulating it each time the package is run. Simply right-click on the Drop Table(s) SQL Task 1 box and choose Delete. Confirm you want to delete it.

2. Right-click on the Preparation SQL Task 1 and choose Edit. The Execute SQL Task editor comes up, and in it you can see all aspects of this SQL task. Click the SQL statement property within this window (where you see the CREATE TABLE statement) and then click the ... icon to the right of the CREATE TABLE statement. This opens an editor window that contains the full SQL statement. Now, change this CREATE TABLE

statement to a TRUNCATE TABLE statement for the same table on the destination SQL Server instance:

```
TRUNCATE TABLE [UnleashedDataMart].[dbo].[HotCustomersPlus]
GO
```

This statement is clearly shown in Figure 47.32. After updating the SQL statement to a TRUNCATE, change the BypassPrepare True/False flag to False. Then click OK and click Parse Query to make sure the SQL statement is valid. You can now rename this task to something more appropriate by just clicking the Name property of this task and changing it to something like Clear out all rows in Destination Table. If all is well, click OK to exit this window. Now this task clears out the destination table before it repopulates it with new data instead of re-creating the destination table over and over.

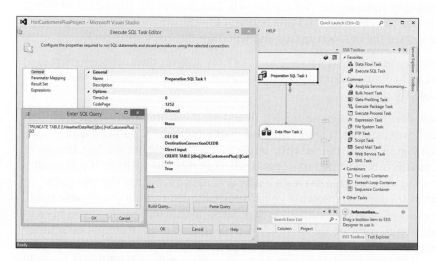

FIGURE 47.32   Modifying the Execute SQL Task from a CREATE TABLE statement to a TRUNCATE TABLE statement.

3. Rename the existing Data Flow task that pulls data out of the source SQL Server tables via a SELECT statement and populates the destination table. To do so, click this current data flow task and choose Rename. After you have renamed this task, right-click on the task and choose Edit or click on the Data Flow tab. You now see the multiple steps within this data flow. Right-click on the first step of the data flow (which has the name property Source - Query) and rename it Select Orders from AdventureWorks2014. Now, right-click on the destination task (Destination - HotCustomersPlus) and rename it Populate Destination Table - HotCustomersPlus, as shown in Figure 47.33.

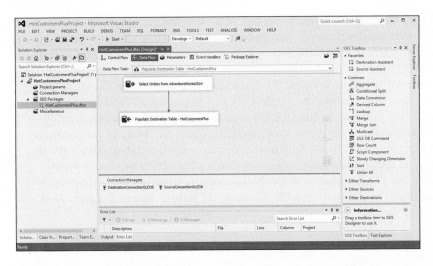

FIGURE 47.33   Modifying the data flow task within the SSIS package.

4. Now, we need to add a new data flow task that will read the sales order data from the destination table being populated from the source tables and then write out an Excel flat file with this new data. From the Control Flow tab of this SSIS package, drag a new data flow task (from the SSIS Toolbox on the right) out to the Control Flow designer pane and then modify its name property to be Read from Destination Table, Populate Excel Flat File, as shown in Figure 47.34.

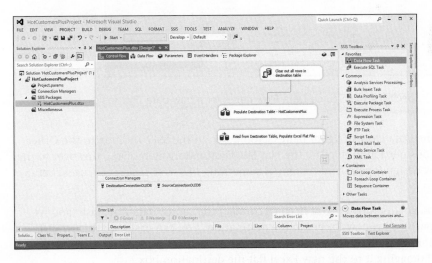

FIGURE 47.34   Creating a new data flow task to write data out to an Excel flat file.

5. Click the Data Flow tab, and you are in the Data Flow designer pane. Also note that the SSIS Toolbox entries change when you click this tab (they are now all the data flow task items). Drag an OLE DB Source item from the SSIS Toolbox over to the Data Flow designer pane (under Other Sources). You will use this to get the data from the destination table. Rename this Data Flow step something like `Pull data from Destination Table` and then right-click this new `Data Flow` source task and choose Edit. This puts you in the OLE DB Source Editor, where you can identify which connection manager to use (`DestinationConnectionOLEDB`, in this example) and what table you want to get data from (`HotCustomersPlus` table). You want the whole table, so specify the Table or View option for the access mode (see Figure 47.35). Click the Preview button at the bottom of this editor to verify that you will get all data from the destination table. Clicking OK returns you to the Data Flow designer pane.

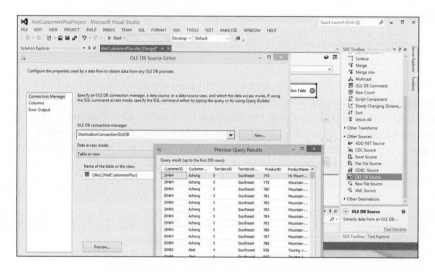

FIGURE 47.35   Specifying the Source Data Flow items for a new data flow task.

6. Back in the Data Flow designer pane, scroll down in the SSIS Toolbox to the Other Destinations portion and locate the Flat File Destinations item. Drag this over to the Data Flow designer pane and rename it something like `Write data to Excel Flat file`.

7. Before you go any further, you need to connect the source data flow task (and its data output) to this new Excel flat file destination. You can easily do this by just clicking the source data flow task's outbound arrow (that is just below the box and is blue) and dragging it to the new Excel flat file destination box.

   A full arrow is redrawn that connects these two data flow tasks (as you can see in Figure 47.36).

FIGURE 47.36   Connecting the data source to the data destination for the new data flow task.

8. Right-click this new data flow task item (Excel Flat file Destination) and choose Edit. This again puts you in an editor where you can specify the flat file destination file properties you want. This starts with identifying the connection manager and the flat file to be used. Click New here and choose the Delimited format for the destination flat file and click OK. Now, specify a location and filename for the destination flat file (`HotCustomersPlus.csv`). Figure 47.37 shows this complete flat file destination specification. Click the Preview button to make sure this data will be retrieved properly (column names appear across the top of the preview dialog; because the file is empty, no data shows).

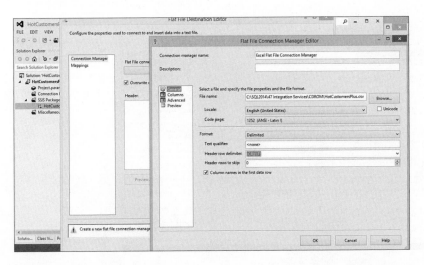

FIGURE 47.37   Specifying the flat file destination data flow items for a new data flow task.

You can also click the Mappings option in the Flat File Destination Editor dialog. As you can see in Figure 47.38, each of the columns in the source table (the HotCustomersPlus table) will be mapped, one to one, to the flat file columns with the same names.

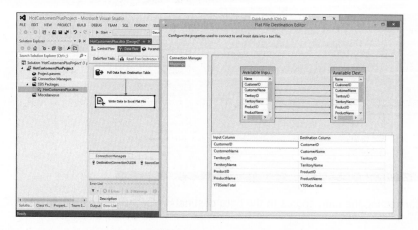

FIGURE 47.38   Source and destination column mappings.

9. Return to the Control Flow pane of the SSIS package and connect the new data flow task to the prior one. You do this by clicking the original data flow task and grabbing its control of flow arrow beneath the box and dragging it to the new data flow task you just created, as shown in Figure 47.39. Note that the Flat File Destination connection manager now appears under the connection manager pane, and you should have zero errors in the error list. At this point, save the package by clicking the disk icon or selecting File, Save.

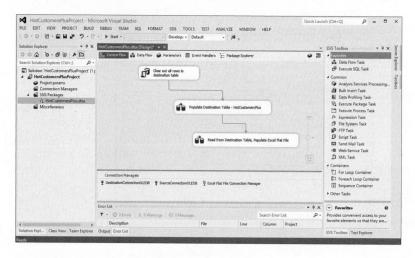

FIGURE 47.39   Control of flow between the old data flow and new data flow tasks.

10. To execute the package, right-click the `.dtsx` file within Visual Studio, choose Execute Package, and the package executes and shows detail step processing information of all results in the execution Results pane, as shown in Figure 47.40. That's it: You have populated the data mart and created data in a flat file for distribution to the sales team. You can deploy this in an Integration Services catalog on a SQL Server instance of your choice or simply use the package execution utility to execute it from a command line anytime you want.

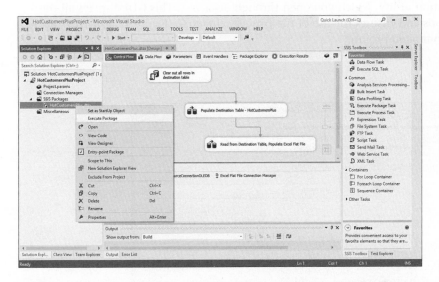

FIGURE 47.40   Executing the SSIS package from within Visual Studio.

> **NOTE**
>
> You could also execute this new package by using the `dtexec` utility (the Package Execution Utility) at a command prompt:
>
> ```
> C:> dtexec /FILE "C:\HotCustomerPlus.dtsx"
> ```

The Package Execution Utility

The `dtsrun` utility in SQL Server 2000 is no longer used within SQL Server 2014. It has been replaced by the `dtexec` utility, which is bigger and better and has more options and values to serve your every SSIS package execution need. Before you begin to use the `dtexec` utility, you should execute it at a command prompt with the help option set only and pipe the results into a text file:

```
c:> dtexec /? > dtexec.txt
```

You will quickly see all the main options and how similar this is to dtsrun (in SQL Server 2000). Some dtsrun command-line options have direct dtexec equivalents, such as the options for providing a server name or package name or for setting the value of a variable. Other dtsrun command-line options don't have direct dtexec equivalents. In addition, some dtexec command-line options support features in SSIS, such as the options to pass in connection strings and manage checkpoints.

You can create new command-line dtexec executions visually with the assistance of the Package Execution utility, which you open through dtexecui. This GUI displays all the available options and ensures the use of the correct syntax (see Figure 47.41). You start it up from the command prompt:

```
c:> dtexecui
```

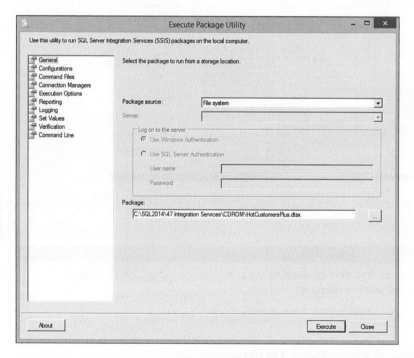

FIGURE 47.41   The user interface for executing and configuring SSIS packages.

Using this Package Execution utility is really the best way to create new command-line executions for SSIS packages and to run them easily. Figure 47.42 shows the Package Execution Progress console during a package execution. You can choose to stop the execution from here.

When you double-click any filesystem-stored SSIS package (that is, .dtsx file), you are always placed in this dtexecui environment (just as you automatically start up Microsoft Word when you double-click a Word document).

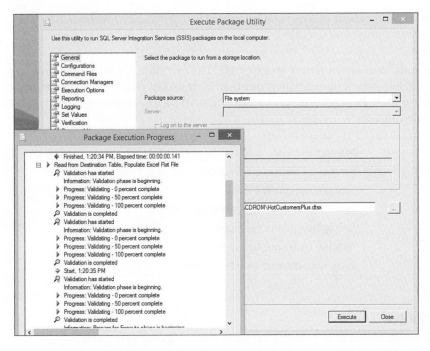

FIGURE 47.42   The Package Execution Progress console in the Execute Package utility.

The `dtexec` Utility

You use the `dtexec` command-line utility to configure and execute SSIS packages. The
`dtexec` utility provides access to all the package configuration and execution features, such
as connections, properties, variables, logging, and progress indicators. The `dtexec` utility
lets you load packages from three sources:

▶ A Microsoft SQL Server database

▶ The SSIS service (package store)

▶ The filesystem itself

The `dtexec` utility proceeds through four phases as it executes:

1. **Command sourcing phase**—The command prompt reads the list of options and
   arguments specified. All subsequent phases are skipped if a `/?` or `/H[ELP]` option is
   encountered.

2. **Package-loading phase**—The package specified by the `/SQL`, `/FILE`, or `/DTS` option is
   loaded.

3. **Configuration phase**—These options are processed in the following order: process
   options that set package flags, variables, and properties; process options that verify
   the package version and build; and process options that configure the runtime
   behavior of the utility, such as reporting.

4. Validation and execution phase—The package is run or validated without running if the /VALIDATE option was specified.

When a package runs, dtexec can return an exit code. The exit code is used to populate the ERRORLEVEL variable—the value of which can then be tested in conditional statements or branching logic within an operating system batch file. The dtexec utility can set the following exit code values:

Exit Code Value	Description
0	Successful package execution.
1	Package execution failure.
3	User-canceled package execution.
4	Package could not be found.
5	Package could not be loaded.
6	Utility encountered an internal error.

Running Packages

The dtexec options are additive. Depending on what you are trying to do, you are able to string one or more options and their values together in the following form:

```
dtexec /option [value] [/option [value]] ...
```

To show available options for dtexec, you use '/?' or '/H' or '/Help'. Alternatively, you can see the details for a particular option by using the available options indicator followed by the option name ('/?' [option name]). This invokes SQL Server Books online for that particular option. Note that a dash (-) may be substituted for / in this command.

The dtexec package execution options include the following:

▶ **/~Ca[llerInfo]**—This option specifies additional information for a package execution. Typically used when packages are run using SQL Server Agent.

▶ **/~CheckF[ile] filespec**—This option sets the CheckpointFileName property on the package to the path and file specified in filespec. This file is used when the package restarts.

▶ **/~CheckP[ointing] {on\off}**—The value on specifies that a failed package is to be rerun. When the failed package is rerun, the runtime engine uses the checkpoint file to restart the package from the point of failure. The default value is on if the option is declared without a value. Package execution fails if the value is set to on and the checkpoint file cannot be found. If this option is not specified, the value set in the package is retained.

> **NOTE**
>
> Using the /CheckPointing on option of dtexec is equivalent to setting the SaveCheckpoints property of the package to True and the CheckpointUsage property to Always.

▶ **/~Com[mandFile] filespec**—This option specifies that during the command sourcing phase of the utility, the file specified in filespec is opened, and options from the file are read until the EOF is found in the file. filespec is a text file that contains additional dtexec command options. The filespec argument specifies the filename and path of the command file to associate with the execution of the package.

▶ **/~Conf[igFile] filespec**—This option specifies a configuration file to extract values from. Using this option, you can set a runtime configuration that differs from the configuration specified for the package at design time.

▶ **/~Conn[ection] id_or_name;connection_string [[;id_or_name;connection_string]...]**—This option specifies the connection manager name or GUID and the specific connection string to use. This option requires that both parameters be specified.

▶ **/~Cons[oleLog] [[displayoptions];[list_options;src_name_or_guid]...]**—This option displays specified log entries to the console during package execution.

The displayoptions values are N (name), C (computer), O (operator), S (source name), G (source GUID), X (execution GUID), M (message), and T (time start and end).

One list_options value is I, which specifies the inclusion list. With this value set, only the source names or GUIDs that are specified are logged. The value E specifies the exclusion list. With this value set, the source names or GUIDs that are specified are not logged. The src_name_or_guid parameter specified for inclusion or exclusion is an event name, a source name, or a source GUID.

▶ **/~D[ts]package_path**—This option is used to load a package from the SSIS package store. The package_path argument specifies the relative path of the SSIS package, starting at the root of the SSIS package store, and includes the name of the SSIS package. The /DTS option cannot be used together with the /File or /SQL option.

▶ **/~De[crypt] password**—This option provides the decryption password used when you load a package with password encryption.

▶ **/~Dump error code**—This option creates the debug dump files, .mdmp and .tmp.

▶ **/~DumpOnError**—(Optional) Creates the debug dump files when any error occurs.

▶ **/~Env[reference] environment reference ID**—Sets the environment reference (ID) that is used by the package execution, for a package that is deployed to the Integration Services server. The parameters configured to bind to variables will use the values of the variables that are contained in the environment. You use the /Env[Reference] option together with the /ISServer and the /Server options. This parameter is used by SQL Server Agent.

47

▶ **/~F[ile] filespec**—This option is used to load a package saved at the filesystem level. The `filespec` argument specifies the path and filename of the package.

▶ **/~H[elp]**—This option is used to display help for the options. DTEXEC starts SQL Server Books Online.

▶ **/~ISServer packagepath**—Runs a package that is deployed to the Integration Services server.

```
\<catalog name>\<folder name>\<project name>\package filename
```

▶ **/~L[ogger] classid_orprogid;configstring**—This option associates one or more log providers with the execution of an SSIS package. The `classid_orprogid` parameter specifies the log provider and can be specified as a class GUID. `configstring` is the string used to configure the log provider.

Following are the available log providers:

```
Text file:
 ProgID: DTS.LogProviderTextFile.1
 ClassID: {59B2C6A5-663F-4C20-8863-C83F9B72E2EB}
SQL Server Profiler:
 ProgID: DTS.LogProviderSQLProfiler.1
 ClassID: {5C0B8D21-E9AA-462E-BA34-30FF5F7A42A1}
SQL Server:
 ProgID: DTS.LogProviderSQLServer.1
 ClassID: {6AA833A1-E4B2-4431-831B-DE695049DC61}
Windows Event Log:
 ProgID: DTS.LogProviderEventLog.1
 ClassID: {97634F75-1DC7-4F1F-8A4C-DAF0E13AAA22}
XML File:
 ProgID: DTS.LogProviderXMLFile.1
 ClassID: {AFED6884-619C-484F-9A09-F42D56E1A7EA}
```

▶ **/~M[axConcurrent] concurrent_executables**—This option is used to identify the number of executable files the package can run concurrently. The value specified must be either a non-negative integer or -1. With a value of -1, SSIS allows a maximum number of concurrently running executables equal to the total number of processors on the computer executing the package, plus two.

▶ **/~Pack[age] PackageName**—This option specifies the package that is to be executed.

▶ **/~P[assword] password**—This option is used together with the /User option to retrieve the package from SQL Server. If the /Password option is omitted and the /User option is used, a blank password is used.

▶ **/~Par[ameter] [$Package:....]**—This option specifies package parameters and is used only with the /ISServer option.

▶ **/~Proj[ect] ProjectFile**—This option specifies the project from which to retrieve the package that is to be executed. The `ProjectFile` argument specifies the `.ispac` filename.

▶ **/~Rem comment**—This option creates a comment on the command prompt or in command files. The comment is a string that must be enclosed in quotation marks, and it must contain no whitespace.

▶ **/~Rep[orting] level [;event_guid_or_name[;event_guid_or_name[...]]**—This option identifies what types of messages to report. Available reporting option levels are N (no reporting), E (errors are reported), W (warnings are reported), I (informational messages are reported), C (custom events are reported), D (data flow task events are reported), P (progress is reported), and V (verbose reporting; all details of each type). If the /Reporting option is not specified, the default level is E, W, and P.

▶ **/~Res[tart] {deny | force | ifPossible}**—This option enables you to set a new value for the `CheckpointUsage` property on the package. The possible values are Deny (sets the `CheckpointUsage` property to DTSCU_NEVER), Force (sets the `CheckpointUsage` property to DTSCU_ALWAYS), and ifPossible (sets the `CheckpointUsage` property to DTSCU_IFEXISTS).

▶ **/~Set propertyPath;value**—This option overrides the configuration of a variable, property, container, log provider, Foreach enumerator, or connection within a package. When this option is used, /SET changes the `propertyPath` argument to the value specified. You can specify more than one /SET option at a time.

▶ **/~Ser[ver] server**—This option identifies the name of the server from which to retrieve the package. If you do not specify the /Server option, the package execution is attempted against the local server. The /Ser[ver] option is required when the /ISServer option is specified

▶ **/~SQ[L] package_path**—This option is used to load a package stored in SQL Server (in the msdb database).

▶ **/~Su[m]**—This option displays the incremental counter that contains the number of rows that will be received by the next package component.

▶ **/~U[ser] user_name**—This option identifies the SQL Server user ID needed to retrieve the package.

▶ **/~Va[lidate]**—This option is used to complete the validation phase of package execution only. The package is not executed.

▶ **/~VerifyB[uild] major[;minor[;build]]**—This option is a verification of the build number of a package against the build numbers specified during the verification phase in the major, minor, and build arguments. If a mismatch occurs, the package does not execute. These values are long integers.

▶ **/~VerifyP[ackageID] packageID**—This option verifies the GUID of the package to be executed by comparing it to the value specified in the package_id argument.

47

▶ **/~VerifyS[igned]**—If specified, this option causes the package to fail if the package is not signed.

▶ **/~VerifyV[ersionID] versioned**—This option verifies the version GUID of a package to be executed by comparing it to the value specified in the `version_id` argument during the package validation phase.

▶ **/~VLog [Filespec]**—If specified, writes all package events to the log provider. If you provide a path and file name, it will log to a text file.

▶ **/~W[arnAsError]**—This option causes the package to consider a warning as an error. In other words, the package fails if a warning occurs during validation. If no warnings occur during validation and the `/Validate` option is not specified, the package is executed.

▶ **/~X86**—Causes SQL Server Agent to run the package in 32-bit mode on a 64-bit computer.

Running Package Examples

To execute an SSIS package saved to SQL Server using Windows authentication, you use the following code:

```
dtexec /SQL UnleashedPackage1SQL /SER DXD001\SQL2014DXD01
```

To execute an SSIS package saved to the package store (on the filesystem), you use the following code:

```
dtexec /DTS "\File System\UnleashedPackage99PS"
```

To execute an SSIS package saved in the filesystem, you use the following code:

```
C:> dtexec /FILE "C:\HotCustomerPlus.dtsx"
    /MAXCONCURRENT " -1 " /CHECKPOINTING OFF  /REPORTING EWCDI
```

Figure 47.43 shows the command prompt and subsequent execution of the `HotCustomersPlus.dtsx` SSIS package. Now, the package can be set up for regular batch execution using SQL Agent or any scheduling software.

To execute an SSIS package saved in the filesystem and specify logging options, you use the following code:

```
C:> dtexec /FILE "C:\HotCustomerPlus.dtsx"
    /l "DTS.LogProviderTextFile;c:\log.txt"
```

To execute a package that uses Windows authentication and is saved to the default local instance of SQL Server, and to verify the version before it is executed, you use the following code:

```
dtexec /sq UnleashedPackage1 /verifyv {b399e360-38c5-11c5-99x1-ae62-08002b2b79ef}
```

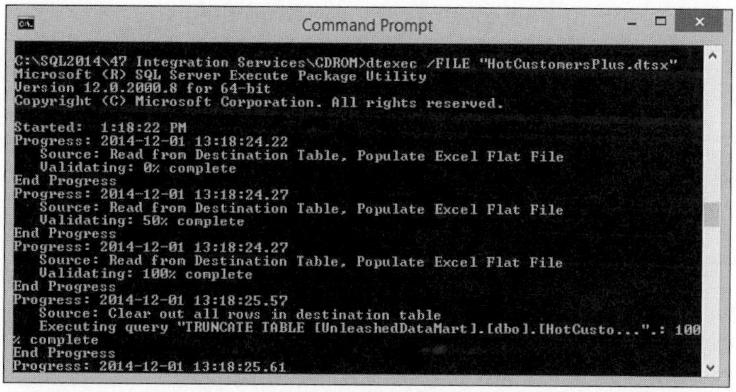

FIGURE 47.43   `dtexec` utility execution.

The `dtutil` Utility

You use the `dtutil` command-line utility to copy, move, delete, or verify the existence of a package. These actions can be performed on any SSIS package, regardless of whether it is stored in a Microsoft SQL Server database, the SSIS package store, or at the filesystem.

The `dtutil` options are additive. Depending on what you are trying to do, you string one or more options and their values together in the following form:

```
dtutil /option [value] [/option [value]] ...
```

To show available options for dtutil, you use `'/?'` or `'/H'` or `'/Help'`, as follows:

```
c:> dtutil /?
```

Note that a dash (-) may be substituted for / in this command.

Alternatively, you can see the details for a particular option by using the available options indicator followed by the option name (`'/?'` [option name]). This invokes SQL Server Books online for that particular option.

The `dtutil` options include the following:

▶ `/~C[opy] [StorageLocation];[PackageName]`—This option identifies where the package is to be stored (`StorageLocation` value of `DTS`, `FILE`, or `SQL`) and the full destination path and filename of the package (`PackageName`). When the Copy action encounters an existing package at the destination, `dtutil` prompts you to confirm package deletion. `Y` overwrites the package, and `N` aborts the overwrite of the destination package. If you include the `/Q` (quiet) option, no prompt appears, and the existing destination package is overwritten.

▶ `/~Dec[rypt] Password`—This option sets the decryption password used when loading a package with password encryption.

▶ `/~Del[ete]`—This option deletes the package specified by the `SQL`, `DTS`, or `FILE` option.

▶ `/~DestP[assword] Password`—This option specifies the password used with the `SQL` option to connect to a destination SQL Server instance using SQL Server authentication.

▶ `/~DestS[erver] Server`—This option specifies the server name used with any action that causes a destination to be saved to SQL Server or a nonlocal or nondefault server when saving an SSIS package.

▶ `/~DestU[ser] User name`—This option specifies the SQL Server username at the destination SQL Server instance.

▶ `/~Dump processID`—This option creates the debug dump files, `.mdmp` and `.tmp`. Find the process ID via the Windows Task Manager.

▶ `/~DT[S] PackagePath`—This option specifies that the SSIS package referenced is located in the SSIS package store, and the `PackagePath` argument is a relative path that commences at the root of the SSIS package store.

▶ `/~En[crypt] [StorageLocation];[;Path;ProtectionLevel[;Password]`—This option encrypts the loaded package with the specified protection level and password and saves it to the location specified in `Path`. `StorageLocation` types are `DTS`, `FILE`, and `SQL`. `ProtectionLevel` determines whether a password is required.

The possible `ProtectionLevel` values are `0` (strips sensitive information), `1` (sensitive information is encrypted using local user credentials), `2` (sensitive information is encrypted using the required password), `3` (package is encrypted using the required password), `4` (package is encrypted using local user credentials), and `5` (package uses SQL Server storage encryption).

▶ `/~Ex[ists]`—This option is used to determine whether a package exists.

▶ `/~FC[reate] [StorageLocation];FolderPath;NewFolderName`—This option creates a new folder with the name specified by `NewFolderName`. `StorageLocation` is `SQL` or `DTS` only. The location of the new folder is indicated by `FolderPath`.

▶ `/~FDe[lete] [StorageLocation] ExistingFolderPath;ExistingFolderName`—This option deletes the folder specified by the name in `ExistingFolderName` from SQL Server (`SQL`) or SSIS (`DTS`). `StorageLocation` is `SQL` or `DTS` only. The location of the folder to delete is indicated by `ExistingFolderPath`.

▶ `/~FDi[rectory] [StorageLocation] FolderPath[;S]]`—This option lists the contents, both folders and packages, in a folder on SSIS (`DTS`) or SQL Server (`SQL`). The optional `ExistingFolderPath` parameter specifies the folder whose contents you want to view. `StorageLocation` is `SQL` or `DTS` only. The optional `s` parameter specifies that you want to view a listing of the contents of the subfolders for the folder specified in `ExistingFolderPath`.

▶ `/~FE[xists] [StorageLocation] ExistingFolderPath`—This option verifies whether the specified folder exists on SSIS (`DTS`) or SQL Server (`SQL`). The `ExistingFolderPath` parameter is the path and name of the folder for which you need to verify its existence. `StorageLocation` is `SQL` or `DTS` only.

▶ **/~Fi[le] filespec**—This option specifies that the SSIS package to be operated on is located in the file system.

▶ **/~FR[ename] [StorageLocation]; ExistingFolderPath; ExistingFolderName; NewFolder**Name—This option renames a folder on the SSIS (DTS) or SQL Server (SQL). StorageLocation is SQL or DTS only. ExistingFolderPath is the location (path) of the folder to rename. ExistingFolderName is the name of the folder to be renamed, and NewFolderName is the new name to give the folder.

▶ **/~H[elp]**—This option displays text help on the dtutil options and descries their use.

▶ **/~I[DRegenerate]**—This option creates a new GUID for the package and updates the package ID property.

▶ **/~M[ove] [StorageLocation]; PathandName**—This option specifies a move action for an SSIS package. StorageLocation may be DTS, FILE, or SQL. PathandName indicates the package path (location) and/or package name: SQL uses the package path and package name, FILE uses a UNC or local path, and DTS uses a location relative to the root of the SSIS package store. If an existing package at the destination has the same name, dtutil prompts you to answer Y to overwrite this existing package or N to not do the move. If you specify the /Q (quiet) option, no prompt appears when an existing package may exist at the move destination, and it is just overwritten.

▶ **/~Q[uiet]**—This option disables the Y/N prompts when a package with the same name as the specified package already exists at the destination location or if the specified package is already signed.

▶ **/~R[emark] [Text]**—This option is a comment to the command line. There can be multiple remarks in a command line.

▶ **/~Si[gn] [StorageLocation]; ExistingPath; Hash**—This option signs an SSIS package. StorageLocation may be DTS, FILE, or SQL. ExistingPath specifies the path (location) of the package to be signed. Hash specifies a certificate identifier expressed as a hexadecimal string of varying length.

▶ **/~SourceP[assword] Password**—This option provides the password used with the SQL and SOURCEUSER options to connect to a SQL Server instance that uses SQL Server authentication.

▶ **/~SourceS[erver] Server**—This option provides the name of the server where the package is to be stored.

▶ **/~SourceU[ser] User Name**—This option provides the SQL Server username to use to access the SSIS package.

▶ **/~SQ[L] PathName**—This option specifies the path (location) of the SSIS package stored in the msdb database.

Next, let's look at various examples of running dtutil.

47

dtutil **Examples**

The following example copies an existing package in SQL to the SSIS package store:

```
C:> Dtutil /SQL ExistingPackage /COPY DTS;destPackage
```

The following example copies an existing package from one location on the filesystem to another location on the filesystem:

```
C:> dtutil /FILE c:\Unleashed\HotCustomersPlus.dtsx /COPY
    FILE;c:\UnleashedProduction\HotCustomersPlus.dtsx
```

The following example creates a new GUID (usually after you copy a package):

```
C:> dtutil /I /FILE HotCustomersPlus.dtsx
```

The following example deletes a package stored in the local server (msdb database):

```
C:> dtutil /SQL HotCustomersPlus /SOURCEUSER PBertucci
    /SOURCEPASSWORD xyz  /DELETE
```

The following example deletes a package stored in the filesystem:

```
c:> dtutil /FILE c:\UnleashedProduction\HotCustomersPlus.dtsx /DELETE
```

The following example verifies whether a package exists in a local server (msdb database):

```
C:> dtutil SQL HotCustomersPlus /SOURCEUSER Pbertucci /SOURCEPASSWORD xyz /EXISTS
```

The following example verifies whether a package exists on the local filesystem:

```
C:> dtutil /FILE c:\UnleashedProduction\HotCustomersPlus.dtsx /EXISTS
```

The following example moves a package from one server (msdb database) to another server (msdb database):

```
C:> dtutil /SQL HotCustomersPlus /SOURCEUSER Pbertucci
    /SOURCEPASSWORD xyz /MOVE SQL;HotCustomersPlus
    /DESTUSER sa /DESTPASSWORD zwx
```

The following example moves a package from one filesystem location to another:

```
c:> dtutil /FILE c:\Unleashed\HotCustomersPlus.dtsx /MOVE
    FILE;c:\UnleashedProduction\HotCustomersPlus.dtsx
```

The following example signs a package on the filesystem:

```
dtutil /FILE c:\Unleashed\HotCustomersPlus.dtsx /SIGN FILE;
    c:\Unleashed\HotCustomersPlus.dtsx;987377773999af33df399999333
```

SSIS tidbits: If you are on Windows 8, all programs are pushed to your Windows 8 Start surface (see Figure 47.44).

FIGURE 47.44   SQL Server Data Tools, Package Execution utility and others on the Windows 8 start surface.

As you know, SSIS Designer is fully integrated within the Visual Studio Framework. This makes it super easy to do builds, deployment, release management, and code debugging. Figure 47.45 shows the debugging options for the package we developed.

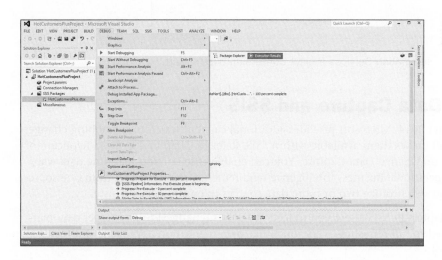

FIGURE 47.45   SSIS package debugging framework within Visual Studio.

And last but not least, Figure 47.46 shows the start of the Integration Services Project Conversion Wizard that will aid you generating the project deployment file (.ispac) from a set of packages and configurations. This is a compiled project, consisting of packages and parameters. Once converted, you can deploy to an Integration Services catalog on an instance of SQL Server. It is also useful in converting older packages (like from 2008) into the 2014 release level.

FIGURE 47.46   Integration Services Project Conversion Wizard start.

Change Data Capture and SSIS

With SQL Server 2014, Microsoft provides additional capabilities around grabbing changes from tables and makes them available within SSIS. Refer to Chapter 43, "Data Replication" for full details on Change Data Capture. You can enable efficient and real-time data warehousing, set operational business intelligence requirements, replicate data from one source to another, and synchronize two or more data sources to ensure data consistency.

These CDC adapters in SSIS allow you to feed the deltas (changes) to any target data platform as opposed to full refreshes—very much like data replication approaches but via SSIS package control.

Using bcp

As you have seen in this chapter, it is fairly easy to create and implement SSIS packages to do data transformations from one or more data sources to one or more data destinations.

However, many organizations still really just need a vanilla and very fast mechanism to export data out of SQL Server or import data into SQL Server. bcp fills this need well (and has done so from the beginning of SQL Server).

The following sections outline the primary execution methods of bcp, the many switches of bcp, the format file, and ways to improve performance when using bcp. By the end of these sections, you will be able to optimally execute bcp successfully for several common production scenarios. Microsoft has added a new execution switch that generates an XML format file. Most other features of bcp have remained the same.

First, you need to see whether you have the right version of bcp. A quick check of your version of bcp guarantees that you won't run into any limitations from older versions of bcp that might be left on your servers. You can do this by executing bcp at the command prompt with the -v option and no other parameters. (Note that all bcp switch options are case sensitive; for example, -v and -V are two very different switches.) Here's an example:

```
C:>bcp -v
BCP - Bulk Copy Program for Microsoft SQL Server.
Copyright (C) Microsoft Corporation. All Rights Reserved.
Version: 12.0.2000.8
```

This is version 12.0, which is distributed with MS SQL Server 2014 (SQL Server 12.0). If a version other than 12.x is present here, you must re-install bcp immediately.

At any time, you can see the proper usage and bcp switch options available by executing bcp at the command prompt with a question mark (?):

```
C:> bcp ?
usage: bcp {dbtable | query} {in | out | queryout | format} datafile
[-m maxerrors]          [-f formatfile]          [-e errfile]
.   .   .
```

You use the following syntax for bcp, along with one or more switches:

```
bcp {dbtable | query} {in | out | queryout | format} datafile
```

In this syntax, dbtable is the database_name, schema, and table_name | view_name (for example, AdventureWorks2014Production.Product or "AdventureWorks2014.Production. Product"):

▶ **database_name**—This is the name of the database in which the specified table or view resides. If not specified, this is the default database for the user.

▶ **owner**—This is the name of the schema of the table or view.

▶ **table_name | view_name**—This is the name of the destination table or view when copying data into SQL Server (in), and it is the name of the source table when copying data from SQL Server (out).

47

query is a T-SQL query that returns a result set. queryout must also be specified when bulk-copying data from a query.

in | out | queryout | format specifies the direction of the bulk copy (in copies from a file in to the database table or view, out copies from the database table or view to a file). queryout must be specified when bulk-copying data from a query. format creates a format file based on the switch specified (-n, -c, -w, -V, or -N) and the table or view delimiters. If format is used, the -f option must be specified as well.

data_file is the data file used when bulk-copying a table or view into or out of SQL Server.

All the available bcp switches are listed in Table 47.1.

TABLE 47.1   bcp Switches

Switch	Description	Example
-m	Specifies the maximum number of errors to allow before stopping the transfer. The default is 10.	[-m max_errors]
-f	Specifies the format file used to customize the load or unload data in a specific style.	[-f format_file]
-e	Specifies the file to write error messages to.	[-e err_file]
-F	Specifies the first row in the data file to start copying from when importing. The default is 1.	[-F first_row]
-L	Specifies the last row in the data file to end copying with when importing. The default is 0, which indicates the last row in the file.	[-L last_row]
-b	Specifies the number of rows to include in each committed batch. By default, all data rows in a file are copied in one batch.	[-b batch_size]
-n	Specifies that native (database) data type formats are to be used for the data.	[-n]
-c	Specifies that character data type format is to be used for the data. In addition, \t (tab character) is used as the field separator, and \n (newline character) is used as the row terminator.	[-c]
-w	Specifies that the Unicode data type format is to be used for the data. In addition, \t (tab character) is used as the field separator, and \n (newline character) is used as the row terminator.	[-w]
-N	Specifies to use Unicode for character data and native format for all others. This can be used as an alternative to the -w switch.	[-N]
-V	Specifies to use data type formats from earlier versions of SQL Server.	[-V (70 | 80|90)]

Switch	Description	Example
-q	Tells bcp to use quoted identifiers when dealing with table and column names.	[-q]
-C	If you are loading extended characters, allows you to specify the code page of the data in the data file.	[-C code_page]
-t	Specifies the terminating character(s) for fields. The default is \t (tab character).	[-t field_term]
-r	Specifies the terminating character(s) for rows. The default is \n (newline character).	[-r row_term]
-i	Specifies a file for redirecting input into bcp (the response file containing the responses to the command prompts).	[-i input_file]
-o	Specifies the file for receiving redirected output from bcp.	[-o output_file]
-a	Specifies the network packet size (in bytes) used to send to or receive from SQL Server. Can be between 4,096 and 65,535 bytes. The default size is 4,096.	[-a packet_size]
-S	Specifies the SQL Server name to connect to. Local is the default.	[-S server_name | server_name\instance_name]
-U	Specifies the user account to log in as; this account must have sufficient privileges to carry out either a read or a write of the table.	[-U login_id]
-P	Specifies the password associated with the user account.	[-P password]
-T	Makes a trusted connection to the server, using the network user/security credentials instead of the login_id/password.	[-T]
-v	Displays the bcp version information.	[-v]
-R	Uses the regional format for currency, date, and time data, as defined by the locale settings of the client computer.	[-R]
-k	Overrides a column's default and enforces NULL values being loaded into the columns as part of the bcp operation.	[-k]
-E	Uses the identity values in the import file rather than generating new ones.	[-E]
-h	Specifies special hints to be used during the bcp operation. They include the following: the sort order of the data file, number of rows of data per batch, number of kilobytes of data per batch, whether to acquire a table-level lock, whether to check constraints, and whether to fire insert triggers.	[-h hint_type,..]

47

Fundamentals of Exporting and Importing Data

One of the great things about bcp is its ease of use. This section runs through a couple simple examples and provides full explanations. All tables used here can be found in the AdventureWorks2014 sample database supplied by Microsoft in Codeplex for SQL Server 2014.

Let's start by exporting product data from AdventureWorks2014 that may be needed by a sales team for reference in Excel format (a .csv file). To do this, you simply export the Product table data into a comma-delimited file. You need to specify the following with bcp in this case:

▶ The full table name (in this case, AdventureWorks2014.Production.Product)

▶ The direction of bcp (OUT in this case because it is exporting data out)

▶ Data filename to hold the exported data (in this case, products.dat)

▶ The server name DXD001\SQL2014DXD01 for this example (in this case, -S DXD001\SQL2014DXD01)

▶ The username SA (in this case, -U sa)

▶ The password (in this case, -P xyz)

▶ A comma as the column delimiter (in this case, -t ",")

▶ That this should be exported in character data format (in this case, -c)

At the command prompt, you execute the following:

```
C:>bcp AdventureWorks2014.Production.Product OUT products.dat
-S DXD001\SQL2014DXD01 -U sa -P bjhl -t "," -c

Starting copy...
SQLState = S1000, NativeError = 0
Error = [Microsoft][SQL Server Native Client 11.0]Warning: BCP import with a
format file will convert empty strings in delimited columns to NULL.

504 rows copied.
Network packet size (bytes): 4096
Clock Time (ms.) Total     : 1      Average : (504000.00 rows per sec.)
```

Here's a sample of the data in the Products.dat file that was just exported:

```
1,Adjustable Race,AR-5381,0,0,,
2,Bearing Ball,BA-8327,0,0,,
3,BB Ball Bearing,BE-2349,1,0,,
4,Headset Ball Bearings,BE-2908,0,0,,
. . .
```

Now let's look at importing data into SQL Server 2014.

Let's say that each salesperson is providing a flat file that contains his or her new sales orders summaries. These files are emailed to a person in the ordering department and need to be imported into SQL Server every week. The file that you will import will be a comma-delimited file (.csv) that the salesperson created using Excel. The new entries will be the salesperson's hottest customer's totals. A sample input data file (named BCPHotCustomersPlus.csv) is included in the sample files and code listings folder for this chapter on the Web. Another file that can create the target table on SQL Server is also included in the sample files and code listings folder for this chapter on the Web. That file-name is CreateHotCustomersPlusTable.sql. So, if you haven't done this yet, go create this table so you can load data into it.

Now, you will need to specify the following with bcp:

▶ The full table name (in this case, AdventureWorks2014.Sales.HotCustomersPlus).

▶ The direction of bcp (IN in this case because it is importing data).

▶ The names of the data files that contain the import data (in this case, BCPHotCustomersPlus.csv). The following is a sample of the input data file (BCPHotCustomersPlus.csv):

```
268,Cycle Parts and Accessories,S,9,Australia,954,Touring-1000
Yellow,7152.210000
268,Cycle Parts and Accessories,S,9,Australia,955,Touring-1000
Yellow,7152.210000
268,Cycle Parts and Accessories,S,9,Australia,956,Touring-1000
Yellow,5721.768000
268,Cycle Parts and Accessories,S,9,Australia,968,Touring-1000 Blue,5721.768000
. . .
```

▶ The server name (in this case, -S DXD001\SQL2014DXD01)

▶ The username SA (in this case, -U sa).

▶ The password (in this case, -P xyz).

▶ A comma as the column delimiter (in this case, -t ",").

▶ That this should be exported in character data format (in this case, -c).

▶ The -q option (in this case, -q), to be sure quoted identifiers are handled properly.

At the command prompt, you execute the following:

```
C:> BCP AdventureWorks2012.dbo.HotCustomersPlus IN BCPHotCustomersPlus.csv
    -S DXD001\SQL2014DXD01 -U sa -P xyz -t "," -c -q
Starting copy...

4 rows copied.
Network packet size (bytes): 4096
Clock Time (ms.): total : 31  Average : (129.03 rows per sec.)
```

A quick SELECT * from the HotCustomersPlus table shows the success of this operation:

```
CustomerID     CustomerName        CustomerType        TerritoryID      TerritoryName
268      Cycle Parts and Accessories    S    9     Australia    954
268      Cycle Parts and Accessories    S    9     Australia    955
268      Cycle Parts and Accessories    S    9     Australia    956
268      Cycle Parts and Accessories    S    9     Australia    968
. . .
```

The sales team can now send in their sales orders as they make sales. This brief example illustrates the beauty and power of using bcp.

The following sections look at how bcp can work with basic data representations (character, native, or Unicode), the use of a format file, and a few other extended bcp capabilities.

File Data Types

bcp can handle data in one of three forms: character (ASCII), native, or Unicode. You have the choice of which character format is used, depending on the source or destination of the data file:

▶ The character format (-c) is the most commonly used of the three data types because it reads or writes using ASCII characters and carries out the appropriate data type conversion for the SQL Server representations. The CHAR data type is the default storage type; it uses tabs as field separators and the newline character as the row terminator.

▶ The native format (-n) is used for copying data between servers. This format allows bcp to read and write using the same data types used by the server, which results in a performance gain. This format does, however, render the data file unreadable by any other means.

▶ The Unicode option (-w) uses Unicode characters rather than ASCII characters. The NCHAR data type is the default storage type; it uses tabs as field separators and the newline character as the row terminator.

Format Files

By using a format file, you can customize the data file created by bcp or specify complex field layouts for data loads. There are two ways to create a format file: by using interactive bcp and by using the format switch.

Customizing a Format File by Using Interactive bcp

If you do not specify one of the -n, -c, or -w data type format switches, bcp (in or out) prompts you for the following information for each column in the data set:

▶ File storage type

▶ Prefix length

▶ Field length

▶ Field terminator

`bcp` offers a default for each of these prompts that you can either accept or reject. If you accept all the defaults, you wind up with the same format file you would have by specifying the native format (with the –n switch). The prompts look like this:

```
Enter the file storage type of field au_id [char]:
Enter prefix length of field au_id [0]:
Enter length of field au_id [11]:
Enter field terminator [none]:
```

or like this:

```
Enter the file storage type of field ProductID [int]:
Enter prefix length of field ProductID [0]:
Enter field terminator [none]:
```

By pressing the Enter key at the prompt, you accept the default. Alternatively, you can type your own value at the prompt if you know the new value and it is different from the default.

Creating a Format File by Using the `format` Switch

By using the `format` option, you can create a format file without actually transferring any data. Here is an example of creating a format file for the `SalesOrderHeader` table in the `AdventureWorks2014` database:

```
C:> BCP AdventureWorks2014.Sales.SalesOrderHeader format orders.dat
    -S DXD001\SQL2014DXD01
        -U sa -P xyz -f orders.fmt -c
```

	Prefix Length=0	Prefix Length=1, 2, 4
No Terminator	stringSstringS	PstringSPstringS
Terminator	stringSTstringST	PstringSTPstringST
No terminator	stringSstringS	PstringPstring
Terminator	stringTstringT	PstringTPstringT

The format file created looks like this:

```
11.0
26
1       SQLCHAR         0       12      "\t"    1       SalesOrderID        ""
2       SQLCHAR         0       5       "\t"    2       RevisionNumber      ""
3       SQLCHAR         0       24      "\t"    3       OrderDate           ""
4       SQLCHAR         0       24      "\t"    4       DueDate             ""
```

5	SQLCHAR	0	24	"\t"	5	ShipDate	""
6	SQLCHAR	0	5	"\t"	6	Status	""
7	SQLCHAR	0	1	"\t"	7	OnlineOrderFlag	""
8	SQLCHAR	0	50	"\t"	8	SalesOrderNumber	SQL_Latin1_General_CP1_CI_AS
9	SQLCHAR	0	50	"\t"	9	PurchaseOrderNumber	SQL_Latin1_General_CP1_CI_AS
10	SQLCHAR	0	30	"\t"	10	AccountNumber	SQL_Latin1_General_CP1_CI_AS
11	SQLCHAR	0	12	"\t"	11	CustomerID	""
12	SQLCHAR	0	12	"\t"	12	SalesPersonID	""
13	SQLCHAR	0	12	"\t"	13	TerritoryID	""
14	SQLCHAR	0	12	"\t"	14	BillToAddressID	""
15	SQLCHAR	0	12	"\t"	15	ShipToAddressID	""
16	SQLCHAR	0	12	"\t"	16	ShipMethodID	""
17	SQLCHAR	0	12	"\t"	17	CreditCardID	""
18	SQLCHAR	0	15	"\t"	18	CreditCardApprovalCode	SQL_Latin1_General_CP1_CI_AS
19	SQLCHAR	0	12	"\t"	19	CurrencyRateID	""
20	SQLCHAR	0	30	"\t"	20	SubTotal	""
21	SQLCHAR	0	30	"\t"	21	TaxAmt	""
22	SQLCHAR	0	30	"\t"	22	Freight	""
23	SQLCHAR	0	30	"\t"	23	TotalDue	""
24	SQLCHAR	0	256	"\t"	24	Comment	SQL_Latin1_General_CP1_CI_AS
25	SQLCHAR	0	37	"\t"	25	rowguid	""
26	SQLCHAR	0	24	"\r\n"	26	ModifiedDate	""

The following is a description of the lines and columns in the preceding format file example:

▶ The first line shows the version of bcp.

▶ The second line shows the number of columns.

▶ The third line, first column shows the data field position.

▶ The third line, second column shows the data type.

▶ The third line, third column shows the prefix.

▶ The third line, fourth column shows the data file field length.

▶ The third line, fifth column shows the field or row terminator.

▶ The third line, sixth column shows the column position.

▶ The third line, seventh column shows the column name.

▶ The third line, eighth column shows the column collation.

You get different format files depending on your table and whether you chose character, native, or Unicode as the data type. As you can see in the preceding example, only the last two columns in the format file relate to the actual table; the remaining columns specify properties of the data file.

File Storage Types

The storage type is a description of how the data is stored in the data file. Table 47.2 lists the definitions used during interactive bcp and what appears in the format file. The storage type allows data to be copied as its base type (native format), as implicitly converted between types (tinyint to smallint), or as a string (in character or Unicode format).

TABLE 47.2   Storage Data Types

File Storage Type	Interactive Prompt	Host File Data Type
char	c[har]	SQLCHAR
varchar	c[har]	SQLCHAR
nchar	w	SQLNCHAR
nvarchar	w	SQLNCHAR
text	T[ext]	SQLCHAR
ntext	W	SQLNCHAR
binary	x	SQLBINARY
varbinary	x	SQLBINARY
image	I[mage]	SQLBINARY
datetime	d[ate]	SQLDATETIME
smalldatetime	D	SQLDATETIM4
decimal	n	SQLDECIMAL
numeric	n	SQLNUMERIC
float	f[loat]	SQLFLT8
real	r	SQLFLT4
int	i[nt]	SQLINT
smallint	s[mallint]	SQLSMALLINT
tinyint	t[inyint]	SQLTINYINT
money	m[oney]	SQLMONEY
smallmoney	M	SQLMONEY4
bit	b[it]	SQLBIT
uniqueidentifier	u	SQLUNIQUEID
timestamp	x	SQLBINARY

47

> **NOTE**
>
> If the table makes use of user-defined data types, these customized data types appear in the format file as their base data type.

If you are having problems loading certain fields into your table, you can try the following tricks:

▶ Copy the data in as `char` data types and force SQL Server to do the conversion for you.

▶ Duplicate the table and replace all the SQL Server data types with `char` or `varchar` of a length sufficient to hold the value. This trick allows you to further manipulate the data with T-SQL after it is loaded.

Prefix Lengths

To maintain compactness in native data files, `bcp` precedes each field with a prefix length that indicates the length of the data stored. The space for storing this information is specified in characters and is called the *prefix length*.

Table 47.3 indicates the value to specify for prefix length for each of the data types.

TABLE 47.3   Prefix Length Values

Prefix	Data Types to Use Length
0	Non-null data of type bit or numerics (`int`, `real`, and so on). Use this value when no prefix characters are wanted. This value causes the field to be padded with spaces to the size indicated for the field length.
1	Non-null data of type `binary` or `varbinary` or `null` data, with the exception of `text`, `ntext`, and `image`. Use this value for any data (except `bit`, `binary`, `varbinary`, `text`, `ntext`, and `image`) that you want stored using a character-based data type.
2	When storing the data types `binary` or `varbinary` as character-based data types, 2 bytes of `char` file storage and 4 bytes of `nchar` file storage are required for each byte of binary table data.
4	For the data types `text`, `ntext`, and `image`.

Prefix lengths are likely to exist only within data files created using `bcp`. It is unlikely that you will encounter a reason to change the defaults `bcp` has chosen for you.

Field Lengths

When using either the native or character data format, you must specify the maximum length of each field. When converting data types to strings, `bcp` suggests lengths large enough to store the entire range of values for each particular data type. Table 47.4 lists the default values for each of the data formats.

TABLE 47.4   Default Field Lengths for Data Formats

Data Type	Length (/c)	Length (/n)
bit	1	1
binary	Column length 2	Column length
datetime	24	8
smalldatetime	24	4
float	30	8
real	30	4
int	12	4
smallint	7	2
tinyint	5	1
money	30	8
smallmoney	30	4
decimal	41	up to 17
numeric	41	up to 17
uniqueidentifier	37	16

NOTE

You must specify a field length that is long enough for the data being stored. bcp error messages regarding overflows indicate that the data value has been truncated in at least one of the fields. If the operation is a load, an overflow error usually results in bcp terminating. However, if you are dumping the data to a file, the data is truncated without error messages.

The field length value is used *only* when the prefix length is 0 and you have specified no terminators. In essence, you are doing a fixed-length data copy. bcp uses exactly the amount of space stated by the field length for each field; unused space within the field is padded out.

NOTE

Pre-existing spaces in the data are not distinguished from added padding.

Field Terminators

If you are not making use of fixed-width fields or length prefixes, you must use a field terminator to indicate the character(s) that separates fields; for the last field in the data row, you must also indicate which character(s) ends the line.

bcp recognizes the indicators for special characters shown in Table 47.5.

47

TABLE 47.5   bcp Indicators for Special Characters

Terminator	Escape Code
Tab	\t
Backslash	\\
Null terminator	\0
Newline	\n
Carriage return	\r

You cannot use spaces as terminators, but you can use any other printable characters. You should choose field and row terminators that make sense for your data. Obviously, you should not use any character you are trying to load. You must combine the \r and \n characters to get your data into an ASCII data file with each row on its own line.

> **TIP**
>
> By specifying the -t and -r switches, you can override the defaults that appear for the prompts during interactive bcp.

> **NOTE**
>
> You can specify terminators for data copied in native format. You should be careful if you decide to go this route; the accepted approach is to use lengthy prefixes.

The prefix length, field length, and terminator values interact with one another. In the following examples, T indicates the terminator character(s), P indicates the prefix length, and s indicates space padding.

The next few sections examine how to load data into tables when there are differences in column number and layout.

Different Numbers of Columns in a File and Table

If you want to load data into tables when you have fewer fields in the data file than in the table, you have to "dummy up" an extra line in your format file.

Let's suppose you want to load a data file that is missing most of the address information for each customer (into a customer table of some kind that has full address columns in it). To do this, you create a format file for this table by using the format option with bcp. With this format file, you can still load this abbreviated data easily. Suppose that the data file looks like this:

```
WELLI    Wellington Importadora    Jane Graham    Sales (14)555-8122
         (14)555-8111
WHITC    White Clover Markets    Donald Bertucci    Owner (206)555-4112
         (206)555-4113
```

To introduce a dummy value for the missing ones, in the format file, you need to make the prefix and data lengths 0 and set the field terminator to nothing (""). The modified format file should look like this:

```
11.0
11
1      SQLCHAR 0    10    "\t"    1    CustomerID     SQL_Latin1_General_
       CP1_CI_AS
2      SQLCHAR 0    80    "\t"    2    CompanyName    SQL_Latin1_General_
       CP1_CI_AS
3      SQLCHAR 0    60    "\t"    3    ContactName    SQL_Latin1_General_
       CP1_CI_AS
4      SQLCHAR 0    60    "\t"    4    ContactTitle   SQL_Latin1_General_
       CP1_CI_AS
5      SQLCHAR 0    0     ""      5    Address        SQL_Latin1_General_
       CP1_CI_AS
6      SQLCHAR 0    0     ""      6    City           SQL_Latin1_General_
       CP1_CI_AS
7      SQLCHAR 0    0     ""      7    Region         SQL_Latin1_General_
       CP1_CI_AS
8      SQLCHAR 0    0     ""      8    PostalCode     SQL_Latin1_General_
       CP1_CI_AS
9      SQLCHAR 0    0     ""      9    Country        SQL_Latin1_General_
       CP1_CI_AS
10     SQLCHAR 0    48    "\t"    10   Phone          SQL_Latin1_General_
       CP1_CI_AS
11     SQLCHAR 0    48    "\r\n"  11   Fax            SQL_Latin1_General_
       CP1_CI_AS
```

Now bcp can load the data file by using this new format file, with the Address, City, Region, PostalCode, and Country columns containing NULL values for the new rows.

For data files that have more fields than the table has columns, you change the format file to add additional lines of information. Suppose that your customer data file contains an additional CreditStatus value at the end:

```
WELLI   Wellington Importadora    Martin Sommer  Sales Manager Rua do Mercado,
        12    Resende   SP    08737-363    Uraguay    (14) 555-8122    NULL 1
WELP    Well Drilling P   Donny Bertucci    Sales Manager    Rue de Vaugirard,
        997    Paris    FR    08737-363    France    (11) 555-8122    NULL 1
WF      WF Enterprises    Yves Moison    Sales Manager    Rue de Sevres,
        4123   Paris    FR    08737-363    France    (14) 555-8122    NULL 1
WGZR    Wellsley Granite    Jack McElreath    Sales Manager    Hillsboro,
        131    Hillsboro    MA    08737-363    USA    (781) 555-8122    NULL 1
WHITC   White Clover Markets    Scott Smith    Owner    305 - 14th Ave. S.
        Suite 3B    Boston    MA    98128    USA (508) 555-4112  (508) 555-4115 2
```

You need to modify a format file in two important areas: You change the second line to reflect the actual number of values, and you add new lines for the extra column in the file that is not in the table (from 11 to 12 entries). Notice that the column position has a value of 0 to indicate the absence of a column in the table. The result is that your source data file will import all data into the table, except the extra field (that is, the CreditStatus field).

Thus, the modified format file looks like this:

```
11.0
12
1       SQLCHAR 0    10    "\t"  1   CustomerID      SQL_Latin1_General_
        CP1_CI_AS
2       SQLCHAR 0    80    "\t"  2   CompanyName     SQL_Latin1_General_
        CP1_CI_AS
3       SQLCHAR 0    60    "\t"  3   ContactName     SQL_Latin1_General_
        CP1_CI_AS
4       SQLCHAR 0    60    "\t"  4   ContactTitle    SQL_Latin1_General_
        CP1_CI_AS
5       SQLCHAR 0    120   "\t"  5   Address         SQL_Latin1_General_
        CP1_CI_AS
6       SQLCHAR 0    30    "\t"  6   City            SQL_Latin1_General_
        CP1_CI_AS
7       SQLCHAR 0    30    "\t"  7   Region          SQL_Latin1_General_
        CP1_CI_AS
8       SQLCHAR 0    20    "\t"  8   PostalCode      SQL_Latin1_General_
        CP1_CI_AS
9       SQLCHAR 0    30    "\t"  9   Country         SQL_Latin1_General_
        CP1_CI_AS
10      SQLCHAR 0    48    "\t"  10  Phone           SQL_Latin1_General_
        CP1_CI_AS
11      SQLCHAR 0    48    "\t"  11  Fax             SQL_Latin1_General_
        CP1_CI_AS
12      SQLCHAR 0    1   "\r\n"  0   CreditStatus    SQL_Latin1_General_
        CP1_CI_AS
```

These two examples show you the possibilities that the format file offers for customizing the loading and unloading of data.

Renumbering Columns

Using the techniques described in the section, "Different Numbers of Columns in a File and Table," you can also handle data file fields that are in different orders than the target tables. All you need to do is change the column order number to reflect the desired sequence of the columns in the table. The fields are then automatically mapped to the corresponding columns in the table.

For example, suppose that a customer data file you got from another source system came with the fields in this order:

1. Address

2. City

3. Country

4. PostalCode

5. Region

6. CompanyName

7. ContactName

8. ContactTitle

9. Fax

10. Phone

11. CustomerID

The SQL Server table has columns in a different order. To load your data file into this table, you modify the format file to look like this:

```
11.0
11
1       SQLCHAR 0    10    "\t"   11   CustomerID     SQL_Latin1_General_
        CP1_CI_AS
2       SQLCHAR 0    80    "\t"   6    CompanyName    SQL_Latin1_General_
        CP1_CI_AS
3       SQLCHAR 0    60    "\t"   7    ContactName    SQL_Latin1_General_
        CP1_CI_AS
4       SQLCHAR 0    60    "\t"   8    ContactTitle   SQL_Latin1_General_
        CP1_CI_AS
5       SQLCHAR 0    120   "\t"   1    Address        SQL_Latin1_General_
        CP1_CI_AS
6       SQLCHAR 0    30    "\t"   2    City           SQL_Latin1_General_
        CP1_CI_AS
7       SQLCHAR 0    30    "\t"   5    Region         SQL_Latin1_General_
        CP1_CI_AS
8       SQLCHAR 0    20    "\t"   4    PostalCode     SQL_Latin1_General_
        CP1_CI_AS
9       SQLCHAR 0    30    "\t"   3    Country        SQL_Latin1_General_
        CP1_CI_AS
10      SQLCHAR 0    48    "\t"   10   Phone          SQL_Latin1_General_
        CP1_CI_AS
11      SQLCHAR 0    48    "\r\n" 9    Fax            SQL_Latin1_General_
        CP1_CI_AS
```

47

The principal point to remember with the format file is that all but the last three columns deal with the data file. The last three columns deal with the database table.

Using Views

`bcp` can use views to export data from a database. This means an export of data can be a result set of data from multiple tables (and with distributed queries, even multiple servers).

You can also use a view with `bcp` to load data back into tables. However, as is the case with normal T-SQL inserts, you can load into only one of the underlying tables at a time.

Logged and Nonlogged Operations

Bulk-copy operations can occur in two modes: logged and nonlogged (also known as slow and fast `bcp`, respectively). The ideal situation is to operate in nonlogged mode because this arrangement dramatically decreases the load time and consumption of other system resources, such as memory, processor use, and disk access. However, the default runs the load in logged mode, which causes the log to grow rapidly for large volumes of data.

To achieve a nonlogged operation, the target table must not be replicated (the replication log reader needs the log records to relay the changes made). The database holding the target table must also have its SELECT INTO/BULK COPY option set, and finally, the TABLOCK hint must be specified.

> **NOTE**
>
> Remember that setting the SELECT INTO/BULK COPY option disables the capability to back up the transaction log until a full database backup has been performed. Transaction log dumps are disabled because if the database had to be restored, the transaction log would not contain a record of the new data.

Although you can still perform fast loads against tables that have indexes, it is advisable to drop and re-create the indexes after the data transfer operation is complete. In other words, the total load time includes the loading of the data and index creation time. If there is existing data in the table, the operation is logged; you achieve a nonlogged operation only if the table is initially empty.

Generally, you get at least a 50% drop in transfer speed if the table has an index. The more indexes, the greater the performance degradation. This is due to the logging factor: More log records are being generated, and index pages are being loaded into the cache and modified. This can also cause the log to grow, possibly filling it (depending on the log file settings).

> **NOTE**
>
> Despite the name, even a nonlogged operation logs some things. In the case of indexes, index page changes and allocations are logged, but the main area of logging is of extent allocations every time the table is extended for additional storage space for the new rows.

Batches

By default, bcp puts all the rows that are inserted into the target table into a single trans-action. bcp calls this a *batch*. This arrangement reduces the amount of work the log must deal with; however, it locks down the transaction log by keeping a large part of it active, which can make truncating or backing up the transaction log impossible or unproductive. By using the bcp batch (-b) switch, you can control the number of rows in each batch (or, effectively, each transaction). This switch controls the frequency of commits; although it can increase the activity in the log, it enables you to trim the size of the transaction log. You should tune the batch size in relation to the size of the data rows, transaction log size, and total number of rows to be loaded. The value you use for one load might not neces-sarily be the right value for all other loads.

Note that if a subsequent batch fails, the prior batches are committed, and those rows become part of the table. However, any rows copied up to the point of failure in the failing batch are rolled back.

Parallel Loading

A great enhancement of bcp is that you can now use it to do parallel loads of tables. If you want to take advantage of this feature, the following must be true:

▶ The bulk-copy operation must be nonlogged; all requirements specified in the previ-ous discussion on nonlogged operations must be met.

▶ There must be no indexes on the target table.

Only applications using the ODBC or SQL OLE DB-based APIs can perform parallel data loads into a single table.

The procedure is straightforward. After you ascertain that the target table has no indexes (which could involve dropping primary or unique constraints) and is not being replicated, you must set the database option SELECT INTO/BULK COPY to true. The requirement to drop all indexes has to do with the locking that must occur to load the data. Although the table itself can have a shared lock, the index pages are an area of contention that prevents parallel access.

Now all that is required is to set up the parallel bcp loads to load the data into the table. You can use the -F and -L switches to specify the range of the data you want each parallel bcp to load into the table if you are using the same data file. Using these switches removes the need to manually break up the file. Here is an example of the command switches involved for a parallel load with bcp for the customers table:

```
bcp AdventureWorks2014.Sales.SalesOrderHeader IN SalesOrders10000.dat -T
  -S servername -c -F 1
-L 10000 -h "TABLOCK"

bcp AdventureWorks2014.Sales.SalesOrderHeader IN SalesOrders20000.dat -T
  -S servername -c -F 10001
-L 20000 -h "TABLOCK"
```

47

The TABLOCK hint (-h switch) provides improved performance by removing contention from other users while the load takes place. If you do not use the hint, the load takes place using row-level locks, and this is considerably slower.

SQL Server 2014 allows parallel loads without affecting performance by making each bcp connection create extents in nonoverlapping ranges. The ranges are then linked into the table's page chain.

After the table is loaded, it is also possible to create multiple nonclustered indexes in parallel. If there is a clustered index, you work with that one first, followed by the parallel nonclustered index.

Supplying Hints to bcp

The SQL Server 2014 version of bcp enables you to further control the speed of data loading, to invoke constraints, and to have insert triggers fired during loads. To take advantage of these capabilities, you use hint switches to specify one or more hints at a time. Following is the syntax:

```
-h "hint [, hint]"
```

The query processor optimizes data loads and unloads for OLE database rowsets that the latest versions of bcp and BULK INSERT can generate.

The following sections describe the various hints you can specify with the -h switch.

The ROWS_PER_BATCH Hint

The ROWS_PER_BATCH hint is used to tell SQL Server the total number of rows in the data file. This hint helps SQL Server optimize the entire load operation. This hint and the -b switch heavily influence the logging operations that occur with data inserts. If you specify both this hint and the -b switch, they must have the same values, or you get an error message.

When you use the ROWS_PER_BATCH hint, you copy the entire result set as a single transaction. SQL Server automatically optimizes the load operation, using the batch size you specify. The value you specify does not have to be accurate, but you should be aware of the practical limit, based on the database's transaction log.

> **TIP**
>
> Do not be confused by the name of the ROWS_PER_BATCH hint. You are specifying the *total file size* and *not* the batch size (as is the case with the -b switch).

The CHECK_CONSTRAINTS Hint

The CHECK_CONSTRAINTS hint controls whether check constraints are executed as part of the bcp operation. With bcp, the default is that check constraints are not executed. This hint option allows you to turn the feature on (to have check constraints executed for each insert). If you do not use this option, you should either be very sure of your data or rerun the same logic as in the check constraints you deferred after the data has been loaded.

The FIRE_TRIGGER Hint

The FIRE_TRIGGER hint controls whether the insert trigger on the target table is executed as part of the bcp operation. With bcp, the default is that no triggers are executed. This hint option allows you to turn the feature on (to have insert triggers executed for each insert). As you can imagine, when this option is used, it slows down the bcp load operation. However, the business reasons to have the insert trigger fired might outweigh the slower loading.

The ORDER Hint

If the data you want to load is already in the same sequence as the clustered index on the receiving table, you can use the ORDER hint. The syntax for this hint is as follows:

```
ORDER( {column [ASC | DESC] [,...n]})
```

There must be a clustered index on the same columns in the same key sequence as specified in the ORDER hint. Using a sorted data file (in the same order as the clustering index) helps SQL Server place the data into the table with minimal overhead.

The KILOBYTES_PER_BATCH Hint

The KILOBYTES_PER_BATCH hint gives the size, in kilobytes, of the data in each batch. This is an estimate that SQL Server uses internally to optimize the data load and logging areas of the bcp operation.

The TABLOCK Hint

The TABLOCK hint is used to place a table-level lock for the bcp load duration. This hint gives you increased performance at a loss of concurrency, as described in the section, "Parallel Loading," earlier in this chapter.

47

Summary

It is fairly easy to create and implement a typical data export, data import, or complex data transformation by using SSIS. You can either use the wizard for basic data transformation needs or the SSIS Designer for massively complex transformations (which may have multiple data sources and/or multiple data destinations). This very robust environment has adopted a very formal, managed code rigor. With the SSIS capabilities, you get a self-contained place to build these data transformation solutions, and you can do so very rapidly. SSIS is completely integrated into the Visual Studio environment as well, making it that much easier to start producing rock-solid implementations. And with Change Data Capture for SSIS, a new dimension of trickling data changes to various platforms becomes available with SSIS processing.

This chapter also shows how to bulk-load data into and out of SQL Server by using the `bcp` utility. The multitude of switches `bcp` offers are very comprehensive and address most, if not all, importing and exporting situations. More importantly, with the advent of some additional switches, such as ORDER (within hints), TABLOCK (within hints), batches (-b), network packet sizes (-a), and others, it is significantly easier to increase the performance of `bcp` in a big way. `bcp` has been around for a long time, and it will continue to be the workhorse of bulk data loading and unloading.

Chapter 48, "SQL Server 2014 Reporting Services" discusses this significant SQL Server capability and how to maximize its use for a production environment.

> **NOTE**
>
> Chapters 48-51 are available online for readers of the printed edition. You can register your book and access them here: informit.com/title/9780672337291.

Index

Numbers

A

C

D

E

F

M

O

P

R

S

T

U

V

X-Y

Z